North American Radio-TV Station Guide

Fifteenth Edition

Vane Jones is engaged in many activities, but his first love is this book. Whenever possible, he is in his study, with a television set and two or three radios all operating at once. He can recite call letters and tell you the history of stations by the hour. Since the publication of his first station guide in 1958, his list of followers has grown with each edition, primarily because of the personal attention he gives each entry and the hairline accuracy for which he is famous.

North American Radio-TV Station Guide

Fifteenth Edition

by

Vane A. Jones

Howard W. Sams & Co., Inc.
4300 WEST 62ND ST. INDIANAPOLIS, INDIANA 46268 USA

FIFTEENTH EDITION
FIRST PRINTING—1984

International Standard Book Number: 0-672-22296-5
Library of Congress Catalog Card Number: 63-23371

Printed in the United States of America.

Preface

This book has been prepared from official information, and every effort has been made to provide listings that are as complete, accurate, and easy to use as possible. Television, fm, and am stations in the United States, Canada, Cuba, Mexico and the West Indies are indexed by geographic location, frequency, and call letters. All stations currently on the air, plus those that have temporarily ceased operation and those that hold construction permits, are listed.

The frequencies of broadcast stations are assigned by individual governments in accordance with international agreements. In this book, the assigned frequencies of am stations are given in kilohertz (kHz), and the frequencies of fm stations are given in megahertz (MHz). (One kilohertz is one thousand cycles per second, and one megahertz is one million cycles per second.) In keeping with the most widely used practice, the frequencies of television stations are given in terms of channel numbers rather than actual frequencies.

The frequencies (sometimes called "channels") for am stations are classified according to the intended coverage areas of the stations assigned to each frequency. Local channels are for use by low-power stations that serve limited areas. Regional channels are for use by medium-power stations that serve somewhat larger areas. Clear channels are primarily for use by high-power stations that cover wide areas; however, other stations are often assigned to a clear channel when they do not interfere with the dominant stations on the channel. In the list of am stations arranged by frequency, the classification of each channel is included in the frequency heading. In the case of clear channels, the country or countries having priority of use of the channel are indicated.

The am listings include day and night power (in watts). Because of the action of a layer of the upper atmosphere called the ionosphere, the signals of am stations travel much greater distances at night than during the day. For this reason, interference between stations is a greater problem during nighttime hours. To minimize the possibility of interference, many stations are prohibited from operating at night; some are permitted only limited nighttime hours of operation; still others are permitted to operate unlimited hours but with reduced power at night. The schedule notes identify stations that operate with these restrictions.

As in many other areas of communication, there are several basic changes coming in television, am, and fm broadcasting. In tv—We are already experiencing the wonders of tv cable and tv satellites, neither of which adds much to the thrill of receiving distant stations via direct broadcast. A few more stations, however, are to be squeezed into the vhf band, and more stations are being added to the uhf band, plus pay-for-viewing will soon be available from several new or existing tv stations. Possibly the biggest change is the 1000 or more (some say 4000) low-power tv stations now being granted construction permits. These 5–10 watt stations will be programming and originating their own shows; unlike the nearly 5000 translator stations now on the air. It should make receiving long-distance tv during times of skip much more difficult, or interesting.

Changes in am—Just recently, the FCC has granted almost blanket authority to all daytime am stations to operate for 2 hours before sunrise and 2 hours after sunset, but at reduced power—so low that, again, there is little chance to receive the signal unless you can see the station's tower from your site. As low as 5 watts will get you nowhere these days. (Although I still treasure a 15-watt verification received from Greenville, Texas back in the '30s.) It is doubtful with such low power just before sunrise and after sunset that many stations will choose to extend their broadcast day. Also to be added are more than 100 unlimited-time am frequencies available as soon as the FCC grants the permits.

For fm—another 1000 commercial frequencies will be available in the 88–108 MHz band for use as soon as the FCC can rule on each application. In the meantime, the FCC is encouraging existing fm stations in Class A, B, and C to raise their power to the maximum for their class (most have already done this). Also, the low-power 10-watt educational stations are being urged to up their power and move to any other frequency they can fit into. This should make for some great DXing until the whole band is too crowded.

It is expected that some of these changes will be included in the next edition of the *North American Radio-TV Station Guide.* Be sure to complete your reminder form at the back of the book and mail it so you will be sure not to miss getting your copy. Suggestions for improving the book are invited and you may add your ideas when you send in your reminder form.

In the United States, fm stations are classified according to the areas they serve. Class A stations are intended to cover local areas and have a maximum power of 3000 watts. Class B and C stations are intended to serve larger areas. Class B stations are assigned in most of the northeastern United States, in Puerto Rico and the Virgin Islands, and in all of California except the northern part. They are permitted a maximum power of 50,000 watts. Class C stations are assigned in the remainder of the United States. They have a maximum power of 100,000 watts. Class D stations are 10-watt noncommercial educational stations. (Some fm stations, authorized before the present rules went into effect, have powers in excess of the maximums stated.)

In the United States, the frequencies from 88.1 through 91.9 MHz are reserved for the use of noncommercial educational fm stations. Class A, B, C, or D stations may be assigned to any of these frequencies. In the remainder of the fm band, certain frequencies are allocated for class A stations, and others are allocated for class B and C stations. These are identified by letters after the frequency headings in the list of fm stations arranged by frequency. The frequency headings also contain the channel numbers used by the Federal Communications Commission to identify the fm frequencies.

Affiliations with the major networks are shown for tv stations. Symbols are used to identify noncommercial educational stations, stations not currently on the air, am stations scheduled to change their facilities, and stations that share time on the same frequency. Satellite television stations are indicated, and their parent stations are identified. An explanation of the format of the listings and the symbols used can be found inside the front and back covers.

The completely integrated alphabetical call-letter list is an important feature of this book. It provides a comprehensive one-source reference to the am, fm, and tv broadcast stations of North America.

The information for each station has been checked and rechecked, and the final lists have been assembled by computer for even greater accuracy, but in a work of this magnitude some errors are inevitable. The listings in this edition include over 3500 changes based on information received up to January 1, 1984. If you are aware of any changes that occurred prior to that date but were missed in this edition, I would appreciate having the information. Comments from users of this book are always welcome.

VANE A. JONES

Contents

TV Stations by Geographic Location

UNITED STATES

Alabama

City	Station		
Anniston	----	40	
	WHMA-TV	40	C
Birmingham	WBRC-TV	6	A
	* WBIQ	10	P
	WVTM-TV	13	N
	WTTO	21	
	WBMG	42	C
	† WCAJ	68	
Decatur	WAFF	48	N
Demopolis	* WIIQ	41	
Dothan	WTVY	4	C
	WDHN	18	A
	† ----	60	
Dozier	* WDIQ	2	P
Florence	WOWL-TV	15	N
	* WFIQ	36	P
Gadsden	† WTJP	44	
Huntsville	WHNT-TV	19	C
	* WHIQ	25	P
	WAAY-TV	31	A
	† ----	54	
Louisville	* WGIQ	43	P
Mobile	WKRG-TV	5	C
	WALA-TV	10	N
	† ----	15	
	† WMPV-TV	21	
	* WEIQ	42	P
Montgomery	WSFA-TV	12	N
	WCOV-TV	20	C
	* WAIQ	26	
	WKAB-TV	32	A
	WMCF-TV	45	
Munford	* WCIQ	7	P
Opelika	WSWS	66	
Selma	WSLA	8	C
Tuscaloosa	† ----	17	
	† WCFT-TV	33	C

Alaska

City	Station		
Anchorage	KTUU-TV	2	N
	† KTBY	4	
	* KAKM	7	P
	KTVA	11	C
	KIMO	13	A
Bethel	* KYUK-TV	4	P
Fairbanks	KTTU-TV	2	AN
	† ----	7	
	* KUAC-TV	9	P
	KTVF	11	CA
	† KATN	13	
Juneau	†* KTOO-TV	3	
	KJUD	8	NA
North Pole	KJNP-TV	4	
Sitka	KTNL	13	CA

Arizona

City	Station		
Flagstaff	KNAZ	2	N
Phoenix	KTVK	3	A
	KPHO-TV	5	
	* KAET	8	P
	KTSP-TV	10	C
	KPNX-TV	12	N
	KNXV-TV	15	
	KPAZ-TV	21	
	KTVW-TV	33	
Prescott	KUSK	7	
Sierra Vista	† KCCA	58	
Tucson	KVOA-TV	4	N
	* KUAT-TV	6	P
	KGUN-TV	9	A
	KOLD-TV	13	C
	† KDTU	18	
	† ----	27	
	† ----	40	
Yuma	† KCAA	11	
	KYEL-TV	13	NC

Arkansas

City	Station		
Arkadelphia	* KETG	9	P
El Dorado	KTVE	10	A
Fayetteville	* KAFT	13	P
	KTVP	29	A
Ft. Smith	KFSM-TV	5	C
	KPOM-TV	24	N
	KHBS	40	A
Hot Springs	† ----	26	
Jonesboro	KAIT-TV	8	A
	* KTEJ	19	P
Little Rock	* KETS	2	P
	KARK-TV	4	N
	KATV	7	A
	KTHV	11	C
	† KLRT	16	
Mountain View	* KEMV	6	
Newark	†* KLEP	17	
Pine Bluff	† KMJD-TV	38	

California

City	Station		
Anaheim	† KDOC	56	
Bakersfield	KPWR-TV	17	N
	KERO-TV	23	C
	KBAK-TV	29	A
Chico	KHSL-TV	12	C
	† KCPM	24	
Clovis	† ----	43	
Concord	† KBSC-TV	42	
Corona	KBSC-TV	52	
Cotati	†* KRCB-TV	22	
El Centro	KECY	9	C
Eureka	KIEM-TV	3	CN
	KVIQ-TV	6	A
	* KEET	13	P
Fresno	* KMTF	18	P
	KSEE	24	N
	KFSN-TV	30	C
	KJEO	47	A
	KAIL	53	
Hanford	KFTV	21	
Huntington Beach	* KOCE-TV	50	P
Los Angeles	KNXT	2	C
	KNBC	4	N
	KTLA	5	
	KABC-TV	7	A
	KHJ-TV	9	
	KTTV	11	
	KCOP	13	
	KWHY-TV	22	
	* KCET	28	P
	KMEX-TV	34	
	* KLCS	58	P
	†* KDDE	68	
Modesto	KCSO	19	
Monterey	KMST	46	C
Ontario	KIHS-TV	46	
Oroville	† ----	28	
Oxnard	† KTIE	63	
Palm Springs	KMIR-TV	36	N
	KESQ	42	A
Redding	KRCR-TV	7	A
	* KIXE-TV	9	P
Riverside	† ----	62	
Sacramento	KCRA-TV	3	N
	* KVIE	6	P
	KXTV	10	C
	KRBK	31	
	KTXL	40	
Salinas	KSBW-TV	8	N
	KCBA	35	A
San Bernardino	KSCI	18	
	* KVCR-TV	24	P
	† KHOF-TV	30	
San Diego	KFMB-TV	8	C
	KGTV	10	A
	* KPBS-TV	15	P
	KCST-TV	39	N
	KUSI	51	
	KTTY	69	
San Francisco	KTVU	2	
	KRON-TV	4	N
	KPIX	5	C
	KGO-TV	7	A
	* KQED	9	P
	* KDTV	14	
	KTZO	20	
	KTSF-TV	26	
	* KQEC	32	P
	† KVOF-TV	38	
	KBHK-TV	44	
San Jose	KNTV	11	A
	KICU	36	
	KSTS	48	
	* KTEH-TV	54	P
	† KLXV	65	
San Luis Obispo	KSBY-TV	6	N
	† ----	33	
San Mateo	* KCSM-TV	60	P
Santa Ana	KTBN-TV	40	
Santa Barbara	KEYT	3	A
Santa Maria	KCOY-TV	12	C
Santa Rosa	KFTY	50	
Stockton	KOVR	13	A
	† KSCH	58	
	† ----	64	
Visalia	KMPH	26	

Colorado

City	Station		
Boulder	† KTVJ	14	
Broomfield	* KBDI-TV	12	P
Colorado Springs	KKTV	11	C
	KRDO-TV	13	A
	† KXRM-TV	21	
Denver	KWGN-TV	2	
	KCNC-TV	4	N
	* KRMA-TV	6	P
	KMGH-TV	7	C
	KBTV	9	A
	† KDVR	31	
Durango	KREZ-TV	6	
Glenwood Springs	KCWS	3	
Grand Junction	KREX-TV	5	C
	KJCT	8	A
Montrose	KREY-TV	10	S
Pueblo	KOAA-TV	5	N
	* KTSC	8	P
Sterling	KTVS	3	CA

Connecticut

City	Station		
Bridgeport	† WBCT	43	
	* WEDW	49	P
Hartford	WFSB	3	C
	WHCT-TV	18	
	* WEDH	24	P
		61	
New Britain	WVIT	30	
New Haven	WTNH-TV	8	A
	† WTVU	59	
	* WEDY	65	P
New London	† WLCT	26	
Norwich	* WEDN	53	P
Waterbury	WATR-TV	20	

Delaware

City	Station		
Seaford	* WDPB	64	P
Wilmington	* WHTY-TV	12	P
	† WDVI	61	

District of Columbia

City	Station		
Washington	WRC-TV	4	N
	WTTG	5	

Washington (Cont)
WJLA-TV 7 A
WDVM-TV 9 C
WDCA-TV 20
* WETA-TV 26 P
* WHMM 32 P
† WCQR 50

Florida

Clearwater
WCLF 22
Cocoa
†* ---- 18
WTGL 52
Daytona Beach
WESH-TV 2 N
† ---- 26
Ft. Lauderdale
WKID 51
Ft. Myers
WINK-TV 11 C
WBBH-TV 20 N
* WSFP-TV 30
Ft. Pierce
WTVX 34 C
Ft. Walton Beach
† WPAN 35
† WQAC 53
Gainesville
* WUFT 5 P
WCJB 20 A
Hollywood
† ---- 69
Jacksonville
WJXT 4 C
* WJCT 7 P
WTLV 12 A
WJKS-TV 17 N
WAWS-TV 30
WNFT 47
Key West
† WQHJ
† WTKW 16
Lakeland
† ---- 32
Leesburg
WIYE 55
Melbourne
† WMOD 43
† WSCT 56
Miami
#* WPBT 2 P
#* WTHS-TV 2 P
WTVJ 4 C
WCIX 6
WSVN 7 N
WPLG 10 A
* WLRN-TV 17 P
WLTV 23
† WBFS-TV 33
WDZL 39
WHFT 45
Naples
WEVU 26 A
Ocala
† WBSP 51
Orange Park
† ---- 25
Orlando
WCPX 6 C
WFTV 9 A
* WMFE-TV 24 P
WOFL 35
Palm Beach
† WFGC 63
Panama City
WJHG-TV 7 N
WMBB 13 A
† WMJA 28
Pensacola
WEAR-TV 3 A
* WSRE 23 P
† ---- 33
† ---- 44
Sarasota
WXLT-TV 40 A
St. Petersburg
WTSP-TV 10 A

St. Petersburg (Cont)
† ---- 38
WTOG 44
Tallahassee
* WFSU-TV 11 P
WECA 27 A
† WTWC 40
Tampa
* WEDU 3 P
WXFL 8 N
WTVT 13 C
* WUSF-TV 16 P
WFTS 28
† ---- 50
West Palm Beach
WPTV 5 N
WPEC 12 A
WFLX 29
†* WHRS 42 P

Georgia

Albany
WALB-TV 10 N
† WJFT-TV 19
† WTSG 31
Athens
* WGTV 8 P
Atlanta
WSB-TV 2 A
WAGA-TV 5 C
WXIA-TV 11 N
WTBS 17
* WETV 30 P
WATL-TV 36
WANX-TV 46
WVEU 69
Augusta
WJBF 6 A
WRDW-TV 12 C
WATU-TV 26 N
† WXTX 54
Chatsworth
* WCLP-TV 18 P
Cochran
* WDCO-TV 15 P
Columbus
WRBL 3 C
WTVM 9 A
* WJSP-TV 28 P
WLTZ 38 N
† WXTX 54
Dawson
* WACS-TV 25 P
Macon
WMAZ-TV 13 C
WGXA 24 A
WMGT 41 N
Pelham
* WABW-TV 14 P
Savannah
WSAV-TV 3 A
* WVAN-TV 9 P
WTOC-TV 11 C
WJCL 22 N
Thomasville
WCTV 6 C
Toccoa
† WNEG-TV 32
Valdosta
WVGA 44 A
Waycross
* WXGA-TV 8 P
Wrens
* WCES-TV 20 P

Hawaii

Hilo
KGMD 9 S
KHAW-TV 11 S
KHVO 13 S
† KOHA 27
Honolulu
KHON-TV 2 N
KITV 4 A
KGMB-TV 9 C
* KHET 11 P
KIKU-TV 13
† KPRR 14

Honolulu (Cont)
† KHAI-TV 20
KSHO 26
† ---- 32
Kailua
† ---- 6
Wailuku
KGMV 3 S
KAII-TV 7 S
* KMEB 10 S
KMAU 12 S

Idaho

Boise
KBCI-TV 2 C
* KAID 4 P
KTVB 7 N
† KWHP 14
Idaho Falls
KID-TV 3 C
KIFI-TV 8 N
Lewiston
KLEW-TV 3 S
Moscow
* KUID-TV 12 P
Nampa
KIVI 6 A
KTRV 12
Pocatello
KPVI 6 A
* KBGL-TV 10 P
Twin Falls
KMVT 11 CNA

Illinois

Aurora
†# WPWR 60
Bloomington
WBLN 43
Carbondale
* WSIU-TV 8 P
Champaign
WCIA 3 C
WICD 15 N
Chicago
WBBM-TV 2 C
WMAQ-TV 5 N
WLS-TV 7 A
WGN-TV 9
* WTTW 11 P
* WYCC 20 P
WCIU-TV 26
WFLD-TV 32
WCFC-TV 38
WSNS 44
Decatur
WAND 17 A
Freeport
WIFR-TV 23 C
Harrisburg
WSIL-TV 3 A
Jacksonville
†* WJPT 14
Joliet
WFBN 66
Lasalle
† WWTO-TV 35
Marion
WDDD-TV 27
Mc Comb
†* ---- 22
Moline
WQAD-TV 8 A
†* WQPT 24 P
Mount Vernon
WCEE 13
Olney
* WUSI-TV 16 P
Peoria
WRAU-TV 19 A
WEEK-TV 25 N
WMBD-TV 31 C
* WTVP 47 P
Quincy
WGEM-TV 10 N
† WTJR 16
Rock Island
WHBF-TV 4 C

Rockford
WREX-TV 13 A
WTVO 17 N
WQRF-TV 39
Springfield
WICS 20 N
WRSP 55
Urbana
* WILL-TV 12 P
West Chicago
†# WBBS-TV 60

Indiana

Angola
WXJC 63
Bloomington
* WTIU 30 P
Elkhart
WSJV 28 A
Evansville
WTVW 7 A
* WNIN 9 P
WFIE-TV 14 N
WEHT 25 C
WEVV 44
Ft. Wayne
WANE-TV 15 C
WPTA 21 A
WKJG-TV 33 N
WFFT 55
Gary
† WDAI 56
Indianapolis
WTTV 4
WRTV 6 A
WISH-TV 8 C
WTHR 13 N
* WFYI 20 P
WHMB-TV 40
WPDS-TV 59
Lafayette
WLFI-TV 18 C
Muncie
* WIPB 49 P
Richmond
WKOI 43
South Bend
WNDU-TV 16 N
WSBT-TV 22 C
* WNIT 34 P
WHME-TV 46
St. John
† WCAE 50
Terre Haute
WTWO 2 N
WTHI-TV 10 C
†* WISU-TV 26
WBAK-TV 38 A
Vincennes
* WVUT 22 P

Iowa

Ames
WOI-TV 5 A
Cedar Rapids
KGAN 2 C
KCRG-TV 9 A
Council Bluffs
* KBIN 32 P
Davenport
WOC-TV 6 N
† ---- 18
† WDAV 30
Des Moines
KCCI-TV 8 C
* KDIN-TV 11 P
WHO-TV 13 N
KCBR 17
† ---- 63
Dubuque
KDUB-TV 40 A
Ft. Dodge
* KTIN 21 P
Iowa City
* KIIN-TV 12
Mason City
KIMT 3 C

Mason City (Cont)
* KYIN 24 P
Red Oak
* KHIN 36 P
Sioux City
KTIV 4 N
KCAU-TV 9 A
KMEG 14 C
* KSIN 27 P
Waterloo
KWWL 7 N
† ---- 22
* KRIN 32

Kansas
Colby
† KLBY 4
Dodge City
KTVC 6 C
Garden City
KSNG 11 N
KUPK-TV 13 A
Goodland
KLOE-TV 10 S
Great Bend
KCKT 2 N
Hays
KAYS-TV 7 C
* KOOD 9 P
Hutchinson
* KPTS 8 P
KWCH-TV 12 C
Lawrence
† ---- 62
Pittsburg
KOAM-TV 7 C
Salina
† ---- 18
Topeka
* KTWU 11 P
WIBW-TV 13 C
KSNT 27 N
KLDH 49 A
Wichita
KSNW 3 N
KAKE-TV 10 A
†* KPTW 15
† ---- 33

Kentucky
Ashland
* WKAS 25 S
WTSF 61
Beattyville
WLJC 65
Bowling Green
WBKO 13 A
† WQQB 40
* WKGB 53 S
Campbellsville
† WGRB 34
Covington
* WCVN 54 S
Danville
† WDKY-TV 56
Elizabethtown
* WKZT 23 S
Hazard
* WKHA 35 S
WKYH-TV 57 N
Hopkinsville
† WNKJ-TV 51
Lexington
WLEX-TV 18 N
WKYT-TV 27 C
WTVQ 36 A
* WKLE 46 P
† ---- 62
Louisville
WAVE-TV 3 N
WHAS-TV 11 C
* WKPC-TV 15 P
† ---- 21
WLKY 32 A
WDRB-TV 41
* WKMJ 68 S
Madisonville
† WLCN 19

Madisonville (Cont)
* WKMA 35 S
Morehead
* WKMR 38 S
† ---- 67
Murray
* WKMU 21 S
Newport
WXIX-TV 19
Owensboro
* WKOH 31
† WPMJ 48
Owenton
* WKON 52 S
Paducah
WPSD-TV 6 N
* WKPD 29
Paintsville
† ---- 69
Pikeville
* WKPI 22 S
Somerset
† ---- 16
* WKSO 29 S

Louisiana
Alexandria
KALB-TV 5 N
* KLPA 25 P
KLAX-TV 31
Baton Rouge
WBRZ 2 A
WAFB-TV 9 C
* WLPB 27 P
WRBT 33 N
Houma
† ---- 11
Lafayette
KATC 3 A
KLFY-TV 10 C
KADN 15
* KLPB 24 P
Lake Charles
KPLC-TV 7 N
* KLTL-TV 18 P
KVHP 29
Monroe
KNOE-TV 8 C
* KLTM 13 P
New Orleans
WWL-TV 4 C
WDSU-TV 6 N
WVUE 8 A
* WYES-TV 12 P
† WULT-TV 20
WGNO-TV 26
† WLAE-TV 32
† WNOL-TV 38
† ---- 49
Shreveport
KTBS-TV 3 A
KTAL-TV 6 N
KSLA-TV 12 C
* KLTS 24
West Monroe
KARD 14 N
† KMCT-TV 39

Maine
Augusta
* WCBB 10 P
Bangor
WLBZ-TV 2 N
WABI-TV 5 C
WVII-TV 7 A
Biddeford
* WMEG-TV 26 P
Calais
* WMED-TV 13 P
Orono
* WMEB-TV 12 P
Portland
WCSH-TV 6 N
WMTW-TV 8 A
WGME 13 C
† ---- 38
† WHSI 51

Presque Isle
WAGM-TV 8 C
* WMEM-TV 10 P

Maryland
Annapolis
* WAPB 22 P
Baltimore
WMAR-TV 2 N
WBAL-TV 11 C
WJZ-TV 13 A
† WKJL 24
WBFF 45
WNUV-TV 54
* WMPB 67 P
Hagerstown
WHAG-TV 25 N
* WWPB 31 P
Salisbury
WBOC-TV 16 CN
* WCPB 28 P
WMDT 47 A

Massachusetts
Adams
WCDC 19 A
Boston
* WGBH-TV 2 P
WBZ-TV 4 N
WCVB-TV 5 A
WNEV-TV 7 C
WXNE 25
WSBK-TV 38
* WGBX-TV 44
WQTV 68
Cambridge
WLVI-TV 56
Greenfield
† WRLP 32
Lawrence
† ---- 62
Marlborough
WGTR-TV 66
New Bedford
WLNE 6 C
† WFDG 28
Pittsfield
† ---- 51
Springfield
WWLP 22 N
WGGB-TV 40 A
* WGBY-TV 57 P
Worcester
WSMW-TV 27

Michigan
Alpena
* WCML-TV 6
WBKB-TV 11 C
Ann Arbor
WIHT 31
Battle Creek
WUHQ-TV 41 A
Bay City
WNEM-TV 5 N
* WUCM-TV 19 P
† WVCI 61
Cadillac
WWTV 9 C
†* WCMV 27
Cheboygan
WTOM-TV 4 N
Detroit
WJBK-TV 2 C
WDIV 4 N
WXYZ-TV 7 A
WXON 20
WKBD 50
* WTVS 56 P
WGPR-TV 62
East Lansing
* WKAR-TV 23 P
Escanaba
WJMN-TV 3 A
Flint
WJRT-TV 12 A
* WFUM 28 P

Grand Rapids
WOTV 8 N
WZZM-TV 13 A
WXMI 17
* WGVC 35 P
Iron Mountain
† WIIM-TV 8
Jackson
WILX-TV 10 N
Kalamazoo
WKZO-TV 3 C
†* ---- 52
† WLLA 64
Lansing
WJIM-TV 6 C
* WFSL 47
† WLAJ 53
Manistee
†* WCMW 21
Marquette
WLUC-TV 6 CA
* WNMU-TV 13 P
Mt. Pleasant
* WCMU-TV 14 P
Muskegon
† WMKT 54
Saginaw
WEYI-TV 25 C
† WAQP 49
Sault Ste. Marie
WGTQ 8 S
WWUP-TV 10 C
Traverse City
WPBN-TV 7 N
WGTU 29 A

Minnesota
Alexandria
KCMT 7 CA
Appleton
* KWCM-TV 10 P
Austin
KAAL 6 A
* KAVT-TV 15 P
Bemidji
* KAWE 9 P
† KXBJ 26
Duluth
KDLH-TV 3 C
* WDSE-TV 8 P
WDIO-TV 10 A
Hibbing
WIRT 13 A
International Falls
† KITF 11
Mankato
KEYC-TV 12 C
Minneapolis
WCCO-TV 4 C
KMSP-TV 9
WTCN-TV 11 N
WFBT 29
Rochester
KTTC 10 N
† KXLT 47
St Cloud
KXLI 41
St. Paul
* KTCA-TV 2 P
KSTP-TV 5 A
* KTCI-TV 17 P
KTMA-TV 23
† ---- 45
Thief River Falls
† KONY 10
Walker
KNMT 12 CA

Mississippi
Ackerman
* WMAB 2
Biloxi
WLOX-TV 13 A
* WMAH 19
Booneville
* WMAE 12
Brookhaven
* WMAU 17

Columbus
WCBI-TV 4 C
Greenville
WXVT 15 C
Greenwood
WABG-TV 6 A
⋆ WMAO 23
Gulfport
† ---- 25
Hattiesburg
WDAM-TV 7 N
† WLHT 22
Jackson
WLBT-TV 3 N
WJTV 12 C
WAPT 16 A
⋆ WMAA 29 P
† WDBD 40
Laurel
† ---- 18
Meridian
WTOK-TV 11 A
⋆ WMAW 14
WHTV 24 CN
WLBM 30
Natchez
† ---- 48
Oxford
⋆ WMAV 18
Tupelo
WTVA 9 NA
West Point
WVSB 27

Missouri

Cape Girardeau
KFVS-TV 12 C
KBSI 23
Columbia
KOMU-TV 8 NA
KCBJ-TV 17 N
Hannibal
KHQA-TV 7 C
Jefferson City
KRCG 13 C
† KBBM-TV 36
Joplin
KODE-TV 12 A
KSNF 16 N
Kansas City
WDAF-TV 4 N
KCTV 5 C
KMBC-TV 9 A
⋆ KCPT 19 P
KSHB-TV 41
KYFC 50
† KEKR 62
Kirksville
KTVO 3 A
Poplar Bluff
KPOB-TV 15 A
Sikeston
† KDCQ 45
Springfield
KYTV 3 N
KOLR-TV 10 C
⋆ KOZK 21 P
KMTC 27 A
KSPR 33
St. Joseph
KQTV 2 A
† ---- 16
† KTAJ 16
St. Louis
KTVI 2 A
KMOX-TV 4 C
KSDK 5 N
⋆ KETC 9 P
KPLR-TV 11
† KNLC 24
KDNL-TV 30
†⋆ KUCU 40
Warrensburg
⋆ KMOS-TV 6 P

Montana

Billings
KTVQ 2 CN
Billings (Cont)
KULR-TV 8 A
Bozeman
† KCTZ 7
†⋆ ---- 9
Butte
KXLF-TV 4 AC
KTVM 6 N
Glendive
KXGN-TV 5 C
Great Falls
KRTV 3 CN
KFBB-TV 5 AC
Hardin
KOUS-TV 4 N
Helena
KTVG 12 N
Kalispell
KCFW-TV 9 N
Miles City
KYUS-TV 3 N
Missoula
KPAX-TV 8 AC
KECI-TV 13 N
† 17

Nebraska

Albion
KBGT-TV 8 A
Alliance
⋆ KTNE-TV 13 S
Bassett
⋆ KMNE-TV 7 S
Grand Island
KGIN-TV 11 C
Hastings
KHAS-TV 5 N
⋆ KHNE-TV 29 S
Hayes Center
KWNB-TV 6 A
Kearney
KHGI-TV 13 A
Lexington
⋆ KLNE-TV 3 S
Lincoln
KOLN-TV 10 C
⋆ KUON-TV 12 P
†⋆ KGNQ 51
Mc Cook
KSNK 8 N
Merriman
⋆ KRNE-TV 12 S
Norfolk
⋆ KXNE-TV 19 S
North Platte
KNOP-TV 2 N
⋆ KPNE-TV 9 S
Omaha
KMTV 3 N
WOWT 6 C
KETV 7 A
⋆ KYNE-TV 26 S
Scottsbluff
KDUH-TV 4 N
KSTF 10 CA
† ---- 16
Superior
KSNB-TV 4 A

Nevada

Henderson
KVVU 5
Las Vegas
KVBC 3 N
KLAS-TV 8 C
⋆ KLVX 10 P
KTNV-TV 13 A
† KRLR 21
Reno
KTVN 2 C
KCRL-TV 4 N
KNPB 5
KOLO-TV 8 A
KAME-TV 21
† KREN 43
Winnemucca
† KQJA 7

New Hampshire

Berlin
⋆ WEDB-TV 40 P
Concord
† WNHT 21
Derry
† WNDS 50
Durham
⋆ WENH-TV 11 P
Hanover
⋆ WHED-TV 15
Keene
⋆ WEKW-TV 52
Littleton
⋆ WLED-TV 49 P
Manchester
WMUR-TV 9 A
Merrimack
† ---- 60

New Jersey

Atlantic City
WWAC-TV 53
Camden
⋆ WNJS 23
Linden
WNJU-TV 47
Montclair
⋆ WNJM 50
New Brunswick
⋆ WNJB 58
Newark
WWHT 68
Paterson
WXTV 41
Secaucus
WOR-TV 9
Trenton
⋆ WNJT 52 P
Vineland
WRBV 65
Wildwood
WAAT 40 N

New Mexico

Albuquerque
KOB-TV 4 N
⋆ KNME-TV 5 P
KOAT-TV 7 A
KGGM-TV 13 C
KGSW 14
KNAT 23
Carlsbad
KAVE-TV 6 A
† KKSG 25
Clovis
KMCC 12 A
Farmington
KOBF 12 N
Hobbs
† KHFT 29
Las Cruces
⋆ KRWG-TV 22 P
† ---- 43
Portales
⋆ KENW 3 P
Roswell
KSWS-TV 8 N
KBIM-TV 10 C
Sante Fe
† KSAF-TV 2
† ---- 11
Silver City
† ---- 6

New York

Albany
WTEN 10 A
WNYT 13 N
WXXA 23
Binghamton
WBNG-TV 12 C
WMGC-TV 34 A
WICZ-TV 40 N
⋆ WERZ 46 P
Buffalo
WGRZ 2 N
WIVB-TV 4 C
Buffalo (Cont)
WKBW-TV 7 A
⋆ WNED-TV 17 P
WUTV 29
† ---- 49
Elmira
WETM-TV 18 N
WENY-TV 36 A
Garden City
⋆ WLIW 21 P
Ithaca
† ---- 52
Kingston
† WTZA 23
† ---- 63
New York
WCBS-TV 2 C
WNBC-TV 4 N
WNEW-TV 5
WABC-TV 7 A
WOR-TV 9
WPIX 11
⋆ WNET 13 P
⋆ WNYE-TV 25 P
⋆ WNYC-TV 31 P
Norwood
⋆ WNPI 18 P
Plattsburgh
WPTZ 5 N
⋆ WCFE-TV 57 P
Poughkeepsie
† WTBY 54
Riverhead
† WLIG 55
Rochester
WROC-TV 8 N
WHEC-TV 10 C
WOKR 13 A
⋆ WXXI 21 P
WUHF 31
Schenectady
WRGB 6 N
⋆ WMHT 17 P
† WUSV 45
Smithtown
WSNL-TV 67
Syracuse
WSTM-TV 3 N
WTVH 5 C
WIXT 9 A
⋆ WCNY-TV 24 P
† WFWY 43
† WKAF 62
Utica
WKTV 2 N
WUTR 20 A
† WTUV 33
Watertown
WWNY-TV 7 CN
⋆ WNPE 16 P

North Carolina

Asheville
WLOS-TV 13 A
WHNS 21
⋆ WUNF-TV 33 S
Burlington
† WRDG 16
Chapel Hill
⋆ WUNC-TV 4 P
Charlotte
WBTV 3 C
WSOC-TV 9 A
WCCB 18 A
WPCQ-TV 36 N
⋆ WTVI 42 P
Columbia
⋆ WUND-TV 2 S
Concord
⋆ WUNG-TV 58 S
Durham
WTVD 11 C
WPTF-TV 28 N
Fayetteville
WKFT 40
† WFCT 62
Forest City
† WSAY-TV 66

Station	Channel	Network
Greensboro		
WFMY-TV	2	C
WGGT	48	
WLXI-TV	61	
Greenville		
WNCT-TV	9	C
† ----	14	
★ WUNK-TV	25	S
† ----	38	
Greeville		
WLXI-TV	61	
Hickory		
WHKY-TV	14	N
High Point		
WGHP-TV	8	A
† WIUW	67	
Jacksonville		
★ WUNM-TV	19	
Lexington		
† WEJC	20	
Linville		
★ WUNE-TV	17	S
New Bern		
WCTI	12	A
Raleigh		
WRAL-TV	5	A
WLFL-TV	22	
Washington		
WITN-TV	7	N
Wilmington		
WWAY-TV	3	A
WECT	6	N
† WJKA	26	
★ WUNJ-TV	39	S
Winston Salem		
WXII	12	N
★ WUNL-TV	26	S
WJTM	45	

North Dakota

Station	Channel	Network
Bismarck		
★ KBME	3	P
†★ KBME	3	
KFYR-TV	5	N
KXMB-TV	12	CA
Bismark		
★ KBME	3	
Devils Lake		
WDAZ-TV	8	N
Dickinson		
KNDX	2	C
KQCD-TV	7	AN
†★ KDSE	9	
Fargo		
WDAY-TV	6	N
KTHI-TV	11	A
★ KFME	13	P
KVNJ	15	
Grand Forks		
★ KGFE	2	S
Minot		
★ KSRE	6	
KMOT	10	N
KXMC-TV	13	C
Pembina		
† KWBA	12	
Valley City		
KXJB-TV	4	C
Williston		
†★ KWSE	4	
KUMV-TV	8	N
KXMD-TV	11	CA

Ohio

Station	Channel	Network
Akron		
WAKR-TV	23	A
★ WEAO	49	
† ----	56	
Alliance		
★ WNEO-TV	45	P
Athens		
★ WOUB-TV	20	P
Bowling Green		
★ WBGU-TV	27	P
Cambridge		
★ WOUC-TV	44	P
Canton		
WDTN	2	A
Canton (Cont)		
KDLI	17	
WOAC	67	
Cincinnati		
WLWT	5	N
WCPO-TV	9	C
WKRC-TV	12	A
★ WCET	48	P
WBTI	64	
Cleveland		
WKYC-TV	3	N
WEWS	5	A
WJKW-TV	8	C
★ WVIZ-TV	25	P
WCLQ-TV	61	
Columbus		
WCMH-TV	4	N
WTVN-TV	6	A
WBNS-TV	10	C
† WTTE	28	
★ WOSU-TV	34	P
Dayton		
WHIO-TV	7	C
★ WPTD	16	P
WKEF	22	N
† ----	45	
Defiance		
† ----	65	
Lima		
WLIO	35	N
WTLW	44	
Lorain		
WUAB-TV	43	
Narajito		
† ----	64	
Newark		
WSFJ	51	
Oxford		
★ WPTO	14	P
Portsmouth		
★ WPBO-TV	42	
Sandusky		
WGGN-TV	52	
Shaker Heights		
† WOIO	19	
Springfield		
WTJC	26	
Steubenville		
WTOV-TV	9	NA
Toledo		
WTOL-TV	11	C
WTVG	13	N
WDHO-TV	24	A
★ WGTE-TV	30	P
† WDMA-TV	36	
Youngstown		
WFMJ-TV	21	N
WKBN-TV	27	C
WYTV	33	A
Zanesville		
WHIZ-TV	18	N

Oklahoma

Station	Channel	Network
Ada		
KTEN	10	A
Ardmore		
KXII	12	NC
Bartlesville		
† KDOR	17	
Cheyenne		
†★ KWET	12	
Enid		
† KEQO	20	
Eufaula		
★ KOET	3	
Lawton		
KSWO-TV	7	A
KQOL-TV	45	
Muskogee		
† ----	19	
Norman		
† ----	46	
Oklahoma City		
KTVY	4	N
KOCO-TV	5	A
KWTV	9	C
★ KETA	13	P
KTBO	14	
Oklahoma City (Cont)		
KOKH-TV	25	
KGMC	34	
KAUT	43	
† KSBI	52	
† ----	62	
Sayre		
KVIJ-TV	8	S
Shawnee		
† KCVT	30	
Tulsa		
KJRH	2	N
KOTV	6	C
KTUL-TV	8	A
★ KOED-TV	11	P
KOKI	23	
KGCT-TV	41	
† KBJH	47	

Oregon

Station	Channel	Network
Bend		
★ KOAB-TV	3	P
KTVZ	21	CN
Coos Bay		
KCBY	11	N
Corvallis		
★ KOAC-TV	7	P
Eugene		
KEZI-TV	9	A
KVAL	13	C
KMTR	16	N
Klamath Falls		
KOTI	2	C
La Grande		
★ KTVR	13	
Medford		
KOBI	5	C
★ KSYS	8	P
KTVL	10	C
† KDRV	12	
Portland		
KATU	2	A
KOIN-TV	6	C
KGW-TV	8	N
†★ KOAP-TV	10	P
KPTV	12	
† KTDZ	24	
Roseburg		
KPIC	4	S
Salem		
† KECH	22	

Pennsylvania

Station	Channel	Network
Allentown		
★ WLVT-TV	39	P
WFMZ-TV	69	
Altoona		
WTAJ-TV	10	C
WOPC	23	A
Clearfield		
★ WPSX-TV	3	P
Erie		
WICU-TV	12	N
WJET-TV	24	A
WSEE	35	C
★ WQLN	54	P
Greensburg		
WPCB-TV	40	
Harrisburg		
WHP-TV	21	C
WHTM-TV	27	A
★ WITF-TV	33	P
Hazleton		
† WERF	56	
Johnstown		
WJAC-TV	6	N
WFAT	19	
Lancaster		
WGAL-TV	8	N
WLYH-TV	15	C
Lebanon		
† WGGF	59	
Philadelphia		
KYW-TV	3	N
WPVI	6	A
WCAU-TV	10	C
WPHL-TV	17	
WTAF-TV	29	
Philadelphia (Cont)		
WWSG	57	
Pittsburgh		
KDKA-TV	2	C
WTAE-TV	4	A
WPXI	11	N
★ WQED	13	P
★ WQEX	16	P
WPTT-TV	22	
WPGH-TV	53	
Reading		
WTVE	51	
Red Lion		
WGCB-TV	49	
Scranton		
WNEP-TV	16	A
WDAU-TV	22	C
★ WVIA-TV	44	P
State College		
† ----	29	
Wilkes Barre		
WBRE-TV	28	N
† WSWB	38	
York		
WPMT	43	

Puerto Rico

Station	Channel	Network
Aguadilla		
WOLE-TV	12	
† ----	32	
WVEO	44	
Arelibo		
WATX	54	
Caguas		
WKBM-TV	11	
†★ WUJA	58	
Cidra		
† WCNT	46	
Fajardo		
† WSTE	13	
† WMTJ	40	
Humacao		
† ----	68	
Mayaguez		
★ WIPM-TV	3	P
WORA-TV	5	
† WTRA	16	
† WNJX-TV	22	
Narajito		
† WART	22	
† ----	64	
Ponce		
WLUZ	7	
WSUR-TV	9	
† WTIN	14	
† WNRP	20	
† ----	48	
San German		
† WUIA-TV	42	
San Juan		
WKAQ-TV	2	
WAPA-TV	4	
★ WIPR-TV	6	P
† WSJU	18	
† WSJN	24	
† WRWR	30	
San Sebastian		
† ----	38	

Rhode Island

Station	Channel	Network
Providence		
WJAR-TV	10	N
WPRI-TV	12	A
★ WSBE-TV	36	P
WSTG	64	

South Carolina

Station	Channel	Network
Allendale		
★ WEBA-TV	14	
Anderson		
WAXA	40	
Beaufort		
★ WJWJ-TV	16	
Charleston		
WCBD	2	A
WCIV	4	N
WCSC-TV	5	C
★ WITV	7	

Columbia
WIS-TV 10 N
WLTX 19 C
WOLO-TV 25 A
★ WRLK-TV 35
WCCT-TV 57
Conway
★ WHMC 23
Florence
WBTW 13 C
WPDE-TV 15 A
† WSMF 21
★ WJPM-TV 33
Greenville
WYFF-TV 4 N
WGGS-TV 16
★ WNTV-TV 29
Greenwood
† WCGC 48
Hardeeville
WTGS 28
Myrtle Beach
† WGSE 43
Rock Hill
† ---- 30
Spartanburg
WSPA-TV 7 C
★ WRET-TV 39 P
Sumter
★ WRJA-TV 27 P

South Dakota

Aberdeen
KABY-TV 9 A
★ KDSD-TV 16 P
Brookings
★ KESD-TV 8 P
Eagle Butte
★ KPSD-TV 13
Lead
KIVV-TV 5 C
KHSD-TV 11 N
Lowry
★ KQSD-TV 11
Martin
★ KZSD-TV 8
Mitchell
KXON 5 A
Pierre
KPRY-TV 4 A
★ KTSD-TV 10
Rapid City
KOTA-TV 3 N
KEVN-TV 7 AC
★ KBHE-TV 9
Reliance
KPLO-TV 6 S
Sioux Falls
KELO-TV 11 C
KSFY-TV 13 A
Vermillion
★ KUSD-TV 2 P
Watertown
KDLO-TV 3 S

Tennessee

Chattanooga
WRCB-TV 3 N
WTVC 9 A
WDEF-TV 12 C
★ WTCI 45 P
WDSI-TV 61
Cookeville
★ WCTE 22
† WKWR 28
Crossville
WINT 20
Greenville
† WOQF 39
Jackson
WBBJ-TV 7 A
† WUAA 16
Johnson City
WJHL-TV 11 C
Kingsport
WKPT-TV 19 A
Knoxville
WATE-TV 6 A

Knoxville (Cont)
WBIR-TV 10 C
WTVK 26 N
† WKCH 43
Lexington
★ WLJT-TV 11 P
Memphis
WREG-TV 3 C
WMC-TV 5 N
★ WKNO-TV 10 P
WHBQ-TV 13 A
WPTY-TV 24
† WMKW 30
Murfreesboro
† WFYZ 39
Nashville
WKRN-TV 2 A
WSMV 4 N
WTVF 5 C
★ WDCN 8 P
WZTV 17
† WCAY-TV 30
Sneedville
★ WSJK-TV 2 P
Tullahoma
† WBGY-TV 64

Texas

Abilene
KRBC-TV 9 N
† KSUZ-TV 15
KTAB-TV 32
Alvin
† ---- 67
Amarillo
KAMR 4 N
KVII-TV 7 A
KFDA-TV 10 C
KJTV 14
Austin
KTBC-TV 7 C
★ KLRU 18
KVUE-TV 24 A
KTVV 36 N
† KBVO 42
Beaumont
KFDM-TV 6 C
KBMT 12 A
Belton
★ KNCT 46 P
Big Spring
KWAB 4 N
Brownsville
KVEO 23 N
Bryan
KBTX-TV 3 AC
College Station
★ KAMU 15 P
Corpus Christi
KIII 3 A
KRIS-TV 6 N
KZTV 10 C
★ KEDT 16 P
KORO 28
† ---- 38
Dallas
KDFW-TV 4 C
WFAA-TV 8 A
★ KERA-TV 13 P
KTWS 27
KNBN-TV 33
KXTX 39
Del Rio
† ---- 10
Denison
† KOAV 20
El Paso
KDBC-TV 4 C
KVIA-TV 7 A
KTSM-TV 9 N
★ KCOS 13
KCIK 14
KINT-TV 26
Farwell
† ---- 18
Ft. Worth
KXAS-TV 5 N
KTVT 11

Ft. Worth (Cont)
KTXA 21
Garland
† ---- 23
Gaveston
† ---- 48
Harlingen
KGBT-TV 4 C
†★ KLUJ 44
★ KZLN 60
Houston
KPRC-TV 2 N
★ KUHT 8 P
KHOU-TV 11 C
KTRK 13 A
†★ ---- 14
KTXH 20
KRIV-TV 26
KHTV 39
Irving
† KLTJ 49
Kerrville
† ---- 35
Laredo
KGNS-TV 8 N
KVTV 13 C
† ---- 27
Longview
KLMG 51
Lubbock
★ KTXT-TV 5 P
KCBD-TV 11 N
KLBK-TV 13 C
KAMC 28 A
KJAA 34
Lufkin
KTRE-TV 9 AN
Marshall
† KMLT-TV 35
Mc Allen
† ---- 48
Midland
KDCD-TV 18
Monahans
KTPX 9 N
Nacogdoches
† KDOG 19
Negerland
† KTGC 21
Odessa
KMID-TV 2 A
KOSA-TV 7 C
† ---- 24
Paris
† KLPH 42
Port Arthur
KJAC-TV 4 N
San Angelo
KACB-TV 3 N
† KIDV 6
KLST 8 C
San Antonio
KMOL-TV 4 N
KENS-TV 5 C
★ KLRN 9 P
KSAT-TV 12 A
† ---- 29
KWEX-TV 41
Sweetwater
KTXS-TV 12 A
Temple
KCEN-TV 6 N
Tyler
KLTV 7 A
† KCKU 14
Victoria
KXIX 19 A
KAVU 25 N
† KVTX 31
Waco
KWTX-TV 10 AC
† KWKT 44
Weslaco
KRGV-TV 5 A
Wichita Falls
KFDX-TV 3 N
KAUZ-TV 6 C
★ KIDZ-TV 24

Utah

Ogden
† ---- 24
† KOOG-TV 30
Provo
★ KBYU-TV 11 P
Salt Lake City
KUTV 2 N
KTVX 4 A
KSL-TV 5 C
★ KUED 7 P
KSTU 20

Vermont

Burlington
WCAX-TV 3 C
WVNY 22 A
★ WETK 33 P
Hartford
WNNE 31 N
Rutland
★ WVER 28
St. Johnsbury
★ WVTB 20
Windsor
★ WVTA 41

Virgin Islands

Charlotte Amalie
WBNB-TV 10 CN
★ WJTX-TV 12 P
Christiansted
WSVI 8 A
† ---- 15

Virginia

Annandale
★ WNVT 53 P
Bluefield
† WRJK 40
Bristol
WCYB-TV 5 N
Charlottesville
WVIR-TV 29 N
Fairfax
★ WNVC 56
Harrisonburg
WHSV-TV 3 A
Lynchburg
WSET-TV 13 A
† WJPR 21
Manassas
WTKK 66
Marion
★ WMSY 52 P
Norfolk
WTKR 3 C
WVEC-TV 13 A
★ WHRO-TV 15 P
WTVZ 33
★ WUHX 49
Norton
★ WSVN-TV 47 P
Petersburg
WXEX-TV 8 A
Portsmouth
WAVY-TV 10 N
WYAH-TV 27
Richmond
WTVR-TV 6 C
WWBT 12 N
★ WCVE-TV 23 P
WRLH 35
★ WCVW 57
WTLL 63
Roanoke
WDBJ 7 C
WSLS-TV 10 N
★ WBRA-TV 15 P
† WEFC 27
† ---- 38
Staunton
★ WVPT 51 P

Washington

Anacortes
† ---- 24

Bellingham
KVOS-TV 12 C
Centralia
KCKA 15
Everett
† ---- 16
Kennewick
KVEW 42 S
Pasco
KEPR-TV 19 C
Pullman
* KWSU-TV 10 P
Richland
KNDU 25 N
Seattle
KOMO-TV 4 A
KING-TV 5 N
KIRO-TV 7 C
* KCTS-TV 9 P
† KTTZ 22
Spokane
KREM-TV 2 C
KXLY-TV 4 A
KHQ-TV 6 N
* KSPS-TV 7 P
† KSKN 22
KAYU 28
Tacoma
KSTW 11
KCPQ 13
KQFB 20
* KTPS 28 P
Vancouver
† KPDX 49
Walla Walla
† KOBK 14
Wenatchee
† KWCT 27
Yakima
KNDO-TV 23 N
KIMA-TV 29 C
KAPP 35 A
* KYVE-TV 47 P

West Virginia

Bluefield
WVVA 6 N
Charleston
WCHS-TV 8 C
WVAH 23
Clarksburg
WBOY-TV 12 N
WLYJ 46
Grandview
* WSWP-TV 9 P
Huntington
WSAZ-TV 3 N
WOWK 13 A
* WPBY 33 P
Morgantown
* WNPB 24 P
Oak Hill
WOAY-TV 4 A
Parkersburg
WTAP-TV 15 N
† ---- 39
Weston
WDTV 5 C
Wheeling
WTRF-TV 7 CA

Wisconsin

Appleton
† WBUD 32
Eau Claire
WEAU-TV 13 N
WQOW-TV 18 A
Green Bay
WBAY-TV 2 C
WFRV-TV 5 A
WLUK-TV 11
WLRE 26
* WPNE 38 P
Kanosha
† ---- 55
La Crosse
WKBT 8 C
WXOW-TV 19 A
La Crosse (Cont)
† WWQI 25
* WHLA-TV 31 P
Madison
WISC-TV 3 C
WMTV 15 N
* WHA-TV 21 P
WKOW-TV 27 A
† WMSN-TV 47
Marshfield
† WWTL 39
Menomonie
* WHWC-TV 28 P
Milwaukee
WTMJ-TV 4 N
WITI-TV 6 C
* WMVS 10 P
WISN-TV 12 A
WVTV 18
WCGV-TV 24
† WVCY 30
* WMVT 36
Oshkosh
† ---- 22
Park Falls
* WLEF-TV 36
Racine
† WJJA 49
† ---- 55
Rhinelander
WAEO-TV 12 N
Superior
KBJR-TV 6 N
Suring
† WSCO 14
Tomah
† WTMB-TV 43
Wausau
WSAW 7 C
WAOW-TV 9 A
* WHRM-TV 20 P

Wyoming

Casper
KTWO-TV 2 AN
KCWY-TV 14 C
Cheyenne
KYCU-TV 5 C
† KLWY 27
Lander
* KCWC-TV 4 P
KOWY 5 CR
Rawlins
† KRWY 11
Riverton
KTNW 10 N
Rock Springs
KWWY 13 C
Sheridan
KSGW-TV 12 N

CANADA

Alberta

Ashmont
CFRN-TV-4 12 S
Athabasca
CBXT-1 8 S
Bonneville
CKSA-TV-2 6 S
Calgary
CFAC-TV 2
CFCN-TV 4 X
CBRT 9 Y
Coronation
CKRD-TV-1 10 S
Drumheller
CFCN-TV-1 12 S
Edmonton
CFRN-TV 3 X
CBXT 5 Y
CBXFT 11 Z
CITV 13
Ft. Mc Murray
CBXFT-6 11
Grand Prairie
CBXAT 10 Y
CFRN-TV-1 13 S
CBXFT-8 19
High Prairie
CBXAT-2 2 S
CFRN-TV-8 18
Lethbridge
CFAC-TV-7 7
CFCN-TV-5 13 S
Lloydminster
CKSA-TV 2 Y
CITL-TV 4
Lougheed
CFRN-TV-7 7 S
Manning
CBXAT-3 12 S
Medicine Hat
CHAT-TV 6 Y
CFCN-TV-8 8 S
Nogales
KZAZ 11
Peace River
CFRN-TV-2 3 S
Pivot
CHAT-TV-1 4 S
Red Deer
CKRD-TV 6 Y
CFRN-TV-6 8 S
Slave Lake
CFRN-TV-9 9
Whitecourt
CBXT-2 9 S

British Columbia

Campbell River
CHEK-TV-5 13 S
Canal Flats
CBUBT-1 12 S
Courtenay
CHAN-TV-4 11 S
Cranbrook
CBUBT 10 Y
Dawson Creek
CJDC-TV 5 Y
Kamloops
CFJC-TV 4 Y
CHKM-TV 6 S
CBUFT-2 50 S
Kelowna
CHBC-TV 2 Y
CHKL-TV 5 S
Oliver
CKKM-TV 3
One Hundred Mile House
CITM-TV 3
Pentilton
CHKL-TV-1 10
Prince George
CKPG-TV 2 Y
CIFG-TV 12
Santa Rosa
CKSR-TV 33
Terrace
CFTK-TV 3 Y
CBUFT-3 11 S
Trail
CKTN-TV 8
CBUAT 11 Y
Vancouver
CBUT 2 Y
CHAN-TV 8 X
CKVU 21
CBUFT 26 Z
Victoria
CHEK-TV 6 X

Manitoba

Brandon
CKYB-TV 4 S
CKX-TV 5 Y
CBWFT-10 21 S
Dauphin
CBWST-TV 8
Fisher Branch
CBWGT 10 Y
Flin Flon
CBWBT 10 Y
Foxwarren
CKX-TV-1 11 S
Lac Du Bonnet
CBWT-2 4 S
Mafeking
CBWYT 2 S
Minnedosa
† CKND-TV-2 2
Ste Rose Du Lac
CBWFT-4 3 S
Winnipeg
CBWFT 3 Z
CBWT 6 Y
CKY-TV 7 X
CKND 9

New Brunswick

Bon Accord
CHSJ-TV-1 6 S
Campbellton
CHCR-TV 4
CKCD-TV 7
Edmundston
CBAFT-2 13 S
Moncton
CKCW-TV 2
CHMT-TV 7
CBAFT 11 Z
St. John
CHSJ-TV 4 Y
CKLT-TV 9
Upsalaquitch Lake
CKAM-TV 12 Y

Newfoundland

Argentia
CJAP-TV 3 X
Baie Verte
CBNAT-1 3 S
Bonne Bay
CBYT-3 2 S
Corner Brook
CBYT 5 Y
CJWN-TV 10 S
Deer Lake
CBYAT 12
Goose Bay
CFLA-TV 8 Y
Grand Bank
CJOX-TV 2
Grand Falls
CJCN-TV 4
CBNAT 11 Y
Labrador City
* CBNLT 13 Y
Marystown
CBNT-3 5 S
Mt. St. Margaret
CBNAT-9 9 S
Placentia
CBNT-2 12 S
Port Rexton
CBNT-1 13 S
St. Anthony
CBNAT-4 6 S
St. John's
CJON-TV 6 X
CBNT 8 Y
Stephenville
CBYT-1 8 S

Northwest Territories

Inuvik
CHAK-TV 6 Y
Pine Point
CBTE-TV 4 Y
Yellowknife
CFYK-TV 8 Y

Nova Scotia

Antigonish
CJCB-TV-2 9 S
Caledonia
CJCH-TV-6 6 S
Canning
CJCH-TV-1 10 S

Cheticamp
- CBIT-2 2 S
- CBHFT-4 10 S

Halifax
- CBHT 3 Y
- CJCH-TV 5 X
- CBHFT 13 Z

Inverness
- CJCB-TV-1 6 S

Mulgrave
- CBHFT-2 7 S
- CBIT-1 12 S

Sheet Harbour
- CBHT-4 11 S

Sydney
- CJCB-TV 4 X
- CBIT 5 Y
- CBHFT-3 13 S

Yarmouth
- CBHFT-1 3 S
- CBHT-3 11 S

Ontario

Bancroft
- CKGN-TV-2 2 S

Barrie
- CKVR-TV 3 Y

Chatham
- CICO-TV-59 59 S

Cornwall
- CJOH-TV-8 8 S

Doseronto
- CJOH-TV-6 6 S

Dryden
- CBWDT 9 Y

Elliot Lake
- CICI-TV-1 3 S
- CKNC-TV-1 7 S
- CBLFT-6 12 S

Ft. Frances
- CBWCT 5 Y

Geraldton
- CBLAT 13 Y

Hamilton
- CHCH-TV 11

Hearst
- CBOFT-2 7 S

Kapuskasing
- CBLFT-4 12 S

Kearns
- CITO-TV-2 11 S

Kenora
- CBWAT 8 Y

Kingston
- CKWS-TV 11 Y

Kitchener
- CKCO-TV 13 X
- CICO-TV-28 28 S

London
- CFPL-TV 10 Y
- CICO-TV-18 18 S

Manitouwadge
- CBLAT-1 8 S

Marathon
- CBLAT-4 11 S

Muskokas
- CKCO-TV-4 11 S

North Bay
- CHNB-TV 4 Y
- CKNY-TV 10 B

Ottawa
- CBOT 4 Y
- CKGN-TV-6 6 S
- CBOFT 9 Z
- CJOH-TV 13 X
- CICO-TV-24 24

Paris
- CKGN-TV 6

Pembroke
- CHRO-TV 5 Y

Peterborough
- CHEX-TV 12 Y

Sarnia
- CKCO-TV-3 42

Sault Ste. Marie
- CKCY-TV 2 B
- CJIC-TV 5 Y
- CICO-TV-20 20

Sturgeon Falls
- CBLFT-1 7 Z

Sudbury
- CICI-TV 5 B
- CKNC-TV 9 Y
- CBLFT-2 13 S
- CICO-TV-19 19 S

Thunder Bay
- CKPR-TV 2
- CHFD-TV 4
- CICO-TV-9 9 S

Timmins
- CICO-TV 3 B
- CFCL-TV 6 Y
- CBLFT-3 9 Z

Toronto
- CBLT 5 Y
- CFTO-TV 9 X
- * CICA-TV 19
- CBLFT 25 Z
- CFMT-TV 47
- CITY-TV 79

Uxbridge
- CKGN-TV-22 22 S

Wawa
- CBLAT-3 9 S

Wiarton
- CKCO-TV-2 2 S

Windsor
- CBET 9 Y
- CICO-TV-32 32 S
- CBEFT 54 Z

Wingham
- CKNX-TV 8 Y

Prince Edward Island

Charlottetown
- CKCW-TV-1 8 S
- CBCT 13 Y

Quebec

Baie-trimite
- CIVF-TV 12

Bearn
- CKRN-TV-3 35 S

Chicoutimi
- CJPM-TV 6
- CIVU-TV 8 B
- CBJET 58 S

Gaspe/norb
- CFER-TV 5

Hull
- CIVO 30 S
- CHOT-TV 40

Iles De La Madeleine
- CBIMT 12 S

Jonquiere
- CKRS-TV 12 Z

La Tuque
- CBVT-2 3 S

Lithiums Mines
- CJDG-TV 7

Malartic
- CFCL-TV-5 5 S

Matane
- CBGAT 9 Z

Mont Laurier
- CBFT-2 3 S

Montreal
- CBFT 2 Z
- CBMT 6 Y
- CFTM-TV 10
- CFCF-TV 12 X
- CIVM-TV 17

New Carlisle
- CHAU-TV 5 Z

Quebec
- CFCM-TV 4
- CKMI-TV 5 Y
- CBVT 11 Z
- CIVQ-TV 15

Rimouski
- CJBR-TV 3 Z
- CFER-TV 11
- CIVR-TV 22

Riviere Du Loup
- CKRT-TV 7 Z
- CIMT-TV 9

Roberval
- CKRS-TV-3 8 S

Rouyn
- CKRN-TV 4 Z
- CIVN-TV 8

Sept Isles
- * CIVG-TV 9
- CFER-TV-1 11 S
- CBST 13 Z

Sherbrooke
- CHLT-TV 7
- CKSH-TV 9 Z
- CIVS-TV 24

Temiscaming
- CBFST-2 12 S

Three Rivers
- CHEM-TV 8 Y
- CKTM-TV 13 Z
- CIVC-TV 45

Val D'or
- CIVA-TV 12

Saskatchewan

Bellegarde
- CBKFT-9 26

Carlyle Lake
- CIEW-TV 7 Z

Colgate
- CKCK-TV-1 12 S

Cypress Hills
- CBCP-TV-2 2 S

Debden
- CBKFT-3 22

Gavelbourg
- CBKFT-6 39

Greenwater Lake
- CKBI-TV-3 4 S

Marquis
- CKMJ-TV 7

Melfort
- CKBQ-TV 2

Moose Jaw
- CBKMT 4 Y

Nipawin
- CBKI-TV-4 10

North Battleford
- CFOC-TV-2 6 S

Pontiex
- CBCP-TV-3 3

Prince Albert
- CKBI-TV 5

Regina
- CKCK-TV 2
- CBKT 9 Y
- CBKFT 13 Z

Saskatoon
- CFQC-TV 8
- CBKST 11 Y
- CKMC-TV 12 S

Shaunavon
- CBCP-TV-1 7 S

St. Brieux
- CBKFT-4 7

Stranraer
- CFQC-TV-1 3 S
- CBKST-1 9 S

Swift Current
- CJFB-TV 5

Willow Bunch
- CKCK-TV-2 6 S
- CBKT-2 10 S

Wynyard
- CHSS-TV 6
- CICC-TV-1 12 S

Yorkton
- CKOS-TV 5 Y
- CICC-TV 10

Zenon Park
- CBKFT-5 21 Z

Yukon Territory

Keno Hill
- CBKHT 13 Y

Whitehorse
- CFWH-TV 6 Y

WEST INDIES

Antigua

St. Johns
- ZAL-TV 10

Bahamas

Freeport
- † 8

Nassau
- ZNS-TV 13

Barbados

St. Thomas
- CBC-TV 3

Bermuda

Hamilton
- ZBF-TV 8 A
- ZBM-TV 10 C

Cuba

Baracoa
- . . . . 7 S

Camaguey
- CMJ-TV 4
- CMJL-TV 6 S

Ciego De Avila
- 2
- CMFD-TV 7 S

Guantanamo
- 13

Havana
- CMBF-TV 2
- 4
- CMQ-TV 6
- 13

Holguin
- CMKJ-TV 3 S
- CMLD-TV 8 S

Matanzas
- CMGQ-TV 9 S
- CMGH-TV 11 S
- CMG-TV 13

Pinar Del Rio
- . . . . 12 S

San Cristobol
- . . . . 7 S

Santa Clara
- CMH-TV 5 S
- CMRA-TV 8

Santiago De Cuba
- CMKU-TV 2 S
- CMLB-TV 5

Dominican Rep.

Romano
- † 12

Santiago
- 2
- 7

Santo Domingo
- HISD-TV 4
- HIN-TV 7
- 9

Haiti

Port Au Prince
- 4VMR 5

Jamaica

Coopers Hill
- . . . . 7 S

Kingston
- 11

Montego Bay
- 11

Morant Point
- 13

Oracabessa
- 12

Port Antonio
- 8

Spur Tree
- 13

Yallahs
- 9

Montserrat

Plymouth

....	7

Netherlands Antilles

Aruba

PJA-TV	13

Curacao

PJC-TV	8

St. Martin

....	8

Trinidad

Port Of Spain

....	2
....	13

Virgin Is. (British)

Roadtown, Tortula, Br V I

ZBTV	5

MEXICO

Baja California

Mexicali

XHBC-TV	3
XHAQ-TV	5

Tijuana

XETV	6
XEWT-TV	12

Baja California Sur

La Paz

XHK-TV	10

Campeche

Campeche

XHAN-TV	12

Chiapas

Tapachula

XHAA-TV	7

Tuxtla

XHTX-TV	8

Chihuahua

Chihuahua

XHCH-TV	2

Chihuahua (Cont)

XHIT-TV	4
XHFI-TV	5

Ciudad Juarez

XEPM-TV	2
XEJ-TV	5

Jimenez

XHBU-TV	8

Parral

XHMA-TV	3

Coahuila

Monclova

XHBW	9

Piedras Negras

XEPN	3

Saltillo

XHAE-TV	5
XHAD-TV	7

Torreon

XHIA-TV	2
XELN-TV	4
XHO-TV	11

Colima

Colima

XHQ-TV	3
XHCC-TV	5
XHBZ-TV	7

Distrito Federal

Mexico City

XEW-TV	2
XHTV	4
XHGC-TV	5
XEX-TV	7
XHTM-TV	8
XEQ-TV	9
* XEIPN-TV	11
XHDF-TV	13

Durango

Durango

XHA-TV	10

Guanajuato

Guanajuato

XEZ-TV	3
XHZ-TV	6

Leon

XHL-TV	10

Guererro

Acapulco

XHAP-TV	2

Chilpancingo

XHAK-TV	12

Jalisco

Guadalajara

XEWO-TV	2
XHG-TV	4
XEHL-TV	6

Michoacan

Morelia

XHKW-TV	10

Nayarit

Tepic

XHCB-TV	10

Nuevo Leon

Monterrey

XEFB-TV	3
XET-TV	6
XHX-TV	10
XHAW-TV	12

Oaxaca

Oaxaca

XHBN-TV	7

Puebla

Puebla

XHP-TV	3

Queretaro

Queretaro

XHTO-TV	9

Sinaloa

Culiacan

XHQTV	3
XHBT-TV	7
XHBL-TV	13

Los Mochis

XHBS-TV	4
XHCG-TV	12

Mazatlan

XHMZ-TV	7
XHOW-TV	12

Sonora

Ciudad Obregon

XHI-TV	2
XHBS-TV	4

Hermosillo

XHCC-TV	5
XEWH-TV	6
XHUS-TV	8
XHTH-TV	10
XHAK-TV	12

Nogales

XHFA-TV	2

Tabasco

Villahermosa

XHLL-TV	13

Tamaulipas

Ciudad Victoria

XHTK-TV	11

Matamoros

XRIO-TV	2
XHAB	7

Nuevo Laredo

XEFE-TV	2
XHBR-TV	11

Reynosa

XERV	9

Tampico

XHD-TV	4

Veracruz

Coatzacoalcos

XHCV-TV	3

Las Lajas

XHAJ-TV	6
XHAH-TV	8
XHAI-TV	10

Veracruz

XHFM-TV	2

Yucatan

Merida

XHY-TV	3
XHTP-TV	9
XHST-TV	13

Zacatecas

Zacatecas

XHBQ-TV	8 A

TV Stations by Channels

2

Call	City	Network
★ WDIQ	Dozier, Ala.	P
KTUU-TV	Anchorage, Alas.	N
KTTU-TV	Fairbanks, Alas.	AN
KNAZ	Flagstaff, Ariz.	N
★ KETS	Little Rock, Ark.	P
KNXT	Los Angeles, Calif.	C
KTVU	San Francisco, Calif.	
KWGN-TV	Denver, Colo.	
WESH-TV	Daytona Beach, Fla.	N
#★ WTHS-TV	Miami, Fla.	P
#★ WPBT	Miami, Fla.	P
WSB-TV	Atlanta, Ga.	A
KHON-TV	Honolulu, Haw.	N
KBCI-TV	Boise, Id.	C
WBBM-TV	Chicago, Ill.	C
WTWO	Terre Haute, Ind.	N
KGAN	Cedar Rapids, Ia.	C
KCKT	Great Bend, Kan.	N
WBRZ	Baton Rouge, La.	A
WLBZ-TV	Bangor, Me.	N
WMAR-TV	Baltimore, Md.	N
★ WGBH-TV	Boston, Mass.	P
WJBK-TV	Detroit, Mich.	C
★ KTCA-TV	St. Paul, Minn.	P
★ WMAB	Ackerman, Miss.	
KQTV	St. Joseph, Mo.	A
KTVI	St. Louis, Mo.	A
KTVQ	Billings, Mont.	CN
KNOP-TV	North Platte, Neb.	N
KTVN	Reno, Nev.	C
† KSAF-TV	Sante Fe, N.M.	
WGRZ	Buffalo, N.Y.	N
WCBS-TV	New York, N.Y.	C
WKTV	Utica, N.Y.	N
★ WUND-TV	Columbia, N.C.	S
WFMY-TV	Greensboro, N.C.	C
KNDX	Dickinson, N.D.	C
★ KGFE	Grand Forks, N.D.	S
WDTN	Canton, O.	A
KJRH	Tulsa, Okla.	N
KOTI	Klamath Falls, Ore.	C
KATU	Portland, Ore.	A
KDKA-TV	Pittsburgh, Pa.	C
WKAQ-TV	San Juan, P.R.	
WCBD	Charleston, S.C.	A
★ KUSD-TV	Vermillion, S.D.	P
WKRN-TV	Nashville, Tenn.	A
★ WSJK-TV	Sneedville, Tenn.	P
KPRC-TV	Houston, Tex.	N
KMID-TV	Odessa, Tex.	A
KUTV	Salt Lake City, Utah	N
KREM-TV	Spokane, Wash.	C
WBAY-TV	Green Bay, Wis.	C
KTWO-TV	Casper, Wyo.	AN
CFAC-TV	Calgary, Alta.	
CBXAT-2	High Prairie, Alta.	S
CKSA-TV	Lloydminster, Alta.	Y
CHBC-TV	Kelowna, B.C.	Y
CKPG-TV	Prince George, B.C.	Y
CBUT	Vancouver, B.C.	Y
CBWYT	Mafeking, Man.	S
† CKND-TV-2	Minnedosa, Man.	
CKCW-TV	Moncton, N.B.	
CBYT-3	Bonne Bay, Nfld.	S
CJOX-TV	Grand Bank, Nfld.	
CBIT-2	Cheticamp, N.S.	S
CKGN-TV-2	Bancroft, Ont.	S
CKCY-TV	Sault Ste. Marie, Ont.	
CKPR-TV	Thunder Bay, Ont.	
CKCO-TV-2	Wiarton, Ont.	S
CBFT	Montreal, Que.	Z
CBCP-TV-2	Cypress Hills, Sask.	S
CKBQ-TV	Melfort, Sask.	
CKCK-TV	Regina, Sask.	
XHCH-TV	Chihuahua, Chih.	
XEPM-TV	Ciudad Juarez, Chih.	
XHIA-TV	Torreon, Coah.	
XEW-TV	Mexico City, D.F.	
XHAP-TV	Acapulco, Gro.	
XEWO-TV	Guadalajara, Jal.	
XHI-TV	Ciudad Obregon, Son.	
XHFA-TV	Nogales, Son.	
XRIO-TV	Matamoros, Tams.	
XEFE-TV	Nuevo Laredo, Tams.	
XHFM-TV	Veracruz, Ver.	
....	Ciego De Avila, Cuba	
CMBF-TV	Havana, Cuba	
CMKU-TV	Santiago De Cuba, Cuba	S
....	Santiago, Dom. Rep.	
....	Port Of Spain, Trinidad	

3

Call	City	Network
†★ KTOO-TV	Juneau, Alas.	
KTVK	Phoenix, Ariz.	A
KIEM-TV	Eureka, Calif.	CN
KCRA-TV	Sacramento, Calif.	N
KEYT	Santa Barbara, Calif.	A
KCWS	Glenwood Springs, Colo.	
KTVS	Sterling, Colo.	CA
WFSB	Hartford, Conn.	C
WEAR-TV	Pensacola, Fla.	A
★ WEDU	Tampa, Fla.	P
WRBL	Columbus, Ga.	C
WSAV-TV	Savannah, Ga.	A
KGMV	Wailuku, Haw.	S
KID-TV	Idaho Falls, Id.	C
KLEW-TV	Lewiston, Id.	S
WCIA	Champaign, Ill.	C
WSIL-TV	Harrisburg, Ill.	A
KIMT	Mason City, Ia.	C
KSNW	Wichita, Kan.	N
WAVE-TV	Louisville, Ky.	N
KATC	Lafayette, La.	A
KTBS-TV	Shreveport, La.	A
WJMN-TV	Escanaba, Mich.	A
WKZO-TV	Kalamazoo, Mich.	C
KDLH-TV	Duluth, Minn.	C
WLBT-TV	Jackson, Miss.	N
KTVO	Kirksville, Mo.	A
KYTV	Springfield, Mo.	N
KRTV	Great Falls, Mont.	CN
KYUS-TV	Miles City, Mont.	N
★ KLNE-TV	Lexington, Neb.	S
KMTV	Omaha, Neb.	N
KVBC	Las Vegas, Nev.	N
★ KENW	Portales, N.M.	P
WSTM-TV	Syracuse, N.Y.	N
WBTV	Charlotte, N.C.	C
WWAY-TV	Wilmington, N.C.	A
†★ KBME	Bismarck, N.D.	
★ KBME	Bismarck, N.D.	P
★ KBME	Bismark, N.D.	
WKYC-TV	Cleveland, O.	N
★ KOET	Eufaula, Okla.	
★ KOAB-TV	Bend, Ore.	P
★ WPSX-TV	Clearfield, Pa.	P
KYW-TV	Philadelphia, Pa.	N
★ WIPM-TV	Mayaguez, P.R.	P
KOTA-TV	Rapid City, S.D.	N
KDLO-TV	Watertown, S.D.	S
WRCB-TV	Chattanooga, Tenn.	N
WREG-TV	Memphis, Tenn.	C
KBTX-TV	Bryan, Tex.	AC
KIII	Corpus Christi, Tex.	A
KACB-TV	San Angelo, Tex.	N
KFDX-TV	Wichita Falls, Tex.	N
WCAX-TV	Burlington, Vt.	C
WHSV-TV	Harrisonburg, Va.	A
WTKR	Norfolk, Va.	C
WSAZ-TV	Huntington, W.V.	N
WISC-TV	Madison, Wis.	C
CFRN-TV	Edmonton, Alta.	X
CFRN-TV-2	Peace River, Alta.	S
CKKM-TV	Oliver, B.C.	
CITM-TV	One Hundred Mile House, B.C.	
CFTK-TV	Terrace, B.C.	Y
CBWFT-4	Ste Rose Du Lac, Man.	S
CBWFT	Winnipeg, Man.	Z
CJAP-TV	Argentia, Nfld.	X
CBNAT-1	Baie Verte, Nfld.	S

CBHT	Halifax, N.S.	Y
CBHFT-1	Yarmouth, N.S.	S
CKVR-TV	Barrie, Ont.	Y
CICI-TV-1	Elliot Lake, Ont.	S
CICO-TV	Timmins, Ont.	
CBVT-2	La Tuque, Que.	S
CBFT-2	Mont Laurier, Que.	S
CJBR-TV	Rimouski, Que.	Z
CBCP-TV-3	Pontiex, Sask.	
CFQC-TV-1	Stranraer, Sask.	S
XHBC-TV	Mexicali, B.C.	
XHMA-TV	Parral, Chih.	
XEPN	Piedras Negras, Coah.	
XHQ-TV	Colima, Col.	
XEZ-TV	Guanajuato, Gto.	
XEFB-TV	Monterrey, N.L.	
XHP-TV	Puebla, Pue.	
XHQTV	Culiacan, Sin.	
XHCV-TV	Coatzacoalcos, Ver.	
XHY-TV	Merida, Yuc.	
CBC-TV	St. Thomas, Barb.	
CMKJ-TV	Holguin, Cuba	S

4

WTVY	Dothan, Ala.	C
† KTBY	Anchorage, Alas.	
★ KYUK-TV	Bethel, Alas.	P
KJNP-TV	North Pole, Alas.	
KVOA-TV	Tucson, Ariz.	N
KARK-TV	Little Rock, Ark.	N
KNBC	Los Angeles, Calif.	N
KRON-TV	San Francisco, Calif.	N
KCNC-TV	Denver, Colo.	N
WRC-TV	Washington, D. C.	N
WJXT	Jacksonville, Fla.	C
WTVJ	Miami, Fla.	C
KITV	Honolulu, Haw.	A
★ KAID	Boise, Id.	P
WHBF-TV	Rock Island, Ill.	C
WTTV	Indianapolis, Ind.	
KTIV	Sioux City, Ia.	N
† KLBY	Colby, Kan.	
WWL-TV	New Orleans, La.	C
WBZ-TV	Boston, Mass.	N
WTOM-TV	Cheboygan, Mich.	N
WDIV	Detroit, Mich.	N
WCCO-TV	Minneapolis, Minn.	C
WCBI-TV	Columbus, Miss.	C
WDAF-TV	Kansas City, Mo.	N
KMOX-TV	St. Louis, Mo.	C
KXLF-TV	Butte, Mont.	AC
KOUS-TV	Hardin, Mont.	N
KDUH-TV	Scottsbluff, Neb.	N
KSNB-TV	Superior, Neb.	A
KCRL-TV	Reno, Nev.	N
KOB-TV	Albuquerque, N.M.	N
WIVB-TV	Buffalo, N.Y.	C
WNBC-TV	New York, N.Y.	N
★ WUNC-TV	Chapel Hill, N.C.	P
KXJB-TV	Valley City, N.D.	C
†★ KWSE	Williston, N.D.	
WCMH-TV	Columbus, O.	N
KTVY	Oklahoma City, Okla.	N
KPIC	Roseburg, Ore.	S
WTAE-TV	Pittsburgh, Pa.	A
WAPA-TV	San Juan, P.R.	
WCIV	Charleston, S.C.	N
WYFF-TV	Greenville, S.C.	N
KPRY-TV	Pierre, S.D.	A
WSMV	Nashville, Tenn.	N
KAMR	Amarillo, Tex.	N
KWAB	Big Spring, Tex.	N
KDFW-TV	Dallas, Tex.	C
KDBC-TV	El Paso, Tex.	C
KGBT-TV	Harlingen, Tex.	C
KJAC-TV	Port Arthur, Tex.	N
KMOL-TV	San Antonio, Tex.	N
KTVX	Salt Lake City, Utah	A
KOMO-TV	Seattle, Wash.	A
KXLY-TV	Spokane, Wash.	A
WOAY-TV	Oak Hill, W.V.	A
WTMJ-TV	Milwaukee, Wis.	N
★ KCWC-TV	Lander, Wyo.	P
CFCN-TV	Calgary, Alta.	X
CITL-TV	Lloydminster, Alta.	
CHAT-TV-1	Pivot, Alta.	S
CFJC-TV	Kamloops, B.C.	Y
CKYB-TV	Brandon, Man.	S
CBWT-2	Lac Du Bonnet, Man.	S
CHCR-TV	Campbellton, N.B.	
CHSJ-TV	St. John, N.B.	Y
CJCN-TV	Grand Falls, Nfld.	
CBTE-TV	Pine Point, N.W.T.	Y
CJCB-TV	Sydney, N.S.	X
CHNB-TV	North Bay, Ont.	Y
CBOT	Ottawa, Ont.	Y
CHFD-TV	Thunder Bay, Ont.	
CFCM-TV	Quebec, Que.	
CKRN-TV	Rouyn, Que.	Z
CKBI-TV-3	Greenwater Lake, Sask.	S
CBKMT	Moose Jaw, Sask.	Y
XHIT-TV	Chihuahua, Chih.	
XELN-TV	Torreon, Coah.	
XHTV	Mexico City, D.F.	
XHG-TV	Guadalajara, Jal.	
XHBS-TV	Los Mochis, Sin.	
XHBS-TV	Ciudad Obregon, Son.	
XHD-TV	Tampico, Tams.	
CMJ-TV	Camaguey, Cuba	
....	Havana, Cuba	
HSID-TV	Santo Domingo, Dom. Rep.	

5

WKRG-TV	Mobile, Ala.	C
KPHO-TV	Phoenix, Ariz.	
KFSM-TV	Ft. Smith, Ark.	C
KTLA	Los Angeles, Calif.	
KPIX	San Francisco, Calif.	C
KREX-TV	Grand Junction, Colo.	C
KOAA-TV	Pueblo, Colo.	N
WTTG	Washington, D. C.	
★ WUFT	Gainesville, Fla.	P
WPTV	West Palm Beach, Fla.	N
WAGA-TV	Atlanta, Ga.	C
WMAQ-TV	Chicago, Ill.	N
WOI-TV	Ames, Ia.	A
KALB-TV	Alexandria, La.	N
WABI-TV	Bangor, Me.	C
WCVB-TV	Boston, Mass.	A
WNEM-TV	Bay City, Mich.	N
KSTP-TV	St. Paul, Minn.	A
KCTV	Kansas City, Mo.	C
KSDK	St. Louis, Mo.	N
KXGN-TV	Glendive, Mont.	C
KFBB-TV	Great Falls, Mont.	AC
KHAS-TV	Hastings, Neb.	N
KVVU	Henderson, Nev.	
KNPB	Reno, Nev.	
★ KNME-TV	Albuquerque, N.M.	P
WNEW-TV	New York, N.Y.	
WPTZ	Plattsburgh, N.Y.	N
WTVH	Syracuse, N.Y.	C
WRAL-TV	Raleigh, N.C.	A
KFYR-TV	Bismarck, N.D.	N
WLWT	Cincinnati, O.	N
WEWS	Cleveland, O.	A
KOCO-TV	Oklahoma City, Okla.	A
KOBI	Medford, Ore.	C
WORA-TV	Mayaguez, P.R.	
WCSC-TV	Charleston, S.C.	C
KIVV-TV	Lead, S.D.	C
KXON	Mitchell, S.D.	A
WMC-TV	Memphis, Tenn.	N
WTVF	Nashville, Tenn.	C
KXAS-TV	Ft. Worth, Tex.	N
★ KTXT-TV	Lubbock, Tex.	P
KENS-TV	San Antonio, Tex.	C
KRGV-TV	Weslaco, Tex.	A
KSL-TV	Salt Lake City, Utah	C
WCYB-TV	Bristol, Va.	N
KING-TV	Seattle, Wash.	N
WDTV	Weston, W.V.	C
WFRV-TV	Green Bay, Wis.	A
KYCU-TV	Cheyenne, Wyo.	C
KOWY	Lander, Wyo.	CR
CBXT	Edmonton, Alta.	Y
CJDC-TV	Dawson Creek, B.C.	Y
CHKL-TV	Kelowna, B.C.	S
CKX-TV	Brandon, Man.	Y
CBYT	Corner Brook, Nfld.	Y
CBNT-3	Marystown, Nfld.	S
CJCH-TV	Halifax, N.S.	X
CBIT	Sydney, N.S.	Y

Call	City	Net
CBWCT	Ft. Frances, Ont.	Y
CHRO-TV	Pembroke, Ont.	Y
CJIC-TV	Sault Ste. Marie, Ont.	Y
CICI-TV	Sudbury, Ont.	
CBLT	Toronto, Ont.	Y
CFER-TV	Gaspe/norb, Que.	
CFCL-TV-5	Malartic, Que.	S
CHAU-TV	New Carlisle, Que.	Z
CKMI-TV	Quebec, Que.	Y
CKBI-TV	Prince Albert, Sask.	
CJFB-TV	Swift Current, Sask.	
CKOS-TV	Yorkton, Sask.	Y
XHAQ-TV	Mexicali, B.C.	
XHFI-TV	Chihuahua, Chih.	
XEJ-TV	Ciudad Juarez, Chih.	
XHAE-TV	Saltillo, Coah.	
XHCC-TV	Colima, Col.	
XHGC-TV	Mexico City, D.F.	
XHCC-TV	Hermosillo, Son.	
CMH-TV	Santa Clara, Cuba	S
CMLB-TV	Santiago De Cuba, Cuba	
4VMR	Port Au Prince, Haiti	
ZBTV	Roadtown, Tortula, Br VI, Virgin Is.	

6

Call	City	Net
WBRC-TV	Birmingham, Ala.	A
* KUAT-TV	Tucson, Ariz.	P
* KEMV	Mountain View, Ark.	
KVIQ-TV	Eureka, Calif.	A
* KVIE	Sacramento, Calif.	P
KSBY-TV	San Luis Obispo, Calif.	N
* KRMA-TV	Denver, Colo.	P
KREZ-TV	Durango, Colo.	
WCIX	Miami, Fla.	
WCPX	Orlando, Fla.	C
WJBF	Augusta, Ga.	A
WCTV	Thomasville, Ga.	C
† ----	Kailua, Haw.	
KIVI	Nampa, Id.	A
KPVI	Pocatello, Id.	A
WRTV	Indianapolis, Ind.	A
WOC-TV	Davenport, Ia.	N
KTVC	Dodge City, Kan.	C
WPSD-TV	Paducah, Ky.	N
WDSU-TV	New Orleans, La.	N
KTAL-TV	Shreveport, La.	N
WCSH-TV	Portland, Me.	N
WLNE	New Bedford, Mass.	C
* WCML-TV	Alpena, Mich.	
WJIM-TV	Lansing, Mich.	C
WLUC-TV	Marquette, Mich.	CA
KAAL	Austin, Minn.	A
WABG-TV	Greenwood, Miss.	A
* KMOS-TV	Warrensburg, Mo.	P
KTVM	Butte, Mont.	N
KWNB-TV	Hayes Center, Neb.	A
WOWT	Omaha, Neb.	C
KAVE-TV	Carlsbad, N.M.	A
† ----	Silver City, N.M.	
WRGB	Schenectady, N.Y.	N
WECT	Wilmington, N.C.	N
WDAY-TV	Fargo, N.D.	N
* KSRE	Minot, N.D.	
WTVN-TV	Columbus, O.	A
KOTV	Tulsa, Okla.	C
KOIN-TV	Portland, Ore.	C
WJAC-TV	Johnstown, Pa.	N
WPVI	Philadelphia, Pa.	A
* WIPR-TV	San Juan, P.R.	P
KPLO-TV	Reliance, S.D.	S
WATE-TV	Knoxville, Tenn.	A
KFDM-TV	Beaumont, Tex.	C
KRIS-TV	Corpus Christi, Tex.	N
† KIDV	San Angelo, Tex.	
KCEN-TV	Temple, Tex.	N
KAUZ-TV	Wichita Falls, Tex.	C
WTVR-TV	Richmond, Va.	C
KHQ-TV	Spokane, Wash.	N
WVVA	Bluefield, W.V.	N
WITI-TV	Milwaukee, Wis.	C
KBJR-TV	Superior, Wis.	N
CKSA-TV-2	Bonneville, Alta.	S
CHAT-TV	Medicine Hat, Alta.	Y
CKRD-TV	Red Deer, Alta.	Y
CHKM-TV	Kamloops, B.C.	S

Call	City	Net
CHEK-TV	Victoria, B.C.	X
CBWT	Winnipeg, Man.	Y
CHSJ-TV-1	Bon Accord, N.B.	S
CBNAT-4	St. Anthony, Nfld.	S
CJON-TV	St. John's, Nfld.	X
CHAK-TV	Inuvik, N.W.T.	Y
CJCH-TV-6	Caledonia, N.S.	S
CJCB-TV-1	Inverness, N.S.	S
CJOH-TV-6	Doseronto, Ont.	S
CKGN-TV-6	Ottawa, Ont.	S
CKGN-TV	Paris, Ont.	
CFCL-TV	Timmins, Ont.	Y
CJPM-TV	Chicoutimi, Que.	
CBMT	Montreal, Que.	Y
CFOC-TV-2	North Battleford, Sask.	S
CKCK-TV-2	Willow Bunch, Sask.	S
CHSS-TV	Wynyard, Sask.	
CFWH-TV	Whitehorse, Yuk.	Y
XETV	Tijuana, B.C.	
XHZ-TV	Guanajuato, Gto.	
XEHL-TV	Guadalajara, Jal.	
XET-TV	Monterrey, N.L.	
XEWH-TV	Hermosillo, Son.	
XHAJ-TV	Las Lajas, Ver.	
CMJL-TV	Camaguey, Cuba	S
CMQ-TV	Havana, Cuba	

7

Call	City	Net
* WCIQ	Munford, Ala.	P
* KAKM	Anchorage, Alas.	P
† ----	Fairbanks, Alas.	
KUSK	Prescott, Ariz.	
KATV	Little Rock, Ark.	A
KABC-TV	Los Angeles, Calif.	A
KRCR-TV	Redding, Calif.	A
KGO-TV	San Francisco, Calif.	A
KMGH-TV	Denver, Colo.	C
WJLA-TV	Washington, D. C.	A
* WJCT	Jacksonville, Fla.	P
WSVN	Miami, Fla.	N
WJHG-TV	Panama City, Fla.	N
KAII-TV	Wailuku, Haw.	S
KTVB	Boise, Id.	N
WLS-TV	Chicago, Ill.	A
WTVW	Evansville, Ind.	A
KWWL	Waterloo, Ia.	N
KAYS-TV	Hays, Kan.	C
KOAM-TV	Pittsburg, Kan.	C
KPLC-TV	Lake Charles, La.	N
WVII-TV	Bangor, Me.	A
WNEV-TV	Boston, Mass.	C
WZYZ-TV	Detroit, Mich.	A
WPBN-TV	Traverse City, Mich.	N
KCMT	Alexandria, Minn.	CA
WDAM-TV	Hattiesburg, Miss.	N
KHQA-TV	Hannibal, Mo.	C
† KCTZ	Bozeman, Mont.	
* KMNE-TV	Bassett, Neb.	S
KETV	Omaha, Neb.	A
† KQJA	Winnemucca, Nev.	
KOAT-TV	Albuquerque, N.M.	A
WKBW-TV	Buffalo, N.Y.	A
WABC-TV	New York, N.Y.	A
WWNY-TV	Watertown, N.Y.	CN
WITN-TV	Washington, N.C.	N
KQCD-TV	Dickinson, N.D.	AN
WHIO-TV	Dayton, O.	C
KSWO-TV	Lawton, Okla.	A
* KOAC-TV	Corvallis, Ore.	P
WLUZ	Ponce, P.R.	
* WITV	Charleston, S.C.	
WSPA-TV	Spartanburg, S.C.	C
KEVN-TV	Rapid City, S.D.	AC
WBBJ-TV	Jackson, Tenn.	A
KVII-TV	Amarillo, Tex.	A
KTBC-TV	Austin, Tex.	C
KVIA-TV	El Paso, Tex.	A
KOSA-TV	Odessa, Tex.	C
KLTV	Tyler, Tex.	A
* KUED	Salt Lake City, Utah	P
WDBJ	Roanoke, Va.	C
KIRO-TV	Seattle, Wash.	C
* KSPS-TV	Spokane, Wash.	P
WTRF-TV	Wheeling, W.V.	CA
WSAW	Wausau, Wis.	C
CFAC-TV-7	Lethbridge, Alta.	
CFRN-TV-7	Lougheed, Alta.	S

CKY-TV	Winnipeg, Man.	X
CKCD-TV	Campbellton, N.B.	
CHMT-TV	Moncton, N.B.	
CBHFT-2	Mulgrave, N.S.	S
CKNC-TV-1	Elliot Lake, Ont.	S
CBOFT-2	Hearst, Ont.	S
CBLFT-1	Sturgeon Falls, Ont.	Z
CJDG-TV	Lithiums Mines, Que.	
CKRT-TV	Riviere Du Loup, Que.	Z
CHLT-TV	Sherbrooke, Que.	
CIEW-TV	Carlyle Lake, Sask.	Z
CKMJ-TV	Marquis, Sask.	
CBCP-TV-1	Shaunavon, Sask.	S
CBKFT-4	St. Brieux, Sask.	
XHAA-TV	Tapachula, Chis.	
XHAD-TV	Saltillo, Coah.	
XHBZ-TV	Colima, Col.	
XEX-TV	Mexico City, D.F.	
XHBN-TV	Oaxaca, Oax.	
XHBT-TV	Culiacan, Sin.	
XHMZ-TV	Mazatlan, Sin.	
XHAB	Matamoros, Tams.	
....	Baracoa, Cuba	S
CMFD-TV	Ciego De Avila, Cuba	S
....	San Cristobol, Cuba	S
....	Santiago, Dom. Rep.	
HIN-TV	Santo Domingo, Dom. Rep.	
....	Coopers Hill, Jamaica	S
....	Plymouth, Montserrat	

8

WSLA	Selma, Ala.	C
KJUD	Juneau, Alas.	NA
* KAET	Phoenix, Ariz.	P
KAIT-TV	Jonesboro, Ark.	A
KSBW-TV	Salinas, Calif.	N
KFMB-TV	San Diego, Calif.	C
KJCT	Grand Junction, Colo.	A
* KTSC	Pueblo, Colo.	P
WTNH-TV	New Haven, Conn.	A
WXFL	Tampa, Fla.	N
* WGTV	Athens, Ga.	P
* WXGA-TV	Waycross, Ga.	P
KIFI-TV	Idaho Falls, Id.	N
* WSIU-TV	Carbondale, Ill.	P
WQAD-TV	Moline, Ill.	A
WISH-TV	Indianapolis, Ind.	C
KCCI-TV	Des Moines, Ia.	C
* KPTS	Hutchinson, Kan.	P
KNOE-TV	Monroe, La.	C
WVUE	New Orleans, La.	A
WMTW-TV	Portland, Me.	A
WAGM-TV	Presque Isle, Me.	C
WOTV	Grand Rapids, Mich.	N
† WIIM-TV	Iron Mountain, Mich.	
WGTQ	Sault Ste. Marie, Mich.	S
* WDSE-TV	Duluth, Minn.	P
KOMU-TV	Columbia, Mo.	NA
KULR-TV	Billings, Mont.	A
KPAX-TV	Missoula, Mont.	AC
KBGT-TV	Albion, Neb.	A
KSNK	Mc Cook, Neb.	N
KLAS-TV	Las Vegas, Nev.	C
KOLO-TV	Reno, Nev.	A
KSWS-TV	Roswell, N.M.	N
WROC-TV	Rochester, N.Y.	N
WGHP-TV	High Point, N.C.	A
WDAZ-TV	Devils Lake, N.D.	N
KUMV-TV	Williston, N.D.	N
WJKW-TV	Cleveland, O.	C
KVIJ-TV	Sayre, Okla.	S
KTUL-TV	Tulsa, Okla.	A
* KSYS	Medford, Ore.	P
KGW-TV	Portland, Ore.	N
WGAL-TV	Lancaster, Pa.	N
* KESD-TV	Brookings, S.D.	P
* KZSD-TV	Martin, S.D.	
* WDCN	Nashville, Tenn.	P
WFAA-TV	Dallas, Tex.	A
* KUHT	Houston, Tex.	P
KGNS-TV	Laredo, Tex.	N
KLST	San Angelo, Tex.	C
WSVI	Christiansted, V.I.	A
WXEX-TV	Petersburg, Va.	A
WCHS-TV	Charleston, W.V.	C
WKBT	La Crosse, Wis.	C

CBXT-1	Athabasca, Alta.	S
CFCN-TV-8	Medicine Hat, Alta.	S
CFRN-TV-6	Red Deer, Alta.	S
CKTN-TV	Trail, B.C.	B
CHAN-TV	Vancouver, B.C.	X
CBWST-TV	Dauphin, Man.	
CFLA-TV	Goose Bay, Nfld.	Y
CBNT	St. John's, Nfld.	Y
CBYT-1	Stephenville, Nfld.	S
CFYK-TV	Yellowknife, N.W.T.	Y
CJOH-TV-8	Cornwall, Ont.	S
CBWAT	Kenora, Ont.	Y
CBLAT-1	Manitouwadge, Ont.	S
CKNX-TV	Wingham, Ont.	Y
CKCW-TV-1	Charlottetown, P.E.	S
CIVU-TV	Chicoutimi, Que.	
CKRS-TV-3	Roberval, Que.	S
CIVN-TV	Rouyn, Que.	
CHEM-TV	Three Rivers, Que.	Y
CFQC-TV	Saskatoon, Sask.	
XHTX-TV	Tuxtla, Chis.	
XHBU-TV	Jimenez, Chih.	
XHTM-TV	Mexico City, D.F.	
XHUS-TV	Hermosillo, Son.	
XHAH-TV	Las Lajas, Ver.	
XHBQ-TV	Zacatecas, Zac.	
†	Freeport, Bahamas	
ZBF-TV	Hamilton, Bermuda	A
CMLD-TV	Holguin, Cuba	S
CMRA-TV	Santa Clara, Cuba	
....	Port Antonio, Jamaica	
PJC-TV	Curacao, Ne. Antil.	
....	St. Martin, Ne. Antil.	

9

* KUAC-TV	Fairbanks, Alas.	P
KGUN-TV	Tucson, Ariz.	A
* KETG	Arkadelphia, Ark.	P
KECY	El Centro, Calif.	C
KHJ-TV	Los Angeles, Calif.	
* KIXE-TV	Redding, Calif.	P
* KQED	San Francisco, Calif.	P
KBTV	Denver, Colo.	A
WDVM-TV	Washington, D. C.	C
WFTV	Orlando, Fla.	A
WTVM	Columbus, Ga.	A
* WVAN-TV	Savannah, Ga.	P
KGMD	Hilo, Haw.	S
KGMB-TV	Honolulu, Haw.	C
WGN-TV	Chicago, Ill.	
* WNIN	Evansville, Ind.	P
KCRG-TV	Cedar Rapids, Ia.	A
KCAU-TV	Sioux City, Ia.	A
* KOOD	Hays, Kan.	P
WAFB-TV	Baton Rouge, La.	C
WWTV	Cadillac, Mich.	C
* KAWE	Bemidji, Minn.	P
KMSP-TV	Minneapolis, Minn.	
WTVA	Tupelo, Miss.	NA
KMBC-TV	Kansas City, Mo.	A
* KETC	St. Louis, Mo.	P
†* ----	Bozeman, Mont.	
KCFW-TV	Kalispell, Mont.	N
* KPNE-TV	North Platte, Neb.	S
WMUR-TV	Manchester, N.H.	A
WOR-TV	Secaucus, N.J.	
WOR-TV	New York, N.Y.	
WIXT	Syracuse, N.Y.	A
WSOC-TV	Charlotte, N.C.	A
WNCT-TV	Greenville, N.C.	C
†* KDSE	Dickinson, N.D.	
WCPO-TV	Cincinnati, O.	C
WTOV-TV	Steubenville, O.	NA
KWTV	Oklahoma City, Okla.	C
KEZI-TV	Eugene, Ore.	A
WSUR-TV	Ponce, P.R.	
KABY-TV	Aberdeen, S.D.	A
* KBHE-TV	Rapid City, S.D.	
WTVC	Chattanooga, Tenn.	A
KRBC-TV	Abilene, Tex.	N
KTSM-TV	El Paso, Tex.	N
KTRE-TV	Lufkin, Tex.	AN
KTPX	Monahans, Tex.	N
* KLRN	San Antonio, Tex.	P
* KCTS-TV	Seattle, Wash.	P
* WSWP-TV	Grandview, W.V.	P
WAOW-TV	Wausau, Wis.	A

CBRT	Calgary, Alta.	Y
CFRN-TV-9	Slave Lake, Alta.	
CBXT-2	Whitecourt, Alta.	S
CKND	Winnipeg, Man.	
CKLT-TV	St. John, N.B.	
CBNAT-9	Mt. St. Margaret, Nfld.	S
CJCB-TV-2	Antigonish, N.S.	S
CBWDT	Dryden, Ont.	Y
CBOFT	Ottawa, Ont.	Z
CKNC-TV	Sudbury, Ont.	Y
CICO-TV-9	Thunder Bay, Ont.	S
CBLFT-3	Timmins, Ont.	Z
CFTO-TV	Toronto, Ont.	X
CBLAT-3	Wawa, Ont.	S
CBET	Windsor, Ont.	Y
CBGAT	Matane, Que.	Z
CIMT-TV	Riviere Du Loup, Que.	
* CIVG-TV	Sept Isles, Que.	
CKSH-TV	Sherbrooke, Que.	Z
CBKT	Regina, Sask.	Y
CBKST-1	Stranraer, Sask.	S
XHBW	Monclova, Coah.	
XEQ-TV	Mexico City, D.F.	
XHTO-TV	Queretaro, Qro.	
XERV	Reynosa, Tams.	
XHTP-TV	Merida, Yuc.	
CMGQ-TV	Matanzas, Cuba	S
....	Santo Domingo, Dom. Rep.	
....	Yallahs, Jamaica	

10

* WBIQ	Birmingham, Ala.	P
WALA-TV	Mobile, Ala.	N
KTSP-TV	Phoenix, Ariz.	C
KTVE	El Dorado, Ark.	A
KXTV	Sacramento, Calif.	C
KGTV	San Diego, Calif.	A
KREY-TV	Montrose, Colo.	S
WPLG	Miami, Fla.	A
WTSP-TV	St. Petersburg, Fla.	A
WALB-TV	Albany, Ga.	N
* KMEB	Wailuku, Haw.	S
* KBGL-TV	Pocatello, Id.	P
WGEM-TV	Quincy, Ill.	N
WTHI-TV	Terre Haute, Ind.	C
KLOE-TV	Goodland, Kan.	S
KAKE-TV	Wichita, Kan.	A
KLFY-TV	Lafayette, La.	C
* WCBB	Augusta, Me.	P
* WMEM-TV	Presque Isle, Me.	P
WILXTV	Jackson, Mich.	N
WWUP-TV	Sault Ste. Marie, Mich.	C
* KWCM-TV	Appleton, Minn.	P
WDIO-TV	Duluth, Minn.	A
KTTC	Rochester, Minn.	N
† KONY	Thief River Falls, Minn.	
KOLR-TV	Springfield, Mo.	C
KOLN-TV	Lincoln, Neb.	C
KSTF	Scottsbluff, Neb.	CA
* KLVX	Las Vegas, Nev.	P
KBIM-TV	Roswell, N.M.	C
WTEN	Albany, N.Y.	A
WHEC-TV	Rochester, N.Y.	C
KMOT	Minot, N.D.	N
WBNS-TV	Columbus, O.	C
KTEN	Ada, Okla.	A
KTVL	Medford, Ore.	C
†* KOAP-TV	Portland, Ore.	P
WTAJ-TV	Altoona, Pa.	C
WCAU-TV	Philadelphia, Pa.	C
WJAR-TV	Providence, R.I.	N
WIS-TV	Columbia, S.C.	N
* KTSD-TV	Pierre, S.D.	
WBIR-TV	Knoxville, Tenn.	C
* WKNO-TV	Memphis, Tenn.	P
KFDA-TV	Amarillo, Tex.	C
KZTV	Corpus Christi, Tex.	C
† ----	Del Rio, Tex.	
KWTX-TV	Waco, Tex.	AC
WBNB-TV	Charlotte Amalie, V.I.	CN
WAVY-TV	Portsmouth, Va.	N
WSLS-TV	Roanoke, Va.	N
* KWSU-TV	Pullman, Wash.	P
* WMVS	Milwaukee, Wis.	P
KTNW	Riverton, Wyo.	N
CKRD-TV-1	Coronation, Alta.	S

CBXAT	Grand Prairie, Alta.	Y
CBUBT	Cranbrook, B.C.	Y
CHKL-TV-1	Pentilton, B.C.	
CBWGT	Fisher Branch, Man.	Y
CBWBT	Flin Flon, Man.	Y
CJWN-TV	Corner Brook, Nfld.	S
CJCH-TV-1	Canning, N.S.	S
CBHFT-4	Cheticamp, N.S.	S
CFPL-TV	London, Ont.	Y
CKNY-TV	North Bay, Ont.	
CFTM-TV	Montreal, Que.	
CBKI-TV-4	Nipawin, Sask.	
CBKT-2	Willow Bunch, Sask.	S
CICC-TV	Yorkton, Sask.	
XHK-TV	La Paz, B.C.S.	
XHA-TV	Durango, Dgo.	
XHL-TV	Leon, Gto.	
XHKW-TV	Morelia, Mich.	
XHCB-TV	Tepic, Nay.	
XHX-TV	Monterrey, N.L.	
XHTH-TV	Hermosillo, Son.	
XHAI-TV	Las Lajas, Ver.	
ZAL-TV	St. Johns, Anti.	
ZBM-TV	Hamilton, Bermuda	C

11

KTVA	Anchorage, Alas.	C
KTVF	Fairbanks, Alas.	CA
† KCAA	Yuma, Ariz.	
KTHV	Little Rock, Ark.	C
KTTV	Los Angeles, Calif.	
KNTV	San Jose, Calif.	A
KKTV	Colorado Springs, Colo.	C
WINK-TV	Ft. Myers, Fla.	C
* WFSU-TV	Tallahassee, Fla.	P
WXIA-TV	Atlanta, Ga.	N
WTOC-TV	Savannah, Ga.	C
KHAW-TV	Hilo, Haw.	S
* KHET	Honolulu, Haw.	P
KMVT	Twin Falls, Id.	CNA
* WTTW	Chicago, Ill.	P
* KDIN-TV	Des Moines, Ia.	P
KSNG	Garden City, Kan.	N
* KTWU	Topeka, Kan.	P
WHAS-TV	Louisville, Ky.	C
† ----	Houma, La.	
WBAL-TV	Baltimore, Md.	C
WBKB-TV	Alpena, Mich.	C
† KITF	International Falls, Minn.	
WTCN-TV	Minneapolis, Minn.	N
WTOK-TV	Meridian, Miss.	A
KPLR-TV	St. Louis, Mo.	
KGIN-TV	Grand Island, Neb.	C
* WENH-TV	Durham, N.H.	P
† ----	Sante Fe, N.M.	
WPIX	New York, N.Y.	
WTVD	Durham, N.C.	C
KTHI-TV	Fargo, N.D.	A
KXMD-TV	Williston, N.D.	CA
WTOL-TV	Toledo, O.	C
* KOED-TV	Tulsa, Okla.	P
KCBY	Coos Bay, Ore.	N
WPXI	Pittsburgh, Pa.	N
WKBM-TV	Caguas, P.R.	
KHSD-TV	Lead, S.D.	N
* KQSD-TV	Lowry, S.D.	
KELO-TV	Sioux Falls, S.D.	C
WJHL-TV	Johnson City, Tenn.	C
* WLJT-TV	Lexington, Tenn.	P
KTVT	Ft. Worth, Tex.	
KHOU-TV	Houston, Tex.	C
KCBD-TV	Lubbock, Tex.	N
* KBYU-TV	Provo, Utah	P
KSTW	Tacoma, Wash.	
WLUK-TV	Green Bay, Wis.	
† KRWY	Rawlins, Wyo.	
CBXFT	Edmonton, Alta.	Z
CBXFT-6	Ft. Mc Murray, Alta.	
KZAZ	Nogales, Alta.	
CHAN-TV-4	Courtenay, B.C.	S
CBUFT-3	Terrace, B.C.	S
CBUAT	Trail, B.C.	Y
CKX-TV-1	Foxwarren, Man.	S
CBAFT	Moncton, N.B.	Z
CBNAT	Grand Falls, Nfld.	Y
CBHT-4	Sheet Harbour, N.S.	S

CBHT-3	Yarmouth, N.S.	S
CHCH-TV	Hamilton, Ont.	
CITO-TV-2	Kearns, Ont.	S
CKWS-TV	Kingston, Ont.	Y
CBLAT-4	Marathon, Ont.	S
CKCO-TV-4	Muskokas, Ont.	S
CBVT	Quebec, Que.	Z
CFER-TV	Rimouski, Que.	
CFER-TV-1	Sept Isles, Que.	S
CBKST	Saskatoon, Sask.	Y
XHO-TV	Torreon, Coah.	
* XEIPN-TV	Mexico City, D.F.	
XHTK-TV	Ciudad Victoria, Tams.	
XHBR-TV	Nuevo Laredo, Tams.	
CMGH-TV	Matanzas, Cuba	S
....	Kingston, Jamaica	
....	Montego Bay, Jamaica	

12

WSFA-TV	Montgomery, Ala.	N
KPNX-TV	Phoenix, Ariz.	N
KHSL-TV	Chico, Calif.	C
KCOY-TV	Santa Maria, Calif.	C
* KBDI-TV	Broomfield, Colo.	P
* WHTY-TV	Wilmington, Del.	P
WTLV	Jacksonville, Fla.	A
WPEC	West Palm Beach, Fla.	A
WRDW-TV	Augusta, Ga.	C
KMAU	Wailuku, Haw.	S
* KUID-TV	Moscow, Id.	P
KTRV	Nampa, Id.	
* WILL-TV	Urbana, Ill.	P
* KIIN-TV	Iowa City, Ia.	
KWCH-TV	Hutchinson, Kan.	C
* WYES-TV	New Orleans, La.	P
KSLA-TV	Shreveport, La.	C
* WMEB-TV	Orono, Me.	P
WJRT-TV	Flint, Mich.	A
KEYC-TV	Mankato, Minn.	C
KNMT	Walker, Minn.	CA
* WMAE	Booneville, Miss.	
WJTV	Jackson, Miss.	C
KFVS-TV	Cape Girardeau, Mo.	C
KODE-TV	Joplin, Mo.	A
KTVG	Helena, Mont.	N
* KUON-TV	Lincoln, Neb.	P
* KRNE-TV	Merriman, Neb.	S
KMCC	Clovis, N.M.	A
KOBF	Farmington, N.M.	N
WBNG-TV	Binghamton, N.Y.	C
WCTI	New Bern, N.C.	A
WXII	Winston Salem, N.C.	N
KXMB-TV	Bismarck, N.D.	CA
† KWBA	Pembina, N.D.	
WKRC-TV	Cincinnati, O.	A
KXII	Ardmore, Okla.	NC
†* KWET	Cheyenne, Okla.	
† KDRV	Medford, Ore.	
KPTV	Portland, Ore.	
WICU-TV	Erie, Pa.	N
WOLE-TV	Aguadilla, P.R.	
WPRI-TV	Providence, R.I.	A
WDEF-TV	Chattanooga, Tenn.	C
KBMT	Beaumont, Tex.	A
KSAT-TV	San Antonio, Tex.	A
KTXS-TV	Sweetwater, Tex.	A
* WJTX-TV	Charlotte Amalie, V.I.	P
WWBT	Richmond, Va.	N
KVOS-TV	Bellingham, Wash.	C
WBOY-TV	Clarksburg, W.V.	N
WISN-TV	Milwaukee, Wis.	A
WAEO-TV	Rhinelander, Wis.	N
KSGW-TV	Sheridan, Wyo.	N
CFRN-TV-4	Ashmont, Alta.	S
CFCN-TV-1	Drumheller, Alta.	S
CBXAT-3	Manning, Alta.	S
CBUBT-1	Canal Flats, B.C.	S
CIFG-TV	Prince George, B.C.	B
CKAM-TV	Upsalaquitch Lake, N.B.	Y
CBYAT	Deer Lake, Nfld.	
CBNT-2	Placentia, Nfld.	S
CBIT-1	Mulgrave, N.S.	S
CBLFT-6	Elliot Lake, Ont.	S
CBLFT-4	Kapuskasing, Ont.	S
CHEX-TV	Peterborough, Ont.	Y
CIVF-TV	Baie-trimite, Que.	

CBIMT	Iles De La Madeleine, Que.	S
CKRS-TV	Jonquiere, Que.	Z
CFCF-TV	Montreal, Que.	X
CBFST-2	Temiscaming, Que.	S
CIVA-TV	Val D'or, Que.	
CKCK-TV-1	Colgate, Sask.	S
CKMC-TV	Saskatoon, Sask.	S
CICC-TV-1	Wynyard, Sask.	S
XEWT-TV	Tijuana, B.C.	
XHAN-TV	Campeche, Cam.	
XHAK-TV	Chilpancingo, Gro.	
XHAW-TV	Monterrey, N.L.	
XHCG-TV	Los Mochis, Sin.	
XHOW-TV	Mazatlan, Sin.	
XHAK-TV5	Hermosillo, Son.	
....	Pinar Del Rio, Cuba	S
†	Romano, Dom. Rep.	
....	Oracabessa, Jamaica	

13

WVTM-TV	Birmingham, Ala.	N
KIMO	Anchorage, Alas.	A
† KATN	Fairbanks, Alas.	
KTNL	Sitka, Alas.	CA
KOLD-TV	Tucson, Ariz.	C
KYEL-TV	Yuma, Ariz.	NC
* KAFT	Fayetteville, Ark.	P
* KEET	Eureka, Calif.	P
KCOP	Los Angeles, Calif.	
KOVR	Stockton, Calif.	A
KRDO-TV	Colorado Springs, Colo.	A
WMBB	Panama City, Fla.	A
WTVT	Tampa, Fla.	C
WMAZ-TV	Macon, Ga.	C
KHVO	Hilo, Haw.	S
KIKU-TV	Honolulu, Haw.	
WCEE	Mount Vernon, Ill.	
WREX-TV	Rockford, Ill.	A
WTHR	Indianapolis, Ind.	N
WHO-TV	Des Moines, Ia.	N
KUPK-TV	Garden City, Kan.	A
WIBW-TV	Topeka, Kan.	C
WBKO	Bowling Green, Ky.	A
* KLTM	Monroe, La.	P
* WMED-TV	Calais, Me.	P
WGME	Portland, Me.	C
WJZ-TV	Baltimore, Md.	A
WZZM-TV	Grand Rapids, Mich.	A
* WNMU-TV	Marquette, Mich.	P
WIRT	Hibbing, Minn.	A
WLOX-TV	Biloxi, Miss.	A
KRCG	Jefferson City, Mo.	C
KECI-TV	Missoula, Mont.	N
* KTNE-TV	Alliance, Neb.	S
KHGI-TV	Kearney, Neb.	A
KTNV-TV	Las Vegas, Nev.	A
KGGM-TV	Albuquerque, N.M.	C
WNYT	Albany, N.Y.	N
* WNET	New York, N.Y.	P
WOKR	Rochester, N.Y.	A
WLOS-TV	Asheville, N.C.	A
* KFME	Fargo, N.D.	P
KXMC-TV	Minot, N.D.	C
WTVG	Toledo, O.	N
* KETA	Oklahoma City, Okla.	P
KVAL	Eugene, Ore.	C
* KTVR	La Grande, Ore.	
* WQED	Pittsburgh, Pa.	P
† WSTE	Fajardo, P.R.	
WBTW	Florence, S.C.	C
* KPSD-TV	Eagle Butte, S.D.	
KSFY-TV	Sioux Falls, S.D.	A
WHBQ-TV	Memphis, Tenn.	A
* KERA-TV	Dallas, Tex.	P
* KCOS	El Paso, Tex.	
KTRK	Houston, Tex.	A
KVTV	Laredo, Tex.	C
KLBK-TV	Lubbock, Tex.	C
WSET-TV	Lynchburg, Va.	A
WVEC-TV	Norfolk, Va.	A
KCPQ	Tacoma, Wash.	
WOWK	Huntington, W.V.	A
WEAU-TV	Eau Claire, Wis.	N
KWWY	Rock Springs, Wyo.	C
CITV	Edmonton, Alta.	
CFRN-TV-1	Grand Prairie, Alta.	S

	Station	Location	
	CFCN-TV-5	Lethbridge, Alta.	S
	CHEK-TV-5	Campbell River, B.C.	S
	CBAFT-2	Edmundston, N.B.	S
*	CBNLT	Labrador City, Nfld.	Y
	CBNT-1	Port Rexton, Nfld.	S
	CBHFT	Halifax, N.S.	Z
	CBHFT-3	Sydney, N.S.	S
	CBLAT	Geraldton, Ont.	Y
	CKCO-TV	Kitchener, Ont.	X
	CJOH-TV	Ottawa, Ont.	X
	CBLFT-2	Sudbury, Ont.	S
	CBCT	Charlottetown, P.E.	Y
	CBST	Sept Isles, Que.	Z
	CKTM-TV	Three Rivers, Que.	Z
	CBKFT	Regina, Sask.	Z
	CBKHT	Keno Hill, Yuk.	Y
	XHDF-TV	Mexico City, D.F.	
	XHBL-TV	Culiacan, Sin.	
	XHLL-TV	Villahermosa, Tab.	
	XHST-TV	Merida, Yuc.	
	ZNS-TV	Nassau, Bahamas	
	....	Guantanamo, Cuba	
	....	Havana, Cuba	
	CMG-TV	Matanzas, Cuba	
	....	Morant, Jamaica	
	....	Spur Tree, Jamaica	
	PJA-TV	Aruba, Ne. Antil.	
	....	Port of Spain, Trinidad	

14

	Station	Location	
*	KDTV	San Francisco, Calif.	
†	KTVJ	Boulder, Colo.	
*	WABW-TV	Pelham, Ga.	P
†	KPRR	Honolulu, Haw.	
†	KWHP	Boise, Id.	
†*	WJPT	Jacksonville, Ill.	
	WFIE-TV	Evansville, Ind.	N
	KMEG	Sioux City, Ia.	C
	KARD	West Monroe, La.	N
*	WCMU-TV	Mt. Pleasant, Mich.	P
*	WMAW	Meridian, Miss.	
	KGSW	Albuquerque, N.M.	
†	----	Greenville, N.C.	
	WHKY-TV	Hickory, N.C.	N
*	WPTO	Oxford, O.	P
	KTBO	Oklahoma City, Okla.	
†	WTIN	Ponce, P.R.	
*	WEBA-TV	Allendale, S.C.	
	KJTV	Amarillo, Tex.	
	KCIK	El Paso, Tex.	
†*	----	Houston, Tex.	
†	KCKU	Tyler, Tex.	
†	KOBK	Walla Walla, Wash.	
†	WSCO	Suring, Wis.	
	KCWY-TV	Casper, Wyo.	C

15

	Station	Location	
	WOWL-TV	Florence, Ala.	N
†	----	Mobile, Ala.	
	KNXV-TV	Phoenix, Ariz.	
*	KPBS-TV	San Diego, Calif.	P
*	WDCO-TV	Cochran, Ga.	P
	WICD	Champaign, Ill.	N
	WANE-TV	Ft. Wayne, Ind.	C
†*	KPTW	Wichita, Kan.	
*	WKPC-TV	Louisville, Ky.	P
	KADN	Lafayette, La.	
*	KAVT-TV	Austin, Minn.	P
	WXVT	Greenville, Miss.	C
	KPOB-TV	Poplar Bluff, Mo.	A
*	WHED-TV	Hanover, N.H.	
	KVNJ	Fargo, N.D.	
	WLYH-TV	Lancaster, Pa.	C
	WPDE-TV	Florence, S.C.	A
†	KSUZ-TV	Abilene, Tex.	
*	KAMU	College Station, Tex.	P
†	----	Christiansted, V.I.	
*	WHRO-TV	Norfolk, Va.	P
*	WBRA-TV	Roanoke, Va.	P
	KCKA	Centralia, Wash.	
	WTAP-TV	Parkersburg, W.V.	N
	WMTV	Madison, Wis.	N
	CIVQ-TV	Quebec, Que.	

16

	Station	Location	
†	KLRT	Little Rock, Ark.	
†	WTKW	Key West, Fla.	
*	WUSF-TV	Tampa, Fla.	P
*	WUSI-TV	Olney, Ill.	P
†	WTJR	Quincy, Ill.	
	WNDU-TV	South Bend, Ind.	N
†	----	Somerset, Ky.	
	WBOC-TV	Salisbury, Md.	CN
	WAPT	Jackson, Miss.	A
	KSNF	Joplin, Mo.	N
†	----	St. Joseph, Mo.	
†	KTAJ	St. Joseph, Mo.	
†	----	Scottsbluff, Neb.	
*	WNPE	Watertown, N.Y.	P
†	WRDG	Burlington, N.C.	
*	WPTD	Dayton, O.	P
	KMTR	Eugene, Ore.	N
*	WQEX	Pittsburgh, Pa.	P
	WNEP-TV	Scranton, Pa.	A
†	WTRA	Mayaguez, P.R.	
*	WJWJ-TV	Beaufort, S.C.	
	WGGS-TV	Greenville, S.C.	
*	KDSD-TV	Aberdeen, S.D.	P
†	WUAA	Jackson, Tenn.	
*	KEDT	Corpus Christi, Tex.	P
†	----	Everett, Wash.	

17

	Station	Location	
†		Tuscaloosa, Ala.	
†*	KLEP	Newark, Ark.	
	KPWR-TV	Bakersfield, Calif.	N
	WJKS-TV	Jacksonville, Fla.	N
*	WLRN-TV	Miami, Fla.	P
	WTBS	Atlanta, Ga.	
	WAND	Decatur, Ill.	A
	WTVO	Rockford, Ill.	N
	KCBR	Des Moines, Ia.	
	WXMI	Grand Rapids, Mich.	
*	KTCI-TV	St. Paul, Minn.	P
*	WMAU	Brookhaven, Miss.	
	KCBJ-TV	Columbia, Mo.	N
†	----	Missoula, Mont.	
*	WNED-TV	Buffalo, N.Y.	P
*	WMHT	Schenectady, N.Y.	P
*	WUNE-TV	Linville, N.C.	S
	KDLI	Canton, O.	
†	KDOR	Bartlesville, Okla.	
	WPHL-TV	Philadelphia, Pa.	
	WZTV	Nashville, Tenn.	
	CIVM-TV	Montreal, Que.	

18

	Station	Location	
	WDHN	Dothan, Ala.	A
†	KDTU	Tucson, Ariz.	
*	KMTF	Fresno, Calif.	P
	KSCI	San Bernardino, Calif.	
	WHCT-TV	Hartford, Conn.	
†*	----	Cocoa, Fla.	
*	WCLP-TV	Chatsworth, Ga.	P
	WLFI-TV	Lafayette, Ind.	C
†	----	Davenport, Ia.	
†	----	Salina, Kan.	
	WLEX-TV	Lexington, Ky.	N
*	KLTL-TV	Lake Charles, La.	P
†	----	Laurel, Miss.	
*	WMAV	Oxford, Miss.	
	WETM-TV	Elmira, N.Y.	N
*	WNPI	Norwood, N.Y.	P
	WCCB	Charlotte, N.C.	A
	WHIZ-TV	Zanesville, O.	N
†	WSJU	San Juan, P.R.	
*	KLRU	Austin, Tex.	
†	----	Farwell, Tex.	
	KDCD-TV	Midland, Tex.	
	WQOW-TV	Eau Claire, Wis.	A
	WVTV	Milwaukee, Wis.	
	CFRN-TV-8	High Prairie, Alta.	
	CICO-TV-18	London, Ont.	S

19

	Station	Location	
	WHNT-TV	Huntsville, Ala.	C
*	KTEJ	Jonesboro, Ark.	P
	KCSO	Modesto, Calif.	

†	WJFT-TV	Albany, Ga.	
	WRAU-TV	Peoria, Ill.	A
†	WLCN	Madisonville, Ky.	
	WXIX-TV	Newport, Ky.	
	WCDC	Adams, Mass.	A
⋆	WUCM-TV	Bay City, Mich.	P
⋆	WMAH	Biloxi, Miss.	
⋆	KCPT	Kansas City, Mo.	P
⋆	KXNE-TV	Norfolk, Neb.	S
⋆	WUNM-TV	Jacksonville, N.C.	
†	WOIO	Shaker Heights, O.	
†	----	Muskogee, Okla.	
	WFAT	Johnstown, Pa.	
	WLTX	Columbia, S.C.	C
	WKPT-TV	Kingsport, Tenn.	A
†	KDOG	Nacogdoches, Tex.	
	KXIX	Victoria, Tex.	A
	KEPR-TV	Pasco, Wash.	C
	WXOW-TV	La Crosse, Wis.	A
	CBXFT-8	Grand Prairie, Alta.	
	CICO-TV-19	Sudbury, Ont.	S
⋆	CICA-TV	Toronto, Ont.	

20

	WCOV-TV	Montgomery, Ala.	C
	KTZO	San Francisco, Calif.	
	WATR-TV	Waterbury, Conn.	
	WDCA-TV	Washington, D. C.	
	WBBH-TV	Ft. Myers, Fla.	N
	WCJB	Gainesville, Fla.	A
⋆	WCES-TV	Wrens, Ga.	P
†	KHAI-TV	Honolulu, Haw.	
⋆	WYCC	Chicago, Ill.	P
	WICS	Springfield, Ill.	N
⋆	WFYI	Indianapolis, Ind.	P
†	WULT-TV	New Orleans, La.	
	WXON	Detroit, Mich.	
	WUTR	Utica, N.Y.	A
†	WEJC	Lexington, N.C.	
⋆	WOUB-TV	Athens, O.	P
†	KEQO	Enid, Okla.	
†	WNRP	Ponce, P.R.	
	WINT	Crossville, Tenn.	
†	KOAV	Denison, Tex.	
	KTXH	Houston, Tex.	
	KSTU	Salt Lake City, Utah	
⋆	WVTB	St. Johnsbury, Vt.	
	KQFB	Tacoma, Wash.	
⋆	WHRM-TV	Wausau, Wis.	P
	CICO-TV-20	Sault Ste. Marie, Ont.	

21

	WTTO	Birmingham, Ala.	
†	WMPV-TV	Mobile, Ala.	
	KPAZ-TV	Phoenix, Ariz.	
	KFTV	Hanford, Calif.	
†	KXRM-TV	Colorado Springs, Colo.	
	WPTA	Ft. Wayne, Ind.	A
⋆	KTIN	Ft. Dodge, Ia.	P
†	----	Louisville, Ky.	
⋆	WKMU	Murray, Ky.	S
†⋆	WCMW	Manistee, Mich.	
⋆	KOZK	Springfield, Mo.	P
†	KRLR	Las Vegas, Nev.	
	KAME-TV	Reno, Nev.	
†	WNHT	Concord, N.H.	
⋆	WLIW	Garden City, N.Y.	P
⋆	WXXI	Rochester, N.Y.	P
	WHNS	Asheville, N.C.	
	WFMJ-TV	Youngstown, O.	N
	KTVZ	Bend, Ore.	CN
	WHP-TV	Harrisburg, Pa.	C
†	WSMF	Florence, S.C.	
	KTXA	Ft. Worth, Tex.	
†	KTGC	Negerland, Tex.	
†	WJPR	Lynchburg, Va.	
⋆	WHA-TV	Madison, Wis.	P
	CKVU	Vancouver, B.C.	
	CBWFT-10	Brandon, Man.	S
	CBKFT-5	Zenon Park, Sask.	Z

22

†⋆	KRCB-TV	Cotati, Calif.	
	KWHY-TV	Los Angeles, Calif.	
	WCLF	Clearwater, Fla.	
	WJCL	Savannah, Ga.	N
†⋆	----	Mc Comb, Ill.	
	WSBT-TV	South Bend, Ind.	C
⋆	WVUT	Vincennes, Ind.	P
†	----	Waterloo, Ia.	
⋆	WKPI	Pikeville, Ky.	S
⋆	WAPB	Annapolis, Md.	P
	WWLP	Springfield, Mass.	N
†	WLHT	Hattiesburg, Miss.	
⋆	KRWG-TV	Las Cruces, N.M.	P
	WLFL-TV	Raleigh, N.C.	
	WKEF	Dayton, O.	N
†	KECH	Salem, Ore.	
	WPTT-TV	Pittsburgh, Pa.	
	WDAU-TV	Scranton, Pa.	C
†	WNJX-TV	Mayaguez, P.R.	
†	WART	Narajito, P.R.	
⋆	WCTE	Cookeville, Tenn.	
	WVNY	Burlington, Vt.	A
†	KTTZ	Seattle, Wash.	
†	KSKN	Spokane, Wash.	
†	----	Oshkosh, Wis.	
	CKGN-TV-22	Uxbridge, Ont.	S
	CIVR-TV	Rimouski, Que.	
	CBKFT-3	Debden, Sask.	

23

	KERO-TV	Bakersfield, Calif.	C
	WLTV	Miami, Fla.	
⋆	WSRE	Pensacola, Fla.	P
	WIFR-TV	Freeport, Ill.	C
⋆	WKZT	Elizabethtown, Ky.	S
⋆	WKAR-TV	East Lansing, Mich.	P
	KTMA-TV	St. Paul, Minn.	
⋆	WMAO	Greenwood, Miss.	
	KBSI	Cape Girardeau, Mo.	
⋆	WNJS	Camden, N.J.	
	KNAT	Albuquerque, N.M.	
	WXXA	Albany, N.Y.	
†	WTZA	Kingston, N.Y.	
	WAKR-TV	Akron, O.	A
	KOKI	Tulsa, Okla.	
	WOPC	Altoona, Pa.	A
⋆	WHMC	Conway, S.C.	
	KVEO	Brownsville, Tex.	N
†	----	Garland, Tex.	
⋆	WCVE-TV	Richmond, Va.	P
	KNDO-TV	Yakima, Wash.	N
	WVAH	Charleston, W.V.	

24

	KPOM-TV	Ft. Smith, Ark.	N
†	KCPM	Chico, Calif.	
	KSEE	Fresno, Calif.	N
⋆	KVCR-TV	San Bernardino, Calif.	P
⋆	WEDH	Hartford, Conn.	P
⋆	WMFE-TV	Orlando, Fla.	P
	WGXA	Macon, Ga.	A
†⋆	WQPT	Moline, Ill.	P
⋆	KYIN	Mason City, Ia.	P
⋆	KLPB	Lafayette, La.	P
⋆	KLTS	Shreveport, La.	
†	WKJL	Baltimore, Md.	
	WHTV	Meridian, Miss.	CN
†	KNLC	St. Louis, Mo.	
⋆	WCNY-TV	Syracuse, N.Y.	P
	WDHO-TV	Toledo, O.	A
†	KTDZ	Portland, Ore.	
	WJET-TV	Erie, Pa.	A
†	WSJN	San Juan, P.R.	
	WPTY-TV	Memphis, Tenn.	
	KVUE-TV	Austin, Tex.	A
†	----	Odessa, Tex.	
⋆	KIDZ-TV	Wichita Falls, Tex.	
†	----	Ogden, Utah	
†	----	Anacortes, Wash.	
⋆	WNPB	Morgantown, W.V.	P
	WCGV-TV	Milwaukee, Wis.	
	CICO-TV-24	Ottawa, Ont.	
	CIVS-TV	Sherbrooke, Que.	

25

⋆	WHIQ	Huntsville, Ala.	P
†	----	Orange Park, Fla.	
⋆	WACS-TV	Dawson, Ga.	P

	Station	City	
	WEEK-TV	Peoria, Ill.	N
	WEHT	Evansville, Ind.	C
*	WKAS	Ashland, Ky.	S
*	KLPA	Alexandria, La.	P
	WHAG-TV	Hagerstown, Md.	N
	WXNE	Boston, Mass.	
	WEYI-TV	Saginaw, Mich.	C
†	----	Gulfport, Miss.	
†	KKSG	Carlsbad, N.M.	
*	WNYE-TV	New York, N.Y.	P
*	WUNK-TV	Greenville, N.C.	S
*	WVIZ-TV	Cleveland, O.	P
	KOKH-TV	Oklahoma City, Okla.	
	WOLO-TV	Columbia, S.C.	A
	KAVU	Victoria, Tex.	N
	KNDU	Richland, Wash.	N
†	WWQI	La Crosse, Wis.	
	CBLFT	Toronto, Ont.	Z

26

	Station	City	
*	WAIQ	Montgomery, Ala.	
†	----	Hot Springs, Ark.	
	KTSF-TV	San Francisco, Calif.	
	KMPH	Visalia, Calif.	
†	WLCT	New London, Conn.	
*	WETA-TV	Washington, D. C.	P
†	----	Daytona Beach, Fla.	
	WEVU	Naples, Fla.	A
	WATU-TV	Augusta, Ga.	N
	KSHO	Honolulu, Haw.	
	WCIU-TV	Chicago, Ill.	
†*	WISU-TV	Terre Haute, Ind.	
	WGNO-TV	New Orleans, La.	
*	WMEG-TV	Biddeford, Me.	P
†	KXBJ	Bemidji, Minn.	
*	KYNE-TV	Omaha, Neb.	S
†	WJKA	Wilmington, N.C.	
*	WUNL-TV	Winston Salem, N.C.	S
	WTJC	Springfield, O.	
	WTVK	Knoxville, Tenn.	N
	KINT-TV	El Paso, Tex.	
	KRIV-TV	Houston, Tex.	
	WLRE	Green Bay, Wis.	
	CBUFT	Vancouver, B.C.	Z
	CBKFT-9	Bellegarde, Sask.	

27

	Station	City	
†	----	Tucson, Ariz.	
	WECA	Tallahassee, Fla.	A
†	KOHA	Hilo, Haw.	
	WDDD-TV	Marion, Ill.	
*	KSIN	Sioux City, Ia.	P
	KSNT	Topeka, Kan.	N
	WKYT-TV	Lexington, Ky.	C
*	WLPB	Baton Rouge, La.	P
	WSMW-TV	Worcester, Mass.	
†*	WCMV	Cadillac, Mich.	
	WVSB	West Point, Miss.	
	KMTC	Springfield, Mo.	A
*	WBGU-TV	Bowling Green, O.	P
	WKBN-TV	Youngstown, O.	C
	WHTM-TV	Harrisburg, Pa.	A
*	WRJA-TV	Sumter, S.C.	P
	KTWS	Dallas, Tex.	
†	----	Laredo, Tex.	
	WYAH-TV	Portsmouth, Va.	
†	WEFC	Roanoke, Va.	
†	KWCT	Wenatchee, Wash.	
	WKOW-TV	Madison, Wis.	A
†	KLWY	Cheyenne, Wyo.	

28

	Station	City	
*	KCET	Los Angeles, Calif.	P
†	----	Oroville, Calif.	
†	WMJA	Panama City, Fla.	
	WFTS	Tampa, Fla.	
*	WJSP-TV	Columbus, Ga.	P
	WSJV	Elkhart, Ind.	A
*	WCPB	Salisbury, Md.	P
†	WFDG	New Bedford, Mass.	
*	WFUM	Flint, Mich.	P
	WPTF-TV	Durham, N.C.	N
†	WTTE	Columbus, O.	
	WBRE-TV	Wilkes Barre, Pa.	N
	WTGS	Hardeeville, S.C.	
†	WKWR	Cookeville, Tenn.	
	KORO	Corpus Christi, Tex.	
	KAMC	Lubbock, Tex.	A
*	WVER	Rutland, Vt.	
	KAYU	Spokane, Wash.	
*	KTPS	Tacoma, Wash.	P
*	WHWC-TV	Menomonie, Wis.	P
	CICO-TV-28	Kitchener, Ont.	S

29

	Station	City	
	KTVP	Fayetteville, Ark.	A
	KBAK-TV	Bakersfield, Calif.	A
	WFLX	West Palm Beach, Fla.	
*	WKPD	Paducah, Ky.	
*	WKSO	Somerset, Ky.	S
	KVHP	Lake Charles, La.	
	WGTU	Traverse City, Mich.	A
	WFBT	Minneapolis, Minn.	
*	WMAA	Jackson, Miss.	P
*	KHNE-TV	Hastings, Neb.	S
†	KHFT	Hobbs, N.M.	
	WUTV	Buffalo, N.Y.	
	WTAF-TV	Philadelphia, Pa.	
†	----	State College, Pa.	
*	WNTV-TV	Greenville, S.C.	
†	----	San Antonio, Tex.	
	WVIR-TV	Charlottesville, Va.	N
	KIMA-TV	Yakima, Wash.	C

30

	Station	City	
	KFSN-TV	Fresno, Calif.	C
†	KHOF-TV	San Bernardino, Calif.	
	WVIT	New Britain, Conn.	
*	WSFP-TV	Ft. Myers, Fla.	
	WAWS-TV	Jacksonville, Fla.	
*	WETV	Atlanta, Ga.	P
*	WTIU	Bloomington, Ind.	P
†	WDAV	Davenport, Ia.	
	WLBM	Meridian, Miss.	
	KDNL-TV	St. Louis, Mo.	
*	WGTE-TV	Toledo, O.	P
†	KCVT	Shawnee, Okla.	
†	WRWR	San Juan, P.R.	
†	----	Rock Hill, S.C.	
†	WMKW	Memphis, Tenn.	
†	WCAY-TV	Nashville, Tenn.	
†	KOOG-TV	Ogden, Utah	
†	WVCY	Milwaukee, Wis.	
	CIVO	Hull, Que.	S

31

	Station	City	
	WAAY-TV	Huntsville, Ala.	A
	KRBK	Sacramento, Calif.	
†	KDVR	Denver, Colo.	
†	WTSG	Albany, Ga.	
	WMBD-TV	Peoria, Ill.	C
*	WKOH	Owensboro, Ky.	
	KLAX-TV	Alexandria, La.	
*	WWPB	Hagerstown, Md.	P
	WIHT	Ann Arbor, Mich.	
*	WNYC-TV	New York, N.Y.	P
	WUHF	Rochester, N.Y.	
†	KVTX	Victoria, Tex.	
	WNNE	Hartford, Vt.	N
*	WHLA-TV	La Crosse, Wis.	P

32

	Station	City	
	WKAB-TV	Montgomery, Ala.	A
*	KQEC	San Francisco, Calif.	P
*	WHMM	Washington, D. C.	P
†	----	Lakeland, Fla.	
†	WNEG-TV	Toccoa, Ga.	
†	----	Honolulu, Haw.	
	WFLD-TV	Chicago, Ill.	
*	KBIN	Council Bluffs, Ia.	P
*	KRIN	Waterloo, Ia.	
	WLKY	Louisville, Ky.	A
†	WLAE-TV	New Orleans, La.	
†	WRLP	Greenfield, Mass.	
†	----	Aguadilla, P.R.	
	KTAB-TV	Abilene, Tex.	
†	WBUD	Appleton, Wis.	
	CICO-TV-32	Windsor, Ont.	S

33

†	WCFT-TV	Tuscaloosa, Ala.	C
	KTVW-TV	Phoenix, Ariz.	
†	----	San Luis Obispo, Calif.	
†	WBFS-TV	Miami, Fla.	
†	----	Pensacola, Fla.	
	WKJG-TV	Ft. Wayne, Ind.	N
†	----	Wichita, Kan.	
	WRBT	Baton Rouge, La.	N
	KSPR	Springfield, Mo.	
†	WTUV	Utica, N.Y.	
*	WUNF-TV	Asheville, N.C.	S
	WYTV	Youngstown, O.	A
*	WITF-TV	Harrisburg, Pa.	P
*	WJPM-TV	Florence, S.C.	
	KNBN-TV	Dallas, Tex.	
*	WETK	Burlington, Vt.	P
	WTVZ	Norfolk, Va.	
*	WPBY	Huntington, W.V.	P
	CKSR-TV	Santa Rosa, B.C.	

34

	KMEX-TV	Los Angeles, Calif.	
	WTVX	Ft. Pierce, Fla.	C
*	WNIT	South Bend, Ind.	P
†	WGRB	Campbellsville, Ky.	
	WMGC-TV	Binghamton, N.Y.	A
*	WOSU-TV	Columbus, O.	P
	KGMC	Oklahoma City, Okla.	
	KJAA	Lubbock, Tex.	

35

	KCBA	Salinas, Calif.	A
†	WPAN	Ft. Walton Beach, Fla.	
	WOFL	Orlando, Fla.	
†	WWTO-TV	Lasalle, Ill.	
*	WKHA	Hazard, Ky.	S
*	WKMA	Madisonville, Ky.	S
*	WGVC	Grand Rapids, Mass.	P
	WLIO	Lima, O.	N
	WSEE	Erie, Pa.	C
*	WRLK-TV	Columbia, S.C.	
†	----	Kerrville, Tex.	
†	KMLT-TV	Marshall, Tex.	
	WRLH	Richmond, Va.	
	KAPP	Yakima, Wash.	A
	CKRN-TV-3	Bearn, Que.	S

36

*	WFIQ	Florence, Ala.	P
	KMIR-TV	Palm Springs, Calif.	N
	KICU	San Jose, Calif.	
	WATL-TV	Atlanta, Ga.	
*	KHIN	Red Oak, Ia.	P
	WTVQ	Lexington, Ky.	A
†	KBBM-TV	Jefferson City, Mo.	
	WENY-TV	Elmira, N.Y.	A
	WPCQ-TV	Charlotte, N.C.	N
†	WDMA-TV	Toledo, O.	
*	WSBE-TV	Providence, R.I.	P
	KTVV	Austin, Tex.	N
*	WMVT	Milwaukee, Wis.	
*	WLEF-TV	Park Falls, Wis.	

38

†	KMJD-TV	Pine Bluff, Ark.	
†	KVOF-TV	San Francisco, Calif.	
†	----	St. Petersburg, Fla.	
	WLTZ	Columbus, Ga.	N
	WCFC-TV	Chicago, Ill.	
	WBAK-TV	Terre Haute, Ind.	A
*	WKMR	Morehead, Ky.	S
†	WNOL-TV	New Orleans, La.	
†	----	Portland, Me.	
	WSBK-TV	Boston,	
†		Greenville, N.C.	
†	WSWB	Wilkes Barre, Pa.	
†	----	San Sebastian, P.R.	
†	----	Corpus Christi, Tex.	
†	----	Roanoke, Va.	
*	WPNE	Green Bay, Wis.	P

39

	KCST-TV	San Diego, Calif.	N
	WDZL	Miami, Fla.	
	WQRF-TV	Rockford, Ill.	
†	KMCT-TV	West Monroe, La.	
*	WUNJ-TV	Wilmington, N.C.	S
*	WLVT-TV	Allentown, Pa.	P
*	WRET-TV	Spartanburg, S.C.	P
†	WOQF	Greenville, Tenn.	
†	WFYZ	Murfreesboro, Tenn.	
	KXTX	Dallas, Tex.	
	KHTV	Houston, Tex.	
†	----	Parkersburg, W.V.	
†	WWTL	Marshfield, Wis.	
	CBKFT-6	Gavelbourg, Sask.	

40

	WHMA-TV	Anniston, Ala.	C
	----	Anniston, Ala.	
†	----	Tucson, Ariz.	
	KHBS	Ft. Smith, Ark.	A
	KTXL	Sacramento, Calif.	
	KTBN-TV	Santa Ana, Calif.	
	WXLT-TV	Sarasota, Fla.	A
†	WTWC	Tallahassee, Fla.	
	WHMB-TV	Indianapolis, Ind.	
	KDUB-TV	Dubuque, Ia.	A
†	WQQB	Bowling Green, Ky.	
	WGGB-TV	Springfield,	A
†	WDBD	Jackson, Miss.	
†*	KUCU	St. Louis, Mo.	
*	WEDB-TV	Berlin, N.H.	P
	WAAT	Wildwood, N.J.	N
	WICZ-TV	Binghamton, N.Y.	N
	WKFT	Fayetteville, N.C.	
	WPCB-TV	Greensburg, Pa.	
†	WMTJ	Fajardo, P.R.	
	WAXA	Anderson, S.C.	
†	WRJK	Bluefield, Va.	
	CHOT-TV	Hull, Que.	

41

*	WIIQ	Demopolis, Ala.	
	WMGT	Macon, Ga.	N
	WDRB-TV	Louisville, Ky.	
	WUHQ-TV	Battle Creek, Mass.	A
	KXLI	St Cloud, Minn.	
	KSHB-TV	Kansas City, Mo.	
	WXTV	Paterson, N.J.	
	KGCT-TV	Tulsa, Okla.	
	KWEX-TV	San Antonio, Tex.	
*	WVTA	Windsor, Vt.	

42

	WBMG	Birmingham, Ala.	C
*	WEIQ	Mobile, Ala.	P
†	KBSC-TV	Concord, Calif.	
	KESQ	Palm Springs, Calif.	A
†*	WHRS	West Palm Beach, Fla.	P
*	WTVI	Charlotte, N.C.	P
*	WPBO-TV	Portsmouth, O.	
†	WUIA-TV	San German, P.R.	
†	KBVO	Austin, Tex.	
†	KLPH	Paris, Tex.	
	KVEW	Kennewick, Wash.	S
	CKCO-TV-3	Sarnia, Ont.	

43

*	WGIQ	Louisville, Ala.	P
†	----	Clovis, Calif.	
†	WBCT	Bridgeport, Conn.	
†	WMOD	Melbourne, Fla.	
	WBLN	Bloomington, Ill.	
	WKOI	Richmond, Ind.	
†	KREN	Reno, Nev.	
†	----	Las Cruces, N.M.	
†	WFWY	Syracuse, N.Y.	
	WUAB-TV	Lorain, O.	
	KAUT	Oklahoma City, Okla.	
	WPMT	York, Pa.	
†	WGSE	Myrtle Beach, S.C.	
†	WKCH	Knoxville, Tenn.	
†	WTMB-TV	Tomah, Wis.	

44

	Station	City	
†	WTJP	Gadsden, Ala.	
	KBHK-TV	San Francisco, Calif.	
†	----	Pensacola, Fla.	
	WTOG	St. Petersburg, Fla.	
	WVGA	Valdosta, Ga.	A
	WSNS	Chicago, Ill.	
	WEVV	Evansville, Ind.	
*	WGBX-TV	Boston, Mass.	
*	WOUC-TV	Cambridge, O.	P
	WTLW	Lima, O.	
*	WVIA-TV	Scranton, Pa.	P
	WVEO	Aguadilla, P.R.	
†*	KLUJ	Harlingen, Tex.	
†	KWKT	Waco, Tex.	

45

	Station	City	
	WMCF-TV	Montgomery, Ala.	
	WHFT	Miami, Fla.	
	WBFF	Baltimore, Md.	
†	----	St. Paul, Minn.	
†	KDCQ	Sikeston, Mo.	
†	WUSV	Schenectady, N.Y.	
	WJTM	Winston Salem, N.C.	
*	WNEO-TV	Alliance, O.	P
†	----	Dayton, O.	
	KQOL-TV	Lawton, Okla.	
*	WTCI	Chattanooga, Tenn.	P
	CIVC-TV	Three Rivers, Que.	

46

	Station	City	
	KMST	Monterey, Calif.	C
	KIHS-TV	Ontario, Calif.	
	WANX-TV	Atlanta, Ga.	
	WHME-TV	South Bend, Ind.	
*	WKLE	Lexington, Ky.	P
*	WERZ	Binghamton, N.Y.	P
†	----	Norman, Okla.	
†	WCNT	Cidra, P.R.	
*	KNCT	Belton, Tex.	P
	WLYJ	Clarksburg, W.V.	

47

	Station	City	
	KJEO	Fresno, Calif.	A
	WNFT	Jacksonville, Fla.	
*	WTVP	Peoria, Ill.	P
	WMDT	Salisbury, Md.	A
*	WFSL	Lansing, Mich.	
†	KXLT	Rochester, Minn.	
	WNJU-TV	Linden, N.J.	
†	KBJH	Tulsa, Okla.	
*	WSVN-TV	Norton, Va.	P
*	KYVE-TV	Yakima, Wash.	P
†	WMSN-TV	Madison, Wis.	
	CFMT-TV	Toronto, Ont.	

48

	Station	City	
	WAFF	Decatur, Ala.	N
	KSTS	San Jose, Calif.	
†	WPMJ	Owensboro, Ky.	
†	----	Natchez, Miss.	
	WGGT	Greensboro, N.C.	
*	WCET	Cincinnati, O.	P
†	----	Ponce, P.R.	
†	WCGC	Greenwood, S.C.	
†	----	Gaveston, Tex.	
†	----	Mc Allen, Tex.	

49

	Station	City	
*	WEDW	Bridgeport, Conn.	P
*	WIPB	Muncie, Ind.	P
	KLDH	Topeka, Kan.	A
†	----	New Orleans, La.	
†	WAQP	Saginaw, Mich.	
*	WLED-TV	Littleton, N.H.	P
†	----	Buffalo, N.Y.	
*	WEAO	Akron, O.	
	WGCB-TV	Red Licn, Pa.	
†	KLTJ	Irving, Tex.	
*	WUHX	Norfolk, Va.	
†	KPDX	Vancouver, Wash.	
†	WJJA	Racine, Wis.	

50

	Station	City	
*	KOCE-TV	Huntington Beach, Calif.	P
	KFTY	Santa Rosa, Calif.	
†	WCQR	Washington, D. C.	
†	----	Tampa, Fla.	
†	WCAE	St. John, Ind.	
	WKBD	Detroit, Mich.	
	KYFC	Kansas City, Mo.	
†	WNDS	Derry, N.H.	
*	WNJM	Montclair, N.J.	
	CBUFT-2	Kamloops, B.C.	S

51

	Station	City	
	KUSI	San Diego, Calif.	
	WKID	Ft. Lauderdale, Fla.	
†	WBSP	Ocala, Fla.	
†	WNKJ-TV	Hopkinsville, Ky.	
†	WHSI	Portland, Me.	
†	----	Pittsfield, Mass.	
†*	KGNQ	Lincoln, Neb.	
	WSFJ	Newark, O.	
	WTVE	Reading, Pa.	
	KLMG	Longview, Tex.	
*	WVPT	Staunton, Va.	P

52

	Station	City	
	KBSC-TV	Corona, Calif.	
	WTGL	Cocoa, Fla.	
*	WKON	Owenton, Ky.	S
†*	----	Kalamazoo, Mich.	
*	WEKW-TV	Keene, N.H.	
*	WNJT	Trenton, N.J.	P
†	----	Ithaca, N.Y.	
	WGGN-TV	Sandusky, O.	
†	KSBI	Oklahoma City, Okla.	
*	WMSY	Marion, Va.	P

53

	Station	City	
	KAIL	Fresno, Calif.	
*	WEDN	Norwich, Conn.	P
†	WQAC	Ft. Walton Beach, Fla.	
*	WKGB	Bowling Green, Ky.	S
†	WLAJ	Lansing, Mich.	
	WWAC-TV	Atlantic City, N.J.	
	WPGH-TV	Pittsburgh, Pa.	
*	WNVT	Annandale, Va.	P

54

	Station	City	
†		Huntsville, Ala.	
*	KTEH-TV	San Jose, Calif.	P
†	WXTX	Augusta, Ga.	
†	WXTX	Columbus, Ga.	
*	WCVN	Covington, Ky.	S
	WNUV-TV	Baltimore, Md.	
†	WMKT	Muskegon, Mich.	
†	WTBY	Poughkeepsie, N.Y.	
*	WQLN	Erie, Pa.	P
	WATX	Arelibo, P.R.	
	CBEFT	Windsor, Ont.	Z

55

	Station	City	
	WIYE	Leesburg, Fla.	
	WRSP	Springfield, Ill.	
	WFFT	Ft. Wayne, Ind.	
†	WLIG	Riverhead, N.Y.	
†	----	Kanosha, Wis.	
†	----	Racine, Wis.	

56

	Station	City	
†	KDOC	Anaheim, Calif.	
†	WSCT	Melbourne, Fla.	
†	WDAI	Gary, Ind.	
†	WDKY-TV	Danville, Ky.	
	WLVI-TV	Cambridge,	
*	WTVS	Detroit, Mich.	P
†	----	Akron, O.	
†	WERF	Hazleton, Pa.	
*	WNVC	Fairfax, Va.	

57

	Station	City	
	WKYH-TV	Hazard, Ky.	N
*	WGBY-TV	Springfield, Mass.	P
*	WCFE-TV	Plattsburgh, N.Y.	P
	WWSG	Philadelphia, Pa.	
	WCCT-TV	Columbia, S.C.	
*	WCVW	Richmond, Va.	

58

	Station	City	
†	KCCA	Sierra Vista, Ariz.	
*	KLCS	Los Angeles, Calif.	P
†	KSCH	Stockton, Calif.	
*	WNJB	New Brunswick, N.J.	
*	WUNG-TV	Concord, N.C.	S
†*	WUJA	Caguas, P.R.	
	CBJET	Chicoutimi, Que.	S

59

	Station	City	
†	WTVU	New Haven, Conn.	
	WPDS-TV	Indianapolis, Ind.	
†	WGGF	Lebanon, Pa.	
	CICO-TV-59	Chatham, Ont.	S

60

	Station	City	
†	----	Dothan, Ala.	
*	KCSM-TV	San Mateo, Calif.	P
†#	WPWR	Aurora, Ill.	
†#	WBBS-TV	West Chicago, Ill.	
†	----	Merrimack, N.H.	
*	KZLN	Harlingen, Tex.	

61

	Station	City	
		Hartford, Conn.	
†	WDVI	Wilmington, Del.	
	WTSF	Ashland, Ky.	
†	WVCI	Bay City, Mich.	
	WLXI-TV	Greensboro, N.C.	
	WLXI-TV	Greeville, N.C.	
	WCLQ-TV	Cleveland, O.	
	WDSI-TV	Chattanooga, Tenn.	

62

	Station	City	
†	----	Riverside, Calif.	
†	----	Lawrence, Kan.	
†	----	Lexington, Ky.	
†	----	Lawrence, Mass.	
	WGPR-TV	Detroit, Mich.	
†	KEKR	Kansas City, Mo.	
†	WKAF	Syracuse, N.Y.	
†	WFCT	Fayetteville, N.C.	
†	----	Oklahoma City, Okla.	

63

	Station	City	
†	KTIE	Oxnard, Calif.	
†	WFGC	Palm Beach, Fla.	
	WXJC	Angola, Ind.	
†	----	Des Moines, Ia.	
†	----	Kingston, N.Y.	
	WTLL	Richmond, Va.	

64

	Station	City	
†	----	Stockton, Calif.	
*	WDPB	Seaford, Del.	P
†	WLLA	Kalamazoo, Mich.	
	WBTI	Cincinnati, O.	
†	----	Narajito, O.	
†	----	Narajito, P.R.	
	WSTG	Providence, R.I.	
†	WBGY-TV	Tullahoma, Tenn.	

65

	Station	City	
†	KLXV	San Jose, Calif.	
*	WEDY	New Haven, Conn.	P
	WLJC	Beattyville, Ky.	
	WRBV	Vineland, N.J.	
†	----	Defiance, O.	

66

	Station	City	
	WSWS	Opelika, Ala.	
	WFBN	Joliet, Ill.	
	WGTR-TV	Marlborough, Mass.	
†	WSAY-TV	Forest City, N.C.	
	WTKK	Manassas, Va.	

67

	Station	City	
†	----	Morehead, Ky.	
*	WMPB	Baltimore, Md.	P
	WSNL-TV	Smithtown, N.Y.	
†	WIUW	High Point, N.C.	
	WOAC	Canton, O.	
†	----	Alvin, Tex.	

68

	Station	City	
†	WCAJ	Birmingham, Ala.	
†*	KDDE	Los Angeles, Calif.	
*	WKMJ	Louisville, Ky.	S
	WQTV	Boston, Mass.	
	WWHT	Newark, N.J.	
†	----	Humacao, P.R.	

69

	Station	City	
	KTTY	San Diego, Calif.	
†	----	Hollywood, Fla.	
	WVEU	Atlanta, Ga.	
†	----	Paintsville, Ky.	
	WFMZ-TV	Allentown, Pa.	

79

	Station	City	
	CITY-TV	Toronto, Ont.	

FM Stations by Geographic Location

UNITED STATES

Alabama

Abbeville
WXLE 94.3
Albertville
WQSB 105.1
Alexander City
WRFS-FM 106.1
Andalusia
WKYD-FM 98.1
Anniston
WHMA-FM 100.5
Arab
WCRQ-FM 92.7
Ashland
† WASZ 95.3
Athens
WZYP 104.3
Atmore
WSKR 104.1
Auburn
* WEGL 91.1
WFRI 97.7
Bay Minette
WWSM 105.5
Birmingham
WAPI-FM 94.5
* WBHM 90.3
WDJC 93.7
WENN-FM 107.7
†* WGIB 91.9
* WJSR 91.1
WKXX 106.9
WMJJ 96.5
WRKK 99.5
* WVSU-FM 91.1
WZZK 104.7
Brewton
WKNU 106.3
Butler
WQGL 93.5
Camden
† WODB 102.3
Carrollton
WAQT 94.1
Chickasaw
† WJQY 98.3
Clanton
WEZZ 97.7
Cullman
WFMH-FM 101.1
WKLN 92.1
Decatur
* WBQM 91.7
WDRM 102.1
WRSA 96.9
Demopolis
WNAN 106.3
Dothan
WOOF-FM 99.7
WTVY-FM 95.5
Enterprise
WKMX 106.7
WLHQ 96.9
Eufaula
WKQK 92.7
Evergreen
† WEGN-FM 93.5
Fairhope
WZEW 92.1
Fayette
WHKW 98.1
Florence
WQLT 107.3
Gadsden
* WEXP 91.5
WQEN 103.7
Geneva
WGEA-FM 93.5
Greenville
WKXN 95.9
Guntersville
WTWX 95.9
Haleyville
WJBB-FM 92.7
Hamilton
WERH-FM 92.1
Huntsville
†* WAED 90.9
WAHR 99.1
* WLRH 89.3
WNDA 95.1
* WOGC 90.1
Jackson
WHOD-FM 104.9
Jacksonville
* WLJS-FM 91.9
Jasper
WWWB-FM 102.5
Marion
† WJAM-FM 103.9
Mobile
WABB-FM 97.5
WBLX 92.9
* WHIL-FM 91.3
WKRG-FM 99.9
WKSJ-FM 94.9
WLPR 96.1
‡* WTOH 90.5
†* WTOH 105.9
Monroeville
WMFC-FM 99.3
Montgomery
WBAM-FM 98.9
WHHY-FM 101.9
†* WLBF 89.1
WLWI 92.3
WREZ 103.3
†* WVAS 90.7
Muscle Shoals
WLAY-FM 105.5
Oneonta
WKLD 97.7
Opp
WAMI-FM 102.3
Ozark
WOAB 104.9
WORJ 103.9
Phenix City
WEIZ 100.1
Prattville
WQIM 95.3
Reform
WVRT 101.7
Roanoke
† WELR-FM 102.3
‡ WELR-FM 95.3
Scottsboro
WKEA-FM 98.3
Selma
WALX 100.9
WTUN 100.1
Sheffield
WBTG 106.3
Stevenson
WVSV 101.7
Sylacauga
WMLS-FM 98.3
Talladega
WHTB 92.7
Thomasville
WJDB-FM 95.3
Troy
WIGC 105.7
* WTSU 89.9
Tuscaloosa
WACT-FM 105.5
WTUG 92.7
* WUAL-FM 91.5
WUOA 95.7
* WVUA-FM 90.7
Tuscumbia
WVNA-FM 100.3
Tuskegee
WBIL-FM 95.9
Union Springs
WSCA 100.9
York
WSLY 99.3

Alaska

Anchorage
KCMG 100.5
KGOT 101.3
† KKLV 104.1
‡ KKLV 103.9
† KNIK-FM 105.3
‡ KNIK-FM 105.5
KRKN 102.1
* KSKA 103.1
KWHL 106.5
Bethel
KJBA 100.1
Fairbanks
† ---- 95.3
† KAYY 101.1
† KQRZ 102.5
* KUAC-FM 104.7
Haines
* KHNS 102.3
Homer
KGTL-FM 103.5
Juneau
* KTOO 104.3
Kenai
KQOK 100.1
Ketchikan
* KRBD 105.9
Kodiak
KMXT 100.1
Naknek
† KTTH 100.9
Nome
KICY-FM 100.3
North Pole
KJNP-FM 103.3
Petersburg
* KFSK 100.9
Sitka
* KCAW 104.7
Wrangell
* KSTK 101.7
Yakutat
†* KJFP 103.9

Arizona

Apache Jct
KCTM 107.1
Benson
KAVV 97.7
Bisbee
KZMK 92.1
Bullhead City
KRHS-FM 102.7
Casa Grande
KSAA 105.5
Chandler
KMLE 107.9
Coolidge
KQEZ-FM 103.9
Cottonwood
KSMK-FM 95.9
Douglas
KKRK 95.3
Eager
† ---- 92.5
Eloy
† KKAF 106.3
Flagstaff
KAFF 92.9
†* KNAU 88.7
‡* KNAU 88.5
KSOJ 93.9
Glendale
KEZC 92.3
Globe
KIKO-FM 100.3
Green Valley
KEZG 92.1
Kingman
† ---- 100.1
KZZZ 94.7
Lake Havasu City
KBBC 101.1
†* KNLB 91.1
Marana
† KOPO 98.3
Mesa
KDKB 93.3
KZZP-FM 104.7
Nogales
* KAYN 98.3
Oracle
† KTTZ 103.1
Page
† KXAZ 93.5
Parker
KMDX 99.3
Payson
KPSN 103.9
Phoenix
KHEP-FM 101.5
†* KIAI 89.5
KKLT 98.7
* KMCR-FM 91.5
KMEO-FM 96.9
KNIX-FM 102.5
KNNN 99.9
KOOL-FM 94.5
KQYT 95.5
Prescott
KAHM 103.9
KNOT-FM 98.3
Safford
KXKQ 94.1
Scottsdale
KOPA-FM 100.7
Sedona
† KOST 100.1
Show Low
† KRFM 96.5
KVWM-FM 93.5
Sierra Vista
KTAZ-FM 100.9
Sun City
KMZK 106.3
Tempe
KUPD-FM 97.9
Thatcher
KFMM 99.1
Tsaile
* KNCC 91.9
Tucson
† ---- 107.5
KJYK 94.9
KLPX 96.1
KNDE 99.5
KRQQ 93.7
* KUAT-FM 90.5
KWFM 92.9
†* KXCI 91.7
Whiteriver
†* KNNB 88.1
Wickenburg
† WHBC 105.5
Willcox
KWCX 98.3
Winslow
† KRIM 95.1
Yuma
KJOK 93.1
KTTI 95.1

Arkansas

Arkadelphia
KDEL-FM 100.9
* KSWH 91.1
Ashdown
KMLA 103.9

Augusta	
KABK-FM	97.7
Bald Knob	
† ----	107.1
Batesville	
★ KGED	88.1
KZLE	93.1
Benton	
KAKI	107.1
Bentonville	
† KBCV	98.3
Berryville	
KSCC	107.1
Blytheville	
† KHLS	96.3
‡ KHLS	96.1
Booneville	
KJON	92.1
Brinkley	
KBRI-FM	102.3
Camden	
KWEH	97.1
Cave City	
★ KZIG	89.9
Cherokee Village	
KFCM	100.9
Clarksville	
KLYR-FM	92.7
Clinton	
† KHPQ	92.1
Conway	
† ----	92.7
★ KHDX	93.1
KMJX	105.1
★ KUCA	91.3
Corning	
† KBKG	93.5
Crossett	
KAGH-FM	104.9
Dardanelle	
KWKK	102.3
De Queen	
KDQN-FM	92.7
De Witt	
KDEW-FM	96.7
Dumas	
KDDA-FM	107.1
El Dorado	
KAYZ	103.1
† KCAJ	95.9
KLBQ	99.3
Fairfield Bay	
KFFB	106.3
Fayetteville	
KEZA	107.9
KKEG	92.1
KKIX	103.9
★ KUAF	88.9
Fordyce	
KQEW	101.7
Forrest City	
KBFC	93.5
Ft. Smith	
KFPW-FM	100.9
KISR	93.7
KMAG	99.1
KTCS-FM	99.9
Greenwood	
KAJJ	106.3
Harrison	
KCWD	96.7
KHOZ-FM	102.9
Heber Springs	
KAWW-FM	96.7
Helena	
KCRI-FM	103.1
Hope	
KHPA	104.9
Hot Springs	
KACQ	106.3
†★ KSBC	90.1
KSPA	96.7
KWBO	97.5
Huntsville	
† KRRA	95.9
Jacksonville	
KEZQ	100.3
Jonesboro	
★ KASU	91.9
KBTM-FM	101.9
KFIN	107.9
Lake Village	
KLVA	95.9
Little Rock	
†★ KABF	88.3
KKYK	103.7
KLAZ	98.5
KLPQ	94.1
★ KLRE-FM	90.5
KSSN	95.7
†★ KUAR	89.1
Lonoke	
† KTWD	106.3
Magnolia	
KVMA-FM	107.9
Mammoth Spring	
KAMS	95.1
Marshall	
† KZRO	104.3
Mena	
KUOL	101.7
Monticello	
KHBM-FM	93.5
Morrilton	
KVOM-FM	101.7
Mountain Home	
† ----	105.5
KTLO-FM	98.3
Mountain View	
KWOZ	103.3
Murfreesboro	
KJKK	95.3
Nashville	
KNAS	105.5
Newark	
†★ KLLN	90.9
Newport	
KOKR	105.5
Osceola	
KHFO	98.1
Ozark	
KZRK-FM	96.7
Paragould	
KDXY	104.9
† KLQZ	107.1
Paris	
KEED	95.3
Piggott	
† KTEI	105.5
Pine Bluff	
KADL	94.9
KFXE	92.3
Pocahontas	
KCYN	103.9
Rogers	
KAMO-FM	94.3
Russellville	
† ----	100.9
Salem	
KSAR	95.9
Searcy	
KSER	99.3
Sheridan	
KKBE	102.3
Siloam Springs	
†★ KLRC	90.3
KMCK	105.7
Springdale	
KCIZ	104.9
Stamps	
KMSL	100.1
Stuttgart	
† ----	105.5
Texarkana	
KADO-FM	107.1
Van Buren	
† KXXI-FM	102.3
Waldron	
KRWA-FM	103.1
Walnut Ridge	
KCAZ	106.3
Warren	
KWRF-FM	105.5
West Helena	
† KQEE	104.9
Wynne	
KWYN-FM	92.7
Yellville	
† ----	97.7

California

Alameda	
KJAZ	92.7
Alturas	
† KBGX	94.5
Anaheim	
KEZY	95.9
Anderson	
† KEWB	94.3
Angwin	
★ KCDS	89.9
Apple Valley	
KAPV	102.3
Arcadia	
KMAX	107.1
Arcata	
†★ KAHS	95.1
‡★ KAHS	91.5
†★ KHSU-FM	91.5
‡★ KHSU-FM	90.5
† KXGO	93.1
‡ KXGO	93.5
Atascadero	
KIQO	104.5
Atherton	
KCEA	89.1
Auburn	
KHYL	101.1
Bakersfield	
KGFM	101.5
KHIS-FM	96.5
KKXX	107.9
KLYD	94.1
Barstow	
KZNS	94.3
Berkeley	
★ KALX	90.7
KBLX	102.9
★ KPFA	94.1
★ KPFB	89.3
Big Bear Lake	
KTOT	101.7
Bishop	
KIOQ-FM	100.7
Blythe	
★ KERU	88.5
KJMB-FM	100.3
Borrego Springs	
★ KBSH	88.9
Brawley	
KSIQ	96.1
Buena Park	
★ KBPK	90.1
Burney	
† KARZ	106.1
Calexico	
† KQVO	97.7
Camarillo	
KZTR	95.9
Carlsbad	
KKOS	95.9
Carmel	
KWST	101.7
Carnelian Bay	
† KHTX	103.7
‡ KHTX	101.7
Carpenteria	
KGFT	101.7
Cathedral City	
KWXY-FM	98.5
Ceres	
★ KBES	89.5
Chico	
★ KCHO	91.1
KFMF	93.7
KPAY-FM	95.1
Chualar	
★ KUBO	90.9
Claremont	
★ KSPC	88.7
Coachella	
KCHV	93.7
Compton	
KJLH	102.3
Concord	
★ KVHS	90.5
Copperopolis	
† KZDO	105.5
Covelo	
†★ KPAU	90.7
Crescent City	
KCRE-FM	94.3
Cupertino	
★ KKUP	91.5
Davis	
★ KDVS	90.3
KYLO	105.5
Delano	
KDNO	98.5
† KZAY	105.3
Delhi	
† KNTO	95.9
Dinuba	
KOJY	98.9
El Cajon	
KECR	93.3
El Centro	
KXO-FM	107.5
El Cerrito	
★ KECG	88.1
Escondido	
KOWN-FM	92.1
Eureka	
† KEKA	101.5
KFMI	96.3
KPDJ	92.3
Fallbrook	
KAVO	107.1
Fort Bragg	
† KOTZ	95.3
Fowler	
KTED	96.7
Fremont	
KBRG	104.9
★ KOHL	89.3
Fresno	
★ KFCF	88.1
KFIG	101.1
KFRY	101.9
†★ KFSR	90.7
KFYE	93.7
KKDJ	105.9
KKNU	102.7
KNAX	97.9
★ KSJV	91.5
★ KVPR-FM	89.3
† KYNO-FM	95.7
‡ KYNO-FM	95.5
Garberville	
KERG	100.1
Garden Grove	
KIKF	94.3
Gilroy	
KWSS	94.5
Glendale	
KUTE	101.9
Goleta	
KMGQ	106.3
Grass Valley	
KNCO-FM	94.3
Grover City	
† KLOI	107.1
Hanford	
KKYS	107.5
KMCX	103.7
Hayward	
★ KCRH	89.9
Healdsburg	
KREO	92.9
Hemet	
KHYE	105.5
Hollister	
KHIP	93.5
Holtville	
KGBA	100.1
Hoopa	
★ KIDE	91.3
Imperial	
KOZN	99.3

Inglewood
KACE 103.9
Irvine
* KUCI 89.9
Jackson
KNGT 94.3
King City
KLFA 92.1
Lake Arrowhead
KBON 103.9
Lakeport
† KQEF 99.5
Lancaster
KOTE 106.3
Legrande
†* KEFR 89.9
Lemoore
† KQYZ 104.9
Livermore
KKIQ 101.7
Livingston
† KNTO 95.9
Lodi
KWIN 97.7
Loma Linda
* KEMR 88.3
Lompoc
KLPC-FM 92.7
KRQK 100.9
Long Beach
* KLON 88.1
KNAC 105.5
KNOB 97.9
* KSUL 90.1
Los Altos
* KFJC 89.7
KPEN 97.7
Los Angeles
KBIG 104.3
KFAC-FM 92.3
KFSG 96.3
† KHOF 99.5
KHTZ 97.1
KIIS-FM 102.7
KIQQ 100.3
KJOI 98.7
KKGO 105.1
KKHR 93.1
KLOS 95.5
KLVE 107.5
KMET 94.7
KMGG 105.9
KOST 103.5
* KPFK 90.7
KRTH 101.1
* KUSC 91.5
* KXLU 88.9
KZLA-FM 93.9
Los Banos
KSNN 104.7
Los Gatos
KRVE 95.3
Madera
* KUUL 92.1
Mammoth Lakes
KMMT 106.3
Manteca
KORY 96.7
Marina
KBOQ 92.7
Mariposa
KUBB 96.3
Marysville
KRFD 99.9
Mendocino
KMFB-FM 92.7
Merced
KAMB 101.5
* KBDR 89.1
KMYT 97.5
Mission Viejo
* KSBR 88.5
Modesto
KBEE-FM 103.3
* KBHI-FM 89.9
* KDHS 90.5
KFIV-FM 102.3
KHOP 104.1

Modesto (Cont)
†* KMPO 88.7
Mojave
KDOL-FM 97.7
Monte Rio
KRJB 97.7
Monterey
KWAV 96.9
Moraga
* KSMC 89.5
Mountain Pass
KXVR 99.5
Mountain View
* KSFH 90.5
Mt. Shasta
KEDY 95.3
Needles
† KJMM 97.9
Nevada City
* KVMR 89.5
Newport Beach
KOCM 103.1
Northridge
KCSN 88.5
Oakdale
KOKQ 95.1
Oakhurst
KAAT 107.1
Oceanside
KEZL-FM 102.1
Ojai
KOVA 105.5
Ontario
KNTF 93.5
Oroville
KEWE 97.7
Oxnard
KCAQ 104.7
KDAR 98.3
Pacific Grove
KAZU 90.3
KOCN 104.9
Palm Desert
KEZN 103.1
Palm Springs
KDES-FM 104.7
† KPLM 106.1
* KPSH-FM 88.3
KPSI-FM 100.9
Paradise
KNVR 96.7
† KRIJ 92.7
Pasadena
* KPCC 89.3
KROQ-FM 106.7
Paso Robles
KDDB 92.5
Patterson
KOSO 93.1
Pebble Beach
†* KSPB 91.9
*‡ KSPB 91.5
Pismo Beach
KPGA 95.3
Placerville
KHTN 92.1
Porterville
KIOO 99.7
Quincy
† KNXN 101.9
Red Bluff
KALF 95.9
† KRBQ 102.3
Redding
KSHA 104.3
KVIP-FM 98.1
Redlands
KCAL-FM 96.7
* KUOR-FM 89.1
Redondo Beach
KFOX 93.5
Ridgecrest
KFIO 104.9
KZIQ-FM 92.7
Rio Vista
†* KRVH 101.5
‡* KRVH 90.9

Riverside
KDUO 97.5
KGGI 99.1
* KSGN 89.7
* KUCR 88.1
KWDJ 92.7
Rosamond
† KCRP 105.5
Roseville
KPOP 93.5
Sacramento
KAER 92.5
KCTC 96.1
KEBR 100.5
KEWT 105.1
KROY 96.9
KWOD 106.5
KXOA-FM 107.9
†* KXPR 90.9
‡* KXPR 89.5
* KYDS 91.5
KZAP 98.5
Salinas
KDON-FM 102.5
KRAY-FM 103.9
KWYT-FM 100.7
San Bernardino
KOLA 99.9
KQLH 95.1
* KVCR 91.9
San Clemente
KWVE 107.9
San Diego
KBZT 94.9
KCBQ-FM 105.3
KFMB-FM 100.7
KFSD-FM 94.1
KGB-FM 101.5
KJQY 103.7
* KPBS-FM 89.5
KPRI 106.5
KSDO-FM 102.9
* KSDS 88.3
KSON-FM 97.3
KYXY 96.5
San Fernando
KGIL-FM 94.3
San Francisco
KABL-FM 98.1
* KALW 91.7
KDFC 102.1
KEAR 106.9
KFOG 104.5
KGO-FM 103.7
KIOI 101.3
KITS 105.3
KKHI-FM 95.7
KYA 93.3
KMEL 106.1
KOIT-FM 96.5
* KPOO 89.5
KQAK 98.9
* KQED-FM 88.5
KRQR 97.3
KSAN-FM 94.9
* KUSF 90.3
KYUU 99.7
San Jose
KBAY 100.3
KEZR 106.5
* KLEL 89.3
KOME 98.5
KSJO 92.3
* KSJS 90.7
San Luis Obispo
† KKUG 98.1
* KCBX 90.1
* KCPR 91.3
KUNA 96.1
KZOZ 93.3
San Mateo
* KCSM 91.1
KSOL 107.7
San Rafael
* KSRH 88.1
KTIM-FM 100.9
Santa Ana
KWIZ-FM 96.7

Santa Ana (Cont)
KYMS 106.3
Santa Barbara
* KCSB-FM 91.9
KDB-FM 93.7
KRUZ 103.3
* KSCA 88.7
KTMS-FM 97.5
KTYD 99.9
Santa Clara
KARA 105.7
* KSCU 103.3
Santa Cruz
KSCO-FM 99.1
* KUSP 88.9
* KZSC 88.1
Santa Maria
KSNI-FM 102.5
KXFM 99.1
Santa Monica
* KCRW 89.9
KSRF 103.1
Santa Paula
KKBZ-FM 96.7
Santa Rosa
* KBBF 89.1
* KCLB 91.9
KVRE-FM 101.7
KZST 100.1
Seaside
KMBY 107.1
Shafter
KIYD-FM 97.7
Solvag
KSYV 96.7
Sonora
KROG 92.7
†* KTUO 99.1
‡* KTUO 91.5
South Lake Tahoe
† KRLT 100.1
‡ KRLT 93.9
† KZFR 102.9
‡ KZFR 103.1
St. Helena
KVYN 99.3
Stanford
* KZSU 90.1
Stockton
* KCJH 90.1
KFMR 100.1
KJAX 99.3
* KSJC-FM 89.3
KSTN-FM 107.3
* KUOP 91.3
Susanville
KSUE-FM 92.7
Taft
† ---- 103.9
Tahoe City
† ---- 96.5
Tehachapi
KTPI 103.1
Temecula
* KRTM 88.9
Thousand Oaks
* KCPB 91.1
KNJO 92.7
Torrance
* KNHS 89.7
Tracy
KYBB 100.9
Travis A F B
* KVIK 91.5
Tulare
KBOS 94.9
KJUG 106.7
Turlock
* KBDG 90.9
* KCSS 91.9
KMIX 98.3
Twentynine Palms
KQYN 95.7
Ukiah
KIAH 103.3
KWNE 94.5
Vacaville
KUIC 95.3

Ventura
† ---- 107.1
KBBY 95.1
KHAY 100.7
Victorville
KVVQ 103.1
Visalia
KONG-FM 92.9
Walnut
★ KSAK 90.1
Walnut Creek
†★ ---- 100.5
KINQ 92.1
Weed
KSQU 100.9
West Covina
KBOB 98.3
West Sacramento
★ KWHS 91.7
Willows
† KIQS-FM 105.5
Woodlake
†★ KUFW 90.5
Woodland
KSFM 102.5
Yermo
KRXV 98.1
Yreka
† KYRE 97.7
Yuba City
KXEZ 103.9
Yucca Valley
† ---- 106.9

Colorado

Alamosa
KALQ-FM 93.5
★ KASF 90.9
†★ KRZA 88.7
Aspen
KSPN 97.7
Boulder
KBCO 97.3
KBVL 94.7
★ KGNU 88.5
Breckenridge
KLGT 102.3
Brush
† KBUL 107.1
Burlington
KNAB-FM 104.1
Canon City
KRLN-FM 103.9
Carbondale
†★ KDNK 90.5
Castle Rock
KRKY 92.1
Colorado Springs
★ KAFA 89.7
★ KEPC 90.5
KILO 93.9
KKCS-FM 101.9
KKFM 96.5
★ KRCC 91.5
KRDO-FM 95.1
KSPZ 92.9
Cortez
KISZ 97.9
† KRTZ 96.7
Craig
KQZR 102.5
KXRC 93.7
Delta
KDTA-FM 95.3
Denver
KAZY 106.7
KBPI 105.9
KBRQ-FM 105.1
★ KCFR 90.1
★ KUVO 89.3
KLIR 100.3
KOAQ 103.5
KOSI-FM 101.1
KPKE 95.7
KVOD 99.5
KYGO 98.5
Durango
★ KDUR 91.9
Durango (Cont)
KIQX 101.3
KRSJ 100.5
Eagle
† ---- 101.5
Ft. Collins
KCOL-FM 107.9
†★ KCSU-FM 90.5
‡★ KCSU-FM 90.9
KTCL 93.3
Ft. Morgan
KBRU 101.7
Fruita
† KEKB 99.9
Glenwood Springs
KMTS 92.7
Grand Juction
†★ KPRN 89.5
Grand Junction
★ KCIC 88.5
★ KJOL 90.3
★ KMSA 91.3
KQIX 93.1
KREX-FM 92.3
Greeley
KGBS 96.1
KGRE 92.5
★ KUNC-FM 91.5
Gunnison
† KGUC-FM 98.3
KVLE 102.7
†★ KWSB-FM 91.1
‡★ KWSB-FM 91.9
Ignacio
★ KSUT 91.3
Kremmling
† KSKE 106.3
La Junta
† KBLJ 92.1
Lakewood
KPPL 107.5
Lamar
KSEC 93.3
Leadville
† KLMC 93.5
Longmont
★ KCDC 90.7
KLMO-FM 104.3
Loveland
KLOV-FM 102.3
Manitou Springs
★ KCME 88.1
KIIQ-FM 102.7
Montrose
KUBC-FM 94.1
KWDE 96.1
Morrison
★ KWBI 91.1
Oak Creek
KFMU 103.9
Paonia
★ KVNF 90.9
Pueblo
† KCCY 96.9
‡ KCCY 97.9
KKMG 98.9
KRMX-FM 107.1
†★ KTSC-FM 89.7
‡★ KTSC-FM 89.5
KVUU 99.9
KZLO 100.7
Rifle
† KDBL 105.3
Rocky Ford
KAVI-FM 95.9
Salida
KVRH-FM 92.1
Security
KWYD 105.5
Silverton
† KDRW 103.9
Snowmas Village
† KTUS 103.9
Steamboat Springs
KSBT 96.7
Sterling
KSTC-FM 104.7
† KVRS 105.5
Telluride
★ KOTO 91.7
Trinidad
KCRT-FM 92.7
Vail
KVMT 104.7
Windsor
KUAD-FM 99.1
Wray
† KRZQ-FM 98.3
Yuma
KJCO 100.9

Connecticut

Berlin
★ WERB 89.9
Bridgeport
WEZN 99.9
★ WPKN 89.5
Brookfield
WRKI 95.1
Cornwall
†★ WKKA 90.9
Danbury
WDAQ 98.3
†★ WFAR 93.3
‡★ WFAR 88.5
★ WXCI 91.7
Derby
★ WLNV 90.1
Fairfield
★ WSHU 91.1
★ WVOF 88.5
Groton
WQGN-FM 105.5
Hamden
WKCI 101.3
†★ WQAQ 98.1
‡★ WQAQ 88.3
Hartford
WCCC-FM 106.9
WDRC-FM 102.9
WHCN 105.9
★ WJMJ 88.9
WLVH 93.7
★ WQTQ 89.9
★ WRTC-FM 89.3
WTIC-FM 96.5
Meriden
WKSS 95.7
†★ WPBH 90.5
‡★ WPBH 90.5
Middlefield
†★ WPBH 90.5
‡★ WPBH 90.5
Middletown
★ WESU 88.1
WIHS 104.9
Monroe
★ WMNR 88.1
New Britain
†★ WFCS 97.9
‡★ WFCS 90.1
WRCH-FM 100.5
New Canaan
★ WSLX 91.9
New Haven
WPLR 99.1
WYBC-FM 94.3
New London
†★ WCNI 91.5
‡★ WCNI 91.1
WTYD 100.9
Norwalk
WLYQ 95.9
Norwich
WCTY 97.7
Somers
†★ WDJW 105.3
‡★ WDJW 89.7
Stamford
WYRS 96.7
Stonington
† WFAN 102.3
Storrs
★ WHUS 91.7
Wallingford
★ WWEB 89.9
Waterbury
WIOF 104.1
WWYZ-FM 92.5
West Hartford
★ WWUH 91.3
West Haven
★ WNHU 88.7
Westport
WDJF 107.9
★ WWPT 90.3
Willimantic
†★ WECS 90.1
WNOU 98.3

Delaware

Bethany Beach
WWTR-FM 95.9
Dover
WDSD 94.7
Georgetown
WSEA 93.5
Hockessin
★ WZZE 88.1
Milford
WAFL-FM 97.7
Newark
★ WXDR 91.3
Rehoboth Beach
WGMD 92.7
Seaford
WSUX-FM 98.3
Wilmington
WJBR-FM 99.5
★ WMPH 91.7
WSTW 93.7

District of Columbia

Washington
★ WAMU-FM 88.5
WASH 97.1
★ WDCU 90.1
★ WETA-FM 90.9
WGAY-FM 99.5
WGMS-FM 103.5
WHUR-FM 96.3
WKYS 93.9
WMZQ 98.7
† WOOK 100.3
★ WPFW 89.3
WRQX 107.3
WWDC-FM 101.1

Florida

Apopka
WTLN-FM 95.3
Arcadia
WOKD 98.3
Atlantic Beach
WFYV 104.5
Avon Park
WWOJ 106.3
Belle Glade
WSWN-FM 93.5
Big Pine Key
WWUS 104.7
Blountstown
WRTM 102.3
Boca Raton
WKQS 99.9
†★ WWOG 88.1
Bonifay
† WTTB 97.7
Bonita Springs
WLEQ 95.9
Boynton Beach
★ WHRS-FM 90.7
★ WRMB 89.3
Bradenton
WDUV 103.3
Cape Coral
WRCC 103.9
Clearwater
WMGG 95.7
WZNE 97.9
Clewiston
WAFC 106.3
Cocoa
WEZY-FM 99.3

City	Station	Frequency
Cocoa (Cont)		
	†* WMIE-FM	91.5
Cocoa Beach		
	WCKS	101.1
	WRKT-FM	104.1
Coral Gables		
	* WVUM	90.5
	WEZI	105.1
Crestview		
	WAAZ-FM	104.9
Crystal River		
	WRYO	98.5
Daytona Beach		
	WDOQ	101.9
	WWLV	94.5
De Funiak Springs		
	WQUH	103.1
De Land		
	WELE-FM	105.9
Destin		
	WMMK	92.1
Dunnellon		
	WTRS-FM	102.3
Ft Lauderdale		
	* WAFG	90.3
Ft. Lauderdale		
	WAXY	105.9
	WEWZ	106.7
	WHYI	100.7
	WSHE-FM	103.5
Ft. Myers		
	†* WFSP	90.1
	WHEW	101.9
	WINK-FM	96.9
	† WQEZ	99.3
	* WSOR	95.3
Ft. Pierce		
	WIZD	98.7
	WOVV	95.5
	†* WQCS	88.3
Ft. Walton Beach		
	WFTW-FM	96.5
Gainesville		
	WMFM	100.9
	WRUF-FM	103.7
	* WUFT-FM	89.1
	WYKS	105.5
Goulds		
	WGLY	98.3
Green Cove Springs		
	WSVE	92.7
Havana		
	† WHFL	104.9
Hialeah		
	WCMQ-FM	92.1
High Springs		
	† WKAE	104.9
Holiday		
	WVTY	106.3
Homosassa Springs		
	† WOOT	95.3
Immokalee		
	† WIKX	98.3
Jacksonville		
	WAIV-FM	96.9
	WCRJ-FM	107.3
	†* WFAM	90.9
	‡* WFAM	91.1
	WIVY-FM	102.9
	WJAX-FM	95.1
	* WJCT-FM	89.9
	WKTZ-FM	96.1
	WQIK-FM	99.1
Jensen Beach		
	WHLG	102.3
Jupiter		
	WVSI-FM	96.7
Key West		
	WFYN-FM	92.5
	WIIS	107.1
	WVFK	95.5
Labelle		
	WVHG	92.1
Lake City		
	WQPD	94.3
Lakeland		
	* WCIE	91.3
	WVFM	94.1
Leesburg		
	WHLY	106.7
Lehigh Acres		
	WOOJ-FM	107.1
Live Oak		
	WQHL	98.1
Mac Clenny		
	WBKF	92.1
Madison		
	† WIMV	104.9
Marathon		
	WMUM	94.3
Marco		
	† WEIB	101.1
Marianna		
	WJAQ	100.9
Melbourne		
	WCIF	106.3
	* WFIT	89.5
	WLLV	107.1
	WYRL	102.3
Miami		
	WAIA	97.3
	* WDNA	88.9
	WEDR	99.1
	* WLRN-FM	91.3
	WLYF	101.5
	* WMCU	89.7
	WQBA-FM	107.5
	WTMI	93.1
Miami Beach		
	WINZ-FM	94.9
	WWWL	93.9
Milton		
	WXBM-FM	102.7
Mt. Dora		
	WORJ-FM	107.7
Naples		
	WCVU	94.5
	WRGI	93.5
	WSGL	97.7
New Port Richey		
	†* WLPJ	91.5
	WGUL-FM	105.5
Ocala		
	WFUZ	93.7
	WMFQ	92.7
Okeechobee		
	WLMC	103.1
	†* ----	91.9
Orlando		
	WBJW	105.1
	WDIZ-FM	100.3
	* WGAG-FM	89.3
	WHOO-FM	96.5
	* WMFE-FM	90.7
	* WUCF-FM	89.9
	WWKA	92.3
Palatka		
	WNFI	99.9
Palm Beach		
	WRMF	97.9
Panama City		
	WGNE-FM	98.5
	* WKGC-FM	90.7
	WPAP-FM	92.5
	WPFM	107.9
Pensacola		
	WJLQ	100.7
	WMEZ	94.1
	WOWW	107.3
	* WPCS	89.3
	WTKX	101.5
	* WUWF	88.1
Plantation Key		
	WXOS	100.3
	† WFKZ	103.1
Pompano Beach		
	WCKO	102.7
Port Charlotte		
	WEEJ	100.1
Port St. Joe		
	† WJST	94.5
	‡ WJST	93.5
Punta Gorda		
	WQLM-FM	92.7
Quincy		
	WWSD	101.7
Riviera Beach		
	WNJY	94.3
Safety Harbor		
	† WXCR	92.1
Sarasota		
	* WKZM	105.5
	WMLO	106.3
	WSRZ	102.5
Sebring		
	WSKP-FM	105.5
St. Augustine		
	WFOY-FM	97.7
	WMKM	105.5
St. Petersburg		
	WKES	101.5
	WQYK-FM	99.5
	WWBA	107.3
Starke		
	WPXE-FM	106.3
	†* WTLG	88.3
Stuart		
	WRIT	92.7
Sunrise		
	* WKPX	88.5
Tallahassee		
	‡* WAMF	90.5
	†* WAMF	90.3
	WBGM	98.9
	WTNT-FM	94.9
	* WFSU-FM	91.5
	WGLF	104.1
	† WMNX	95.9
	WOWD	103.1
Tampa		
	WIQI	100.7
	* WMNF	88.5
	WOJC	93.3
	WRBQ-FM	104.7
	* WUSF	89.7
	WYNF	94.9
Titusville		
	WAJX	98.3
	* WPIO	89.1
Venice		
	WARV	92.1
Vero Beach		
	WAVW	105.5
	WGYL	93.5
West Palm Beach		
	WEAT-FM	104.5
	* WHRS	90.7
	WIRK-FM	107.9
	WNGS	92.1
Williston		
	† WJRQ	92.1
Winter Haven		
	WPCV	97.5
Winter Park		
	WLOQ	103.1
	* WPFL	88.9
	* WPRK	91.5

Georgia

City	Station	Frequency
Adel		
	WDDQ	92.1
Albany		
	WGPC-FM	104.5
	WJIZ	96.3
	WKAK	101.7
Americus		
	WADZ	94.3
	WPUR	97.7
Athens		
	WAGQ	104.7
	WNGC	95.5
	* WUOG	90.5
Atlanta		
	* WABE	90.1
	* WCLK	91.9
	WKLS-FM	96.1
	WPCH	94.9
	* WRAS	88.5
	* WREK	91.1
	* WRFG	89.3
	WRMM	99.7
	WSB-FM	98.5
	WVEE	103.3
	WZGC	92.9
Augusta		
	* WACG-FM	90.7
	WBBQ-FM	104.3
	WGUS-FM	102.3
	WYMX	105.7
	WZZW	103.1
Bainbridge		
	WJAD	97.3
Baxley		
	† WBYZ	94.5
Blackshear		
	WKUB	104.9
Blakely		
	† WBBK-FM	93.5
Blue Ridge		
	WPPL	103.9
Brunswick		
	WPIQ	101.5
	WGIG-FM	100.7
Buford		
	WGCO	102.3
Cairo		
	† WTGQ	102.3
Camilla		
	WOFF	105.5
Canton		
	WCHK-FM	105.5
Carrollton		
	WBTR-FM	92.1
	* WWGC	90.7
Cartersville		
	† WCCV.	
Chatsworth		
	WQMT	99.3
Claxton		
	WCLA-FM	107.1
Cochran		
	†* WDCO-FM	89.7
	WVMG-FM	96.7
Columbus		
	WCGQ	107.3
	†* ----	90.5
	WFXE	104.9
	†* ----	91.7
	WVOC	102.9
Cordele		
	WFAV	98.3
Cornelia		
	WCON-FM	99.3
Cumming		
	†* WWEV	91.5
Dawson		
	WAZE	92.1
Donalsonville		
	WGMK	106.3
Douglas		
	WDMG-FM	99.5
	WOKA-FM	106.7
Dublin		
	WKKZ	92.7
	WQZY	95.9
Eastman		
	WUFF-FM	92.1
Elberton		
	WWRK	92.1
Forsyth		
	WFNE	100.1
Fort Valley		
	†* WHGW	91.3
	WQBZ	106.3
Gainesville		
	* WBCX	89.1
	WFOX	97.1
	WWLT	106.7
Glennville		
	WKIG-FM	106.3
Gordon		
	WQXM-FM	107.1
Greensboro		
	WGRG	103.9
Griffin		
	WKEU-FM	97.7
Hawkinsville		
	WCEH-FM	103.9
Hazlehurst		
	WVOH-FM	93.5
Hinesville		
	WBLU	92.1

Homerville
WBTY 105.5
Jackson
WJGA-FM 92.1
Jessup
WIFO-FM 105.5
WSOJ 98.3
La Grange
WJYF 104.1
†* WOAK 90.9
Louisville
WPEH-FM 92.1
Macon
WDEN-FM 105.3
WMAZ-FM 99.1
WPEZ 107.9
Manchester
WVFJ-FM 93.3
Marietta
* WGHR 102.5
WKHX 101.5
Martinez
† WMTZ 94.3
Mc Rae
WDAX-FM 95.3
Mcdonough
†* WMVV 90.7
Metter
WHCG 104.9
Milan
† WMCG 104.9
Milledgeville
WKZR 102.3
* WXGC 88.9
Moultrie
WMTM-FM 93.9
Newnan
WRNG 96.7
Ocilla
† WKAA.
Perry
WPGA-FM 100.9
Rockmart
WZOT 107.1
Rome
WKCX 97.7
WQTU 102.3
Rossville
WOWE 105.5
Sandersville
WSNT-FM 93.5
Savannah
WAEV 97.3
WCHY 94.1
WEAS-FM 93.1
* WHCJ 88.5
WIXV 95.5
WJCL-FM 96.5
* WSVH 91.1
WZAT 102.1
Smyrna
WQXI-FM 94.1
Soperton
WMPZ-FM 101.7
Springfield
WGEC 103.9
St. Mary's
† WLKC 93.5
St. Simons Island
† ---- 92.7
Statesboro
WMCD 100.1
* WVGS 107.7
Swainsboro
WJAT-FM 98.3
WXRS-FM 103.9
Thomaston
† WTGA 95.3
Thomasville
WTUF 107.1
Thomson
WTHO-FM 101.7
Tifton
†* WABR-FM 107.5
‡* WABR-FM 90.5
WCUP 100.3
Toccoa
WLET-FM 106.1
Toccoa Falls
* WRAF 90.9
Valdosta
WAFT 101.1
WGOV-FM 92.9
WLGA 95.9
* WVVS 90.9
Vidalia
WTCQ 97.7
Warm Springs
†* ---- 88.1
Warner Robbins
WRBN-FM 101.7
Washington
WLOV-FM 100.1
Waycross
† ---- 97.7
WACL-FM 103.3
WQCW 102.5
Waynesboro
WWGA 100.9
West Point
WCJM 100.9
Wrens
WRNZ 96.7

Hawaii

Hilo
† KWXX 94.7
† KFSH 97.1
KKBG 97.9
Honolulu
KAIM-FM 95.5
* KHPR 88.1
KPIG 93.9
KPOI-FM 97.5
KQMQ 93.1
* KTUH 90.3
KUMU-FM 94.7
Kahului
† ---- 99.9
Kailua
KSHO-FM 96.3
Kealakekua
† KOAS 92.1
Lihue
KIPO-FM 93.5
† KJAD 92.7
Mukawao
KVIB 94.3
Poauilo
† KHCR 95.9
Wailuku
KAOI 95.1
Waipahu
KULA 92.3

Idaho

Blackfoot
KBLI-FM 97.7
Boise
KBBK-FM 92.3
KBOI-FM 97.9
* KBSU 91.3
† KIDQ 104.3
KJOT 105.1
Burley
KMVC 98.3
Caldwell
KBXL 94.1
Coeur D' Alene
KCDA 103.1
Emmett
KMFE 101.7
Grangeville
KORT-FM 92.7
Idaho Falls
KID-FM 96.1
KQPI-FM 99.1
Jerome
KFMA 102.9
Kellogg
† KCJF 104.3
Lewiston
†* KJLC 97.7
‡* KJLC 89.9
†* KLHS-FM 88.9
‡* KLHS-FM 89.1
Lewiston (Cont)
† KMOK 106.9
‡ KOZE-FM 96.5
‡ KOZE-FM 96.7
Moscow
KRPL-FM 103.9
* KUID 91.7
* KUOI-FM 89.3
Mountain Home
KQKZ 99.3
Nampa
KBNY 96.9
KFXD-FM 94.9
New Plymouth
KIZN 93.1
Orofino
KLER-FM 95.3
Payette
† KWBJ 100.3
‡ KWBJ 100.1
Pocatello
* KBGL 89.5
KPKY 94.9
† KRBU 102.5
‡ KRBU 104.9
KZBQ 93.7
Preston
† KACH-FM 96.7
Rexburg
KADQ 94.3
† KKQT 98.3
†* KRIC 100.5
‡* KRIC 90.1
Rupert
KNAQ 92.1
Salmon
KSRA-FM 92.7
Sandpoint
KPND 95.3
Soda Springs
KFIS 100.1
Sun Valley
KSKI-FM 93.5
Twin Falls
†* KCIR 90.7
KEZJ 95.7
KMTW 96.5
Weiser
† KWEI-FM 100.9

Illinois

Aledo
WRMJ 102.3
Alton
WZEN 100.3
Anna
WRAJ-FM 92.7
Arlington Heights
WSEX 92.7
Aurora
WAUR 107.9
WKKD-FM 95.9
Ava
WXAN 103.9
Barrington
* WBPR 88.5
Beardstown
WRMS-FM 94.3
Belvedere
WYBR-FM 104.9
Benton
WQRL 106.3
Bloomington
WBNQ 101.5
* WESN 88.1
Cahokia
* WRTE 89.5
Canton
† WBOD 100.9
WBYS-FM 98.3
Carbondale
WCIL-FM 101.5
* WSIU 91.9
Carlinville
* WIBI 91.1
Carmi
WRUL 97.3
Carthage
WCAZ-FM 92.1
Centralia
WRXX 95.3
Champaign
* WBGL 91.7
WDWS-FM 97.5
* WEFT 90.1
WLRW 94.5
* WPCD 88.7
Charleston
WEIC-FM 92.1
* WEIU 88.9
Chicago
WBBM-FM 96.3
* WBEZ 91.5
* WBHI 88.5
* WCRX 88.1
* WCYC 88.7
WFMT-FM 98.7
† WFYR 103.5
WGCI-FM 107.5
* WHPK-FM 88.3
WJEZ 104.3
* WKKC 89.3
WKQX 101.1
WLAK 93.9
WLOO 100.3
WLS-FM 94.7
WLUP 97.9
* WLUW 88.7
* WMBI-FM 90.1
WMET 95.5
WNIB 97.1
* WOUI 88.9
* WSSD 88.1
WUSN 99.5
WXRT 93.1
* WZRD 88.3
Chillicothe
WTXR 94.3
Clinton
WHOW-FM 95.9
Columbia
WCBW 104.9
Covington
†* ---- 90.3
Crest Hill
WCCQ 98.3
Crete
WTAS 102.3
Danville
WDNL 102.1
WIAI 99.1
De Kalb
WDEK 92.5
* WNIU-FM 89.5
Decatur
WDZQ 95.1
†* WJMU 89.5
‡* WJMU 89.0
WSOY-FM 102.9
Des Plaines
WYEN 106.7
Dixon
WIXN-FM 101.7
Downers Grove
* WDGC-FM 88.3
Du Quoin
WDQN-FM 95.9
Dundee
WCRM 103.9
East Moline
†* WDLM-FM 89.3
WLLR 101.3
East St. Louis
WMRY 101.1
Edwardsville
* WSIE 88.7
Effingham
WBFG 97.7
WCRC 95.7
Eldorado
WKSI 102.3
Elgin
* WEPS 90.9
WJKL 94.3

Elmhurst
★ WRSE-FM 88.7
Elmwood Park
WXFM 105.9
Elsah
★ WTPC 89.7
Evanston
★ WNUR 89.3
WOJO 105.1
Fairfield
WFIW-FM 104.9
Farmer City
† WZRO 98.3
Flora
WNOI 103.9
Flossmoor
★ WHFH 88.5
Freeport
WFPS 92.1
WXXQ 98.5
Galesburg
WAAG 94.9
WGBQ 92.7
★ WVKC 90.5
Geneseo
WGEN-FM 104.9
Gibson City
† WGCY 106.3
Glen Ellyn
★ WDCB 90.9
Glenview
★ WMWA 88.9
Godfrey
†★ WLCA 89.9
Granite City
KWK-FM 106.5
Greenville
† ---- 101.7
†★ WGRN 89.5
‡★ WGRN 89.3
Harrisburg
WEBQ-FM 99.9
Havana
WDUK 99.3
Highland Park
WVVX 103.1
Hinsdale
★ WHSD 88.5
Hoopeston
WHPO 100.9
Jacksonville
WEAI 100.5
Jerseyville
WJBM-FM 104.1
Joliet
WAJP 93.5
WLLI-FM 96.7
Kankakee
WBYG 99.9
★ WKOC 88.3
Kewanee
WJRE 92.1
La Grange
★ WLTL 88.1
La Salle
WAJK 99.3
Lake Forest
★ WMXM 88.9
Lansing
WLNR 106.3
Lawrenceville
WAKO-FM 103.1
Le Roy
WMLA 92.7
Lincoln
★ WLNX 88.9
WLRX 100.1
Litchfield
WSMI-FM 106.1
Lockport
†★ WLRA 88.1
Loves Park
WLUV-FM 96.7
Macomb
★ WIUM 91.3
★ WIUS 88.3
WJEQ 103.1
WKAI-FM 100.1

Marion
WDDD 107.3
Mattoon
WLBH-FM 96.9
★ WLKL 89.9
Mendota
WGLC-FM 100.1
Metropolis
† WRIK 98.3
Moline
WXLP 96.9
Monmouth
WDRL 97.7
Monticello
WVLJ 105.5
Morris
WCSJ-FM 104.7
Morton
WTAZ 102.3
Mt. Carmel
★ WVJC 89.1
WYER-FM 94.9
Mt. Vernon
WMIX-FM 94.1
Mt. Zion
WLVO 99.3
Murphysboro
WTAO 104.9
Naperville
★ WONC 89.1
Normal
★ WGLT 89.1
WIHN 96.7
Oak Park
WBMX 102.7
Olney
WSEI 92.9
Ottawa
WRKX 95.3
Pana
WKXK 100.9
Paris
WACF 98.5
Park Forest
★ WRHS 88.1
Park Ridge
★ WMTH 88.5
Paxton
† WOKO 104.9
Pekin
†★ WCIC 91.5
WGLO 95.3
WKQA 104.9
Peoria
★ WCBU 89.9
WKZW 93.3
WSWT 106.9
WWCT 105.7
Peru
WIVQ 100.9
Pittsfield
WBBA-FM 97.7
Plano
WSPY 107.1
Pontiac
WPOK-FM 103.1
Princeton
WZOE-FM 98.3
Quincy
WGEM-FM 105.1
WQCY 99.5
★ WWQC 90.3
Rantoul
WRTL-FM 95.3
River Grove
★ WRRG 88.9
Robinson
WTAY-FM 101.7
Rochelle
WRHL-FM 102.3
Rock Island
WHBF-FM 98.9
★ WVIK 90.1
Rockford
WQFL 100.9
WZOK 97.5
Rockton
WRWC 103.1

Salem
WJBD-FM 100.1
Savanna
WCCI 100.1
Shelbyville
WSHY-FM 104.9
Skokie
WCLR 101.9
Springfield
WDBR 103.7
WFMB 104.5
WNNS 98.7
†★ WQNA 88.3
‡★ WQNA 89.9
★ WSSR 91.9
WVEM 101.9
Sterling
WJVM 94.3
Streator
WLAX 97.7
Sullivan
WSAK 106.3
Summit
★ WARG 88.9
Taylorville
WTJY 92.7
Tuscola
WITT 93.5
Urbana
★ WILL-FM 90.9
WKIO 103.9
WPGU 107.1
Vandalia
WKRV 107.1
Virden
WRVI 96.7
Watseka
WGFA-FM 94.1
Waukegan
WXLC 102.3
West Frankfort
WFRX-FM 97.7
Wheaton
★ WETN 88.1
Wilmington
WDND 105.5
Winnebago
WYFE-FM 95.3
Winnetka
★ WNTH 88.1
Woodstock
WXRD 105.5
Zion
WNIZ-FM 96.9

Indiana

Alexandria
WAXT 96.7
Anderson
WLHN 97.9
Angola
★ WEAX 88.3
WLKI 100.1
Auburn
WIFF-FM 105.5
Aurora
WSCH 99.3
Batesville
WRBI 103.9
Bedford
WBIF 105.5
Bloomington
WBWB 96.7
★ WFIU 103.7
WGTC 92.3
Bluffton
WCRD 100.1
Boonville
WBNL-FM 107.1
Brazil
WBDJ-FM 97.7
Carmel
★ WHJE 91.3
Chesterton
†★ WDSO 89.7
‡★ WDSO 89.1
Columbia City
WKSY 106.3

Columbus
WCSI-FM 101.5
WWWY 104.9
Connersville
WCNB-FM 100.3
Covington
†★ WFOF 90.3
WVWV 103.1
Crawfordsville
WLFQ 103.9
WNDY 106.3
Crown Point
WFLM 103.9
Danville
WGRT 107.1
Decatur
WADM-FM 92.7
Earl Park
† WIBN 98.3
Elkhart
WFRN 104.7
★ WVPE 88.1
WYEZ 100.7
Elwood
WBMP 101.7
Evansville
WIKY-FM 104.1
★ WNIN-FM 88.3
★ WPSR 90.7
★ WUEV 91.5
WYNG 105.3
Frankfort
WSHW 99.7
Franklin
†★ WFCI 89.5
‡★ WFCI 89.3
WGAQ 95.9
French Lick
WFLQ 100.1
Ft. Wayne
★ WBCL 90.3
★ WBNI 89.1
WEZV 101.7
WFWQ 95.1
★ WLHI 88.3
WMEE 97.3
WXKE 103.9
Gary
★ WGVE 88.7
Gaston
†★ WDHS 90.9
‡★ WDHS 91.1
Goshen
★ WGCS 91.1
WZOW 97.7
Greencastle
★ WGRE 91.5
WJNZ 94.3
Greenfield
WZPL 99.5
Greensburg
WRZQ 107.3
Hammond
WYCA 92.3
Hartford City
† WWHC 93.5
‡ WWHC 104.9
Howe
★ WHWE 89.7
Huntingburg
WBDC 100.9
Huntington
WHUZ 103.1
★ WVSH 91.9
Indianapolis
† ---- 107.9
★ WAJC 104.5
★ WBDG 90.9
★ WEDM 91.1
WFBQ 94.7
WFMS 95.5
★ WIAN 90.1
★ WICR 88.7
†★ WJEL 89.3
‡★ WJEL 89.1
WNAP 93.1
★ WRFT 91.5

Station	Frequency
Indianapolis (Cont)	
WTLC	105.7
WXTZ	103.3
Jasper	
WITZ-FM	104.7
Jeffersonville	
WQMF	95.7
Kendallville	
WAWK-FM	93.3
Knox	
WKVI-FM	99.3
Kokomo	
†⋆ WHSK	98.9
‡⋆ WHSK	89.1
WWKI	100.5
† WZWZ	92.7
‡ WZWZ	93.5
La Porte	
WCOE	96.7
Lafayette	
WASK-FM	105.3
WAZY-FM	96.5
⋆ WJEF	91.9
† WXUS	93.5
‡ WXUS	92.7
Lebanon	
WNON	100.9
Linton	
WQTY	93.5
Logansport	
WSAL-FM	102.3
Loogootee	
† WKMD	94.3
Lowell	
WLCL-FM	107.1
Madison	
WCJC	96.7
Marion	
WMRI	106.9
Martinsville	
WCBK-FM	102.3
Michigan City	
WEFM	95.9
Monticello	
WWET	95.3
Muncie	
† ----	104.9
†⋆ WBST	92.1
‡⋆ WBST	90.7
WLBC-FM	104.1
†⋆ WWDS	90.5
⋆ WWHI	91.5
New Albany	
⋆ WNAS	88.1
New Castle	
WMDH	102.5
North Manchester	
⋆ WBKE-FM	89.5
North Vernon	
WHVI-FM	106.1
Notre Dame	
⋆ WSND-FM	88.9
Paoli	
WUME-FM	95.3
Pendleton	
⋆ WEEM	91.7
Peru	
WARU-FM	98.3
Plainfield	
WXIR	98.3
Plymouth	
WNZE	94.3
Portland	
WPGW-FM	100.9
Princeton	
WRAY-FM	98.1
Rensselaer	
WLOJ	97.7
⋆ WPUM	90.5
Richmond	
†⋆ WECI	89.7
‡⋆ WECI	91.5
WQLK	96.1
WRIA	101.3
Rochester	
WROI	92.1
Rockville	
WAXI	104.9
Rushville	
WRCR	94.3
Salem	
WSLM-FM	98.9
Scottsburg	
WMPI	100.9
Seymour	
WJCD-FM	93.7
Shelbyville	
WENS	97.1
South Bend	
⋆ WETL	91.7
WHME	103.1
WNDU-FM	92.9
WTHQ	101.5
WXMG	103.9
Spencer	
† WLSO	92.7
Sullivan	
WNDI-FM	95.3
Terre Haute	
⋆ WISU	89.7
⋆ WMHD-FM	90.5
WPFR-FM	102.7
WTHI-FM	99.9
WVTS	100.7
WZZQ	107.5
Valparaiso	
WLJE	105.5
†⋆ WVUR-FM	95.1
‡⋆ WVUR-FM	89.5
Versailles	
† WOVR	103.1
Vevay	
WAVV	95.9
Vincennes	
WRTB	96.7
⋆ WVUB	91.1
Wabash	
WKUZ	95.9
Warsaw	
WRSW-FM	107.3
Washington	
WFML	106.5
West Terre Haute	
WWVR	105.5
Winchester	
WZZY	98.3

Iowa

Station	Frequency
Algona	
KLGA-FM	92.7
Ames	
KCCQ	107.1
†⋆ KUSR	91.5
‡⋆ KUSR	91.9
REZT	104.1
⋆ WOI-FM	90.1
Ankeny	
KJJY	106.3
Atlantic	
KJAN-FM	103.7
Bettendorf	
† KBQC	93.5
Bloomfield	
† KXOF	106.3
Boone	
⋆ KFGQ-FM	99.3
KWBG-FM	98.3
Burlington	
KDWD	93.5
KGRS	107.3
Carroll	
KKRL	93.7
Cedar Falls	
⋆ KHKE	89.5
⋆ KUNI	90.9
Cedar Rapids	
⋆ KCCK-FM	88.3
⋆ KCOE-FM	90.3
KHAK-FM	98.1
⋆ KOJC	89.7
KQCR	102.9
KTOF	104.5
WMT-FM	96.5
Centerville	
KMGO	98.7
Chariton	
KYRS	105.5
Charles City	
KCHA-FM	95.9
Cherokee	
KCHE-FM	102.3
Clarinda	
KQIS	106.3
Clarion	
KRIT	96.9
Clear Lake	
KZEV	103.1
Clinton	
KNJY	97.7
KSAY	96.1
Council Bluffs	
†⋆ KIWR	89.7
KQKQ-FM	98.5
Creston	
KITR	101.7
Davenport	
⋆ KALA	88.5
KIIK	103.7
KRVR	106.5
Decorah	
⋆ KLCD	89.5
Denison	
KDSN-FM	107.1
Des Moines	
KDMI	97.3
⋆ KDPS	88.1
KGGO	94.9
KLYF	100.3
KMGK	93.3
KRNQ	102.5
†⋆ KUCB-FM	89.3
Dubuque	
KFMD	92.9
KLXL	102.3
KLYV	105.3
Emmetsburg	
KEMB	98.3
Estherville	
KILR-FM	95.9
Fairfield	
KBCT	95.9
Forest City	
KIOW	102.3
Ft. Dodge	
⋆ KICB	88.1
KKEZ	94.5
KSMX	92.1
⋆ KTPR	91.1
Ft. Madison	
KBKB-FM	101.7
Garanavillo	
KCTN	100.1
Grinnell	
⋆ KDIC	88.5
Grundy Center	
† KGCI	97.7
Hampton	
† KQHJ-FM	104.9
Harlan	
KWGG	105.5
Humboldt	
KHBT	97.7
Ida Grove	
KIDA	92.7
Independence	
KOUR-FM	95.3
Iowa City	
†⋆ ----	89.7
KKRQ	100.7
KRNA	93.9
⋆ KSUI	91.7
Iowa Falls	
KIFG-FM	95.3
Keokuk	
KIMI	95.3
Knoxville	
KRLS	92.1
KTAV	92.1
Le Mars	
KZZL	99.5
Maquoketa	
KMAQ-FM	95.3
Marshalltown	
KFJB-FM	101.1
Mason City	
KCMR	98.3
KLSS	106.1
Mt. Pleasant	
KILJ	105.5
Mt. Vernon	
⋆ KRNL-FM	89.7
Muscatine	
KFMH	99.7
Newton	
KLVN	95.9
Oelwein	
KOEL-FM	92.3
Osage	
KOSG	92.7
Osceola	
KJJC	107.1
Oskaloosa	
KBOE-FM	104.9
⋆ KIGC	88.7
Ottumwa	
KLEE-FM	97.7
† KTWA	92.7
Pella	
⋆ KCUI	89.1
KXJX	103.3
Perry	
KDLS-FM	104.9
Red Oak	
KOAK-FM	95.3
Sheldon	
KIWA-FM	105.5
Sioux Center	
⋆ KDCR	88.5
KVDB-FM	94.3
Sioux City	
KGLI	95.5
⋆ KMSC	88.3
KSEZ	97.9
KTFC	103.3
⋆ KWIT	90.3
Spencer	
KICD-FM	107.7
KRGS	104.9
Storm Lake	
KAYL-FM	101.5
Twin Lakes	
KTLB	105.5
Washington	
KCII-FM	95.3
Waterloo	
⋆ KBBG	88.1
KCNB	105.7
KFMW	107.9
⋆ KNWS-FM	101.9
Waukon	
KNEI-FM	103.9
Waverly	
⋆ KWAR	89.1
KWAY	99.3
Webster City	
KQWC-FM	95.9
West Des Moines	
⋆ KWDM	88.9

Kansas

Station	Frequency
Abilene	
KABI-FM	98.3
Arkansas City	
KBUZ	106.5
Baldwin City	
†⋆ KNBU	92.5
‡⋆ KNBU	88.9
Baxter Springs	
KBLT	107.1
Belleville	
† ----	92.1
Beloit	
KVSV-FM	105.5
Chanute	
KQSM	105.5
Clay Center	
KCLY	100.9
Coffeyville	
† KQQF	92.1

City	Station	Frequency
Colby		
	* KTCC	91.9
	KXXX-FM	100.3
Columbus		
	KCCU	98.3
Concordia		
	KCKS	95.3
	* KVCO	88.3
Derby		
	KAKZ-FM	95.9
Dodge City		
	KDCK	95.5
	* KINF	91.9
	KTTL	93.9
El Dorado		
	KSPG	99.3
Emporia		
	KLRF	104.9
Fort Scott		
	KOMB	103.9
Ft. Scott		
	† KFTS	101.7
Garden City		
	* KANZ	91.1
	KBUF-FM	97.3
Goodland		
	† KGKS	102.5
Great Bend		
	* KBJC	91.9
	KVGB-FM	104.3
Hays		
	KJLS	103.3
Hiawatha		
	KNZA	103.9
Holsington		
	KHOK	100.7
Huboton		
	† KHUQ	106.7
Hutchinson		
	* KHCC-FM	90.1
	KHUT	102.9
	KSKU	102.1
Independence		
	KIND-FM	101.7
Iola		
	KIOL	99.3
Junction City		
	KJCK-FM	94.5
Kansas City		
	KFKF-FM	94.1
	KUDL	98.1
Larned		
	KANS-FM	96.7
Lawrence		
	* KANU	91.5
	* KJHK	90.7
	KLZR	105.9
Leavenworth		
	KZZC	98.9
Leoti		
	† KWKR	99.9
Liberal		
	† KWNR	102.7
	† KSCB-FM	107.5
	‡ KSCB-FM	105.5
	KSLS	101.5
Lyons		
	KLFQ	106.1
Manhattan		
	* KMKF	101.7
	* KSDB-FM	88.1
Marysville		
	KNDY-FM	103.1
Mc Pherson		
	KNEX-FM	96.7
Newton		
	KOEZ	92.3
Oberlin		
	KFNF	101.1
Ogden		
	† ----	103.1
Osage City		
	KZOC	92.7
Ottawa		
	KKKX	95.7
	* KTJO-FM	88.1
Parsons		
	KLKC-FM	93.5
Phillipsburg		
	† KBMG	92.5
Pittsburg		
	KDBQ	96.9
Pratt		
	KGLS	93.1
Russell		
	KRSL-FM	95.9
Salina		
	KSKG	99.9
	KYEZ	93.7
Scott City		
	KEZU	94.5
Topeka		
	KDVV	100.3
	KMAJ	107.7
	KTPK	106.9
	WIBW-FM	97.3
Wellington		
	† KZED	93.5
Wichita		
	KBRA	97.9
	KEYN-FM	103.7
	KFDI-FM	101.3
	KICT	95.1
	KKRD	107.3
	* KMUW	89.1
	* KSOP	91.1
Winfield		
	* KSWC	100.3
	KWKS	105.5

Kentucky

City	Station	Frequency
Albany		
	WANY-FM	106.3
Ashland		
	WAMX	93.7
Barbourville		
	WYWY-FM	93.5
Bardstown		
	WOKH	96.7
Beattyville		
	WLJC	102.3
Benton		
	WCBL-FM	102.3
Bowling Green		
	WDNS	98.3
	* WKYU-FM	88.9
	WLBJ-FM	96.7
Brandenburg		
	WMMG	93.5
Cadiz		
	WKDZ-FM	106.3
Campbellsville		
	WCKQ-FM	103.9
Carrollton		
	WIKI	100.1
Catlettsburg		
	WCAK	92.7
Central City		
	WKYA	101.9
Columbia		
	WAIN-FM	93.5
Corbin		
	WCTT-FM	107.1
	WYGO-FM	99.3
Cynthiana		
	WCYN-FM	102.3
Danville		
	WMGE	107.1
Elizabethtown		
	WQXE	100.1
Elkhorn City		
	WECL	103.1
Erlanger		
	WHKK	100.9
Falmouth		
	WIOK	95.3
Frankfort		
	WKYW	104.9
	†* ----	89.9
Ft. Campbell		
	WABD-FM	107.9
Ft. Knox		
	WWKK	105.5
Fulton		
	WWKF	99.3
Georgetown		
	WAXU-FM	103.1
	†* WRVG	89.9
	‡* WRVG	90.1
Glasgow		
	WGGC	95.1
	WOVO	105.5
Grayson		
	* WKCC	96.7
	WUGO	102.3
Greensburg		
	WGRK-FM	103.1
Greenup		
	WLGC	105.5
Greenville		
	WGKY-FM	105.5
Hardinsburg		
	WHIC-FM	94.3
Harrodsburg		
	WHBN-FM	99.3
Hartford		
	WLLS-FM	106.3
Hazard		
	WSGS	101.1
Henderson		
	WHKC	103.1
	WKDQ	99.5
Highland Hgts.		
	†* WNKU	89.7
Hindman		
	WKCB-FM	107.1
Hodgenville		
	WKMO	106.3
Hopkinsville		
	WHOP-FM	98.7
	WKOA-FM	100.3
	* WNKJ	89.3
Jackson		
	WJSN-FM	97.7
Jamestown		
	WJRS	104.9
Jeffersontown		
	WJYL	101.7
Jenkins		
	WIFX-FM	94.3
Keavy		
	†* WVCT	91.5
Lebanon		
	WLSK	100.9
Leitchfield		
	WKHG	104.9
Lexington		
	* WBKY	91.3
	WKQQ	98.1
	WLAP-FM	94.5
	WVLK-FM	92.9
Liberty		
	WKDO-FM	105.5
London		
	WWEL	103.9
Louisville		
	WAMZ	97.5
	* WFPK	91.9
	* WFPL	89.3
	WKJJ-FM	99.7
	WLRS	102.3
	* WUOL	90.5
	WVEZ	106.9
	WXLN	103.9
Madisonville		
	WKTG	93.9
	* WSOF-FM	89.9
Manchester		
	WWXL-FM	103.1
Mayfield		
	WXID	94.7
Maysville		
	WFTM-FM	95.9
Middlesboro		
	WMIK-FM	92.7
Monticello		
	WKYM	101.7
Morehead		
	* WMKY-FM	90.3
	WMOR-FM	92.1
Morganfield		
	WMSK-FM	95.3
Mt. Sterling		
	WMST-FM	105.5
Munfordville		
	WLOC-FM	102.3
Murray		
	WAAW	103.7
	* WKMS-FM	91.3
Owensboro		
	WBKR	92.5
	* WKWC	90.3
	WSTO	96.1
Owingsville		
	† WKCA	107.1
Paducah		
	WDDJ	96.9
	WKYQ	93.3
Paintsville		
	WSIP-FM	98.9
Paris		
	WNCW	96.7
Pikeville		
	WDHR	92.1
Pineville		
	WTJM	106.3
Prestonburg		
	WPRT-FM	105.5
	WQHY	95.5
Princeton		
	WPKY-FM	104.9
Providence		
	WHRZ	97.7
Richmond		
	WCBR-FM	101.7
	* WEKU-FM	88.9
Russellville		
	WAKQ	101.1
Scottsville		
	WLCK-FM	99.3
Somerset		
	†* WDCL	89.7
	†* WSCC	92.1
	‡* WSCC	90.7
	WSEK	96.7
St. Matthews		
	WRKA	103.1
Stanford		
	WRSL-FM	95.9
Stanton		
	WSKV	104.9
Tomkinsville		
	WTKY-FM	92.1
Vanceburg		
	† WKKS-FM	104.9
Versailles		
	WJMM	106.3
Whitesburg		
	†* WMMT	88.7
	WXKQ	103.9
Winchester		
	WKDJ	100.1

Louisiana

City	Station	Frequency
Abbeville		
	KASC	104.9
Alexandria		
	†* KDEI	88.3
	KQID	93.1
	KRRV	100.3
	KTIZ	96.9
Bastrop		
	KJBS	100.1
	KTRY-FM	94.3
Baton Rouge		
	†* KLSU	91.1
	‡* KLSU	107.3
	WAFB-FM	98.1
	†* WBRH	90.3
	‡* WBRH	90.1
	WFMF	102.5
	WQXY-FM	100.7
	* WRKF	89.3
	WYNK-FM	101.5
Bayou Vista		
	KWKI	95.3
Benton		
	† KDKS	92.1
Boyce		
	KBCE	102.3

Clinton
WQCK 92.7
Columbia
KCTO-FM 103.1
Crowley
KAJN-FM 102.9
De Ridder
KEAZ 101.7
Donaldsonville
KSMI-FM 104.9
Dubach
† ---- 97.7
Eunice
KJJB 105.5
Farmerville
KWJM 92.7
Ferriday
KFNV-FM 107.1
Franklin
KFRA-FM 105.5
Galliano
KZZQ 94.3
Grambling
★ KGRM 91.3
Hammond
★ KSLU 90.9
WHMD 107.1
WTGI 103.3
Haynesville
† KLUV 105.5
Houma
KCIL 107.1
KHOM 104.1
Jena
KJNA 99.3
Jennings
KJEF-FM 92.7
Jesup
KWLV 107.1
Jonesboro
KJBQ 104.9
Kaplan
KMDL 97.7
La Place
WCKW 92.3
Lafayette
†★ KRVS 88.7
‡★ KRVS 88.1
KSMB 94.5
KTDY 99.9
Lake Charles
KBIU 103.7
KHEZ 99.5
KYKZ 96.1
Lake Providence
KLPL-FM 92.7
Leesville
KJAE 92.7
KVVP 105.5
Mansfield
KJVC 92.7
Marksville
KWLB-FM 97.7
Minden
KASO-FM 95.3
Monroe
KNAN 106.1
★ KNLU 88.7
KNOE-FM 101.9
KWEZ 104.1
Moreauville
† KLIL 92.1
Morgan City
KFXY 96.7
Natchitoches
KDBH 97.7
★ KNWD 91.7
New Iberia
KDEA 99.1
New Orleans
WAJY 101.9
★ WBSN-FM 89.1
WBYU 95.7
WEZB-FM 97.1
WNOE-FM 101.1
WQUE-FM 93.3
★ WRBH 88.3
WRNO 99.5

New Orleans (Cont)
★ WTUL-FM 91.5
★ WWNO-FM 89.9
★ WWOZ 90.7
WYLD-FM 98.5
New Roads
KQXL-FM 106.3
Oak Grove
KWCL-FM 96.7
Oakdale
KGBM-FM 104.9
Opelousas
KOGM 107.1
Port Sulphur
† KHHA 106.7
Rayville
† ---- 92.1
Ruston
★ KLPI 89.1
KXKZ 107.5
Shreveport
KCOZ 100.1
†★ KDAQ 89.9
KVKI 96.5
KMBQ 93.7
KRMD-FM 101.1
KROK 94.5
★ KSCL 91.3
Slidell
WAIL 105.3
Springhill
KTKC 92.7
Sulphur
KTQQ 100.9
Thibodaux
★ KVFG 91.3
KXOR 106.3
Ville Platte
KVPI-FM 93.5
West Monroe
KYEA 98.3
Winnfield
KVCL-FM 92.1
Winnsboro
KMAR-FM 95.9

Maine

Auburn
WKZS 99.9
Augusta
WKCG 101.3
† WRDO-FM 92.3
‡ WRDO-FM 92.1
Bangor
WBGW 97.1
★ WHCF 88.5
★ WHSN 89.3
★ WMEH 90.9
WPBC 92.9
Bath
WIGY 105.9
★ WMOS 95.3
Biddeford
★ WDOF 91.7
WBYC-FM 94.3
Boothbay Harbor
† WCME 96.7
Brewer
WGUY-FM 100.9
Brunswick
★ WBOR 91.1
WCLZ 98.9
Calais
†★ WMED 89.7
WQDY-FM 92.7
Camden
† ---- 102.5
Dover Foxcroft
WDME-FM 103.1
Eastport
†★ WSHD 91.7
Ellsworth
WWMJ 95.7
† WKSQ 94.5
‡ WKSQ 94.3
Farmington
WKTJ-FM 99.3
†★ WUMF-FM 92.3

Farmington (Cont)
‡★ WUMF-FM 91.9
Ft. Kent
†★ WUFK 92.1
‡★ WUFK 90.3
Gardiner
WABK-FM 104.3
Gorham
†★ WMPG 90.9
‡★ WMPG 91.1
Houlton
WHOU-FM 100.1
Lewiston
WAYU 93.9
WBLM 107.5
★ WRBC 91.5
Lincoln
WLKN-FM 99.3
Machias
WALZ 95.3
Millinocket
WKTR 97.7
Norway
WOXO-FM 92.7
Orono
†★ WMEB-FM 91.9
Portland
WGAN-FM 102.9
WJBQ 97.9
★ WMEA 90.1
WMGX 93.1
WPOR-FM 101.9
Presque Isle
WDHP 96.9
★ WMEM 106.1
WOZI 101.7
WTMS 96.1
★ WUPI 92.1
Rockland
WMCM 93.5
Rumford
WWMR 96.3
Saco
† WPIG 95.9
Sanford
WEBI 92.1
Scarborough
WDCS 106.3
Skowhegan
WTOS 105.1
Springvale
★ WNCY 91.1
Standish
†★ ---- 90.9
Waterville
†★ WMEW 91.3
†★ WMHB 90.5
‡★ WMHB 91.5
WTVL-FM 98.3
Westbrook
WYNZ-FM 100.9

Maryland

Annapolis
WFSI 107.9
WHFS 99.1
†★ WRNV 89.7
Arnold
★ WACC 89.9
Baltimore
★ WBJC 91.5
WBSB 104.3
★ WEAA 88.9
WIYY 97.9
★ WJHU 88.1
WLIF 101.9
WMAR-FM 106.5
WPOC 93.1
WRBS 95.1
†★ WBYQ 96.7
‡★ WBYQ 88.1
WXYV 102.7
WYST-FM 92.3
Bel Air
★ WHFC 99.1
Berlin
WOCQ 103.9

Bethesda
WLTT 94.7
WTKS 102.3
Braddock Heights
WZYQ-FM 103.9
Cambridge
WCEM-FM 106.3
Catonsville
WKTK 105.7
College Park
★ WMUC 88.1
Cumberland
WKGO 106.1
WROG 102.9
Easton
WCEI-FM 96.7
Elkton
★ WOEL-FM 89.9
Emmitsburg
★ WMTB-FM 89.9
Federalsburg
WCTD-FM 107.1
Frederick
WFRE 99.9
Frostburg
WFRB-FM 105.3
Glen Burnie
WWIN-FM 95.9
Grasonville
WBEY 103.1
Hagerstown
WKCS 106.9
WWMD 104.7
Halfway
WQCM 96.7
Havre De Grace
WHDG 103.7
La Plata
WXTR-FM 104.1
Lexington Park
WMDM-FM 97.7
Morningside
WPGC-FM 95.5
Oakland
WXIE 92.1
Ocean City
WKHI 99.9
WQHQ 104.7
Prince Frederick
WMJS 92.7
Princess Anne
WOLC 102.5
Salisbury
WICO-FM 94.3
WKYZ 105.5
Takoma Park
★ WGTS-FM 91.9
Towson
★ WCVT 89.7
Westminster
WTTR-FM 100.7
Williamsport
★ WCRH 90.5
WYII 95.9
Worton
★ WKHS 90.5

Massachusetts

Acton
★ WHAB 89.1
Amherst
★ WAMH 89.5
★ WFCR 88.5
★ WMUA 91.1
Andover
★ WPAA 91.7
Barnstable
WQRC 99.9
Boston
WBCN 104.1
★ WBUR 90.9
WCOZ 94.5
★ WERS 88.9
★ WGBH 89.7
WHTT 103.3
WHUE-FM 100.7
WJIB 96.9
WMJX 106.7

City	Station	Frequency
Boston (Cont)		
	★ WRBB	104.9
	WROR	98.5
	★ WUMB-FM	91.9
Boxford		
	★ WBMT	88.3
Bridgewater		
	★ WBIM-FM	91.5
Brockton		
	WCAV	97.7
	†★ WMCI	90.5
Brookline		
	WBOS	92.9
Cambridge		
	WHRB	95.3
	★ WMBR	88.1
Charlton		
	★ WBPV	90.1
Concord		
	★ WIQH	88.3
Deerfield		
	★ WGAJ	91.7
Dudley		
	★ WNRC	95.1
Duxbury		
	†★ WDBY	91.7
Easton		
	★ WSHL-FM	91.3
Falmouth		
	† ----	100.9
	WCIB	101.9
Fitchburg		
	WFMP	104.5
Framingham		
	★ WDJM-FM	91.3
	WVBF	105.7
Franklin		
	★ WGAO	88.3
Gardner		
	★ WMWC	91.7
Gloucester		
	WVCA-FM	104.9
Greenfield		
	WHAI-FM	98.3
	WRSI	95.3
Haverhill		
	WLYT	92.5
Holliston		
	★ WHHB	91.5
Holyoke		
	★ WCCH	103.5
Hyannis		
	WCOD-FM	106.1
Lawrence		
	WCGY	93.7
Lowell		
	★ WJUL	91.5
	WSSH	99.5
Lynn		
	WFNX	101.7
Marshfield		
	WATD	95.9
Maynard		
	★ WAVM	91.7
Medford		
	★ WMFO	91.5
	WXKS-FM	107.9
Milton		
	★ WMLN-FM	91.5
Nantucket		
	WGTF	96.3
New Bedford		
	WJFD-FM	97.3
	WMYS	98.1
Newbury		
	★ WQLI	88.7
Newton		
	★ WZBC	90.3
North Adams		
	★ WJJW	91.1
	WMNB-FM	100.1
North Dartmouth		
	★ WUSM	90.5
Northampton		
	WHMP-FM	99.3
	†★ WOZQ	91.9
Northfield		
	†★ WNMH	91.5
Orleans		
	WKPE	104.7
Pittsfield		
	WBEC-FM	105.5
	★ WTBR-FM	89.7
	WUPE	95.9
	WXTQ-FM	101.7
Plymouth		
	WPLM-FM	99.1
Provincetown		
	★ WOMR	91.9
Rockland		
	★ WRPS	91.5
Salem		
	★ WMWM	91.7
Sandwich		
	★ WSDH	91.5
Sheffield		
	★ WBSL	91.7
South Hadley		
	★ WMHC	91.5
Southbridge		
	WQVR	100.1
Springfield		
	★ WAIC	91.9
	WAQY	102.1
	WHYN-FM	93.1
	WMAS-FM	94.7
	★ WNEK-FM	97.5
	★ WSCB	89.9
	★ WTCC	90.7
Stockbridge		
	★ WCWL	91.3
Sudbury		
	★ WYAJ	88.1
Taunton		
	WSNE	93.3
Tisbury		
	WMVY	92.7
Walpole		
	★ WSRB	91.5
Waltham		
	★ WBRS	91.7
	WCRB	102.5
Wellesley		
	★ WZLY	91.5
West Barnstable		
	★ WKKL	90.7
West Yarmouth		
	WSOX-FM	94.9
Westfield		
	★ WSKB	91.5
Weston		
	★ WRSB	88.3
Williamstown		
	★ WCFM	91.9
Winchendon		
	WINQ	97.7
Winchester		
	★ WHSR-FM	91.9
Worcester		
	WAAF	107.3
	†★ WAYW	91.9
	★ WCHC	89.1
	★ WCUW	91.3
	★ WICN	90.5
	WSRS	96.1

Michigan

City	Station	Frequency
Adrian		
	WLEN	103.9
	WQTE	95.3
	★ WVAC	107.9
Albion		
	WUFN	96.7
Allendale		
	★ WGVC-FM	88.5
Alma		
	WFYC-FM	104.9
Alpena		
	WATZ-FM	93.5
	★ WCML-FM	91.7
	WHSB	107.7
Ann Arbor		
	★ WCBN-FM	88.3
	WIQB	102.9
	WPAG-FM	107.1
	★ WUOM	91.7
Auburn Heights		
	★ WAHS	89.5
Bad Axe		
	WLEW-FM	92.1
Battle Creek		
	WDFP	95.3
	WKFR-FM	103.3
Bay City		
	★ WCHW-FM	91.3
	WGER-FM	102.5
	WHNN	96.1
Beaverton		
	WMRX-FM	97.7
Benton Harbor		
	WHFB-FM	99.9
Berrien Springs		
	★ WAUS	90.7
Big Rapids		
	WAAQ	102.3
	WBRN-FM	100.9
Birmingham		
	WMJC	94.7
Bloomfield Hills		
	★ WBFH	88.1
Boyne City		
	WCLX	93.5
Cadillac		
	† ----	107.1
	WEVZ	96.7
	WKJF-FM	92.9
Caro		
	WKYO-FM	104.9
Charlevoix		
	WKHQ	105.9
Charlotte		
	WMMQ	92.7
Cheboygan		
	WQLZ	105.1
Clare		
	WRNN	95.3
Coldwater		
	WNWN	98.5
Dearborn		
	†★ WHFR	89.3
	WNIC-FM	100.3
Detroit		
	WABX	99.5
	WCXI-FM	92.3
	WCZY	95.5
	★ WDET-FM	101.9
	WDRQ	93.1
	★ WDTR	90.9
	WGPR	107.5
	WHYT	96.3
	WJLB	97.9
	WJOI	97.1
	WJZZ	105.9
	WLLZ	98.7
	WMUZ	103.5
	WOMC	104.3
	WQRS-FM	105.1
	WRIF	101.1
	WWWW	106.7
Dowagiac		
	WDOW-FM	92.1
East Lansing		
	WFMK	99.1
	★ WKAR-FM	90.5
Elsie		
	★ WOES	91.3
Escanaba		
	WGLQ	97.1
	WYKX	104.7
Farmington Hills		
	★ WORB	90.3
Flint		
	WDZZ-FM	92.7
	★ WFBE	95.1
	WGMZ	107.9
	WWCK	105.5
Frankfort		
	WBNZ	99.3
Fremont		
	WSHN-FM	100.1
Gaylord		
	†★ ----	90.5
	WEGS	95.3
	WWRM	106.7
Gladwin		
	WGMM	103.1
Grand Haven		
	WGHN-FM	92.1
Grand Rapids		
	★ WCSG	91.3
	WCUZ-FM	101.3
	★ WEHB	89.9
	WFUR-FM	102.9
	†★ WGNR	88.9
	WGRD-FM	97.9
	WJFM	93.7
	WLAV-FM	96.9
	WOOD-FM	105.7
	★ WVGR	104.1
	WZZR-FM	95.7
Grayling		
	WQON	100.1
Greenville		
	WPLB-FM	107.3
Hancock		
	WZRK	93.5
Harrison		
	WKKM	92.1
Hart		
	† WCXT	105.3
Hastings		
	WBCH-FM	100.1
Highland Park		
	★ WHPR	88.1
Hillsdale		
	WCSR-FM	92.1
Holland		
	WYXX	96.1
	WJBL-FM	94.5
Houghton		
	★ WGGL-FM	91.1
	WHUH	97.7
Houghton Lake		
	WJGS	98.5
Howell		
	WHMI-FM	93.5
Interlochen		
	★ WIAA	88.3
Iron Mountain		
	† WIMK	93.1
	WJNR-FM	101.5
Iron River		
	WIKB	99.3
Ironwood		
	WIMI	99.7
	WUPM	106.9
Ishpeming		
	† WJPD-FM	92.3
	WMQT	107.1
Jackson		
	WIBM-FM	94.1
	WJXQ	106.1
Kalamazoo		
	★ WIDR	89.1
	★ WKDS	89.9
	★ WMUK	102.1
	WQLR	106.5
Kalkaska		
	WKLT	97.7
Lakeview		
	† ----	106.3
Lansing		
	WILS-FM	101.7
	WITL-FM	100.7
	WJIM-FM	97.5
	WVIC-FM	94.9
Lapeer		
	WDEY-FM	103.1
Ludington		
	WKLA-FM	106.3
Manistee		
	WRRK	97.7
Marquette		
	WHWL	95.7
	★ WNMU-FM	90.1
	WUUN	100.1
Marshall		
	WELL-FM	104.9
Menominee		
	† ----	106.3
Midland		
	WRCI	93.5

Midland (Cont)
WUGN 99.7
Monroe
* WEJY 89.5
WTWR 98.3
Mt. Clemens
WLBS 102.7
Mt. Pleasant
WCEN-FM 94.5
* WCMU-FM 89.5
* WMHW-FM 91.5
Munising
WQXO-FM 98.3
Muskegon
WMUS-FM 106.9
WQWQ-FM 104.5
Muskegon Heights
WABM 101.7
Newberry
WNBY-FM 93.5
Niles
WAOR 95.3
North Muskegon
† 98.3
Novi
* WOVI 89.5
Oak Park
* WOPR 90.3
Olivet
* WOCR 89.7
Ontonagon
* WOAS 88.5
Ontonogan
† WONT 98.3
Orchard Lake
* WBLD 89.3
Otsego
WAOP 104.9
Owosso
WOAP-FM 103.9
Petoskey
WJML-FM 98.9
WMBN-FM 96.3
Pinconning
† WFXZ 100.9
Plymouth
* WSDP 88.1
Port Huron
* WORW 91.9
WSAQ 107.1
* WSGR-FM 91.3
Portage
† ---- 107.7
Rogers City
† WOEA 97.7
Saginaw
WIOG 106.3
WKCQ 98.1
WWWS 107.1
Sandusky
WTGV-FM 97.7
Sault Ste. Marie
WLXX 99.5
WSUE 101.3
Scottville
WKZC 95.9
South Haven
WCSY-FM 98.3
Southfield
* WSHJ 88.3
Spring Arbor
* WSAE 89.3
St. Ignace
† WMKC 102.9
St. Johns
WKLH 92.1
St. Joseph
WIRX 107.1
Sturgis
WSTR-FM 99.3
Tawas City
WDBI-FM 101.7
WKJC 103.9
Three Rivers
WLKM-FM 95.9
Traverse City
WLDR 101.9
WMZK 92.1

Traverse (Cont)
* WNCM-FM 90.9
WTCM-FM 103.5
Twin Lake
†* WBLV 90.3
Warren
* WPHS 91.5
West Branch
WBMI 105.5
Whitehall
WCNF 95.3
Wyoming
†* WYCE 88.1
Ypsilanti
* WEMU 89.1
Zeeland
WZND 99.3

Minnesota

Aitkin
KEZZ 94.3
Albert Lea
KCPI-FM 95.3
Alexandria
KCMT-FM 100.7
† KSTQ 99.3
KXRA-FM 92.7
Anoka
KGBB 107.9
Austin
KAUS-FM 99.9
* KAVT-FM 91.3
Bemidji
KBHP 101.1
* KBSB 89.7
†* KCRB-FM 88.5
† KKBJ-FM 103.7
Benson
KBMO-FM 93.5
Blue Earth
† KJLY 100.9
Brainerd
KLIZ-FM 107.5
WJJY 106.7
Breckenridge
KKIB 105.1
Breezy Point
† KLKS 95.3
Cambridge
KXLV-FM 105.5
Cloquet
WKLK-FM 100.9
Collegeville
* KSJR-FM 90.1
* KSJU 89.1
Crookston
* KCUM-FM 91.5
KYZK 97.1
Detroit Lakes
KVLR 95.3
Duluth
†* KDNW 90.5
KQDS-FM 94.9
* KUMD-FM 103.3
WAKX-FM 98.9
WAVC 105.1
* WSCD-FM 92.9
East Grand Forks
KRRK-FM 103.9
Eveleth
WEVE-FM 100.1
Fairmont
KFMC 106.5
Faribault
KDHL-FM 95.9
Fergus Falls
KBRF-FM 103.3
KJJK 96.5
Forest Lake
WLKX-FM 95.9
Fosston
KEHG-FM 107.1
Glenwood
† KZZA 107.1
Golden Valley
KQRS 92.5
Grand Rapids
* KAXE 91.7

Grand Rapids (Cont)
KNNS 96.9
Hibbing
WMFG 106.3
Hutchinson
KDUZ-FM 107.1
International Falls
* KICC 91.5
KSDM 94.3
Litchfield
KLFD-FM 95.3
Little Falls
WYRQ 92.1
Luverne
KLQL 101.1
Madison
† KLQF 92.1
Mankato
KEEZ-FM 99.1
* KMSU 89.7
KYSM-FM 103.5
Marshall
KCCK 100.1
Minneapolis
* KBEM-FM 88.5
KFAI 90.3
* KMOJ 89.9
KTCR-FM 97.1
* KTIS-FM 98.5
WAYL 93.7
WLTE 102.9
WCTS-FM 100.3
WLOL 99.5
Montevideo
KMGM 105.5
Moorhead
* KCCM-FM 91.1
KQWB-FM 98.7
KVOX-FM 99.9
Morris
KKOK-FM 95.7
* KUMM 89.7
New Ulm
KXLP 93.1
Northfield
* KRLX 90.3
* WCAL-FM 89.3
Olivia
† KOLV 101.7
Ortonville
† KBAA 106.3
† KCGN 101.5
Owatonna
KRFO-FM 104.9
* KRPC 90.5
Park Rapids
KPRM-FM 97.5
Pequot Lakes
KTIG 100.1
Pine City
WCMP-FM 92.1
Pipestone
KLOH-FM 98.7
Preston
KFIL-FM 103.1
Princeton
WQPM-FM 106.3
Red Wing
KWNG 105.5
Redwood Falls
KLGR-FM 97.7
Richfield
KDWB-FM 101.3
Rochester
* KFSI 88.5
†* KLSX-FM 90.7
KNXR 97.5
KRCH 101.7
KROC-FM 106.9
* KRPR 89.9
KWWK 96.7
Rushford
* KLSE-FM 91.7
Sauk Center
KMSR 94.3
Sauk Rapids
WHMH-FM 101.7

Spring Grove
† KQYB 98.3
St. Cloud
KCLD-FM 104.7
* KVSC 88.1
WWJO 98.1
St. James
KXAX 104.9
St. Louis Park
* KDXL 91.7
KJJO 104.1
St. Paul
KEEY-FM 102.1
KNOF 95.3
* KSJN-FM 91.1
KSTP-FM 94.5
* WMCN 91.7
St. Peter
KRBI-FM 105.5
†* KSCG 90.5
Thief River Falls
* KSRQ 90.1
KSNR 99.3
Virginia
WHLB-FM 107.1
Wadena
KKWS 105.9
Walker
† ---- 99.3
Waseca
KQDE-FM 92.1
Willmar
KQIC 102.5
Windom
KDOM-FM 94.3
Winona
KAGE-FM 95.3
* KQAL 89.5
†* KSMR 92.5
‡* KSMR 90.9
Worthington
* KRSW 91.7
KWOA-FM 95.1

Mississippi

Aberdeen
WHAY 105.5
Ackerman
† WFCA 107.9
Amory
WAFM 95.3
Baldwyn
WESE 95.9
Batesville
WBLE 95.9
Bay Springs
WXIY 93.5
Biloxi
†* WMAH-FM 90.3
WQID 93.7
Booneville
WBIP-FM 99.3
†* WMAE-FM 89.5
Brandon
WRJH 97.7
Brookhaven
WMRQ 92.1
Bude
†* WMAU-FM 88.9
Canton
WZXQ 101.7
Carthage
WWYN 98.3
Centreville
WZZB 104.9
Clarksdale
WAID 106.3
WJBI 101.7
Cleveland
WCLD-FM 103.9
WQAZ 92.7
Clinton
* WHJT 93.5
Coldwater
WVIM-FM
Collins
WKNZ

Columbia
WFFF-FM 96.7
Columbus
WACR-FM 103.9
WJWF 103.1
★ WMUW 89.5
Corinth
WADI 95.3
★ WALP 90.5
WKCU-FM 94.3
Drew
WKZB 95.3
Ellisville
WBSJ 102.3
Eupora
WEXA 101.7
Fayette
WTYJ 97.7
Forest
WQST 92.5
Fulton
WFTA 101.7
Goodman
★ WVTH 89.5
Greenville
WBAQ 97.9
WDMS 100.7
Greenwood
†★ WMAO-FM 90.9
WSWG-FM 99.1
Grenada
WQXB 100.1
Gulfport
WGCM 102.3
WGUF-FM 96.7
WZKX 107.1
Hattiesburg
WHER 103.7
WHSY-FM 104.5
† WJMG 92.1
★ WMSU 88.5
Hazlehurst
WMDC-FM 100.9
Heidelberg
WEEZ 99.3
Holly Springs
WKRA-FM 92.7
Houston
WCPC-FM 93.3
Indianola
WNLA-FM 105.5
Iuka
WTIB 104.9
Jackson
WJMI 99.7
★ WJSU 88.5
WLIN 95.5
†★ WMAA-FM 91.3
★ WMPR 90.1
WMSI 102.9
WTYX 94.7
★ WWCJ 89.3
WYYN 96.3
Kosciusko
WKOZ-FM 105.1
Laurel
WNSL 100.3
Leland
† ---- 102.3
WBAD 94.3
Lexington
WLTD 106.3
Louisville
WLSM-FM 107.1
Lumberton
† WLUN 95.3
Magee
WSJC-FM 107.5
Mc Comb
WAKH 105.7
WCCA 94.1
Meridian
WJDQ 101.3
†★ WMAW-FM 88.1
WOKK 97.1
Mississippi State
†★ WMAB-FM 96.7
★ WMSB 89.1
Moss Point
WKKY 104.9
Natchez
WQNZ 95.1
New Albany
WOKM 103.5
Newton
WMYQ-FM 106.3
Ocean Springs
WOSM 103.1
Oxford
†★ WMAV-FM 90.3
WOOR 97.5
Pascagoula
WGUD 106.3
WPMO 99.1
Philadelphia
WWSL 102.3
Picayune
WJOJ 106.3
Pontotoc
WSEL-FM 96.7
Poplarville
WRPM-FM 107.9
Prentiss
WJDR 98.3
Quitman
WYKK 98.3
Ripley
WTXI 102.3
Senatobia
★ WNJC-FM 88.9
Starkville
WKOR-FM 92.1
WSMU-FM 106.3
Tupelo
WZLQ 98.5
Tylertown
WTYL-FM 97.7
Vicksburg
WKYV-FM 106.7
WQMV 98.7
Waynesboro
WABO-FM 105.5
Wesson
† WCLL-FM 92.9
West Point
WKBB 100.9
Winona
WONA-FM 96.7
Yazoo City
WJNS-FM 92.1

Missouri

Aurora
KELE 100.1
Ballwin
★ KYMC 89.7
Bethany
KAAN-FM 95.9
Birch Tree
† ---- 107.1
Bolivar
KYOO-FM 106.3
Boonville
KDBX 99.3
Bowling Green
KPCR-FM 100.9
Branson
KRZK 106.3
Brookfield
KQMO 97.7
Buffalo
★ KBFL 90.3
Butler
KMOE 92.1
Cabool
KVVC-FM 106.3
California
† KZMO-FM 94.3
Canton
KQCA 102.3
Cape Girardeau
KEZS-FM 102.9
KGMO-FM 100.7
★ KRCU 90.9
Carrollton
KMZU 101.1
Carthage
KRGK 104.9
Caruthersville
KCRV-FM 103.1
Centralia
† ---- 92.1
Chillicothe
KCHI-FM 103.9
Clayton
★ KFUO-FM 99.1
★ KHRU 88.1
★ KWUR 90.3
Clinton
KDKD-FM 95.3
Columbia
KARO 101.7
★ KBIA 91.3
KCMQ 96.7
★ KCOU 88.1
KFMZ 98.3
★ KOPN 89.5
★ KWWC-FM 90.5
Crestwood
KSHE 94.7
Desoto
KOLS 100.1
Dexter
KDEX-FM 102.3
Doniphan
KOEA 97.7
El Dorado Springs
KESM-FM 105.5
Eldon
KLDN 92.7
Farmington
KTJJ 98.5
Ferguson
★ KCFV 89.5
Florissant
KCPM 97.1
Fulton
KKCA 97.7
Gordonville
KJAQ-FM 99.3
Greenfield
KRFG 93.5
Hannibal
KGRC 92.9
Harrisonville
KCFX 100.7
Houston
KSCM-FM 99.3
Ironton
† KYLS 92.7
Jefferson City
KJMO 100.1
★ KLUM-FM 88.9
KTXY 106.9
Joplin
KKUZ 102.5
★ KOBC 90.7
KSYN 92.5
Kansas City
KBEQ 104.3
KCMO-FM 94.9
★ KCUR-FM 89.3
★ KLJC 88.5
KLSI 93.3
KMBR 99.7
KPRS 103.3
★ KTSR 90.1
KXTR 96.5
KYYS 102.1
Kennett
KTMO 98.9
Kirksville
KRXL 94.5
KTUF 93.5
Knob Noster
† KLUK 105.5
Lebanon
KIRK 103.7
KLWT-FM 92.1
Lexington
KBEK 107.3
Liberty
KKCI-FM 106.5
★ KWPB 91.9
Louisana
† KJFM 101.7
Malden
KMAL 92.7
Mansfield
KTRI-FM 95.9
Marshall
KMFL-FM 102.9
★ KNOS 91.7
Marshfield
KOSC-FM 104.9
Maryville
KNIM-FM 99.3
★ KXCV 90.5
Memphis
KMEM 96.7
Mexico
KWWR 95.7
Moberly
KRES 104.7
Monett
KKBL 95.9
Monroe City
KLCQ 106.3
Montgomery City
KVCM 103.9
Mountain Grove
KLRS-FM 92.7
Mountain View
† KAIG 96.7
Nevada
† KNMO-FM 97.7
Osage Beach
KYLC 93.5
Overland
★ KRSH 90.1
Palmyra
KIDS 98.3
Parkville
★ KGSP 90.3
Point Lookout
★ KSOZ 91.7
Poplar Bluff
KJEZ 95.5
KPBM-FM 94.5
Portageville
KMIS-FM 106.3
Rolla
KCLU-FM 94.3
★ KMNR 89.7
★ KUMR 88.5
§ KZNN 105.3
Salem
KSMO-FM 95.9
Sedalia
KCBW 92.1
Sikeston
KSTG 97.7
Springfield
★ KSMU 91.1
KTTS-FM 94.7
KTXR 101.5
KWFC 97.3
KWTO-FM 98.7
St. Charles
★ KCLC 89.1
St. Joseph
KSFT 105.1
St. Louis
KADI-FM 96.3
★ KBDY 89.9
KEZK 102.5
KHTR 103.3
KMJM 107.7
KSD-FM 93.7
★ KSLH 91.5
KSLQ 98.1
†★ KTOD 88.1
★ KWMU 90.7
WIL-FM 92.3
Ste. Genevieve
KSGM-FM 105.7
Steelville
† KNSX 96.7
Sullivan
† KTUI-FM 100.9
Tarkio
KTRX 93.5

Trenton
KTTN-FM 92.1
Union
KLPW 101.7
Vandalia
† KMWR 100.1
Warrensburg
* KCMW-FM 90.9
Warsaw
KAYQ 97.7
Waynesville
KFBD-FM 97.7
KJPW-FM 102.3
Webb City
† ---- 94.3
West Plains
† KKDY 102.3
KWPM-FM 93.9

Montana

Anaconda
KGLM-FM 97.7
Baker
† KFLN-FM 100.9
Belgrade
KZDQ 96.7
Billings
* KEMC 91.7
KIDX 98.5
KOOK-FM 102.9
* KRER-FM 88.9
KYYA 93.3
KZLS 97.1
Bozeman
† ---- 93.1
KBOZ-FM 93.7
* KGLT 91.1
Browning
†* KBFT 88.7
Butte
* KMSM-FM 91.5
KOPR 94.1
KQUY 95.5
Chinook
† KRYK 101.3
Cut Bank
† KCTB-FM 102.7
Dillon
KDLN 98.3
Forsythe
KXXE 101.3
Glasgow
KLAN 93.5
Glendive
KIVE 96.5
Great Falls
†* ---- 89.9
KAAK 98.9
KLFM 92.9
KNUW 94.5
KOOZ 106.3
Hamilton
KLYQ FM 95.9
Hardin
KHDN-FM 95.3
Havre
* KNOG 90.1
KPQX 92.5
Helena
KBLL-FM 92.1
KCAP-FM 103.1
* KHTC 89.5
Kalispell
KALS 97.1
KBBZ 98.5
Lewistown
KLCM 95.9
Livingston
KYBS 97.5
Malta
KMMR 100.1
Miles City
† KMCM-FM 92.7
Missoula
KDXT 93.3
* KUFM 89.1
KYSS-FM 94.9
KZOQ 100.1
Plentywood
KATQ-FM 100.1
Ronan
KQRR 92.3
Scobey
KCGM 95.7
Shelby
KZIN-FM 96.3
Sidney
KGCH-FM 93.1
KSDY 95.1
Wolf Point
KYZZ 92.7

Nebraska

Ainsworth
KBRB-FM 92.7
Alliance
KPNY 92.1
Auburn
KAUB 105.5
KIAE 103.1
Aurora
KIAE 103.1
Beatrice
KMAZ 92.9
KMAZ 92.9
Blair
KBWH 106.3
* KDVC-FM 91.1
* KDVC-FM 91.1
Broken Bow
KBBN-FM 98.3
Chadron
KQSK 97.5
Columbus
KOXI 101.1
* KTLX 91.9
KTTT-FM 93.5
Cozad
† KOOC 104.5
Crete
KTAP 103.9
Crookston
* KINI 96.1
Elko
KLKO 93.5
Ely
† ---- 92.7
Fairbury
† KCIE 99.3
Falls City
KTNC-FM 95.3
Fremont
KHUB-FM 105.5
Gordon
KSDZ 95.5
Grand Island
KRGI-FM 96.5
KROA 95.7
KSYZ-FM 107.7
Hastings
* KCNT 88.1
† KEZH 101.5
‡ KEZH 93.5
Henderson
KMZQ-FM 100.5
Holdrege
KUVR-FM 97.7
Incline Village
† KLKT 100.1
Kearney
KQKY 105.9
KRNY-FM 98.9
* KSCV 91.3
Lexington
KRVN-FM 93.1
Lincoln
KFMQ 101.9
KFRX 102.7
KHAT 106.3
KLIN-FM 107.3
* KRNU 90.3
* KUCV 90.9
KXSS 95.3
* KZUM 89.5
Mc Cook
KICX-FM 95.9
Mc Cook (Cont)
KXMC 105.3
Nebraska City
KNCY-FM 97.7
Norfolk
KEXL 106.7
KNEN 94.7
North Platte
KELN 97.1
KODY-FM 94.9
KXNP 103.5
O' Neill
KBRX-FM 102.9
Ogallala
KMCX 106.5
KOGA-FM 99.7
Omaha
KEFM 96.1
KESY-FM 104.5
KEZO 92.3
* KGBI-FM 100.7
KGOR 99.9
* KIOS-FM 91.5
* KVNO 90.7
WOW-FM 94.1
Ord
KNLV-FM 103.9
Scottsbluff
KMOR 92.9
KNEB-FM 94.1
Seward
KSRD 96.9
Sidney
KSID-FM 95.3
Superior
KRFS-FM 103.9
Terrytown
KCMI 103.9
Wayne
KTCH-FM 104.9
* KWSC 91.9
York
KAWL-FM 104.9

Nevada

Battle Mountain
* KLME 88.1
Boulder City
KRRI 105.5
Carson City
KKBC 97.3
KNIS 94.7
Elko
KLKO 93.5
KRJC 95.3
Ely
† KBXS 92.7
Fallon
KVLV-FM 99.3
Gerlach
* KGLH 91.5
Henderson
KILA 95.5
KMZQ-FM 100.5
KXTZ 94.1
Incline Village
† KLKT 100.1
Las Vegas
* KCEP 88.1
KFMS 101.9
KLUC 98.5
* KNPR 89.5
KOMP 92.3
KEER 97.1
KITT 96.3
KUDO 93.1
* KUNV 91.5
Reno
KNEV 95.5
KOZZ 105.7
KRNO 106.9
KSRN 104.5
* KUNR 88.7
Sparks
† KNAA 100.9
Tonopah
KPAH 92.7
Winnemucca
KWNA-FM 92.7

New Hampshire

Berlin
WXLQ 103.7
Claremont
WECM 106.1
Concord
* WEVO 89.1
† WJYY 105.5
WKXL-FM 102.3
* WSPS 90.5
Conway
WMWV 93.5
Dover
WOKQ 97.5
Durham
* WUNH 91.3
Exeter
WERZ 107.1
* WPEA 90.5
Hanover
WFRD 99.3
Henniker
* WNEC-FM 91.7
Keene
* WKNH 89.1
WNBX-FM 103.7
Laconia
WLNH-FM 98.3
Littleton
† ---- 106.3
Manchester
†* WANH-FM 90.7
WGIR-FM 101.1
WZID 95.7
Mt. Washington
WHOM 94.9
Nashua
WOTW-FM 106.3
Newport
WCNL-FM 101.7
Peterborough
WMDK 92.1
Plymouth
* WPCR-FM 91.7
WPNH-FM 100.1
Portsmouth
WHEB-FM 100.3
Rochester
WXKZ 96.7
Wolfeboro
† WLKZ 104.9

New Jersey

Asbury Park
WJLK-FM 94.3
Atlantic City
WAYV 95.1
WFPG 96.9
WMGM 103.7
Avalon
WWOC 94.3
Blackwood
* WDBK 91.5
Blairstown
WFMV 106.3
Brick Town
* WBGD 91.9
Bridgeton
WSNJ-FM 107.7
Camden
WKDN-FM 106.9
Canton
WNNN 107.1
Cape May
WSJL 102.3
Cherry Hill
* WBEK 88.1
†* WEEE 89.5
Dover
WDHA-FM 105.5
East Orange
* WFMU 91.1
Eatontown
WHTG-FM 106.3

Egg Harbor	WRDR	104.9
Flemington	★ WCVH	90.5
Franklin	WSUS	102.3
Franklin Lakes	★ WRRH	88.7
Glassboro	★ WGLS-FM	89.7
Hackettstown	★ WNTI	91.9
Hazlet	★ WVRM	89.3
Highland Park	★ WVHP-FM	90.3
Lawrenceville	★ WWRC	88.5
Lincroft	★ WBJB-FM	90.5
Long Branch	WMJY	107.1
Madison	★ WMNJ	88.9
Mahwah	★ WRPR	90.3
Manahawkin	WJRZ	100.1
Millville	WMVB	97.3
Morristown	★ WJSV	90.5
New Brunswick	WMGQ	98.3
	★ WRSU-FM	88.7
Newark	★ WBGO	88.3
	WFME	94.7
	† WHBI	105.9
	WHTZ	100.3
Newton	WIXL-FM	103.7
Ocean City	WDVR	98.3
	WSLT	106.3
Paterson	WPAT-FM	93.1
Piscataway	★ WVPH	90.3
Pleasantville	WLQF	99.3
Point Pleasant	WADB	95.9
Princeton	WPRB	103.3
Princeton Junction	★ WWPH	107.9
South Orange	★ WSOU	89.5
Teaneck	★ WFDU	89.1
Toms River	WOBM-FM	92.7
Trenton	WCHR	94.5
	WKXW	101.5
	WPST	97.5
	★ WTSR	91.3
	★ WWFM	89.1
Union	★ WKNJ	90.3
Upper Montclair	★ WMSC	101.5
Vineland	WKQV	92.1
West Long Branch	★ WMCX	88.1
Whippany	★ WHPH	90.5
Wildwood	WNBR	100.7
Zarephath	WAWZ-FM	99.1

New Mexico

Alamogordo	KINN-FM	105.5
Alamogordo (Cont)	KKEE	94.3
Albuquerque	★ KANW	89.1
	★ KFLQ	91.5
	KFMG	107.9
	KHFM	96.3
	KKJY-FM	100.3
	★ KLYT	88.3
	KOB-FM	93.3
	KRST	92.3
	★ KUNM	90.1
	KWXL	94.1
	KZZX	99.5
Artesia	KTZA	92.9
Aztec	KWYK-FM	94.9
Bayard	KLCJ	92.7
Belen	† KMLW	97.7
Carlsbad	KATK	92.1
Clovis	KCLV-FM	99.1
	† KICA	107.5
	† KCPK	107.5
	KTQM-FM	99.9
Deming	KDEM	94.3
Espanola	KEVR	102.3
Farmington	★ KNMI	88.9
	KRAZ	96.9
	KRWN	92.9
Gallup	KOVO	94.5
	KQNM	93.7
Grants	KLLT	95.3
Hobbs	KPER	95.7
	KZOR	94.1
La Luz	† KALG-FM	92.7
Las Cruces	KASK	103.1
	KGRT-FM	103.9
	★ KRWG	90.7
Las Vegas	★ KEDP	91.1
	KLVF	100.9
Los Alamos	KRSN-FM	98.5
Lovington	KLEA-FM	101.7
Maljamar	†★ ----	88.9
Mesilla Park	KOPE	104.9
Portales	★ KENW-FM	89.5
	KNIT	95.3
Ramah	★ KTDB	89.7
Raton	KRTN-FM	94.3
Rio Rancho	† KZIA-FM	101.7
Roswell	KBIM-FM	94.9
	KRIZ	97.1
Rudioso	KTNT	93.5
Santa Fe	KAFE-FM	97.3
	† KLSK	104.1
	† KNMQ	105.9
	KSNM	95.5
Taos	KVNM	101.7
Tucumcari	KQAY-FM	92.7
Zuni	★ KSHI	90.9

New York

Albany	★ WAMC	90.3
	★ WCDB	90.9
	WGNA	107.7
	WHRL	103.1
	WPYX	106.5
	WROW-FM	95.5
	WWOM	100.9
Alfred	★ WALF	89.7
	★ WETD	90.9
Amsterdam	WMVQ	97.7
Auburn	★ WDWN	88.9
	WPCX	106.9
Babylon	WBAB-FM	102.3
Baldwinsville	★ WBXL	90.5
	WSEN-FM	92.1
Bath	† WCIK	103.1
	WVIN-FM	98.3
Binghamton	WAAL	99.1
	★ WHRW	90.5
	WHWK	98.1
	★ WSKG-FM	89.3
Brentwood	★ WXBA	88.1
Briarcliff Manor	WZFM	107.1
Brockport	★ WBKT	93.3
	★ WBSU	88.9
Brooklyn	★ WKRB	103.1
Brookville	★ WCWP	88.1
Buffalo	WBEN-FM	102.5
	★ WBFO	88.7
	†★ WBNY	91.3
	WBUF	92.9
	WDCX	99.5
	WGRQ	96.9
	WJYE	96.1
	★ WNED-FM	94.5
	WNYS-FM	104.1
	WPHD	103.3
	WYRK	106.5
Canandaigua	WFLC	102.3
Canton	★ WSLU	96.7
Carthage	† ----	103.1
Cazenovia	★ WITC	90.9
Central Square	★ WCSQ	89.3
Cherry Valley	WJIV	101.9
Clifton Park	† WIAK	96.7
Clinton	★ WHCL-FM	88.7
Cobleskill	† ----	103.5
Corinth	WSCG	93.5
Corning	★ WCEB	91.9
	WZKZ	106.1
Cortland	WOKW	99.9
	★ WSUC-FM	90.5
De Pew	WBLK-FM	93.7
De Ruyter	WOIV	105.1
Dix Hills	★ WHHJ	88.9
Dundee	WFLR-FM	95.9
Ellenville	WDRE	99.3
Elmira	★ WECW	88.1
	WLEZ	92.7
	WLVY	94.3
Endicott	WMRV	105.7
Frankfurt	† ----	105.5
Fredonia	★ WCVF-FM	88.9
Fulton	WKFM	104.7
Garden City	#★ WBAU	90.3
	#★ WHPC	90.3
	WLIR	92.7
Geneseo	★ WGSU	89.3
Geneva	WECQ	101.7
	★ WEOS-FM	89.7
Glens Falls	★ WGFR	92.1
	WYLR-FM	95.9
Gouverneur	WIGS-FM	95.3
Greece	★ WGMC	90.1
Hamilton	★ WRCU-FM	90.1
Hampton Bays	WWHB	107.1
Hempstead	WKJY	98.3
	★ WRHU	88.7
Henrietta	★ WITR	89.7
	★ WRHR	90.5
Herkimer	WYUT-FM	92.7
Hornell	WCKR	92.1
	WKPQ	105.3
Horseheads	WQIX	100.9
Houghton	★ WJSL	90.3
Hudson	WRVW	93.5
Hudson Falls	† WENU	101.7
	WNIQ-FM	107.1
Hyde Park	WJJB	97.7
Ithaca	WHCU-FM	97.3
	★ WICB	91.7
	WQNY	103.7
	WVBR-FM	93.5
Jamestown	WHUG	101.7
	★ WJWK	91.5
	WWSE	93.3
Johnstown	WIZR-FM	104.9
Kingston	WBPM	94.3
	†★ WFGB	89.7
Lake Placid	WLPW	105.5
Lake Ronkonkoma	★ WSHR	91.9
Lake Success	WAPP	103.5
Liberty	WVOS-FM	95.9
Loudonville	★ WVCR-FM	88.3
Manlius	WAQX	95.3
Middle Island	†★ ----	88.5
Middletown	WKGL	92.7
Monticello	WSUL	98.3

Montour Falls
WNGZ 104.9
Mount Kisco
WVIP-FM 106.3
New Rochelle
WRTN 93.5
New York
* WBAI 99.5
WBLS 107.5
WCBS-FM 101.1
WEVD 97.9
* WFUV 90.7
†* WHCR-FM 90.3
* WKCR-FM 89.9
WKHK 106.7
WKTU 92.3
WNCN 104.3
WNEW-FM 102.7
* WNYC-FM 93.9
* WNYE 91.5
* WNYU-FM 89.1
WPIX-FM 101.9
WPLJ 95.5
WQXR-FM 96.3
WRFM 105.1
WRKS-FM 98.7
WYNY 97.1
Newburgh
WFMN 103.1
Niagara Falls
WZIR 98.5
North Syracuse
WSCY 100.9
Norwich
WXKZ 93.9
Nyack
* WNYK 88.7
Ogdensburg
WPAC 92.7
Olean
WBJZ 100.9
WEBF 95.7
Oneida
WMCR-FM 106.3
Oneonta
* WONY 90.9
* WRHO 89.5
WSRK 103.9
WZOZ 103.1
Ossining
* WOSS 90.3
Oswego
* WRVO 89.9
WSGO-FM 105.5
Owego
WWWT 101.7
Patchogue
WALK-FM 97.5
WBLI 106.1
Patterson
* WRVH 105.5
Paul Smith's
* WPSA 89.1
Peekskill
WHUD 100.7
Plainview
* WPOB 88.5
Plattsburgh
WGFB 99.9
* WPLT 93.9
Port Henry
* WHRC 92.1
Port Jervis
WDLC-FM 96.7
Potsdam
WSNN 99.3
* WTSC-FM 91.1
Poughkeepsie
WPDH 101.5
WSPK 104.7
* WVKR-FM 91.3
Remsen
WAES-FM 93.5
Rensselaer
WQBK-FM 103.9
Riverhead
WRCN-FM 103.9

Rochester
WCMF 96.5
WDKX 103.9
WEZO 101.3
WHFM 98.9
* WIRQ 90.9
WMJQ 92.5
WPXY-FM 97.9
* WRUR-FM 88.5
WVOR-FM 100.5
* WXXI-FM 91.5
Rome
WKAL-FM 95.9
† WUUU 102.5
Sag Harbor
WLNG-FM 92.1
Saratoga Springs
WASM 102.3
* WSPN 91.1
Schenectady
WGFM 99.5
* WMHT-FM 89.1
* WRUC 89.7
Seneca Falls
WSFW-FM 99.3
Sidney
† WSID 100.9
Smithtown
WCTO 94.3
Sodus
* WSCS 89.5
South Bristol
WYLF 95.1
Southampton
* WPBX 91.3
WSBH 95.3
Southold
* WBAZ 101.7
St. Bonaventura
* WSBU 88.3
Staten Island
* WSIA 88.9
Stony Brook
* WUSB 90.1
Syosset
* WKWZ 88.5
Syracuse
* WAER 88.3
* WCNY-FM 91.3
WMHR-FM 102.9
WNTQ 93.1
WRRB 107.9
WYYY 94.5
Ticonderoga
WXTY 103.9
Troy
WFLY 92.3
* WRPI 91.5
Tupper Lake
WTPL-FM 102.3
Utica
†* ---- 89.5
WIBQ 98.7
WKGW 104.3
WOUR 96.9
* WPNR-FM 90.7
WRCK 107.3
Valhalla
* WARY 88.5
Walton
WDLA-FM 92.1
Watertown
†* ---- 90.9
WNCQ 97.5
Waverly
WAVR 102.3
West Point
†* WKDT 89.3
Wethersfield
WUWU 107.7
White Plains
WFAS-FM 103.9
Woodstock
WDST 100.1

North Carolina

Ahoskie
WQDK 99.3
Albemarle
WABZ-FM 100.9
Asheboro
WCSE 92.3
Asheville
* WBMU-FM 91.3
WLOS 99.9
* WUNF-FM 88.1
Belhaven
WKJA 92.1
Black Mountain
WMIT 106.9
Boiling Springs
* WGWG 88.3
Boone
* WASU-FM 90.5
Bridgeton
WSFL 106.5
Buie's Creek
* WCCE 90.1
Burgaw
WVBS-FM 99.9
Burlington
WBAG 93.9
WPCM 101.1
Carrington
† ---- 97.7
Chapel Hill
* WUNC 91.5
* WXYC 89.3
Charlotte
WBCY 107.9
WEZC 104.7
* WFAE 90.7
WROQ 95.1
WSOC-FM 103.7
Clinton
WRRZ-FM 107.1
Columbia
WTHD 105.7
Concord
WPEG 97.9
Cullowhee
* WWCU 90.5
Dallas
* WSGE 91.7
Davidson
* WDAV 89.9
Dunn
WIDO 103.1
Durham
* WAFR 90.3
WDBS 107.1
WDCG 105.1
†* WXDU 88.7
Eden
WSRQ 94.5
Edenton
WBXB 100.1
† WZBO-FM 102.3
Elizabeth City
WMYK 93.7
Elkin
WIFM-FM 100.9
Elon College
* WSOE 89.3
Fairmont
WZYZ 100.9
Farmville
WRQR 94.3
Fayetteville
* WFSS 89.1
WQSM 98.1
Forest City
WBBO-FM 93.3
Franklin
WRFR 96.7
Fuquay Springs
WAKS-FM 103.9
Gastonia
WZXI 101.9
Goldsboro
WEQR 96.9
WOKN 102.3
Greensboro
* WNAA 90.5
* WQFS 90.9
WQMG 97.1

Greensboro (Cont)
WRQK 98.7
* WUAG 106.1
Greenville
†* ---- 88.3
WNCT-FM 107.9
* WZMB 91.3
Grifton
† WNBB 99.3
Havelock
WMSQ 104.9
Henderson
WYFL 92.5
Hendersonville
WKIT 102.5
Hickory
WHKY-FM 102.9
WXRC 95.7
High Point
WGLD-FM 100.3
WHPE-FM 95.5
WMAG 99.5
* WWIH 90.3
Jacksonville
WRCM 92.1
WXQR 105.5
Kannapolis
WJZR 99.7
Kinston
* WKNS 90.5
WQDW 97.7
WRNS 95.1
Laurinburg
WSTS 96.5
Lexington
WLXN 94.1
Lumberton
WGSS 95.7
WJSK 102.3
Mars Hill
* WVMH-FM 90.5
Morehead City
WMBJ-FM 95.9
Morganton
WQXX 92.1
Moyock
WOFM 92.1
Murfreesboro
WBCG 98.3
New Bern
WAZZ 101.9
WSFL 106.5
* WTEB 89.5
New Port
† WZYC 103.3
North Wilkesboro
WKBC-FM 97.3
Plymouth
WKLX 95.9
Raleigh
* WCPE 89.7
* WKNC-FM 88.1
WQDR 94.7
WRAL 101.5
* WSHA 88.9
WYYD 96.1
Reidsville
WWMO 102.1
Roanoke Rapids
* WPGT 90.1
WPTM 102.3
Rockingham
* WRSH 91.1
Rocky Mount
WFMA 100.7
WRSV 92.1
Roxboro
WKRX 96.7
Salisbury
* WNDN-FM 102.5
WRDX 106.5
Sanford
* WDCC 90.5
WFJA 105.5
Shallotte
† WPGO 106.3
WDZD 93.5

Shelby
WXIK 96.1
Southern Pines
WIOZ 107.1
Southport
WJYW 107.1
Statesville
WFMX 105.7
WLVV 96.9
Swan Quarter
WHYC 88.5
Tabor City
WKSM 104.9
Tarboro
WKTC 104.3
Thomasville
WTNC-FM 98.3
Wallace
WZKB 94.3
Wanchese
WOBR-FM 95.3
Warrenton
* WVSP 90.9
Washington
WITN-FM 93.3
Waynesville
WQNS 104.9
Whiteville
WQTR 99.1
Wilkesboro
* WSIF 94.7
Williamston
WSEC 103.7
Wilmington
WGNI 102.7
†* WHQR 91.3
WHSL 97.3
WWQQ-FM 100.9
Wilson
WXYY 106.1
Windsor
† WDJB 97.7
Winston Salem
* WFDD-FM 88.5
WKZL 107.5
WSEZ 93.1
* WSNC 89.3
WTQR 104.1

North Dakota

Belcourt
* KEYA 88.5
Bismarck
* KCND 90.5
KQDY 94.5
KYYY 92.9
Bottineau
KBTO 101.9
Carrington
† KDAK-FM 97.7
Devils Lake
KDVL 102.5
† KZZY 103.5
Dickinson
KRRB 92.1
Fargo
† KRRZ 101.9
* KDSU 91.9
KFNW-FM 97.9
WDAY-FM 93.7
Grafton
† KXPO-FM 100.9
Grand Forks
* KFJM-FM 89.3
KKXL-FM 92.9
KYTN 94.7
Jamestown
† KQDJ-FM 95.5
KSJM 93.3
Mandan
KNDR 104.9
Mayville
KMAV-FM 101.7
Minot
† KZPR 105.3
† KBQQ 99.9
KCJB-FM 97.1
KIZZ 93.7
Minot (Cont)
†* KMPR 89.9
New Town
†* KMHA 91.3
Villey City
† KKVC 100.9
Williston
† ---- 98.5
KYYZ 96.1

Ohio

Akron
WAEZ 97.5
* WAPS 89.1
* WAUP 88.1
WKDD 96.5
Alliance
WDJQ 92.5
* WRMU 91.1
Archbold
WHFD 95.9
Ashland
WNCO-FM 101.3
* WRDL 88.9
Ashtabula
WREO-FM 97.1
Athens
* WOUB-FM 91.3
WXTQ 105.5
Bainbridge
* WKHR 88.3
Batavia
* WCNE 88.7
* WOBO 88.1
Beaver Creek
WYMJ-FM 103.9
Bellaire
* WBHR 88.7
WOMP-FM 100.5
Bellefontaine
WTOO-FM 98.3
Bellevue
WNRR 92.1
Belpre
WNUS 102.1
Berea
* WBWC 88.3
Bowling Green
* WBGU 88.1
WRQN 93.5
Bryan
WBNO-FM 100.9
Bucyrus
WBCO-FM 92.7
Byesville
†* ---- 91.7
Cadiz
† ---- 106.3
Cambridge
WILE-FM 96.7
Canton
WHBC-FM 94.1
WOOS-FM 106.9
WTOF 98.1
Castalia
WGGN 97.7
Cedarville
* WCDR-FM 90.3
Celina
WCSM-FM 96.7
WKKI 94.3
Centerville
* WCWT-FM 92.1
Chillicothe
WFCB 94.3
WKKJ 93.3
Cincinnati
* WAIF 88.3
* WAKW 93.3
WEBN 102.7
* WGUC 90.9
* WJVS 88.3
WKRQ 101.9
WRRM 98.5
WSAI-FM 94.1
WUBE-FM 105.1
* WVXU-FM 91.7
WWEZ 92.5
Circleville
WNRE-FM 107.1
Cleveland
WCLV 95.5
* WCPN 90.3
* WCRF 103.3
* WCSB 89.3
WDMT 107.9
WDOK 102.1
WGCL 98.5
WKSW 99.5
WMJI 105.7
WMMS 100.7
WQAL 104.1
* WRUW-FM 91.1
* WUJC 88.7
WZAK 93.1
WZZP 106.5
Cleveland Heights
WRQC 92.3
Clyde
WMEX 100.9
Columbus
WBNS-FM 97.1
* WCBE 90.5
WLVQ 96.3
WNCI 97.9
* WOSU-FM 89.7
WRMZ 99.7
WSNY 94.7
WXGT 92.3
Conneaut
WGOJ 105.5
Coshocton
WTNS-FM 99.3
Dayton
* WCXL 89.3
WDAO 107.7
* WDPS 89.3
* WGXM 97.3
WHIO-FM 99.1
* WSMR 89.3
WTUE 104.7
De Graff
* WDEQ-FM 91.1
Delaware
* WSLN 91.1
Delphos
WDOH 107.1
Dover
WJER-FM 101.7
East Liverpool
WELA 104.3
Eaton
WJAI 92.9
Elyria
WBEA 107.3
Fairborn
* WWSU 106.9
Fairfield
WLLT 94.9
Findlay
WHMQ 100.5
* WLFC 88.3
Fostoria
WFOB-FM 96.7
Fremont
WFRO-FM 99.1
Gahanna
WCVO 104.9
Galion
WQLX 102.3
Gallipolis
WYPC 101.5
Gambier
* WKCO 91.9
Georgetown
WURD 97.7
Granville
†* WDUB 91.1
‡* WDUB 90.9
Greenville
†* WGVO 91.5
‡* WGVO 91.7
WLSN 106.5
Hamilton
WBLZ 103.5
* WHSS 89.5
Hamilton (Cont)
WSKS 96.5
Hillsboro
WSRW-FM 106.7
Holland
WPOS-FM 102.3
Ironton
WITO 107.1
Jackson
WCJO 97.7
WWWJ 103.1
Kent
* WKSU-FM 89.7
WNIR 100.1
Kenton
WKTN 95.3
Kettering
* WKET 89.5
WVUD-FM 99.9
Lancaster
WHOK 95.5
Lima
* WGLE 90.7
WIMT 102.1
WLSR 104.9
WTGN 97.7
Logan
WLGN-FM 98.3
London
WSYX 106.3
Lorain
WZLE 104.9
Mansfield
WCLW-FM 105.3
* WVMC 90.7
WVNO-FM 106.1
Marietta
* WCMO 98.5
WEYQ 94.3
* WMRT 88.3
Marion
WDIF 94.3
WMRN-FM 106.9
Medina
WDBN 94.9
Miamisburg
WFCJ 93.7
* WRSF 89.9
Middleport
WMPO-FM 92.1
Middletown
WPBF-FM 105.9
Milford
WLYK 107.1
Morrow
* WLMH 89.1
Mt. Vernon
WMVO-FM 93.7
Napoleon
WNDH 103.1
New Concord
* WMCO 90.7
New Lexington
WWJM 106.3
New Philadelphia
WNPQ 95.9
Newark
WCLT-FM 100.3
WNKO 101.7
Norwalk
WLKR-FM 95.3
Oberlin
* WOBC-FM 88.7
Ottawa
WPNM 106.3
Oxford
* WMUB 88.5
WOXY 97.7
Piqua
WPTW-FM 95.7
Port Clinton
WOSE 94.5
Portsmouth
WNXT-FM 99.3
WPAY-FM 104.1
Reading
* WRCJ 89.3

City	Station	Frequency
Salem		
	WQXX	105.1
Sandusky		
	WCPZ	102.7
Shelby		
	WSWR	100.1
Sidney		
	WMVR-FM	105.5
Springfield		
	WAZU	102.9
	WEEC	100.7
	★ WUSO	89.1
Steubenville		
	WRKY	103.5
Streetsboro		
	★ WSTB	91.5
Struthers		
	★ WKTL	90.7
Sylvania		
	WWWM	93.3
Tiffin		
	★ WHEI	88.9
	WTTF-FM	103.7
Toledo		
	★ WAMP-FM	88.3
	★ WGTE-FM	91.3
	WIOT	104.7
	WKLR	99.9
	WLQR	101.5
	WMHE	92.5
Upper Sandusky		
	WYAN-FM	95.9
Urbana		
	WCOM-FM	101.7
	★ WUHS	91.7
Van Wert		
	WERT-FM	98.9
Wapakoneta		
	WAXC	92.1
Washington Court House		
	WCHO-FM	105.5
Waverly		
	WXIZ	100.9
Wellston		
	WKOV-FM	96.7
West Carrollton		
	★ WQRP	88.1
West Chester		
	★ WLHS	89.9
West Union		
	WRAC	103.1
Westerville		
	WBBY	103.9
	★ WOBN	105.7
Wilberforce		
	★ WCSU-FM	88.9
Wilmington		
	WSWO	102.3
Wooster		
	★ WCWS	91.9
	WQKT	104.5
Xenia		
	WBZI	95.3
Yellow Springs		
	★ WYSO	91.3
Youngstown		
	WKBN-FM	98.9
	WQOD	93.3
	WSRD	101.1
	★ WYSU	88.5
Zanesville		
	WHIZ-FM	102.5

Oklahoma

City	Station	Frequency
Ada		
	KASX	96.7
	KTEN-FM	93.3
Altus		
	KWHW-FM	93.5
Alva		
	† KRKA	104.7
	KXLS	99.7
Anadarko		
	KRPT-FM	103.7
Ardmore		
	KELS	92.1
	KKAJ	95.7
	KRRO	92.1
Atoka		
	† KEOR-FM	103.1
Bartlesville		
	KYFM	100.1
Bethany		
	KJIL	104.9
Bristow		
	KREK	104.9
Broken Arrow		
	†★ KNYD	90.5
	KSNE	92.1
Broken Bow		
	† KKBI	106.3
Chickasha		
	KXXK	105.5
Claremore		
	★ KNGX	91.3
Clinton		
	KCLI	95.3
	KKCC-FM	106.9
Commanche		
	† ----	96.7
Duncan		
	KRHD-FM	102.3
Durant		
	† KEYD	97.7
	★ KHIB	91.9
	KLBC	107.1
Edmond		
	★ KCSC	90.1
	KKLR	97.7
	★ KOKF	90.9
Elk City		
	KECO	96.5
Enid		
	KNID	96.9
	KUAL	103.1
Eufaula		
	KCES	102.3
Frederick		
	KYBE	95.9
Goodwell		
	★ KPSU	91.7
Grove		
	KGVE	99.3
Guymon		
	† KKBS	92.7
Henryetta		
	KGCG-FM	99.5
Hobart		
	KQTZ	105.9
Hugo		
	† KITX	95.3
Idabel		
	KWDG	96.7
Langston		
	★ KALU	90.7
Lawton		
	KLAW	101.5
	† KMGZ	95.3
	KRLG	98.1
Mc Alester		
	KMCO	101.3
Miami		
	KORS	100.9
Muskogee		
	KAYI	106.9
	† KRLQ	97.1
Norman		
	KGOU	106.3
Nowata		
	KNFB	94.3
Oklahoma City		
	KAEZ	107.7
	KATT-FM	100.5
	KEBC	94.7
	KJYO	102.7
	KKNG	92.5
	KLNK	98.9
	KLTE	101.9
	★ KOCC	88.5
	KOFM	104.1
	KXXY	96.1
Okmulgee		
	KQBC	94.3
Owasso		
	KCMA	106.1
Pauls Valley		
	KGOK	97.7
Ponca City		
	KLOR-FM	99.3
	KPNC-FM	100.9
Poteau		
	KINB	107.3
	KLUP	97.9
Pryor		
	KMYZ-FM	104.5
Sallisaw		
	KAZZ	95.9
Sapulpa		
	KXOJ-FM	100.9
Seminole		
	KSLE	105.5
Stillwater		
	★ KOSU-FM	91.7
	KSPI-FM	93.9
	KVRO	105.5
Sulphur		
	KSDW	100.9
Tahlequah		
	KEOK	101.7
Tonkawa		
	★ KAYE-FM	90.7
Tulsa		
	KBEZ	92.9
	KCFO	98.5
	KMOD-FM	97.5
	KRAV	96.5
	KTFX	103.3
	KWEN	95.5
	★ KWGS	89.5
Vinita		
	KITO	95.9
Weatherford		
	KWEY-FM	97.3
Woodward		
	† ----	102.3
	† KDAA	92.1
	KSIW-FM	93.5
	† KWOX	101.1

Oregon

City	Station	Frequency
Albany		
	KHPE	107.9
	KRKT-FM	99.9
Ashland		
	KCMX-FM	101.7
	★ KSOR	90.1
Astoria		
	KBKN	92.9
	†★ KMUN	91.9
Baker		
	† KBKR-FM	95.3
Beaverton		
	KTJA	103.3
Bend		
	† ----	105.7
	KICE	100.7
	† KLNR	97.5
	KXIQ	94.1
Brookings		
	KURY-FM	95.3
Central Point		
	★ KCHC	91.7
Coos Bay		
	KYNG-FM	105.5
	KYTT-FM	98.3
Coquille		
	KSHR-FM	102.3
Corvallis		
	★ KBVR	88.7
	KEJO	101.5
	KLOO-FM	106.1
Creswell		
	† KRNN	95.3
Eagle Point		
	★ KEPO	92.1
Eugene		
	KBMC	94.5
	★ KLCC	89.7
	KPNW-FM	99.1
	★ KRVM	91.9
	KUGN-FM	97.9
	★ KWAX	91.1
	KZEL-FM	96.1
Florence		
	KDUK	104.7
Gold Beach		
	† KGBR	92.7
Gold Hill		
	KRWQ	100.3
Grants Pass		
	KFMJ	96.9
Gresham		
	†★ KMHD	88.5
Hermiston		
	KOHU-FM	99.3
Hood River		
	KCGB	105.5
Klamath Falls		
	KAGO-FM	98.5
	KJSN	92.5
	† KKRB	95.9
	★ KTEC	89.5
La Grande		
	★ KEOL	91.7
	KLBM-FM	98.3
Lake Oswego		
	KMJK	106.7
Lebanon		
	KIQY	103.7
Lincoln City		
	KCRF	96.7
Mc Minnville		
	★ KSLC	90.3
Medford		
	KBOY-FM	95.3
	KTMT	93.7
Newport		
	KNPT-FM	102.5
North Bend		
	KOOS	100.9
Ontario		
	KXBQ	96.1
Pendleton		
	KFMT	103.5
	★ KRBM	90.9
	KUMA-FM	107.7
Portland		
	★ KBOO	90.7
	★ KBPS-FM	89.9
	KCNR-FM	97.1
	KGON	92.3
	KINK	101.9
	KJIB	99.5
	★ KOAP-FM	91.5
	KPDQ-FM	93.7
	KRKZ	100.3
	KRCK	101.1
	KUPL-FM	98.5
	KXL-FM	95.5
Prineville		
	KIJK	95.3
Redmond		
	† KPRB-FM	102.9
	† KPUP	107.5
Roseburg		
	KRSB	103.1
Salem		
	KSKD	105.1
Springfield		
	KSND	93.1
Sweet Home		
	KBYQ	107.1
The Dalles		
	KCIV	104.5
Tillamook		
	KTIL-FM	104.1
Toledo		
	KCEL	107.1
Warm Springs		
	† KWSI	96.5

Pennsylvania

City	Station	Frequency
Allentown		
	WFMZ	100.7
	★ WMUH	89.7
	WXKW	104.1
Altoona		
	WFBG-FM	98.1
	WPRR	100.1
Beaver Falls		
	★ WGEV	88.3

City	Station	Frequency
Beaver Falls (Cont)		
	WWKS	106.7
Bedford		
	WRAX	100.9
Bellwood		
	WHGM	103.9
Bethlehem		
	* WLVR	91.3
	WZZO	95.1
Blairsville		
	WCQO	106.3
Bloomsburg		
	WHLM-FM	106.5
Boyertown		
	WBYO	107.5
Braddock		
	WHYW-FM	96.9
Brookville		
	WMKX	95.9
Butler		
	WLER-FM	97.7
California		
	* WVCS	91.9
Canton		
	WKAD	100.1
Carbondale		
	WCDL-FM	94.3
Carlisle		
	* WDCV-FM	88.3
	WZUE	102.3
Carolina		
	†* WIDA-FM	90.5
Central City		
	WWZE	101.7
Chambersburg		
	WIKZ	95.1
Charleroi		
	WESA-FM	98.3
Chester		
	* WDNR	89.5
Clarion		
	* WCUC-FM	91.7
Clearfield		
	WQYX	93.5
Cresson		
	WBXQ	94.3
Danville		
	WPGM-FM	96.7
Du Bois		
	WDBA	107.3
	WOWQ	102.1
East Stroudsburg		
	* WESS	90.3
Easton		
	* WJRH	90.5
	WLEV	96.1
	WQQQ	99.9
Ebensburg		
	WIYQ	99.1
Edinboro		
	* WFSE	88.9
Ellwood City		
	WFEM	92.1
Emporium		
	† WQKY	92.7
Ephrata		
	WIOV	105.1
Erie		
	WCCK	103.7
	* WERG	89.9
	WLVU	99.9
	* WQLN-FM	91.3
Exeter		
	†* WASD	88.1
Folsom		
	† WRSD	94.9
Franklin		
	WVEN	99.3
Freeland		
	WQEQ	103.1
Gettysburg		
	WGTY	107.7
	* WZBT	91.1
Girard		
	†* WGAE	88.3
Greencastle		
	WKSL	94.3
Greensburg		
	WOKU-FM	107.1
Greenville		
	WGRP-FM	107.1
	* WTGP	88.1
Grove City		
	WEDA-FM	95.1
	* WSAJ-FM	89.5
Hanover		
	WYCR	98.5
Harrisburg		
	WHP-FM	97.3
	* WITF-FM	89.5
	* WMSP	94.9
	WSFM	99.3
	WTPA-FM	104.1
Havertown		
	* WHHS	89.3
Hazleton		
	WVCD	97.9
Hershey		
	WRKZ	106.7
Hollidaysburg		
	WHPA	104.9
Honesdale		
	WDNH-FM	95.3
Huntingdon		
	* WKVR-FM	103.5
	WRLR	106.3
Indiana		
	* WIUP-FM	90.1
	WQMU	103.1
Jenkintown		
	WIBF-FM	103.9
Jersey Shore		
	WSQV	97.7
Johnstown		
	WGLU	92.1
	WKYE	95.5
	WJNL-FM	96.5
Kane		
	WRXZ	103.9
Lancaster		
	WDAC	94.5
	* WFNM	89.1
	WLAN-FM	96.9
	WNCE	101.3
	* WPTG	90.3
Lebanon		
	WUFM	100.1
Lehman		
	* WPSU	89.1
Lewisburg		
	* WVBU-FM	90.5
Lewistown		
	WMRF-FM	95.9
Linesville		
	WVCC	101.7
Lock Haven		
	WCNM	92.1
Mansfield		
	* WNTE	89.5
Martinsburg		
	WJSM-FM	92.7
Mc Kean		
	WSEG	102.3
Meadville		
	* WARC	90.3
	WZPR	100.3
Mechanicsburg		
	WKCD	93.5
Media		
	WKSZ	100.3
Mercer		
	WWIZ	103.9
Mercersburg		
	WGLL	92.1
Middletown		
	* WMSS	91.1
Mifflinburg		
	WWMC-FM	98.3
Millersville		
	* WIXQ	91.7
Milton		
	WOEZ-FM	100.9
Montrose		
	WPEL-FM	96.5
Muncy		
	† WJKR	103.9
Nanticoke		
	WMJW	92.1
New Kensington		
	WNUF	100.7
New Wilmington		
	* WWNW	88.9
North East		
	WHYP-FM	100.9
Oil City		
	WRJS	98.5
Oxford		
	* WLIU	88.7
Palmyra		
	WCTX	92.1
Philadelphia		
	WCAU-FM	98.1
	WDAS-FM	105.3
	WEAZ	101.1
	WFLN-FM	95.7
	* WHYY-FM	90.9
	WXTU	92.5
	WIOQ	102.1
	* WKDU	91.7
	WMGK	102.9
	WMMR	93.3
	* WPEB	88.1
	* WPWT	91.7
	* WRTI	90.1
	WSNI-FM	104.5
	WUSL	98.9
	WWDB	96.5
	WWSH	106.1
	* WXPN	88.9
	WYSP	94.1
Pittsburgh		
	WAMO-FM	105.9
	WBZZ	93.7
	WDSY	107.9
	* WDUQ	90.5
	WDVE	102.5
	†* WEBB	88.1
	WHTX	96.1
	WPIT-FM	101.5
	WPNT	92.9
	* WQED-FM	89.3
	* WRCT	88.3
	WSHH	99.7
	WWSW-FM	94.5
	WYDD	104.7
	* WYEP-FM	91.3
Pittston		
	WTLQ	102.3
Pottsville		
	WAVT-FM	101.9
Punxsutawney		
	WPXZ-FM	105.5
Reading		
	WRFY-FM	102.5
	* WXAC	91.3
Red Lion		
	WGCB-FM	96.1
Ridgeway		
	WKBI-FM	94.3
Russell		
	† ----	103.1
Saegertown		
	WEOZ	94.3
Schencksville		
	†* WXLV	90.3
Scottdale		
	WLSW	103.9
Scranton		
	WEZX	107.1
	WGBI-FM	101.3
	* WVIA-FM	89.9
	* WVMW-FM	91.5
	WWDL-FM	104.9
Selinsgrove		
	* WQSU	88.9
Shamokin		
	WSPI	95.3
Sharon		
	WYFM	102.9
Sharpsville		
	WMGZ-FM	95.9
Shippensburg		
	* WSYC-FM	88.7
Slippery Rock		
	* WSRU	90.1
Somerset		
	WVSC-FM	97.7
South Williamsport		
	WFXX-FM	99.3
Starview		
	WHTF	92.7
State College		
	* WDFM	91.1
	WQWK	96.7
	* WTLR	89.9
	WXLR	103.1
Stroudsburg		
	WSBG	93.5
Sunbury		
	WQKX	94.1
Swarthmore		
	* WSRN-FM	91.5
Tamaqua		
	WZTA	105.5
Telford		
	* WBMR	91.7
Towanda		
	WTTC-FM	95.3
Tyrone		
	WGMR	101.1
Union City		
	WCTL	106.3
Uniontown		
	WPQR-FM	99.3
Warminster		
	* WCSD-FM	89.3
Warren		
	WRRN	92.3
Washington		
	* WJCR	92.1
	WYTX	95.3
Waynesboro		
	WAYZ-FM	101.5
	* WCYJ-FM	88.7
Waynesburg		
	WANB-FM	103.1
Wellsboro		
	WNBT-FM	104.5
Wilkes Barre		
	* WCLH	90.7
	WKRZ-FM	98.5
	* WRKC	88.5
	WYZZ	92.9
Williamsport		
	WILQ	105.1
	WKSB	102.7
	* WRLC	91.7
	* WWAS	88.1
York		
	WQXA	105.7
	WSBA-FM	103.3
	* WVYC	88.1

Puerto Rico

City	Station	Frequency
Aguada		
	WRFE	105.5
Aguadilla		
	WIVA-FM	100.3
	WTPM	92.9
Anasco		
	†* WVID	90.3
Arecibo		
	WCMN-FM	107.3
	WNIK-FM	106.5
Bayamon		
	WGSX	94.7
	WXYX	100.7
Caguas		
	WVJP-FM	103.3
Camuy		
	WCHQ-FM	102.9
Carolina		
	WVOZ-FM	107.7
Cidra		
	WBRQ	97.7
Corozal		
	WORO	92.5
Fajardo		
	WDOY	96.5

Guayama
† * WCRP 88.1
WSRA 106.9
Hormigueros
WGIT 92.1
Isabela
WKSA-FM 101.5
Levittown
* WJDZ 89.9
Luquillo
WZOL 92.1
Manati
WMLD 96.9
Mayaguez
WAEL-FM 96.1
WIOA 97.5
WKJB-FM 99.1
WOYE-FM 94.1
Ponce
† WEUC 101.1
WIOC 105.1
WOQI 93.3
WZAR 101.9
Quebradillas
WREI 98.3
Rio Piedras
WFID 95.7
San German
WRPC 95.1
San Juan
WCAD 105.7
WIAC-FM 102.5
WIOB 99.9
* WIPR-FM 91.3
WKAQ-FM 104.7
WPRM-FM 98.5
* WRTU 89.7
WZNT 93.7
Utuado
WERR 104.1
Vieques
* WLID 98.9

Rhode Island

Coventry
* WCVY 91.5
Kingston
* WRIU 90.3
Middletown
WOTB 107.1
Portsmouth
* WJHD 90.7
Providence
WBRU 95.5
* WDOM 91.3
WHJY 94.1
WLKW-FM 101.5
WPJB-FM 105.1
WPRO-FM 92.3
Smithfield
* WJMF 88.7
Westerly
WERI-FM 103.7
Woonsocket
WWON-FM 106.3

South Carolina

Aiken
WNEZ 99.3
WPBM-FM 95.9
Allendale
† WYXZ 93.5
Anderson
WANS-FM 107.3
WCKN-FM 101.1
Bamberg
WWBD-FM 92.7
Barnwell
WBAW-FM 101.7
Batesburg
WKWQ-FM 92.1
Beaufort
* WJWJ-FM 89.9
WQLO 98.7
Camden
WPUB-FM 94.3
Cayce
WZLD 96.7
Charleston
* WCEW 90.9
WEZL 103.5
WKTM 102.5
* WSCI 89.3
WSSX-FM 95.1
WXTC 96.9
Cheraw
WPDZ 103.1
Chester
WDZK 99.3
Clemson
* WSBF-FM 88.1
Columbia
WCEZ 93.5
WCOS-FM 97.9
WDPN 103.1
* WLTR 91.3
* WMHK 89.7
WNOK-FM 104.7
WSCQ 100.1
* WUSC-FM 90.5
Conway
WLAT-FM 104.1
Darlington
WDAR-FM 105.5
Dillon
WDSC-FM 92.9
Easley
WELP-FM 103.9
Florence
WSTN 106.3
Gaffney
WAGI 105.3
* WYFG 91.1
Georgetown
WAZX 106.3
WGMB 97.7
Goose Creek
† WBJX 94.3
Gray Court
WSSL 100.5
Greenville
* WEPR 90.1
WESC-FM 92.5
WFBC-FM 93.7
* WLFJ 89.3
WMUU-FM 94.5
* WPLS-FM 96.5
Greenwood
WSCZ 96.7
Hampton
WJBW-FM 103.1
Hemingway
† * WLGI 90.9
Hilton Head Island
WHHR 106.3
Honea Path
WRIX 103.1
Kingstree
WWKT-FM 98.3
Ladson
* WKCL 91.5
Lake City
WGFG-FM 100.1
Lancaster
WPAJ-FM 107.1
Laurens
WSSL 100.5
Manning
WTWE 92.1
Marion
WATP-FM 94.3
Moncks Corner
WLVW 105.5
Mullins
WCIG 107.1
Myrtle Beach
WJYR 92.1
WKZQ 101.7
North Myrtle Beach
WNMB 105.5
Orangeburg
† * WFCM 91.9
WIGL 106.7
WORG-FM 103.9
Orangeburg (Cont)
† * WSSB-FM 90.3
Pageland
WCPL-FM 102.3
Rock Hill
* WNSC-FM 88.9
Seneca
WBFM 98.1
Spartanburg
WSPA-FM 98.9
St. Andrews
† WTOX 102.3
St. George
WKQB 107.5
Summerville
* WWWZ 93.5
Sumter
* WRJA-FM 88.1
WWDM 101.3
Surfside Beach
WYAK-FM 103.1
Walterboro
WALD-FM 100.9

South Dakota

Aberdeen
KQAA 94.9
KSDN-FM 94.1
Bellefourche
† KKEB 95.9
Brookings
* KESD 88.3
KGKG 94.3
Deadwood
KSQY 95.1
Garden City
† * KEJA 89.3
Gregory
KKSD 101.5
Hot Springs
KOBH-FM 96.7
Huron
KURO 92.1
Madison
KJAM-FM 103.1
Milbank
† ---- 104.3
Mitchell
KMIT 105.9
KQRN 107.3
Mobridge
KOLY-FM 99.5
Pierpont
† * ---- 90.9
Pierre
KGFX-FM 92.7
KNEY 95.3
Porcupine
* KILI 90.1
Rapid City
KGGG-FM 100.3
KKLS-FM 93.9
* KTEQ 91.3
KVSR 97.9
Reliance
† * KASD-FM 90.1
Sioux Falls
* KAUR 89.1
* KCFS 90.1
KELO-FM 92.5
KIOV 104.7
KKRC-FM 93.5
* KNWC-FM 96.5
KPAT 97.3
Sisseton
† ---- 102.9
Spearfish
† KEZV 101.1
* KBHU-FM 89.1
† KSLT 107.3
Springfield
* KSTI 90.1
Sturgis
KRCS 93.1
Vermillion
* KUSD-FM 89.7
KVRF 102.3
Volga
† KRAA 102.3
Watertown
KDLO-FM 96.9
KIXX 96.1
Winner
KWYR-FM 93.7
Yankton
* KKYA 93.1
KQHU 104.1

Tennessee

Athens
WJSQ 101.7
Bolivar
WQKZ 96.7
Bristol
* WHBC 91.5
Brownsville
WTBG 95.3
Camden
WRJB 98.3
Carthage
WRKM-FM 102.3
Centerville
WHLP-FM 96.7
Chattanooga
WDEF-FM 92.3
WDOD-FM 96.5
* WDYN 89.7
* WMBW 88.9
WSKZ 106.5
WSMC-FM 90.5
* WUTC 88.1
Cleveland
WALV 98.3
WUSY 100.7
Clinton
WNKX 95.3
Columbia
WKOM 101.7
Cookeville
WGSQ 94.3
WHUB-FM 98.3
* WTTU 88.5
Covington
WKBL-FM 93.5
Crossville
WXVL 99.3
Dayton
WNFM 104.9
Dickson
WTNQ 102.3
Dyersburg
WASL 100.1
Elizabethton
WIDD-FM 99.3
Erwin
WXIS 103.9
Etowah
* WCPH-FM 103.1
Fayetteville
WYTM-FM 105.5
Franklin
WIZO-FM 100.1
Gallatin
* WVCP 88.5
WWKX 104.5
Gatlinburg
WVTN 105.5
Germantown
WLVS 94.3
Greeneville
WIKQ 94.9
Harriman
WHBT 92.7
Henderson
* WFHC 91.5
† WFKX 95.9
Hendersonville
WMAK-FM 92.1
Humboldt
WZDQ 102.3
Huntingdon
WPBE 100.9
Jackson
WJHR 103.1
WKIR 104.1

Jamestown
WDEB-FM 103.9
Jefferson City
WKJQ 99.3
Johnson City
* WETS 89.5
WQUT 101.5
Kingsport
* WCSK 90.3
WTFM 98.5
WZXY 104.9
Knoxville
WEZK 97.5
WIMZ 103.5
WIVK-FM 107.7
* WKCS 91.1
* WUOT 91.9
* WUTK 90.3
La Follette
WQLA 104.9
Lawrenceburg
WDXE-FM 95.9
Lebanon
* WFMQ 91.5
* WLCH 88.7
WYHY 107.3
Lenoir City
WLIL-FM 93.5
Lewisburg
WJJM-FM 94.3
Lexington
WZLT 99.3
Livingston
WXKG 95.9
Lobelville
WIST 94.3
Manchester
WMSR-FM 99.7
Martin
WCMT-FM 101.7
* WUTM-FM 90.3
Mc Kenzie
WKTA 106.9
Mc Minnville
WBMC-FM 103.9
Memphis
KRNB 101.1
* WEVL 90.3
WGKX 105.9
WHRK 97.1
* WKNO-FM 91.1
* WLYX 89.5
WMC-FM 99.7
* WQOX 88.5
WRVR 104.5
* WSMS 91.7
WZXR 102.7
Milan
WYNU 92.3
Minor Hill
† WLLX 92.1
Morristown
WAZI 95.9
Murfreesboro
WKOS 96.3
* WMOT 89.5
Nashville
WKDF 103.3
WLAC-FM 105.9
* WNAZ-FM 89.1
* WPLN 90.3
* WRFN 88.1
* WRVU 91.1
WSIX-FM 97.9
WSM-FM 95.5
WZEZ 92.9
Oak Ridge
WETQ 94.3
WOKI-FM 100.3
Olive Hill
* WDNX 89.1
Oneida
WBNT-FM 105.5
Paris
WTPR-FM 105.5
Pikeville
†* WIKU 91.3
Pulaski
* WMGL 98.3
Red Bank
WJTT 94.3
Savannah
WKWX 93.5
WORM-FM 101.7
Sevierville
WMYU 102.1
Sewanee
* WUTS 91.5
Shelbyville
WYCQ 102.9
Signal Mountain
* WCSO 91.5
Smithville
WJLE-FM 101.7
Soddy Daisy
WCHU-FM 102.3
Sparta
WSMT-FM 105.5
Springfield
WDBL-FM 94.3
Summertown
* WUTZ 88.3
Sweetwater
WDEH-FM 95.3
Trenton
WLOT 97.7
Tullahoma
WBGY-FM 93.3
Union City
WALR-FM 104.9
Waverly
WVRY 104.9

Texas

Abilene
KEAN-FM 105.1
§ KFMN-FM 107.9
†* KGNZ 88.1
KORQ 100.7
Alamo
KJAV 104.9
Alice
KBIC 102.3
KDSI 92.1
Alvin
* KACC 91.3
Amarillo
* KACV-FM 89.9
KBUY-FM 94.1
KGNC-FM 97.9
KMML 98.7
KQIZ-FM 93.1
KWAS 101.9
Andrews
KACT-FM 105.5
Anson
† ---- 103.1
Arlington
KWJS 94.9
Atlanta
KPYN 99.3
Austin
KASE 100.7
†* KAZI 88.7
KHFI-FM 98.3
KLBJ-FM 93.7
* KMFA 89.5
KOKE-FM 95.5
KPEZ 102.3
* KUT-FM 90.5
Ballinger
KRUN-FM 103.1
Bandera
KQRK 98.3
Beaumont
KAYD 97.5
KQXY 94.1
* KVLU 91.3
KWIC 107.7
KZZB 95.1
Beeville
KCWW 104.9
Belton
KTON-FM 106.3
Big Spring
KWKI 95.3
Bishop
KFLZ 107.1
Bonham
KFYZ-FM 98.3
Borger
KDKQ 104.3
Brady
KIXV 95.3
Breckenridge
KRDO 93.5
Brenham
KWHI-FM 106.3
Bridgeport
KWCS 96.7
Brownsville
* KBNR 88.3
KTXF 100.3
KRIX 99.5
Brownwood
KOXE 101.5
KPSM 99.3
KXYL-FM 104.1
Bryan
† ---- 104.9
KORA-FM 98.3
Burnet
KMRB 107.1
Cameron
† KCRM 103.1
Canadian
† ---- 103.1
Canyon
KHBQ 107.1
* KWTS 91.1
Carthage
† ---- 98.9
Center
KLCR 102.3
Clear Lake City
KMJQ 102.1
Coleman
KSTA-FM 107.1
College Station
* KAMU-FM 90.9
KTAW 92.1
Colorado City
† KAUM 106.3
Columbus
KULM 98.3
Commerce
KEMM 92.1
* KETR 88.9
Conroe
KJOJ 106.9
Copperas Cove
KOOV 103.1
Corpus Christi
† KBCB 99.1
KEXX-FM 93.9
†* KFLV 91.9
KIOU 96.5
* KKED-FM 90.3
KOUL 103.3
KZFM 95.5
Corsicana
KXCL 107.9
Crockett
KCKR 93.5
KIVY-FM 92.7
Crystal City
† KHER 94.3
Dalhart
KXIT-FM 95.9
Dallas
KAFM 92.5
* KCBI 89.3
* KERA-FM 90.1
KKDA-FM 104.5
KLVU 98.7
KMEZ-FM 100.3
KMGC 102.9
* KNON 90.9
KOAX 105.3
* KRSM 88.5
KVIL-FM 103.7
* KVTT 91.7
Dallas (Cont)
KZEW 97.9
WRR 101.1
Del Rio
KLKE 94.3
Denison
KDSQ 101.7
* KGCC 89.7
† KALK 104.9
Denton
KIXK 106.1
* KNTU 88.1
Devine
† KDCI 92.1
Diboll
KIPR-FM 95.5
Dumas
KMRE 95.3
Eagle Pass
KINL 92.7
Eastland
KVMX 96.7
Edinburg
KBFM 104.1
†* KOIR 88.5
KVLY 107.9
El Campo
KXGC-FM 96.9
El Paso
†* ---- 89.5
KAMZ 93.1
KEZB 93.9
KFIM 92.3
KHEY-FM 96.3
KLAQ 95.5
KLOZ 102.1
KSET-FM 94.7
KSYR-FM 97.5
* KTEP 88.5
KTSM-FM 99.9
Fabens
KLMF-FM 103.1
Fairfield
† KNES 92.1
Falfurrias
† KPSO-FM 106.3
Farwell
† ---- 98.3
† KIJN-FM 92.3
Floresville
KWCB 94.3
Fredericksburg
KFAN 101.1
Freeport
† ---- 103.3
Freer
† ---- 95.9
Ft. Stockton
KPJH 94.3
Ft. Worth
KEGL 97.1
KESS 94.1
KNOK-FM 107.5
KPLX 99.5
KSCS 96.3
* KTCU-FM 88.7
KTXQ 102.1
Gainesville
KGAF-FM 94.5
Galveston
KXKX 106.5
Gatesville
KPEP 98.3
Georgetown
KGTN-FM 96.7
Gilmer
KNIF 95.3
Graham
KWKQ 107.1
Greenville
KIKT 93.5
Groves
† KTFA 92.1
Harlingen
KELT 94.5
KIWW 96.1
Haskell
KVRP-FM 95.5

Station	Frequency
Henderson	
KGRI-FM	100.1
Hereford	
KPAN-FM	106.3
Hillsboro	
KJNE	102.5
Hooks	
† KFFR	95.9
Houston	
KFMK	97.9
KHCB-FM	105.7
KIKK-FM	95.7
KILT-FM	100.3
KLEF	94.5
KLOL	101.1
KODA	99.1
⋆ KPFT	90.1
KQUE	102.9
KRBE-FM	104.1
KRLY	93.7
KSRR	96.5
⋆ KTRU	91.7
⋆ KTSU	90.9
⋆ KUHF	88.7
Humble	
†⋆ KSBJ	88.1
Huntsville	
KHUN	101.7
⋆ KSHU	89.3
Jacksonville	
KOOI	106.5
Jasper	
KWYX	102.3
Keene	
⋆ KSUC	88.3
Kennedy	
KTNR	92.1
Kerrville	
KPFM	94.3
Kilgore	
KKTX	95.9
Killeen	
KIXS-FM	93.3
⋆ KNCT-FM	91.3
Kingsville	
KINE-FM	97.7
KODK	92.7
⋆ KTAI	91.1
La Grange	
KMUZ	104.9
Lake Jackson	
KGOL	107.5
Lamesa	
KIOF	104.7
Lampasas	
KLTD	99.3
LaredO	
KRRG	98.1
Laredo	
KFIX	92.7
KOYE	94.9
Levelland	
KHOC	105.5
Livingston	
KETX-FM	92.1
Llano	
† KFQX	104.9
Longview	
KYKX	105.7
Lorenzo	
† ----	98.3
Lubbock	
KFMX	94.5
KLLL	96.3
⋆ KOHM	89.1
KRLB-FM	99.5
KRUX	102.5
KSEL-FM	93.7
KTEZ	101.1
⋆ KTXT-FM	88.1
Lufkin	
KDEY	99.3
KYKS	105.1
Malakoff	
† KCKL	95.9
KRUX	102.5
Marlin	
KLMT	96.7
Marshall	
⋆ KBWC	91.1
KMHT-FM	103.9
Mc Allen	
KQXX	98.5
KVMV	96.9
Mc Kinney	
KMMK	95.3
Memphis	
KLSR-FM	105.3
Mercedes	
KGAR	106.3
Merkel	
KMIO-FM	102.3
Mexia	
† ----	104.9
Midland	
KBAT	93.3
KNFM	92.3
KWMJ	103.3
Mineola	
KMOO-FM	96.7
Mineral Wells	
KYXS-FM	95.9
Mission	
† KITM	105.5
Monahans	
KGEE	99.9
KWES	102.1
Mt. Pleasant	
KPXI	100.7
Muleshoe	
KMUL-FM	103.1
Nacogdoches	
KJCS	103.3
⋆ KSAU	90.1
KTBC	92.1
New Braunfels	
KNBT	92.1
Odessa	
KKKK	99.1
⋆ KOCV	91.3
KQIP	96.9
KUFO	97.9
Orange	
KIOC	106.1
KZOM	104.5
Ozona	
KRCT	94.3
Palestine	
KLIS	96.7
KYYK	98.3
Pampa	
KOMX	100.3
Paris	
KTXU	99.3
Pasadena	
⋆ KJIC	89.3
KKBQ-FM	92.5
Pearsall	
† KVWG-FM	95.3
Pecos	
KPTX	98.3
Perryton	
KEYE-FM	95.9
Plains	
⋆ KPLN-FM	90.3
Plainview	
KATX	97.3
⋆ KWLD	91.5
Pleasanton	
KBOP-FM	98.3
Port Arthur	
KHYS	98.5
KYKR-FM	93.3
Port Lavaca	
KAOC-FM	93.3
Portland	
KITE	105.5
Prairie View	
⋆ KPVU	91.3
Premont	
† KMFM	104.9
Quanah	
KIXC-FM	100.9
Raymondville	
† KSOX-FM	101.7
Refugio	
KYOT	106.3
Richardson	
†⋆ KSLL	88.1
Rio Grande City	
KCTM	103.1
Robstown	
KROB-FM	99.9
Roma	
KBMI	97.7
Rosenberg	
KFRD-FM	104.9
Round Rock	
⋆ KHCH-FM	88.1
Rusk	
KWRW	97.7
San Angelo	
KBIL	92.9
KGKL-FM	97.5
KIXY-FM	94.7
KWLW	93.9
San Antonio	
KAJA	97.3
KBUC-FM	107.5
KISS	99.5
KITY	92.9
KLLS-FM	100.3
†⋆ KPAC	90.9
KQXT	101.9
⋆ KRTU	91.7
KSAQ	96.1
⋆ KSYM-FM	90.1
KTFM	102.7
⋆ KURU	89.1
KVAR	104.5
San Marcos	
KEYI	103.5
Seabrook	
† ----	92.1
Seguin	
KWED-FM	105.3
Seminole	
KIKZ-FM	106.3
Seymour	
KSEY-FM	94.3
Shamrock	
† ----	92.7
Sherman	
KZXL-FM	96.7
Silsbee	
KWDX	101.7
Sinton	
KNCN	101.3
KOUL	103.7
Slaton	
KJAK	92.7
Snyder	
KSNY-FM	101.7
Sonora	
KVRN-FM	92.1
Spearman	
KRDF-FM	90.3
Stephenville	
KWWM	105.7
Sulphur Springs	
KDXE	95.9
Sweetwater	
KXOX-FM	96.7
Taylor	
KRGT	92.1
Temple	
KPLE	104.9
Terrell	
KTLR-FM	107.1
Terrell Hills	
KESI	106.3
Texarkana	
KOSY-FM	102.5
KTAL-FM	98.1
†⋆ KTXK	91.5
Tulla	
----	104.9
Tye	
† KTYE	99.3
Tyler	
KNUE	101.5
KROZ	92.1
KTYL-FM	93.1
Tyler (Cont)	
†⋆ KVNE	89.5
Uvalde	
KYUF	104.9
Vernon	
KVWC-FM	102.3
Victoria	
KCWM	95.1
KTXN-FM	98.7
KZEU	107.9
Waco	
KHOO	99.9
KNFO	95.5
⋆ KWBU	107.1
KWTX-FM	97.5
White House	
† KFML	99.3
Wichita Falls	
KKQV	103.3
KLUR	99.9
KNIN-FM	92.9
Winnsboro	
† KWNS	104.9
Yorkum	
† KYOC	102.3

Utah

Station	Frequency
Beaver	
⋆ KBBD	90.1
Brigham City	
KFRZ	107.1
Cedar City	
KBRE-FM	94.9
⋆ KGSU-FM	91.1
KSUB-FM	92.5
Centerville	
KCGL	105.5
Gunnison	
⋆ KGVH	91.7
Kanab	
† ----	101.1
Logan	
KBLQ-FM	92.9
KMXL	94.5
⋆ KUSU-FM	91.5
Manti	
KMXU	105.1
⋆ KSME	90.7
Midvale	
† ----	102.7
Moab	
KKLX	96.7
Mt. Pleasant	
⋆ KMTP	91.1
Neola	
⋆ KUUU	88.1
Ogden	
KDAB	101.1
KQPD	101.9
KJQN-FM	95.5
⋆ KWC-FM	88.1
KZAN	97.9
Orem	
KUUT	107.5
⋆ KOHS	91.7
Park City	
⋆ KPCW	91.9
Pleasant Grove	
⋆ KPGR	88.1
Price	
KARB	98.3
Provo	
⋆ KBYU-FM	88.9
KFMY	96.1
KLRZ	94.9
Richfield	
KKWZ	93.7
Roy	
† KRGQ-FM	107.9
Salt Lake City	
KCPX-FM	98.7
KISN	97.1
KLCY	94.1
⋆ KRCL	90.9
KRSP-FM	103.5
KSFI	100.3
KSOP-FM	104.3
⋆ KUER	90.1

Station	Frequency
Salt Lake City (Cont)	
KWHO-FM	93.3
Smithfield	
† KVEX	103.9
Spanish Fork	
KBHV	106.3
St. George	
* KRDC-FM	99.3
KZEZ	93.5
Tooele	
KTLE-FM	92.1
Tremont	
† KBXN-FM	104.9
Vernal	
KUIN	92.7

Vermont

Station	Frequency
Barre	
WORK	107.1
Bellows Falls	
† WBFL	107.1
Bennington	
WHGC	94.3
Brattleboro	
WKVT-FM	92.7
WMMJ	96.7
Burlington	
WEZF	92.9
WQCR	98.9
* WRUV	90.1
WVPS	107.9
Castleton	
* WIUV	91.3
Colchester	
* WWPV-FM	88.7
Johnson	
* WJSC-FM	90.7
Lyndonville	
* WWLR	91.5
Manchester	
† WEQX	102.7
Middlebury	
WCVM	100.9
* WRMC-FM	91.7
Montpelier	
WNCS	96.7
Northfield	
* WNUB-FM	89.1
Plainfield	
* WGDR	91.1
Randolph	
WCVR-FM	102.3
Randolph Center	
* WVTC	90.7
Rutland	
WHWB-FM	98.1
WRUT	97.1
Springfield	
WCFR-FM	93.5
St. Albans	
WLFE	102.3
Stowe	
* WMTF	91.5
WRFB	101.7
Vergennes	
† WIZN	106.3
Waterbury	
† WVRS	103.1
White River Junction	
WNHV-FM	95.3
Windsor	
* WVPR	89.5

Virgin Islands

Station	Frequency
Charlotte Amalie	
WCRN	101.1
WIBS	97.9
Christiansted	
† WJKC	95.1
WIVI-FM	99.5
Fredericksted, St. Croix	
WVIS	106.1
St. Thomas	
* WIUJ	88.9

Virginia

Station	Frequency
Abingdon	
WABN-FM	92.7
Altavista	
WKDE-FM	105.5
Amherst	
WCNV	107.9
Appomattox	
WTTX-FM	107.1
Arlington	
WAVA	105.1
Ashland	
WYFJ	100.1
Berryville	
WWOO	105.5
Big Stone Gap	
WLSD-FM	93.5
Blacksburg	
* WUVT-FM	90.7
WVVV	104.9
Blackstone	
WBBC	93.5
Bluefield	
WBDY-FM	106.3
Bristol	
WXBQ-FM	96.9
Buena Vista	
WWZD	96.7
Cape Charles	
† ----	96.1
Charlottesville	
WQMC	95.3
* WTJU	91.3
WUVA	92.7
WWWV	97.5
Chesapeake	
* WFOS	90.3
Chester	
WDYL	92.1
Clifton Forge	
WXCF-FM	103.9
Covington	
WIQO-FM	100.9
Crewe	
WSVS-FM	104.7
Crozet	
WPED-FM	102.3
Culpeper	
WCUL	103.1
Danville	
WAKG	103.3
Exmore	
WKRE-FM	107.5
Farmville	
WFLO-FM	95.7
* WUTA	90.1
Fredericksburg	
WFLS-FM	93.3
WFVA-FM	101.5
†* WJYJ	90.5
Front Royal	
WFFV	99.3
WIXV	95.3
Galax	
WBOB-FM	98.1
Gretna	
WMNA-FM	106.3
Grundy	
WMJD	97.7
Hampden Sydney	
* WWHS-FM	91.7
Hampton	
* WHOV	88.3
WWDE-FM	101.3
Harrisonburg	
* WEMC	91.7
WJSY	104.3
* WMRA	90.7
WQPO	100.7
Highland Springs	
* WHCE	91.1
Kilmarnock	
WKWI	101.7
Lexington	
* WLUR	91.5
Lorton	
†* WDCJ	88.1
Louisa	
WLSA	105.5
Luray	
WLCC	106.3
Luray (Cont)	
WQAA	103.9
Lynchburg	
WGOL	98.3
WJJS-FM	101.7
WKZZ	100.1
* WRVL	88.3
* WWLC	90.3
Manassas	
WEZR	106.7
Marion	
WMEV-FM	93.9
WOLD-FM	102.3
Martinsville	
WMVA-FM	96.3
Newport News	
WNSY-FM	97.3
Norfolk	
WCMS-FM	100.5
* WHRO-FM	89.5
WLTY	95.7
WNOR-FM	98.7
* WNSB	91.1
WNVZ	104.5
WOWI	102.9
WYFI	99.7
Norton	
WNVA-FM	106.3
Onancock	
WESR-FM	103.3
Orange	
WJMA-FM	96.7
Pennington Gap	
WSWV-FM	105.5
Petersburg	
WPLZ	99.3
WPVA-FM	95.3
Portsmouth	
* WNHS	88.7
WXRI	105.3
Pound	
WWLH	102.3
Pulaski	
WPSK	107.1
Radford	
WRIQ	101.7
* WVRU	89.9
Richlands	
WGTH	105.5
Richmond	
* WDCE	90.1
WEZS	103.7
* WRFK-FM	106.5
WRVQ	94.5
WRXL	102.1
WVTF	89.1
Roanoke	
WPVR	94.9
WSLQ	99.1
* WVWR-FM	89.1
WXLK	92.3
Salem	
WJLM	93.5
South Boston	
WJLC-FM	97.5
South Hill	
WSHV	105.5
Staunton	
WSGM	93.5
Suffolk	
WFOG-FM	92.9
Sweet Briar	
* WUDZ	91.5
Tappahannock	
WRAR-FM	105.5
Tazewell	
WTZE-FM	100.1
Virginia Beach	
WWRN	94.9
Warrenton	
WQRA	94.3
WWWK	107.7
Warsaw	
WNNT-FM	100.9
Williamsburg	
* WCWM	89.1
WQKS	96.5
Winchester	
WQUS	92.5
WUSQ	102.5
Woodbridge	
WPKX-FM	105.9
Yorktown	
WKEZ	94.1
* WYCS	91.5

Washington

Station	Frequency
Aberdeen	
KDUX-FM	104.7
KJMD	99.3
Auburn	
* KGRG	89.9
Bellevue	
* KASB	89.3
* KBCS	91.3
KLSY	92.5
Bellingham	
KISM	92.9
KNWR	104.3
* KUGS	89.3
Bremerton	
KWWA	106.9
Centralia	
* KCED	91.3
KMNT	102.9
Chelan	
KOZI-FM	93.5
Cheney	
* KEWC-FM	89.9
Clarkston	
KCLK-FM	94.1
Colville	
KCRK-FM	92.1
Deer Park	
† KNOI	107.1
East Wenatchee	
KTRW	97.7
Edmonds	
KBIQ	105.3
Ellensburg	
† KQBE	103.1
KXLE-FM	95.3
Ephrata	
KTRJ	95.9
Forks	
† KLLM	103.9
Grandcoulee	
† KEYF	98.5
Hoquiam	
KGHO-FM	95.3
Kennewick	
KONA-FM	105.3
Longview	
KLYK	105.5
Lynden	
KLYN-FM	106.5
Mercer Island	
* KMIH	90.1
Moses Lake	
KSEM-FM	99.3
KWIQ-FM	100.3
Mt. Vernon	
* KSVR	90.1
Newport	
* KUBS	91.5
Olympia	
* KAOS	89.3
Omak	
KOMW-FM	92.7
Opportunity	
KKPL	96.1
Pasco	
* KOLU	90.1
Prosser	
KACA	101.7
Pullman	
KQQQ-FM	104.9
* KZUU	90.7
Quincy	
† KLLH	96.7
Raymond	
† ----	97.7
Richland	
†* KFAE	89.1
KHWK	106.3

Richland (Cont)
KIOK 94.9
KZZK-FM 102.7
Seattle
* KCMU 90.5
KEZX 98.9
KING-FM 98.1
KISW 99.9
KIXI-FM 95.7
KMPS-FM 94.1
* KNHC 89.5
KPLZ 101.5
* KRAB 107.7
KSEA 100.7
KUBE 93.3
* KUOW 94.9
KYYX 96.5
KZOK-FM 102.5
Spokane
KDRK 93.7
KEZE-FM 105.7
KHQ-FM 98.1
KICN 98.9
* KMBI-FM 107.9
* KPBX-FM 91.1
KREM-FM 92.9
* KSFC 91.9
* KWRS 90.3
KXLY-FM 99.9
Sunnyside
KREW-FM 96.7
Tacoma
KBRD 103.7
KNBQ 97.3
* KPLU-FM 88.5
KRPM-FM 106.1
* KTOY 91.7
* KUPS 90.1
* KVTI 90.9
Toppenish
KENE-FM 92.7
Walla Walla
KEXI 93.3
* KGTS 91.3
KSXT 97.1
KUJ-FM 95.7
* KWCW 90.5
Wenatchee
KPQ-FM 102.1
KYJR 104.9
Yakima
KATS 94.5
* KDNA 91.9
KFFM 107.3
KRSE 98.3
KXDD 104.1
* KYSC 88.5

West Virginia

Beckley
WBKW 99.5
WCIR-FM 103.7
* WVPB 91.7
Berkeley Springs
WCST-FM 93.5
Bethany
* WVBC 88.1
Bluefield
WHAJ 104.5
Buckhannon
* WVPW 88.9
* WVWC 92.1
Ceredo
† WCKV 94.9
Charles Town
WZFM 98.3
Charleston
WBES 96.1
WQBE-FM 97.5
WVAF 99.9
* WVPN 88.5
WYSR 102.7
Charlestown
WXVA-FM 98.3
Clarksburg
WKKW 106.5
WPDX-FM 104.9
WVHF-FM 92.7
Elkins
* WCDE 90.3
† WDNE-FM 99.3
† WELK 95.3
Fairmont
WFGM 97.9
Fort Gay
* WFGH 90.7
Grafton
WTBZ 95.9
Hinton
† WMTD-FM 102.3
Huntington
WEMM 107.9
* WHPW-FM 89.9
WKEE-FM 100.5
* WMUL 88.1
WTCR 103.3
Institute
†* WEYS 90.9
Keyser
WQZP-FM 94.1
Lancaster
WAXL 97.7
Lewisburg
WKCJ 105.5
Logan
WVOW-FM 101.9
Martinsburg
WKMZ 97.5
Miami
† WVCM 107.1
Milton
† WNST-FM 106.3
Morgantown
WCLG-FM 100.1
WVAQ 101.9
* WVPM 90.9
WWVU-FM 91.7
Mt. Hope
WTNJ 105.9
Mullens
WPMW 92.7
New Martinsville
WKGI 103.9
Oak Hill
WRJL 94.1
Parkersburg
WIBZ 99.3
WQAW 103.1
†* WVPG 90.3
WXIL 95.1
Phillipi
* WQAB 92.1
Princeton
WAEY-FM 95.9
† WKMY 100.9
Rainelle
WRRL-FM 96.7
Ripley
WCEF 98.3
Romney
* WJGF 91.5
Ronceverte
WRON-FM 97.7
Salem
* WITB-FM 91.1
Shepherdstown
* WSHC 88.7
Shepherstown
* WSHC 93.7
St. Albans
WKLC-FM 105.1
St. Marys
† WRRR-FM 101.7
Summerville
† WCWV 92.9
Sutton
† WCKA 97.1
Weston
WSSN 102.3
Westover
WJCF 100.9
Wheeling
WANJ 107.5
WCPI 98.7
WKWK-FM 97.3
* WPHP 91.9
Wheeling (Cont)
†* WVNP 89.9
Williamson
WXCC 96.5

Wisconsin

Antigo
WRLO-FM 105.3
Appleton
WAPL-FM 105.7
* WLFM 91.1
Ashland
WATW-FM 95.9
Baraboo
WLVE 94.9
Beaver Dam
WXRO 95.3
Beloit
* WBCR-FM 90.3
Berlin
WISS-FM 102.3
Brule
* WHSA 89.9
Burlington
* WBSD 89.1
Chippewa Falls
WCFW 105.5
Clintonville
† WFCL-FM 92.1
De Pere
† WJLW 95.9
Delafield
* WHAD 90.7
Dodgeville
WDMP-FM 99.3
Durand
WRDN-FM 95.9
Eagle River
WERL-FM 94.3
Eau Claire
WAXX 104.5
WBIZ 100.7
WIAL 94.1
* WUEC 89.7
Fond Du Lac
WFON 107.1
Fort Atkinson
WSJY 107.3
Green Bay
WDUZ-FM 98.5
* WGBP-FM 90.1
* WGBW 91.5
WIXX 101.1
* WPNE-FM 89.3
Hartford
WTKM-FM 104.9
Hayward
WHSM-FM 101.7
WRLS-FM 92.1
Highland
* WHHI 91.3
Janesville
WJVL 99.9
Kaukauna
WKAU-FM 104.9
Kenosha
* WGTD 91.1
WJZQ 95.1
Kewaunee
WAUN 92.7
La Crosse
* WHLA 90.3
WIZM-FM 93.3
* WLSU 88.9
WLXR-FM 104.9
WSPL 95.9
Ladysmith
† WLDY-FM 92.7
WWIB 103.7
Lancaster
†* WJTY 88.1
Madison
* WERN 88.7
WIBA-FM 101.5
WMGN 98.1
WNWC 102.5
Madison (Cont)
* WORT 89.9
WZEE 104.1
Manitowoc
WKKB 92.1
Marinette
WLST 95.1
Marshfield
WLJY 106.5
Mauston
WRJC-FM 92.1
Medford
WIGM-FM 99.3
Menasha
WEMI 100.1
Menomonee Falls
WFMR 98.3
Menomonie
* WHWC 88.3
WMEQ 92.1
* WVSS 90.7
Merrill
WJMT-FM 93.5
Middleton
WWQM-FM 106.3
Milwaukee
WBCS-FM 102.9
WKTI 94.5
WLPX 97.3
WLUM 102.1
WMGF 96.5
* WMSE 91.7
WMYX 99.1
WQFM 93.3
* WUWM 89.7
WVCY 107.7
* WYMS 88.9
WZUU-FM 95.7
Minocqua
WWMH 95.9
Monroe
WEKZ-FM 93.7
Neenah
WROE 99.3
Neillsville
WCCN-FM 107.5
New London
WNBK 93.5
New Richmond
WIXK-FM 107.1
Oconto
WOCO-FM 107.1
Oshkosh
WAHC 96.7
WOSH 103.9
* WRST-FM 90.3
Park Falls
WNBI-FM 98.3
Platteville
WKPL 107.1
* WSUP 90.5
Port Washington
WGLB-FM 100.1
Portage
WDDC 100.1
Prairie Du Chien
WPRE-FM 94.3
Racine
WFNY 92.1
WRKR-FM 100.7
Reedsburg
WRDB-FM 104.9
Reserve
* WOJB 88.9
Rhinelander
WRHN 107.9
†* WXPR 91.7
Rice Lake
WAQE-FM 97.7
WJMC-FM 96.3
Richland Center
WRCO-FM 100.9
Ripon
* WRPN-FM 90.1
WYUR-FM 95.9
River Falls
WEVR-FM 106.3
* WRFW 88.7

Sauk City
WSEY 96.7
Schofield
* WESD 89.1
Shawano
WOWN-FM 99.3
Sheboygan
* WSHS 91.7
WWJR 97.7
Shell Lake
WGMO 95.3
Sparta
WCOW-FM 97.1
Stevens Point
WSPT 97.9
* WWSP 89.9
Sturgeon Bay
WDOR-FM 93.9
WSBW 100.1
Sun Prairie
WMAD 92.1
Superior
KZIO 102.5
* WSSU 99.1
Suring
WRVM 102.7
Tomah
WTMB-FM 98.9
Tomahawk
† WRJQ 92.7
Two Rivers
WQTC-FM 102.3
Viroqua
WGBM 102.3
Washburn
WBWA 105.9
†* WHIJ-FM 90.5
Watertown
†* WBII 91.5
WMLW 94.1
Waukesha
* WCCX 104.5
WMIL 106.1
Waupaca
WDUX-FM 92.7
Waupun
WGGQ 99.3
Wausau
† WXCO-FM 107.9
WDEZ 101.9
* WHRM 90.9
WIFC 95.5
Wauwatosa
WEZW 103.7
West Bend
WBKV-FM 92.5
West Salem
WISQ 100.1
Whitehall
WHTL-FM 102.3
Whitewater
* WSUW 91.7
Wisconsin Dells
WNNO-FM 107.1
Wisconsin Rapids
WWRW 103.3

Wyoming

Afton
† ---- 98.3
Buffalo
† KLGM 92.7
Casper
KAWY 94.5
† KOLT 103.7
KTRS 95.5
Cheyenne
KFBQ 97.9
KKAZ 100.7
† KLEN 106.3
Cody
KTAG 97.9
* KYDZ 90.1
Douglas
KATH-FM 99.3
Ethete
†* KIEA 89.7
* KIEA 89.7
Evanston
KOTB 106.3
Gillette
† KGWY 100.7
KOLL-FM 96.9
Greybull
† KZMK 100.3
Jackson
KMTN 96.9
Lander
KDLY 97.5
Laramie
† ---- 95.1
KIOZ 102.9
* KUWR 91.9
Powell
† KNWY 104.1
KPCQ-FM 92.5
Rawlins
KIQZ 92.7
Riverton
* KCWC 88.1
KTAK 93.9
Rock Springs
KQSW 96.5
KSIT 104.5
Saratoga
KWND 99.9
Sheridan
KLWD 96.5
KROE-FM 94.9
Thermopolis
† KLYX 98.3
Torrington
KERM 98.3
Worland
KENB-FM 95.9

CANADA

Alberta

Banff
CJAY-1 95.1
Calgary
CBR-FM 102.1
CBRF-FM 103.9
CHFM 95.9
* CJAY-FM 92.1
CKO-FM-5 103.1
* CKUA-FM-1 93.7
Edmonton
CIRK 97.3
CISN 103.9
CJAX 92.5
CKO-FM-6 101.9
CKRA 96.3
* CKUA-FM 94.9
CKXM 100.3
Grand Prairie
* CKUA-FM-4 100.9
Lethbridge
CBRX-FM 100.1
CHFA-1 104.3
CILA 107.7
* CKUA-FM-2 99.3
Medicine Hat
* CKUA-FM-3 97.3
Peace River
* CKUA-FM-5 96.9
Red Deer
CFRC 98.9
CKUA-FM-6 101.3

British Columbia

Kamloops
CBYK 94.1
CBUF-6 96.5
CFFM 98.3
CHNL-FM 97.5
Kelowna
CHIM 104.7
New Westminster
CFMI 101.1
Penticton
CIGV-FM 100.7
CHMY 97.1
Squamish
CISQ 104.9
Trail
CBTA 106.7
Vancouver
CBU-FM 105.7
CBUF 97.7
CFOX 99.3
* CFRO 102.7
CHQM-FM 103.5
CJAZ-FM 92.1
CKO-FM-4 96.1
Victoria
CFMS 98.5

Manitoba

Baldy Mountain
CBWW 105.3
Brandon
CBWV 97.9
CJCM 96.1
CKSB-8 99.5
Fairford
CBWZ 104.3
Fisher Branch
CBWX-FM 95.7
Jackhead
CBWY 92.7
Selkirk
CFQX-FM 92.9
Thompson
CBWK 100.9
Winnipeg
CBW-FM 98.3
CHIQ 94.3
CHMM 97.5
CITI 92.1
* CJUM 101.5
CKO-FM-7 99.1
CKWG 103.1

New Brunswick

Fredericton
CBD-FM 91.3
Moncton
CFQM-FM 103.9
St. John
CBAF 102.3
CBZ-FM 101.5
CJYC 98.9
CKO-FM-9 99.7

Newfoundland

Argentia
CFOZ 100.3
Bonavista
CJOZ 92.1
Corner Brook
CKOZ 92.3
Marystown
CIOZ 96.3
Rattling Brook
CHOS 95.9
Red Rocks
CKSS 96.9
St. John's
CBN-FM 106.9
* CHOZ 93.9
CKO-FM-10 101.9
Stephenville
* COIS 98.5

Nova Scotia

Halifax
CBH-FM 102.7
CBHA 90.5
CHFX-FM 101.9
CIOO 100.1
Kentville
CKWM-FM 97.7
Liverpool
† CKBW-1 94.5
Shelburn
CKBW-2 93.1
Sydney
CBI-FM 105.9
CKPE 94.9
Truro
CKTO 100.9

Ontario

Barrie
CHAY 93.1
Belleville
CIGL 97.1
Brampton
CFNY 102.1
Brantford
CKPC-FM 92.1
Brockville
CBOB-FM 100.3
CBOF-7 102.1
Burlington
CING 107.9
Chatham
CBEE-FM 95.1
Cobourg
CFMX 103.1
Cornwall
CBOF-6 98.1
CFLG 104.5
Guelph
CKLA 106.1
Hamilton
CKDS 95.3
Kenora
CBQX 98.7
Kingston
CFLY 98.3
CFMK 96.3
Kitchener
CFCA-FM 105.3
CKGL 96.7
London
CBBL 100.5
CBCL 93.5
CFPL-FM 95.9
CJBC-FM-20 99.3
CJBX 92.7
CKO-FM-3 97.5
North Bay
CKAT 101.9
Orillia
CBCO 105.9
Oshawa
CKQT 94.9
Ottawa
CBO-FM 103.3
CBOF-FM 102.5
CFMO 93.9
CHEZ 106.1
CKBY 105.3
CKCU 93.1
CKO-FM 106.9
CKO-FM-1 106.9
Penetanguishene
CBCM 107.5
CJBC-3-FM 96.5
Peterborough
CFMP 101.5
CJBC-5-FM 106.3
* CKQM-FM 105.1
Port Hope
CHWC 103.1
Sarnia
CBEG-FM 106.3
CJFI 99.9
Sault Ste. Marie
CHAS 100.5
CJQM 104.3
Smith's Falls
CKUE 101.1
St. Catherines
CHRE 105.7
CJQR 97.7
Sudbury
CBCS 99.9
CBON 98.1
CIGM 92.7
CJMX 105.3
Thunder Bay
CJSD 94.3
Tillsonburg
CKOT-FM 101.3

Timmins

CFTI	92.1

Toronto

CBL-FM	94.1
CHFI	98.1
CHIN-FM	100.7
CHUM-FM	104.5
CILQ	107.1
* CJRT-FM	91.1
CKFM	99.9
CKO-FM-2	99.1

Windsor

CBE-FM	89.9
CJOM-FM	88.7
CKJY	93.9

Wingham

CKNX-FM	101.7

Prince Edward Island

Charlottetown

CBCT	96.9
CHLQ	93.1

Quebec

Bale Comeau

CBMI	99.7

Chicoutimi

CBJ-FM	100.9
CBJE	107.9

Drummondville

CBF-FM-1	104.3

Hull

CIMF	94.9

Iles De-la-madeleine

CBIM	93.5

La Pocatiere

CHGB-FM	102.9

Laval

CFGL	105.7

Lithiums Mines

CHLM-1	103.5

Longueuil

CIEL	98.5

Montreal

CBF-FM	100.7
CBM-FM	93.5
CFQR	92.5
CHOM	97.7
CITE	107.3
CJFM	95.9
CKMF	94.3

Quebec

CBVE-FM	104.7
CHOI	98.1
CJMF	95.3
CKIK	98.9
CKRL	89.1

Rimouski

CJBR-FM	101.5

Rouyn

CHLM	96.5

Sept Iles

CIMH	94.1

Sherbrooke

CITE-1	102.7

Ste. Adele

CIME	99.5

Three Rivers

CBF-8	100.1
CFCQ-FM	93.9

Verdun

CKOI	96.9

Saskatchewan

Prince Albert

CFMM	99.1

Regina

CBK-FM	96.9
CBKF	97.7
CFMQ	92.1
CIZL	98.9
CKIT	104.9
CKO-FM-8	94.5

Saskatoon

CBKS	105.5
CFMC	103.9
* CJUS-FM	89.7

Swift Current

CJGL	94.1

MEXICO

Baja California

Mexicali

XHJC-FM	91.5
XHMC-FM	104.9
XHMMP	92.3
XHPF-FM	101.9
XHVG-FM	103.3

Tijuana

XETRA-FM	91.1
XHFG-FM	107.3
XHIS-FM	90.3
XHQF-FM	98.9
XHQS-FM	95.7
XHRM	92.5

Chihuahua

Chihuahua

XHUA	90.1

Ciudad Juarez

XHEM-FM	103.5

Coahuila

Ciudad Acuna

XHRG-FM	95.5

Piedras Negras

XHRE-FM	105.5
XHSG-FM	99.9
XHSL-FM	99.1
XHTA-FM	94.5

Sabinas

XHEC-FM	91.9

Nuevo Leon

Monterey

XET-FM	94.1
XHQQ-FM	93.3

Tamaulipas

Matamoros

XHMLS	101.5

Nuevo Laredo

XHNOE	94.1

WEST INDIES

Bermuda

Hamilton

ZBM-FM	89.1
ZFB-FM	94.9

FM Stations by Frequency

88.1 (201)

	Call	Location
†★	KNNB	Whiteriver, Ariz.
★	KGED	Batesville, Ark.
★	KECG	El Cerrito, Calif.
★	KFCF	Fresno, Calif.
★	KLON	Long Beach, Calif.
★	KUCR	Riverside, Calif.
★	KSRH	San Rafael, Calif.
★	KZSC	Santa Cruz, Calif.
★	KCME	Manitou Springs, Colo.
★	WESU	Middletown, Conn.
★	WMNR	Monroe, Conn.
★	WZZE	Hockessin, Del.
†★	WWOG	Boca Raton, Fla.
★	WUWF	Pensacola, Fla.
†★	----	Warm Springs, Ga.
★	KHPR	Honolulu, Haw.
★	WESN	Bloomington, Ill.
★	WCRX	Chicago, Ill.
★	WSSD	Chicago, Ill.
★	WLTL	La Grange, Ill.
†★	WLRA	Lockport, Ill.
★	WRHS	Park Forest, Ill.
★	WETN	Wheaton, Ill.
★	WNTH	Winnetka, Ill.
★	WVPE	Elkhart, Ind.
★	WNAS	New Albany, Ind.
★	KDPS	Des Moines, Ia.
★	KICB	Ft. Dodge, Ia.
★	KBBG	Waterloo, Ia.
★	KSDB-FM	Manhattan, Kan.
★	KTJO-FM	Ottawa, Kan.
‡★	KRVS	Lafayette, La.
★	WJHU	Baltimore, Md.
‡★	WBYQ	Baltimore, Md.
★	WMUC	College Park, Md.
★	WMBR	Cambridge,
★	WYAJ	Sudbury, Mass.
★	WBFH	Bloomfield Hills, Mich.
★	WHPR	Highland Park, Mich.
★	WSDP	Plymouth, Mich.
†★	WYCE	Wyoming, Mich.
★	KVSC	St. Cloud, Minn.
†★	WMAW-FM	Meridian, Miss.
★	KHRU	Clayton, Mo.
★	KCOU	Columbia, Mo.
†★	KTOD	St. Louis, Mo.
★	KCNT	Hastings, Neb.
★	KLME	Battle Mountain, Nev.
★	KCEP	Las Vegas, Nev.
★	WBEK	Cherry Hill, N.J.
★	WMCX	West Long Branch, N.J.
★	WXBA	Brentwood, N.Y.
★	WCWP	Brookville, N.Y.
★	WECW	Elmira, N.Y.
★	WUNF-FM	Asheville, N.C.
★	WKNC-FM	Raleigh, N.C.
★	WAUP	Akron, O.
★	WOBO	Batavia, O.
★	WBGU	Bowling Green, O.
★	WQRP	West Carrollton, O.
†★	WASD	Exeter, Pa.
★	WTGP	Greenville, Pa.
★	WPEB	Philadelphia, Pa.
†★	WEBB	Pittsburgh, Pa.
★	WWAS	Williamsport, Pa.
★	WVYC	York, Pa.
†★	WCRP	Guayama, P.R.
★	WSBF-FM	Clemson, S.C.
★	WRJA-FM	Sumter, S.C.
★	WUTC	Chattanooga, Tenn.
★	WRFN	Nashville, Tenn.
†★	KGNZ	Abilene, Tex.
★	KNTU	Denton, Tex.
†★	KSBJ	Humble, Tex.
★	KTXT-FM	Lubbock, Tex.
†★	KSLL	Richardson, Tex.
★	KHCH-FM	Round Rock, Tex.
★	KUUU	Neola, Utah
★	KWC-FM	Ogden, Utah
★	KPGR	Pleasant Grove, Utah
†★	WDCJ	Lorton, Va.
★	WVBC	Bethany, W.V.
★	WMUL	Huntington, W.V.
†★	WJTY	Lancaster, Wis.
★	KCWC	Riverton, Wyo.

88.3 (202)

	Call	Location
†★	KABF	Little Rock, Ark.
★	KEMR	Loma Linda, Calif.
★	KPSH-FM	Palm Springs, Calif.
★	KSDS	San Diego, Calif.
‡★	WQAQ	Hamden, Conn.
†★	WQCS	Ft. Pierce, Fla.
†★	WTLG	Starke, Fla.
★	WHPK-FM	Chicago, Ill.
★	WZRD	Chicago, Ill.
★	WDGC-FM	Downers Grove, Ill.
★	WKOC	Kankakee, Ill.
★	WIUS	Macomb, Ill.
†★	WQNA	Springfield, Ill.
★	WEAX	Angola, Ind.
★	WNIN-FM	Evansville, Ind.
★	WLHI	Ft. Wayne, Ind.
★	KCCK-FM	Cedar Rapids, Ia.
★	KMSC	Sioux City, Ia.
★	KVCO	Concordia, Kan.
†★	KDEI	Alexandria, La.
★	WRBH	New Orleans, La.
★	WBMT	Boxford, Mass.
★	WIZH	Concord, Mass.
★	WGAO	Franklin, Mass.
★	WRSB	Weston, Mass.
★	WCBN-FM	Ann Arbor, Mich.
★	WIAA	Interlochen, Mich.
★	WSHJ	Southfield, Mich.
★	WBGO	Newark, N.J.
★	KLYT	Albuquerque, N.M.
★	WVCR-FM	Loudonville, N.Y.
★	WSBU	St. Bonaventura, N.Y.
★	WAER	Syracuse, N.Y.
★	WGWG	Boiling Springs, N.C.
†★	----	Greenville, N.C.
★	WKHR	Bainbridge, O.
★	WBWC	Berea, O.
★	WAIF	Cincinnati, O.
★	WJVS	Cincinnati, O.
★	WLFC	Findlay, O.
★	WMRT	Marietta, O.
★	WAMP-FM	Toledo, O.
★	WGEV	Beaver Falls, Pa.
★	WDCV-FM	Carlisle, Pa.
†★	WGAE	Girard, Pa.
★	WRCT	Pittsburgh, Pa.
★	KESD	Brookings, S.D.
★	WUTZ	Summertown, Tenn.
★	KBNR	Brownsville, Tex.
★	KSUC	Keene, Tex.
★	WHOV	Hampton, Va.
★	WRVL	Lynchburg, Va.
★	WHWC	Menomonie, Wis.

88.5 (203)

	Call	Location
‡★	KNAU	Flagstaff, Ariz.
★	KERU	Blythe, Calif.
★	KSBR	Mission Viejo, Calif.
	KCSN	Northridge, Calif.
★	KQED-FM	San Francisco, Calif.
★	KGNU	Boulder, Colo.
★	KCIC	Grand Junction, Colo.
‡★	WFAR	Danbury, Conn.
★	WVOF	Fairfield, Conn.
★	WAMU-FM	Washington, D. C.
★	WKPX	Sunrise, Fla.
★	WMNF	Tampa, Fla.
★	WRAS	Atlanta, Ga.
★	WHCJ	Savannah, Ga.
★	WBPR	Barrington, Ill.
★	WBHI	Chicago, Ill.
★	WHFH	Flossmoor, Ill.
★	WHSD	Hinsdale, Ill.
★	WMTH	Park Ridge, Ill.
★	KALA	Davenport, Ia.
★	KDIC	Grinnell, Ia.
★	KDCR	Sioux Center, Ia.
★	WHCF	Bangor, Me.
★	WFCR	Amherst, Mass.
★	WGVC-FM	Allendale, Mich.
★	WOAS	Ontonagon, Mich.
†★	KCRB-FM	Bemidji, Minn.
★	KBEM-FM	Minneapolis, Minn.
★	KFSI	Rochester, Minn.
★	WMSU	Hattiesburg, Miss.
★	WJSU	Jackson, Miss.
★	KLJC	Kansas City, Mo.
★	KUMR	Rolla, Mo.
★	WWRC	Lawrenceville, N.J.
†★	----	Middle Island, N.Y.
★	WPOB	Plainview, N.Y.
★	WRUR-FM	Rochester, N.Y.
★	WKWZ	Syosset, N.Y.
★	WARY	Valhalla, N.Y.
	WHYC	Swan Quarter, N.C.
★	WFDD-FM	Winston Salem, N.C.
★	KEYA	Belcourt, N.D.
★	WMUB	Oxford, O.
★	WYSU	Youngstown, O.
★	KOCC	Oklahoma City, Okla.
†★	KMHD	Gresham, Ore.
★	WRKC	Wilkes Barre, Pa.
★	WTTU	Cookeville, Tenn.
★	WVCP	Gallatin, Tenn.
★	WQOX	Memphis, Tenn.
★	KRSM	Dallas, Tex.
†★	KOIR	Edinburg, Tex.
★	KTEP	El Paso, Tex.
★	KPLU-FM	Tacoma, Wash.
★	KYSC	Yakima, Wash.
★	WVPN	Charleston, W.V.

88.7 (204)

	Call	Location
†★	KNAU	Flagstaff, Ariz.
★	KSPC	Claremont, Calif.
†★	KMPO	Modesto, Calif.
★	KSCA	Santa Barbara, Calif.
†★	KRZA	Alamosa, Colo.
★	WNHU	West Haven, Conn.
★	WPCD	Champaign, Ill.
★	WCYC	Chicago, Ill.
★	WLUW	Chicago, Ill.
★	WSIE	Edwardsville, Ill.
★	WRSE-FM	Elmhurst, Ill.
★	WGVE	Gary, Ind.
★	WICR	Indianapolis, Ind.
★	KIGC	Oskaloosa, Ia.
†★	WMMT	Whitesburg, Ky.
†★	KRVS	Lafayette, La.
★	KNLU	Monroe, La.
★	WQLI	Newbury, Mass.
†★	KBFT	Browning, Mont.
★	KUNR	Reno, Nev.
★	WRRH	Franklin Lakes, N.J.
★	WRSU-FM	New Brunswick, N.J.
★	WBFO	Buffalo, N.Y.
★	WHCL-FM	Clinton, N.Y.
★	WRHU	Hempstead, N.Y.
★	WNYK	Nyack, N.Y.
†★	WXDU	Durham, N.C.

*	WCNE	Batavia, O.
*	WBHR	Bellaire, O.
*	WUJC	Cleveland, O.
*	WOBC-FM	Oberlin, O.
*	KBVR	Corvallis, Ore.
*	WLIU	Oxford, Pa.
*	WSYC-FM	Shippensburg, Pa.
*	WCYJ-FM	Waynesboro, Pa.
*	WJMF	Smithfield, R.I.
*	WLCH	Lebanon, Tenn.
†*	KAZI	Austin, Tex.
*	KTCU-FM	Ft. Worth, Tex.
*	KUHF	Houston, Tex.
*	WWPV-FM	Colchester, Vt.
*	WNHS	Portsmouth, Va.
*	WSHC	Shepherdstown, W.V.
*	WERN	Madison, Wis.
*	WRFW	River Falls, Wis.
	CJOM-FM	Windsor, Ont.

88.9 (205)

*	KUAF	Fayetteville, Ark.
*	KBSH	Borrego Springs, Calif.
*	KXLU	Los Angeles, Calif.
*	KUSP	Santa Cruz, Calif.
*	KRTM	Temecula, Calif.
*	WJMJ	Hartford, Conn.
*	WDNA	Miami, Fla.
*	WPFL	Winter Park, Fla.
*	WXGC	Milledgeville, Ga.
†*	KLHS-FM	Lewiston, Id.
*	WEIU	Charleston, Ill.
*	WOUI	Chicago, Ill.
*	WMWA	Glenview, Ill.
*	WMXM	Lake Forest, Ill.
*	WLNX	Lincoln, Ill.
*	WRRG	River Grove, Ill.
*	WARG	Summit, Ill.
*	WSND-FM	Notre Dame, Ind.
*	KWDM	West Des Moines, Ia.
‡*	KNBU	Baldwin City, Kan.
*	WKYU-FM	Bowling Green, Ky.
*	WEKU-FM	Richmond, Ky.
*	WEAA	Baltimore, Md.
*	WERS	Boston, Mass.
†*	WGNR	Grand Rapids, Mich.
†*	WMAU-FM	Bude, Miss.
*	WNJC-FM	Senatobia, Miss.
*	KLUM-FM	Jefferson City, Mo.
*	KRER-FM	Billings, Mont.
*	WMNJ	Madison, N.J.
*	KNMI	Farmington, N.M.
†*	----	Maljamar, N.M.
*	WDWN	Auburn, N.Y.
*	WBSU	Brockport, N.Y.
*	WHHJ	Dix Hills, N.Y.
*	WCVF-FM	Fredonia, N.Y.
*	WSIA	Staten Island, N.Y.
*	WSHA	Raleigh, N.C.
*	WRDL	Ashland, O.
*	WHEI	Tiffin, O.
*	WCSU-FM	Wilberforce, O.
*	WFSE	Edinboro, Pa.
*	WWNW	New Wilmington, Pa.
*	WXPN	Philadelphia, Pa.
*	WQSU	Selinsgrove, Pa.
*	WNSC-FM	Rock Hill, S.C.
*	WMBW	Chattanooga, Tenn.
*	KETR	Commerce, Tex.
*	KBYU-FM	Provo, Utah
*	WIUJ	St. Thomas, V.I.
*	WVPW	Buckhannon, W.V.
*	WLSU	La Crosse, Wis.
*	WYMS	Milwaukee, Wis.
*	WOJB	Reserve, Wis.

89.1 (206)

†*	WLBF	Montgomery, Ala.
†*	KUAR	Little Rock, Ark.
	KCEA	Atherton, Calif.
*	KBDR	Merced, Calif.
*	KUOR-FM	Redlands, Calif.
*	KBBF	Santa Rosa, Calif.
*	WUFT-FM	Gainesville, Fla.
*	WPIO	Titusville, Fla.
*	WBCX	Gainesville, Ga.
‡*	KLHS-FM	Lewiston, Id.
*	WVJC	Mt. Carmel, Ill.
*	WONC	Naperville, Ill.
*	WGLT	Normal, Ill.
‡*	WDSO	Chesterton, Ind.
*	WBNI	Ft. Wayne, Ind.
‡*	WJEL	Indianapolis, Ind.
‡*	WHSK	Kokomo, Ind.
*	KCUI	Pella, Ia.
*	KWAR	Waverly, Ia.
*	KMUW	Wichita, Kan.
*	WBSN-FM	New Orleans, La.
*	KLPI	Ruston, La.
*	WHAB	Acton, Mass.
*	WCHC	Worcester, Mass.
*	WIDR	Kalamazoo, Mich.
*	WEMU	Ypsilanti, Mich.
*	KSJU	Collegeville, Minn.
*	WMSB	Mississippi State, Miss.
*	KCLC	St. Charles, Mo.
*	KUFM	Missoula, Mont.
*	WEVO	Concord, N.H.
*	WKNH	Keene, N.H.
*	WFDU	Teaneck, N.J.
*	WWFM	Trenton, N.J.
*	KANW	Albuquerque, N.M.
*	WNYU-FM	New York, N.Y.
*	WPSA	Paul Smith's, N.Y.
*	WMHT-FM	Schenectady, N.Y.
*	WFSS	Fayetteville, N.C.
*	WAPS	Akron, O.
*	WLMH	Morrow, O.
*	WUSO	Springfield, O.
*	WFNM	Lancaster, Pa.
*	WPSU	Lehman, Pa.
*	KAUR	Sioux Falls, S.D.
*	KBHU-FM	Spearfish, S.D.
*	WNAZ-FM	Nashville, Tenn.
*	WDNX	Olive Hill, Tenn.
*	KOHM	Lubbock, Tex.
*	KURU	San Antonio, Tex.
*	WNUB-FM	Northfield, Vt.
	WVTF	Richmond, Va.
*	WVWR-FM	Roanoke, Va.
*	WCWM	Williamsburg, Va.
†*	KFAE	Richland, Wash.
*	WBSD	Burlington, Wis.
*	WESD	Schofield, Wis.
	CKRL	Quebec, Que.
	ZBM-FM	Hamilton, Bermuda

89.3 (207)

*	WLRH	Huntsville, Ala.
*	KPFB	Berkeley, Calif.
*	KOHL	Fremont, Calif.
*	KVPR-FM	Fresno, Calif.
*	KPCC	Pasadena, Calif.
*	KLEL	San Jose, Calif.
*	KSJC-FM	Stockton, Calif.
*	KUVO	Denver, Colo.
*	WRTC-FM	Hartford, Conn.
*	WPFW	Washington, D. C.
*	WRMB	Boynton Beach, Fla.
*	WGAG-FM	Orlando, Fla.
*	WPCS	Pensacola, Fla.
*	WRFG	Atlanta, Ga.
*	KUOI-FM	Moscow, Id.
*	WKKC	Chicago, Ill.
†*	WDLM-FM	East Moline, Ill.
*	WNUR	Evanston, Ill.
‡*	WGRN	Greenville, Ill.
‡*	WFCI	Franklin, Ind.
†*	WJEL	Indianapolis, Ind.
†*	KUCB-FM	Des Moines, Ia.
*	WNKJ	Hopkinsville, Ky.
*	WFPL	Louisville, Ky.
*	WRKF	Baton Rouge, La.
*	WHSN	Bangor, Me.
†*	WHFR	Dearborn, Mich.
*	WBLD	Orchard Lake, Mich.
*	WSAE	Spring Arbor, Mass.
*	WCAL-FM	Northfield, Minn.
*	WWCJ	Jackson, Miss.
*	KCUR-FM	Kansas City, Mo.
*	WVRM	Hazlet, N.J.
*	WSKG-FM	Binghamton, N.Y.
*	WCSQ	Central Square, N.Y.
*	WGSU	Geneseo, N.Y.
††	WKDT	West Point, N.Y.
*	WXYC	Chapel Hill, N.C.
*	WSOE	Elon College, N.C.
*	WSNC	Winston Salem, N.C.
*	KFJM-FM	Grand Forks, N.D.
*	WCSB	Cleveland, O.
*	WCXL	Dayton, O.
*	WDPS	Dayton, O.
*	WSMR	Dayton, O.
*	WRCJ	Reading, O.
*	WHHS	Havertown, Pa.
*	WQED-FM	Pittsburgh, Pa.
*	WCSD-FM	Warminster, Pa.
*	WSCI	Charleston, S.C.
*	WLFJ	Greenville, S.C.
†*	KEJA	Garden City, S.D.
*	KCBI	Dallas, Tex.
*	KSHU	Huntsville, Tex.
*	KJIC	Pasadena, Tex.
*	KASB	Bellevue, Wash.
*	KUGS	Bellingham, Wash.
*	KAOS	Olympia, Wash.
*	WPNE-FM	Green Bay, Wis.

89.5 (208)

†*	KIAI	Phoenix, Ariz.
*	KBES	Ceres, Calif.
*	KSMC	Moraga, Calif.
*	KVMR	Nevada City, Calif.
‡*	KXPR	Sacramento, Calif.
*	KPBS-FM	San Diego, Calif.
*	KPOO	San Francisco, Calif.
†*	KPRN	Grand Juction, Colo.
‡*	KTSC-FM	Pueblo, Colo.
*	WPKN	Bridgeport, Conn.
*	WFIT	Melbourne, Fla.
*	KBGL	Pocatello, Id.
*	WRTE	Cahokia, Ill.
*	WNIU-FM	De Kalb, Ill.
†*	WJMU	Decatur, Ill.
†*	WGRN	Greenville, Ill.
†*	WFCI	Franklin, Ind.
*	WBKE-FM	North Manchester, Ind.
‡*	WVUR-FM	Valparaiso, Ind.
*	KHKE	Cedar Falls, Ia.
*	KLCD	Decorah, Ia.
*	WAMH	Amherst, Mass.
*	WAHS	Auburn Heights, Mich.
*	WEJY	Monroe, Mich.
*	WCMU-FM	Mt. Pleasant, Mich.
*	WOVI	Novi, Mich.
*	KQAL	Winona, Minn.
†*	WMAE-FM	Booneville, Miss.
*	WMUW	Columbus, Miss.
*	WVTH	Goodman, Miss.
*	KOPN	Columbia, Mo.
*	KCFV	Ferguson, Mo.
*	KHTC	Helena, Mont.
*	KZUM	Lincoln, Neb.
*	KNPR	Las Vegas, Nev.
†*	WEEE	Cherry Hill, N.J.
*	WSOU	South Orange, N.J.
*	KENW-FM	Portales, N.M.
*	WRHO	Oneonta, N.Y.
*	WSCS	Sodus, N.Y.
†*	----	Utica, N.Y.
*	WTEB	New Bern, N.C.
*	WHSS	Hamilton, O.
*	WKET	Kettering, O.
*	KWGS	Tulsa, Okla.

★	KTEC	Klamath Falls, Ore.
★	WDNR	Chester, Pa.
★	WSAJ-FM	Grove City, Pa.
★	WITF-FM	Harrisburg, Pa.
★	WNTE	Mansfield, Pa.
★	WETS	Johnson City, Tenn.
★	WLYX	Memphis, Tenn.
★	WMOT	Murfreesboro, Tenn.
★	KMFA	Austin, Tex.
†★	----	El Paso, Tex.
†★	KVNE	Tyler, Tex.
★	WVPR	Windsor, Vt.
★	WHRO-FM	Norfolk, Va.
★	KNHC	Seattle, Wash.

89.7 (209)

★	KFJC	Los Altos, Calif.
★	KSGN	Riverside, Calif.
★	KNHS	Torrance, Calif.
★	KAFA	Colorado Springs, Colo.
†★	KTSC-FM	Pueblo, Colo.
‡★	WDJW	Somers, Conn.
★	WMCU	Miami, Fla.
★	WUSF	Tampa, Fla.
†★	WDCO-FM	Cochran, Ga.
★	WTPC	Elsah, Ill.
†★	WDSO	Chesterton, Ind.
†★	WHWE	Howe, Ind.
†★	WECI	Richmond, Ind.
★	WISU	Terre Haute, Ind.
★	KOJC	Cedar Rapids, Ia.
†★	KIWR	Council Bluffs, Ia.
†★	----	Iowa City, Ia.
★	KRNL-FM	Mt. Vernon, Ia.
†★	WNKU	Highland Hgts., Ky.
†★	WDCL	Somerset, Ky.
†★	WMED	Calais, Me.
†★	WRNV	Annapolis, Md.
★	WCVT	Towson, Md.
★	WGBH	Boston, Mass.
★	WTBR-FM	Pittsfield, Mass.
★	WOCR	Olivet, Mich.
★	KBSB	Bemidji, Minn.
★	KMSU	Mankato, Minn.
★	KUMM	Morris, Minn.
★	KYMC	Ballwin, Mo.
★	KMNR	Rolla, Mo.
★	WGLS-FM	Glassboro, N.J.
★	KTDB	Ramah, N.M.
★	WALF	Alfred, N.Y.
★	WEOS-FM	Geneva, N.Y.
★	WITR	Henrietta, N.Y.
†★	WFGB	Kingston, N.Y.
★	WRUC	Schenectady, N.Y.
★	WCPE	Raleigh, N.C.
★	WOSU-FM	Columbus, O.
★	WKSU-FM	Kent, O.
★	KLCC	Eugene, Ore.
★	WMUH	Allentown, Pa.
★	WRTU	San Juan, P.R.
★	WMHK	Columbia, S.C.
★	KUSD-FM	Vermillion, S.D.
★	WDYN	Chattanooga, Tenn.
★	KGCC	Denison, Tex.
★	WUEC	Eau Claire, Wis.
★	WUWM	Milwaukee, Wis.
★	KIEA	Ethete, Wyo.
†★	KIEA	Ethete, Wyo.
★	CJUS-FM	Saskatoon, Sask.

89.9 (210)

★	WTSU	Troy, Ala.
★	KZIG	Cave City, Ark.
★	KCDS	Angwin, Calif.
★	KCRH	Hayward, Calif.
★	KUCI	Irvine, Calif.
†★	KEFR	Legrande, Calif.
★	KBHI-FM	Modesto, Calif.
★	KCRW	Santa Monica, Calif.
★	WERB	Berlin, Conn.
★	WQTQ	Hartford, Conn.
★	WWEB	Wallingford, Conn.
★	WJCT-FM	Jacksonville, Fla.
★	WUCF-FM	Orlando, Fla.
‡★	KJLC	Lewiston, Id.
‡★	WJMU	Decatur, Ill.
†★	WLCA	Godfrey, Ill.
★	WLKL	Mattoon, Ill.
★	WCBU	Peoria, Ill.
‡★	WQNA	Springfield, Ill.
†★	----	Frankfort, Ky.
†★	WRVG	Georgetown, Ky.
★	WSOF-FM	Madisonville, Ky.
★	WWNO-FM	New Orleans, La.
†★	KDAQ	Shreveport, La.
★	WACC	Arnold, Md.
★	WOEL-FM	Elkton, Md.
★	WMTB-FM	Emmitsburg, Md.
★	WSCB	Springfield, Mass.
★	WEHB	Grand Rapids, Mich.
★	WKDS	Kalamazoo, Mich.
★	KMOJ	Minneapolis, Minn.
★	KRPR	Rochester, Minn.
★	KBDY	St. Louis, Mo.
†★	----	Great Falls, Mont.
★	WKCR-FM	New York, N.Y.
★	WRVO	Oswego, N.Y.
★	WDAV	Davidson, N.C.
†★	KMPR	Minot, N.D.
★	WRSF	Miamisburg, O.
★	WLHS	West Chester, O.
★	KBPS-FM	Portland, Ore.
★	WERG	Erie, Pa.
★	WVIA-FM	Scranton, Pa.
★	WTLR	State College, Pa.
★	WJDZ	Levittown, P.R.
★	WJWJ-FM	Beaufort, S.C.
★	KACV-FM	Amarillo, Tex.
★	WVRU	Radford, Va.
★	KGRG	Auburn, Wash.
★	KEWC-FM	Cheney, Wash.
★	WHPW-FM	Huntington, W.V.
†★	WVNP	Wheeling, W.V.
★	WHSA	Brule, Wis.
★	WORT	Madison, Wis.
★	WWSP	Stevens Point, Wis.
	CBE-FM	Windsor, Ont.

90.1 (211)

★	WOGC	Huntsville, Ala.
†★	KSBC	Hot Springs, Ark.
★	KBPK	Buena Park, Calif.
★	KSUL	Long Beach, Calif.
★	KCBX	San Luis Obispo, Calif.
★	KZSU	Stanford, Calif.
★	KCJH	Stockton, Calif.
★	KSAK	Walnut, Calif.
★	KCFR	Denver, Colo.
★	WLNV	Derby, Conn.
‡★	WFCS	New Britain, Conn.
†★	WECS	Willimantic, Conn.
★	WDCU	Washington, D. C.
†★	WFSP	Ft. Myers, Fla.
★	WABE	Atlanta, Ga.
‡★	KRIC	Rexburg, Id.
★	WEFT	Champaign, Ill.
★	WMBI-FM	Chicago, Ill.
★	WVIK	Rock Island, Ill.
★	WIAN	Indianapolis, Ind.
★	WOI-FM	Ames, Ia.
★	KHCC-FM	Hutchinson, Kan.
‡★	WRVG	Georgetown, Ky.
‡★	WBRH	Baton Rouge, La.
★	WMEA	Portland, Me.
★	WBPV	Charlton, Mass.
★	WNMU-FM	Marquette, Mich.
★	KSJR-FM	Collegeville, Minn.
★	KSRQ	Thief River Falls, Minn.
★	WMPR	Jackson, Miss.
★	KTSR	Kansas City, Mo.
★	KRSH	Overland, Mo.
★	KNOG	Havre, Mont.
★	KUNM	Albuquerque, N.M.
★	WGMC	Greece, N.Y.
★	WRCU-FM	Hamilton, N.Y.
★	WUSB	Stony Brook, N.Y.
★	WCCE	Buie's Creek, N.C.
★	WPGT	Roanoke Rapids, N.C.
★	KCSC	Edmond, Okla.
★	KSOR	Ashland, Ore.
★	WIUP-FM	Indiana, Pa.
★	WRTI	Philadelphia, Pa.
★	WSRU	Slippery Rock, Pa.
★	WEPR	Greenville, S.C.
★	KILI	Porcupine, S.D.
†★	KASD-FM	Reliance, S.D.
★	KCFS	Sioux Falls, S.D.
★	KSTI	Springfield, S.D.
★	KERA-FM	Dallas, Tex.
★	KPFT	Houston, Tex.
★	KSAU	Nacogdoches, Tex.
★	KSYM-FM	San Antonio, Tex.
★	KBBD	Beaver, Utah
★	KUER	Salt Lake City, Utah
★	WRUV	Burlington, Vt.
★	WUTA	Farmville, Va.
★	WDCE	Richmond, Va.
★	KMIH	Mercer Island, Wash.
★	KSVR	Mt. Vernon, Wash.
★	KOLU	Pasco, Wash.
★	KUPS	Tacoma, Wash.
★	WGBP-FM	Green Bay, Wis.
★	WRPN-FM	Ripon, Wis.
★	KYDZ	Cody, Wyo.
	XHUA	Chihuahua, Chih.

90.3 (212)

★	WBHM	Birmingham, Ala.
†★	KLRC	Siloam Springs, Ark.
★	KDVS	Davis, Calif.
★	KAZU	Pacific Grove, Calif.
★	KUSF	San Francisco, Calif.
★	KJOL	Grand Junction, Colo.
★	WWPT	Westport, Conn.
★	WAFG	Ft Lauderdale, Fla.
†★	WAMF	Tallahassee, Fla.
★	KTUH	Honolulu, Haw.
†★		Covington, Ill.
★	WWQC	Quincy, Ill.
†★	WFOF	Covington, Ind.
★	WBCL	Ft. Wayne, Ind.
★	KCOE-FM	Cedar Rapids, Ia.
★	KWIT	Sioux City, Ia.
★	WMKY-FM	Morehead, Ky.
★	WKWC	Owensboro, Ky.
†★	WBRH	Baton Rouge, La.
‡★	WUFK	Ft. Kent, Me.
★	WZBC	Newton, Mass.
★	WORB	Farmington Hills, Mich.
★	WOPR	Oak Park, Mich.
†★	WBLV	Twin Lake, Mich.
	KFAI	Minneapolis, Minn.
★	KRLX	Northfield, Minn.
†★	WMAH-FM	Biloxi, Miss.
†★	WMAV-FM	Oxford, Miss.
★	KBFL	Buffalo, Mo.
★	KWUR	Clayton, Mo.
★	KGSP	Parkville, Mo.
★	KRNU	Lincoln, Neb.
★	WVHP-FM	Highland Park, N.J.
★	WRPR	Mahwah, N.J.
★	WVPH	Piscataway, N.J.
★	WKNJ	Union, N.J.
★	WAMC	Albany, N.Y.
#★	WHPC	Garden City, N.Y.
#★	WBAU	Garden City, N.Y.
★	WJSL	Houghton, N.Y.
†★	WHCR-FM	New York, N.Y.
★	WOSS	Ossining, N.Y.
★	WAFR	Durham, N.C.
★	WWIH	High Point, N.C.
★	WCDR-FM	Cedarville, O.
★	WCPN	Cleveland, O.
★	KSLC	Mc Minnville, Ore.
★	WESS	East Stroudsburg, Pa.
★	WPTG	Lancaster, Pa.

* WARC Meadville, Pa.
†* WXLV Schencksville, Pa.
†* WVID Anasco, P.R.
* WRIU Kingston, R.I.
†* WSSB-FM Orangeburg, S.C.
* WCSK Kingsport, Tenn.
* WUTK Knoxville, Tenn.
* WUTM-FM Martin, Tenn.
* WEVL Memphis, Tenn.
* WPLN Nashville, Tenn.
* KKED-FM Corpus Christi, Tex.
* KPLN-FM Plains, Tex.
* WFOS Chesapeake, Va.
* WWLC Lynchburg, Va.
* KWRS Spokane, Wash.
* WCDE Elkins, W.V.
†* WVPG Parkersburg, W.V.
* WBCR-FM Beloit, Wis.
* WHLA La Crosse, Wis.
* WRST-FM Oshkosh, Wis.
XHIS-FM Tijuana, B.C.

90.5 (213)

†* WTOH Mobile, Ala.
* KUAT-FM Tucson, Ariz.
* KLRE-FM Little Rock, Ark.
‡* KHSU-FM Arcata, Calif.
* KVHS Concord, Calif.
* KDHS Modesto, Calif.
* KSFH Mountain View, Calif.
†* KUFW Woodlake, Calif.
†* KDNK Carbondale, Colo.
* KEPC Colorado Springs, Colo.
†* KCSU-FM Ft. Collins, Colo.
‡* WPBH Meriden, Conn.
†* WPBH Meriden, Conn.
†* WPBH Middlefield, Conn.
‡* WPBH Middlefield, Conn.
* WVUM Coral Gables, Fla.
‡* WAMF Tallahassee, Fla.
* WUOG Athens, Ga.
†* ---- Columbus, Ga.
‡* WABR-FM Tifton, Ga.
* WVKC Galesburg, Ill.
†* WWDS Muncie, Ind.
* WPUM Rensselaer, Ind.
* WMHD-FM Terre Haute, Ind.
* WUOL Louisville, Ky.
†* WMHB Waterville, Me.
* WCRH Williamsport, Md.
* WKHS Worton, Md.
†* WMCI Brockton,
* WUSM North Dartmouth, Mass.
* WICN Worcester, Mass.
* WKAR-FM East Lansing, Mich.
†* ---- Gaylord, Mich.
†* KDNW Duluth, Minn.
* KRPC Owatonna, Minn.
†* KSCG St. Peter, Minn.
* WALP Corinth, Miss.
* KWWC-FM Columbia, Mo.
* KXCV Maryville, Mo.
* WSPS Concord, N.H.
* WPEA Exeter, N.H.
* WCVH Flemington, N.J.
* WBJB-FM Lincroft, N.J.
* WJSV Morristown, N.J.
* WHPH Whippany, N.J.
* WBXL Baldwinsville, N.Y.
* WHRW Binghamton, N.Y.
* WSUC-FM Cortland, N.Y.
* WRHR Henrietta, N.Y.
* WASU-FM Boone, N.C.
* WWCU Cullowhee, N.C.
* WNAA Greensboro, N.C.
* WKNS Kinston, N.C.
* WVMH-FM Mars Hill, N.C.
* WDCC Sanford, N.C.
* KCND Bismarck, N.D.
* WCBE Columbus, O.
†* KNYD Broken Arrow, Okla.
†* WIDA-FM Carolina, Pa.
* WJRH Easton, Pa.
* WVBU-FM Lewisburg, Pa.
* WDUQ Pittsburgh, Pa.
* WUSC-FM Columbia, S.C.
WSMC-FM Chattanooga, Tenn.
* KUT-FM Austin, Tex.
†* WJYJ Fredericksburg, Va.
* KCMU Seattle, Wash.
* KWCW Walla Walla, Wash.
* WSUP Platteville, Wis.
†* WHIJ-FM Washburn, Wis.
CBHA Halifax, N.S.

90.7 (214)

†* WVAS Montgomery, Ala.
* WVUA-FM Tuscaloosa, Ala.
* KALX Berkeley, Calif.
†* KPAU Covelo, Calif.
†* KFSR Fresno, Calif.
* KPFK Los Angeles, Calif.
* KSJS San Jose, Calif.
* KCDC Longmont, Colo.
* WHRS-FM Boynton Beach, Fla.
* WMFE-FM Orlando, Fla.
* WKGC-FM Panama City, Fla.
* WHRS West Palm Beach, Fla.
* WACG-FM Augusta, Ga.
* WWGC Carrollton, Ga.
†* WMVV Mcdonough, Ga.
†* KCIR Twin Falls, Id.
* WPSR Evansville, Ind.
‡* WBST Muncie, Ind.
* KJHK Lawrence, Kan.
‡* WSCC Somerset, Ky.
* WWOZ New Orleans, La.
* WTCC Springfield, Mass.
* WKKL West Barnstable, Mass.
* WAUS Berrien Springs, Mich.
†* KLSX-FM Rochester, Minn.
* KOBC Joplin, Mo.
* KWMU St. Louis, Mo.
* KVNO Omaha, Neb.
†* WANH-FM Manchester, N.H.
* KRWG Las Cruces, N.M.
* WFUV New York, N.Y.
* WPNR-FM Utica, N.Y.
* WFAE Charlotte, N.C.
* WGLE Lima, O.
* WVMC Mansfield, O.
* WMCO New Concord, O.
* WKTL Struthers, O.
* KALU Langston, Okla.
* KAYE-FM Tonkawa, Okla.
* KBOO Portland, Ore.
* WCLH Wilkes Barre, Pa.
* WJHD Portsmouth, R.I.
* KSME Manti, Utah
* WJSC-FM Johnson, Vt.
* WVTC Randolph Center, Vt.
* WUVT-FM Blacksburg, Va.
* WMRA Harrisonburg, Va.
* KZUU Pullman, Wash.
* WFGH Fort Gay, W.V.
* WHAD Delafield, Wis.
* WVSS Menomonie, Wis.

90.9 (215)

†* WAED Huntsville, Ala.
†* KLLN Newark, Ark.
* KUBO Chualar, Calif.
‡* KRVH Rio Vista, Calif.
†* KXPR Sacramento, Calif.
* KBDG Turlock, Calif.
* KASF Alamosa, Colo.
‡* KCSU-FM Ft. Collins, Colo.
* KVNF Paonia, Colo.
†* WKKA Cornwall, Conn.
* WETA-FM Washington, D. C.
†* WFAM Jacksonville, Fla.
†* WOAK La Grange, Ga.
* WRAF Toccoa Falls, Ga.
* WVVS Valdosta, Ga.
* WEPS Elgin, Ill.
* WDCB Glen Ellyn, Ill.
* WILL-FM Urbana, Ill.
†* WDHS Gaston, Ind.
* WBDG Indianapolis, Ind.
* KUNI Cedar Falls, Ia.
* KSLU Hammond, La.
* WMEH Bangor, Me.
†* WMPG Gorham, Me.
†* ---- Standish, Me.
* WBUR Boston, Mass.
* WDTR Detroit, Mich.
* WNCM-FM Traverse City, Mich.
‡* KSMR Winona, Minn.
†* WMAO-FM Greenwood, Miss.
* KRCU Cape Girardeau, Mo.
* KCMW-FM Warrensburg, Mo.
* KUCV Lincoln, Neb.
* KSHI Zuni, N.M.
* WCDB Albany, N.Y.
* WETD Alfred, N.Y.
* WITC Cazenovia, N.Y.
* WONY Oneonta, N.Y.
* WIRQ Rochester, N.Y.
†* ---- Watertown, N.Y.
* WQFS Greensboro, N.C.
* WVSP Warrenton, N.C.
* WGUC Cincinnati, O.
‡* WDUB Granville, O.
* KOKF Edmond, Okla.
* KRBM Pendleton, Ore.
* WHYY-FM Philadelphia, Pa.
* WCEW Charleston, S.C.
†* WLGI Hemingway, S.C.
†* ---- Pierpont, S.D.
* KAMU-FM College Station, Tex.
* KNON Dallas, Tex.
* KTSU Houston, Tex.
†* KPAC San Antonio, Tex.
* KRCL Salt Lake City, Utah
* KVTI Tacoma, Wash.
†* WEYS Institute, W.V.
* WVPM Morgantown, W.V.
* WHRM Wausau, Wis.

91.1 (216)

* WEGL Auburn, Ala.
* WJSR Birmingham, Ala.
* WVSU-FM Birmingham, Ala.
†* KNLB Lake Havasu City, Ariz.
* KSWH Arkadelphia, Ark.
* KCHO Chico, Calif.
* KCSM San Mateo, Calif.
* KCPB Thousand Oaks, Calif.
†* KWSB-FM Gunnison, Colo.
* KWBI Morrison, Colo.
* WSHU Fairfield, Conn.
‡* WCNI New London, Conn.
‡* WFAM Jacksonville, Fla.
* WREK Atlanta, Ga.
* WSVH Savannah, Ga.
* WIBI Carlinville, Ill.
‡* WDHS Gaston, Ind.
* WGCS Goshen, Ind.
* WEDM Indianapolis, Ind.
* WVUB Vincennes, Ind.
* KTPR Ft. Dodge, Ia.
* KANZ Garden City, Kan.
* KSOP Wichita, Kan.
†* KLSU Baton Rouge, La.
* WBOR Brunswick, Me.
‡* WMPG Gorham, Me.
* WNCY Springvale, Me.
* WMUA Amherst, Mass.
* WJJW North Adams, Mass.
* WGGL-FM Houghton, Mich.
* KCCM-FM Moorhead, Minn.
* KSJN-FM St. Paul, Minn.
* KSMU Springfield, Mo.
* KGLT Bozeman, Mont.
* KDVC-FM Blair, Neb.
* KDVC-FM Blair, Neb.

*	WFMU	East Orange, N.J.
*	KEDP	Las Vegas, N.M.
*	WTSC-FM	Potsdam, N.Y.
*	WSPN	Saratoga Springs, N.Y.
*	WRSH	Rockingham, N.C.
*	WRMU	Alliance, O.
*	WRUW-FM	Cleveland, O.
*	WDEQ-FM	De Graff, O.
*	WSLN	Delaware, O.
†*	WDUB	Granville, O.
*	KWAX	Eugene, Ore.
*	WZBT	Gettysburg, Pa.
*	WMSS	Middletown, Pa.
*	WDFM	State College, Pa.
*	WYFG	Gaffney, S.C.
*	WKCS	Knoxville, Tenn.
*	WKNO-FM	Memphis, Tenn.
*	WRVU	Nashville, Tenn.
*	KWTS	Canyon, Tex.
*	KTAI	Kingsville, Tex.
*	KBWC	Marshall, Tex.
*	KGSU-FM	Cedar City, Utah
*	KMTP	Mt. Pleasant, Utah
*	WGDR	Plainfield, Vt.
*	WHCE	Highland Springs, Va.
*	WNSB	Norfolk, Va.
*	KPBX-FM	Spokane, Wash.
*	WITB-FM	Salem, W.V.
*	WLFM	Appleton, Wis.
*	WGTD	Kenosha, Wis.
*	CJRT-FM	Toronto, Ont.
	XETRA-FM	Tijuana, B.C.

91.3 (217)

*	WHIL-FM	Mobile, Ala.
*	KUCA	Conway, Ark.
*	KIDE	Hoopa, Calif.
*	KCPR	San Luis Obispo, Calif.
*	KUOP	Stockton, Calif.
*	KMSA	Grand Junction, Colo.
*	KSUT	Ignacio, Colo.
*	WWUH	West Hartford, Conn.
*	WXDR	Newark, Del.
*	WCIE	Lakeland, Fla.
*	WLRN-FM	Miami, Fla.
†*	WHGW	Fort Valley, Ga.
*	KBSU	Boise, Id.
*	WIUM	Macomb, Ill.
*	WHJE	Carmel, Ind.
*	WBKY	Lexington, Ky.
*	WKMS-FM	Murray, Ky.
*	KGRM	Grambling, La.
*	KSCL	Shreveport, La.
*	KVFG	Thibodaux, La.
†*	WMEW	Waterville, Me.
*	WSHL-FM	Easton, Mass.
*	WDJM-FM	Framingham, Mass.
*	WCWL	Stockbridge, Mass.
*	WCUW	Worcester, Mass.
*	WCHW-FM	Bay City, Mich.
*	WOES	Elsie, Mich.
*	WCSG	Grand Rapids, Mich.
*	WSGR-FM	Port Huron, Mich.
*	KAVT-FM	Austin, Minn.
†*	WMAA-FM	Jackson, Miss.
*	KBIA	Columbia, Mo.
*	KSCV	Kearney, Neb.
*	WUNH	Durham, N.H.
*	WTSR	Trenton, N.J.
†*	WBNY	Buffalo, N.Y.
*	WVKR-FM	Poughkeepsie, N.Y.
*	WPBX	Southampton, N.Y.
*	WCNY-FM	Syracuse, N.Y.
*	WBMU-FM	Asheville, N.C.
*	WZMB	Greenville, N.C.
†*	WHQR	Wilmington, N.C.
†*	KMHA	New Town, N.D.
*	WOUB-FM	Athens, O.
*	WGTE-FM	Toledo, O.
*	WYSO	Yellow Springs, O.

*	KNGX	Claremore, Okla.
*	WLVR	Bethlehem, Pa.
*	WQLN-FM	Erie, Pa.
*	WYEP-FM	Pittsburgh, Pa.
*	WXAC	Reading, Pa.
*	WIPR-FM	San Juan, P.R.
*	WDOM	Providence, R.I.
*	WLTR	Columbia, S.C.
*	KTEQ	Rapid City, S.D.
†*	WIKU	Pikeville, Tenn.
*	KACC	Alvin, Tex.
*	KVLU	Beaumont, Tex.
*	KNCT-FM	Killeen, Tex.
*	KOCV	Odessa, Tex.
*	KPVU	Prairie View, Tex.
*	WIUV	Castleton, Vt.
*	WTJU	Charlottesville, Va.
*	KBCS	Bellevue, Wash.
*	KCED	Centralia, Wash.
*	KGTS	Walla Walla, Wash.
*	WHHI	Highland, Wis.
	CBD-FM	Fredericton, N.B.

91.5 (218)

*	WEXP	Gadsden, Ala.
*	WUAL-FM	Tuscaloosa, Ala.
*	KMCR-FM	Phoenix, Ariz.
‡*	KAHS	Arcata, Calif.
†*	KHSU-FM	Arcata, Calif.
*	KKUP	Cupertino, Calif.
*	KSJV	Fresno, Calif.
*	KUSC	Los Angeles, Calif.
*‡	KSPB	Pebble Beach, Calif.
*	KYDS	Sacramento, Calif.
†*	KTUO	Sonora, Calif.
*	KVIK	Travis A F B, Calif.
*	KRCC	Colorado Springs, Colo.
*	KUNC-FM	Greeley, Colo.
†*	WCNI	New London, Conn.
†*	WMIE-FM	Cocoa, Fla.
†*	WLPJ	New Port Richey, Fla.
*	WFSU-FM	Tallahassee, Fla.
*	WPRK	Winter Park, Fla.
†*	WWEV	Cumming, Ga.
*	WBEZ	Chicago, Ill.
†*	WCIC	Pekin, Ill.
*	WUEV	Evansville, Ind.
*	WGRE	Greencastle, Ind.
*	WRFT	Indianapolis, Ind.
*	WWHI	Muncie, Ind.
‡*	WECI	Richmond, Ind.
†*	KUSR	Ames, Ia.
*	KANU	Lawrence, Kan.
†*	WVCT	Keavy, Ky.
*	WTUL-FM	New Orleans, La.
*	WRBC	Lewiston, Me.
‡*	WMHB	Waterville, Me.
*	WBJC	Baltimore, Md.
*	WBIM-FM	Bridgewater, Mass.
*	WHHB	Holliston, Mass.
*	WJUL	Lowell, Mass.
*	WMFO	Medford, Mass.
*	WMLN-FM	Milton, Mass.
†*	WNMH	Northfield, Mass.
*	WRPS	Rockland, Mass.
*	WSDH	Sandwich, Mass.
*	WMHC	South Hadley, Mass.
*	WSRB	Walpole, Mass.
*	WZLY	Wellesley, Mass.
*	WSKB	Westfield, Mass.
*	WMHW-FM	Mt. Pleasant, Mich.
*	WPHS	Warren, Mich.
*	KCUM-FM	Crookston, Minn.
*	KICC	International Falls, Minn.
*	KSLH	St. Louis, Mo.
*	KMSM-FM	Butte, Mont.
*	KIOS-FM	Omaha, Neb.
*	KGLH	Gerlach, Nev.
*	KUNV	Las Vegas, Nev.
*	WDBK	Blackwood, N.J.
*	KFLQ	Albuquerque, N.M.
*	WJWK	Jamestown, N.Y.
*	WNYE	New York, N.Y.

*	WXXI-FM	Rochester, N.Y.
*	WRPI	Troy, N.Y.
*	WUNC	Chapel Hill, N.C.
†*	WGVO	Greenville, O.
*	WSTB	Streetsboro, O.
*	KOAP-FM	Portland, Ore.
*	WVMW-FM	Scranton, Pa.
*	WSRN-FM	Swarthmore, Pa.
*	WCVY	Coventry, R.I.
*	WKCL	Ladson, S.C.
*	WHBC	Bristol, Tenn.
*	WFHC	Henderson, Tenn.
*	WFMQ	Lebanon, Tenn.
*	WUTS	Sewanee, Tenn.
*	WCSO	Signal Mountain, Tenn.
*	KWLD	Plainview, Tex.
†*	KTXK	Texarkana, Tex.
*	KUSU-FM	Logan, Utah
*	WWLR	Lyndonville, Vt.
*	WMTF	Stowe, Vt.
*	WLUR	Lexington, Va.
*	WUDZ	Sweet Briar, Va.
*	WYCS	Yorktown, Va.
*	KUBS	Newport, Wash.
*	WJGF	Romney, W.V.
*	WGBW	Green Bay, Wis.
†*	WBII	Watertown, Wis.
	XHJC-FM	Mexicali, B.C.

91.7 (219)

*	WBQM	Decatur, Ala.
†*	KXCI	Tucson, Ariz.
*	KALW	San Francisco, Calif.
*	KWHS	West Sacramento, Calif.
*	KOTO	Telluride, Colo.
*	WXCI	Danbury, Conn.
*	WHUS	Storrs, Conn.
*	WMPH	Wilmington, Del.
†*	----	Columbus, Ga.
*	KUID	Moscow, Id.
*	WBGL	Champaign, Ill.
*	WEEM	Pendleton, Ind.
*	WETL	South Bend, Ind.
*	KSUI	Iowa City, Ia.
*	KNWD	Natchitoches, La.
*	WBSF	Biddeford, Me.
†*	WSHD	Eastport, Me.
*	WPAA	Andover, Mass.
*	WGAJ	Deerfield, Mass.
†*	WDBY	Duxbury, Mass.
*	WMWC	Gardner, Mass.
*	WAVM	Maynard, Mass.
*	WMWM	Salem, Mass.
*	WBSL	Sheffield, Mass.
*	WBRS	Waltham, Mass.
*	WCML-FM	Alpena, Mich.
*	WUOM	Ann Arbor, Mich.
*	KAXE	Grand Rapids, Minn.
*	KLSE-FM	Rushford, Minn.
*	KDXL	St. Louis Park, Minn.
*	WMCN	St. Paul, Minn.
*	KRSW	Worthington, Minn.
*	KNOS	Marshall, Mo.
*	KSOZ	Point Lookout, Mo.
*	KEMC	Billings, Mont.
*	WNEC-FM	Henniker, N.H.
*	WPCR-FM	Plymouth, N.H.
*	WICB	Ithaca, N.Y.
*	WSGE	Dallas, N.C.
†*		Byesville, O.
*	WVXU-FM	Cincinnati, O.
‡*	WGVO	Greenville, O.
*	WUHS	Urbana, O.
*	KPSU	Goodwell, Okla.
*	KOSU-FM	Stillwater, Okla.
*	KCHC	Central Point, Ore.
*	KEOL	La Grande, Ore.
*	WCUC-FM	Clarion, Pa.
*	WIXQ	Millersville, Pa.
*	WPWT	Philadelphia, Pa.
*	WKDU	Philadelphia, Pa.

★	WBMR	Telford, Pa.
★	WRLC	Williamsport, Pa.
★	WSMS	Memphis, Tenn.
★	KVTT	Dallas, Tex.
★	KTRU	Houston, Tex.
★	KRTU	San Antonio, Tex.
★	KGVH	Gunnison, Utah
★	KOHS	Orem, Utah
★	WRMC-FM	Middlebury, Vt.
★	WWHS-FM	Hampden Sydney, Va.
★	WEMC	Harrisonburg, Va.
★	KTOY	Tacoma, Wash.
★	WVPB	Beckley, W.V.
	WWVU-FM	Morgantown, W.V.
★	WMSE	Milwaukee, Wis.
†★	WXPR	Rhinelander, Wis.
★	WSHS	Sheboygan, Wis.
★	WSUW	Whitewater, Wis.

91.9 (220)

†★	WGIB	Birmingham, Ala.
★	WLJS-FM	Jacksonville, Ala.
★	KNCC	Tsaile, Ariz.
★	KASU	Jonesboro, Ark.
†★	KSPB	Pebble Beach, Calif.
★	KVCR	San Bernardino, Calif.
★	KCSB-FM	Santa Barbara, Calif.
★	KCLB	Santa Rosa, Calif.
★	KCSS	Turlock, Calif.
★	KDUR	Durango, Colo.
‡★	KWSB-FM	Gunnison, Colo.
★	WSLX	New Canaan, Conn.
†★	----	Okeechobee, Fla.
★	WCLK	Atlanta, Ga.
★	WSIU	Carbondale, Ill.
★	WSSR	Springfield, Ill.
★	WVSH	Huntington, Ind.
★	WJEF	Lafayette, Ind.
‡★	KUSR	Ames, Ia.
★	KTCC	Colby, Kan.
★	KINF	Dodge City, Kan.
★	KBJC	Great Bend, Kan.
★	WFPK	Louisville, Ky.
‡★	WUMF-FM	Farmington, Me.
†★	WMEB-FM	Orono, Me.
★	WGTS-FM	Takoma Park, Md.
★	WUMB-FM	Boston, Mass.
†★	WOZQ	Northampton, Mass.
★	WOMR	Provincetown, Mass.
★	WAIC	Springfield, Mass.
★	WCFM	Williamstown, Mass.
★	WHSR-FM	Winchester, Mass.
†★	WAYW	Worcester, Mass.
★	WORW	Port Huron, Mich.
★	KWPB	Liberty, Mo.
★	KTLX	Columbus, Neb.
★	KWSC	Wayne, Neb.
★	WBGD	Brick Town, N.J.
★	WNTI	Hackettstown, N.J.
★	WCEB	Corning, N.Y.
★	WSHR	Lake Ronkonkoma, N.Y.
★	KDSU	Fargo, N.D.
★	WKCO	Gambier, O.
★	WCWS	Wooster, O.
★	KHIB	Durant, Okla.
†★	KMUN	Astoria, Ore.
★	KRVM	Eugene, Ore.
★	WVCS	California, Pa.
†★	WFCM	Orangeburg, S.C.
★	WUOT	Knoxville, Tenn.
†★	KFLV	Corpus Christi, Tex.
★	KPCW	Park City, Utah
★	KSFC	Spokane, Wash.
★	KDNA	Yakima, Wash.
★	WPHP	Wheeling, W.V.
★	KUWR	Laramie, Wyo.
	XHEC-FM	Sabinas, Coah.

92.1 (221) A

	WKLN	Cullman, Ala.
	WZEW	Fairhope, Ala.
	WERH-FM	Hamilton, Ala.
	KZMK	Bisbee, Ariz.
	KEZG	Green Valley, Ariz.
	KJON	Booneville, Ark.
†	KHPQ	Clinton, Ark.
	KKEG	Fayetteville, Ark.
	KOWN-FM	Escondido, Calif.
	KLFA	King City, Calif.
★	KUUL	Madera, Calif.
	KHTN	Placerville, Calif.
	KINQ	Walnut Creek, Calif.
	KRKY	Castle Rock, Colo.
†	KBLJ	La Junta, Colo.
	KVRH-FM	Salida, Colo.
	WMMK	Destin, Fla.
	WCMQ-FM	Hialeah, Fla.
	WVHG	Labelle, Fla.
	WBKF	Mac Clenny, Fla.
†	WXCR	Safety Harbor, Fla.
	WARV	Venice, Fla.
	WNGS	West Palm Beach, Fla.
†	WJRQ	Williston, Fla.
	WDDQ	Adel, Ga.
	WBTR-FM	Carrollton, Ga.
	WAZE	Dawson, Ga.
	WUFF-FM	Eastman, Ga.
	WWRK	Elberton, Ga.
	WBLU	Hinesville, Ga.
	WJGA-FM	Jackson, Ga.
	WPEH-FM	Louisville, Ga.
†	KOAS	Kealakekua, Haw.
	KNAQ	Rupert, Id.
	WCAZ-FM	Carthage, Ill.
	WEIC-FM	Charleston, Ill.
	WFPS	Freeport, Ill.
	WJRE	Kewanee, Ill.
†★	WBST	Muncie, Ind.
	WROI	Rochester, Ind.
	KSMX	Ft. Dodge, Ia.
	KTAV	Knoxville, Ia.
	KRLS	Knoxville, Ia.
†	----	Belleville, Kan.
†	KQQF	Coffeyville, Kan.
	WMOR-FM	Morehead, Ky.
	WDHR	Pikeville, Ky.
†★	WSCC	Somerset, Ky.
	WTKY-FM	Tomkinsville, Ky.
†	KDKS	Benton, La.
†	KLIL	Moreauville, La.
†	----	Rayville, La.
	KVCL-FM	Winnfield, La.
‡	WRDO-FM	Augusta, Me.
†★	WUFK	Ft. Kent, Me.
★	WUPI	Presque Isle, Me.
	WEBI	Sanford, Me.
	WXIE	Oakland, Md.
	WLEW-FM	Bad Axe, Mich.
	WDOW-FM	Dowagiac, Mich.
	WGHN-FM	Grand Haven, Mich.
	WKKM	Harrison, Mich.
	WCSR-FM	Hillsdale, Mich.
	WKLH	St. Johns, Mich.
	WMZK	Traverse City, Mich.
	WYRQ	Little Falls, Minn.
†	KLQF	Madison, Minn.
	WCMP-FM	Pine City, Minn.
	KQDE-FM	Waseca, Minn.
	WMRQ	Brookhaven, Miss.
†	WJMG	Hattiesburg, Miss.
	WKOR-FM	Starkville, Miss.
	WJNS-FM	Yazoo City, Miss.
	KMOE	Butler, Mo.
†	----	Centralia, Mo.
	KLWT-FM	Lebanon, Mo.
	KCBW	Sedalia, Mo.
	KTTN-FM	Trenton, Mo.
	KBLL-FM	Helena, Mont.
	KPNY	Alliance, Neb.
	WMDK	Peterborough, N.H.
	WKQV	Vineland, N.J.
	KATK	Carlsbad, N.M.
	WSEN-FM	Baldwinsville, N.Y.
★	WGFR	Glens Falls, N.Y.
	WCKR	Hornell, N.Y.
★	WHRC	Port Henry, N.Y.
	WLNG-FM	Sag Harbor, N.Y.
	WDLA-FM	Walton, N.Y.
	WKJA	Belhaven, N.C.
	WRCM	Jacksonville, N.C.
	WQXX	Morganton, N.C.
	WOFM	Moyock, N.C.
	WRSV	Rocky Mount, N.C.
	KRRB	Dickinson, N.D.
	WNRR	Bellevue, O.
★	WCWT-FM	Centerville, O.
	WMPO-FM	Middleport, O.
	WAXC	Wapakoneta, O.
	KELS	Ardmore, Okla.
	KRRO	Ardmore, Okla.
	KSNE	Broken Arrow, Okla.
†	KDAA	Woodward, Okla.
★	KEPO	Eagle Point, Ore.
	WFEM	Ellwood City, Pa.
	WGLU	Johnstown, Pa.
	WCNM	Lock Haven, Pa.
	WGLL	Mercersburg, Pa.
	WMJW	Nanticoke, Pa.
	WCTX	Palmyra, Pa.
★	WJCR	Washington, Pa.
	WGIT	Hormigueros, P.R.
	WZOL	Luquillo, P.R.
	WKWQ-FM	Batesburg, S.C.
	WTWE	Manning, S.C.
	WJYR	Myrtle Beach, S.C.
	KURO	Huron, S.D.
	WMAK-FM	Hendersonville, Tenn.
†	WLLX	Minor Hill, Tenn.
	KDSI	Alice, Tex.
	KTAW	College Station, Tex.
	KEMM	Commerce, Tex.
†	KDCI	Devine, Tex.
†	KNES	Fairfield, Tex.
†	KTFA	Groves, Tex.
	KTNR	Kennedy, Tex.
	KETX-FM	Livingston, Tex.
	KTBC	Nacogdoches, Tex.
	KNBT	New Braunfels, Tex.
†	----	Seabrook, Tex.
	KVRN-FM	Sonora, Tex.
	KRGT	Taylor, Tex.
	KROZ	Tyler, Tex.
	KTLE-FM	Tooele, Utah
	WDYL	Chester, Va.
	KCRK-FM	Colville, Wash.
★	WVWC	Buckhannon, W.V.
★	WQAB	Phillipi, W.V.
†	WFCL-FM	Clintonville, Wis.
	WRLS-FM	Hayward, Wis.
	WKKB	Manitowoc, Wis.
	WRJC-FM	Mauston, Wis.
	WMEQ	Menomonie, Wis.
	WFNY	Racine, Wis.
	WMAD	Sun Prairie, Wis.
★	CJAY-FM	Calgary, Alta.
	CJAZ-FM	Vancouver, B.C.
	CITI	Winnipeg, Man.
	CJOZ	Bonavista, Nfld.
	CKPC-FM	Brantford, Ont.
	CFTI	Timmins, Ont.
	CFMQ	Regina, Sask.

92.3 (222) BC

	WLWI	Montgomery, Ala.
	KEZC	Glendale, Ariz.
	KFXE	Pine Bluff, Ark.
	KPDJ	Eureka, Calif.
	KFAC-FM	Los Angeles, Calif.
	KSJO	San Jose, Calif.
	KREX-FM	Grand Junction, Colo.
	WWKA	Orlando, Fla.
	KULA	Waipahu, Haw.
	KBBK-FM	Boise, Id.
	WGTC	Bloomington, Ind.
	WYCA	Hammond, Ind.
	KOEL-FM	Oelwein, Ia.
	KOEZ	Newton, Kan.
	WCKW	La Place, La.
†	WRDO-FM	Augusta, Me.
†★	WUMF-FM	Farmington, Me.

WYST-FM Baltimore, Md.
WCXI-FM Detroit, Mich.
† WJPD-FM Ishpeming, Mich.
WIL-FM St. Louis, Mo.
KQRR Ronan, Mont.
KEZO Omaha, Neb.
KOMP Las Vegas, Nev.
KRST Albuquerque, N.M.
WKTU New York, N.Y.
WFLY Troy, N.Y.
WCSE Asheboro, N.C.
WRQC Cleveland Heights, O.
WXGT Columbus, O.
KGON Portland, Ore.
WRRN Warren, Pa.
WPRO-FM Providence, R.I.
WDEF-FM Chattanooga, Tenn.
WYNU Milan, Tenn.
KFIM El Paso, Tex.
† KIJN-FM Farwell, Tex.
KNFM Midland, Tex.
WXLK Roanoke, Va.
CKOZ Corner Brook, Nfld.
XHMMP Mexicali, B.C.

92.5 (223) BC

† ---- Eager, Ariz.
KDDB Paso Robles, Calif.
KAER Sacramento, Calif.
KGRE Greeley, Colo.
WWYZ-FM Waterbury, Conn.
WFYN-FM Key West, Fla.
WPAP-FM Panama City, Fla.
WDEK De Kalb, Ill.
†* KNBU Baldwin City, Kan.
† KBMG Phillipsburg, Kan.
WBKR Owensboro, Ky.
WLYT Haverhill, Mass.
KQRS Golden Valley, Minn.
†* KSMR Winona, Minn.
WQST Forest, Miss.
KSYN Joplin, Mo.
KPQX Havre, Mont.
WMJQ Rochester, N.Y.
WYFL Henderson, N.C.
WDJQ Alliance, O.
WWEZ Cincinnati, O.
WMHE Toledo, O.
KKNG Oklahoma City, Okla.
KJSN Klamath Falls, Ore.
WXTU Philadelphia, Pa.
WORO Corozal, P.R.
WESC-FM Greenville, S.C.
KELO-FM Sioux Falls, S.D.
KAFM Dallas, Tex.
KKBQ-FM Pasadena, Tex.
KSUB-FM Cedar City, Utah
WQUS Winchester, Va.
KLSY Bellevue, Wash.
WBKV-FM West Bend, Wis.
KPCQ-FM Powell, Wyo.
CJAX Edmonton, Alta.
CFQR Montreal, Que.
XHRM Tijuana, B.C.

92.7 (224) A

WCRQ-FM Arab, Ala.
WKQK Eufaula, Ala.
WJBB-FM Haleyville, Ala.
WHTB Talladega, Ala.
WTUG Tuscaloosa, Ala.
KLYR-FM Clarksville, Ark.
† ---- Conway, Ark.
KDQN-FM De Queen, Ark.
KWYN-FM Wynne, Ark.
KJAZ Alameda, Calif.
KLPC-FM Lompoc, Calif.
KBOQ Marina, Calif.
KMFB-FM Mendocino, Calif.
† KRIJ Paradise, Calif.
KZIQ-FM Ridgecrest, Calif.
KWDJ Riverside, Calif.
KROG Sonora, Calif.
KSUE-FM Susanville, Calif.
KNJO Thousand Oaks, Calif.
KMTS Glenwood Springs, Colo.
KCRT-FM Trinidad, Colo.
WGMD Rehoboth Beach, Del.
WSVE Green Cove Springs, Fla.
WMFQ Ocala, Fla.
WQLM-FM Punta Gorda, Fla.
WRIT Stuart, Fla.
WKKZ Dublin, Ga.
† ---- St. Simons Island, Ga.
† KJAD Lihue, Haw.
KORT-FM Grangeville, Id.
KSRA-FM Salmon, Id.
WRAJ-FM Anna, Ill.
WSEX Arlington Heights, Ill.
WGBQ Galesburg, Ill.
WMLA Le Roy, Ill.
WTJY Taylorville, Ill.
WADM-FM Decatur, Ind.
† WZWZ Kokomo, Ind.
‡ WXUS Lafayette, Ind.
† WLSO Spencer, Ind.
KLGA-FM Algona, Ia.
KIDA Ida Grove, Ia.
KOSG Osage, Ia.
† KTWA Ottumwa, Ia.
KZOC Osage City, Kan.
WCAK Catlettsburg, Ky.
WMIK-FM Middlesboro, Ky.
WQCK Clinton, La.
KWJM Farmerville, La.
KJEF-FM Jennings, La.
KLPL-FM Lake Providence, La.
KJAE Leesville, La.
KJVC Mansfield, La.
KTKC Springhill, La.
WQDY-FM Calais, Me.
WOXO-FM Norway, Me.
WMJS Prince Frederick, Md.
WMVY Tisbury, Mass.
WMMQ Charlotte, Mich.
WDZZ-FM Flint, Mich.
KXRA-FM Alexandria, Minn.
WQAZ Cleveland, Miss.
WKRA-FM Holly Springs, Miss.
KLDN Eldon, Mo.
† KYLS Ironton, Mo.
KMAL Malden, Mo.
KLRS-FM Mountain Grove, Mo.
† KMCM-FM Miles City, Mont.
KYZZ Wolf Point, Mont.
KBRB-FM Ainsworth, Neb.
† ---- Ely, Neb.
† KBXS Ely, Nev.
KPAH Tonopah, Nev.
KWNA-FM Winnemucca, Nev.
WOBM-FM Toms River, N.J.
KLCJ Bayard, N.M.
† KALG-FM La Luz, N.M.
KQAY-FM Tucumcari, N.M.
WLEZ Elmira, N.Y.
WLIR Garden City, N.Y.
WYUT-FM Herkimer, N.Y.
WKGL Middletown, N.Y.
WPAC Ogdensburg, N.Y.
WBCO-FM Bucyrus, O.
† KKBS Guymon, Okla.
† KGBR Gold Beach, Ore.
† WQKY Emporium, Pa.
WJSM-FM Martinsburg, Pa.
WHTF Starview, Pa.
WWBD-FM Bamberg, S.C.
KGFX-FM Pierre, S.D.
WHBT Harriman, Tenn.
KIVY-FM Crockett, Tex.
KINL Eagle Pass, Tex.
KODK Kingsville, Tex.
KFIX Laredo, Tex.
† ---- Shamrock, Tex.
KJAK Slaton, Tex.
KUIN Vernal, Utah
WKVT-FM Brattleboro, Vt.
WABN-FM Abingdon, Va.
WUVA Charlottesville, Va.
KOMW-FM Omak, Wash.
KENE-FM Toppenish, Wash.
WVHF-FM Clarksburg, W.V.
WPMW Mullens, W.V.
WAUN Kewaunee, Wis.
† WLDY-FM Ladysmith, Wis.
† WRJQ Tomahawk, Wis.
WDUX-FM Waupaca, Wis.
† KLGM Buffalo, Wyo.
KIQZ Rawlins, Wyo.
CBWY Jackhead, Man.
CJBX London, Ont.
CIGM Sudbury, Ont.

92.9 (225) BC

WBLX Mobile, Ala.
KAFF Flagstaff, Ariz.
KWFM Tucson, Ariz.
KREO Healdsburg, Calif.
KONG-FM Visalia, Calif.
KSPZ Colorado Springs, Colo.
WZGC Atlanta, Ga.
WGOV-FM Valdosta, Ga.
WSEI Olney, Ill.
WNDU-FM South Bend, Ind.
KFMD Dubuque, Ia.
WVLK-FM Lexington, Ky.
WPBC Bangor, Me.
WBOS Brookline, Mass.
WKJF-FM Cadillac, Mich.
* WSCD-FM Duluth, Minn.
† WCLL-FM Wesson, Miss.
KGRC Hannibal, Mo.
KLFM Great Falls, Mont.
KMAZ Beatrice, Neb.
KMAZ Beatrice, Neb.
KMOR Scottsbluff, Neb.
KTZA Artesia, N.M.
KRWN Farmington, N.M.
WBUF Buffalo, N.Y.
KYYY Bismarck, N.D.
KKXL-FM Grand Forks, N.D.
WJAI Eaton, O.
KBEZ Tulsa, Okla.
KBKN Astoria, Ore.
WPNT Pittsburgh, Pa.
WYZZ Wilkes Barre, Pa.
WTPM Aguadilla, P.R.
WDSC-FM Dillon, S.C.
WZEZ Nashville, Tenn.
KBIL San Angelo, Tex.
KITY San Antonio, Tex.
KNIN-FM Wichita Falls, Tex.
KBLQ-FM Logan, Utah
WEZF Burlington, Vt.
WFOG-FM Suffolk, Va.
KISM Bellingham, Wash.
KREM-FM Spokane, Wash.
† WCWV Summerville, W.V.
CFQX-FM Selkirk, Man.

93.1 (226) BC

KJOK Yuma, Ariz.
KZLE Batesville, Ark.
* KHDX Conway, Ark.
† KXGO Arcata, Calif.
KKHR Los Angeles, Calif.
KOSO Patterson, Calif.
KQIX Grand Junction, Colo.
WTMI Miami, Fla.
WEAS-FM Savannah, Ga.
KQMQ Honolulu, Haw.
KIZN New Plymouth, Id.
WXRT Chicago, Ill.
WNAP Indianapolis, Ind.

KGLS	Pratt, Kan.
KQID	Alexandria, La.
WMGX	Portland, Me.
WPOC	Baltimore, Md.
WHYN-FM	Springfield, Mass.
WDRQ	Detroit, Mich.
† WIMK	Iron Mountain, Mich.
KXLP	New Ulm, Minn.
† ----	Bozeman, Mont.
KGCH-FM	Sidney, Mont.
KRVN-FM	Lexington, Neb.
KUDO	Las Vegas, Nev.
WPAT-FM	Paterson, N.J.
WNTQ	Syracuse, N.Y.
WSEZ	Winston Salem, N.C.
WZAK	Cleveland, O.
KSND	Springfield, Ore.
KRCS	Sturgis, S.D.
* KKYA	Yankton, S.D.
KQIZ-FM	Amarillo, Tex.
KAMZ	El Paso, Tex.
KTYL-FM	Tyler, Tex.
CKBW-2	Shelburn, N.S.
CHAY	Barrie, Ont.
CKCU	Ottawa, Ont.
CHLQ	Challottetown, P.E.

93.3 (227) BC

KDKB	Mesa, Ariz.
KECR	El Cajon, Calif.
KYA	San Francisco, Calif.
KZOZ	San Luis Obispo, Calif.
KTCL	Ft. Collins, Colo.
KSEC	Lamar, Colo.
†* WFAR	Danbury, Conn.
WOJC	Tampa, Fla.
WVFJ-FM	Manchester, Ga.
WKZW	Peoria, Ill.
WAWK-FM	Kendallville, Ind.
KMGK	Des Moines, Ia.
WKYQ	Paducah, Ky.
WQUE-FM	New Orleans, La.
WSNE	Taunton, Mass.
WCPC-FM	Houston, Miss.
KLSI	Kansas City, Mo.
KYYA	Billings, Mont.
KDXT	Missoula, Mont.
KOB-FM	Albuquerque, N.M.
* WBKT	Brockport, N.Y.
WWSE	Jamestown, N.Y.
WBBO-FM	Forest City, N.C.
WITN-FM	Washington, N.C.
KSJM	Jamestown, N.D.
WKKJ	Chillicothe, O.
* WAKW	Cincinnati, O.
WWWM	Sylvania, O.
WQOD	Youngstown, O.
KTEN-FM	Ada, Okla.
WMMR	Philadelphia, Pa.
WOQI	Ponce, P.R.
WBGY-FM	Tullahoma, Tenn.
KIXS-FM	Killeen, Tex.
KBAT	Midland, Tex.
KYKR-FM	Port Arthur, Tex.
KAOC-FM	Port Lavaca, Tex.
KWHO-FM	Salt Lake City, Utah
WFLS-FM	Fredericksburg, Va.
KUBE	Seattle, Wash.
KEXI	Walla Walla, Wash.
WIZM-FM	La Crosse, Wis.
WQFM	Milwaukee, Wis.
XHQQ-FM	Monterrey, N.L.

93.5 (228) A

WQGL	Butler, Ala.
† WEGN-FM	Evergreen, Ala.
WGEA-FM	Geneva, Ala.
† KXAZ	Page, Ariz.
KVWM-FM	Show Low, Ariz.
† KBKG	Corning, Ark.
KBFC	Forrest City, Ark.
KHBM-FM	Monticello, Ark.
‡ KXGO	Arcata, Calif.
KHIP	Hollister, Calif.
KNTF	Ontario, Calif.
KFOX	Redondo Beach, Calif.
KPOP	Roseville, Calif.
KALQ-FM	Alamosa, Colo.
† KLMC	Leadville, Colo.
WSEA	Georgetown, Del.
WSWN-FM	Belle Glade, Fla.
WRGI	Naples, Fla.
‡ WJST	Port St. Joe, Fla.
WGYL	Vero Beach, Fla.
† WBBK-FM	Blakely, Ga.
WVOH-FM	Hazlehurst, Ga.
WSNT-FM	Sandersville, Ga.
† WLKC	St. Mary's, Ga.
KIPO-FM	Lihue, Haw.
KSKI-FM	Sun Valley, Id.
WAJP	Joliet, Ill.
WITT	Tuscola, Ill.
† WWHC	Hartford City, Ind.
‡ WZWZ	Kokomo, Ind.
† WXUS	Lafayette, Ind.
WQTY	Linton, Ind.
† KBQC	Bettendorp, Ia.
KDWD	Burlington, Ia.
KLKC-FM	Parsons, Kan.
† KZED	Wellington, Kan.
WYWY-FM	Barbourville, Ky.
WMMG	Brandenburg, Ky.
WAIN-FM	Columbia, Ky.
KVPI-FM	Ville Platte, La.
WMCM	Rockland, Me.
WATZ-FM	Alpena, Mich.
WCLX	Boyne City, Mich.
WZRK	Hancock, Mich.
WHMI-FM	Howell, Mich.
WRCI	Midland, Mich.
WNBY-FM	Newberry, Mich.
KBMO-FM	Benson, Minn.
WXIY	Bay Springs, Miss.
* WHJT	Clinton, Miss.
KRFG	Greenfield, Mo.
KTUF	Kirksville, Mo.
KYLC	Osage Beach, Mo.
KTRX	Tarkio, Mo.
KLAN	Glasgow, Mont.
KTTT-FM	Columbus, Neb.
KLKO	Elko, Neb.
‡ KEZH	Hastings, Neb.
KLKO	Elko, Nev.
WMWV	Conway, N.H.
KTNT	Rudioso, N.M.
WSCG	Corinth, N.Y.
WRVW	Hudson, N.Y.
WVBR-FM	Ithaca, N.Y.
WRTN	New Rochelle, N.Y.
WAES-FM	Remsen, N.Y.
WDZD	Shallotte, N.C.
WRQN	Bowling Green, O.
KWHW-FM	Altus, Okla.
KSIW-FM	Woodward, Okla.
WQYX	Clearfield, Pa.
WKCD	Mechanicsburg, Pa.
WSBG	Stroudsburg, Pa.
† WYXZ	Allendale, S.C.
WCEZ	Columbia, S.C.
* WWWZ	Summerville, S.C.
KKRC-FM	Sioux Falls, S.D.
WKBL-FM	Covington, Tenn.
WLIL-FM	Lenoir City, Tenn.
WKWX	Savannah, Tenn.
KRDO	Breckenridge, Tex.
KCKR	Crockett, Tex.
KIKT	Greenville, Tex.
KZEZ	St. George, Utah
WCFR-FM	Springfield, Vt.
WLSD-FM	Big Stone Gap, Va.
WBBC	Blackstone, Va.
WJLM	Salem, Va.
WSGM	Staunton, Va.
KOZI-FM	Chelan, Wash.
WCST-FM	Berkeley Springs, W.V.
WJMT-FM	Merrill, Wis.
WNBK	New London, Wis.
CBCL	London, Ont.
CBIM	Iles De-la-madeleine, Que.
CBM-FM	Montreal, Que.

93.7 (229) BC

WDJC	Birmingham, Ala.
KRQQ	Tucson, Ariz.
KISR	Ft. Smith, Ark.
KFMF	Chico, Calif.
KCHV	Coachella, Calif.
KFYE	Fresno, Calif.
KDB-FM	Santa Barbara, Calif.
KXRC	Craig, Colo.
WLVH	Hartford, Conn.
WSTW	Wilmington, Del.
WFUZ	Ocala, Fla.
KZBQ	Pocatello, Id.
WJCD-FM	Seymour, Ind.
KKRL	Carroll, Ia.
KYEZ	Salina, Kan.
WAMX	Ashland, Ky.
KMBQ	Shreveport, La.
WCGY	Lawrence, Mass.
WJFM	Grand Rapids, Mich.
WAYL	Minneapolis, Minn.
WQID	Biloxi, Miss.
KSD-FM	St. Louis, Mo.
KBOZ-FM	Bozeman, Mont.
KQNM	Gallup, N.M.
WBLK-FM	De Pew, N.Y.
WMYK	Elizabeth City, N.C.
WDAY-FM	Fargo, N.D.
KIZZ	Minot, N.D.
WFCJ	Miamisburg, O.
WMVO-FM	Mt. Vernon, O.
KTMT	Medford, Ore.
KPDQ-FM	Portland, Ore.
WBZZ	Pittsburgh, Pa.
WZNT	San Juan, P.R.
WFBC-FM	Greenville, S.C.
KWYR-FM	Winner, S.D.
KLBJ-FM	Austin, Tex.
KRLY	Houston, Tex.
KSEL-FM	Lubbock, Tex.
KKWZ	Richfield, Utah
KDRK	Spokane, Wash.
* WSHC	Shepherstown, W.V.
WEKZ-FM	Monroe, Wis.
* CKUA-FM-1	Calgary, Alta.

93.9 (230) BC

KSOJ	Flagstaff, Ariz.
KZLA-FM	Los Angeles, Calif.
‡ KRLT	South Lake Tahoe, Calif.
KILO	Colorado Springs, Colo.
WKYS	Washington, D. C.
WWWL	Miami Beach, Fla.
WMTM-FM	Moultrie, Ga.
KPIG	Honolulu, Haw.
WLAK	Chicago, Ill.
KRNA	Iowa City, Ia.
KTTL	Dodge City, Kan.
WKTG	Madisonville, Ky.
WAYU	Lewiston, Me.
KWPM-FM	West Plains, Mo.
* WNYC-FM	New York, N.Y.
WXKZ	Norwich, N.Y.
* WPLT	Plattsburgh, N.Y.
WBAG	Burlington, N.C.
KSPI-FM	Stillwater, Okla.
KKLS-FM	Rapid City, S.D.
KEXX-FM	Corpus Christi, Tex.
KEZB	El Paso, Tex.
KWLW	San Angelo, Tex.
WMEV-FM	Marion, Va.
WDOR-FM	Sturgeon Bay, Wis.
KTAK	Riverton, Wyo.
* CHOZ	St. John's, Nfld.

CFMO	Ottawa, Ont.
CKJY	Windsor, Ont.
CFCQ-FM	Three Rivers, Que.

94.1 (231) BC

WAQT	Carrollton, Ala.
KXKQ	Safford, Ariz.
KLPQ	Little Rock, Ark.
KLYD	Bakersfield, Calif.
* KPFA	Berkeley, Calif.
KFSD-FM	San Diego, Calif.
KUBC-FM	Montrose, Colo.
WVFM	Lakeland, Fla.
WMEZ	Pensacola, Fla.
WCHY	Savannah, Ga.
WQXI-FM	Smyrna, Ga.
KBXL	Caldwell, Id.
WMIX-FM	Mt. Vernon, Ill.
WGFA-FM	Watseka, Ill.
KFKF-FM	Kansas City, Kan.
WIBM-FM	Jackson, Mich.
WCCA	Mc Comb, Miss.
KOPR	Butte, Mont.
WOW-FM	Omaha, Neb.
KNEB-FM	Scottsbluff, Neb.
KXTZ	Henderson, Nev.
KWXL	Albuquerque, N.M.
KZOR	Hobbs, N.M.
WLXN	Lexington, N.C.
WHBC-FM	Canton, O.
WSAI-FM	Cincinnati, O.
KXIQ	Bend, Ore.
WYSP	Philadelphia, Pa.
WQKX	Sunbury, Pa.
WOYE-FM	Mayaguez, P.R.
WHJY	Providence, R.I.
KSDN-FM	Aberdeen, S.D.
KBUY-FM	Amarillo, Tex.
KQXY	Beaumont, Tex.
KESS	Ft. Worth, Tex.
KLCY	Salt Lake City, Utah
WKEZ	Yorktown, Va.
KCLK-FM	Clarkston, Wash.
KMPS-FM	Seattle, Wash.
WQZP-FM	Keyser, W.V.
WRJL	Oak Hill, W.V.
WIAL	Eau Claire, Wis.
WMLW	Watertown, Wis.
CBYK	Kamloops, B.C.
CBL-FM	Toronto, Ont.
CIMH	Sept Iles, Que.
CJGL	Swift Current, Sask.
XET-FM	Monterrey, N.L.
XHNOE	Nuevo Laredo, Tams.

94.3 (232) A

WXLE	Abbeville, Ala.
KAMO-FM	Rogers, Ark.
† KEWB	Anderson, Calif.
KZNS	Barstow, Calif.
KCRE-FM	Crescent City, Calif.
KIKF	Garden Grove, Calif.
KNCO-FM	Grass Valley, Calif.
KNGT	Jackson, Calif.
KGIL-FM	San Fernando, Calif.
WYBC-FM	New Haven, Conn.
WQPD	Lake City, Fla.
WMUM	Marathon, Fla.
WNJY	Riviera Beach, Fla.
WADZ	Americus, Ga.
† WMTZ	Martinez, Ga.
KVIB	Mukawao, Haw.
KADQ	Rexburg, Id.
WRMS-FM	Beardstown, Ill.
WTXR	Chillicothe, Ill.
WJKL	Elgin, Ill.
WJVM	Sterling, Ill.
WJNZ	Greencastle, Ind.
† WKMD	Loogootee, Ind.
WNZE	Plymouth, Ind.
WRCR	Rushville, Ind.
KVDB-FM	Sioux Center, Ia.
WHIC-FM	Hardinsburg, Ky.
WIFX-FM	Jenkins, Ky.
KTRY-FM	Bastrop, La.
KZZQ	Galliano, La.
WBYC-FM	Biddeford, Me.
‡ WKSQ	Ellsworth, Me.
WICO-FM	Salisbury, Md.
KEZZ	Aitkin, Minn.
KSDM	International Falls, Minn.
KMSR	Sauk Center, Minn.
KDOM-FM	Windom, Minn.
WKCU-FM	Corinth, Miss.
WBAD	Leland, Miss.
† KZMO-FM	California, Mo.
KCLU-FM	Rolla, Mo.
† ----	Webb City, Mo.
WJLK-FM	Asbury Park, N.J.
WWOC	Avalon, N.J.
KKEE	Alamogordo, N.M.
KDEM	Deming, N.M.
KRTN-FM	Raton, N.M.
WLVY	Elmira, N.Y.
WBPM	Kingston, N.Y.
WCTO	Smithtown, N.Y.
WRQR	Farmville, N.C.
WZKB	Wallace, N.C.
WKKI	Celina, O.
WFCB	Chillicothe, O.
WEYQ	Marietta, O.
WDIF	Marion, O.
KNFB	Nowata, Okla.
KQBC	Okmulgee, Okla.
WCDL-FM	Carbondale, Pa.
WBXQ	Cresson, Pa.
WKSL	Greencastle, Pa.
WKBI-FM	Ridgeway, Pa.
WEOZ	Saegertown, Pa.
WPUB-FM	Camden, S.C.
† WBJX	Goose Creek, S.C.
WATP-FM	Marion, S.C.
KGKG	Brookings, S.D.
WGSQ	Cookeville, Tenn.
WLVS	Germantown, Tenn.
WJJM-FM	Lewisburg, Tenn.
WIST	Lobelville, Tenn.
WETQ	Oak Ridge, Tenn.
WJTT	Red Bank, Tenn.
WDBL-FM	Springfield, Tenn.
† KHER	Crystal City, Tex.
KLKE	Del Rio, Tex.
KWCB	Floresville, Tex.
KPJH	Ft. Stockton, Tex.
KPFM	Kerrville, Tex.
KRCT	Ozona, Tex.
KSEY-FM	Seymour, Tex.
WHGC	Bennington, Vt.
WQRA	Warrenton, Va.
WERL-FM	Eagle River, Wis.
WPRE-FM	Prairie Du Chien, Wis.
CHIQ	Winnipeg, Man.
CJSD	Thunder Bay, Ont.
CKMF	Montreal, Que.

94.5 (233) BC

WAPI-FM	Birmingham, Ala.
KOOL-FM	Phoenix, Ariz.
† KBGX	Alturas, Calif.
KWSS	Gilroy, Calif.
KWNE	Ukiah, Calif.
WWLV	Daytona Beach, Fla.
WCVU	Naples, Fla.
† WJST	Port St. Joe, Fla.
† WBYZ	Baxley, Ga.
WLRW	Champaign, Ill.
KKEZ	Ft. Dodge, Ia.
KJCK-FM	Junction City, Kan.
KEZU	Scott City, Kan.
WLAP-FM	Lexington, Ky.
KSMB	Lafayette, La.
KROK	Shreveport, La.
† WKSQ	Ellsworth, Me.
WCOZ	Boston, Mass.
WJBL-FM	Holland, Mich.
WCEN-FM	Mt. Pleasant, Mass.
KSTP-FM	St. Paul, Minn.
KRXL	Kirksville, Mo.
KPBM-FM	Poplar Bluff, Mo.
KNUW	Great Falls, Mont.
WCHR	Trenton, N.J.
KOVO	Gallup, N.M.
* WNED-FM	Buffalo, N.Y.
WYYY	Syracuse, N.Y.
WSRQ	Eden, N.C.
KQDY	Bismarck, N.D.
WOSE	Port Clinton, O.
KBMC	Eugene, Ore.
WDAC	Lancaster, Pa.
WWSW-FM	Pittsburgh, Pa.
WMUU-FM	Greenville, S.C.
KGAF-FM	Gainesville, Tex.
KELT	Harlingen, Tex.
KLEF	Houston, Tex.
KFMX	Lubbock, Tex.
KMXL	Logan, Utah
WRVQ	Richmond, Va.
KATS	Yakima, Wash.
WKTI	Milwaukee, Wis.
KAWY	Casper, Wyo.
† CKBW-1	Liverpool, N.S.
CKO-FM-8	Regina, Sask.
XHTA-FM	Piedras Negras, Coah.

94.7 (234) BC

KZZZ	Kingman, Ariz.
KMET	Los Angeles, Calif.
KBVL	Boulder, Colo.
WDSD	Dover, Del.
† KWXX	Hilo, Haw.
KUMU-FM	Honolulu, Haw.
WLS-FM	Chicago, Ill.
WFBQ	Indianapolis, Ind.
WXID	Mayfield, Ky.
WLTT	Bethesda, Md.
WMAS-FM	Springfield, Mass.
WMJC	Birmingham, Mich.
WTYX	Jackson, Miss.
KSHE	Crestwood, Mo.
KTTS-FM	Springfield, Mo.
KNEN	Norfolk, Neb.
KNIS	Carson City, Nev.
WFME	Newark, N.J.
WQDR	Raleigh, N.C.
* WSIF	Wilkesboro, N.C.
KYTN	Grand Forks, N.D.
WSNY	Columbus, O.
KEBC	Oklahoma City, Okla.
WGSX	Bayamon, P.R.
KSET-FM	El Paso, Tex.
KIXY-FM	San Angelo, Tex.

94.9 (235) BC

WKSJ-FM	Mobile, Ala.
KJYK	Tucson, Ariz.
KADL	Pine Bluff, Ark.
KBZT	San Diego, Calif.
KSAN-FM	San Francisco, Calif.
KBOS	Tulare, Calif.
WINZ-FM	Miami Beach, Fla.
WTNT-FM	Tallahassee, Fla.
WYNF	Tampa, Fla.
WPCH	Atlanta, Ga.
KFXD-FM	Nampa, Id.
KPKY	Pocatello, Id.
WAAG	Galesburg, Ill.
WYER-FM	Mt. Carmel, Ill.
KGGO	Des Moines, Ia.
WSOX-FM	West Yarmouth, Mass.
WVIC-FM	Lansing, Mich.
KQDS-FM	Duluth, Minn.
KCMO-FM	Kansas City, Mo.
KYSS-FM	Missoula, Mont.
KODY-FM	North Platte, Neb.
WHOM	Mt. Washington, N.H.

KWYK-FM Aztec, N.M.
KBIM-FM Roswell, N.M.
WLLT Fairfield, O.
WDBN Medina, O.
† WRSD Folsom, Pa.
* WMSP Harrisburg, Pa.
KQAA Aberdeen, S.D.
WIKQ Greeneville, Tenn.
KWJS Arlington, Tex.
KOYE Laredo, Tex.
KBRE-FM Cedar City, Utah
KLRZ Provo, Utah
WPVR Roanoke, Va.
WWRN Virginia Beach, Va.
KIOK Richland, Wash.
* KUOW Seattle, Wash.
† WCKV Ceredo, W.V.
WLVE Baraboo, Wis.
KROE-FM Sheridan, Wyo.
* CKUA-FM Edmonton, Alta.
CKPE Sydney, N.S.
CKQT Oshawa, Ont.
CIMF Hull, Que.
ZFB-FM Hamilton, Bermuda

95.1 (236) BC

WNDA Huntsville, Ala.
† KRIM Winslow, Ariz.
KTTI Yuma, Ariz.
KAMS Mammoth Spring, Ark.
†* KAHS Arcata, Calif.
KPAY-FM Chico, Calif.
KOKQ Oakdale, Calif.
KQLH San Bernardino, Calif.
KBBY Ventura, Calif.
KRDO-FM Colorado Springs, Colo.
WRKI Brookfield, Conn.
WJAX-FM Jacksonville, Fla.
KAOI Wailuku, Haw.
WDZQ Decatur, Ill.
WFWQ Ft. Wayne, Ind.
†* WVUR-FM Valparaiso, Ind.
KICT Wichita, Kan.
WGGC Glasgow, Ky.
WRBS Baltimore, Md.
* WNRC Dudley, Mass.
* WFBE Flint, Mich.
KWOA-FM Worthington, Minn.
WQNZ Natchez, Miss.
KSDY Sidney, Mont.
WAYV Atlantic City, N.J.
WYLF South Bristol, N.Y.
WROQ Charlotte, N.C.
WRNS Kinston, N.C.
WZZO Bethlehem, Pa.
WIKZ Chambersburg, Pa.
WEDA-FM Grove City, Pa.
WRPC San German, P.R.
WSSX-FM Charleston, S.C.
KSQY Deadwood, S.D.
KZZB Beaumont, Tex.
KCWM Victoria, Tex.
† WJKC Christiansted, V.I.
WXIL Parkersburg, W.V.
WJZQ Kenosha, Wis.
WLST Marinette, Wis.
† ---- Laramie, Wyo.
CJAY-1 Banff, Alta.
CBEE-FM Chatham, Ont.

95.3 (237) A

† WASZ Ashland, Ala.
WQIM Prattville, Ala.
‡ WELR-FM Roanoke, Ala.
WJDB-FM Thomasville, Ala.
† ---- Fairbanks, Alas.
KKRK Douglas, Ariz.
KJKK Murfreesboro, Ark.
KEED Paris, Ark.
† KOTZ Fort Bragg, Calif.
KRVE Los Gatos, Calif.
KEDY Mt. Shasta, Calif.
KPGA Pismo Beach, Calif.
KUIC Vacaville, Calif.
KDTA-FM Delta, Colo.
WTLN-FM Apopka, Fla.
* WSOR Ft. Myers, Fla.
† WOOT Homosassa Springs, Fla.
WDAX-FM Mc Rae, Ga.
† WTGA Thomaston, Ga.
KLER-FM Orofino, Id.
KPND Sandpoint, Id.
WRXX Centralia, Ill.
WRKX Ottawa, Ill.
WGLO Pekin, Ill.
WRTL-FM Rantoul, Ill.
WYFE-FM Winnebago, Ill.
WWET Monticello, Ind.
WUME-FM Paoli, Ind.
WNDI-FM Sullivan, Ind.
KOUR-FM Independence, Ia.
KIFG-FM Iowa Falls, Ia.
KIMI Keokuk, Ia.
KMAQ-FM Maquoketa, Ia.
KOAK-FM Red Oak, Ia.
KCII-FM Washington, Ia.
KCKS Concordia, Kan.
WIOK Falmouth, Ky.
WMSK-FM Morganfield, Ky.
KWKI Bayou Vista, La.
KASO-FM Minden, La.
* WMOS Bath, Me.
WALZ Machias, Me.
WHRB Cambridge, Mass.
WRSI Greenfield, Mass.
WQTE Adrian, Mich.
WDFP Battle Creek, Mich.
WRNN Clare, Mich.
WEGS Gaylord, Mich.
WAOR Niles, Mich.
WCNF Whitehall, Mich.
KCPI-FM Albert Lea, Minn.
† KLKS Breezy Point, Minn.
KVLR Detroit Lakes, Minn.
KLFD-FM Litchfield, Minn.
KNOF St. Paul, Minn.
KAGE-FM Winona, Minn.
WAFM Amory, Miss.
WVIM-FM Coldwater, Miss.
WADI Corinth, Miss.
WKZB Drew, Miss.
† WLUN Lumberton, Miss.
KDKD-FM Clinton, Mo.
KHDN-FM Hardin, Mont.
KTNC-FM Falls City, Neb.
KXSS Lincoln, Neb.
KSID-FM Sidney, Neb.
KRJC Elko, Nev.
KLLT Grants, N.M.
KNIT Portales, N.M.
WIGS-FM Gouverneur, N.Y.
WAQX Manlius, N.Y.
WSRH Southampton, N.Y.
WOBR-FM Wanchese, N.C.
WKTN Kenton, O.
WLKR-FM Norwalk, O.
WBZI Xenia, O.
KCLI Clinton, Okla.
† KITX Hugo, Okla.
† KMGZ Lawton, Okla.
† KBKR-FM Baker, Ore.
KURY-FM Brookings, Ore.
† KRNN Creswell, Ore.
KBOY-FM Medford, Ore.
KIJK Prineville, Ore.
WDNH-FM Honesdale, Pa.
WSPI Shamokin, Pa.
WTTC-FM Towanda, Pa.
WYTX Washington, Pa.
KNEY Pierre, S.D.
WTBG Brownsville, Tenn.
WNKX Clinton, Tenn.
WDEH-FM Sweetwater, Tenn.
KWKI Big Spring, Tex.
KIXV Brady, Tex.
KMRE Dumas, Tex.
KNIF Gilmer, Tex.
KMMK Mc Kinney, Tex.
† KVWG-FM Pearsall, Tex.
WNHV-FM White River Junction, Vt.
WQMC Charlottesville, Va.
WIXV Front Royal, Va.
WPVA-FM Petersburg, Va.
KXLE-FM Ellensburg, Wash.
KGHO-FM Hoquiam, Wash.
† WELK Elkins, W.V.
WXRO Beaver Dam, Wis.
WGMO Shell Lake, Wis.
CKDS Hamilton, Ont.
CJMF Quebec, Que.

95.5 (238) BC

WTVY-FM Dothan, Ala.
KQYT Phoenix, Ariz.
‡ KYNO-FM Fresno, Calif.
KLOS Los Angeles, Calif.
WOVV Ft. Pierce, Fla.
WVFK Key West, Fla.
WNGC Athens, Ga.
WIXV Savannah, Ga.
KAIM-FM Honolulu, Haw.
WMET Chicago, Ill.
WFMS Indianapolis, Ind.
KGLI Sioux City, Ia.
KDCK Dodge City, Kan.
WQHY Prestonburg, Ky.
WPGC-FM Morningside, Md.
WCZY Detroit, Mich.
WLIN Jackson, Miss.
KJEZ Poplar Bluff, Mo.
KQUY Butte, Mont.
KSDZ Gordon, Neb.
KILA Henderson, Nev.
KNEV Reno, Nev.
KSNM Santa Fe, N.M.
WROW-FM Albany, N.Y.
WPLJ New York, N.Y.
WHPE-FM High Point, N.C.
† KQDJ-FM Jamestown, N.D.
WCLV Cleveland, O.
WHOK Lancaster, O.
KWEN Tulsa, Okla.
KXL-FM Portland, Ore.
WKYE Johnstown, Pa.
WBRU Providence, R.I.
WSM-FM Nashville, Tenn.
KOKE-FM Austin, Tex.
KZFM Corpus Christi, Tex.
KIPR-FM Diboll, Tex.
KLAQ El Paso, Tex.
KVRP-FM Haskell, Tex.
KNFO Waco, Tex.
KJQN-FM Ogden, Utah
WIFC Wausau, Wis.
KTRS Casper, Wyo.
XHRG-FM Ciudad Acuna, Coah.

95.7 (239) BC

WUOA Tuscaloosa, Ala.
KSSN Little Rock, Ark.
† KYNO-FM Fresno, Calif.
KKHI-FM San Francisco, Calif.
KQYN Twentynine Palms, Calif.
KPKE Denver, Colo.
WKSS Meriden, Conn.
WMGG Clearwater, Fla.
KEZJ Twin Falls, Id.
WCRC Effingham, Ill.
WQMF Jeffersonville, Ind.
KKKX Ottawa, Kan.
WBYU New Orleans, La.
WWMJ Ellsworth, Me.
WZZR-FM Grand Rapids, Mich.
WHWL Marquette, Mich.
KKOK-FM Morris, Minn.
KWWR Mexico, Mo.
KCGM Scobey, Mont.
KROA Grand Island, Neb.

WZID	Manchester, N.H.
KPER	Hobbs, N.M.
WEBF	Olean, N.Y.
WXRC	Hickory, N.C.
WGSS	Lumberton, N.C.
WPTW-FM	Piqua, O.
KKAJ	Ardmore, Okla.
WFLN-FM	Philadelphia, Pa.
WFID	Rio Piedras, P.R.
KIKK-FM	Houston, Tex.
WFLO-FM	Farmville, Va.
WLTY	Norfolk, Va.
KIXI-FM	Seattle, Wash.
KUJ-FM	Walla Walla, Wash.
WZUU-FM	Milwaukee, Wis.
CBWX-FM	Fisher Branch, Man.
XHQS-FM	Tijuana, B.C.

95.9 (240) A

WKXN	Greenville, Ala.
WTWX	Guntersville, Ala.
WBIL-FM	Tuskegee, Ala.
KSMK-FM	Cottonwood, Ariz.
† KCAJ	El Dorado, Ark.
† KRRA	Huntsville, Ark.
KLVA	Lake Village, Ark.
KSAR	Salem, Ark.
KEZY	Anaheim, Calif.
KZTR	Camarillo, Calif.
KKOS	Carlsbad, Calif.
† KNTO	Delhi, Calif.
† KNTO	Livingston, Calif.
KALF	Red Bluff, Calif.
KAVI-FM	Rocky Ford, Colo.
WLYQ	Norwalk, Conn.
WWTR-FM	Bethany Beach, Del.
WLEQ	Bonita Springs, Fla.
† WMNX	Tallahassee, Fla.
WQZY	Dublin, Ga.
WLGA	Valdosta, Ga.
† KHCR	Poauilo, Haw.
WKKD-FM	Aurora, Ill.
WHOW-FM	Clinton, Ill.
WDQN-FM	Du Quoin, Ill.
WGAQ	Franklin, Ind.
WEFM	Michigan City, Ind.
WAVV	Vevay, Ind.
WKUZ	Wabash, Ind.
KCHA-FM	Charles City, Ia.
KILR-FM	Estherville, Ia.
KBCT	Fairfield, Ia.
KLVN	Newton, Ia.
KQWC-FM	Webster City, Ia.
KAKZ-FM	Derby, Kan.
KRSL-FM	Russell, Kan.
WFTM-FM	Maysville, Ky.
WRSL-FM	Stanford, Ky.
KMAR-FM	Winnsboro, La.
† WPIG	Saco, Me.
WWIN-FM	Glen Burnie, Md.
WYII	Williamsport, Md.
WATD	Marshfield, Mass.
WUPE	Pittsfield, Mass.
WKZC	Scottville, Mich.
WLKM-FM	Three Rivers, Mich.
KDHL-FM	Faribault, Minn.
WLKX-FM	Forest Lake, Minn.
WESE	Baldwyn, Miss.
WBLE	Batesville, Miss.
KAAN-FM	Bethany, Mo.
KTRI-FM	Mansfield, Mo.
KKBL	Monett, Mo.
KSMO-FM	Salem, Mo.
KLYQ-FM	Hamilton, Mont.
KLCM	Lewistown, Mont.
KICX-FM	Mc Cook, Neb.
WADB	Point Pleasant, N.J.
WFLR-FM	Dundee, N.Y.
WYLR-FM	Glens Falls, N.Y.
WVOS-FM	Liberty, N.Y.
WKAL-FM	Rome, N.Y.
WMBJ-FM	Morehead City, N.C.
WKLX	Plymouth, N.C.
WHFD	Archbold, O.
WNPQ	New Philadelphia, O.
WYAN-FM	Upper Sandusky, O.
KYBE	Frederick, Okla.
KAZZ	Sallisaw, Okla.
KITO	Vinita, Okla.
† KKRB	Klamath Falls, Ore.
WMKX	Brookville, Pa.
WMRF-FM	Lewistown, Pa.
WMGZ-FM	Sharpsville, Pa.
WPBM-FM	Aiken, S.C.
† KKEB	Bellefourche, S.D.
† WFKX	Henderson, Tenn.
WDXE-FM	Lawrenceburg, Tenn.
WXKG	Livingston, Tenn.
WAZI	Morristown, Tenn.
KXIT-FM	Dalhart, Tex.
† ----	Freer, Tex.
† KFFR	Hooks, Tex.
KKTX	Kilgore, Tex.
† KCKL	Malakoff, Tex.
KYXS-FM	Mineral Wells, Tex.
KEYE-FM	Perryton, Tex.
KDXE	Sulphur Springs, Tex.
KTRJ	Ephrata, Wash.
WTBZ	Grafton, W.V.
WAEY-FM	Princeton, W.V.
WATW-FM	Ashland, Wis.
† WJLW	De Pere, Wis.
WRDN-FM	Durand, Wis.
WSPL	La Crosse, Wis.
WWMH	Minocqua, Wis.
WYUR-FM	Ripon, Wis.
KENB-FM	Worland, Wyo.
CHFM	Calgary, Alta.
CHOS	Rattling Brook, Nfld.
CFPL-FM	London, Ont.
CJFM	Montreal, Que.

96.1 (241) BC

WLPR	Mobile, Ala.
KLPX	Tucson, Ariz.
‡ KHLS	Blytheville, Ark.
KSIQ	Brawley, Calif.
~~KCTC~~	~~Sacramento, Calif.~~
KUNA	San Luis Obispo, Calif.
KGBS	Greeley, Colo.
KWDE	Montrose, Colo.
WKTZ-FM	Jacksonville, Fla.
WKLS-FM	Atlanta, Ga.
KID-FM	Idaho Falls, Id.
WQLK	Richmond, Ind.
KSAY	Clinton, Ia.
WSTO	Owensboro, Ky.
KYKZ	Lake Charles, La.
WTMS	Presque Isle, Me.
WSRS	Worcester, Mass.
WHNN	Bay City, Mich.
WYXX	Holland, Mich.
* KINI	Crookston, Neb.
KEFM	Omaha, Neb.
WJYE	Buffalo, N.Y.
WYYD	Raleigh, N.C.
WXIK	Shelby, N.C.
KYYZ	Williston, N.D.
KXXY	Oklahoma City, Okla.
KZEL-FM	Eugene, Ore.
KXBQ	Ontario, Ore.
WLEV	Easton, Pa.
WHTX	Pittsburgh, Pa.
WGCB-FM	Red Lion, Pa.
WAEL-FM	Mayaguez, P.R.
KIXX	Watertown, S.D.
KIWW	Harlingen, Tex.
KSAQ	San Antonio, Tex.
KFMY	Provo, Utah
† ----	Cape Charles, Va.
KKPL	Opportunity, Wash
WBES	Charleston, W.V.
CKO-FM-4	Vancouver, B.C.
CJCM	Brandon, Man.

96.3 (242) BC

† KHLS	Blytheville, Ark.
KFMI	Eureka, Calif.
KFSG	Los Angeles, Calif.
KUBB	Mariposa, Calif.
WHUR-FM	Washington, D. C.
WJIZ	Albany, Ga.
KSHO-FM	Kailua, Haw.
WBBM-FM	Chicago, Ill.
WWMR	Rumford, Me.
WGTF	Nantucket, Mass.
WHYT	Detroit, Mich.
WMBN-FM	Petoskey Mich.
WYYN	Jackson, Miss.
KADI-FM	St. Louis, Mo.
KZIN-FM	Shelby, Mont.
KITT	Las Vegas, Nev.
KHFM	Albuquerque, N.M.
WQXR-FM	New York, N.Y.
WLVQ	Columbus, O.
WKOS	Murfreesboro, Tenn.
KHEY-FM	El Paso, Tex.
KSCS	Ft. Worth, Tex.
KLLL	Lubbock, Tex.
WMVA-FM	Martinsville, Va.
WJMC-FM	Rice Lake, Wis.
CKRA	Edmonton, Alta.
CIOZ	Marystown, Nfld.
CFMK	Kingston, Ont.

96.5 (243) BC

WMJJ	Birmingham, Ala.
† KRFM	Show Low, Ariz.
KHIS-FM	Bakersfield, Calif.
KYXY	San Diego, Calif.
KOIT-FM	San Francisco, Calif.
~~† ----~~	~~Tahoe City, Calif.~~
KKFM	Colorado Springs, Colo.
WTIC-FM	Hartford, Conn.
WFTW-FM	Ft. Walton Beach, Fla.
WHOO-FM	Orlando, Fla.
WJCL-FM	Savannah, Ga.
‡ KOZE-FM	Lewiston, Id.
KMTW	Twin Falls, Id.
WAZY-FM	Lafayette, Ind.
WMT-FM	Cedar Rapids, Ia.
KVKI	Shreveport, La.
KJJK	Fergus Falls, Minn.
KXTR	Kansas City, Mo.
KIVE	Glendive, Mont.
KRGI-FM	Grand Island, Neb.
WCMF	Rochester, N.Y.
WSTS	Laurinburg, N.C.
WKDD	Akron, O.
WSKS	Hamilton, O.
KECO	Elk City, Okla.
KRAV	Tulsa, Okla.
† KWSI	Warm Springs, Ore.
WJNL-FM	Johnstown, Pa.
WPEL-FM	Montrose, Pa.
WWDB	Philadelphia, Pa.
WDOY	Fajardo, P.R.
* WPLS-FM	Greenville, S.C.
* KNWC-FM	Sioux Falls, S.D.
WDOD-FM	Chattanooga, Tenn.
KIOU	Corpus Christi, Tex.
KSRR	Houston, Tex.
WQKS	Williamsburg, Va.
KYYX	Seattle, Wash.
WXCC	Williamson, W.V.
WMGF	Milwaukee, Wis.
KQSW	Rock Springs, Wyo.
KLWD	Sheridan, Wyo.
CBUF-6	Kamloops, B.C.
CJBC-3-FM	Penetanguishene, Ont.
CHLM	Rouyn, Que.

96.7 (244) A

	Call	Location
	KDEW-FM	De Witt, Ark.
	KCWD	Harrison, Ark.
	KAWW-FM	Heber Springs, Ark.
	KSPA	Hot Springs, Ark.
	KZRK-FM	Ozark, Ark.
	KTED	Fowler, Calif.
	KORY	Manteca, Calif.
	KNVR	Paradise, Calif.
	KCAL-FM	Redlands, Calif.
	KWIZ-FM	Santa Ana, Calif.
	KKBZ-FM	Santa Paula, Calif.
	KSYV	Solvag, Calif.
†	KRTZ	Cortez, Colo.
	KSBT	Steamboat Springs, Colo.
	WYRS	Stamford, Conn.
	WVSI-FM	Jupiter, Fla.
	WVMG-FM	Cochran, Ga.
	WRNG	Newnan, Ga.
	WRNZ	Wrens, Ga.
‡	KOZE-FM	Lewiston, Id.
†	KACH-FM	Preston, Id.
	WLLI-FM	Joliet, Ill.
	WLUV-FM	Loves Park, Ill.
	WIHN	Normal, Ill.
	WRVI	Virden, Ill.
	WAXT	Alexandria, Ind.
	WBWB	Bloomington, Ind.
	WCOE	La Porte, Ind.
	WCJC	Madison, Ind.
	WRTB	Vincennes, Ind.
	KANS-FM	Larned, Kan.
	KNEX-FM	Mc Pherson, Kan.
	WOKH	Bardstown, Ky.
	WLBJ-FM	Bowling Green, Ky.
*	WKCC	Grayson, Ky.
	WNCW	Paris, Ky.
	WSEK	Somerset, Ky.
	KFXY	Morgan City, La.
	KWCL-FM	Oak Grove, La.
†	WCME	Boothbay Harbor, Me.
†*	WBYQ	Baltimore, Md.
	WCEI-FM	Easton, Md.
	WQCM	Halfway, Md.
	WUFN	Albion, Mich.
	WEVZ	Cadillac, Mich.
	KWWK	Rochester, Minn.
	WFFF-FM	Columbia, Miss.
	WGUF-FM	Gulfport, Miss.
†*	WMAB-FM	Mississippi State, Miss.
	WSEL-FM	Pontotoc, Miss.
	WONA-FM	Winona, Miss.
	KCMQ	Columbia, Mo.
	KMEM	Memphis, Mo.
†	KAIG	Mountain View, Mo.
†	KNSX	Steelville, Mo.
	KZDQ	Belgrade, Mont.
	WXKZ	Rochester, N.H.
*	WSLU	Canton, N.Y.
†	WIAK	Clifton Park, N.Y.
	WDLC-FM	Port Jervis, N.Y.
	WRFR	Franklin, N.C.
	WKRX	Roxboro, N.C.
	WILE-FM	Cambridge, O.
	WCSM-FM	Celina, O.
	WFOB-FM	Fostoria, O.
	WKOV-FM	Wellston, O.
	KASX	Ada, Okla.
†	----	Commanche, Okla.
	KWDG	Idabel, Okla.
	KCRF	Lincoln City, Ore.
	WPGM-FM	Danville, Pa.
	WQWK	State College, Pa.
	WZLD	Cayce, S.C.
	WSCZ	Greenwood, S.C.
	KOBH-FM	Hot Springs, S.D.
	WQKZ	Bolivar, Tenn.
	WHLP-FM	Centerville, Tenn.
	KWCS	Bridgeport, Tex.
	KVMX	Eastland, Tex.
	KGTN-FM	Georgetown, Tex.
	KLMT	Marlin, Tex.
	KMOO-FM	Mineola, Tex.
	KLIS	Palestine, Tex.
	KZXL-FM	Sherman, Tex.
	KXOX-FM	Sweetwater, Tex.
	KKLX	Moab, Utah
	WMMJ	Brattleboro, Vt.
	WNCS	Montpelier, Vt.
	WWZD	Buena Vista, Va.
	WJMA-FM	Orange, Va.
†	KLLH	Quincy, Wash.
	KREW-FM	Sunnyside, Wash.
	WRRL-FM	Rainelle, W.V.
	WAHC	Oshkosh, Wis.
	WSEY	Sauk City, Wis.
	CKGL	Kitchener, Ont.

96.9 (245) BC

	Call	Location
	WRSA	Decatur, Ala.
	WLHQ	Enterprise, Ala.
	KMEO-FM	Phoenix, Ariz.
	KWAV	Monterey, Calif.
	KROY	Sacramento, Calif.
†	KCCY	Pueblo, Colo.
	WINK-FM	Ft. Myers, Fla.
	WAIV-FM	Jacksonville, Fla.
	KBNY	Nampa, Id.
	WLBH-FM	Mattoon, Ill.
	WXLP	Moline, Ill.
	WNIZ-FM	Zion, Ill.
	KRIT	Clarion, Ia.
	KDBQ	Pittsburg, Kan.
	WDDJ	Paducah, Ky.
	KTIZ	Alexandria, La.
	WDHP	Presque Isle, Me.
	WJIB	Boston, Mass.
	WLAV-FM	Grand Rapids, Mich.
	KNNS	Grand Rapids, Minn.
	KSRD	Seward, Neb.
	WFPG	Atlantic City, N.J.
	KRAZ	Farmington, N.M.
	WGRQ	Buffalo, N.Y.
	WOUR	Utica, N.Y.
	WEQR	Goldsboro, N.C.
	WLVV	Statesville, N.C.
	KNID	Enid, Okla.
	KFMJ	Grants Pass, Ore.
	WHYW-FM	Braddock, Pa.
	WLAN-FM	Lancaster, Pa.
	WMLD	Manati, P.R.
	WXTC	Charleston, S.C.
	KDLO-FM	Watertown, S.D.
	KXGC-FM	El Campo, Tex.
	KVMV	Mc Allen, Tex.
	KQIP	Odessa, Tex.
	WXBQ-FM	Bristol, Va.
	KMTN	Jackson, Wyo.
	KOLL-FM	Gillette, Wyo.
*	CKUA-FM-5	Peace River, Alta.
	CKSS	Red Rocks, Nfld.
	CBCT	Charlottetown, P.E.
	CKOI	Verdun, Que.
	CBK-FM	Regina, Sask.

97.1 (246) BC

	Call	Location
	KWEH	Camden, Ark.
	KHTZ	Los Angeles, Calif.
	WASH	Washington, D. C.
	WFOX	Gainesville, Ga.
†	KFSH	Hilo, Haw.
	WNIB	Chicago, Ill.
	WENS	Shelbyville, Ind.
	WEZB-FM	New Orleans, La.
	WBGW	Bangor, Me.
	WJOI	Detroit, Mich.
	WGLQ	Escanaba, Mich.
	KYZK	Crookston, Minn.
	KTCR-FM	Minneapolis, Minn.
	WOKK	Meridian, Miss.
	KCPM	Florissant, Mo.
	KZLS	Billings, Mont.
	KALS	Kalispell, Mont.
	KELN	North Platte, Neb.
	KEER	Las Vegas, Nev.
	KRIZ	Roswell, N.M.
	WYNY	New York, N.Y.
	WQMG	Greensboro, N.C.
	KCJB-FM	Minot, N.D.
	WREO-FM	Ashtabula, O.
	WBNS-FM	Columbus, O.
†	KRLQ	Muskogee, Okla.
	KCNR-FM	Portland, Ore.
	WHRK	Memphis, Tenn.
	KEGL	Ft. Worth, Tex.
	KISN	Salt Lake City, Utah
	WRUT	Rutland, Vt.
	KSXT	Walla Walla, Wash.
†	WCKA	Sutton, W.V.
	WCOW-FM	Sparta, Wis.
	CHMY	Penticton, B.C.
	CIGL	Belleville, Ont.

97.3 (247) BC

	Call	Location
	KSON-FM	San Diego, Calif.
	KRQR	San Francisco, Calif.
	KBCO	Boulder, Colo.
	WAIA	Miami, Fla.
	WJAD	Bainbridge, Ga.
	WAEV	Savannah, Ga.
	WRUL	Carmi, Ill.
	WMEE	Ft. Wayne, Ind.
	KDMI	Des Moines, Ia.
	KBUF-FM	Garden City, Kan.
	WIBW-FM	Topeka, Kan.
	WJFD-FM	New Bedford, Mass.
	KWFC	Springfield, Mo.
	KKBC	Carson City, Nev.
	WMVB	Millville, N.J.
	KAFE-FM	Santa Fe, N.M.
	WHCU-FM	Ithaca, N.Y.
	WKBC-FM	North Wilkesboro, N.C.
	WHSL	Wilmington, N.C.
*	WGXM	Dayton, O.
	KWEY-FM	Weatherford, Okla.
	WHP-FM	Harrisburg, Pa.
	KPAT	Sioux Falls, S.D.
	KATX	Plainview, Tex.
	KAJA	San Antonio, Tex.
	WNSY-FM	Newport News, Va.
	KNBQ	Tacoma, Wash.
	WKWK-FM	Wheeling, W.V.
	WLPX	Milwaukee, Wis.
	CIRK	Edmonton, Alta.
*	CKUA-FM-3	Medicine Hat, Alta.

97.5 (248) BC

	Call	Location
	WABB-FM	Mobile, Ala.
	KWBO	Hot Springs, Ark.
	KMYT	Merced, Calif.
	KDUO	Riverside, Calif.
	KTMS-FM	Santa Barbara, Calif.
	WPCV	Winter Haven, Fla.
	KPOI-FM	Honolulu, Haw.
	WDWS-FM	Champaign, Ill.
	WZOK	Rockford, Ill.
	WAMZ	Louisville, Ky.
*	WNEK-FM	Springfield, Mass.
	WJIM-FM	Lansing, Mich.
	KPRM-FM	Park Rapids, Minn.
	KNXR	Rochester, Minn.
	WOOR	Oxford, Miss.
	KYBS	Livingston, Mont.
	KQSK	Chadron, Neb.
	WOKQ	Dover, N.H.
	WPST	Trenton, N.J.
	WALK-FM	Patchogue, N.Y.
	WNCQ	Watertown, N.Y.
	WAEZ	Akron, O.
	KMOD-FM	Tulsa, Okla.
†	KLNR	Bend, Ore.
	WIOA	Mayaguez, P.R.
	WEZK	Knoxville, Tenn.
	KAYD	Beaumont, Tex.
	KSYR-FM	El Paso, Tex.
	KGKL-FM	San Angelo, Tex.
	KWTX-FM	Waco, Tex.
	WWWV	Charlottesville, Va.

	WJLC-FM	South Boston, Va.
	WQBE-FM	Charleston, W.V.
	WKMZ	Martinsburg, W.V.
	KDLY	Lander, Wyo.
	CHNL-FM	Kamloops, B.C.
	CHMM	Winnipeg, Man.
	CKO-FM-3	London, Ont.

97.7 (249) A

	WFRI	Auburn, Ala.
	WEZZ	Clanton, Ala.
	WKLD	Oneonta, Ala.
	KAVV	Benson, Ariz.
	KABK-FM	Augusta, Ark.
†	----	Yellville, Ark.
†	KQVO	Calexico, Calif.
	KWIN	Lodi, Calif.
	KPEN	Los Altos, Calif.
	KDOL-FM	Mojave, Calif.
	KRJB	Monte Rio, Calif.
	KEWE	Oroville, Calif.
	KIYD-FM	Shafter, Calif.
†	KYRE	Yreka, Calif.
	KSPN	Aspen, Colo.
	WCTY	Norwich, Conn.
	WAFL-FM	Milford, Del.
†	WTTB	Bonifay, Fla.
	WSGL	Naples, Fla.
	WFOY-FM	St. Augustine, Fla.
	WPUR	Americus, Ga.
	WKEU-FM	Griffin, Ga.
	WKCX	Rome, Ga.
	WTCQ	Vidalia, Ga.
†	----	Waycross, Ga.
	KBLI-FM	Blackfoot, Id.
†*	KJLC	Lewiston, Id.
	WBFG	Effingham, Ill.
	WDRL	Monmouth, Ill.
	WBBA-FM	Pittsfield, Ill.
	WLAX	Streator, Ill.
	WFRX-FM	West Frankfort, Ill.
	WBDJ-FM	Brazil, Ind.
	WZOW	Goshen, Ind.
	WLOJ	Rensselaer, Ind.
	KNJY	Clinton, Ia.
†	KGCI	Grundy Center, Ia.
	KHBT	Humboldt, Ia.
	KLEE-FM	Ottumwa, Ia.
	WJSN-FM	Jackson, Ky.
	WHRZ	Providence, Ky.
†	----	Dubach, La.
	KMDL	Kaplan, La.
	KWLB-FM	Marksville, La.
	KDBH	Natchitoches, La.
	WKTR	Millinocket, Me.
	WMDM-FM	Lexington Park, Md.
	WCAV	Brockton, Mass.
	WINQ	Winchendon, Mass.
	WMRX-FM	Beaverton, Mich.
	WHUH	Houghton, Mich.
	WKLT	Kalkaska, Mich.
	WRRK	Manistee, Mich.
†	WOEA	Rogers City, Mich.
	WTGV-FM	Sandusky, Mich.
	KLGR-FM	Redwood Falls, Minn.
	WRJH	Brandon, Miss.
	WTYJ	Fayette, Miss.
	WTYL-FM	Tylertown, Miss.
	KQMO	Brookfield, Mo.
	KOEA	Doniphan, Mo.
	KKCA	Fulton, Mo.
†	KNMO-FM	Nevada, Mo.
	KSTG	Sikeston, Mo.
	KAYQ	Warsaw, Mo.
	KFBD-FM	Waynesville, Mo.
	KGLM-FM	Anaconda, Mont.
	KUVR-FM	Holdrege, Neb.
	KNCY-FM	Nebraska City, Neb.
†	KMLW	Belen, N.M.
	WMVQ	Amsterdam, N.Y.
	WJJB	Hyde Park, N.Y.
†	----	Carrington, N.C.
	WQDW	Kinston, N.C.
†	WDJB	Windsor, N.C.
†	KDAK-FM	Carrington, N.D.
	WGGN	Castalia, O.
	WURD	Georgetown, O.
	WCJO	Jackson, O.
	WTGN	Lima, O.
	WOXY	Oxford, O.
†	KEYD	Durant, Okla.
	KKLR	Edmond, Okla.
	KGOK	Pauls Valley, Okla.
	WLER-FM	Butler, Pa.
	WSQV	Jersey Shore, Pa.
	WVSC-FM	Somerset, Pa.
	WBRQ	Cidra, P.R.
	WGMB	Georgetown, S.C.
	WLOT	Trenton, Tenn.
	KINE-FM	Kingsville, Tex.
	KBMI	Roma, Tex.
	KWRW	Rusk, Tex.
	WMJD	Grundy, Va.
	KTRW	East Wenatchee, Wash.
†	----	Raymond, Wash.
	WAXL	Lancaster, W.V.
	WRON-FM	Ronceverte, W.V.
	WAQE-FM	Rice Lake, Wis.
	WWJR	Sheboygan, Wis.
	CBUF	Vancouver, B.C.
	CKWM-FM	Kentville, N.S.
	CJQR	St. Catherines, Ont.
	CHOM	Montreal, Que.
	CBKF	Regina, Sask.

97.9 (250) BC

	KUPD-FM	Tempe, Ariz.
	KNAX	Fresno, Calif.
	KNOB	Long Beach, Calif.
†	KJMM	Needles, Calif.
	KISZ	Cortez, Colo.
‡	KCCY	Pueblo, Colo.
†*	WFCS	New Britain, Conn.
	WZNE	Clearwater, Fla.
	WRMF	Palm Beach, Fla.
	KKBG	Hilo, Haw.
	KBOI-FM	Boise, Id.
	WLUP	Chicago, Ill.
	WLHN	Anderson, Ind.
	KSEZ	Sioux City, Ia.
	KBRA	Wichita, Kan.
	WJBQ	Portland, Me.
	WIYY	Baltimore, Md.
	WJLB	Detroit, Mich.
	WGRD-FM	Grand Rapids, Mich.
	WBAQ	Greenville, Miss.
	WEVD	New York, N.Y.
	WPXY-FM	Rochester, N.Y.
	WPEG	Concord, N.C.
	KFNW-FM	Fargo, N.D.
	WNCI	Columbus, O.
	KLUP	Poteau, Okla.
	KUGN-FM	Eugene, Ore.
	WVCD	Hazleton, Pa.
	WCOS-FM	Columbia, S.C.
	KVSR	Rapid City, S.D.
	WSIX-FM	Nashville, Tenn.
	KGNC-FM	Amarillo, Tex.
	KZEW	Dallas, Tex.
	KFMK	Houston, Tex.
	KUFO	Odessa, Tex.
	KZAN	Ogden, Utah
	WIBS	Charlotte Amalie, V.I.
	WFGM	Fairmont, W.V.
	WSPT	Stevens Point, Wis.
	KFBQ	Cheyenne, Wyo.
	KTAG	Cody, Wyo.
	CBWV	Brandon, Man.

98.1 (251) BC

	WKYD-FM	Andalusia, Ala.
	WHKW	Fayette, Ala.
	KHFO	Osceola, Ark.
	KVIP-FM	Redding, Calif.
	KABL-FM	San Francisco, Calif.
†	KKUG	San Luis Obispo, Calif.
	KRXV	Yermo, Calif.
†*	WQAQ	Hamden, Conn.
	WQHL	Live Oak, Fla.
	WRAY-FM	Princeton, Ind.
	KHAK-FM	Cedar Rapids, Ia.
	KUDL	Kansas City, Kan.
	WKQQ	Lexington, Ky.
	WAFB-FM	Baton Rouge, La.
	WMYS	New Bedford, Mass.
	WKCQ	Saginaw, Mich.
	WWJO	St. Cloud, Minn.
	KSLQ	St. Louis, Mo.
	WHWK	Binghamton, N.Y.
	WQSM	Fayetteville, N.C.
	WTOF	Canton, O.
	KRLG	Lawton, Okla.
	WFBG-FM	Altoona, Pa.
	WCAU-FM	Philadelphia, Pa.
	WBFM	Seneca, S.C.
	KRRG	Lared0, Tex.
	KTAL-FM	Texarkana, Tex.
	WHWB-FM	Rutland, Vt.
	WBOB-FM	Galax, Va.
	KING-FM	Seattle, Wash.
	KHQ-FM	Spokane, Wash.
	WMGN	Madison, Wis.
	CBOF-6	Cornwall, Ont.
	CBON	Sudbury, Ont.
	CHFI	Toronto, Ont.
	CHOI	Quebec, Que.

98.3 (252) A

†	WJQY	Chickasaw, Ala.
	WKEA-FM	Scottsboro, Ala.
	WMLS-FM	Sylacauga, Ala.
†	KOPO	Marana, Ariz.
*	KAYN	Nogales, Ariz.
	KNOT-FM	Prescott, Ariz.
	KWCX	Willcox, Ariz.
†	KBCV	Bentonville, Ark.
	KTLO-FM	Mountain Home, Ark.
	KDAR	Oxnard, Calif.
	KMIX	Turlock, Calif.
	KBOB	West Covina, Calif.
†	KGUC-FM	Gunnison, Colo.
†	KRZQ-FM	Wray, Colo.
	WDAQ	Danbury, Conn.
	WNOU	Willimantic, Conn.
	WSUX-FM	Seaford, Del.
	WOKD	Arcadia, Fla.
	WGLY	Goulds, Fla.
†	WIKX	Immokalee, Fla.
	WAJX	Titusville, Fla.
	WFAV	Cordele, Ga.
	WSOJ	Jessup, Ga.
	WJAT-FM	Swainsboro, Ga.
	KMVC	Burley, Id.
†	KKQT	Rexburg, Id.
	WBYS-FM	Canton, Ill.
	WCCQ	Crest Hill, Ill.
†	WZRO	Farmer City, Ill.
†	WRIK	Metropolis, Ill.
	WZOE-FM	Princeton, Ill.
†	WIBN	Earl Park, Ind.
	WARU-FM	Peru, Ind.
	WXIR	Plainfield, Ind.
	WZZY	Winchester, Ind.
	KWBG-FM	Boone, Ia.
	KEMB	Emmetsburg, Ia.
	KCMR	Mason City, Ia.
	KABI-FM	Abilene, Kan.
	KCCU	Columbus, Kan.
	WDNS	Bowling Green, Ky.
	KYEA	West Monroe, La.
	WTVL-FM	Waterville, Me.
	WHAI-FM	Greenfield, Mass.
	WTWR	Monroe, Mich.
	WQXO-FM	Munising, Mich.
†	----	North Muskegon, Mich.
†	WONT	Ontonogan, Mich.
	WCSY-FM	South Haven, Mich.
†	KQYB	Spring Grove, Minn.

WWYN	Carthage, Miss.
WJDR	Prentiss, Miss.
WYKK	Quitman, Miss.
KFMZ	Columbia, Mo.
KIDS	Palmyra, Mo.
KDLN	Dillon, Mont.
KBBN-FM	Broken Bow, Neb.
WLNH-FM	Laconia, N.H.
WMGQ	New Brunswick, N.J.
WDVR	Ocean City, N.J.
WVIN-FM	Bath, N.Y.
WKJY	Hempstead, N.Y.
WSUL	Monticello, N.Y.
WBCG	Murfreesboro, N.C.
WTNC-FM	Thomasville, N.C.
WTOO-FM	Bellefontaine, O.
WLGN-FM	Logan, O.
KYTT-FM	Coos Bay, Ore.
KLBM-FM	La Grande, Ore.
WESA-FM	Charleroi, Pa.
WWMC-FM	Mifflinburg, Pa.
WREI	Quebradillas, P.R.
WWKT-FM	Kingstree, S.C.
WRJB	Camden, Tenn.
WALV	Cleveland, Tenn.
WHUB-FM	Cookeville, Tenn.
* WMGL	Pulaski, Tenn.
KHFI-FM	Austin, Tex.
KQRK	Bandera, Tex.
KFYZ-FM	Bonham, Tex.
KORA-FM	Bryan, Tex.
KULM	Columbus, Tex.
† ----	Farwell, Tex.
KPEP	Gatesville, Tex.
† ----	Lorenzo, Tex.
KYYK	Palestine, Tex.
KPTX	Pecos, Tex.
KBOP-FM	Pleasanton, Tex.
KRDF-FM	Spearman, Tex.
KARB	Price, Utah
WGOL	Lynchburg, Va.
KRSE	Yakima, Wash.
WZFM	Charles Town, W.V.
WXVA-FM	Charlestown, W.V.
WCEF	Ripley, W.V.
WFMR	Menomonee Falls, Wis.
WNBI-FM	Park Falls, Wis.
† ----	Afton, Wyo.
† KLYX	Thermopolis, Wyo.
KERM	Torrington, Wyo.
CFFM	Kamloops, B.C.
CBW-FM	Winnipeg, Man.
CFLY	Kingston, Ont.

98.5 (253) BC

KLAZ	Little Rock, Ark.
KWXY-FM	Cathedral City, Calif.
KDNO	Delano, Calif.
KZAP	Sacramento, Calif.
KOME	San Jose, Calif.
KYGO	Denver, Colo.
WRYO	Crystal River, Fla.
WGNE-FM	Panama City, Fla.
WSB-FM	Atlanta, Ga.
WXXQ	Freeport, Ill.
WACF	Paris, Ill.
KQKQ-FM	Council Bluffs, Ia.
WYLD-FM	New Orleans, La.
WROR	Boston, Mass.
WNWN	Coldwater, Mich.
WJGS	Houghton Lake, Mich.
* KTIS-FM	Minneapolis, Minn.
WZLQ	Tupelo, Miss.
KTJJ	Farmington, Mo.
KIDX	Billings, Mont.
KBBZ	Kalispell, Mont.
KLUC	Las Vegas, Nev.
KRSN-FM	Los Alamos, N.M.
WZIR	Niagara Falls, N.Y.
† ----	Williston, N.D.
WRRM	Cincinnati, O.
WGCL	Cleveland, O.
* WCMO	Marietta, O.
KCFO	Tulsa, Okla.
KAGO-FM	Klamath Falls, Ore.
KUPL-FM	Portland, Ore.
WYCR	Hanover, Pa.
WRJS	Oil City, Pa.
WKRZ-FM	Wilkes Barre, Pa.
WPRM-FM	San Juan, P.R.
WTFM	Kingsport, Tenn.
KQXX	Mc Allen, Tex.
KHYS	Port Arthur, Tex.
† KEYF	Grandcoulee, Wash.
WDUZ-FM	Green Bay, Wis.
CFMS	Victoria, B.C.
* COIS	Stephenville, Nfld.
CIEL	Longueuil, Que.

98.7 (254) BC

KKLT	Phoenix, Ariz.
KJOI	Los Angeles, Calif.
WMZQ	Washington, D. C.
WIZD	Ft. Pierce, Fla.
WFMT-FM	Chicago, Ill.
WNNS	Springfield, Ill.
KMGO	Centerville, Ia.
WHOP-FM	Hopkinsville, Ky.
WLLZ	Detroit, Mass.
KQWB-FM	Moorhead, Minn.
KLOH-FM	Pipestone, Minn.
WQMV	Vicksburg, Miss.
KWTO-FM	Springfield, Mo.
WRKS-FM	New York, N.Y.
WIBQ	Utica, N.Y.
WRQK	Greensboro, N.C.
WQLO	Beaufort, S.C.
KMML	Amarillo, Tex.
KLVU	Dallas, Tex.
KTXN-FM	Victoria, Tex.
KCPX-FM	Salt Lake City, Utah
WNOR-FM	Norfolk, Va.
WCPI	Wheeling, W.V.
CBQX	Kenora, Ont.

98.9 (255) BC

WBAM-FM	Montgomery, Ala.
KOJY	Dinuba, Calif.
KQAK	San Francisco, Calif.
KKMG	Pueblo, Colo.
WBGM	Tallahassee, Fla.
WHBF-FM	Rock Island, Ill.
†* WHSK	Kokomo, Ind.
WSLM-FM	Salem, Ind.
KZZC	Leavenworth, Kan.
WSIP-FM	Paintsville, Ky.
WCLZ	Brunswick, Me.
WJML-FM	Petoskey, Mich.
WAKX-FM	Duluth, Minn.
KTMO	Kennett, Mo.
KAAK	Great Falls, Mont.
KRNY-FM	Kearney, Neb.
WHFM	Rochester, N.Y.
WERT-FM	Van Wert, O.
WKBN-FM	Youngstown, O.
KLNK	Oklahoma City, Okla.
WUSL	Philadelphia, Pa.
* WLID	Vieques, P.R.
WSPA-FM	Spartanburg, S.C.
† ----	Carthage, Tex.
WQCR	Burlington, Vt.
KEZX	Seattle, Wash.
KICN	Spokane, Wash.
WTMB-FM	Tomah, Wis.
CFRC	Red Deer, Alta.
CJYC	St. John, N.B.
CKIK	Quebec, Que.
CIZL	Regina, Sask.
XHQF-FM	Tijuana, B.C.

99.1 (256) BC

WAHR	Huntsville, Ala.
KFMM	Thatcher, Ariz.
KMAG	Ft. Smith, Ark.
KGGI	Riverside, Calif.
KSCO-FM	Santa Cruz, Calif.
KXFM	Santa Maria, Calif.
†* KTUO	Sonora, Calif.
KUAD-FM	Windsor, Colo.
WPLR	New Haven, Conn.
WQIK-FM	Jacksonville, Fla.
WEDR	Miami, Fla.
WMAZ-FM	Macon, Ga.
KQPI-FM	Idaho Falls, Id.
WIAI	Danville, Ill.
KDEA	New Iberia, La.
WHFS	Annapolis, Md.
* WHFC	Bel Air, Md.
WPLM-FM	Plymouth, Mass.
WFMK	East Lansing, Mich.
KEEZ-FM	Mankato, Minn.
WSWG-FM	Greenwood, Miss.
WPMO	Pascagoula, Miss.
* KFUO-FM	Clayton, Mo.
WAWZ-FM	Zarephath, N.J.
KCLV-FM	Clovis, N.M.
WAAL	Binghamton, N.Y.
WQTR	Whiteville, N.C.
WHIO-FM	Dayton, O.
WFRO-FM	Fremont, O.
KPNW-FM	Eugene, Ore.
WIYQ	Ebensburg, Pa.
WKJB-FM	Mayaguez, P.R.
† KBCB	Corpus Christi, Tex.
KODA	Houston, Tex.
KKKK	Odessa, Tex.
WSLQ	Roanoke, Va.
WMYX	Milwaukee, Wis.
* WSSU	Superior, Wis.
CKO-FM-7	Winnipeg, Man.
CKO-FM-2	Toronto, Ont.
CFMM	Prince Albert, Sask.
XHSL-FM	Piedras Negras, Coah.

99.3 (257) A

WMFC-FM	Monroeville, Ala.
WSLY	York, Ala.
KMDX	Parker, Ariz.
KLBQ	El Dorado, Ark.
KSER	Searcy, Ark.
KOZN	Imperial, Calif.
KVYN	St. Helena, Calif.
KJAX	Stockton, Calif.
WEZY-FM	Cocoa, Fla.
† WQEZ	Ft. Myers, Fla.
WQMT	Chatsworth, Ga.
WCON-FM	Cornelia, Ga.
KQKZ	Mountain Home, Id.
WDUK	Havana, Ill.
WAJK	La Salle, Ill.
WLVO	Mt. Zion, Ill.
WSCH	Aurora, Ind.
WKVI-FM	Knox, Ind.
* KFGQ-FM	Boone, Ia.
KWAY	Waverly, Ia.
KSPG	El Dorado, Kan.
KIOL	Iola, Kan.
WYGO-FM	Corbin, Ky.
WWKF	Fulton, Ky.
WHBN-FM	Harrodsburg, Ky.
WLCK-FM	Scottsville, Ky.
KJNA	Jena, La.
WKTJ-FM	Farmington, Me.
WLKN-FM	Lincoln, Me.
WHMP-FM	Northampton, Mass.
WBNZ	Frankfort, Mich.
WIKB	Iron River, Mich.
WSTR-FM	Strugis, Mich.
WZND	Zeeland, Mich.
† KSTQ	Alexandria, Minn.
KSNR	Thief River Falls, Minn.
† ----	Walker, Minn.
WBIP-FM	Booneville, Miss.
WEEZ	Heidelberg, Miss.
KDBX	Boonville, Mo.
KJAQ-FM	Gordonville, Mo.

	KSCM-FM	Houston, Mo.
	KNIM-FM	Maryville, Mo.
†	KCIE	Fairbury, Neb.
	KVLV-FM	Fallon, Nev.
	WFRD	Hanover, N.H.
	WLQF	Pleasantville, N.J.
	WDRE	Ellenville, N.Y.
	WSNN	Potsdam, N.Y.
	WSFW-FM	Seneca Falls, N.Y.
	WQDK	Ahoskie, N.C.
†	WNBB	Grifton, N.C.
	WTNS-FM	Coshocton, O.
	WNXT-FM	Portsmouth, O.
	KGVE	Grove, Okla.
	KLOR-FM	Ponca City, Okla.
	KOHU-FM	Hermiston, Ore.
	WVEN	Franklin, Pa.
	WSFM	Harrisburg, Pa.
	WFXX-FM	South Williamsport, Pa.
	WPQR-FM	Uniontown, Pa.
	WNEZ	Aiken, S.C.
	WDZK	Chester, S.C.
	WXVL	Crossville, Tenn.
	WIDD-FM	Elizabethton, Tenn.
	WKJQ	Jefferson City, Tenn.
	WZLT	Lexington, Tenn.
	KPYN	Atlanta, Tex.
	KPSM	Brownwood, Tex.
	KLTD	Lampasas, Tex.
	KDEY	Lufkin, Tex.
	KTXU	Paris, Tex.
†	KTYE	Tye, Tex.
†	KFML	White House, Tex.
*	KRDC-FM	St. George, Utah
	WFFV	Front Royal, Va.
	WPLZ	Petersburg, Va.
	KJMD	Aberdeen, Wash.
	KSEM-FM	Moses Lake, Wash.
†	WDNE-FM	Elkins, W.V.
	WIBZ	Parkersburg, W.V.
	WDMP-FM	Dodgeville, Wis.
	WIGM-FM	Medford, Wis.
	WROE	Neenah, Wis.
	WOWN-FM	Shawano, Wis.
	WGGQ	Waupun, Wis.
	KATH-FM	Douglas, Wyo.
*	CKUA-FM-2	Lethbridge, Alta.
	CFOX	Vancouver, B.C.
	CJBC-FM-20	London, Ont.

99.5 (258) BC

	WRKK	Birmingham, Ala.
	KNDE	Tucson, Ariz.
†	KQEF	Lakeport, Calif.
†	KHOF	Los Angeles, Calif.
	KXVR	Mountain Pass, Calif.
	KVOD	Denver, Colo.
	WJBR-FM	Wilmington, Del.
	WGAY-FM	Washington, D. C.
	WQYK-FM	St. Petersburg, Fla.
	WDMG-FM	Douglas, Ga.
	WUSN	Chicago, Ill.
	WQCY	Quincy, Ill.
	WZPL	Greenfield, Ind.
	KZZL	Le Mars, Ia.
	WKDQ	Henderson, Ky.
	KHEZ	Lake Charles, La.
	WRNO	New Orleans, La.
	WSSH	Lowell, Mass.
	WABX	Detroit, Mich.
	WLXX	Sault Ste. Marie Mich.
	WLOL	Minneapolis, Minn.
	KZZX	Albuquerque, N.M.
	WDCX	Buffalo, N.Y.
*	WBAI	New York, N.Y.
	WGFM	Schenectady, N.Y.
	WMAG	High Point, N.C.
	WKSW	Cleveland, O.
	KGCG-FM	Henryetta, Okla.
	KJIB	Portland, Ore.
	KOLY-FM	Mobridge, S.D.
	KRIX	Brownsville, Tex.
	KPLX	Ft. Worth, Tex.
	KRLB-FM	Lubbock, Tex.
	KISS	San Antonio, Tex.
	WIVI-FM	Christiansted, V.I.
	WBKW	Beckley, W.V.
	CKSB-8	Brandon, Man.
	CIME	Ste. Adele, Que.

99.7 (259) BC

	WOOF-FM	Dothan, Ala.
	KIOO	Porterville, Calif.
	KYUU	San Francisco, Calif.
	WRMM	Atlanta, Ga.
	WSHW	Frankfort, Ind.
	KFMH	Muscatine, Ia.
	WKJJ-FM	Louisville, Ky.
	WIMI	Ironwood, Mich.
	WUGN	Midland, Mich.
	WJMI	Jackson, Miss.
	KMBR	Kansas City, Mo.
	KOGA-FM	Ogallala, Neb.
	WJZR	Kannapolis, N.C.
	WRMZ	Columbus, O.
	KXLS	Alva, Okla.
	WSHH	Pittsburgh, Pa.
	WMSR-FM	Manchester, Tenn.
	WMC-FM	Memphis, Tenn.
	WYFI	Norfolk, Va.
	CKO-FM-9	St. John, N.B.
	CBMI	Bale Comeau, Que.

99.9 (260) BC

	WKRG-FM	Mobile, Ala.
	KNNN	Phoenix, Ariz.
	KTCS-FM	Ft. Smith, Ark.
	KRFD	Marysville, Calif.
	KOLA	San Bernardino, Calif.
	KTYD	Santa Barbara, Calif.
†	KEKB	Fruita, Colo.
	KVUU	Pueblo, Colo.
	WEZN	Bridgeport, Conn.
	WKQS	Boca Raton, Fla.
	WNFI	Palatka, Fla.
†	----	Kahului, Haw.
	WEBQ-FM	Harrisburg, Ill.
	WBYG	Kankakee, Ill.
	WTHI-FM	Terre Haute, Ind.
†	KWKR	Leoti, Kan.
	KSKG	Salina, Kan.
	KTDY	Lafayette, La.
	WKZS	Auburn, Me.
	WFRE	Frederick, Md.
	WKHI	Ocean City, Md.
	WQRC	Barnstable, Mass.
	WHFB-FM	Benton Harbor, Mich.
	KAUS-FM	Austin, Minn.
	KVOX-FM	Moorhead, Minn.
	KGOR	Omaha, Neb.
	KTQM-FM	Clovis, N.M.
	WOKW	Cortland, N.Y.
	WGFB	Plattsburgh, N.Y.
	WLOS	Asheville, N.C.
	WVBS-FM	Burgaw, N.C.
†	KBQQ	Minot, N.D.
	WVUD-FM	Kettering, O.
	WKLR	Toledo, O.
	KRKT-FM	Albany, Ore.
	WQQQ	Easton, Pa.
	WLVU	Erie, Pa.
	WIOB	San Juan, P.R.
	KTSM-FM	El Paso, Tex.
	KGEE	Monahans, Tex.
	KROB-FM	Robstown, Tex.
	KHOO	Waco, Tex.
	KLUR	Wichita Falls, Tex.
	KISW	Seattle, Wash.
	KXLY-FM	Spokane, Wash.
	WVAF	Charleston, W.V.
	WJVL	Janesville, Wis.
	KWND	Saratoga, Wyo.
	CJFI	Sarnia, Ont.
	CBCS	Sudbury, Ont.
	CKFM	Toronto, Ont.
	XHSG-FM	Piedras Negras, Coah.

100.1 (261) A

	WEIZ	Phenix City, Ala.
	WTUN	Selma, Ala.
	KJBA	Bethel, Alas.
	KQOK	Kenai, Alas.
	KMXT	Kodiak, Alas.
†	----	Kingman, Ariz.
†	KOST	Sedona, Ariz.
	KMSL	Stamps, Ark.
	KERG	Garberville, Calif.
	KGBA	Holtville, Calif.
	KZST	Santa Rosa, Calif.
†	KRLT	South Lake Tahoe, Calif.
	KFMR	Stockton, Calif.
	WEEJ	Port Charlotte, Fla.
	WFNE	Forsyth, Ga.
	WMCD	Statesboro, Ga.
	WLOV-FM	Washington, Ga.
‡	KWBJ	Payette, Id.
	KFIS	Soda Springs, Id.
	WLRX	Lincoln, Ill.
	WKAI-FM	Macomb, Ill.
	WGLC-FM	Mendota, Ill.
	WJBD-FM	Salem, Ill.
	WCCI	Savanna, Ill.
	WLKI	Angola, Ind.
	WCRD	Bluffton, Ind.
	WFLQ	French Lick, Ind.
	KCTN	Garanavillo, Ia.
	WIKI	Carrollton, Ky.
	WQXE	Elizabethtown, Ky.
	WKDJ	Winchester, Ky.
	KJBS	Bastrop, La.
	KCOZ	Shreveport, La.
	WHOU-FM	Houlton, Me.
	WMNB-FM	North Adams, Mass.
	WQVR	Southbridge, Mass.
	WSHN-FM	Fremont, Mich.
	WQON	Grayling, Mich.
	WBCH-FM	Hastings, Mich.
	WUUN	Marquette, Mich.
	WEVE-FM	Eveleth, Minn.
	KCCK	Marshall, Minn.
	KTIG	Pequot Lakes, Minn.
	WQXB	Grenada, Miss.
	KELE	Aurora, Mo.
	KOLS	Desoto, Mo.
	KJMO	Jefferson City, Mo.
†	KMWR	Vandalia, Mo.
	KMMR	Malta, Mont.
	KZOQ	Missoula, Mont.
	KATQ-FM	Plentywood, Mont.
†	KLKT	Incline Village, Neb.
†	KLKT	Incline Village, Nev.
	WPNH-FM	Plymouth, N.H.
	WJRZ	Manahawkin, N.J.
	WDST	Woodstock, N.Y.
	WBXB	Edenton, N.C.
	WNIR	Kent, O.
	WSWR	Shelby, O.
	KYFM	Bartlesville, Okla.
	WPRR	Altoona, Pa.
	WKAD	Canton, Pa.
	WUFM	Lebanon, Pa.
	WSCQ	Columbia, S.C.
	WGFG-FM	Lake City, S.C.
	WASL	Dyersburg, Tenn.
	WIZO-FM	Franklin, Tenn.
	KGRI-FM	Henderson, Tex.
	WYFJ	Ashland, Va.
	WKZZ	Lynchburg, Va.
	WTZE-FM	Tazewell, Va.
	WCLG-FM	Morgantown, W.V.
	WEMI	Menasha, Wis.
	WGLB-FM	Port Washington, Wis.
	WDDC	Portage, Wis.
	WSBW	Sturgeon Bay, Wis.
	WISQ	West Salem, Wis.

CBRX-FM	Lethbridge, Alta.
CIOO	Halifax, N.S.
CBF-8	Three Rivers, Que.

100.3 (262) BC

WVNA-FM	Tuscumbia, Ala.
KICY-FM	Nome, Alas.
KIKO-FM	Globe, Ariz.
KEZQ	Jacksonville, Ark.
KJMB-FM	Blythe, Calif.
KIQQ	Los Angeles, Calif.
KBAY	San Jose, Calif.
KLIR	Denver, Colo.
† WOOK	Washington, D. C.
WDIZ-FM	Orlando, Fla.
WXOS	Plantation Key, Fla.
WCUP	Tifton, Ga.
† KWBJ	Payette, Id.
WZEN	Alton, Ill.
WLOO	Chicago, Ill.
WCNB-FM	Connersville, Ind.
KLYF	Des Moines, Ia.
KXXX-FM	Colby, Kan.
KDVV	Topeka, Kan.
* KSWC	Winfield, Kan.
WKOA-FM	Hopkinsville, Ky.
KRRV	Alexandria, La.
WNIC-FM	Dearborn, Mich.
WCTS-FM	Minneapolis, Minn.
WNSL	Laurel, Miss.
WHEB-FM	Portsmouth, N.H.
WHTZ	Newark, N.J.
KKJY-FM	Albuquerque, N.M.
WGLD-FM	High Point, N.C.
WCLT-FM	Newark, O.
KRWQ	Gold Hill, Ore.
KRKZ	Portland, Ore.
WZPR	Meadville, Pa.
WKSZ	Media, Pa.
WIVA-FM	Aguadilla, P.R.
KGGG-FM	Rapid City, S.D.
WOKI-FM	Oak Ridge, Tenn.
KTXF	Brownsville, Tex.
KMEZ-FM	Dallas, Tex.
KILT-FM	Houston, Tex.
KOMX	Pampa, Tex.
KLLS-FM	San Antonio, Tex.
KSFI	Salt Lake City, Utah
KWIQ-FM	Moses Lake, Wash.
† KZMK	Greybull, Wyo.
CKXM	Edmonton, Alta.
CFOZ	Argentia, Nfld.
CBOB-FM	Brockville, Ont.

100.5 (263) BC

WHMA-FM	Anniston, Ala.
KCMG	Anchorage, Alas.
KEBH	Sacramento, Calif.
†* ----	Walnut Creek, Calif.
KRSJ	Durango, Colo.
WRCH-FM	New Britain, Conn.
†* KRIC	Rexburg, Id.
WEAI	Jacksonville, Ill.
WWKI	Kokomo, Ind.
KMZQ-FM	Henderson, Neb.
KMZQ-FM	Henderson, Nev.
WVOR-FM	Rochester, N.Y.
WOMP-FM	Bellaire, O.
WHMQ	Findlay, O.
KATT-FM	Oklahoma City, Okla.
WSSL	Gray Court, S.C.
WSSL	Laurens, S.C.
WCMS-FM	Norfolk, Va.
WKEE-FM	Huntington, W.V.
CBBL	London, Ont.
CHAS	Sault Ste. Marie, Ont.

100.7 (264) BC

KOPA-FM	Scottsdale, Ariz.
KIOQ-FM	Bishop, Calif.
KWYT-FM	Salinas, Calif.
KFMB-FM	San Diego, Calif.
KHAY	Ventura, Calif.
KZLO	Pueblo, Colo.
WHYI	Ft. Lauderdale, Fla.
WJLQ	Pensacola, Fla.
WIQI	Tampa, Fla.
WGIG-FM	Brunswick, Ga.
WYEZ	Elkhart, Ind.
WVTS	Terre Haute, Ind.
KKRQ	Iowa City, Ia.
KHOK	Holsington, Kan.
WQXY-FM	Baton Rouge, La.
WTTR-FM	Westminster, Md.
WHUE-FM	Boston, Mass.
WITL-FM	Lansing, Mich.
KCMT-FM	Alexandria, Minn.
WDMS	Greenville, Miss.
KGMO-FM	Cape Girardeau, Mo.
KCFX	Harrisonville, Mo.
* KGBI-FM	Omaha, Neb.
WNBR	Wildwood, N.J.
WHUD	Peekskill, N.Y.
WFMA	Rocky Mount, N.C.
WMMS	Cleveland, O.
WEEC	Springfield, O.
KICE	Bend, Ore.
WFMZ	Allentown, Pa.
WNUF	New Kensington, Pa.
WXYX	Bayamon, P.R.
WUSY	Cleveland, Tenn.
KORQ	Abilene, Tex.
KASE	Austin, Tex.
KPXI	Mt. Pleasant, Tex.
WQPO	Harrisonburg, Va.
KSEA	Seattle, Wash.
WBIZ	Eau Claire, Wis.
WRKR-FM	Racine, Wis.
KKAZ	Cheyenne, Wyo.
† KGWY	Gillette, Wyo.
CIGV-FM	Penticton, B.C.
CHIN-FM	Toronto, Ont.
CBF-FM	Montreal, Que.

100.9 (265) A

WALX	Selma, Ala.
WSCA	Union Springs, Ala.
† KTTH	Naknek, Alas.
* KFSK	Petersburg, Alas.
KTAZ-FM	Sierra Vista, Ariz.
KDEL-FM	Arkadelphia, Ark.
KFCM	Cherokee Village, Ark.
KFPW-FM	Ft. Smith, Ark.
† ----	Russellville, Ark.
KRQK	Lompoc, Calif.
KPSI-FM	Palm Springs, Calif.
KTIM-FM	San Rafael, Calif.
KYBB	Tracy, Calif.
KSQU	Weed, Calif.
KJCO	Yuma, Colo.
WTYD	New London, Conn.
WMFM	Gainesville, Fla.
WJAQ	Marianna, Fla.
WPGA-FM	Perry, Ga.
WWGA	Waynesboro, Ga.
WCJM	West Point, Ga.
† KWEI-FM	Weiser, Id.
† WBOD	Canton, Ill.
WHPO	Hoopeston, Ill.
WKXK	Pana, Ill.
WIVQ	Peru, Ill.
WQFL	Rockford, Ill.
WBDC	Huntingburg, Ind.
WNON	Lebanon, Ind.
WPGW-FM	Portland, Ind.
WMPI	Scottsburg, Ind.
KCLY	Clay Center, Kan.
WHKK	Erlanger, Ky.
WLSK	Lebanon, Ky.
KTQQ	Sulphur, La.
WGUY-FM	Brewer, Me.
WYNZ-FM	Westbrook, Me.
† ----	Falmouth, Mass.
WBRN-FM	Big Rapids, Mich.
† WFXZ	Pinconning, Mich.
† KJLY	Blue Earth, Minn.
WKLK-FM	Cloquet, Minn.
WMDC-FM	Hazlehurst, Miss.
WKBB	West Point, Miss.
KPCR-FM	Bowling Green, Mo.
† KTUI-FM	Sullivan, Mo.
† KFLN-FM	Baker, Mont.
† KNAA	Sparks, Nev.
KLVF	Las Vegas, N.M.
WWOM	Albany, N.Y.
WQIX	Horseheads, N.Y.
WSCY	North Syracuse, N.Y.
WBJZ	Olean, N.Y.
† WSID	Sidney, N.Y.
WABZ-FM	Albemarle, N.C.
WIFM-FM	Elkin, N.C.
WZYZ	Fairmont, N.C.
WWQQ-FM	Wilmington, N.C.
† KXPO-FM	Grafton, N.D.
† KKVC	Villey City, N.D.
WBNO-FM	Bryan, O.
WMEX	Clyde, O.
WXIZ	Waverly, O.
KORS	Miami, Okla.
KPNC-FM	Ponca City, Okla.
KXOJ-FM	Sapulpa, Okla.
KSDW	Sulphur, Okla.
KOOS	North Bend, Ore.
WRAX	Bedford, Pa.
WOEZ-FM	Milton, Pa.
WHYP-FM	North East, Pa.
WALD-FM	Walterboro, S.C.
WPBE	Huntingdon, Tenn.
KIXC-FM	Quanah, Tex.
WCVM	Middlebury, Vt.
WIQO-FM	Covington, Va.
WNNT-FM	Warsaw, Va.
† WKMY	Princeton, W.V.
WJCF	Westover, W.V.
WRCO-FM	Richland Center, Wis.
* CKUA-FM-4	Grand Prairie, Alta.
CBWK	Thompson, Man.
CKTO	Truro, N.S.
CBJ-FM	Chicoutimi, Que.

101.1 (266) BC

WFMH-FM	Cullman, Ala.
† KAYY	Fairbanks, Alas.
KBBC	Lake Havasu City, Ariz.
KHYL	Auburn, Calif.
KFIG	Fresno, Calif.
KRTH	Los Angeles, Calif.
KOSI-FM	Denver, Colo.
WWDC-FM	Washington, D. C.
WCKS	Cocoa Beach, Fla.
† WEIB	Marco, Fla.
WAFT	Valdosta, Ga.
WKQX	Chicago, Ill.
WMRY	East St. Louis, Ill.
KFJB-FM	Marshalltown, Ia.
KFNF	Oberlin, Kan.
WSGS	Hazard, Ky.
WAKQ	Russellville, Ky.
WNOE-FM	New Orleans, La.
KRMD-FM	Shreveport, La.
WRIF	Detroit, Mich.
KBHP	Bemidji, Minn.
KLQL	Luverne, Minn.
KMZU	Carrollton, Mo.
KOXI	Columbus, Neb.
WGIR-FM	Manchester, N.H.
WCBS-FM	New York, N.Y.
WPCM	Burlington, N.C.
WSRD	Youngstown, O.
† KWOX	Woodward, Okla.
KRCK	Portland, Ore.
WEAZ	Philadelphia, Pa.
WGMR	Tyrone, Pa.
† WEUC	Ponce, P.R.
WCKN-FM	Anderson, S.C.
† KEZV	Spearfish, S.D.

KRNB Memphis, Tenn.
WRR Dallas, Tex.
KFAN Fredericksburg, Tex.
KLOL Houston, Tex.
KTEZ Lubbock, Tex.
† ---- Kanab, Utah
KDAB Ogden, Utah
WCRN Charlotte Amalie, V.I.
WIXX Green Bay, Wis.
CFMI New Westminster, B.C.
CKUE Smith's Falls, Ont.

101.3 (267) BC

KGOT Anchorage, Alas.
KIOI San Francisco, Calif.
KIQX Durango, Colo.
WKCI Hamden, Conn.
WLLR East Moline, Ill.
WRIA Richmond, Ind.
KFDI-FM Wichita, Kan.
WKCG Augusta, Me.
WCUZ-FM Grand Rapids, Mich.
WSUE Sault St. Marie, Mich.
KDWB-FM Richfield, Minn.
WJDQ Meridian, Miss.
† KRYK Chinook, Mont.
KXXE Forsythe, Mont.
WEZO Rochester, N.Y.
WNCO-FM Ashland, O.
KMCO Mc Alester, Okla.
WNCE Lancaster, Pa.
WGBI-FM Scranton, Pa.
WWDM Sumter, S.C.
KNCN Sinton, Tex.
WWDE-FM Hampton, Va.
CKUA-FM-6 Red Deer, Alta.
CKOT-FM Tillsonburg, Ont.

101.5 (268) BC

KHEP-FM Phoenix, Ariz.
KGFM Bakersfield, Calif.
† KEKA Eureka, Calif.
KAMB Merced, Calif.
†⋆ KRVH Rio Vista, Calif.
KGB-FM San Diego, Calif.
† ---- Eagle, Colo.
WLYF Miami, Fla.
WTKX Pensacola, Fla.
WKES St. Petersburg, Fla.
WPIQ Brunswick, Ga.
WKHX Marietta, Ga.
WBNQ Bloomington, Ill.
WCIL-FM Carbondale, Ill.
WCSI-FM Columbus, Ind.
WTHQ South Bend, Ind.
KAYL-FM Storm Lake, Ia.
KSLS Liberal, Kan.
WYNK-FM Baton Rouge, La.
WJNR-FM Iron Mountain, Mich.
† KCGN Ortonville, Minn.
KTXR Springfield, Mo.
† KEZH Hastings, Neb.
WKXW Trenton, N.J.
⋆ WMSC Upper Montclair, N.J.
WPDH Poughkeepsie, N.Y.
WRAL Raleigh, N.C.
WYPC Gallipolis, O.
WLQR Toledo, O.
KLAW Lawton, Okla.
KEJO Corvallis, Ore.
WPIT-FM Pittsburgh, Pa.
WAYZ-FM Waynesboro, Pa.
WKSA-FM Isabela, P.R.
WLKW-FM Providence, R.I.
KKSD Gregory, S.D.
WQUT Johnson City, Tenn.
KOXE Brownwood, Tex.
KNUE Tyler, Tex.
WFVA-FM Fredericksburg, Va.
KPLZ Seattle, Wash.
WIBA-FM Madison, Wis.
⋆ CJUM Winnipeg, Man.
CBZ-FM St. John, N.B.
CFMP Peterborough, Ont.
CJBR-FM Rimouski, Que.
XHMLS Matamoros, Tams.

101.7 (269) A

WVRT Reform, Ala.
WVSV Stevenson, Ala.
⋆ KSTK Wrangell, Alas.
KQEW Fordyce, Ark.
KUOL Mena, Ark.
KVOM-FM Morrilton, Ark.
KTOT Big Bear Lake, Calif.
KWST Carmel, Calif.
‡ KHTX Carnelian Bay, Calif.
KGFT Carpenteria, Calif.
KKIQ Livermore, Calif.
KVRE-FM Santa Rosa, Calif.
KBRU Ft. Morgan, Colo.
WWSD Quincy, Fla.
WKAK Albany, Ga.
WMPZ-FM Soperton, Ga.
WTHO-FM Thomson, Ga.
WRBN-FM Warner Robbins, Ga.
KMFE Emmett, Id.
WIXN-FM Dixon, Ill.
† ---- Greenville, Ill.
WTAY-FM Robinson, Ill.
WBMP Elwood, Ind.
WEZV Ft. Wayne, Ind.
KITR Creston, Ia.
KBKB-FM Ft. Madison, Ia.
† KFTS Ft. Scott, Kan.
KIND-FM Independence, Kan.
⋆ KMKF Manhattan, Kan.
WJYL Jeffersontown, Ky.
WKYM Monticello, Ky.
WCBR-FM Richmond, Ky.
KEAZ De Ridder, La.
WOZI Presque Isle, Me.
WFNX Lynn, Mass.
WXTQ-FM Pittsfield, Mass.
WILS-FM Lansing, Mich.
WABM Muskegon Heights, Mich.
WDBI-FM Tawas City, Mich.
† KOLV Olivia, Minn.
KRCH Rochester, Minn.
WHMH-FM Sauk Rapids, Minn.
WZXQ Canton, Miss.
WJBI Clarksdale, Miss.
WKNZ Collins, Miss.
WEXA Eupora, Miss.
WFTA Fulton, Miss.
KARO Columbia, Mo.
† KJFM Louisana, Mo.
KLPW Union, Mo.
WCNL-FM Newport, N.H.
KLEA-FM Lovington, N.M.
† KZIA-FM Rio Rancho, N.M.
KVNM Taos, N.M.
WBTF Attica, N.Y.
WECQ Geneva, N.Y.
† WENU Hudson Falls, N.Y.
WHUG Jamestown, N.Y.
WWWT Owego, N.Y.
⋆ WBAZ Southold, N.Y.
KMAV-FM Mayville, N.D.
WJER-FM Dover, O.
WNKO Newark, O.
WCOM-FM Urbana, O.
KEOK Tahlequah, Okla.
KCMX-FM Ashland, Ore.
WWZE Central City, Pa.
WVCC Linesville, Pa.
WBAW-FM Barnwell, S.C.
WKZQ Myrtle Beach, S.C.
WJSQ Athens, Tenn.
WKOM Columbia, Tenn.
WCMT-FM Martin, Tenn.
WORM-FM Savannah, Tenn.
WJLE-FM Smithville, Tenn.
KDSQ Denison, Tex.
KHUN Huntsville, Tex.
† KSOX-FM Raymondville, Tex.
KWDX Silsbee, Tex.
KSNY-FM Snyder, Tex.
WRFB Stowe, Vt.
WKWI Kilmarnock, Va.
WJJS-FM Lynchburg, Va.
WRIQ Radford, Va.
KACA Prosser, Wash.
† WRRR-FM St. Marys, W.V.
WHSM-FM Hayward, Wis.
CKNX-FM Wingham, Ont.

101.9 (270) BC

WHHY-FM Montgomery, Ala.
KBTM-FM Jonesboro, Ark.
KFRY Fresno, Calif.
KUTE Glendale, Calif.
† KNXN Quincy, Calif.
KKCS-FM Colorado Springs, Colo.
WDOQ Daytona Beach, Fla.
WHEW Ft. Myers, Fla.
WCLR Skokie, Ill.
WVEM Springfield, Ill.
⋆ KNWS-FM Waterloo, Ia.
WKYA Central City, Ky.
KNOE-FM Monroe, La.
WAJY New Orleans, La.
WPOR-FM Portland, Me.
WLIF Baltimore, Md.
WCIB Falmouth, Mass.
⋆ WDET-FM Detroit, Mich.
WLDR Traverse City, Mich.
KFMQ Lincoln, Neb.
KFMS Las Vegas, Nev.
WJIV Cherry Valley, N.Y.
WPIX-FM New York, N.Y.
WZXI Gastonia, N.C.
WAZZ New Bern, N.C.
KBTO Bottineau, N.D.
† KRRZ Fargo, N.D.
WKRQ Cincinnati, O.
KLTE Oklahoma City, Okla.
KINK Portland, Ore.
WAVT-FM Pottsville, Pa.
WZAR Ponce, P.R.
KWAS Amarillo, Tex.
KQXT San Antonio, Tex.
KQPD Ogden, Utah
WVOW-FM Logan, W.V.
WVAQ Morgantown, W.V.
WDEZ Wausau, Wis.
CKO-FM-6 Edmonton, Alta.
CKO-FM-10 St. John's, Nfld.
CHFX-FM Halifax, N.S.
CKAT North Bay, Ont.
XHPF-FM Mexicali, B.C.

102.1 (271) BC

WDRM Decatur, Ala.
KRKN Anchorage, Alas.
KEZL-FM Oceanside, Calif.
KDFC San Francisco, Calif.
WZAT Savannah, Ga.
WDNL Danville, Ill.
KSKU Hutchinson, Kan.
WAQY Springfield, Mass.
⋆ WMUK Kalamazoo, Mich.
KEEY-FM St. Paul, Minn.
KYYS Kansas City, Mo.
WWMO Reidsville, N.C.
WNUS Belpre, O.
WDOK Cleveland, O.
WIMT Lima, O.
WOWQ Du Bois, Pa.
WIOQ Philadelphia, Pa.
WMYU Sevierville, Tenn.
KMJQ Clear Lake City, Tex.
KLOZ El Paso, Tex.

	KTXQ	Ft. Worth, Tex.
	KWES	Monahans, Tex.
	WRXL	Richmond, Va.
	KPQ-FM	Wenatchee, Wash.
	WLUM	Milwaukee, Wis.
	CBR-FM	Calgary, Alta.
	CFNY	Brampton, Ont.
	CBOF-7	Brockville, Ont.

102.3 (272) A

†	WODB	Camden, Ala.
	WAMI-FM	Opp, Ala.
†	WELR-FM	Roanoke, Ala.
*	KHNS	Haines, Alas.
	KBRI-FM	Brinkley, Ark.
	KWKK	Dardanelle, Ark.
	KKBE	Sheridan, Ark.
†	KXXI-FM	Van Buren, Ark.
	KAPV	Apple Valley, Calif.
	KJLH	Compton, Calif.
	KFIV-FM	Modesto, Calif.
†	KRBQ	Red Bluff, Calif.
	KLGT	Breckenridge, Colo.
	KLOV-FM	Loveland, Colo.
†	WFAN	Stonington, Conn.
	WRTM	Blountstown, Fla.
	WTRS-FM	Dunnellon, Fla.
	WHLG	Jensen Beach, Fla.
	WYRL	Melbourne, Fla.
	WGUS-FM	Augusta, Ga.
	WGCO	Buford, Ga.
†	WTGQ	Cairo, Ga.
	WKZR	Milledgeville, Ga.
	WQTU	Rome, Ga.
	WRMJ	Aledo, Ill.
	WTAS	Crete, Ill.
	WKSI	Eldorado, Ill.
	WTAZ	Morton, Ill.
	WRHL-FM	Rochelle, Ill.
	WXLC	Waukegan, Ill.
	WSAL-FM	Logansport, Ind.
	WCBK-FM	Martinsville, Ind.
	KCHE-FM	Cherokee, Ia.
	KLXL	Dubuque, Ia.
	KIOW	Forest City, Ia.
	WLJC	Beattyville, Ky.
	WCBL-FM	Benton, Ky.
	WCYN-FM	Cynthiana, Ky.
	WUGO	Grayson, Ky.
	WLRS	Louisville, Ky.
	WLOC-FM	Munfordville, Ky.
	KBCE	Boyce, La.
	WTKS	Bethesda, Md.
	WAAQ	Big Rapids, Mich.
	WBSJ	Ellisville, Miss.
	WGCM	Gulfport, Miss.
†	----	Leland, Miss.
	WWSL	Philadelphia, Miss.
	WTXI	Ripley, Miss.
	KUCA	Canton, Mo.
	KDEX-FM	Dexter, Mo.
	KJPW-FM	Waynesville, Mo.
†	KKDY	West Plains, Mo.
	WKXL-FM	Concord, N.H.
	WSJL	Cape May, N.J.
	WSUS	Franklin, N.J.
	KEVR	Espanola, N.M.
	WBAB-FM	Babylon, N.Y.
	WFLC	Canandaigua, N.Y.
	WASM	Saratoga Springs, N.Y.
	WTPL-FM	Tupper Lake, N.Y.
	WAVR	Waverly, N.Y.
†	WZBO-FM	Edenton, N.C.
	WOKN	Goldsboro, N.C.
	WJSK	Lumberton, N.C.
	WPTM	Roanoke Rapids, N.C.
	WQLX	Galion, O.
	WPOS-FM	Holland, O.
	WSWO	Wilmington, O.
	KRHD-FM	Duncan, Okla.
	KCES	Eufaula, Okla.
†	----	Woodward, Okla.
	KSHR-FM	Coquille, Ore.
	WZUE	Carlisle, Pa.
	WSEG	Mc Kean, Pa.
	WTLQ	Pittston, Pa.
	WCPL-FM	Pageland, S.C.
†	WTOX	St. Andrews, S.C.
	KVRF	Vermillion, S.D.
†	KRAA	Volga, S.D.
	WRKM-FM	Carthage, Tenn.
	WTNQ	Dickson, Tenn.
	WZDQ	Humboldt, Tenn.
	WCHU-FM	Soddy Daisy, Tenn.
	KBIC	Alice, Tex.
	KPEZ	Austin, Tex.
	KLCR	Center, Tex.
	KWYX	Jasper, Tex.
	KMIO-FM	Merkel, Tex.
	KVWC-FM	Vernon, Tex.
†	KYOC	Yorkum, Tex.
	WCVR-FM	Randolph, Vt.
	WLFE	St. Albans, Vt.
	WPED-FM	Crozet, Va.
	WOLD-FM	Marion, Va.
	WWLH	Pound, Va.
†	WMTD-FM	Hinton, W.V.
	WSSN	Weston, W.V.
	WISS-FM	Berlin, Wis.
	WQTC-FM	Two Rivers, Wis.
	WGBM	Viroqua, Wis.
	WHTL-FM	Whitehall, Wis.
	CBAF	St. John, N.B.

102.5 (273) BC

	WWWB-FM	Jasper, Ala.
†	KQRZ	Fairbanks, Alas.
	KNIX-FM	Phoenix, Ariz.
	KDON-FM	Salinas, Calif.
	KSNI-FM	Santa Maria, Calif.
	~~KSFM~~	~~Woodland, Calif.~~
	KQZR	Craig, Colo.
	WSRZ	Sarasota, Fla.
*	WGHR	Marietta, Ga.
	WQCW	Waycross, Ga.
†	KRBU	Pocatello, Id.
	WMDH	New Castle, Ind.
	KRNQ	Des Moines, Ia.
†	KGKS	Goodland, Kan.
	WFMF	Baton Rouge, La.
†	----	Camden, Me.
	WOLC	Princess Anne, Md.
	WCRB	Waltham, Mass.
	WGER-FM	Bay City, Mich.
	KQIC	Willmar, Minn.
	KKUZ	Joplin, Mo.
	KEZK	St. Louis, Mo.
	WBEN-FM	Buffalo, N.Y.
†	WUUU	Rome, N.Y.
	WKIT	Hendersonville, N.C.
*	WNDN-FM	Salisbury, N.C.
	KDVL	Devils Lake, N.D.
	WHIZ-FM	Zanesville, O.
	KNPT-FM	Newport, Ore.
	WDVE	Pittsburgh, Pa.
	WRFY-FM	Reading, Pa.
	WIAC-FM	San Juan, P.R.
	WKTM	Charleston, S.C.
	KJNE	Hillsboro, Tex.
	KRUX	Lubbock, Tex.
	KRUX	Malakoff, Tex.
	KOSY-FM	Texarkana, Tex.
	WUSQ	Winchester, Va.
	KZOK-FM	Seattle, Wash.
	WNWC	Madison, Wis.
	KZIO	Superior, Wis.
	CBOF-FM	Ottawa, Ont.

102.7 (274) BC

	KRHS-FM	Bullhead City, Ariz.
	KKNU	Fresno, Calif.
	KIIS-FM	Los Angeles, Calif.
	KVLE	Gunnison, Colo.
	KIIQ-FM	Manitou Springs, Colo.
	WXBM-FM	Milton, Fla.
	WCKO	Pompano Beach, Fla.
	WBMX	Oak Park, Ill.
	WPFR-FM	Terre Haute, Ind.
†	KWNR	Liberal, Kan.
	WXYV	Baltimore, Md.
	WLBS	Mt. Clemens, Mich.
†	KCTB-FM	Cut Bank, Mont.
	KFRX	Lincoln, Neb.
	WNEW-FM	New York, N.Y.
	WGNI	Wilmington, N.C.
	WEBN	Cincinnati, O.
	WCPZ	Sandusky, O.
	KJYO	Oklahoma City, Okla.
	WKSB	Williamsport, Pa.
	WZXR	Memphis, Tenn.
	KTFM	San Antonio, Tex.
†	----	Midvale, Utah
†	WEQX	Manchester, Vt.
	KZZK-FM	Richland, Wash.
	WYSR	Charleston, W.V.
	WRVM	Suring, Wis.
*	CFRO	Vancouver, B.C.
	CBH-FM	Halifax, N.S.
	CITE-1	Sherbrooke, Que.

102.9 (275) BC

	KHOZ-FM	Harrison, Ark.
	KBLX	Berkeley, Calif.
	KSDO-FM	San Diego, Calif.
†	KZFR	South Lake Tahoe, Calif.
	WDRC-FM	Hartford, Conn.
	WIVY-FM	Jacksonville, Fla.
	WVOC	Columbus, Ga.
	KFMA	Jerome, Id.
	WSOY-FM	Decatur, Ill.
	KQCR	Cedar Rapids, Ia.
	KHUT	Hutchinson, Kan.
	KAJN-FM	Crowley, La.
	WGAN-FM	Portland, Me.
	WROG	Cumberland, Md.
	WIQB	Ann Arbor, Mich.
	WFUR-FM	Grand Rapids, Mich.
†	WMKC	St. Ignace, Mich.
	WLTE	Minneapolis, Minn.
	WMSI	Jackson, Miss.
	KEZS-FM	Cape Girardeau, Mo.
	KMFL-FM	Marshall, Mo.
	KOOK-FM	Billings, Mont.
	KBRX-FM	O' Neill, Neb.
	WMHR-FM	Syracuse, N.Y.
	WHKY-FM	Hickory, N.C.
	WAZU	Springfield, O.
†	KPRB-FM	Redmond, Ore.
	WMGK	Philadelphia, Pa.
	WYFM	Sharon, Pa.
	WCHQ-FM	Camuy, P.R.
†	----	Sisseton, S.D.
	WYCQ	Shelbyville, Tenn.
	KMGC	Dallas, Tex.
	KQUE	Houston, Tex.
	WOWI	Norfolk, Va.
	KMNT	Centralia, Wash.
	WBCS-FM	Milwaukee, Wis.
	KIOZ	Laramie, Wyo.
	CHGB-FM	La Pocatiere, Que.

103.1 (276) A

*	KSKA	Anchorage, Alas.
†	KTTZ	Oracle, Ariz.
	KAYZ	El Dorado, Ark.
	KCRI-FM	Helena, Ark.
	KRWA-FM	Waldron, Ark.
	KOCM	Newport Beach, Calif.
	KEZN	Palm Desert, Calif.

	Call	Location
	KSRF	Santa Monica, Calif.
‡	KZFR	South Lake Tahoe, Calif.
	KTPI	Tehachapi, Calif.
	KVVQ	Victorville, Calif.
	WQUH	De Funiak Springs, Fla.
	WLMC	Okeechobee, Fla.
†	WFKZ	Plantation Key, Fla.
	WOWD	Tallahassee, Fla.
	WLOQ	Winter Park, Fla.
	WZZW	Augusta, Ga.
	KCDA	Coeur D' Alene, Id.
	WVVX	Highland Park, Ill.
	WAKO-FM	Lawrenceville, Ill.
	WJEQ	Macomb, Ill.
	WPOK-FM	Pontiac, Ill.
	WRWC	Rockton, Ill.
	WVWV	Covington, Ind.
	WHUZ	Huntington, Ind.
	WHME	South Bend, Ind.
†	WOVR	Versailles, Ind.
	KZEV	Clear Lake, Ia.
	KNDY-FM	Marysville, Kan.
†	----	Ogden, Kan.
	WECL	Elkhorn City, Ky.
	WAXU-FM	Georgetown, Ky.
	WGRK-FM	Greensburg, Ky.
	WHKC	Henderson, Ky.
	WWXL-FM	Manchester, Ky.
	WRKA	St. Matthews, Ky.
	KCTO-FM	Columbia, La.
	WDME-FM	Dover Foxcroft, Me.
	WBEY	Grasonville, Md.
	WGMM	Gladwin, Mich.
	WDEY-FM	Lapeer, Mich.
	KFIL-FM	Preston, Minn.
	WJWF	Columbus, Miss.
	WOSM	Ocean Springs, Miss.
	KCRV-FM	Caruthersville, Mo.
	KCAP-FM	Helena, Mont.
	KIAE	Auburn, Neb.
	KIAE	Aurora, Neb.
	KASK	Las Cruces, N.M.
	WHRL	Albany, N.Y.
†	WCIK	Bath, N.Y.
*	WKRB	Brooklyn, N.Y.
†	----	Carthage, N.Y.
	WFMN	Newburgh, N.Y.
	WZOZ	Oneonta, N.Y.
	WIDO	Dunn, N.C.
	WWWJ	Jackson, O.
	WNDH	Napoleon, O.
	WRAC	West Union, O.
†	KEOR-FM	Atoka, Okla.
	KUAL	Enid, Okla.
	KRSB	Roseburg, Ore.
	WQEQ	Freeland, Pa.
	WQMU	Indiana, Pa.
†	----	Russell, Pa.
	WXLR	State College, Pa.
	WANB-FM	Waynesburg, Pa.
	WPDZ	Cheraw, S.C.
	WDPN	Columbia, S.C.
	WJBW-FM	Hampton, S.C.
	WRIX	Honea Path, S.C.
	WYAK-FM	Surfside Beach, S.C.
	KJAM-FM	Madison, S.D.
*	WCPH-FM	Etowah, Tenn.
	WJHR	Jackson, Tenn.
†	----	Anson, Tex.
	KRUN-FM	Ballinger, Tex.
†	KCRM	Cameron, Tex.
†	----	Canadian, Tex.
	KOOV	Copperas Cove, Tex.
	KLMF-FM	Fabens, Tex.
	KMUL-FM	Muleshoe, Tex.
	KCTM	Rio Grande City, Tex.
†	WVRS	Waterbury, Vt.
	WCUL	Culpeper, Va.
†	KQBE	Ellensburg, Wash.
	WQAW	Parkersburg, W.V.
	CKO-FM-5	Calgary, Alta.
	CKWG	Winnipeg, Man.
	CFMX	Cobourg, Ont.
	CHWC	Port Hope, Ont.

103.3 (277) BC

	Call	Location
	WREZ	Montgomery, Ala.
	KJNP-FM	North Pole, Alas.
	KWOZ	Mountain View, Ark.
	KBEE-FM	Modesto, Calif.
	KRUZ	Santa Barbara, Calif.
*	KSCU	Santa Clara, Calif.
	KIAH	Ukiah, Calif.
	WDUV	Bradenton, Fla.
	WVEE	Atlanta, Ga.
	WACL-FM	Waycross, Ga.
	WXTZ	Indianapolis, Ind.
	KXJX	Pella, Ia.
	KTFC	Sioux City, Ia.
	KJLS	Hays, Kan.
	WTGI	Hammond, La.
	WHTT	Boston, Mass.
	WKFR-FM	Battle Creek, Mich.
*	KUMD-FM	Duluth, Minn.
	KBRF-FM	Fergus Falls, Minn.
	KPRS	Kansas City, Mo.
	KHTR	St. Louis, Mo.
	WPRB	Princeton, N.J.
	WPHD	Buffalo, N.Y.
†	WZYC	New Port, N.C.
*	WCRF	Cleveland, O.
	KTFX	Tulsa, Okla.
	KTJA	Beaverton, Ore.
	WSBA-FM	York, Pa.
	WVJP-FM	Caguas, P.R.
	WKDF	Nashville, Tenn.
	KOUL	Corpus Christi, Tex.
†	----	Freeport, Tex.
	KWMJ	Midland, Tex.
	KJCS	Nacogdoches, Tex.
	KKQV	Wichita Falls, Tex.
	WAKG	Danville, Va.
	WESR-FM	Onancock, Va.
	WTCR	Huntington, W.V.
	WWRW	Wisconsin Rapids, Wis.
	CBO-FM	Ottawa, Ont.
	XHVG-FM	Mexicali, B.C.

103.5 (278) BC

	Call	Location
	KGTL-FM	Homer, Alas.
	KOST	Los Angeles, Calif.
	KOAQ	Denver, Colo.
	WGMS-FM	Washington, D. C.
	WSHE-FM	Ft. Lauderdale, Fla.
†	WFYR	Chicago, Ill.
†	WCCH	Holyoke, Mass.
	WMUZ	Detroit, Mich.
	WTCM-FM	Traverse City, Mich.
	KYSM-FM	Mankato, Minn.
	WOKM	New Albany, Miss.
	KXNP	North Platte, Neb.
†	----	Cobleskill, N.Y.
	WAPP	Lake Success, N.Y.
†	KZZY	Devils Lake, N.D.
	WBLZ	Hamilton, O.
	WRKY	Steubenville, O.
	KFMT	Pendleton, Ore.
*	WKVR-FM	Huntingdon, Pa.
	WEZL	Charleston, S.C.
	WIMZ	Knoxville, Tenn.
	KEYI	San Marcos, Tex.
	KRSP-FM	Salt Lake City, Utah
	CHQM-FM	Vancouver, B.C.
	CHLM-1	Lithiums Mines, Que.
	XHEM-FM	Ciudad Juarez, Chih.

103.7 (279) BC

	Call	Location
	WQEN	Gadsden, Ala.
	KKYK	Little Rock, Ark.
†	KHTX	Carnelian Bay, Calif.
	KMCX	Hanford, Calif.
	KJQY	San Diego, Calif.
	KGO-FM	San Francisco, Calif.
	WRUF-FM	Gainesville, Fla.
	WDBR	Springfield, Ill.
*	WFIU	Bloomington, Ind.
	KJAN-FM	Atlantic, Ia.
	KIIK	Davenport, Ia.
	KEYN-FM	Wichita, Kan.
	WAAW	Murray, Ky.
	KBIU	Lake Charles, La.
	WHDG	Havre De Grace, Md.
†	KKBJ-FM	Bemidji, Minn.
	WHER	Hattiesburg, Miss.
	KIRK	Lebanon, Mo.
	WXLQ	Berlin, N.H.
	WNBX-FM	Keene, N.H.
	WMGM	Atlantic City, N.J.
	WIXL-FM	Newton, N.J.
	WQNY	Ithaca, N.Y.
	WSOC-FM	Charlotte, N.C.
	WSEC	Williamston, N.C.
	WTTF-FM	Tiffin, O.
	KRPT-FM	Anadarko, Okla.
	KIQY	Lebanon, Ore.
	WCCK	Erie, Pa.
	WERI-FM	Westerly, R.I.
	KVIL-FM	Dallas, Tex.
	KOUL	Sinton, Tex.
	WEZS	Richmond, Va.
	KBRD	Tacoma, Wash.
	WCIR-FM	Beckley, W.V.
	WWIB	Ladysmith, Wis.
	WEZW	Wauwatosa, Wis.
†	KOLT	Casper, Wyo.

103.9 (280) A

	Call	Location
†	WJAM-FM	Marion, Ala.
	WORJ	Ozark, Ala.
‡	KKLV	Anchorage, Alas.
†*	KJFP	Yakutat, Alas.
	KQEZ-FM	Coolidge, Ariz.
	KPSN	Payson, Ariz.
	KAHM	Prescott, Ariz.
	KMLA	Ashdown, Ark.
	KKIX	Fayetteville, Ark.
	KCYN	Pocahontas, Ark.
	KACE	Inglewood, Calif.
	KBON	Lake Arrowhead, Calif.
	KRAY-FM	Salinas, Calif.
†	----	Taft, Calif.
	KXEZ	Yuba City, Calif.
	KRLN-FM	Canon City, Colo.
	KFMU	Oak Creek, Colo.
†	KDRW	Silverton, Colo.
†	KTUS	Snowmas Village, Colo.
	WRCC	Cape Coral, Fla.
	WPPL	Blue Ridge, Ga.
	WGRG	Greensboro, Ga.
	WCEH-FM	Hawkinsville, Ga.
	WGEC	Springfield, Ga.
	WXRS-FM	Swainsboro, Ga.
	KRPL-FM	Moscow, Id.
	WXAN	Ava, Ill.
	WCRM	Dundee, Ill.
	WNOI	Flora, Ill.
	WKIO	Urbana, Ill.
	WRBI	Batesville, Ind.
	WLFQ	Crawfordsville, Ind.
	WFLM	Crown Point, Ind.
	WXKE	Ft. Wayne, Ind.
	WXMG	South Bend, Ind.
	KNEI-FM	Waukon, Ia.
	KOMB	Fort Scott, Kan.
	KNZA	Hiawatha, Kan.
	WCKQ-FM	Campbellsville, Ky.
	WWEL	London, Ky.
	WXLN	Louisville, Ky.
	WXKQ	Whitesburg, Ky.
	WOCQ	Berlin, Md.
	WZYQ-FM	Braddock Heights, Md.

WLEN Adrian, Mich.
WOAP-FM Owosso, Mich.
WKJC Tawas City, Mich.
KRRK-FM East Grand Forks, Minn.
WCLD-FM Cleveland, Miss.
WACR-FM Columbus, Miss.
KCHI-FM Chillicothe, Mo.
KVCM Montgomery City, Mo.
KTAP Crete, Neb.
KNLV-FM Ord, Neb.
KRFS-FM Superior, Neb.
KCMI Terrytown, Neb.
KGRT-FM Las Cruces, N.M.
WSRK Oneonta, N.Y.
WQBK-FM Rensselaer, N.Y.
WRCN-FM Riverhead, N.Y.
WDKX Rochester, N.Y.
WXTY Ticonderoga, N.Y.
WFAS-FM White Plains, N.Y.
WAKS-FM Fuquay Springs, N.C.
WYMJ-FM Beaver Creek, O.
WBBY Westerville, O.
WHGM Bellwood, Pa.
WIBF-FM Jenkintown, Pa.
WRXZ Kane, Pa.
WWIZ Mercer, Pa.
† WJKR Muncy, Pa.
WLSW Scottdale, Pa.
WELP-FM Easley, S.C.
WORG-FM Orangeburg, S.C.
WXIS Erwin, Tenn.
WDEB-FM Jamestown, Tenn.
WBMC-FM Mc Minnville, Tenn.
KMHT-FM Marshall, Tex.
† KVEX Smithfield, Utah
WXCF-FM Clifton Forge, Va.
WQAA Luray, Va.
† KLLM Forks, Wash.
WKGI New Martinsville, W.V.
WOSH Oshkosh, Wis.
CBRF-FM Calgary, Alta.
CISN Edmonton, Alta.
CFQM-FM Moncton, N.B.
CFMC Saskatoon, Sask.

104.1 (281) BC

WSKR Atmore, Ala.
† KKLV Anchorage, Alas.
KHOP Modesto, Calif.
KNAB-FM Burlington, Colo.
WIOF Waterbury, Conn.
WRKT-FM Cocoa Beach, Fla.
WGLF Tallahassee, Fla.
WJYF La Grange, Ga.
WJBM-FM Jerseyville, Ill.
WIKY-FM Evansville, Ind.
WLBC-FM Muncie, Ind.
REZT Ames, Ia.
KHOM Houma, La.
KWEZ Monroe, La.
WXTR-FM La Plata, Md.
WBCN Boston, Mass.
* WVGR Grand Rapids, Mich.
KJJO St. Louis Park, Minn.
† KLSK Santa Fe, N.M.
WNYS-FM Buffalo, N.Y.
WTQR Winston Salem, N.C.
WQAL Cleveland, O.
WPAY-FM Portsmouth, O.
KOFM Oklahoma City, Okla.
KTIL-FM Tillamook, Ore.
WXKW Allentown, Pa.
WTPA-FM Harrisburg, Pa.
WERR Utuado, P.R.
WLAT-FM Conway, S.C.
KQHU Yankton, S.D.
WKIR Jackson, Tenn.
KXYL-FM Brownwood, Tex.

KBFM Edinburg, Tex.
KRBE-FM Houston, Tex.
KXDD Yakima, Wash.
WZEE Madison, Wis.
† KNWY Powell, Wyo.

104.3 (282) BC

WZYP Athens, Ala.
* KTOO Juneau, Alas.
† KZRO Marshall, Ark.
KBIG Los Angeles, Calif.
KSHA Redding, Calif.
KLMO-FM Longmont, Colo.
WBBQ-FM Augusta, Ga.
† KIDQ Boise, Id.
† KCJF Kellogg, Id.
WJEZ Chicago, Ill.
KVGB-FM Great Bend, Kan.
WABK-FM Gardiner, Me.
WBSB Baltimore, Md.
WOMC Detroit, Mich.
KBEQ Kansas City, Mo.
WNCN New York, N.Y.
WKGW Utica, N.Y.
WKTC Tarboro, N.C.
WELA East Liverpool, O.
† ---- Milbank, S.D.
KDKQ Borger, Tex.
KSOP-FM Salt Lake City, Utah
WJSY Harrisonburg, Va.
KNWR Bellingham, Wash.
CHFA-1 Lethbridge, Alta.
CBWZ Fairford, Man.
CJQM Sault Ste. Marie, Ont.
CBF-FM-1 Drummondville, Que.

104.5 (283) BC

KIQO Atascadero, Calif.
KFOG San Francisco, Calif.
WFYV Atlantic Beach, Fla.
WEAT-FM West Palm Beach, Fla.
WGPC-FM Albany, Ga.
WFMB Springfield, Ill.
* WAJC Indianapolis, Ind.
KTOF Cedar Rapids, Ia.
WFMP Fitchburg, Mass.
WQWQ-FM Muskegon, Mich.
WHSY-FM Hattiesburg, Miss.
† KOOC Cozad, Neb.
KESY-FM Omaha, Neb.
KSRN Reno, Nev.
WQKT Wooster, O.
KMYZ-FM Pryor, Okla.
KCIV The Dalles, Ore.
WSNI-FM Philadelphia, Pa.
WNBT-FM Wellsboro, Pa.
WWKX Gallatin, Tenn.
WRVR Memphis, Tenn.
KKDA-FM Dallas, Tex.
KZOM Orange, Tex.
KVAR San Antonio, Tex.
WNVZ Norfolk, Va.
WHAJ Bluefield, W.V.
WAXX Eau Claire, Wis.
* WCCX Waukesha, Wis.
KSIT Rock Springs, Wyo.
CFLG Cornwall, Ont.
CHUM-FM Toronto, Ont.

104.7 (284) BC

WZZK Birmingham, Ala.
* KUAC-FM Fairbanks, Alas.
* KCAW Sitka, Alas.
KZZP-FM Mesa, Ariz.

KSNN Los Banos, Calif.
KCAQ Oxnard, Calif.
KDES-FM Palm Springs, Calif.
KSTC-FM Sterling, Colo.
KVMT Vail, Colo.
WWUS Big Pine Key, Fla.
WRBQ-FM Tampa, Fla.
WAGQ Athens, Ga.
WCSJ-FM Morris, Ill.
WFRN Elkhart, Ind.
WITZ-FM Jasper, Ind.
WWMD Hagerstown, Md.
WQHQ Ocean City, Md.
WKPE Orleans, Mass.
WYKX Escanaba, Mich.
KCLD-FM St. Cloud, Minn.
KRES Moberly, Mo.
WKFM Fulton, N.Y.
WSPK Poughkeepsie, N.Y.
WEZC Charlotte, N.C.
WTUE Dayton, O.
WIOT Toledo, O.
† KRKA Alva, Okla.
KDUK Florence, Ore.
WYDD Pittsburgh, Pa.
WKAQ-FM San Juan, P.R.
WNOK-FM Columbia, S.C.
KIOV Sioux Falls, S.D.
KIOF Lamesa, Tex.
WSVS-FM Crewe, Va.
KDUX-FM Aberdeen, Wash.
CHIM Kelowna, B.C.
CBVE-FM Quebec, Que.

104.9 (285) A

WHOD-FM Jackson, Ala.
WOAB Ozark, Ala.
KAGH-FM Crossett, Ark.
KHPA Hope, Ark.
KDXY Paragould, Ark.
KCIZ Springdale, Ark.
† KQEE West Helena, Ark.
KBRG Fremont, Calif.
† KQYZ Lemoore, Calif.
KOCN Pacific Grove, Calif.
KFIO Ridgecrest, Calif.
WIHS Middletown, Conn.
WAAZ-FM Crestview, Fla.
† WHFL Havana, Fla.
† WKAE High Springs, Fla.
† WIMV Madison, Fla.
WKUB Blackshear, Ga.
WFXE Columbus, Ga.
WHCG Metter, Ga.
† WMCG Milan, Ga.
‡ KRBU Pocatello, Id.
WYBR-FM Belvedere, Ill.
WCBW Columbia, Ill.
WFIW-FM Fairfield, Ill.
WGEN-FM Geneseo, Ill.
WTAO Murphysboro, Ill.
† WOKO Paxton, Ill.
WKQA Pekin, Ill.
WSHY-FM Shelbyville, Ill.
WWWY Columbus, Ind.
‡ WWHC Hartford City, Ind.
† ---- Muncie, Ind.
WAXI Rockville, Ind.
† KQHJ-FM Hampton, Ia.
KBOE-FM Oskaloosa, Ia.
KDLS-FM Perry, Ia.
KRGS Spencer, Ia.
KLRF Emporia, Kan.
WKYW Frankfort, Ky.
WJRS Jamestown, Ky.
WKHG Leitchfield, Ky.
WPKY-FM Princeton, Ky.
WSKV Stanton, Ky.
† WKKS-FM Vanceburg, Ky.
KASC Abbeville, La.
KSMI-FM Donaldsonville, La.
KJBQ Jonesboro, La.
KGBM-FM Oakdale, La.
* WRBB Boston, Mass.
WVCA-FM Gloucester, Mass.
WFYC-FM Alma, Mich.

WKYO-FM Caro, Mich.
WELL-FM Marshall, Mass.
WAOP Otsego, Mich.
KRFO-FM Owatonna, Minn.
KXAX St. James, Minn.
WZZB Centreville, Miss.
WTIB Iuka, Miss.
WKKY Moss Point, Miss.
KRGK Carthage, Mo.
KOSC-FM Marshfield, Mo.
KTCH-FM Wayne, Neb.
KAWL-FM York, Neb.
† WLKZ Wolfeboro, N.H.
WRDR Egg Harbor, N.J.
KOPE Mesilla Park, N.M.
WIZR-FM Johnstown, N.Y.
WNGZ Montour Falls, N.Y.
WMSQ Havelock, N.C.
WKSM Tabor City, N.C.
WQNS Waynesville, N.C.
KNDR Mandan, N.D.
WCVO Gahanna, O.
WLSR Lima, O.
WZLE Lorain, O.
KJIL Bethany, Okla.
KREK Bristow, Okla.
WHPA Hollidaysburg, Pa.
WWDL-FM Scranton, Pa.
WNFM Dayton, Tenn.
WZXY Kingsport, Tenn.
WQLA La Follette, Tenn.
WALR-FM Union City, Tenn.
WVRY Waverly, Tenn.
KJAV Alamo, Tex.
KCWW Beeville, Tex.
† ---- Bryan, Tex.
† KALK Denison, Tex.
KMUZ La Grange, Tex.
† KFQX Llano, Tex.
† ---- Mexia, Tex.
† KMFM Premont, Tex.
KFRD-FM Rosenberg, Tex.
KPLE Temple, Tex.
---- Tulla, Tex.
KYUF Uvalde, Tex.
† KWNS Winnsboro, Tex.
† KBXN-FM Tremont, Utah
WVVV Blacksburg, Va.
KQQQ-FM Pullman, Wash.
KYJR Wenatchee, Wash.
WPDX-FM Clarksburg, W.V.
WTKM-FM Hartford, Wis.
WKAU-FM Kaukauna, Wis.
WLXR-FM La Crosse, Wis.
WRDB-FM Reedsburg, Wis.
CISQ Squamish, B.C.
CKIT Regina, Sask.
XHMC-FM Mexicali, B.C.

105.1 (286) BC

WQSB Albertville, Ala.
KMJX Conway, Ark.
KKGO Los Angeles, Calif.
KEWT Sacramento, Calif.
KBRQ-FM Denver, Colo.
WEZI Coral Gables, Fla.
WBJW Orlando, Fla.
KJOT Boise, Id.
WOJO Evanston, Ill.
WGEM-FM Quincy, Ill.
WTOS Skowhegan, Me.
WQLZ Cheboygan, Mich.
WQRS-FM Detroit, Mich.
KKIB Breckenridge, Minn.
WAVC Duluth, Minn.
WKOZ-FM Kosciusko, Miss.
KSFT St. Joseph, Mo.
WOIV De Ruyter, N.Y.
WRFM New York, N.Y.
WDCG Durham, N.C.
WUBE-FM Cincinnati, O.
WQXX Salem, O.
KSKD Salem, Ore.
WIOV Ephrata, Pa.
WILQ Williamsport, Pa.
WIOC Ponce, P.R.
WPJB-FM Providence, R.I.
KEAN-FM Abilene, Tex.
KYKS Lufkin, Tex.
KMXU Manti, Utah
WAVA Arlington, Va.
WKLC-FM St. Albans, W.V.
* CKQM-FM Peterborough, Ont.

105.3 (287) BC

† KNIK-FM Anchorage, Alas.
† KZAY Delano, Calif.
KCBQ-FM San Diego, Calif.
KITS San Francisco, Calif.
† KDBL Rifle, Colo.
†* WDJW Somers, Conn.
WDEN-FM Macon, Ga.
WYNG Evansville, Ind.
WASK-FM Lafayette, Ind.
KLYV Dubuque, Ia.
WAIL Slidell, La.
WFRB-FM Frostburg, Md.
† WCXT Hart, Mich.
KZNN Rolla, Mo.
KXMC Mc Cook, Neb.
WKPQ Hornell, N.Y.
† KZPR Minot, N.D.
WCLW-FM Mansfield, O.
WDAS-FM Philadelphia, Pa.
WAGI Gaffney, S.C.
KOAX Dallas, Tex.
KLSR-FM Memphis, Tex.
KWED-FM Seguin, Tex.
WXRI Portsmouth, Va.
KBIQ Edmonds, Wash.
KONA-FM Kennewick, Wash.
WRLO-FM Antigo, Wis.
CBWW Baldy Mountain, Man.
CFCA-FM Kitchener, Ont.
CKBY Ottawa, Ont.
CJMX Sudbury, Ont.

105.5 (288) A

WWSM Bay Minette, Ala.
WLAY-FM Muscle Shoals, Ala.
WACT-FM Tuscaloosa, Ala.
‡ KNIK-FM Anchorage, Alas.
KSAA Casa Grande, Ariz.
† WHBC Wickenburg, Ariz.
† ---- Mountain Home, Ark.
KNAS Nashville, Ark.
KOKR Newport, Ark.
† KTEI Piggott, Ark.
† ---- Stuttgart, Ark.
KWRF-FM Warren, Ark.
† KZDO Copperopolis, Calif.
KYLO Davis, Calif.
KHYE Hemet, Calif.
KNAC Long Beach, Calif.
KOVA Ojai, Calif.
† KCRP Rosamond, Calif.
† KIQS-FM Willows, Calif.
KWYD Security, Colo.
† KVRS Sterling, Colo.
WQGN-FM Groton, Conn.
WYKS Gainesville, Fla.
WGUL-FM New Port Richey, Fla.
* WKZM Sarasota, Fla.
WSKP-FM Sebring, Fla.
WMKM St. Augustine, Fla.
WAVW Vero Beach, Fla.
WOFF Camilla, Ga.
WCHK-FM Canton, Ga.
WBTY Homerville, Ga.
WIFO-FM Jessup, Ga.
WOWE Rossville, Ga.
WVLJ Monticello, Ill.
WDND Wilmington, Ill.
WXRD Woodstock, Ill.
WIFF-FM Auburn, Ind.
WBIF Bedford, Ind.
WLJE Valparaiso, Ind.
WWVR West Terre Haute, Ind.
KYRS Chariton, Ia.
KWGG Harlan, Ia.
KILJ Mt. Pleasant, Ia.
KIWA-FM Sheldon, Ia.
KTLB Twin Lakes, Ia.
KVSV-FM Beloit, Kan.
KQSM Chanute, Kan.
‡ KSCB-FM Liberal, Kan.
KWKS Winfield, Kan.
WWKK Ft. Knox, Ky.
WOVO Glasgow, Ky.
WLGC Greenup, Ky.
WGKY-FM Greenville, Ky.
WKDO-FM Liberty, Ky.
WMST-FM Mt. Sterling, Ky.
WPRT-FM Prestonburg, Ky.
KJJB Eunice, La.
KFRA-FM Franklin, La.
† KLUV Haynesville, La.
KVVP Leesville, La.
WKYZ Salisbury, Md.
WBEC-FM Pittsfield, Mass.
WWCK Flint, Mich.
WBMI West Branch, Mich.
KXLV-FM Cambridge, Minn.
KMGM Montevideo, Minn.
KWNG Red Wing, Minn.
KRBI-FM St. Peter, Minn.
WHAY Aberdeen, Miss.
WNLA-FM Indianola, Miss.
WABO-FM Waynesboro, Miss.
KESM-FM El Dorado Springs, Mo.
† KLUK Knob Noster, Mo.
KAUB Auburn, Neb.
KHUB-FM Fremont, Neb.
KRRI Boulder City, Nev.
† WJYY Concord, N.H.
WDHA-FM Dover, N.J.
KINN-FM Alamogordo, N.M.
† ---- Frankfurt, N.Y.
WLPW Lake Placid, N.Y.
WSGO-FM Oswego, N.Y.
* WRVH Patterson, N.Y.
WXQR Jacksonville, N.C.
WFJA Sanford, N.C.
WXTQ Athens, O.
WGOJ Conneaut, O.
WMVR-FM Sidney, O.
WCHO-FM Washington Court House, O.
KXXK Chickasha, Okla.
KSLE Seminole, Okla.
KVRO Stillwater, Okla.
KYNG-FM Coos Bay, Ore.
KCGB Hood River, Ore.
WPXZ-FM Punxsutawney, Pa.
WZTA Tamaqua, Pa.
WRFE Aguada, P.R.
WDAR-FM Darlington, S.C.
WLVW Moncks Corner, S.C.
WNMB North Myrtle Beach, S.C.
WYTM-FM Fayetteville, Tenn.
WVTN Gatlinburg, Tenn.
WBNT-FM Oneida, Tenn.
WTPR-FM Paris, Tenn.
WSMT-FM Sparta, Tenn.
KACT-FM Andrews, Tex.
KHOC Levelland, Tex.
† KITM Mission, Tex.
KITE Portland, Tex.
KCGL Centerville, Utah
WKDE-FM Altavista, Va.
WWOO Berryville, Va.
WLSA Louisa, Va.
WSWV-FM Pennington Gap, Va.
WGTH Richlands, Va.
WSHV South Hill, Va.
WRAR-FM Tappahannock, Va.
KLYK Longview, Wash.
WKCJ Lewisburg, W.V.
WCFW Chippewa Falls, Wis.

	CBKS	Saskatoon, Sask.
	XHRE-FM	Piedras Negras, Coah.

105.7 (289) BC

	WIGC	Troy, Ala.
	KMCK	Siloam Springs, Ark.
	KARA	Santa Clara, Calif.
	WYMX	Augusta, Ga.
	WWCT	Peoria, Ill.
	WTLC	Indianapolis, Ind.
	KCNB	Waterloo, Ia.
	WKTK	Catonsville, Md.
	WVBF	Framingham, Mass.
	WOOD-FM	Grand Rapids, Mich.
	WAKH	Mc Comb, Miss.
	KSGM-FM	Ste. Genevieve, Mo.
	KOZZ	Reno, Nev.
	WMRV	Endicott, N.Y.
	WTHD	Columbia, N.C.
	WFMX	Statesville, N.C.
	WMJI	Cleveland, O.
*	WOBN	Westerville, O.
†	----	Bend, Ore.
	WQXA	York, Pa.
	WCAD	San Juan, P.R.
	KHCB-FM	Houston, Tex.
	KYKX	Longview, Tex.
	KWWM	Stephenville, Tex.
	KEZE-FM	Spokane, Wash.
	WAPL-FM	Appleton, Wis.
	CBU-FM	Vancouver, B.C.
	CHRE	St. Catherines, Ont.
	CFGL	Laval, Que.

105.9 (290) BC

†*	WTOH	Mobile, Ala.
*	KRBD	Ketchikan, Alas.
	KKDJ	Fresno, Calif.
	KMGG	Los Angeles, Calif.
	KBPI	Denver, Colo.
	WHCN	Hartford, Conn.
	WELE-FM	De Land, Fla.
	WAXY	Ft. Lauderdale, Fla.
	WXFM	Elmwood Park, Ill.
	KLZR	Lawrence, Kan.
	WIGY	Bath, Me.
	WKHQ	Charlevoix, Mich.
	WJZZ	Detroit, Mich.
	KKWS	Wadena, Minn.
	KQKY	Kearney, Neb.
†	WHBI	Newark, N.J.
†	KNMQ	Santa Fe, N.M.
	WPBF-FM	Middletown, O.
	KQTZ	Hobart, Okla.
	WAMO-FM	Pittsburgh, Pa.
	KMIT	Mitchell, S.D.
	WGKX	Memphis, Tenn.
	WLAC-FM	Nashville, Tenn.
	WPKX-FM	Woodbridge, Va.
	WTNJ	Mt. Hope, W.V.
	WBWA	Washburn, Wis.
	CBI-FM	Sydney, N.S.
	CBCO	Orillia, Ont.

106.1 (291) BC

	WRFS-FM	Alexander City, Ala.
†	KARZ	Burney, Calif.
†	KPLM	Palm Springs, Calif.
	KMEL	San Francisco, Calif.
	WLET-FM	Toccoa, Ga.
	WSMI-FM	Litchfield, Ill.
	WHVI-FM	North Vernon, Ind.
	KLSS	Mason City, Ia.
	KLFQ	Lyons, Kan.
	KNAN	Monroe, La.
*	WMEM	Presque Isle, Me.
	WKGO	Cumberland, Md.
	WCOD-FM	Hyannis, Mass.
	WJXQ	Jackson, Mich.
	WECM	Claremont, N.H.
	WZKZ	Corning, N.Y.
	WBLI	Patchogue, N.Y.
*	WUAG	Greensboro, N.C.
	WXYY	Wilson, N.C.
	WVNO-FM	Mansfield, O.
	KCMA	Owasso, Okla.
	KLOO-FM	Corvallis, Ore.
	WWSH	Philadelphia, Pa.
	KIXK	Denton, Tex.
	KIOC	Orange, Tex.
	WVIS	Fredericksted, St. Croix, V.I.
	KRPM-FM	Tacoma, Wash.
	WMIL	Waukesha, Wis.
	CKLA	Guelph, Ont.
	CHEZ	Ottawa, Ont.

106.3 (292) A

	WKNU	Brewton, Ala.
	WNAN	Demopolis, Ala.
	WBTG	Sheffield, Ala.
†	KKAF	Eloy, Ariz.
	KMZK	Sun City, Ariz.
	KFFB	Fairfield Bay, Ark.
	KAJJ	Greenwood, Ark.
	KACQ	Hot Springs, Ark.
†	KTWD	Lonoke, Ark.
	KCAZ	Walnut Ridge, Ark.
	KMGQ	Goleta, Calif.
	KOTE	Lancaster, Calif.
	KMMT	Mammoth Lakes, Calif.
	KYMS	Santa Ana, Calif.
†	KSKE	Kremmling, Colo.
	WWOJ	Avon Park, Fla.
	WAFC	Clewiston, Fla.
	WVTY	Holiday, Fla.
	WCIF	Melbourne, Fla.
	WMLO	Sarasota, Fla.
	WPXE-FM	Starke, Fla.
	WGMK	Donalsonville, Ga.
	WQBZ	Fort Valley, Ga.
	WKIG-FM	Glennville, Ga.
	WQRL	Benton, Ill.
†	WGCY	Gibson City, Ill.
	WLNR	Lansing, Ill.
	WSAK	Sullivan, Ill.
	WKSY	Columbia City, Ind.
	WNDY	Crawfordsville, Ind.
	KJJY	Ankeny, Ia.
†	KXOF	Bloomfield, Ia.
	KQIS	Clarinda, Ia.
	WANY-FM	Albany, Ky.
	WKDZ-FM	Cadiz, Ky.
	WLLS-FM	Hartford, Ky.
	WKMO	Hodgenville, Ky.
	WTJM	Pineville, Ky.
	WJMM	Versailles, Ky.
	KQXL-FM	New Roads, La.
	KXOR	Thibodaux, La.
	WDCS	Scarborough, Me.
	WCEM-FM	Cambridge, Md.
†	----	Lakeview, Mich.
	WKLA-FM	Ludington, Mich.
†	----	Menominee, Mich.
	WIOG	Saginaw, Mich.
	WMFG	Hibbing, Minn.
†	KBAA	Ortonville, Minn.
	WQPM-FM	Princeton, Minn.
	WAID	Clarksdale, Miss.
	WLTD	Lexington, Miss.
	WMYQ-FM	Newton, Miss.
	WGUD	Pascagoula, Miss.
	WJOJ	Picayune, Miss.
	WSMU-FM	Starkville, Miss.
	KYOO-FM	Bolivar, Mo.
	KRZK	Branson, Mo.
	KVVC-FM	Cabool, Mo.
	KLCQ	Monroe City, Mo.
	KMIS-FM	Portageville, Mo.
	KOOZ	Great Falls, Mont.
	KBWH	Blair, Neb.
	KHAT	Lincoln, Neb.
†		Littleton, N.H.
	WOTW-FM	Nashua, N.H.
	WFMV	Blairstown, N.J.
	WHTG-FM	Eatontown, N.J.
	WSLT	Ocean City, N.J.
	WVIP-FM	Mount Kisco, N.Y.
	WMCR-FM	Oneida, N.Y.
†	WPGO	Shallotte, N.C.
†	----	Cadiz, O.
	WSYX	London, O.
	WWJM	New Lexington, O.
	WPNM	Ottawa, O.
†	KKBI	Broken Bow, Okla.
	KGOU	Norman, Okla.
	WCQO	Blairsville, Pa.
	WRLR	Huntingdon, Pa.
	WCTL	Union City, Pa.
	WWON-FM	Woonsocket, R.I.
	WSTN	Florence, S.C.
	WAZX	Georgetown, S.C.
	WHHR	Hilton Head Island, S.C.
	KTON-FM	Belton, Tex.
	KWHI-FM	Brenham, Tex.
†	KAUM	Colorado City, Tex.
†	KPSO-FM	Falfurrias, Tex.
	KPAN-FM	Hereford, Tex.
	KGAR	Mercedes, Tex.
	KYOT	Refugio, Tex.
	KIKZ-FM	Seminole, Tex.
	KESI	Terrell Hills, Tex.
	KBHV	Spanish Fork, Utah
†	WIZN	Vergennes, Vt.
	WBDY-FM	Bluefield, Va.
	WMNA-FM	Gretna, Va.
	WLCC	Luray, Va.
	WNVA-FM	Norton, Va.
	KHWK	Richland, Wash.
†	WNST-FM	Milton, W.V.
	WWQM-FM	Middleton, Wis.
	WEVR-FM	River Falls, Wis.
†	KLEN	Cheyenne, Wyo.
	KOTB	Evanston, Wyo.
	CJBC-5-FM	Peterborough, Ont.
	CBEG-FM	Sarnia, Ont.

106.5 (293) BC

	KWHL	Anchorage, Alas.
	KWOD	Sacramento, Calif.
	KPRI	San Diego, Calif.
	KEZR	San Jose, Calif.
	KWK-FM	Granite City, Ill.
	WFML	Washington, Ind.
	KRVR	Davenport, Ia.
	KBUZ	Arkansas City, Kan.
	WMAR-FM	Baltimore, Md.
	WQLR	Kalamazoo, Mich.
	KFMC	Fairmont, Minn.
	KKCI-FM	Liberty, Mo.
	KMCX	Ogallala, Neb.
	WPYX	Albany, N.Y.
	WYRK	Buffalo, N.Y.
	WSFL	Bridgeton, N.C.
	WSFL	New Bern, N.C.
	WRDX	Salisbury, N.C.
	WZZP	Cleveland, O.
	WLSN	Greenville, O.
	WHLM-FM	Bloomsburg, Pa.
	WNIK-FM	Arecibo, P.R.
	WSKZ	Chattanooga, Tenn.
	KXKX	Galveston, Tex.
	KOOI	Jacksonville, Tex.
*	WRFK-FM	Richmond, Va.
	KLYN-FM	Lynden, Wash.
	WKKW	Clarksburg, W.V.
	WLJY	Marshfield, Wis.

106.7 (294) BC

	WKMX	Enterprise, Ala.
	KROQ-FM	Pasadena, Calif.
	KJUG	Tulare, Calif.
	KAZY	Denver, Colo.
	WEWZ	Ft. Lauderdale, Fla.
	WHLY	Leesburg, Fla.
	WOKA-FM	Douglas, Ga.
	WWLT	Gainesville, Ga.

WYEN Des Plaines, Ill.
† KHUQ Huboton, Kan.
† KHHA Port Sulphur, La.
WMJX Boston, Mass.
WWWW Detroit, Mich.
WWRM Gaylord, Mich.
WJJY Brainerd, Minn.
WKYV-FM Vicksburg, Miss.
KEXL Norfolk, Neb.
WKHK New York, N.Y.
WSRW-FM Hillsboro, O.
KMJK Lake Oswego, Ore.
WWKS Beaver Falls, Pa.
WRKZ Hershey, Pa.
WIGL Orangeburg, S.C.
WEZR Manassas, Va.
CBTA Trail, B.C.

106.9 (295) BC

WKXX Birmingham, Ala.
KEAR San Francisco, Calif.
† ---- Yucca Valley, Calif.
WCCC-FM Hartford, Conn.
† KMOK Lewiston, Id.
WSWT Peoria, Ill.
WMRI Marion, Ind.
KTPK Topeka, Kan.
WVEZ Louisville, Ky.
WKCS Hagerstown, Md.
WUPM Ironwood, Mich.
WMUS-FM Muskegon, Mich.
KROC-FM Rochester, Minn.
KTXY Jefferson City, Mo.
KRNO Reno, Nev.
WKDN-FM Camden, N.J.
WPCX Auburn, N.Y.
WMIT Black Mountain, N.C.
WOOS-FM Canton, O.
* WWSU Fairborn, O.
WMRN-FM Marion, O.
KKCC-FM Clinton, Okla.
KAYI Muskogee, Okla.
WSRA Guayama, P.R.
WKTA Mc Kenzie, Tenn.
KJOJ Conroe, Tex.
KWWA Bremerton, Wash.
CBN-FM St. John's, Nfld.
CKO-FM Ottawa, Ont.
CKO-FM-1 Ottawa, Ont.

107.1 (296) A

KSTM Apache Jct, Ariz.
† ---- Bald Knob, Ark.
KAKI Benton, Ark.
KSCC Berryville, Ark.
KDDA-FM Dumas, Ark.
† KLQZ Paragould, Ark.
KADO-FM Texarkana, Ark.
KMAX Arcadia, Calif.
KAVO Fallbrook, Calif.
† KLOI Grover City, Calif.
KAAT Oakhurst, Calif.
KMBY Seaside, Calif.
† ---- Ventura, Calif.
† KBUL Brush, Colo.
KRMX-FM Pueblo, Colo.
WIIS Key West, Fla.
WOOJ-FM Lehigh Acres, Fla.
WLLV Melbourne, Fla.
WCLA-FM Claxton, Ga.
WQXM-FM Gordon, Ga.
WZOT Rockmart, Ga.
WTUF Thomasville, Ga.
WSPY Plano, Ill.
WPGU Urbana, Ill.
WKRV Vandalia, Ill.
WBNL-FM Boonville, Ind.
WGRT Danville, Ind.
WLCL-FM Lowell, Ind.
KCCQ Ames, Ia.
KDSN-FM Denison, Ia.
KJJC Osceola, Ia.
KBLT Baxter Springs, Kan.
WCTT-FM Corbin, Ky.
WMGE Danville, Ky.
WKCB-FM Hindman, Ky.
† WKCA Owingsville, Ky.
KFNV-FM Ferriday, La.
WHMD Hammond, La.
KCIL Houma, La.
KWLV Jesup, La.
KOGM Opelousas, La.
WCTD-FM Federalsburg, Md.
WPAG-FM Ann Arbor, Mich.
† ---- Cadillac, Mich.
WMQT Ishpeming, Mich.
WSAQ Port Huron, Mich.
WWWS Saginaw, Mich.
WIRX St. Joseph, Mich.
KEHG-FM Fosston, Minn.
† KZZA Glenwood, Minn.
KDUZ-FM Hutchinson, Minn.
WHLB-FM Virginia, Minn.
WZKX Gulfport, Miss.
WLSM-FM Louisville, Miss.
† ---- Birch Tree, Mo.
WERZ Exeter, N.H.
WNNN Canton, N.J.
WMJY Long Branch, N.J.
WZFM Briarcliff Manor, N.Y.
WWHB Hampton Bays, N.Y.
WNIQ-FM Hudson Falls, N.Y.
WRRZ-FM Clinton, N.C.
WDBS Durham, N.C.
WIOZ Southern Pines, N.C.
WJYW Southport, N.C.
WNRE-FM Circleville, O.
WDOH Delphos, O.
WITO Ironton, O.
WLYK Milford, O.
KLBC Durant, Okla.
KBYQ Sweet Home, Ore.
KCEL Toledo, Ore.
WOKU-FM Greensburg, Pa.
WGRP-FM Greenville, Pa.
WEZX Scranton, Pa.
WOTB Middletown, R.I.
WPAJ-FM Lancaster, S.C.
WCIG Mullins, S.C.
KFLZ Bishop, Tex.
KMRB Burnet, Tex.
KHBQ Canyon, Tex.
KSTA-FM Coleman, Tex.
KWKQ Graham, Tex.
KTLR-FM Terrell, Tex.
* KWBU Waco, Tex.
KFRZ Brigham City, Utah
WORK Barre, Vt.
† WBFL Bellows Falls, Vt.
WTTX-FM Appomattox, Va.
WPSK Pulaski, Va.
† KNOI Deer Park, Wash.
† WVCM Miami, W.V.
WFON Fond Du Lac, Wis.
WIXK-FM New Richmond, Wis.
WOCO-FM Oconto, Wis.
WKPL Platteville, Wis.
WNNO-FM Wisconsin Dells, Wis.
CILQ Toronto, Ont.

107.3 (297) BC

WQLT Florence, Ala.
KSTN-FM Stockton, Calif.
WRQX Washington, D. C.
WCRJ-FM Jacksonville, Fla.
WOWW Pensacola, Fla.
WWBA St. Petersburg, Fla.
WCGQ Columbus, Ga.
WDDD Marion, Ill.
WRZQ Greensburg, Ind.
WRSW-FM Warsaw, Ind.
KGRS Burlington, Ia.
KKRD Wichita, Kan.
†* KLSU Baton Rouge, La.
WAAF Worcester, Mass.
WPLB-FM Greenville, Mich.
KBEK Lexington, Mo.
KLIN-FM Lincoln, Neb.
WRCK Utica, N.Y.
WBEA Elyria, O.
KINB Poteau, Okla.
WDBA Du Bois, Pa.
WCMN-FM Arecibo, P.R.
WANS-FM Anderson, S.C.
KQRN Mitchell, S.D.
† KSLT Spearfish, S.D.
WYHY Lebanon, Tenn.
KFFM Yakima, Wash.
WSJY Fort Atkinson, Wis.
CITE Montreal, Que.
XHFG-FM Tijuana, B.C.

107.5 (298) BC

† ---- Tucson, Ariz.
KXO-FM El Centro, Calif.
KKYS Hanford, Calif.
KLVE Los Angeles, Calif.
KPPL Lakewood, Colo.
WQBA-FM Miami, Fla.
†* WABR-FM Tifton, Ga.
WGCI-FM Chicago, Ill.
WZZQ Terre Haute, Ind.
† KSCB-FM Liberal, Kan.
KXKZ Ruston, La.
WBLM Lewiston, Me.
WGPR Detroit, Mich.
KLIZ-FM Brainerd, Minn.
WSJC-FM Magee, Miss.
† KICA Clovis, N.M.
† KCPK Clovis, N.M.
WBLS New York, N.Y.
WKZL Winston Salem, N.C.
† KPUP Redmond, Ore.
WBYO Boyertown, Pa.
WKQB St. George, S.C.
KNOK-FM Ft. Worth, Tex.
KGOL Lake Jackson, Tex.
KBUC-FM San Antonio, Tex.
KUUT Orem, Utah
WKRE-FM Exmore, Va.
WANJ Wheeling, W.V.
WCCN-FM Neillsville, Wis.
CBCM Penetanguishene, Ont.

107.7 (299) BC

WENN-FM Birmingham, Ala.
KSOL San Mateo, Calif.
WORJ-FM Mt. Dora, Fla.
* WVGS Statesboro, Ga.
KICD-FM Spencer, Ia.
KMAJ Topeka, Kan.
WHSB Alpena, Mich.
† ---- Portage, Mich.
KMJM St. Louis, Mo.
KSYZ-FM Grand Island, Neb.
WSNJ-FM Bridgeton, N.J.
WGNA Albany, N.Y.
WUWU Wethersfield, N.Y.
WDAO Dayton, O.
KAEZ Oklahoma City, Okla.
KUMA-FM Pendleton, Ore.
WGTY Gettysburg, Pa.
WVOZ-FM Carolina, P.R.
WIVK-FM Knoxville, Tenn.
KWIC Beaumont, Tex.
WWWK Warrenton, Va.
* KRAB Seattle, Wash.
WVCY Milwaukee, Wis.
CILA Lethbridge, Alta.

107.9 (300) BC

KMLE Chandler, Ariz.
KEZA Fayetteville, Ark.

	KFIN	Jonesboro, Ark.
	KVMA-FM	Magnolia, Ark.
	KKXX	Bakersfield, Calif.
	KXOA-FM	Sacramento, Calif.
	KWVE	San Clemente, Calif.
	KCOL-FM	Ft. Collins, Colo.
	WDJF	Westport, Conn.
	WPFM	Panama City, Fla.
	WIRK-FM	West Palm Beach, Fla.
	WPEZ	Macon, Ga.
	WAUR	Aurora, Ill.
†	----	Indianapolis, Inc.
	KFMW	Waterloo, Ia.
	WABD-FM	Ft. Campbell, Ky.
	WFSI	Annapolis, Md.
	WXKS-FM	Medford, Mass.
*	WVAC	Adrian, Mich.
	WGMZ	Flint, Mich.
	KGBB	Anoka, Minn.
†	WFCA	Ackerman, Miss.
	WRPM-FM	Poplarville, Miss.
*	WWPH	Princeton Junction, N.J.
	KFMG	Albuquerque, N.M.
	WRRB	Syracuse, N.Y.
	WBCY	Charlotte, N.C.
	WNCT-FM	Greenville, N.C.
	WDMT	Cleveland, O.
	KHPE	Albany, Ore.
	WDSY	Pittsburgh, Pa.
	KFMN-FM	Abilene, Tex.
	KXCL	Corsicana, Tex.
	KVLY	Edinburg, Tex.
	KZEU	Victoria, Tex.
†	KRGQ-FM	Roy, Utah
	WVPS	Burlington, Vt.
	WCNV	Amherst, Va.
*	KMBI-FM	Spokane, Wash.
	WEMM	Huntington, W.V.
	WRHN	Rhinelander, Wis.
†	WXCO-FM	Wausau, Wis.
	CING	Burlington, Ont.
	CBJE	Chicoutimi, Que.

AM Stations by Geographic Location

UNITED STATES

ALABAMA

Location	Station	Frequency	Power
Abbeville			
	WARI	1480	1000 d
Alabaster			
	WQMS	1500	1000 d
Albertville			
	WAVU	630	1000 d
	WXBX	1090	2500 d
Alexander City			
	WACD	1590	1000 d
	WRFS	1050	1000 d
Andalusia			
	WAAO	1530	1000 d
	WKYD	920	5000 -
	† WTCG	1400	1000 -
Anniston			
	WANA	1490	1000 -
	WDNG	1450	1000 -
	WHMA	1390	5000 -
Arab			
	WRAB	1380	1000 d
Athens			
	‡ WJMW	730	1000 d
	† WJMW	770	10000 -
	WKAC	1080	5000 d
Atmore			
	WASG	1140	10000 d
	WATM	1590	5000 d
Auburn			
	WAUD	1230	1000 -
Bay Minette			
	WBCA	1110	10000 d
Bessemer			
	WSMQ	1450	1000 -
Birmingham			
	WAGG	1320	5000 d
	WAPI	1070	50000 -
	WATV	900	1000 d
	WCRT	1260	5000 c
	WERC	960	5000
	WSGN	610	5000 -
	WTWG	1220	1000 d
	WVOK	690	50000 d
	WYDE	850	50000 -
Boaz			
	WBSA	1300	1000 d
Brewton			
	WEBJ	1240	1000 -
Bridgeport			
	WBTS	1480	1000 d
Butler			
	† WPRN	1330	5000 d
	‡ WPRN	1240	1000 -
Calera			
	WBYE	1370	1000 d
Camden			
	WCOX	1450	1000 -
Carrollton			
	WRAG	590	1000 d
Centre			
	WAGC	1560	1000 d
	WEIS	990	250 d
Centreville			
	WBIB	1110	1000 d
Clanton			
	WKLF	980	1000 d
Cullman			
	WFMH	1460	5000 -
	WKUL	1340	1000 -
Dadeville			
	WDLK	1450	1000p -
Decatur			
	WAJF	1490	1000 -
	WHOS	800	1000 d
	WMSL	1400	1000 -
Demopolis			
	WXAL	1400	1000 -
Dora			
	WPYK	1010	500 d
Dothan			
	WDBM	1320	1000
Dothan (Cont)			
	WOOF	560	5000 d
	WWNT	1450	1000 -
Elba			
	WELB	1350	1000 d
Enterprise			
	WIRB	600	1000 d
Eufaula			
	WULA	1240	1000 -
Evergreen			
	WEGN	1470	1000 d
Fairhope			
	WABF	1220	1000 d
Fayette			
	WWWF	990	1000 d
Flomaton			
	WPIK	990	500 d
Florala			
	WKWL	1230	1000 -
Florence			
	WBCF	1240	1000 -
	WXOR	1340	1000 -
Foley			
	WHEP	1310	1000 d
Fort Payne			
	WFPA	1400	1000 -
	WZOB	1250	1000 d
Gadsden			
	WAAX	570	5000 -
	WGAD	1350	5000 -
	WJBY	930	5000 -
Geneva			
	WGEA	1150	1000 d
Greenville			
	WGYV	1380	1000 d
Guntersville			
	WGSV	1270	1000 d
Haleyville			
	WJBB	1230	1000 -
Hamilton			
	WERH	970	5000 d
Hartselle			
	WHRT	860	250 d
Homewood			
	WJLD	1400	1000 -
Huntsville			
	WAAY	1550	50000 -
	WBHP	1230	1000 -
	WEUP	1600	5000 -
	WFIX	1450	1000 -
	WTAK	1000	10000 d
Irondale			
	WLPH	1480	5000 d
Jackson			
	WHOD	1230	1000 -
Jacksonville			
	WJXL	810	50000 -
Jasper			
	WARF	1240	1000 -
	WWWB	1360	1000 d
Lafayette			
	WTXN	910	1000 d
Lanett			
	WRLD	1490	1000 -
Lexington			
	WWLX	620	5000 d
Lineville			
	WZZX	1540	1000 d
Luverne			
	WLVN	1080	500 d
Madison			
	† WABT	1360	500 d
Marion			
	WAJQ	1310	5000 d
Mobile			
	WABB	1480	5000
	WGOK	900	1000 d
	WKRG	710	1000 -
	WMOB	1360	5000 d
	WMOO	1550	50000 d
Mobile (Cont)			
	WWAX	840	1000 d
Monroeville			
	WMFC	1360	1000 d
Montgomery			
	WBAM	740	50000 d
	WCOV	1170	10000 -
	WHHY	1440	5000 -
	WLSQ	950	1000
	WMGY	800	1000 d
	WXVI	1600	5000 -
	WZTN	1000	5000 d
Moulton			
	WHIY	1190	1000 d
Muscle Shoals			
	WLAY	1450	1000 -
Oneonta			
	WCRL	1570	1000 d
Opelika			
	WAOA	1520	5000 d
	WJHO	1400	1000 -
Opp			
	WAMI	860	1000 d
	WOPP	1290	2500 -
Ozark			
	WAYD	1190	1000 d
	WOZK	900	1000 d
Parrish			
	† WKIJ	1130	1000 d
Pell City			
	WFHK	1430	5000r dk
Phenix City			
	WPNX	1460	5000 -
Piedmont			
	WPID	1280	1000 d
Prattville			
	WIQR	1410	5000
Prichard			
	WKSJ	1270	1000 d
Rainsville			
	WVSM	1500	1000 d
Red Bay			
	WRMG	1430	1000 d
Roanoke			
	WELR	1360	1000 d
Russellville			
	WKAX	1500	1000 d
	WWWR	920	1000 d
Scottsboro			
	WCRI	1050	250 d
	WKEA	1330	5000 d
Selma			
	WHBB	1490	1000 -
	WMRK	1340	1000 -
	WTQX	1570	5000 d
Sheffield			
	WSHF	1290	1000 d
Sumiton			
	WRSM	1540	1000 d
Sylacauga			
	WFEB	1340	1000 -
	WYEA	1290	1000 d
Talladega			
	WEYY	1580	2500 dk
	WNUZ	1230	1000 -
Tallassee			
	WACQ	1130	1000 d
	WTLS	1300	1000 d
Thomasville			
	WJDB	630	1000 d
Troy			
	WTBF	970	5000 -
Tuscaloosa			
	WACT	1420	5000 d
	WJRD	1150	5000 -
	WNPT	1280	5000 -
	WTBC	1230	1000 -
	WTSK	790	2500 d
Tuscumbia			
	WVNA	1590	5000 -
	WZZA	1410	500 d

City	Station	Frequency	Power
Tuskegee			
	WBIL	580	500 d
Vernon			
	WVSA	1380	1000 d
Wetumpka			
	WETU	1250	5000 d
Winfield			
	WEZQ	1300	5000 d
York			
	WYLS	1350	5000 d

ALASKA

City	Station	Frequency	Power
Anchorage			
	KBYR	700	1000 d
	KENI	550	5000
	KFQD	750	50000
	KHAR	590	5000
	KTNX	1080	10000
	KYAK	650	50000
Barrow			
	* KBRW	680	10000
Bethel			
	* KYUK	580	5000
Cordova			
	KLAM	1450	250 f
Dillingham			
	* KDLG	670	5000
Fairbanks			
	† KCBF	820	10000 -
	‡ KCBF	900	10000
	KFAR	660	10000
	KIAK	970	5000
Glennallen			
	KCAM	790	5000
Homer			
	* KBBI	1250	5000
	KGTL	620	5000
Juneau			
	KINY	800	5000
	KJNO	630	1000 -
Ketchikan			
	† KETH	1290	5000 -
	KTKN	930	5000 -
Kodiak			
	KVOK	560	1000
	WCVQ	960	250
Kotzebue			
	* KOTZ	720	5000
Long Island			
	KABN	830	10000
Mc Grath			
	* KSKO	870	5000
Nenana			
	† KIAM	1270	5000
Nome			
	KICY	850	10000
	* KNOM	780	10000
North Pole			
	KJNP	1170	50000
Petersburg			
	† KHSA	580	5000
Seward			
	KRXA	950	1000
Sitka			
	KIFW	1230	1000 -
Soldatna			
	KSRM	920	5000
Unalaska			
	† KIAL	1450	50

ARIZONA

City	Station	Frequency	Power
Bisbee			
	KBZB	1230	1000 -
Black Canyon City			
	KUET	710	1000
Bullhead City			
	KBAS	1490	1000 -
	† KRHS	1000	1000 d
Casa Grande			
	KPIN	1260	1000 d
	† KWLL	1460	2500 -
Clifton			
	KCUZ	1490	1000
Coolidge			
	KCKY	1150	5000r -k
Cottonwood			
	KVRD	1600	1000 d
Douglas			
	KAPR	930	2500 dk
	KDAP	1450	1000 -
Flagstaff			
	KCLS	600	5000 -
	KFLG	930	5000 d
	KZKZ	690	1000 -
Florence			
	† ----	1300	5000 -
Glendale			
	KLFF	1360	5000 -
Globe			
	KSML	1240	1000 -
Green Valley			
	KGVY	1080	1000 d
Holbrook			
	KDJI	1270	5000 d
Kingman			
	KAAA	1230	1000 -
Lake Havasu City			
	KFWJ	980	1000 d
Marana			
	† KCOT	1110	2500 d
Mesa			
	KDJQ	1510	10000 d
	KZZP	1310	5000 -
Miami			
	KIKO	1340	1000 -
Nogales			
	KFBR	1340	250
Page			
	KPGE	1340	1000 -
Parker			
	KZUL	1380	2500 d
Payson			
	† KMOG	1420	2500 -
Phoenix			
	KASA	1540	10000 d
	KFLR	1230	1000 -
	KHEP	1280	1000 d
	KJJJ	910	5000
	KMEO	740	1000 d
	KOOL	960	5000
	KOY	550	5000 -
	KPHX	1480	1000 dk
	KSUN	1400	1000 -
	KTAR	620	5000
	KVVA	860	1000 d
	KXEG	1010	1000 -
Prescott			
	KNOT	1450	1000 -
	KYCA	1490	1000 -
Safford			
	KATO	1230	1000 -
Scottsdale			
	KOPA	1440	5000 d
Sedona			
	KAZM	780	5000 -
Show Low			
	KVSL	1450	1000 -
	KVWM	970	5000 d
Sierra Vista			
	KSVA	1470	2500 -
	KTAN	1420	1000 -
Springville			
	KRVZ	1400	1000 -
Tempe			
	KNIX	1580	50000 -
	KUKQ	1060	5000 -
Tolleson			
	KRDS	1190	5000 -
Tuba City			
	KTBA	1050	5000 d
Tucson			
	KAIR	1490	1000 -k
	KCEE	790	5000 -
	KCUB	1290	5000 -k
	KFLT	1450	1000 -
	KHYT	1330	5000
	KIKX	580	5000 -
	KNST	940	1000 -
	KTKT	990	10000 -
	KTUC	1400	1000 -
	* KUAT	1550	50000 d
	KVOI	690	250 d
	KXEW	1600	1000
Wickenburg			
	KUUK	1250	1000 d
Willcox			
	KHIL	1250	5000 d
Williams			
	KDAN	1180	10000 -
Window Rock			
	† ----	660	50000
	KHAC	1110	10000 d
Winslow			
	KINO	1230	1000 -
Yuma			
	* KAWC	1320	1000 d
	KBLU	560	1000
	KVOY	1400	1000 -

ARKANSAS

City	Station	Frequency	Power
Arkadelphia			
	KVRC	1240	1000 -k
Augusta			
	KMCW	1190	500 d
Bald Knob			
	KAPZ	710	250 d
Batesville			
	KAAB	1130	250 d
	KBTA	1340	1000 -
Benton			
	KBBA	690	250 d
	KGKO	850	1000 d
Bentonville			
	KJEM	1190	5000 d
Berryville			
	KTHS	1480	5000 d
Blytheville			
	KLCN	910	5000 d
Brinkley			
	KBRI	1570	250 d
Cabot			
	KBOT	1350	2500 d
Camden			
	KAMD	910	5000 -
	KJWH	1450	1000 -
Clarksville			
	KLYR	1360	500 d
Clinton			
	KGFL	1110	1000 d
Conway			
	KCON	1230	1000 -
	KTOD	1330	500 d
Corning			
	KCCB	1260	1000 d
Crossett			
	KAGH	800	250 d
Dardanelle			
	KCAB	980	1000 d
De Queen			
	KDQN	1390	500 d
De Witt			
	KDEW	1470	500 d
Dermott			
	KAKA	1110	10000 d
Dumas			
	KDDA	1560	500 d
El Dorado			
	KDMS	1290	5000 d
	KELD	1400	1000 -
England			
	KELC	1530	250 d
Fayetteville			
	KFAY	1250	1000 d
	KHOG	1440	1000 d
Fordyce			
	KBJT	1570	250 d
Forrest City			
	KXJK	950	5000 d
Ft. Smith			
	KFPW	1230	1000 -
	KFSA	950	1000 -
	KTCS	1410	1000 d
	KWHN	1320	5000
Glenwood			
	† KWXI	670	5000 d
	‡ KWXI	1470	2500 d
Greenwood			
	KACJ	1510	1000 d
Hardy			
	KSRB	1570	1000 d
Harrison			
	KHOZ	900	1000 d

Heber Springs
KAWW 1370 1000 d
Helena
KFFA 1360 1000
Hope
KXAR 1490 1000 -
Horseshoe Bend
KHAM 1000 250 d
Hot Springs
KBHS 590 5000
KXOW 1420 5000 d
KZNG 1340 1000 -
Jacksonville
KIEL 1500 1000 d
Jonesboro
KBTM 1230 1000 -
KNEA 970 1000 d
Little Rock
KAAY 1090 50000
KARN 920 5000
KITA 1440 5000 d
KLRA 1010 10000 -
KOKY 1250 1000 -
KSOH 1050 1000
Magnolia
KVMA 630 1000 d
Malvern
KBOK 1310 1000 d
Marianna
KZOT 1460 500 d
Marked Tree
KPCA 1580 250 d
Marshall
KCGS 1600 5000 dk
Mc Gehee
KVSA 1220 1000 d
Mena
KENA 1450 1000 -
Monette
KBIB 1560 250 d
Monticello
KHBM 1430 1000 d
Morrilton
KVOM 800 250 d
Mountain Home
KTLO 1240 1000 -
Nashville
KBHC 1260 500 d
Newport
KNBY 1280 1000 d
North Little Rock
KAUL 1380 5000 -
KBOX 1150 5000 -
Osceola
KOSE 860 1000 d
Ozark
KZRK 1540 500 d
Paragould
KDRS 1490 1000 -
Paris
KCCL 1460 500 d
Pine Bluff
KABS 1270 5000 d
KCAT 1340 1000 -
KCLA 1400 1000 -
KOTN 1490 1000 -
KYDE 1590 5000r kc
Pocahontas
KPOC 1420 1000 d
Prescott
KTPA 1370 1000 d
Rogers
KAMO 1390 1000 d
KURM 790 1000 d
Russellville
KARV 610 1000 -
Searcy
KWCK 1300 5000 d
Sheridan
KKDI 1540 250 d
Sherwood
† KMTL 760 5000 d
Siloam Springs
KUOA 1290 5000 d
Springdale
KBRS 1340 1000 -
KQXK 1590 2500r dk

Stuttgart
KWAK 1240 1000 -
Texarkana
KOSY 790 1000 -
Trumann
KXRQ 1530 250 d
Van Buren
KAYR 1060 500 d
KFDF 1580 1000 d
Walnut Ridge
KRLW 1320 1000 d
Warren
KWRF 860 250 d
West Helena
KCRI 1600 1000 d
West Memphis
KSUD 730 250 d
Wynne
KWYN 1400 1000 -
Yellville
KCTT 1530 1000 d

CALIFORNIA

Alturas
KCNO 570 5000 d
Anaheim
KNWZ 1190 10000r -k
Apple Valley
KAVR 960 5000 d
Aptos Capitola
KMFO 1540 10000 d
Arcata
KATA 1340 1000 -
Arroyo Grande
KKAL 1280 5000 -
Auburn
KAHI 950 5000
Avalon
KBRT 740 10000 d
Bakersfield
KAFY 550 1000
KERN 1410 1000
KGEO 1230 1000 -
KHIS 800 250 d
KLYD 1350 1000 d
KPMC 1560 10000
KUZZ 970 1000
KWAC 1490 1000 -
Banning
KGUD 1490 1000 -
Barstow
KIOT 1310 5000 d
KPRO 1230 1000 -
Berkeley
KRE 1400 1000 -
Big Bear Lake
KBBV 1050 250 d
Bishop
KIBS 1230 1000 -
Blythe
KJMB 1450 1000 -
Brawley
KROP 1300 1000 -
Burbank
KROQ 1500 10000 -
Burney
KAVA 1450 1000 -
Calexico
KICO 1490 1000 -
Carmel
KRML 1410 5000
Carmichael
KFIA 710 10000
Cathedral City
KWXY 1340 1000 -
Ceres
KLOC 920 2500
Chico
KHSL 1290 5000
KPAY 1060 10000
Clovis
KXQR 790 500 d
Coachella
KVIM 970 5000 -
Coalinga
KOLI 1470 500 d
Concord
KWUN 1480 500 d

Corona
KWRM 1370 5000 -
Crescent City
KCRE 1310 1000 d
KPOD 1240 1000 -
Delano
KCHJ 1010 5000 -
Dinuba
KRDU 1130 1000
El Cajon
KMJC 910 5000
El Centro
KAMP 1430 1000 d
KXO 1230 1000
Escondido
KOWN 1450 1000 -
Eureka
KEKA 790 5000
KINS 980 5000 -
KRED 1480 5000 -
Fortuna
KNCR 1090 10000 d
Fowler
KLIP 1220 250 d
Fresno
KARM 1430 5000
KBIF 900 1000 d
KEAP 980 500 d
KFRE 940 50000
KGST 1600 5000
KIRV 1510 10000 dk
KMAK 1340 1000 -
KMJ 580 5000
KXEX 1550 5000 dk
KYNO 1300 5000 -
Ft. Bragg
KDAC 1230 1000 -
Gilroy
KAZA 1290 5000 d
Glendale
KIEV 870 5000 c
Gonzales
† ---- 880 5000 -
Grass Valley
KNCO 1250 500 kc
Hanford
KNGS 620 1000
Hemet
KHSJ 1320 500 d
Hesperia
† ---- 540 1000 d
† KHSP 910 1000 -
Hollister
KMPG 1520 500 d
Independence
KESR 600 500 d
Indio
KRCQ 1400 1000 -
Inglewood
KTYM 1460 5000 -
King City
KRKC 1490 1000 -
Lake Isabella
KVLI 1140 500 d
Lakeport
† KBLC 840 1000 -
‡ KBLC 1270 500 d
Lancaster
KAVL 610 1000 -
KOTE 1380 1000 d
Lemoore
KJOP 1240 250
KQIQ 1320 1000 d
Lodi
KCVR 1570 5000 d
Lompoc
KLOM 1330 1000 d
KLVV 1410 500 d
KNEZ 960 500
Long Beach
KFRN 1280 1000
KGER 1390 5000
Los Angeles
KABC 790 5000
KFAC 1330 5000
KFI 640 50000
KFWB 980 5000
KGFJ 1230 1000 -

Station	Frequency	Power
Los Angeles (Cont)		
KHJ	930	5000
KLAC	570	5000
KMPC	710	50000 -
KNX	1070	50000
KPRZ	1150	5000
KTNQ	1020	50000
KZLA	1540	50000 -
Los Banos		
KLBS	1330	500 d
Madera		
KHOT	1250	500 d
Marysville		
KMYC	1410	5000
Mc Farland		
KXEM	1590	500 d
Mendocino		
KPMD	1300	5000 d
Merced		
KLOQ	1580	1000 d
KYOS	1480	5000
Modesto		
KFIV	1360	5000 -
KHYV	970	1000
KTRB	860	10000 -
Mojave		
KDOL	1340	1000 -
Monterey		
KIDD	630	1000
KNRY	1240	1000 -
Morro Bay		
KBAI	1150	5000
Mt. Shasta		
KWSD	620	1000 d
Napa		
KVON	1440	5000 -
Needles		
KSFE	1340	1000 -f
Oakland		
KABL	960	5000
KDIA	1310	5000
KNEW	910	5000
Oceanside		
KEZL	1320	500
Ontario		
KNSE	1510	10000 -
Oroville		
KORV	1340	1000 -
Oxnard		
KOXR	910	5000 -
Palm Desert		
KGUY	1270	1000 d
Palm Springs		
‡ KCMJ	1010	1000 -
† KCMJ	1140	10000 -
KDES	920	5000 -
KPSI	1450	1000 -
Palmdale		
KUTY	1470	5000 -c
Palo Alto		
KIBE	1220	5000 d
Paradise		
KEWQ	930	500 d
Pasadena		
KPPC	1240	100 df
KRLA	1110	50000 -
KWKW	1300	5000 -
Paso Robles		
KPRL	1230	1000 -
Petaluma		
KTOB	1490	1000 -
Pittsburg		
KKIS	990	5000
Pomona		
KTSJ	1220	250 d
KWOW	1600	5000 -
Port Hueneme		
KACY	1520	50000 -
Porterville		
KTIP	1450	1000 -
Quincy		
KPCO	1370	500 d
Red Bluff		
KBLF	1490	1000 -
Redding		
KCLM	1330	5000 d
KQMS	1400	1000 -
KRDG	1230	1000 -
Redding (Cont)		
KSXO	600	1000
KVIP	540	1000 d
Redlands		
KCAL	1410	5000 -k
Ridgecrest		
KLOA	1240	1000 -
KZIQ	1360	1000 d
Riverside		
KMAY	1570	5000 d
KPRO	1440	1000
Roseville		
KPIP	1110	500
Sacramento		
KENZ	1240	1000 -
KFBK	1530	50000
KGMS	1380	5000
KGNR	1320	5000 k
KJAY	1430	500 d
KRAK	1140	50000
KXOA	1470	5000 -
Salinas		
KCTY	980	1000 d
KDON	1460	5000
KTOM	1380	5000
KXES	1570	5000p d
San Bernardino		
KCKC	1350	5000 -
KDIG	1240	1000 -
KFXM	590	1000
KMEN	1290	5000
San Diego		
KCBQ	1170	50000 -
KFMB	760	5000
KOGO	600	5000
KPQP	1360	5000 -
KSDO	1130	50000 -
KSON	1240	1000 -
San Fernando		
KGIL	1260	5000
San Francisco		
KCBS	740	50000
KEST	1450	1000 -
KFAX	1100	50000
KFRC	610	5000
KGO	810	50000
KIOT	1260	5000 -
KKHI	1550	10000
KNBR	680	50000
KSFO	560	5000 -
San Gabriel		
KALI	1430	5000
San Jose		
KEEN	1370	5000
KHTT	1500	10000 -
KLIV	1590	5000
KLOK	1170	50000 -
San Luis Obispo		
KATY	1340	1000 -
KSLY	1400	1000 -
KVEC	920	1000 -
San Mateo		
KOFY	1050	1000 d
San Rafael		
KTIM	1510	1000 d
Santa Ana		
KWIZ	1480	5000 -
Santa Barbara		
KBLS	990	1000 d
KDB	1490	1000 -
KIST	1340	1000 -
KTMS	1250	2500 -
KXXN	1290	500 d
Santa Clara		
KNTA	1430	1000
Santa Cruz		
KSCO	1080	10000 -
Santa Maria		
KSBQ	1480	1000 d
KSMA	1240	1000 -
KUHL	1440	5000 -
KZON	1600	500 d
Santa Monica		
KDAY	1580	50000
Santa Paula		
KQTE	1400	1000 -
Santa Rosa		
KPLS	1150	5000 -
Santa Rosa (Cont)		
KSRO	1350	5000
KVRE	1460	1000 d
Simi Valley		
† KWNK	670	1000
Solvang		
† ----	1550	1000 d
Sonora		
KVML	1450	1000 -
South Lake Tahoe		
KOWL	1490	1000 -
KTHO	590	2500 -
Stockton		
KJOY	1280	1000
KSTN	1420	5000 -
KWG	1230	1000 -
Sunnyvale		
KIQI	1010	50000 -c
Susanville		
KSUE	1240	1000 -
Taft		
KTKR	1310	1000 d
Thousand Oaks		
KGOE	850	500
Truckee		
KTRT	1400	1000 -
Tulare		
KCOK	1270	5000 -
KGEN	1370	1000 d
Turlock		
KCEY	1390	5000
Twentynine Palms		
KDHI	1250	1000 d
Ukiah		
KUKI	1400	1000 -
Vallejo		
KNBA	1190	1000 d
Ventura		
KBBQ	1590	5000
KVEN	1450	1000 -
Victorville		
KCIN	1590	500 d
Visalia		
KONG	1400	1000 -
Vista		
KMLO	1000	5000 -k
Wasco		
KWSO	1180	10000
Watsonville		
KOMY	1340	1000 -
West Covina		
KGRB	900	500
Willits		
† KLLK	1250	2500 -
Willows		
KIQS	1560	250 d
Yreka		
KSYC	1490	1000 -
Yuba City		
KOBO	1450	500 -
KUBA	1600	5000 -
Yucca Valley		
† KSES	1420	1000 -

COLORADO

Station	Frequency	Power
Alamosa		
KGIW	1450	1000 -
Arvada		
KQXI	1550	10000 d
Aspen		
KSNO	1260	5000 d
Aurora		
KEZW	1430	5000
KKBB	1090	50000 -
Boulder		
KADE	1190	5000 d
KBOL	1490	1000 -
Breen		
† ----	1500	10000 d
Brighton		
KLTT	800	1000 d
Brush		
KCMP	1010	5000 d
Burlington		
KNAB	1140	1000 d
Canon City		
KRLN	1400	1000 -

Station	Freq	Power
Colorado Springs		
KCMN	1530	1000 d
KPIK	1580	5000 d
KRDO	1240	1000 -
KSSS	740	1000 -
KVOR	1300	5000 -
KYSN	1460	1000 -
Cortez		
KVFC	740	1000 -
Craig		
KRAI	550	5000 -
Deer Trail		
KTMG	1370	5000 d
Delta		
KDTA	1400	1000 -
Denver		
KBNO	1220	1000 d
KBRQ	1280	5000
KDEN	1340	1000 -
KHOW	630	5000
KIMN	950	5000
KJJZ	1390	5000 -
KLZ	560	5000
KNUS	710	5000
KOA	850	50000
* KPOF	910	5000 -
KRKS	990	5000 d
Durango		
KDGO	1240	1000 -
KIUP	930	5000 -
Englewood		
KRZN	1150	5000 -
Estes Park		
KSIR	1470	1000 d
Ft. Collins		
KCOL	1410	1000
KIIX	600	5000 c
Ft. Morgan		
KFTM	1400	1000 -
Glenwood Springs		
KGLN	980	1000 d
Grand Junction		
KEXO	1230	1000 -
KQIL	1340	1000 -
KREX	1100	50000 -
KSTR	620	5000 d
Greeley		
KFKA	1310	5000 -
KYOU	1450	1000 -
Gunnison		
KGUC	1490	1000 -
Hayden		
KRDZ	1000	10000 -
La Junta		
KBZZ	1400	1000 -
Lakewood		
KLAK	1600	5000
Lamar		
KLMR	920	5000 -
Leadville		
KLRR	1230	1000 -
Limon		
† ----	1120	250 d
Littleton		
KDKO	1510	5000
Longmont		
KLMO	1060	10000 d
Loveland		
KLOV	1570	1000 d
Manitou Springs		
KIIQ	1490	500 -
Meeker		
KMKR	1450	1000 -
Monte Vista		
KSLV	1240	1000 -
Montrose		
KUBC	580	5000 -
Pagosa Springs		
KPAG	1400	1000 -
Pueblo		
KAYK	1480	1000 d
KCSJ	590	1000
KDZA	1230	1000 -
KFEL	970	1000 d
KIDN	1350	5000 -
KRMX	690	250 d
Rifle		
KWSR	810	1000 d
Rocky Ford		
KAVI	1320	1000 d
Salida		
KVRH	1340	1000 -
Silt		
† KRMW	700	50000 -
Silverton		
KDRW	1450	1000 -
Steamboat Springs		
KBCR	1230	1000 -
Sterling		
KSTC	1230	1000 -
Trinidad		
KCRT	1240	250 f
Walsenburg		
KFLJ	1380	1000 d
Windsor		
KUAD	1170	1000 d
Wray		
† KRDZ	1440	5000 d
‡ KRDZ	1470	1000 d

CONNECTICUT

Station	Freq	Power
Ansonia		
WADS	690	1000 d
Bloomfield		
WMLB	1550	5000 -
Bridgeport		
WDJZ	1530	5000 d
WICC	600	1000 -
WNAB	1450	1000 -
Bristol		
WBIS	1440	500 d
Brookfield		
WINE	940	1000 d
Danbury		
WLAD	800	1000 d
Greenwich		
WGCH	1490	1000 -
Groton		
WSUB	980	1000 d
Hamden		
WSCR	1220	1000 d
Hartford		
WCCC	1290	5000 d
WDRC	1360	5000
WPOP	1410	5000
WTIC	1080	50000
Manchester		
WINF	1230	1000 -
Meriden		
WMMW	1470	2500 hc
Middletown		
WCNX	1150	2500r dk
Milford		
WFIF	1500	5000 d
Naugatuck		
WNVR	1380	5000 -
New Britain		
WRCQ	910	5000
WRYM	840	1000 d
New Haven		
WAVZ	1300	1000
WELI	960	5000
WNHC	1340	1000 -
New London		
WNLC	1510	10000 -
Norwalk		
WNLK	1350	1000 -
Norwich		
WICH	1310	5000
Old Saybrook		
WLIS	1420	5000 -
Putnam		
WINY	1350	1000 d
Ridgefield		
WVFR	850	500 d
Southington		
WNTY	990	500 d
Stamford		
WSTC	1400	1000 -
Torrington		
WSNG	610	1000 -
Vernon		
WRTT	1170	1000 d
Waterbury		
WATR	1320	5000 -
WQQW	1590	5000
Waterbury (Cont)		
WWCO	1240	1000 -
Westport		
WMMM	1260	1000 d
Willimantic		
WILI	1400	1000 -
Windsor		
WKND	1480	500 d

DELAWARE

Station	Freq	Power
Dover		
WDOV	1410	5000
WKEN	1600	5000 -
Georgetown		
WJWL	900	1000 d
Milford		
WYUS	930	500 d
Newark		
WNRK	1260	1000 d
Seaford		
WSUX	1280	1000 d
Wilmington		
WAMS	1380	5000 -
WDEL	1150	5000
WILM	1450	1000 -
WJBR	1290	1000 d

DISTRICT OF COLUMBIA

Station	Freq	Power
Washington		
WGMS	570	5000 -
WMAL	630	5000
WOL	1450	1000 -
WRC	980	5000
WTOP	1500	50000
WUST	1120	5000r dk
WWDC	1260	5000
WYCB	1340	1000 -

FLORIDA

Station	Freq	Power
Apopka		
WTLN	1520	5000 d
Arcadia		
WAPG	1480	1000 d
Atlantic Beach		
WJNJ	1600	5000 d
Auburndale		
WTWB	1570	5000 d
Avon Park		
WAPR	1390	1000 d
Bartow		
WBAR	1460	1000 d
WPUL	1130	2500 -c
Belle Glade		
WSWN	900	1000 d
Blountstown		
WKMK	1000	1000 d
Boca Raton		
WSBR	740	1000 d
Boynton Beach		
† WKAO	1040	10000 -
‡ WKAO	1510	1000 d
Bradenton		
WBRD	1420	1000 d
WTRL	1490	1000 -
Brooksville		
WWJB	1450	1000 -
Chattahoochee		
WENO	1580	5000 d
Chiefland		
WLQH	940	1000 dk
Chipley		
WBGC	1240	1000 -
Clearwater		
WAMA	860	1000
WTAN	1340	1000 -
Cocoa		
WEZY	1350	5000r -c
WKKO	860	1000 d
Cocoa Beach		
WRKT	1300	5000 -
Coral Gables		
WRHC	1550	10000 -
WVCG	1080	50000 -
Crescent City		
WBAS	1330	1000 d
Crestview		
WCNU	1010	10000r dk
WJSB	1050	5000 d

Cross City
† WDKA 1240 1000 -
Cypress Gardens
WGTO 540 50000 -k
WYXY 1360 5000 -
Dade City
WDCF 1350 1000 -
Daytona Beach
WMFJ 1450 1000 -
WNDB 1150 1000
WROD 1340 1000 -
De Funiak Springs
WGTX 1280 5000 d
WZEP 1460 1000 d
De Land
WDLF 1310 5000 d
WXVQ 1490 1000 -
Delray Beach
WDBF 1420 5000 -
Dunedin
WFNN 1470 5000 d
Dunnellon
WTRS 920 500 d
Englewood
WENG 1530 1000 d
Eustis
WLCO 1240 1000 -
Fernandina Beach
WHOG 1570 5000 d
Ft. Lauderdale
WAVS 1190 5000 d
WFTL 1400 1000 -
WSRF 1580 10000 -
Ft. Myers
WCAI 1350 1000 d
WINK 1240 1000 -
WMYR 1410 5000
Ft. Pierce
WFTP 1330 1000 -
WIRA 1400 1000 -
Ft. Walton Beach
WFTW 1260 2500 d
WNUE 1400 1000 -
Gainesville
WDVH 980 5000 d
WGGG 1230 1000 -
WKGR 1390 5000 d
WRUF 850 5000
Haines City
WFXI 930 500 d
Hollywood
WLQY 1320 5000
Homestead
WQDI 1430 500
Immokalee
WKEM 1490 1000 -
Indian Rocks Beach
WGNB 1520 1000 d
Inverness
WYSE 1560 5000
Jacksonville
WAPE 690 50000 -
WCGL 1360 5000 d
WCRJ 1530 50000 d
WERD 1400 1000 -
WEXI 1280 5000 d
WJAX 930 5000
WKTZ 1220 5000 d
WOKV 600 5000
WOZN 970 1000 d
WPDQ 1460 5000
WQIK 1320 5000
WROS 1050 5000 d
Jacksonville Beach
WBIX 1010 10000 d
Jupiter
WVSI 1000 1000 d
Key West
WKIZ 1500 250
WKWF 1600 500
Kissimmee
WFIV 1080 10000 d
WMJK 1220 1000 d
Lake City
WDSR 1340 1000 -
WGRO 960 1000
Lake Wales
WIPC 1280 1000

Lake Worth
WLIZ 1380 1000 d
Lakeland
WLKF 1430 5000 -
WONN 1230 1000 -
WWAB 1330 1000 d
Largo
WSST 800 250 d
Leesburg
WLBE 790 5000 -
WZST 1410 5000 d
Lehigh Acres
WOOJ 1440 5000 -
Live Oak
WNER 1250 1000 d
Madison
WMAF 1230 1000 -
Marathon
‡ WFFG 1300 500
† WFFG 1300 2500
Marathon Key
VOA 1180 50000
Marco Island
WMIB 1510 1000 d
Marianna
WTOT 980 1000 d
WTYS 1340 1000 -
Melbourne
WMEL 920 1000
WMMB 1240 1000 -
WTAI 1560 5000 d
Miami
WCMQ 1220 1000 d
WGBS 710 50000
WHTT 1260 5000
WINZ 940 50000 -
WIOD 610 10000
WOCN 1450 1000 -
WQAM 560 5000 -
WQBA 1140 10000 -
Miami Beach
WKAT 1360 5000 -
WMBM 1490 1000 -
Milton
WCKC 1490 1000 -
WAVX 1330 5000 d
Monticello
WMFL 1090 1000 d
Mt. Dora
WQTK 1580 5000 d
Naples
WNOG 1270 500
New Port Richey
WGUL 1500 250 d
New Smyrna Beach
WCCZ 1550 250 d
WSBB 1230 1000 -
Oakland Park
WEXY 1520 1000 d
Ocala
WMOP 900 5000 d
WOCA 1370 5000 d
WTMC 1290 5000 -
Ocoee
WVCF 1480 1000 d
Okeechobee
WOKC 1570 1000 d
Orange Park
WAYR 550 1000 d
Orlando
WCOT 950 5000
WDBO 580 5000
WHOO 990 50000 -
WKIS 740 5000 -
WORL 1270 5000 -c
Ormond Beach
WDAT 1380 5000 -
Palatka
WIYD 1260 1000 -
WSUZ 800 1000 d
Palm Beach
WPBR 1340 1000 -
Palm City
† ---- 760 5000 -
Panama City
WDLP 590 1000
WWWQ 1430 5000

Panama City Beach
WKGC 1480 500 d
WPCF 1290 500 d
Pensacola
WBOP 980 1000 d
WBSR 1450 1000 -
WCOA 1370 5000
WHYM 610 500 d
WNVY 1230 1000 -
WPFA 790 1000 d
Perry
WGKR 1310 1000 d
WPRY 1400 1000 -
Pine Castle
WHHL 1190 1000 d
Pinellas Park
† WHBO 1040 5000 -
WPLP 570 1000
Plant City
WPLA 910 1000
Pompano Beach
WBSS 980 5000r -k
WRBD 1470 5000 -
Port St. Joe
WJBU 1080 1000 d
Punta Gorda
WCCF 1580 1000 d
Quincy
WCNH 1230 1000 -
Riviera Beach
WPOM 1600 1000
Rockledge
WWBC 1510 1000 d
Sanford
WWJZ 1400 1000 -
Sarasota
WKXY 930 1000 -
WQSA 1220 1000 d
WSPB 1450 1000 -
WWZZ 1280 500 d
Sebring
WJCM 960 1000 d
WSEB 1340 1000 -
South Daytona
WZIP 1590 1000 d
South Miami
WNWS 790 5000
St. Augustine
WAOC 1420 1000 d
WFOY 1240 1000 -
St. Petersburg
WRBQ 1380 5000
WSUN 620 5000
WWLF 680 1000 d
St. Petersburg Beach
WRXB 1590 1000 d
Starke
WPXE 1490 1000 -
Stuart
WSTU 1450 1000 -
Tallahassee
WANM 1070 10000 d
WCVC 1330 5000 d
WKQE 1410 5000 d
WTAL 1450 1000 -
WTNT 1270 5000
Tampa
WCBF 1010 50000 d
WDAE 1250 5000
WFLA 970 5000
‡ WHBO 1050 250 d
WTIS 1110 10000 d
WTMP 1150 5000 -
WTYM 1300 5000 -k
WYOU 1550 10000 d
Titusville
WAMT 1060 10000 -
Valparaiso
WFSH 1340 1000 -
Venice
WAMR 1320 5000 -
Vero Beach
WAXE 1370 1000 d
WTTB 1490 1000 -
Wauchula
WAUC 1310 5000 d
West Palm Beach
WEAT 850 1000

West Palm Beach (Cont)
WJNO 1230 1000 -
WPCK 1290 50000r k
Winter Garden
WOKB 1600 5000
Winter Haven
WSIR 1490 1000 -
Winter Park
WAJL 1440 5000 -
Zephyr Hills
WPAS 1400 1000 -

GEORGIA

Adel
WBIT 1470 1000 d
Albany
WALG 1590 5000 -
WGPC 1450 1000 -
WJAZ 960 5000 d
WQDE 1250 1000 d
Alma
WULF 1400 1000 -
Alpharetta
† WVNF 1400 1000 -
Americus
WDEC 1290 1000 d
WISK 1390 5000 d
Ashburn
WMES 1570 1000 d
Athens
WCCD 1470 1000 d
WGAU 1340 1000 -
WRFC 960 5000 -
Atlanta
WAEC 860 5000 d
WAOK 1380 5000
WCNN 680 50000w -k
WGKA 1190 5000 d
WGST 920 5000 -
WGUN 1010 50000 d
WIGO 1340 1000 -
WKLS 970 5000 d
WPLO 590 5000
WQXI 790 5000 -
WSB 750 50000
WYZE 1480 5000 d
Augusta
WBBQ 1340 1000 -
WCKJ 1230 1000 -
WGAC 580 5000 -
WGUS 1380 1000 d
WHGI 1050 5000 d
WRDW 1480 5000
WTHB 1550 5000 d
Austell
WCKZ 1600 1000 d
Bainbridge
WAZA 1360 5000 -
WMGR 930 5000
Barnesville
WBAF 1090 1000 d
Baxley
WUFE 1260 5000 d
Blackshear
WGIA 1350 2500 d
Blakely
WBBK 1260 1000 d
Bremen
WWCC 1440 2500 d
Brunswick
WBGA 1440 5000 -
WMOG 1490 1000 -
WYNR 790 500 d
Buford
WDYX 1460 5000 d
Cairo
WGRA 790 1000 d
Calhoun
WEBS 1110 250 d
Camilla
WCLB 1220 1000 d
Canton
WCHK 1290 5000 -k
Carrollton
† ---- 1100 1000 d
WPPI 1330 500 d
Cartersville
WBHF 1450 1000 -

Cartersville (Cont)
WYXC 1270 500 d
Cedartown
WGAA 1340 1000 -
Clarkesville
WIAF 1500 5000 d
Claxton
WCLA 1470 1000 d
Clayton
WGHC 1570 1000 d
Cleveland
WRWH 1350 1000 d
Cochran
WVMG 1440 1000 d
College Park
† ---- 890 2500 d
Columbus
WCLS 1580 1000
WDAK 540 5000 -
WHYD 1270 5000 d
WOKS 1340 1000 -
WRCG 1420 5000
Commerce
WJJC 1270 5000 d
Conyers
WCGA 1050 1000 d
Cordele
WMJM 1490 1000 -
Cornelia
WCON 1450 1000 -
Covington
WGFS 1430 1000 d
Cumming
WHNE 1170 1000 d
Cuthbert
WCUG 850 500 d
Dahlonega
† WDGR 1210 10000 d
‡ WDGR 1520 500 d
Dallas
WKRP 1500 1000 d
Dalton
WBLJ 1230 1000 -
WRCD 1430 1000 d
WTTI 1530 10000
Dawson
WDWD 990 1000 d
Decatur
WAVO 1420 1000 d
WXLL 1310 500 d
Donalsonville
WSEM 1500 1000 d
Douglas
WDMG 860 5000
WOKA 1310 1000 d
Douglasville
WDGL 1520 1000 d
Dublin
WMLT 1330 5000 -
WXLI 1230 1000 -
East Point
WTJH 1260 5000 d
Eastman
WUFF 710 1000 d
Eatonton
WXPQ 1520 1000 d
Elberton
WSGC 1400 1000 -
Ellijay
WLEJ 1560 1000 d
Fitzgerald
WBHB 1240 1000 -
Ft. Valley
WXKO 1150 1000 d
Gainesville
WDUN 550 5000 -
WGGA 1240 1000 -
WLBA 1130 10000 d
Garden City
WNMT 1520 1000 d
Glennville
WKIG 1580 1000 d
Gordon
† WQXM 1120 5000 d
‡ WQXM 1560 5000 d
Griffin
WGRI 1410 1000 d
WHIE 1320 5000 d

Griffin (Cont)
WKEU 1450 1000 -
Hartwell
WKLY 980 1000 d
Hawkinsville
WCEH 610 500 d
Hazlehurst
WVOH 920 500 d
Hinesville
WGML 990 250 d
Jasper
† WYYZ 1490 1000 -
Jessup
WLOP 1370 5000 d
La Grange
WLAG 1240 1000 -
WTRP 620 1000 d
Lafayette
WLFA 1590 5000 d
Lawrenceville
WLAW 1360 1000 d
Louisville
WPEH 1420 1000 d
Lyons
WBBT 1340 1000 -
Macon
WBML 900 250 d
WDDO 1240 1000 -
WIBB 1280 5000 d
WMAZ 940 50000 -
WNEX 1400 1000 -
WPTC 1500 1000 d
Madison
WYTH 1250 1000 d
Manchester
WVFJ 1370 1000 d
Marietta
WFOM 1230 1000 -
WJYA 1080 10000 d
Mc Donough
WZAL 1540 2500 dk
Mc Rae
WDAX 1410 1000 d
Metter
WMAC 1360 500 d
Milledgeville
WKGQ 1060 1000 d
WMVG 1450 1000 -
Millen
WGSR 1570 1000 d
Monroe
WKUN 1580 1000 d
WRED 1490 1000 -
Montezuma
WMNZ 1050 250 d
Morrow
WSSA 1570 5000 d
Moultrie
WMGA 1130 10000 -
WMTM 1300 5000 d
Nashville
WNGA 1600 1000 d
Newnan
WCOH 1400 1000 -
WNEA 1300 500 d
Ochlochnee
† WJEP 1020 10000 d
Ocilla
WSIZ 1380 5000 d
Perry
WPGA 980 1000 d
Quitman
WSFB 1490 1000 -
Reidsville
WTNL 1390 500 d
Rockmart
WPLK 1220 500 d
Rome
WIYN 1360 500 d
WLAQ 1410 1000
WRGA 1470 5000
WROM 710 1000 d
Rossville
WRIP 980 500
Royston
WBLW 810 250 d
Sandersville
WSNT 1490 1000 -

Savannah
WKBX 630 5000
WQCN 1450 1000 -
WSGA 1400 1000 -
WSOK 1230 1000 -
WWJD 900 5000 d
WWSA 1290 5000
Smyrna
WYNX 1550 10000 -
Soperton
WMPZ 1000 1000 d
Statesboro
WPTB 850 1000
WWNS 1240 1000 -
Summerville
WGTA 950 5000 d
Swainsboro
WJAT 800 1000 d
WXRS 1590 2500 d
Sylvania
WSYL 1490 1000 -
Sylvester
WRSG 1540 1000 d
Tallapoosa
WKNG 1060 5000 d
Thomaston
WSFT 1220 250 d
WTGA 1590 500 d
Thomasville
WLOR 730 5000 d
WPAX 1240 1000 -
Thomson
WTWA 1240 1000 -
Tifton
WTIF 1340 1000 -
WWGS 1430 5000 -
Toccoa
WLET 1420 5000 d
WNEG 630 500 d
Trenton
† WADX 1420 500 d
Valdosta
WGAF 910 5000
WGOV 950 5000 -
WJEM 1150 1000 d
WVLD 1450 1000 -
Vidalia
WVOP 970 5000 d
Vienna
WWWN 1550 250 d
Warner Robbins
WAVC 1350 5000 d
WRBN 1600 2500 -k
Washington
WLOV 1370 1000 d
Waycross
WACL 570 5000 -
WAYX 1230 1000 -
Waynesboro
WBRO 1310 1000 d
West Point
WZZZ 1310 1000 d
Winder
WIMO 1300 1000 d
Young Harris
† WZEL 1380 500 d

HAWAII

Eleele
KUAI 720 5000
Hilo
KHLO 850 5000
KIPA 620 5000
KPUA 670 5000
Honolulu
KAIM 870 50000
KCCN 1420 5000
KGU 760 10000
† KHNL 1310 5000
KHVH 990 5000
KIKI 830 10000
KIOE 1080 5000
KISA 1540 5000
KKUA 690 10000
KNDI 1270 5000
KOHO 1170 5000
KORL 650 10000
KPOI 1040 10000
Honolulu (Cont)
KSSK 590 5000
KUMU 1500 10000u k
KZOO 1210 1000
Kahului
KNUI 900 5000
Kailua
KLEI 1130 10000
Kealakekua
KKON 790 5000
Kihei
KHEI 1110 5000
Lihue
KIVM 1350 5000
Pearl City
† KLNI 1380 5000
Wailuku
KMVI 550 5000 -k
Waipahu
KDEO 940 10000

IDAHO

Blackfoot
KBLI 690 1000 d
Boise
KBOI 670 50000
KGEM 1140 10000
KIDO 630 5000
KSPD 790 1000 d
† KTOX 730 500 d
‡ KTOX 740 500 d
Bonners Ferry
KBFI 1450 1000 -
Burley
KBAR 1230 1000 -
Caldwell
KBGN 1060 10000 d
KCID 1490 1000 -
Coeur D' Alene
KVNI 1080 10000 -
Grangeville
KORT 1230 1000 -
Hailey
KSKI 1340 1000 -
Idaho Falls
KID 590 5000 -
KTEE 1260 5000
KUPI 980 1000 d
Jerome
KART 1400 1000 f
Lewiston
KOZE 950 5000 -
KRLC 1350 5000 -
Mc Call
KMCL 1240 500 -
Meridian
KKIC 950 5000 dc
Montpelier
KVSI 1450 1000 -
Moscow
KRPL 1400 1000 -
Mountain Home
KJCY 1240 1000 -
Nampa
KFXD 580 5000
KXTC 1340 1000 -
Orofino
KLER 950 1000
Payette
KYET 1450 250
Pocatello
KSEI 930 5000
KWIK 1240 1000 -
KZBQ 1290 1000 d
Preston
KACH 1340 1000 -
Rexburg
KRXK 1230 1000 -
Rupert
KAYT 970 2500 d
Salmon
KSRA 960 1000 d
Sandpoint
KSPT 1400 1000 -
Soda Springs
KBRV 790 5000 d
St. Anthony
KIGO 1400 1000 -
St. Maries
KOFE 1490 1000 -
Twin Falls
KEEP 1450 1000 -
KLIX 1310 2500 -
KTLC 1270 5000 -
Wallace
KWAL 620 1000
Weiser
KWEI 1260 1000 d

ILLINOIS

Alton
WOKZ 1570 1000 d
Anna
WRAJ 1440 500 d
Aurora
WKKD 1580 250 d
WMRO 1280 2500 -k
Beardstown
WRMS 790 500 d
Belleville
WIBV 1260 5000
Bloomington
WJBC 1230 1000 -
Cairo
WKRO 1490 1000 -
Canton
WBYS 1560 250 d
Carbondale
WCIL 1020 1000 d
Carmi
WROY 1460 1000 d
Carthage
WCAZ 990 1000 d
Casey
WKZI 800 250 d
Centralia
WILY 1210 1000 d
Champaign
WDWS 1400 1000 -
Charleston
WEIC 1270 1000 -
Chester
KSGM 980 1000 -
Chicago
WAIT 820 5000 f
WBBM 780 50000
WCFL 1000 50000
WCRW 1240 1000 -
WEDC 1240 1000 -
WGCI 1390 5000
WGN 720 50000
WIND 560 5000
WJJD 1160 50000 f
WJPC 950 5000 -
WLS 890 50000
WMAQ 670 50000
* WMBI 1110 5000 f
WSBC 1240 1000 -
Chicago Heights
WCGO 1600 1000 d
WMPP 1470 1000 c
Cicero
WCEV 1450 1000 -
WXOL 1450 1000 -
Clinton
WHOW 1520 5000 d
Crystal Lake
WIVS 850 500 d
Danville
WDAN 1490 1000 -
WITY 980 1000
De Kalb
WLBK 1360 1000 d
Decatur
WDZ 1050 1000 d
WSOY 1340 1000 -
Dixon
WIXN 1460 1000 d
Du Quoin
WDQN 1580 250 d
East Moline
* WDLM 960 1000 d
East St. Louis
WESL 1490 1000 -
Effingham
WCRA 1090 1000 d

Elgin		
WRMN	1410	1000 -
Elmhurst		
WKDC	1530	250 d
Evanston		
WEAW	1330	5000 d
WONX	1590	1000 d
Fairfield		
WFIW	1390	1000 d
Freeport		
WFRL	1570	5000 d
Galesburg		
WAIK	1590	5000 d
WGIL	1400	1000 -
Geneseo		
WGEN	1500	250 d
Geneva		
WFXW	1480	1000 -
Granite City		
WGNU	920	500
Harrisburg		
WEBQ	1240	1000 -
Harvard		
WMCW	1600	500 d
Harvey		
WBEE	1570	1000 d
Herrin		
WHPI	1340	1000 -
Highland		
WINU	1510	1000 d
Highland Park		
WEEF	1430	1000 c
Jacksonville		
WJIL	1550	1000 d
WLDS	1180	1000 d
Jerseyville		
WJBM	1480	500 d
Johnston City		
WDDW	810	250 d
Joliet		
WJOL	1340	1000 -
WJRC	1510	500 d
Kankakee		
WKAN	1320	1000 -
Kewanee		
WKEI	1450	500 -
La Grange		
WTAQ	1300	5000 -
La Salle		
WLPO	1220	1000 d
Lawrenceville		
WAKO	910	500 d
Lincoln		
WPRC	1370	1000 d
Litchfield		
WSMI	1540	1000 d
Loves Park		
WLUV	1520	500 d
Macomb		
WKAI	1510	1000 d
Marion		
WGGH	1150	5000 d
Mattoon		
WLBH	1170	5000 dk
Mc Leansboro		
WMCL	1060	2500 d
Mendota		
WGLC	1090	250 d
Metropolis		
WMOK	920	1000 d
Moline		
WMRZ	1230	1000 -
Monmouth		
WRAM	1330	1000 d
Morris		
WCSJ	1550	250 d
Mt. Carmel		
WYER	1360	500 d
Mt. Vernon		
WMIX	940	5000 -
Murphysboro		
WINI	1420	500 d
Normal		
WRBA	1440	1000 -
Oak Park		
WOPA	1490	1000 -
Olney		
WVLN	740	250 d
Ottawa		
WCMY	1430	500 d
Paris		
WPRS	1440	1000 d
Pekin		
WVEL	1140	5000 d
Peoria		
WIRL	1290	5000
WMBD	1470	5000
WPEO	1020	1000 d
WXCL	1350	1000
Pittsfield		
WBBA	1580	250 d
Pontiac		
WPOK	1080	1000 d
Princeton		
WZOE	1490	1000 -
Quincy		
WGEM	1440	5000 -
WTAD	930	5000 -
Rantoul		
WRTL	1460	500 d
Robinson		
WTAY	1570	250 d
Rochelle		
WRHL	1060	250 d
Rock Island		
WHBF	1270	5000
Rockford		
WKKN	1150	1000 d
WROK	1440	5000 -
WXTA	1330	1000 d
Salem		
WJBD	1350	500 d
Shelbyville		
WSHY	1560	500 d
Sparta		
WHCO	1230	1000 -
Springfield		
WCVS	1450	1000 -
WMAY	970	1000 -
WTAX	1240	1000 -
Sterling		
WSDR	1240	500 -
Streator		
WIZZ	1250	500 d
Sycamore		
WSQR	1560	250 d
Taylorville		
WTIM	1410	1000 c
Urbana		
WCCR	1580	250 d
* WILL	580	5000 d
Vandalia		
WPMB	1500	250 d
Watseka		
WGFA	1360	1000 d
Waukegan		
WKRS	1220	1000 d
West Frankfort		
WFRX	1300	1000 d
Wood River		
WRTH	590	1000
Zion		
WNIZ	1500	250 d

INDIANA

Anderson		
WHBU	1240	1000 -
WHUT	1470	1000 d
Auburn		
WIFF	1570	500 d
Bedford		
WBIW	1340	1000 -
Beech Grove		
WNTS	1590	5000 -
Bloomington		
WTTS	1370	5000 -
Boonville		
WBNL	1540	250 d
Brazil		
WWCM	1130	500 d
Columbus		
WCSI	1010	500 d
Connersville		
WIFE	1580	250 d
Corydon		
WJDW	1550	250 d
Crawfordsville		
WCVL	1550	250
Decatur		
WADM	1540	250 d
Elkhart		
WCMR	1270	5000 -
WTRC	1340	1000 -
Evansville		
WGBF	1280	5000 -
WROZ	1400	1000 -
* WSWI	820	250 d
WVHI	1330	5000 -
Frankfort		
WILO	1570	250 d
Ft. Wayne		
WAFX	1450	1000 -
WFCV	1090	1000 d
WGL	1250	1000
WOWO	1190	50000
WQHK	1380	5000
Gary		
WLTH	1370	1000 -
WWCA	1270	1000
Goshen		
WKAM	1460	1000 -
Greensburg		
WTRE	1330	500 d
Hammond		
WJOB	1230	1000 -
Huntington		
WHLT	1300	500 d
Indianapolis		
WATI	810	250 d
WBRI	1500	5000 d
WIBC	1070	50000 -
WIRE	1430	5000
WMLF	1310	5000 -
WNDE	1260	5000
WXLW	950	5000 -c
Jasper		
WITZ	990	1000 d
Jeffersonville		
WXVW	1450	1000 -
Kendallville		
WAWK	1140	250 d
Knox		
WKVI	1520	250 d
Kokomo		
WIOU	1350	5000 -
La Porte		
WLOI	1540	250 d
Lafayette		
WASK	1450	1000 -
WFTE	1410	1000 d
Linton		
WBTO	1600	500 d
Logansport		
WSAL	1230	1000 -
Madison		
WORX	1270	1000 d
Marion		
WBAT	1400	1000 -
WGOM	860	1000 d
Martinsville		
WCBK	1540	250 d
Michigan City		
WIMS	1420	5000
Mishawaka		
† WLPD	910	1000 -
Mount Vernon		
WPCO	1590	500 d
Muncie		
WERK	990	250 d
WLBC	1340	1000 -
New Albany		
WDGS	1290	500 d
WOBS	1570	1000 d
New Castle		
WCTW	1550	250
Newburgh		
† WJJN	1180	500 d
Noblesville		
WFBM	1110	1000 d
North Vernon		
WNVI	1460	1000 d
Paoli		
WKKX	1560	250 d

City	Station	Freq.	Power
Peru			
	WARU	1600	1000 d
Plymouth			
	WTCA	1050	250 d
Portland			
	WPGW	1440	500 d
Princeton			
	WRAY	1250	1000 d
Rensselaer			
	WRIN	1560	1000 d
Richmond			
	WHON	930	500 d
	WKBV	1490	1000 -
Salem			
	WSLM	1220	5000 d
Seymour			
	WJCD	1390	1000 d
Shelbyville			
	WSVL	1520	1000 -
South Bend			
	WAMJ	1580	1000 d
	WNDU	1490	1000 -
	WSBT	960	5000
Sullivan			
	WNDI	1550	250 d
Tell City			
	WTCJ	1230	1000 -
Terre Haute			
	WBOW	1230	1000 -
	WPFR	1300	500 d
	WTHI	1480	5000 -
Valparaiso			
	WAKE	1500	1000 d
	WNWI	1080	250 d
Vincennes			
	WAOV	1450	1000 -
Wabash			
	WAYT	1510	250 d
Warsaw			
	WRSW	1480	1000 -
Washington			
	WAMW	1580	250 d
West Lafayette			
	★ WBAA	920	5000 -
Winamac			
	WAOB	1280	500 d

IOWA

City	Station	Freq.	Power
Albia			
	KLBA	1370	500 d
Algona			
	KLGA	1600	5000 d
Ames			
	KASI	1430	1000 d
	★ WOI	640	5000 d
Anamosa			
	KLEH	1290	500 d
Atlantic			
	KJAN	1220	250 d
Boone			
	★ KFGQ	1260	1000 d
	KWBG	1590	1000 -
Burlington			
	KBUR	1490	1000 -
	KCPS	1150	500 d
Carroll			
	KCIM	1380	1000
Cedar Falls			
	KCFI	1250	500 -
Cedar Rapids			
	KCDR	1450	1000 -
	KCRG	1600	5000
	KHAK	1360	1000 d
	WMT	600	5000
Centerville			
	KCOG	1400	500 -
Charles City			
	KCHA	1580	500 d
Cherokee			
	KCHE	1440	500 d
Clinton			
	KLNT	1390	1000 d
	KROS	1340	1000 -
Council Bluffs			
	KLNG	1560	1000 d
Creston			
	KSIB	1520	1000 d
Davenport			
	KSTT	1170	1000
	KXRK	1580	500 d
	WOC	1420	5000
Decorah			
	† KDEC	1200	1000
	‡# KDEC	1240	1000 -
	★# KWLC	1240	1000 -
Denison			
	KDSN	1530	500 d
Des Moines			
	KIOA	940	10000 -
	KMRY	1390	1000
	KRNT	1350	5000
	KSO	1460	5000
	KWKY	1150	1000
	WHO	1040	50000
Dubuque			
	KDTH	1370	5000
	WDBQ	1490	1000 -
Elkader			
	† KADR	1400	1000 -
Estherville			
	KILR	1070	250 d
Fairfield			
	KMCD	1570	250 d
Ft. Dodge			
	KVFD	1400	1000 -
	KWMT	540	5000 d
Ft. Madison			
	KBKB	1360	1000 d
Grinnell			
	KGRN	1410	500 d
Independence			
	KOUR	1220	250 d
Indianola			
	KBAB	1490	500 -
Iowa City			
	KCJJ	1560	1000 f
	KXIC	800	1000 d
	★ WSUI	910	5000
Iowa Falls			
	KIFG	1510	1000 d
Keokuk			
	KOKX	1310	1000 -
Knoxville			
	KNIA	1320	500 d
Le Mars			
	KLEM	1410	1000 d
Maquoketa			
	KMAQ	1320	500 d
Marshalltown			
	KDAO	1190	250 d
	KFJB	1230	1000 -
Mason City			
	KGLO	1300	5000
	KRIB	1490	1000 -
	KSMN	1010	1000 d
Mt. Pleasant			
	KKSI	1130	250 d
Muscatine			
	KWPC	860	250 d
Newton			
	KCOB	1280	1000 d
Oelwein			
	KOEL	950	5000 -
Oskaloosa			
	KBOE	740	250 d
Ottumwa			
	KBIZ	1240	1000 -
	KLEE	1480	500 d
Perry			
	KDLS	1310	500 d
Red Oak			
	KOAK	1080	250 d
Sheldon			
	KIWA	1550	500 d
Shenandoah			
	KMA	960	5000
	KYFR	920	5000 -
Sioux Center			
	KVDB	1090	500 d
Sioux City			
	KMNS	620	1000
	KSCJ	1360	5000
	KWSL	1470	5000
Spencer			
	KICD	1240	1000 -
Storm Lake			
	KAYL	990	250 d
Washington			
	KCII	1380	500 d
Waterloo			
	KLEU	850	500 d
	★ KNWS	1090	1000 d
	KWLO	1330	5000
	KXEL	1540	50000
Waukon			
	KNEI	1140	1000 d
Waverly			
	KWAY	1470	1000 d
Webster City			
	KQWC	1570	250 d

KANSAS

City	Station	Freq.	Power
Abilene			
	KABI	1560	250 d
Arkansas City			
	KSOK	1280	1000 -
Atchison			
	KARE	1470	1000
Beloit			
	KVSV	1190	2500 d
Chanute			
	KKOY	1460	1000 d
Coffeyville			
	KGGF	690	10000 -
Colby			
	KXXX	790	5000 d
Concordia			
	KNCK	1390	500 d
Dodge City			
	KEDD	1550	1000 d
	KGNO	1370	5000 -
El Dorado			
	KOYY	1360	500 d
Emporia			
	KVOE	1400	1000 -
Fairway			
	KCNW	1380	5000 -
Fort Scott			
	KMDO	1600	1000 d
Garden City			
	KBUF	1050	5000 d
	KIUL	1240	1000 -
Goodland			
	KLOE	730	1000 d
Great Bend			
	KVGB	1590	5000
Hays			
	KAYS	1400	1000 -
Hutchinson			
	KWBW	1450	1000 -
	KWHK	1260	1000 -
Independence			
	KIND	1010	250 d
Iola			
	KIKS	1370	500 d
Junction City			
	KJCK	1420	1000 d
Kansas City			
	KFKF	1340	1000 -
Larned			
	KANS	1510	1000 d
Lawrence			
	#★ KFKU	1250	5000
	KLWN	1320	500 d
Leavenworth			
	KCLO	1410	5000
Liberal			
	KLIB	1470	1000 d
	KSCB	1270	1000 -
Manhattan			
	KMAN	1350	500 d
	★ KSAC	580	5000 -
Marysville			
	KNDY	1570	250 d
Mc Pherson			
	KNEX	1540	250 d
Mission			
	KBEA	1480	1000 -
Newton			
	KJRG	950	500 d
Norton			
	KQNK	1530	1000 d

Ottawa		
KOFO	1220	250 d
Parsons		
KLKC	1540	250 d
Phillipsburg		
KKAN	1490	1000 -
Pittsburg		
KKOW	860	10000 -
KSEK	1340	1000 -
Pratt		
KWLS	1290	5000 -
Russell		
KRSL	990	250 d
Salina		
KFRM	550	5000 d
KINA	910	500 d
KSAL	1150	5000
Scott City		
KFLA	1310	500 d
Topeka		
KSKX	1440	5000 -
KTOP	1490	1000 -
WIBW	580	5000
# WREN	1250	5000
Ulysses		
KULY	1420	1000 -
Wellington		
KLEY	1130	250 d
Wichita		
KAKZ	1240	1000 -
KFDI	1070	10000 -
KFH	1330	5000
KLEO	1480	5000 -
KQAM	1410	5000 -
KSGL	900	250 d
Winfield		
KNIC	1550	250 d

KENTUCKY

Albany		
WANY	1390	1000 d
Ashland		
WCMI	1340	1000 -
Barbourville		
WYWY	950	1000 d
Bardstown		
WBRT	1320	1000 d
Benton		
WCBL	1290	5000 d
Berea		
WKXO	1500	250 d
Bowling Green		
WBGN	1340	1000 -
WKCT	930	5000 -
WLBJ	1410	5000 -
Buffalo		
WLCB	1430	500 d
Burkesville		
WKYR	1570	1000 d
Burnside		
† WKEQ	910	500 d
Cadiz		
WKDZ	1110	1000 d
Campbellsville		
WKXJ	1450	1000 -
Cave City		
WKVE	800	250 d
Central City		
WNES	1050	1000q dk
WMTA	1380	500 d
Columbia		
WAIN	1270	1000 d
Corbin		
WCTT	680	1000
WYGO	1330	5000 d
Covington		
WCLU	1320	500 d
Cumberland		
WCPM	1280	1000 d
Cynthiana		
WCYN	1400	500 -
Danville		
WHIR	1230	1000 -
WKLO	1000	1000 d
Eddyville		
WEAK	900	250 d
Elizabethtown		
WIEL	1400	1000 -
Elkhorn City		
WBPA	1460	1000 d
Elkton		
WSRG	1070	250 d
Eminence		
WSTL	1600	500 d
Flemingsburg		
WFLE	1060	1000 d
Frankfort		
WFKY	1490	1000 -
WKED	1130	500 d
Franklin		
WFKN	1220	250 d
Ft. Campbell		
WABD	1370	1000 d
Ft. Knox		
WSAC	1470	1000 d
Fulton		
WFUL	1270	1000 d
Georgetown		
WBBE	1580	10000 d
Glasgow		
WCDS	1440	5000 d
WKAY	1490	1000 -
Grayson		
WGOH	1370	5000 d
Greensburg		
WGRK	1540	1000 d
Hardinsburg		
WHIC	1520	250 d
Harlan		
WFSR	1470	5000 d
WHLN	1410	5000 d
Harrodsburg		
WHBN	1420	1000 d
Hartford		
WLLS	1600	1000 d
Hawesville		
‡ WKCM	1140	2500 d
† WKCM	1160	2500 -
Hazard		
WKIC	1390	5000 d
Henderson		
WSON	860	500 d
Hindman		
WKCB	1340	1000 -
Hopkinsville		
WHOP	1230	1000 -
WKOA	1480	1000 d
Hyden		
WSLK	1600	1000 d
Inez		
WFJT	1590	1000 d
Irvine		
WIRV	1550	1000 d
Jackson		
WEKG	810	1000 d
Jamestown		
WJKY	1060	2500 d
Jenkins		
WIFX	1000	1000 d
Lancaster		
WIXI	1280	1000 d
Lebanon		
WLBN	1590	1000 d
Leitchfield		
WMTL	1580	250 d
Lexington		
WLAP	630	5000 -
WTKC	1300	2500
WVLK	590	5000 -
Liberty		
WKDO	1560	250 d
London		
† WFTG	980	1000 d
‡ WFTG	1400	1000 -
Louisa		
WVKY	1270	1000 d
Louisville		
WAKY	790	5000 -
WAVG	970	5000
WCII	1080	10000 -
WFIA	900	1000 d
WHAS	840	50000
WINN	1240	1000 -
WLOU	1350	5000 -c
WTMT	620	500 d
Madisonville		
WFMW	730	500 d
WTTL	1310	1000 -
Manchester		
WKLB	1290	5000 d
WWXL	1450	1000 -
Marion		
WMJL	1500	250 d
Martin		
† WMDJ	1440	2500 d
Mayfield		
WNGO	1320	1000 d
WYMC	1430	1000 d
Maysville		
WFTM	1240	1000 -
Middlesboro		
WFXY	1490	1000 -
WMIK	560	500 d
Monticello		
WFLW	1360	1000 d
Morehead		
WMOR	1330	1000 d
Morganfield		
WMSK	1550	250 d
Morgantown		
WLBQ	1570	1000p dk
Mt. Sterling		
WMST	1150	500 d
Mt. Vernon		
WRVK	1460	500 d
Munfordville		
WLOC	1150	1000 d
Murray		
WNBS	1340	1000 -
WSJP	1130	1000p -c
Neon		
WNKY	1480	5000 d
Newport		
WNOP	740	1000 d
Nicholasville		
WNVL	1250	500 d
Owensboro		
WOMI	1490	1000 -
WVJS	1420	5000 -
Paducah		
WDXR	1450	1000 -
WKYX	570	1000 -
WPAD	1560	10000 -
Paintsville		
WSIP	1490	1000 -
Paris		
WBGR	1440	1000 d
Pikeville		
WLSI	900	5000 d
WPKE	1240	1000 -
Pineville		
WANO	1230	1000 -
Pittsburg		
WLPQ	980	1000 d
Prestonburg		
WDOC	1310	5000 d
WPRT	960	5000 d
Princeton		
WPKY	1580	250 d
Radcliff		
† ----	1220	500 d
Richmond		
WCBR	1110	250 d
WEKY	1340	1000 -
Russell Springs		
† WIDS	1190	1000 d
Russellville		
WRUS	610	5000q dk
Saylersville		
WRLV	1140	1000 d
Scottsville		
WLCK	1250	500 d
Shelbyville		
WCND	940	250 d
Somerset		
WSFC	1240	1000 -
WTLO	1480	1000 d
Stanford		
WRSL	1520	500 d
Stanton		
WBFC	1470	1000 d
Tomkinsville		
WTKY	1370	2500 d

Vanceburg
WKKS 1570 1000 d
Vancleve
WMTC 730 5000 d
West Liberty
WLKS 1450 1000 -
Whitesburg
WTCW 920 5000 d
Whitley City
WEQO 1220 1000 d
Wickliffe
‡ WBCE 1010 250 d
† WBCE 1100 1000 d
Williamsburg
WEKC 710 1000 d
WEZJ 1440 1000 d
Winchester
WWKY 1380 1000 d

LOUISIANA

Abbeville
KROF 960 1000 d
Alexandria
KALB 580 5000 -
KDBS 1410 1000 d
KSYL 970 1000
Amite
WABL 1570 500 d
Bastrop
KTRY 730 250 d
KVOB 1340 1000 -
Baton Rouge
WIBR 1300 5000 -
WJBO 1150 5000
WLCS 910 1000
WLUX 1550 5000 d
WTKL 1260 1000 d
WXOK 1460 5000 -
WYNK 1380 5000 d
Bayou Vista
KDLP 1170 500 d
Bogalusa
WBOX 920 1000 d
WIKC 1490 1000 -
Columbia
KCTO 1540 1000 d
Coushatta
KRRP 950 500 d
Covington
WARB 730 250 d
Crowley
KAJN 1560 1000 d
KSIG 1450 1000 -
De Ridder
KDLA 1010 1000 d
Denham Springs
WLBI 1220 250 d
Eunice
KEUN 1490 1000 -
Farmerville
KTDL 1470 1000 d
Ferriday
KFNV 1600 1000
Franklin
KFRA 1390 500 d
Franklinton
WFCG 1110 1000 d
Garyville
WKQT 1010 500 d
Golden Meadow
KLEB 1600 1000 d
Gonzales
WSLG 1090 10000 d
Gretna
KGLA 1540 500 d
Hammond
WFPR 1400 1000 -
Haynesville
KLUV 1580 1000 d
Houma
KJIN 1490 1000 -
Jena
KCKW 1480 500 d
Jennings
KJEF 1290 1000 d
Jonesboro
KTOC 920 1000 d

Lafayette
† KJCB 770 1000
KPEL 1420 1000 -
KVOL 1330 5000 -
KXKW 1520 10000 -
Lake Charles
KAOK 1400 1000 -
KLCL 1470 5000
KLOU 1580 1000
Lake Providence
KLPL 1050 250 d
Leesville
KLLA 1570 1000 d
Mansfield
KDXI 1360 1000 d
Many
KWLA 1400 1000 -
Marksville
KAPB 1370 1000 d
Minden
KASO 1240 1000 -
Monroe
KLIC 1230 1000 -
KMLB 1440 5000 -
KNOE 540 5000 -
Morgan City
KMRC 1430 500 d
Natchitoches
KNOC 1450 1000 -
New Iberia
KANE 1240 1000 -
KNIR 1360 1000 d
New Orleans
WBOK 1230 1000 -
WNNR 990 250 d
WNOE 1060 50000 -
WQUE 1280 5000
WSHO 800 1000 d
WSMB 1350 5000
WTIX 690 10000 -
WVOG 600 1000 d
WWIW 1450 1000 -
WWL 870 50000
WYLD 940 10000 -
New Roads
KQXL 1500 1000 d
Oak Grove
KWCL 1280 1000 d
Oakdale
KREH 900 250 d
Opelousas
KSLO 1230 1000 -
Pineville
† ---- 680 250 d
KPAL 1110 500 d
Port Sulphur
KAGY 1510 1000 d
Rayville
KXLA 990 1000 -
Ruston
KRUS 1490 1000 -
Shreveport
KBCL 1220 250 d
KCIJ 980 5000 d
KEEL 710 50000 -
KFLO 1300 5000q dk
KJOE 1480 1000 d
KOKA 1550 10000 -
KRMD 1340 1000 -
KWKH 1130 50000
Slidell
WSDL 1560 1000 d
Springhill
KBSF 1460 1000 d
Sulphur
KEZM 1310 500 d
Tallulah
KTLD 1360 500 d
Thibodaux
‡ KTIB 630 500 d
† KTIB 640 5000 -
Ville Platte
KVPI 1050 250 d
Vivian
KNCB 1320 5000 d
Washington
KNEK 1190 250 d

West Monroe
KUZN 1310 1000 d
White Castle
KKAY 1590 1000 d
Winnfield
KVCL 1270 1000 d
Winnsboro
KMAR 1570 1000 d

MAINE

Auburn
WRXV 1530 1000 d
Augusta
WFAU 1340 1000 -
WRDO 1400 1000 -
Bangor
WABI 910 5000
WMLI 1250 5000 c
WZON 620 5000
Bath
WJTO 730 1000 d
Belfast
WBME 1230 250
Biddeford
WIDE 1400 1000 -
Brunswick
WKXA 900 1000 d
Calais
WQDY 1230 1000 -
Caribou
WFST 600 5000 d
Dover Foxcroft
WDME 1340 1000 -
Ellsworth
WDEA 1370 5000
Farmington
WKTJ 1380 1000 d
Ft. Kent
WLVC 1340 250
Gardiner
WABK 1280 5000
Gorham
WDCI 1590 5000 -
Houlton
WHOU 1340 1000 -
Lewiston
WCOU 1240 1000 -
WLAM 1470 5000
Lincoln
WLKN 1450 1000 -
Machias
WMCS 1400 1000 -
Madawaska
WSJR 1230 1000 -
Millinocket
WMKR 1240 1000 -
Monticello
WOZW 710 2500 -
Portland
WCSH 970 5000
WGAN 560 5000
WLOB 1310 5000
WPOR 1490 1000 -
Presque Isle
WEGP 1390 5000
WKZX 950 5000
Rockland
WRKD 1450 1000 -
Rumford
WRUM 790 1000 d
Sanford
WSME 1220 1000 d
Skowhegan
WQMR 1150 5000 d
South Paris
WOXO 1450 1000 -
Waterville
WTVL 1490 1000 -
Westbrook
WMER 1440 5000

MARYLAND

Aberdeen
WAMD 970 500
Annapolis
WANN 1190 10000 d
WNAV 1430 5000 -
WYRE 810 250 d

Station	Freq	Power
Baltimore		
WAYE	860	5000r dk
WBAL	1090	50000
WBMD	750	1000 d
WCAO	600	5000
WCBM	680	10000 -
WEBB	1360	5000 d
WFBR	1300	5000
WITH	1230	1000 -
WWIN	1400	1000
WYST	1010	1000 d
Bel Air		
WVOB	1520	250 d
Brunswick		
WTRI	1520	500 d
Cambridge		
WCEM	1240	1000 -
Chestertown		
WCTR	1530	250 d
Cumberland		
WALI	1230	1000 -
WCBC	1270	5000 -
WTBO	1450	1000 -
Easton		
WCEI	1460	1000 -
Elkton		
WSER	1550	1000 d
Frederick		
WFMD	930	5000 -
WZYQ	1370	500 d
Frostburg		
WFRB	560	5000 d
Gaithersburg		
WJOK	1150	1000
Glen Burnie		
WJRO	1590	1000
Hagerstown		
WARK	1490	1000 -
WJEJ	1240	1000 -
Halfway		
WHAG	1410	1000 d
Havre De Grace		
WASA	1330	5000 -
La Plata		
WSMD	1560	25000 dk
Laurel		
WLMD	900	1000 d
Leonardtown		
WKIK	1370	1000
Lexington Park		
WPTX	920	5000 -
Morningside		
WPGC	1580	10000 d
Oakland		
WMSG	1050	500 d
Ocean City		
WETT	1590	1000 -
Pocomoke City		
WDMV	540	500 d
Potomac		
WCTN	950	1000 d
Rockville		
WINX	1600	1000 -
Salisbury		
WICO	1320	1000 d
WJDY	1470	5000 d
WSBY	960	5000 -
Silver Spring		
WGAY	1050	1000 d
Thurmont		
WTHU	1450	500 -
Towson		
WTOW	1570	5000 d
Westminster		
WTTR	1470	1000 d
Wheaton		
WMDO	1540	1000 d

MASSACHUSETTS

Station	Freq	Power
Amherst		
WTTT	1430	5000 d
Attleboro		
WARA	1320	1000
Beverly		
WBVD	1570	500 d
Boston		
WBZ	1030	50000
Boston (Cont)		
WEEI	590	5000
WEZE	1260	5000
WHDH	850	50000
WHUE	1150	5000
WILD	1090	5000 d
WMRE	1510	50000
WRKO	680	50000
WROL	950	5000 d
Brockton		
WAMK	1410	1000 d
WBET	1460	5000 -
Brookline		
WUNR	1600	5000
Cambridge		
WCAS	740	250 d
Chicopee		
WACE	730	5000 d
E. Longmeadow		
WIXY	1600	5000 -c
Fall River		
WALE	1400	1000 -
WSAR	1480	5000
Fitchburg		
WEIM	1280	5000 -
WFGL	960	1000
Framingham		
WKOX	1190	1000 d
Gardner		
WGAW	1340	1000 -
Great Barrington		
WSBS	860	250 d
Greenfield		
WHAI	1240	1000 -
WPOE	1520	10000 d
Haverhill		
WHAV	1490	1000 -
Holyoke		
WREB	930	500 d
Lawrence		
WCCM	800	1000 d
Leicester		
† ----	760	5000 d
Leominster		
WLMS	1000	1000 d
Lowell		
WCAP	980	5000
WLLH	1400	1000 -
Lynn		
WLYN	1360	1000 d
Marlboro		
WSRO	1470	5000
Medford		
WXKS	1430	5000 d
Middleboro		
† ----	1530	250 d
Milford		
WMRC	1490	1000 -
Natick		
WTTP	1060	25000 -
New Bedford		
WBSM	1420	5000 -
WNBH	1340	1000 -
Newburyport		
WCEK	1470	500 d
Newton		
WNTN	1550	10000 d
Norfolk		
WJMQ	1170	1000 d
North Adams		
WMNB	1230	1000 -
Northampton		
WHMP	1400	1000 -
Orange		
† WCAT	700	1000 d
‡ WCAT	1390	1000 d
Orleans		
WVLC	1170	1000 d
Pittsfield		
WBEC	1420	1000
WBRK	1340	1000 -
WUHN	1110	1000 d
Plymouth		
WPLM	1390	5000
Quincy		
WJDA	1300	1000 d
Salem		
WESX	1230	1000 -
Southbridge		
WESO	970	1000 d
Springfield		
WHYN	560	5000 -
WMAS	1450	1000 -
WSPR	1270	5000 -
Taunton		
WPEP	1570	1000 d
Waltham		
WDLW	1330	5000
Ware		
WARE	1250	5000 -
Webster		
WGKP	940	1000p dk
West Springfield		
WACM	1490	1000 -
West Yarmouth		
WSOX	1240	1000 -
Westfield		
WLDM	1570	2500 d
Worcester		
WFTQ	1440	5000
WNEB	1230	1000 -
WORC	1310	5000 -
WTAG	580	5000

MICHIGAN

Station	Freq	Power
Adrian		
WABJ	1490	1000 -
Albion		
WELL	1260	1000 -
Alma		
WFYC	1280	1000 d
Alpena		
WATZ	1450	1000 -
Ann Arbor		
WAAM	1600	5000
WPAG	1050	5000 d
Bad Axe		
WLEW	1340	1000 -
Battle Creek		
WBCK	930	5000 -
WKNR	1400	1000 -
WWKQ	1500	1000 d
Bay City		
WBCM	1440	5000 -
WTCX	1250	1000 d
Benton Harbor		
WHFB	1060	5000 d
Big Rapids		
WBRN	1460	5000 -
Cadillac		
WATT	1240	1000 -
WKJF	1370	5000 -
Caro		
WKYO	1360	1000 -
Charlevoix		
WVOY	1270	5000
Charlotte		
WGWY	1390	5000 d
Cheboygan		
WCBY	1240	1000 -
Clare		
WSDM	990	250 d
Coldwater		
WTVB	1590	5000 -
Dearborn		
WNIC	1310	5000
Detroit		
WCXI	1130	50000 -
WJR	760	50000
WLQV	1500	50000 -
WQBH	1400	1000 -
WWJ	950	5000
WXYZ	1270	5000
Dimondale		
WDTB	1170	1000 d
Dowagiac		
WDOW	1440	1000 d
East Lansing		
* WKAR	870	10000 d
WVIC	730	500 d
Elmwood Twp		
† WLJN	1400	1000 -
Escanaba		
WBDN	600	1000 d
WDBC	680	10000 -

Flint		
WFDF	910	5000 -
WFLT	1420	500 d
WKMF	1470	5000 -
WTAC	600	1000 -
WTRX	1330	5000 -
WWMN	1570	1000 d
Fremont		
WSHN	1550	1000 d
Gaylord		
WZXM	900	1000 d
Gladwin		
WJEB	1350	1000
Grand Haven		
WGHN	1370	500 d
Grand Rapids		
WCUZ	1230	1000 -
WFUR	1570	1000 d
‡ WMAX	1480	5000 d
WOOD	1300	5000
WXQT	1410	1000 d
Grayling		
WGRY	1590	1000 d
Greenville		
WPLB	1380	1000 -
Hancock		
WMPL	920	1000 d
Hastings		
WBCH	1220	250 d
Hillsdale		
WCSR	1340	500 -
Holland		
WHTC	1450	1000 -
WWJQ	1260	5000 -
Houghton		
WCCY	1400	1000 -
Houghton Lake		
WHGR	1290	5000
Howell		
WHMI	1350	500 d
Inkster		
WCHB	1440	1000
Ionia		
WION	1430	5000 d
Iron Mountain		
WMIQ	1450	1000 -
Iron River		
WIKB	1230	1000 -
Ironwood		
WJMS	590	5000 -
Ishpeming		
WJPD	1240	1000 -
WMVN	970	5000 d
Jackson		
WDJD	1510	5000 d
WKHM	970	1000
WXCM	1450	1000 -
Kalamazoo		
WKLZ	1470	500 d
WKMI	1360	5000 -
WKPR	1420	1000 d
WKZO	590	5000
Kalkaska		
WTGE	1420	500 d
Kentwood		
WKWM	1140	5000 d
† WMAX	1480	5000
Lansing		
WILS	1320	5000 -
WITL	1010	500 d
WJIM	1240	1000 -
Lapeer		
WDEY	1530	5000 d
* WMPC	1230	1000 -
Livonia		
WCAR	1090	250 h
Ludington		
WKLA	1450	1000 -
Manistee		
WMTE	1340	1000 -
Manistique		
WTIQ	1490	1000 -
Marine City		
WSMA	1590	1000 d
Marquette		
WDMJ	1320	5000 -
Mason		
* WUNN	1110	1000 d
Menominee		
WAGN	1340	1000 -
Midland		
WMPX	1490	1000 -
Monroe		
WHND	560	500 d
Mt. Clemens		
WWHK	1430	500
Mt. Pleasant		
WCEN	1150	1000 -
Munising		
WQXO	1400	1000 -
Muskegon		
WKBZ	850	1000
WMUS	1090	1000 d
WTRU	1600	5000
Muskegon Heights		
WKJR	1520	10000 -
Newberry		
WNBY	1450	1000 -
Niles		
WNIL	1290	500 d
Otsego		
WOAM	980	1000 d
Owosso		
WOAP	1080	1000 d
Petoskey		
WJML	1110	10000 d
WWPZ	1340	1000 -
Pontiac		
WPON	1460	1000 -
Port Huron		
WHLS	1450	1000 -
WPHM	1380	5000
Portage		
WBUK	1560	1000 d
Reed City		
WDEE	1500	250 -
Rockford		
WJPW	810	500 d
Rogers City		
WHAK	960	5000 d
Royal Oak		
WEXL	1340	1000 -
Saginaw		
WKNX	1210	10000 d
WSAM	1400	1000 -
WSGW	790	5000 -
Saline		
WNRS	1290	500 d
Sandusky		
WMIC	1560	1000 d
Sault Ste. Marie		
WSOO	1230	1000 -
South Haven		
WCSY	940	1000 d
St. Ignace		
WIDG	940	5000 d
St. Johns		
WVGO	1580	1000 d
St. Joseph		
WSJM	1400	1000 -
St. Louis		
WMLM	1540	1000 d
Sturgis		
WSTR	1230	1000 -
Tawas City		
WIOS	1480	1000 d
Three Rivers		
WLKM	1510	500 d
Traverse City		
WCCW	1310	5000 d
WTCM	580	5000q -k
West Branch		
WBMB	1060	1000 d
Whitehall		
WPBK	1490	1000 -
Wyoming		
WYGR	1530	500 d
Ypsilanti		
WSDS	1480	1000q kch
WYFC	1520	250 d

MINNESOTA

Aitkin		
KKIN	930	1000 d
Albany		
KASM	1150	1000 d
Albert Lea		
KATE	1450	1000 -
Alexandria		
KXRA	1490	1000 -
Anoka		
KKKC	1470	1000 d
Austin		
KAUS	1480	1000
KQAQ	970	5000 -
Bemidji		
KBUN	1450	1000 -
KKBJ	1360	5000 -
Benson		
KBMO	1290	500 d
Blue Earth		
KBEW	1560	1000 d
Brainerd		
KLIZ	1380	5000
KVBR	1340	1000 -
Breckenridge		
KBMW	1450	1000 -
Buffalo		
KRWC	1360	500 d
Cloquet		
WKLK	1230	1000 -
Crookston		
KROX	1260	1000 -
Detroit Lakes		
KDLM	1340	1000 -
Duluth		
KDAL	610	5000
WEBC	560	5000
WNLT	1390	500 d
WWJC	850	10000 d
East Grand Forks		
KRRK	1590	5000 -
Ely		
WELY	1450	1000 -
Eveleth		
WEVE	1340	1000 -
Fairmont		
KSUM	1370	1000
Faribault		
KDHL	920	5000
Fergus Falls		
KBRF	1250	5000 -
Fosston		
KEHG	1480	5000 -
Glencoe		
† KQPM	1550	500 d
Golden Valley		
KGLD	1440	5000 -
KUXL	1570	2500 d
Grand Rapids		
KOZY	1320	5000
Hastings		
KDWA	1460	1000 d
Hibbing		
WGGR	1240	1000 -
‡ WKKQ	1060	5000 d
† WKKQ	1080	10000
Hutchinson		
KDUZ	1260	1000 d
International Falls		
KGHS	1230	500 -
Jackson		
KKOJ	1190	5000 d
Litchfield		
KLFD	1410	500 d
Little Falls		
KLTF	960	5000 d
Long Prairie		
KEYL	1400	1000 -
Luverne		
KQAD	800	500 d
Mankato		
KTOE	1420	5000
KYSM	1230	1000 -
Maplewood		
WMIN	1010	250 d
Marshall		
KMHL	1400	1000 -
Minneapolis		
KKSS	980	5000
* KSJN	1330	5000
KTCR	690	500 d
* KTIS	900	2500 d
* KUOM	770	5000

Minneapolis (Cont)			
	WCCO	830	50000
	WDGY	1130	50000
	WWTC	1280	5000
Montevideo			
	KDMA	1460	1000
Monticello			
	KMOM	1070	10000q -
Moorhead			
	KVOX	1280	5000 -
Morris			
	KMRS	1230	1000 -
New Prague			
	KCHK	1350	500 d
New Ulm			
	KNUJ	860	1000 d
Northfield			
	KYMN	1080	1000 d
	* WCAL	770	5000
Ortonville			
	KDIO	1350	1000 d
Owatonna			
	KRFO	1390	500 d
Park Rapids			
	† KPRM	870	2500 -
	‡ KPRM	1270	5000 d
Pine City			
	WCMP	1350	1000 d
Pipestone			
	KLOH	1050	1000 d
Preston			
	KFIL	1060	1000 d
Princeton			
	WQPM	1300	1000 d
Red Wing			
	KCUE	1250	1000 d
Redwood Falls			
	KLGR	1490	1000 -
Rochester			
	KOLM	1520	10000 d
	KROC	1340	1000 -
	KWEB	1270	5000 -
Roseau			
	KRWB	1410	1000
Sauk Rapids			
	WVAL	800	250 d
Shakopee			
	KSMM	1530	500 d
South St. Paul			
	KMAP	1370	500 d
St. Cloud			
	KNSI	1450	1000 -
	WJON	1240	1000 -
St. Louis Park			
	KRSI	950	1000
St. Paul			
	KDWB	630	5000 -
	KLBB	1400	1000 -
	KSTP	1500	50000
St. Peter			
	KRBI	1310	1000 d
Staples			
	† KNSP	1430	1000 d
Stillwater			
	WVLE	1220	5000 d
Thief River Falls			
	KKAQ	1460	500 d
	KTRF	1230	1000 -
Virginia			
	WHLB	1400	1000 -
Wabasha			
	KWMB	1190	1000 d
Wadena			
	KWAD	920	1000
Waite Park			
	KKCM	1390	2500 -
Walker			
	KLLR	1600	1000 d
Waseca			
	KOWO	1170	1000 d
Willmar			
	KDJS	1590	1000 d
	KWLM	1340	1000 -
Windom			
	KDOM	1580	1000 d
Winona			
	KAGE	1380	1000 d
	KWNO	1230	1000 -
Worthington			
	KWOA	730	1000 d

MISSISSIPPI

Aberdeen			
	WMPA	1240	1000 -
Amory			
	WAMY	1580	5000 d
	WZBR	1520	500 d
Batesville			
	WBLE	1290	1000 d
Bay Springs			
	WHII	1570	1000 d
Bay St. Louis			
	WXGR	1190	5000 d
Belzoni			
	WELZ	1460	1000 d
Biloxi			
	WLOX	1490	1000 -
	WVMI	570	5000 -
Booneville			
	WBIP	1400	1000 -
Brandon			
	WRKN	970	1000 d
Brookhaven			
	WCHJ	1470	1000 d
	WJMB	1340	1000 -f
Calhoun City			
	WJRL	1530	250 d
Canton			
	WMGO	1370	1000 d
Carthage			
	WECP	1080	5000 d
Centreville			
	WSSL	1580	250 d
Clarksdale			
	WROX	1450	1000 -
Cleveland			
	WCLD	1490	1000 -
	WRDC	1410	1000 d
Clinton			
	† WTWZ	1150	500 d
Columbia			
	WCJU	1450	1000 -
	WFFF	1360	1000 d
Columbus			
	WACR	1050	1000 d
	WCBI	550	1000 -
	WMBC	1400	1000 -
Corinth			
	WCMA	1230	1000 -
	WKCU	1350	1000 d
Crystal Springs			
	WCSP	1520	1000 d
Eupora			
	WEPA	710	2500 d
Forest			
	WJYV	850	10000 d
Fulton			
	WFTO	1330	5000 d
Greenville			
	WDDT	900	1000 d
	WGVM	1260	5000 d
	WNIX	1330	1000 -
Greenwood			
	WABG	960	1000 -
	WGRM	1240	1000 -
Grenada			
	WYKC	1400	1000 -
Gulfport			
	WGUF	1130	500 d
	WROA	1390	5000
	WTAM	1240	1000 -
Hattiesburg			
	WBKH	950	5000 d
	WFOR	1400	1000 -
	WHSY	1230	1000 -
	WKOJ	1310	1000 d
	WORV	1580	1000 d
Hazlehurst			
	WMDC	1220	250 d
Holly Springs			
	WKRA	1110	1000 d
Houston			
	WCPC	940	50000 -
Indianola			
	WNLA	1380	500 d
Iuka			
	WVOM	1270	1000 d
Jackson			
	WCCL	1590	5000 -
	WJDX	620	5000 -
	WJQS	1400	1000 -
	WJXN	1450	1000 -
	WKXI	1300	5000 -
	WOKJ	1550	50000 -
	WSLI	930	5000
Kosciusko			
	WKOZ	1340	1000 -
Laurel			
	WAML	1340	1000 -
	WLAU	1430	5000 d
	WQIS	1260	5000 d
Leland			
	WESY	1580	1000 d
Lexington			
	WXTN	1000	5000 d
Louisville			
	WLSM	1270	5000 d
Lucedale			
	WRBE	1440	5000 d
Magee			
	WSJC	810	50000 -
Marion			
	† WJDQ	1240	1000 -
Marks			
	WQMA	1520	250 d
Mc Comb			
	WAKK	1140	500 d
	WAPF	980	5000 d
	WHNY	1250	5000 -
Meridian			
	WALT	910	5000 -
	WFEZ	1390	5000 d
	‡ WJDQ	1330	5000 d
	WMOX	1010	10000 -
	WQIC	1450	1000 -
Monticello			
	WMLC	1270	1000 d
Moss Point			
	WJKX	1460	500 d
Natchez			
	WMIS	1240	1000 -
	WNAT	1450	1000 -
New Albany			
	WKXC	1470	500
Newton			
	WMYQ	1410	500 d
Oxford			
	WSUH	1420	1000 d
Pascagoula			
	WPMP	1580	5000 d
Pearl			
	WKKE	1180	10000 -
Philadelphia			
	WHOC	1490	1000 -
Picayune			
	WRJW	1320	5000 d
Pontotoc			
	WSEL	1440	1000 d
Poplarville			
	WRPM	1530	10000 d
Port Gibson			
	WKPG	1320	500 d
Prentiss			
	WKPO	1510	1000 d
Quitman			
	WBFN	1500	1000
Ripley			
	WCSA	1260	500 d
Sardis			
	WRDS	1500	500 d
Senatobia			
	WSAO	1140	5000 d
Starkville			
	WKOR	980	1000 d
	WSSO	1230	1000 -
Tupelo			
	WCFB	1060	250 d
	WELO	580	1000 -
	WTUP	1490	1000 -
Tylertown			
	WTYL	1290	1000 d
Vicksburg			
	WJFL	1490	1000 -

Location / Station	Frequency	Power
Vicksburg (Cont)		
WQBC	1420	5000r -
Walnut		
WLRC	850	250 d
Water Valley		
WVLY	1320	500 d
Waynesboro		
WABO	990	1000 d
West Point		
WROB	1450	1000 -
Wiggins		
WIGG	1420	5000r dk
Winona		
WONA	1570	1000 d
Yazoo City		
WAZF	1230	1000 -
WJNS	1530	250 d

MISSOURI

Location / Station	Frequency	Power
Aurora		
KSWM	940	500 d
Ava		
KSOA	1430	500 d
Birch Tree		
KBMV	1310	1000q d
Bolivar		
KYOO	1130	250 d
Boonville		
KWRT	1370	1000 d
Bowling Green		
KPCR	1530	1000 d
Branson		
KLCO	1220	1000 d
Brookfield		
KGHM	1470	500 d
Butler		
KMAM	1530	500 d
California		
† KZMO	1420	5000 d
Cameron		
KMRN	1360	500 d
Cape Girardeau		
KEWI	1550	5000 d
KGIR	960	5000 -
KZYM	1220	250 d
Carrollton		
KAOL	1430	500 d
Carthage		
KDMO	1490	1000 -
Caruthersville		
KCRV	1370	1000 d
Charleston		
KCHR	1350	1000 d
Chillicothe		
KCHI	1010	250 d
Clayton		
⋆ KFUO	850	5000 d
KSIV	1320	5000 d
Clinton		
KDKD	1280	1000 d
Columbia		
KFRU	1400	1000 -
KTGR	1580	250 d
Cuba		
KBCC	1410	1000 d
De Soto		
KHAD	1190	5000 d
Dexter		
KDEX	1590	1000 d
Doniphan		
KDFN	1500	1000 d
East Prairie		
KYMO	1080	500 d
El Dorado Springs		
KESM	1580	500 d
Excelsior Springs		
KEXS	1090	1000 d
Farmington		
KREI	800	1000 d
Festus		
KJCF	1400	1000 -
Flat River		
KFMO	1240	1000 -
Fredericktown		
KFTW	1450	1000 -
Fulton		
KFAL	900	1000 d
Hannibal		
KHMO	1070	5000 -
Houston		
KBTC	1250	1000 d
Independence		
KCCV	1510	1000 d
Ironton		
KPIA	1480	5000 d
Jackson		
KJAS	1170	250 d
Jefferson City		
KLIK	950	5000 -
KWOS	1240	1000 -
Joplin		
KFSB	1310	5000 -
KODE	1230	1000 -
KQYX	1560	10000 d
WMBH	1450	1000 -
Kansas City		
KCMO	810	50000 -
KJLA	1190	1000 -
KMBZ	980	5000
KPRT	1590	1000 d
WDAF	610	5000
WHB	710	10000 -
Kennett		
KBOA	830	1000 d
KBXM	1540	1000 d
Kirksville		
KIRX	1450	1000 -
Lebanon		
KJEL	1080	250 d
KLWT	1230	1000 -
Lexington		
KLEX	1570	250 d
Liberty		
KKCI	1140	500 d
Macon		
KLTI	1560	1000p d
Malden		
KTCB	1470	1000 d
Marshall		
KMMO	1300	1000 d
Marshfield		
KOSC	1510	250 d
Maryville		
KNIM	1580	250 d
Mexico		
KXEO	1340	1000 -
Moberly		
KWIX	1230	1000 -
Monett		
KRMO	990	250 d
Mountain Grove		
KLRS	1360	1000 d
Neosho		
KBTN	1420	1000r -k
Nevada		
KNEM	1240	1000 -k
New Hampton		
† KAAN	870	250 d
Osage Beach		
KRMS	1150	1000 d
Piedmont		
KPWB	1140	1000 d
Poplar Bluff		
KLID	1340	1000 -
KWOC	930	5000 -
Portageville		
KMIS	1050	1000 d
Potosi		
KYRO	1280	500 d
Rolla		
KCLU	1590	1000 d
KTTR	1490	1000 -
Salem		
† KFPS	1440	500 d
KSMO	1340	1000 -
Sedalia		
KDRO	1490	1000 -
KSIS	1050	1000 d
Sikeston		
KMPL	1520	5000 -
KSIM	1400	1000 -
Southwest City		
KCTE	1140	250 d
Springfield		
KGBX	1260	5000
Springfield (Cont)		
KICK	1340	1000 -
KLFJ	1550	500 d
KLSM	1060	500 d
KTTS	1400	1000 -
KWTO	560	5000
St. Charles		
KIRL	1460	5000 -
St. Joseph		
KFEQ	680	5000
KGNM	1270	1000 d
KKJO	1550	5000
St. Louis		
KATZ	1600	5000
KMOX	1120	50000
KSD	550	5000
KSTL	690	1000 d
KWK	1380	5000
KXEN	1010	50000 d
KXOK	630	5000
WEW	770	1000 d
WIL	1430	5000
Sullivan		
KTUI	1560	1000 d
Thayer		
KALM	1290	1000 d
Trenton		
KTTN	1600	500 d
Union		
KLPW	1220	1000 d
Warrensburg		
KOKO	1450	1000 -
Warrenton		
KWRE	730	1000 d
Waynesville		
KJPW	1390	1000 d
KOZQ	1270	500 d
Webb City		
† ----	1100	5000 d
West Plains		
KWPM	1450	1000 -
Willow Springs		
KUKU	1330	1000 d

MONTANA

Location / Station	Frequency	Power
Anaconda		
KANA	580	1000 d
Baker		
KFLN	960	5000 d
Belgrade		
‡ KGVW	630	1000 d
† KGVW	640	10000 -
Billings		
KBMY	1240	1000 -
KGHL	790	5000
KOOK	970	5000
KOYN	910	1000 d
KURL	730	500 d
Bozeman		
KBMN	1230	1000 -
KBOZ	1090	5000
KXXL	1450	1000 -
Butte		
KBOW	550	5000 -
KXLF	1370	5000
Deer Lodge		
KDRG	1400	1000 -
Dillon		
KDBM	1490	1000 -
East Missoula		
† KYSS	930	5000 -
Glasgow		
KLTZ	1240	1000 -
Glendive		
KGLE	590	500 d
KXGN	1400	1000 -
Great Falls		
KARR	1400	1000 -
KEIN	1310	5000 -
KMON	560	5000
KQDI	1450	1000 -
Hamilton		
KLYQ	1240	1000 -
Hardin		
KHDN	1230	1000 -
Havre		
KOJM	610	1000

City / Station	Freq	Power
Helena		
KBLL	1240	1000 -
KCAP	1340	1000 -
KMTX	950	5000
Kalispell		
KGEZ	600	5000 -
KOFI	1180	10000
Laurel		
KLYC	1490	1000 -
Lewistown		
KXLO	1230	1000 -
Libby		
KLCB	1230	1000 -
Livingston		
KPRK	1340	1000 -f
Miles City		
KATL	1340	1000 -
Missoula		
KGRZ	1450	1000 -
KGVO	1290	5000
KYLT	1340	1000 -
‡ KYSS	930	5000 d
Plentywood		
† KATQ	1070	5000 d
Polson		
† KERR	750	50000 -
‡ KERR	1070	25000 -
Red Lodge		
KRBN	1450	1000 -
Shelby		
KSEN	1150	5000
Sidney		
KGCX	1480	5000
West Yellowstone		
KWYS	920	1000 d
Whitefish		
KJJR	880	10000 -
KTXX	1450	1000 -
Wolf Point		
KVCK	1450	1000 -

NEBRASKA

City / Station	Freq	Power
Ainsworth		
KBRB	1400	1000 -
Alliance		
KCOW	1400	1000 -
Beatrice		
KWBE	1450	1000 -
Broken Bow		
KCNI	1280	1000 d
Chadron		
KCSR	610	1000 d
Columbus		
KJSK	900	1000 d
KTTT	1510	1000 d
Cozad		
KAMI	1580	1000 d
Fairbury		
KGMT	1310	500 d
Falls City		
KTNC	1230	500 -
Fremont		
KHUB	1340	500 -
Grand Island		
KMMJ	750	10000 d
KRGI	1430	5000 -
Hastings		
KHAS	1230	1000 -
KICS	1550	500 d
Holdrege		
KUVR	1380	500 d
Kearney		
KGFW	1340	1000 -
KRNY	1460	5000 d
Kimball		
KIMB	1260	1000 d
Lexington		
KRVN	880	50000
Lincoln		
KECK	1530	5000 d
KFOR	1240	1000 -
KLIN	1400	1000 -
KLMS	1480	5000 -
Mc Cook		
KBRL	1300	5000 d
KICX	1360	1000 d
Nebraska City		
KNCY	1600	500 d
Norfolk		
WJAG	780	1000 d
North Platte		
KJLT	970	5000 d
KODY	1240	1000 -
KOOQ	1410	5000 -
O' Neill		
KBRX	1350	1000 d
Ogallala		
KOGA	930	500
Omaha		
KCRO	660	1000 d
KFAB	1110	50000
KOIL	1290	5000
KOOO	1420	1000 d
KYNN	1490	1000 -
WOW	590	5000
Ord		
KNLV	1060	1000 d
Plattsmouth		
KOTD	1000	250 d
Scottsbluff		
KNEB	960	1000 -
KOLT	1320	5000 -
Sidney		
KSID	1340	1000 -
Superior		
KRFS	1600	500 d
Terrytown		
KEYR	690	1000 d
Valentine		
KVSH	940	5000 d
Wayne		
KTCH	1590	2500 d
York		
KAWL	1370	500 d

NEVADA

City / Station	Freq	Power
Carson City		
KPTL	1300	5000 -
Elko		
KELK	1240	1000 -
Ely		
KELY	1230	250 f
Fallon		
KVLV	980	5000 d
Henderson		
KVOV	1280	5000 d
Las Vegas		
KDWN	720	50000 -
KENO	1460	5000 -
KLAV	1230	1000 -
KMJJ	1140	10000 -
KNUU	970	5000 -
KORK	920	5000 -
KRAM	1340	1000 -
KVEG	1410	5000
Reno		
KBET	1340	1000 -
KCBN	1230	1000 -
† ----	1550	10000 d
KOH	630	5000 -
KOLO	920	5000 -
KONE	1450	1000 -
KROW	780	50000
Sparks		
KROI	1270	5000r c
Winnemucca		
KWNA	1400	1000 -f

NEW HAMPSHIRE

City / Station	Freq	Power
Berlin		
WBRL	1400	1000 -
WMOU	1230	1000 -
Claremont		
WTSV	1230	1000 -
Concord		
WKXL	1450	1000 -
Conway		
WBNC	1050	1000 d
Derry		
WDER	1320	5000 -
Dover		
WTSN	1270	5000
Exeter		
WMYF	1540	5000r d
Franklin		
WFTN	1240	1000 -
Hanover		
WDCR	1340	1000 -
WTSL	1400	1000 -
Keene		
WKBK	1220	1000 d
WKNE	1290	5000
Laconia		
WEMJ	1490	1000 -
WKZU	1350	5000 d
Littleton		
WLTN	1400	1000 -
Manchester		
WFEA	1370	5000
WGIR	610	5000 -
WKBR	1250	5000
Nashua		
WOTW	900	1000 d
WSMN	1590	5000
Newport		
WCNL	1010	250 d
Peterborough		
WRPT	1050	1000 d
Plymouth		
WPNH	1300	5000 d
Portsmouth		
WBBX	1380	1000
WHEB	750	1000 d
Rochester		
WWNH	930	5000
Salem		
WVNH	1110	5000 d
Wolfeboro		
WASR	1420	5000 d

NEW JERSEY

City / Station	Freq	Power
Asbury Park		
WJLK	1310	2500 -
Atlantic City		
WIIN	1450	1000 -
WMID	1340	1000 -
WUSS	1490	1000 -
Bridgeton		
WSNJ	1240	1000 -
Camden		
WSSJ	1310	1000 -
WTMR	800	5000 d
Dover		
WRAN	1510	10000 -
Eatontown		
WHTG	1410	500 d
Elizabeth		
WJDM	1530	500 d
Hackensack		
WWDJ	970	5000
Hackettstown		
WRNJ	1000	2500 d
Hammondton		
WTYO	1580	1000 d
Lakewood		
WHLW	1170	5000 d
Millville		
WREY	1440	1000 d
Morristown		
WMTR	1250	5000 d
Mount Holly		
WJJZ	1460	5000 d
New Brunswick		
WCTC	1450	1000 -
Newark		
† WNJR	1430	5000
WSKQ	620	5000
Newton		
WNNJ	1360	1000 d
Ocean City		
WIBG	1520	1000 d
Parsippany		
WXMC	1310	1000 d
Paterson		
WPAT	930	5000
Plainfield		
WERA	1590	500 c
Pleasantville		
WOND	1400	1000 -
Pompton Lakes		
WKER	1500	1000 d
Princeton		
WHWH	1350	5000

Salem			
	WJIC	1510	2500 d
Somerville			
	WBRW	1170	500 d
Stirling			
	WKMB	1070	2500 d
Trenton			
	WBUD	1260	5000 -
	WIMG	1300	5000 -
	WTTM	920	1000
Vineland			
	WDVL	1270	500 d
	WWBZ	1360	1000
Washington			
	WCRV	1580	1000 d
Wildwood			
	WCMC	1230	1000 -
Zarephath			
	# WAWZ	1380	5000

NEW MEXICO

Alamogordo			
	KINN	1270	1000 d
	KPSA	1230	1000 -
Albuquerque			
	KABQ	1350	5000 -
	KAMX	1520	1000 d
	KDAZ	730	1000 d
	KDEF	1150	5000 -
	KKIM	1000	10000 d
	KLTN	1240	1000 -
	KOB	770	50000
	KQEO	920	1000 -
	KRKE	610	5000
	† KRZY	1090	50000 -
	‡ KRZY	1450	1000 -
	KXKS	1190	1000 d
	KZIA	1580	10000 d
Artesia			
	KSVP	990	1000 -
Aztec			
	KKBK	1340	1000 -
Bayard			
	KNFT	950	5000 d
Belen			
	KARS	860	250 d
Carlsbad			
	KAMQ	1240	1000 -
	KBAD	740	1000 d
	KCCC	930	1000 d
Clayton			
	KLMX	1450	1000 -
Clovis			
	KCLV	1240	1000 -
	KICA	980	1000
	KWKA	680	500
Corrales			
	† KXAK	1310	1000 d
Deming			
	KOTS	1230	1000 -
Espanola			
	KDCE	970	1000 d
Farmington			
	KENN	1390	5000 -
	KNDN	960	5000 d
	KRZE	1280	5000 d
Gallup			
	KGAK	1330	5000 -
	KYVA	1230	1000 -
Grants			
	KMIN	980	1000 d
Hobbs			
	KHOB	1390	5000 d
	KUUX	1480	5000 -
Humble City			
	KYKK	1110	1000 d
Las Cruces			
	KGRT	570	5000 d
	KOBE	1450	1000 -
Las Vegas			
	KFUN	1230	1000 -
	KNMX	540	5000 d
Los Alamos			
	KRSN	1490	1000 -
Lovington			
	KLEA	630	500 d
Magdalena			
	*† KABR	1500	1000 d
Portales			
	KENM	1450	1000 -
Raton			
	KRTN	1490	1000 -f
Roswell			
	KBCQ	1020	50000
	KBIM	910	5000 -
	KCRX	1430	5000 -
	KRDD	1320	1000 d
	KRSY	1230	1000 -
Ruidoso			
	† KOAW	1490	1000 -
	KREE	1360	5000 d
Santa Fe			
	KAFE	810	5000 d
	KTRC	1400	1000 -
	KVSF	1260	5000 -k
Santa Rosa			
	KSYX	1340	1000 -
Silver City			
	KSIL	1340	1000 -
Socorro			
	KSRC	1290	1000 d
Taos			
	KKIT	1340	1000 -
Truth Or Consequences			
	KCHS	1400	250
Tucumcari			
	KTNM	1400	1000 -

NEW YORK

Albany			
	WABY	1400	1000 -
	WOKO	1460	5000
	WPTR	1540	50000
	WROW	590	5000 -
Amherst			
	WUFO	1080	1000 d
Amsterdam			
	WCSS	1490	1000 -
	WKOL	1570	1000 d
Attica			
	§ WBTF	1017	1250
Auburn			
	WAUB	1590	500 d
	WMBO	1340	1000 -
Babylon			
	WGLI	1290	5000 -
	WNYG	1440	1000 d
Baldwinsville			
	WSEN	1050	1000 d
Batavia			
	WBTA	1490	500 -
Bath			
	WVIN	1380	500 d
Beacon			
	WBNR	1260	1000 d
Binghamton			
	WINR	680	1000 -
	WKOP	1360	5000 -
	WNBF	1290	5000
Boonville			
	WBRV	900	1000 d
Brewster			
	WPUT	1510	1000 d
Brockport			
	WJBT	1590	1000
Buffalo			
	WBEN	930	5000
	* WEBR	970	5000
	WGR	550	5000
	WKBW	1520	50000
	WNYS	1120	1000 d
	WYSL	1400	1000 -
Canandaigua			
	WCGR	1550	250 d
Catskill			
	WCKL	560	1000 d
Cheektowaga			
	WECK	1230	1000 -
Cobelskill			
	WSCM	1190	500 d
Corning			
	WCBA	1350	1000 d
	WCLI	1450	1000 -
Cornwall			
	WCRR	1170	1000 d
Cortland			
	WKRT	920	1000 -
Dansville			
	WDNY	1400	500 -
Dundee			
	WFLR	1570	1000 d
Dunkirk			
	WDOE	1410	1000 -
East Syracuse			
	WSIV	1540	1000 d
Ellenville			
	WELV	1370	5000 d
Elmira			
	WELM	1410	1000 -
	WENY	1230	1000 -
Elmira Heights			
	WEHH	1590	500 d
Endicott			
	WENE	1430	5000
Fredonia			
	WBUZ	1570	250 d
Freeport			
	WGBB	1240	1000 -
Fulton			
	WOSC	1300	1000 d
Geneva			
	WGVA	1240	1000 -
Glens Falls			
	WBZA	1410	1000 d
	WWSC	1450	1000 -
Gloversville			
	WENT	1340	1000 -
Gouverneur			
	WIGS	1230	1000 -
Hempstead			
	WHLI	1100	10000 d
Herkimer			
	WRMV	1420	1000 d
Hornell			
	WHHO	1320	5000
	WLEA	1480	2500 d
Horseheads			
	WIQT	1000	5000 d
Hudson			
	WHUC	1230	1000 -
Huntington			
	WGSM	740	25000 d
Hyde Park			
	WHVW	950	500 d
Islip			
	WLIX	540	250 d
Ithaca			
	WHCU	870	5000 -
	WTKO	1470	5000
Jamestown			
	WJTN	1240	500 -
	WKSN	1340	250
Johnstown			
	WMYL	930	1000 d
Kingston			
	WGHQ	920	5000 -c
	WKNY	1490	1000 -
Lake Placid			
	WIRD	920	5000 d
Lancaster			
	WXRL	1300	1000 hc
Liberty			
	WVOS	1240	1000 -
Little Falls			
	WLFH	1230	1000 -
Lockport			
	WLVL	1340	1000 -
Malone			
	WICY	1490	1000 -
Massena			
	WMSA	1340	1000 -
	WYBG	1050	1000 d
Mechanicville			
	WMVI	1170	250 d
Middletown			
	WALL	1340	1000 -
Mineola			
	WTHE	1520	1000 d
Mount Kisco			
	WVIP	1310	5000 d
New City			
	WRKL	910	1000 c

Location / Station	Frequency	Power
New Rochelle		
WVOX	1460	500 d
New York		
WABC	770	50000
WADO	1280	5000
# WBNX	1380	5000
WCBS	880	50000
WHN	1050	50000
WINS	1010	50000
WJIT	1480	5000
WLIB	1190	10000 f
WMCA	570	5000
WNBC	660	50000
WNEW	1130	50000
⋆ WNYC	830	1000 d
WNYM	1330	5000
WOR	710	50000
WPOW	1330	5000
WQXR	1560	50000
WWRL	1600	5000
Newark		
WACK	1420	500
Newburgh		
WGNY	1220	5000 d
Niagara Falls		
WHLD	1270	5000 d
WJJL	1440	1000 d
North Syracuse		
WSOQ	1220	1000 d
Norwich		
WCHN	970	1000 d
Ogdensburg		
WSLB	1400	1000 -
Olean		
WHDL	1450	1000 -
WMNS	1360	1000 d
Oneida		
WMCR	1600	1000 d
Oneonta		
WDOS	730	1000 d
Oswego		
WSGO	1440	1000 d
Owego		
WEBO	1330	5000 d
Patchogue		
WALK	1370	500 d
WLIM	1580	10000 d
Peekskill		
WLNA	1420	5000 c
Pennyan		
WOZO	850	500 d
Plattsburgh		
WEAV	960	5000
WIRY	1340	1000 -
WKDR	1070	5000 d
Port Jervis		
WDLC	1490	1000 -
Potsdam		
WPDM	1470	1000 d
Poughkeepsie		
WEOK	1390	5000 d
WKIP	1450	1000 -
Remsen		
WADR	1480	5000 d
Rensselaer		
WQBK	1300	5000 d
Riverhead		
WRHD	1570	1000 d
WRIV	1390	1000 d
Rochester		
----	990	1000 -
WBBF	950	1000
WHAM	1180	50000
WPXY	1280	5000
WRTK	1370	5000
WWWG	1460	5000
Rome		
WKAL	1450	1000 -
WRNY	1350	500 d
Sag Harbor		
WLNG	1600	500 d
Salamanca		
WGGO	1590	5000 d
Sandy Creek		
WSCP	1070	2500 d
Saranac Lake		
WNBZ	1240	1000 -
Saratoga Springs		
WKAJ	900	500 d
Schenectady		
WGY	810	50000
WWWD	1240	1000 -
Seneca Falls		
WSFW	1110	1000 d
Sidney		
WCDO	1490	250
Spring Valley		
WGRC	1300	500 d
Syracuse		
WFBL	1390	5000
WHEN	620	5000 -
WNDR	1260	5000
WOLF	1490	1000 -
WSYR	570	5000
Ticonderoga		
WIPS	1250	1000 d
Troy		
WHAZ	1330	1000 d
WTRY	980	5000
Utica		
WIBX	950	5000
WRUN	1150	5000 -
WTLB	1310	1000 -
WUTQ	1550	1000 d
Walton		
WDLA	1270	5000 d
Warsaw		
WCJW	1140	1000 d
Warwick		
WTBQ	1110	250 d
Watertown		
WATN	1240	1000 -
WOTT	1410	5000 -
WTNY	790	1000
Watkins Glen		
WGMF	1500	250 d
Wellsville		
WLSV	790	1000 d
White Plains		
WFAS	1230	1000 -

NORTH CAROLINA

Location / Station	Frequency	Power
Aberdeen		
WANC	1350	2500 d
Ahoskie		
WRCS	970	1000 d
Albemarle		
WWWX	1010	1000 d
WZKY	1580	250 d
Ashboro		
WZOO	710	1000 d
Asheboro		
WGWR	1260	5000 -
Asheville		
WISE	1310	5000 -
WRAQ	1380	5000 -
WSKY	1230	1000 -
WWNC	570	5000
Beaufort		
WBTB	1400	1000 -
Belmont		
WCGC	1270	1000 -
Benson		
WPYB	1130	1000 d
Black Mountain		
WFGW	1010	50000 d
WONO	1350	1000q d
Boone		
WATA	1450	1000 -
Brevard		
WPNF	1240	1000 -
Bryson City		
WBHN	1590	500 d
Burgaw		
WVBS	1470	1000 d
Burlington		
WBBB	920	5000 d
WQRB	1150	1000 d
Burnsville		
WKYK	940	5000 -
Camp Lejeune		
WJIK	1580	10000 d
Canton		
WPTL	920	500 d
WWIT	970	5000 d
Chadbourn		
WVOE	1590	1000 d
Chapel Hill		
WCHL	1360	5000 -
WRBX	1530	10000 d
Charlotte		
WAME	1480	5000
WAYS	610	5000 -
WBT	1110	50000
WGIV	1600	2500
WGSP	1310	1000 d
WHVN	1240	1000 -
WQCC	1540	1000 d
WSOC	930	5000 -
Cherryville		
WCSL	1590	500 d
China Grove		
WRNA	1140	250 d
Claremont		
† ----	1170	5000 -
Clayton		
WHPY	1590	5000 d
Clinton		
WCLN	1170	5000 d
WRRZ	880	1000 d
Concord		
WEGO	1410	1000 d
Dallas		
WAAK	960	1000 -k
Dobson		
WYZD	1560	1000 d
Dunn		
WCKB	780	1000 d
Durham		
WDNC	620	5000 -
WDUR	1490	1000 -
WSRC	1410	5000 d
WTIK	1310	5000 -
Eden		
WCBX	1130	1000 k
WLOE	1490	1000 -
Edenton		
WCDJ	1260	1000 d
Elizabeth City		
WCNC	1240	1000 -
WGAI	560	1000 -
Elizabethtown		
WBLA	1440	5000 d
Elkin		
WJOS	1540	1000 d
Fair Bluff		
WWKO	1480	1000 d
Fairmont		
WFMO	860	1000 d
Farmville		
WGHB	1250	5000 -
Fayetteville		
WFAI	1230	1000 -
WFLB	1490	1000 -
WFNC	940	50000 -
WIDU	1600	1000 d
Forest City		
WAGY	1320	1000 -c
WBBO	780	1000 d
Franklin		
WFSC	1050	1000 d
WLTM	1480	5000 d
Fuquay Springs		
WAKS	1460	5000 d
Garner		
WKBQ	1000	1000 d
Gastonia		
WGNC	1450	1000 -
WLTC	1370	5000 d
Goldsboro		
WFMC	730	1000 d
WGBR	1150	5000
WSSG	1300	1000 d
Graham		
WSML	1190	1000 d
Granite Falls		
WKJK	900	250 d
Greensboro		
WBIG	1470	5000 d
WCOG	1320	5000
WEAL	1510	1000 d
WKEW	1400	1000 -
WPET	950	500 d

Greenville		
WBZQ	1550	1000 d
WNCT	1070	10000
WOOW	1340	1000 -
Hamlet		
WKDX	1250	1000 d
Havelock		
WCPQ	1330	1000 d
Henderson		
WHNC	890	1000 d
WIZS	1450	1000 -
Hendersonville		
WHKP	1450	1000 -
WHVL	1600	5000 d
Hickory		
WHKY	1290	5000 -
WIRC	630	1000 d
WSPF	1000	5000 d
High Point		
WGOS	1070	1000 d
WMFR	1230	1000 -
WOKX	1590	1000 d
Icard Township		
WUIV	1580	5000 d
Jacksonville		
WIIZ	1290	1000 d
WJNC	1240	1000 -
WLAS	910	5000
Kannapolis		
WGTL	870	1000 d
WRKB	1460	500 d
King		
WKTE	1090	1000 d
Kings Mountain		
WKMT	1220	1000 d
Kinston		
WELS	1010	1000 d
WFTC	960	5000 -
WISP	1230	1000 -
Laurinburg		
WEWO	1460	5000
WLNC	1300	500 hc
Lenoir		
WJRI	1340	1000 -
WKGX	1080	5000 d
Lexington		
WBUY	1440	5000 -
Lillington		
WLLN	1370	2500 d
Lincolnton		
WLON	1050	1000 d
Louisburg		
WYRN	1480	500 d
Lumberton		
WAGR	580	500 d
WTSB	1340	1000 -
Marion		
WBRM	1250	5000 d
Marshall		
WMMH	1460	500 d
Mayodan		
WMYN	1420	500 d
Mebane		
WHNI	1060	1000 d
Mocksville		
WDSL	1520	5000 d
Monroe		
† WDEX	1430	2500
WIXE	1190	1000 d
WMAP	1060	1000 d
Mooresville		
WHIP	1350	1000 d
Morehead City		
WMBL	740	1000 d
Morganton		
WMNC	1430	5000 -
Mt. Airy		
WPAQ	740	10000 d
WSYD	1300	5000 -
Mt. Olive		
WDJS	1430	1000 d
Murfreesboro		
WYCM	1080	1000 d
Murphy		
WCVP	600	1000 d
WKRK	1320	5000 d
New Bern		
WJQI	1450	1000 -

New Barn (Cont)		
WRNB	1490	1000 -
WWMG	1380	5000 d
Newland		
WJTP	1130	1000 d
Newton		
WNNC	1230	1000 -
North Wilkesboro		
WKBC	810	1000 d
Oxford		
WCBQ	1340	1000 -
Pembroke		
† ----	940	10000 d
Pinehurst		
WDLV	550	1000 d
Plymouth		
WPNC	1470	5000 d
Raeford		
WSMR	1400	1000 -
Raleigh		
WKIX	850	50000r -k
WLLE	570	500 d
WPJL	1240	1000 -
WPTF	680	50000
WSES	1550	1000 d
Red Springs		
WYRU	1520	5000 d
Reidsville		
WREV	1220	1000 d
WRNC	1600	1000
Roanoke Rapids		
WCBT	1230	1000 -
Rockingham		
WAYN	900	1000 d
WLWL	1500	500 d
Rocky Mount		
WCEC	810	1000 d
WEED	1390	5000 -
WRMT	1490	1000 -
Rose Hill		
WEGG	710	250 d
Roxboro		
WRXO	1430	1000 d
Rutherfordton		
WCAB	590	500 d
Salisbury		
WSAT	1280	1000
WSTP	1490	1000 -
Sanford		
WSBL	1290	1000 d
WWGP	1050	1000 d
Scotland Neck		
WYAL	1280	5000 d
Selma		
WBZB	1090	1000 d
Shallotte		
WVCB	1410	500 d
Shelby		
WADA	1390	1000 -
WOHS	730	1000 d
Siler City		
WNCA	1570	1000 d
Smithfield		
WMPM	1270	5000 d
South Gastonia		
WGAS	1420	500 d
Southern Pines		
WEEB	990	5000 d
Sparta		
WCOK	1060	250 d
Spindale		
WGMA	1520	500 d
Spring Lake		
WRZK	1450	1000 -
Spruce Pine		
WTOE	1470	5000 d
St. Pauls		
WNCR	1080	5000 d
Statesville		
WDRV	550	500 d
WSIC	1400	1000 -
Sylva		
WRGC	680	1000 -
Tabor City		
WTAB	1370	5000 d
Tarboro		
WCPS	760	1000 d

Taylorsville		
WQXZ	860	250 d
WTLK	1570	500 d
Thomasville		
WTNC	790	1000 d
Troy		
WJRM	1390	1000 d
Tryon		
† WTYN	1160	10000 -
‡ WTYN	1550	1000 d
Valdese		
WSVM	1490	1000 -
Wadesboro		
WADE	1210	1000 d
Wallace		
WLSE	1400	1000 -
Wanchese		
WOBR	1530	250 d
Warrenton		
WARR	1520	1000 d
Warsaw		
WTRQ	1560	10000 d
Washington		
WITN	930	5000 -
WWGN	1320	500 d
Waynesville		
WHCC	1400	1000 -
Weldon		
WSMY	1400	1000 -
West Jefferson		
WKSK	580	1000 -
Whiteville		
WENC	1220	5000 d
WTXY	1540	1000 d
Wilkesboro		
WWWC	1240	500 -
Williamston		
WIAM	900	1000 d
Wilmington		
WAAV	1340	1000 -
WKLM	980	5000 d
WMFD	630	1000
WWIL	1490	1000 -
Wilson		
WGTM	590	5000
WLLY	1350	1000 d
WVOT	1420	1000 -
Windsor		
WBTE	990	1000 d
Winston Salem		
WAAA	980	1000 d
WAIR	1340	1000 -
WBFJ	1550	1000 d
WSJS	600	5000
WSMX	1500	10000 d
WTOB	1380	5000 -
Yadkinville		
WYDK	1480	1000 d
Yanceyville		
WYNC	1540	1000 d
Zebulon		
WETC	540	5000 d

NORTH DAKOTA

Beulah		
KHOL	1410	1000 d
Bismarck		
KBMR	1130	50000r c
KBOM	1270	1000 -
KFYR	550	5000
Bowman		
KPOK	1340	1000 -
Carrington		
KDAK	1600	500 d
Devils Lake		
KDLR	1240	1000 -
Dickinson		
KDIX	1230	1000 -
KLTC	1460	5000
Fargo		
KFGO	790	5000
⋆ KFNW	1200	10000 -
KQWB	1550	10000 -
WDAY	970	5000
Grafton		
KXPO	1340	1000 -
Grand Forks		
⋆ KFJM	1370	1000 d

Location	Station	kHz	Watts
Grand Forks (Cont)			
	KKXL	1440	1000 -
	KNOX	1310	5000
Harvey			
	KHND	1540	500 d
Hettinger			
	KNDC	1490	1000 -f
Jamestown			
	KQDJ	1400	1000 -
	KSJB	600	5000
Langdon			
	KNDK	1080	1000 d
Mayville			
	KMAV	1520	2500 d
Minot			
	KCJB	910	5000 -
	KHRT	1320	2500 d
	KKOA	1390	5000 -
	KTYN	1430	5000 d
Oakes			
	KDDR	1220	1000 d
Rugby			
	KGCA	1450	1000 -
Tioga			
	KTGO	1090	1000 d
Valley City			
	KOVC	1490	1000 -
Williston			
	KEYZ	1360	5000

OHIO

Location	Station	kHz	Watts
Akron			
	WAKR	1590	5000
	WCUE	1150	1000 -
	WHLO	640	1000 -
	WSLR	1350	5000
Alliance			
	WFAH	1310	1000 d
Ashland			
	WNCO	1340	1000 -
Ashtabula			
	WFUN	970	5000 -
Athens			
	WATH	970	1000 d
	⋆ WOUB	1340	500
Bellaire			
	WOMP	1290	1000 d
Bellefontaine			
	WOHP	1390	500 d
Bowling Green			
	WJYM	730	1000 d
Bryan			
	WQCT	1520	500 d
Bucyrus			
	WBCO	1540	500 d
Cambridge			
	WILE	1270	1000 d
Campbell			
	WHOT	1330	5000 -
Canton			
	WHBC	1480	5000
	WINW	1520	1000 d
	WNYN	900	500
	WRCW	1060	5000 d
Celina			
	WCSM	1350	500 d
Chardon			
	WBKC	1560	1000 d
Chillicothe			
	WBEX	1490	1000 -
	WCHI	1350	1000 d
Cincinnati			
	WCIN	1480	5000 -
	WCKY	1530	50000
	WKRC	550	5000 -
	WLW	700	50000
	WMLX	1230	1000 -
	WSAI	1360	5000
	WTSJ	1050	1000 d
Circleville			
	WNRE	1540	1000 d
Cleveland			
	WABQ	1540	1000 d
	WBBG	1260	5000
	WERE	1300	5000
	WGAR	1220	50000
	WHK	1420	5000
Cleveland (Cont)			
	WJW	850	10000 -
	WWWE	1100	50000
Cleveland Heights			
	WJMO	1490	1000 -
Columbus			
	WBNS	1460	5000 -
	WCOL	1230	1000 -
	WMNI	920	1000 -
	⋆ WOSU	820	5000 f
	WTVN	610	5000
	WVKO	1580	1000 d
Conneaut			
	WWOW	1360	500 d
Coshocton			
	WTNS	1560	1000 d
Dayton			
	WAVI	1210	1000 d
	WHIO	1290	5000
	WING	1410	5000
	WONE	980	5000
Defiance			
	WONW	1280	1000 -
Delaware			
	WDLR	1550	500 d
Dover			
	WJER	1450	1000 -
East Liverpool			
	WOHI	1490	1000 -
Eaton			
	WCTM	1130	250 d
Elyria			
	WEOL	930	1000
Fairfield			
	WCNW	1560	5000 d
Findlay			
	WFIN	1330	1000 d
Fostoria			
	WFOB	1430	1000
Fremont			
	WFRO	900	500 d
Galion			
	WGLX	1570	250 d
Gallipolis			
	WJEH	990	1000 d
Hamilton			
	WMOH	1450	1000 -
Heath			
	WHTH	790	1000 d
Hillsboro			
	WSRW	1590	500 d
Ironton			
	WIRO	1230	1000 -
Jackson			
	WLMJ	1280	1000 d
Kent			
	WKNT	1520	1000 d
Lancaster			
	WLOH	1320	1000 d
Lima			
	WCIT	940	250 d
	WIMA	1150	1000
Logan			
	WLGN	1510	1000 d
Lorain			
	WLRO	1380	500 d
Mansfield			
	WCLW	1140	250 d
	WMAN	1400	1000 -
Marietta			
	WBRJ	910	5000 d
	WMOA	1490	1000 -
Marion			
	WMRN	1490	1000 -
Marysville			
	† WUCO	1270	500
Massillon			
	WTIG	990	250 d
Middletown			
	WPFB	910	1000 -
Mt. Vernon			
	WMVO	1300	500 d
Nelsonville			
	WYNO	1120	2500 d
New Boston			
	WIOI	1010	1000 d
Newark			
	WCLT	1430	500 d
Niles			
	WNIO	1540	500 d
Norwalk			
	WLKR	1510	500 d
Oberlin			
	WOBL	1320	1000
Painesville			
	WPVL	1460	1000 -
Parma			
	WSUM	1000	500 d
Piqua			
	WPTW	1570	250 d
Pomeroy			
	WMPO	1390	5000 d
Portsmouth			
	WNXT	1260	5000 -
	WPAY	1400	1000 -
Salem			
	WSOM	600	500 d
Sandusky			
	WLEC	1450	1000 -
Sidney			
	WMVR	1080	250 d
Springfield			
	WBLY	1600	1000 d
	WIZE	1340	1000 -
Steubenville			
	WLIT	950	1000 d
	WSTV	1340	1000 -
Tiffin			
	WTTF	1600	500 d
Toledo			
	WCWA	1230	1000 -
	WOHO	1470	1000
	WSPD	1370	5000
	WTOD	1560	5000 d
	WVOI	1520	1000
Troy			
	† WTRJ	1510	250 d
Uhrichsville			
	WBTC	1540	250 d
Van Wert			
	WERT	1220	250 d
Warren			
	WOKG	1570	500 d
	WRRO	1440	5000
Washington Court House			
	WOFR	1250	500 d
Waverly			
	WXIC	1380	1000 d
Wellston			
	WKOV	1330	500 d
Willoughby			
	WELW	1330	500 d
Wilmington			
	WKFI	1090	1000
Wooster			
	WWST	960	1000 d
Worthington			
	WRFD	880	5000 d
Xenia			
	WELX	1110	250 d
	WGIC	1500	500 d
Youngstown			
	WBBW	1240	1000 -
	WFMJ	1390	5000
	WGFT	1500	500 d
	WKBN	570	5000
Zanesville			
	WHIZ	1240	1000 -

OKLAHOMA

Location	Station	kHz	Watts
Ada			
	KADA	1230	1000 -
Altus			
	KWHW	1450	1000 -
Alva			
	KALV	1430	500
Anadarko			
	KRPT	850	500 d
Ardmore			
	KVSO	1240	1000 -
Atoka			
	KEOR	1110	5000 d
Bartlesville			
	KWON	1400	1000 -
Blackwell			
	KLTR	1580	1000 d

City / Station	Freq	Power
Chickasha		
KWCO	1560	1000 -
Claremore		
KOKN	1270	1000 d
Clinton		
KKCC	1320	1000 d
Cushing		
KUSH	1600	1000 d
Duncan		
KRHD	1350	250 -
Durant		
KSEO	750	250 d
El Reno		
KCAN	1460	500 d
Elk City		
KADS	1240	1000 -
Enid		
KCRC	1390	1000
KGWA	960	1000
Frederick		
KTAT	1570	250 d
Guthrie		
KOKC	1490	500 -
Guymon		
KGYN	1210	10000
Henryetta		
KGCG	1590	500 d
Hobart		
KTJS	1420	1000 d
Holdenville		
KVYL	1370	500 d
Hugo		
KIHN	1340	1000 -
Idabel		
KBEL	1240	1000 -
Lawton		
KCCO	1050	250 d
KSWO	1380	1000
Madill		
KMAD	1550	1000 dk
Mc Alester		
KNED	1150	1000 -
KTMC	1400	1000 -
Miami		
KGLC	910	1000
Midwest City		
KRMC	1220	250 d
Muskogee		
KBIX	1490	1000 -
KMUS	1380	1000 -
Norman		
KNOR	1400	1000 -
WWLS	640	1000 d
Oklahoma City		
KATT	1140	1000 d
KBYE	890	1000 d
KOCY	1340	1000 -
KOMA	1520	50000
KQCV	800	250 d
KTOK	1000	5000
WKY	930	5000
Okmulgee		
KOKL	1240	1000 -
Pauls Valley		
KVLH	1470	1000 d
Pawhuska		
KXVQ	1500	5000 d
Ponca City		
WBBZ	1230	1000 -
Poteau		
KLCO	1280	1000 d
Pryor		
KMYZ	1570	1000 d
Sallisaw		
KKID	1560	250 d
Sand Springs		
KTOW	1340	500 -
Sapulpa		
KXOJ	1550	500 d
Shawnee		
KGFF	1450	1000 -
Stillwater		
KSPI	780	250 d
Tahlequah		
KTLQ	1350	1000 d
Tulsa		
KAKC	970	2500 -
KBBJ	1300	5000 -
Tulsa (Cont)		
KELI	1430	5000
KGTO	1050	1000 d
KRMG	740	50000 -
KVOO	1170	50000
Vinita		
KVIN	1470	500 d
Wagoner		
KWOK	1530	500 d
Weatherford		
KWEY	1590	1000 d
Wewoka		
KWSH	1260	1000
Woodward		
KSIW	1450	1000 -

OREGON

City / Station	Freq	Power
Albany		
KRKT	990	250 d
KWIL	790	1000
Ashland		
KCMX	580	1000
† KDOV	1230	1000 -
‡ KDOV	1350	1000 d
Astoria		
KAST	1370	1000
KVAS	1230	1000 -
Baker		
KBKR	1490	1000 -
Bend		
KBND	1110	10000 -
KGRL	940	1000 d
Brookings		
KURY	910	1000 d
Burns		
KRNS	1230	1000 -f
Cave Jct		
KLVR	1400	1000 -
Coos Bay		
KHSN	1230	1000 -
KYNG	1420	1000 d
Coquille		
KSHR	630	5000 -c
Corvallis		
KFLY	1240	1000 -
KLOO	1340	1000 -
⋆ KOAC	550	5000
Cottage Grove		
KNND	1400	1000 -f
Dallas		
KWIP	880	5000 -
Enterprise		
KWVR	1340	1000 -
Eugene		
KASH	1600	5000 -
KBDF	1280	5000 -
KEED	1450	1000 -
KPNW	1120	50000
KQDQ	1320	1000 d
KUGN	590	5000 -
Grants Pass		
KAGI	930	5000 -
KAJO	1270	5000 d
Gresham		
KRDR	1230	1000 -
Hermiston		
KOHU	1360	1000
Hillsboro		
KUIK	1360	1000 d
Hood River		
KIHR	1340	1000
John Day		
KJDY	1400	1000 -f
Klamath Falls		
KAGO	1150	5000 -
KFLS	1450	1000 -
KLAD	960	5000
La Grande		
KLBM	1450	1000 -
Lake Oswego		
KLIQ	1290	5000 c
Lakeview		
KQIK	1230	1000 -f
Lebanon		
KGAL	920	1000
Lincoln City		
KBCH	1400	1000 -
Mc Minnville		
KCYX	1260	1000
Medford		
KHUG	1300	5000 d
KISD	880	1000 d
KMED	1440	5000 -
KRVC	730	1000 d
KYJC	1230	1000 -
Milwaukee		
† ----	1010	250
Myrtle Creek		
KROR	1360	5000 d
Newport		
KNPT	1310	5000 -
North Bend		
KBBR	1340	1000 -
Ontario		
KSRV	1380	5000 -
Oregon City		
KYXI	1520	50000 -
Pendleton		
KTIX	1240	1000 -
KUMA	1290	5000
Portland		
⋆ KBPS	1450	1000 -
KCNR	1410	5000 d
KEX	1190	50000
KGW	620	5000
KKEY	1150	5000 d
KPDQ	800	1000 d
KUPL	1330	5000
KWJJ	1080	50000 -
KXL	750	50000 -
KYTE	970	5000
Prineville		
KRCO	690	1000 d
Redmond		
KPRB	1240	1000 -
Reedsport		
KDUN	1470	5000 d
Roseburg		
KQEN	1240	1000 -
KRNR	1490	1000 -
KYES	950	1000 d
Salem		
KBZY	1490	1000 -
KCCS	1220	1000 d
KGAY	1430	5000 d
KSLM	1390	5000 -
Seaside		
KSWB	930	1000
Springfield		
KORE	1050	1000 d
St. Helens		
KOHI	1600	1000 d
Sweet Home		
KFIR	1370	1000 d
The Dalles		
KACI	1300	1000 d
KODL	1440	5000 -
Tillamook		
KTIL	1590	5000 -
Toledo		
KTDO	1230	1000 -
Umatilla		
KLWJ	1090	2500 d
Winston		
† KGRV	700	1000 d
Woodburn		
KWRC	940	250 d

PENNSYLVANIA

City / Station	Freq	Power
Allentown		
WAEB	790	1000
WHOL	1600	500 d
WKAP	1320	5000 -
WSAN	1470	5000
Altoona		
WFBG	1290	5000 -
WRTA	1240	1000 -
WVAM	1430	5000 -
Ambridge		
WMBA	1460	500 d
Annville		
WAHT	1510	5000 d
Apollo		
WAVL	910	5000 d

City	Station	Frequency	Power
Barnesboro			
	WNCC	950	500 d
Beaver Falls			
	WBVP	1230	1000 -
Bedford			
	WAYC	1600	5000 d
	WBFD	1310	5000 d
Bellefonte			
	WBLF	970	1000 d
Berwick			
	WBRX	1280	1000 d
Bethlehem			
	WGPA	1100	250 d
Bloomsburg			
	WCNR	930	1000 c
	WHLM	550	1000
Braddock			
	WJLY	1550	1000 d
Bradford			
	WESB	1490	1000 -
Brownsville			
	WASP	1130	5000 d
Butler			
	WBUT	1050	500 d
	WISR	680	250 d
Canonsburg			
	WARO	540	250 d
Carbondale			
	WCDL	1440	5000 d
Carlisle			
	WHYL	960	5000 d
	WIOO	1000	1000 d
Carnegie			
	WPLW	1590	1000 d
Chambersburg			
	WCBG	1590	5000 -
	WCHA	800	1000 d
Charleroi			
	WESA	940	250 d
Chester			
	WQIQ	1590	1000
	WVCH	740	1000 d
Clarion			
	WWCH	1300	1000 d
Clearfield			
	WCPA	900	1000 d
Coatesville			
	WCOJ	1420	5000
Columbia			
	† WHEX	1580	500 d
Connellsville			
	WCVI	1340	1000 -
Corry			
	WWCB	1370	1000 -
Coudersport			
	WFRM	600	1000 d
Danville			
	WPGM	1570	2500 dk
Doylestown			
	WBUX	1570	5000 d
Du Bois			
	WCED	1420	5000 -
Easton			
	WEEX	1230	1000 -
	WEST	1400	1000 -
Ebensburg			
	WAJE	1580	1000 d
Elizabethtown			
	WPDC	1600	500 d
Emporium			
	WLEM	1250	2500 d
Ephrata			
	WGSA	1310	5000 d
Erie			
	WEYZ	1450	1000 -
	WJET	1400	1000 -
	WLKK	1260	5000
	WRIE	1330	5000
Everett			
	† WSKE	1040	10000 d
	‡ WSKE	1050	1000 dk
Farrell			
	WMGZ	1470	1000 -
Franklin			
	WFRA	1450	1000 -
Gettysburg			
	WGET	1320	1000 -
Greensburg			
	WHJB	620	2500 -
Greenville			
	WGRP	940	1000 d
Grove City			
	⋆ WSAJ	1340	100 f
Hanover			
	WHVR	1280	5000 -
Harrisburg			
	WCMB	1460	5000
	WFEC	1400	1000 -
	WHP	580	5000
	WKBO	1230	1000 -
Hazleton			
	WAZL	1490	1000 -
Homer City			
	WRID	1160	5000 d
Honesdale			
	WDNH	1590	2500 -
Huntingdon			
	WHUN	1150	5000 d
	WQRO	1080	1000 d
Indiana			
	WDAD	1450	1000 -
Jeanette			
	WBCW	1530	1000 d
Jersey Shore			
	† WJSA	1600	1000 d
Johnstown			
	WCRO	1230	1000 -
	WJAC	850	10000
	WJNL	1490	1000 -
Kane			
	WKZA	960	1000 d
Kittanning			
	WACB	1380	1000 d
Lancaster			
	WLAN	1390	5000 -
	WLPA	1490	1000 -
Lansdale			
	WNPV	1440	500
Lansford			
	WLSH	1410	5000 d
Latrobe			
	WCNS	1480	1000 c
	† WQTW	890	1000 d
	‡ WQTW	1570	1000 d
Lebanon			
	WLBR	1270	5000 -
	WVLV	940	1000 d
Lehighton			
	WYNS	1150	1000 d
Levittown			
	WBCB	1490	1000 -
Lewisburg			
	WTGC	1010	1000 d
Lewistown			
	WKVA	920	1000 -
	WMRF	1490	1000 -
Lock Haven			
	WBPZ	1230	1000 -
Loretto			
	WAMQ	1400	1000 -
Lykens			
	WQIN	1290	1000 d
Martinsburg			
	WJSM	1110	1000 d
Mc Connellsburg			
	WVFC	1530	1000 d
Mc Keesport			
	WEDO	810	1000 d
	WIXZ	1360	5000 -
Meadville			
	WMGW	1490	1000 -
Mexico			
	WJUN	1220	1000 d
Milton			
	WMLP	1380	1000 d
Monroeville			
	WRUA	1510	250 d
Montrose			
	WPEL	1250	1000 d
Mt. Carmel			
	WMIM	1590	1000 d
Mt. Pocono			
	WPCN	960	1000 d
Nanticoke			
	WNAK	730	1000 d
New Castle			
	WBZY	1140	5000 d
	WKST	1280	1000
New Kensington			
	WKPA	1150	1000 d
Norristown			
	WNAR	1110	2500 dk
North East			
	WHYP	1530	1000 d
Oil City			
	† WKQW	1120	250 d
	WOYL	1340	1000 -
Philadelphia			
	KYW	1060	50000
	WCAU	1210	50000
	WDAS	1480	5000 -
	WFIL	560	5000
	WFLN	900	1000 d
	WHAT	1340	1000 -
	WIP	610	5000
	WPEN	950	5000
	WSNI	1540	50000 d
	WTEL	860	10000 d
	WZZD	990	50000 -
Philipsburg			
	WPHB	1260	5000 d
Phoenixville			
	WYIS	690	1000 d
Pittsburgh			
	KDKA	1020	50000
	KQV	1410	5000
	WAMO	860	1000 d
	WEEP	1080	50000 d
	WJAS	1320	5000
	WPIT	730	5000 d
	WTAE	1250	5000
	WTKN	970	5000
Pittston			
	WARD	1540	1000 d
Portage			
	WRML	1470	500 d
Pottstown			
	WPAZ	1370	1000 d
Pottsville			
	WPAM	1450	1000 -
	WPPA	1360	5000 -
Punxsutawney			
	WPXZ	1540	5000 d
Reading			
	WEEU	850	1000
	WHUM	1240	1000 -
	WRAW	1340	1000 -
Red Lion			
	WGCB	1440	1000 d
Roaring Spring			
	WKMC	1370	5000 d
Sayre			
	WATS	960	1000 d
Scranton			
	WARM	590	5000
	WBQW	1320	1000 -
	WEJL	630	500 d
	WGBI	910	1000 -
	WICK	1400	1000 -
Selinsgrove			
	WSEW	1240	1000 -
Shamokin			
	WISL	1480	1000
Sharon			
	WPIC	790	1000 d
Shenandoah			
	WMBT	1530	2500 d
Shippensburg			
	WSHP	1480	500 d
Somerset			
	WADJ	1330	5000r dk
	WVSC	990	5000 d
South Williamsport			
	WFXX	1450	1000 -
St. Marys			
	WKBI	1400	1000 -
State College			
	WMAJ	1450	1000 -
	WRSC	1390	2500 -c
Stroudsburg			
	WVPO	840	250 d
Sunbury			
	WKOK	1070	10000 -

Titusville
WTIV 1230 1000 -
Towanda
WTTC 1550 500
Troy
† WJOZ 1310 500 d
Tyrone
WTRN 1340 1000 -
Uniontown
WMBS 590 1000
Warren
WNAE 1310 5000 d
Washington
WJPA 1450 1000 -
WKEG 1110 1000 d
Waynesboro
WAYZ 1380 1000 d
WBZT 1130 1000 d
Waynesburg
WANB 1580 1000 d
Wellsboro
WNBT 1490 1000 -
West Chester
WCHE 1520 250 d
West Hazleton
WXPX 1300 5000 d
Wilkes Barre
WBAX 1240 1000 -
WILK 980 5000 -
WKRZ 1340 1000 -
Williamsport
WLYC 1050 1000 d
WRAK 1400 1000 -
WWPA 1340 1000 -
Windber
WWBR 1350 2500 d
York
WNOW 1250 1000 d
WOYK 1350 5000 -
WSBA 910 5000 -

PUERTO RICO

Aguadilla
WABA 850 500
WUNA 1340 250
Arecibo
WCMN 1280 5000 -
WMIA 1070 500
WNIK 1230 1000 -
Barceloneta
WBQN 1160 1000
Barranquitas
WOLA 1380 500
Bayamon
WLUZ 1600 1000
WRSJ 1560 5000 -
Cabo Rojo
WEKO 930 500
Caguas
WNEL 1430 5000 -
WVJP 1110 250
Camuy
WCHQ 1360 1000 -
Carolina
WIDA 1400 1000 -
Cayey
WLEY 1080 250
Coama
WCPR 1450 1000 -
Fajardo
WMDD 1480 5000
Guayama
WBJA 1540 250 d
WXRF 1590 1000
Hatillo
WMSW 1120 1000 -
Humacao
WALO 1240 1000 -
Isabela
WISA 1390 1000 -
Juana Diaz
WCGB 1050 5000r -c
Juncos
WFAB 1460 500 d
Lajas
† WIVD 1510 1000
Lares
WGDL 1200 250 d
Manati
WMNT 1500 1000 -
Mayaguez
WAEL 600 1000
WKJB 710 5000 -
WORA 760 5000
WPRA 990 1000
WTIL 1300 1000
Moca
WCXQ 1040 250 d
Morovis
WGFW 1580 1000
Orocovis
WKCK 1470 1000
Penuelas
WENA 1330 1000 -
WPPC 1570 1000 d
Ponce
* WEUC 1420 1000
WISO 1260 1000
WLEO 1170 250
WPAB 550 5000 -
WPRP 910 5000 -
WZBS 1490 1000 -
Quebradillas
WJYT 960 1000
Sabana Granda
† WPRX 880 1000
Salinas
WHOY 1210 5000 -
San German
WBOZ 1090 250
San Juan
WAPA 680 10000
WBMJ 1190 10000 -
WIAC 740 10000
* WIPR 940 10000
WKAQ 580 5000
WKVM 810 50000 -
WOSO 1030 10000
WQBS 630 5000
WQII 1140 10000
WRAI 1520 10000
WUNO 1320 5000 -
WVOZ 870 5000
San Sebastian
WFBA 1460 500
† WRSS 1410 1000 d
Utuado
WUPR 1530 1000 -
Vega Baja
WEGA 1350 500
Vieques
WIVV 1370 1000 -
Yabucoa
WXEW 840 5000 -
Yauco
WKFE 1550 250

RHODE ISLAND

Newport
WADK 1540 1000 d
Pawtucket
WGNG 550 1000 -
Providence
WEAN 790 5000
WHIM 1110 5000 d
WHJJ 920 5000
WLKW 990 50000 d
WPRO 630 5000
WRCP 1290 5000 -
WRIB 1220 1000 d
Warwick
WARV 1590 5000
West Warwick
WKRI 1450 1000 -
Westerly
WERI 1230 1000 -
Wickford
WMYD 1370 500 d
Woonsocket
WNRI 1380 1000 d
WWON 1240 1000 -

SOUTH CAROLINA

Abbeville
WABV 1590 1000 d
Aiken
WAKN 990 1000 d
WPBM 1300 1000q dk
Allendale
WDOG 1460 1000 d
Anderson
WAIM 1230 1000 -
WANS 1280 5000 -
Bamberg
WWBD 790 1000 d
Barnwell
WBAW 740 1000 d
Batesburg
WBLR 1430 5000 d
Beaufort
WBEU 960 1000 d
† WVGB 1490 500 -
Belton
WHPB 1390 1000 d
Bennettsville
WBSC 1550 10000 -
Bishopville
WAGS 1380 1000 d
Burnettown
WVAP 1510 1000 d
Camden
WCAM 1590 1000 d
WCCG 1130 1000 d
Cayce
WLFF 620 500 d
Charleston
WCSC 1390 5000
WGCA 1450 1000 -
WOKE 1340 1000 -
WPAL 730 1000 d
WTMA 1250 5000 -
Cheraw
WCRE 1420 1000 d
Chester
WGCD 1490 1000 -
Clemson
WCCP 1560 1000 d
Clinton
WPCC 1410 1000 d
Columbia
WCOS 1400 1000 -
WIS 560 5000 -
WNOK 1230 1000 -
WOIC 1320 5000 -
WQXL 1470 5000 d
Conway
WJXY 1050 5000 d
WLAT 1330 5000 -
Darlington
WKGE 1350 1000 d
Dillon
WDSC 800 1000 d
Easley
WELP 1360 1000 d
Elloree
WOOL 1370 5000 d
Florence
WJMX 970 5000 -
WOLS 1230 1000 -
WYNN 540 250 d
Fountain Inn
WFIS 1600 1000 d
Gaffney
WEAC 1500 1000 d
WFGN 1570 250 d
Georgetown
WGMB 1470 1000 d
WGTN 1400 1000 -
Greenville
WESC 660 10000 d
WFBC 1330 5000
WGLV 1440 5000
WHYZ 1070 50000 d
WMRB 1490 1000 -
WMUU 1260 5000 d
Greenwood
WCRS 1450 1000 -
WGSW 1350 1000 d
WMTY 1090 1000
Greer
WCKI 1300 1000 d
WEAB 800 250 d

Station	Frequency	Power
Hampton		
WBHC	1270	1000 d
Hartsville		
WHSC	1450	1000 -
WSDC	1490	1000 -k
Hemingway		
WKYB	1000	10000 d
Hilton Head Island		
† WHHQ	1130	10000 d
Holly Hill		
WKHJ	1440	1000
Johnston		
WJES	1190	1000 d
Kershaw		
WKSC	1300	500 d
Kingstree		
WDKD	1310	5000 d
WKSP	1090	5000 d
Lake City		
WJOT	1260	1000 d
Lancaster		
WAGL	1560	50000 d
WLCM	1360	1000 d
Laurens		
WLBG	860	1000 d
Loris		
WLSC	1570	5000 dk
Manning		
WYMB	1410	1000 d
Marion		
WATP	1430	1000 d
Moncks Corner		
WBER	950	500 d
Mt. Pleasant		
WIXR	1500	1000 d
Mullins		
WJAY	1280	5000 d
Myrtle Beach		
WQOK	1450	1000 -
WTGR	1520	5000 d
Newberry		
WKDK	1240	1000 -k
WKMG	1520	1000
North Augusta		
WKZK	1600	500 d
North Charleston		
WKCN	910	500 d
North Myrtle Beach		
† WGSN	900	500 d
Orangeburg		
WDIX	1150	5000 -
WORG	1580	1000 d
WTND	920	5000r d
Pageland		
WCPL	1510	500 d
Pickens		
WPKZ	1540	10000 d
Ridgeland		
WJMR	1430	1000 d
Rock Hill		
WRHI	1340	1000 -
WTYC	1150	1000 d
Seneca		
WSNW	1150	1000 d
Spartanburg		
WASC	1530	1000 d
WKDY	1400	1000 -
WORD	910	5000 -
WSPA	950	5000
St. George		
WQIZ	810	5000 d
St. Matthews		
WQKI	710	1000 d
Summerville		
WAZS	980	1000 d
Sumter		
WDXY	1240	1000 -
WFIG	1290	1000
WSSC	1340	1000 -
Surfside Beach		
WYAK	1270	5000 d
Travelers Rest		
WBBR	1580	5000 dk
Union		
WBCU	1460	1000
Walhalla		
WGOG	1000	1000 d
Walterboro		
‡ WALD	1060	1000 d
† WALD	1080	2500 d
Winnsboro		
WCKM	1250	500 d
Woodruff		
WSJW	1510	1000 d
York		
WBZK	980	1000 d

SOUTH DAKOTA

Station	Frequency	Power
Aberdeen		
KGIM	1420	1000 d
KKAA	1560	10000 -
KSDN	930	5000 -
Belle Fourche		
KBFS	1450	1000 -
Brookings		
KBRK	1430	1000 d
Deadwood		
KDSJ	980	5000 -
Hot Springs		
KOBH	580	500 d
Huron		
KIJV	1340	1000 -
KOKK	1190	500 d
Lemmon		
KBJM	1400	1000 -
Madison		
KJAM	1390	500 d
Milbank		
KMSD	1510	5000 d
Mitchell		
KORN	1490	1000 -
Mobridge		
KOLY	1300	5000 d
Pierre		
KCCR	1240	1000 -
KGFX	1060	10000 -
Rapid City		
KIMM	1150	5000 d
KKLS	920	5000 d
KOTA	1380	5000
KTOQ	1340	1000 -
Redfield		
KQKD	1380	500 d
Sioux Falls		
KELO	1320	5000
⋆ KNWC	1270	2500
KRSS	1520	500 d
KSOO	1140	10000 -
KXRB	1000	10000 d
KYKC	1230	1000 -
Sturgis		
KBHB	810	5000 d
Vermillion		
⋆ KUSD	690	1000 d
KVRA	1570	500 d
Volga		
KVAA	910	1000 -
Watertown		
KLSC	1480	1000 d
KWAT	950	1000
Winner		
KWYR	1260	5000 d
Yankton		
KYNT	1450	1000 -
WNAX	570	5000

TENNESSEE

Station	Frequency	Power
Adamsville		
WLIC	1540	2500 d
Alamo		
† ANFC	810	250 d
† WCTA	1280	500
Alcoa		
WEAG	1470	1000 d
Algood		
WWRT	1590	500 d
Ardmore		
WSLV	1110	1000
Arlington		
† WGSF	1220	1000 d
Ashland City		
WAJN	790	250 d
Athens		
WLAR	1450	1000 -
WYXI	1390	2500 d
Benton		
WBIN	1540	250 d
Bolivar		
WBOL	1560	250 d
Brentwood		
† WTBN	560	500 d
Bristol		
WBCV	1550	5000r d
WOPI	1490	1000 -
Brownsville		
WBHT	1520	250 d
Camden		
WFWL	1220	250 d
Carthage		
WRKM	1350	1000 d
Centerville		
WHLP	1570	5000 d
Chattanooga		
WDEF	1370	5000
WDOD	1310	5000
WDXB	1490	1000 -
WGOW	1150	5000 -
WNOO	1260	5000 d
WZRA	1450	1000 -
Church Hill		
WMCH	1260	1000 d
Clarksville		
WDXN	540	1000 d
WJZM	1400	1000 -
WKVL	1550	1000 -
Cleveland		
WBAC	1340	1000 -
WCLE	1570	2500 d
Clinton		
WYSH	1380	1000 d
Collierville		
† WMSO	640	10000 d
‡ WMSO	1590	500 d
Columbia		
WKRM	1340	1000 -
WMCP	1280	5000 -
Cookeville		
WHUB	1400	1000 -
WPTN	1550	250 d
Copper Hill		
WLSB	1400	1000 -
Covington		
WKBL	1250	1000 -
Cowan		
WZYX	1440	5000r dk
Crossville		
WAEW	1330	1000 d
WCSV	1490	1000 -
Dayton		
WDNT	1280	1000 d
WKOE	1520	5000 d
Dickson		
WDKN	1260	5000r dk
Donelson		
† WAMB	1160	50000
Donelson		
‡ WAMB	1170	25000 d
Dunlap		
WSVC	1190	5000 d
Dyersburg		
WDSG	1450	1000 -
WTRO	1330	500 d
Elizabethton		
WBEJ	1240	1000 -
WIDD	1520	1000 d
Englewood		
WENR	1090	1000 d
Erwin		
WEMB	1420	5000 d
Etowah		
WCPH	1220	1000 d
Fairview		
† WBLP	850	1000 d
Fayetteville		
WEKR	1240	1000 -
WIXC	1140	5000 d
Franklin		
WAKM	950	1000 d
WIZO	1380	5000 d
Gallatin		
WAMG	1130	2500 d
WHIN	1010	5000 d

Gatlinburg
† ---- 1230 1000 -
Greeneville
WGRV 1340 1000 -
WSMG 1450 1000 -
Harriman
WKCE 1230 250
WKJS 1600 5000 d
Harrogate
WSVQ 740 1000p dk
Hartsville
WJKM 1090 1000 d
Henderson
WHHM 1580 250 d
Hohenwald
WMLR 1230 1000 -
Humboldt
† WHMT 1160 1000
‡ WHMT 1190 500 d
WIRJ 740 250 d
Huntingdon
WJPJ 1530 1000 d
Jackson
WDXI 1310 5000 -
WJAK 1460 1000 d
WTJS 1390 5000 -
Jamestown
WCLC 1260 1000 d
WDEB 1500 1000 d
Jefferson City
WJFC 1480 500 d
Jellico
WJJT 1540 1000 d
Johnson City
WETB 790 5000 d
WJCW 910 5000 -
Jonesboro
WJSO 1590 5000
Kingsport
WGOC 1090 1000 d
WKIN 1320 5000 -
WKPT 1400 1000 -
Kingston
WYLQ 1410 1000 h
Knoxville
WBMK 1430 1000 d
WHEL 1240 1000 -
WITA 1490 1000 -
WIVK 850 50000 d
WKGN 1340 1000 -
WKXV 900 1000 d
WNOX 990 10000
WRJZ 620 5000
WSKT 1580 5000 d
La Follette
WLAF 1450 1000 -
WWBR 960 250 d
Lafayette
WEEN 1460 1000 d
Lawrenceburg
† WCMG 1520 500 d
WDXE 1070 1000 d
Lebanon
WCOR 900 500 d
WQDQ 1600 500 d
Lenoir City
WBLC 1360 1000 d
WLIL 730 1000 d
Lewisburg
WAXO 1220 1000 d
WJJM 1490 1000 -
Lexington
WDXL 1490 1000 -
Livingston
WLIV 920 1000 d
London
WLNT 1140 1000 d
Lookout Mountain
WFLI 1070 50000 -
Lynchburg
WTNX 1290 1000 d
Madison
WJRB 1430 5000 -
Madisonville
WRKQ 1250 500 d
Manchester
WMSR 1320 5000 d

Martin
WCMT 1410 1000 d
Maryville
WGAP 1400 1000 -
Mc Kenzie
WHDM 1440 5000 dk
Mc Minnville
WAKI 1230 1000 -
WBMC 960 500 d
Memphis
KWAM 990 10000 d
WDIA 1070 50000 -
WHBQ 560 5000 -
WKDJ 680 10000 -
WLOK 1340 1000 -
WMC 790 5000
WMQM 1480 5000 d
WREC 600 5000
WWEE 1430 1000 d
Milan
WKBJ 1600 1000 d
† WKXY 1360 5000 -
Millington
WTNN 1380 2500 -
Morristown
WCRK 1150 5000r -k
WMTN 1300 5000 d
Mountain City
WMCT 1390 1000 d
Mt. Juliet
† WMJT 1330 500 d
Mt. Pleasant
† WXRQ 1460 5000 d
Murfreesboro
WGNS 1450 1000 -
WMTS 810 5000 d
Nashville
WKDA 1240 1000 -
WLAC 1510 50000
WLUY 1300 5000
† WMDB 880 2500 d
WNAH 1360 1000 d
WSIX 980 5000
WSM 650 50000
WVOL 1470 5000 -
WWGM 1560 10000 d
Newport
WLIK 1270 5000 -
WNPC 1060 1000 d
Oak Ridge
WATO 1290 5000 -
WORI 1550 1000 d
Oliver Springs
† WBTZ 1080 2500 d
Oneida
WBNT 1310 1000 d
Paris
WMUF 1000 500 d
WTPR 710 250 d
Parsons
WTBP 1550 1000 d
Pikeville
WUAT 1110 250 d
Portland
WQSI 1270 1000 d
Powell
† ---- 1040 5000 d
Pulaski
WKSR 1420 1000
Ripley
WTRB 1570 1000 d
Rockwood
WOFE 580 1000 d
Rogersville
WRGS 1370 1000 d
Savannah
WORM 1010 250 d
Selmer
WDTM 1130 1000 d
Sevierville
WSEV 930 5000 d
Shelbyville
WHAL 1400 1000 -
WLIJ 1580 1000 d
Smithville
WJLE 1480 1000 d
Smyrna
WSVT 710 250 d

Soddy Daisy
WCHU 1550 1000 d
WSDT 1240 1000 -
Somerville
† WJED 1410 500
South Pittsburg
WEPG 910 5000r d
Sparta
WSMT 1050 1000 d
WTZX 860 1000 d
Spring City
WXQK 970 500 d
Springfield
WDBL 1590 1000 d
WSGI 1190 250 d
Sweetwater
WDEH 800 1000 d
Tazewell
WNTT 1250 500 d
Thompson Station
† WAAS 1100 1000 d
Trenton
WTNE 1530 250 d
Tullahoma
WCWY 740 250 d
Union City
WENK 1240 1000 -
Wartburg
WECO 940 1000 d
Waverly
WPHC 1060 1000 d
Waynesboro
WNBG 1400 1000 -
White Bluff
WBDX 1030 1000 -
Winchester
WCDT 1340 1000 -
Woodbury
WBRY 1540 500 d

TEXAS

Abilene
KEAN 1280 500 d
KFMN 1560 500 d
KRBC 1470 5000 -
KWKC 1340 1000 -
Alamo Heights
KDRY 1110 2500r -c
Alice
KOPY 1070 1000
Alpine
KVLF 1240 1000 -
Alvin
KTEK 1110 500 d
Amarillo
KDJW 1010 5000 -
KGNC 710 10000
KIXZ 940 5000 -
KPUR 1440 5000 -
KQIZ 1360 500 d
KZIP 1310 1000 d
Andrews
KACT 1360 1000 d
Athens
KBUD 1410 1000 d
Atlanta
KALT 900 1000 d
Austin
KIXL 970 1000 c
KLBJ 590 5000 -
KMMM 1370 1000 d
KNOW 1490 1000 -
KVET 1300 5000 -
Ballinger
KRUN 1400 1000 -
Bay City
KIOX 1270 1000
Baytown
KBUK 1360 1000
Beaumont
KAYC 1450 1000 -
KIEZ 1380 1000 d
KLVI 560 5000
KTRM 990 1000
Beeville
KIBL 1490 1000 -
Bellville
KACO 1090 250 d

Belton			
	KTON	940	1000 d
Big Lake			
	KWGH	1290	1000 d
Big Spring			
	KBST	1490	1000 -
	KBYG	1400	1000 -
	KHEM	1270	1000 d
Boerne			
	KNCI	1500	250 d
Bonham			
	KFYN	1420	250 d
Borger			
	KBBB	1600	5000 d
	KQTY	1490	1000 -
Bowie			
	KBAN	1410	500 d
Brady			
	KNEL	1490	1000 -
Breckenridge			
	KSTB	1430	1000 -c
Brenham			
	KTTX	1280	1000 d
Brownfield			
	KKUB	1300	1000 d
Brownsville			
	KBOR	1600	1000
Brownwood			
	KBWD	1380	1000 -
	KXYL	1240	1000 -
Bryan			
	KAGC	1510	500 d
	KTAM	1240	1000 -
Burnet			
	KHLB	1340	1000 -
Cameron			
	KMIL	1330	500 d
Canyon			
	KHBJ	1550	1000 d
Carrizo Springs			
	KBEN	1450	1000 -
Carthage			
	KGAS	1590	2500 d
Center			
	KDET	930	1000 d
Childress			
	KCTX	1510	250 d
Clarksville			
	KCAR	1350	500 d
Cleburne			
	KCLE	1120	250 d
Cleveland			
	KJCH	1410	1000
Coleman			
	KSTA	1000	250 d
College Station			
	WTAW	1150	1000 -
Colorado City			
	† KJUM	1560	2500 d
	KVMC	1320	1000 d
Comanche			
	KCOM	1550	250 d
Conroe			
	KIKR	900	500 d
	KSKS	1140	250 d
Corpus Christi			
	KCCT	1150	1000 -
	KCTA	1030	50000 d
	KEYS	1440	1000
	KRYS	1360	1000
	KSIX	1230	1000 -
	KUNO	1400	1000 -
Corsicana			
	KAND	1340	1000 -
Crane			
	KXOI	810	1000 -
Crockett			
	KIVY	1290	2500 d
Cuero			
	KEWS	1600	500 d
Daingerfield			
	KEGG	1560	1000 d
Dalhart			
	KXIT	1240	1000 -
Dallas			
	KAAM	1310	5000
	KBOX	1480	5000 -
	KLIF	1190	50000 -
Dallas (Cont)			
	KPBC	1040	1000 d
	KRLD	1080	50000
	KSKY	660	10000 d
	WFAA	570	5000
Del Rio			
	KDLK	1230	1000 -
	KWMC	1490	1000 -k
Denison			
	KDSX	950	500
Denton			
	KDNT	1440	5000 -
Diboll			
	KIPR	1260	1000 d
Dimmitt			
	KDHN	1470	500 d
Dumas			
	KDDD	800	250 d
Eagle Pass			
	KEPS	1270	1000 d
Eastland			
	KEAS	1590	500 d
Edinburg			
	KURV	710	1000 -
Edna			
	KQTI	1130	2500 d
El Campo			
	KULP	1390	500 d
El Paso			
	KAMA	1060	10000 d
	KELP	1590	1000 d
	KHEY	690	10000
	KISO	1150	1000 d
	KROD	600	5000
	KSET	1340	1000 -
	KTSM	1380	5000 -
	KYSR	920	1000 -
Elgin			
	KELG	1440	500
Falfurrias			
	KPSO	1260	500 d
Farwell			
	‡ KIJN	1060	
	† KIJN	1570	250 d
Floydada			
	KFBA	900	250 d
Fredericksburg			
	KNAF	910	1000 d
Freeport			
	KBRZ	1460	500 d
Ft. Stockton			
	KFST	860	250 d
Ft. Worth			
	KJIM	870	250 d
	KNOK	970	1000 d
	KSSA	1270	5000
	KUQQ	1540	50000 -
	KXOL	1360	5000 -
	WBAP	820	50000
Gainesville			
	KGAF	1580	250
Galveston			
	KGBC	1540	1000 -
	KILE	1400	1000 -
Georgetown			
	KGTN	1530	1000 d
Gilmer			
	KHYM	1060	10000 d
Gladewater			
	KEES	1430	5000 -
Gonzales			
	KCTI	1450	250
Graham			
	KSWA	1330	500 d
Granbury			
	KPAR	1420	500
Grand Prairie			
	KKDA	730	500 d
Greenville			
	KGVL	1400	1000 -
Hallettsville			
	KRJH	1520	250 d
Hamilton			
	KCLW	900	250 d
Harlingen			
	KGBT	1530	50000 -
Hemphill			
	KAWS	1240	1000 -
Henderson			
	KGRI	1000	250 d
	KWRD	1470	500 d
Hereford			
	KPAN	860	250 d
Highland Park			
	KVIL	1150	1000 d
Hillsboro			
	KHBR	1560	250 d
Hondo			
	KRME	1460	500 d
Houston			
	KCOH	1430	1000 d
	KEYH	850	10000 d
	KILT	610	5000
	KKBQ	790	5000
	KLAT	1010	5000
	KNUZ	1230	1000 -
	KPRC	950	5000
	KRBE	1070	10000 -
	KTRH	740	50000
	KXYZ	1320	5000
	KYOK	1590	5000
Humble			
	† KTUN	1180	1000
Huntsville			
	KNNX	1400	1000
	KSAM	1490	1000 -
Jacksonville			
	KEBE	1400	1000 -
Jasper			
	KTXJ	1350	5000 d
Junction			
	KMBL	1450	1000 -
Kenedy			
	KAML	990	250 d
Kermit			
	KERB	600	1000 d
Kerrville			
	KERV	1230	1000 -
Kilgore			
	KOCA	1240	1000 -
Killeen			
	KIIZ	1050	250 d
Kingsville			
	KINE	1330	1000 d
La Grange			
	KVLG	1570	250 d
Lamesa			
	KPET	690	250
Lampasas			
	KCYL	1450	1000 -
Laredo			
	KLAR	1300	1000
	KVOZ	1490	1000 -
Levelland			
	KLVT	1230	1000 -
Liberty			
	KPXE	1050	250 d
Littlefield			
	KZZN	1490	1000 -
Livingston			
	KETX	1440	5000 d
Lockhart			
	KHJK	1060	250 d
Longview			
	KFRO	1370	1000
	KLUE	1280	1000 d
Lubbock			
	KBBL	1340	1000 -
	KEND	1590	1000
	KFYO	790	5000 -
	KLFB	1420	500
	KRLB	580	500 d
	KSEL	950	5000 -
	KTLK	1460	1000 d
Lufkin			
	KLNX	1420	5000 -
	KRBA	1340	1000 -
Madisonville			
	† ----	880	5000 -
Marshall			
	KCUL	1410	500 d
	KMHT	1450	1000 -
Mc Allen			
	KRIO	910	5000
Mc Kinney			
	KXVI	1600	5000 c

City	Station	Frequency	Power
Memphis			
	KLSR	1130	1000 d
Merkel			
	KMIO	1500	1000
Mexia			
	KBUS	1590	500 d
Midland			
	KCRS	550	5000 -
	KJBC	1150	1000 d
	KMND	1510	500 d
	KWEL	1070	2500 d
Mineola			
	KMOO	1510	500 d
Mineral Wells			
	KYXS	1140	250 d
Mission			
	KIRT	1580	1000 d
Monahans			
	KVKM	1330	5000 -
Morton			
	KRAN	1280	500 d
Mt. Pleasant			
	KIMP	960	1000 d
Muleshoe			
	KMUL	1380	1000 d
Nacogdoches			
	KEEE	1230	1000 -
	KSFA	860	1000 d
Navasota			
	KWBC	1550	250 d
Nederland			
	KOVE	1510	5000 d
New Boston			
	KNBO	1530	2500r -c
New Braunfels			
	KGNB	1420	1000 d
Odessa			
	KJJT	1000	250 d
	KOYL	1310	1000 d
	KOZA	1230	1000 -
	KRIG	1410	1000
	KYXX	920	1000 -
Orange			
	KOGT	1600	1000
Palestine			
	KNET	1450	1000 -
Pampa			
	KGRO	1230	1000 -
	KSZN	1340	1000 -
Paris			
	KPLT	1490	1000 -
	KPRE	1250	500 d
Pasadena			
	KIKK	650	250 d
	KLVL	1480	1000 -
Pearsall			
	KVWG	1280	500 d
Pecos			
	KIUN	1400	1000 -
Perryton			
	KEYE	1400	1000 -
Pharr			
	† KJTA	840	50000 -
Plainview			
	KKYN	1090	5000
	KVOP	1400	1000 -
Pleasanton			
	KBOP	1380	1000 d
Port Arthur			
	KOLE	1340	1000 -
	KTXC	1250	5000 -
Port Lavaca			
	KGUL	1560	500 d
Port Neches			
	KDLF	1150	500 d
Post			
	KPOS	1370	1000 d
Quanah			
	KIXC	1150	500 d
Ralls			
	KCLR	1530	5000 d
Raymondville			
	KSOX	1240	1000 -
Robstown			
	KROB	1510	500 d
Rosenberg			
	KFRD	980	1000 d
Rusk			
	KTLU	1580	500 d
San Angelo			
	KGKL	960	5000 -
	KHOS	1420	1000 d
	KQSA	1260	1000 d
	KTEO	1340	1000 -
San Antonio			
	KAPE	1480	500 d
	KBUC	1310	5000 d
	KCOR	1350	5000
	KEDA	1540	5000 -
	KFHM	1150	1000 d
	KKYX	680	50000 -
	KONO	860	5000 -
	† KSJL	760	5000 d
	KSLR	630	5000
	KTSA	550	5000
	KUKA	1250	1000
	WOAI	1200	50000
San Marcos			
	KCNY	1470	250 d
San Saba			
	KBAL	1410	500 d
Seguin			
	KWED	1580	1000 d
Seminole			
	KIKZ	1250	1000 d
Seymour			
	KSEY	1230	1000 -f
Shamrock			
	KBYP	1580	250 d
Sherman			
	KIKM	910	1000
	KTXO	1500	1000 d
Silsbee			
	KKAS	1300	500 d
Sinton			
	KIKN	1590	1000 -
Slaton			
	KCAS	1050	250 d
Snyder			
	KSNY	1450	1000 -
Sonora			
	KVRN	980	1000 d
Stamford			
	KDWT	1400	1000 -
Stephenville			
	KSTV	1510	500 d
Sulphur Springs			
	KSST	1230	1000 -
Sweetwater			
	KXOX	1240	1000 -
Taylor			
	KTAE	1260	1000 d
Temple			
	KTEM	1400	1000 -
Terrell			
	KTER	1570	250 d
Terrell Hills			
	KLLS	930	5000 -
Texarkana			
	KADO	940	2500 d
	KCMC	740	1000
	KTFS	1400	1000 -
Texas City			
	KYST	920	5000 -
Tulia			
	KTUE	1260	1000 d
Tyler			
	KDOK	1490	1000 -
	KTBB	600	1000
	KTYL	1330	1000
	KZEY	690	1000 d
Uvalde			
	KVOU	1400	1000 -
Vernon			
	KVWC	1490	1000 -
Victoria			
	KCWM	1340	1000 -
	KNAL	1410	500
Waco			
	KBBW	1010	10000 -
	KRZI	1580	1000 -
	KWTX	1230	1000 -
	WACO	1460	1000
Waxahachee			
	KBEC	1390	500 d
Weatherford			
	KZEE	1220	500 d
Weslaco			
	KRGV	1290	5000
West Lake Hills			
	KTXZ	1560	2500
Wharton			
	KANI	1500	500
Wichita Falls			
	KGTM	990	10000 -
	KTRN	1290	5000 -
	KWFT	620	5000
Winters			
	KPUB	1060	2500r dk
Woodville			
	KVLL	1220	250 d

UTAH

City	Station	Frequency	Power
Blanding			
	KUTA	790	1000 d
Bountiful			
	‡ KFAM	680	1000 d
Brigham City			
	KBUH	800	500 d
Cedar City			
	KBRE	940	10000 d
	KSUB	590	5000 -
Centerville			
	KBBX	1600	5000 -
Delta			
	KNAK	540	1000 d
Heber City			
	KLVR	1340	500 -
Logan			
	KBLQ	1390	5000 -
	KVNU	610	5000 -
Manti			
	KMTI	1590	5000 -
Moab			
	KURA	1450	1000 -
Murray			
	KLAF	1230	1000 -
North Salt Lake City			
	† KFAM	680	50000 d
Ogden			
	KANN	1090	5000 d
	KJQN	1490	1000 -
	KLO	1430	5000
	KSVN	730	1000 d
Price			
	KOAL	1230	1000 -
	KRPX	1080	2500 d
Provo			
	KDOT	960	5000 -
	KEYY	1450	1000 -
	KFTN	1400	1000 -
Richfield			
	KSVC	980	5000 -
Roosevelt			
	KNEU	1250	5000 d
Salt Lake City			
	KALL	910	5000 -
	KBUG	1320	5000
	KDYL	1280	5000 -
	KLUB	570	5000
	KSL	1160	50000
	KWHO	860	1000 d
Sandy			
	KSXX	630	1000 -
South Salt Lake City			
	KRSP	1060	10000 -
	KSOP	1370	1000 -
Spanish Fork			
	KONI	1480	1000 d
St. George			
	† ANJ	890	50000
	‡ KDXU	1450	1000 -
Tooele			
	‡ KTLE	990	1000 d
	† KTLE	1010	50000 d
Tremonton			
	† KBXN	1470	5000 d
Vernal			
	KVEL	920	5000
Washington			
	KCLG	1210	10000 -
West Jordan			
	KZZI	1510	10000 d

West Valley City
KRGO 1550 10000 -

VERMONT

Barre
WSNO 1450 1000 -
Bennington
WBTN 1370 1000 d
Brattleboro
WKVT 1490 1000 -
WTSA 1450 1000 -
Burlington
WDOT 1390 5000 -
WJOY 1230 1000 -
WVMT 620 5000
Middlebury
WFAD 1490 1000 -
Montpelier
WSKI 1240 1000 -
Newport
WIKE 1490 1000 -
Poultney
WVNR 1340 1000 -
Randolph
WCVR 1320 1000 d
Rutland
WHWB 1000 1000 d
WSYB 1380 5000 -
Springfield
WCFR 1480 5000 d
St. Albans
WWSR 1420 1000 d
St. Johnsbury
WSTJ 1340 1000 -
Waterbury
WDEV 550 5000 -
Wells River
WYKR 1490 1000 -
White River Junction
WNHV 910 1000 d

VIRGIN ISLANDS

Charlotte Amalie
WSTA 1340 250
WVWI 1000 5000 -
Christiansted
WSTX 970 5000 -
Fredericksted. St. Croi
WRRA 1290 500

VIRGINIA

Abingdon
WBBI 1230 1000 -
Alexandria
WRMR 730 5000 d
Altavista
WKDE 1000 1000 d
Amherst
WAMV 1420 1000 d
Appomattox
WTTX 1280 2500r dk
Arlington
WABS 780 1000 d
WEAM 1390 5000
Ashland
WIVE 1430 1000 d
Bassett
WODY 900 500 d
Bedford
WBLT 1350 1000 d
Big Stone Gap
WLSD 1220 1000 d
Blacksburg
WKEX 1430 1000 d
WQBX 710 5000 d
Blackstone
WKLV 1440 5000 d
Bluefield
WBDY 1190 10000 d
Bristol
WFHG 980 5000 -
WZAP 690 10000 d
Broadway
WBTX 1470 5000 d
Brookneal
WODI 1230 1000 -f
Charlottesville
WINA 1070 5000

Charlottesville (Cont)
WVCH 1260 5000 -
WXAM 1400 1000 -
Chase City
WMEK 980 500 d
Chatham
WKBY 1080 1000 d
Chesapeake
WCPK 1600 5000 d
Chester
WGGM 1410 5000 d
Christiansburg
WJJJ 1260 2500 d
Churchville
WNLR 1150 1000 d
Clifton Forge
WXCF 1230 1000 -
Clinchco
WDIC 1430 5000 d
Collinsville
WFIC 1530 1000 d
Colonial Heights
WPVA 1290 5000 d
Covington
WKEY 1340 1000 -
Crewe
WSVS 800 5000 d
Crozet
WPED 810 500 d
Culpeper
WCVA 1490 1000 -
Danville
WBTM 1330 5000 -
WDVA 1250 5000
WILA 1580 1000 d
WYPR 970 1000 d
Emporia
WEVA 860 1000 d
Exmore
WKRE 1520 5000 d
Fairfax
WEEL 1310 5000 -
Falls Church
WFAX 1220 5000 d
Farmville
WFLO 870 1000 d
WPAK 1490 1000 -
Franklin
WYSR 1250 1000 d
Fredericksburg
WFLS 1350 1000 d
WFVA 1230 1000 -
Front Royal
WFTR 1450 1000 -
Galax
WBOB 1360 5000 d
Gate City
WGAT 1050 1000 d
Gloucester
WDDY 1420 1000 d
Gretna
WMNA 730 1000 d
Grundy
WNRG 940 5000 d
Hampton
WPEX 1490 1000 -
Harrisonburg
WHBG 1360 5000 d
WKCY 1300 5000 d
WSVA 550 5000 -
Herndon
WVBK 1440 1000 d
Highland Springs
WNWZ 1450 1000 -
Hillsville
WHHV 1400 1000 -
Hopewell
WHAP 1340 1000 -
Hot Springs
† WWES 1270 500 d
Lawrenceville
WLES 580 500 d
Lebanon
WLRV 1380 1000 d
Leesburg
WAGE 1290 1000 d
Lexington
WREL 1450 1000 -

Luray
WRAA 1330 1000 d
Lynchburg
WBRG 1050 1000 d
WLGM 1320 1000 d
WLLL 930 5000 d
WLVA 590 1000
WWOD 1390 5000 -
Manassas
WPRW 1460 5000
Marion
WMEV 1010 1000 d
WOLD 1330 1000 d
Martinsville
WHEE 1370 5000 d
WMVA 1450 1000 -
Mount Jackson
WSIG 790 1000 d
Narrows
WNRV 990 5000 d
Newport News
WNSV 1310 5000
WOKT 1270 1000
Norfolk
WCMS 1050 5000 d
WNOR 1230 1000 -
WRAP 850 5000 -
WTAR 790 5000
WZAM 1110 50000 d
Norton
WNVA 1350 5000 d
Onley
WESR 1330 5000 d
Orange
WJMA 1340 1000 -
Pennington Gap
WSWV 1570 1000 d
Petersburg
WSSV 1240 1000 -
Portsmouth
WNIS 1350 5000 e
WPCE 1400 1000 -
WPMH 1010 5000 d
Pulaski
WBLB 1510 1000 d
WPUV 1580 5000 d
Quantico
WPWC 1480 500
Radford
WRAD 1460 5000 -
Richlands
WRIC 540 1000 d
Richmond
WANT 990 1000 d
WBBL 1480 5000
WEET 1320 5000 d
WFTH 1590 5000 d
WKIE 1540 10000 d
WLEE 1480 5000
WRNL 910 5000
WRVA 1140 50000
WTVR 1380 5000
WXGI 950 5000 d
Roanoke
WFIR 960 5000
WRIS 1410 5000 d
WROV 1240 1000 -
WSLC 610 5000 -
WTOY 910 1000 d
Rocky Mount
WNLB 1290 1000 d
WYTI 1570 1000 d
Salem
WUEZ 1480 5000 d
Saltville
WKGK 1600 5000 d
Smithfield
WKGM 940 10000 d
South Boston
WHLF 1400 1000 -
WSBV 1560 2500 d
South Hill
WJWS 1370 5000 d
St. Paul
WSPC 1140 1000 d
Staunton
WKDW 900 1000 d
WTON 1240 1000 -

Stuart			
	WHEO	1270	5000 dk
Suffolk			
	WLPM	1450	1000 -
Tappahannock			
	WRAR	1000	500 d
Tazewell			
	WTZE	1470	5000 d
Vinton			
	WKBA	1550	10000 d
Virginia Beach			
	WVAB	1550	5000 d
Warrenton			
	WKCW	1420	5000 d
	WPRZ	1250	5000 d
Warsaw			
	WNNT	690	250 d
Waynesboro			
	WANV	970	5000 -
	WAYB	1490	1000 -
Williamsburg			
	WMBG	740	500 d
Winchester			
	WINC	1400	1000 -
	WVAI	610	500
Woodstock			
	WAAM	1230	1000 -
Wytheville			
	WYVE	1280	2500 d

WASHINGTON

Aberdeen			
	KAYO	1450	1000 -
	KXRO	1320	5000 -
Anacortes			
	KAGT	1340	1000 -
Auburn			
	KASY	1220	2500 d
Bellevue			
	KJZZ	1540	5000
Bellingham			
	KGMI	790	5000 -
	KPUG	1170	10000 -
Blaine			
	KARI	550	5000 -k
Bremerton			
	KBRO	1490	1000 -
Burien			
	KQIN	800	500 d
Centralia			
	KITI	1420	5000
Chehalis			
	KELA	1470	5000 -
Chelan			
	KOZI	1230	1000 -
Clarkston			
	KCLK	1430	500 d
Colfax			
	KCLX	1450	1000 -
Colville			
	KCVL	1270	1000 d
Dishman			
	† KSPO	1050	5000 d
Edmonds			
	KGDN	630	5000 -
Ellensburg			
	KXLE	1240	1000 -
Enumclaw			
	KENU	1330	500 d
Ephrata			
	KTRQ	810	10000 d
Everett			
	KRKO	1380	5000
	KWYZ	1230	1000 -
Ferndale			
	KBFW	930	1000 d
	KOQT	1550	10000
Forks			
	KVAC	1490	1000 -
Goldendale			
	† KLCK	1400	1000 -
Grand Coulee			
	KEYG	1490	1000 -
Hoquiam			
	KGHO	1560	1000 d
Kelso			
	KLOG	1490	1000 -
Kennewick			
	KOTY	1340	1000 -
Kirkland			
	KGAA	1460	5000 -
Lakewood			
	KLAY	1480	1000 d
Longview			
	KBAM	1270	5000 d
	KEDO	1400	1000 -
Millwood			
	KCKO	1380	5000 -
Moses Lake			
	KSEM	1470	5000 -
	† KWIQ	1020	5000 -
	‡ KWIQ	1260	1000 d
Mountlake Terrace			
	KKNW	1510	250 d
Mt. Vernon			
	KAPS	1470	500 d
	KBRC	1430	5000 -
Newport			
	† KMTI	700	1000 d
Olympia			
	KGY	1240	1000 -
	KQEU	920	1000 -
Omak			
	KOMW	680	5000 d
Opportunity			
	KGGR	630	1000 d
Othello			
	KRSC	1400	1000 -
Pasco			
	KONA	610	5000
	† KORD	870	10000 -
	‡ KORD	910	1000 d
Port Angeles			
	KAPY	1290	1000 d
	KONP	1450	250
Prosser			
	KARY	1310	5000 d
Pullman			
	KQQQ	1150	1000 d
	* KWSU	1250	5000
Puyallup			
	KJUN	1450	1000 -
Quincy			
	KWNC	1370	1000 d
Raymond			
	KAPA	1340	1000 -
Renton			
	KSCR	1420	500 d
Richland			
	KALE	960	5000 -
Seattle			
	KBLE	1050	5000 d
	KING	1090	50000
	KIRO	710	50000
	KIXI	910	50000 -
	KJET	1590	5000
	KJR	950	5000
	KKFX	1250	5000
	KMPS	1300	5000
	KOMO	1000	50000
	KSPL	1150	5000
	KVI	570	5000
	KXA	770	50000r
Selah			
	† KYXE	1020	10000 -
Shelton			
	KMAS	1280	5000 d
Spokane			
	KGA	1510	50000
	KHQ	590	5000
	KJRB	790	5000
	KKER	1230	1000 -
	* KMBI	1330	5000 d
	KREM	970	5000 -
	KUDY	1280	5000 d
	KXLY	920	5000
	KXXR	1440	5000 d
Sumner			
	KFWY	1560	250 d
Sunnyside			
	† KREW	1210	10000 -
	‡ KREW	1230	1000 -
Tacoma			
	KAMT	1360	5000
	KPMA	1400	1000 -
Tacoma (Cont)			
	KTAC	850	10000 -
Toppenish			
	KENE	1490	1000 -
Vancouver			
	KAAR	1480	2500 k
	KKSN	910	5000
	KVAN	1550	10000
Walla Walla			
	KHIT	1320	1000 d
	KTEL	1490	1000 -
	KUJ	1420	5000
Wenatchee			
	KPQ	560	5000
	KUEN	900	1000 d
	KWWW	1340	1000 -
Yakima			
	KBBO	1390	1000 -
	KIT	1280	5000 -
	KMWX	1460	5000
	KUTI	980	5000 -c
	KVGM	930	1000 d

WEST VIRGINIA

Beckley			
	WJKK	1070	10000 d
	WJLS	560	5000 -
	WWNR	620	1000 -
Berkeley Springs			
	WCST	1010	250 d
Bluefield			
	WHIS	1440	5000 -
	WKOY	1240	1000 -
Buckhannon			
	WBUC	1460	5000 d
Charles Town			
	WXVA	1550	5000 d
Charleston			
	WCAW	680	50000 -
	WCHS	580	5000
	WQBE	950	5000 -
	WTIP	1240	1000 -
	WXIT	1490	1000 -
Clarksburg			
	WHAR	1340	1000 -
	WPDX	750	1000 d
	WPQZ	1400	1000 -
Elkins			
	WDNE	1240	1000 -
Fairmont			
	WMMN	920	5000
	WTCS	1490	1000 -
Fisher			
	WELD	690	500 d
Frost			
	WVMR	1370	2500 d
Grafton			
	WKGA	1260	500 d
Hinton			
	WMTD	1380	1000 d
Huntington			
	WGNT	930	5000 -
	WKEE	800	5000 d
	WWHY	1470	5000 d
Hurricane			
	WZTQ	1080	5000 d
Kenova			
	WTCR	1420	5000 -
Keyser			
	WKLP	1390	1000 d
Kingwood			
	WFSP	1560	1000 d
Logan			
	WLOG	1230	1000 -
	WVOW	1290	5000 -
Madison			
	WWBB	1450	1000 -
Martinsburg			
	WEPM	1340	1000 -
	WRNR	740	500 d
Matewan			
	WHJC	1360	1000 d
Milton			
	WNST	1600	5000 d
Montgomery			
	WMON	1340	1000 -
Morgantown			
	WAJR	1440	5000 -

Morgantown (Cont)		
WCLG	1300	2500 d
Moundsville		
WEIF	1370	5000 d
New Martinsville		
WETZ	1330	1000 d
Oak Hill		
WOAY	860	10000 d
Parkersburg		
WADC	1050	5000 d
WIKS	1450	1000 -
WKYG	1230	1000 -
Pineville		
WWYO	970	1000 d
Princeton		
WAEY	1490	1000 -
Rainelle		
WRRL	1130	1000 d
Ravenswood		
WMOV	1360	1000 d
Richwood		
WVAR	600	1000 d
Ronceverte		
WRON	1400	1000 -
Rupert		
† WYKM	1250	500 d
South Charleston		
WSCW	1410	5000 d
Spencer		
WVRC	1400	1000 -
St. Albans		
WKAZ	1300	1000 d
St. Marys		
† WRRR	1570	1000 d
Sutton		
WSGB	1490	1000 -
Weirton		
WEIR	1430	1000
Welch		
WELC	1150	5000 d
WXEE	1340	1000 -
Weston		
WHAW	980	1000 d
Wheeling		
WANR	1600	5000 d
WKWK	1400	1000 -
WWVA	1170	50000
White Sulphur Springs		
WSLW	1310	5000 d
Williamson •		
WBTH	1400	1000 -

WISCONSIN

Amery		
WXCE	1260	5000
Antigo		
WATK	900	250 d
Appleton		
WHBY	1230	1000 -
WVMS	1570	1000 d
Ashland		
WATW	1400	1000 -
Auburndale		
⋆ WLBL	930	5000 d
Baraboo		
WRPQ	740	250 d
Beaver Dam		
WBEV	1430	1000
Beloit		
WBEL	1380	5000
WGEZ	1490	1000 -
Berlin		
WISS	1090	500 d
Black River Falls		
WWIS	1260	1000 d
Chilton		
†⋆ WMBE	1530	250 d
Chippewa Falls		
WAYY	1150	5000 d
Clintonville		
WFCL	1380	5000 -
Cornell		
† WOGO	680	2500 d
Dodgeville		
WDMP	810	250 d
Durand		
WRDN	1430	1000 d
Eagle River		
WERL	950	1000 d
Eau Claire		
WEAQ	790	5000
WJJK	1400	1000 -
WOKL	1050	1000 d
Fond Du Lac		
KFIZ	1450	1000 -
Fort Atkinson		
WFAW	940	500 d
Green Bay		
WDUZ	1400	1000 -
WGEE	1360	5000
WNFL	1440	5000 -
Greenfield		
WLZZ	1290	5000
Hartford		
WTKM	1540	500 d
Hayward		
WHSM	910	5000 d
Hudson		
† ----	740	500 d
Jackson		
WYLO	540	250 d
Janesville		
WCLO	1230	1000 -
Kaukauna		
WKAU	1050	1000 d
Kenosha		
WLIP	1050	250 d
Kimberly		
WYNE	1150	5000
La Crosse		
WIZM	1410	5000
WKTY	580	5000 -
WLXR	1490	1000 -
Ladysmith		
WLDY	1340	1000 -
Lake Geneva		
WMIR	1550	1000 d
Lancaster		
WGLR	1280	500 d
Madison		
⋆ WHA	970	5000 d
WHIT	1550	5000 d
WIBA	1310	5000
WISM	1480	5000
WTSO	1070	10000 -
Manitowoc		
WCUB	980	5000 d
WOMT	1240	1000 -
Marinette		
WCJL	1300	1000 d
WMAM	570	250 -
Marshfield		
WDLB	1450	1000 -
Mauston		
WRJC	1270	500 d
Medford		
WIGM	1490	1000 -
Menomonie		
WMNE	1360	1000 d
Merrill		
WJMT	730	1000 d
Milwaukee		
WEMP	1250	5000
WISN	1130	50000 -
WMKE	1340	1000 -
WNOV	860	250 d
WOKY	920	5000 -
WTMJ	620	5000
Minocqua		
WFBZ	1570	2500 d
Monroe		
WEKZ	1260	1000 d
Neenah		
WNAM	1280	5000 -
Neillsville		
WCCN	1370	5000 d
New Richmond		
WIXK	1590	5000 d
Oconto		
WOCO	1260	1000 d
Oshkosh		
WCKK	690	250 d
WYTL	1490	1000 -
Park Falls		
WNBI	980	1000 d
Pewaukee		
‡ WGNW	1370	500 d
Platteville		
WTOQ	1590	1000 -
Plymouth		
WPLY	1420	500 d
Port Washington		
WGLB	1560	250 d
Portage		
WPDR	1350	1000 d
Poynette		
WIBU	1240	1000 -
Prairie Du Chien		
WPRE	980	1000 d
Racine		
WRJN	1400	1000 -
WRKR	1460	500 d
Reedsburg		
WRDB	1400	1000 -
Rhinelander		
WOBT	1240	1000 -
Rice Lake		
WAQE	1090	5000 d
WJMC	1240	1000 -
Richland Center		
WRCO	1450	1000 -
Ripon		
WCWC	1600	5000
River Falls		
WEVR	1550	1000 d
Shawano		
WOWN	960	1000
Sheboygan		
WHBL	1330	5000
WKTS	950	500 d
Shell Lake		
WCSW	940	1000 d
Sparta		
WCOW	1290	5000 d
Stevens Point		
WXYQ	1010	1000 d
Sturgeon Bay		
WDOR	910	1000 d
Sun Prairie		
WERU	1190	1000 d
Superior		
KXTP	970	1000 d
WDSM	710	10000 -
Sussex		
† WGNW	1370	500
Tomah		
WTMB	1460	1000 d
Tomahawk		
WJJQ	810	10000 d
Two Rivers		
WRTR	1590	1000 -
Viroqua		
WISV	1360	1000 d
Watertown		
WTTN	1580	1000 d
Waukesha		
WAUK	1510	10000 d
Waupaca		
WDUX	800	5000 d
Waupun		
WGZS	1170	1000 d
Wausau		
WRIG	1400	1000 -
WSAU	550	5000
WXCO	1230	1000 -
West Allis		
WAWA	1590	1000 d
West Bend		
WBKV	1470	2500r dk
Wisconsin Dells		
WNNO	900	1000 d
Wisconsin Rapids		
WFHR	1320	5000 -

WYOMING

Buffalo		
KBBS	1450	1000 -
Casper		
KATI	1400	1000 -
KTWO	1030	50000
KVOC	1230	1000 -
Cheyenne		
KFBC	1240	1000 -

Location	Station	Frequency	Power
Cheyenne (Cont)			
	KRAE	1480	1000 d
	KSHY	1370	1000 d
	KUUY	1530	10000 -
Cody			
	KODI	1400	1000 -
Douglas			
	KWIV	1470	1000 -
Evanston			
	KEVA	1240	1000 -
Gillette			
	KIML	1270	5000 -
Green River			
	KUGR	1490	1000 -
Greybull			
	KMMZ	1140	10000 d
Jackson			
	KSGT	1340	1000 -
Kemmerer			
	KMER	950	5000 dk
Lander			
	KOVE	1330	5000 -
Laramie			
	† KOJO	1210	25000 -
	‡ KOJO	1490	500 -
	KOWB	1290	5000 -
Newcastle			
	KASL	1240	1000 -
Powell			
	KPOW	1260	5000 -
Rawlins			
	KRAL	1240	1000 -
Riverton			
	KVOW	1450	1000 -
Rock Springs			
	KRKK	1360	1000 -
Sheridan			
	KROE	930	5000 d
	KWYO	1410	5000 -
St. Stepmen			
	†⋆ ----	1550	2500 -
Thermopolis			
	KRTR	1490	250
	KTHE	1240	1000 -
Torrington			
	KGOS	1490	1000 -
Wheatland			
	KYCN	1340	250
Worland			
	KWOR	1340	1000 -

CANADA

ALBERTA

Location	Station	Frequency	Power
Blairmore			
	CJPR	1490	1000 -
Brooks			
	CIBQ	1340	1000 -
Calgary			
	CBR	1010	50000
	CFAC	960	50000
	CFCN	1060	50000
	CHQR	810	50000
	CKXL	1140	50000
Camrose			
	CFCW	790	50000
Drumheller			
	CKDQ	910	5000
Edmonton			
	CBX	740	50000
	CFRN	1260	50000
	CHED	630	50000
	CHFA	680	10000
	CHQT	1110	50000
	CJCA	930	50000
	CKER	1480	10000
	⋆ CKUA	580	10000
Edson			
	CJYR	970	10000
Fort Mc Murray			
	CJOK	1230	1000 -
Grand Centre			
	CIOK-1	1340	250
Grand Prairie			
	CFGP	1050	10000
	CJXX	1430	10000
High River			
	CHRB	1280	10000
Jasper			
	CKYR	1450	100
Lethbridge			
	CHEC	1090	5000
	CJOC	1220	10000 -
Lloydminster			
	CKSA	1080	10000
Medicine Hat			
	CHAT	1270	10000
	CJCY	1390	10000
	CJMH	1460	10000
Peace River			
	CKYL	610	10000
Red Deer			
	CKGY	1170	10000 -
	CKRD	850	10000 -
St. Albert			
	CKST	1070	10000
St. Paul			
	CHLO	1310	10000
Stettler			
	CKSQ	1400	1000 -
Taber			
	CKTA	1570	5000
Westlock			
	CFOK	1370	10000
Wetaskiwin			
	CJOI	1440	10000

BRITISH COLUMBIA

Location	Station	Frequency	Power
100 Mile House			
	CKBX	1240	1000
Abbotsford			
	CFVR	850	10000
Burns Lake			
	CFLD	1400	1000 -
Campbell River			
	CFWB	1490	1000
Castlegar			
	CKQR	1230	1000
Chetwynd			
	CHET	1450	1000 -
Chilliwack			
	CHWK	1270	10000
Clearwater			
	CHNL-1	1400	1000 -
Courtenay			
	CFCP	1440	1000
Cranbrook			
	CKEK	570	10000 -
Creston			
	CFKC	1340	250
Dawson Creek			
	CJDC	1350	1000
Duncan			
	CKAY	1500	10000 -
Fernie			
	CFEK	1240	1000 -
Fort Nelson			
	CFNL	590	250
Fort St. John			
	CKNL	560	1000
Golden			
	CKGR	1400	1000 -
Grand Forks			
	CKGF	1340	1000 -
Hope			
	CKGO	1240	1000 -
Kamloops			
	CFJC	550	25000 -
	CHNL	610	25000 -
Kelowna			
	CKIQ	1150	10000
	CKOV	630	5000 -k
Kitimat			
	CKTK	1230	1000 -
Langley			
	CJJC	800	10000
Mackenzie			
	CKMK	1240	1000 -
Merritt			
	CJNL	1230	1000 -
Nanaimo			
	CHUB	1570	10000
	CKEG	1350	10000
Nelson			
	CKKC	1390	1000
New Westminster			
	CKNW	980	50000
Osoyoos			
	CKOO	1240	1000 -
Parksville			
	CHPQ	1370	1000
Penticton			
	CKOK	800	10000
Port Alberni			
	CJAV	1240	1000 -
Port Hardy			
	CFNI	1240	1000 -
Powell River			
	CHQB	1280	1000
Prince George			
	CJCI	620	10000
	CKPG	550	10000
Prince Rupert			
	CFPR	860	10000
	CHTK	560	1000 -
Princeton			
	CINL	1400	1000 -
Quesnel			
	CKCQ	920	10000 -
Revelstoke			
	CKCR	1340	1000
Richmond			
	CISL	940	2500
Salmon Arm			
	CKXR	580	10000
Smithers			
	CFBV	1230	1000 -
Summerland			
	CKSP	1450	1000 -
Terrace			
	CFTK	590	1000
Trail			
	CJAT	610	10000
Vancouver			
	CBU	690	50000
	CFUN	1410	50000
	CHQM	1320	50000
	CJOR	600	10000
	CJVB	1470	50000
	CKLG	730	50000
	CKWX	1130	50000
Vanderhoof			
	CIVH	1340	1000 -
Vernon			
	CJIB	940	10000
	CKAL	1050	10000 -
Victoria			
	CFAX	1070	10000
	CJVI	900	10000
	CKDA	1220	50000
Williams Lake			
	CKWL	570	1000

MANITOBA

Location	Station	Frequency	Power
Altona			
	CFAM	950	10000
Boissevain			
	CJRB	1220	10000
Brandon			
	CKLQ	1570	10000
	CKX	1150	50000 -
Churchill			
	CHFC	1230	250
Dauphin			
	CKDM	730	10000 -
Flin Flon			
	CFAR	590	10000 -
Morden			
	CISV	1530	10000 -
Portage La Prairie			
	CFRY	920	10000
St. Boniface			
	CKSB	1050	10000
Steinbach			
	CHSM	1250	10000
The Pas			
	CJAR	1240	1000 -
Thompson			
	CHTM	610	1000
Winnipeg			
	CBW	990	50000

Winnipeg (Cont)

	CFRW	1290	10000
	CJOB	680	50000
	CKJS	810	10000
	CKRC	630	10000
	CKY	580	50000

NEW BRUNSWICK

Bathurst			
	CKBC	1350	10000
Campbellton			
	CKNB	950	10000 -
Caraquet			
	CJVA	810	10000
Edmundston			
	CJEM	570	5000 -
Fredericton			
	CBZ	970	10000
	CFNB	550	50000
	CIHI	1260	10000
Grand Falls			
	CKMV	1480	5000 d
Moncton			
	CBA	1070	50000
	CBAF	1300	5000
	CHLR	1380	10000
	CKCW	1220	25000
Newcastle			
	CFAN	790	5000 -
St. John			
	CBD	1110	10000
	CFBC	930	50000
	CHSJ	1150	10000 -
Sussex			
	CJCW	590	1000 -
Woodstock			
	CJCJ	920	10000 -

NEWFOUNDLAND

Baie Verte			
	CKIM	1240	1000 -
Bonavista Bay			
	CBGY	750	10000
Clarenceville			
	CKVO	710	10000
Corner Brook			
	CBY	990	10000
	CFCB	570	1000
Gander			
	CBG	1450	1000
	† CFYQ	850	1000
	‡ CFYQ	1350	1000
	CKGA	730	1000
Goose Bay			
	CFGB	1340	1000
	CFLN	1230	1000 -
Grand Bank			
	CKYQ	610	1000
Grand Falls			
	CBT	540	10000
	CIYQ	680	10000
	CKCM	620	10000
Hawkesbury			
	† ----	1110	1000 d
Lac Etchemin			
	† ----	920	1000
Marystown			
	CHCM	560	10000 -
Musgravetown			
	CHYQ	670	10000
Port Aux Basques			
	CFGN	1230	250
Port Aux Choix			
	CFNW	790	1000
Spainard's Bay			
	† CHVO	850	5000
St. John's			
	CBN	640	10000
	CJYQ	930	50000
	⋆ VOAR	1230	100
	VOCM	590	10000
	⋆ VOWR	800	5000 -
Stephenville			
	CFSX	910	500
Wabush			
	CBDQ	1490	1000 -
	CFLW	1340	250

NORTHWEST TERRITORIES

Frobisher Bay			
	CFFB	1210	1000
Inuvik			
	CHAK	860	1000
Tuktoyaktuk			
	CFCT	600	1000
Yellowknife			
	CFYK	1340	1000

NOVA SCOTIA

Amherst			
	CKDH	900	1000
Antigonish			
	CJFX	580	10000
Bridgewater			
	CKBW	1000	10000
Dartmouth			
	CFDR	680	50000 -
Digby			
	CKDY	1420	1000
Halifax			
	CBH	860	10000
	CHNS	960	10000
	CJCH	920	25000
Kentville			
	CKEN	1490	1000 -
Middleton			
	CKAD	1350	1000
New Glasgow			
	CKEC	1320	5000
Pt. Hawkesbury			
	CIGO	1410	10000
Sydney			
	CBI	1140	10000
	CHER	950	10000
	CJCB	1270	10000
Truro			
	CKCL	600	10000 -
Windsor			
	CFAB	1450	250
Yarmouth			
	CJLS	1340	5000

ONTARIO

Ajax			
	CHOO	1390	10000
Atikokan			
	CFAK	1240	250
Bancroft			
	CJNH	1240	1000 -
Barrie			
	CKBB	950	10000 -
Belleville			
	CJBQ	800	10000
Blind River			
	CJNR	730	1000 -
Brampton			
	CKMW	790	5000
Brantford			
	CKPC	1380	10000
Brockville			
	CFJR	1450	1000 -
Cambridge			
	CFTJ	960	1000
Chatham			
	CFCO	630	10000 -
Cobourg			
	CHUC	1450	1000
Collingwood			
	CKCB	1400	1000 -
Cornwall			
	CFIX	1170	10000 d
	CJSS	1220	1000
Dryden			
	CKDR	900	1000 -
Elliot Lake			
	CKNR	1340	1000 -
Espanola			
	CKNS	930	10000
Ft. Frances			
	CFOB	800	1000 -
Guelph			
	CJOY	1460	10000
Hamilton			
	CHAM	1280	10000
	CHML	900	50000
	CKOC	1150	50000
Hawkesbury			
	CHPR	1110	250 d
Hearst			
	CFLH	1340	1000 -
Huntsville			
	CFBK	630	1000
Kapuskasing			
	CFLK	1230	100
	CKAP	580	10000 -
Kenora			
	CJRL	1220	1000
Kingston			
	⋆ CFRC	1490	100
	CKLC	1380	10000
	CKWS	960	10000 -
Kirkland Lake			
	CJKL	560	5000
Kitchener			
	CHYM	570	10000
	CKKW	1090	10000
Leamington			
	CHIR	730	0 n
	CHYR	710	10000 d
Lindsay			
	CKLY	910	10000 -
London			
	CFPL	980	10000 -
	CJBK	1290	10000
	CKSL	1410	10000
Midland			
	CKMP	1230	1000 -
Mississauga			
	CJMR	1190	10000 d
New Liskeard			
	CJTT	1230	1000 -
Newmarket			
	CKAN	1480	10000
Niagara Falls			
	CJRN	710	5000 -
North Bay			
	CFCH	600	10000 -
	CHUR	1100	10000
Oakville			
	CHWO	1250	10000 -
Orillia			
	CFOR	1570	10000 -
Oshawa			
	CKAR	1350	10000 -
Ottawa			
	CBO	920	50000
	CBOF	1250	50000
	CFGO	1440	50000
	CFRA	580	50000 -
	CJRC	1150	50000 -
	CJSB	540	50000 -
	CKOY	1310	50000
Owen Sound			
	CFOS	560	5000 -
Parry Sound			
	CFBQ	1340	250
Pembroke			
	CHOV	1350	1000
Peterborough			
	CHEX	980	10000 -
	CKPT	1420	10000 -
Port Elgin			
	CFPS	1490	1000 -
Red Lake			
	CXRE	1340	250
Renfrew			
	CKOB	1400	1000 -
Richmond Hill			
	CFGM	1320	50000
Sarnia			
	CHOK	1070	10000
	CKJD	1110	10000 -
Sault Ste. Marie			
	CFYN	1050	10000 -
	CKCY	920	10000 -
Simcoe			
	CHNR	1600	10000
Smith's Falls			
	CJET	630	10000
St. Catherines			
	CHSC	1220	1000
	CKTB	610	10000 -
St. Thomas			
	CHLO	1570	10000

Stratford
CJCS 1240 500 -
Sudbury
CFBR 900 10000 -
CHNO 550 50000 -
CKSO 790 50000
Thunder Bay
CBQ 800 10000 -
CJLB 1230 1000 -
CKPR 580 5000 -
Tillsonburg
CKOT 1510 1000 d
Timmins
CFCL 620 10000 -
‡ CKGB 680 10000
† CKGB 730 25000
Toronto
CBL 740 50000
CFRB 1010 50000
CFTR 680 25000
CHIN 1540 50000
CHUM 1050 50000
CJBC 860 50000
CJCL 1430 50000
CKEY 590 10000
Trenton
CJTN 1270 1000
Wawa
CJWA 1240 1000 -
Welland
CHOW 1470 10000
Windsor
CBE 1550 10000
CBEF 540 2500 h
CKLW 800 50000
CKWW 580 500
Wingham
CKNX 920 10000 -
Woodstock
CKDK 1340 10000 -k

PRINCE EDWARD ISLAND

Charlottetown
CFCY 630 10000
CHTN 1190 10000
Summerside
CJRW 1240 250

QUEBEC

Alma
CFGT 1270 10000
Amos
CHAD 1340 1000 -
Amqui
CFVM 1220 5000
Asbestos
CJAN 1340 1000 -
Baie Comeau
CKBH 790 1000
Cabano
CJAF 1240 1000
Causapscal
CJBM 1450 1000 -
Chapais
CFED 1340 250
Chibougamau
CJMD 1240 1000
Chicoutimi
CBJ 1580 10000
CJMT 1420 10000
Dolbeau
CHVD 1230 1000 -
Drummondville
CHRD 1480 10000
CKVR 1400 250
Forestville
CFRP 620 1000
Granby
CHEF 1450 10000 -
Hautervie
CHLC 580 5000 -
Hull
CKCH 970 10000
Joliette
CJLM 1350 10000 -
Jonquiere
CKRS 590 10000 -
L'annonciaton
CKLR 1490 1000 -
La Pocatiere
CHGB 1310 10000 -
La Sarre
CKLS 1240 1000 -
La Tuque
CFLM 1240 1000 -
Lac Etchemin
CIRB 1240 1000 -
Lac Megantic
CKFL 1400 1000 -
Lachute
CJLA 630 500 h
Laval
CKLM 1570 50000
Levis
CFLS 920 10000
Longueuil
CHRS 1090 10000 d
Matane
CBGA 1250 10000 -
CHRM 1290 10000
Mont Laurier
CKML 610 1000 -
Montmagny
CKBM 1490 2500 -
Montreal
CBF 690 50000
CBM 940 50000
CFCF 600 5000
CFMB 1410 10000
CJAD 800 50000 -
CJMS 1280 50000
CKAC 730 50000
CKGM 980 10000
New Carlisle
CHNC 610 10000 -
Plessisville
CKTL 1420 1000
Pointe Claire
CFOX 1470 10000 -
Port Cartier
CIPC 710 1000
Quebec
CBV 980 50000
CFOM 1340 250
CHRC 800 50000
CJRP 1060 50000
CKCV 1280 50000
Rimouski
CFLP 1000 10000
CJBR 900 10000
Riviere Du Loup
CJFP 1400 10000 -
Roberval
CHRL 910 10000
Rouyn
CKRN 1400 1000 -
Seven Islands
CKCN 560 10000 -
Shawinigan Falls
CKSM 1220 10000 -
Sherbrooke
CHLT 630 10000 -
CJRS 1510 10000
CKTS 900 10000
Sorel
CJSO 1320 10000 -
St. Eleuthere
CHRT 1450 1000 -
St. Georges De Beauce
CKRB 1460 10000 -
St. Hyacinthe
CKBS 1240 250
St. Jerome
CJER 900 1000
St. Pamphile
CHAL 1350 1000
Ste. Agathe Des Monts
CJSA 1230 1000 -
Ste. Anne Des Monts
CBGA-7 1340 1000 -
CBGN 1490 1000 -
Ste. Marie De Beauce
CJVL 1360 10000
Temiscaming
CKVT 1340 1000 -
Thetford Mines
CKLD 1330 10000
Three Rivers
CHLN 550 10000 -
CJTR 1140 10000 -
Val D' Or
CKVD 900 10000 -
Valleyfield
CFLV 1370 10000 -
Verdun
CKVL 850 50000 -
Victoriaville
CFDA 1380 10000
Ville Degelis
CFVD 1370 1000
Ville Marie
CKVM 710 10000 -

SASKATCHEWAN

Estevan
CJSL 1280 10000
Gravelbourg
CFGR 1230 0 n
CFRG 710 5000 d
Meadow Lake
CJNS 1240 1000 -
Melfort
CJVR 1420 10000
Moose Jaw
CHAB 800 10000
North Battleford
CJNB 1050 10000
Prince Albert
CKBI 900 10000
Regina
CBK 540 50000
CJME 1300 10000
CKCK 620 10000
CKRM 980 10000 -
Rosetown
CKKR 1330 10000
Saskatoon
CFNS 860 10000
CFQC 600 10000
CJWW 1370 10000
CKOM 1250 10000
Shaunavon
CJSN 1490 1000 -
Swift Current
CKSW 570 10000
Weyburn
CFSL 1190 10000 -
Yorkton
CJGX 940 10000

YUKON TERRITORY

Whitehorse
CFWH 570 1000
CKRW 610 1000

ST. PIERRE

St. Pierre & Miquelon
.... 1375 4000

MEXICO

AGUASCALIENTES

Aguascalientes
† ---- 1370 250 d
XEAC 1400 500 -
† XEAGA 1590 250 d
XEBI 790 1000 -
† XEDC 1080 250 d
XENM 1320 1000
XERO 1490 250
XEUAA 1370 500 d
XEUVA 1170 1000 d
XEYZ 1450 1000 -
Calvillo
XECAA 1020 1000 -
El Puertecito
XELTZ 740 3300 h
Pebellon
XEPLA 860 4000 -

BAJA CALIFORNIA

Location / Station	Freq	Power
Ensenada		
XEDX	1010	500 -
XEEP	1500	500 d
XEHC	920	2500 -
XEPF	1400	250
XESCT	1230	1000
XESS	1450	1000 -
Guerrero Negro		
† XEZO	1070	1000 d
Mexicali		
XEAA	1340	1000 -
XEAD	910	1000 -
XECL	990	5000
XED	1050	10000 -
XEHG	1370	500 d
XEYX	1590	10000 -
XEMBC	1190	1000 -
XERM	1150	1000 -
XESU	790	1000 d
XEWV	940	1000 d
XEZF	850	250 d
Rosarito		
XEPRS	1090	50000
San Felipe		
† ----	540	1000 d
Tecate		
XEHA	560	250
XEKT	1380	250 -
Tijuana		
XEBBC	1470	5000
XEBG	1550	1000
XEC	1310	250
XECAL	1270	5000
XEGM	950	10000 -
XEMMM	800	500 d
XEMO	860	5000
XETRA	690	50000
XEXX	1420	2000

BAJA CALIFORNIA SUR

Location / Station	Freq	Power
Cabo San Lucas		
† ----	1540	5000 d
Ciudad Morelos		
XEDY	1080	500 d
XEMCA	1480	500 -
Ensenada		
XEHC	1590	1000
La Paz		
† ----	1040	500 d
† ----	1100	250 d
XEHZ	990	5000 -
XELPZ	1310	10000 d
XENT	790	5000 -
XEPAB	1380	250
Loreto		
† ----	1200	5000 -
San Jose Del Cabo		
† XEKA	1420	250
Santa Rosalia		
† XERLA	930	1000 -
XESR	1320	500 -
Todas Santos		
XEIB	1490	1000 -
Villa Constitucion		
XEVSD	1440	1000 -

CAMPECHE

Location / Station	Freq	Power
Becal		
XEBAL	1470	1000 d
Campeche		
† ----	1140	250 d
XEA	1370	1000
XECAM	1280	500
XECUC	840	500 d
XERAC	1430	250
Carmen		
XEBCC	1340	5000 -
XEIT	1070	1000 -
XEMAB	950	1000
XEUJ	1460	250
Champoton		
XESE	1560	5000 d
Escarcega		
XEESC	820	750 d
Hopelchen		
† ----	920	1000 d
Palizada		
XETH	1290	250 -

CHIAPAS

Location / Station	Freq	Power
Arriaga		
XEGJ	1190	250 d
XEMG	1250	1000 -
Chiapa De Corzo		
XEVV	920	5000 -
Cintalapa		
XEIN	810	1000 d
Comitan		
† ----	1580	1000 d
XEUI	1320	1000 -
Hidalgo		
XEZW	1380	5000 -
XEZZZ	590	1000
Huixtla		
† XEMK	930	5000 -
XEKY	1280	1000 -
Motozintla		
† ----	1030	10000 d
Palenque		
† ----	1480	1000 -
XEPAC	600	500 -
Pichucalco		
XEOB	1080	1500 -
Reforma		
† ----	1470	500 d
San Cristobal		
† ----	950	1000
† ----	1430	300 -
XERA	760	8000 -
XEWM	640	1000 d
Tapachula		
XETAC	1000	1000
† ----	1580	500 d
XEKQ	680	5000 -
XEOE	810	1000 -
XETAK	1100	750 d
XETAP	890	1000 d
XETS	630	3000 -
Tonala		
XEDB	860	1000 -
Tuxtla		
† ----	1120	250 d
† ----	1180	1000 d
† XEDG	1300	1000 d
† XEIO	840	10000 d
XELM	1240	1000 -
XEON	710	3000 -
XESX	1390	5000 d
XETG	990	10000
XEUD	1360	3500 -
XEUE	580	1000
Venustiano Carranza		
† ----	1070	1000 -
Villa Flores		
† ----	870	500 d
† ----	1040	2500 d
XEVF	1540	500 d
Yajalon		
XEYS	1350	1000

CHIHUAHUA

Location / Station	Freq	Power
Camargo		
XEACC	1520	1000 d
XECC	960	1000 -
XEFCD	1440	5000 -
XEOH	1270	1000 -
Chihuahua		
† ----	1530	250 d
XEBU	620	5000 -
XEBW	1280	1000 -
XEDG	1490	1000 -
XEDI	1360	1000 -
XEES	1110	1000 -
XEFA	950	500 -
XEFI	580	5000 -
XEFO	680	1000 d
XELO	1010	1000 d
XEM	850	5000 -
XEQD	920	1000 -
XERPC	790	5000 -
XERU	1310	1000 -
XEV	1390	1000 -
Ciudad Jimenez		
† ----	1460	5000 -
Ciudad Juarez		
XECJC	1490	1000
XEF	1420	5000 -
XEFV	1000	1000 d
XEJ	970	10000 -
XEP	1300	1000 -
XEPZ	1190	1000 d
XEROK	800	150000
XEWG	1240	1000 -
XEWR	1110	500 d
XEYC	1460	1000
XEZOL	860	1000 -
Ciudad Madero		
XESW	1300	1000 d
Ciudad Saucillio		
† ----	1190	250 d
Cuahutemoc		
† ----	740	5000 -
† ----	1490	1000 -
XEDP	710	5000 d
† XEDT	1080	1000 d
† XEEA	1130	1000 d
XEER	990	1000 -
XEPL	550	500 -
XEQZ	1560	750 -
Delicias		
XEACB	660	500 d
XEBN	1240	1000 -
† XEDCH	1540	1000 d
XEHM	1470	1000 d
XEJK	1340	1000 -
Jimenez		
XEJZ	1320	1000 -
Meoqui		
XEBZ	1590	1000 -
Nuevo Casas Grandes		
† ----	1140	250 d
XETX	1010	1000 -
Ojinaga		
XEOG	1260	1000 -
XEQU	1450	1000
XERCH	1340	1000 -
Parral		
† ----	1000	1000 d
XEAT	1250	250
XEGD	1400	1000 -
XEJR	1490	1000 -
XEJS	1150	1000 -
San Francisco, Del Oro		
XEHB	770	500 d
Santa Barbara		
XESB	820	750 d
Zaragoza		
XEJPV	1560	1000 d

COAHUILA

Location / Station	Freq	Power
Allende		
XEIA	1430	1000 -
XEVD	1380	5000 -
Buenaventura		
† ----	1300	1000 d
Ciudad Acuna		
XEAE	1600	5000
XEDH	1340	1000
XEKD	1010	500 -
XERF	1570	250000
Francisco I. Madero		
XEYD	1410	1000 -
Matamoros		
XETOR	670	1000 d
Monclova		
XEMDA	1170	500 d
XEMF	1260	1000 -
XEPU	1110	250 d
XEQX	970	1000 -
XEWQ	1330	1000 -
Muzquiz		
XEPQ	710	5000 -
Nueva Rosita		
XEABA	1300	1000 -
XEARO	1400	1000 -
XENR	980	5000 -
XEPD	1460	1000 d
XEYJ	950	10000 -
Parras		
XEAY	1470	1000 -
XEJQ	1500	250 d

Station	kHz	Power
Piedras Negras		
XEIK	1360	500 -
XEMJ	920	1000 -
XEMU	580	5000 -
XEVM	1240	250 -
Ramos Arispe		
† ----	1300	1000 d
Sabinas		
XEBX	610	3000 -
XESC	1250	1000
Saltillo		
XEAJ	1080	1000
XEDE	1400	500 -
XEIM	810	500 d
XEKS	960	500 -
† XESAC	1580	250 d
† XESHT	1430	500 d
XESJ	1250	1000 -
San Pedro		
XEBF	1150	1000 -
XEOT	980	1000
Torreon		
† ----	1090	500 d
† ----	1540	250 d
XEDN	600	1000
† XELZ	1600	1000 d
XEQN	1310	10000 -
XETAA	920	5000 -
XETB	1350	5000 -
XETC	1240	500 -
XETJ	570	1000 -
XEVK	1010	5000 -
Villa Frontera		
XEDP	920	1000 -
XEXU	1480	1000 -
Villa Union		
XEVUC	1520	1000 d
Zaragoza		
XEZR	860	1000 n

COLIMA

Station	kHz	Power
Armeria		
XELS	1360	1000 -
Colima		
XECOC	1430	1500 -
XEDS	1470	5000
XERL	710	10000
XEUU	910	500 -
† XEVE	1040	250 d
Manzanillo		
XEAL	860	5000 -
XECS	960	1000 -
† XEMAC	1330	500 d
Tecoman		
XETY	1390	5000 -

DISTRITO FEDERAL

Station	kHz	Power
Mexico City		
XEAI	1440	5000 -
XEB	1220	100000
XEBS	1410	5000
XECMQ	1320	10000
XECO	1380	5000
XEDA	1290	10000 -
XEDF	970	10000 -
XEEP	1060	50000
XEFAJ	1560	20000
XEFR	1180	1000
XEJP	1150	10000
XEL	1260	10000 -
XELA	830	10000 -
XEMP	710	1000
XEN	690	20000 -
XENK	620	10000
XEOC	560	1000
XEOY	1000	10000
XEPH	590	5000
XEQ	940	150000
XEQK	1350	1000
XEQR	1030	10000 -
XERC	790	10000 -
XERED	1110	50000
XERH	1500	20000
XERPM	660	50000 -
XESM	1470	10000 -
XEUN	860	45000 -
XEUR	1530	3000 h
XEVOZ	1590	10000 -
Mexico City (Cont)		
XEW	900	250000
XEX	730	100000

DURANGO

Station	kHz	Power
Durango		
† ----	1330	1000 d
XECAV	1470	1000 -
XECK	620	1000 -
XEDGO	760	1000 -
† XEDRD	1540	250 d
XEDU	860	1000 -
XEE	590	1000 -
XEHD	1270	1000 d
XERPU	1370	1000 -
† XEWX	660	250 d
Gomez Palacio		
XEEP	1450	1000 -
XEGZ	790	1000 -
XERS	1380	500 -
XEWN	1270	500
Guadalupe Victoria		
† ----	1460	200 d
Santiago Papasquiaro		
† ----	560	1000 d

GUANAJUATO

Station	kHz	Power
Acambaro		
† ----	1440	250 d
XEAK	1600	500 -
XEVW	1160	1000 d
Apaseo El Grande		
XEAF	1580	1000 d
Arperos		
XEGTO	600	5000
Celaya		
XEFG	840	1000
XEITC	1200	1000
XENC	1540	1000 -
XEY	1360	1000 -
XEZN	780	500 d
Cortazar		
XEFY	950	500 -
XEOF	1510	5000 d
Dolores Hidalgo		
XEJE	1370	1000
Guanajuato		
XEFL	1500	1000
XEUG	970	500 d
Irapuato		
XEAMO	870	1000
XEBO	1330	5000 -
XECN	1080	1000 d
† XEIRG	1590	250 d
XEWE	1420	10000 -
XEYA	1470	1000 d
Leon		
† ----	1350	250 d
XELEO	1110	5000
XELG	680	10000 -
XERPL	1270	5000 -
XERW	1390	10000 -
XERZ	1240	1000 -
† XEX-1	710	500 -
XEXF	1140	5000 -
Moroleon		
XEBV	1100	500 d
XETN	700	1000
Salamanca		
XEEMM	1210	250 d
XEMAS	1560	1000 -
† XESAG	1040	1000 d
XEZH	1260	500 d
Salvatierra		
XEFAC	920	2000 -
XEMC	1480	250 d
XERE	1290	1000
San Francisco Del Rincon		
XEAGN	910	100 d
XEXV	1300	20000 -
San Luis De La Paz		
XEGX	1480	500
San Miguel Allende		
XESQ	1280	500 -
Silao		
XESD	1530	1000 -

GUERRERO

Station	kHz	Power
Acapulco		
† ----	1460	1000 d
† ----	1520	500 d
XEACA	630	5000 -
XEACD	550	500 -
XEACG	1600	500
XEAGR	810	1000 -
XEBB	600	5000 -
XECI	1340	1000 -
XEKJ	1400	750 -
XEKU	710	500 -
XERY	1450	1000 -
XEVMA	1430	1000 d
XEVP	1030	1500 d
Atoyac		
† ----	660	500 d
† XERAA	1240	500 -
Chilapa		
† ----	1200	1000 d
Chilpancingo		
† ----	1300	1000 d
† XECHG	1130	1000 d
XELI	1580	1000 -
Ciudad Altimirano		
XEXY	780	1000 d
Coyuca De Benitez		
† ----	1540	10000 d
Cozumel		
† XERB	1510	500 d
Iguala		
† KEYL	1510	10000
XEIG	1430	1000 -
XEKF	1360	1000 -
XEYL	1170	50000 -
Las Cruces		
XEKOK	750	1000 d
Ometepec		
† ----	1100	5000 -
Petalan		
XEHJ	1310	250
Taxco		
† ----	1270	250 -
† ----	1310	400 d
XEXC	1480	1000 -
Tecpan		
† ----	1480	250 d
Teloloapan		
† ----	1270	2000 d
Tixtla		
XEPI	1250	1000 -
Tlapa		
XEZV	800	1000 d
Zihuatenejo		
† ----	1070	2000 d
† ----	1280	500 d
† ----	1410	500 d
† ----	1600	500 -
XEUQ	960	1000 -

HIDALGO

Station	kHz	Power
Huejutla		
XECY	1320	1000 -
Ixmiquilpan		
† ----	1140	250 d
XEQH	1270	1000 -
XEZG	1510	1000
Mixquiahuala		
† XEXH	1390	100 d
Pachuca		
† ----	1550	1000 d
XEPK	1190	1000
XERD	1420	1000
Tlanchinol		
† ----	1470	1000 d
Tulancingo		
XENQ	1580	5000 -
XEQB	1340	500 -

JALISCO

Station	kHz	Power
Ameca		
XEED	1490	1000 -
Arandas		
XERAL	1560	250 d
Atemajac		
XEKB	1410	8000 -
Autlan		
XELD	780	5000 -

Autlan (Cont)		
XEQA	1600	1000 d
Ciudad Guzman		
XEBC	990	1000 -
XEGUZ	550	1000 -
XEIS	670	5000 d
XELW	1510	5000
Cocula		
† ----	1580	250 d
El Grullo		
XEJY	1350	1000 -
Encarnacion		
XEKB	1410	8000 -
Guadalajara		
XEAD	1150	1000 -
XEAV	580	10000 -
XEBA	820	10000 -
XEDK	1250	5000 -
XEDKR	700	1000 d
XEDKT	1340	1000 -
XEGAJ	1520	1000 d
XEHK	960	1000
XEHL	1010	50000 -
* XEJB	630	10000 -
XELT	920	20000 -
XEQP	1280	1000 -
XETIA	1310	5000 -
XEUNO	1120	500 d
XEWK	1190	50000
La Barca		
XELB	1090	250 d
Lagos		
† ----	990	250 h
XELJ	1030	1000 d
XEQZ	720	1000 d
Mascota		
XEMST	910	1000
XEMTJ	1430	1000 d
Ocotlan		
XEAN	790	25000 -
XENP	1430	250 h
Pihuamo		
† ----	1590	500 d
Puerto Vallarta		
† ----	1080	5000 d
† ----	1260	1000
† ----	1510	500 d
† ----	1600	250 d
XEEJ	740	1000 -
† XEPVJ	1110	1000 d
San Juan		
† ----	720	500 d
Sayula		
XEWP	1420	500 d
Tala		
XECX	1040	250 d
Tamazula		
† ----	1270	500 d
XEQJ	1400	1000 d
Tepatitlan		
XEZK	1600	1000 -
Tequila		
† ----	1590	100 d
Tiaquepaque		
† ----	1400	10000 d
XEMIA	850	1000
XEPJ	1370	1000 -
XESP	1070	10000 -
Tonala		
† ----	1550	500 d
XECCC	1440	5000 -
XEZZ	760	5000 d
Tuxpan		
† ----	1140	3000 d
Zacoalco		
XEJTF	1450	250
Zapopan		
† ----	1550	500 d
XEBBB	1040	5000 -
XETZ	880	10000 d
XEZJ	1480	500 -

MEXICO

Atlacomulco		
XERLK	1340	500 d
XEATL	1520	1000 d
El Oro		
XEDV	1550	500 d
Ixtapan De La Sal		
XEXI	1400	250
Toluca		
XECH	1490	250
XEGEM	1600	2000 d
XEQY	1360	1000
Valle De Bravo		
XEVAB	1580	250 d

MICHOACAN

Apatzingan		
XETZI	550	5000 -
† ----	1590	250 d
† XEAPM	1380	1000 -
XECJ	970	5000 -
XEML	770	1000 d
Cheran		
XEMCH	830	1000 d
Ciudad Hidalgo		
XESOL	1190	500 d
Coahiueyana		
† ----	1540	500 d
Huetamo		
XEKN	1490	250
Jiquilpan		
† ----	950	500 d
XEIX	1290	1000 -
La Piedad		
XELC	980	5000 -
XELP	1170	250 -
Lazaro Cardenas		
† XELAC	1560	5000 -
XELCM	930	500 d
XEOJ	1400	1000 -
Los Reyes		
XEABC	760	20000 -
XEGO	1530	1000 -
Melchor Ocampo De Balsas		
† ----	1120	500 d
† ----	1510	500 d
Morelia		
XEREL	1550	1000
† XECGP	1520	500 d
XECR	1340	250
XEI	1400	1000 -
XEKW	1300	500
† XELIA	1140	250 d
XELQ	570	1000
XELY	870	1000 d
XEMM	960	500 -
XERPA	1240	500 -
† XESV	1370	500 d
XEYM	810	1000 d
Nueva Italia		
XENI	1320	1000 -
Patzcuaro		
XEPAT	1050	5000 d
XEXL	1020	1000 d
Purepero		
XERCP	1600	200 d
Puruandiro		
† ----	1250	250 d
Sahuayo		
XEGC	1450	1000 -
Tacambaro		
XEMBA	750	1000
† ----	990	1000 d
Uruapan		
XEFN	1130	1000 d
† XEIP	1480	500 d
XEIW	1160	1000 d
XEUF	610	5000 -
XEURM	1440	5000 d
Yurecuaro		
† ----	1350	500 d
Zacapu		
XECAP	790	1000
XEZI	1200	1000 d
XEZU	1270	1000 -
Zamora		
† ----	1410	1000 d
XEGT	1490	1000 -
XEQL	1580	1000 -
XEZM	650	5000 d
Zitacuaro		
† ----	1080	500 -
XETA	600	500 -

MORELOS

Cuernavaca		
† XEIC	1540	1000
XEJC	1340	1000 -
XEWF	1420	500 -
Jojutila		
XEDO	1190	1000
Zacatepec		
XEART	1590	1000

NAYARIT

Acaponeta		
XELH	1400	1000 -
Ahuacatlan		
XENAY	1470	600 -
Compostela		
XEEF	1050	5000 d
Ixtlan		
XERIO	1560	5000 d
XEVR	1030	1000
Ruiz		
XESK	1490	250
Santiago Ixcuintla		
† ----	950	1000
XESI	1240	1000 -
XEZE	1340	250
Tecuala		
XETD	1450	250
Tepic		
† ----	1380	1000 -
† ----	1460	1000 d
XENF	680	250 d
XEOO	620	1000 -
† XEPNA	1590	250 d
XERK	710	1000 -
XETEY	840	500 d
XETNC	550	10000 -
XEXT	980	1000
Tuxpan		
XEUX	810	10000 -

NUEVO LEON

Linares		
XELE	1400	250 -
XELN	790	1000 -
XER	1260	1000 -
Montemorelos		
† ----	1230	1000 d
XEDD	1560	500 -
XERN	950	5000 -
XESF	1320	1000 -
Monterrey		
† ----	660	10000 -
† ----	760	5000 d
XEACH	1590	5000 -
XEAU	1090	2500 -
XEAW	1280	5000 -
XEBJB	570	5000 -
XECT	1190	500 d
XEFB	630	10000
XEFZ	740	500
XEG	1050	150000
XEH	1420	5000 -
XEIZ	1240	500 -
XEJM	1450	500 -
XEMN	600	5000 -
XEMON	1370	10000
XEMR	1140	50000
XENL	860	5000 -
XENV	1340	1000 -
XEOK	920	1000 -
XEQI	1510	10000 d
XERG	690	2500 -
XET	990	50000
XEVB	1310	1000 -
XEWA-1	540	500
Sabinas Hidalgo		
XESH	1400	1000
Santa Catarina		
† XESTN	1540	5000 d
Villa De Guadalupe		
XETKR	1480	5000 -

OAXACA

Cosolapa		
† ----	1200	1000

Location / Station	Frequency	Power
Huajuapan De Leon		
XEOU	1480	500 d
Ixtepec		
† ----	740	1000 d
† ----	1080	5000 d
† ----	1600	500 d
XECA	1430	1000 -
Juchitan		
† ----	670	5000 d
† ----	770	5000 d
† ----	970	500 d
XEAH	1330	500
Loma Bonita		
XEQF	750	5000 d
Matias Romero		
XEYG	660	250 d
Miahuatlan		
† ----	780	250 d
Oaxaca		
† ----	1020	2000 d
† ----	1460	1000 d
XEAX	1270	5000 -
XECE	1240	500 -
XEIU	990	1000 -
† XEIV	1190	500 d
XEKC	1460	1000 d
XEOA	570	5000 -
XERPO	710	1000 -
XEUBJ	1400	1000 -
XEZB	950	1000 -
† XEZYB	1530	500 d
Ocotlan		
† ----	1090	250 d
Pinotepa		
† XETEP	1450	500 d
Puerto Angel		
† ----	1600	1000 d
XEPX	1340	1000 -
Puerto Escondido		
† ----	1550	1000 d
XEACC	870	500 h
Salina Cruz		
† ----	1510	1000 d
Tehuantepec		
XEJI	1390	2500 -
XEKZ	610	1000 -
XEUC	550	1000 -
Tlaxiaco		
† ----	930	700 d
Tuxtepec		
----	1110	2000 -
XEUH	1320	1000 -
XEXP	1150	5000 -

PUEBLA

Location / Station	Frequency	Power
Atlixco		
† ----	1480	1000 d
XEXD	1450	500 -
Cholula		
† XESZ	1520	250 d
Cuidad Serdan		
XELU	1340	250
Huauchinango		
XENG	1240	1000 -
Izucar De Matamoros		
----	1020	500 d
XEEV	1330	1000
XEFS	1400	350 d
Libres		
† ----	1350	500 d
Puebla		
† ----	1570	1000 d
XECD	1170	1000
XEHIT	1310	500 -
XEHR	1090	500 -
XEPA	1370	5000 -
XEPOP	1490	500
XEZT	1250	500 -
San Diego		
† ----	830	200 h
San Martin		
XERTF	1600	500 d
Tehuacan		
† ----	1390	250 d
XEATP	1520	1000
XEGY	1070	1000 -
† XEJCP	1600	250 d
XETE	1140	1000 d
Tehuacan (Cont)		
XEWJ	1420	1000 -
Tezultlan		
XEOL	990	1000 -

QUERETARO

Location / Station	Frequency	Power
Cozumel		
XERB	1170	5000 -
Jalpan		
XEJAQ	1040	250 d
Queretaro		
† ----	1130	1000 d
XEJX	1250	1000 -
† XEKH	1020	500 d
XENA	1450	1000 -
XEQG	980	1000 -
† XEW-2	900	1000 d
XEXE	1490	1000 -
San Juan Del Rio		
XEVI	1400	1000 -
Villa De La Corregidora		
XEHY	1310	5000 -
Villa Del Pueblito		
XEGV	1120	500 d
Villa Juarez		
† XEVJP	570	250 d

QUINTANA ROO

Location / Station	Frequency	Power
Cancun		
† ----	1080	1000 d
† ----	1120	1000 d
----	1480	250 d
XEYI	580	500 d
Carillo Puerto		
XECPQ	1460	1000 d
XEKX	620	1000 -
Chetumal		
† XEEN	1540	250 d
† XEQAA	560	200 d
XEROO	960	1000 -
XEUO	1250	250
XEWO	1020	1000 d
Cozumel		
† ----	810	5000
† ----	1000	100 d
XERB	1170	5000 d
Isla Mujeres		
† ----	1210	1000 d
Kantunil Kin		
† ----	1260	250 d
Morelos		
† ----	1350	1000
Tihosuco		
† ----	1300	150 d
Tulum		
† ----	1150	200 d

SAN LUIS POTOSI

Location / Station	Frequency	Power
Cerritos		
† XEZW	1560	500 d
Ciudad Valles		
† ----	580	1000 -
† ----	700	1000 d
XECV	610	1000 -
XEIR	1410	1000 d
XETR	1120	5000 -
XEVAL	1360	5000 d
XEXR	1260	1000 d
Matehuala		
† ----	1540	1000 d
† ----	1590	1000 -
XEFF	1490	1000 -
XEIE	1450	1000 -
XEWU	1400	250 -
Rio Verde		
XEEM	880	1000 d
XEIY	1290	1000 d
XETUN	1430	250 d
San Luis Potosi		
† ----	1600	1000 -
XEBM	920	5000 -
XECZ	960	500 -
† XEEI	1070	250 d
XEEQ	760	250 d
XEPO	1310	500 -
XESL	1340	1000 -
† XESMR	1380	1000
XEWA	540	150000
San Luis Potosi (Cont)		
XEXQ	1460	1000 -
Tamazunchale		
† ----	700	250 d
XEGI	1160	500 d
XEGK	770	1000 d

SINALOA

Location / Station	Frequency	Power
Culiacan		
† ----	960	500 -
† ----	1040	1000 -
XEBL	710	5000 -
XECQ	920	5000 -
† XECSI	1590	250 d
XEEX	1400	1000 -
XENW	860	1000 -
XENZ	570	1000 -
XESA	1260	1000 -
XEUAS	1150	10000 -
XEWS	1010	5000 -
† XEWT	1200	1000 d
El Fuerte		
† ----	1170	1000 d
XEGU	1450	1000 -
XEORF	950	5000 -
Escuinapa		
XEQE	1340	250
Guamuchil		
† ----	1390	1000 -
XEJL	1300	1000 -
Guasave		
† ----	1560	1000 d
XEGS	610	1000 -
XEORO	680	1000
XEVP	1490	500 -
Los Mochis		
XELMS	1000	1000 d
† ----	1080	1000 d
XECF	1410	1000 -
XECU	1470	1000 -
XECW	1340	1000 -
XEHS	1280	250
XEMOS	1130	500 d
XEMV	770	2500 d
XEPNK	880	5000 d
XETNT	650	500 d
Mazatlan		
XEMMS	1000	1000 d
† ----	1070	1000 d
† ----	1170	1000 d
XEACE	1470	1000 -
XENH	870	1000 d
XENX	1290	10000 -
XEVOX	970	10000 -
XERJ	600	5000 -
XEST	1580	250 d
XETK	630	1000 -
XEVU	1350	850 -
XEW-1	900	5000 d
Navolato		
XEVQ	830	1000 d
Rosario		
XEHW	1440	1000 -
San Blas		
XEREY	1240	1000 -

SONORA

Location / Station	Frequency	Power
Agua Prieta		
† ----	1390	1000 -
XEAQ	1490	1000 -
XEFH	1310	1000 -
Benjamin Hill		
† ----	1490	500 -
Caborca		
XEANA	1280	500 d
XEEZ	970	500 -
XEIB	1170	250 d
† XESN	1250	500 d
XEUK	1470	500 d
Cananea		
† ----	630	750 d
XEFQ	980	500
Ciudad Obregon		
† ----	610	1000 -
† ----	1590	250 d
XEAP	1290	1000 -
XEHO	910	1000 -
XEIQ	960	1000 -

City	Call	Freq	Power
Ciudad Obregon (Cont)			
	XEOBS	1370	10000 -
	XEOS	1340	250
	XEOX	1430	5000 -
	XERSV	810	5000 -
	XESO	1150	5000 -
Empalme			
	† ----	1520	1000 d
	† XEPE	1450	250
	XEPS	710	1000 d
Esperanza			
	XEEB	1010	500 -
Guaymas			
	XEBQ	1240	1000 -
	XEDR	1490	1000 -
	XEFX	630	1000 -
	† XEGYS	1560	250 d
Hermosillo			
	† ----	740	1000 -
	† ----	1200	1000 d
	† ----	1450	1000 d
	† ----	1480	1000 d
	XEBH	920	5000 -
	XEDL	1250	1000 -
	XEDM	1580	50000
	XEHOS	1540	5000
	XEHQ	590	1500
	XELV	680	250 d
	XEPB	1400	1000
	XEUS	850	1000
	XEYH	1170	1000 -
Huatabampo			
	XEYO	560	1000 -
Magdalena			
	XEDJ	1450	250 -
	XESY	1320	200 d
Nacozari			
	† ----	1460	250 d
	† XENAZ	1600	1000 d
	XETM	1350	1000
Navojoa			
	† ----	1540	500 d
	† ----	1600	500 d
	XEGL	1270	1000 -
	XEKE	980	1000 -
	XEKI	1510	500 d
	XENAS	1400	500 -
	XENS	1480	1000
	XESON	1110	1000 d
Nogales			
	XECG	1240	1000 -
	XEHF	1370	5000
	XEHN	1130	1000 d
	XENY	1270	1000 -
	XEPE	1600	1000 d
	XEVN	1190	500 d
	XEXW	1300	5000 -
Puerto Penasco			
	XEQC	1390	1000 d
San Luis			
	XECB	1450	250
	XEEH	1520	1000 d
	XELBL	1350	500 -
	XEMW	1260	1000 -
Santa Ana			
	XEAB	1400	1000 -
Topolobampo			
	XEZA	740	1000 -
Ures			
	XEXN	1010	500 -
Villa De Seris			
	XEVS	1110	1000 d
	XEVSS	1340	1000 d

TABASCO

City	Call	Freq	Power
Cardenas			
	† ----	1320	150 d
	XEJAC	1110	1000
Comalcalco			
	† ----	1200	250 d
	XEVX	570	1000 -
Huimanguillo			
	XEZQ	1520	1000 -
Muacuspana			
	XECUS	1020	1000
	XENB	660	1000 d
	XERTM	1150	1000 -
Nacajuca			
	† ----	1440	500 d
Teapa			
	XEQQQ	880	9000 -
Tenosique			
	† ----	1120	1000 d
	† ----	1520	250 d
	XEZX	860	1000 -
Villahermosa			
	XETVH	1230	5000 -
	† ----	1540	5000 d
	† ----	1600	250 d
	XEACM	620	5000 -k
	XEKV	740	1000 -
	XETAB	1410	5000 -
	XEUV	1500	500
	XEVA	790	10000 -
	XEVT	970	5000 -

TAMAULIPAS

City	Call	Freq	Power
Altamira			
	XEOLA	1460	5000
Camargo			
	XEZD	1350	250
Ciudad Madero			
	† ----	1030	1000 -
	† ----	1190	500 d
	† XEMTS	1590	1000 d
	XERP	1330	10000 -
	XEPRT	1270	5000 -
Ciudad Mante			
	† ----	950	1000 d
	XECM	1450	1000 -
	XEGG	1490	250 -
	XEMY	840	1000 -
	XEXO	1390	5000 -
Ciudad Miguel Aleman			
	XEHI	1470	1000 -
	XEWD	1430	2000 -
Ciudad Victoria			
	XEBJ	970	1000 -
	XEGW	1380	5000 -
	XEHP	580	1000 -
	XERCM	1410	1000 -
	XERPV	1340	1000 -
	† XETAM	1550	500 d
El Limon			
	XEYP	1520	1000 d
Matamoros			
	XEAM	1310	1000 -
	XEEW	1420	1000
	XEMS	1490	1000 -
	XEMT	1340	1000 -
	XEMV	1000	1000
	XEO	970	1000
Nuevo Laredo			
	XENLT	1000	1000 d
	XEAS	1410	1000 -
	XEBK	1340	500 -
	XEFE	790	1000 -
	XEGNK	1370	250 d
	XEK	960	5000 -
	XENU	1550	5000 d
	XEWL	1090	1000 d
Reynosa			
	XEOR	1390	1000
	XERI	810	1000 d
	XERKS	940	1000
	XERT	1170	5000 -
Rio Bravo			
	XEFD	590	5000 -
	XEGH	620	250 d
	XEOQ	1110	5000 -
Tampico			
	XEAR	930	1000 -
	XEFW	810	50000
	XELE	1300	1000 -
	XES	1240	1000 -
	XETO	1400	1000 -
	† XETOT	1190	5000 -
	XETU	980	10000 -
	XETW	860	500 d
Valle Hermosa			
	XEVH	1450	1000 -
Xicotencatl			
	† ----	1080	1000 d

TLAXCALA

City	Call	Freq	Power
Apizaco			
	† ----	980	10000 d
	† ----	1010	1000 -
Huamantla			
	XEHT	810	500 d
Panzacola			
	† ----	1520	500 d
	XEEG	1280	1000 -
Tlaxcala			
	XETT	1430	800 d

VERACRUZ

City	Call	Freq	Power
Acayucan			
	† ----	1190	1000 d
	XEVZ	1490	1000 -
Alamo			
	XEID	1230	1000
Alvarado			
	† XEAVR	1540	5000 -
Boca Del Rio			
	XEOD	1090	1000
Cardel			
	XEJPM	1510	1000
Ciudad Mendoza			
	XEAGV	1360	1000
Coatepec			
	XEGR	1040	1000 d
Coatzacoalcos			
	† ----	1000	1000
	† ----	1200	2000 -
	XEGB	960	1000 -
	XEOM	1340	5000 -
	XEZS	1170	500 -
Coatzintla			
	† ----	780	250 d
Cordoba			
	† ----	770	250 d
	† ----	1410	500 d
	XEAG	1280	1000
	XEDZ	580	1000 -
	XEVC	700	500 d
Cosamaloapan			
	XEFU	630	5000 -
	XEQO	980	5000
	XEYB	1380	1000
El Higo			
	† ----	1600	250 d
Fortin De Las Flores			
	XEKG	820	1000 d
Gutierrez Zomora			
	XEGF	1420	1000 -
Huatusco			
	XEYV	1180	1000
Huayacocotla			
	† ----	1370	250 d
Jalapa			
	XEJA	610	1000 -
	XEJH	1460	500 d
	XEKL	550	1000 -
	XEOZ	960	1000
	XERUV	1550	10000
	XEZL	1130	10000
Jaltipan			
	XEJV	1420	1000 -
Las Choapas			
	XEUY	1580	250 -
Martinez De La Torre			
	XEFBF	1360	500 -
	XEHU	1300	5000 -
	XEUZ	1330	1000 -
Minatitlan			
	XEKM	1450	500 -
	XEMI	1070	500 -
	XEMTV	1260	1000
Misantla			
	XEPT	1590	1000 -
Nadlingo			
	† ----	640	1000
	† ----	1260	250 d
	† XETP	1380	3000 d
Naranjos			
	† ----	1110	250 d
	† ----	1560	1000 d
Orizaba			
	† ----	880	250 d
	XEOV	1240	250 -
	XEPP	1450	1000 -

Orizaba (Cont)
XETQ 850 100000 -
Panuco
† ---- 1510 1000 d
† XEMCA 1090 5000 d
† XEPAV 1540 1000 d
Papantla
† XEEU 1170 250 d
XEPV 1270 1000 -
Perote
XEBD 1100 1000 d
XEBE 1160 1000 d
Piedras Negras
XEGN 1500 1000
Poza Rica
† ---- 1600 1000 d
† XEGP 1540 1000 d
XEJD 1450 1000 -
XEPR 1480 10000 -
XEPW 1200 1000
XEXK 1080 500 d
Rio Blanco
† ---- 1480 250 d
San Andres Tuxtla
XEDQ 1360 1000 -
XEGA 1300 500
San Rafael
XEVO 1520 250
Tantoyucah
† ---- 1070 1000 -
Teocelo
XEYT 1490 250 -
Tierra Blanca
XEJF 1350 1000 -
† XETBV 1580 1000 d
Tlapacoyan
† ---- 1400 250 d
XEEC 1440 250 -
Tuxpan
† ---- 920 1000 d
XEBY 1340 250 -
XETL 1390 5000 -
† XETVR 1150 250 d
Veracruz
XEFM 1010 5000 -
XEHV 1310 1000
XELL 1430 5000 -
XEPG 1400 250 -
XEQT 1600 500 -
XETF 1250 1000 -
XEU 930 5000 -
XEWB 900 50000 -

YUCATAN

Buctzoz
† ---- 1440 1000 -
Merida
XEMY 1000 1000 d
XEFC 1330 5000 -
XEMH 970 1000 -
XEMQ 1240 5000 -
XEPY 1450 1000 -
XEQW 550 2000 -
XERRF 1150 1000 -
XERUY 1390 10000 -
XEVG 650 1000 -
XEZ 600 5000 -
Motul
XEYK 1540 1000 -
Peto
XEYAA 740 10000 d
Progreso
† XEHA 1560 1000 d
XETRN 690 50000
XEUL 1360 1000
Tizimin
† ---- 1280 1000 d
† ---- 1420 500 -
XEUP 1310 1000
Uman
XEYW 1270 2500 -
Valladolid
† ---- 1100 2000 d
XECP 1590 10000 d
XEME 1490 5000 -
XEUM 990 1000 -
Yogope
† ---- 920 1000 d

ZACATECAS

Concepcion Oro
XECNO 760 1000 d
Fresnillo
† ---- 1540 1000 d
XEEL 610 5000 -
XEIH 930 5000 -
XEMA 690 5000 -
XEQS 980 4000 -
XEYQ 1500 1000 d
Jalapa
XEEY 1260 1000
XEFP 1290 10000 -
Jerez
† ---- 660 1000 d
XEXM 1360 1000 -
Juchipila
† ---- 970 1000
Loreto
XELTZ 740 5000 -
Miguel Auza
XEMAU 890 10000 d
Ojo Caliente
XEOCE 570 250 d
Rio Grande
† ---- 1180 1000
XEHE 1450 500 -
XEZC 810 1000 -
Sombrerete
XESOM 720 2500 d
Tlaltenango
XETGO 1350 2000 d
Zacatecas
XECAS 1090 1000 -
† ---- 1210 5000 d
XELK 830 1000 -
XEPC 1240 1000 d
XEUA 830 1000 d
XEXZ 1150 1000 -
XEZAZ 1120 250 d
Zapopan
XEBBB 1040 5000 d

WEST INDIES

ANGUILLA

The Valley
.... 1505 500

ANTIGUA

Ottos
.... 620 500
St. Johns
ZDK 1100 50000 k

BAHAMAS

Nassau
ZNS-1 1540 10000
ZNS-2 1240 250

BARBADOS

Bridgetown
.... 900 10000

BERMUDA

Hamilton
ZBM-1 1230 1000
ZBM-2 1340 1000
Pembroke West
ZFB-1 960 1000

CARRIACOU ISLAND

Hillsborough
.... 1045 100

CUBA

Artemisa
CMAD 1160 1000
Banes
CMDO 1150 250
Baracoa
CMDX 1420 1000
CMKG 1059 1000
Bayamo
CMDD 1310 1000

Bayamo (Cont)
CMDE 1260 250
CMKX 1390 1000
Camaguey
CMFA 1030 5000
CMJB 910 1000
CMJE 810 1000
CMJG 1270 1000
CMJK 1140 1000
CMJL 740 10000
CMJN 784 60000
Cardenas
CMGB 1560 250
CMGE 1470 250
Ciego De Avila
CMJD 1300 250
CMJM 580 500
CMJP 1190 1000
CMJT 700 1000 -
CMJV 900 1000
CMJY 860 1000
Cienfuegos
CMHN 680 5000 -
CMHU 1100 1000
Colon
CMGN 720 30000
Consolacion Del Sur
CMAG 1260 1000
Cruces
CMHK 1307 250
Florida
CMJI 1400 250
Guane
CMAP 1000 250
Guantanamo
CMDJ 950 1000
CMDN 870 10000
CMDW 1130 1000
CMKA 1250 250
CMKS 1290 1000
Havana
CMBC 690 50000
CMBF 950 10000
CMBG 1360 250
CMBL 870 1000
CMBQ 1060 5000
CMCA 830 10000
CMCH 790 10000
CMCI 760 10000
CMCK 980 5000
CMQ 640 50000
CMW 590 150000 -
Holguin
CMDL 1120 1000
CMKJ 730 10000
CMKM 1011 5000
CMKV 851 50000
Jaguey Grande
CMGM 1230 1000
Las Mercedes
CMDT 840 1000
Manzanillo
CMDF 1590 250
Matanzas
CMGW 1240 1000
CMGX 930 1000
Moron
CMJX 1210 250
Nuevitas
CMJQ 1300 250
Palma Soriano
CMKZ 1430 250
Perico
CMGY 1220 5000
Pinar Del Rio
CMAF 670 10000
CMAN 550 30000
CMAQ 730 1000
CMAS 1010 250
Puerto Padre
CMKY 1350 250
San Cristobal
CMAC 1019 1000
San Pedro De Cacocum
CMKP 670 50000
Sancti Spiritus
CMHB 960 1000
CMHT 990 1000

Santa Clara			
	CMHA	1130	1000
	CMHD	890	1000
	CMHG	660	10000
	CMHI	570	10000
	CMHM	1280	1000
	CMHW	840	10000
Santa Cruz Del Sur			
	CMJW	1450	1000
Santa Fe, Isla De Pinos			
	CMBM	1080	1000
Santiago De Cuba			
	CMDB	680	1000 -
	CMDV	1550	250
	CMDZ	890	250
	CMKC	850	2000
	CMKN	960	1000
	CMKU	650	2000
	CMKW	1370	1000
Trinidad			
	CMHV	610	1000
Victoria De Las Tunas			
	CMDP	1280	250
	CMKE	1240	250
	CMKT	1520	1000

DOMINICA

Roseau			
	....	590	10000
	....	695	500

DOMINICAN REP.

Azua			
	HIBM	920	500
Bani			
	HIAV	1320	500
Barahona			
	HICV	1240	250
	HISD	1370	1000
	HIUA	1370	1000
Bonoa			
	HIVM	1290	1000
Cotui			
	HIBR	630	500 -
	HIDE	1160	500 -
Dajabon			
	HIUB	1300	1000
El Seibo			
	HISD	1310	1000
Hato Mayor Del Rey			
	HIAN	1460	500
Higuey			
	HIRM	1250	250
La Romana			
	HIBB	1240	500 -
	HIBP	1400	500 -
La Vega			
	HIAL	1400	250
	HIDL	1000	500 -
	HIMH	1100	250
	HISD	1360	1000
	HIVG	1430	3000
Moca			
	HIAP	1490	250
	HIBK	1310	1000 -
	HIBX	640	1000 -
	HICP	1210	1000 -
Monte Cristi			
	HIAF	630	1000
Nagua			
	HICF	800	1000 -
	HIFS	1440	1000
Neyba			
	HIFU	1580	1000
Puerto Plata			
	HIAB	590	500
	HIAU	1300	2000
	HIBN	1400	1000 -
	HIFF	960	1000
Salcedo			
	HIAC	1450	500
Samana			
	HIWJ	1580	500
San Cristobal			
	HIAR	1450	500
San Francisco De Macoris			
	HIBC	1250	5000 -
	HIBI	1070	1000 -
	HICJ	1210	1000 -
San Francisco De Macoris (Cont)			
	HIFS	600	250 -
	HIPT	1340	250
San Juan			
	HIAD	1440	500
	HIBZ	1340	1000 -
	HIUA	1390	1000
San Pedro De Macoris			
	HIBS	1600	1000
	HIDB	1450	1000
	HIHD	1320	1000
Santiago			
	HIAA	560	500
	HIAG	1470	500
	HIAM	660	2000
	HIAQ	720	1000
	HIAZ	820	3000
	HIBA	1590	1000
	HICB	1050	1000
	HICK	920	2000
	HIDA	1590	1000
	HIDB	1330	1000
	HIGB	750	1000 -
	HIJC	1560	5000
	HIJM	1410	500
	HIRL	1130	1000 -
	HISA	980	3000
	HIST	1380	5000 -
	HIUA	1270	1000
Santo Domingo			
	HIAE	1420	1000
	HIAH	1490	250
	HIAJ	1570	1000
	HIAK	1440	1000 -
	HIAS	1150	5000 -
	HIAT	650	10000 -
	HIAW	690	5000
	HIBA	910	500
	HIBE	1180	50000 -
	HIBJ	830	50000 -
	HIBK	770	1000 -
	HIBL	1510	10000
	HIBW	540	5000 -
	HICN	1120	1000
	HIFA	1600	5000
	HIFB	1540	1000
	HIG	950	2000
	HIJP	1010	50000 -
	HIKQ	1300	500
	HIL	790	5000
	HILR	860	50000
	HIMC	1100	1000
	HIMS	570	10000 -
	HIPJ	890	5000
	HISD	620	50000 -
	HIT	1260	500
	HIXZ	1350	1000 -
	HIZ	730	5000 -
Valverde			
	HIBU	1240	500
	HIBY	880	1000 -
	HIDC	700	1000

GRENADA

St. Georges			
	....	535	500
Basse Terre			
	....	640	20000
	....	1420	4000

HAITI

Aux Cayes			
	4VI	760	20000
Cap Haitien			
	4VEA	1460	1000
	4VEC	1035	10000
	4VEF	830	2500
	4VWA	1550	1000
Jeremie			
	4VAE	1190	150
	4VIE	780	500
Les Gonaives			
	4VJS	930	250
Port Au Prince			
	4VA	1080	1500
	4VAA	880	200
	4VAB	1150	1000
	4VCD	960	300
	4VCPS	1000	200
	4VDS	860	500
Port Au Prince (Cont)			
	4VF	1120	200
	4VGM	1430	1000
	4VM	1250	600
	4VOC	1500	350
	4VRD	1170	250
	4VS	1380	1000
	4VUE	660	5000
	4VW	1330	1500
	† AQW	910	10000

JAMAICA

Kingston			
	....	560	5000
	ZQI	720	5000
Mandeville			
	....	770	5000
Montego Bay			
	....	550	5000
	....	700	5000
Point Galina			
	....	580	5000
	....	750	5000
Spur Tree			
	....	620	5000

MARTINIQUE

Fort De France			
	....	1310	50000

MONTSERRAT

Plymouth			
	ZGB	885	1000
Riverfield			
	....	640	25000
	....	930	200000

NETHERLANDS ANTILLES

Aruba			
	PJA-10	1330	1000
	PJA5	1435	1000
	PJA6	920	10000
	PJA8	1270	1000
Bonaire			
	PJB	800	500000
	PJB2	1380	1000
Curacao			
	PJC2	855	5000
	PJC7	1010	1000
	PJC7A	1500	1000
	PJL	1540	1000
	PJL3	1230	250
St. Martin			
	PJD2	1295	50000

ST. KITTS

Springfield			
	ZIZ	570	660

ST. LUCIA

Castries			
	....	840	10000

ST. VINCENT

Kingstown			
	....	705	500

TRINIDAD

Port Of Spain			
	VP4RD	730	20000
	VPL6	610	10000
	WVDI	570	250

VIRGIN IS. (BRITISH)

Roadtown, Tortula, Br VI			
	ZBVI	780	10000

CENTRAL AMERICA

COSTA RICA

San Jose			
	TIRICA	625	100000

GUATEMALA

Guatemala City			
	TGW	640	20000

NICARAGUA

Managua			
	YNX	750	50000

AM Stations by Frequency

535

....	St. Georges, Gren.	500	500

540 (CANADIAN CLEAR)

† ----	Hesperia, Calif.	1000	
KVIP	Redding, Calif.	1000	
WGTO	Cypress Gardens, Fla.	50000	1000
WDAK	Columbus, Ga.	5000	500
KWMT	Ft. Dodge, Ia.	5000	
KNOE	Monroe, La.	5000	1000
WDMV	Pocomoke City, Md.	500	
KNMX	Las Vegas, N.M.	5000	
WLIX	Islip, N.Y.	250	
WETC	Zebulon, N.C.	5000	
WARO	Canonsburg, Pa.	250	
WYNN	Florence, S.C.	250	
WDXN	Clarksville, Tenn.	1000	
KNAK	Delta, Utah	1000	
WRIC	Richlands, Va.	1000	
WYLO	Jackson, Wis.	250	
CBT	Grand Falls, Nfld.	10000	10000
CJSB	Ottawa, Ont.	50000	10000
CBEF	Windsor, Ont.	2500	5000
CBK	Regina, Sask.	50000	50000
† ----	San Felipe, B.C.	1000	
XEWA-1	Monterrey, N.L.	500	500
XEWA	San Luis Potosi, S.L.P.	150000	150000
HIBW	Santo Domingo, Dom. Rep.	5000	1000

550 (REGIONAL)

KENI	Anchorage, Alas.	5000	5000
KOY	Phoenix, Ariz.	5000	1000
KAFY	Bakersfield, Calif.	1000	1000
KRAI	Craig, Colo.	5000	500
WAYR	Orange Park, Fla.	1000	
WDUN	Gainesville, Ga.	5000	500
KMVI	Wailuku, Haw.	5000	5000
KFRM	Salina, Kan.	5000	
WCBI	Columbus, Miss.	1000	500
KSD	St. Louis, Mo.	5000	5000
KBOW	Butte, Mont.	5000	1000
WGR	Buffalo, N.Y.	5000	5000
WDLV	Pinehurst, N.C.	1000	
WDRV	Statesville, N.C.	500	
KFYR	Bismarck, N.D.	5000	5000
WKRC	Cincinnati, O.	5000	1000
* KOAC	Corvallis, Ore.	5000	5000
WHLM	Bloomsburg, Pa.	1000	1000
WPAB	Ponce, P.R.	5000	1000
WGNG	Pawtucket, R.I.	1000	500
KCRS	Midland, Tex.	5000	1000
KTSA	San Antonio, Tex.	5000	5000
WDEV	Waterbury, Vt.	5000	1000
WSVA	Harrisonburg, Va.	5000	1000
KARI	Blaine, Wash.	5000	2500
WSAU	Wausau, Wis.	5000	5000
CFJC	Kamloops, B.C.	25000	5000
CKPG	Prince George, B.C.	10000	10000
CFNB	Fredericton, N.B.	50000	50000
CHNO	Sudbury, Ont.	50000	10000
CHLN	Three Rivers, Que.	10000	5000
XEPL	Cuahutemoc, Chih.	500	150
XEACD	Acapulco, Gro.	500	250
XEGUZ	Ciudad Guzman, Jal.	1000	100
XETZI	Apatzingan, Mich.	5000	1000
XETNC	Tepic, Nay.	10000	1000
XEUC	Tehuantepec, Oax.	1000	250
XEKL	Jalapa, Ver.	1000	250
XEQW	Merida, Yuc.	2000	350
CMAN	Pinar Del Rio, Cuba	30000	30000
....	Montego Bay, Jamaica	5000	5000

560 (REGIONAL)

WOOF	Dothan, Ala.	5000	
KVOK	Kodiak, Alas.	1000	1000
KBLU	Yuma, Ariz.	1000	1000
KSFO	San Francisco, Calif.	5000	1000
KLZ	Denver, Colo.	5000	5000
WQAM	Miami, Fla.	5000	1000
WIND	Chicago, Ill.	5000	5000
WMIK	Middlesboro, Ky.	500	
WGAN	Portland, Me.	5000	5000
WFRB	Frostburg, Md.	5000	
WHYN	Springfield, Mass.	5000	1000
WHND	Monroe, Mich.	500	
WEBC	Duluth, Minn.	5000	5000
KWTO	Springfield, Mo.	5000	5000
KMON	Great Falls, Mont.	5000	5000
WCKL	Catskill, N.Y.	1000	
WGAI	Elizabeth City, N.C.	1000	500
WFIL	Philadelphia, Pa.	5000	5000
WIS	Columbia, S.C.	5000	5000
† WTBN	Brentwood, Tenn.	500	
WHBQ	Memphis, Tenn.	5000	1000
KLVI	Beaumont, Tex.	5000	5000
KPQ	Wenatchee, Wash.	5000	5000
WJLS	Beckley, W.V.	5000	500
CKNL	Fort St. John, B.C.	1000	1000
CHTK	Prince Rupert, B.C.	1000	250
CHCM	Marystown, Nfld.	10000	5000
CJKL	Kirkland Lake, Ont.	5000	5000
CFOS	Owen Sound, Ont.	5000	1000
CKCN	Seven Islands, Que.	10000	5000
XEHA	Tecate, B.C.	250	250
XEOC	Mexico City, D.F.	1000	1000
† ----	Santiago Papasquiaro, Dgo.	1000	500
† XEQAA	Chetumal, Q.R.	200	
XEYO	Huatabampo, Son.	1000	500
HIAA	Santiago, Dom. Rep.	500	500
....	Kingston, Jamaica	5000	5000

570 (REGIONAL)

WAAX	Gadsden, Ala.	5000	500
KCNO	Alturas, Calif.	5000	
KLAC	Los Angeles, Calif.	5000	5000
WGMS	Washington, D. C.	5000	1000
WPLP	Pinellas Park, Fla.	1000	1000
WACL	Waycross, Ga.	5000	1000
WKYX	Paducah, Ky.	1000	500
WVMI	Biloxi, Miss.	5000	1000
KGRT	Las Cruces, N.M.	5000	
WMCA	New York, N.Y.	5000	5000
WSYR	Syracuse, N.Y.	5000	5000
WWNC	Asheville, N.C.	5000	5000
WLLE	Raleigh, N.C.	500	
WKBN	Youngstown, O.	5000	5000
WNAX	Yankton, S.D.	5000	5000
WFAA	Dallas, Tex.	5000	5000
KLUB	Salt Lake City, Utah	5000	5000
KVI	Seattle, Wash.	5000	5000
WMAM	Marinette, Wis.	250	100
CKEK	Cranbrook, B.C.	10000	1000

	CKWL	Williams Lake, B.C.	1000	1000
	CJEM	Edmundston, N.B.	5000	1000
	CFCB	Corner Brook, Nfld.	1000	1000
	CHYM	Kitchener, Ont.	10000	10000
	CKSW	Swift Current, Sask.	10000	10000
	CFWH	Whitehorse, Yuk.	1000	1000
	XETJ	Torreon, Coah.	1000	250
	XELQ	Morelia, Mich.	1000	1000
	XEBJB	Monterrey, N.L.	5000	250
	XEOA	Oaxaca, Oax.	5000	250
†	XEVJP	Villa Juarez, Qro.	250	
	XENZ	Culiacan, Sin.	1000	250
	XEVX	Comalcalco, Tab.	1000	250
	XEOCE	Ojo Caliente, Zac.	250	
	CMHI	Santa Clara, Cuba	10000	10000
	HIMS	Santo Domingo, Dom. Rep.	10000	1000
	ZIZ	Springfield, St. Kitts	660	660
	WVDI	Port Of Spain, Trinidad	250	250

580 (REGIONAL)

	WBIL	Tuskegee, Ala.	500	
*	KYUK	Bethel, Alas.	5000	5000
†	KRSA	Petersburg, Alas.	5000	5000
	KIKX	Tucson, Ariz.	5000	500
	KMJ	Fresno, Calif.	5000	5000
	KUBC	Montrose, Colo.	5000	1000
	WDBO	Orlando, Fla.	5000	5000
	WGAC	Augusta, Ga.	5000	1000
	KFXD	Nampa, Id.	5000	5000
*	WILL	Urbana, Ill.	5000	
*	KSAC	Manhattan, Kan.	5000	500
	WIBW	Topeka, Kan.	5000	5000
	KALB	Alexandria, La.	5000	1000
	WTAG	Worcester, Mass.	5000	5000
	WTCM	Traverse City, Mich.	5000q	500
	WELO	Tupelo, Miss.	1000	500
	KANA	Anaconda, Mont.	1000	
	WAGR	Lumberton, N.C.	500	
	WKSK	West Jefferson, N.C.	1000	500
	KCMX	Ashland, Ore.	1000	1000
	WHP	Harrisburg, Pa.	5000	5000
	WKAQ	San Juan, P.R.	5000	5000
	KOBH	Hot Springs, S.D.	500	
	WOFE	Rockwood, Tenn.	1000	
	KRLB	Lubbock, Tex.	500	
	WLES	Lawrenceville, Va.	500	
	WCHS	Charleston, W.V.	5000	5000
	WKTY	La Crosse, Wis.	5000	1000
*	CKUA	Edmonton, Alta.	10000	10000
	CKXR	Salmon Arm, B.C.	10000	10000
	CKY	Winnipeg, Man.	50000	50000
	CJFX	Antigonish, N.S.	10000	10000
	CKAP	Kapuskasing, Ont.	10000	1000
	CFRA	Ottawa, Ont.	50000	10000
	CKPR	Thunder Bay, Ont.	5000	1000
	CKWW	Windsor, Ont.	500	500
	CHLC	Hautervie, Que.	5000	2500
	XEUE	Tuxtla, Chis.	1000	1000
	XEFI	Chihuahua, Chih.	5000	250
	XEMU	Piedras Negras, Coah.	5000	250
	XEAV	Guadalajara, Jal.	10000	1000
	XEYI	Cancun, Q.R.	500	
†	----	Ciudad Valles, S.L.P.	1000	250
	XEHP	Ciudad Victoria, Tams.	1000	150
	XEDZ	Cordoba, Ver.	1000	450
	CMJM	Ciego De Avila, Cuba	500	500
	....	Point Galina, Jamaica	5000	5000

590 (REGIONAL)

	WRAG	Carrollton, Ala.	1000	
	KHAR	Anchorage, Alas.	5000	5000
	KBHS	Hot Springs, Ark.	5000	1000
	KFXM	San Bernardino, Calif.	1000	1000
	KTHO	South Lake Tahoe, Calif.	2500	500
	KCSJ	Pueblo, Colo.	1000	1000
	WDLP	Panama City, Fla.	1000	1000
	WPLO	Atlanta, Ga.	5000	5000
	KSSK	Honolulu, Haw.	5000	5000
	KID	Idaho Falls, Id.	5000	1000
	WRTH	Wood River, Ill.	1000	1000
	WVLK	Lexington, Ky.	5000	1000
	WEEI	Boston, Mass.	5000	5000
	WJMS	Ironwood, Mich.	5000	1000
	WKZO	Kalamazoo, Mich.	5000	5000
	KGLE	Glendive, Mont.	500	
	WOW	Omaha, Neb.	5000	5000
	WROW	Albany, N.Y.	5000	1000
	WCAB	Rutherfordton, N.C.	500	
	WGTM	Wilson, N.C.	5000	5000
	KUGN	Eugene, Ore.	5000	1000
	WARM	Scranton, Pa.	5000	5000
	WMBS	Uniontown, Pa.	1000	1000
	KLBJ	Austin, Tex.	5000	1000
	KSUB	Cedar City, Utah	5000	1000
	WLVA	Lynchburg, Va.	1000	1000
	KHQ	Spokane, Wash.	5000	5000
	CFNL	Fort Nelson, B.C.	250	250
	CFTK	Terrace, B.C.	1000	1000
	CFAR	Flin Flon, Man.	10000	1000
	CJCW	Sussex, N.B.	1000	250
	VOCM	St. John's, Nfld.	10000	10000
	CKEY	Toronto, Ont.	10000	10000
	CKRS	Jonquiere, Que.	10000	5000
	XEZZZ	Hidalgo, Chis.	1000	1000
	XEPH	Mexico City, D.F.	5000	5000
	XEE	Durango, Dgo.	1000	500
	XEHQ	Hermosillo, Son.	1500	1500
	XEFD	Rio Bravo, Tams.	5000	250
	CMW	Havana, Cuba	150000	150000
	....	Roseau, Dom.	10000	10000
	HIAB	Puerto Plata, Dom. Rep.	500	500

600 (REGIONAL)

	WIRB	Enterprise, Ala.	1000	
	KCLS	Flagstaff, Ariz.	5000	500
	KESR	Independence, Calif.	500	
	KSXO	Redding, Calif.	1000	1000
	KOGO	San Diego, Calif.	5000	5000
	KIIX	Ft. Collins, Colo.	5000	500
	WICC	Bridgeport, Conn.	1000	500
	WOKV	Jacksonville, Fla.	5000	5000
	WMT	Cedar Rapids, Ia.	5000	5000
	WVOG	New Orleans, La.	1000	
	WFST	Caribou, Me.	5000	
	WCAO	Baltimore, Md.	5000	5000
	WBDN	Escanaba, Mich.	1000	
	WTAC	Flint, Mich.	1000	500
	KGEZ	Kalispell, Mont.	5000	1000
	WCVP	Murphy, N.C.	1000	
	WSJS	Winston Salem, N.C.	5000	5000
	KSJB	Jamestown, N.D.	5000	5000
	WSOM	Salem, O.	500	
	WFRM	Coudersport, Pa.	1000	
	WAEL	Mayaguez, P.R.	1000	1000
	WREC	Memphis, Tenn.	5000	5000
	KROD	El Paso, Tex.	5000	5000
	KERB	Kermit, Tex.	1000	
	KTBB	Tyler, Tex.	1000	1000
	WVAR	Richwood, W.V.	1000	
	CJOR	Vancouver, B.C.	10000	10000
	CFCT	Tuktoyaktuk, N.W.T.	1000	1000
	CKCL	Truro, N.S.	10000	1000
	CFCH	North Bay, Ont.	10000	5000
	CFCF	Montreal, Que.	5000	5000
	CFQC	Saskatoon, Sask.	10000	10000
	XEPAC	Palenque, Chis.	500	100
	XEDN	Torreon, Coah.	1000	1000
	XEGTO	Arperos, Gto.	5000	250
	XEBB	Acapulco, Gro.	5000	1000
	XETA	Zitacuaro, Mich.	500	150
	XEMN	Monterrey, N.L.	5000	250

XERJ	Mazatlan, Sin.	5000	1000
XEZ	Merida, Yuc.	5000	1000
HIFS	San Francisco De Macoris, Dom. Rep.	250	100

610 (REGIONAL)

WSGN	Birmingham, Ala.	5000	1000
KARV	Russellville, Ark.	1000	500
KAVL	Lancaster, Calif.	1000	500
KFRC	San Francisco, Calif.	5000	5000
WSNG	Torrington, Conn.	1000	500
WIOD	Miami, Fla.	10000	5000
WHYM	Pensacola, Fla.	500	
WCEH	Hawkinsville, Ga.	500	
WRUS	Russellville, Ky.	5000q	
KDAL	Duluth, Minn.	5000	5000
WDAF	Kansas City, Mo.	5000	5000
KOJM	Havre, Mont.	1000	1000
KCSR	Chadron, Neb.	1000	
WGIR	Manchester, N.H.	5000	1000
KRKE	Albuquerque, N.M.	5000	5000
WAYS	Charlotte, N.C.	5000	1000
WTVN	Columbus, O.	5000	5000
WIP	Philadelphia, Pa.	5000	5000
KILT	Houston, Tex.	5000	5000
KVNU	Logan, Utah	5000	1000
WSLC	Roanoke, Va.	5000	1000
WVAI	Winchester, Va.	500	500
KONA	Pasco, Wash.	5000	5000
CKYL	Peace River, Alta.	10000	10000
CHNL	Kamloops, B.C.	25000	5000
CJAT	Trail, B.C.	10000	1000
CHTM	Thompson, Man.	1000	1000
CKYQ	Grand Bank, Nfld.	1000	1000
CKTB	St. Catherines, Ont.	10000	5000
CKML	Mont Laurier, Que.	1000	250
CHNC	New Carlisle, Que.	10000	5000
CKRW	Whitehorse, Yuk.	1000	1000
XEBX	Sabinas, Coah.	3000	500
XEUF	Uruapan, Mich.	5000	1000
XEKZ	Tehuantepec, Oax.	1000	500
XECV	Ciudad Valles, S.L.P.	1000	250
XEGS	Guasave, Sin.	1000	500
† ----	Ciudad Obregon, Son.	1000	250
XEJA	Jalapa, Ver.	1000	500
XEEL	Fresnillo, Zac.	5000	1000
CMHV	Trinidad, Cuba	1000	1000
VPL6	Port Of Spain, Trinidad	10000	10000

620 (REGIONAL)

WWLX	Lexington, Ala.	5000	
KGTL	Homer, Alas.	5000	
KTAR	Phoenix, Ariz.	5000	5000
KNGS	Hanford, Calif.	1000	1000
KWSD	Mt. Shasta, Calif.	1000	
KSTR	Grand Junction, Colo.	5000	
WSUN	St. Petersburg, Fla.	5000	5000
WTRP	La Grange, Ga.	1000	
KIPA	Hilo, Haw.	5000	5000
KWAL	Wallace, Id.	1000	1000
KMNS	Sioux City, Ia.	1000	1000
WTMT	Louisville, Ky.	500	
WZON	Bangor, Me.	5000	5000
WJDX	Jackson, Miss.	5000	1000
WSKQ	Newark, N.J.	5000	5000
WHEN	Syracuse, N.Y.	5000	1000
WDNC	Durham, N.C.	5000	1000
KGW	Portland, Ore.	5000	5000
WHJB	Greensburg, Pa.	2500	500
WLFF	Cayce, S.C.	500	
WRJZ	Knoxville, Tenn.	5000	5000
KWFT	Wichita Falls, Tex.	5000	5000
WVMT	Burlington, Vt.	5000	5000
WWNR	Beckley, W.V.	1000	500
WTMJ	Milwaukee, Wis.	5000	5000
CJCI	Prince George, B.C.	10000	10000
CKCM	Grand Falls, Nfld.	10000	10000
CFCL	Timmins, Ont.	10000	5000
CFRP	Forestville, Que.	1000	1000
CKCK	Regina, Sask.	10000	10000
XEBU	Chihuahua, Chih.	5000	250
XENK	Mexico City, D.F.	10000	5000
XECK	Durango, Dgo.	1000	100
XEOO	Tepic, Nay.	1000	250
XEKX	Carillo Puerto, Q.R.	1000	250
XEACM	Villahermosa, Tab.	5000	100
XEGH	Rio Bravo, Tams.	250	
....	Ottos, Anti.	500	500
HISD	Santo Domingo, Dom. Rep.	50000	2500
....	Spur Tree, Jamaica	5000	5000

625

TIRICA	San Jose, Costa Rica	100000	100000

630 (REGIONAL)

WAVU	Albertville, Ala.	1000	
WJDB	Thomasville, Ala.	1000	
KJNO	Juneau, Alas.	1000	500
KVMA	Magnolia, Ark.	1000	
KIDD	Monterey, Calif.	1000	1000
KHOW	Denver, Colo.	5000	5000
WMAL	Washington, D. C.	5000	5000
WKBX	Savannah, Ga.	5000	5000
WNEG	Toccoa, Ga.	500	
KIDO	Boise, Id.	5000	5000
WLAP	Lexington, Ky.	5000	1000
‡ KTIB	Thibodaux, La.	500	1000
KDWB	St. Paul, Minn.	5000	500
KXOK	St. Louis, Mo.	5000	5000
‡ KGVW	Belgrade, Mont.	1000	
KOH	Reno, Nev.	5000	1000
KLEA	Lovington, N.M.	500	
WIRC	Hickory, N.C.	1000	
WMFD	Wilmington, N.C.	1000	1000
KSHR	Coquille, Ore.	5000	1000
WEJL	Scranton, Pa.	500	
WQBS	San Juan, P.R.	5000	5000
WPRO	Providence, R.I.	5000	5000
KSLR	San Antonio, Tex.	5000	5000
KSXX	Sandy, Utah	1000	500
KGDN	Edmonds, Wash.	5000	2500
KGGR	Opportunity, Wash.	1000	
CHED	Edmonton, Alta.	50000	50000
CKOV	Kelowna, B.C.	5000	1000
CKRC	Winnipeg, Man.	10000	10000
CFCO	Chatham, Ont.	10000	1000
CFBK	Huntsville, Ont.	1000	1000
CJET	Smith's Falls, Ont.	10000	10000
CFCY	Charlottetown, P.E.	10000	10000
CJLA	Lachute, Que.	500	1000
CHLT	Sherbrooke, Que.	10000	5000
XETS	Tapachula, Chis.	3000	500
XEACA	Acapulco, Gro.	5000	250
★ XEJB	Guadalajara, Jal.	10000	500
XEFB	Monterrey, N.L.	10000	10000
XETK	Mazatlan, Sin.	1000	250
† ----	Cananea, Son.	750	
XEFX	Guaymas, Son.	1000	250
XEFU	Cosamaloapan, Ver.	5000	1000
HIBR	Cotui, Dom. Rep.	500	250
HIAF	Monte Cristi, Dom. Rep.	1000	1000

640 (CLEAR)

KFI	Los Angeles, Calif.	50000	50000
★ WOI	Ames, Ia.	5000	

†	KTIB	Thibodaux, La.	5000	
†	KGVW	Belgrade, Mont.	10000	1000
	WHLO	Akron, O.	1000	500
	WWLS	Norman, Okla.	1000	
†	WMSO	Collierville, Tenn.	10000	
	CBN	St. John's, Nfld.	10000	10000
	XEWM	San Cristobal, Chis.	1000	
†	----	Nadlingo, Ver.	1000	1000
	CMQ	Havana, Cuba	50000	50000
	HIBX	Moca, Dom. Rep.	1000	250
	....	Basse Terre, Gren.	20000	20000
	....	Riverfield, Montserrat	25000	25000
	TGW	Guatemala City, Guatemala	20000	20000

650 (CLEAR)

	KYAK	Anchorage, Alas.	50000	25000
	KORL	Honolulu, Haw.	10000	10000
	WSM	Nashville, Tenn.	50000	50000
	KIKK	Pasadena, Tex.	250	
	XEZM	Zamora, Mich.	5000	
	XETNT	Los Mochis, Sin.	500	
	XEVG	Merida, Yuc.	1000	500
	CMKU	Santiago De Cuba, Cuba	2000	2000
	HIAT	Santo Domingo, Dom. Rep.	10000	2000

660 (CLEAR)

	KFAR	Fairbanks, Alas.	10000	10000
†	----	Window Rock, Ariz.	50000	50000
	KCRO	Omaha, Neb.	1000	
	WNBC	New York, N.Y.	50000	50000
	WESC	Greenville, S.C.	10000	
	KSKY	Dallas, Tex.	10000	
	XEACB	Delicias, Chih.	500	
	XERPM	Mexico City, D.F.	50000	5000
†	XEWX	Durango, Dgo.	250	
†	----	Atoyac, Gro.	500	
†	----	Monterrey, N.L.	10000	250
	XEYG	Matias Romero, Oax.	250	
	XENB	Muacuspana, Tab.	1000	
†	----	Jerez, Zac.	1000	
	CMHG	Santa Clara, Cuba	10000	10000
	HIAM	Santiago, Dom. Rep.	2000	2000
	4VUE	Port Au Prince, Haiti	5000	5000

670 (CLEAR)

*	KDLG	Dillingham, Alas.	5000	5000
†	KWXI	Glenwood, Ark.	5000	
†	KWNK	Simi Valley, Calif.	1000	
	KPUA	Hilo, Haw.	5000	5000
	KBOI	Boise, Id.	50000	50000
	WMAQ	Chicago, Ill.	50000	50000
	CHYQ	Musgravetown, Nfld.	10000	10000
	XETOR	Matamoros, Coah.	1000	
	XEIS	Ciudad Guzman, Jal.	5000	
†	----	Juchitan, Oax.	5000	
	CMAF	Pinar Del Rio, Cuba	10000	10000
	CMKP	San Pedro De Cacocum, Cuba	50000	50000

680 (CLEAR)

*	KBRW	Barrow, Alas.	10000	5000
	KNBR	San Francisco, Calif.	50000	50000
	WWLF	St. Petersburg, Fla.	1000	
	WCNN	Atlanta, Ga.	50000w	10000
	WCTT	Corbin, Ky.	1000	1000
†	----	Pineville, La.	250	
	WCBM	Baltimore, Md.	10000	5000
	WRKO	Boston, Mass.	50000	50000
	WDBC	Escanaba, Mich.	10000	1000
	KFEQ	St. Joseph, Mo.	5000	5000
	KWKA	Clovis, N.M.	500	500
	WINR	Binghamton, N.Y.	1000	500
	WPTF	Raleigh, N.C.	50000	50000
	WRGC	Sylva, N.C.	1000	250
	WISR	Butler, Pa.	250	
	WAPA	San Juan, P.R.	10000	10000
	WKDJ	Memphis, Tenn.	10000	5000
	KKYX	San Antonio, Tex.	50000	10000
‡	KFAM	Bountiful, Utah	1000	
†	KFAM	North Salt Lake City, Utah	50000	
	KOMW	Omak, Wash.	5000	
	WCAW	Charleston, W.V.	50000	250
†	WOGO	Cornell, Wis.	2500	
	CHFA	Edmonton, Alta.	10000	10000
	CJOB	Winnipeg, Man.	50000	50000
	CIYQ	Grand Falls, Nfld.	10000	10000
	CFDR	Dartmouth, N.S.	50000	10000
‡	CKGB	Timmins, Ont.	10000	10000
	CFTR	Toronto, Ont.	25000	25000
	XEKQ	Tapachula, Chis.	5000	500
	XEFO	Chihuahua, Chih.	1000	
	XELG	Leon, Gto.	10000	5000
	XENF	Tepic, Nay.	250	
	XEORO	Guasave, Sin.	1000	1000
	XELV	Hermosillo, Son.	250	
	CMHN	Cienfuegos, Cuba	5000	500
	CMDB	Santiago De Cuba, Cuba	1000	1000

690 (CANADIAN CLEAR)

	WVOK	Birmingham, Ala.	50000	
	KZKZ	Flagstaff, Ariz.	1000	500
	KVOI	Tucson, Ariz.	250	
	KBBA	Benton, Ark.	250	
	KRMX	Pueblo, Colo.	250	
	WADS	Ansonia, Conn.	1000	
	WAPE	Jacksonville, Fla.	50000	10000
	KKUA	Honolulu, Haw.	10000	10000
	KBLI	Blackfoot, Id.	1000	
	KGGF	Coffeyville, Kan.	10000	5000
	WTIX	New Orleans, La.	10000	5000
	KTCR	Minneapolis, Minn.	500	
	KSTL	St. Louis, Mo.	1000	
	KEYR	Terrytown, Neb.	1000	
	KRCO	Prineville, Ore.	1000	
	WYIS	Phoenixville, Pa.	1000	
*	KUSD	Vermillion, S.D.	1000	
	KHEY	El Paso, Tex.	10000	10000
	KPET	Lamesa, Tex.	250	250
	KZEY	Tyler, Tex.	1000	
	WZAP	Bristol, Va.	10000	
	WNNT	Warsaw, Va.	250	
	WELD	Fisher, W.V.	500	
	WCKK	Oshkosh, Wis.	250	
	CBU	Vancouver, B.C.	50000	50000
	CBF	Montreal, Que.	50000	50000
	XETRA	Tijuana, B.C.	50000	50000
	XEN	Mexico City, D.F.	20000	5000
	XERG	Monterrey, N.L.	2500	500
	XETRN	Progreso, Yuc.	50000	50000
	XEMA	Fresnillo, Zac.	5000	250
	CMBC	Havana, Cuba	50000	50000
	HIAW	Santo Domingo, Dom. Rep.	5000	5000

695

	....	Roseau, Dom.	500	500

700 (CLEAR)

	KBYR	Anchorage, Alas.	1000	500
†	KRMW	Silt, Colo.	50000	1000
†	WCAT	Orange,	1000	
	WLW	Cincinnati, O.	50000	50000
†	KGRV	Winston, Ore.	1000	
†	KMTI	Newport, Wash.	1000	
	XETN	Moroleon, Gto.	1000	1000

XEDKR	Guadalajara, Jal.	1000	
† ----	Ciudad Valles, S.L.P.	1000	
† ----	Tamazunchale, S.L.P.	250	
XEVC	Cordoba, Ver.	500	
CMJT	Ciego De Avila, Cuba	1000	1000
HIDC	Valverde, Dom. Rep.	1000	1000
....	Montego Bay, Jamaica	5000	5000

705

....	Kingstown, St. Vin.	500	500

710 (CLEAR)

WKRG	Mobile, Ala.	1000	500
KUET	Black Canyon City, Ariz.	1000	1000
KAPZ	Bald Knob, Ark.	250	
KFIA	Carmichael, Calif.	10000	25000
KMPC	Los Angeles, Calif.	50000	10000
KNUS	Denver, Colo.	5000	5000
WGBS	Miami, Fla.	50000	50000
WUFF	Eastman, Ga.	1000	
WROM	Rome, Ga.	1000	
WEKC	Williamsburg, Ky.	1000	
KEEL	Shreveport, La.	50000	5000
WOZW	Monticello, Me.	2500	
WEPA	Eupora, Miss.	2500	
WHB	Kansas City, Mo.	10000	5000
WOR	New York, N.Y.	50000	50000
WZOO	Ashboro, N.C.	1000	
WEGG	Rose Hill, N.C.	250	
WKJB	Mayaguez, P.R.	5000	500
WQKI	St. Matthews, S.C.	1000	
WTPR	Paris, Tenn.	250	
WSVT	Smyrna, Tenn.	250	
KGNC	Amarillo, Tex.	10000	10000
KURV	Edinburg, Tex.	1000	250
WQBX	Blacksburg, Va.	5000	
KIRO	Seattle, Wash.	50000	50000
WDSM	Superior, Wis.	10000	5000
CKVO	Clarenceville, Nfld.	10000	10000
CHYR	Leamington, Ont.	10000	
CJRN	Niagara Falls, Ont.	5000	2500
CIPC	Port Cartier, Que.	1000	1000
CKVM	Ville Marie, Que.	10000	1000
CFRG	Gravelbourg, Sask.	5000	
XEON	Tuxtla, Chis.	3000	1000
XEDP	Cuahutemoc, Chih.	5000	
XEPQ	Muzquiz, Coah.	5000	1000
XERL	Colima, Col.	10000	10000
XEMP	Mexico City, D.F.	1000	1000
† XEX-1	Leon, Gto.	500	200
XEKU	Acapulco, Gro.	500	150
XERK	Tepic, Nay.	1000	175
XERPO	Oaxaca, Oax.	1000	100
XEBL	Culiacan, Sin.	5000	250
XEPS	Empalme, Son.	1000	250

720 (CLEAR)

* KOTZ	Kotzebue, Alas.	5000	5000
KUAI	Eleele, Haw.	5000	5000
WGN	Chicago, Ill.	50000	50000
KDWN	Las Vegas, Nev.	50000	10000
XEQZ	Lagos, Jal.	1000	
† ----	San Juan, Jal.	500	
XESOM	Sombrerete, Zac.	2500	
CMGN	Colon, Cuba	30000	30000
HIAQ	Santiago, Dom. Rep.	1000	1000
ZQI	Kingston, Jamaica	5000	5000

730 (MEXICAN CLEAR)

‡ WJMW	Athens, Ala.	1000	
KSUD	West Memphis, Ark.	250	
WLOR	Thomasville, Ga.	5000	
† KTOX	Boise, Id.	500	
KLOE	Goodland, Kan.	1000	
WFMW	Madisonville, Ky.	500	
WMTC	Vancleve, Ky.	5000	
KTRY	Bastrop, La.	250	
WARB	Covington, La.	250	
WJTO	Bath, Me.	1000	
WACE	Chicopee, Mass.	5000	
WVIC	East Lansing, Mich.	500	
KWOA	Worthington, Minn.	1000	
KWRE	Warrenton, Mo.	1000	
KURL	Billings, Mont.	500	
KDAZ	Albuquerque, N.M.	1000	
WDOS	Oneonta, N.Y.	1000	
WFMC	Goldsboro, N.C.	1000	
WOHS	Shelby, N.C.	1000	
WJYM	Bowling Green, O.	1000	
KRVC	Medford, Ore.	1000	
WNAK	Nanticoke, Pa.	1000	
WPIT	Pittsburgh, Pa.	5000	
WPAL	Charleston, S.C.	1000	
WLIL	Lenoir City, Tenn.	1000	
KKDA	Grand Prairie, Tex.	500	
KSVN	Ogden, Utah	1000	
WRMR	Alexandria, Va.	5000	
WMNA	Gretna, Va.	1000	
WJMT	Merrill, Wis.	1000	
CKLG	Vancouver, B.C.	50000	50000
CKDM	Dauphin, Man.	10000	5000
CKGA	Gander, Nfld.	1000	1000
CJNR	Blind River, Ont.	1000	500
CHIR	Leamington, Ont.	0	500
† CKGB	Timmins, Ont.	25000	25000
CKAC	Montreal, Que.	50000	50000
XEX	Mexico City, D.F.	100000	100000
CMKJ	Holguin, Cuba	10000	10000
CMAQ	Pinar Del Rio, Cuba	1000	1000
HIZ	Santo Domingo, Dom. Rep.	5000	1000
VP4RD	Port Of Spain, Trinidad	20000	20000

740 (CANADIAN CLEAR)

WBAM	Montgomery, Ala.	50000	
KMEO	Phoenix, Ariz.	1000	
KBRT	Avalon, Calif.	10000	
KCBS	San Francisco, Calif.	50000	50000
KSSS	Colorado Springs, Colo.	1000	250
KVFC	Cortez, Colo.	1000	250
WSBR	Boca Raton, Fla.	1000	500
WKIS	Orlando, Fla.	5000	1000
‡ KTOX	Boise, Id.	500	
WVLN	Olney, Ill.	250	
KBOE	Oskaloosa, Ia.	250	
WNOP	Newport, Ky.	1000	
WCAS	Cambridge, Mass.	250	
KBAD	Carlsbad, N.M.	1000	250
WGSM	Huntington, N.Y.	25000	
WMBL	Morehead City, N.C.	1000	
WPAQ	Mt. Airy, N.C.	10000	
KRMG	Tulsa, Okla.	50000	25000
WVCH	Chester, Pa.	1000	
WIAC	San Juan, P.R.	10000	10000
WBAW	Barnwell, S.C.	1000	
WSVQ	Harrogate, Tenn.	1000p	
WIRJ	Humboldt, Tenn.	250	
WCWY	Tullahoma, Tenn.	250	
KTRH	Houston, Tex.	50000	50000
KCMC	Texarkana, Tex.	1000	1000
WMBG	Williamsburg, Va.	500	
WRNR	Martinsburg, W.V.	500	
WRPQ	Baraboo, Wis.	250	
† ----	Hudson, Wis.	500	

Call	Location	Day	Night
CBX	Edmonton, Alta.	50000	50000
CBL	Toronto, Ont.	50000	50000
XELTZ	El Puertecito, Ags.	3300	5000
† ----	Cuahutemoc, Chih.	5000	250
XEEJ	Puerto Vallarta, Jal.	1000	1000
XEFZ	Monterrey, N.L.	500	500
† ----	Ixtepec, Oax.	1000	
† ----	Hermosillo, Son.	1000	250
XEZA	Topolobampo, Son.	1000	500
XEKV	Villahermosa, Tab.	1000	250
XEYAA	Peto, Yuc.	10000	
XELTZ	Loreto, Zac.	5000	250
CMJL	Camaguey, Cuba	10000	10000

750 (CLEAR)

Call	Location	Day	Night
KFQD	Anchorage, Alas.	50000	10000
WSB	Atlanta, Ga.	50000	50000
WBMD	Baltimore, Md.	1000	
† KERR	Polson, Mont.	50000	1000
KMMJ	Grand Island, Neb.	10000	
WHEB	Portsmouth, N.H.	1000	
KSEO	Durant, Okla.	250	
KXL	Portland, Ore.	50000	1000
WPDX	Clarksburg, W.V.	1000	
CBGY	Bonavista Bay, Nfld.	10000	10000
XEKOK	Las Cruces, Gro.	1000	
XEMBA	Tacambaro, Mich.	1000	1000
XEQF	Loma Bonita, Oax.	5000	1000
HIGB	Santiago, Dom. Rep.	1000	250
----	Point Galina, Jamaica	5000	5000
YNX	Managua, Nicaragua	50000	50000

760 (CLEAR)

Call	Location	Day	Night
† KMTL	Sherwood, Ark.	5000	
KFMB	San Diego, Calif.	5000	5000
† ----	Palm City, Fla.	5000	250
KGU	Honolulu, Haw.	10000	10000
† ----	Leicester, Mass.	5000	
WJR	Detroit, Mich.	50000	50000
WCPS	Tarboro, N.C.	1000	
WORA	Mayaguez, P.R.	5000	5000
† KSJL	San Antonio, Tex.	5000	
XERA	San Cristobal, Chis.	8000	1000
XEDGO	Durango, Dgo.	1000	500
XEZZ	Tonala, Jal.	5000	
XEABC	Los Reyes, Mich.	20000	5000
† ----	Monterrey, N.L.	5000	
XEEQ	San Luis Potosi, S.L.P.	250	
XECNO	Concepcion Oro, Zac.	1000	
CMCI	Havana, Cuba	10000	10000
4VI	Aux Cayes, Haiti	20000	20000

770 (CLEAR)

Call	Location	Day	Night
† WJMW	Athens, Ala.	10000	500
† KJCB	Lafayette, La.	1000	
* KUOM	Minneapolis, Minn.	5000	
* WCAL	Northfield, Minn.	5000	
WEW	St. Louis, Mo.	1000	
KOB	Albuquerque, N.M.	50000	50000
WABC	New York, N.Y.	50000	50000
KXA	Seattle, Wash.	50000r	500000
XEHB	San Francisco, Del Oro, Chih.	500	
XEML	Apatzingan, Mich.	1000	
† ----	Juchitan, Oax.	5000	
XEGK	Tamazunchale, S.L.P.	1000	
XEMV	Los Mochis, Sin.	2500	
† ----	Cordoba, Ver.	250	
HIBK	Santo Domingo, Dom. Rep.	1000	100
....	Mandeville, Jamaica	5000	5000

780 (CLEAR)

Call	Location	Day	Night
* KNOM	Nome, Alas.	10000	5000
KAZM	Sedona, Ariz.	5000	250
WBBM	Chicago, Ill.	50000	50000
WJAG	Norfolk, Neb.	1000	
KROW	Reno, Nev.	50000	50000
WCKB	Dunn, N.C.	1000	
WBBO	Forest City, N.C.	1000	
KSPI	Stillwater, Okla.	250	
WABS	Arlington, Va.	1000	
XEZN	Celaya, Gto.	500	
XEXY	Ciudad Altimirano, Gro.	1000	1000
XELD	Autlan, Jal.	5000	1000
† ----	Miahuatlan, Oax.	250	
† ----	Coatzintla, Ver.	250	
4VIE	Jeremie, Haiti	500	500
ZBVI	Roadtown, Tortula, Br V I, Virgin Is.	10000	10000
CMJN	Camaguey, Cuba	60000	60000

790 (REGIONAL)

Call	Location	Day	Night
WTSK	Tuscaloosa, Ala.	2500	
KCAM	Glennallen, Alas.	5000	5000
KCEE	Tucson, Ariz.	5000	500
KURM	Rogers, Ark.	1000	
KOSY	Texarkana, Ark.	1000	500
KXQR	Clovis, Calif.	500	
KEKA	Eureka, Calif.	5000	5000
KABC	Los Angeles, Calif.	5000	5000
WLBE	Leesburg, Fla.	5000	1000
WPFA	Pensacola, Fla.	1000	
WNWS	South Miami, Fla.	5000	5000
WQXI	Atlanta, Ga.	5000	1000
WYNR	Brunswick, Ga.	500	
WGRA	Cairo, Ga.	1000	
KKON	Kealakekua, Haw.	5000	5000
KSPD	Boise, Id.	1000	
KBRV	Soda Springs, Id.	5000	
WRMS	Beardstown, Ill.	500	
KXXX	Colby, Kan.	5000	
WAKY	Louisville, Ky.	5000	1000
WRUM	Rumford, Me.	1000	
WSGW	Saginaw, Mich.	5000	1000
KGHL	Billings, Mont.	5000	5000
WTNY	Watertown, N.Y.	1000	1000
WLSV	Wellsville, N.Y.	1000	
WTNC	Thomasville, N.C.	1000	
KFGO	Fargo, N.D.	5000	5000
WHTH	Heath, O.	1000	
KWIL	Albany, Ore.	1000	1000
WAEB	Allentown, Pa.	1000	1000
WPIC	Sharon, Pa.	1000	
WEAN	Providence, R.I.	5000	5000
WWBD	Bamberg, S.C.	1000	
WAJN	Ashland City, Tenn.	250	
WETB	Johnson City, Tenn.	5000	
WMC	Memphis, Tenn.	5000	5000
KKBQ	Houston, Tex.	5000	5000
KFYO	Lubbock, Tex.	5000	1000
KUTA	Blanding, Utah	1000	
WSIG	Mount Jackson, Va.	1000	
WTAR	Norfolk, Va.	5000	5000
KGMI	Bellingham, Wash.	5000	1000
KJRB	Spokane, Wash.	5000	5000
WEAQ	Eau Claire, Wis.	5000	5000
CFCW	Camrose, Alta.	50000	50000
CFAN	Newcastle, N.B.	5000	1000

CFNW	Port Aux Choix, Nfld.	1000	1000
CKMW	Brampton, Ont.	5000	5000
CKSO	Sudbury, Ont.	50000	50000
CKBH	Baie Comeau, Que.	1000	1000
XEBI	Aguascalientes, Ags.	1000	250
XESU	Mexicali, B.C.	1000	
XENT	La Paz, B.C.S.	5000	750
XERPC	Chihuahua, Chih.	5000	400
XERC	Mexico City, D.F.	10000	1000
XEGZ	Gomez Palacio, Dgo.	1000	250
XEAN	Ocotlan, Jal.	25000	175
XECAP	Zacapu, Mich.	1000	1000
XELN	Linares, N.L.	1000	250
XEVA	Villahermosa, Tab.	10000	500
XEFE	Nuevo Laredo, Tams.	1000	500
CMCH	Havana, Cuba	10000	10000
HIL	Santo Domingo, Dom. Rep.	5000	5000

800 (MEXICAN CLEAR)

WHOS	Decatur, Ala.	1000	
WMGY	Montgomery, Ala.	1000	
KINY	Juneau, Alas.	5000	5000
KAGH	Crossett, Ark.	250	
KVOM	Morrilton, Ark.	250	
KHIS	Bakersfield, Calif.	250	
KLTT	Brighton, Colo.	1000	
WLAD	Danbury, Conn.	1000	
WSST	Largo, Fla.	250	
WSUZ	Palatka, Fla.	1000	
WJAT	Swainsboro, Ga.	1000	
WKZI	Casey, Ill.	250	
KXIC	Iowa City, Ia.	1000	
WKVE	Cave City, Ky.	250	
WSHO	New Orleans, La.	1000	
WCCM	Lawrence, Mass.	1000	
KQAD	Luverne, Minn.	500	
WVAL	Sauk Rapids, Minn.	250	
KREI	Farmington, Mo.	1000	
WTMR	Camden, N.J.	5000	
KQCV	Oklahoma City, Okla.	250	
KPDQ	Portland, Ore.	1000	
WCHA	Chambersburg, Pa.	1000	
WDSC	Dillon, S.C.	1000	
WEAB	Greer, S.C.	250	
WDEH	Sweetwater, Tenn.	1000	
KDDD	Dumas, Tex.	250	
KBUH	Brigham City, Utah	500	
WSVS	Crewe, Va.	5000	
KQIN	Burien, Wash.	500	
WKEE	Huntington, W.V.	5000	
WDUX	Waupaca, Wis.	5000	
CJJC	Langley, B.C.	10000	10000
CKOK	Penticton, B.C.	10000	10000
* VOWR	St. John's, Nfld.	5000	2500
CJBQ	Belleville, Ont.	10000	10000
CFOB	Ft. Frances, Ont.	1000	500
CBQ	Thunder Bay, Ont.	10000	5000
CKLW	Windsor, Ont.	50000	50000
CJAD	Montreal, Que.	50000	10000
CHRC	Quebec, Que.	50000	50000
CHAB	Moose Jaw, Sask.	10000	10000
XEMMM	Tijuana, B.C.	500	
XEROK	Ciudad Juarez, Chih.	150000	150000
XEZV	Tlapa, Gro.	1000	
HICF	Nagua, Dom. Rep.	1000	250
PJB	Bonaire, Ne. Antil.	500000	500000

810 (CLEAR)

WJXL	Jacksonville, Ala.	50000	500
KGO	San Francisco, Calif.	50000	50000
KWSR	Rifle, Colo.	1000	
WBLW	Royston, Ga.	250	
WDDW	Johnston City, Ill.	250	
WATI	Indianapolis, Ind.	250	
WEKG	Jackson, Ky.	1000	
WYRE	Annapolis, Md.	250	
WJPW	Rockford, Mich.	500	
WSJC	Magee, Miss.	50000	500
KCMO	Kansas City, Mo.	50000	5000
KAFE	Santa Fe, N.M.	5000	
WGY	Schenectady, N.Y.	50000	50000
WKBC	North Wilkesboro, N.C.	1000	
WCEC	Rocky Mount, N.C.	1000	
WEDO	Mc Keesport, Pa.	1000	
WKVM	San Juan, P.R.	50000	50000
WQIZ	St. George, S.C.	5000	
KBHB	Sturgis, S.D.	5000	
† ----	Alamo, Tenn.	250	
WMTS	Murfreesboro, Tenn.	5000	
KXOI	Crane, Tex.	1000	500
WPED	Crozet, Va.	500	
KTRQ	Ephrata, Wash.	10000	
WDMP	Dodgeville, Wis.	250	
WJJQ	Tomahawk, Wis.	10000	
CHQR	Calgary, Alta.	50000	50000
CKJS	Winnipeg, Man.	10000	10000
CJVA	Caraquet, N.B.	10000	
XEIN	Cintalapa, Chis.	1000	
XEOE	Tapachula, Chis.	1000	250
XEIM	Saltillo, Coah.	500	
XEAGR	Acapulco, Gro.	1000	150
XEYM	Morelia, Mich.	1000	
XEUX	Tuxpan, Nay.	10000	250
† ----	Cozumel, Q.R.	5000	5000
XERSV	Ciudad Obregon, Son.	5000	250
XERI	Reynosa, Tams.	1000	250
XEFW	Tampico, Tams.	50000	50000
XEHT	Huamantla, Tlax.	500	
XEZC	Rio Grande, Zac.	1000	125
CMJE	Camaguey, Cuba	1000	1000

820 (CLEAR)

† KCBF	Fairbanks, Alas.	10000	1000
WAIT	Chicago, Ill.	5000	5000 f
* WSWI	Evansville, Ind.	250	
* WOSU	Columbus, O.	5000	5000 f
WBAP	Ft. Worth, Tex.	50000	50000
XEESC	Escarcega, Cam.	750	
XESB	Santa Barbara, Chih.	750	
XEBA	Guadalajara, Jal.	10000	1000
XEKG	Fortin De Las Flores, Ver.	1000	
HIAZ	Santiago, Dom. Rep.	3000	3000

830 (CLEAR)

KABN	Long Island, Alas.	10000	10000
KIKI	Honolulu, Haw.	10000	10000
WCCO	Minneapolis, Minn.	50000	50000
KBOA	Kennett, Mo.	1000	
* WNYC	New York, N.Y.	1000	50000
XELA	Mexico City, D.F.	10000	10000
XEMCH	Cheran, Mich.	1000	
† ----	San Diego, Pue.	200	250
XEVQ	Navolato, Sin.	1000	
XELK	Zacatecas, Zac.	1000	100
XEUA	Zacatecas, Zac.	1000	
CMCA	Havana, Cuba	10000	10000
HIBJ	Santo Domingo, Dom. Rep.	50000	1000
4VEF	Cap Haitien, Haiti	2500	2500

840 (CLEAR)

WWAX	Mobile, Ala.	1000	
† KBLC	Lakeport, Calif.	1000	500
WRYM	New Britain, Conn.	1000	
WHAS	Louisville, Ky.	50000	50000

WVPO	Stroudsburg, Pa.	250	
WXEW	Yabucoa, P.R.	5000	5000
† KJTA	Pharr, Tex.	50000	1000
XECUC	Campeche, Cam.	500	
† XEIO	Tuxtla, Chis.	10000	
XEFG	Celaya, Gto.	1000	1000
XETEY	Tepic, Nay.	500	
XEMY	Ciudad Mante, Tams.	1000	1000
CMDT	Las Mercedes, Cuba	1000	1000
CMHW	Santa Clara, Cuba	10000	10000
....	Castries, St. Luc.	10000	10000

850 (CLEAR)

WYDE	Birmingham, Ala.	50000	1000
KICY	Nome, Alas.	10000	10000
KGKO	Benton, Ark.	1000	
KGOE	Thousand Oaks, Calif.	500	500
KOA	Denver, Colo.	50000	50000
WVFR	Ridgefield, Conn.	500	
WRUF	Gainesville, Fla.	5000	5000
WEAT	West Palm Beach, Fla.	1000	1000
WCUG	Cuthbert, Ga.	500	
WPTB	Statesboro, Ga.	1000	1000
KHLO	Hilo, Haw.	5000	1000
WIVS	Crystal Lake, Ill.	500	
KLEU	Waterloo, Ia.	500	
WHDH	Boston, Mass.	50000	50000
WKBZ	Muskegon, Mich.	1000	1000
WWJC	Duluth, Minn.	10000	
WJYV	Forest, Miss.	10000	
WLRC	Walnut, Miss.	250	
* KFUO	Clayton, Mo.	5000	
WOZO	Pennyan, N.Y.	500	
WKIX	Raleigh, N.C.	50000r	5000
WJW	Cleveland, O.	10000	5000
KRPT	Anadarko, Okla.	500	
WJAC	Johnstown, Pa.	10000	10000
WEEU	Reading, Pa.	1000	1000
WABA	Aguadilla, P.R.	500	5000
† WBLP	Fairview, Tenn.	1000	
WIVK	Knoxville, Tenn.	50000	
KEYH	Houston, Tex.	10000	
WRAP	Norfolk, Va.	5000	1000
KTAC	Tacoma, Wash.	10000	1000
CKRD	Red Deer, Alta.	10000	1000
CFVR	Abbotsford, B.C.	10000	10000
† CFYQ	Gander, Nfld.	1000	1000
† CHVO	Spainard's Bay, Nfld.	5000	5000
CKVL	Verdun, Que.	50000	10000
XEZF	Mexicali, B.C.	250	
XEM	Chihuahua, Chih.	5000	250
XEMIA	Tlaquepaque, Jal.	1000	1000
XEUS	Hermosillo, Son.	1000	1000
XETQ	Orizaba, Ver.	100000	50000
CMKC	Santiago De Cuba, Cuba	2000	2000
CMKV	Holguin, Cuba	50000	50000

855

PJC2	Curacao, Ne. Antil.	5000	5000

860 (CANADIAN CLEAR)

WHRT	Hartselle, Ala.	250	
WAMI	Opp, Ala.	1000	
KVVA	Phoenix, Ariz.	1000	
KOSE	Osceola, Ark.	1000	
KWRF	Warren, Ark.	250	
KTRB	Modesto, Calif.	10000	1000
WAMA	Clearwater, Fla.	1000	500
WKKO	Cocoa, Fla.	1000	
WAEC	Atlanta, Ga.	5000	
WDMG	Douglas, Ga.	5000	5000
WGOM	Marion, Ind.	1000	
KWPC	Muscatine, Ia.	250	
KKOW	Pittsburg, Kan.	10000	5000
WSON	Henderson, Ky.	500	
WAYE	Baltimore, Md.	5000r	
WSBS	Great Barrington, Mass.	250	
KNUJ	New Ulm, Minn.	1000	
KARS	Belen, N.M.	250	
WFMO	Fairmont, N.C.	1000	
WQXZ	Taylorsville, N.C.	250	
WTEL	Philadelphia, Pa.	10000	
WAMO	Pittsburgh, Pa.	1000	
WLBG	Laurens, S.C.	1000	
WTZX	Sparta, Tenn.	1000	
KFST	Ft. Stockton, Tex.	250	
KPAN	Hereford, Tex.	250	
KSFA	Nacogdoches, Tex.	1000	
KONO	San Antonio, Tex.	5000	1000
KWHO	Salt Lake City, Utah	1000	
WEVA	Emporia, Va.	1000	
WOAY	Oak Hill, W.V.	10000	
WNOV	Milwaukee, Wis.	250	
CFPR	Prince Rupert, B.C.	10000	10000
CHAK	Inuvik, N.W.T.	1000	1000
CBH	Halifax, N.S.	10000	10000
CJBC	Toronto, Ont.	50000	50000
CFNS	Saskatoon, Sask.	10000	10000
XEPLA	Pebellon, Ags.	4000	1000
XEMO	Tijuana, B.C.	5000	5000
XEDB	Tonala, Chis.	1000	250
XEZOL	Ciudad Juarez, Chih.	1000	500
XEZR	Zaragoza, Coah.	1000	250
XEAL	Manzanillo, Col.	5000	100
XEUN	Mexico City, D.F.	45000	25000
XEDU	Durango, Dgo.	1000	500
XENL	Monterrey, N.L.	5000	2000
XENW	Culiacan, Sin.	1000	250
XEZX	Tenosique, Tab.	1000	150
XETW	Tampico, Tams.	500	
CMJY	Ciego De Avila, Cuba	1000	1000
HILR	Santo Domingo, Dom. Rep.	50000	5000
4VDS	Port Au Prince, Haiti	500	500

870 (CLEAR)

* KSKO	Mc Grath, Alas.	5000	1000
KIEV	Glendale, Calif.	5000	1000
KAIM	Honolulu, Haw.	50000	50000
WWL	New Orleans, La.	50000	50000
* WKAR	East Lansing, Mich.	10000	
† KPRM	Park Rapids, Minn.	2500	1000
† KAAN	New Hampton, Mo.	250	
WHCU	Ithaca, N.Y.	5000	1000
WGTL	Kannapolis, N.C.	1000	
WVOZ	San Juan, P.R.	5000	5000
KJIM	Ft. Worth, Tex.	250	
WFLO	Farmville, Va.	1000	
† KORD	Pasco, Wash.	10000	250
† ----	Villa Flores, Chis.	500	
XEAMO	Irapuato, Gto.	1000	1000
† ----	Salamanca, Gto.	1000	
XELY	Morelia, Mich.	1000	
XEACC	Puerto Escondido, Oax.	500	1000
XENH	Mazatlan, Sin.	1000	500
CMDN	Guantanamo, Cuba	10000	10000
CMBL	Havana, Cuba	1000	1000

880 (CLEAR)

† ----	Gonzales, Calif.	5000	1000
KJJR	Whitefish, Mont.	10000	500
KRVN	Lexington, Neb.	50000	50000
WCBS	New York, N.Y.	50000	50000
WRRZ	Clinton, N.C.	1000	

	WRFD	Worthington, O.	5000	
	KWIP	Dallas, Ore.	5000	1000
	KISD	Medford, Ore.	1000	
†	WPRX	Sabana Granda, P.R.	1000	1000
†	WMDB	Nashville, Tenn.	2500	
†	----	Madisonville, Tex.	5000	1000
	XETZ	Zapopan, Jal.	10000	
	XEEM	Rio Verde, S.L.P.	1000	
	XEPNK	Los Mochis, Sin.	5000	
	XEQQQ	Teapa, Tab.	9000	250
†	----	Orizaba, Ver.	250	
	HIBY	Valverde, Dom. Rep.	1000	250
	4VAA	Port Au Prince, Haiti	200	200

885

	ZGB	Plymouth, Montserrat	1000	1000

890 (CLEAR)

†	----	College Park, Ga.	2500	
	WLS	Chicago, Ill.	50000	50000
	WHNC	Henderson, N.C.	1000	
	KBYE	Oklahoma City, Okla.	1000	
†	WQTW	Latrobe, Pa.	1000	
†	----	St. George, Utah	50000	50000
	XETAP	Tapachula, Chis.	1000	
	XEMAU	Miguel Auza, Zac.	10000	
	CMHD	Santa Clara, Cuba	1000	1000
	CMDZ	Santiago De Cuba, Cuba	250	250
	HIPJ	Santo Domingo, Dom. Rep.	5000	5000

900 (MEXICAN CLEAR)

	WATV	Birmingham, Ala.	1000	
	WGOK	Mobile, Ala.	1000	
	WOZK	Ozark, Ala.	1000	
‡	KCBF	Fairbanks, Alas.	10000	10000
	KHOZ	Harrison, Ark.	1000	
	KBIF	Fresno, Calif.	1000	
	KGRB	West Covina, Calif.	500	
	WJWL	Georgetown, Del.	1000	
	WSWN	Belle Glade, Fla.	1000	
	WMOP	Ocala, Fla.	5000	
	WBML	Macon, Ga.	250	
	WWJD	Savannah, Ga.	5000	
	KNUI	Kahului, Haw.	5000	25000
	KSGL	Wichita, Kan.	250	
	WEAK	Eddyville, Ky.	250	
	WFIA	Louisville, Ky.	1000	
	WLSI	Pikeville, Ky.	5000	
	KREH	Oakdale, La.	250	
	WKXA	Brunswick, Me.	1000	
	WLMD	Laurel, Md.	1000	
	WZXM	Gaylord, Mich.	1000	
⋆	KTIS	Minneapolis, Minn.	2500	
	WDDT	Greenville, Miss.	1000	
	KFAL	Fulton, Mo.	1000	
	KJSK	Columbus, Neb.	1000	
	WOTW	Nashua, N.H.	1000	
	WBRV	Boonville, N.Y.	1000	
	WKAJ	Saratoga Springs, N.Y.	500	
	WKJK	Granite Falls, N.C.	250	
	WAYN	Rockingham, N.C.	1000	
	WIAM	Williamston, N.C.	1000	
	WNYN	Canton, O.	500	500
	WFRO	Fremont, O.	500	
	WCPA	Clearfield, Pa.	1000	
	WFLN	Philadelphia, Pa.	1000	
†	WGSN	North Myrtle Beach, S.C.	500	
	WKXV	Knoxville, Tenn.	1000	
	WCOR	Lebanon, Tenn.	500	
	KALT	Atlanta, Tex.	1000	
	KIKR	Conroe, Tex.	500	
	KFBA	Floydada, Tex.	250	
	KCLW	Hamilton, Tex.	250	
	WODY	Bassett, Va.	500	
	WKDW	Staunton, Va.	1000	
	KUEN	Wenatchee, Wash.	1000	
	WATK	Antigo, Wis.	250	
	WNNO	Wisconsin Dells, Wis.	1000	
	CJVI	Victoria, B.C.	10000	10000
	CKDH	Amherst, N.S.	1000	1000
	CKDR	Dryden, Ont.	1000	250
	CHML	Hamilton, Ont.	50000	50000
	CFBR	Sudbury, Ont.	10000	1000
	CJBR	Rimouski, Que.	10000	10000
	CKTS	Sherbrooke, Que.	10000	10000
	CJER	St. Jerome, Que.	1000	1000
	CKVD	Val D' Or, Que.	10000	2500
	CKBI	Prince Albert, Sask.	10000	10000
	XEW	Mexico City, D.F.	250000	250000
†	XEW-2	Queretaro, Qro.	1000	
	XEW-1	Mazatlan, Sin.	5000	
	XEWB	Veracruz, Ver.	50000	10000
	....	Bridgetown, Barb.	10000	10000
	CMJV	Ciego De Avila, Cuba	1000	1000

910 (REGIONAL)

	WTXN	Lafayette, Ala.	1000	
	KJJJ	Phoenix, Ariz.	5000	5000
	KLCN	Blytheville, Ark.	5000	
	KAMD	Camden, Ark.	5000	500
	KMJC	El Cajon, Calif.	5000	5000
†	KHSP	Hesperia, Calif.	1000	500
	KNEW	Oakland, Calif.	5000	5000
	KOXR	Oxnard, Calif.	5000	1000
⋆	KPOF	Denver, Colo.	5000	1000
	WRCQ	New Britain, Conn.	5000	5000
	WPLA	Plant City, Fla.	1000	1000
	WGAF	Valdosta, Ga.	5000	5000
	WAKO	Lawrenceville, Ill.	500	
†	WLPD	Mishawaka, Ind.	1000	
⋆	WSUI	Iowa City, Ia.	5000	5000
	KINA	Salina, Kan.	500	
†	WKEQ	Burnside, Ky.	500	
	WLCS	Baton Rouge, La.	1000	1000
	WABI	Bangor, Me.	5000	5000
	WFDF	Flint, Mich.	5000	1000
	WALT	Meridian, Miss.	5000	1000
	KOYN	Billings, Mont.	1000	
	KBIM	Roswell, N.M.	5000	500
	WRKL	New City, N.Y.	1000	1000
	WLAS	Jacksonville, N.C.	5000	5000
	KCJB	Minot, N.D.	5000	1000
	WBRJ	Marietta, O.	5000	
	WPFB	Middletown, O.	1000	100
	KGLO	Miami, Okla.	1000	1000
	KURY	Brookings, Ore.	1000	
	WAVL	Apollo, Pa.	5000	
	WGBI	Scranton, Pa.	1000	500
	WSBA	York, Pa.	5000	1000
	WPRP	Ponce, P.R.	5000	500
	WKCN	North Charleston, S.C.	500	
	WORD	Spartanburg, S.C.	5000	1000
	KVAA	Volga, S.D.	1000	500
	WJCW	Johnson City, Tenn.	5000	1000
	WEPG	South Pittsburg, Tenn.	5000r	
	KNAF	Fredericksburg, Tex.	1000	
	KRIO	Mc Allen, Tex.	5000	5000
	KIKM	Sherman, Tex.	1000	1000
	KALL	Salt Lake City, Utah	5000	1000
	WNHV	White River Junction, Vt.	1000	
	WRNL	Richmond, Va.	5000	5000
	WTOY	Roanoke, Va.	1000	
‡	KORD	Pasco, Wash.	1000	
	KIXI	Seattle, Wash.	50000	10000
	KKSN	Vancouver, Wash.	5000	5000
	WHSM	Hayward, Wis.	5000	

WDOR	Sturgeon Bay, Wis.	1000	
CKDQ	Drumheller, Alta.	5000	10000
CFSX	Stephenville, Nfld.	500	500
CKLY	Lindsay, Ont.	10000	5000
CHRL	Roberval, Que.	10000	10000
XEAD	Mexicali, B.C.	1000	250
XEUU	Colima, Col.	500	100
XEAGN	San Francisco Del Rincon, Gto.	100	
XEMST	Mascota, Jal.	1000	1000
XEHO	Ciudad Obregon, Son.	1000	250
CMJB	Camaguey, Cuba	1000	1000
HIBA	Santo Domingo, Dom. Rep.	500	500
† ----	Port Au Prince, Haiti	10000	10000

920 (REGIONAL)

WKYD	Andalusia, Ala.	5000	500
WWWR	Russellville, Ala.	1000	
KSRM	Soldatna, Alas.	5000	5000
KARN	Little Rock, Ark.	5000	5000
KLOC	Ceres, Calif.	2500	2500
KDES	Palm Springs, Calif.	5000	1000
KVEC	San Luis Obispo, Calif.	1000	500
KLMR	Lamar, Colo.	5000	500
WTRS	Dunnellon, Fla.	500	
WMEL	Melbourne, Fla.	1000	1000
WGST	Atlanta, Ga.	5000	1000
WVOH	Hazlehurst, Ga.	500	
WGNU	Granite City, Ill.	500	500
WMOK	Metropolis, Ill.	1000	
* WBAA	West Lafayette, Ind.	5000	1000
KYFR	Shenandoah, Ia.	5000	2500
WTCW	Whitesburg, Ky.	5000	
WBOX	Bogalusa, La.	1000	1000
KTOC	Jonesboro, La.	1000	
WPTX	Lexington Park, Md.	5000	1000
WMPL	Hancock, Mich.	1000	
KDHL	Faribault, Minn.	5000	5000
KWAD	Wadena, Minn.	1000	1000
KWYS	West Yellowstone, Mont.	1000	
KORK	Las Vegas, Nev.	5000	500
KOLO	Reno, Nev.	5000	1000
WTTM	Trenton, N.J.	1000	1000
KQEO	Albuquerque, N.M.	1000	500
WKRT	Cortland, N.Y.	1000	500
WGHQ	Kingston, N.Y.	5000	500
WIRD	Lake Placid, N.Y.	5000	
WBBB	Burlington, N.C.	5000	
WPTL	Canton, N.C.	500	
WMNI	Columbus, O.	1000	500
KGAL	Lebanon, Ore.	1000	1000
WKVA	Lewistown, Pa.	1000	500
WHJJ	Providence, R.I.	5000	5000
WTND	Orangeburg, S.C.	5000r	
KKLS	Rapid City, S.D.	5000	
WLIV	Livingston, Tenn.	1000	
KYSR	El Paso, Tex.	1000	500
KYXX	Odessa, Tex.	1000	500
KYST	Texas City, Tex.	5000	1000
KVEL	Vernal, Utah	5000	1000
KQEU	Olympia, Wash.	1000	500
KXLY	Spokane, Wash.	5000	5000
WMMN	Fairmont, W.V.	5000	5000
WOKY	Milwaukee, Wis.	5000	1000
CKCQ	Quesnel, B.C.	10000	1000
CFRY	Portage La Prairie, Man.	10000	10000
CJCJ	Woodstock, N.B.	10000	1000
† ----	Lac Etchemin, Nfld.	1000	1000
CJCH	Halifax, N.S.	25000	25000
CBO	Ottawa, Ont.	50000	50000
CKCY	Sault Ste. Marie, Ont.	10000	5000
CKNX	Wingham, Ont.	10000	1000
CFLS	Levis, Que.	10000	10000
XEHC	Ensenada, B.C.	2500	200
† ----	Hopelchen, Cam.	1000	
XEVV	Chiapa De Corzo, Chis.	5000	250
XEQD	Chihuahua, Chih.	1000	250
XEMJ	Piedras Negras, Coah.	1000	250
XETAA	Torreon, Coah.	5000	200
XEDP	Villa Frontera, Coah.	1000	250
XEFAC	Salvatierra, Gto.	2000	1000
XELT	Guadalajara, Jal.	20000	250
XEOK	Monterrey, N.L.	1000	250
XEBM	San Luis Potosi, S.L.P.	5000	1000
XECQ	Culiacan, Sin.	5000	100
XEBH	Hermosillo, Son.	5000	1000
† ----	Tuxpan, Ver.	1000	
† ----	Yogope, Yuc.	1000	
HIBM	Azua, Dom. Rep.	500	500
HICK	Santiago, Dom. Rep.	2000	2000
PJA6	Aruba, Ne. Antil.	10000	10000

930 (REGIONAL)

WJBY	Gadsden, Ala.	5000	500
KTKN	Ketchikan, Alas.	5000	1000
KAPR	Douglas, Ariz.	2500	
KFLG	Flagstaff, Ariz.	5000	
KHJ	Los Angeles, Calif.	5000	5000
KEWQ	Paradise, Calif.	500	
KIUP	Durango, Colo.	5000	1000
WYUS	Milford, Del.	500	
WFXI	Haines City, Fla.	500	
WJAX	Jacksonville, Fla.	5000	5000
WKXY	Sarasota, Fla.	1000	500
WMGR	Bainbridge, Ga.	5000	5000
KSEI	Pocatello, Id.	5000	5000
WTAD	Quincy, Ill.	5000	1000
WHON	Richmond, Ind.	500	
WKCT	Bowling Green, Ky.	5000	500
WFMD	Frederick, Md.	5000	1000
WREB	Holyoke, Mass.	500	
WBCK	Battle Creek, Mich.	5000	1000
KKIN	Aitkin, Minn.	1000	
WSLI	Jackson, Miss.	5000	5000
KWOC	Poplar Bluff, Mo.	5000	500
† KYSS	East Missoula, Mont.	5000	1000
‡ KYSS	Missoula, Mont.	5000	
KOGA	Ogallata, Neb.	500	500
WWNH	Rochester, N.H.	5000	5000
WPAT	Paterson, N.J.	5000	5000
KCCC	Carlsbad, N.M.	1000	
WBEN	Buffalo, N.Y.	5000	5000
WMYL	Johnstown, N.Y.	1000	
WSOC	Charlotte, N.C.	5000	1000
WITN	Washington, N.C.	5000	1000
WEOL	Elyria, O.	1000	1000
WKY	Oklahoma City, Okla.	5000	5000
KAGI	Grants Pass, Ore.	5000	1000
KSWB	Seaside, Ore.	1000	1000
WCNR	Bloomsburg, Pa.	1000	1000
WEKO	Cabo Rojo, P.R.	500	500
KSDN	Aberdeen, S.D.	5000	1000
WSEV	Sevierville, Tenn.	5000	
KDET	Center, Tex.	1000	
KLLS	Terrell Hills, Tex.	5000	1000
WLLL	Lynchburg, Va.	5000	
KBFW	Ferndale, Wash.	1000	
KVGM	Yakima, Wash.	1000	
WGNT	Huntington, W.V.	5000	1000
* WLBL	Auburndale, Wis.	5000	
KROE	Sheridan, Wyo.	5000	
CJCA	Edmonton, Alta.	50000	50000
CFBC	St. John, N.B.	50000	50000
CJYQ	St. John's, Nfld.	50000	25000
CKNS	Espanola, Ont.	10000	10000
† XERLA	Santa Rosalia, B.C.S.	1000	250
† XEMK	Huixtla, Chis.	5000	500
XELCM	Lazaro Cardenas, Mich.	500	
† ----	Tlaxiaco, Oax.	700	

XEAR	Tampico, Tams.	1000	500
XEU	Veracruz, Ver.	5000	1000
XEIH	Fresnillo, Zac.	5000	200
CMGX	Matanzas, Cuba	1000	1000
4VJS	Les Gonaives, Haiti	250	250
....	Riverfield, Montserrat	200000	200000

940 (MEXICAN & CANADIAN CLEAR)

KNST	Tucson, Ariz.	1000	250
KFRE	Fresno, Calif.	50000	50000
WINE	Brookfield, Conn.	1000	
WLQH	Chiefland, Fla.	1000	
WINZ	Miami, Fla.	50000	25000
WMAZ	Macon, Ga.	50000	10000
KDEO	Waipahu, Haw.	10000	10000
WMIX	Mt. Vernon, Ill.	5000	500
KIOA	Des Moines, Ia.	10000	5000
WCND	Shelbyville, Ky.	250	
WYLD	New Orleans, La.	10000	500
WGKP	Webster, Mass.	1000p	
WCSY	South Haven, Mich.	1000	
WIDG	St. Ignace, Mich.	5000	
WCPC	Houston, Miss.	50000	250
KSWM	Aurora, Mo.	500	
KVSH	Valentine, Neb.	5000	
WKYK	Burnsville, N.C.	5000	250
WFNC	Fayetteville, N.C.	50000	1000
† ----	Pembroke, N.C.	10000	
WCIT	Lima, O.	250	
KGRL	Bend, Ore.	1000	
KWRC	Woodburn, Ore.	250	
WESA	Charleroi, Pa.	250	
WGRP	Greenville, Pa.	1000	
WVLV	Lebanon, Pa.	1000	
* WIPR	San Juan, P.R.	10000	10000
WECO	Wartburg, Tenn.	1000	
KIXZ	Amarillo, Tex.	5000	1000
KTON	Belton, Tex.	1000	
KADO	Texarkana, Tex.	2500	
KBRE	Cedar City, Utah	10000	
WNRG	Grundy, Va.	5000	
WKGM	Smithfield, Va.	10000	
WFAW	Fort Atkinson, Wis.	500	
WCSW	Shell Lake, Wis.	1000	
CISL	Richmond, B.C.	2500	2500
CJIB	Vernon, B.C.	10000	10000
CBM	Montreal, Que.	50000	50000
CJGX	Yorkton, Sask.	10000	10000
XEWV	Mexicali, B.C.	1000	
XEQ	Mexico City, D.F.	150000	50000
XERKS	Reynosa, Tams.	1000	1000

950 (REGIONAL)

WLSQ	Montgomery, Ala.	1000	1000
KRXA	Seward, Alas.	1000	1000
KXJK	Forrest City, Ark.	5000	
KFSA	Ft. Smith, Ark.	1000	500
KAHI	Auburn, Calif.	5000	5000
KIMN	Denver, Colo.	5000	5000
WCOT	Orlando, Fla.	5000	5000
WGTA	Summerville, Ga.	5000	
WGOV	Valdosta, Ga.	5000	1000
KOZE	Lewiston, Id.	5000	1000
KKIC	Meridian, Id.	5000	5000
KLER	Orofino, Id.	1000	1000
WJPC	Chicago, Ill.	5000	1000
WXLW	Indianapolis, Ind.	5000	500
KOEL	Oelwein, Ia.	5000	500
KJRG	Newton, Kan.	500	
WYWY	Barbourville, Ky.	1000	
KRRP	Coushatta, La.	500	
WKZX	Presque Isle, Me.	5000	5000
WCTN	Potomac, Md.	1000	
WROL	Boston, Mass.	5000	
WWJ	Detroit, Mich.	5000	5000
KRSI	St. Louis Park, Minn.	1000	1000
WBKH	Hattiesburg, Miss.	5000	
KLIK	Jefferson City, Mo.	5000	500
KMXT	Helena, Mont.	5000	5000
KNFT	Bayard, N.M.	5000	
WHVW	Hyde Park, N.Y.	500	
WBBF	Rochester, N.Y.	1000	1000
WIBX	Utica, N.Y.	5000	5000
WPET	Greensboro, N.C.	500	
WLIT	Steubenville, O.	1000	
KYES	Roseburg, Ore.	1000	
WNCC	Barnesboro, Pa.	500	
WPEN	Philadelphia, Pa.	5000	5000
WBER	Moncks Corner, S.C.	500	
WSPA	Spartanburg, S.C.	5000	5000
KWAT	Watertown, S.D.	1000	1000
WAKM	Franklin, Tenn.	1000	
KDSX	Denison, Tex.	500	500
KPRC	Houston, Tex.	5000	5000
KSEL	Lubbock, Tex.	5000	500
WXGI	Richmond, Va.	5000	
KJR	Seattle, Wash.	5000	5000
WQBE	Charleston, W.V.	5000	1000
WERL	Eagle River, Wis.	1000	
WKTS	Sheboygan, Wis.	500	
KMER	Kemmerer, Wyo.	5000	
CFAM	Altona, Man.	10000	10000
CKNB	Campbellton, N.B.	10000	1000
CHER	Sydney, N.S.	10000	10000
CKBB	Barrie, Ont.	10000	2500
XEGM	Tijuana, B.C.	10000	5000
XEMAB	Carmen, Cam.	1000	1000
† ----	San Cristobal, Chis.	1000	1000
XEFA	Chihuahua, Chih.	500	250
XEYJ	Nueva Rosita, Coah.	10000	10000
XEFY	Cortazar, Gto.	500	250
† ----	Jiquilpan, Mich.	500	
† ----	Santiago Ixcuintla, Nay.	1000	1000
XERN	Montemorelos, N.L.	5000	255
XEZB	Oaxaca, Oax.	1000	100
XEORF	El Fuerte, Sin.	5000	500
† ----	Ciudad Mante, Tams.	1000	
CMDJ	Guantanamo, Cuba	1000	1000
CMBF	Havana, Cuba	10000	10000
HIG	Santo Domingo, Dom. Rep.	2000	2000

960 (REGIONAL)

WERC	Birmingham, Ala.	5000	5000
WCVQ	Kodiak, Alas.	250	250
KOOL	Phoenix, Ariz.	5000	5000
KAVR	Apple Valley, Calif.	5000	
KNEZ	Lompoc, Calif.	500	500
KABL	Oakland, Calif.	5000	5000
WELI	New Haven, Conn.	5000	5000
WGRO	Lake City, Fla.	1000	1000
WJCM	Sebring, Fla.	1000	
WJAZ	Albany, Ga.	5000	
WRFC	Athens, Ga.	5000	500
KSRA	Salmon, Id.	1000	
* WDLM	East Moline, Ill.	1000	
WSBT	South Bend, Ind.	5000	5000
KMA	Shenandoah, Ia.	5000	5000
WPRT	Prestonburg, Ky.	5000	
KROF	Abbeville, La.	1000	
WSBY	Salisbury, Md.	5000	1000
WFGL	Fitchburg, Mass.	1000	1000
WHAK	Rogers City, Mich.	5000	
KLTF	Little Falls, Minn.	5000	
WABG	Greenwood, Miss.	1000	500
KGIR	Cape Girardeau, Mo.	5000	500
KFLN	Baker, Mont.	5000	
KNEB	Scottsbluff, Neb.	1000	500
KNDN	Farmington, N.M.	5000	
WEAV	Plattsburgh, N.Y.	5000	5000
WAAK	Dallas, N.C.	1000	500
WFTC	Kinston, N.C.	5000	1000
WWST	Wooster, O.	1000	
KGWA	Enid, Okla.	1000	1000

Call	Location	Day	Night
KLAD	Klamath Falls, Ore.	5000	5000
WHYL	Carlisle, Pa.	5000	
WKZA	Kane, Pa.	1000	
WPCN	Mt. Pocono, Pa.	1000	
WATS	Sayre, Pa.	1000	
WJYT	Quebradillas, P.R.	1000	1000
WBEU	Beaufort, S.C.	1000	
WWBR	La Follette, Tenn.	250	
WBMC	Mc Minnville, Tenn.	500	
KIMP	Mt. Pleasant, Tex.	1000	
KGKL	San Angelo, Tex.	5000	1000
KDOT	Provo, Utah	5000	1000
WFIR	Roanoke, Va.	5000	5000
KALE	Richland, Wash.	5000	1000
WOWN	Shawano, Wis.	1000	1000
CFAC	Calgary, Alta.	50000	50000
CHNS	Halifax, N.S.	10000	10000
CFTJ	Cambridge, Ont.	1000	1000
CKWS	Kingston, Ont.	10000	5000
XECC	Camargo, Chih.	1000	250
XEKS	Saltillo, Coah.	500	100
XECS	Manzanillo, Col.	1000	200
XEUQ	Zihuatenejo, Gro.	1000	250
XEHK	Guadalajara, Jal.	1000	1000
XEMM	Morelia, Mich.	500	200
XEROO	Chetumal, Q.R.	1000	500
XECZ	San Luis Potosi, S.L.P.	500	250
† ----	Culiacan, Sin.	500	250
XEIQ	Ciudad Obregon, Son.	1000	500
XEK	Nuevo Laredo, Tams.	5000	1000
XEGB	Coatzacoalcos, Ver.	1000	500
XEOZ	Jalapa, Ver.	1000	250
ZFB-1	Pembroke West, Bermuda	1000	1000
CMHB	Sancti Spiritus, Cuba	1000	1000
CMKN	Santiago De Cuba, Cuba	1000	1000
HIFF	Puerto Plata, Dom. Rep.	1000	1000
4VCD	Port Au Prince, Haiti	300	300

970 (REGIONAL)

Call	Location	Day	Night
WERH	Hamilton, Ala.	5000	
WTBF	Troy, Ala.	5000	500
KIAK	Fairbanks, Alas.	5000	5000
KVWM	Show Low, Ariz.	5000	
KNEA	Jonesboro, Ark.	1000	
KUZZ	Bakersfield, Calif.	1000	1000
KVIM	Coachella, Calif.	5000	1000
KHYV	Modesto, Calif.	1000	1000
KFEL	Pueblo, Colo.	1000	
WOZN	Jacksonville, Fla.	1000	
WFLA	Tampa, Fla.	5000	5000
WKLS	Atlanta, Ga.	5000	
WVOP	Vidalia, Ga.	5000	
KAYT	Rupert, Id.	2500	
WMAY	Springfield, Ill.	1000	500
WAVG	Louisville, Ky.	5000	5000
KSYL	Alexandria, La.	1000	1000
WCSH	Portland, Me.	5000	5000
WAMD	Aberdeen, Md.	500	500
WESO	Southbridge, Mass.	1000	
WMVN	Ishpeming, Mich.	5000	
WKHM	Jackson, Mich.	1000	1000
KQAQ	Austin, Minn.	5000	500
WRKN	Brandon, Miss.	1000	
KOOK	Billings, Mont.	5000	5000
KJLT	North Platte, Neb.	5000	
KNUU	Las Vegas, Nev.	5000	500
WWDJ	Hackensack, N.J.	5000	5000
KDCE	Espanola, N.M.	1000	
* WEBR	Buffalo, N.Y.	5000	5000
WCHN	Norwich, N.Y.	1000	
WRCS	Ahoskie, N.C.	1000	
WWIT	Canton, N.C.	5000	
WDAY	Fargo, N.D.	5000	5000
WFUN	Ashtabula, O.	5000	1000
WATH	Athens, O.	1000	
KAKC	Tulsa, Okla.	2500	1000
KYTE	Portland, Ore.	5000	5000
WBLF	Bellefonte, Pa.	1000	
WTKN	Pittsburgh, Pa.	5000	5000
WJMX	Florence, S.C.	5000	1000
WXQK	Spring City, Tenn.	500	
KIXL	Austin, Tex.	1000	1000
KNOK	Ft. Worth, Tex.	1000	
WSTX	Christiansted, V.I.	5000	1000
WYPR	Danville, Va.	1000	
WANV	Waynesboro, Va.	5000	1000
KREM	Spokane, Wash.	5000	1000
WWYO	Pineville, W.V.	1000	
* WHA	Madison, Wis.	5000	
KXTP	Superior, Wis.	1000	
CJYR	Edson, Alta.	10000	10000
CBZ	Fredericton, N.B.	10000	10000
CKCH	Hull, Que.	10000	10000
XEJ	Ciudad Juarez, Chih.	10000	5000
XEQX	Monclova, Coah.	1000	250
XEDF	Mexico City, D.F.	10000	5000
XEUG	Guanajuato, Gto.	500	
XECJ	Apatzingan, Mich.	5000	250
† ----	Juchitan, Oax.	500	
XEVOX	Mazatlan, Sin.	10000	500
XEEZ	Caborca, Son.	500	100
XEVT	Villahermosa, Tab.	5000	400
XEBJ	Ciudad Victoria, Tams.	1000	200
XEO	Matamoros, Tams.	1000	1000
XEMH	Merida, Yuc.	1000	100
† ----	Juchipila, Zac.	1000	1000

980 (REGIONAL)

Call	Location	Day	Night
WKLF	Clanton, Ala.	1000	
KFWJ	Lake Havasu City, Ariz.	1000	
KCAB	Dardanelle, Ark.	1000	
KINS	Eureka, Calif.	5000	500
KEAP	Fresno, Calif.	500	
KFWB	Los Angeles, Calif.	5000	5000
KCTY	Salinas, Calif.	1000	
KGLN	Glenwood Springs, Colo.	1000	
WSUB	Groton, Conn.	1000	
WRC	Washington, D. C.	5000	5000
WDVH	Gainesville, Fla.	5000	
WTOT	Marianna, Fla.	1000	
WBOP	Pensacola, Fla.	1000	
WBSS	Pompano Beach, Fla.	5000r	1000
WKLY	Hartwell, Ga.	1000	
WPGA	Perry, Ga.	1000	
WRIP	Rossville, Ga.	500	500
KUPI	Idaho Falls, Id.	1000	
KSGM	Chester, Ill.	1000	500
WITY	Danville, Ill.	1000	1000
† WFTG	London, Ky.	1000	
WLPQ	Pittsburg, Ky.	1000	
KCIJ	Shreveport, La.	5000	
WCAP	Lowell, Mass.	5000	5000
WOAM	Otsego, Mich.	1000	
KKSS	Minneapolis, Minn.	5000	5000
WAPF	Mc Comb, Miss.	5000	
WKOR	Starkville, Miss.	1000	
KMBZ	Kansas City, Mo.	5000	5000
KVLV	Fallon, Nev.	5000	
KICA	Clovis, N.M.	1000	1000
KMIN	Grants, N.M.	1000	
WTRY	Troy, N.Y.	5000	5000
WKLM	Wilmington, N.C.	5000	
WAAA	Winston Salem, N.C.	1000	
WONE	Dayton, O.	5000	5000
WILK	Wilkes Barre, Pa.	5000	1000
WAZS	Summerville, S.C.	1000	
WBZK	York, S.C.	1000	
KDSJ	Deadwood, S.D.	5000	1000
WSIX	Nashville, Tenn.	5000	5000
KFRD	Rosenberg, Tex.	1000	
KVRN	Sonora, Tex.	1000	
KSVC	Richfield, Utah	5000	1000
WFHG	Bristol, Va.	5000	1000
WMEK	Chase City, Va.	500	

Call	Location	Day	Night
KUTI	Yakima, Wash.	5000	500
WHAW	Weston, W.V.	1000	
WCUB	Manitowoc, Wis.	5000	
WNBI	Park Falls, Wis.	1000	
WPRE	Prairie Du Chien, Wis.	1000	
CKNW	New Westminster, B.C.	50000	50000
CFPL	London, Ont.	10000	5000
CHEX	Peterborough, Ont.	10000	5000
CKGM	Montreal, Que.	10000	10000
CBV	Quebec, Que.	50000	50000
CKRM	Regina, Sask.	10000	5000
XENR	Nueva Rosita, Coah.	5000	500
XEOT	San Pedro, Coah.	1000	600
XELC	La Piedad, Mich.	5000	200
XEXT	Tepic, Nay.	1000	1000
XEQG	Queretaro, Qro.	1000	150
XEFQ	Cananea, Son.	500	500
XEKE	Navojoa, Son.	1000	250
XETU	Tampico, Tams.	10000	1000
† ----	Apizaco, Tlax.	10000	
XEQO	Cosamaloapan, Ver.	5000	5000
XEQS	Fresnillo, Zac.	4000	100
CMCK	Havana, Cuba	5000	5000
HISA	Santiago, Dom. Rep.	3000	3000

990 (CANADIAN CLEAR)

Call	Location	Day	Night
WEIS	Centre, Ala.	250	
WWWF	Fayette, Ala.	1000	
WPIK	Flomaton, Ala.	500	
KTKT	Tucson, Ariz.	10000	1000
KKIS	Pittsburg, Calif.	5000	5000
KBLS	Santa Barbara, Calif.	1000	
KRKS	Denver, Colo.	5000	
WNTY	Southington, Conn.	500	
WHOO	Orlando, Fla.	50000	5000
WDWD	Dawson, Ga.	1000	
WGML	Hinesville, Ga.	250	
KHVH	Honolulu, Haw.	5000	5000
WCAZ	Carthage, Ill.	1000	
WITZ	Jasper, Ind.	1000	
WERK	Muncie, Ind.	250	
KAYL	Storm Lake, Ia.	250	
KRSL	Russell, Kan.	250	
WNNR	New Orleans, La.	250	
KXLA	Rayville, La.	1000	250
WSDM	Clare, Mich.	250	
WABO	Waynesboro, Miss.	1000	
KRMO	Monett, Mo.	250	
KSVP	Artesia, N.M.	1000	250
----	Rochester, N.Y.	1000	250
WEEB	Southern Pines, N.C.	5000	
WBTE	Windsor, N.C.	1000	
WJEH	Gallipolis, O.	1000	
WTIG	Massillon, O.	250	
KRKT	Albany, Ore.	250	
WZZD	Philadelphia, Pa.	50000	10000
WVSC	Somerset, Pa.	5000	
WPRA	Mayaguez, P.R.	1000	1000
WLKW	Providence, R.I.	50000	
WAKN	Aiken, S.C.	1000	
WNOX	Knoxville, Tenn.	10000	10000
KWAM	Memphis, Tenn.	10000	
KTRM	Beaumont, Tex.	1000	1000
KAML	Kenedy, Tex.	250	
KGTM	Wichita Falls, Tex.	10000	1000
‡ KTLE	Tooele, Utah	1000	
WNRV	Narrows, Va.	5000	
WANT	Richmond, Va.	1000	
CBW	Winnipeg, Man.	50000	50000
CBY	Corner Brook, Nfld.	10000	10000
XECL	Mexicali, B.C.	5000	5000
XEHZ	La Paz, B.C.S.	5000	500
XETG	Tuxtla, Chis.	10000	10000
XEER	Cuahutemoc, Chih.	1000	200
XEBC	Ciudad Guzman, Jal.	1000	100
† ----	Lagos, Jal.	250	1000
† ----	Tacambaro, Mich.	1000	
XET	Monterrey, N.L.	50000	50000
XEIU	Oaxaca, Oax.	1000	250
XEOL	Tezultlan, Pue.	1000	200
XEUM	Valladolid, Yuc.	1000	250
CMHT	Sancti Spiritus, Cuba	1000	1000

1000 (USA & MEXICAN CLEAR)

Call	Location	Day	Night
WTAK	Huntsville, Ala.	10000	
WZTN	Montgomery, Ala.	5000	
† KRHS	Bullhead City, Ariz.	1000	
KHAM	Horseshoe Bend, Ark.	250	
KMLO	Vista, Calif.	5000	1000
KRDZ	Hayden, Colo.	10000	
WKMK	Blountstown, Fla.	1000	
WVSI	Jupiter, Fla.	1000	
WMPZ	Soperton, Ga.	1000	
WCFL	Chicago, Ill.	50000	50000
WKLO	Danville, Ky.	1000	
WIFX	Jenkins, Ky.	1000	
WLMS	Leominster, Mass.	1000	
WXTN	Lexington, Miss.	5000	
KOTD	Plattsmouth, Neb.	250	
WRNJ	Hackettstown, N.J.	2500	
KKIM	Albuquerque, N.M.	10000	
WIQT	Horseheads, N.Y.	5000	
WKBQ	Garner, N.C.	1000	
WSPF	Hickory, N.C.	5000	
WSUM	Parma, O.	500	
KTOK	Oklahoma City, Okla.	5000	5000
WIOO	Carlisle, Pa.	1000	
WKYB	Hemingway, S.C.	10000	
WGOG	Walhalla, S.C.	1000	
KXRB	Sioux Falls, S.D.	10000	
WMUF	Paris, Tenn.	500	
KSTA	Coleman, Tex.	250	
KGRI	Henderson, Tex.	250	
KJJT	Odessa, Tex.	250	
WHWB	Rutland, Vt.	1000	
WVWI	Charlotte Amalie, V.I.	5000	1000
WKDE	Altavista, Va.	1000	
WRAR	Tappahannock, Va.	500	
KOMO	Seattle, Wash.	50000	50000
CKBW	Bridgewater, N.S.	10000	10000
CFLP	Rimouski, Que.	10000	10000
XETAC	Tapachula, Chis.	1000	1000
XEFV	Ciudad Juarez, Chih.	1000	
† ----	Parral, Chih.	1000	250
XEOY	Mexico City, D.F.	10000	10000
† ----	Cozumel, Q.R.	100	
XELMS	Los Mochis, Sin.	1000	1000
XEMMS	Mazatlan, Sin.	1000	500
XEMV	Matamoros, Tams.	1000	1000
XENLT	Nuevo Laredo, Tams.	1000	250
† ----	Coatzacoalcos, Ver.	1000	1000
XEMY	Merida, Yuc.	1000	500
CMAP	Guane, Cuba	250	250
HIDL	La Vega, Dom. Rep.	500	100
4VCPS	Port Au Prince, Haiti	200	200

1010 (CANADIAN & CUBAN CLEAR)

Call	Location	Day	Night
WPYK	Dora, Ala.	500	
KXEG	Phoenix, Ariz.	1000	250
KLRA	Little Rock, Ark.	10000	5000
KCHJ	Delano, Calif.	5000	1000
‡ KCMJ	Palm Springs, Calif.	1000	500
KIQI	Sunnyvale, Calif.	50000	5000
KCMP	Brush, Colo.	5000	

WCNU	Crestview, Fla.	10000r	
WBIX	Jacksonville Beach, Fla.	10000	
WCBF	Tampa, Fla.	50000	
WGUN	Atlanta, Ga.	50000	
WCSI	Columbus, Ind.	500	
KSMN	Mason City, Ia.	1000	
KIND	Independence, Kan.	250	
‡ WBCE	Wickliffe, Ky.	250	
KDLA	De Ridder, La.	1000	
WKQT	Garyville, La.	500	
WYST	Baltimore, Md.	1000	
WITL	Lansing, Mich.	500	
WMIN	Maplewood, Minn.	250	
WMOX	Meridian, Miss.	10000	1000
KCHI	Chillicothe, Mo.	250	
KXEN	St. Louis, Mo.	50000	
WCNL	Newport, N.H.	250	
WINS	New York, N.Y.	50000	50000
WWWX	Albemarle, N.C.	1000	
WFGW	Black Mountain, N.C.	50000	
WELS	Kinston, N.C.	1000	
WIOI	New Boston, O.	1000	
† ----	Milwaukee, Ore.	250	250
WTGC	Lewisburg, Pa.	1000	
WHIN	Gallatin, Tenn.	5000	
WORM	Savannah, Tenn.	250	
KDJW	Amarillo, Tex.	5000	500
KLAT	Houston, Tex.	5000	5000
KBBW	Waco, Tex.	10000	2500
† KTLE	Tooele, Utah	50000	1000
WMEV	Marion, Va.	1000	
WPMH	Portsmouth, Va.	5000	
WCST	Berkeley Springs, W.V.	250	
WXYQ	Stevens Point, Wis.	1000	
CBR	Calgary, Alta.	50000	50000
CFRB	Toronto, Ont.	50000	50000
XEDX	Ensenada, B.C.	500	250
XELO	Chihuahua, Chih.	1000	
XETX	Nuevo Casas Grandes, Chih.	1000	250
XEKD	Ciudad Acuna, Coah.	500	250
XEVK	Torreon, Coah.	5000	100
XEHL	Guadalajara, Jal.	50000	5000
XEWS	Culiacan, Sin.	5000	250
XEEB	Esperanza, Son.	500	250
XEXN	Ures, Son.	500	200
† ----	Apizaco, Tlax.	1000	500
XEFM	Veracruz, Ver.	5000	1000
CMKM	Holguin, Cuba	5000	5000
CMAS	Pinar Del Rio, Cuba	250	250
CMAC	San Cristobal, Cuba	1000	1000
HIJP	Santo Domingo, Dom. Rep.	50000	250
PJC7	Curacao, Ne. Antil.	1000	1000

1020 (CLEAR)

KTNQ	Los Angeles, Calif.	50000	50000
† WJEP	Ochlochnee, Ga.	10000	
WCIL	Carbondale, Ill.	1000	
WPEO	Peoria, Ill.	1000	
KBCQ	Roswell, N.M.	50000	50000
KDKA	Pittsburgh, Pa.	50000	50000
† KWIQ	Moses Lake, Wash.	5000	500
† KYXE	Selah, Wash.	10000	250
XECAA	Calvillo, Ags.	1000	100
XEXL	Patzcuaro, Mich.	1000	
† ----	Oaxaca, Oax.	2000	
† ----	Izucar De Matamoros, Pue.	500	
† XEKH	Queretaro, Qro.	500	
XEWO	Chetumal, Q.R.	1000	
XECUS	Muacuspana, Tab.	1000	1000

1030 (CLEAR)

WBZ	Boston,	50000	50000
WOSO	San Juan, P.R.	10000	10000
WBDX	White Bluff, Tenn.	1000	250
KCTA	Corpus Christi, Tex.	50000	
KTWO	Casper, Wyo.	50000	50000
† ----	Motozintla, Chis.	10000	
XEQR	Mexico City, D.F.	10000	1000
XEVP	Acapulco, Gro.	1500	
XELJ	Lagos, Jal.	1000	
XEVR	Ixtlan, Nay.	1000	1000
† ----	Ciudad Madero, Tams.	1000	500
CMFA	Camaguey, Cuba	5000	5000

1035

4VEC	Cap Haitien, Haiti	10000	10000

1040 (CLEAR)

† WKAO	Boynton Beach, Fla.	10000	1000
† WHBO	Pinellas Park, Fla.	5000	1000
KPOI	Honolulu, Haw.	10000	10000
WHO	Des Moines, Ia.	50000	50000
† WSKE	Everett, Pa.	10000	
WCXQ	Moca, P.R.	250	
† ----	Powell, Tenn.	5000	
KPBC	Dallas, Tex.	1000	
† ----	La Paz, B.C.S.	500	
† ----	Villa Flores, Chis.	2500	
† XEVE	Colima, Col.	250	
† XESAG	Salamanca, Gto.	1000	
XECX	Tala, Jal.	250	
XEBBB	Zapopan, Jal.	5000	1000
XEJAQ	Jalpan, Qro.	250	
† ----	Culiacan, Sin.	1000	500
XEGR	Coatepec, Ver.	1000	
XEBBB	Zapopan, Zac.	5000	

1045

BKH	Hillsborough, Car. Is.	100	100

1050 (MEXICAN CLEAR)

WRFS	Alexander City, Ala.	1000	
WCRI	Scottsboro, Ala.	250	
KTBA	Tuba City, Ariz.	5000	
KSOH	Little Rock, Ark.	1000	
KBBV	Big Bear Lake, Calif.	250	
KOFY	San Mateo, Calif.	1000	
WJSB	Crestview, Fla.	5000	
WROS	Jacksonville, Fla.	5000	
‡ WHBO	Tampa, Fla.	250	
WHGI	Augusta, Ga.	5000	
WCGA	Conyers, Ga.	1000	
WMNZ	Montezuma, Ga.	250	
WDZ	Decatur, Ill.	1000	
WTCA	Plymouth, Ind.	250	
KBUF	Garden City, Kan.	5000	
WNES	Central City, Ky.	1000q	
KLPL	Lake Providence, La.	250	
KVPI	Ville Platte, La.	250	
WMSG	Oakland, Md.	500	
WGAY	Silver Spring, Md.	1000	
WPAG	Ann Arbor, Mich.	5000	
KLOH	Pipestone, Minn.	1000	
WACR	Columbus, Miss.	1000	
KMIS	Portageville, Mo.	1000	
KSIS	Sedalia, Mo.	1000	
WBNC	Conway, N.H.	1000	
WRPT	Peterborough, N.H.	1000	

Call	Location	Day	Night
WSEN	Baldwinsville, N.Y.	1000	
WYBG	Massena, N.Y.	1000	
WHN	New York, N.Y.	50000	50000
WFSC	Franklin, N.C.	1000	
WLON	Lincolnton, N.C.	1000	
WWGP	Sanford, N.C.	1000	
WTSJ	Cincinnati, O.	1000	
KCCO	Lawton, Okla.	250	
KGTO	Tulsa, Okla.	1000	
KORE	Springfield, Ore.	1000	
WBUT	Butler, Pa.	500	
‡ WSKE	Everett, Pa.	1000	
WLYC	Williamsport, Pa.	1000	
WCGB	Juana Diaz, P.R.	5000r	500
WJXY	Conway, S.C.	5000	
WSMT	Sparta, Tenn.	1000	
KIIZ	Killeen, Tex.	250	
KPXE	Liberty, Tex.	250	
KCAS	Slaton, Tex.	250	
WGAT	Gate City, Va.	1000	
WBRG	Lynchburg, Va.	1000	
WCMS	Norfolk, Va.	5000	
† KSPO	Dishman, Wash.	5000	
KBLE	Seattle, Wash.	5000	
WADC	Parkersburg, W.V.	5000	
WOKL	Eau Claire, Wis.	1000	
WKAU	Kaukauna, Wis.	1000	
WLIP	Kenosha, Wis.	250	
CFGP	Grand Prairie, Alta.	10000	10000
CKAL	Vernon, B.C.	10000	1000
CKSB	St. Boniface, Man.	10000	10000
CFYN	Sault Ste. Marie, Ont.	10000	2500
CHUM	Toronto, Ont.	50000	50000
CJNB	North Battleford, Sask.	10000	10000
XED	Mexicali, B.C.	10000	1000
XEPAT	Patzcuaro, Mich.	5000	250
XEEF	Compostela, Nay.	5000	
XEG	Monterrey, N.L.	150000	150000
HICB	Santiago, Dom. Rep.	1000	1000

1060 (USA & MEXICAN CLEAR)

Call	Location	Day	Night
KUKQ	Tempe, Ariz.	5000	500
KAYR	Van Buren, Ark.	500	
KPAY	Chico, Calif.	10000	10000
KLMO	Longmont, Colo.	10000	
WAMT	Titusville, Fla.	10000	5000
WKGQ	Milledgeville, Ga.	1000	
WKNG	Tallapoosa, Ga.	5000	
KBGN	Caldwell, Id.	10000	
WMCL	Mc Leansboro, Ill.	2500	
WRHL	Rochelle, Ill.	250	
WFLE	Flemingsburg, Ky.	1000	
WJKY	Jamestown, Ky.	2500	
WNOE	New Orleans, La.	50000	5000
WTTP	Natick, Mass.	25000	2500
WHFB	Benton Harbor, Mich.	5000	
WBMB	West Branch, Mich.	1000	
‡ WKKQ	Hibbing, Minn.	5000	
KFIL	Preston, Minn.	1000	
WCFB	Tupelo, Miss.	250	
KLSM	Springfield, Mo.	500	
KNLV	Ord, Neb.	1000	
WHNI	Mebane, N.C.	1000	
WMAP	Monroe, N.C.	1000	
WCOK	Sparta, N.C.	250	
WRCW	Canton, O.	5000	
KYW	Philadelphia, Pa.	50000	50000
‡ WALD	Walterboro, S.C.	1000	
WNPC	Newport, Tenn.	1000	
WPHC	Waverly, Tenn.	1000	
KAMA	El Paso, Tex.	10000	
‡ KIJN	Farwell, Tex.		
KHYM	Gilmer, Tex.	10000	
KHJK	Lockhart, Tex.	250	
KPUB	Winters, Tex.	2500r	
KRSP	South Salt Lake City, Utah	10000	1000
CFCN	Calgary, Alta.	50000	50000
CJRP	Quebec, Que.	50000	10000
XEEP	Mexico City, D.F.	50000	50000
CMMM	Baracoa, Cuba	1000	1000
CMBQ	Havana, Cuba	5000	5000

1070 (USA & CANADIAN CLEAR)

Call	Location	Day	Night
WAPI	Birmingham, Ala.	50000	5000
KNX	Los Angeles, Calif.	50000	50000
WANM	Tallahassee, Fla.	10000	
WIBC	Indianapolis, Ind.	50000	10000
KILR	Estherville, Ia.	250	
KFDI	Wichita, Kan.	10000	1000
WSRG	Elkton, Ky.	250	
KMOM	Monticello, Minn.	10000q	2500
KHMO	Hannibal, Mo.	5000	1000
† KATQ	Plentywood, Mont.	5000	
‡ KERR	Polson, Mont.	25000	1000
WKMB	Stirling, N.J.	2500	
WKDR	Plattsburgh, N.Y.	5000	
WSCP	Sandy Creek, N.Y.	2500	
WNCT	Greenville, N.C.	10000	10000
WGOS	High Point, N.C.	1000	
WKOK	Sunbury, Pa.	10000	1000
WMIA	Arecibo, P.R.	500	500
WHYZ	Greenville, S.C.	50000	
WFLI	Lookout Mountain, Tenn.	50000	1000
WDIA	Memphis, Tenn.	50000	5000
KOPY	Alice, Tex.	1000	1000
KRBE	Houston, Tex.	10000	5000
KWEL	Midland, Tex.	2500	
WINA	Charlottesville, Va.	5000	5000
WJKK	Beckley, W.V.	10000	
WTSO	Madison, Wis.	10000	5000
CKST	St. Albert, Alta.	10000	10000
CFAX	Victoria, B.C.	10000	10000
CBA	Moncton, N.B.	50000	50000
CHOK	Sarnia, Ont.	10000	10000
† XEZO	Guerrero Negro, B.C.	1000	
XEIT	Carmen, Cam.	1000	250
† ----	Venustiano Carranza, Chis.	1000	100
† ----	Zihuatenejo, Gro.	2000	
XESP	Tlaquepaque, Jal.	10000	1000
XEGY	Tehuacan, Pue.	1000	250
† XEEI	San Luis Potosi, S.L.P.	250	
† ----	Mazatlan, Sin.	1000	
XEMI	Minatitlan, Ver.	500	100
† ----	Tantoyucah, Ver.	1000	500
HIBI	San Francisco De Macoris, Dom. Rep.	1000	250

1080 (CLEAR)

Call	Location	Day	Night
WKAC	Athens, Ala.	5000	
WLVN	Luverne, Ala.	500	
KTNX	Anchorage, Alas.	10000	10000
KGVY	Green Valley, Ariz.	1000	
KSCO	Santa Cruz, Calif.	10000	5000
WTIC	Hartford, Conn.	50000	50000
WVCG	Coral Gables, Fla.	50000	10000
WFIV	Kissimmee, Fla.	10000	
WJBU	Port St. Joe, Fla.	1000	
WJYA	Marietta, Ga.	10000	
KIOE	Honolulu, Haw.	5000	5000
KVNI	Coeur D' Alene, Id.	10000	1000
WPOK	Pontiac, Ill.	1000	
WNWI	Valparaiso, Ind.	250	
KOAK	Red Oak, Ia.	250	
WCII	Louisville, Ky.	10000	1000
WOAP	Owosso, Mich.	1000	
† WKKQ	Hibbing, Minn.	10000	10000
KYMN	Northfield, Minn.	1000	
WECP	Carthage, Miss.	5000	

Call	Location	Power	Power
KYMO	East Prairie, Mo.	500	
KJEL	Lebanon, Mo.	250	
WUFO	Amherst, N.Y.	1000	
WKGX	Lenoir, N.C.	5000	
WYCM	Murfreesboro, N.C.	1000	
WNCR	St. Pauls, N.C.	5000	
KNDK	Langdon, N.D.	1000	
WMVR	Sidney, O.	250	
KWJJ	Portland, Ore.	50000	10000
WQRO	Huntingdon, Pa.	1000	
WEEP	Pittsburgh, Pa.	50000	
WLEY	Cayey, P.R.	250	250
† WALD	Walterboro, S.C.	2500	
† WBTZ	Oliver Springs, Tenn.	2500	
KRLD	Dallas, Tex.	50000	50000
KRPX	Price, Utah	2500	
WKBY	Chatham, Va.	1000	
WZTQ	Hurricane, W.V.	5000	
CKSA	Lloydminster, Alta.	10000	10000
† XEDC	Aguascalientes, Ags.	250	
XEDY	Ciudad Morelos, B.C.S.	500	
XEOB	Pichucalco, Chis.	1500	150
† XEDT	Cuahutemoc, Chih.	1000	
XEAJ	Saltillo, Coah.	1000	250
XECN	Irapuato, Gto.	1000	
† ----	Puerto Vallarta, Jal.	5000	
† ----	Zitacuaro, Mich.	500	150
† ----	Ixtepec, Oax.	5000	
† ----	Cancun, Q.R.	1000	500
† ----	Los Mochis, Sin.	1000	
† ----	Xicotencatl, Tams.	1000	
XEXK	Poza Rica, Ver.	500	
CMBM	Santa Fe, Isla De Pinos, Cuba	1000	1000
4VA	Port Au Prince, Haiti	1500	1500

1090 (USA & MEXICAN CLEAR)

Call	Location	Power	Power
WXBX	Albertville, Ala.	2500	
KAAY	Little Rock, Ark.	50000	50000
KNCR	Fortuna, Calif.	10000	
KKBB	Aurora, Colo.	50000	500
WMFL	Monticello, Fla.	1000	
WBAF	Barnesville, Ga.	1000	
WCRA	Effingham, Ill.	1000	
WGLC	Mendota, Ill.	250	
WFCV	Ft. Wayne, Ind.	1000	
KVDB	Sioux Center, Ia.	500	
* KNWS	Waterloo, Ia.	1000	
WSLG	Gonzales, La.	10000	
WBAL	Baltimore, Md.	50000	50000
WILD	Boston, Mass.	5000	
WCAR	Livonia, Mich.	250	500
WMUS	Muskegon, Mich.	1000	
KEXS	Excelsior Springs, Mo.	1000	
KBOZ	Bozeman, Mont.	5000	5000
† KRZY	Albuquerque, N.M.	50000	1000
WKTE	King, N.C.	1000	
WBZB	Selma, N.C.	1000	
KTGO	Tioga, N.D.	1000	
WKFI	Wilmington, O.	1000	
KLWJ	Umatilla, Ore.	2500	
WBOZ	San German, P.R.	250	250
WMTY	Greenwood, S.C.	1000	
WKSP	Kingstree, S.C.	5000	
WENR	Englewood, Tenn.	1000	
WJKM	Hartsville, Tenn.	1000	
WGOC	Kingsport, Tenn.	1000	
KACO	Bellville, Tex.	250	
KKYN	Plainview, Tex.	5000	500
KANN	Ogden, Utah	5000	
KING	Seattle, Wash.	50000	50000
WISS	Berlin, Wis.	500	
WAQE	Rice Lake, Wis.	5000	
CHEC	Lethbridge, Alta.	5000	5000
CKKW	Kitchener, Ont.	10000	10000
CHRS	Longueuil, Que.	10000	
XEPRS	Rosarito, B.C.	50000	50000
† ----	Torreon, Coah.	500	
XELB	La Barca, Jal.	250	
XEAU	Monterrey, N.L.	2500	250
† ----	Ocotlan, Oax.	250	
XEHR	Puebla, Pue.	500	250
XEWL	Nuevo Laredo, Tams.	1000	
XEOD	Boca Del Rio, Ver.	1000	1000
† XEMCA	Panuco, Ver.	5000	
XECAS	Zacatecas, Zac.	1000	250

1100 (CLEAR)

Call	Location	Power	Power
KFAX	San Francisco, Calif.	50000	50000
KREX	Grand Junction, Colo.	50000	10000
† ----	Carrollton, Ga.	1000	
† WBCE	Wickliffe, Ky.	1000	
† ----	Webb City, Mo.	5000	
WHLI	Hempstead, N.Y.	10000	
WWWE	Cleveland, O.	50000	50000
WGPA	Bethlehem, Pa.	250	
† WAAS	Thompson Station, Tenn.	1000	
CHUR	North Bay, Ont.	10000	
† ----	La Paz, B.C.S.	250	
XETAK	Tapachula, Chis.	750	
XEBV	Moroleon, Gto.	500	
† ----	Ometepec, Gro.	5000	1000
XEBD	Perote, Ver.	1000	
† ----	Valladolid, Yuc.	2000	
ZDK	St. Johns, Anti.	50000	50000
CMHU	Cienfuegos, Cuba	1000	1000
HIMH	La Vega, Dom. Rep.	250	250
HIMC	Santo Domingo, Dom. Rep.	1000	1000

1110 (CLEAR)

Call	Location	Power	Power
WBCA	Bay Minette, Ala.	10000	
WBIB	Centreville, Ala.	1000	
† KCOT	Marana, Ariz.	2500	
KHAC	Window Rock, Ariz.	10000	
KGFL	Clinton, Ark.	1000	
KAKA	Dermott, Ark.	10000	
KRLA	Pasadena, Calif.	50000	10000
KPIP	Roseville, Calif.	500	500
WTIS	Tampa, Fla.	10000	
WEBS	Calhoun, Ga.	250	
KHEI	Kihei, Haw.	5000	5000
* WMBI	Chicago, Ill.	5000	5000 f
WFBM	Noblesville, Ind.	1000	
WKDZ	Cadiz, Ky.	1000	
WCBR	Richmond, Ky.	250	
WFCG	Franklinton, La.	1000	
KPAL	Pineville, La.	500	
WUHN	Pittsfield, Mass.	1000	
* WUNN	Mason, Mich.	1000	
WJML	Petoskey, Mich.	10000	
WKRA	Holly Springs, Miss.	1000	
KFAB	Omaha, Neb.	50000	50000
WVNH	Salem, N.H.	5000	
KYKK	Humble City, N.M.	1000	
WSFW	Seneca Falls, N.Y.	1000	
WTBQ	Warwick, N.Y.	250	
WBT	Charlotte, N.C.	50000	50000
WELX	Xenia, O.	250	
KEOR	Atoka, Okla.	5000	
KBND	Bend, Ore.	10000	1000
WJSM	Martinsburg, Pa.	1000	
WNAR	Norristown, Pa.	2500	
WKEG	Washington, Pa.	1000	
WVJP	Caguas, P.R.	250	500
WHIM	Providence, R.I.	5000	5000
WSLV	Ardmore, Tenn.	1000	
WUAT	Pikeville, Tenn.	250	

	Call	Location	Power	
	KDRY	Alamo Heights, Tex.	2500r	1000
	KTEK	Alvin, Tex.	500	
	WZAM	Norfolk, Va.	50000	
	CHQT	Edmonton, Alta.	50000	50000
	CBD	St. John, N.B.	10000	
†	----	Hawkesbury, Nfld.	1000	
	CHPR	Hawkesbury, Ont.	250	
	CKJD	Sarnia, Ont.	10000	1000
	XEES	Chihuahua, Chih.	1000	250
	XEWR	Ciudad Juarez, Chih.	500	
	XEPU	Monclova, Coah.	250	
	XERED	Mexico City, D.F.	50000	50000
	XELEO	Leon, Gto.	5000	5000
†	XEPVJ	Puerto Vallarta, Jal.	1000	
	----	Tuxtepec, Oax.	2000	1000
	XESON	Navojoa, Son.	1000	
	XEVS	Villa De Seris, Son.	1000	
	XEJAC	Cardenas, Tab.	1000	1000
	XEOQ	Rio Bravo, Tams.	5000	250
†	----	Naranjos, Ver.	250	

1120 (CLEAR)

	Call	Location	Power	
†	----	Limon, Colo.	250	
	WUST	Washington, D. C.	5000r	
†	WQXM	Gordon, Ga.	5000	
	KMOX	St. Louis, Mo.	50000	50000
	WNYS	Buffalo, N.Y.	1000	
	WYNO	Nelsonville, O.	2500	
	KPNW	Eugene, Ore.	50000	50000
†	WKQW	Oil City, Pa.	250	
	WMSW	Hatillo, P.R.	1000	1000
	KCLE	Cleburne, Tex.	250	
†	----	Tuxtla, Chis.	250	
	XEUNO	Guadalajara, Jal.	500	
†	----	Melchor Ocampo De Balsas, Mich.	500	
	XEGV	Villa Del Pueblito, Qro.	500	
†	----	Cancun, Q.R.	1000	500
	XETR	Ciudad Valles, S.L.P.	5000	500
†	----	Tenosique, Tab.	1000	
	XEZAZ	Zacatecas, Zac.	250	
	CMDL	Holguin, Cuba	1000	1000
	HICN	Santo Domingo, Dom. Rep.	1000	1000
	4VF	Port Au Prince, Haiti	200	200

1130 (USA & CANADIAN CLEAR)

	Call	Location	Power	
†	WKIJ	Parrish, Ala.	1000	
	WACQ	Tallassee, Ala.	1000	
	KAAB	Batesville, Ark.	250	
	KRDU	Dinuba, Calif.	1000	1000
	KSDO	San Diego, Calif.	50000	10000
	WPUL	Bartow, Fla.	2500	500
	WLBA	Gainesville, Ga.	10000	
	WMGA	Moultrie, Ga.	10000	250
	KLEI	Kailua, Haw.	10000	10000
	WWCM	Brazil, Ind.	500	
	KKSI	Mt. Pleasant, Ia.	250	
	KLEY	Wellington, Kan.	250	
	WKED	Frankfort, Ky.	500	
	WSJP	Murray, Ky.	1000p	250
	KWKH	Shreveport, La.	50000	50000
	WCXI	Detroit, Mich.	50000	10000
	WDGY	Minneapolis, Minn.	50000	50000
	WGUF	Gulfport, Miss.	500	
	KYOO	Bolivar, Mo.	250	
	WNEW	New York, N.Y.	50000	50000
	WPYB	Benson, N.C.	1000	
	WCBX	Eden, N.C.	1000	
	WJTP	Newland, N.C.	1000	
	KBMR	Bismarck, N.D.	50000r	50000
	WCTM	Eaton, O.	250	
	WASP	Brownsville, Pa.	5000	
	WBZT	Waynesboro, Pa.	1000	
	WCCG	Camden, S.C.	1000	
†	WHHQ	Hilton Head Island, S.C.	10000	
	WAMG	Gallatin, Tenn.	2500	
	WDTM	Selmer, Tenn.	1000	
	KQTI	Edna, Tex.	2500	
	KLSR	Memphis, Tex.	1000	
	WRRL	Rainelle, W.V.	1000	
	WISN	Milwaukee, Wis.	50000	10000
	CKWX	Vancouver, B.C.	50000	50000
†	XEEA	Cuahutemoc, Chih.	1000	
†	XECHG	Chilpancingo, Gro.	1000	
	XEFN	Uruapan, Mich.	1000	
†	----	Queretaro, Qro.	1000	
	XEMOS	Los Mochis, Sin.	500	
	XEHN	Nogales, Son.	1000	
	XEZL	Jalapa, Ver.	10000	10000
	CMDW	Guantanamo, Cuba	1000	1000
	CMHA	Santa Clara, Cuba	1000	1000
	HIRL	Santiago, Dom. Rep.	1000	250

1140 (USA & MEXICAN CLEAR)

	Call	Location	Power	
	WASG	Atmore, Ala.	10000	
	KVLI	Lake Isabella, Calif.	500	
†	KCMJ	Palm Springs, Calif.	10000	5000
	KRAK	Sacramento, Calif.	50000	50000
	KNAB	Burlington, Colo.	1000	
	WQBA	Miami, Fla.	10000	5000
	KGEM	Boise, Id.	10000	10000
	WVEL	Pekin, Ill.	5000	
	WAWK	Kendallville, Ind.	250	
	KNEI	Waukon, Ia.	1000	
‡	WKCM	Hawesville, Ky.	2500	
	WRLV	Saylersville, Ky.	1000	
	WKWM	Kentwood, Mich.	5000	
	WAKK	Mc Comb, Miss.	500	
	WSAO	Senatobia, Miss.	5000	
	KKCI	Liberty, Mo.	500	
	KPWB	Piedmont, Mo.	1000	
	KCTE	Southwest City, Mo.	250	
	KMJJ	Las Vegas, Nev.	10000	2500
	WCJW	Warsaw, N.Y.	1000	
	WRNA	China Grove, N.C.	250	
	WCLW	Mansfield, O.	250	
	KATT	Oklahoma City, Okla.	1000	
	WBZY	New Castle, Pa.	5000	
	WQII	San Juan, P.R.	10000	10000
	KSOO	Sioux Falls, S.D.	10000	5000
	WIXC	Fayetteville, Tenn.	5000	
	WLNT	London, Tenn.	1000	
	KSKS	Conroe, Tex.	250	
	KYXS	Mineral Wells, Tex.	250	
	WRVA	Richmond, Va.	50000	50000
	WSPC	St. Paul, Va.	1000	
	KMMZ	Greybull, Wyo.	10000	
	CKXL	Calgary, Alta.	50000	50000
	CBI	Sydney, N.S.	10000	10000
	CJTR	Three Rivers, Que.	10000	10000
†	----	Campeche, Cam.	250	
†	----	Nuevo Casas Grandes, Chih.	250	
	XEXF	Leon, Gto.	5000	1000
†	----	Ixmiquilpan, Hgo.	250	
†	----	Tuxpan, Jal.	3000	
†	XELIA	Morelia, Mich.	250	
	XEMR	Monterrey, N.L.	50000	50000
	XETE	Tehuacan, Pue.	1000	
	CMJK	Camaguey, Cuba	1000	1000

1150 (REGIONAL)

	Call	Location	Power	
	WGEA	Geneva, Ala.	1000	

	WJRD	Tuscaloosa, Ala.	5000	1000
	KCKY	Coolidge, Ariz.	5000r	1000
	KBOX	North Little Rock, Ark.	5000	1000
	KPRZ	Los Angeles, Calif.	5000	5000
	KBAI	Morro Bay, Calif.	5000	5000
	KPLS	Santa Rosa, Calif.	5000	500
	KRZN	Englewood, Colo.	5000	1000
	WCNX	Middletown, Conn.	2500r	
	WDEL	Wilmington, Del.	5000	5000
	WNDB	Daytona Beach, Fla.	1000	1000
	WTMP	Tampa, Fla.	5000	2500
	WXKO	Ft. Valley, Ga.	1000	
	WJEM	Valdosta, Ga.	1000	
	WGGH	Marion, Ill.	5000	
	WKKN	Rockford, Ill.	1000	
	KCPS	Burlington, Ia.	500	
	KWKY	Des Moines, Ia.	1000	1000
	KSAL	Salina, Kan.	5000	5000
	WMST	Mt. Sterling, Ky.	500	
	WLOC	Munfordville, Ky.	1000	
	WJBO	Baton Rouge, La.	5000	5000
	WQMR	Skowhegan, Me.	5000	
	WJOK	Gaithersburg, Md.	1000	1000
	WHUE	Boston, Mass.	5000	5000
	WCEN	Mt. Pleasant, Mich.	1000	500
	KASM	Albany, Minn.	1000	
†	WTWZ	Clinton, Miss.	500	
	KRMS	Osage Beach, Mo.	1000	
	KSEN	Shelby, Mont.	5000	5000
	KDEF	Albuquerque, N.M.	5000	500
	WRUN	Utica, N.Y.	5000	1000
	WQRB	Burlington, N.C.	1000	
	WGBR	Goldsboro, N.C.	5000	5000
	WCUE	Akron, O.	1000	500
	WIMA	Lima, O.	1000	1000
	KNED	Mc Alester, Okla.	1000	500
	KAGO	Klamath Falls, Ore.	5000	1000
	KKEY	Portland, Ore.	5000	
	WHUN	Huntingdon, Pa.	5000	
	WYNS	Lehighton, Pa.	1000	
	WKPA	New Kensington, Pa.	1000	
	WDIX	Orangeburg, S.C.	5000	500
	WTYC	Rock Hill, S.C.	1000	
	WSNW	Seneca, S.C.	1000	
	KIMM	Rapid City, S.D.	5000	
	WGOW	Chattanooga, Tenn.	5000	1000
	WCRK	Morristown, Tenn.	5000r	500
	WTAW	College Station, Tex.	1000	500
	KCCT	Corpus Christi, Tex.	1000	500
	KISO	El Paso, Tex.	1000	
	KVIL	Highland Park, Tex.	1000	
	KJBC	Midland, Tex.	1000	
	KDLF	Port Neches, Tex.	500	
	KIXC	Quanah, Tex.	500	
	KFHM	San Antonio, Tex.	1000	
	WNLR	Churchville, Va.	1000	
	KQQQ	Pullman, Wash.	1000	
	KSPL	Seattle, Wash.	5000	5000
	WELC	Welch, W.V.	5000	
	WAYY	Chippewa Falls, Wis.	5000	
	WYNE	Kimberly, Wis.	5000	5000
	CKIQ	Kelowna, B.C.	10000	10000
	CKX	Brandon, Man.	50000	10000
	CHSJ	St. John, N.B.	10000	5000
	CKOC	Hamilton, Ont.	50000	50000
	CJRC	Ottawa, Ont.	50000	5000
	XERM	Mexicali, B.C.	1000	500
	XEJS	Parral, Chih.	1000	500
	XEBF	San Pedro, Coah.	1000	250
	XEJP	Mexico City, D.F.	10000	10000
	XEAD	Guadalajara, Jal.	1000	125
	XEXP	Tuxtepec, Oax.	5000	1000
†	----	Tulum, Q.R.	200	
	XEUAS	Culiacan, Sin.	10000	125
	XESO	Ciudad Obregon, Son.	5000	300
	XERTM	Muacuspana, Tab.	1000	125
†	XETVR	Tuxpan, Ver.	250	
	XERRF	Merida, Yuc.	1000	350
	XEXZ	Zacatecas, Zac.	1000	200
	CMDO	Banes, Cuba	250	250
	HIAS	Santo Domingo, Dom. Rep.	5000	1000
	4VAB	Port Au Prince, Haiti	1000	1000

1160 (CLEAR)

	WJJD	Chicago, Ill.	50000	50000 f
†	WKCM	Hawesville, Ky.	2500	1000
†	WTYN	Tryon, N.C.	10000	1000
	WRID	Homer City, Pa.	5000	
	WBQN	Barceloneta, P.R.	1000	1000
†	WAMB	Donelson, Tenn.	50000	50000
†	WHMT	Humboldt, Tenn.	1000	1000
	KSL	Salt Lake City, Utah	50000	50000
	XEVW	Acambaro, Gto.	1000	
	XEIW	Uruapan, Mich.	1000	
	XEGI	Tamazunchale, S.L.P.	500	
	XEBE	Perote, Ver.	1000	
	CMAD	Artemisa, Cuba	1000	1000
	HIDE	Cotui, Dom. Rep.	500	100

1170 (CLEAR)

	WCOV	Montgomery, Ala.	10000	1000
	KJNP	North Pole, Alas.	50000	50000
	KCBQ	San Diego, Calif.	50000	5000
	KLOK	San Jose, Calif.	50000	5000
	KUAD	Windsor, Colo.	1000	
	WRTT	Vernon, Conn.	1000	
	WHNE	Cumming, Ga.	1000	
	KOHO	Honolulu, Haw.	5000	5000
	WLBH	Mattoon, Ill.	5000	
	KSTT	Davenport, Ia.	1000	1000
	KDLP	Bayou Vista, La.	500	
	WJMQ	Norfolk, Mass.	1000	
	WVLC	Orleans, Mass.	1000	
	WDTB	Dimondale, Mich.	1000	
	KOWO	Waseca, Minn.	1000	
	KJAS	Jackson, Mo.	250	
	WHLW	Lakewood, N.J.	5000	
	WBRW	Somerville, N.J.	500	
	WCRR	Cornwall, N.Y.	1000	
	WMVI	Mechanicville, N.Y.	250	
†	----	Claremont, N.C.	5000	1000
	WCLN	Clinton, N.C.	5000	
	KVOO	Tulsa, Okla.	50000	50000
	WLEO	Ponce, P.R.	250	250
‡	WAMB	Donelson, Tenn.	25000	
	KPUG	Bellingham, Wash.	10000	5000
	WWVA	Wheeling, W.V.	50000	50000
	WGZS	Waupun, Wis.	1000	
	CKGY	Red Deer, Alta.	10000	5000
	CFIX	Cornwall, Ont.	10000	
	XEUVA	Aguascalientes, Ags.	1000	
	XEMDA	Monclova, Coah.	500	
	XEYL	Iguala, Gro.	50000	10000
	XELP	La Piedad, Mich.	250	100
	XECD	Puebla, Pue.	1000	1000
	XERB	Cozumel, Qro.	5000	100
	XERB	Cozumel, Q.R.	5000	1000
†	----	El Fuerte, Sin.	1000	500
†	----	Mazatlan, Sin.	1000	
	XEIB	Caborca, Son.	250	
	XEYH	Hermosillo, Son.	1000	250
	XERT	Reynosa, Tams.	5000	250
	XEZS	Coatzacoalcos, Ver.	500	250
†	XEEU	Papantla, Ver.	250	
	4VRD	Port Au Prince, Haiti	250	250

1180 (CLEAR)

	KDAN	Williams, Ariz.	10000	250

	KWSO	Wasco, Calif.	10000	1000
	VOA	Marathon Key, Fla.	50000	50000
	WLDS	Jacksonville, Ill.	1000	
†	WJJN	Newburgh, Ind.	500	
	WKKE	Pearl, Miss.	10000	5000
	KOFI	Kalispell, Mont.	10000	10000
	WHAM	Rochester, N.Y.	50000	50000
†	KTUN	Humble, Tex.	1000	1000
†	----	Tuxtla, Chis.	1000	
	XEFR	Mexico City, D.F.	1000	1000
	XEYV	Huatusco, Ver.	1000	1000
†	----	Rio Grande, Zac.	1000	500
	HIBE	Santo Domingo, Dom. Rep.	50000	1000

1190 (USA & MEXICAN CLEAR)

	WHIY	Moulton, Ala.	1000	2500
	WAYD	Ozark, Ala.	1000	
	KRDS	Tolleson, Ariz.	5000	250
	KMCW	Augusta, Ark.	500	
	KJEM	Bentonville, Ark.	5000	
	KNWZ	Anaheim, Calif.	10000r	1000
	KNBA	Vallejo, Calif.	1000	
	KADE	Boulder, Colo.	5000	
	WAVS	Ft. Lauderdale, Fla.	5000	
	WHHL	Pine Castle, Fla.	1000	
	WGKA	Atlanta, Ga.	5000	
	WOWO	Ft. Wayne, Ind.	50000	50000
	KDAO	Marshalltown, Ia.	250	
	KVSV	Beloit, Kan.	2500	
†	WIDS	Russell Springs, Ky.	1000	
	KNEK	Washington, La.	250	
	WANN	Annapolis, Md.	10000	
	WKOX	Framingham, Mass.	1000	
	KKOJ	Jackson, Minn.	5000	
	KWMB	Wabasha, Minn.	1000	
	WXGR	Bay St. Louis, Miss.	5000	
	KHAD	De Soto, Mo.	5000	
	KJLA	Kansas City, Mo.	1000	250
	KXKS	Albuquerque, N.M.	1000	
	WSCM	Cobelskill, N.Y.	500	
	WLIB	New York, N.Y.	10000	10000 f
	WSML	Graham, N.C.	1000	
	WIXE	Monroe, N.C.	1000	
	KEX	Portland, Ore.	50000	50000
	WBMJ	San Juan, P.R.	10000	5000
	WJES	Johnston, S.C.	1000	
	KOKK	Huron, S.D.	500	
	WSVC	Dunlap, Tenn.	5000	
‡	WHMT	Humboldt, Tenn.	500	
	WSGI	Springfield, Tenn.	250	
	KLIF	Dallas, Tex.	50000	5000
	WBDY	Bluefield, Va.	10000	
	WERU	Sun Prairie, Wis.	1000	
	CJMR	Mississauga, Ont.	10000	
	CHTN	Charlottetown, P.E.	10000	10000
	CFSL	Weyburn, Sask.	10000	5000
	XEMBC	Mexicali, B.C.	1000	250
	XEGJ	Arriaga, Chis.	250	
	XEPZ	Ciudad Juarez, Chih.	1000	
†	----	Ciudad Saucillio, Chih.	250	
	XEPK	Pachuca, Hgo.	1000	1000
	XEWK	Guadalajara, Jal.	50000	50000
	XESOL	Ciudad Hidalgo, Mich.	500	
	XEDO	Jojutila, Mor.	1000	1000
	XECT	Monterrey, N.L.	500	
†	XEIV	Oaxaca, Oax.	500	
	XEVN	Nogales, Son.	500	
†	----	Ciudad Madero, Tams.	500	
†	XETOT	Tampico, Tams.	5000	250
†	----	Acayucan, Ver.	1000	1000
	CMJP	Ciego De Avila, Cuba	1000	1000
	4VAE	Jeremie, Haiti	150	150

1200 (CLEAR)

†	KDEC	Decorah, Ia.	1000	
*	KFNW	Fargo, N.D.	10000	1000
	WGDL	Lares, P.R.	250	
	WOAI	San Antonio, Tex.	50000	50000
†	----	Loreto, B.C.S.	5000	500
	XEITC	Celaya, Gto.	1000	1000
†	----	Chilapa, Gro.	1000	
	XEZI	Zacapu, Mich.	1000	
†	----	Cosolapa, Oax.	1000	1000
†	XEWT	Culiacan, Sin.	1000	
†	----	Hermosillo, Son.	1000	
†	----	Comalcalco, Tab.	250	
†	----	Coatzacoalcos, Ver.	2000	1000
	XEPW	Poza Rica, Ver.	1000	1000

1210 (CLEAR)

†	WDGR	Dahlonega, Ga.	10000	
	KZOO	Honolulu, Haw.	1000	1000
	WILY	Centralia, Ill.	1000	
	WKNX	Saginaw, Mass.	10000	
	WADE	Wadesboro, N.C.	1000	
	WAVI	Dayton, O.	1000	
	KGYN	Guymon, Okla.	10000	10000
	WCAU	Philadelphia, Pa.	50000	50000
	WHOY	Salinas, P.R.	5000	1000
	KCLG	Washington, Utah	10000	250
†	KREW	Sunnyside, Wash.	10000	1000
†	KOJO	Laramie, Wyo.	25000	1000
	CFFB	Frobisher Bay, N.W.T.	1000	250
	XEEMM	Salamanca, Gto.	250	
†	----	Isla Mujeres, Q.R.	1000	500
†	----	Zacatecas, Zac.	5000	
	CMJX	Moron, Cuba	250	250
	HICP	Moca, Dom. Rep.	1000	250
	HICJ	San Francisco De Macoris, Dom. Rep.	1000	100

1220 (MEXICAN CLEAR)

	WTWG	Birmingham, Ala.	1000	
	WABF	Fairhope, Ala.	1000	
	KVSA	Mc Gehee, Ark.	1000	
	KLIP	Fowler, Calif.	250	
	KIBE	Palo Alto, Calif.	5000	
	KTSJ	Pomona, Calif.	250	
	KBNO	Denver, Colo.	1000	
	WSCR	Hamden, Conn.	1000	
	WKTZ	Jacksonville, Fla.	5000	
	WMJK	Kissimmee, Fla.	1000	
	WCMQ	Miami, Fla.	1000	
	WQSA	Sarasota, Fla.	1000	
	WCLB	Camilla, Ga.	1000	
	WPLK	Rockmart, Ga.	500	
	WSFT	Thomaston, Ga.	250	
	WLPO	La Salle, Ill.	1000	
	WKRS	Waukegan, Ill.	1000	
	WSLM	Salem, Ind.	5000	
	KJAN	Atlantic, Ia.	250	
	KOUR	Independence, Ia.	250	
	KOFO	Ottawa, Kan.	250	
	WFKN	Franklin, Ky.	250	
†	----	Radcliff, Ky.	500	
	WEQO	Whitley City, Ky.	1000	
	WLBI	Denham Springs, La.	250	
	KBCL	Shreveport, La.	250	
	WSME	Sanford, Me.	1000	
	WBCH	Hastings, Mich.	250	
	WVLE	Stillwater, Minn.	5000	
	WMDC	Hazlehurst, Miss.	250	
	KLCO	Branson, Mo.	1000	
	KZYM	Cape Girardeau, Mo.	250	
	KLPW	Union, Mo.	1000	
	WKBK	Keene, N.H.	1000	
	WGNY	Newburgh, N.Y.	5000	
	WSOQ	North Syracuse, N.Y.	1000	
	WKMT	Kings Mountain, N.C.	1000	
	WREV	Reidsville, N.C.	1000	

WENC	Whiteville, N.C.	5000	
KDDR	Oakes, N.D.	1000	
WGAR	Cleveland, O.	50000	50000
WERT	Van Wert, O.	250	
KRMC	Midwest City, Okla.	250	
KCCS	Salem, Ore.	1000	
WJUN	Mexico, Pa.	1000	
WRIB	Providence, R.I.	1000	
† WGSF	Arlington, Tenn.	1000	
WFWL	Camden, Tenn.	250	
WCPH	Etowah, Tenn.	1000	
WAXO	Lewisburg, Tenn.	1000	
KZEE	Weatherford, Tex.	500	
KVLL	Woodville, Tex.	250	
WLSD	Big Stone Gap, Va.	1000	
WFAX	Falls Church, Va.	5000	
KASY	Auburn, Wash.	2500	
CJOC	Lethbridge, Alta.	10000	5000
CKDA	Victoria, B.C.	50000	50000
CJRB	Boissevain, Man.	10000	10000
CKCW	Moncton, N.B.	25000	25000
CJSS	Cornwall, Ont.	1000	1000
CJRL	Kenora, Ont.	1000	1000
CHSC	St. Catherines, Ont.	1000	10000
CFVM	Amqui, Que.	5000	5000
CKSM	Shawinigan Falls, Que.	10000	2500
XEB	Mexico City, D.F.	100000	100000
CMGY	Perico, Cuba	5000	5000

1230 (LOCAL)

WAUD	Auburn, Ala.	1000	250
WKWL	Florala, Ala.	1000	250
WJBB	Haleyville, Ala.	1000	250
WBHP	Huntsville, Ala.	1000	250
WHOD	Jackson, Ala.	1000	250
WNUZ	Talladega, Ala.	1000	250
WTBC	Tuscaloosa, Ala.	1000	250
KIFW	Sitka, Alas.	1000	250
KBZB	Bisbee, Ariz.	1000	250
KAAA	Kingman, Ariz.	1000	250
KFLR	Phoenix, Ariz.	1000	250
KATO	Safford, Ariz.	1000	250
KINO	Winslow, Ariz.	1000	250
KCON	Conway, Ark.	1000	250
KFPW	Ft. Smith, Ark.	1000	250
KBTM	Jonesboro, Ark.	1000	250
KGEO	Bakersfield, Calif.	1000	250
KPRO	Barstow, Calif.	1000	250
KIBS	Bishop, Calif.	1000	250
KXO	El Centro, Calif.	1000	250
KDAC	Ft. Bragg, Calif.	1000	250
KGFJ	Los Angeles, Calif.	1000	250
KPRL	Paso Robles, Calif.	1000	250
KRDG	Redding, Calif.	1000	250
KWG	Stockton, Calif.	1000	250
KEXO	Grand Junction, Colo.	1000	250
KLRR	Leadville, Colo.	1000	250
KDZA	Pueblo, Colo.	1000	250
KBCR	Steamboat Springs, Colo.	1000	250
KSTC	Sterling, Colo.	1000	250
WINF	Manchester, Conn.	1000	250
WGGG	Gainesville, Fla.	1000	250
WONN	Lakeland, Fla.	1000	250
WMAF	Madison, Fla.	1000	250
WSBB	New Smyrna Beach, Fla.	1000	250
WNVY	Pensacola, Fla.	1000	250
WCNH	Quincy, Fla.	1000	250
WJNO	West Palm Beach, Fla.	1000	250
WCKJ	Augusta, Ga.	1000	250
WBLJ	Dalton, Ga.	1000	250
WXLI	Dublin, Ga.	1000	250
WFOM	Marietta, Ga.	1000	250
WSOK	Savannah, Ga.	1000	250
WAYX	Waycross, Ga.	1000	250
KBAR	Burley, Id.	1000	250
KORT	Grangeville, Id.	1000	250
KRXK	Rexburg, Id.	1000	250
WJBC	Bloomington, Ill.	1000	250
WMRZ	Moline, Ill.	1000	250
WHCO	Sparta, Ill.	1000	250
WJOB	Hammond, Ind.	1000	250
WSAL	Logansport, Ind.	1000	250
WTCJ	Tell City, Ind.	1000	250
WBOW	Terre Haute, Ind.	1000	250
KFJB	Marshalltown, Ia.	1000	250
WHIR	Danville, Ky.	1000	250
WHOP	Hopkinsville, Ky.	1000	250
WANO	Pineville, Ky.	1000	250
KLIC	Monroe, La.	1000	250
WBOK	New Orleans, La.	1000	250
KSLO	Opelousas, La.	1000	250
WBME	Belfast, Me.	250	250
WQDY	Calais, Me.	1000	250
WSJR	Madawaska, Me.	1000	250
WITH	Baltimore, Md.	1000	250
WALI	Cumberland, Md.	1000	250
WMNB	North Adams, Mass.	1000	250
WESX	Salem, Mass.	1000	250
WNEB	Worcester, Mass.	1000	250
WCUZ	Grand Rapids, Mich.	1000	250
WIKB	Iron River, Mich.	1000	250
* WMPC	Lapeer, Mich.	1000	250
WSOO	Sault Ste. Marie, Mich.	1000	250
WSTR	Sturgis, Mich.	1000	250
WKLK	Cloquet, Minn.	1000	250
KGHS	International Falls, Minn.	500	250
KYSM	Mankato, Minn.	1000	250
KMRS	Morris, Minn.	1000	250
KTRF	Thief River Falls, Minn.	1000	250
KWNO	Winona, Minn.	1000	250
WCMA	Corinth, Miss.	1000	250
WHSY	Hattiesburg, Miss.	1000	250
WSSO	Starkville, Miss.	1000	250
WAZF	Yazoo City, Miss.	1000	250
KODE	Joplin, Mo.	1000	250
KLWT	Lebanon, Mo.	1000	250
KWIX	Moberly, Mo.	1000	250
KBMN	Bozeman, Mont.	1000	250
KHDN	Hardin, Mont.	1000	250
KXLO	Lewistown, Mont.	1000	250
KLCB	Libby, Mont.	1000	250
KTNC	Falls City, Neb.	500	250
KHAS	Hastings, Neb.	1000	250
KELY	Ely, Nev.	250	250 f
KLAV	Las Vegas, Nev.	1000	250
KCBN	Reno, Nev.	1000	250
WMOU	Berlin, N.H.	1000	250
WTSV	Claremont, N.H.	1000	250
WCMC	Wildwood, N.J.	1000	250
KPSA	Alamogordo, N.M.	1000	250
KOTS	Deming, N.M.	1000	250
KYVA	Gallup, N.M.	1000	250
KFUN	Las Vegas, N.M.	1000	250
KRSY	Roswell, N.M.	1000	250
WECK	Cheektowaga, N.Y.	1000	250
WENY	Elmira, N.Y.	1000	250
WIGS	Gouverneur, N.Y.	1000	250
WHUC	Hudson, N.Y.	1000	250
WLFH	Little Falls, N.Y.	1000	250
WFAS	White Plains, N.Y.	1000	250
WSKY	Asheville, N.C.	1000	250
WFAI	Fayetteville, N.C.	1000	250
WMFR	High Point, N.C.	1000	250
WISP	Kinston, N.C.	1000	250
WNNC	Newton, N.C.	1000	250
WCBT	Roanoke Rapids, N.C.	1000	250
KDIX	Dickinson, N.D.	1000	250
WMLX	Cincinnati, O.	1000	250
WCOL	Columbus, O.	1000	250
WIRO	Ironton, O.	1000	250
WCWA	Toledo, O.	1000	250
KADA	Ada, Okla.	1000	250
WBBZ	Ponca City, Okla.	1000	250
† KDOV	Ashland, Ore.	1000	250
KVAS	Astoria, Ore.	1000	250
KRNS	Burns, Ore.	1000	250 -f
KHSN	Coos Bay, Ore.	1000	250

Call	Location	Day	Night
KRDR	Gresham, Ore.	1000	250
KQIK	Lakeview, Ore.	1000	250 -f
KYJC	Medford, Ore.	1000	250
KTDO	Toledo, Ore.	1000	250
WBVP	Beaver Falls, Pa.	1000	250
WEEX	Easton, Pa.	1000	250
WKBO	Harrisburg, Pa.	1000	250
WCRO	Johnstown, Pa.	1000	250
WBPZ	Lock Haven, Pa.	1000	250
WTIV	Titusville, Pa.	1000	250
WNIK	Arecibo, P.R.	1000	250
WERI	Westerly, R.I.	1000	250
WAIM	Anderson, S.C.	1000	250
WNOK	Columbia, S.C.	1000	250
WOLS	Florence, S.C.	1000	250
KYKC	Sioux Falls, S.D.	1000	250
† ----	Gatlinburg, Tenn.	1000	250
WKCE	Harriman, Tenn.	250	250
WMLR	Hohenwald, Tenn.	1000	250
WAKI	Mc Minnville, Tenn.	1000	250
KSIX	Corpus Christi, Tex.	1000	250
KDLK	Del Rio, Tex.	1000	250
KNUZ	Houston, Tex.	1000	250
KERV	Kerrville, Tex.	1000	250
KLVT	Levelland, Tex.	1000	250
KEEE	Nacogdoches, Tex.	1000	250
KOZA	Odessa, Tex.	1000	250
KGRO	Pampa, Tex.	1000	250
KSEY	Seymour, Tex.	1000	250 -f
KSST	Sulphur Springs, Tex.	1000	250
KWTX	Waco, Tex.	1000	250
KLAF	Murray, Utah	1000	250
KOAL	Price, Utah	1000	250
WJOY	Burlington, Vt.	1000	250
WBBI	Abingdon, Va.	1000	250
WODI	Brookneal, Va.	1000	250 -f
WXCF	Clifton Forge, Va.	1000	250
WFVA	Fredericksburg, Va.	1000	250
WNOR	Norfolk, Va.	1000	250
WAAM	Woodstock, Va.	1000	250
KOZI	Chelan, Wash.	1000	250
KWYZ	Everett, Wash.	1000	250
KKER	Spokane, Wash.	1000	250
‡ KREW	Sunnyside, Wash.	1000	250
WLOG	Logan, W.V.	1000	250
WKYG	Parkersburg, W.V.	1000	250
WHBY	Appleton, Wis.	1000	250
WCLO	Janesville, Wis.	1000	250
WXCO	Wausau, Wis.	1000	250
KVOC	Casper, Wyo.	1000	250
CJOK	Fort Mc Murray, Alta.	1000	500
CKQR	Castlegar, B.C.	1000	250
CKTK	Kitimat, B.C.	1000	250
CJNL	Merritt, B.C.	1000	250
CFBV	Smithers, B.C.	1000	250
CHFC	Churchill, Man.	250	250
CFLN	Goose Bay, Nfld.	1000	250
CFGN	Port Aux Basques, Nfld.	250	250
• VOAR	St. John's, Nfld.	100	100
CFLK	Kapuskasing, Ont.	100	100
CKMP	Midland, Ont.	1000	250
CJTT	New Liskeard, Ont.	1000	250
CJLB	Thunder Bay, Ont.	1000	250
CHVD	Dolbeau, Que.	1000	250
CJSA	Ste. Agathe Des Monts, Que.	1000	250
CFGR	Gravelbourg, Sask.	0	250
XESCT	Ensenada, B.C.	1000	250
† ----	Montemorelos, N.L.	1000	
XETVH	Villahermosa, Tab.	5000	500 -
XEID	Alamo, Ver.	1000	1000
ZBM-1	Hamilton, Bermuda	1000	1000
CMGM	Jaguey Grande, Cuba	1000	1000
PJL3	Curacao, Ne. Antil.	250	250

1240 (LOCAL)

Call	Location	Day	Night
WEBJ	Brewton, Ala.	1000	250
‡ WPRN	Butler, Ala.	1000	250
WULA	Eufaula, Ala.	1000	250
WBCF	Florence, Ala.	1000	250
WARF	Jasper, Ala.	1000	250
KSML	Globe, Ariz.	1000	250
KVRC	Arkadelphia, Ark.	1000	250
KTLO	Mountain Home, Ark.	1000	250
KWAK	Stuttgart, Ark.	1000	250
KPOD	Crescent City, Calif.	1000	250
KJOP	Lemoore, Calif.	250	250
KNRY	Monterey, Calif.	1000	250
KPPC	Pasadena, Calif.	100	f
KLOA	Ridgecrest, Calif.	1000	250
KENZ	Sacramento, Calif.	1000	250
KDIG	San Bernardino, Calif.	1000	250
KSON	San Diego, Calif.	1000	250
KSMA	Santa Maria, Calif.	1000	250
KSUE	Susanville, Calif.	1000	250
KRDO	Colorado Springs, Colo.	1000	250
KDGO	Durango, Colo.	1000	250
KSLV	Monte Vista, Colo.	1000	250
KCRT	Trinidad, Colo.	250	250 f
WWCO	Waterbury, Conn.	1000	250
WBGC	Chipley, Fla.	1000	250
† WDKA	Cross City, Fla.	1000	250
WLCO	Eustis, Fla.	1000	250
WINK	Ft. Myers, Fla.	1000	250
WMMB	Melbourne, Fla.	1000	250
WFOY	St. Augustine, Fla.	1000	250
WBHB	Fitzgerald, Ga.	1000	250
WGGA	Gainesville, Ga.	1000	250
WLAG	La Grange, Ga.	1000	250
WDDO	Macon, Ga.	1000	250
WWNS	Statesboro, Ga.	1000	250
WPAX	Thomasville, Ga.	1000	250
WTWA	Thomson, Ga.	1000	250
KMCL	Mc Call, Id.	500	250
KJCY	Mountain Home, Id.	1000	250
KWIK	Pocatello, Id.	1000	250
WSBC	Chicago, Ill.	1000	250
WCRW	Chicago, Ill.	1000	250
WEDC	Chicago, Ill.	1000	250
WEBQ	Harrisburg, Ill.	1000	250
WTAX	Springfield, Ill.	1000	250
WSDR	Sterling, Ill.	500	250
WHBU	Anderson, Ind.	1000	250
‡# KDEC	Decorah, Ia.	1000	250
•# KWLC	Decorah, Ia.	1000	250
KBIZ	Ottumwa, Ia.	1000	250
KICD	Spencer, Ia.	1000	250
KIUL	Garden City, Kan.	1000	250
KAKZ	Wichita, Kan.	1000	250
WINN	Louisville, Ky.	1000	250
WFTM	Maysville, Ky.	1000	250
WPKE	Pikeville, Ky.	1000	250
WSFC	Somerset, Ky.	1000	250
KASO	Minden, La.	1000	250
KANE	New Iberia, La.	1000	250
WCOU	Lewiston, Me.	1000	250
WMKR	Millinocket, Me.	1000	250
WCEM	Cambridge, Md.	1000	250
WJEJ	Hagerstown, Md.	1000	250
WHAI	Greenfield, Mass.	1000	250
WSOX	West Yarmouth, Mass.	1000	250
WATT	Cadillac, Mich.	1000	250
WCBY	Cheboygan, Mich.	1000	250
WJPD	Ishpeming, Mich.	1000	250
WJIM	Lansing, Mich.	1000	250
WGGR	Hibbing, Minn.	1000	250
WJON	St. Cloud, Minn.	1000	250
WMPA	Aberdeen, Miss.	1000	250
WGRM	Greenwood, Miss.	1000	250
WTAM	Gulfport, Miss.	1000	250
† WJDQ	Marion, Miss.	1000	250
WMIS	Natchez, Miss.	1000	250
KFMO	Flat River, Mo.	1000	250

KWOS	Jefferson City, Mo.	1000	250
KNEM	Nevada, Mo.	1000	250
KBMY	Billings, Mont.	1000	250
KLTZ	Glasgow, Mont.	1000	250
KLYQ	Hamilton, Mont.	1000	250
KBLL	Helena, Mont.	1000	250
KFOR	Lincoln, Neb.	1000	250
KODY	North Platte, Neb.	1000	250
KELK	Elko, Nev.	1000	250
WFTN	Franklin, N.H.	1000	250
WSNJ	Bridgeton, N.J.	1000	250
KLTN	Albuquerque, N.M.	1000	250
KAMQ	Carlsbad, N.M.	1000	250
KCLV	Clovis, N.M.	1000	250
WGBB	Freeport, N.Y.	1000	250
WGVA	Geneva, N.Y.	1000	250
WJTN	Jamestown, N.Y.	500	250
WVOS	Liberty, N.Y.	1000	250
WNBZ	Saranac Lake, N.Y.	1000	250
WWWD	Schenectady, N.Y.	1000	250
WATN	Watertown, N.Y.	1000	250
WPNF	Brevard, N.C.	1000	250
WHVN	Charlotte, N.C.	1000	250
WCNC	Elizabeth City, N.C.	1000	250
WJNC	Jacksonville, N.C.	1000	250
WPJL	Raleigh, N.C.	1000	250
WWWC	Wilkesboro, N.C.	500	250
KDLR	Devils Lake, N.D.	1000	250
WBBW	Youngstown, O.	1000	250
WHIZ	Zanesville, O.	1000	250
KVSO	Ardmore, Okla.	1000	250
KADS	Elk City, Okla.	1000	250
KBEL	Idabel, Okla.	1000	250
KOKL	Okmulgee, Okla.	1000	250
KFLY	Corvallis, Ore.	1000	250
KTIX	Pendleton, Ore.	1000	250
KPRB	Redmond, Ore.	1000	250
KQEN	Roseburg, Ore.	1000	250
WRTA	Altoona, Pa.	1000	250
WHUM	Reading, Pa.	1000	250
WSEW	Selinsgrove, Pa.	1000	250
WBAX	Wilkes Barre, Pa.	1000	250
WALO	Humacao, P.R.	1000	250
WWON	Woonsocket, R.I.	1000	250
WKDK	Newberry, S.C.	1000	250
WDXY	Sumter, S.C.	1000	250
KCCR	Pierre, S.D.	1000	250
WBEJ	Elizabethton, Tenn.	1000	250
WEKR	Fayetteville, Tenn.	1000	250
WHEL	Knoxville, Tenn.	1000	250
WKDA	Nashville, Tenn.	1000	250
WSDT	Soddy Daisy, Tenn.	1000	250
WENK	Union City, Tenn.	1000	250
KVLF	Alpine, Tex.	1000	250
KXYL	Brownwood, Tex.	1000	250
KTAM	Bryan, Tex.	1000	250
KXIT	Dalhart, Tex.	1000	500
KAWS	Hemphill, Tex.	1000	250
KOCA	Kilgore, Tex.	1000	250
KSOX	Raymondville, Tex.	1000	250
KXOX	Sweetwater, Tex.	1000	250
WSKI	Montpelier, Vt.	1000	250
WSSV	Petersburg, Va.	1000	250
WROV	Roanoke, Va.	1000	250
WTON	Staunton, Va.	1000	250
KXLE	Ellensburg, Wash.	1000	250
KGY	Olympia, Wash.	1000	250
WKOY	Bluefield, W.V.	1000	250
WTIP	Charleston, W.V.	1000	250
WDNE	Elkins, W.V.	1000	250
WOMT	Manitowoc, Wis.	1000	250
WIBU	Poynette, Wis.	1000	250
WOBT	Rhinelander, Wis.	1000	250
WJMC	Rice Lake, Wis.	1000	250
KFBC	Cheyenne, Wyo.	1000	250
KEVA	Evanston, Wyo.	1000	250
KASL	Newcastle, Wyo.	1000	250
KRAL	Rawlins, Wyo.	1000	250
KTHE	Thermopolis, Wyo.	1000	250
CKBX	100 Mile House, B.C.	1000	1000
CFEK	Fernie, B.C.	1000	500
CKGO	Hope, B.C.	1000	250
CKMK	Mackenzie, B.C.	1000	250
CKOO	Osoyoos, B.C.	1000	500
CJAV	Port Alberni, B.C.	1000	250
CFNI	Port Hardy, B.C.	1000	250
CJAR	The Pas, Man.	1000	250
CKIM	Baie Verte, Nfld.	1000	500
CFAK	Atikokan, Ont.	250	250
CJNH	Bancroft, Ont.	1000	250
CJCS	Stratford, Ont.	500	250
CJWA	Wawa, Ont.	1000	250
CJRW	Summerside, P.E.	250	250
CJAF	Cabano, Que.	1000	250
CJMD	Chibougamau, Que.	1000	250
CKLS	La Sarre, Que.	1000	250
CFLM	La Tuque, Que.	1000	250
CIRB	Lac Etchemin, Que.	1000	250
CKBS	St. Hyacinthe, Que.	250	250
CJNS	Meadow Lake, Sask.	1000	250
XELM	Tuxtla, Chis.	1000	500
XEWG	Ciudad Juarez, Chih.	1000	250
XEBN	Delicias, Chih.	1000	250
XEVM	Piedras Negras, Coah.	250	200
XETC	Torreon, Coah.	500	250
XERZ	Leon, Gto.	1000	500
† XERAA	Atoyac, Gro.	500	250
XERPA	Morelia, Mich.	500	100
XESI	Santiago Ixcuintla, Nay.	1000	300
XEIZ	Monterrey, N.L.	500	250
XECE	Oaxaca, Oax.	500	250
XENG	Huauchinango, Pue.	1000	200
XEREY	San Blas, Sin.	1000	250
XEBQ	Guaymas, Son.	1000	250
XECG	Nogales, Son.	1000	250
XES	Tampico, Tams.	1000	250
XEOV	Orizaba, Ver.	250	175
XEMQ	Merida, Yuc.	5000	500
XEPC	Zacatecas, Zac.	1000	
ZNS-2	Nassau, Bahamas	250	250
CMGW	Matanzas, Cuba	1000	1000
CMKE	Victoria De Las Tunas, Cuba	250	250
HICV	Barahona, Dom. Rep.	250	250
HIBB	La Romana, Dom. Rep.	500	250
HIBU	Valverde, Dom. Rep.	500	500

1250 (REGIONAL)

WZOB	Fort Payne, Ala.	1000	
WETU	Wetumpka, Ala.	5000	
* KBBI	Homer, Alas.	5000	5000
KUUK	Wickenburg, Ariz.	1000	
KHIL	Willcox, Ariz.	5000	
KFAY	Fayetteville, Ark.	1000	
KOKY	Little Rock, Ark.	1000	500
KNCO	Grass Valley, Calif.	500	1000
KHOT	Madera, Calif.	500	
KTMS	Santa Barbara, Calif.	2500	1000
KDHI	Twentynine Palms, Calif.	1000	
† KLLK	Willits, Calif.	2500	1000
WNER	Live Oak, Fla.	1000	
WDAE	Tampa, Fla.	5000	5000
WQDE	Albany, Ga.	1000	
WYTH	Madison, Ga.	1000	
WIZZ	Streator, Ill.	500	
WGL	Ft. Wayne, Ind.	1000	1000
WRAY	Princeton, Ind.	1000	
KCFI	Cedar Falls, Ia.	500	500
#* KFKU	Lawrence, Kan.	5000	5000
# WREN	Topeka, Kan.	5000	5000
WNVL	Nicholasville, Ky.	500	
WLCK	Scottsville, Ky.	500	
WMLI	Bangor, Me.	5000	5000

WARE	Ware, Mass.	5000	2500
WTCX	Bay City, Mich.	1000	
KBRF	Fergus Falls, Minn.	5000	1000
KCUE	Red Wing, Minn.	1000	
WHNY	Mc Comb, Miss.	5000	1000
KBTC	Houston, Mo.	1000	
WKBR	Manchester, N.H.	5000	5000
WMTR	Morristown, N.J.	5000	
WIPS	Ticonderoga, N.Y.	1000	
WGHB	Farmville, N.C.	5000	2500
WKDX	Hamlet, N.C.	1000	
WBRM	Marion, N.C.	5000	
WOFR	Washington Court House, O.	500	
WLEM	Emporium, Pa.	2500	
WPEL	Montrose, Pa.	1000	
WTAE	Pittsburgh, Pa.	5000	5000
WNOW	York, Pa.	1000	
WTMA	Charleston, S.C.	5000	1000
WCKM	Winnsboro, S.C.	500	
WKBL	Covington, Tenn.	1000	500
WRKQ	Madisonville, Tenn.	500	
WNTT	Tazewell, Tenn.	500	
KPRE	Paris, Tex.	500	
KTXC	Port Arthur, Tex.	5000	1000
KUKA	San Antonio, Tex.	1000	1000
KIKZ	Seminole, Tex.	1000	
KNEU	Roosevelt, Utah	5000	
WDVA	Danville, Va.	5000	5000
WYSR	Franklin, Va.	1000	
WPRZ	Warrenton, Va.	5000	
* KWSU	Pullman, Wash.	5000	5000
KKFX	Seattle, Wash.	5000	5000
† WYKM	Rupert, W.V.	500	
WEMP	Milwaukee, Wis.	5000	5000
CHSM	Steinbach, Man.	10000	10000
CHWO	Oakville, Ont.	10000	5000
CBOF	Ottawa, Ont.	50000	50000
CBGA	Matane, Que.	10000	5000
CKOM	Saskatoon, Sask.	10000	10000
XEMG	Arriaga, Chis.	1000	250
XEAT	Parral, Chih.	250	250
XESC	Sabinas, Coah.	1000	1000
XESJ	Saltillo, Coah.	1000	500
XEPI	Tixtla, Gro.	1000	100
XEDK	Guadalajara, Jal.	5000	1000
† ----	Puruandiro, Mich.	250	
XEZT	Puebla, Pue.	500	100
XEJX	Queretaro, Qro.	1000	250
XEUO	Chetumal, Q.R.	250	250
† XESN	Caborca, Son.	500	
XEDL	Hermosillo, Son.	1000	500
XETF	Veracruz, Ver.	1000	500
CMKA	Guantanamo, Cuba	250	250
HIRM	Higuey, Dom. Rep.	250	250
HIBC	San Francisco De Macoris, Dom Rep.	5000	500
4VM	Port Au Prince, Haiti	600	600

1260 (REGIONAL)

WCRT	Birmingham, Ala.	5000	1000
KPIN	Casa Grande, Ariz.	1000	
KCCB	Corning, Ark.	1000	
KBHC	Nashville, Ark.	500	
KGIL	San Fernando, Calif.	5000	5000
KIOT	San Francisco, Calif.	5000	1000
KSNO	Aspen, Colo.	5000	
WMMM	Westport, Conn.	1000	
WNRK	Newark, Del.	1000	
WWDC	Washington, D. C.	5000	5000
WFTW	Ft. Walton Beach, Fla.	2500	
WHTT	Miami, Fla.	5000	5000
WIYD	Palatka, Fla.	1000	500
WUFE	Baxley, Ga.	5000	
WBBK	Blakely, Ga.	1000	
WTJH	East Point, Ga.	5000	
KTEE	Idaho Falls, Id.	5000	
KWEI	Weiser, Id.	1000	
WIBV	Belleville, Ill.	5000	5000
WNDE	Indianapolis, Ind.	5000	5000
* KFGQ	Boone, Ia.	1000	
KWHK	Hutchinson, Kan.	1000	500
WTKL	Baton Rouge, La.	1000	
WEZE	Boston, Mass.	5000	5000
WELL	Albion, Mich.	1000	500
WWJQ	Holland, Mich.	5000	1000
KROX	Crookston, Minn.	1000	500
KDUZ	Hutchinson, Minn.	1000	
WGVM	Greenville, Miss.	5000	
WQIS	Laurel, Miss.	5000	
WCSA	Ripley, Miss.	500	
KGBX	Springfield, Mo.	5000	5000
KIMB	Kimball, Neb.	1000	
WBUD	Trenton, N.J.	5000	1000
KVSF	Santa Fe, N.M.	5000	1000
WBNR	Beacon, N.Y.	1000	
WNDR	Syracuse, N.Y.	5000	5000
WGWR	Asheboro, N.C.	5000	500
WCDJ	Edenton, N.C.	1000	
WBBG	Cleveland, O.	5000	5000
WNXT	Portsmouth, O.	5000	1000
KWSH	Wewoka, Okla.	1000	1000
KCYX	Mc Minnville, Ore.	1000	1000
WLKK	Erie, Pa.	5000	5000
WPHB	Philipsburg, Pa.	5000	
WISO	Ponce, P.R.	1000	1000
WMUU	Greenville, S.C.	5000	
WJOT	Lake City, S.C.	1000	
KWYR	Winner, S.D.	5000	
WNOO	Chattanooga, Tenn.	5000	
WMCH	Church Hill, Tenn.	1000	
WDKN	Dickson, Tenn.	5000r	
WCLC	Jamestown, Tenn.	1000	
KIPR	Diboll, Tex.	1000	
KPSO	Falfurrias, Tex.	500	
KQSA	San Angelo, Tex.	1000	
KTAE	Taylor, Tex.	1000	
KTUE	Tulia, Tex.	1000	
WVCH	Charlottesville, Va.	5000	2500r
WJJJ	Christiansburg, Va.	2500	
‡ KWIQ	Moses Lake, Wash.	1000	
WKGA	Grafton, W.V.	500	
WXCE	Amery, Wis.	5000	5000
WWIS	Black River Falls, Wis.	1000	
WEKZ	Monroe, Wis.	1000	
WOCO	Oconto, Wis.	1000	
KPOW	Powell, Wyo.	5000	1000
CFRN	Edmonton, Alta.	50000	50000
CIHI	Fredericton, N.B.	10000	10000
XEOG	Ojinaga, Chih.	1000	250
XEMF	Monclova, Coah.	1000	250
XEL	Mexico City, D.F.	10000	500
XEZH	Salamanca, Gto.	500	
† ----	Puerto Vallarta, Jal.	1000	1000
XER	Linares, N.L.	1000	250
† ----	Kantunil Kin, Q.R.	250	
XEXR	Ciudad Valles, S.L.P.	1000	
XESA	Culiacan, Sin.	1000	500
XEMW	San Luis, Son.	1000	250
XEMTV	Minatitlan, Ver.	1000	1000
† ----	Nadlingo, Ver.	250	
XEEY	Jalapa, Zac.	1000	1000
CMDE	Bayamo, Cuba	250	250
CMAG	Consolacion Del Sur, Cuba	1000	1000
HIT	Santo Domingo, Dom. Rep.	500	500

1270 (REGIONAL)

WGSV	Guntersville, Ala.	1000	
WKSJ	Prichard, Ala.	1000	
† KIAM	Nenana, Alas.	5000	5000
KDJI	Holbrook, Ariz.	5000	
KABS	Pine Bluff, Ark.	5000	
‡ KBLC	Lakeport, Calif.	500	
KGUY	Palm Desert, Calif.	1000	

Call	Location	Day	Night
KCOK	Tulare, Calif.	5000	1000
WNOG	Naples, Fla.	500	500
WORL	Orlando, Fla.	5000	5000
WTNT	Tallahassee, Fla.	5000	5000
WYXC	Cartersville, Ga.	500	
WHYD	Columbus, Ga.	5000	
WJJC	Commerce, Ga.	5000	
KNDI	Honolulu, Haw.	5000	5000
KTLC	Twin Falls, Id.	5000	1000
WEIC	Charleston, Ill.	1000	500
WHBF	Rock Island, Ill.	5000	5000
WCMR	Elkhart, Ind.	5000	1000
WWCA	Gary, Ind.	1000	1000
WORX	Madison, Ind.	1000	
KSCB	Liberal, Kan.	1000	500
WAIN	Columbia, Ky.	1000	
WFUL	Fulton, Ky.	1000	
WVKY	Louisa, Ky.	1000	
KVCL	Winnfield, La.	1000	
WCBC	Cumberland, Md.	5000	1000
WSPR	Springfield, Mass.	5000	1000
WVOY	Charlevoix, Mich.	5000	5000
WXYZ	Detroit, Mich.	5000	5000
‡ KPRM	Park Rapids, Minn.	5000	
KWEB	Rochester, Minn.	5000	1000
WVOM	Iuka, Miss.	1000	
WLSM	Louisville, Miss.	5000	
WMLC	Monticello, Miss.	1000	
KGNM	St. Joseph, Mo.	1000	
KOZQ	Waynesville, Mo.	500	
KROI	Sparks, Nev.	5000r	5000
WTSN	Dover, N.H.	5000	5000
WDVL	Vineland, N.J.	500	
KINN	Alamogordo, N.M.	1000	
WHLD	Niagara Falls, N.Y.	5000	
WDLA	Walton, N.Y.	5000	
WCGC	Belmont, N.C.	1000	500
WMPM	Smithfield, N.C.	5000	
KBOM	Bismarck, N.D.	1000	250
WILE	Cambridge, O.	1000	
† WUCO	Marysville, O.	500	
KOKN	Claremore, Okla.	1000	
KAJO	Grants Pass, Ore.	5000	
WLBR	Lebanon, Pa.	5000	1000
WBHC	Hampton, S.C.	1000	
WYAK	Surfside Beach, S.C.	5000	
★ KNWC	Sioux Falls, S.D.	2500	2500
WLIK	Newport, Tenn.	5000	500
WQSI	Portland, Tenn.	1000	
KIOX	Bay City, Tex.	1000	1000
KHEM	Big Spring, Tex.	1000	
KEPS	Eagle Pass, Tex.	1000	
KSSA	Ft. Worth, Tex.	5000	5000
† WWES	Hot Springs, Va.	500	
WOKT	Newport News, Va.	1000	1000
WHEO	Stuart, Va.	5000	
KCVL	Colville, Wash.	1000	
KBAM	Longview, Wash.	5000	
WRJC	Mauston, Wis.	500	
KIML	Gillette, Wyo.	5000	1000
CHAT	Medicine Hat, Alta.	10000	10000
CHWK	Chilliwack, B.C.	10000	10000
CJCB	Sydney, N.S.	10000	10000
CJTN	Trenton, Ont.	1000	1000
CFGT	Alma, Que.	10000	5000
XECAL	Tijuana, B.C.	5000	5000
XEOH	Camargo, Chih.	1000	150
XEHD	Durango, Dgo.	1000	500
XEWN	Gomez Palacio, Dgo.	500	150
XERPL	Leon, Gto.	5000	150
† ----	Taxco, Gro.	250	100
† ----	Teloloapan, Gro.	2000	
XEQH	Ixmiquilpan, Hgo.	1000	100
† ----	Tamazula, Jal.	500	
XEZU	Zacapu, Mich.	1000	250
XEAX	Oaxaca, Oax.	5000	500
XEGL	Navojoa, Son.	1000	500
XENY	Nogales, Son.	1000	250
XEPRT	Ciudad Madero, Tams.	5000	500
XEPV	Papantla, Ver.	1000	250
XEYW	Uman, Yuc.	2500	500
CMJG	Camaguey, Cuba	1000	1000
HIUA	Santiago, Dom. Rep.	1000	1000
PJA8	Aruba, Ne. Antil.	1000	1000

1280 (REGIONAL)

Call	Location	Day	Night
WPID	Piedmont, Ala.	1000	
WNPT	Tuscaloosa, Ala.	5000	500
KHEP	Phoenix, Ariz.	1000	
KNBY	Newport, Ark.	1000	
KKAL	Arroyo Grande, Calif.	5000	2500
KFRN	Long Beach, Calif.	1000	1000
KJOY	Stockton, Calif.	1000	1000
KBRQ	Denver, Colo.	5000	5000
WSUX	Seaford, Del.	1000	
WGTX	De Funiak Springs, Fla.	5000	
WEXI	Jacksonville, Fla.	5000	
WIPC	Lake Wales, Fla.	1000	500
WWZZ	Sarasota, Fla.	500	
WIBB	Macon, Ga.	5000	
WMRO	Aurora, Ill.	2500	500
WGBF	Evansville, Ind.	5000	1000
WAOB	Winamac, Ind.	500	
KCOB	Newton, Ia.	1000	
KSOK	Arkansas City, Kan.	1000	100
WCPM	Cumberland, Ky.	1000	
WIXI	Lancaster, Ky.	1000	
WQUE	New Orleans, La.	5000	5000
KWCL	Oak Grove, La.	1000	
WABK	Gardiner, Me.	5000	5000
WEIM	Fitchburg, Mass.	5000	1000
WFYC	Alma, Mich.	1000	
WWTC	Minneapolis, Minn.	5000	5000
KVOX	Moorhead, Minn.	5000	1000
KDKD	Clinton, Mo.	1000	
KYRO	Potosi, Mo.	500	
KCNI	Broken Bow, Neb.	1000	
KVOV	Henderson, Nev.	5000	
KRZE	Farmington, N.M.	5000	
WADO	New York, N.Y.	5000	5000
WPXY	Rochester, N.Y.	5000	5000
WSAT	Salisbury, N.C.	1000	1000
WYAL	Scotland Neck, N.C.	5000	
WONW	Defiance, O.	1000	500
WLMJ	Jackson, O.	1000	
KLCO	Poteau, Okla.	1000	
KBDF	Eugene, Ore.	5000	1000
WBRX	Berwick, Pa.	1000	
WHVR	Hanover, Pa.	5000	500
WKST	New Castle, Pa.	1000	1000
WCMN	Arecibo, P.R.	5000	1000
WANS	Anderson, S.C.	5000	1000
WJAY	Mullins, S.C.	5000	
† WCTA	Alamo, Tenn.	500	
WMCP	Columbia, Tenn.	5000	500
WDNT	Dayton, Tenn.	1000	
KEAN	Abilene, Tex.	500	
KTTX	Brenham, Tex.	1000	
KLUE	Longview, Tex.	1000	
KRAN	Morton, Tex.	500	
KVWG	Pearsall, Tex.	500	
KDYL	Salt Lake City, Utah	5000	500
WTTX	Appomattox, Va.	2500r	
WYVE	Wytheville, Va.	2500	
KMAS	Shelton, Wash.	5000	
KUDY	Spokane, Wash.	5000	
KIT	Yakima, Wash.	5000	1000
WGLR	Lancaster, Wis.	500	
WNAM	Neenah, Wis.	5000	1000
CHRB	High River, Alta.	10000	10000
CHQB	Powell River, B.C.	1000	1000
CHAM	Hamilton, Ont.	10000	10000
CJMS	Montreal, Que.	50000	50000
CKCV	Quebec, Que.	50000	50000
CJSL	Estevan, Sask.	10000	10000
XECAM	Campeche, Cam.	500	200
XEKY	Huixtla, Chis.	1000	100
XEBW	Chihuahua, Chih.	1000	600
XESQ	San Miguel Allende, Gto.	500	250
† ----	Zihuatenejo, Gro.	500	
XEQP	Guadalajara, Jal.	1000	250

† ----	Acaponeta, Nay.	1000	500
XEAW	Monterrey, N.L.	5000	500
XEHS	Los Mochis, Sin.	250	250
XEANA	Caborca, Son.	500	
XEEG	Panzacola, Tlax.	1000	250
XEAG	Cordoba, Ver.	1000	1000
† ----	Tizimin, Yuc.	1000	
CMHM	Santa Clara, Cuba	1000	1000
CMDP	Victoria De Las Tunas, Cuba	250	250

1290 (REGIONAL)

WOPP	Opp, Ala.	2500	500
WSHF	Sheffield, Ala.	1000	
WYEA	Sylacauga, Ala.	1000	
† KETH	Ketchikan, Alas.	5000	1000
KCUB	Tucson, Ariz.	5000	1000
KDMS	El Dorado, Ark.	5000	
KUOA	Siloam Springs, Ark.	5000	
KHSL	Chico, Calif.	5000	5000
KAZA	Gilroy, Calif.	5000	
KMEN	San Bernardino, Calif.	5000	5000
KXXN	Santa Barbara, Calif.	500	
WCCC	Hartford, Conn.	5000	
WJBR	Wilmington, Del.	1000	
WTMC	Ocala, Fla.	5000	1000
WPCF	Panama City Beach, Fla.	500	
WPCK	West Palm Beach, Fla.	50000r	1000
WDEC	Americus, Ga.	1000	
WCHK	Canton, Ga.	5000	500
WWSA	Savannah, Ga.	5000	5000
KZBQ	Pocatello, Id.	1000	
WIRL	Peoria, Ill.	5000	5000
WDGS	New Albany, Ind.	500	
KLEH	Anamosa, Ia.	500	
KWLS	Pratt, Kan.	5000	500
WCBL	Benton, Ky.	5000	
WKLB	Manchester, Ky.	5000	
KJEF	Jennings, La.	1000	
WHGR	Houghton Lake, Mich.	5000	5000
WNIL	Niles, Mich.	500	
WNRS	Saline, Mich.	500	
KBMO	Benson, Minn.	500	
WBLE	Batesville, Miss.	1000	
WTYL	Tylertown, Miss.	1000	
KALM	Thayer, Mo.	1000	
KGVO	Missoula, Mont.	5000	5000
KOIL	Omaha, Neb.	5000	5000
WKNE	Keene, N.H.	5000	5000
KSRC	Socorro, N.M.	1000	
WGLI	Babylon, N.Y.	5000	1000
WNBF	Binghamton, N.Y.	5000	1000
WHKY	Hickory, N.C.	5000	1000
WIIZ	Jacksonville, N.C.	1000	
WSBL	Sanford, N.C.	1000	
WOMP	Bellaire, O.	1000	
WHIO	Dayton, O.	5000	5000
KLIQ	Lake Oswego, Ore.	5000	5000
KUMA	Pendleton, Ore.	5000	5000
WFBG	Altoona, Pa.	5000	1000
WQIN	Lykens, Pa.	1000	
WRCP	Providence, R.I.	5000	1000
WFIG	Sumter, S.C.	1000	1000
WTNX	Lynchburg, Tenn.	1000	
WATO	Oak Ridge, Tenn.	5000	500
KWGH	Big Lake, Tex.	1000	
KIVY	Crockett, Tex.	2500	
KRGV	Weslaco, Tex.	5000	5000
KTRN	Wichita Falls, Tex.	5000	1000
WRRA	Fredericksted, St. Croi, V.I.	500	
WPVA	Colonial Heights, Va.	5000	
WAGE	Leesburg, Va.	1000	
WNLB	Rocky Mount, Va.	1000	
KAPY	Port Angeles, Wash.	1000	
WVOW	Logan, W.V.	5000	1000
WLZZ	Greenfield, Wis.	5000	5000
WCOW	Sparta, Wis.	5000	
KOWB	Laramie, Wyo.	5000	1000
CFRW	Winnipeg, Man.	10000	10000
CJBK	London, Ont.	10000	10000
CHRM	Matane, Que.	10000	10000
XETH	Palizada, Cam.	250	100
XEDA	Mexico City, D.F.	10000	1000
XERE	Salvatierra, Gto.	1000	1000
XEIX	Jiquilpan, Mich.	1000	100
XEIY	Rio Verde, S.L.P.	1000	500
XENX	Mazatlan, Sin.	10000	250
XEAP	Ciudad Obregon, Son.	1000	100
XEFP	Jalapa, Zac.	10000	5000
CMKS	Guantanamo, Cuba	1000	1000
HIVM	Bonoa, Dom. Rep.	1000	1000

1295

PJD2	St. Martin, Ne. Antil.	50000	50000

1300 (REGIONAL)

WBSA	Boaz, Ala.	1000	
WTLS	Tallassee, Ala.	1000	
WEZQ	Winfield, Ala.	5000	
† ----	Florence, Ariz.	5000	250
KWCK	Searcy, Ark.	5000	
KROP	Brawley, Calif.	1000	500
KYNO	Fresno, Calif.	5000	1000
KPMD	Mendocino, Calif.	5000	
KWKW	Pasadena, Calif.	5000	1000
KVOR	Colorado Springs, Colo.	5000	1000
WAVZ	New Haven, Conn.	1000	1000
WRKT	Cocoa Beach, Fla.	5000	1000
‡ WFFG	Marathon, Fla.	500	500
† WFFG	Marathon, Fla.	2500	2500
WTYM	Tampa, Fla.	5000	1000
WMTM	Moultrie, Ga.	5000	
WNEA	Newnan, Ga.	500	
WIMO	Winder, Ga.	1000	
WTAQ	La Grange, Ill.	5000	500
WFRX	West Frankfort, Ill.	1000	
WHLT	Huntington, Ind.	500	
WPFR	Terre Haute, Ind.	500	
KGLO	Mason City, Ia.	5000	5000
WTKC	Lexington, Ky.	2500	2500
WIBR	Baton Rouge, La.	5000	1000
KFLO	Shreveport, La.	5000q	
WFBR	Baltimore, Md.	5000	5000
WJDA	Quincy, Mass.	1000	
WOOD	Grand Rapids, Mich.	5000	5000
WQPM	Princeton, Minn.	1000	
WKXI	Jackson, Miss.	5000	1000
KMMO	Marshall, Mo.	1000	
KBRL	Mc Cook, Neb.	5000	
KPTL	Carson City, Nev.	5000	500
WPNH	Plymouth, N.H.	5000	
WIMG	Trenton, N.J.	5000	2500
WOSC	Fulton, N.Y.	1000	
WXRL	Lancaster, N.Y.	1000	2500
WQBK	Rensselaer, N.Y.	5000	
WGRC	Spring Valley, N.Y.	500	
WSSG	Goldsboro, N.C.	1000	
WLNC	Laurinburg, N.C.	500	5000
WSYD	Mt. Airy, N.C.	5000	1000
WERE	Cleveland, O.	5000	5000
WMVO	Mt. Vernon, O.	500	
KBBJ	Tulsa, Okla.	5000	1000
KHUG	Medford, Ore.	5000	
KACI	The Dalles, Ore.	1000	
WWCH	Clarion, Pa.	1000	
WXPX	West Hazleton, Pa.	5000	
WTIL	Mayaguez, P.R.	1000	1000
WPBM	Aiken, S.C.	1000q	
WCKI	Greer, S.C.	1000	
WKSC	Kershaw, S.C.	500	
KOLY	Mobridge, S.D.	5000	
WMTN	Morristown, Tenn.	5000	
WLUY	Nashville, Tenn.	5000	5000

KVET	Austin, Tex.	5000	1000
KKUB	Brownfield, Tex.	1000	
KLAR	Laredo, Tex.	1000	500
KKAS	Silsbee, Tex.	500	
WKCY	Harrisonburg, Va.	5000	
KMPS	Seattle, Wash.	5000	5000
WCLG	Morgantown, W.V.	2500	
WKAZ	St. Albans, W.V.	1000	
WCJL	Marinette, Wis.	1000	
CBAF	Moncton, N.B.	5000	5000
CJME	Regina, Sask.	10000	10000
† XEDG	Tuxtla, Chis.	1000	
XEP	Ciudad Juarez, Chih.	1000	500
XESW	Ciudad Madero, Chih.	1000	
† ----	Buenaventura, Coah.	1000	
XEABA	Nueva Rosita, Coah.	1000	100
† ----	Ramos Arispe, Coah.	1000	
XEXV	San Francisco Del Rincon, Gto.	20000	100
† ----	Chilpancingo, Gro.	1000	
XEKW	Morelia, Mich.	500	500
† ----	Tihosuco, Q.R.	150	
XEJL	Guamuchil, Sin.	1000	250
XEXW	Nogales, Son.	5000	100
XELE	Tampico, Tams.	1000	150
XEHU	Martinez De La Torre, Ver.	5000	100
XEGA	San Andres Tuxtla, Ver.	500	500
CMJD	Ciego De Avila, Cuba	250	250
CMJQ	Nuevitas, Cuba	250	250
HIUB	Dajabon, Dom. Rep.	1000	1000
HIAU	Puerto Plata, Dom. Rep.	2000	2000
HIKQ	Santo Domingo, Dom. Rep.	500	500

1310 (REGIONAL)

WHEP	Foley, Ala.	1000	
WAJQ	Marion, Ala.	5000	
KZZP	Mesa, Ariz.	5000	500
KBOK	Malvern, Ark.	1000	
KIOT	Barstow, Calif.	5000	
KCRE	Crescent City, Calif.	1000	
KDIA	Oakland, Calif.	5000	5000
KTKR	Taft, Calif.	1000	
KFKA	Greeley, Colo.	5000	1000
WICH	Norwich, Conn.	5000	5000
WDLF	De Land, Fla.	5000	
WGKR	Perry, Fla.	1000	
WAUC	Wauchula, Fla.	5000	
WXLL	Decatur, Ga.	500	
WOKA	Douglas, Ga.	1000	
WBRO	Waynesboro, Ga.	1000	
WZZZ	West Point, Ga.	1000	
† KHNL	Honolulu, Haw.	5000	
KLIX	Twin Falls, Id.	2500	2500
WMLF	Indianapolis, Ind.	5000	1000
KOKX	Keokuk, Ia.	1000	500
KDLS	Perry, Ia.	500	
KFLA	Scott City, Kan.	500	
WTTL	Madisonville, Ky.	1000	500
WDOC	Prestonburg, Ky.	5000	
KEZM	Sulphur, La.	500	
KUZN	West Monroe, La.	1000	
WLOB	Portland, Me.	5000	5000
WORC	Worcester, Mass.	5000	1000
WNIC	Dearborn, Mich.	5000	5000
WCCW	Traverse City, Mich.	5000	
KRBI	St. Peter, Minn.	1000	
WKOJ	Hattiesburg, Miss.	1000	
KBMV	Birch Tree, Mo.	1000q	
KFSB	Joplin, Mo.	5000	1000
KEIN	Great Falls, Mont.	5000	1000
KGMT	Fairbury, Neb.	500	
WJLK	Asbury Park, N.J.	2500	500
WSSJ	Camden, N.J.	1000	250
WXMC	Parsippany, N.J.	1000	
† KXAK	Corrales, N.M.	1000	
WVIP	Mount Kisco, N.Y.	5000	
WTLB	Utica, N.Y.	1000	500
WISE	Asheville, N.C.	5000	1000
WGSP	Charlotte, N.C.	1000	
WTIK	Durham, N.C.	5000	1000
KNOX	Grand Forks, N.D.	5000	5000
WFAH	Alliance, O.	1000	
KNPT	Newport, Ore.	5000	1000
WBFD	Bedford, Pa.	5000	
WGSA	Ephrata, Pa.	5000	
† WJOZ	Troy, Pa.	500	
WNAE	Warren, Pa.	5000	
WDKD	Kingstree, S.C.	5000	
WDOD	Chattanooga, Tenn.	5000	5000
WDXI	Jackson, Tenn.	5000	1000
WBNT	Oneida, Tenn.	1000	
KZIP	Amarillo, Tex.	1000	
KAAM	Dallas, Tex.	5000	5000
KOYL	Odessa, Tex.	1000	
KBUC	San Antonio, Tex.	5000	
WEEL	Fairfax, Va.	5000	500
WNSV	Newport News, Va.	5000	5000
KARY	Prosser, Wash.	5000	
WSLW	White Sulphur Springs, W.V.	5000	
WIBA	Madison, Wis.	5000	5000
CHLO	St. Paul, Alta.	10000	10000
CKOY	Ottawa, Ont.	50000	50000
CHGB	La Pocatiere, Que.	10000	1000
XEC	Tijuana, B.C.	250	250
XELPZ	La Paz, B.C.S.	10000	
XERU	Chihuahua, Chih.	1000	250
XEQN	Torreon, Coah.	10000	250
XEHJ	Petalan, Gro.	250	250
† ----	Taxco, Gro.	400	
XETIA	Guadalajara, Jal.	5000	250
XEVB	Monterrey, N.L.	1000	250
XEHIT	Puebla, Pue.	500	100
XEHY	Villa De La Corregidora, Qro.	5000	1000
XEPO	San Luis Potosi, S.L.P.	500	250
XEFH	Agua Prieta, Son.	1000	100
XEAM	Matamoros, Tams.	1000	250
XEHV	Veracruz, Ver.	1000	1000
XEUP	Tizimin, Yuc.	1000	1000
CMDD	Bayamo, Cuba	1000	1000
HISD%	El Seibo, Dom. Rep.	1000	1000
HIBK	Moca, Dom. Rep.	1000	250
....	Fort De France, Marti.	50000	50000

1320 (REGIONAL)

WAGG	Birmingham, Ala.	5000	
WDBM	Dothan, Ala.	1000	1000
* KAWC	Yuma, Ariz.	1000	
KWHN	Ft. Smith, Ark.	5000	5000
KRLW	Walnut Ridge, Ark.	1000	
KHSJ	Hemet, Calif.	500	
KQIQ	Lemoore, Calif.	1000	
KEZL	Oceanside, Calif.	500	500
KGNR	Sacramento, Calif.	5000	5000
KAVI	Rocky Ford, Colo.	1000	
WATR	Waterbury, Conn.	5000	1000
WLQY	Hollywood, Fla.	5000	5000
WQIK	Jacksonville, Fla.	5000	5000
WAMR	Venice, Fla.	5000	1000
WHIE	Griffin, Ga.	5000	
WKAN	Kankakee, Ill.	1000	500
KNIA	Knoxville, Ia.	500	
KMAQ	Maquoketa, Ia.	500	
KLWN	Lawrence, Kan.	500	
WBRT	Bardstown, Ky.	1000	
WCLU	Covington, Ky.	500	
WNGO	Mayfield, Ky.	1000	
KNCB	Vivian, La.	5000	
WICO	Salisbury, Md.	1000	

WARA	Attleboro, Mass.	1000	1000
WILS	Lansing, Mich.	5000	1000
WDMJ	Marquette, Mich.	5000	1000
KOZY	Grand Rapids, Minn.	5000	5000
WRJW	Picayune, Miss.	5000	
WKPG	Port Gibson, Miss.	500	
WVLY	Water Valley, Miss.	500	
KSIV	Clayton, Mo.	5000	
KOLT	Scottsbluff, Neb.	5000	1000
WDER	Derry, N.H.	5000	1000
KRDD	Roswell, N.M.	1000	
WHHO	Hornell, N.Y.	5000	
WAGY	Forest City, N.C.	1000	500
WCOG	Greensboro, N.C.	5000	5000
WKRK	Murphy, N.C.	5000	
WWGN	Washington, N.C.	500	
KHRT	Minot, N.D.	2500	
WLOH	Lancaster, O.	1000	
WOBL	Oberlin, O.	1000	1000
KKCC	Clinton, Okla.	1000	
KQDQ	Eugene, Ore.	1000	
WKAP	Allentown, Pa.	5000	1000
WGET	Gettysburg, Pa.	1000	500
WJAS	Pittsburgh, Pa.	5000	5000
WBQW	Scranton, Pa.	1000	500
WUNO	San Juan, P.R.	5000	1000
WOIC	Columbia, S.C.	5000	2500
KELO	Sioux Falls, S.D.	5000	5000
WKIN	Kingsport, Tenn.	5000	500
WMSR	Manchester, Tenn.	5000	
KVMC	Colorado City, Tex.	1000	
KXYZ	Houston, Tex.	5000	5000
KBUG	Salt Lake City, Utah	5000	5000
WCVR	Randolph, Vt.	1000	
WLGM	Lynchburg, Va.	1000	
WEET	Richmond, Va.	5000	
KXRO	Aberdeen, Wash.	5000	1000
KHIT	Walla Walla, Wash.	1000	
WFHR	Wisconsin Rapids, Wis.	5000	500
CHQM	Vancouver, B.C.	50000	50000
CKEC	New Glasgow, N.S.	5000	5000
CFGM	Richmond Hill, Ont.	50000	50000
CJSO	Sorel, Que.	10000	5000
XENM	Aguascalientes, Ags.	1000	1000
XESR	Santa Rosalia, B.C.S.	500	250
XEUI	Comitan, Chis.	1000	500
XEJZ	Jimenez, Chih.	1000	250
XECMQ	Mexico City, D.F.	10000	1000
XECY	Huejutla, Hgo.	1000	250
XENI	Nueva Italia, Mich.	1000	250
XESF	Montemorelos, N.L.	1000	100
XEUH	Tuxtepec, Oax.	1000	100
XESY	Magdalena, Son.	200	
† ----	Cardenas, Tab.	150	
HIAV	Bani, Dom. Rep.	500	500
HIHD	San Pedro De Macoris, Dom. Rep.	1000	1000

1330 (REGIONAL)

† WPRN	Butler, Ala.	5000	
WKEA	Scottsboro, Ala.	5000	
KHYT	Tucson, Ariz.	5000	5000
KTOD	Conway, Ark.	500	
KLOM	Lompoc, Calif.	1000	
KFAC	Los Angeles, Calif.	5000	5000
KLBS	Los Banos, Calif.	500	
KCLM	Redding, Calif.	5000	
WBAS	Crescent City, Fla.	1000	
WFTP	Ft. Pierce, Fla.	1000	500
WWAB	Lakeland, Fla.	1000	
WAVX	Milton, Fla.	5000	
WCVC	Tallahassee, Fla.	5000	
WPPI	Carrollton, Ga.	500	
WMLT	Dublin, Ga.	5000	500
WEAW	Evanston, Ill.	5000	
WRAM	Monmouth, Ill.	1000	
WXTA	Rockford, Ill.	1000	
WVHI	Evansville, Ind.	5000	1000
WTRE	Greensburg, Ind.	500	
KWLO	Waterloo, Ia.	5000	5000
KFH	Wichita, Kan.	5000	5000
WYGO	Corbin, Ky.	5000	
WMOR	Morehead, Ky.	1000	
KVOL	Lafayette, La.	5000	1000
WASA	Havre De Grace, Md.	5000	500
WDLW	Waltham, Mass.	5000	5000
WTRX	Flint, Mich.	5000	1000
* KSJN	Minneapolis, Minn.	5000	5000
WFTO	Fulton, Miss.	5000	
WNIX	Greenville, Miss.	1000	500
‡ WJDQ	Meridian, Miss.	5000	
KUKU	Willow Springs, Mo.	1000	
KGAK	Gallup, N.M.	5000	1000
WPOW	New York, N.Y.	5000	5000
WNYM	New York, N.Y.	5000	5000
WEBO	Owego, N.Y.	5000	
WHAZ	Troy, N.Y.	1000	
WCPQ	Havelock, N.C.	1000	
WHOT	Campbell, O.	5000	500
WFIN	Findlay, O.	1000	
WKOV	Wellston, O.	500	
WELW	Willoughby, O.	500	
KUPL	Portland, Ore.	5000	5000
WRIE	Erie, Pa.	5000	5000
WADJ	Somerset, Pa.	5000r	
WENA	Penuelas, P.R.	1000	500
WLAT	Conway, S.C.	5000	500
WFBC	Greenville, S.C.	5000	5000
WAEW	Crossville, Tenn.	1000	
WTRO	Dyersburg, Tenn.	500	
† WMJT	Mt. Juliet, Tenn.	500	
KMIL	Cameron, Tex.	500	
KSWA	Graham, Tex.	500	
KINE	Kingsville, Tex.	1000	
KVKM	Monahans, Tex.	5000	1000
KTYL	Tyler, Tex.	1000	1000
WBTM	Danville, Va.	5000	1000
WRAA	Luray, Va.	1000	
WOLD	Marion, Va.	1000	
WESR	Onley, Va.	5000	
KENU	Enumclaw, Wash.	500	
* KMBI	Spokane, Wash.	5000	
WETZ	New Martinsville, W.V.	1000	
WHBL	Sheboygan, Wis.	5000	1000
KOVE	Lander, Wyo.	5000	1000
CKLD	Thetford Mines, Que.	10000	10000
CKKR	Rosetown, Sask.	10000	10000
XEWQ	Monclova, Coah.	1000	250
† XEMAC	Manzanillo, Col.	500	
† ----	Durango, Dgo.	1000	
XEBO	Irapuato, Gto.	5000	1000
XEAH	Juchitan, Oax.	500	500
XEEV	Izucar De Matamoros, Pue.	1000	1000
XERP	Ciudad Madero, Tams.	10000	100
XEUZ	Martinez De La Torre, Ver.	1000	100
XEFC	Merida, Yuc.	5000	1000
HIDB	Santiago, Dom. Rep.	1000	1000
4VW	Port Au Prince, Haiti	1500	1500
PJA-10	Aruba, Ne. Antil.	1000	1000

1340 (LOCAL)

WKUL	Cullman, Ala.	1000	250
WXOR	Florence, Ala.	1000	250
WMRK	Selma, Ala.	1000	250
WFEB	Sylacauga, Ala.	1000	250
KIKO	Miami, Ariz.	1000	250

KFBR	Nogales, Ariz.	250	250
KPGE	Page, Ariz.	1000	250
KBTA	Batesville, Ark.	1000	250
KZNG	Hot Springs, Ark.	1000	250
KCAT	Pine Bluff, Ark.	1000	250
KBRS	Springdale, Ark.	1000	250
KATA	Arcata, Calif.	1000	250
KWXY	Cathedral City, Calif.	1000	250
KMAK	Fresno, Calif.	1000	250
KDOL	Mojave, Calif.	1000	250
KSFE	Needles, Calif.	1000	250 -f
KORV	Oroville, Calif.	1000	250
KATY	San Luis Obispo, Calif.	1000	250
KIST	Santa Barbara, Calif.	1000	250
KOMY	Watsonville, Calif.	1000	250
KDEN	Denver, Colo.	1000	250
KQIL	Grand Junction, Colo.	1000	250
KVRH	Salida, Colo.	1000	250
WNHC	New Haven, Conn.	1000	250
WYCB	Washington, D. C.	1000	250
WTAN	Clearwater, Fla.	1000	250
WROD	Daytona Beach, Fla.	1000	250
WDSR	Lake City, Fla.	1000	250
WTYS	Marianna, Fla.	1000	250
WPBR	Palm Beach, Fla.	1000	250
WSEB	Sebring, Fla.	1000	250
WFSH	Valparaiso, Fla.	1000	250
WGAU	Athens, Ga.	1000	250
WIGO	Atlanta, Ga.	1000	250
WBBQ	Augusta, Ga.	1000	250
WGAA	Cedartown, Ga.	1000	250
WOKS	Columbus, Ga.	1000	250
WBBT	Lyons, Ga.	1000	250
WTIF	Tifton, Ga.	1000	250
KSKI	Hailey, Id.	1000	250
KXTC	Nampa, Id.	1000	250
KACH	Preston, Id.	1000	250
WSOY	Decatur, Ill.	1000	250
WHPI	Herrin, Ill.	1000	250
WJOL	Joliet, Ill.	1000	250
WBIW	Bedford, Ind.	1000	250
WTRC	Elkhart, Ind.	1000	250
WLBC	Muncie, Ind.	1000	250
KROS	Clinton, Ia.	1000	250
KFKF	Kansas City, Kan.	1000	250
KSEK	Pittsburg, Kan.	1000	250
WCMI	Ashland, Ky.	1000	250
WBGN	Bowling Green, Ky.	1000	250
WKCB	Hindman, Ky.	1000	250
WNBS	Murray, Ky.	1000	250
WEKY	Richmond, Ky.	1000	250
KVOB	Bastrop, La.	1000	250
KRMD	Shreveport, La.	1000	250
WFAU	Augusta, Me.	1000	250
WDME	Dover Foxcroft, Me.	1000	250
WLVC	Ft. Kent, Me.	250	250
WHOU	Houlton, Me.	1000	250
WGAW	Gardner, Mass.	1000	250
WNBH	New Bedford, Mass.	1000	250
WBRK	Pittsfield, Mass.	1000	250
WLEW	Bad Axe, Mich.	1000	250
WCSR	Hillsdale, Mich.	500	250
WMTE	Manistee, Mich.	1000	250
WAGN	Menominee, Mich.	1000	250
WWPZ	Petoskey, Mich.	1000	250
WEXL	Royal Oak, Mich.	1000	250
KVBR	Brainerd, Minn.	1000	250
KDLM	Detroit Lakes, Minn.	1000	250
WEVE	Eveleth, Minn.	1000	250
KROC	Rochester, Minn.	1000	250
KWLM	Willmar, Minn.	1000	250
WJMB	Brookhaven, Miss.	1000	250 -f
WKOZ	Kosciusko, Miss.	1000	250
WAML	Laurel, Miss.	1000	250
KXEO	Mexico, Mo.	1000	250
KLID	Poplar Bluff, Mo.	1000	250
KSMO	Salem, Mo.	1000	250
KICK	Springfield, Mo.	1000	250
KCAP	Helena, Mont.	1000	250

KPRK	Livingston, Mont.	1000	250 -f
KATL	Miles City, Mont.	1000	250
KYLT	Missoula, Mont.	1000	250
KHUB	Fremont, Neb.	500	250
KGFW	Kearney, Neb.	1000	250
KSID	Sidney, Neb.	1000	250
KRAM	Las Vegas, Nev.	1000	250
KBET	Reno, Nev.	1000	250
WDCR	Hanover, N.H.	1000	250
WMID	Atlantic City, N.J.	1000	250
KKBK	Aztec, N.M.	1000	250
KSYX	Santa Rosa, N.M.	1000	250
KSIL	Silver City, N.M.	1000	250
KKIT	Taos, N.M.	1000	250
WMBO	Auburn, N.Y.	1000	250
WENT	Gloversville, N.Y.	1000	250
WKSN	Jamestown, N.Y.	250	250
WLVL	Lockport, N.Y.	1000	250
WMSA	Massena, N.Y.	1000	250
WALL	Middletown, N.Y.	1000	250
WIRY	Plattsburgh, N.Y.	1000	250
WOOW	Greenville, N.C.	1000	250
WJRI	Lenoir, N.C.	1000	250
WTSB	Lumberton, N.C.	1000	250
WCBQ	Oxford, N.C.	1000	250
WAAV	Wilmington, N.C.	1000	250
WAIR	Winston Salem, N.C.	1000	250
KPOK	Bowman, N.D.	1000	250
KXPO	Grafton, N.D.	1000	250
WNCO	Ashland, O.	1000	250
* WOUB	Athens, O.	500	250
WIZE	Springfield, O.	1000	250
WSTV	Steubenville, O.	1000	250
KIHN	Hugo, Okla.	1000	250
KOCY	Oklahoma City, Okla.	1000	250
KTOW	Sand Springs, Okla.	500	250
KLOO	Corvallis, Ore.	1000	250
KWVR	Enterprise, Ore.	1000	250
KIHR	Hood River, Ore.	1000	250
KBBR	North Bend, Ore.	1000	250
WCVI	Connellsville, Pa.	1000	250
* WSAJ	Grove City, Pa.	100	100 f
WOYL	Oil City, Pa.	1000	250
WHAT	Philadelphia, Pa.	1000	250
WRAW	Reading, Pa.	1000	250
WTRN	Tyrone, Pa.	1000	250
WKRZ	Wilkes Barre, Pa.	1000	250
WWPA	Williamsport, Pa.	1000	250
WUNA	Aguadilla, P.R.	250	250
WOKE	Charleston, S.C.	1000	250
WRHI	Rock Hill, S.C.	1000	250
WSSC	Sumter, S.C.	1000	250
KIJV	Huron, S.D.	1000	250
KTOQ	Rapid City, S.D.	1000	250
WBAC	Cleveland, Tenn.	1000	250
WKRM	Columbia, Tenn.	1000	250
WGRV	Greeneville, Tenn.	1000	250
WKGN	Knoxville, Tenn.	1000	250
WLOK	Memphis, Tenn.	1000	250
WCDT	Winchester, Tenn.	1000	250
KWKC	Abilene, Tex.	1000	250
KHLB	Burnet, Tex.	1000	250
KAND	Corsicana, Tex.	1000	250
KSET	El Paso, Tex.	1000	250
KBBL	Lubbock, Tex.	1000	250
KRBA	Lufkin, Tex.	1000	250
KSZN	Pampa, Tex.	1000	250
KOLE	Port Arthur, Tex.	1000	250
KTEO	San Angelo, Tex.	1000	250
KCWM	Victoria, Tex.	1000	250
KLVR	Heber City, Utah	500	250
WVNR	Poultney, Vt.	1000	250
WSTJ	St. Johnsbury, Vt.	1000	250
WSTA	Charlotte Amalie, V.I.	250	250
WKEY	Covington, Va.	1000	250
WHAP	Hopewell, Va.	1000	250
WJMA	Orange, Va.	1000	250
KAGT	Anacortes, Wash.	1000	250
KOTY	Kennewick, Wash.	1000	250
KAPA	Raymond, Wash.	1000	250
KWWW	Wenatchee, Wash.	1000	250
WHAR	Clarksburg, W.V.	1000	250
WEPM	Martinsburg, W.V.	1000	250
WMON	Montgomery, W.V.	1000	250

WXEE	Welch, W.V.	1000	250
WLDY	Ladysmith, Wis.	1000	250
WMKE	Milwaukee, Wis.	1000	250
KSGT	Jackson, Wyo.	1000	250
KYCN	Wheatland, Wyo.	250	250
KWOR	Worland, Wyo.	1000	250
CIBQ	Brooks, Alta.	1000	250
CIOK-1	Grand Centre, Alta.	250	250
CFKC	Creston, B.C.	250	250
CKGF	Grand Forks, B.C.	1000	250
CKCR	Revelstoke, B.C.	1000	1000
CIVH	Vanderhoof, B.C.	1000	500
CFGB	Goose Bay, Nfld.	1000	1000
CFLW	Wabush, Nfld.	250	250
CFYK	Yellowknife, N.W.T.	1000	1000
CJLS	Yarmouth, N.S.	5000	1000
CKNR	Elliot Lake, Ont.	1000	250
CFLH	Hearst, Ont.	1000	250
CFBQ	Parry Sound, Ont.	250	250
CXRE	Red Lake, Ont.	250	250
CKDK	Woodstock, Ont.	10000	1000
CHAD	Amos, Que.	1000	250
CJAN	Asbestos, Que.	1000	250
CFED	Chapais, Que.	250	250
CFOM	Quebec, Que.	250	250
CBGA-7	Ste. Anne Des Monts, Que.	1000	250
CKVT	Temiscaming, Que.	1000	250
XEAA	Mexicali, B.C.	1000	250
XEBCC	Carmen, Cam.	5000	500
XEJK	Delicias, Chih.	1000	250
XERCH	Ojinaga, Chih.	1000	100
XEDH	Ciudad Acuna, Coah.	1000	250
XECI	Acapulco, Gro.	1000	250
XEQB	Tulancingo, Hgo.	500	250
XEDKT	Guadalajara, Jal.	1000	250
XERLK	Atlacomulco, Mex.	500	
XECR	Morelia, Mich.	250	250
XEJC	Cuernavaca, Mor.	1000	600
XEZE	Santiago Ixcuintla, Nay.	250	200
XENV	Monterrey, N.L.	1000	250
XEPX	Puerto Angel, Oax.	1000	200
XELU	Cuidad Serdan, Pue.	250	250
XESL	San Luis Potosi, S.L.P.	1000	500
XEQE	Escuinapa, Sin.	250	250
XECW	Los Mochis, Sin.	1000	200
XEOS	Ciudad Obregon, Son.	250	250
XEVSS	Villa De Seris, Son.	1000	
XERPV	Ciudad Victoria, Tams.	1000	250
XEMT	Matamoros, Tams	1000	250
XEBK	Nuevo Laredo, Tams.	500	250
XEOM	Coatzacoalcos, Ver.	5000	500
XEBY	Tuxpan, Ver.	250	150
ZBM-2	Hamilton, Bermuda	1000	1000
HIPT	San Francisco De Macoris, Dom. Rep.	250	250
HIBZ	San Juan, Dom. Rep.	1000	250

1350 (REGIONAL)

WELB	Elba, Ala.	1000	
WGAD	Gadsden, Ala.	5000	1000
WYLS	York, Ala.	5000	
KBOT	Cabot, Ark.	2500	
KLYD	Bakersfield, Calif.	1000	
KCKC	San Bernardino, Calif.	5000	500
KSRO	Santa Rosa, Calif.	5000	5000
KIDN	Pueblo, Colo.	5000	1000
WNLK	Norwalk, Conn.	1000	500
WINY	Putnam, Conn.	1000	
WEZY	Cocoa, Fla.	5000r	500
WDCF	Dade City, Fla.	1000	500
WCAI	Ft. Myers, Fla.	1000	
WGIA	Blackshear, Ga.	2500	
WRWH	Cleveland, Ga.	1000	
WAVC	Warner Robbins, Ga.	5000	
KIVM	Lihue, Haw.	5000	5000
KRLC	Lewiston, Id.	5000	1000
WXCL	Peoria, Ill.	1000	1000
WJBD	Salem, Ill.	500	
WIOU	Kokomo, Ind.	5000	1000
KRNT	Des Moines, Ia.	5000	5000
KMAN	Manhattan, Kan.	500	
WLOU	Louisville, Ky.	5000	500
WSMB	New Orleans, La.	5000	5000
WJEB	Gladwin, Mich.	1000	1000
WHMI	Howell, Mich.	500	
KCHK	New Prague, Minn.	500	
KDIO	Ortonville, Minn.	1000	
WCMP	Pine City, Minn.	1000	
WKCU	Corinth, Miss.	1000	
KCHR	Charleston, Mo.	1000	
KBRX	O' Neill, Neb.	1000	
WKZU	Laconia, N.H.	5000	
WHWH	Princeton, N.J.	5000	5000
KABQ	Albuquerque, N.M.	5000	500
WCBA	Corning, N.Y.	1000	
WRNY	Rome, N.Y.	500	
WANC	Aberdeen, N.C.	2500	
WONO	Black Mountain, N.C.	1000q	
WHIP	Mooresville, N.C.	1000	
WLLY	Wilson, N.C.	1000	
WSLR	Akron, O.	5000	5000
WCSM	Celina, O.	500	
WCHI	Chillicothe, O.	1000	
KRHD	Duncan, Okla.	250	100
KTLQ	Tahlequah, Okla.	1000	
‡ KDOV	Ashland, Ore.	1000	
WWBR	Windber, Pa.	2500	
WOYK	York, Pa.	5000	1000
WEGA	Vega Baja, P.R.	500	500
WKGE	Darlington, S.C.	1000	
WGSW	Greenwood, S.C.	1000	
WRKM	Carthage, Tenn.	1000	
KCAR	Clarksville, Tex.	500	
KTXJ	Jasper, Tex.	5000	
KCOR	San Antonio, Tex.	5000	5000
WBLT	Bedford, Va.	1000	
WFLS	Fredericksburg, Va.	1000	
WNVA	Norton, Va.	5000	
WNIS	Portsmouth, Va.	5000	5000
WPDR	Portage, Wis.	1000	
CJDC	Dawson Creek, B.C.	1000	1000
CKEG	Nanaimo, B.C.	10000	5000
CKBC	Bathurst, N.B.	10000	10000
‡ CFYQ	Gander, Nfld.	1000	1000
CKAD	Middleton, N.S.	1000	1000
CKAR	Oshawa, Ont.	10000	5000
CHOV	Pembroke, Ont.	1000	1000
CJLM	Joliette, Que.	10000	1000
CHAL	St. Pamphile, Que.	1000	1000
XEYS	Yajalon, Chis.	1000	1000
XETB	Torreon, Coah.	5000	500
XEQK	Mexico City, D.F.	1000	1000
† ----	Leon, Gto.	250	
XEJY	El Grullo, Jal.	1000	100
† ----	Yurecuaro, Mich.	500	
† ----	Libres, Pue.	500	
† ----	Morelos, Q.R.	1000	1000
XEVU	Mazatlan, Sin.	850	125
XETM	Nacozari, Son.	1000	1000
XELBL	San Luis, Son.	500	100
XEZD	Camargo, Tams.	250	250
XEJF	Tierra Blanca, Ver.	1000	100
XETGO	Tlaltenango, Zac.	2000	
CMKY	Puerto Padre, Cuba	250	250
HIXZ	Santo Domingo, Dom. Rep.	1000	250

1360 (REGIONAL)

WWWB	Jasper, Ala.	1000	
† WABT	Madison, Ala.	500	
WMOB	Mobile, Ala.	5000	
WMFC	Monroeville, Ala.	1000	
WELR	Roanoke, Ala.	1000	
KLFF	Glendale, Ariz.	5000	500
KLYR	Clarksville, Ark.	500	
KFFA	Helena, Ark.	1000	1000
KFIV	Modesto, Calif.	5000	1000
KZIQ	Ridgecrest, Calif.	1000	
KPQP	San Diego, Calif.	5000	1000
WDRC	Hartford, Conn.	5000	5000
WYXY	Cypress Gardens, Fla.	5000	2500
WCGL	Jacksonville, Fla.	5000	
WKAT	Miami Beach, Fla.	5000	1000
WAZA	Bainbridge, Ga.	5000	1000
WLAW	Lawrenceville, Ga.	1000	
WMAC	Metter, Ga.	500	
WIYN	Rome, Ga.	500	
WLBK	De Kalb, Ill.	1000	
WYER	Mt. Carmel, Ill.	500	
WGFA	Watseka, Ill.	1000	
KHAK	Cedar Rapids, Ia.	1000	
KBKB	Ft. Madison, Ia.	1000	
KSCJ	Sioux City, Ia.	5000	5000
KOYY	El Dorado, Kan.	500	
WFLW	Monticello, Ky.	1000	
KDXI	Mansfield, La.	1000	
KNIR	New Iberia, La.	1000	
KTLD	Tallulah, La.	500	
WEBB	Baltimore, Md.	5000	
WLYN	Lynn, Mass.	1000	
WKYO	Caro, Mich.	1000	500
WKMI	Kalamazoo, Mich.	5000	1000
KKBJ	Bemidji, Minn.	5000	2500
KRWC	Buffalo, Minn.	500	
WFFF	Columbia, Miss.	1000	
KMRN	Cameron, Mo.	500	
KLRS	Mountain Grove, Mo.	1000	
KICX	Mc Cook, Neb.	1000	
WNNJ	Newton, N.J.	1000	
WWBZ	Vineland, N.J.	1000	1000
KREE	Ruidoso, N.M.	5000	
WKOP	Binghamton, N.Y.	5000	500
WMNS	Olean, N.Y.	1000	
WCHL	Chapel Hill, N.C.	5000	2500
KEYZ	Williston, N.D.	5000	5000
WSAI	Cincinnati, O.	5000	5000
WWOW	Conneaut, O.	500	
KOHU	Hermiston, Ore.	1000	1000
KUIK	Hillsboro, Ore.	1000	
KROR	Myrtle Creek, Ore.	5000	
WIXZ	Mc Keesport, Pa.	5000	1000
WPPA	Pottsville, Pa.	5000	500
WCHQ	Camuy, P.R.	1000	500
WELP	Easley, S.C.	1000	
WLCM	Lancaster, S.C.	1000	
WBLC	Lenoir City, Tenn.	1000	
† WKXY	Milan, Tenn.	5000	500
WNAH	Nashville, Tenn.	1000	
KQIZ	Amarillo, Tex.	500	
KACT	Andrews, Tex.	1000	
KBUK	Baytown, Tex.	1000	1000
KRYS	Corpus Christi, Tex.	1000	1000
KXOL	Ft. Worth, Tex.	5000	1000
WBOB	Galax, Va.	5000	
WHBG	Harrisonburg, Va.	5000	
KAMT	Tacoma, Wash.	5000	5000
WHJC	Matewan, W.V.	1000	
WMOV	Ravenswood, W.V.	1000	
WGEE	Green Bay, Wis.	5000	5000
WMNE	Menomonie, Wis.	1000	
WISV	Viroqua, Wis.	1000	
KRKK	Rock Springs, Wyo.	1000	1000
CJVL	Ste. Marie De Beauce, Que.	10000	5000
XEUD	Tuxtla, Chis.	3500	1000
XEDI	Chihuahua, Chih.	1000	200
XEIK	Piedras Negras, Coah.	500	250
XELS	Armeria, Col.	1000	250
XEY	Celaya, Gto.	1000	250
XEKF	Iguala, Gro.	1000	500
XEQY	Toluca, Mex.	1000	1000
XEVAL	Ciudad Valles, S.L.P.	5000	
XEAGV	Ciudad Mendoza, Ver.	1000	1000
XEFBF	Martinez De La Torre, Ver.	500	100
XEDQ	San Andres Tuxtla, Ver.	1000	100
XEUL	Progreso, Yuc.	1000	1000
XEXM	Jerez, Zac.	1000	100
CMBG	Havana, Cuba	250	250
HISD	La Vega, Dom. Rep.	1000	1000

1370 (REGIONAL)

WBYE	Calera, Ala.	1000	
KAWW	Heber Springs, Ark.	1000	
KTPA	Prescott, Ark.	1000	
KWRM	Corona, Calif.	5000	2500
KPCO	Quincy, Calif.	500	
KEEN	San Jose, Calif.	5000	5000
KGEN	Tulare, Calif.	1000	
KTMG	Deer Trail, Colo.	5000	
WOCA	Ocala, Fla.	5000	
WCOA	Pensacola, Fla.	5000	5000
WAXE	Vero Beach, Fla.	1000	
WLOP	Jessup, Ga.	5000	
WVFJ	Manchester, Ga.	1000	
WLOV	Washington, Ga.	1000	
WPRC	Lincoln, Ill.	1000	
WTTS	Bloomington, Ind.	5000	500
WLTH	Gary, Ind.	1000	500
KLBA	Albia, Ia.	500	
KDTH	Dubuque, Ia.	5000	5000
KGNO	Dodge City, Kan.	5000	1000
KIKS	Iola, Kan.	500	
WABD	Ft. Campbell, Ky.	1000	
WGOH	Grayson, Ky.	5000	
WTKY	Tomkinsville, Ky.	2500	
KAPB	Marksville, La.	1000	
WDEA	Ellsworth, Me.	5000	5000
WZYQ	Frederick, Md.	500	
WKIK	Leonardtown, Md.	1000	1000
WKJF	Cadillac, Mich.	5000	1000
WGHN	Grand Haven, Mich.	500	
KSUM	Fairmont, Minn.	1000	1000
KMAP	South St. Paul, Minn.	500	
WMGO	Canton, Miss.	1000	
KWRT	Boonville, Mo.	1000	
KCRV	Caruthersville, Mo.	1000	
KXLF	Butte, Mont.	5000	5000
KAWL	York, Neb.	500	
WFEA	Manchester, N.H.	5000	5000
WELV	Ellenville, N.Y.	5000	
WALK	Patchogue, N.Y.	500	
WRTK	Rochester, N.Y.	5000	5000
WLTC	Gastonia, N.C.	5000	
WLLN	Lillington, N.C.	2500	
WTAB	Tabor City, N.C.	5000	
* KFJM	Grand Forks, N.D.	1000	
WSPD	Toledo, O.	5000	5000
KVYL	Holdenville, Okla.	500	
KAST	Astoria, Ore.	1000	1000
KFIR	Sweet Home, Ore.	1000	
WWCB	Corry, Pa.	1000	500
WPAZ	Pottstown, Pa.	1000	
WKMC	Roaring Spring, Pa.	5000	
WIVV	Vieques, P.R.	1000	1000
WMYD	Wickford, R.I.	500	
WSOL	Elloree, S.C.	5000	
WDEF	Chattanooga, Tenn.	5000	5000
WDXE	Lawrenceburg, Tenn.	1000	
WRGS	Rogersville, Tenn.	1000	
KMMM	Austin, Tex.	1000	
KFRO	Longview, Tex.	1000	1000
KPOS	Post, Tex.	1000	
KSOP	South Salt Lake		

		City, Utah	1000	500
	WBTN	Bennington, Vt.	1000	
	WHEE	Martinsville, Va.	5000	
	WJWS	South Hill, Va.	5000	
	KWNC	Quincy, Wash.	1000	
	WVMR	Frost, W.V.	2500	
	WEIF	Moundsville, W.V.	5000	
	WCCN	Neillsville, Wis.	5000	
‡	WGNW	Pewaukee, Wis.	500	
†	WGNW	Sussex, Wis.	500	500
	KSHY	Cheyenne, Wyo.	1000	
	CFOK	Westlock, Alta.	10000	10000
	CHPQ	Parksville, B.C.	1000	1000
	CFLV	Valleyfield, Que.	10000	5000
	CFVD	Ville Degelis, Que.	1000	1000
	CJWW	Saskatoon, Sask.	10000	10000
†	----	Aguascalientes, Ags.	250	
	XEUAA	Aguascalientes, Ags.	500	
	XEHG	Mexicali, B.C.	500	
	XEA	Campeche, Cam.	1000	1000
	XERPU	Durango, Dgo.	1000	100
	XEJE	Dolores Hidalgo, Gto.	1000	1000
	XEPJ	Tlaquepaque, Jal.	1000	500
†	XESV	Morelia, Mich.	500	
	XEMON	Monterrey, N.L.	10000	10000
	XEPA	Puebla, Pue.	5000	1000
	XEOBS	Ciudad Obregon, Son.	10000	5000
	XEHF	Nogales, Son.	5000	5000
	XEGNK	Nuevo Laredo, Tams.	250	
†	----	Huayacocotla, Ver.	250	
	CMKW	Santiago De Cuba, Cuba	1000	1000
	HISD	Barahona, Dom. Rep.	1000	1000
	HIUA	Barahona, Dom. Rep.	1000	1000

1375

	....	St. Pierre & Miquelon,	4000	4000

1380 (REGIONAL)

	WRAB	Arab, Ala.	1000	
	WGYV	Greenville, Ala.	1000	
	WVSA	Vernon, Ala.	1000	
	KZUL	Parker, Ariz.	2500	
	KAUL	North Little Rock, Ark.	5000	2500
	KOTE	Lancaster, Calif.	1000	
	KGMS	Sacramento, Calif.	5000	5000
	KTOM	Salinas, Calif.	5000	5000
	KFLJ	Walsenburg, Colo.	1000	
	WNVR	Naugatuck, Conn.	5000	500
	WAMS	Wilmington, Del.	5000	1000
	WLIZ	Lake Worth, Fla.	1000	
	WDAT	Ormond Beach, Fla.	5000	2500
	WRBQ	St. Petersburg, Fla.	5000	5000
	WAOK	Atlanta, Ga.	5000	5000
	WGUS	Augusta, Ga.	1000	
	WSIZ	Ocilla, Ga.	5000	
†	WZEL	Young Harris, Ga.	500	
†	KLNI	Pearl City, Haw.	5000	5000
	WQHK	Ft. Wayne, Ind.	5000	5000
	KCIM	Carroll, Ia.	1000	1000
	KCII	Washington, Ia.	500	
	KCNW	Fairway, Kan.	5000	1000
	WMTA	Central City, Ky.	500	
	WWKY	Winchester, Ky.	1000	
	WYNK	Baton Rouge, La.	5000	
	WKTJ	Farmington, Me.	1000	
	WPLB	Greenville, Mich.	1000	500
	WPHM	Port Huron, Mich.	5000	5000
	KLIZ	Brainerd, Minn.	5000	5000
	KAGE	Winona, Minn.	1000	
	WNLA	Indianola, Miss.	500	
	KWK	St. Louis, Mo.	5000	5000
	KUVR	Holdrege, Neb.	500	
	WBBX	Portsmouth, N.H.	1000	1000
#	WAWZ	Zarephath, N.J.	5000	5000
	WVIN	Bath, N.Y.	500	
#	WBNX	New York, N.Y.	5000	5000
	WRAQ	Asheville, N.C.	5000	1000
	WWMG	New Bern, N.C.	5000	
	WTOB	Winston Salem, N.C.	5000	1000
	WLRO	Lorain, O.	500	
	WXIC	Waverly, O.	1000	
	KSWO	Lawton, Okla.	1000	1000
	KMUS	Muskogee, Okla.	1000	500
	KSRV	Ontario, Ore.	5000	1000
	WACB	Kittanning, Pa.	1000	
	WMLP	Milton, Pa.	1000	
	WAYZ	Waynesboro, Pa.	1000	
	WOLA	Barranquitas, P.R.	500	500
	WNRI	Woonsocket, R.I.	1000	
	WAGS	Bishopville, S.C.	1000	
	KOTA	Rapid City, S.D.	5000	5000
	KQKD	Redfield, S.D.	500	
	WYSH	Clinton, Tenn.	1000	
	WIZO	Franklin, Tenn.	5000	
	WTNN	Millington, Tenn.	2500	1000
	KIEZ	Beaumont, Tex.	1000	
	KBWD	Brownwood, Tex.	1000	500
	KTSM	El Paso, Tex.	5000	500
	KMUL	Muleshoe, Tex.	1000	
	KBOP	Pleasanton, Tex.	1000	
	WSYB	Rutland, Vt.	5000	1000
	WLRV	Lebanon, Va.	1000	
	WTVR	Richmond, Va.	5000	5000
	KRKO	Everett, Wash.	5000	5000
	KCKO	Millwood, Wash.	5000	2500
	WMTD	Hinton, W.V.	1000	
	WBEL	Beloit, Wis.	5000	5000
	WFCL	Clintonville, Wis.	5000	2500
	CHLR	Moncton, N.B.	10000	
	CKPC	Brantford, Ont.	10000	10000
	CKLC	Kingston, Ont.	10000	10000
	CFDA	Victoriaville, Que.	10000	10000
	XEKT	Tecate, B.C.	250	100
	XEPAB	La Paz, B.C.S.	250	250
	XEZW	Hidalgo, Chis.	5000	500
	XEVD	Allende, Coah.	5000	1000
	XECO	Mexico City, D.F.	5000	5000
	XERS	Gomez Palacio, Dgo.	500	250
†	XEAPM	Apatzingan, Mich.	1000	100
†	----	Tepic, Nay.	1000	500
†	XESMR	San Luis Potosi, S.L.P.	1000	1000
	XEGW	Ciudad Victoria, Tams.	5000	150
	XEYB	Cosamaloapan, Ver.	1000	1000
†	XETP	Nadlingo, Ver.	3000	1000
	HIST	Santiago, Dom. Rep.	5000	1000
	4VC	Port Au Prince, Haiti	1000	1000
	PJB2	Bonaire, Ne. Antil.	1000	1000

1390 (REGIONAL)

	WHMA	Anniston, Ala.	5000	1000
	KDQN	De Queen, Ark.	500	
	KAMO	Rogers, Ark.	1000	
	KGER	Long Beach, Calif.	5000	5000
	KCEY	Turlock, Calif.	5000	5000
	KJJZ	Denver, Colo.	5000	1000
	WAPR	Avon Park, Fla.	1000	
	WKGR	Gainesville, Fla.	5000	
	WISK	Americus, Ga.	5000	
	WTNL	Reidsville, Ga.	500	
	WGCI	Chicago, Ill.	5000	5000
	WFIW	Fairfield, Ill.	1000	
	WJCD	Seymour, Ind.	1000	
	KLNT	Clinton, Ia.	1000	
	KMRY	Des Moines, Ia.	1000	1000
	KNCK	Concordia, Kan.	500	
	WANY	Albany, Ky.	1000	
	WKIC	Hazard, Ky.	5000	
	KFRA	Franklin, La.	500	
	WEGP	Presque Isle, Me.	5000	5000
‡	WCAT	Orange, Mass.	1000	

WPLM	Plymouth, Mass.	5000	5000
WGWY	Charlotte, Mich.	5000	
WNLT	Duluth, Minn.	500	
KRFO	Owatonna, Minn.	500	
KKCM	Waite Park, Minn.	2500	1000
WROA	Gulfport, Miss.	5000	5000
WFEZ	Meridian, Miss.	5000	
KJPW	Waynesville, Mo.	1000	
KENN	Farmington, N.M.	5000	1000
KHOB	Hobbs, N.M.	5000	
WEOK	Poughkeepsie, N.Y.	5000	
WRIV	Riverhead, N.Y.	1000	
WFBL	Syracuse, N.Y.	5000	5000
WEED	Rocky Mount, N.C.	5000	1000
WADA	Shelby, N.C.	1000	500
WJRM	Troy, N.C.	1000	
KKOA	Minot, N.D.	5000	1000
WOHP	Bellefontaine, O.	500	
WMPO	Pomeroy, O.	5000	
WFMJ	Youngstown, O.	5000	5000
KCRC	Enid, Okla.	1000	1000
KSLM	Salem, Ore.	5000	1000
WLAN	Lancaster, Pa.	5000	1000
WRSC	State College, Pa.	2500	1000
WISA	Isabela, P.R.	1000	500
WHPB	Belton, S.C.	1000	
WCSC	Charleston, S.C.	5000	5000
KJAM	Madison, S.D.	500	
WYXI	Athens, Tenn.	2500	
WTJS	Jackson, Tenn.	5000	1000
WMCT	Mountain City, Tenn.	1000	
KULP	El Campo, Tex.	500	
KBEC	Waxahachee, Tex.	500	
KBLQ	Logan, Utah	5000	500
WDOT	Burlington, Vt.	5000	5000
WEAM	Arlington, Va.	5000	5000
WWOD	Lynchburg, Va.	5000	1000
KBBO	Yakima, Wash.	1000	500
WKLP	Keyser, W.V.	1000	
CJCY	Medicine Hat, Alta.	10000	
CKKC	Nelson, B.C.	1000	1000
CHOO	Ajax, Ont.	10000	10000
XESX	Tuxtla, Chis.	5000	
XEV	Chihuahua, Chih.	1000	500
XETY	Tecoman, Col.	5000	200
XERW	Leon, Gto.	10000	250
† XEXH	Mixquiahuala, Hgo.	100	
XEJI	Tehuantepec, Oax.	2500	350
† ----	Tehuacan, Pue.	250	
† ----	Guamuchil, Sin.	1000	100
† ----	Agua Prieta, Son.	1000	250
XEQC	Puerto Penasco, Son.	1000	250
XEXO	Ciudad Mante, Tams.	5000	100
XEOR	Reynosa, Tams.	1000	1000
XETL	Tuxpan, Ver.	5000	1000
XERUY	Merida, Yuc.	10000	1000
CMKX	Bayamo, Cuba	1000	1000
HIUA	San Juan, Dom. Rep.	1000	1000

1400 (LOCAL)

† WTCG	Andalusia, Ala.	1000	250
WMSL	Decatur, Ala.	1000	250
WXAL	Demopolis, Ala.	1000	250
WFPA	Fort Payne, Ala.	1000	250
WJLD	Homewood, Ala.	1000	250
WJHO	Opelika, Ala.	1000	250
KSUN	Phoenix, Ariz.	1000	250
KRVZ	Springville, Ariz.	1000	250
KTUC	Tucson, Ariz.	1000	250
KVOY	Yuma, Ariz.	1000	250
KELD	El Dorado, Ark.	1000	250
KCLA	Pine Bluff, Ark.	1000	250
KWYN	Wynne, Ark.	1000	250
KRE	Berkeley, Calif.	1000	250
KRCQ	Indio, Calif.	1000	250
KQMS	Redding, Calif.	1000	250
KSLY	San Luis Obispo, Calif.	1000	250
KQTE	Santa Paula, Calif.	1000	250
KTRT	Truckee, Calif.	1000	250
KUKI	Ukiah, Calif.	1000	250
KONG	Visalia, Calif.	1000	250
KRLN	Canon City, Colo.	1000	250
KDTA	Delta, Colo.	1000	250
KFTM	Ft. Morgan, Colo.	1000	250
KBZZ	La Junta, Colo.	1000	250
KPAG	Pagosa Springs, Colo.	1000	250
WSTC	Stamford, Conn.	1000	250
WILI	Willimantic, Conn.	1000	250
WFTL	Ft. Lauderdale, Fla.	1000	250
WIRA	Ft. Pierce, Fla.	1000	250
WNUE	Ft. Walton Beach, Fla.	1000	250
WERD	Jacksonville, Fla.	1000	250
WPRY	Perry, Fla.	1000	250
WWJZ	Sanford, Fla.	1000	250
WPAS	Zephyr Hills, Fla.	1000	250
WULF	Alma, Ga.	1000	250
† WVNF	Alpharetta, Ga.	1000	250
WSGC	Elberton, Ga.	1000	250
WNEX	Macon, Ga.	1000	250
WCOH	Newnan, Ga.	1000	250
WSGA	Savannah, Ga.	1000	250
KART	Jerome, Id.	1000	250 f
KRPL	Moscow, Id.	1000	250
KSPT	Sandpoint, Id.	1000	250
KIGO	St. Anthony, Id.	1000	250
WDWS	Champaign, Ill.	1000	250
WGIL	Galesburg, Ill.	1000	250
WROZ	Evansville, Ind.	1000	250
WBAT	Marion, Ind.	1000	250
KCOG	Centerville, Ia.	500	250
† KADR	Elkader, Ia.	1000	250
KVFD	Ft. Dodge, Ia.	1000	250
KVOE	Emporia, Kan.	1000	250
KAYS	Hays, Kan.	1000	250
WCYN	Cynthiana, Ky.	500	250
WIEL	Elizabethtown, Ky.	1000	250
‡ WFTG	London, Ky.	1000	250
WFPR	Hammond, La.	1000	250
KAOK	Lake Charles, La.	1000	250
KWLA	Many, La.	1000	250
WRDO	Augusta, Me.	1000	250
WIDE	Biddeford, Me.	1000	250
WMCS	Machias, Me.	1000	250
WWIN	Baltimore, Md.	1000	250
WALE	Fall River, Mass.	1000	250
WLLH	Lowell, Mass.	1000	250
WHMP	Northampton, Mass.	1000	250
WKNR	Battle Creek, Mich.	1000	250
WQBH	Detroit, Mich.	1000	250
† WLJN	Elmwood Twp, Mich.	1000	250
WCCY	Houghton, Mich.	1000	250
WQXO	Munising, Mich.	1000	250
WSAM	Saginaw, Mich.	1000	250
WSJM	St. Joseph, Mich.	1000	250
KEYL	Long Prairie, Minn.	1000	250
KMHL	Marshall, Minn.	1000	250
KLBB	St. Paul, Minn.	1000	250
WHLB	Virginia, Minn.	1000	250
WBIP	Booneville, Miss.	1000	250
WMBC	Columbus, Miss.	1000	250
WYKC	Grenada, Miss.	1000	250
WFOR	Hattiesburg, Miss.	1000	250
WJQS	Jackson, Miss.	1000	250
KFRU	Columbia, Mo.	1000	250
KJCF	Festus, Mo.	1000	250
KSIM	Sikeston, Mo.	1000	250
KTTS	Springfield, Mo.	1000	250
KDRG	Deer Lodge, Mont.	1000	250
KXGN	Glendive, Mont.	1000	250
KARR	Great Falls, Mont.	1000	250
KBRB	Ainsworth, Neb.	1000	250
KCOW	Alliance, Neb.	1000	250
KLIN	Lincoln, Neb.	1000	250
KWNA	Winnemucca, Nev.	1000	250 -f
WBRL	Berlin, N.H.	1000	250
WTSL	Hanover, N.H.	1000	250
WLTN	Littleton, N.H.	1000	250

WOND	Pleasantville, N.J.	1000	250
KTRC	Santa Fe, N.M.	1000	250
KCHS	Truth Or Consequences, N.M.	250	250
KTNM	Tucumcari, N.M.	1000	250
WABY	Albany, N.Y.	1000	250
WYSL	Buffalo, N.Y.	1000	250
WDNY	Dansville, N.Y.	500	250
WSLB	Ogdensburg, N.Y.	1000	250
WBTB	Beaufort, N.C.	1000	250
WKEW	Greensboro, N.C.	1000	250
WSMR	Raeford, N.C.	1000	250
WSIC	Statesville, N.C.	1000	250
WLSE	Wallace, N.C.	1000	250
WHCC	Waynesville, N.C.	1000	250
WSMY	Weldon, N.C.	1000	250
KQDJ	Jamestown, N.D.	1000	250
WMAN	Mansfield, O.	1000	250
WPAY	Portsmouth, O.	1000	250
KWON	Bartlesville, Okla.	1000	250
KTMC	Mc Alester, Okla.	1000	250
KNOR	Norman, Okla.	1000	250
KLVR	Cave Jct, Ore.	1000	250
KNND	Cottage Grove, Ore.	1000	250 -f
KJDY	John Day, Ore.	1000	250 -f
KBCH	Lincoln City, Ore.	1000	250
WEST	Easton, Pa.	1000	250
WJET	Erie, Pa.	1000	250
WFEC	Harrisburg, Pa.	1000	250
WAMQ	Loretto, Pa.	1000	250
WICK	Scranton, Pa.	1000	250
WKBI	St. Marys, Pa.	1000	250
WRAK	Williamsport, Pa.	1000	250
WIDA	Carolina, P.R.	1000	250
WCOS	Columbia, S.C.	1000	250
WGTN	Georgetown, S.C.	1000	250
WKDY	Spartanburg, S.C.	1000	250
KBJM	Lemmon, S.D.	1000	250
WJZM	Clarksville, Tenn.	1000	250
WHUB	Cookeville, Tenn.	1000	250
WLSB	Copper Hill, Tenn.	1000	250
WKPT	Kingsport, Tenn.	1000	250
WGAP	Maryville, Tenn.	1000	250
WHAL	Shelbyville, Tenn.	1000	250
WNBG	Waynesboro, Tenn.	1000	250
KRUN	Ballinger, Tex.	1000	250
KBYG	Big Spring, Tex.	1000	250
KUNO	Corpus Christi, Tex.	1000	250
KILE	Galveston, Tex.	1000	250
KGVL	Greenville, Tex.	1000	250
KNNX	Huntsville, Tex.	1000	250
KEBE	Jacksonville, Tex.	1000	250
KIUN	Pecos, Tex.	1000	250
KEYE	Perryton, Tex.	1000	250
KVOP	Plainview, Tex.	1000	250
KDWT	Stamford, Tex.	1000	250
KTEM	Temple, Tex.	1000	250
KTFS	Texarkana, Tex.	1000	250
KVOU	Uvalde, Tex.	1000	250
KFTN	Provo, Utah	1000	250
WXAM	Charlottesville, Va.	1000	250
WHHV	Hillsville, Va.	1000	250
WPCE	Portsmouth, Va.	1000	250
WHLF	South Boston, Va.	1000	250
WINC	Winchester, Va.	1000	250
† KLCK	Goldendale, Wash.	1000	250
KEDO	Longview, Wash.	1000	250
KRSC	Othello, Wash.	1000	250
KPMA	Tacoma, Wash.	1000	250
WPQZ	Clarksburg, W.V.	1000	250
WRON	Ronceverte, W.V.	1000	250
WVRC	Spencer, W.V.	1000	250
WKWK	Wheeling, W.V.	1000	250
WBTH	Williamson, W.V.	1000	250
WATW	Ashland, Wis.	1000	250
WJJK	Eau Claire, Wis.	1000	250
WDUZ	Green Bay, Wis.	1000	250
WRJN	Racine, Wis.	1000	250
WRDB	Reedsburg, Wis.	1000	250
WRIG	Wausau, Wis.	1000	250
KATI	Casper, Wyo.	1000	250
KODI	Cody, Wyo.	1000	250
CKSQ	Stettler, Alta.	1000	250
CFLD	Burns Lake, B.C.	1000	250
CHNL-1	Clearwater, B.C.	1000	250
CKGR	Golden, B.C.	1000	250
CINL	Princeton, B.C.	1000	250
CKCB	Collingwood, Ont.	1000	250
CKOB	Renfrew, Ont.	1000	250
CKVR	Drummondville, Que.	250	250
CKFL	Lac Megantic, Que.	1000	250
CJFP	Riviere Du Loup, Que.	10000	5000
CKRN	Rouyn, Que.	1000	250
XEAC	Aguascalientes, Ags.	500	200
XEPF	Ensenada, B.C.	250	250
XEGD	Parral, Chih.	1000	200
XEARO	Nueva Rosita, Coah.	1000	250
XEDE	Saltillo, Coah.	500	250
XEKJ	Acapulco, Gro.	750	250
XEQJ	Tamazula, Jal.	1000	
† ----	Tlaquepaque, Jal.	10000	
XEXI	Ixtapan De La Sal, Mex.	250	250
XEOJ	Lazaro Cardenas, Mich.	1000	100
XEI	Morelia, Mich.	1000	250
XELH	Acaponeta, Nay.	1000	250
XELE	Linares, N.L.	250	100
XESH	Sabinas Hidalgo, N.L.	1000	250
XEUBJ	Oaxaca, Oax.	1000	200
XEFS	Izucar De Matamoros, Pue.	350	
XEVI	San Juan Del Rio, Qro.	1000	200
XEWU	Matehuala, S.L.P.	250	200
XEEX	Culiacan, Sin.	1000	150
XEPB	Hermosillo, Son.	1000	1000
XENAS	Navojoa, Son.	500	200
XEAB	Santa Ana, Son.	1000	250
XETO	Tampico, Tams.	1000	250
† ----	Tlapacoyan, Ver.	250	
XEPG	Veracruz, Ver.	250	100
CMJI	Florida, Cuba	250	250
HIBP	La Romana, Dom. Rep.	500	250
HIAL	La Vega, Dom. Rep.	250	250
HIBN	Puerto Plata, Dom. Rep.	1000	250

1410 (REGIONAL)

WUNI	Mobile, Ala.	5000	5000
WIQR	Prattville, Ala.	5000	1000
WZZA	Tuscumbia, Ala.	500	
KTCS	Ft. Smith, Ark.	1000	
KERN	Bakersfield, Calif.	1000	1000
KRML	Carmel, Calif.	5000	5000
KLVV	Lompoc, Calif.	500	
KMYC	Marysville, Calif.	5000	5000
KCAL	Redlands, Calif.	5000	1000
KCOL	Ft. Collins, Colo.	1000	1000
WPOP	Hartford, Conn.	5000	5000
WDOV	Dover, Del.	5000	5000
WMYR	Ft. Myers, Fla.	5000	5000
WZST	Leesburg, Fla.	5000	
WKQE	Tallahassee, Fla.	5000	
WGRI	Griffin, Ga.	1000	
WDAX	Mc Rae, Ga.	1000	
WLAQ	Rome, Ga.	1000	1000
WRMN	Elgin, Ill.	1000	500
WTIM	Taylorville, Ill.	1000	1000
WFTE	Lafayette, Ind.	1000	
KGRN	Grinnell, Ia.	500	
KLEM	Le Mars, Ia.	1000	
KCLO	Leavenworth, Kan.	5000	5000
KQAM	Wichita, Kan.	5000	1000
WLBJ	Bowling Green, Ky.	5000	1000
WHLN	Harlan, Ky.	5000	
KDBS	Alexandria, La.	1000	
WHAG	Halfway, Md.	1000	
WAMK	Brockton, Mass.	1000	

	Call	Location	Day	Night
	WXQT	Grand Rapids, Mich.	1000	
	KLFD	Litchfield, Minn.	500	
	KRWB	Roseau, Minn.	1000	1000
	WRDC	Cleveland, Miss.	1000	
	WMYQ	Newton, Miss.	500	
	KBCC	Cuba, Mo.	1000	
	KOOQ	North Platte, Neb.	5000	500
	KVEG	Las Vegas, Nev.	5000	5000
	WHTG	Eatontown, N.J.	500	
	WDOE	Dunkirk, N.Y.	1000	500
	WELM	Elmira, N.Y.	1000	500
	WBZA	Glens Falls, N.Y.	1000	
	WOTT	Watertown, N.Y.	5000	1000
	WEGO	Concord, N.C.	1000	
	WSRC	Durham, N.C.	5000	
	WVCB	Shallotte, N.C.	500	
	KHOL	Beulah, N.D.	1000	
	WING	Dayton, O.	5000	5000
	KCNR	Portland, Ore.	5000	
	WLSH	Lansford, Pa.	5000	
	KQV	Pittsburgh, Pa.	5000	5000
†	WRSS	San Sebastian, P.R.	1000	
	WPCC	Clinton, S.C.	1000	
	WYMB	Manning, S.C.	1000	
	WYLQ	Kingston, Tenn.	1000	
	WCMT	Martin, Tenn.	1000	
†	WJED	Somerville, Tenn.	500	500
	KBUD	Athens, Tex.	1000	
	KBAN	Bowie, Tex.	500	
	KJCH	Cleveland, Tex.	1000	1000
	KCUL	Marshall, Tex.	500	
	KRIG	Odessa, Tex.	1000	1000
	KBAL	San Saba, Tex.	500	
	KNAL	Victoria, Tex.	500	500
	WGGM	Chester, Va.	5000	
	WRIS	Roanoke, Va.	5000	
	WSCW	South Charleston, W.V.	5000	
	WIZM	La Crosse, Wis.	5000	5000
	KWYO	Sheridan, Wyo.	5000	500
	CFUN	Vancouver, B.C.	50000	50000
	CIGO	Pt. Hawkesbury, N.S.	10000	10000
	CKSL	London, Ont.	10000	10000
	CFMB	Montreal, Que.	10000	10000
	XEYD	Francisco I. Madero, Coah.	1000	100
	XEBS	Mexico City, D.F.	5000	1000
†	----	Zihuatenejo, Gro.	500	
	XEKB	Atemajac, Jal.	8000	1000
	XEKB	Encarnacion, Jal.	8000	150
†	----	Zamora, Mich.	1000	
	XEIR	Ciudad Valles, S.L.P.	1000	
	XECF	Los Mochis, Sin.	1000	500
	XETAB	Villahermosa, Tab.	5000	500
	XERCM	Ciudad Victoria, Tams.	1000	150
	XEAS	Nuevo Laredo, Tams.	1000	250
†	----	Cordoba, Ver.	500	
	HIJM	Santiago, Dom. Rep.	500	500

1420 (REGIONAL)

	Call	Location	Day	Night
	WACT	Tuscaloosa, Ala.	5000	
†	KMOG	Payson, Ariz.	2500	500
	KTAN	Sierra Vista, Ariz.	1000	500
	KXOW	Hot Springs, Ark.	5000	
	KPOC	Pocahontas, Ark.	1000	
	KSTN	Stockton, Calif.	5000	1000
†	KSES	Yucca Valley, Calif.	1000	
	WLIS	Old Saybrook, Conn.	5000	500
	WBRD	Bradenton, Fla.	1000	
	WDBF	Delray Beach, Fla.	5000	500
	WAOC	St. Augustine, Fla.	1000	
	WRCG	Columbus, Ga.	5000	5000
	WAVO	Decatur, Ga.	1000	
	WPEH	Louisville, Ga.	1000	
	WLET	Toccoa, Ga.	5000	
†	WADX	Trenton, Ga.	500	
	KCCN	Honolulu, Haw.	5000	5000
	WINI	Murphysboro, Ill.	500	500
	WIMS	Michigan City, Ind.	5000	500
	WOC	Davenport, Ia.	5000	5000
	KJCK	Junction City, Kan.	1000	
	KULY	Ulysses, Kan.	1000	500
	WHBN	Harrodsburg, Ky.	1000	
	WVJS	Owensboro, Ky.	5000	1000
	KPEL	Lafayette, La.	1000	500
	WBSM	New Bedford, Mass.	5000	1000
	WBEC	Pittsfield, Mass.	1000	1000
	WFLT	Flint, Mich.	500	
	WKPR	Kalamazoo, Mich.	1000	
	WTGE	Kalkaska, Mich.	500	
	KTOE	Mankato, Minn.	5000	5000
	WSUH	Oxford, Miss.	1000	
	WQBC	Vicksburg, Miss.	5000r	500
	WIGG	Wiggins, Miss.	5000r	
†	KZMO	California, Mo.	5000	
	KBTN	Neosho, Mo.	1000r	500
	KOOO	Omaha, Neb.	1000	
	WASR	Wolfeboro, N.H.	5000	
	WRMV	Herkimer, N.Y.	1000	
	WACK	Newark, N.Y.	500	500
	WLNA	Peekskill, N.Y.	5000	5000
	WMYN	Mayodan, N.C.	500	
	WGAS	South Gastonia, N.C.	500	
	WVOT	Wilson, N.C.	1000	500
	WHK	Cleveland, O.	5000	5000
	KTJS	Hobart, Okla.	1000	
	KYNG	Coos Bay, Ore.	1000	
	WCOJ	Coatesville, Pa.	5000	5000
	WCED	Du Bois, Pa.	5000	500
*	WEUC	Ponce, P.R.	1000	1000
	WCRE	Cheraw, S.C.	1000	
	KGIM	Aberdeen, S.D.	1000	
	WEMB	Erwin, Tenn.	5000	
	WKSR	Pulaski, Tenn.	1000	1000
	KFYN	Bonham, Tex.	250	
	KPAR	Granbury, Tex.	500	500
	KLFB	Lubbock, Tex.	500	500
	KLNX	Lufkin, Tex.	5000	1000
	KGNB	New Braunfels, Tex.	1000	
	KHOS	San Angelo, Tex.	1000	
	WWSR	St. Albans, Vt.	1000	
	WAMV	Amherst, Va.	1000	
	WDDY	Gloucester, Va.	1000	
	WKCW	Warrenton, Va.	5000	
	KITI	Centralia, Wash.	5000	5000
	KSCR	Renton, Wash.	500	
	KUJ	Walla Walla, Wash.	5000	5000
	WTCR	Kenova, W.V.	5000	1000
	WPLY	Plymouth, Wis.	500	
	CKDY	Digby, N.S.	1000	1000
	CKPT	Peterborough, Ont.	10000	5000
	CJMT	Chicoutimi, Que.	10000	2500
	CKTL	Plessisville, Que.	1000	500
	CJVR	Melfort, Sask.	10000	10000
	XEXX	Tijuana, B.C.	2000	2000
†	XEKA	San Jose Del Cabo, B.C.S.	250	250
	XEF	Ciudad Juarez, Chih.	5000	500
	XEWE	Irapuato, Gto.	10000	1000
	XERD	Pachuca, Hgo.	1000	1000
	XEWP	Sayula, Jal.	500	
	XEWF	Cuernavaca, Mor.	500	250
	XEH	Monterrey, N.L.	5000	1000
	XEWJ	Tehuacan, Pue.	1000	250
	XEEW	Matamoros, Tams.	1000	1000
	XEGF	Gutierrez Zomora, Ver.	1000	500
	XEJV	Jaltipan, Ver.	1000	250
†	----	Tizimin, Yuc.	500	250
	CMDX	Baracoa, Cuba	1000	1000
	HIAE	Santo Domingo, Dom. Rep.	1000	1000
	....	Basse Terre, Gren.	4000	4000

1430 (REGIONAL)

Call	Location	Day	Night
WFHK	Pell City, Ala.	5000r	
WRMG	Red Bay, Ala.	1000	
KHBM	Monticello, Ark.	1000	
KAMP	El Centro, Calif.	1000	
KARM	Fresno, Calif.	5000	5000
KJAY	Sacramento, Calif.	500	
KALI	San Gabriel, Calif.	5000	5000
KNTA	Santa Clara, Calif.	1000	1000
KEZW	Aurora, Colo.	5000	5000
WQDI	Homestead, Fla.	500	500
WLKF	Lakeland, Fla.	5000	1000
WWWQ	Panama City, Fla.	5000	5000
WGFS	Covington, Ga.	1000	
WRCD	Dalton, Ga.	1000	
WWGS	Tifton, Ga.	5000	1000
WEEF	Highland Park, Ill.	1000	1000
WCMY	Ottawa, Ill.	500	
WIRE	Indianapolis, Ind.	5000	5000
KASI	Ames, Ia.	1000	
WLCB	Buffalo, Ky.	500	
WYMC	Mayfield, Ky.	1000	
KMRC	Morgan City, La.	500	
WNAV	Annapolis, Md.	5000	1000
WTTT	Amherst, Mass.	5000	
WXKS	Medford, Mass.	5000	
WION	Ionia, Mich.	5000	
WWHK	Mt. Clemens, Mich.	500	500
† KNSP	Staples, Minn.	1000	
WLAU	Laurel, Miss.	5000	
KSOA	Ava, Mo.	500	
KAOL	Carrollton, Mo.	500	
WIL	St. Louis, Mo.	5000	5000
KRGI	Grand Island, Neb.	5000	1000
† WNJR	Newark, N.J.	5000	5000
KCRX	Roswell, N.M.	5000	1000
WENE	Endicott, N.Y.	5000	5000
† WDEX	Monroe, N.C.	2500	2500
WMNC	Morganton, N.C.	5000	1000
WDJS	Mt. Olive, N.C.	1000	
WRXO	Roxboro, N.C.	1000	
KTYN	Minot, N.D.	5000	
WFOB	Fostoria, O.	1000	1000
WCLT	Newark, O.	500	
KALV	Alva, Okla.	500	500
KELI	Tulsa, Okla.	5000	5000
KGAY	Salem, Ore.	5000	
WVAM	Altoona, Pa.	5000	1000
WNEL	Caguas, P.R.	5000	500
WBLR	Batesburg, S.C.	5000	
WATP	Marion, S.C.	1000	
WJMR	Ridgeland, S.C.	1000	
KBRK	Brookings, S.D.	1000	
WBMK	Knoxville, Tenn.	1000	
WJRB	Madison, Tenn.	5000	1000
WWEE	Memphis, Tenn.	1000	
KSTB	Breckenridge, Tex.	1000	500
KEES	Gladewater, Tex.	5000	1000
KCOH	Houston, Tex.	1000	
KLO	Ogden, Utah	5000	5000
WIVE	Ashland, Va.	1000	
WKEX	Blacksburg, Va.	1000	
WDIC	Clinchco, Va.	5000	
KCLK	Clarkston, Wash.	500	
KBRC	Mt. Vernon, Wash.	5000	1000
WEIR	Weirton, W.V.	1000	1000
WBEV	Beaver Dam, Wis.	1000	1000
WRDN	Durand, Wis.	1000	
CJXX	Grand Prairie, Alta.	10000	10000
CJCL	Toronto, Ont.	50000	50000
XERAC	Campeche, Cam.	250	250
† ----	San Cristobal, Chis.	300	100
XEIA	Allende, Coah.	1000	250
† XESHT	Saltillo, Coah.	500	
XECOC	Colima, Col.	1500	1000
XEVMA	Acapulco, Gro.	1000	
XEIG	Iguala, Gro.	1000	100
XEMTJ	Mascota, Jal.	1000	
XENP	Ocotlan, Jal.	250	500
XECA	Ixtepec, Oax.	1000	200
XETUN	Rio Verde, S.L.P.	250	
XEOX	Ciudad Obregon, Son.	5000	500
XEWD	Ciudad Miguel Aleman, Tams.	2000	150
XETT	Tlaxcala, Tlax.	800	
XELL	Veracruz, Ver.	5000	250
CMKZ	Palma Soriano, Cuba	250	250
HIVG	La Vega, Dom. Rep.	3000	3000
4VGM	Port Au Prince, Haiti	1000	1000

1435

Call	Location	Day	Night
PJA5	Aruba, Ne. Antil.	1000	1000

1440 (REGIONAL)

Call	Location	Day	Night
WHHY	Montgomery, Ala.	5000	1000
KOPA	Scottsdale, Ariz.	5000	
KHOG	Fayetteville, Ark.	1000	
KITA	Little Rock, Ark.	5000	
KVON	Napa, Calif.	5000	1000
KPRO	Riverside, Calif.	1000	1000
KUHL	Santa Maria, Calif.	5000	1000
† KRDZ	Wray, Colo.	5000	
WBIS	Bristol, Conn.	500	
WOOJ	Lehigh Acres, Fla.	5000	1000
WAJL	Winter Park, Fla.	5000	1000
WWCC	Bremen, Ga.	2500	
WBGA	Brunswick, Ga.	5000	1000
WVMG	Cochran, Ga.	1000	
WRAJ	Anna, Ill.	500	
WRBA	Normal, Ill.	1000	500
WPRS	Paris, Ill.	1000	
WGEM	Quincy, Ill.	5000	1000
WROK	Rockford, Ill.	5000	500
WPGW	Portland, Ind.	500	
KCHE	Cherokee, Ia.	500	
KSKX	Topeka, Kan.	5000	1000
WCDS	Glasgow, Ky.	5000	
† WMDJ	Martin, Ky.	2500	
WBGR	Paris, Ky.	1000	
WEZJ	Williamsburg, Ky.	1000	
KMLB	Monroe, La.	5000	1000
WMER	Westbrook, Me.	5000	5000
WFTQ	Worcester, Mass.	5000	5000
WBCM	Bay City, Mich.	5000	2500
WDOW	Dowagiac, Mich.	1000	
WCHB	Inkster, Mich.	1000	1000
KGLD	Golden Valley, Minn.	5000	500
WRBE	Lucedale, Miss.	5000	
WSEL	Pontotoc, Miss.	1000	
† KFPS	Salem, Mo.	500	
WREY	Millville, N.J.	1000	
WNYG	Babylon, N.Y.	1000	
WJJL	Niagara Falls, N.Y.	1000	
WSGO	Oswego, N.Y.	1000	
WBLA	Elizabethtown, N.C.	5000	
WBUY	Lexington, N.C.	5000	1000
KKXL	Grand Forks, N.D.	1000	500
WRRO	Warren, O.	5000	5000
KMED	Medford, Ore.	5000	1000
KODL	The Dalles, Ore.	5000	1000
WCDL	Carbondale, Pa.	5000	
WNPV	Lansdale, Pa.	500	500
WGCB	Red Lion, Pa.	1000	
WGLV	Greenville, S.C.	5000	5000
WKHJ	Holly Hill, S.C.	1000	1000
WZYX	Cowan, Tenn.	5000r	
WHDM	Mc Kenzie, Tenn.	5000	
KPUR	Amarillo, Tex.	5000	1000
KEYS	Corpus Christi, Tex.	1000	1000
KDNT	Denton, Tex.	5000	500
KELG	Elgin, Tex.	500	500
KETX	Livingston, Tex.	5000	
WKLV	Blackstone, Va.	5000	
WVBK	Herndon, Va.	1000	
KXXR	Spokane, Wash.	5000	
WHIS	Bluefield, W.V.	5000	500

WAJR	Morgantown, W.V.	5000	500
WNFL	Green Bay, Wis.	5000	500
CJOI	Wetaskiwin, Alta.	10000	10000
CFCP	Courtenay, B.C.	1000	1000
CFGO	Ottawa, Ont.	50000	50000
XEVSD	Villa Constitucion, B.C.S.	1000	150
XEFCD	Camargo, Chih.	5000	1000
XEAI	Mexico City, D.F.	5000	1000
† ----	Acambaro, Gto.	250	
XECCC	Tonala, Jal.	5000	1000
XEURM	Uruapan, Mich.	5000	
XEHW	Rosario, Sin.	1000	250
† ----	Nacajuca, Tab.	500	
XEEC	Tlapacoyan, Ver.	250	
† ----	Buctzoz, Yuc.	1000	1000
HIFS	Nagua, Dom. Rep.	1000	1000
HIAD	San Juan, Dom. Rep.	500	500
HIAK	Santo Domingo, Dom. Rep.	1000	250

1450 (LOCAL)

WDNG	Anniston, Ala.	1000	250
WSMQ	Bessemer, Ala.	1000	250
WCOX	Camden, Ala.	1000	250
WDLK	Dadeville, Ala.	1000p	250
WWNT	Dothan, Ala.	1000	250
WFIX	Huntsville, Ala.	1000	250
WLAY	Muscle Shoals, Ala.	1000	250
KLAM	Cordova, Alas.	250	250 f
† KIAL	Unalaska, Alas.	50	
KDAP	Douglas, Ariz.	1000	250
KNOT	Prescott, Ariz.	1000	250
KVSL	Show Low, Ariz.	1000	250
KFLT	Tucson, Ariz.	1000	250
KJWH	Camden, Ark.	1000	250
KENA	Mena, Ark.	1000	250
KJMB	Blythe, Calif.	1000	250
KAVA	Burney, Calif.	1000	250
KOWN	Escondido, Calif.	1000	250
KPSI	Palm Springs, Calif.	1000	250
KTIP	Porterville, Calif.	1000	250
KEST	San Francisco, Calif.	1000	250
KVML	Sonora, Calif.	1000	250
KVEN	Ventura, Calif.	1000	250
KOBO	Yuba City, Calif.	500	250
KGIW	Alamosa, Colo.	1000	250
KYOU	Greeley, Colo.	1000	250
KMKR	Meeker, Colo.	1000	250
KDRW	Silverton, Colo.	1000	250
WNAB	Bridgeport, Conn.	1000	250
WILM	Wilmington, Del.	1000	250
WOL	Washington, D. C.	1000	250
WWJB	Brooksville, Fla.	1000	250
WMFJ	Daytona Beach, Fla.	1000	250
WOCN	Miami, Fla.	1000	250
WBSR	Pensacola, Fla.	1000	250
WSPB	Sarasota, Fla.	1000	250
WSTU	Stuart, Fla.	1000	250
WTAL	Tallahassee, Fla.	1000	250
WGPC	Albany, Ga.	1000	250
WBHF	Cartersville, Ga.	1000	250
WCON	Cornelia, Ga.	1000	250
WKEU	Griffin, Ga.	1000	250
WMVG	Milledgeville, Ga.	1000	250
WQCN	Savannah, Ga.	1000	250
WVLD	Valdosta, Ga.	1000	250
KBFI	Bonners Ferry, Id.	1000	250
KVSI	Montpelier, Id.	1000	250
KYET	Payette, Id.	250	250
KEEP	Twin Falls, Id.	1000	250
WXOL	Cicero, Ill.	1000	250
WCEV	Cicero, Ill.	1000	250
WKEI	Kewanee, Ill.	500	250
WCVS	Springfield, Ill.	1000	250
WAFX	Ft. Wayne, Ind.	1000	250
WXVW	Jeffersonville, Ind.	1000	250
WASK	Lafayette, Ind.	1000	250
WAOV	Vincennes, Ind.	1000	250
KCDR	Cedar Rapids, Ia.	1000	250
KWBW	Hutchinson, Kan.	1000	250
WKXJ	Campbellsville, Ky.	1000	250
WWXL	Manchester, Ky.	1000	250
WDXR	Paducah, Ky.	1000	250
WLKS	West Liberty, Ky.	1000	250
KSIG	Crowley, La.	1000	250
KNOC	Natchitoches, La.	1000	250
WWIW	New Orleans, La.	1000	250
WLKN	Lincoln, Me.	1000	250
WRKD	Rockland, Me.	1000	250
WOXO	South Paris, Me.	1000	250
WTBO	Cumberland, Md.	1000	250
WTHU	Thurmont, Md.	500	100
WMAS	Springfield, Mass.	1000	250
WATZ	Alpena, Mich.	1000	250
WHTC	Holland, Mich.	1000	250
WMIQ	Iron Mountain, Mich.	1000	250
WXCM	Jackson, Mich.	1000	250
WKLA	Ludington, Mich.	1000	250
WNBY	Newberry, Mich.	1000	250
WHLS	Port Huron, Mich.	1000	250
KATE	Albert Lea, Minn.	1000	250
KBUN	Bemidji, Minn.	1000	250
KBMW	Breckenridge, Minn.	1000	250
WELY	Ely, Minn.	1000	250
KNSI	St. Cloud, Minn.	1000	250
WROX	Clarksdale, Miss.	1000	250
WCJU	Columbia, Miss.	1000	250
WJXN	Jackson, Miss.	1000	250
WQIC	Meridian, Miss.	1000	250
WNAT	Natchez, Miss.	1000	250
WROB	West Point, Miss.	1000	250
KFTW	Fredericktown, Mo.	1000	250
WMBH	Joplin, Mo.	1000	250
KIRX	Kirksville, Mo.	1000	250
KOKO	Warrensburg, Mo.	1000	250
KWPM	West Plains, Mo.	1000	250
KXXL	Bozeman, Mont.	1000	250
KQDI	Great Falls, Mont.	1000	250
KGRZ	Missoula, Mont.	1000	250
KRBN	Red Lodge, Mont.	1000	250
KTXX	Whitefish, Mont.	1000	250
KVCK	Wolf Point, Mont.	1000	250
KWBE	Beatrice, Neb.	1000	250
KONE	Reno, Nev.	1000	250
WKXL	Concord, N.H.	1000	250
WIIN	Atlantic City, N.J.	1000	250
WCTC	New Brunswick, N.J.	1000	250
‡ KRZY	Albuquerque, N.M.	1000	250
KLMX	Clayton, N.M.	1000	250
KOBE	Las Cruces, N.M.	1000	250
KENM	Portales, N.M.	1000	250
WCLI	Corning, N.Y.	1000	250
WWSC	Glens Falls, N.Y.	1000	250
WHDL	Olean, N.Y.	1000	250
WKIP	Poughkeepsie, N.Y.	1000	250
WKAL	Rome, N.Y.	1000	250
WATA	Boone, N.C.	1000	250
WGNC	Gastonia, N.C.	1000	250
WIZS	Henderson, N.C.	1000	250
WHKP	Hendersonville, N.C.	1000	250
WJQI	New Bern, N.C.	1000	250
WRZK	Spring Lake, N.C.	1000	250
KGCA	Rugby, N.D.	1000	250
WJER	Dover, O.	1000	250
WMOH	Hamilton, O.	1000	250
WLEC	Sandusky, O.	1000	250
KWHW	Altus, Okla.	1000	250
KGFF	Shawnee, Okla.	1000	250
KSIW	Woodward, Okla.	1000	250
KEED	Eugene, Ore.	1000	250
KFLS	Klamath Falls, Ore.	1000	250
KLBM	La Grande, Ore.	1000	250
* KBPS	Portland, Ore.	1000	250
WEYZ	Erie, Pa.	1000	250
WFRA	Franklin, Pa.	1000	250
WDAD	Indiana, Pa.	1000	250
WPAM	Pottsville, Pa.	1000	250
WFXX	South Williamsport, Pa.	1000	250

WMAJ	State College, Pa.	1000	250
WJPA	Washington, Pa.	1000	250
WCPR	Coama, P.R.	1000	250
WKRI	West Warwick, R.I.	1000	250
WGCA	Charleston, S.C.	1000	250
WCRS	Greenwood, S.C.	1000	250
WHSC	Hartsville, S.C.	1000	250
WQOK	Myrtle Beach, S.C.	1000	250
KBFS	Belle Fourche, S.D.	1000	250
KYNT	Yankton, S.D.	1000	250
WLAR	Athens, Tenn.	1000	250
WZRA	Chattanooga, Tenn.	1000	250
WDSG	Dyersburg, Tenn.	1000	250
WSMG	Greeneville, Tenn.	1000	250
WLAF	La Follette, Tenn.	1000	250
WGNS	Murfreesboro, Tenn.	1000	250
KAYC	Beaumont, Tex.	1000	250
KBEN	Carrizo Springs, Tex.	1000	250
KCTI	Gonzales, Tex.	250	250
KMBL	Junction, Tex.	1000	250
KCYL	Lampasas, Tex.	1000	250
KMHT	Marshall, Tex.	1000	250
KNET	Palestine, Tex.	1000	250
KSNY	Snyder, Tex.	1000	250
KURA	Moab, Utah	1000	250
KEYY	Provo, Utah	1000	250
‡ KDXU	St. George, Utah	1000	250
WSNO	Barre, Vt.	1000	250
WTSA	Brattleboro, Vt.	1000	250
WFTR	Front Royal, Va.	1000	250
WNWZ	Highland Springs, Va.	1000	250
WREL	Lexington, Va.	1000	250
WMVA	Martinsville, Va.	1000	250
WLPM	Suffolk, Va.	1000	250
KAYO	Aberdeen, Wash.	1000	250
KCLX	Colfax, Wash.	1000	250
KONP	Port Angeles, Wash.	250	250
KJUN	Puyallup, Wash.	1000	250
WWBB	Madison, W.V.	1000	250
WIKS	Parkersburg, W.V.	1000	250
KFIZ	Fond Du Lac, Wis.	1000	250
WDLB	Marshfield, Wis.	1000	250
WRCO	Richland Center, Wis.	1000	250
KBBS	Buffalo, Wyo.	1000	250
KVOW	Riverton, Wyo.	1000	250
CKYR	Jasper, Alta.	100	100
CHET	Chetwynd, B.C.	1000	250
CKSP	Summerland, B.C.	1000	250
CBG	Gander, Nfld.	1000	500
CFAB	Windsor, N.S.	250	250
CFJR	Brockville, Ont.	1000	250
CHUC	Cobourg, Ont.	1000	1000
CJBM	Causapscal, Que.	1000	250
CHEF	Granby, Que.	10000	5000
CHRT	St. Eleuthere, Que.	1000	250
XEYZ	Aguascalientes, Ags.	1000	500
XESS	Ensenada, B.C.	1000	200
XEQU	Ojinaga, Chih.	1000	250
XEEP	Gomez Palacio, Dgo.	1000	250
XERY	Acapulco, Gro.	1000	100
XEJTF	Zacoalco, Jal.	250	250
XEGC	Sahuayo, Mich.	1000	250
XETD	Tecuala, Nay.	250	250
XEJM	Monterrey, N.L.	500	250
† XETEP	Pinotepa, Oax.	500	
XEXD	Atlixco, Pue.	500	250
XENA	Queretaro, Qro.	1000	500
XEIE	Matehuala, S.L.P.	1000	200
XEGU	El Fuerte, Sin.	1000	250
† XEPE	Empalme, Son.	250	250
† ----	Hermosillo, Son.	250	
XEDJ	Magdalena, Son.	250	100
XECB	San Luis, Son.	250	250
XECM	Ciudad Mante, Tams.	1000	250
XEVH	Valle Hermosa, Tams.	1000	250
XEKM	Minatitlan, Ver.	500	250
XEPP	Orizaba, Ver.	1000	250
XEJD	Poza Rica, Ver.	1000	250
XEPY	Merida, Yuc.	1000	250
XEHE	Rio Grande, Zac.	500	250
CMJW	Santa Cruz Del Sur, Cuba	1000	1000
HIAC	Salcedo, Dom. Rep.	500	500
HIAR	San Cristobal, Dom. Rep.	500	500
HIDB	San Pedro De Macoris, Dom. Rep.	1000	1000

1460 (REGIONAL)

WFMH	Cullman, Ala.	5000	500
WPNX	Phenix City, Ala.	5000	1000
† KWLL	Casa Grande, Ariz.	2500	1000
KZOT	Marianna, Ark.	500	
KCCL	Paris, Ark.	500	
KTYM	Inglewood, Calif.	5000	500
KDON	Salinas, Calif.	5000	5000
KVRE	Santa Rosa, Calif.	1000	
KYSN	Colorado Springs, Colo.	1000	500
WBAR	Bartow, Fla.	1000	
WZEP	De Funiak Springs, Fla.	1000	
WPDQ	Jacksonville, Fla.	5000	5000
WDYX	Buford, Ga.	5000	
WROY	Carmi, Ill.	1000	
WIXN	Dixon, Ill.	1000	
WRTL	Rantoul, Ill.	500	
WKAM	Goshen, Ind.	1000	500
WNVI	North Vernon, Ind.	1000	
KSO	Des Moines, Ia.	5000	5000
KKOY	Chanute, Kan.	1000	
WBPA	Elkhorn City, Ky.	1000	
WRVK	Mt. Vernon, Ky.	500	
WXOK	Baton Rouge, La.	5000	1000
KBSF	Springhill, La.	1000	
WCEI	Easton, Md.	1000	500
WBET	Brockton, Mass.	5000	1000
WBRN	Big Rapids, Mich.	5000	2500
WPON	Pontiac, Mich.	1000	500
KDWA	Hastings, Minn.	1000	
KDMA	Montevideo, Minn.	1000	1000
KKAQ	Thief River Falls, Minn.	500	
WELZ	Belzoni, Miss.	1000	
WJKX	Moss Point, Miss.	500	
KIRL	St. Charles, Mo.	5000	500
KRNY	Kearney, Neb.	5000	
KENO	Las Vegas, Nev.	5000	1000
WJJZ	Mount Holly, N.J.	5000	5000
WOKO	Albany, N.Y.	5000	5000
WVOX	New Rochelle, N.Y.	500	
WWWG	Rochester, N.Y.	5000	5000
WAKS	Fuquay Springs, N.C.	5000	
WRKB	Kannapolis, N.C.	500	
WEWO	Laurinburg, N.C.	5000	5000
WMMH	Marshall, N.C.	500	
KLTC	Dickinson, N.D.	5000	5000
WBNS	Columbus, O.	5000	1000
WPVL	Painesville, O.	1000	500
KCAN	El Reno, Okla.	500	
WMBA	Ambridge, Pa.	500	
WCMB	Harrisburg, Pa.	5000	5000
WFAB	Juncos, P.R.	500	500
WFBA	San Sebastian, P.R.	500	500
WDOG	Allendale, S.C.	1000	
WBCU	Union, S.C.	1000	1000
WJAK	Jackson, Tenn.	1000	
WEEN	Lafayette, Tenn.	1000	
† WXRQ	Mt. Pleasant, Tenn.	5000	
KBRZ	Freeport, Tex.	500	
KRME	Hondo, Tex.	500	
KTLK	Lubbock, Tex.	1000	
WACO	Waco, Tex.	1000	1000
WPRW	Manassas, Va.	5000	5000
WRAD	Radford, Va.	5000	500

	KGAA	Kirkland, Wash.	5000	2500
	KMWX	Yakima, Wash.	5000	5000
	WBUC	Buckhannon, W.V.	5000	
	WRKR	Racine, Wis.	500	
	WTMB	Tomah, Wis.	1000	
	CJMH	Medicine Hat, Alta.	10000	10000
	CJOY	Guelph, Ont.	10000	10000
	CKRB	St. Georges De Beauce, Que.	10000	5000
	XEUJ	Carmen, Cam.	250	250
†	----	Ciudad Jimenez, Chih.	5000	250
	XEYC	Ciudad Juarez, Chih.	1000	1000
	XEPD	Nueva Rosita, Coah.	1000	
†	----	Guadalupe Victoria, Dgo.	200	100
†	----	Acapulco, Gro.	1000	
†	----	Tepic, Nay.	1000	
	XEKC	Oaxaca, Oax.	1000	
†	----	Oaxaca, Oax.	1000	
	XECPQ	Carillo Puerto, Q.R.	1000	500
	XEXQ	San Luis Potosi, S.L.P.	1000	250
†	----	Nacozari, Son.	250	
	XEOLA	Altamira, Tams.	5000	1000
	XEJH	Jalapa, Ver.	500	
	HIAN	Hato Mayor Del Rey, Dom. Rep.	500	500
	4VEA	Cap Haitien, Haiti	1000	1000

1470 (REGIONAL)

	WEGN	Evergreen, Ala.	1000	
	KSVA	Sierra Vista, Ariz.	2500	
	KDEW	De Witt, Ark.	500	
‡	KWXI	Glenwood, Ark.	2500	
	KOLI	Coalinga, Calif.	500	
	KUTY	Palmdale, Calif.	5000	500
	KXOA	Sacramento, Calif.	5000	1000
	KSIR	Estes Park, Colo.	1000	
‡	KRDZ	Wray, Colo.	1000	
	WMMW	Meriden, Conn.	2500	5000
	WFNN	Dunedin, Fla.	5000	
	WRBD	Pompano Beach, Fla.	5000	2500
	WBIT	Adel, Ga.	1000	
	WCCD	Athens, Ga.	1000	
	WCLA	Claxton, Ga.	1000	
	WRGA	Rome, Ga.	5000	5000
	WMPP	Chicago Heights, Ill.	1000	1000
	WMBD	Peoria, Ill.	5000	5000
	WHUT	Anderson, Ind.	1000	
	KWSL	Sioux City, Ia.	5000	5000
	KWAY	Waverly, Ia.	1000	
	KARE	Atchison, Kan.	1000	1000
	KLIB	Liberal, Kan.	1000	
	WSAC	Ft. Knox, Ky.	1000	
	WFSR	Harlan, Ky.	5000	
	WBFC	Stanton, Ky.	1000	
	KTDL	Farmerville, La.	1000	
	KLCL	Lake Charles, La.	5000	5000
	WLAM	Lewiston, Me.	5000	5000
	WJDY	Salisbury, Md.	5000	
	WTTR	Westminster, Md.	1000	
	WSRO	Marlboro, Mass.	5000	5000
	WCEK	Newburyport, Mass.	500	
	WKMF	Flint, Mich.	5000	1000
	WKLZ	Kalamazoo, Mich.	500	
	KKKC	Anoka, Minn.	1000	
	WCHJ	Brookhaven, Miss.	1000	
	WKXC	New Albany, Miss.	500	500
	KGHM	Brookfield, Mo.	500	
	KTCB	Malden, Mo.	1000	
	WTKO	Ithaca, N.Y.	5000	500
	WPDM	Potsdam, N.Y.	1000	
	WVBS	Burgaw, N.C.	1000	
	WBIG	Greensboro, N.C.	5000	5000
	WPNC	Plymouth, N.C.	5000	
	WTOE	Spruce Pine, N.C.	5000	
	WOHO	Toledo, O.	1000	1000
	KVLH	Pauls Valley, Okla.	1000	
	KVIN	Vinita, Okla.	500	
	KDUN	Reedsport, Ore.	5000	
	WSAN	Allentown, Pa.	5000	5000
	WMGZ	Farrell, Pa.	1000	500
	WRML	Portage, Pa.	500	
	WKCK	Orocovis, P.R.	1000	1000
	WQXL	Columbia, S.C.	5000	
	WGMB	Georgetown, S.C.	1000	
	WEAG	Alcoa, Tenn.	1000	
	WVOL	Nashville, Tenn.	5000	1000
	KRBC	Abilene, Tex.	5000	1000
	KDHN	Dimmitt, Tex.	500	
	KWRD	Henderson, Tex.	500	
	KCNY	San Marcos, Tex.	250	
†	KBXN	Tremonton, Utah	5000	
	WBTX	Broadway, Va.	5000	
	WTZE	Tazewell, Va.	5000	
	KELA	Chehalis, Wash.	5000	1000
	KSEM	Moses Lake, Wash.	5000	1000
	KAPS	Mt. Vernon, Wash.	500	
	WWHY	Huntington, W.V.	5000	
	WBKV	West Bend, Wis.	2500r	
	KWIV	Douglas, Wyo.	1000	500
	CJVB	Vancouver, B.C.	50000	50000
	CHOW	Welland, Ont.	10000	10000
	CFOX	Pointe Claire, Que.	10000	5000
	XEBBC	Tijuana, B.C.	5000	5000
	XEBAL	Becal, Cam.	1000	
†	----	Reforma, Chis.	500	
	XEHM	Delicias, Chih.	1000	
	XEAY	Parras, Coah.	1000	250
	XEDS	Colima, Col.	5000	5000
	XESM	Mexico City, D.F.	10000	5000
	XECAV	Durango, Dgo.	1000	500
	XEYA	Irapuato, Gto.	1000	
†	----	Tlanchinol, Hgo.	1000	
	XENAY	Ahuacatlan, Nay.	600	150
	XECU	Los Mochis, Sin.	1000	250
	XEACE	Mazatlan, Sin.	1000	100
	XEUK	Caborca, Son.	500	
	XEHI	Ciudad Miguel Aleman, Tams.	1000	250
	CMGE	Cardenas, Cuba	250	250
	HIAG	Santiago, Dom. Rep.	500	500

1480 (REGIONAL)

	WARI	Abbeville, Ala.	1000	
	WBTS	Bridgeport, Ala.	1000	
	WLPH	Irondale, Ala.	5000	
	WABB	Mobile, Ala.	5000	5000
	KPHX	Phoenix, Ariz.	1000	
	KTHS	Berryville, Ark.	5000	
	KWUN	Concord, Calif.	500	500
	KRED	Eureka, Calif.	5000	1000
	KYOS	Merced, Calif.	5000	5000
	KWIZ	Santa Ana, Calif.	5000	1000
	KSBQ	Santa Maria, Calif.	1000	
	KAYK	Pueblo, Colo.	1000	
	WKND	Windsor, Conn.	500	
	WAPG	Arcadia, Fla.	1000	
	WVCF	Ocoee, Fla.	1000	
	WKGC	Panama City Beach, Fla.	500	
	WYZE	Atlanta, Ga.	5000	
	WRDW	Augusta, Ga.	5000	5000
	WFXW	Geneva, Ill.	1000	500
	WJBM	Jerseyville, Ill.	500	
	WTHI	Terre Haute, Ind.	5000	1000
	WRSW	Warsaw, Ind.	1000	500
	KLEE	Ottumwa, Ia.	500	
	KBEA	Mission, Kan.	1000	500
	KLEO	Wichita, Kan.	5000	1000
	WKOA	Hopkinsville, Ky.	1000	
	WNKY	Neon, Ky.	5000	
	WTLO	Somerset, Ky.	1000	
	KCKW	Jena, La.	500	
	KJOE	Shreveport, La.	1000	
	WSAR	Fall River, Mass.	5000	5000
‡	WMAX	Grand Rapids, Mich.	5000	
†	WMAX	Kentwood, Mich.	5000	5000
	WIOS	Tawas City, Mich.	1000	
	WSDS	Ypsilanti, Mich.		5000
	KAUS	Austin, Minn.	1000	1000

Call	Location	Day	Night
KEHG	Fosston, Minn.	5000	2500
KPIA	Ironton, Mo.	5000	
KGCX	Sidney, Mont.	5000	5000
KLMS	Lincoln, Neb.	5000	1000
KUUX	Hobbs, N.M.	5000	1000
WLEA	Hornell, N.Y.	2500	
WJIT	New York, N.Y.	5000	5000
WADR	Remsen, N.Y.	5000	
WAME	Charlotte, N.C.	5000	5000
WWKO	Fair Bluff, N.C.	1000	
WLTM	Franklin, N.C.	5000	
WYRN	Louisburg, N.C.	500	
WYDK	Yadkinville, N.C.	1000	
WHBC	Canton, O.	5000	5000
WCIN	Cincinnati, O.	5000	500
WCNS	Latrobe, Pa.	1000	
WDAS	Philadelphia, Pa.	5000	1000
WISL	Shamokin, Pa.	1000	1000
WSHP	Shippensburg, Pa.	500	
WMDD	Fajardo, P.R.	5000	5000
KLSC	Watertown, S.D.	1000	
WJFC	Jefferson City, Tenn.	500	
WMQM	Memphis, Tenn.	5000	
WJLE	Smithville, Tenn.	1000	
KBOX	Dallas, Tex.	5000	1000
KLVL	Pasadena, Tex.	1000	500
KAPE	San Antonio, Tex.	500	
KONI	Spanish Fork, Utah	1000	
WCFR	Springfield, Vt.	5000	
WPWC	Quantico, Va.	500	500
# WBBL	Richmond, Va.	5000	5000
# WLEE	Richmond, Va.	5000	5000
WUEZ	Salem, Va.	5000	
KLAY	Lakewood, Wash.	1000	
KAAR	Vancouver, Wash.	2500	2500
WISM	Madison, Wis.	5000	5000
KRAE	Cheyenne, Wyo.	1000	
CKER	Edmonton, Alta.	10000	10000
CKMV	Grand Falls, N.B.	5000	
CKAN	Newmarket, Ont.	10000	10000
CHRD	Drummondville, Que.	10000	10000
XEMCA	Ciudad Morelos, B.C.S.	500	100
† ----	Palenque, Chis.	1000	1000
XEXU	Villa Frontera, Coah.	1000	100
XEMC	Salvatierra, Gto.	250	
XEGX	San Luis De La Paz, Gto.	500	100
XEXC	Taxco, Gro.	1000	125
† ----	Tecpan, Gro.	250	
XEZJ	Zapopan, Jal.	500	200
† XEIP	Uruapan, Mich.	500	
XETKR	Villa De Guadalupe, N.L.	5000	500
XEOU	Huajuapan De Leon, Oax.	500	
† ----	Atlixco, Pue.	1000	
----	Cancun, Q.R.	250	
† ----	Hermosillo, Son.	1000	
XENS	Navojoa, Son.	1000	1000
XEPR	Poza Rica, Ver.	10000	500
† ----	Rio Blanco, Ver.	250	

1490 (LOCAL)

Call	Location	Day	Night
WANA	Anniston, Ala.	1000	250
WAJF	Decatur, Ala.	1000	250
WRLD	Lanett, Ala.	1000	250
WHBB	Selma, Ala.	1000	250
KBAS	Bullhead City, Ariz.	1000	250
KCUZ	Clifton, Ariz.	1000	250
KYCA	Prescott, Ariz.	1000	250
KAIR	Tucson, Ariz.	1000	250
KXAR	Hope, Ark.	1000	250
KDRS	Paragould, Ark.	1000	250
KOTN	Pine Bluff, Ark.	1000	250
KWAC	Bakersfield, Calif.	1000	250
KGUD	Banning, Calif.	1000	250
KICO	Calexico, Calif.	1000	250
KRKC	King City, Calif.	1000	250
KTOB	Petaluma, Calif.	1000	250
KBLF	Red Bluff, Calif.	1000	250
KDB	Santa Barbara, Calif.	1000	250
KOWL	South Lake Tahoe, Calif.	1000	250
KSYC	Yreka, Calif.	1000	250
KBOL	Boulder, Colo.	1000	250
KGUC	Gunnison, Colo.	1000	250
KIIQ	Manitou Springs, Colo.	500	250
WGCH	Greenwich, Conn.	1000	250
WTRL	Bradenton, Fla.	1000	250
WXVQ	De Land, Fla.	1000	250
WKEM	Immokalee, Fla.	1000	250
WMBM	Miami Beach, Fla.	1000	250
WCKC	Milton, Fla.	1000	
WPXE	Starke, Fla.	1000	250
WTTB	Vero Beach, Fla.	1000	250
WSIR	Winter Haven, Fla.	1000	250
WMOG	Brunswick, Ga.	1000	250
WMJM	Cordele, Ga.	1000	250
† WYYZ	Jasper, Ga.	1000	250
WRED	Monroe, Ga.	1000	250
WSFB	Quitman, Ga.	1000	250
WSNT	Sandersville, Ga.	1000	250
WSYL	Sylvania, Ga.	1000	250
KCID	Caldwell, Id.	1000	250
KOFE	St. Maries, Id.	1000	250
WKRO	Cairo, Ill.	1000	250
WDAN	Danville, Ill.	1000	250
WESL	East St. Louis, Ill.	1000	250
WOPA	Oak Park, Ill.	1000	250
WZOE	Princeton, Ill.	1000	250
WKBV	Richmond, Ind.	1000	250
WNDU	South Bend, Ind.	1000	250
KBUR	Burlington, Ia.	1000	250
WDBQ	Dubuque, Ia.	1000	250
KBAB	Indianola, Ia.	500	250
KRIB	Mason City, Ia.	1000	250
KKAN	Phillipsburg, Kan.	1000	250
KTOP	Topeka, Kan.	1000	250
WFKY	Frankfort, Ky.	1000	250
WKAY	Glasgow, Ky.	1000	250
WFXY	Middlesboro, Ky.	1000	250
WOMI	Owensboro, Ky.	1000	250
WSIP	Paintsville, Ky.	1000	250
WIKC	Bogalusa, La.	1000	250
KEUN	Eunice, La.	1000	250
KJIN	Houma, La.	1000	250
KRUS	Ruston, La.	1000	250
WPOR	Portland, Me.	1000	250
WTVL	Waterville, Me.	1000	250
WARK	Hagerstown, Md.	1000	250
WHAV	Haverhill, Mass.	1000	250
WMRC	Milford, Mass.	1000	250
WACM	West Springfield, Mass.	1000	250
WABJ	Adrian, Mich.	1000	250
WTIQ	Manistique, Mich.	1000	250
WMPX	Midland, Mich.	1000	250
WPBK	Whitehall, Mich.	1000	250
KXRA	Alexandria, Minn.	1000	250
KLGR	Redwood Falls, Minn.	1000	250
WLOX	Biloxi, Miss.	1000	250
WCLD	Cleveland, Miss.	1000	250
WHOC	Philadelphia, Miss.	1000	250
WTUP	Tupelo, Miss.	1000	250
WJFL	Vicksburg, Miss.	1000	250
KDMO	Carthage, Mo.	1000	250
KTTR	Rolla, Mo.	1000	250
KDRO	Sedalia, Mo.	1000	250
KDBM	Dillon, Mont.	1000	250
KLYC	Laurel, Mont.	1000	250
KYNN	Omaha, Neb.	1000	250
WEMJ	Laconia, N.H.	1000	250
WUSS	Atlantic City, N.J.	1000	250
KRSN	Los Alamos, N.M.	1000	250
KRTN	Raton, N.M.	1000	250 -f
† KOAW	Ruidoso, N.M.	1000	250
WCSS	Amsterdam, N.Y.	1000	250
WBTA	Batavia, N.Y.	500	250
WKNY	Kingston, N.Y.	1000	250
WICY	Malone, N.Y.	1000	250
WDLC	Port Jervis, N.Y.	1000	250
WCDO	Sidney, N.Y.	250	250
WOLF	Syracuse, N.Y.	1000	250
WDUR	Durham, N.C.	1000	250
WLOE	Eden, N.C.	1000	250

WFLB	Fayetteville, N.C.	1000	250
WRNB	New Bern, N.C.	1000	250
WRMT	Rocky Mount, N.C.	1000	250
WSTP	Salisbury, N.C.	1000	250
WSVM	Valdese, N.C.	1000	250
WWIL	Wilmington, N.C.	1000	250
KNDC	Hettinger, N.D.	1000	250 -f
KOVC	Valley City, N.D.	1000	250
WBEX	Chillicothe, O.	1000	250
WJMO	Cleveland Heights, O.	1000	250
WOHI	East Liverpool, O.	1000	250
WMOA	Marietta, O.	1000	250
WMRN	Marion, O.	1000	250
KOKC	Guthrie, Okla.	500	250
KBIX	Muskogee, Okla.	1000	250
KBKR	Baker, Ore.	1000	250
KRNR	Roseburg, Ore.	1000	250
KBZY	Salem, Ore.	1000	250
WESB	Bradford, Pa.	1000	250
WAZL	Hazleton, Pa.	1000	250
WJNL	Johnstown, Pa.	1000	250
WLPA	Lancaster, Pa.	1000	250
WBCB	Levittown, Pa.	1000	250
WMRF	Lewistown, Pa.	1000	250
WMGW	Meadville, Pa.	1000	250
WNBT	Wellsboro, Pa.	1000	250
WZBS	Ponce, P.R.	1000	250
† WVGB	Beaufort, S.C.	500	250
WGCD	Chester, S.C.	1000	250
WMRB	Greenville, S.C.	1000	250
WSDC	Hartsville, S.C.	1000	250
KORN	Mitchell, S.D.	1000	250
WOPI	Bristol, Tenn.	1000	250
WDXB	Chattanooga, Tenn.	1000	250
WCSV	Crossville, Tenn.	1000	250
WITA	Knoxville, Tenn.	1000	250
WJJM	Lewisburg, Tenn.	1000	250
WDXL	Lexington, Tenn.	1000	250
KNOW	Austin, Tex.	1000	250
KIBL	Beeville, Tex.	1000	250
KBST	Big Spring, Tex.	1000	250
KQTY	Borger, Tex.	1000	250
KNEL	Brady, Tex.	1000	250
KWMC	Del Rio, Tex.	1000	250
KSAM	Huntsville, Tex.	1000	250
KVOZ	Laredo, Tex.	1000	250
KZZN	Littlefield, Tex.	1000	250
KPLT	Paris, Tex.	1000	250
KDOK	Tyler, Tex.	1000	250
KVWC	Vernon, Tex.	1000	250
KJQN	Ogden, Utah	1000	250
WKVT	Brattleboro, Vt.	1000	250
WFAD	Middlebury, Vt.	1000	250
WIKE	Newport, Vt.	1000	250
WYKR	Wells River, Vt.	1000	250
WCVA	Culpeper, Va.	1000	250
WPAK	Farmville, Va.	1000	250
WPEX	Hampton, Va.	1000	250
WAYB	Waynesboro, Va.	1000	250
KBRO	Bremerton, Wash.	1000	250
KVAC	Forks, Wash.	1000	250
KEYG	Grand Coulee, Wash.	1000	250
KLOG	Kelso, Wash.	1000	250
KENE	Toppenish, Wash.	1000	250
KTEL	Walla Walla, Wash.	1000	250
WXIT	Charleston, W.V.	1000	250
WTCS	Fairmont, W.V.	1000	250
WAEY	Princeton, W.V.	1000	250
WSGB	Sutton, W.V.	1000	250
WGEZ	Beloit, Wis.	1000	250
WLXR	La Crosse, Wis.	1000	250
WIGM	Medford, Wis.	1000	250
WYTL	Oshkosh, Wis.	1000	250
KUGR	Green River, Wyo.	1000	250
‡ KOJO	Laramie, Wyo.	500	250
KRTR	Thermopolis, Wyo.	250	250
KGOS	Torrington, Wyo.	1000	250
CJPR	Blairmore, Alta.	1000	250
CFWB	Campbell River, B.C.	1000	1000
CBDQ	Wabush, Nfld.	1000	250
CKEN	Kentville, N.S.	1000	500
• CFRC	Kingston, Ont.	100	100
CFPS	Port Elgin, Ont.	1000	250
CKLR	L'annonciaton, Que.	1000	250
CKBM	Montmagny, Que.	1000	250
CBGN	Ste. Anne Des Monts, Que.	1000	250
CJSN	Shaunavon, Sask.	1000	250
XERO	Aguascalientes, Ags.	250	250
XEIB	Todas Santos, B.C.S.	1000	500
XEDG	Chihuahua, Chih.	1000	250
XECJC	Ciudad Juarez, Chih.	1000	250
† ----	Cuahutemoc, Chih.	1000	100
XEJR	Parral, Chih.	1000	200
XEED	Ameca, Jal.	1000	250
XECH	Toluca, Mex.	250	250
XEKN	Huetamo, Mich.	250	250
XEGT	Zamora, Mich.	1000	250
XESK	Ruiz, Nay.	250	250
XEPOP	Puebla, Pue.	500	250
XEXE	Queretaro, Qro.	1000	200
XEFF	Matehuala, S.L.P.	1000	250
XEVP	Guasave, Sin.	500	200
XEAQ	Agua Prieta, Son.	1000	250
† ----	Benjamin Hill, Son.	500	100
XEDR	Guaymas, Son.	1000	250
XEGG	Ciudad Mante, Tams.	250	100
XEMS	Matamoros, Tams.	1000	250
XEVZ	Acayucan, Ver.	1000	200
XEYT	Teocelo, Ver.	250	100
XEME	Valladolid, Yuc.	5000	500
HIAP	Moca, Dom. Rep.	250	250
HIAH	Santo Domingo, Dom. Rep.	250	250

1500 (CLEAR)

WQMS	Alabaster, Ala.	1000	
WVSM	Rainsville, Ala.	1000	
WKAX	Russellville, Ala.	1000	
KIEL	Jacksonville, Ark.	1000	
KROQ	Burbank, Calif.	10000	1000
KHTT	San Jose, Calif.	10000	5000
† ----	Breen, Colo.	10000	
WFIF	Milford, Conn.	5000	
WTOP	Washington, D. C.	50000	50000
WKIZ	Key West, Fla.	250	250
WGUL	New Port Richey, Fla.	250	
WIAF	Clarkesville, Ga.	5000	
WKRP	Dallas, Ga.	1000	
WSEM	Donalsonville, Ga.	1000	
WPTC	Macon, Ga.	1000	
KUMU	Honolulu, Haw.	10000u	10000u
WGEN	Geneseo, Ill.	250	
WPMB	Vandalia, Ill.	250	
WNIZ	Zion, Ill.	250	
WBRI	Indianapolis, Ind.	5000	
WAKE	Valparaiso, Ind.	1000	
WKXO	Berea, Ky.	250	
WMJL	Marion, Ky.	250	
KQXL	New Roads, La.	1000	
WWKQ	Battle Creek, Mich.	1000	
WLQV	Detroit, Mich.	50000	5000
WDEE	Reed City, Mich.	250	
KSTP	St. Paul, Minn.	50000	50000
WBFN	Quitman, Miss.	1000	
WRDS	Sardis, Miss.	500	
KDFN	Doniphan, Mo.	1000	
WKER	Pompton Lakes, N.J.	1000	
•† KABR	Magdalena, N.M.	1000	
WGMF	Watkins Glen, N.Y.	250	
WLWL	Rockingham, N.C.	500	
WSMX	Winston Salem, N.C.	10000	
WGIC	Xenia, O.	500	
WGFT	Youngstown, O.	500	
KXVQ	Pawhuska, Okla.	5000	
WMNT	Manati, P.R.	1000	250
WEAC	Gaffney, S.C.	1000	
WIXR	Mt. Pleasant, S.C.	1000	

WDEB	Jamestown, Tenn.	1000	
KNCI	Boerne, Tex.	250	
KMIO	Merkel, Tex.	1000	
KTXO	Sherman, Tex.	1000	
KANI	Wharton, Tex.	500	500
CKAY	Duncan, B.C.	10000	1000
XEEP	Ensenada, B.C.	500	
XEJQ	Parras, Coah.	250	
XERH	Mexico City, D.F.	20000	20000
XEFL	Guanajuato, Gto.	1000	1000
XEUV	Villahermosa, Tab.	500	250
XEGN	Piedras Negras, Ver.	1000	1000
XEYQ	Fresnillo, Zac.	1000	
4VOC	Port Au Prince, Haiti	350	350
PJC7A	Curacao, Ne. Antil.	1000	1000

1505

....	The Valley, Angu.	500	500

1510 (CLEAR)

KDJQ	Mesa, Ariz.	10000	
KACJ	Greenwood, Ark.	1000	
KIRV	Fresno, Calif.	10000	
KNSE	Ontario, Calif.	10000	1000
KTIM	San Rafael, Calif.	1000	
KDKO	Littleton, Colo.	5000	5000
WNLC	New London, Conn.	10000	5000
‡ WKAO	Boynton Beach, Fla.	1000	
WMIB	Marco Island, Fla.	1000	
WWBC	Rockledge, Fla.	1000	
WINU	Highland, Ill.	1000	
WJRC	Joliet, Ill.	500	
WKAI	Macomb, Ill.	1000	
WAYT	Wabash, Ind.	250	
KIFG	Iowa Falls, Ia.	1000	
KANS	Larned, Kan.	1000	
KAGY	Port Sulphur, La.	1000	
WMRE	Boston, Mass.	50000	50000
WDJD	Jackson, Mich.	5000	
WLKM	Three Rivers, Mich.	500	
WKPO	Prentiss, Miss.	1000	
KCCV	Independence, Mo.	1000	
KOSC	Marshfield, Mo.	250	
KTTT	Columbus, Neb.	1000	
WRAN	Dover, N.J.	10000	500
WJIC	Salem, N.J.	2500	
WPUT	Brewster, N.Y.	1000	
WEAL	Greensboro, N.C.	1000	
WLGN	Logan, O.	1000	
WLKR	Norwalk, O.	500	
† WTRJ	Troy, O.	250	
WAHT	Annville, Pa.	5000	
WRUA	Monroeville, Pa.	250	
† WIVD	Lajas, P.R.	1000	1000
WVAP	Burnettown, S.C.	1000	
WCPL	Pageland, S.C.	500	
WSJW	Woodruff, S.C.	1000	
KMSD	Milbank, S.D.	5000	
WLAC	Nashville, Tenn.	50000	50000
KAGC	Bryan, Tex.	500	
KCTX	Childress, Tex.	250	
KMND	Midland, Tex.	500	
KMOO	Mineola, Tex.	500	
KOVE	Nederland, Tex.	5000	
KROB	Robstown, Tex.	500	
KSTV	Stephenville, Tex.	500	
KZZI	West Jordan, Utah	10000	
WBLB	Pulaski, Va.	1000	
KKNW	Mountlake Terrace, Wash.	250	
KGA	Spokane, Wash.	50000	50000
WAUK	Waukesha, Wis.	10000	
CKOT	Tillsonburg, Ont.	1000	
CJRS	Sherbrooke, Que.	10000	10000
XEOF	Cortazar, Gto.	5000	
† XERB	Cozumel, Gro.	500	
† KEYL	Iguala, Gro.	10000	10000
XEZG	Ixmiquilpan, Hgo.	1000	1000
XELW	Ciudad Guzman, Jal.	5000	5000
† ----	Puerto Vallarta, Jal.	500	
† ----	Melchor Ocampo De Balsas, Mich.	500	
XEQI	Monterrey, N.L.	10000	
† ----	Salina Cruz, Oax.	1000	
XEKI	Navojoa, Son.	500	
XEJPM	Cardel, Ver.	1000	1000
† ----	Panuco, Ver.	1000	
HIBL	Santo Domingo, Dom. Rep.	10000	10000

1520 (CLEAR)

WAOA	Opelika, Ala.	5000	
KMPG	Hollister, Calif.	500	
KACY	Port Hueneme, Calif.	50000	1000
WTLN	Apopka, Fla.	5000	
WGNB	Indian Rocks Beach, Fla.	1000	
WEXY	Oakland Park, Fla.	1000	
‡ WDGR	Dahlonega, Ga.	500	
WDGL	Douglasville, Ga.	1000	
WXPQ	Eatonton, Ga.	1000	
WNMT	Garden City, Ga.	1000	
WHOW	Clinton, Ill.	5000	
WLUV	Loves Park, Ill.	500	
WKVI	Knox, Ind.	250	
WSVL	Shelbyville, Ind.	1000	250
KSIB	Creston, Ia.	1000	
WHIC	Hardinsburg, Ky.	250	
WRSL	Stanford, Ky.	500	
KXKW	Lafayette, La.	10000	500
WVOB	Bel Air, Md.	250	
WTRI	Brunswick, Md.	500	
WPOE	Greenfield, Mass.	10000	
WKJR	Muskegon Heights, Mich.	10000	1000
WYFC	Ypsilanti, Mich.	250	
KOLM	Rochester, Minn.	10000	
WZBR	Amory, Miss.	500	
WCSP	Crystal Springs, Miss.	1000	
WQMA	Marks, Miss.	250	
KMPL	Sikeston, Mo.	5000	500
WIBG	Ocean City, N.J.	1000	
KAMX	Albuquerque, N.M.	1000	
WKBW	Buffalo, N.Y.	50000	50000
WTHE	Mineola, N.Y.	1000	
WDSL	Mocksville, N.C.	5000	
WYRU	Red Springs, N.C.	5000	
WGMA	Spindale, N.C.	500	
WARR	Warrenton, N.C.	1000	
KMAV	Mayville, N.D.	2500	
WQCT	Bryan, O.	500	
WINW	Canton, O.	1000	
WKNT	Kent, O.	1000	
WVOI	Toledo, O.	1000	1000
KOMA	Oklahoma City, Okla.	50000	50000
KYXI	Oregon City, Ore.	50000	10000
WCHE	West Chester, Pa.	250	
WRAI	San Juan, P.R.	10000	10000
WTGR	Myrtle Beach, S.C.	5000	
WKMG	Newberry, S.C.	1000	
KRSS	Sioux Falls, S.D.	500	
WBHT	Brownsville, Tenn.	250	
WKOE	Dayton, Tenn.	5000	
WIDD	Elizabethton, Tenn.	1000	
† WCMG	Lawrenceburg, Tenn.	500	
KRJH	Hallettsville, Tex.	250	
WKRE	Exmore, Va.	5000	
XEACC	Camargo, Chih.	1000	
XEVUC	Villa Union, Coah.	1000	
† ----	Acapulco, Gro.	500	
XEGAJ	Guadalajara, Jal.	1000	
XEATL	Atlacomulco, Mex.	1000	
† XECGP	Morelia, Mich.	500	

	Call	Location	Day	Night
†	XESZ	Cholula, Pue.	250	
	XEATP	Tehuacan, Pue.	1000	1000
†	----	Empalme, Son.	1000	
	XEEH	San Luis, Son.	1000	
	XEZQ	Huimanguillo, Tab.	1000	100
†	----	Tenosique, Tab.	250	
	XEYP	El Limon, Tams.	1000	
†	----	Panzacola, Tlax.	500	
	XEVO	San Rafael, Ver.	250	
	CMKT	Victoria De Las Tunas, Cuba	1000	1000

1530 (CLEAR)

	Call	Location	Day	Night
	WAAO	Andalusia, Ala.	1000	
	KELC	England, Ark.	250	
	KXRQ	Trumann, Ark.	250	
	KCTT	Yellville, Ark.	1000	
	KFBK	Sacramento, Calif.	50000	50000
	KCMN	Colorado Springs, Colo.	1000	
	WDJZ	Bridgeport, Conn.	5000	
	WENG	Englewood, Fla.	1000	
	WCRJ	Jacksonville, Fla.	50000	
	WTTI	Dalton, Ga.	10000	10000
	WKDC	Elmhurst, Ill.	250	
	KDSN	Denison, Ia.	500	
	KQNK	Norton, Kan.	1000	
	WRXV	Auburn, Me.	1000	
	WCTR	Chestertown, Md.	250	
†	----	Middleboro, Mass.	250	
	WDEY	Lapeer, Mich.	5000	
	WYGR	Wyoming, Mich.	500	
	KSMM	Shakopee, Minn.	500	
	WJRL	Calhoun City, Miss.	250	
	WRPM	Poplarville, Miss.	10000	
	WJNS	Yazoo City, Miss.	250	
	KPCR	Bowling Green, Mo.	1000	
	KMAM	Butler, Mo.	500	
	KECK	Lincoln, Neb.	5000	
	WJDM	Elizabeth, N.J.	500	
	WRBX	Chapel Hill, N.C.	10000	
	WOBR	Wanchese, N.C.	250	
	WCKY	Cincinnati, O.	50000	50000
	KWOK	Wagoner, Okla.	500	
	WBCW	Jeanette, Pa.	1000	
	WVFC	Mc Connellsburg, Pa.	1000	
	WHYP	North East, Pa.	1000	
	WMBT	Shenandoah, Pa.	2500	
	WUPR	Utuado, P.R.	1000	250
	WASC	Spartanburg, S.C.	1000	
	WJPJ	Huntingdon, Tenn.	1000	
	WTNE	Trenton, Tenn.	250	
	KGTN	Georgetown, Tex.	1000	
	KGBT	Harlingen, Tex.	50000	10000
	KNBO	New Boston, Tex.	2500r	1000
	KCLR	Ralls, Tex.	5000	
	WFIC	Collinsville, Va.	1000	
†*	WMBE	Chilton, Wis.	250	
	KUUY	Cheyenne, Wyo.	10000	1000
	CISV	Morden, Man.	10000	1000
†	----	Chihuahua, Chih.	250	
	XEUR	Mexico City, D.F.	3000	5000
	XESD	Silao, Gto.	1000	100
	XEGO	Los Reyes, Mich.	1000	100
†	XEZYB	Oaxaca, Oax.	500	

1540 (BAHAMAS CLEAR)

	Call	Location	Day	Night
	WZZX	Lineville, Ala.	1000	
	WRSM	Sumiton, Ala.	1000	
	KASA	Phoenix, Ariz.	10000	
	KZRK	Ozark, Ark.	500	
	KKDI	Sheridan, Ark.	250	
	KMFO	Aptos Capitola, Calif.	10000	
	KZLA	Los Angeles, Calif.	50000	10000
	WZAL	Mc Donough, Ga.	2500	
	WRSG	Sylvester, Ga.	1000	
	KISA	Honolulu, Haw.	5000	5000
	WSMI	Litchfield, Ill.	1000	
	WBNL	Boonville, Ind.	250	
	WADM	Decatur, Ind.	250	
	WLOI	La Porte, Ind.	250	
	WCBK	Martinsville, Ind.	250	
	KXEL	Waterloo, Ia.	50000	50000
	KNEX	Mc Pherson, Kan.	250	
	KLKC	Parsons, Kan.	250	
	WGRK	Greensburg, Ky.	1000	
	KCTO	Columbia, La.	1000	
	KGLA	Gretna, La.	500	
	WMDO	Wheaton, Md.	1000	
	WMLM	St. Louis, Mich.	1000	
	KBXM	Kennett, Mo.	1000	
	WMYF	Exeter, N.H.	5000r	
	WPTR	Albany, N.Y.	50000	50000
	WSIV	East Syracuse, N.Y.	1000	
	WQCC	Charlotte, N.C.	1000	
	WJOS	Elkin, N.C.	1000	
	WTXY	Whiteville, N.C.	1000	
	WYNC	Yanceyville, N.C.	1000	
	KHND	Harvey, N.D.	500	
	WBCO	Bucyrus, O.	500	
	WNRE	Circleville, O.	1000	
	WABQ	Cleveland, O.	1000	
	WNIO	Niles, O.	500	
	WBTC	Uhrichsville, O.	250	
	WSNI	Philadelphia, Pa.	50000	
	WARD	Pittston, Pa.	1000	
	WPXZ	Punxsutawney, Pa.	5000	
	WBJA	Guayama, P.R.	250	
	WADK	Newport, R.I.	1000	
	WPKZ	Pickens, S.C.	10000	
	WLIC	Adamsville, Tenn.	2500	
	WBIN	Benton, Tenn.	250	
	WJJT	Jellico, Tenn.	1000	
	WBRY	Woodbury, Tenn.	500	
	KUQQ	Ft. Worth, Tex.	50000	1000
	KGBC	Galveston, Tex.	1000	250
	KEDA	San Antonio, Tex.	5000	1000
	WKIE	Richmond, Va.	10000	
	KJZZ	Bellevue, Wash.	5000	5000
	WTKM	Hartford, Wis.	500	
	CHIN	Toronto, Ont.	50000	50000
†	----	Cabo San Lucas, B.C.S.	5000	
	XEVF	Villa Flores, Chis.	500	
†	XEDCH	Delicias, Chih.	1000	
†	----	Torreon, Coah.	250	
†	XEDRD	Durango, Dgo.	250	
	XENC	Celaya, Gto.	1000	250
†	----	Coyuca De Benitez, Gro.	50000	
†	----	Coahiueyana, Mich.	500	
†	XEIC	Cuernavaca, Mor.	1000	1000
†	XESTN	Santa Catarina, N.L.	5000	
†	XEEN	Chetumal, Q.R.	250	
†	----	Matehuala, S.L.P.	1000	
	XEHOS	Hermosillo, Son.	5000	5000
†	----	Navojoa, Son.	500	
†	----	Villahermosa, Tab.	5000	
†	XEAVR	Alvarado, Ver.	5000	1000
†	XEPAV	Panuco, Ver.	1000	
†	XEGP	Poza Rica, Ver.	1000	
	XEYK	Motul, Yuc.	1000	100
†	----	Fresnillo, Zac.	1000	
	ZNS-1	Nassau, Bahamas	10000	10000
	HIFB	Santo Domingo, Dom. Rep.	1000	1000
	PJL	Curacao, Ne. Antil.	1000	1000

1550 (MEXICAN CLEAR)

	Call	Location	Day	Night
	WAAY	Huntsville, Ala.	50000	500
	WMOO	Mobile, Ala.	50000	
*	KUAT	Tucson, Ariz.	50000	
	KXEX	Fresno, Calif.	5000	2500
	KKHI	San Francisco, Calif.	10000	10000
†	----	Solvang, Calif.	1000	
	KQXI	Arvada, Colo.	10000	
	WMLB	Bloomfield, Conn.	5000	1000
	WRHC	Coral Gables, Fla.	10000	500

	WCCZ	New Smyrna Beach, Fla.	250	
	WYOU	Tampa, Fla.	10000	
	WTHB	Augusta, Ga.	5000	
	WYNX	Smyrna, Ga.	10000	500
	WWWN	Vienna, Ga.	250	
	WJIL	Jacksonville, Ill.	1000	
	WCSJ	Morris, Ill.	250	
	WJDW	Corydon, Ind.	250	
	WCVL	Crawfordsville, Ind.	250	250
	WCTW	New Castle, Ind.	250	250
	WNDI	Sullivan, Ind.	250	
	KIWA	Sheldon, Ia.	500	
	KEDD	Dodge City, Kan.	1000	
	KNIC	Winfield, Kan.	250	
	WIRV	Irvine, Ky.	1000	
	WMSK	Morganfield, Ky.	250	
	WLUX	Baton Rouge, La.	5000	
	KOKA	Shreveport, La.	10000	500
	WSER	Elkton, Md.	1000	
	WNTN	Newton, Mass.	10000	
	WSHN	Fremont, Mich.	1000	
†	KQPM	Glencoe, Minn.	500	
	WOKJ	Jackson, Miss.	50000	10000
	KEWI	Cape Girardeau, Mo.	5000	
	KLFJ	Springfield, Mo.	500	
	KKJO	St. Joseph, Mo.	5000	5000
	KICS	Hastings, Neb.	500	
†	----	Reno, Nev.	10000	
	WCGR	Canandaigua, N.Y.	250	
	WUTQ	Utica, N.Y.	1000	
	WBZQ	Greenville, N.C.	1000	
	WSES	Raleigh, N.C.	1000	
‡	WTYN	Tryon, N.C.	1000	
	WBFJ	Winston Salem, N.C.	1000	
	KQWB	Fargo, N.D.	10000	5000
	WDLR	Delaware, O.	500	
	KMAD	Madill, Okla.	1000	
	KXOJ	Sapulpa, Okla.	500	
	WJLY	Braddock, Pa.	1000	
	WTTC	Towanda, Pa.	500	500
	WKFE	Yauco, P.R.	250	250
	WBSC	Bennettsville, S.C.	10000	5000
	WBCV	Bristol, Tenn.	5000r	
	WKVL	Clarksville, Tenn.	1000	250
	WPTN	Cookeville, Tenn.	250	
	WORI	Oak Ridge, Tenn.	1000	
	WTBP	Parsons, Tenn.	1000	
	WCHU	Soddy Daisy, Tenn.	1000	
	KHBJ	Canyon, Tex.	1000	
	KCOM	Comanche, Tex.	250	
	KWBC	Navasota, Tex.	250	
	KRGO	West Valley City, Utah	10000	500
	WKBA	Vinton, Va.	10000	
	WVAB	Virginia Beach, Va.	5000	
	KOQT	Ferndale, Wash.	10000	10000
	KVAN	Vancouver, Wash.	10000	10000
	WXVA	Charles Town, W.V.	5000	
	WMIR	Lake Geneva, Wis.	1000	
	WHIT	Madison, Wis.	5000	
	WEVR	River Falls, Wis.	1000	
†*	----	St. Stephen, Wyo.	2500	500
	CBE	Windsor, Ont.	10000	10000
	XEBG	Tijuana, B.C.	1000	1000
†	----	Pachuca, Hgo.	1000	
†	----	Tonala, Jal.	500	
†	----	Zapopan, Jal.	500	
	XEDV	El Oro, Mex.	500	
	XEREL	Morelia, Mich.	1000	1000
†	----	Puerto Escondido, Oax.	1000	
†	XETAM	Ciudad Victoria, Tams.	500	
	XENU	Nuevo Laredo, Tams.	5000	
	XERUV	Jalapa, Ver.	10000	10000
	CMDV	Santiago De Cuba, Cuba	250	250
	4VWA	Cap Haitien, Haiti	1000	1000

1560 (CUBAN CLEAR)

	WAGC	Centre, Ala.	1000	
	KDDA	Dumas, Ark.	500	
	KBIB	Monette, Ark.	250	
	KPMC	Bakersfield, Calif.	10000	10000
	KIQS	Willows, Calif.	250	
	WYSE	Inverness, Fla.	5000	5000
	WTAI	Melbourne, Fla.	5000	
	WLEJ	Ellijay, Ga.	1000	
‡	WQXM	Gordon, Ga.	5000	
	WBYS	Canton, Ill.	250	
	WSHY	Shelbyville, Ill.	500	
	WSQR	Sycamore, Ill.	250	
	WKKX	Paoli, Ind.	250	
	WRIN	Rensselaer, Ind.	1000	
	KLNG	Council Bluffs, Ia.	1000	
	KCJJ	Iowa City, Ia.	1000	1000 f
	KABI	Abilene, Kan.	250	
	WKDO	Liberty, Ky.	250	
	WPAD	Paducah, Ky.	10000	1000
	KAJN	Crowley, La.	1000	
	WSDL	Slidell, La.	1000	
	WSMD	La Plata, Md.	25000	
	WBUK	Portage, Mich.	1000	
	WMIC	Sandusky, Mich.	1000	
	KBEW	Blue Earth, Minn.	1000	
	KQYX	Joplin, Mo.	10000	
	KLTI	Macon, Mo.	1000p	
	KTUI	Sullivan, Mo.	1000	
	WQXR	New York, N.Y.	50000	50000
	WYZD	Dobson, N.C.	1000	
	WTRQ	Warsaw, N.C.	10000	
	WBKC	Chardon, O.	1000	
	WTNS	Coshocton, O.	1000	
	WCNW	Fairfield, O.	5000	
	WTOD	Toledo, O.	5000	
	KWCO	Chickasha, Okla.	1000	250
	KKID	Sallisaw, Okla.	250	
	WRSJ	Bayamon, P.R.	5000	250
	WCCP	Clemson, S.C.	1000	
	WAGL	Lancaster, S.C.	50000	
	KKAA	Aberdeen, S.D.	10000	5000
	WBOL	Bolivar, Tenn.	250	
	WWGM	Nashville, Tenn.	10000	
	KFMN	Abilene, Tex.	500	
†	KJUM	Colorado City, Tex.	2500	
	KEGG	Daingerfield, Tex.	1000	
	KHBR	Hillsboro, Tex.	250	
	KGUL	Port Lavaca, Tex.	500	
	KTXZ	West Lake Hills, Tex.	2500	2500
	WSBV	South Boston, Va.	2500	
	KGHO	Hoquiam, Wash.	1000	
	KFWY	Sumner, Wash.	250	
	WFSP	Kingwood, W.V.	1000	
	WGLB	Port Washington, Wis.	250	
	XESE	Champoton, Cam.	5000	
	XEQZ	Cuahutemoc, Chih.	750	250
	XEJPV	Zaragoza, Chih.	1000	
	XEFAJ	Mexico City, D.F.	20000	10000
	XEMAS	Salamanca, Gto.	1000	250
	XERAL	Arandas, Jal.	250	
†	XELAC	Lazaro Cardenas, Mich.	5000	150
	XERIO	Ixtlan, Nay.	5000	
	XEDD	Montemorelos, N.L.	500	150
†	XEZW	Cerritos, S.L.P.	500	
†	----	Guasave, Sin.	1000	500
†	XEGYS	Guaymas, Son.	250	
†	----	Naranjos, Ver.	1000	500
†	XEHA	Progreso, Yuc.	1000	500
	CMGB	Cardenas, Cuba	250	250
	HIJC	Santiago, Dom. Rep.	5000	5000

1570 (MEXICAN CLEAR)

	WCRL	Oneonta, Ala.	1000	
	WTQX	Selma, Ala.	5000	
	KBRI	Brinkley, Ark.	250	

Call	Location	Power	
KBJT	Fordyce, Ark.	250	
KSRB	Hardy, Ark.	1000	
KCVR	Lodi, Calif.	5000	
KMAY	Riverside, Calif.	5000	
KXES	Salinas, Calif.	5000p	
KLOV	Loveland, Colo.	1000	
WTWB	Auburndale, Fla.	5000	
WHOG	Fernandina Beach, Fla.	5000	
WOKC	Okeechobee, Fla.	1000	
WMES	Ashburn, Ga.	1000	
WGHC	Clayton, Ga.	1000	
WGSR	Millen, Ga.	1000	
WSSA	Morrow, Ga.	5000	
WOKZ	Alton, Ill.	1000	
WFRL	Freeport, Ill.	5000	
WBEE	Harvey, Ill.	1000	
WTAY	Robinson, Ill.	250	
WIFF	Auburn, Ind.	500	
WILO	Frankfort, Ind.	250	
WOBS	New Albany, Ind.	1000	
KMCD	Fairfield, Ia.	250	
KQWC	Webster City, Ia.	250	
KNDY	Marysville, Kan.	250	
WKYR	Burkesville, Ky.	1000	
WLBQ	Morgantown, Ky.	1000p	
WKKS	Vanceburg, Ky.	1000	
WABL	Amite, La.	500	
KLLA	Leesville, La.	1000	
KMAR	Winnsboro, La.	1000	
WTOW	Towson, Md.	5000	
WBVD	Beverly, Mass.	500	
WPEP	Taunton, Mass.	1000	
WLDM	Westfield, Mass.	2500	
WWMN	Flint, Mich.	1000	
WFUR	Grand Rapids, Mich.	1000	
KUXL	Golden Valley, Minn.	2500	
WHII	Bay Springs, Miss.	1000	
WONA	Winona, Miss.	1000	
KLEX	Lexington, Mo.	250	
WKOL	Amsterdam, N.Y.	1000	
WFLR	Dundee, N.Y.	1000	
WBUZ	Fredonia, N.Y.	250	
WRHD	Riverhead, N.Y.	1000	
WNCA	Siler City, N.C.	1000	
WTLK	Taylorsville, N.C.	500	
WGLX	Galion, O.	250	
WPTW	Piqua, O.	250	
WOKG	Warren, O.	500	
KTAT	Frederick, Okla.	250	
KMYZ	Pryor, Okla.	1000	
WPGM	Danville, Pa.	2500	
WBUX	Doylestown, Pa.	5000	
‡ WQTW	Latrobe, Pa.	1000	
WPPC	Penuelas, P.R.	1000	
WFGN	Gaffney, S.C.	250	
WLSC	Loris, S.C.	5000	
KVRA	Vermillion, S.D.	500	
WHLP	Centerville, Tenn.	5000	
WCLE	Cleveland, Tenn.	2500	
WTRB	Ripley, Tenn.	1000	
† KIJN	Farwell, Tex.	250	
KVLG	La Grange, Tex.	250	
KTER	Terrell, Tex.	250	
WSWV	Pennington Gap, Va.	1000	
WYTI	Rocky Mount, Va.	1000	
† WRRR	St. Marys, W.V.	1000	
WVMS	Appleton, Wis.	1000	
WFBZ	Minocqua, Wis.	2500	
CKTA	Taber, Alta.	5000	5000
CHUB	Nanaimo, B.C.	10000	10000
CKLQ	Brandon, Man.	10000	10000
CFOR	Orillia, Ont.	10000	5000
CHLO	St. Thomas, Ont.	10000	10000
CKLM	Laval, Que.	50000	50000
XERF	Ciudad Acuna, Coah.	250000	250000
† ----	Puebla, Pue.	1000	
HIAJ	Santo Domingo, Dom. Rep.	1000	1000

1580 (CANADIAN CLEAR)

Call	Location	Power	
WEYY	Talladega, Ala.	2500	
KNIX	Tempe, Ariz.	50000	10000
KPCA	Marked Tree, Ark.	250	
KFDF	Van Buren, Ark.	1000	
KLOQ	Merced, Calif.	1000	
KDAY	Santa Monica, Calif.	50000	50000
KPIK	Colorado Springs, Colo.	5000	
WENO	Chattahoochee, Fla.	5000	
WSRF	Ft. Lauderdale, Fla.	10000	5000
WQTK	Mt. Dora, Fla.	5000	
WCCF	Punta Gorda, Fla.	1000	
WCLS	Columbus, Ga.	1000	1000
WKIG	Glennville, Ga.	1000	
WKUN	Monroe, Ga.	1000	
WKKD	Aurora, Ill.	250	
WDQN	Du Quoin, Ill.	250	
WBBA	Pittsfield, Ill.	250	
WCCR	Urbana, Ill.	250	
WIFE	Connersville, Ind.	250	
WAMJ	South Bend, Ind.	1000	
WAMW	Washington, Ind.	250	
KCHA	Charles City, Ia.	500	
KXRK	Davenport, Ia.	500	
WBBE	Georgetown, Ky.	10000	
WMTL	Leitchfield, Ky.	250	
WPKY	Princeton, Ky.	250	
KLUV	Haynesville, La.	1000	
KLOU	Lake Charles, La.	1000	1000
WPGC	Morningside, Md.	10000	
WVGO	St. Johns, Mich.	1000	
KDOM	Windom, Minn.	1000	
WAMY	Amory, Miss.	5000	
WSSL	Centreville, Miss.	250	
WORV	Hattiesburg, Miss.	1000	
WESY	Leland, Miss.	1000	
WPMP	Pascagoula, Miss.	5000	
KTGR	Columbia, Mo.	250	
KESM	El Dorado Springs, Mo.	500	
KNIM	Maryville, Mo.	250	
KAMI	Cozad, Neb.	1000	
WTYO	Hammondton, N.J.	1000	
WCRV	Washington, N.J.	1000	
KZIA	Albuquerque, N.M.	10000	
WLIM	Patchogue, N.Y.	10000	
WZKY	Albemarle, N.C.	250	
WJIK	Camp Lejeune, N.C.	10000	
WUIV	Icard Township, N.C.	5000	
WVKO	Columbus, O.	1000	
KLTR	Blackwell, Okla.	1000	
† WHEX	Columbia, Pa.	500	
WAJE	Ebensburg, Pa.	1000	
WANB	Waynesburg, Pa.	1000	
WGFW	Morovis, P.R.	1000	1000
WORG	Orangeburg, S.C.	1000	
WBBR	Travelers Rest, S.C.	5000	
WHHM	Henderson, Tenn.	250	
WSKT	Knoxville, Tenn.	5000	
WLIJ	Shelbyville, Tenn.	1000	
KGAF	Gainesville, Tex.	250	250
KIRT	Mission, Tex.	1000	
KTLU	Rusk, Tex.	500	
KWED	Seguin, Tex.	1000	
KBYP	Shamrock, Tex.	250	
KRZI	Waco, Tex.	1000	500
WILA	Danville, Va.	1000	
WPUV	Pulaski, Va.	5000	
WTTN	Watertown, Wis.	1000	
CBJ	Chicoutimi, Que.	10000	10000
† ----	Comitan, Chis.	1000	
† ----	Tapachula, Chis.	500	
† XESAC	Saltillo, Coah.	250	
XEAF	Apaseo El Grande, Gto.	1000	
XELI	Chilpancingo, Gro.	1000	250
XENQ	Tulancingo, Hgo.	5000	500
† ----	Cocula, Jal.	250	
XEVAB	Valle De Bravo, Mex.	250	
XEQL	Zamora, Mich.	1000	250

XEST	Mazatlan, Sin.	250	
XEDM	Hermosillo, Son.	50000	50000
XEUY	Las Choapas, Ver.	250	100
† XETBV	Tierra Blanca, Ver.	1000	
HIFU	Neyba, Dom. Rep.	1000	1000
HIWJ	Samana, Dom. Rep.	500	500

1590 (REGIONAL)

WACD	Alexander City, Ala.	1000	
WATM	Atmore, Ala.	5000	
WVNA	Tuscumbia, Ala.	5000	1000
KYDE	Pine Bluff, Ark.	5000r	5000
KQXK	Springdale, Ark.	2500r	
KXEM	Mc Farland, Calif.	500	
KLIV	San Jose, Calif.	5000	5000
KBBQ	Ventura, Calif.	5000	5000
KCIN	Victorville, Calif.	500	
WQQW	Waterbury, Conn.	5000	5000
WZIP	South Daytona, Fla.	1000	
WRXB	St. Petersburg Beach, Fla.	1000	
WALG	Albany, Ga.	5000	1000
WLFA	Lafayette, Ga.	5000	
WXRS	Swainsboro, Ga.	2500	
WTGA	Thomaston, Ga.	500	
WONX	Evanston, Ill.	1000	2500
WAIK	Galesburg, Ill.	5000	
WNTS	Beech Grove, Ind.	5000	500
WPCO	Mount Vernon, Ind.	500	
KWBG	Boone, Ia.	1000	500
KVGB	Great Bend, Kan.	5000	5000
WFJT	Inez, Ky.	1000	
WLBN	Lebanon, Ky.	1000	
KKAY	White Castle, La.	1000	
WDCI	Gorham, Me.	5000	2500
WJRO	Glen Burnie, Md.	1000	1000
WETT	Ocean City, Md.	1000	500
WTVB	Coldwater, Mich.	5000	1000
WGRY	Grayling, Mich.	1000	
WSMA	Marine City, Mich.	1000	
KRRK	East Grand Forks, Minn.	5000	1000
KDJS	Willmar, Minn.	1000	
WCCL	Jackson, Miss.	5000	1000
KDEX	Dexter, Mo.	1000	
KPRT	Kansas City, Mo.	1000	
KCLU	Rolla, Mo.	1000	
KTCH	Wayne, Neb.	2500	
WSMN	Nashua, N.H.	5000	5000
WERA	Plainfield, N.J.	500	500
WAUB	Auburn, N.Y.	500	
WJBT	Brockport, N.Y.	1000	1000
WEHH	Elmira Heights, N.Y.	500	
WGGO	Salamanca, N.Y.	5000	
WRHN	Bryson City, N.C.	500	
WVOE	Chadbourn, N.C.	1000	
WCSL	Cherryville, N.C.	500	
WHPY	Clayton, N.C.	5000	
WOKX	High Point, N.C.	1000	
WAKR	Akron, O.	5000	5000
WSRW	Hillsboro, O.	500	
KGCG	Henryetta, Okla.	500	
KWEY	Weatherford, Okla.	1000	
KTIL	Tillamook, Ore.	5000	1000
WPLW	Carnegie, Pa.	1000	
WCBG	Chambersburg, Pa.	5000	1000
WQIQ	Chester, Pa.	1000	1000
WDNH	Honesdale, Pa.	2500	500
WMIM	Mt. Carmel, Pa.	1000	
WXRF	Guayama, P.R.	1000	1000
WARV	Warwick, R.I.	5000	5000
WABV	Abbeville, S.C.	1000	
WCAM	Camden, S.C.	1000	
WWRT	Algood, Tenn.	500	
‡ WMSO	Collierville, Tenn.	500	
WJSO	Jonesboro, Tenn.	5000	5000
WDBL	Springfield, Tenn.	1000	
KGAS	Carthage, Tex.	2500	
KEAS	Eastland, Tex.	500	
KELP	El Paso, Tex.	1000	
KYOK	Houston, Tex.	5000	5000
KEND	Lubbock, Tex.	1000	1000
KBUS	Mexia, Tex.	500	
KIKN	Sinton, Tex.	1000	500
KMTI	Manti, Utah	5000	1000
WFTH	Richmond, Va.	5000	
KJET	Seattle, Wash.	5000	5000
WIXK	New Richmond, Wis.	5000	
WTOQ	Platteville, Wis.	1000	500
WRTR	Two Rivers, Wis.	1000	500
WAWA	West Allis, Wis.	1000	
† XEAGA	Aguascalientes, Ags.	250	
XEYX	Mexicali, B.C.	10000	250
XEHC	Ensenada, B.C.S.	1000	1000
XEBZ	Meoqui, Chih.	1000	250
XEVOZ	Mexico City, D.F.	10000	5000
† XEIRG	Irapuato, Gto.	250	
† ----	Pihuamo, Jal.	500	
† ----	Tequila, Jal.	100	
† ----	Apatzingan, Mich.	250	
XEART	Zacatepec, Mor.	1000	1000
† XEPNA	Tepic, Nay.	250	
XEACH	Monterrey, N.L.	5000	1000
† ----	Matehuala, S.L.P.	1000	500
† XECSI	Culiacan, Sin.	250	
† ----	Ciudad Obregon, Son.	250	
† XEMTS	Ciudad Madero, Tams.	1000	
XEPT	Misantla, Ver.	1000	100
XECP	Valladolid, Yuc.	10000	
CMDF	Manzanillo, Cuba	250	250
HIDA	Santiago, Dom. Rep.	1000	1000
HIBA	Santiago, Dom. Rep.	1000	1000

1600 (REGIONAL)

WEUP	Huntsville, Ala.	5000	500
WXVI	Montgomery, Ala.	5000	1000
KVRD	Cottonwood, Ariz.	1000	
KXEW	Tucson, Ariz.	1000	1000
KCGS	Marshall, Ark.	5000	
KCRI	West Helena, Ark.	1000	
KGST	Fresno, Calif.	5000	5000
KWOW	Pomona, Calif.	5000	500
KZON	Santa Maria, Calif.	500	
KUBA	Yuba City, Calif.	5000	2500
KLAK	Lakewood, Colo.	5000	5000
WKEN	Dover, Del.	5000	1000
WJNJ	Atlantic Beach, Fla.	5000	
WKWF	Key West, Fla.	500	500
WPOM	Riviera Beach, Fla.	1000	1000
WOKB	Winter Garden, Fla.	5000	
WCKZ	Austell, Ga.	1000	
WNGA	Nashville, Ga.	1000	
WRBN	Warner Robbins, Ga.	2500	500
WCGO	Chicago Heights, Ill.	1000	
WMCW	Harvard, Ill.	500	
WBTO	Linton, Ind.	500	
WARU	Peru, Ind.	1000	
KLGA	Algona, Ia.	5000	
KCRG	Cedar Rapids, Ia.	5000	5000
KMDO	Fort Scott, Kan.	1000	
WSTL	Eminence, Ky.	500	
WLLS	Hartford, Ky.	1000	
WSLK	Hyden, Ky.	1000	
KFNV	Ferriday, La.	1000	
KLEB	Golden Meadow, La.	1000	
WINX	Rockville, Md.	1000	500
WUNR	Brookline, Mass.	5000	5000
WIXY	E. Longmeadow, Mass.	5000	2500
WAAM	Ann Arbor, Mich.	5000	5000
WTRU	Muskegon, Mich.	5000	5000
KLLR	Walker, Minn.	1000	
KATZ	St. Louis, Mo.	5000	5000
KTTN	Trenton, Mo.	500	

	Call	Location	Day	Night
	KNCY	Nebraska City, Neb.	500	
	KRFS	Superior, Neb.	500	
	WWRL	New York, N.Y.	5000	5000
	WMCR	Oneida, N.Y.	1000	
	WLNG	Sag Harbor, N.Y.	500	
	WGIV	Charlotte, N.C.	2500	2500
	WIDU	Fayetteville, N.C.	1000	
	WHVL	Hendersonville, N.C.	5000	
	WRNC	Reidsville, N.C.	1000	1000
	KDAK	Carrington, N.D.	500	
	WBLY	Springfield, O.	1000	
	WTTF	Tiffin, O.	500	
	KUSH	Cushing, Okla.	1000	
	KASH	Eugene, Ore.	5000	1000
	KOHI	St. Helens, Ore.	1000	
	WHOL	Allentown, Pa.	500	
	WAYC	Bedford, Pa.	5000	
	WPDC	Elizabethtown, Pa.	500	
†	WJSA	Jersey Shore, Pa.	1000	
	WLUZ	Bayamon, P.R.	1000	1000
	WFIS	Fountain Inn, S.C.	1000	
	WKZK	North Augusta, S.C.	500	
	WKJS	Harriman, Tenn.	5000	
	WQDQ	Lebanon, Tenn.	500	
	WKBJ	Milan, Tenn.	1000	
	KBBB	Borger, Tex.	5000	
	KBOR	Brownsville, Tex.	1000	1000
	KEWS	Cuero, Tex.	500	
	KXVI	Mc Kinney, Tex.	5000	1000
	KOGT	Orange, Tex.	1000	1000
	KBBX	Centerville, Utah	5000	1000
	WCPK	Chesapeake, Va.	5000	
	WKGK	Saltville, Va.	5000	
	WNST	Milton, W.V.	5000	
	WANR	Wheeling, W.V.	5000	
	WCWC	Ripon, Wis.	5000	5000
	CHNR	Simcoe, Ont.	10000	10000
	XEAE	Ciudad Acuna, Coah.	5000	5000
†	XELZ	Torreon, Coah.	1000	
	XEAK	Acambaro, Gto.	500	200
	XEACG	Acapulco, Gro.	500	500
†	----	Zihuatenejo, Gro.	500	150
	XEQA	Autlan, Jal.	1000	
†	----	Puerto Vallarta, Jal.	250	
	XEZK	Tepatitlan, Jal.	1000	250
	XEGEM	Toluca, Mex.	2000	
	XERCP	Purepero, Mich.	200	
†	----	Ixtepec, Oax.	500	
†	----	Puerto Angel, Oax.	1000	
	XERTF	San Martin, Pue.	500	
†	XEJCP	Tehuacan, Pue.	250	
†	----	San Luis Potosi, S.L.P.	1000	500
†	XENAZ	Nacozari, Son.	1000	
†	----	Navojoa, Son.	500	
	XEPE	Nogales, Son.	1000	
†	----	Villahermosa, Tab.	250	
†	----	El Higo, Ver.	250	
†	----	Poza Rica, Ver.	1000	
	XEQT	Veracruz, Ver.	500	250
	HIBS	San Pedro De Macoris, Dom. Rep.	1000	1000
	HIFA	Santo Domingo, Dom. Rep.	5000	5000

AM, FM, and TV Stations by Call Letters

Call Letters	Frequency/Channel	Location
CBA	1070	Moncton, N.B.
CBAF	1300	Moncton, N.B.
CBAF	102.3	St. John, N.B.
CBAFT	11	Moncton, N.B.
CBAFT-2	13	Edmundston, N.B.
CBBL	100.5	London, Ont.
CBC-TV	3	St. Thomas, Barb.
CBCL	93.5	London, Ont.
CBCM	107.5	Penetangui-shene, Ont.
CBCO	105.9	Orillia, Ont.
CBCP-TV-1	7	Shaunavon, Sask.
CBCP-TV-2	2	Cypress Hills, Sask.
CBCP-TV-3	3	Pontiex, Sask.
CBCS	99.9	Sudbury, Ont.
CBCT	13	Charlottetown, P.E.
CBCT	96.9	Challottetown, P.E.
CBD	1110	St. John, N.B.
CBD-FM	91.3	Fredericton, N.B.
CBDQ	1490	Wabush, Nfld.
CBE	1550	Windsor, Ont.
CBE-FM	89.9	Windsor, Ont.
CBEE-FM	95.1	Chatham, Ont.
CBEF	540	Windsor, Ont.
CBEFT	54	Windsor, Ont.
CBEG-FM	106.3	Sarnia, Ont.
CBET	9	Windsor, Ont.
CBF	690	Montreal, Que.
CBF-FM	100.7	Montreal, Que.
CBF-FM-1	104.3	Drummondville, Que.
CBF-8	100.1	Three Rivers, Que.
CBFST-2	12	Temiscaming, Que.
CBFT	2	Montreal, Que.
CBFT-2	3	Mont Laurier, Que.
CBG	1450	Gander, Nfld.
CBGA	1250	Matane, Que.
CBGA-7	1340	Ste. Anne Des Monts, Que.
CBGAT	9	Matane, Que.
CBGN	1490	Ste. Anne Des Monts, Que.
CBGY	750	Bonavista Bay, Nfld.
CBH	860	Halifax, N.S.
CBH-FM	102.7	Halifax, N.S.
CBHA	90.5	Halifax, N.S.
CBHFT	13	Halifax, N.S.
CBHFT-1	3	Yarmouth, N.S.
CBHFT-2	7	Mulgrave, N.S.
CBHFT-3	13	Sydney, N.S.
CBHFT-4	10	Cheticamp, N.S.
CBHT	3	Halifax, N.S.
CBHT-3	11	Yarmouth, N.S.
CBHT-4	11	Sheet Harbour, N.S.
CBI	1140	Sydney, N.S.
CBI-FM	105.9	Sydney, N.S.
CBIM	93.5	Iles De-la-madeleine, Que.
CBIMT	12	Iles De La Madeleine, Que.
CBIT	5	Sydney, N.S.
CBIT-1	12	Mulgrave, N.S.
CBIT-2	2	Cheticamp, N.S.
CBJ	1580	Chicoutimi, Que.
CBJ-FM	100.9	Chicoutimi, Que.
CBJE	107.9	Chicoutimi, Que.
CBJET	58	Chicoutimi, Que.
CBK	540	Regina, Sask.
CBK-FM	96.9	Regina, Sask.
CBKF	97.7	Regina, Sask.
CBKFT	13	Regina, Sask.
CBKFT-3	22	Debden, Sask.
CBKFT-4	7	St. Brieux, Sask.
CBKFT-5	21	Zenon Park, Sask.
CBKFT-6	39	Gavelbourg, Sask.
CBKFT-9	26	Bellegarde, Sask.
CBKHT	13	Keno Hill, Yuk.
CBKI-TV-4	10	Nipawin, Sask.
CBKMT	4	Moose Jaw, Sask.
CBKS	105.5	Saskatoon, Sask.
CBKST	11	Saskatoon, Sask.
CBKST-1	9	Stranraer, Sask.
CBKT	9	Regina, Sask.
CBKT-2	10	Willow Bunch, Sask.
CBL	740	Toronto, Ont.
CBL-FM	94.1	Toronto, Ont.
CBLAT	13	Geraldton, Ont.
CBLAT-1	8	Manitouwadge, Ont.
CBLAT-3	9	Wawa, Ont.
CBLAT-4	11	Marathon, Ont.
CBLFT	25	Toronto, Ont.
CBLFT-1	7	Sturgeon Falls, Ont.
CBLFT-2	13	Sudbury, Ont.
CBLFT-3	9	Timmins, Ont.
CBLFT-4	12	Kapuskasing, Ont.
CBLFT-6	12	Elliot Lake, Ont.
CBLT	5	Toronto, Ont.
CBM	940	Montreal, Que.
CBM-FM	93.5	Montreal, Que.
CBMI	99.7	Bale Comeau, Que.
CBMT	6	Montreal, Que.
CBN	640	St. John's, Nfld.
CBN-FM	106.9	St. John's, Nfld.
CBNAT	11	Grand Falls, Nfld.
CBNAT-1	3	Baie Verte, Nfld.
CBNAT-4	6	St. Anthony, Nfld.
CBNAT-9	9	Mt. St. Margaret, Nfld.
CBNLT	13	Labrador City, Nfld.
CBNT	8	St. John's, Nfld.
CBNT-1	13	Port Rexton, Nfld.
CBNT-2	12	Placentia, Nfld.
CBNT-3	5	Marystown, Nfld.
CBO	920	Ottawa, Ont.
CBO-FM	103.3	Ottawa, Ont.
CBOB-FM	100.3	Brockville, Ont.
CBOF	1250	Ottawa, Ont.
CBOF-FM	102.5	Ottawa, Ont.
CBOF-6	98.1	Cornwall, Ont.
CBOF-7	102.1	Brockville, Ont.
CBOFT	9	Ottawa, Ont.
CBOFT-2	7	Hearst, Ont.
CBON	98.1	Sudbury, Ont.
CBOT	4	Ottawa, Ont.
CBQ	800	Thunder Bay, Ont.
CBQX	98.7	Kenora, Ont.
CBR	1010	Calgary, Alta.
CBR-FM	102.1	Calgary, Alta.
CBRF-FM	103.9	Calgary, Alta.
CBRT	9	Calgary, Alta.
CBRX-FM	100.1	Lethbridge, Alta.
CBST	13	Sept Isles, Que.
CBT	540	Grand Falls, Nfld.
CBTA	106.7	Trail, B.C.
CBTE-TV	4	Pine Point, N.W.T.
CBU	690	Vancouver, B.C.
CBU-FM	105.7	Vancouver, B.C.
CBUAT	11	Trail, B.C.
CBUBT	10	Cranbrook, B.C.
CBUBT-1	12	Canal Flats, B.C.
CBUF	97.7	Vancouver, B.C.
CBUF-6	96.5	Kamloops, B.C.
CBUFT	26	Vancouver, B.C.
CBUFT-2	50	Kamloops, B.C.
CBUFT-3	11	Terrace, B.C.
CBUT	2	Vancouver, B.C.
CBV	980	Quebec, Que.
CBVE-FM	104.7	Quebec, Que.
CBVT	11	Quebec, Que.
CBVT-2	3	La Tuque, Que.
CBW	990	Winnipeg, Man.
CBW-FM	98.3	Winnipeg, Man.
CBWAT	8	Kenora, Ont.
CBWBT	10	Flin Flon, Man.
CBWCT	5	Ft. Frances, Ont.
CBWDT	9	Dryden, Ont.
CBWFT	3	Winnipeg, Man.
CBWFT-10	21	Brandon, Man.
CBWFT-4	3	Ste Rose Du Lac, Man.
CBWGT	10	Fisher Branch, Man.
CBWK	100.9	Thompson, Man.
CBWST-TV	8	Dauphin, Man.
CBWT	6	Winnipeg, Man.
CBWT-2	4	Lac Du Bonnet, Man.
CBWV	97.9	Brandon, Man.
CBWW	105.3	Baldy Mountain, Man.
CBWX-FM	95.7	Fisher Branch, Man.
CBWY	92.7	Jackhead, Man.
CBWYT	2	Mafeking, Man.
CBWZ	104.3	Fairford, Man.
CBX	740	Edmonton, Alta.
CBXAT	10	Grand Prairie, Alta.
CBXAT-2	2	High Prairie, Alta.
CBXAT-3	12	Manning, Alta.
CBXFT	11	Edmonton, Alta.
CBXFT-6	11	Ft. Mc Murray, Alta.
CBXFT-8	19	Grand Prairie, Alta.
CBXT	5	Edmonton, Alta.
CBXT-1	8	Athabasca, Alta.
CBXT-2	9	Whitecourt, Alta.
CBY	990	Corner Brook, Nfld.
CBYAT	12	Deer Lake, Nfld.
CBYK	94.1	Kamloops, B.C.
CBYT	5	Corner Brook, Nfld.
CBYT-1	8	Stephenville, Nfld.
CBYT-3	2	Bonne Bay, Nfld.
CBZ	970	Fredericton, N.B.
CBZ-FM	101.5	St. John, N.B.
CFAB	1450	Windsor, N.S.
CFAC	960	Calgary, Alta.
CFAC-TV	2	Calgary, Alta.
CFAC-TV-7	7	Lethbridge, Alta.
CFAK	1240	Atikokan, Ont.
CFAM	950	Altona, Man.
CFAN	790	Newcastle, N.B.
CFAR	590	Flin Flon, Man.
CFAX	1070	Victoria, B.C.
CFBC	930	St. John, N.B.
CFBK	630	Huntsville, Ont.
CFBQ	1340	Parry Sound, Ont.
CFBR	900	Sudbury, Ont.
CFBV	1230	Smithers, B.C.
CFCA-FM	105.3	Kitchener, Ont.
CFCB	570	Corner Brook, Nfld.
CFCF	600	Montreal, Que.
CFCF-TV	12	Montreal, Que.
CFCH	600	North Bay, Ont.
CFCL	620	Timmins, Ont.
CFCL-TV	6	Timmins, Ont.
CFCL-TV-5	5	Malartic, Que.
CFCM-TV	4	Quebec, Que.
CFCN	1060	Calgary, Alta.
CFCN-TV	4	Calgary, Alta.

CFCN-TV-1	12	Drumheller, Alta.
CFCN-TV-5	13	Lethbridge, Alta.
CFCN-TV-8	8	Medicine Hat, Alta.
CFCO	630	Chatham, Ont.
CFCP	1440	Courtenay, B.C.
CFCQ-FM	93.9	Three Rivers, Que.
CFCT	600	Tuktoyaktuk, N.W.T.
CFCW	790	Camrose, Alta.
CFCY	630	Charlottetown, P.E.
CFDA	1380	Victoriaville, Que.
CFDR	680	Dartmouth, N.S.
CFED	1340	Chapais, Que.
CFEK	1240	Fernie, B.C.
CFER-TV	11	Rimouski, Que.
CFER-TV	5	Gaspe/norb, Que.
CFER-TV-1	11	Sept Isles, Que.
CFFB	1210	Frobisher Bay, N.W.T.
CFFM	98.3	Kamloops, B.C.
CFGB	1340	Goose Bay, Nfld.
CFGL	105.7	Laval, Que.
CFGM	1320	Richmond Hill, Ont.
CFGN	1230	Port Aux Basques, Nfld.
CFGO	1440	Ottawa, Ont.
CFGP	1050	Grand Prairie, Alta.
CFGR	1230	Gravelbourg, Sask.
CFGT	1270	Alma, Que.
CFIX	1170	Cornwall, Ont.
CFJC	550	Kamloops, B.C.
CFJC-TV	4	Kamloops, B.C.
CFJR	1450	Brockville, Ont.
CFKC	1340	Creston, B.C.
CFLA-TV	8	Goose Bay, Nfld.
CFLD	1400	Burns Lake, B.C.
CFLG	104.5	Cornwall, Ont.
CFLH	1340	Hearst, Ont.
CFLK	1230	Kapuskasing, Ont.
CFLM	1240	La Tuque, Que.
CFLN	1230	Goose Bay, Nfld.
CFLP	1000	Rimouski, Que.
CFLS	920	Levis, Que.
CFLV	1370	Valleyfield, Que.
CFLW	1340	Wabush, Nfld.
CFLY	98.3	Kingston, Ont.
CFMB	1410	Montreal, Que.
CFMC	103.9	Saskatoon, Sask.
CFMI	101.1	New Westminster, B.C.
CFMK	96.3	Kingston, Ont.
CFMM	99.1	Prince Albert, Sask.
CFMO	93.9	Ottawa, Ont.
CFMP	101.5	Peterborough, Ont.
CFMQ	92.1	Regina, Sask.
CFMS	98.5	Victoria, B.C.
CFMT-TV	47	Toronto, Ont.
CFMX	103.1	Cobourg, Ont.
CFNB	550	Fredericton, N.B.
CFNI	1240	Port Hardy, B.C.
CFNL	590	Fort Nelson, B.C.
CFNS	860	Saskatoon, Sask.
CFNW	790	Port Aux Choix, Nfld.
CFNY	102.1	Brampton, Ont.
CFOB	800	Ft. Frances, Ont.
CFOC-TV-2	6	North Battleford, Sask.
CFOK	1370	Westlock, Alta.
CFOM	1340	Quebec, Que.
CFOR	1570	Orillia, Ont.
CFOS	560	Owen Sound, Ont.
CFOX	1470	Pointe Claire, Que.
CFOX	99.3	Vancouver, B.C.
CFOZ	100.3	Argentia, Nfld.
CFPL	980	London, Ont.
CFPL-FM	95.9	London, Ont.
CFPL-TV	10	London, Ont.
CFPR	860	Prince Rupert, B.C.
CFPS	1490	Port Elgin, Ont.
CFQC	600	Saskatoon, Sask.
CFQC-TV	8	Saskatoon, Sask.
CFQC-TV-1	3	Stranraer, Sask.
CFQM-FM	103.9	Moncton, N.B.
CFQR	92.5	Montreal, Que.
CFQX-FM	92.9	Selkirk, Man.
CFRA	580	Ottawa, Ont.
CFRB	1010	Toronto, Ont.
CFRC	98.9	Red Deer, Alta.
CFRC	1490	Kingston, Ont.
CFRG	710	Gravelbourg, Sask.
CFRN	1260	Edmonton, Alta.
CFRN-TV	3	Edmonton, Alta.
CFRN-TV-1	13	Grand Prairie, Alta.
CFRN-TV-2	3	Peace River, Alta.
CFRN-TV-4	12	Ashmont, Alta.
CFRN-TV-6	8	Red Deer, Alta.
CFRN-TV-7	7	Lougheed, Alta.
CFRN-TV-8	18	High Prairie, Alta.
CFRN-TV-9	9	Slave Lake, Alta.
CFRO	102.7	Vancouver, B.C.
CFRP	620	Forestville, Que.
CFRW	1290	Winnipeg, Man.
CFRY	920	Portage La Prairie, Man.
CFSL	1190	Weyburn, Sask.
CFSX	910	Stephenville, Nfld.
CFTI	92.1	Timmins, Ont.
CFTJ	960	Cambridge, Ont.
CFTK	590	Terrace, B.C.
CFTK-TV	3	Terrace, B.C.
CFTM-TV	10	Montreal, Que.
CFTO-TV	9	Toronto, Ont.
CFTR	680	Toronto, Ont.
CFUN	1410	Vancouver, B.C.
CFVD	1370	Ville Degelis, Que.
CFVM	1220	Amqui, Que.
CFVR	850	Abbotsford, B.C.
CFWB	1490	Campbell River, B.C.
CFWH	570	Whitehorse, Yuk.
CFWH-TV	6	Whitehorse, Yuk.
CFYK	1340	Yellowknife, N.W.T.
CFYK-TV	8	Yellowknife, N.W.T.
CFYN	1050	Sault Ste. Marie, Ont.
CFYQ	1350	Gander, Nfld.
CFYQ	850	Gander, Nfld.
CHAB	800	Moose Jaw, Sask.
CHAD	1340	Amos, Que.
CHAK	860	Inuvik, N.W.T.
CHAK-TV	6	Inuvik, N.W.T.
CHAL	1350	St. Pamphile, Que.
CHAM	1280	Hamilton, Ont.
CHAN-TV	8	Vancouver, B.C.
CHAN-TV-4	11	Courtenay, B.C.
CHAS	100.5	Sault Ste. Marie, Ont.
CHAT	1270	Medicine Hat, Alta.
CHAT-TV	6	Medicine Hat, Alta.
CHAT-TV-1	4	Pivot, Alta.
CHAU-TV	5	New Carlisle, Que.
CHAY	93.1	Barrie, Ont.
CHBC-TV	2	Kelowna, B.C.
CHCH-TV	11	Hamilton, Ont.
CHCM	560	Marystown, Nfld.
CHCR-TV	4	Campbellton, N.B.
CHEC	1090	Lethbridge, Alta.
CHED	630	Edmonton, Alta.
CHEF	1450	Granby, Que.
CHEK-TV	6	Victoria, B.C.
CHEK-TV-5	13	Campbell River, B.C.
CHEM-TV	8	Three Rivers, Que.
CHER	950	Sydney, N.S.
CHET	1450	Chetwynd, B.C.
CHEX	980	Peterborough, Ont.
CHEX-TV	12	Peterborough, Ont.
CHEZ	106.1	Ottawa, Ont.
CHFA	680	Edmonton, Alta.
CHFA-1	104.3	Lethbridge, Alta.
CHFC	1230	Churchill, Man.
CHFD-TV	4	Thunder Bay, Ont.
CHFI	98.1	Toronto, Ont.
CHFM	95.9	Calgary, Alta.
CHFX-FM	101.9	Halifax, N.S.
CHGB	1310	La Pocatiere, Que.
CHGB-FM	102.9	La Pocatiere, Que.
CHIM	104.7	Kelowna, B.C.
CHIN	1540	Toronto, Ont.
CHIN-FM	100.7	Toronto, Ont.
CHIQ	94.3	Winnipeg, Man.
CHIR	730	Leamington, Ont.
CHKL-TV	5	Kelowna, B.C.
CHKL-TV-1	10	Pentilton, B.C.
CHKM-TV	6	Kamloops, B.C.
CHLC	580	Hautervie, Que.
CHLM	96.5	Rouyn, Que.
CHLM-1	103.5	Lithiums Mines, Que.
CHLN	550	Three Rivers, Que.
CHLO	1570	St. Thomas, Ont.
CHLO	1310	St. Paul, Alta.
CHLQ	93.1	Challottetown, P.E.
CHLR	1380	Moncton, N.B.
CHLT	630	Sherbrooke, Que.
CHLT-TV	7	Sherbrooke, Que.
CHML	900	Hamilton, Ont.
CHMM	97.5	Winnipeg, Man.
CHMT-TV	7	Moncton, N.B.
CHMY	97.1	Penticton, B.C.
CHNB-TV	4	North Bay, Ont.
CHNC	610	New Carlisle, Que.
CHNL	610	Kamloops, B.C.
CHNL-FM	97.5	Kamloops, B.C.
CHNL-1	1400	Clearwater, B.C.
CHNO	550	Sudbury, Ont.
CHNR	1600	Simcoe, Ont.
CHNS	960	Halifax, N.S.
CHOI	98.1	Quebec, Que.
CHOK	1070	Sarnia, Ont.
CHOM	97.7	Montreal, Que.
CHOO	1390	Ajax, Ont.
CHOS	95.9	Rattling Brook, Nfld.
CHOT-TV	40	Hull, Que.
CHOV	1350	Pembroke, Ont.
CHOW	1470	Welland, Ont.
CHOZ	93.9	St. John's, Nfld.
CHPQ	1370	Parksville, B.C.
CHPR	1110	Hawkesbury, Ont.
CHQB	1280	Powell River, B.C.
CHQM	1320	Vancouver, B.C.
CHQM-FM	103.5	Vancouver, B.C.
CHQR	810	Calgary, Alta.
CHQT	1110	Edmonton, Alta.
CHRB	1280	High River, Alta.
CHRC	800	Quebec, Que.
CHRD	1480	Drummondville, Que.
CHRE	105.7	St. Catherines, Ont.
CHRL	910	Roberval, Que.
CHRM	1290	Matane, Que.
CHRO-TV	5	Pembroke, Ont.
CHRS	1090	Longueuil, Que.
CHRT	1450	St. Eleuthere, Que.

CHSC 1220 St. Catherines, Ont.
CHSJ 1150 St. John, N.B.
CHSJ-TV 4 St. John, N.B.
CHSJ-TV-1 6 Bon Accord, N.B.
CHSM 1250 Steinbach, Man.
CHSS-TV 6 Wynyard, Sask.
CHTK 560 Prince Rupert, B.C.
CHTM 610 Thompson, Man.
CHTN 1190 Charlottetown, P.E.
CHUB 1570 Nanaimo, B.C.
CHUC 1450 Cobourg, Ont.
CHUM 1050 Toronto, Ont.
CHUM-FM 104.5 Toronto, Ont.
CHUR 1100 North Bay, Ont.
CHVD 1230 Dolbeau, Que.
CHVO 850 Spainard's Bay, Nfld.
CHWC 103.1 Port Hope, Ont.
CHWK 1270 Chilliwack, B.C.
CHWO 1250 Oakville, Ont.
CHYM 570 Kitchener, Ont.
CHYQ 670 Musgravetown, Nfld.
CHYR 710 Leamington, Ont.
CIBQ 1340 Brooks, Alta.
CICA-TV 19 Toronto, Ont.
CICC-TV 10 Yorkton, Sask.
CICC-TV-1 12 Wynyard, Sask.
CICI-TV 5 Sudbury, Ont.
CICI-TV-1 3 Elliot Lake, Ont.
CICO-TV 3 Timmins, Ont.
CICO-TV-9 9 Thunder Bay, Ont.
CICO-TV-18 18 London, Ont.
CICO-TV-19 19 Sudbury, Ont.
CICO-TV-20 20 Sault Ste. Marie, Ont.
CICO-TV-24 24 Ottawa, Ont.
CICO-TV-28 28 Kitchener, Ont.
CICO-TV-32 32 Windsor, Ont.
CICO-TV-59 59 Chatham, Ont.
CIEL 98.5 Longueuil, Que.
CIEW-TV 7 Carlyle Lake, Sask.
CIFG-TV 12 Prince George, B.C.
CIGL 97.1 Belleville, Ont.
CIGM 92.7 Sudbury, Ont.
CIGO 1410 Pt. Hawkesbury, N.S.
CIGV-FM 100.7 Penticton, B.C.
CIHI 1260 Fredericton, N.B.
CILA 107.7 Lethbridge, Alta.
CILQ 107.1 Toronto, Ont.
CIME 99.5 Ste. Adele, Que.
CIMF 94.9 Hull, Que.
CIMH 94.1 Sept Iles, Que.
CIMT-TV 9 Riviere Du Loup, Que.
CING 107.9 Burlington, Ont.
CINL 1400 Princeton, B.C.
CIOK-1 1340 Grand Centre, Alta.
CIOO 100.1 Halifax, N.S.
CIOZ 96.3 Marystown, Nfld.
CIPC 710 Port Cartier, Que.
CIRB 1240 Lac Etchemin, Que.
CIRK 97.3 Edmonton, Alta.
CISL 940 Richmond, B.C.
CISN 103.9 Edmonton, Alta.
CISQ 104.9 Squamish, B.C.
CISV 1530 Morden, Man.
CITE 107.3 Montreal, Que.
CITE-1 102.7 Sherbrooke, Que.
CITI 92.1 Winnepeg, Man.
CITL-TV 4 Lloydminster, Alta.
CITM-TV 3 One Hundred Mile House
CITO-TV-2 11 Kearns, Ont.
CITV 13 Edmonton, Alta.
CITY-TV 79 Toronto, Ont.
CIVA-TV 12 Val D'or, Que.
CIVC-TV 45 Three Rivers, Que.
CIVF-TV 12 Baie-trimite, Que.
CIVG-TV 9 Sept Isles, Que.
CIVH 1340 Vanderhoof, B.C.
CIVM-TV 17 Montreal, Que.
CIVN-TV 8 Rouyn, Que.
CIVO 30 Hull, Que.
CIVQ-TV 15 Quebec, Que.
CIVR-TV 22 Rimouski, Que.
CIVS-TV 24 Sherbrooke, Que.
CIVU-TV 8 Chicoutimi, Que.
CIYQ 680 Grand Falls, Nfld.
CIZL 98.9 Regina, Sask.
CJAD 800 Montreal, Que.
CJAF 1240 Cabano, Que.
CJAN 1340 Asbestos, Que.
CJAP-TV 3 Argentia, Nfld.
CJAR 1240 The Pas, Man.
CJAT 610 Trail, B.C.
CJAV 1240 Port Alberni, B.C.
CJAX 92.5 Edmonton, Alta.
CJAY-FM 92.1 Calgary, Alta.
CJAY-1 95.1 Banff, Alta.
CJAZ-FM 92.1 Vancouver, B.C.
CJBC 860 Toronto, Ont.
CJBC-FM-20 99.3 London, Ont.
CJBC-3-FM 96.5 Penetanguishene, Ont.
CJBC-5-FM 106.3 Peterborough, Ont.
CJBK 1290 London, Ont.
CJBM 1450 Causapscal, Que.
CJBQ 800 Belleville, Ont.
CJBR 900 Rimouski, Que.
CJBR-FM 101.5 Rimouski, Que.
CJBR-TV 3 Rimouski, Que.
CJBX 92.7 London, Ont.
CJCA 930 Edmonton, Alta.
CJCB 1270 Sydney, N.S.
CJCB-TV 4 Sydney, N.S.
CJCB-TV-1 6 Inverness, N.S.
CJCB-TV-2 9 Antigonish, N.S.
CJCH 920 Halifax, N.S.
CJCH-TV 5 Halifax, N.S.
CJCH-TV-1 10 Canning, N.S.
CJCH-TV-6 6 Caledonia, N.S.
CJCI 620 Prince George, B.C.
CJCJ 920 Woodstock, N.B.
CJCL 1430 Toronto, Ont.
CJCM 96.1 Brandon, Man.
CJCN-TV 4 Grand Falls, Nfld.
CJCS 1240 Stratford, Ont.
CJCW 590 Sussex, N.B.
CJCY 1390 Medicine Hat, Alta.
CJDC 1350 Dawson Creek, B.C.
CJDC-TV 5 Dawson Creek, B.C.
CJDG-TV 7 Lithiums Mines, Que.
CJEM 570 Edmundston, N.B.
CJER 900 St. Jerome, Que.
CJET 630 Smith's Falls, Ont.
CJFB-TV 5 Swift Current, Sask.
CJFI 99.9 Sarnia, Ont.
CJFM 95.9 Montreal, Que.
CJFP 1400 Riviere Du Loup, Que.
CJFX 580 Antigonish, N.S.
CJGL 94.1 Swift Current, Sask.
CJGX 940 Yorkton, Sask.
CJIB 940 Vernon, B.C.
CJIC-TV 5 Sault Ste. Marie, Ont.
CJJC 800 Langley, B.C.
CJKL 560 Kirkland Lake, Ont.
CJLA 630 Lachute, Que.
CJLB 1230 Thunder Bay, Ont.
CJLM 1350 Joliette, Que.
CJLS 1340 Yarmouth, N.S.
CJMD 1240 Chibougamau, Que.
CJME 1300 Regina, Sask.
CJMF 95.3 Quebec, Que.
CJMH 1460 Medicine Hat, Alta.
CJMR 1190 Mississauga, Ont.
CJMS 1280 Montreal, Que.
CJMT 1420 Chicoutimi, Que.
CJMX 105.3 Sudbury, Ont.
CJNB 1050 North Battleford, Sask.
CJNH 1240 Bancroft, Ont.
CJNL 1230 Merritt, B.C.
CJNR 730 Blind River, Ont.
CJNS 1240 Meadow Lake, Sask.
CJOB 680 Winnipeg, Man.
CJOC 1220 Lethbridge, Alta.
CJOH-TV 13 Ottawa, Ont.
CJOH-TV-6 6 Doseronto, Ont.
CJOH-TV-8 8 Cornwall, Ont.
CJOI 1440 Wetaskiwin, Alta.
CJOK 1230 Fort Mc Murray, Alta.
CJOM-FM 88.7 Windsor, Ont.
CJON-TV 6 St. John's, Nfld.
CJOR 600 Vancouver, B.C.
CJOX-TV 2 Grand Bank, Nfld.
CJOY 1460 Guelph, Ont.
CJOZ 92.1 Bonavista, Nfld.
CJPM-TV 6 Chicoutimi, Que.
CJPR 1490 Blairmore, Alta.
CJQM 104.3 Sault Ste. Marie, Ont.
CJQR 97.7 St. Catherines, Ont.
CJRB 1220 Boissevain, Man.
CJRC 1150 Ottawa, Ont.
CJRL 1220 Kenora, Ont.
CJRN 710 Niagara Falls, Ont.
CJRP 1060 Quebec, Que.
CJRS 1510 Sherbrooke, Que.
CJRT-FM 91.1 Toronto, Ont.
CJRW 1240 Summerside, P.E.
CJSA 1230 Ste. Agathe Des Monts, Que.
CJSB 540 Ottawa, Ont.
CJSD 94.3 Thunder Bay, Ont.
CJSL 1280 Estevan, Sask.
CJSN 1490 Shaunavon, Sask.
CJSO 1320 Sorel, Que.
CJSS 1220 Cornwall, Ont.
CJTN 1270 Trenton, Ont.
CJTR 1140 Three Rivers, Que.
CJTT 1230 New Liskeard, Ont.
CJUM 101.5 Winnipeg, Man.
CJUS-FM 89.7 Saskatoon, Sask.
CJVA 810 Caraquet, N.B.
CJVB 1470 Vancouver, B.C.
CJVI 900 Victoria, B.C.
CJVL 1360 Ste. Marie De Beauce, Que.
CJVR 1420 Melfort, Sask.
CJWA 1240 Wawa, Ont.
CJWN-TV 10 Corner Brook, Nfld.
CJWW 1370 Saskatoon, Sask.
CJXX 1430 Grand Prairie, Alta.
CJYC 98.9 St. John, N.B.
CJYQ 930 St. John's, Nfld.
CJYR 970 Edson, Alta.
CKAC 730 Montreal, Que.
CKAD 1350 Middleton, N.S.
CKAL 1050 Vernon, B.C.
CKAM-TV 12 Upsalaquitch Lake, N.B.
CKAN 1480 Newmarket, Ont.

CKAP	580	Kapuskasing, Ont.
CKAR	1350	Oshawa, Ont.
CKAT	101.9	North Bay, Ont.
CKAY	1500	Duncan, B.C.
CKBB	950	Barrie, Ont.
CKBC	1350	Bathurst, N.B.
CKBH	790	Baie Comeau, Que.
CKBI	900	Prince Albert, Sask.
CKBI-TV	5	Prince Albert, Sask.
CKBI-TV-3	4	Greenwater Lake, Sask.
CKBM	1490	Montmagny, Que.
CKBQ-TV	2	Melfort, Sask.
CKBS	1240	St. Hyacinthe, Que.
CKBW	1000	Bridgewater, N.S.
CKBW-1	94.5	Liverpool, N.S.
CKBW-2	93.1	Shelburn, N.S.
CKBX	1240	100 Mile House, B.C.
CKBY	105.3	Ottawa, Ont.
CKCB	1400	Collingwood, Ont.
CKCD-TV	7	Campbellton, N.B.
CKCH	970	Hull, Que.
CKCK	620	Regina, Sask.
CKCK-TV	2	Regina, Sask.
CKCK-TV-1	12	Colgate, Sask.
CKCK-TV-2	6	Willow Bunch, Sask.
CKCL	600	Truro, N.S.
CKCM	620	Grand Falls, Nfld.
CKCN	560	Seven Islands, Que.
CKCO-TV	13	Kitchener, Ont.
CKCO-TV-2	2	Wiarton, Ont.
CKCO-TV-3	42	Sarnia, Ont.
CKCO-TV-4	11	Muskokas, Ont.
CKCQ	920	Quesnel, B.C.
CKCR	1340	Revelstoke, B.C.
CKCU	93.1	Ottawa, Ont.
CKCV	1280	Quebec, Que.
CKCW	1220	Moncton, N.B.
CKCW-TV	2	Moncton, N.B.
CKCW-TV-1	8	Charlottetown, P.E.
CKCY	920	Sault Ste. Marie, Ont.
CKCY-TV	2	Sault Ste. Marie, Ont.
CKDA	1220	Victoria, B.C.
CKDH	900	Amherst, N.S.
CKDK	1340	Woodstock, Ont.
CKDM	730	Dauphin, Man.
CKDQ	910	Drumheller, Alta.
CKDR	900	Dryden, Ont.
CKDS	95.3	Hamilton, Ont.
CKDY	1420	Digby, N.S.
CKEC	1320	New Glasgow, N.S.
CKEG	1350	Nanaimo, B.C.
CKEK	570	Cranbrook, B.C.
CKEN	1490	Kentville, N.S.
CKER	1480	Edmonton, Alta.
CKEY	590	Toronto, Ont.
CKFL	1400	Lac Megantic, Que.
CKFM	99.9	Toronto, Ont.
CKGA	730	Gander, Nfld.
CKGB	680	Timmins, Ont.
CKGB	730	Timmins, Ont.
CKGF	1340	Grand Forks, B.C.
CKGL	96.7	Kitchener, Ont.
CKGM	980	Montreal, Que.
CKGN-TV	6	Paris, Ont.
CKGN-TV-2	2	Bancroft, Ont.
CKGN-TV-22	22	Uxbridge, Ont.
CKGN-TV-6	6	Ottawa, Ont.
CKGO	1240	Hope, B.C.
CKGR	1400	Golden, B.C.
CKGY	1170	Red Deer, Alta.
CKIK	98.9	Quebec, Que.
CKIM	1240	Baie Verte, Nfld.
CKIQ	1150	Kelowna, B.C.
CKIT	104.9	Regina, Sask.
CKJD	1110	Sarnia, Ont.
CKJS	810	Winnipeg, Man.
CKJY	93.9	Windsor, Ont.
CKKC	1390	Nelson, B.C.
CKKM-TV	3	Oliver, B.C.
CKKR	1330	Rosetown, Sask.
CKKW	1090	Kitchener, Ont.
CKLA	106.1	Guelph, Ont.
CKLC	1380	Kingston, Ont.
CKLD	1330	Thetford Mines, Que.
CKLG	730	Vancouver, B.C.
CKLM	1570	Laval, Que.
CKLQ	1570	Brandon, Man.
CKLR	1490	L'annonciaton, Que.
CKLS	1240	La Sarre, Que.
CKLT-TV	9	St. John, N.B.
CKLW	800	Windsor, Ont.
CKLY	910	Lindsay, Ont.
CKMC-TV	12	Saskatoon, Sask.
CKMF	94.3	Montreal, Que.
CKMI-TV	5	Quebec, Que.
CKMJ-TV	7	Marquis, Sask.
CKMK	1240	Mackenzie, B.C.
CKML	610	Mont Laurier, Que.
CKMP	1230	Midland, Ont.
CKMV	1480	Grand Falls, N.B.
CKMW	790	Brampton, Ont.
CKNB	950	Campbellton, N.B.
CKNC-TV	9	Sudbury, Ont.
CKNC-TV-1	7	Elliot Lake, Ont.
CKND	9	Winnipeg, Man.
CKND-TV-2	2	Minnedosa, Man.
CKNL	560	Fort St. John, B.C.
CKNR	1340	Elliot Lake, Ont.
CKNS	930	Espanola, Ont.
CKNW	980	New Westminster, B.C.
CKNX	920	Wingham, Ont.
CKNX-FM	101.7	Wingham, Ont.
CKNX-TV	8	Wingham, Ont.
CKNY-TV	10	North Bay, Ont.
CKO-FM	106.9	Ottawa, Ont.
CKO-FM-1	106.9	Ottawa, Ont.
CKO-FM-2	99.1	Toronto, Ont.
CKO-FM-3	97.5	London, Ont.
CKO-FM-4	96.1	Vancouver, B.C.
CKO-FM-5	103.1	Calgary, Alta.
CKO-FM-6	101.9	Edmonton, Alta.
CKO-FM-7	99.1	Winnipeg, Man.
CKO-FM-8	94.5	Regina, Sask.
CKO-FM-9	99.7	St. John, N.B.
CKO-FM-10	101.9	St. John's, Nfld.
CKOB	1400	Renfrew, Ont.
CKOC	1150	Hamilton, Ont.
CKOI	96.9	Verdun, Que.
CKOK	800	Penticton, B.C.
CKOM	1250	Saskatoon, Sask.
CKOO	1240	Osoyoos, B.C.
CKOS-TV	5	Yorkton, Sask.
CKOT	1510	Tillsonburg, Ont.
CKOT-FM	101.3	Tillsonburg, Ont.
CKOV	630	Kelowna, B.C.
CKOY	1310	Ottawa, Ont.
CKOZ	92.3	Corner Brook, Nfld.
CKPC	1380	Brantford, Ont.
CKPC-FM	92.1	Brantford, Ont.
CKPE	94.9	Sydney, N.S.
CKPG	550	Prince George, B.C.
CKPG-TV	2	Prince George, B.C.
CKPR	580	Thunder Bay, Ont.
CKPR-TV	2	Thunder Bay, Ont.
CKPT	1420	Peterborough, Ont.
CKQM-FM	105.1	Peterborough, Ont.
CKQR	1230	Castlegar, B.C.
CKQT	94.9	Oshawa, Ont.
CKRA	96.3	Edmonton, Alta.
CKRB	1460	St. Georges De Beauce, Que.
CKRC	630	Winnipeg, Man.
CKRD	850	Red Deer, Alta.
CKRD-TV	6	Red Deer, Alta.
CKRD-TV-1	10	Coronation, Alta.
CKRL	89.1	Quebec, Que.
CKRM	980	Regina, Sask.
CKRN	1400	Rouyn, Que.
CKRN-TV	4	Rouyn, Que.
CKRN-TV-3	35	Bearn, Que.
CKRS	590	Jonquiere, Que.
CKRS-TV	12	Jonquiere, Que.
CKRS-TV-3	8	Roberval, Que.
CKRT-TV	7	Riviere Du Loup, Que.
CKRW	610	Whitehorse, Yuk.
CKSA	1080	Lloydminster, Alta.
CKSA-TV	2	Lloydminster, Alta.
CKSA-TV-2	6	Bonneville, Alta.
CKSB	1050	St. Boniface, Man.
CKSB-8	99.5	Brandon, Man.
CKSH-TV	9	Sherbrooke, Que.
CKSL	1410	London, Ont.
CKSM	1220	Shawinigan Falls, Que.
CKSO	790	Sudbury, Ont.
CKSP	1450	Summerland, B.C.
CKSQ	1400	Stettler, Alta.
CKSR-TV	33	Santa Rosa, B.C.
CKSS	96.9	Red Rocks, Nfld.
CKST	1070	St. Albert, Alta.
CKSW	570	Swift Current, Sask.
CKTA	1570	Taber, Alta.
CKTB	610	St. Catherines, Ont.
CKTK	1230	Kitimat, B.C.
CKTL	1420	Plessisville, Que.
CKTM-TV	13	Three Rivers, Que.
CKTN-TV	8	Trail, B.C.
CKTO	100.9	Truro, N.S.
CKTS	900	Sherbrooke, Que.
CKUA	580	Edmonton, Alta.
CKUA-FM	94.9	Edmonton, Alta.
CKUA-FM-1	93.7	Calgary, Alta.
CKUA-FM-2	99.3	Lethbridge, Alta.
CKUA-FM-3	97.3	Medicine Hat, Alta.
CKUA-FM-4	100.9	Grand Prairie, Alta.
CKUA-FM-5	96.9	Peace River, Alta.
CKUA-FM-6	101.3	Red Deer, Alta.
CKUE	101.1	Smith's Falls, Ont.
CKVD	900	Val D' Or, Que.
CKVL	850	Verdun, Que.
CKVM	710	Ville Marie, Que.
CKVO	710	Clarenceville, Nfld.
CKVR	1400	Drummondville, Que.
CKVR-TV	3	Barrie, Ont.
CKVT	1340	Temiscaming, Que.
CKVU	21	Vancouver, B.C.
CKWG	103.1	Winnipeg, Man.
CKWL	570	Williams Lake, B.C.
CKWM-FM	97.7	Kentville, N.S.
CKWS	960	Kingston, Ont.
CKWS-TV	11	Kingston, Ont.
CKWW	580	Windsor, Ont.
CKWX	1130	Vancouver, B.C.
CKX	1150	Brandon, Man.
CKX-TV	5	Brandon, Man.
CKX-TV-1	11	Foxwarren, Man.
CKXL	1140	Calgary, Alta.
CKXM	100.3	Edmonton, Alta.

CKXR	580	Salmon Arm, B.C.
CKY	580	Winnipeg, Man.
CKY-TV	7	Winnipeg, Man.
CKYB-TV	4	Brandon, Man.
CKYL	610	Peace River, Alta.
CKYQ	610	Grand Bank, Nfld.
CKYR	1450	Jasper, Alta.
CMAC	1019	San Cristobal, Cuba
CMAD	1160	Artemisa, Cuba
CMAF	670	Pinar Del Rio, Cuba
CMAG	1260	Consolacion Del Sur, Cuba
CMAN	550	Pinar Del Rio, Cuba
CMAP	1000	Guane, Cuba
CMAQ	730	Pinar Del Rio, Cuba
CMAS	1010	Pinar Del Rio, Cuba
CMBC	690	Havana, Cuba
CMBF	950	Havana, Cuba
CMBF-TV	2	Havana, Cuba
CMBG	1360	Havana, Cuba
CMBL	870	Havana, Cuba
CMBM	1080	Santa Fe, Isla De Pinos, Cuba
CMBQ	1060	Havana, Cuba
CMCA	830	Havana, Cuba
CMCH	790	Havana, Cuba
CMCI	760	Havana, Cuba
CMCK	980	Havana, Cuba
CMDB	680	Santiago De Cuba, Cuba
CMDD	1310	Bayamo, Cuba
CMDE	1260	Bayamo, Cuba
CMDF	1590	Manzanillo, Cuba
CMDJ	950	Guantanamo, Cuba
CMDL	1120	Holguin, Cuba
CMDN	870	Guantanamo, Cuba
CMDO	1150	Banes, Cuba
CMDP	1280	Victoria De Las Tunas, Cuba
CMDT	840	Las Mercedes, Cuba
CMDV	1550	Santiago De Cuba, Cuba
CMDW	1130	Guantanamo, Cuba
CMDX	1420	Baracoa, Cuba
CMDZ	890	Santiago De Cuba, Cuba
CMFA	1030	Camaguey, Cuba
CMFD-TV	7	Ciego De Avila, Cuba
CMG-TV	13	Matanzas, Cuba
CMGB	1560	Cardenas, Cuba
CMGE	1470	Cardenas, Cuba
CMGH-TV	11	Matanzas, Cuba
CMGN	720	Colon, Cuba
CMGQ-TV	9	Matanzas, Cuba
CMGW	1240	Matanzas, Cuba
CMGX	930	Matanzas, Cuba
CMGY	1220	Perico, Cuba
CMH-TV	5	Santa Clara, Cuba
CMHA	1130	Santa Clara, Cuba
CMHB	960	Sancti Spiritus, Cuba
CMHD	890	Santa Clara, Cuba
CMHG	660	Santa Clara, Cuba
CMHI	570	Santa Clara, Cuba
CMHK	1307	Cruces, Cuba
CMHM	1280	Santa Clara, Cuba
CMHN	680	Cienfuegos, Cuba
CMHT	990	Sancti Spiritus, Cuba
CMHU	1100	Cienfuegos, Cuba
CMHV	610	Trinidad, Cuba
CMHW	840	Santa Clara, Cuba
CMJ-TV	4	Camaguey, Cuba
CMJB	910	Camaguey, Cuba
CMJD	1300	Ciego De Avila, Cuba
CMJE	810	Camaguey, Cuba
CMJG	1270	Camaguey, Cuba
CMJI	1400	Florida, Cuba
CMJK	1140	Camaguey, Cuba
CMJL	740	Camaguey, Cuba
CMJL-TV	6	Camaguey, Cuba
CMJM	580	Ciego De Avila, Cuba
CMJN	784	Camaguey, Cuba
CMJP	1190	Ciego De Avila, Cuba
CMJQ	1300	Nuevitas, Cuba
CMJT	700	Ciego De Avila, Cuba
CMJV	900	Ciego De Avila, Cuba
CMJW	1450	Santa Cruz Del Sur, Cuba
CMJX	1210	Moron, Cuba
CMJY	860	Ciego De Avila, Cuba
CMKA	1250	Guantanamo, Cuba
CMKC	850	Santiago De Cuba, Cuba
CMKE	1240	Victoria De Las Tunas, Cuba
CMKG	1059	Baracoa, Cuba
CMKJ	730	Holguin, Cuba
CMKJ-TV	3	Holguin, Cuba
CMKM	1011	Holguin, Cuba
CMKN	960	Santiago De Cuba, Cuba
CMKP	670	San Pedro De Cacocum, Cuba
CMKS	1290	Guantanamo, Cuba
CMKT	1520	Victoria De Las Tunas, Cuba
CMKU	650	Santiago De Cuba, Cuba
CMKU-TV	2	Santiago De Cuba, Cuba
CMKV	851	Holguin, Cuba
CMKW	1370	Santiago De Cuba, Cuba
CMKX	1390	Bayamo, Cuba
CMKY	1350	Puerto Padre, Cuba
CMKZ	1430	Palma Soriano, Cuba
CMLB-TV	5	Santiago De Cuba, Cuba
CMLD-TV	8	Holguin, Cuba
CMQ	640	Havana, Cuba
CMQ-TV	6	Havana, Cuba
CMRA-TV	8	Santa Clara, Cuba
CMW	590	Havana, Cuba
COIS	98.5	Stephenville, Nfld.
CXRE	1340	Red Lake, Ont.
HIAA	560	Santiago, Dom. Rep.
HIAB	590	Puerto Plata, Dom. Rep.
HIAC	1450	Salcedo, Dom. Rep.
HIAD	1440	San Juan, Dom. Rep.
HIAE	1420	Santo Domingo, Dom. Rep.
HIAF	630	Monte Cristi, Dom. Rep.
HIAG	1470	Santiago, Dom. Rep.
HIAH	1490	Santo Domingo, Dom. Rep.
HIAJ	1570	Santo Domingo, Dom. Rep.
HIAK	1440	Santo Domingo, Dòm. Rep.
HIAL	1400	La Vega, Dom. Rep.
HIAM	660	Santiago, Dom. Rep.
HIAN	1460	Hato Mayor Del Rey, Dom. Rep.
HIAP	1490	Moca, Dom. Rep.
HIAQ	720	Santiago, Dom. Rep.
HIAR	1450	San Cristobal, Dom. Rep.
HIAS	1150	Santo Domingo, Dom. Rep.
HIAT	650	Santo Domingo, Dom. Rep.
HIAU	1300	Puerto Plata, Dom. Rep.
HIAV	1320	Bani, Dom. Rep.
HIAW	690	Santo Domingo, Dom. Rep.
HIAZ	820	Santiago, Dom. Rep.
HIBA	910	Santo Domingo, Dom. Rep.
HIBA	1590	Santiago, Dom. Rep.
HIBB	1240	La Romana, Dom. Rep.
HIBC	1250	San Francisco De Macoris, Dom. Rep.
HIBE	1180	Santo Domingo, Dom. Rep.
HIBI	1070	San Francisco De Macoris, Dom. Rep.
HIBJ	830	Santo Domingo, Dom. Rep.
HIBK	1310	Moca, Dom. Rep.
HIBK	770	Santo Domingo, Dom. Rep.
HIBL	1510	Santo Domingo, Dom. Rep.
HIBM	920	Azua, Dom. Rep.
HIBN	1400	Puerto Plata, Dom. Rep.
HIBP	1400	La Romana, Dom. Rep.
HIBR	630	Cotui, Dom. Rep.
HIBS	1600	San Pedro De Macoris, Dom. Rep.
HIBU	1240	Valverde, Dom. Rep.
HIBW	540	Santo Domingo, Dom. Rep.
HIBX	640	Moca, Dom. Rep.
HIBY	880	Valverde, Dom. Rep.
HIBZ	1340	San Juan, Dom. Rep.
HICB	1050	Santiago, Dom. Rep.
HICF	800	Nagua, Dom. Rep.
HICJ	1210	San Francisco De Macoris, Dom. Rep.
HICK	920	Santiago, Dom. Rep.
HICN	1120	Santo Domingo, Dom. Rep.
HICP	1210	Moca, Dom. Rep.
HICV	1240	Barahona, Dom. Rep.
HIDA	1590	Santiago, Dom. Rep.
HIDB	1330	Santiago, Dom. Rep.
HIDB	1450	San Pedro De Macoris, Dom. Rep.

HIDC	700	Valverde, Dom. Rep.
HIDE	1160	Cotui, Dom. Rep.
HIDL	1000	La Vega, Dom. Rep.
HIFA	1600	Santo Domingo, Dom. Rep.
HIFB	1540	Santo Domingo, Dom. Rep.
HIFF	960	Puerto Plata, Dom. Rep.
HIFS	1440	Nagua, Dom. Rep.
HIFS	600	San Francisco De Macoris, Dom. Rep.
HIFU	1580	Neyba, Dom. Rep.
HIG	950	Santo Domingo, Dom. Rep.
HIGB	750	Santiago, Dom. Rep.
HIHD	1320	San Pedro De Macoris, Dom. Rep.
HIJC	1560	Santiago, Dom. Rep.
HIJM	1410	Santiago, Dom. Rep.
HIJP	1010	Santo Domingo, Dom. Rep.
HIKQ	1300	Santo Domingo, Dom. Rep.
HIL	790	Santo Domingo, Dom. Rep.
HILR	860	Santo Domingo, Dom. Rep.
HIMC	1100	Santo Domingo, Dom. Rep.
HIMH	1100	La Vega, Dom. Rep.
HIMS	570	Santo Domingo, Dom. Rep.
HIN-TV	7	Santo Domingo, Dom. Rep.
HIPJ	890	Santo Domingo, Dom. Rep.
HIPT	1340	San Francisco De Macoris, Dom. Rep.
HIRL	1130	Santiago, Dom. Rep.
HIRM	1250	Higuey, Dom. Rep.
HISA	980	Santiago, Dom. Rep.
HISD	620	Santo Domingo, Dom. Rep.
HISD	1360	La Vega, Dom. Rep.
HISD	1310	El Seibo, Dom. Rep.
HISD	1370	Barahona, Dom. Rep.
HISD-TV	4	Santo Domingo, Dom. Rep.
HIST	1380	Santiago, Dom. Rep.
HIT	1260	Santo Domingo, Dom. Rep.
HIUA	1370	Barahona, Dom. Rep.
HIUA	1270	Santiago, Dom. Rep.
HIUA	1390	San Juan, Dom. Rep.
HIUB	1300	Dajabon, Dom. Rep.
HIVG	1430	La Vega, Dom. Rep.
HIVM	1290	Bonoa, Dom. Rep.
HIWJ	1580	Samana, Dom. Rep.
HIXZ	1350	Santo Domingo, Dom. Rep.
HIZ	730	Santo Domingo, Dom. Rep.
KAAA	1230	Kingman, Ariz.
KAAB	1130	Batesville, Ark.
KAAK	98.9	Great Falls, Mont.
KAAL	6	Austin, Minn.
KAAM	1310	Dallas, Tex.
KAAN	870	New Hampton, Mo.
KAAN-FM	95.9	Bethany, Mo.
KAAR	1480	Vancouver, Wash.
KAAT	107.1	Oakhurst, Calif.
KAAY	1090	Little Rock, Ark.
KABC	790	Los Angeles, Calif.
KABC-TV	7	Los Angeles, Calif.
KABF	88.3	Little Rock, Ark.
KABI	1560	Abilene, Kan.
KABI-FM	98.3	Abilene, Kan.
KABK-FM	97.7	Augusta, Ark.
KABL	960	Oakland, Calif.
KABL-FM	98.1	San Francisco, Calif.
KABN	830	Long Island, Alas.
KABQ	1350	Albuquerque, N.M.
KABR	1500	Magdalena, N.M.
KABS	1270	Pine Bluff, Ark.
KABY-TV	9	Aberdeen, S.D.
KACA	101.7	Prosser, Wash.
KACB-TV	3	San Angelo, Tex.
KACC	91.3	Alvin, Tex.
KACE	103.9	Inglewood, Calif.
KACH	1340	Preston, Id.
KACH-FM	96.7	Preston, Id.
KACI	1300	The Dalles, Ore.
KACJ	1510	Greenwood, Ark.
KACO	1090	Bellville, Tex.
KACQ	106.3	Hot Springs, Ark.
KACT	1360	Andrews, Tex.
KACT-FM	105.5	Andrews, Tex.
KACV-FM	89.9	Amarillo, Tex.
KACY	1520	Port Hueneme, Calif.
KADA	1230	Ada, Okla.
KADE	1190	Boulder, Colo.
KADI-FM	96.3	St. Louis, Mo.
KADL	94.9	Pine Bluff, Ark.
KADN	15	Lafayette, La.
KADO	940	Texarkana, Tex.
KADO-FM	107.1	Texarkana, Ark.
KADQ	94.3	Rexburg, Id.
KADR	1400	Elkader, Ia.
KADS	1240	Elk City, Okla.
KAER	92.5	Sacramento, Calif.
KAET	8	Phoenix, Ariz.
KAEZ	107.7	Oklahoma City, Okla.
KAFA	89.7	Colorado Springs, Colo.
KAFE	810	Santa Fe, N.M.
KAFE-FM	97.3	Santa Fe, N.M.
KAFF	92.9	Flagstaff, Ariz.
KAFM	92.5	Dallas, Tex.
KAFT	13	Fayetteville, Ark.
KAFY	550	Bakersfield, Calif.
KAGC	1510	Bryan, Tex.
KAGE	1380	Winona, Minn.
KAGE-FM	95.3	Winona, Minn.
KAGH	800	Crossett, Ark.
KAGH-FM	104.9	Crossett, Ark.
KAGI	930	Grants Pass, Ore.
KAGO	1150	Klamath Falls, Ore.
KAGO-FM	98.5	Klamath Falls, Ore.
KAGT	1340	Anacortes, Wash.
KAGY	1510	Port Sulphur, La.
KAHI	950	Auburn, Calif.
KAHM	103.9	Prescott, Ariz.
KAHS	91.5	Arcata, Calif.
KAHS	95.1	Arcata, Calif.
KAID	4	Boise, Id.
KAIG	96.7	Mountain View, Mo.
KAII-TV	7	Wailuku, Haw.
KAIL	53	Fresno, Calif.
KAIM	870	Honolulu, Haw.
KAIM-FM	95.5	Honolulu, Haw.
KAIR	1490	Tucson, Ariz.
KAIT-TV	8	Jonesboro, Ark.
KAJA	97.3	San Antonio, Tex.
KAJJ	106.3	Greenwood, Ark.
KAJN	1560	Crowley, La.
KAJN-FM	102.9	Crowley, La.
KAJO	1270	Grants Pass, Ore.
KAKA	1110	Dermott, Ark.
KAKC	970	Tulsa, Okla.
KAKE-TV	10	Wichita, Kan.
KAKI	107.1	Benton, Ark.
KAKM	7	Anchorage, Alas.
KAKZ	1240	Wichita, Kan.
KAKZ-FM	95.9	Derby, Kan.
KALA	88.5	Davenport, Ia.
KALB	580	Alexandria, La.
KALB-TV	5	Alexandria, La.
KALE	960	Richland, Wash.
KALF	95.9	Red Bluff, Calif.
KALG-FM	92.7	La Luz, N.M.
KALI	1430	San Gabriel, Calif.
KALK	104.9	Denison, Tex.
KALL	910	Salt Lake City, Utah
KALM	1290	Thayer, Mo.
KALQ-FM	93.5	Alamosa, Colo.
KALS	97.1	Kalispell, Mont.
KALT	900	Atlanta, Tex.
KALU	90.7	Langston, Okla.
KALV	1430	Alva, Okla.
KALW	91.7	San Francisco, Calif.
KALX	90.7	Berkeley, Calif.
KAMA	1060	El Paso, Tex.
KAMB	101.5	Merced, Calif.
KAMC	28	Lubbock, Tex.
KAMD	910	Camden, Ark.
KAME-TV	21	Reno, Nev.
KAMI	1580	Cozad, Neb.
KAML	990	Kenedy, Tex.
KAMO	1390	Rogers, Ark.
KAMO-FM	94.3	Rogers, Ark.
KAMP	1430	El Centro, Calif.
KAMQ	1240	Carlsbad, N.M.
KAMR	4	Amarillo, Tex.
KAMS	95.1	Mammoth Spring, Ark.
KAMT	1360	Tacoma, Wash.
KAMU	15	College Station, Tex.
KAMU-FM	90.9	College Station, Tex.
KAMX	1520	Albuquerque, N.M.
KAMZ	93.1	El Paso, Tex.
KANA	580	Anaconda, Mont.
KAND	1340	Corsicana, Tex.
KANE	1240	New Iberia, La.
KANI	1500	Wharton, Tex.
KANN	1090	Ogden, Utah
KANS	1510	Larned, Kan.
KANS-FM	96.7	Larned, Kan.
KANU	91.5	Lawrence, Kan.
KANW	89.1	Albuquerque, N.M.
KANZ	91.1	Garden City, Kan.
KAOC-FM	93.3	Port Lavaca, Tex.
KAOI	95.1	Wailuku, Haw.
KAOK	1400	Lake Charles, La.
KAOL	1430	Carrollton, Mo.
KAOS	89.3	Olympia, Wash.
KAPA	1340	Raymond, Wash.
KAPB	1370	Marksville, La.
KAPE	1480	San Antonio, Tex.
KAPP	35	Yakima, Wash.
KAPR	930	Douglas, Ariz.
KAPS	1470	Mt. Vernon, Wash.
KAPV	102.3	Apple Valley, Calif.

KAPY	1290	Port Angeles, Wash.
KAPZ	710	Bald Knob, Ark.
KARA	105.7	Santa Clara, Calif.
KARB	98.3	Price, Utah
KARD	14	West Monroe, La.
KARE	1470	Atchison, Kan.
KARI	550	Blaine, Wash.
KARK-TV	4	Little Rock, Ark.
KARM	1430	Fresno, Calif.
KARN	920	Little Rock, Ark.
KARO	101.7	Columbia, Mo.
KARR	1400	Great Falls, Mont.
KARS	860	Belen, N.M.
KART	1400	Jerome, Id.
KARV	610	Russellville, Ark.
KARY	1310	Prosser, Wash.
KARZ	106.1	Burney, Calif.
KASA	1540	Phoenix, Ariz.
KASB	89.3	Bellevue, Wash.
KASC	104.9	Abbeville, La.
KASD-FM	90.1	Reliance, S.D.
KASE	100.7	Austin, Tex.
KASF	90.9	Alamosa, Colo.
KASH	1600	Eugene, Ore.
KASI	1430	Ames, Ia.
KASK	103.1	Las Cruces, N.M.
KASL	1240	Newcastle, Wyo.
KASM	1150	Albany, Minn.
KASO	1240	Minden, La.
KASO-FM	95.3	Minden, La.
KAST	1370	Astoria, Ore.
KASU	91.9	Jonesboro, Ark.
KASX	96.7	Ada, Okla.
KASY	1220	Auburn, Wash.
KATA	1340	Arcata, Calif.
KATC	3	Lafayette, La.
KATE	1450	Albert Lea, Minn.
KATH-FM	99.3	Douglas, Wyo.
KATI	1400	Casper, Wyo.
KATK	92.1	Carlsbad, N.M.
KATL	1340	Miles City, Mont.
KATN	13	Fairbanks, Alas.
KATO	1230	Safford, Ariz.
KATQ	1070	Plentywood, Mont.
KATQ-FM	100.1	Plentywood, Mont.
KATS	94.5	Yakima, Wash.
KATT	1140	Oklahoma City, Okla.
KATT-FM	100.5	Oklahoma City, Okla.
KATU	2	Portland, Ore.
KATV	7	Little Rock, Ark.
KATX	97.3	Plainview, Tex.
KATY	1340	San Luis Obispo, Calif.
KATZ	1600	St. Louis, Mo.
KAUB	105.5	Auburn, Neb.
KAUL	1380	North Little Rock, Ark.
KAUM	106.3	Colorado City, Tex.
KAUR	89.1	Sioux Falls, S.D.
KAUS	1480	Austin, Minn.
KAUS-FM	99.9	Austin, Minn.
KAUT	43	Oklahoma City, Okla.
KAUZ-TV	6	Wichita Falls, Tex.
KAVA	1450	Burney, Calif.
KAVE-TV	6	Carlsbad, N.M.
KAVI	1320	Rocky Ford, Colo.
KAVI-FM	95.9	Rocky Ford, Colo.
KAVL	610	Lancaster, Calif.
KAVO	107.1	Fallbrook, Calif.
KAVR	960	Apple Valley, Calif.
KAVT-FM	91.3	Austin, Minn.
KAVT-TV	15	Austin, Minn.
KAVU	25	Victoria, Tex.
KAVV	97.7	Benson, Ariz.
KAWC	1320	Yuma, Ariz.
KAWE	9	Bemidji, Minn.
KAWL	1370	York, Neb.
KAWL-FM	104.9	York, Neb.
KAWS	1240	Hemphill, Tex.
KAWW	1370	Heber Springs, Ark.
KAWW-FM	96.7	Heber Springs, Ark.
KAWY	94.5	Casper, Wyo.
KAXE	91.7	Grand Rapids, Minn.
KAYC	1450	Beaumont, Tex.
KAYD	97.5	Beaumont, Tex.
KAYE-FM	90.7	Tonkawa, Okla.
KAYI	106.9	Muskogee, Okla.
KAYK	1480	Pueblo, Colo.
KAYL	990	Storm Lake, Ia.
KAYL-FM	101.5	Storm Lake, Ia.
KAYN	98.3	Nogales, Ariz.
KAYO	1450	Aberdeen, Wash.
KAYQ	97.7	Warsaw, Mo.
KAYR	1060	Van Buren, Ark.
KAYS	1400	Hays, Kan.
KAYS-TV	7	Hays, Kan.
KAYT	970	Rupert, Id.
KAYU	28	Spokane, Wash.
KAYY	101.1	Fairbanks, Alas.
KAYZ	103.1	El Dorado, Ark.
KAZA	1290	Gilroy, Calif.
KAZI	88.7	Austin, Tex.
KAZM	780	Sedona, Ariz.
KAZU	90.3	Pacific Grove, Calif.
KAZY	106.7	Denver, Colo.
KAZZ	95.9	Sallisaw, Okla.
KBAA	106.3	Ortonville, Minn.
KBAB	1490	Indianola, Ia.
KBAD	740	Carlsbad, N.M.
KBAI	1150	Morro Bay, Calif.
KBAK-TV	29	Bakersfield, Calif.
KBAL	1410	San Saba, Tex.
KBAM	1270	Longview, Wash.
KBAN	1410	Bowie, Tex.
KBAR	1230	Burley, Id.
KBAS	1490	Bullhead City, Ariz.
KBAT	93.3	Midland, Tex.
KBAY	100.3	San Jose, Calif.
KBBA	690	Benton, Ark.
KBBB	1600	Borger, Tex.
KBBC	101.1	Lake Havasu City, Ariz.
KBBD	90.1	Beaver, Utah
KBBF	89.1	Santa Rosa, Calif.
KBBG	88.1	Waterloo, Ia.
KBBI	1250	Homer, Alas.
KBBJ	1300	Tulsa, Okla.
KBBK-FM	92.3	Boise, Id.
KBBL	1340	Lubbock, Tex.
KBBM-TV	36	Jefferson City, Mo.
KBBN-FM	98.3	Broken Bow, Neb.
KBBO	1390	Yakima, Wash.
KBBQ	1590	Ventura, Calif.
KBBR	1340	North Bend, Ore.
KBBS	1450	Buffalo, Wyo.
KBBV	1050	Big Bear Lake, Calif.
KBBW	1010	Waco, Tex.
KBBX	1600	Centerville, Utah
KBBY	95.1	Ventura, Calif.
KBBZ	98.5	Kalispell, Mont.
KBCB	99.1	Corpus Christi, Tex.
KBCC	1410	Cuba, Mo.
KBCE	102.3	Boyce, La.
KBCH	1400	Lincoln City, Ore
KBCI-TV	2	Boise, Id.
KBCL	1220	Shreveport, La.
KBCO	97.3	Boulder, Colo.
KBCQ	1020	Roswell, N.M.
KBCR	1230	Steamboat Springs, Colo.
KBCS	91.3	Bellevue, Wash.
KBCT	95.9	Fairfield, Ia.
KBCV	98.3	Bentonville, Ark.
KBDF	1280	Eugene, Ore.
KBDG	90.9	Turlock, Calif.
KBDI-TV	12	Broomfield, Colo.
KBDR	89.1	Merced, Calif.
KBDY	89.9	St. Louis, Mo.
KBEA	1480	Mission, Kan.
KBEC	1390	Waxahachee, Tex.
KBEE-FM	103.3	Modesto, Calif.
KBEK	107.3	Lexington, Mo.
KBEL	1240	Idabel, Okla.
KBEM-FM	88.5	Minneapolis, Minn.
KBEN	1450	Carrizo Springs, Tex.
KBEQ	104.3	Kansas City, Mo.
KBES	89.5	Ceres, Calif.
KBET	1340	Reno, Nev.
KBEW	1560	Blue Earth, Minn.
KBEZ	92.9	Tulsa, Okla.
KBFC	93.5	Forrest City, Ark.
KBFI	1450	Bonners Ferry, Id.
KBFL	90.3	Buffalo, Mo.
KBFM	104.1	Edinburg, Tex.
KBFS	1450	Belle Fourche, S.D.
KBFT	88.7	Browning, Mont.
KBFW	930	Ferndale, Wash.
KBGL	89.5	Pocatello, Id.
KBGL-TV	10	Pocatello, Id.
KBGN	1060	Caldwell, Id.
KBGT-TV	8	Albion, Neb.
KBGX	94.5	Alturas, Calif.
KBHB	810	Sturgis, S.D.
KBHC	1260	Nashville, Ark.
KBHE-TV	9	Rapid City, S.D.
KBHI-FM	89.9	Modesto, Calif.
KBHK-TV	44	San Francisco, Calif.
KBHP	101.1	Bemidji, Minn.
KBHS	590	Hot Springs, Ark.
KBHU-FM	89.1	Spearfish, S.D.
KBHV	106.3	Spanish Fork, Utah
KBIA	91.3	Columbia, Mo.
KBIB	1560	Monette, Ark.
KBIC	102.3	Alice, Tex.
KBIF	900	Fresno, Calif.
KBIG	104.3	Los Angeles, Calif
KBIL	92.9	San Angelo, Tex.
KBIM	910	Roswell, N.M.
KBIM-FM	94.9	Roswell, N.M.
KBIM-TV	10	Roswell, N.M.
KBIN	32	Council Bluffs, Ia.
KBIQ	105.3	Edmonds, Wash.
KBIU	103.7	Lake Charles, La.
KBIX	1490	Muskogee, Okla.
KBIZ	1240	Ottumwa, Ia.
KBJC	91.9	Great Bend, Kan.
KBJH	47	Tulsa, Okla.
KBJM	1400	Lemmon, S.D.
KBJR-TV	6	Superior, Wis.
KBJT	1570	Fordyce, Ark.
KBKB	1360	Ft. Madison, Ia.
KBKB-FM	101.7	Ft. Madison, Ia.
KBKG	93.5	Corning, Ark.
KBKN	92.9	Astoria, Ore.
KBKR	1490	Baker, Ore.
KBKR-FM	95.3	Baker, Ore.
KBLC	1270	Lakeport, Calif.
KBLC	840	Lakeport, Calif.
KBLE	1050	Seattle, Wash.
KBLF	1490	Red Bluff, Calif.
KBLI	690	Blackfoot, Id.
KBLI-FM	97.7	Blackfoot, Id.
KBLJ	92.1	La Junta, Colo.
KBLL	1240	Helena, Mont.
KBLL-FM	92.1	Helena, Mont.
KBLQ	1390	Logan, Utah
KBLQ-FM	92.9	Logan, Utah
KBLS	990	Santa Barbara, Calif.
KBLT	107.1	Baxter Springs, Kan.
KBLU	560	Yuma, Ariz.
KBLX	102.9	Berkeley, Calif.

KBMC	94.5	Eugene, Ore.
KBME	3	Bismarck, N.D.
KBME	3	Bismark, N.D.
KBME	3	Bismarck, N.D.
KBMG	92.5	Phillipsburg, Kan.
KBMI	97.7	Roma, Tex.
KBMN	1230	Bozeman, Mont.
KBMO	1290	Benson, Minn.
KBMO-FM	93.5	Benson, Minn.
KBMR	1130	Bismarck, N.D.
KBMT	12	Beaumont, Tex.
KBMV	1310	Birch Tree, Mo.
KBMW	1450	Breckenridge, Minn.
KBMY	1240	Billings, Mont.
KBND	1110	Bend, Ore.
KBNO	1220	Denver, Colo.
KBNR	88.3	Brownsville, Tex.
KBNY	96.9	Nampa, Id.
KBOA	830	Kennett, Mo.
KBOB	98.3	West Covina, Calif.
KBOE	740	Oskaloosa, Ia.
KBOE-FM	104.9	Oskaloosa, Ia.
KBOI	670	Boise, Id.
KBOI-FM	97.9	Boise, Id.
KBOK	1310	Malvern, Ark.
KBOL	1490	Boulder, Colo.
KBOM	1270	Bismarck, N.D.
KBON	103.9	Lake Arrowhead, Calif.
KBOO	90.7	Portland, Ore.
KBOP	1380	Pleasanton, Tex.
KBOP-FM	98.3	Pleasanton, Tex.
KBOQ	92.7	Marina, Calif.
KBOR	1600	Brownsville, Tex.
KBOS	94.9	Tulare, Calif.
KBOT	1350	Cabot, Ark.
KBOW	550	Butte, Mont.
KBOX	1150	North Little Rock, Ark.
KBOX	1480	Dallas, Tex.
KBOY-FM	95.3	Medford, Ore.
KBOZ	1090	Bozeman, Mont.
KBOZ-FM	93.7	Bozeman, Mont.
KBPI	105.9	Denver, Colo.
KBPK	90.1	Buena Park, Calif.
KBPS	1450	Portland, Ore.
KBPS-FM	89.9	Portland, Ore.
KBQC	93.5	Bettendorp, Ia.
KBQQ	99.9	Minot, N.D.
KBRA	97.9	Wichita, Kan.
KBRB	1400	Ainsworth, Neb.
KBRB-FM	92.7	Ainsworth, Neb.
KBRC	1430	Mt. Vernon, Wash.
KBRD	103.7	Tacoma, Wash.
KBRE	940	Cedar City, Utah
KBRE-FM	94.9	Cedar City, Utah
KBRF	1250	Fergus Falls, Minn.
KBRF-FM	103.3	Fergus Falls, Minn.
KBRG	104.9	Fremont, Calif.
KBRI	1570	Brinkley, Ark.
KBRI-FM	102.3	Brinkley, Ark.
KBRK	1430	Brookings, S.D.
KBRL	1300	Mc Cook, Neb.
KBRO	1490	Bremerton, Wash.
KBRQ	1280	Denver, Colo.
KBRQ-FM	105.1	Denver, Colo.
KBRS	1340	Springdale, Ark.
KBRT	740	Avalon, Calif.
KBRU	101.7	Ft. Morgan, Colo.
KBRV	790	Soda Springs, Id.
KBRW	680	Barrow, Alas.
KBRX	1350	O' Neill, Neb.
KBRX-FM	102.9	O' Neill, Neb.
KBRZ	1460	Freeport, Tex.
KBSB	89.7	Bemidji, Minn.
KBSC-TV	52	Corona, Calif.
KBSC-TV	42	Concord, Calif.
KBSF	1460	Springhill, La.
KBSH	88.9	Borrego Springs, Calif.
KBSI	23	Cape Girardeau, Mo.
KBST	1490	Big Spring, Tex.
KBSU	91.3	Boise, Id.
KBTA	1340	Batesville, Ark.
KBTC	1250	Houston, Mo.
KBTM	1230	Jonesboro, Ark.
KBTM-FM	101.9	Jonesboro, Ark.
KBTN	1420	Neosho, Mo.
KBTO	101.9	Bottineau, N.D.
KBTV	9	Denver, Colo.
KBTX-TV	3	Bryan, Tex.
KBUC	1310	San Antonio, Tex.
KBUC-FM	107.5	San Antonio, Tex.
KBUD	1410	Athens, Tex.
KBUF	1050	Garden City, Kan.
KBUF-FM	97.3	Garden City, Kan.
KBUG	1320	Salt Lake City, Utah
KBUH	800	Brigham City, Utah
KBUK	1360	Baytown, Tex.
KBUL	107.1	Brush, Colo.
KBUN	1450	Bemidji, Minn.
KBUR	1490	Burlington, Ia.
KBUS	1590	Mexia, Tex.
KBUY-FM	94.1	Amarillo, Tex.
KBUZ	106.5	Arkansas City, Kan.
KBVL	94.7	Boulder, Colo.
KBVO	42	Austin, Tex.
KBVR	88.7	Corvallis, Ore.
KBWC	91.1	Marshall, Tex.
KBWD	1380	Brownwood, Tex.
KBWH	106.3	Blair, Neb.
KBXL	94.1	Caldwell, Id.
KBXM	1540	Kennett, Mo.
KBXN	1470	Tremonton, Utah
KBXN-FM	104.9	Tremont, Utah
KBXS	92.7	Ely, Nev.
KBYE	890	Oklahoma City, Okla.
KBYG	1400	Big Spring, Tex.
KBYP	1580	Shamrock, Tex.
KBYQ	107.1	Sweet Home, Ore.
KBYR	700	Anchorage, Alas.
KBYU-FM	88.9	Provo, Utah
KBYU-TV	11	Provo, Utah
KBZB	1230	Bisbee, Ariz.
KBZT	94.9	San Diego, Calif.
KBZY	1490	Salem, Ore.
KBZZ	1400	La Junta, Colo.
KCAA	11	Yuma, Ariz.
KCAB	980	Dardanelle, Ark.
KCAJ	95.9	El Dorado, Ark.
KCAL	1410	Redlands, Calif.
KCAL-FM	96.7	Redlands, Calif.
KCAM	790	Glennallen, Alas.
KCAN	1460	El Reno, Okla.
KCAP	1340	Helena, Mont.
KCAP-FM	103.1	Helena, Mont.
KCAQ	104.7	Oxnard, Calif.
KCAR	1350	Clarksville, Tex.
KCAS	1050	Slaton, Tex.
KCAT	1340	Pine Bluff, Ark.
KCAU-TV	9	Sioux City, Ia.
KCAW	104.7	Sitka, Alas.
KCAZ	106.3	Walnut Ridge, Ark.
KCBA	35	Salinas, Calif.
KCBD-TV	11	Lubbock, Tex.
KCBF	820	Fairbanks, Alas.
KCBF	900	Fairbanks, Alas.
KCBI	89.3	Dallas, Tex.
KCBJ-TV	17	Columbia, Mo.
KCBN	1230	Reno, Nev.
KCBQ	1170	San Diego, Calif.
KCBQ-FM	105.3	San Diego, Calif.
KCBR	17	Des Moines, Ia.
KCBS	740	San Francisco, Calif.
KCBW	92.1	Sedalia, Mo.
KCBX	90.1	San Luis Obispo, Calif.
KCBY	11	Coos Bay, Ore.
KCCA	58	Sierra Vista, Ariz.
KCCB	1260	Corning, Ark.
KCCC	930	Carlsbad, N.M.
KCCI-TV	8	Des Moines, Ia.
KCCK	100.1	Marshall, Minn.
KCCK-FM	88.3	Cedar Rapids, Ia.
KCCL	1460	Paris, Ark.
KCCM-FM	91.1	Moorhead, Minn.
KCCN	1420	Honolulu, Haw.
KCCO	1050	Lawton, Okla.
KCCQ	107.1	Ames, Ia.
KCCR	1240	Pierre, S.D.
KCCS	1220	Salem, Ore.
KCCT	1150	Corpus Christi, Tex.
KCCU	98.3	Columbus, Kan.
KCCV	1510	Independence, Mo.
KCCY	97.9	Pueblo, Colo.
KCCY	96.9	Pueblo, Colo.
KCDA	103.1	Coeur D' Alene, Id.
KCDC	90.7	Longmont, Colo.
KCDR	1450	Cedar Rapids, Ia.
KCDS	89.9	Angwin, Calif.
KCEA	89.1	Atherton, Calif.
KCED	91.3	Centralia, Wash.
KCEE	790	Tucson, Ariz.
KCEL	107.1	Toledo, Ore.
KCEN-TV	6	Temple, Tex.
KCEP	88.1	Las Vegas, Nev.
KCES	102.3	Eufaula, Okla.
KCET	28	Los Angeles, Calif.
KCEY	1390	Turlock, Calif.
KCFI	1250	Cedar Falls, Ia.
KCFO	98.5	Tulsa, Okla.
KCFR	90.1	Denver, Colo.
KCFS	90.1	Sioux Falls, S.D.
KCFV	89.5	Ferguson, Mo.
KCFW-TV	9	Kalispell, Mont.
KCFX	100.7	Harrisonville, Mo.
KCGB	105.5	Hood River, Ore.
KCGL	105.5	Centerville, Utah
KCGM	95.7	Scobey, Mont.
KCGN	101.5	Ortonville, Minn.
KCGS	1600	Marshall, Ark.
KCHA	1580	Charles City, Ia.
KCHA-FM	95.9	Charles City, Ia.
KCHC	91.7	Central Point, Ore.
KCHE	1440	Cherokee, Ia.
KCHE-FM	102.3	Cherokee, Ia.
KCHI	1010	Chillicothe, Mo.
KCHI-FM	103.9	Chillicothe, Mo.
KCHJ	1010	Delano, Calif.
KCHK	1350	New Prague, Minn.
KCHO	91.1	Chico, Calif.
KCHR	1350	Charleston, Mo.
KCHS	1400	Truth Or Consequences, N.M.
KCHV	93.7	Coachella, Calif.
KCIC	88.5	Grand Junction, Colo.
KCID	1490	Caldwell, Id.
KCIE	99.3	Fairbury, Neb.
KCII	1380	Washington, Ia.
KCII-FM	95.3	Washington, Ia.
KCIJ	980	Shreveport, La.
KCIK	14	El Paso, Tex.
KCIL	107.1	Houma, La.
KCIM	1380	Carroll, Ia.
KCIN	1590	Victorville, Calif.
KCIR	90.7	Twin Falls, Id.
KCIV	104.5	The Dalles, Ore.
KCIZ	104.9	Springdale, Ark.
KCJB	910	Minot, N.D.
KCJB-FM	97.1	Minot, N.D.
KCJF	104.3	Kellogg, Id.
KCJH	90.1	Stockton, Calif.
KCJJ	1560	Iowa City, Ia.
KCKA	15	Centralia, Wash.
KCKC	1350	San Bernardino, Calif.
KCKL	95.9	Malakoff, Tex.
KCKO	1380	Millwood, Wash.

KCKR	93.5	Crockett, Tex.
KCKS	95.3	Concordia, Kan.
KCKT	2	Great Bend, Kan.
KCKU	14	Tyler, Tex.
KCKW	1480	Jena, La.
KCKY	1150	Coolidge, Ariz.
KCLA	1400	Pine Bluff, Ark.
KCLB	91.9	Santa Rosa, Calif.
KCLC	89.1	St. Charles, Mo.
KCLD-FM	104.7	St. Cloud, Minn.
KCLE	1120	Cleburne, Tex.
KCLG	1210	Washington, Utah
KCLI	95.3	Clinton, Okla.
KCLK	1430	Clarkston, Wash.
KCLK-FM	94.1	Clarkston, Wash.
KCLM	1330	Redding, Calif.
KCLO	1410	Leavenworth, Kan.
KCLR	1530	Ralls, Tex.
KCLS	600	Flagstaff, Ariz.
KCLU	1590	Rolla, Mo.
KCLU-FM	94.3	Rolla, Mo.
KCLV	1240	Clovis, N.M.
KCLV-FM	99.1	Clovis, N.M.
KCLW	900	Hamilton, Tex.
KCLX	1450	Colfax, Wash.
KCLY	100.9	Clay Center, Kan.
KCMA	106.1	Owasso, Okla.
KCMC	740	Texarkana, Tex.
KCME	88.1	Manitou Springs, Colo.
KCMG	100.5	Anchorage, Alas.
KCMI	103.9	Terrytown, Neb.
KCMJ	1140	Palm Springs, Calif.
KCMJ	1010	Palm Springs, Calif.
KCMN	1530	Colorado Springs, Colo.
KCMO	810	Kansas City, Mo.
KCMO-FM	94.9	Kansas City, Mo.
KCMP	1010	Brush, Colo.
KCMQ	96.7	Columbia, Mo.
KCMR	98.3	Mason City, Ia.
KCMT	7	Alexandria, Minn.
KCMT-FM	100.7	Alexandria, Minn.
KCMU	90.5	Seattle, Wash.
KCMW-FM	90.9	Warrensburg, Mo.
KCMX	580	Ashland, Ore.
KCMX-FM	101.7	Ashland, Ore.
KCNB	105.7	Waterloo, Ia.
KCNC-TV	4	Denver, Colo.
KCND	90.5	Bismarck, N.D.
KCNI	1280	Broken Bow, Neb.
KCNO	570	Alturas, Calif.
KCNR	1410	Portland, Ore.
KCNR-FM	97.1	Portland, Ore.
KCNT	88.1	Hastings, Neb.
KCNW	1380	Fairway, Kan.
KCNY	1470	San Marcos, Tex.
KCOB	1280	Newton, Ia.
KCOE-FM	90.3	Cedar Rapids, Ia.
KCOG	1400	Centerville, Ia.
KCOH	1430	Houston, Tex.
KCOK	1270	Tulare, Calif.
KCOL	1410	Ft. Collins, Colo.
KCOL-FM	107.9	Ft. Collins, Colo.
KCOM	1550	Comanche, Tex.
KCON	1230	Conway, Ark.
KCOP	13	Los Angeles, Calif.
KCOR	1350	San Antonio, Tex.
KCOS	13	El Paso, Tex.
KCOT	1110	Marana, Ariz.
KCOU	88.1	Columbia, Mo.
KCOW	1400	Alliance, Neb.
KCOY-TV	12	Santa Maria, Calif.
KCOZ	100.1	Shreveport, La.
KCPB	91.1	Thousand Oaks, Calif.
KCPI-FM	95.3	Albert Lea, Minn.
KCPK	107.5	Clovis, N.M.
KCPM	97.1	Florissant, Mo.
KCPM	24	Chico, Calif.
KCPQ	13	Tacoma, Wash.
KCPR	91.3	San Luis Obispo, Calif.
KCPS	1150	Burlington, Ia.
KCPT	19	Kansas City, Mo.
KCPX-FM	98.7	Salt Lake City, Utah
KCRA-TV	3	Sacramento, Calif.
KCRB-FM	88.5	Bemidji, Minn.
KCRC	1390	Enid, Okla.
KCRE	1310	Crescent City, Calif.
KCRE-FM	94.3	Crescent City, Calif.
KCRF	96.7	Lincoln City, Ore.
KCRG	1600	Cedar Rapids, Ia.
KCRG-TV	9	Cedar Rapids, Ia.
KCRH	89.9	Hayward, Calif.
KCRI	1600	West Helena, Ark.
KCRI-FM	103.1	Helena, Ark.
KCRK-FM	92.1	Colville, Wash.
KCRL-TV	4	Reno, Nev.
KCRM	103.1	Cameron, Tex.
KCRO	660	Omaha, Neb.
KCRP	105.5	Rosamond, Calif.
KCRS	550	Midland, Tex.
KCRT	1240	Trinidad, Colo.
KCRT-FM	92.7	Trinidad, Colo.
KCRV	1370	Caruthersville, Mo.
KCRV-FM	103.1	Caruthersville, Mo.
KCRW	89.9	Santa Monica, Calif.
KCRX	1430	Roswell, N.M.
KCSB-FM	91.9	Santa Barbara, Calif.
KCSC	90.1	Edmond, Okla.
KCSJ	590	Pueblo, Colo.
KCSM	91.1	San Mateo, Calif.
KCSM-TV	60	San Mateo, Calif.
KCSN	88.5	Northridge, Calif.
KCSO	19	Modesto, Calif.
KCSR	610	Chadron, Neb.
KCSS	91.9	Turlock, Calif.
KCST-TV	39	San Diego, Calif.
KCSU-FM	90.9	Ft. Collins, Colo.
KCSU-FM	90.5	Ft. Collins, Colo.
KCTA	1030	Corpus Christi, Tex.
KCTB-FM	102.7	Cut Bank, Mont.
KCTC	96.1	Sacramento, Calif.
KCTE	1140	Southwest City, Mo.
KCTI	1450	Gonzales, Tex.
KCTM	103.1	Rio Grande City, Tex.
KCTN	100.1	Garnavillo, Ia.
KCTO	1540	Columbia, La.
KCTO-FM	103.1	Columbia, La.
KCTS-TV	9	Seattle, Wash.
KCTT	1530	Yellville, Ark.
KCTV	5	Kansas City, Mo.
KCTX	1510	Childress, Tex.
KCTY	980	Salinas, Calif.
KCTZ	7	Bozeman, Mont.
KCUB	1290	Tucson, Ariz.
KCUE	1250	Red Wing, Minn.
KCUI	89.1	Pella, Ia.
KCUL	1410	Marshall, Tex.
KCUM-FM	91.5	Crookston, Minn.
KCUR-FM	89.3	Kansas City, Mo.
KCUZ	1490	Clifton, Ariz.
KCVL	1270	Colville, Wash.
KCVR	1570	Lodi, Calif.
KCVT	30	Shawnee, Okla.
KCWC	88.1	Riverton, Wyo.
KCWC-TV	4	Lander, Wyo.
KCWD	96.7	Harrison, Ark.
KCWM	1340	Victoria, Tex.
KCWM	95.1	Victoria, Tex.
KCWS	3	Glenwood Springs, Colo.
KCWW	104.9	Beeville, Tex.
KCWY-TV	14	Casper, Wyo.
KCYL	1450	Lampasas, Tex.
KCYN	103.9	Pocahontas, Ark.
KCYX	1260	Mc Minnville, Ore.
KDAA	92.1	Woodward, Okla.
KDAB	101.1	Ogden, Utah
KDAC	1230	Ft. Bragg, Calif.
KDAK	1600	Carrington, N.D.
KDAK-FM	97.7	Carrington, N.D.
KDAL	610	Duluth, Minn.
KDAN	1180	Williams, Ariz.
KDAO	1190	Marshalltown, Ia.
KDAP	1450	Douglas, Ariz.
KDAQ	89.9	Shreveport, La.
KDAR	98.3	Oxnard, Calif.
KDAY	1580	Santa Monica, Calif.
KDAZ	730	Albuquerque, N.M.
KDB	1490	Santa Barbara, Calif.
KDB-FM	93.7	Santa Barbara, Calif.
KDBC-TV	4	El Paso, Tex.
KDBH	97.7	Natchitoches, La.
KDBL	105.3	Rifle, Colo.
KDBM	1490	Dillon, Mont.
KDBQ	96.9	Pittsburg, Kan.
KDBS	1410	Alexandria, La.
KDBX	99.3	Boonville, Mo.
KDCD-TV	18	Midland, Tex.
KDCE	970	Espanola, N.M.
KDCI	92.1	Devine, Tex.
KDCK	95.5	Dodge City, Kan.
KDCQ	45	Sikeston, Mo.
KDCR	88.5	Sioux Center, Ia.
KDDA	1560	Dumas, Ark.
KDDA-FM	107.1	Dumas, Ark.
KDDB	92.5	Paso Robles, Calif.
KDDD	800	Dumas, Tex.
KDDE	68	Los Angeles, Calif.
KDDR	1220	Oakes, N.D.
KDEA	99.1	New Iberia, La.
KDEC	1240	Decorah, Ia.
KDEC	1200	Decorah, Ia.
KDEF	1150	Albuquerque, N.M.
KDEI	88.3	Alexandria, La.
KDEL-FM	100.9	Arkadelphia, Ark.
KDEM	94.3	Deming, N.M.
KDEN	1340	Denver, Colo.
KDEO	940	Waipahu, Haw.
KDES	920	Palm Springs, Calif.
KDES-FM	104.7	Palm Springs, Calif.
KDET	930	Center, Tex.
KDEW	1470	De Witt, Ark.
KDEW-FM	96.7	De Witt, Ark.
KDEX	1590	Dexter, Mo.
KDEX-FM	102.3	Dexter, Mo.
KDEY	99.3	Lufkin, Tex.
KDFC	102.1	San Francisco, Calif.
KDFN	1500	Doniphan, Mo.
KDFW-TV	4	Dallas, Tex.
KDGO	1240	Durango, Colo.
KDHI	1250	Twentynine Palms, Calif.
KDHL	920	Faribault, Minn.
KDHL-FM	95.9	Faribault, Minn.
KDHN	1470	Dimmitt, Tex.
KDHS	90.5	Modesto, Calif.
KDIA	1310	Oakland, Calif.
KDIC	88.5	Grinnell, Ia.
KDIG	1240	San Bernardino, Calif.
KDIN-TV	11	Des Moines, Ia.
KDIO	1350	Ortonville, Minn.
KDIX	1230	Dickinson, N.D.
KDJI	1270	Holbrook, Ariz.
KDJQ	1510	Mesa, Ariz.
KDJS	1590	Willmar, Minn.
KDJW	1010	Amarillo, Tex.
KDKA	1020	Pittsburgh, Pa.

Call	Freq.	Location
KDKA-TV	2	Pittsburgh, Pa.
KDKB	93.3	Mesa, Ariz.
KDKD	1280	Clinton, Mo.
KDKD-FM	95.3	Clinton, Mo.
KDKO	1510	Littleton, Colo.
KDKQ	104.3	Borger, Tex.
KDKS	92.1	Benton, La.
KDLA	1010	De Ridder, La.
KDLF	1150	Port Neches, Tex.
KDLG	670	Dillingham, Alas.
KDLH-TV	3	Duluth, Minn.
KDLI	17	Canton, O.
KDLK	1230	Del Rio, Tex.
KDLM	1340	Detroit Lakes, Minn.
KDLN	98.3	Dillon, Mont.
KDLO-FM	96.9	Watertown, S.D.
KDLO-TV	3	Watertown, S.D.
KDLP	1170	Bayou Vista, La.
KDLR	1240	Devils Lake, N.D.
KDLS	1310	Perry, Ia.
KDLS-FM	104.9	Perry, Ia.
KDLY	97.5	Lander, Wyo.
KDMA	1460	Montevideo, Minn.
KDMI	97.3	Des Moines, Ia.
KDMO	1490	Carthage, Mo.
KDMS	1290	El Dorado, Ark.
KDNA	91.9	Yakima, Wash.
KDNK	90.5	Carbondale, Colo.
KDNL-TV	30	St. Louis, Mo.
KDNO	98.5	Delano, Calif.
KDNT	1440	Denton, Tex.
KDNW	90.5	Duluth, Minn.
KDOC	56	Anaheim, Calif.
KDOG	19	Nacogdoches, Tex.
KDOK	1490	Tyler, Tex.
KDOL	1340	Mojave, Calif.
KDOL-FM	97.7	Mojave, Calif.
KDOM	1580	Windom, Minn.
KDOM-FM	94.3	Windom, Minn.
KDON	1460	Salinas, Calif.
KDON-FM	102.5	Salinas, Calif.
KDOR	17	Bartlesville, Okla.
KDOT	960	Provo, Utah
KDOV	1350	Ashland, Ore.
KDOV	1230	Ashland, Ore.
KDPS	88.1	Des Moines, Ia.
KDQN	1390	De Queen, Ark.
KDQN-FM	92.7	De Queen, Ark.
KDRG	1400	Deer Lodge, Mont.
KDRK	93.7	Spokane, Wash.
KDRO	1490	Sedalia, Mo.
KDRS	1490	Paragould, Ark.
KDRV	12	Medford, Ore.
KDRW	1450	Silverton, Colo.
KDRW	103.9	Silverton, Colo.
KDRY	1110	Alamo Heights, Tex.
KDSD-TV	16	Aberdeen, S.D.
KDSE	9	Dickinson, N.D.
KDSI	92.1	Alice, Tex.
KDSJ	980	Deadwood, S.D.
KDSN	1530	Denison, Ia.
KDSN-FM	107.1	Denison, Ia.
KDSQ	101.7	Denison, Tex.
KDSU	91.9	Fargo, N.D.
KDSX	950	Denison, Tex.
KDTA	1400	Delta, Colo.
KDTA-FM	95.3	Delta, Colo.
KDTH	1370	Dubuque, Ia.
KDTU	18	Tucson, Ariz.
KDTV	14	San Francisco, Calif.
KDUB-TV	40	Dubuque, Ia.
KDUH-TV	4	Scottsbluff, Neb.
KDUK	104.7	Florence, Ore.
KDUN	1470	Reedsport, Ore.
KDUO	97.5	Riverside, Calif.
KDUR	91.9	Durango, Colo.
KDUX-FM	104.7	Aberdeen, Wash.
KDUZ	1260	Hutchinson, Minn.
KDUZ-FM	107.1	Hutchinson, Minn.
KDVC-FM	91.1	Blair, Neb.
KDVC-FM	91.1	Blair, Neb.
KDVL	102.5	Devils Lake, N.D.
KDVR	31	Denver, Colo.
KDVS	90.3	Davis, Calif.
KDVV	100.3	Topeka, Kan.
KDWA	1460	Hastings, Minn.
KDWB	630	St. Paul, Minn.
KDWB-FM	101.3	Richfield, Minn.
KDWD	93.5	Burlington, Ia.
KDWN	720	Las Vegas, Nev.
KDWT	1400	Stamford, Tex.
KDXE	95.9	Sulphur Springs, Tex.
KDXI	1360	Mansfield, La.
KDXL	91.7	St. Louis Park, Minn.
KDXT	93.3	Missoula, Mont.
KDXU	1450	St. George, Utah
KDXY	104.9	Paragould, Ark.
KDYL	1280	Salt Lake City, Utah
KDZA	1230	Pueblo, Colo.
KEAN	1280	Abilene, Tex.
KEAN-FM	105.1	Abilene, Tex.
KEAP	980	Fresno, Calif.
KEAR	106.9	San Francisco, Calif.
KEAS	1590	Eastland, Tex.
KEAZ	101.7	De Ridder, La.
KEBC	94.7	Oklahoma City, Okla.
KEBE	1400	Jacksonville, Tex.
KEBR	100.5	Sacramento, Calif.
KECG	88.1	El Cerrito, Calif.
KECH	22	Salem, Ore.
KECK	1530	Lincoln, Neb.
KECO	96.5	Elk City, Okla.
KECR	93.3	El Cajon, Calif.
KECY	9	El Centro, Calif.
KEDA	1540	San Antonio, Tex.
KEDD	1550	Dodge City, Kan.
KEDO	1400	Longview, Wash.
KEDP	91.1	Las Vegas, N.M.
KEDT	16	Corpus Christi, Tex.
KEDY	95.3	Mt. Shasta, Calif.
KEED	1450	Eugene, Ore.
KEED	95.3	Paris, Ark.
KEEE	1230	Nacogdoches, Tex.
KEEL	710	Shreveport, La.
KEEN	1370	San Jose, Calif.
KEEP	1450	Twin Falls, Id.
KEER	97.1	Las Vegas, Nev.
KEES	1430	Gladewater, Tex.
KEET	13	Eureka, Calif.
KEEY-FM	102.1	St. Paul, Minn.
KEEZ-FM	99.1	Mankato, Minn.
KEFM	96.1	Omaha, Neb.
KEFR	89.9	Legrande, Calif.
KEGG	1560	Daingerfield, Tex.
KEGL	97.1	Ft. Worth, Tex.
KEHG	1480	Fosston, Minn.
KEHG-FM	107.1	Fosston, Minn.
KEIN	1310	Great Falls, Mont.
KEJA	89.3	Garden City, S.D.
KEJO	101.5	Corvallis, Ore.
KEKA	101.5	Eureka, Calif.
KEKA	790	Eureka, Calif.
KEKB	99.9	Fruita, Colo.
KEKR	62	Kansas City, Mo.
KELA	1470	Chehalis, Wash.
KELC	1530	England, Ark.
KELD	1400	El Dorado, Ark.
KELE	100.1	Aurora, Mo.
KELG	1440	Elgin, Tex.
KELI	1430	Tulsa, Okla.
KELK	1240	Elko, Nev.
KELN	97.1	North Platte, Neb.
KELO	1320	Sioux Falls, S.D.
KELO-FM	92.5	Sioux Falls, S.D.
KELO-TV	11	Sioux Falls, S.D.
KELP	1590	El Paso, Tex.
KELS	92.1	Ardmore, Okla.
KELT	94.5	Harlingen, Tex.
KELY	1230	Ely, Nev.
KEMB	98.3	Emmetsburg, Ia.
KEMC	91.7	Billings, Mont.
KEMM	92.1	Commerce, Tex.
KEMR	88.3	Loma Linda, Calif.
KEMV	6	Mountain View, Ark.
KENA	1450	Mena, Ark.
KENB-FM	95.9	Worland, Wyo.
KEND	1590	Lubbock, Tex.
KENE	1490	Toppenish, Wash.
KENE-FM	92.7	Toppenish, Wash.
KENI	550	Anchorage, Alas.
KENM	1450	Portales, N.M.
KENN	1390	Farmington, N.M.
KENO	1460	Las Vegas, Nev.
KENS-TV	5	San Antonio, Tex.
KENU	1330	Enumclaw, Wash.
KENW	3	Portales, N.M.
KENW-FM	89.5	Portales, N.M.
KENZ	1240	Sacramento, Calif.
KEOK	101.7	Tahlequah, Okla.
KEOL	91.7	La Grande, Ore.
KEOR	1110	Atoka, Okla.
KEOR-FM	103.1	Atoka, Okla.
KEPC	90.5	Colorado Springs, Colo.
KEPO	92.1	Eagle Point, Ore.
KEPR-TV	19	Pasco, Wash.
KEPS	1270	Eagle Pass, Tex.
KEQO	20	Enid, Okla.
KERA-FM	90.1	Dallas, Tex.
KERA-TV	13	Dallas, Tex.
KERB	600	Kermit, Tex.
KERG	100.1	Garberville, Calif.
KERM	98.3	Torrington, Wyo.
KERN	1410	Bakersfield, Calif.
KERO-TV	23	Bakersfield, Calif.
KERR	1070	Polson, Mont.
KERR	750	Polson, Mont.
KERU	88.5	Blythe, Calif.
KERV	1230	Kerrville, Tex.
KESD	88.3	Brookings, S.D.
KESD-TV	8	Brookings, S.D.
KESI	106.3	Terrell Hills, Tex.
KESM	1580	El Dorado Springs, Mo.
KESM-FM	105.5	El Dorado Springs, Mo.
KESQ	42	Palm Springs, Calif.
KESR	600	Independence, Calif.
KESS	94.1	Ft. Worth, Tex.
KEST	1450	San Francisco, Calif.
KESY-FM	104.5	Omaha, Neb.
KETA	13	Oklahoma City, Okla.
KETC	9	St. Louis, Mo.
KETG	9	Arkadelphia, Ark.
KETH	1290	Ketchikan, Alas.
KETR	88.9	Commerce, Tex.
KETS	2	Little Rock, Ark.
KETV	7	Omaha, Neb.
KETX	1440	Livingston, Tex.
KETX-FM	92.1	Livingston, Tex.
KEUN	1490	Eunice, La.
KEVA	1240	Evanston, Wyo.
KEVN-TV	7	Rapid City, S.D.
KEVR	102.3	Espanola, N.M.
KEWB	94.3	Anderson, Calif.
KEWC-FM	89.9	Cheney, Wash.
KEWE	97.7	Oroville, Calif.
KEWI	1550	Cape Girardeau, Mo.
KEWQ	930	Paradise, Calif.
KEWS	1600	Cuero, Tex.
KEWT	105.1	Sacramento, Calif.
KEX	1190	Portland, Ore.

KEXI	93.3	Walla Walla, Wash.
KEXL	106.7	Norfolk, Neb.
KEXO	1230	Grand Junction, Colo.
KEXS	1090	Excelsior Springs, Mo.
KEXX-FM	93.9	Corpus Christi, Tex.
KEYA	88.5	Belcourt, N.D.
KEYC-TV	12	Mankato, Minn.
KEYD	97.7	Durant, Okla.
KEYE	1400	Perryton, Tex.
KEYE-FM	95.9	Perryton, Tex.
KEYF	98.5	Grandcoulee, Wash.
KEYG	1490	Grand Coulee, Wash.
KEYH	850	Houston, Tex.
KEYI	103.5	San Marcos, Tex.
KEYL	1510	Iguala, Gro.
KEYL	1400	Long Prairie, Minn.
KEYN-FM	103.7	Wichita, Kan.
KEYR	690	Terrytown, Neb.
KEYS	1440	Corpus Christi, Tex.
KEYT	3	Santa Barbara, Calif.
KEYY	1450	Provo, Utah
KEYZ	1360	Williston, N.D.
KEZA	107.9	Fayetteville, Ark.
KEZB	93.9	El Paso, Tex.
KEZC	92.3	Glendale, Ariz.
KEZE-FM	105.7	Spokane, Wash.
KEZG	92.1	Green Valley, Ariz.
KEZH	93.5	Hastings, Neb.
KEZH	101.5	Hastings, Neb.
KEZI-TV	9	Eugene, Ore.
KEZJ	95.7	Twin Falls, Id.
KEZK	102.5	St. Louis, Mo.
KEZL	1320	Oceanside, Calif.
KEZL-FM	102.1	Oceanside, Calif.
KEZM	1310	Sulphur, La.
KEZN	103.1	Palm Desert, Calif.
KEZO	92.3	Omaha, Neb.
KEZQ	100.3	Jacksonville, Ark.
KEZR	106.5	San Jose, Calif.
KEZS-FM	102.9	Cape Girardeau, Mo.
KEZU	94.5	Scott City, Kan.
KEZV	101.1	Spearfish, S.D.
KEZW	1430	Aurora, Colo.
KEZX	98.9	Seattle, Wash.
KEZY	95.9	Anaheim, Calif.
KEZZ	94.3	Aitkin, Minn.
KFAB	1110	Omaha, Neb.
KFAC	1330	Los Angeles, Calif.
KFAC-FM	92.3	Los Angeles, Calif.
KFAE	89.1	Richland, Wash.
KFAI	90.3	Minneapolis, Minn.
KFAL	900	Fulton, Mo.
KFAM	680	North Salt Lake City, Utah
KFAM	680	Bountiful, Utah
KFAN	101.1	Fredericksburg, Tex.
KFAR	660	Fairbanks, Alas.
KFAX	1100	San Francisco, Calif.
KFAY	1250	Fayetteville, Ark.
KFBA	900	Floydada, Tex.
KFBB-TV	5	Great Falls, Mont.
KFBC	1240	Cheyenne, Wyo.
KFBD-FM	97.7	Waynesville, Mo.
KFBK	1530	Sacramento, Calif.
KFBQ	97.9	Cheyenne, Wyo.
KFBR	1340	Nogales, Ariz.
KFCF	88.1	Fresno, Calif.
KFCM	100.9	Cherokee Village, Ark.
KFDA-TV	10	Amarillo, Tex.
KFDF	1580	Van Buren, Ark.
KFDI	1070	Wichita, Kan.
KFDI-FM	101.3	Wichita, Kan.
KFDM-TV	6	Beaumont, Tex.
KFDX-TV	3	Wichita Falls, Tex.
KFEL	970	Pueblo, Colo.
KFEQ	680	St. Joseph, Mo.
KFFA	1360	Helena, Ark.
KFFB	106.3	Fairfield Bay, Ark.
KFFM	107.3	Yakima, Wash.
KFFR	95.9	Hooks, Tex.
KFGO	790	Fargo, N.D.
KFGQ	1260	Boone, Ia.
KFGQ-FM	99.3	Boone, Ia.
KFH	1330	Wichita, Kan.
KFHM	1150	San Antonio, Tex.
KFI	640	Los Angeles, Calif.
KFIA	710	Carmichael, Calif.
KFIG	101.1	Fresno, Calif.
KFIL	1060	Preston, Minn.
KFIL-FM	103.1	Preston, Minn.
KFIM	92.3	El Paso, Tex.
KFIN	107.9	Jonesboro, Ark.
KFIO	104.9	Ridgecrest, Calif.
KFIR	1370	Sweet Home, Ore.
KFIS	100.1	Soda Springs, Id.
KFIV	1360	Modesto, Calif.
KFIV-FM	102.3	Modesto, Calif.
KFIX	92.7	Laredo, Tex.
KFIZ	1450	Fond Du Lac, Wis.
KFJB	1230	Marshalltown, Ia.
KFJB-FM	101.1	Marshalltown, Ia.
KFJC	89.7	Los Altos, Calif.
KFJM	1370	Grand Forks, N.D.
KFJM-FM	89.3	Grand Forks, N.D.
KFKA	1310	Greeley, Colo.
KFKF	1340	Kansas City, Kan.
KFKF-FM	94.1	Kansas City, Kan.
KFKU	1250	Lawrence, Kan.
KFLA	1310	Scott City, Kan.
KFLG	930	Flagstaff, Ariz.
KFLJ	1380	Walsenburg, Colo.
KFLN	960	Baker, Mont.
KFLN-FM	100.9	Baker, Mont.
KFLO	1300	Shreveport, La.
KFLQ	91.5	Albuquerque, N.M.
KFLR	1230	Phoenix, Ariz.
KFLS	1450	Klamath Falls, Ore.
KFLT	1450	Tucson, Ariz.
KFLV	91.9	Corpus Christi, Tex.
KFLY	1240	Corvallis, Ore.
KFLZ	107.1	Bishop, Tex.
KFMA	102.9	Jerome, Id.
KFMB	760	San Diego, Calif.
KFMB-FM	100.7	San Diego, Calif.
KFMB-TV	8	San Diego, Calif.
KFMC	106.5	Fairmont, Minn.
KFMD	92.9	Dubuque, Ia.
KFME	13	Fargo, N.D.
KFMF	93.7	Chico, Calif.
KFMG	107.9	Albuquerque, N.M.
KFMH	99.7	Muscatine, Ia.
KFMI	96.3	Eureka, Calif.
KFMJ	96.9	Grants Pass, Ore.
KFMK	97.9	Houston, Tex.
KFML	99.3	White House, Tex.
KFMM	99.1	Thatcher, Ariz.
KFMN	1560	Abilene, Tex.
KFMN-FM	107.9	Abilene, Tex.
KFMO	1240	Flat River, Mo.
KFMQ	101.9	Lincoln, Neb.
KFMR	100.1	Stockton, Calif.
KFMS	101.9	Las Vegas, Nev.
KFMT	103.5	Pendleton, Ore.
KFMU	103.9	Oak Creek, Colo.
KFMW	107.9	Waterloo, Ia.
KFMX	94.5	Lubbock, Tex.
KFMY	96.1	Provo, Utah
KFMZ	98.3	Columbia, Mo.
KFNF	101.1	Oberlin, Kan.
KFNV	1600	Ferriday, La.
KFNV-FM	107.1	Ferriday, La.
KFNW	1200	Fargo, N.D.
KFNW-FM	97.9	Fargo, N.D.
KFOG	104.5	San Francisco, Calif.
KFOR	1240	Lincoln, Neb.
KFOX	93.5	Redondo Beach, Calif.
KFPS	1440	Salem, Mo.
KFPW	1230	Ft. Smith, Ark.
KFPW-FM	100.9	Ft. Smith, Ark.
KFQD	750	Anchorage, Alas.
KFQX	104.9	Llano, Tex.
KFRA	1390	Franklin, La.
KFRA-FM	105.5	Franklin, La.
KFRC	610	San Francisco, Calif.
KFRD	980	Rosenberg, Tex.
KFRD-FM	104.9	Rosenberg, Tex.
KFRE	940	Fresno, Calif.
KFRM	550	Salina, Kan.
KFRN	1280	Long Beach, Calif.
KFRO	1370	Longview, Tex.
KFRU	1400	Columbia, Mo.
KFRX	102.7	Lincoln, Neb.
KFRY	101.9	Fresno, Calif.
KFRZ	107.1	Brigham City, Utah
KFSA	950	Ft. Smith, Ark.
KFSB	1310	Joplin, Mo.
KFSD-FM	94.1	San Diego, Calif.
KFSG	96.3	Los Angeles, Calif.
KFSH	97.1	Hilo, Haw.
KFSI	88.5	Rochester, Minn.
KFSK	100.9	Petersburg, Alas.
KFSM-TV	5	Ft. Smith, Ark.
KFSN-TV	30	Fresno, Calif.
KFSR	90.7	Fresno, Calif.
KFST	860	Ft. Stockton, Tex.
KFTM	1400	Ft. Morgan, Colo.
KFTN	1400	Provo, Utah
KFTS	101.7	Ft. Scott, Kan.
KFTV	21	Hanford, Calif.
KFTW	1450	Fredericktown, Mo.
KFTY	50	Santa Rosa, Calif.
KFUN	1230	Las Vegas, N.M.
KFUO	850	Clayton, Mo.
KFUO-FM	99.1	Clayton, Mo.
KFVS-TV	12	Cape Girardeau, Mo.
KFWB	980	Los Angeles, Calif.
KFWJ	980	Lake Havasu City, Ariz.
KFWY	1560	Sumner, Wash.
KFXD	580	Nampa, Id.
KFXD-FM	94.9	Nampa, Id.
KFXE	92.3	Pine Bluff, Ark.
KFXM	590	San Bernardino, Calif.
KFXY	96.7	Morgan City, La.
KFYE	93.7	Fresno, Calif.
KFYN	1420	Bonham, Tex.
KFYO	790	Lubbock, Tex.
KFYR	550	Bismarck, N.D.
KFYR-TV	5	Bismarck, N.D.
KFYZ-FM	98.3	Bonham, Tex.
KGA	1510	Spokane, Wash.
KGAA	1460	Kirkland, Wash.
KGAF	1580	Gainesville, Tex.
KGAF-FM	94.5	Gainesville, Tex.
KGAK	1330	Gallup, N.M.
KGAL	920	Lebanon, Ore.
KGAN	2	Cedar Rapids, Ia.

KGAR 106.3 Mercedes, Tex.
KGAS 1590 Carthage, Tex.
KGAY 1430 Salem, Ore.
KGB-FM 101.5 San Diego, Calif.
KGBA 100.1 Holtville, Calif.
KGBB 107.9 Anoka, Minn.
KGBC 1540 Galveston, Tex.
KGBI-FM 100.7 Omaha, Neb.
KGBM-FM 104.9 Oakdale, La.
KGBR 92.7 Gold Beach, Ore.
KGBS 96.1 Greeley, Colo.
KGBT 1530 Harlingen, Tex.
KGBT-TV 4 Harlingen, Tex.
KGBX 1260 Springfield, Mo.
KGCA 1450 Rugby, N.D.
KGCC 89.7 Denison, Tex.
KGCG 1590 Henryetta, Okla.
KGCG-FM 99.5 Henryetta, Okla.
KGCH-FM 93.1 Sidney, Mont.
KGCI 97.7 Grundy Center, Ia.
KGCT-TV 41 Tulsa, Okla.
KGCX 1480 Sidney, Mont.
KGDN 630 Edmonds, Wash.
KGED 88.1 Batesville, Ark.
KGEE 99.9 Monahans, Tex.
KGEM 1140 Boise, Id.
KGEN 1370 Tulare, Calif.
KGEO 1230 Bakersfield, Calif.
KGER 1390 Long Beach, Calif.
KGEZ 600 Kalispell, Mont.
KGFE 2 Grand Forks, N.D.
KGFF 1450 Shawnee, Okla.
KGFJ 1230 Los Angeles, Calif.
KGFL 1110 Clinton, Ark.
KGFM 101.5 Bakersfield, Calif.
KGFT 101.7 Carpenteria, Calif.
KGFW 1340 Kearney, Neb.
KGFX 1060 Pierre, S.D.
KGFX-FM 92.7 Pierre, S.D.
KGGF 690 Coffeyville, Kan.
KGGG-FM 100.3 Rapid City, S.D.
KGGI 99.1 Riverside, Calif.
KGGM-TV 13 Albuquerque, N.M.
KGGR 630 Opportunity, Wash.
KGG0 94.9 Des Moines, Ia.
KGHL 790 Billings, Mont.
KGHM 1470 Brookfield, Mo.
KGHO 1560 Hoquiam, Wash.
KGHO-FM 95.3 Hoquiam, Wash.
KGHS 1230 International Falls, Minn.
KGIL 1260 San Fernando, Calif.
KGIL-FM 94.3 San Fernando, Calif.
KGIM 1420 Aberdeen, S.D.
KGIN-TV 11 Grand Island, Neb.
KGIR 960 Cape Girardeau, Mo.
KGIW 1450 Alamosa, Colo.
KGKG 94.3 Brookings, S.D.
KGKL 960 San Angelo, Tex.
KGKL-FM 97.5 San Angelo, Tex.
KGKO 850 Benton, Ark.
KGKS 102.5 Goodland, Kan.
KGLA 1540 Gretna, La.
KGLC 910 Miami, Okla.
KGLD 1440 Golden Valley, Minn.
KGLE 590 Glendive, Mont.
KGLH 91.5 Gerlach, Nev.
KGLI 95.5 Sioux City, Ia.
KGLM-FM 97.7 Anaconda, Mont.
KGLN 980 Glenwood Springs, Colo.
KGLO 1300 Mason City, Ia.
KGLS 93.1 Pratt, Kan.
KGLT 91.1 Bozeman, Mont.
KGMB-TV 9 Honolulu, Haw.
KGMC 34 Oklahoma City, Okla.
KGMD 9 Hilo, Haw.
KGMI 790 Bellingham, Wash.
KGMO-FM 100.7 Cape Girardeau, Mo.
KGMS 1380 Sacramento, Calif.
KGMT 1310 Fairbury, Neb.
KGMV 3 Wailuku, Haw.
KGNB 1420 New Braunfels, Tex.
KGNC 710 Amarillo, Tex.
KGNC-FM 97.9 Amarillo, Tex.
KGNM 1270 St. Joseph, Mo.
KGNO 1370 Dodge City, Kan.
KGNQ 51 Lincoln, Neb.
KGNR 1320 Sacramento, Calif.
KGNS-TV 8 Laredo, Tex.
KGNU 88.5 Boulder, Colo.
KGNZ 88.1 Abilene, Tex.
KGO 810 San Francisco, Calif.
KGO-FM 103.7 San Francisco, Calif.
KGO-TV 7 San Francisco, Calif.
KGOE 850 Thousand Oaks, Calif.
KGOK 97.7 Pauls Valley, Okla.
KGOL 107.5 Lake Jackson, Tex.
KGON 92.3 Portland, Ore.
KGOR 99.9 Omaha, Neb.
KGOS 1490 Torrington, Wyo.
KGOT 101.3 Anchorage, Alas.
KGOU 106.3 Norman, Okla.
KGRB 900 West Covina, Calif.
KGRC 92.9 Hannibal, Mo.
KGRE 92.5 Greeley, Colo.
KGRG 89.9 Auburn, Wash.
KGRI 1000 Henderson, Tex.
KGRI-FM 100.1 Henderson, Tex.
KGRL 940 Bend, Ore.
KGRM 91.3 Grambling, La.
KGRN 1410 Grinnell, Ia.
KGRO 1230 Pampa, Tex.
KGRS 107.3 Burlington, Ia.
KGRT 570 Las Cruces, N.M.
KGRT-FM 103.9 Las Cruces, N.M.
KGRV 700 Winston, Ore.
KGRZ 1450 Missoula, Mont.
KGSP 90.3 Parkville, Mo.
KGST 1600 Fresno, Calif.
KGSU-FM 91.1 Cedar City, Utah
KGSW 14 Albuquerque, N.M.
KGTL 620 Homer, Alas.
KGTL-FM 103.5 Homer, Alas.
KGTM 990 Wichita Falls, Tex.
KGTN 1530 Georgetown, Tex.
KGTN-FM 96.7 Georgetown, Tex.
KGTO 1050 Tulsa, Okla.
KGTS 91.3 Walla Walla, Wash.
KGTV 10 San Diego, Calif.
KGU 760 Honolulu, Haw.
KGUC 1490 Gunnison, Colo.
KGUC-FM 98.3 Gunnison, Colo.
KGUD 1490 Banning, Calif.
KGUL 1560 Port Lavaca, Tex.
KGUN-TV 9 Tucson, Ariz.
KGUY 1270 Palm Desert, Calif.
KGVE 99.3 Grove, Okla.
KGVH 91.7 Gunnison, Utah
KGVL 1400 Greenville, Tex.
KGVO 1290 Missoula, Mont.
KGVW 640 Belgrade, Mont.
KGVW 630 Belgrade, Mont.
KGVY 1080 Green Valley, Ariz.
KGW 620 Portland, Ore.
KGW-TV 8 Portland, Ore.
KGWA 960 Enid, Okla.
KGWY 100.7 Gillette, Wyo.
KGY 1240 Olympia, Wash.
KGYN 1210 Guymon, Okla.
KHAC 1110 Window Rock, Ariz.
KHAD 1190 De Soto, Mo.
KHAI-TV 20 Honolulu, Haw.
KHAK 1360 Cedar Rapids, Ia.
KHAK-FM 98.1 Cedar Rapids, Ia.
KHAM 1000 Horseshoe Bend, Ark.
KHAR 590 Anchorage, Alas.
KHAS 1230 Hastings, Neb.
KHAS-TV 5 Hastings, Neb.
KHAT 106.3 Lincoln, Neb.
KHAW-TV 11 Hilo, Haw.
KHAY 100.7 Ventura, Calif.
KHBJ 1550 Canyon, Tex.
KHBM 1430 Monticello, Ark.
KHBM-FM 93.5 Monticello, Ark.
KHBQ 107.1 Canyon, Tex.
KHBR 1560 Hillsboro, Tex.
KHBS 40 Ft. Smith, Ark.
KHBT 97.7 Humboldt, Ia.
KHCB-FM 105.7 Houston, Tex.
KHCC-FM 90.1 Hutchinson, Kan.
KHCH-FM 88.1 Round Rock, Tex.
KHCR 95.9 Poauilo, Haw.
KHDN 1230 Hardin, Mont.
KHDN-FM 95.3 Hardin, Mont.
KHDX 93.1 Conway, Ark.
KHEI 1110 Kihei, Haw.
KHEM 1270 Big Spring, Tex.
KHEP 1280 Phoenix, Ariz.
KHEP-FM 101.5 Phoenix, Ariz.
KHER 94.3 Crystal City, Tex.
KHET 11 Honolulu, Haw.
KHEY 690 El Paso, Tex.
KHEY-FM 96.3 El Paso, Tex.
KHEZ 99.5 Lake Charles, La.
KHFI-FM 98.3 Austin, Tex.
KHFM 96.3 Albuquerque, N.M.
KHFO 98.1 Osceola, Ark.
KHFT 29 Hobbs, N.M.
KHGI-TV 13 Kearney, Neb.
KHHA 106.7 Port Sulphur, La.
KHIB 91.9 Durant, Okla.
KHIL 1250 Willcox, Ariz.
KHIN 36 Red Oak, Ia.
KHIP 93.5 Hollister, Calif.
KHIS 800 Bakersfield, Calif.
KHIS-FM 96.5 Bakersfield, Calif.
KHIT 1320 Walla Walla, Wash.
KHJ 930 Los Angeles, Calif.
KHJ-TV 9 Los Angeles, Calif.
KHJK 1060 Lockhart, Tex.
KHKE 89.5 Cedar Falls, Ia.
KHLB 1340 Burnet, Tex.
KHLO 850 Hilo, Haw.
KHLS 96.3 Blytheville, Ark.
KHLS 96.1 Blytheville, Ark.
KHMO 1070 Hannibal, Mo.
KHND 1540 Harvey, N.D.
KHNE-TV 29 Hastings, Neb.
KHNL 1310 Honolulu, Haw.
KHNS 102.3 Haines, Alas.
KHOB 1390 Hobbs, N.M.
KHOC 105.5 Levelland, Tex.
KHOF 99.5 Los Angeles, Calif.
KHOF-TV 30 San Bernardino, Calif.
KHOG 1440 Fayetteville, Ark.
KHOK 100.7 Holsington, Kan.
KHOL 1410 Beulah, N.D.
KHOM 104.1 Houma, La.
KHON-TV 2 Honolulu, Haw.
KHOO 99.9 Waco, Tex.
KHOP 104.1 Modesto, Calif.
KHOS 1420 San Angelo, Tex.
KHOT 1250 Madera, Calif.
KHOU-TV 11 Houston, Tex.
KHOW 630 Denver, Colo.

KHOZ	900	Harrison, Ark.
KHOZ-FM	102.9	Harrison, Ark.
KHPA	104.9	Hope, Ark.
KHPE	107.9	Albany, Ore.
KHPQ	92.1	Clinton, Ark.
KHPR	88.1	Honolulu, Haw.
KHQ	590	Spokane, Wash.
KHQ-FM	98.1	Spokane, Wash.
KHQ-TV	6	Spokane, Wash.
KHQA-TV	7	Hannibal, Mo.
KHRT	1320	Minot, N.D.
KHRU	88.1	Clayton, Mo.
KHSD-TV	11	Lead, S.D.
KHSJ	1320	Hemet, Calif.
KHSL	1290	Chico, Calif.
KHSL-TV	12	Chico, Calif.
KHSN	1230	Coos Bay, Ore.
KHSP	910	Hesperia, Calif.
KHSU-FM	90.5	Arcata, Calif.
KHSU-FM	91.5	Arcata, Calif.
KHTC	89.5	Helena, Mont.
KHTN	92.1	Placerville, Calif.
KHTR	103.3	St. Louis, Mo.
KHTT	1500	San Jose, Calif.
KHTV	39	Houston, Tex.
KHTX	103.7	Carnelian Bay, Calif.
KHTX	101.7	Carnelian Bay, Calif.
KHTZ	97.1	Los Angeles, Calif.
KHUB	1340	Fremont, Neb.
KHUB-FM	105.5	Fremont, Neb.
KHUG	1300	Medford, Ore.
KHUN	101.7	Huntsville, Tex.
KHUQ	106.7	Huboton, Kan.
KHUT	102.9	Hutchinson, Kan.
KHVH	990	Honolulu, Haw.
KHVO	13	Hilo, Haw.
KHWK	106.3	Richland, Wash.
KHYE	105.5	Hemet, Calif.
KHYL	101.1	Auburn, Calif.
KHYM	1060	Gilmer, Tex.
KHYS	98.5	Port Arthur, Tex.
KHYT	1330	Tucson, Ariz.
KHYV	970	Modesto, Calif.
KIAE	103.1	Auburn, Neb.
KIAE	103.1	Aurora, Neb.
KIAH	103.3	Ukiah, Calif.
KIAI	89.5	Phoenix, Ariz.
KIAK	970	Fairbanks, Alas.
KIAL	1450	Unalaska, Alas.
KIAM	1270	Nenana, Alas.
KIBE	1220	Palo Alto, Calif.
KIBL	1490	Beeville, Tex.
KIBS	1230	Bishop, Calif.
KICA	107.5	Clovis, N.M.
KICA	980	Clovis, N.M.
KICB	88.1	Ft. Dodge, Ia.
KICC	91.5	International Falls, Minn.
KICD	1240	Spencer, Ia.
KICD-FM	107.7	Spencer, Ia.
KICE	100.7	Bend, Ore.
KICK	1340	Springfield, Mo.
KICN	98.9	Spokane, Wash.
KICO	1490	Calexico, Calif.
KICS	1550	Hastings, Neb.
KICT	95.1	Wichita, Kan.
KICU	36	San Jose, Calif.
KICX	1360	Mc Cook, Neb.
KICX-FM	95.9	Mc Cook, Neb.
KICY	850	Nome, Alas.
KICY-FM	100.3	Nome, Alas.
KID	590	Idaho Falls, Id.
KID-FM	96.1	Idaho Falls, Id.
KID-TV	3	Idaho Falls, Id.
KIDA	92.7	Ida Grove, Ia.
KIDD	630	Monterey, Calif.
KIDE	91.3	Hoopa, Calif.
KIDN	1350	Pueblo, Colo.
KIDO	630	Boise, Id.
KIDQ	104.3	Boise, Id.
KIDS	98.3	Palmyra, Mo.
KIDV	6	San Angelo, Tex.
KIDX	98.5	Billings, Mont.
KIDZ-TV	24	Wichita Falls, Tex.
KIEA	89.7	Ethete, Wyo.
KIEA	89.7	Ethete, Wyo.
KIEL	1500	Jacksonville, Ark.
KIEM-TV	3	Eureka, Calif.
KIEV	870	Glendale, Calif.
KIEZ	1380	Beaumont, Tex.
KIFG	1510	Iowa Falls, Ia.
KIFG-FM	95.3	Iowa Falls, Ia.
KIFI-TV	8	Idaho Falls, Id.
KIFW	1230	Sitka, Alas.
KIGC	88.7	Oskaloosa, Ia.
KIGO	1400	St. Anthony, Id.
KIHN	1340	Hugo, Okla.
KIHR	1340	Hood River, Ore.
KIHS-TV	46	Ontario, Calif.
KIII	3	Corpus Christi, Tex.
KIIK	103.7	Davenport, Ia.
KIIN-TV	12	Iowa City, Ia.
KIIQ	1490	Manitou Springs, Colo.
KIIQ-FM	102.7	Manitou Springs, Colo.
KIIS-FM	102.7	Los Angeles, Calif.
KIIX	600	Ft. Collins, Colo.
KIIZ	1050	Killeen, Tex.
KIJK	95.3	Prineville, Ore.
KIJN	1570	Farwell, Tex.
KIJN	1060	Farwell, Tex.
KIJN-FM	92.3	Farwell, Tex.
KIJV	1340	Huron, S.D.
KIKF	94.3	Garden Grove, Calif.
KIKI	830	Honolulu, Haw.
KIKK	650	Pasadena, Tex.
KIKK-FM	95.7	Houston, Tex.
KIKM	910	Sherman, Tex.
KIKN	1590	Sinton, Tex.
KIKO	1340	Miami, Ariz.
KIKO-FM	100.3	Globe, Ariz.
KIKR	900	Conroe, Tex.
KIKS	1370	Iola, Kan.
KIKT	93.5	Greenville, Tex.
KIKU-TV	13	Honolulu, Haw.
KIKX	580	Tucson, Ariz.
KIKZ	1250	Seminole, Tex.
KIKZ-FM	106.3	Seminole, Tex.
KILA	95.5	Henderson, Nev.
KILE	1400	Galveston, Tex.
KILI	90.1	Porcupine, S.D.
KILJ	105.5	Mt. Pleasant, Ia.
KILO	93.9	Colorado Springs, Colo.
KILR	1070	Estherville, Ia.
KILR-FM	95.9	Estherville, Ia.
KILT	610	Houston, Tex.
KILT-FM	100.3	Houston, Tex.
KIMA-TV	29	Yakima, Wash.
KIMB	1260	Kimball, Neb.
KIMI	95.3	Keokuk, Ia.
KIML	1270	Gillette, Wyo.
KIMM	1150	Rapid City, S.D.
KIMN	950	Denver, Colo.
KIMO	13	Anchorage, Alas.
KIMP	960	Mt. Pleasant, Tex.
KIMT	3	Mason City, Ia.
KINA	910	Salina, Kan.
KINB	107.3	Poteau, Okla.
KIND	1010	Independence, Kan.
KIND-FM	101.7	Independence, Kan.
KINE	1330	Kingsville, Tex.
KINE-FM	97.7	Kingsville, Tex.
KINF	91.9	Dodge City, Kan.
KING	1090	Seattle, Wash.
KING-FM	98.1	Seattle, Wash.
KING-TV	5	Seattle, Wash.
KINI	96.1	Crookston, Neb.
KINK	101.9	Portland, Ore.
KINL	92.7	Eagle Pass, Tex.
KINN	1270	Alamogordo, N.M.
KINN-FM	105.5	Alamogordo, N.M.
KINO	1230	Winslow, Ariz.
KINQ	92.1	Walnut Creek, Calif.
KINS	980	Eureka, Calif.
KINT-TV	26	El Paso, Tex.
KINY	800	Juneau, Alas.
KIOA	940	Des Moines, Ia.
KIOC	106.1	Orange, Tex.
KIOE	1080	Honolulu, Haw.
KIOF	104.7	Lamesa, Tex.
KIOI	101.3	San Francisco, Calif.
KIOK	94.9	Richland, Wash.
KIOL	99.3	Iola, Kan.
KIOO	99.7	Porterville, Calif.
KIOQ-FM	100.7	Bishop, Calif.
KIOS-FM	91.5	Omaha, Neb.
KIOT	1310	Barstow, Calif.
KIOT	1260	San Francisco, Calif.
KIOU	96.5	Corpus Christi, Tex.
KIOV	104.7	Sioux Falls, S.D.
KIOW	102.3	Forest City, Ia.
KIOX	1270	Bay City, Tex.
KIOZ	102.9	Laramie, Wyo.
KIPA	620	Hilo, Haw.
KIPO-FM	93.5	Lihue, Haw.
KIPR	1260	Diboll, Tex.
KIPR-FM	95.5	Diboll, Tex.
KIQI	1010	Sunnyvale, Calif.
KIQO	104.5	Atascadero, Calif.
KIQQ	100.3	Los Angeles, Calif.
KIQS	1560	Willows, Calif.
KIQS-FM	105.5	Willows, Calif.
KIQX	101.3	Durango, Colo.
KIQY	103.7	Lebanon, Ore.
KIQZ	92.7	Rawlins, Wyo.
KIRK	103.7	Lebanon, Mo.
KIRL	1460	St. Charles, Mo.
KIRO	710	Seattle, Wash.
KIRO-TV	7	Seattle, Wash.
KIRT	1580	Mission, Tex.
KIRV	1510	Fresno, Calif.
KIRX	1450	Kirksville, Mo.
KISA	1540	Honolulu, Haw.
KISD	880	Medford, Ore.
KISM	92.9	Bellingham, Wash.
KISN	97.1	Salt Lake City, Utah
KISO	1150	El Paso, Tex.
KISR	93.7	Ft. Smith, Ark.
KISS	99.5	San Antonio, Tex.
KIST	1340	Santa Barbara, Calif.
KISW	99.9	Seattle, Wash.
KISZ	97.9	Cortez, Colo.
KIT	1280	Yakima, Wash.
KITA	1440	Little Rock, Ark.
KITE	105.5	Portland, Tex.
KITF	11	International Falls, Minn.
KITI	1420	Centralia, Wash.
KITM	105.5	Mission, Tex.
KITO	95.9	Vinita, Okla.
KITR	101.7	Creston, Ia.
KITS	105.3	San Francisco, Calif.
KITT	96.3	Las Vegas, Nev.
KITV	4	Honolulu, Haw.
KITX	95.3	Hugo, Okla.
KITY	92.9	San Antonio, Tex.
KIUL	1240	Garden City, Kan.
KIUN	1400	Pecos, Tex.
KIUP	930	Durango, Colo.
KIVE	96.5	Glendive, Mont.
KIVI	6	Nampa, Id.
KIVM	1350	Lihue, Haw.
KIVV-TV	5	Lead, S.D.
KIVY	1290	Crockett, Tex.
KIVY-FM	92.7	Crockett, Tex.
KIWA	1550	Sheldon, Ia.
KIWA-FM	105.5	Sheldon, Ia.
KIWR	89.7	Council Bluffs, Ia.

KIWW	96.1	Harlingen, Tex.
KIXC	1150	Quanah, Tex.
KIXC-FM	100.9	Quanah, Tex.
KIXE-TV	9	Redding, Calif.
KIXI	910	Seattle, Wash.
KIXI-FM	95.7	Seattle, Wash.
KIXK	106.1	Denton, Tex.
KIXL	970	Austin, Tex.
KIXS-FM	93.3	Killeen, Tex.
KIXV	95.3	Brady, Tex.
KIXX	96.1	Watertown, S.D.
KIXY-FM	94.7	San Angelo, Tex.
KIXZ	940	Amarillo, Tex.
KIYD-FM	97.7	Shafter, Calif.
KIZN	93.1	New Plymouth, Id.
KIZZ	93.7	Minot, N.D.
KJAA	34	Lubbock, Tex.
KJAC-TV	4	Port Arthur, Tex.
KJAD	92.7	Lihue, Haw.
KJAE	92.7	Leesville, La.
KJAK	92.7	Slaton, Tex.
KJAM	1390	Madison, S.D.
KJAM-FM	103.1	Madison, S.D.
KJAN	1220	Atlantic, Ia.
KJAN-FM	103.7	Atlantic, Ia.
KJAQ-FM	99.3	Gordonville, Mo.
KJAS	1170	Jackson, Mo.
KJAV	104.9	Alamo, Tex.
KJAX	99.3	Stockton, Calif.
KJAY	1430	Sacramento, Calif.
KJAZ	92.7	Alameda, Calif.
KJBA	100.1	Bethel, Alas.
KJBC	1150	Midland, Tex.
KJBQ	104.9	Jonesboro, La.
KJBS	100.1	Bastrop, La.
KJCB	770	Lafayette, La.
KJCF	1400	Festus, Mo.
KJCH	1410	Cleveland, Tex.
KJCK	1420	Junction City, Kan.
KJCK-FM	94.5	Junction City, Kan.
KJCO	100.9	Yuma, Colo.
KJCS	103.3	Nacogdoches, Tex.
KJCT	8	Grand Junction, Colo.
KJCY	1240	Mountain Home, Id.
KJDY	1400	John Day, Ore.
KJEF	1290	Jennings, La.
KJEF-FM	92.7	Jennings, La.
KJEL	1080	Lebanon, Mo.
KJEM	1190	Bentonville, Ark.
KJEO	47	Fresno, Calif.
KJET	1590	Seattle, Wash.
KJEZ	95.5	Poplar Bluff, Mo.
KJFM	101.7	Louisana, Mo.
KJFP	103.9	Yakutat, Alas.
KJHK	90.7	Lawrence, Kan.
KJIB	99.5	Portland, Ore.
KJIC	89.3	Pasadena, Tex.
KJIL	104.9	Bethany, Okla.
KJIM	870	Ft. Worth, Tex.
KJIN	1490	Houma, La.
KJJB	105.5	Eunice, La.
KJJC	107.1	Osceola, Ia.
KJJJ	910	Phoenix, Ariz.
KJJK	96.5	Fergus Falls, Minn.
KJJO	104.1	St. Louis Park, Minn.
KJJR	880	Whitefish, Mont.
KJJT	1000	Odessa, Tex.
KJJY	106.3	Ankeny, Ia.
KJJZ	1390	Denver, Colo.
KJKK	95.3	Murfreesboro, Ark.
KJLA	1190	Kansas City, Mo.
KJLC	89.9	Lewiston, Id.
KJLC	97.7	Lewiston, Id.
KJLH	102.3	Compton, Calif.
KJLS	103.3	Hays, Kan.
KJLT	970	North Platte, Neb.
KJLY	100.9	Blue Earth, Minn.
KJMB	1450	Blythe, Calif.
KJMB-FM	100.3	Blythe, Calif.
KJMD	99.3	Aberdeen, Wash.
KJMM	97.9	Needles, Calif.
KJMO	100.1	Jefferson City, Mo.
KJNA	99.3	Jena, La.
KJNE	102.5	Hillsboro, Tex.
KJNO	630	Juneau, Alas.
KJNP	1170	North Pole, Alas.
KJNP-FM	103.3	North Pole, Alas.
KJNP-TV	4	North Pole, Alas.
KJOE	1480	Shreveport, La.
KJOI	98.7	Los Angeles, Calif.
KJOJ	106.9	Conroe, Tex.
KJOK	93.1	Yuma, Ariz.
KJOL	90.3	Grand Junction, Colo.
KJON	92.1	Booneville, Ark.
KJOP	1240	Lemoore, Calif.
KJOT	105.1	Boise, Id.
KJOY	1280	Stockton, Calif.
KJPW	1390	Waynesville, Mo.
KJPW-FM	102.3	Waynesville, Mo.
KJQN	1490	Ogden, Utah
KJQN-FM	95.5	Ogden, Utah
KJQY	103.7	San Diego, Calif.
KJR	950	Seattle, Wash.
KJRB	790	Spokane, Wash.
KJRG	950	Newton, Kan.
KJRH	2	Tulsa, Okla.
KJSK	900	Columbus, Neb.
KJSN	92.5	Klamath Falls, Ore.
KJTA	840	Pharr, Tex.
KJTV	14	Amarillo, Tex.
KJUD	8	Juneau, Alas.
KJUG	106.7	Tulare, Calif.
KJUM	1560	Colorado City, Tex.
KJUN	1450	Puyallup, Wash.
KJVC	92.7	Mansfield, La.
KJWH	1450	Camden, Ark.
KJYK	94.9	Tucson, Ariz.
KJYO	102.7	Oklahoma City, Okla.
KJZZ	1540	Bellevue, Wash.
KKAA	1560	Aberdeen, S.D.
KKAF	106.3	Eloy, Ariz.
KKAJ	95.7	Ardmore, Okla.
KKAL	1280	Arroyo Grande, Calif.
KKAN	1490	Phillipsburg, Kan.
KKAQ	1460	Thief River Falls, Minn.
KKAS	1300	Silsbee, Tex.
KKAY	1590	White Castle, La.
KKAZ	100.7	Cheyenne, Wyo.
KKBB	1090	Aurora, Colo.
KKBC	97.3	Carson City, Nev.
KKBE	102.3	Sheridan, Ark.
KKBG	97.9	Hilo, Haw.
KKBI	106.3	Broken Bow, Okla.
KKBJ	1360	Bemidji, Minn.
KKBJ-FM	103.7	Bemidji, Minn.
KKBK	1340	Aztec, N.M.
KKBL	95.9	Monett, Mo.
KKBQ	790	Houston, Tex.
KKBQ-FM	92.5	Pasadena, Tex.
KKBS	92.7	Guymon, Okla.
KKBZ-FM	96.7	Santa Paula, Calif.
KKCA	97.7	Fulton, Mo.
KKCC	1320	Clinton, Okla.
KKCC-FM	106.9	Clinton, Okla.
KKCI	1140	Liberty, Mo.
KKCI-FM	106.5	Liberty, Mo.
KKCM	1390	Waite Park, Minn.
KKCS-FM	101.9	Colorado Springs, Colo.
KKDA	730	Grand Prairie, Tex.
KKDA-FM	104.5	Dallas, Tex.
KKDI	1540	Sheridan, Ark.
KKDJ	105.9	Fresno, Calif.
KKDY	102.3	West Plains, Mo.
KKEB	95.9	Bellefourche, S.D.
KKED-FM	90.3	Corpus Christi, Tex.
KKEE	94.3	Alamogordo, N.M.
KKEG	92.1	Fayetteville, Ark.
KKER	1230	Spokane, Wash.
KKEY	1150	Portland, Ore.
KKEZ	94.5	Ft. Dodge, Ia.
KKFM	96.5	Colorado Springs, Colo.
KKFX	1250	Seattle, Wash.
KKGO	105.1	Los Angeles, Calif.
KKHI	1550	San Francisco, Calif.
KKHI-FM	95.7	San Francisco, Calif.
KKHR	93.1	Los Angeles, Calif.
KKIB	105.1	Breckenridge, Minn.
KKIC	950	Meridian, Id.
KKID	1560	Sallisaw, Okla.
KKIM	1000	Albuquerque, N.M.
KKIN	930	Aitkin, Minn.
KKIQ	101.7	Livermore, Calif.
KKIS	990	Pittsburg, Calif.
KKIT	1340	Taos, N.M.
KKIX	103.9	Fayetteville, Ark.
KKJO	1550	St. Joseph, Mo.
KKJY-FM	100.3	Albuquerque, N.M.
KKKC	1470	Anoka, Minn.
KKKK	99.1	Odessa, Tex.
KKKX	95.7	Ottawa, Kan.
KKLR	97.7	Edmond, Okla.
KKLS	920	Rapid City, S.D.
KKLS-FM	93.9	Rapid City, S.D.
KKLT	98.7	Phoenix, Ariz.
KKLV	104.1	Anchorage, Alas.
KKLV	103.9	Anchorage, Alas.
KKLX	96.7	Moab, Utah
KKMG	98.9	Pueblo, Colo.
KKNG	92.5	Oklahoma City, Okla.
KKNU	102.7	Fresno, Calif.
KKNW	1510	Mountlake Terrace, Wash.
KKOA	1390	Minot, N.D.
KKOJ	1190	Jackson, Minn.
KKOK-FM	95.7	Morris, Minn.
KKON	790	Kealakekua, Haw.
KKOS	95.9	Carlsbad, Calif.
KKOW	860	Pittsburg, Kan.
KKOY	1460	Chanute, Kan.
KKPL	96.1	Opportunity, Wash.
KKQT	98.3	Rexburg, Id.
KKQV	103.3	Wichita Falls, Tex.
KKRB	95.9	Klamath Falls, Ore.
KKRC-FM	93.5	Sioux Falls, S.D.
KKRD	107.3	Wichita, Kan.
KKRK	95.3	Douglas, Ariz.
KKRL	93.7	Carroll, Ia.
KKRQ	100.7	Iowa City, Ia.
KKSD	101.5	Gregory, S.D.
KKSG	25	Carlsbad, N.M.
KKSI	1130	Mt. Pleasant, Ia.
KKSN	910	Vancouver, Wash.
KKSS	980	Minneapolis, Minn.
KKTV	11	Colorado Springs, Colo.
KKTX	95.9	Kilgore, Tex.
KKUA	690	Honolulu, Haw.
KKUB	1300	Brownfield, Tex.
KKUG	98.1	San Luis Obispo, Calif.
KKUP	91.5	Cupertino, Calif.
KKUZ	102.5	Joplin, Mo.
KKVC	100.9	Villey City, N.D.

KKWS	105.9	Wadena, Minn.
KKWZ	93.7	Richfield, Utah
KKXL	1440	Grand Forks, N.D.
KKXL-FM	92.9	Grand Forks, N.D.
KKXX	107.9	Bakersfield, Calif.
KKYA	93.1	Yankton, S.D.
KKYK	103.7	Little Rock, Ark.
KKYN	1090	Plainview, Tex.
KKYS	107.5	Hanford, Calif.
KKYX	680	San Antonio, Tex.
KLAC	570	Los Angeles, Calif.
KLAD	960	Klamath Falls, Ore.
KLAF	1230	Murray, Utah
KLAK	1600	Lakewood, Colo.
KLAM	1450	Cordova, Alas.
KLAN	93.5	Glasgow, Mont.
KLAQ	95.5	El Paso, Tex.
KLAR	1300	Laredo, Tex.
KLAS-TV	8	Las Vegas, Nev.
KLAT	1010	Houston, Tex.
KLAV	1230	Las Vegas, Nev.
KLAW	101.5	Lawton, Okla.
KLAX-TV	31	Alexandria, La.
KLAY	1480	Lakewood, Wash.
KLAZ	98.5	Little Rock, Ark.
KLBA	1370	Albia, Ia.
KLBB	1400	St. Paul, Minn.
KLBC	107.1	Durant, Okla.
KLBJ	590	Austin, Tex.
KLBJ-FM	93.7	Austin, Tex.
KLBK-TV	13	Lubbock, Tex.
KLBM	1450	La Grande, Ore.
KLBM-FM	98.3	La Grande, Ore.
KLBQ	99.3	El Dorado, Ark.
KLBS	1330	Los Banos, Calif.
KLBY	4	Colby, Kan.
KLCB	1230	Libby, Mont.
KLCC	89.7	Eugene, Ore.
KLCD	89.5	Decorah, Ia.
KLCJ	92.7	Bayard, N.M.
KLCK	1400	Goldendale, Wash.
KLCL	1470	Lake Charles, La.
KLCM	95.9	Lewistown, Mont.
KLCN	910	Blytheville, Ark.
KLCO	1220	Branson, Mo.
KLCO	1280	Poteau, Okla.
KLCQ	106.3	Monroe City, Mo.
KLCR	102.3	Center, Tex.
KLCS	58	Los Angeles, Calif.
KLCY	94.1	Salt Lake City, Utah
KLDH	49	Topeka, Kan.
KLDN	92.7	Eldon, Mo.
KLEA	630	Lovington, N.M.
KLEA-FM	101.7	Lovington, N.M.
KLEB	1600	Golden Meadow, La.
KLEE	1480	Ottumwa, Ia.
KLEE-FM	97.7	Ottumwa, Ia.
KLEF	94.5	Houston, Tex.
KLEH	1290	Anamosa, Ia.
KLEI	1130	Kailua, Haw.
KLEL	89.3	San Jose, Calif.
KLEM	1410	Le Mars, Ia.
KLEN	106.3	Cheyenne, Wyo.
KLEO	1480	Wichita, Kan.
KLEP	17	Newark, Ark.
KLER	950	Orofino, Id.
KLER-FM	95.3	Orofino, Id.
KLEU	850	Waterloo, Ia.
KLEW-TV	3	Lewiston, Id.
KLEX	1570	Lexington, Mo.
KLEY	1130	Wellington, Kan.
KLFA	92.1	King City, Calif.
KLFB	1420	Lubbock, Tex.
KLFD	1410	Litchfield, Minn.
KLFD-FM	95.3	Litchfield, Minn.
KLFF	1360	Glendale, Ariz.
KLFJ	1550	Springfield, Mo.
KLFM	92.9	Great Falls, Mont.
KLFQ	106.1	Lyons, Kan.
KLFY-TV	10	Lafayette, La.
KLGA	1600	Algona, Ia.
KLGA-FM	92.7	Algona, Ia.
KLGM	92.7	Buffalo, Wyo.
KLGR	1490	Redwood Falls, Minn.
KLGR-FM	97.7	Redwood Falls, Minn.
KLGT	102.3	Breckenridge, Colo.
KLHS-FM	89.1	Lewiston, Id.
KLHS-FM	88.9	Lewiston, Id.
KLIB	1470	Liberal, Kan.
KLIC	1230	Monroe, La.
KLID	1340	Poplar Bluff, Mo.
KLIF	1190	Dallas, Tex.
KLIK	950	Jefferson City, Mo.
KLIL	92.1	Moreauville, La.
KLIN	1400	Lincoln, Neb.
KLIP	1220	Fowler, Calif.
KLIQ	1290	Lake Oswego, Ore.
KLIR	100.3	Denver, Colo.
KLIS	96.7	Palestine, Tex.
KLIV	1590	San Jose, Calif.
KLIX	1310	Twin Falls, Id.
KLIZ	1380	Brainerd, Minn.
KLIZ-FM	107.5	Brainerd, Minn.
KLJC	88.5	Kansas City, Mo.
KLKC	1540	Parsons, Kan.
KLKC-FM	93.5	Parsons, Kan.
KLKE	94.3	Del Rio, Tex.
KLKO	93.5	Elko, Nev.
KLKO	93.5	Elko, Neb.
KLKS	95.3	Breezy Point, Minn.
KLKT	100.1	Incline Village, Neb.
KLKT	100.1	Incline Village, Nev.
KLLA	1570	Leesville, La.
KLLH	96.7	Quincy, Wash.
KLLK	1250	Willits, Calif.
KLLL	96.3	Lubbock, Tex.
KLLM	103.9	Forks, Wash.
KLLN	90.9	Newark, Ark.
KLLR	1600	Walker, Minn.
KLLS	930	Terrell Hills, Tex.
KLLS-FM	100.3	San Antonio, Tex.
KLLT	95.3	Grants, N.M.
KLMC	93.5	Leadville, Colo.
KLME	88.1	Battle Mountain, Nev.
KLMF-FM	103.1	Fabens, Tex.
KLMG	51	Longview, Tex.
KLMO	1060	Longmont, Colo.
KLMO-FM	104.3	Longmont, Colo.
KLMR	920	Lamar, Colo.
KLMS	1480	Lincoln, Neb.
KLMT	96.7	Marlin, Tex.
KLMX	1450	Clayton, N.M.
KLNE-TV	3	Lexington, Neb.
KLNG	1560	Council Bluffs, Ia.
KLNI	1380	Pearl City, Haw.
KLNK	98.9	Oklahoma City, Okla.
KLNR	97.5	Bend, Ore.
KLNT	1390	Clinton, Ia.
KLNX	1420	Lufkin, Tex.
KLO	1430	Ogden, Utah
KLOA	1240	Ridgecrest, Calif.
KLOC	920	Ceres, Calif.
KLOE	730	Goodland, Kan.
KLOE-TV	10	Goodland, Kan.
KLOG	1490	Kelso, Wash.
KLOH	1050	Pipestone, Minn.
KLOH-FM	98.7	Pipestone, Minn.
KLOI	107.1	Grover City, Calif.
KLOK	1170	San Jose, Calif.
KLOL	101.1	Houston, Tex.
KLOM	1330	Lompoc, Calif.
KLON	88.1	Long Beach, Calif.
KLOO	1340	Corvallis, Ore.
KLOO-FM	106.1	Corvallis, Ore.
KLOQ	1580	Merced, Calif.
KLOR-FM	99.3	Ponca City, Okla.
KLOS	95.5	Los Angeles, Calif.
KLOU	1580	Lake Charles, La.
KLOV	1570	Loveland, Colo.
KLOV-FM	102.3	Loveland, Colo.
KLOZ	102.1	El Paso, Tex.
KLPA	25	Alexandria, La.
KLPB	24	Lafayette, La.
KLPC-FM	92.7	Lompoc, Calif.
KLPH	42	Paris, Tex.
KLPI	89.1	Ruston, La.
KLPL	1050	Lake Providence, La.
KLPL-FM	92.7	Lake Providence, La.
KLPQ	94.1	Little Rock, Ark.
KLPW	101.7	Union, Mo.
KLPW	1220	Union, Mo.
KLPX	96.1	Tucson, Ariz.
KLQF	92.1	Madison, Minn.
KLQL	101.1	Luverne, Minn.
KLQZ	107.1	Paragould, Ark.
KLRA	1010	Little Rock, Ark.
KLRC	90.3	Siloam Springs, Ark.
KLRE-FM	90.5	Little Rock, Ark.
KLRF	104.9	Emporia, Kan.
KLRN	9	San Antonio, Tex.
KLRR	1230	Leadville, Colo.
KLRS	1360	Mountain Grove, Mo.
KLRS-FM	92.7	Mountain Grove, Mo.
KLRT	16	Little Rock, Ark.
KLRU	18	Austin, Tex.
KLRZ	94.9	Provo, Utah
KLSC	1480	Watertown, S.D.
KLSE-FM	91.7	Rushford, Minn.
KLSI	93.3	Kansas City, Mo.
KLSK	104.1	Santa Fe, N.M.
KLSM	1060	Springfield, Mo.
KLSR	1130	Memphis, Tex.
KLSR-FM	105.3	Memphis, Tex.
KLSS	106.1	Mason City, Ia.
KLST	8	San Angelo, Tex.
KLSU	107.3	Baton Rouge, La.
KLSU	91.1	Baton Rouge, La.
KLSX-FM	90.7	Rochester, Minn.
KLSY	92.5	Bellevue, Wash.
KLTC	1460	Dickinson, N.D.
KLTD	99.3	Lampasas, Tex.
KLTE	101.9	Oklahoma City, Okla.
KLTF	960	Little Falls, Minn.
KLTI	1560	Macon, Mo.
KLTJ	49	Irving, Tex.
KLTL-TV	18	Lake Charles, La.
KLTM	13	Monroe, La.
KLTN	1240	Albuquerque, N.M.
KLTR	1580	Blackwell, Okla.
KLTS	24	Shreveport, La.
KLTT	800	Brighton, Colo.
KLTV	7	Tyler, Tex.
KLTZ	1240	Glasgow, Mont.
KLUB	570	Salt Lake City, Utah
KLUC	98.5	Las Vegas, Nev.
KLUE	1280	Longview, Tex.
KLUJ	44	Harlingen, Tex.
KLUK	105.5	Knob Noster, Mo.
KLUM-FM	88.9	Jefferson City, Mo.
KLUP	97.9	Poteau, Okla.
KLUR	99.9	Wichita Falls, Tex.
KLUV	1580	Haynesville, La.
KLUV	105.5	Haynesville, La.
KLVA	95.9	Lake Village, Ark.
KLVE	107.5	Los Angeles, Calif.
KLVF	100.9	Las Vegas, N.M.
KLVI	560	Beaumont, Tex.
KLVL	1480	Pasadena, Tex.
KLVN	95.9	Newton, Ia.
KLVR	1340	Heber City, Utah

Call	Freq.	Location
KLVR	1400	Cave Jct, Ore.
KLVT	1230	Levelland, Tex.
KLVU	98.7	Dallas, Tex.
KLVV	1410	Lompoc, Calif.
KLVX	10	Las Vegas, Nev.
KLWD	96.5	Sheridan, Wyo.
KLWJ	1090	Umatilla, Ore.
KLWN	1320	Lawrence, Kan.
KLWT	1230	Lebanon, Mo.
KLWT-FM	92.1	Lebanon, Mo.
KLWY	27	Cheyenne, Wyo.
KLXL	102.3	Dubuque, Ia.
KLXV	65	San Jose, Calif.
KLYC	1490	Laurel, Mont.
KLYD	1350	Bakersfield, Calif.
KLYD	94.1	Bakersfield, Calif.
KLYF	100.3	Des Moines, Ia.
KLYK	105.5	Longview, Wash.
KLYN-FM	106.5	Lynden, Wash.
KLYQ	1240	Hamilton, Mont.
KLYQ-FM	95.9	Hamilton, Mont.
KLYR	1360	Clarksville, Ark.
KLYR-FM	92.7	Clarksville, Ark.
KLYT	88.3	Albuquerque, N.M.
KLYV	105.3	Dubuque, Ia.
KLYX	98.3	Thermopolis, Wyo.
KLZ	560	Denver, Colo.
KLZR	105.9	Lawrence, Kan.
KMA	960	Shenandoah, Ia.
KMAD	1550	Madill, Okla.
KMAG	99.1	Ft. Smith, Ark.
KMAJ	107.7	Topeka, Kan.
KMAK	1340	Fresno, Calif.
KMAL	92.7	Malden, Mo.
KMAM	1530	Butler, Mo.
KMAN	1350	Manhattan, Kan.
KMAP	1370	South St. Paul, Minn.
KMAQ	1320	Maquoketa, Ia.
KMAQ-FM	95.3	Maquoketa, Ia.
KMAR	1570	Winnsboro, La.
KMAR-FM	95.9	Winnsboro, La.
KMAS	1280	Shelton, Wash.
KMAU	12	Wailuku, Haw.
KMAV	1520	Mayville, N.D.
KMAV-FM	101.7	Mayville, N.D.
KMAX	107.1	Arcadia, Calif.
KMAY	1570	Riverside, Calif.
KMAZ	92.9	Beatrice, Neb.
KMAZ	92.9	Beatrice, Neb.
KMBC-TV	9	Kansas City, Mo.
KMBI	1330	Spokane, Wash.
KMBI-FM	107.9	Spokane, Wash.
KMBL	1450	Junction, Tex.
KMBQ	93.7	Shreveport, La.
KMBR	99.7	Kansas City, Mo.
KMBY	107.1	Seaside, Calif.
KMBZ	980	Kansas City, Mo.
KMCC	12	Clovis, N.M.
KMCD	1570	Fairfield, Ia.
KMCK	105.7	Siloam Springs, Ark.
KMCL	1240	Mc Call, Id.
KMCM-FM	92.7	Miles City, Mont.
KMCO	101.3	Mc Alester, Okla.
KMCR-FM	91.5	Phoenix, Ariz.
KMCT-TV	39	West Monroe, La.
KMCW	1190	Augusta, Ark.
KMCX	103.7	Hanford, Calif.
KMCX	106.5	Ogallala, Neb.
KMDL	97.7	Kaplan, La.
KMDO	1600	Fort Scott, Kan.
KMDX	99.3	Parker, Ariz.
KMEB	10	Wailuku, Haw.
KMED	1440	Medford, Ore.
KMEG	14	Sioux City, Ia.
KMEL	106.1	San Francisco, Calif.
KMEM	96.7	Memphis, Mo.
KMEN	1290	San Bernardino, Calif.
KMEO	740	Phoenix, Ariz.
KMEO-FM	96.9	Phoenix, Ariz.
KMER	950	Kemmerer, Wyo.
KMET	94.7	Los Angeles, Calif.
KMEX-TV	34	Los Angeles, Calif.
KMEZ-FM	100.3	Dallas, Tex.
KMFA	89.5	Austin, Tex.
KMFB-FM	92.7	Mendocino, Calif.
KMFE	101.7	Emmett, Id.
KMFL-FM	102.9	Marshall, Mo.
KMFM	104.9	Premont, Tex.
KMFO	1540	Aptos Capitola, Calif.
KMGC	102.9	Dallas, Tex.
KMGG	105.9	Los Angeles, Calif.
KMGH-TV	7	Denver, Colo.
KMGK	93.3	Des Moines, Ia.
KMGM	105.5	Montevideo, Minn.
KMGO	98.7	Centerville, Ia.
KMGQ	106.3	Goleta, Calif.
KMGZ	95.3	Lawton, Okla.
KMHA	91.3	New Town, N.D.
KMHD	88.5	Gresham, Ore.
KMHL	1400	Marshall, Minn.
KMHT	1450	Marshall, Tex.
KMHT-FM	103.9	Marshall, Tex.
KMID-TV	2	Odessa, Tex.
KMIH	90.1	Mercer Island, Wash.
KMIL	1330	Cameron, Tex.
KMIN	980	Grants, N.M.
KMIO	1500	Merkel, Tex.
KMIO-FM	102.3	Merkel, Tex.
KMIR-TV	36	Palm Springs, Calif.
KMIS	1050	Portageville, Mo.
KMIS-FM	106.3	Portageville, Mo.
KMIT	105.9	Mitchell, S.D.
KMIX	98.3	Turlock, Calif.
KMJ	580	Fresno, Calif.
KMJC	910	El Cajon, Calif.
KMJD-TV	38	Pine Bluff, Ark.
KMJJ	1140	Las Vegas, Nev.
KMJK	106.7	Lake Oswego, Ore.
KMJM	107.7	St. Louis, Mo.
KMJQ	102.1	Clear Lake City, Tex.
KMJX	105.1	Conway, Ark.
KMKF	101.7	Manhattan, Kan.
KMKR	1450	Meeker, Colo.
KMLA	103.9	Ashdown, Ark.
KMLB	1440	Monroe, La.
KMLE	107.9	Chandler, Ariz.
KMLO	1000	Vista, Calif.
KMLT-TV	35	Marshall, Tex.
KMLW	97.7	Belen, N.M.
KMMJ	750	Grand Island, Neb.
KMMK	95.3	Mc Kinney, Tex.
KMML	98.7	Amarillo, Tex.
KMMM	1370	Austin, Tex.
KMMO	1300	Marshall, Mo.
KMMR	100.1	Malta, Mont.
KMMT	106.3	Mammoth Lakes, Calif.
KMMZ	1140	Greybull, Wyo.
KMND	1510	Midland, Tex.
KMNE-TV	7	Bassett, Neb.
KMNR	89.7	Rolla, Mo.
KMNS	620	Sioux City, Ia.
KMNT	102.9	Centralia, Wash.
KMOD-FM	97.5	Tulsa, Okla.
KMOE	92.1	Butler, Mo.
KMOG	1420	Payson, Ariz.
KMOJ	89.9	Minneapolis, Minn.
KMOK	106.9	Lewiston, Id.
KMOL-TV	4	San Antonio, Tex.
KMOM	1070	Monticello, Minn.
KMON	560	Great Falls, Mont.
KMOO	1510	Mineola, Tex.
KMOO-FM	96.7	Mineola, Tex.
KMOR	92.9	Scottsbluff, Neb.
KMOS-TV	6	Warrensburg, Mo.
KMOT	10	Minot, N.D.
KMOX	1120	St. Louis, Mo.
KMOX-TV	4	St. Louis, Mo.
KMPC	710	Los Angeles, Calif.
KMPG	1520	Hollister, Calif.
KMPH	26	Visalia, Calif.
KMPL	1520	Sikeston, Mo.
KMPO	88.7	Modesto, Calif.
KMPR	89.9	Minot, N.D.
KMPS	1300	Seattle, Wash.
KMPS-FM	94.1	Seattle, Wash.
KMRB	107.1	Burnet, Tex.
KMRC	1430	Morgan City, La.
KMRE	95.3	Dumas, Tex.
KMRN	1360	Cameron, Mo.
KMRS	1230	Morris, Minn.
KMRY	1390	Des Moines, Ia.
KMSA	91.3	Grand Junction, Colo.
KMSC	88.3	Sioux City, Ia.
KMSD	1510	Milbank, S.D.
KMSL	100.1	Stamps, Ark.
KMSM-FM	91.5	Butte, Mont.
KMSP-TV	9	Minneapolis, Minn.
KMSR	94.3	Sauk Center, Minn.
KMST	46	Monterey, Calif.
KMSU	89.7	Mankato, Minn.
KMTC	27	Springfield, Mo.
KMTF	18	Fresno, Calif.
KMTI	700	Newport, Wash.
KMTI	1590	Manti, Utah
KMTL	760	Sherwood, Ark.
KMTN	96.9	Jackson, Wyo.
KMTP	91.1	Mt. Pleasant, Utah
KMTR	16	Eugene, Ore.
KMTS	92.7	Glenwood Springs, Colo.
KMTV	3	Omaha, Neb.
KMTW	96.5	Twin Falls, Id.
KMTX	950	Helena, Mont.
KMUL	1380	Muleshoe, Tex.
KMUL-FM	103.1	Muleshoe, Tex.
KMUN	91.9	Astoria, Ore.
KMUS	1380	Muskogee, Okla.
KMUW	89.1	Wichita, Kan.
KMUZ	104.9	La Grange, Tex.
KMVC	98.3	Burley, Id.
KMVI	550	Wailuku, Haw.
KMVT	11	Twin Falls, Id.
KMWR	100.1	Vandalia, Mo.
KMWX	1460	Yakima, Wash.
KMXL	94.5	Logan, Utah
KMXT	100.1	Kodiak, Alas.
KMXU	105.1	Manti, Utah
KMYC	1410	Marysville, Calif.
KMYT	97.5	Merced, Calif.
KMYZ	1570	Pryor, Okla.
KMYZ-FM	104.5	Pryor, Okla.
KMZK	106.3	Sun City, Ariz.
KMZQ-FM	100.5	Henderson, Nev.
KMZQ-FM	100.5	Henderson, Neb.
KMZU	101.1	Carrollton, Mo.
KNAA	100.9	Sparks, Nev.
KNAB	1140	Burlington, Colo.
KNAB-FM	104.1	Burlington, Colo.
KNAC	105.5	Long Beach, Calif.
KNAF	910	Fredericksburg, Tex.
KNAK	540	Delta, Utah
KNAL	1410	Victoria, Tex.
KNAN	106.1	Monroe, La.
KNAQ	92.1	Rupert, Id.
KNAS	105.5	Nashville, Ark.
KNAT	23	Albuquerque, N.M.
KNAU	88.5	Flagstaff, Ariz.
KNAU	88.7	Flagstaff, Ariz.
KNAX	97.9	Fresno, Calif.
KNAZ	2	Flagstaff, Ariz.
KNBA	1190	Vallejo, Calif.
KNBC	4	Los Angeles, Calif.
KNBN-TV	33	Dallas, Tex.
KNBO	1530	New Boston, Tex.

Call	Freq.	Location
KNBQ	97.3	Tacoma, Wash.
KNBR	680	San Francisco, Calif.
KNBT	92.1	New Braunfels, Tex.
KNBU	88.9	Baldwin City, Kan.
KNBU	92.5	Baldwin City, Kan.
KNBY	1280	Newport, Ark.
KNCB	1320	Vivian, La.
KNCC	91.9	Tsaile, Ariz.
KNCI	1500	Boerne, Tex.
KNCK	1390	Concordia, Kan.
KNCN	101.3	Sinton, Tex.
KNCO	1250	Grass Valley, Calif.
KNCO-FM	94.3	Grass Valley, Calif.
KNCR	1090	Fortuna, Calif.
KNCT	46	Belton, Tex.
KNCT-FM	91.3	Killeen, Tex.
KNCY	1600	Nebraska City, Neb.
KNCY-FM	97.7	Nebraska City, Neb.
KNDC	1490	Hettinger, N.D.
KNDE	99.5	Tucson, Ariz.
KNDI	1270	Honolulu, Haw.
KNDK	1080	Langdon, N.D.
KNDN	960	Farmington, N.M.
KNDO-TV	23	Yakima, Wash.
KNDR	104.9	Mandan, N.D.
KNDU	25	Richland, Wash.
KNDX	2	Dickinson, N.D.
KNDY	1570	Marysville, Kan.
KNDY-FM	103.1	Marysville, Kan.
KNEA	970	Jonesboro, Ark.
KNEB	960	Scottsbluff, Neb.
KNEB-FM	94.1	Scottsbluff, Neb.
KNED	1150	Mc Alester, Okla.
KNEI	1140	Waukon, Ia.
KNEI-FM	103.9	Waukon, Ia.
KNEK	1190	Washington, La.
KNEL	1490	Brady, Tex.
KNEM	1240	Nevada, Mo.
KNEN	94.7	Norfolk, Neb.
KNES	92.1	Fairfield, Tex.
KNET	1450	Palestine, Tex.
KNEU	1250	Roosevelt, Utah
KNEV	95.5	Reno, Nev.
KNEW	910	Oakland, Calif.
KNEX	1540	Mc Pherson, Kan.
KNEX-FM	96.7	Mc Pherson, Kan.
KNEY	95.3	Pierre, S.D.
KNEZ	960	Lompoc, Calif.
KNFB	94.3	Nowata, Okla.
KNFM	92.3	Midland, Tex.
KNFO	95.5	Waco, Tex.
KNFT	950	Bayard, N.M.
KNGS	620	Hanford, Calif.
KNGT	94.3	Jackson, Calif.
KNGX	91.3	Claremore, Okla.
KNHC	89.5	Seattle, Wash.
KNHS	89.7	Torrance, Calif.
KNIA	1320	Knoxville, Ia.
KNIC	1550	Winfield, Kan.
KNID	96.9	Enid, Okla.
KNIF	95.3	Gilmer, Tex.
KNIK-FM	105.5	Anchorage, Alas.
KNIK-FM	105.3	Anchorage, Alas.
KNIM	1580	Maryville, Mo.
KNIM-FM	99.3	Maryville, Mo.
KNIN-FM	92.9	Wichita Falls, Tex.
KNIR	1360	New Iberia, La.
KNIS	94.7	Carson City, Nev.
KNIT	95.3	Portales, N.M.
KNIX	1580	Tempe, Ariz.
KNIX-FM	102.5	Phoenix, Ariz.
KNJO	92.7	Thousand Oaks, Calif.
KNJY	97.7	Clinton, Ia.
KNLB	91.1	Lake Havasu City, Ariz.
KNLC	24	St. Louis, Mo.
KNLU	88.7	Monroe, La.
KNLV	1060	Ord, Neb.
KNLV-FM	103.9	Ord, Neb.
KNME-TV	5	Albuquerque, N.M.
KNMI	88.9	Farmington, N.M.
KNMO-FM	97.7	Nevada, Mo.
KNMQ	105.9	Santa Fe, N.M.
KNMT	12	Walker, Minn.
KNMX	540	Las Vegas, N.M.
KNNB	88.1	Whiteriver, Ariz.
KNND	1400	Cottage Grove, Ore.
KNNN	99.9	Phoenix, Ariz.
KNNS	96.9	Grand Rapids, Minn.
KNNX	1400	Huntsville, Tex.
KNOB	97.9	Long Beach, Calif.
KNOC	1450	Natchitoches, La.
KNOE	540	Monroe, La.
KNOE-FM	101.9	Monroe, La.
KNOE-TV	8	Monroe, La.
KNOF	95.3	St. Paul, Minn.
KNOG	90.1	Havre, Mont.
KNOI	107.1	Deer Park, Wash.
KNOK	970	Ft. Worth, Tex.
KNOK-FM	107.5	Ft. Worth, Tex.
KNOM	780	Nome, Alas.
KNON	90.9	Dallas, Tex.
KNOP-TV	2	North Platte, Neb.
KNOR	1400	Norman, Okla.
KNOS	91.7	Marshall, Mo.
KNOT	1450	Prescott, Ariz.
KNOT-FM	98.3	Prescott, Ariz.
KNOW	1490	Austin, Tex.
KNOX	1310	Grand Forks, N.D.
KNPB	5	Reno, Nev.
KNPR	89.5	Las Vegas, Nev.
KNPT	1310	Newport, Ore.
KNPT-FM	102.5	Newport, Ore.
KNRY	1240	Monterey, Calif.
KNSE	1510	Ontario, Calif.
KNSI	1450	St. Cloud, Minn.
KNSP	1430	Staples, Minn.
KNST	940	Tucson, Ariz.
KNSX	96.7	Steelville, Mo.
KNTA	1430	Santa Clara, Calif.
KNTF	93.5	Ontario, Calif.
KNTO	95.9	Livingston, Calif.
KNTO	95.9	Delhi, Calif.
KNTU	88.1	Denton, Tex.
KNTV	11	San Jose, Calif.
KNUE	101.5	Tyler, Tex.
KNUI	900	Kahului, Haw.
KNUJ	860	New Ulm, Minn.
KNUS	710	Denver, Colo.
KNUU	970	Las Vegas, Nev.
KNUW	94.5	Great Falls, Mont.
KNUZ	1230	Houston, Tex.
KNVR	96.7	Paradise, Calif.
KNWC	1270	Sioux Falls, S.D.
KNWC-FM	96.5	Sioux Falls, S.D.
KNWD	91.7	Natchitoches, La.
KNWR	104.3	Bellingham, Wash.
KNWS	1090	Waterloo, Ia.
KNWS-FM	101.9	Waterloo, Ia.
KNWY	104.4	Powell, Wyo.
KNWZ	1190	Anaheim, Calif.
KNX	1070	Los Angeles, Calif.
KNXN	101.9	Quincy, Calif.
KNXR	97.5	Rochester, Minn.
KNXT	2	Los Angeles, Calif.
KNXV-TV	15	Phoenix, Ariz.
KNYD	90.5	Broken Arrow, Okla.
KNZA	103.9	Hiawatha, Kan.
KOA	850	Denver, Colo.
KOAA-TV	5	Pueblo, Colo.
KOAB-TV	3	Bend, Ore.
KOAC	550	Corvallis, Ore.
KOAC-TV	7	Corvallis, Ore.
KOAK	1080	Red Oak, Ia.
KOAK-FM	95.3	Red Oak, Ia.
KOAL	1230	Price, Utah
KOAM-TV	7	Pittsburg, Kan.
KOAP-FM	91.5	Portland, Ore.
KOAP-TV	10	Portland, Ore.
KOAQ	103.5	Denver, Colo.
KOAS	92.1	Kealakekua, Haw.
KOAT-TV	7	Albuquerque, N.M.
KOAV	20	Denison, Tex.
KOAW	1490	Ruidoso, N.M.
KOAX	105.3	Dallas, Tex.
KOB	770	Albuquerque, N.M.
KOB-FM	93.3	Albuquerque, N.M.
KOB-TV	4	Albuquerque, N.M.
KOBC	90.7	Joplin, Mo.
KOBE	1450	Las Cruces, N.M.
KOBF	12	Farmington, N.M.
KOBH	580	Hot Springs, S.D.
KOBH-FM	96.7	Hot Springs, S.D.
KOBI	5	Medford, Ore.
KOBK	14	Walla Walla, Wash.
KOBO	1450	Yuba City, Calif.
KOCA	1240	Kilgore, Tex.
KOCC	88.5	Oklahoma City, Okla.
KOCE-TV	50	Huntington Beach, Calif.
KOCM	103.1	Newport Beach, Calif.
KOCN	104.9	Pacific Grove, Calif.
KOCO-TV	5	Oklahoma City, Okla.
KOCV	91.3	Odessa, Tex.
KOCY	1340	Oklahoma City, Okla.
KODA	99.1	Houston, Tex.
KODE	1230	Joplin, Mo.
KODE-TV	12	Joplin, Mo.
KODI	1400	Cody, Wyo.
KODK	92.7	Kingsville, Tex.
KODL	1440	The Dalles, Ore.
KODY	1240	North Platte, Neb.
KODY-FM	94.9	North Platte, Neb.
KOEA	97.7	Doniphan, Mo.
KOED-TV	11	Tulsa, Okla.
KOEL	950	Oelwein, Ia.
KOEL-FM	92.3	Oelwein, Ia.
KOET	3	Eufaula, Okla.
KOEZ	92.3	Newton, Kan.
KOFE	1490	St. Maries, Id.
KOFI	1180	Kalispell, Mont.
KOFM	104.1	Oklahoma City, Okla.
KOFO	1220	Ottawa, Kan.
KOFY	1050	San Mateo, Calif.
KOGA	930	Ogallala, Neb.
KOGA-FM	99.7	Ogallala, Neb.
KOGM	107.1	Opelousas, La.
KOGO	600	San Diego, Calif.
KOGT	1600	Orange, Tex.
KOH	630	Reno, Nev.
KOHA	27	Hilo, Haw.
KOHI	1600	St. Helens, Ore.
KOHL	89.3	Fremont, Calif.
KOHM	89.1	Lubbock, Tex.
KOHO	1170	Honolulu, Haw.
KOHS	91.7	Orem, Utah
KOHU	1360	Hermiston, Ore.
KOHU-FM	99.3	Hermiston, Ore.
KOIL	1290	Omaha, Neb.
KOIN-TV	6	Portland, Ore.
KOIR	88.5	Edinburg, Tex.
KOIT-FM	96.5	San Francisco, Calif.
KOJC	89.7	Cedar Rapids, Ia.
KOJM	610	Havre, Mont.
KOJO	1490	Laramie, Wyo.

KOJO	1210	Laramie, Wyo.
KOJY	98.9	Dinuba, Calif.
KOKA	1550	Shreveport, La.
KOKC	1490	Guthrie, Okla.
KOKE-FM	95.5	Austin, Tex.
KOKF	90.9	Edmond, Okla.
KOKH-TV	25	Oklahoma City, Okla.
KOKI	23	Tulsa, Okla.
KOKK	1190	Huron, S.D.
KOKL	1240	Okmulgee, Okla.
KOKN	1270	Claremore, Okla.
KOKO	1450	Warrensburg, Mo.
KOKQ	95.1	Oakdale, Calif.
KOKR	105.5	Newport, Ark.
KOKX	1310	Keokuk, Ia.
KOKY	1250	Little Rock, Ark.
KOLA	99.9	San Bernardino, Calif.
KOLD-TV	13	Tucson, Ariz.
KOLE	1340	Port Arthur, Tex.
KOLI	1470	Coalinga, Calif.
KOLL-FM	96.6	Gillette, Wyo.
KOLM	1520	Rochester, Minn.
KOLN-TV	10	Lincoln, Neb.
KOLO	920	Reno, Nev.
KOLO-TV	8	Reno, Nev.
KOLR-TV	10	Springfield, Mo.
KOLS	100.1	Desoto, Mo.
KOLT	1320	Scottsbluff, Neb.
KOLT	103.7	Casper, Wyo.
KOLU	90.1	Pasco, Wash.
KOLV	101.7	Olivia, Minn.
KOLY	1300	Mobridge, S.D.
KOLY-FM	99.5	Mobridge, S.D.
KOMA	1520	Oklahoma City, Okla.
KOMB	103.9	Fort Scott, Kan.
KOME	98.5	San Jose, Calif.
KOMO	1000	Seattle, Wash.
KOMO-TV	4	Seattle, Wash.
KOMP	92.3	Las Vegas, Nev.
KOMU-TV	8	Columbia, Mo.
KOMW	680	Omak, Wash.
KOMW-FM	92.7	Omak, Wash.
KOMX	100.3	Pampa, Tex.
KOMY	1340	Watsonville, Calif.
KONA	610	Pasco, Wash.
KONA-FM	105.3	Kennewick, Wash.
KONE	1450	Reno, Nev.
KONG	1400	Visalia, Calif.
KONG-FM	92.9	Visalia, Calif.
KONI	1480	Spanish Fork, Utah
KONO	860	San Antonio, Tex.
KONP	1450	Port Angeles, Wash.
KONY	10	Thief River Falls, Minn.
KOOC	104.5	Cozad, Neb.
KOOD	9	Hays, Kan.
KOOG-TV	30	Ogden, Utah
KOOI	106.5	Jacksonville, Tex.
KOOK	970	Billings, Mont.
KOOK-FM	102.9	Billings, Mont.
KOOL	960	Phoenix, Ariz.
KOOL-FM	94.5	Phoenix, Ariz.
KOOO	1420	Omaha, Neb.
KOOQ	1410	North Platte, Neb.
KOOS	100.9	North Bend, Ore.
KOOV	103.1	Copperas Cove, Tex.
KOOZ	106.3	Great Falls, Mont.
KOPA	1440	Scottsdale, Ariz.
KOPA-FM	100.7	Scottsdale, Ariz.
KOPE	104.9	Mesilla Park, N.M.
KOPN	89.5	Columbia, Mo.
KOPO	98.3	Marana, Ariz.
KOPR	94.1	Butte, Mont.
KOPY	1070	Alice, Tex.
KOQT	1550	Ferndale, Wash.
KORA-FM	98.3	Bryan, Tex.
KORD	870	Pasco, Wash.
KORD	910	Pasco, Wash.
KORE	1050	Springfield, Ore.
KORK	920	Las Vegas, Nev.
KORL	650	Honolulu, Haw.
KORN	1490	Mitchell, S.D.
KORO	28	Corpus Christi, Tex.
KORQ	100.7	Abilene, Tex.
KORS	100.9	Miami, Okla.
KORT	1230	Grangeville, Id.
KORT-FM	92.7	Grangeville, Id.
KORV	1340	Oroville, Calif.
KORY	96.7	Manteca, Calif.
KOSA-TV	7	Odessa, Tex.
KOSC	1510	Marshfield, Mo.
KOSC-FM	104.9	Marshfield, Mo.
KOSE	860	Osceola, Ark.
KOSG	92.7	Osage, Ia.
KOSI-FM	101.1	Denver, Colo.
KOSO	93.1	Patterson, Calif.
KOST	103.5	Los Angeles, Calif.
KOST	100.1	Sedona, Ariz.
KOSU-FM	91.7	Stillwater, Okla.
KOSY	790	Texarkana, Ark.
KOSY-FM	102.5	Texarkana, Tex.
KOTA	1380	Rapid City, S.D.
KOTA-TV	3	Rapid City, S.D.
KOTB	106.3	Evanston, Wyo.
KOTD	1000	Plattsmouth, Neb.
KOTE	1380	Lancaster, Calif.
KOTE	106.3	Lancaster, Calif.
KOTI	2	Klamath Falls, Ore.
KOTN	1490	Pine Bluff, Ark.
KOTO	91.7	Telluride, Colo.
KOTS	1230	Deming, N.M.
KOTV	6	Tulsa, Okla.
KOTY	1340	Kennewick, Wash.
KOTZ	720	Kotzebue, Alas.
KOTZ	95.3	Fort Bragg, Calif.
KOUL	103.3	Corpus Christi, Tex.
KOUL	103.7	Sinton, Tex.
KOUR	1220	Independence, Ia.
KOUR-FM	95.3	Independence, Ia.
KOUS-TV	4	Hardin, Mont.
KOVA	105.5	Ojai, Calif.
KOVC	1490	Valley City, N.D.
KOVE	1510	Nederland, Tex.
KOVE	1330	Lander, Wyo.
KOVO	94.5	Gallup, N.M.
KOVR	13	Stockton, Calif.
KOWB	1290	Laramie, Wyo.
KOWL	1490	South Lake Tahoe, Calif.
KOWN	1450	Escondido, Calif.
KOWN-FM	92.1	Escondido, Calif.
KOWO	1170	Waseca, Minn.
KOWY	5	Lander, Wyo.
KOXE	101.5	Brownwood, Tex.
KOXI	101.1	Columbus, Neb.
KOXR	910	Oxnard, Calif.
KOY	550	Phoenix, Ariz.
KOYE	94.9	Laredo, Tex.
KOYL	1310	Odessa, Tex.
KOYN	910	Billings, Mont.
KOYY	1360	El Dorado, Kan.
KOZA	1230	Odessa, Tex.
KOZE	950	Lewiston, Id.
KOZE-FM	96.7	Lewiston, Id.
KOZE-FM	96.5	Lewiston, Id.
KOZI	1230	Chelan, Wash.
KOZI-FM	93.5	Chelan, Wash.
KOZK	21	Springfield, Mo.
KOZN	99.3	Imperial, Calif.
KOZQ	1270	Waynesville, Mo.
KOZY	1320	Grand Rapids, Minn.
KOZZ	105.7	Reno, Nev.
KPAC	90.9	San Antonio, Tex.
KPAG	1400	Pagosa Springs, Colo.
KPAH	92.7	Tonopah, Nev.
KPAL	1110	Pineville, La.
KPAN	860	Hereford, Tex.
KPAN-FM	106.3	Hereford, Tex.
KPAR	1420	Granbury, Tex.
KPAT	97.3	Sioux Falls, S.D.
KPAU	90.7	Covelo, Calif.
KPAX-TV	8	Missoula, Mont.
KPAY	1060	Chico, Calif.
KPAY-FM	95.1	Chico, Calif.
KPAZ-TV	21	Phoenix, Ariz.
KPBC	1040	Dallas, Tex.
KPBM-FM	94.5	Poplar Bluff, Mo.
KPBS-FM	89.5	San Diego, Calif.
KPBS-TV	15	San Diego, Calif.
KPBX-FM	91.1	Spokane, Wash.
KPCA	1580	Marked Tree, Ark.
KPCC	89.3	Pasadena, Calif.
KPCO	1370	Quincy, Calif.
KPCQ-FM	92.5	Powell, Wyo.
KPCR	1530	Bowling Green, Mo.
KPCR-FM	100.9	Bowling Green, Mo.
KPCW	91.9	Park City, Utah
KPDJ	92.3	Eureka, Calif.
KPDQ	800	Portland, Ore.
KPDQ-FM	93.7	Portland, Ore.
KPDX	49	Vancouver, Wash.
KPEL	1420	Lafayette, La.
KPEN	97.7	Los Altos, Calif.
KPEP	98.3	Gatesville, Tex.
KPER	95.7	Hobbs, N.M.
KPET	690	Lamesa, Tex.
KPEZ	102.3	Austin, Tex.
KPFA	94.1	Berkeley, Calif.
KPFB	89.3	Berkeley, Calif.
KPFK	90.7	Los Angeles, Calif.
KPFM	94.3	Kerrville, Tex.
KPFT	90.1	Houston, Tex.
KPGA	95.3	Pismo Beach, Calif.
KPGE	1340	Page, Ariz.
KPGR	88.1	Pleasant Grove, Utah
KPHO-TV	5	Phoenix, Ariz.
KPHX	1480	Phoenix, Ariz.
KPIA	1480	Ironton, Mo.
KPIC	4	Roseburg, Ore.
KPIG	93.9	Honolulu, Haw.
KPIK	1580	Colorado Springs, Colo.
KPIN	1260	Casa Grande, Ariz.
KPIP	1110	Roseville, Calif.
KPIX	5	San Francisco, Calif.
KPJH	94.3	Ft. Stockton, Tex.
KPKE	95.7	Denver, Colo.
KPKY	94.9	Pocatello, Id.
KPLC-TV	7	Lake Charles, La.
KPLE	104.9	Temple, Tex.
KPLM	106.1	Palm Springs, Calif.
KPLN-FM	90.3	Plains, Tex.
KPLO-TV	6	Reliance, S.D.
KPLR-TV	11	St. Louis, Mo.
KPLS	1150	Santa Rosa, Calif.
KPLT	1490	Paris, Tex.
KPLU-FM	88.5	Tacoma, Wash.
KPLX	99.5	Ft. Worth, Tex.
KPLZ	101.5	Seattle, Wash.
KPMA	1400	Tacoma, Wash.
KPMC	1560	Bakersfield, Calif.
KPMD	1300	Mendocino, Calif.
KPNC-FM	100.9	Ponca City, Okla.
KPND	95.3	Sandpoint, Id.
KPNE-TV	9	North Platte, Neb.
KPNW	1120	Eugene, Ore.
KPNW-FM	99.1	Eugene, Ore.
KPNX-TV	12	Phoenix, Ariz.
KPNY	92.1	Alliance, Neb.
KPOB-TV	15	Poplar Bluff, Mo.

KPOC	1420	Pocahontas, Ark.
KPOD	1240	Crescent City, Calif.
KPOF	910	Denver, Colo.
KPOI	1040	Honolulu, Haw.
KPOI-FM	97.5	Honolulu, Haw.
KPOK	1340	Bowman, N.D.
KPOM-TV	24	Ft. Smith, Ark.
KPOO	89.5	San Francisco, Calif.
KPOP	93.5	Roseville, Calif.
KPOS	1370	Post, Tex.
KPOW	1260	Powell, Wyo.
KPPC	1240	Pasadena, Calif.
KPPL	107.5	Lakewood, Colo.
KPQ	560	Wenatchee, Wash.
KPQ-FM	102.1	Wenatchee, Wash.
KPQP	1360	San Diego, Calif.
KPQX	92.5	Havre, Mont.
KPRB	1240	Redmond, Ore.
KPRB-FM	102.9	Redmond, Ore.
KPRC	950	Houston, Tex.
KPRC-TV	2	Houston, Tex.
KPRE	1250	Paris, Tex.
KPRI	106.5	San Diego, Calif.
KPRK	1340	Livingston, Mont.
KPRL	1230	Paso Robles, Calif.
KPRM	1270	Park Rapids, Minn.
KPRM	870	Park Rapids, Minn.
KPRM-FM	97.5	Park Rapids, Minn.
KPRN	89.5	Grand Juction, Colo.
KPRO	1230	Barstow, Calif.
KPRO	1440	Riverside, Calif.
KPRR	14	Honolulu, Haw.
KPRS	103.3	Kansas City, Mo.
KPRT	1590	Kansas City, Mo.
KPRY-TV	4	Pierre, S.D.
KPRZ	1150	Los Angeles, Calif.
KPSA	1230	Alamogordo, N.M.
KPSD-TV	13	Eagle Butte, S.D.
KPSH-FM	88.3	Palm Springs, Calif.
KPSI	1450	Palm Springs, Calif.
KPSI-FM	100.9	Palm Springs, Calif.
KPSM	99.3	Brownwood, Tex.
KPSN	103.9	Payson, Ariz.
KPSO	1260	Falfurrias, Tex.
KPSO-FM	106.3	Falfurrias, Tex.
KPSU	91.7	Goodwell, Okla.
KPTL	1300	Carson City, Nev.
KPTS	8	Hutchinson, Kan.
KPTV	12	Portland, Ore.
KPTW	15	Wichita, Kan.
KPTX	98.3	Pecos, Tex.
KPUA	670	Hilo, Haw.
KPUB	1060	Winters, Tex.
KPUG	1170	Bellingham, Wash.
KPUP	107.5	Redmond, Ore.
KPUR	1440	Amarillo, Tex.
KPVI	6	Pocatello, Id.
KPVU	91.3	Prairie View, Tex.
KPWB	1140	Piedmont, Mo.
KPWR-TV	17	Bakersfield, Calif.
KPXE	1050	Liberty, Tex.
KPXI	100.7	Mt. Pleasant, Tex.
KPYN	99.3	Atlanta, Tex.
KQAA	94.9	Aberdeen, S.D.
KQAD	800	Luverne, Minn.
KQAK	98.9	San Francisco, Calif.
KQAL	89.5	Winona, Minn.
KQAM	1410	Wichita, Kan.
KQAQ	970	Austin, Minn.
KQAY-FM	92.7	Tucumcari, N.M.
KQBC	94.3	Okmulgee, Okla.
KQBE	103.1	Ellensburg, Wash.
KQCA	102.3	Canton, Mo.
KQCD-TV	7	Dickinson, N.D.
KQCR	102.9	Cedar Rapids, Ia.
KQCV	800	Oklahoma City, Okla.
KQDE-FM	92.1	Waseca, Minn.
KQDI	1450	Great Falls, Mont.
KQDJ	1400	Jamestown, N.D.
KQDJ-FM	95.5	Jamestown, N.D.
KQDQ	1320	Eugene, Ore.
KQDS-FM	94.9	Duluth, Minn.
KQDY	94.5	Bismarck, N.D.
KQEC	32	San Francisco, Calif.
KQED	9	San Francisco, Calif.
KQED-FM	88.5	San Francisco, Calif.
KQEE	104.9	West Helena, Ark.
KQEF	99.5	Lakeport, Calif.
KQEN	1240	Roseburg, Ore.
KQEO	920	Albuquerque, N.M.
KQEU	920	Olympia, Wash.
KQEW	101.7	Fordyce, Ark.
KQEZ-FM	103.9	Coolidge, Ariz.
KQFB	20	Tacoma, Wash.
KQHJ-FM	104.9	Hampton, Ia.
KQHU	104.1	Yankton, S.D.
KQIC	102.5	Willmar, Minn.
KQID	93.1	Alexandria, La.
KQIK	1230	Lakeview, Ore.
KQIL	1340	Grand Junction, Colo.
KQIN	800	Burien, Wash.
KQIP	96.9	Odessa, Tex.
KQIQ	1320	Lemoore, Calif.
KQIS	106.3	Clarinda, Ia.
KQIX	93.1	Grand Junction, Colo.
KQIZ	1360	Amarillo, Tex.
KQIZ-FM	93.1	Amarillo, Tex.
KQJA	7	Winnemucca, Nev.
KQKD	1380	Redfield, S.D.
KQKQ-FM	98.5	Council Bluffs, Ia.
KQKY	105.9	Kearney, Neb.
KQKZ	99.3	Mountain Home, Id.
KQLH	95.1	San Bernardino, Calif.
KQMO	97.7	Brookfield, Mo.
KQMQ	93.1	Honolulu, Haw.
KQMS	1400	Redding, Calif.
KQNK	1530	Norton, Kan.
KQNM	93.7	Gallup, N.M.
KQOK	100.1	Kenai, Alas.
KQOL-TV	45	Lawton, Okla.
KQPD	101.9	Ogden, Utah
KQPI-FM	99.1	Idaho Falls, Id.
KQPM	1550	Glencoe, Minn.
KQQF	92.1	Coffeyville, Kan.
KQQQ	1150	Pullman, Wash.
KQQQ-FM	104.9	Pullman, Wash.
KQRK	98.3	Bandera, Tex.
KQRN	107.3	Mitchell, S.D.
KQRR	92.3	Ronan, Mont.
KQRS	92.5	Golden Valley, Minn.
KQRZ	102.5	Fairbanks, Alas.
KQSA	1260	San Angelo, Tex.
KQSD-TV	11	Lowry, S.D.
KQSK	97.5	Chadron, Neb.
KQSM	105.5	Chanute, Kan.
KQSW	96.5	Rock Springs, Wyo.
KQTE	1400	Santa Paula, Calif.
KQTI	1130	Edna, Tex.
KQTV	2	St. Joseph, Mo.
KQTY	1490	Borger, Tex.
KQTZ	105.9	Hobart, Okla.
KQUE	102.9	Houston, Tex.
KQUY	95.5	Butte, Mont.
KQV	1410	Pittsburgh, Pa.
KQVO	97.7	Calexico, Calif.
KQWB	1550	Fargo, N.D.
KQWB-FM	98.7	Moorhead, Minn.
KQWC	1570	Webster City, Ia.
KQWC-FM	95.9	Webster City, Ia.
KQXI	1550	Arvada, Colo.
KQXK	1590	Springdale, Ark.
KQXL	1500	New Roads, La.
KQXL-FM	106.3	New Roads, La.
KQXT	101.9	San Antonio, Tex.
KQXX	98.5	Mc Allen, Tex.
KQXY	94.1	Beaumont, Tex.
KQYB	98.3	Spring Grove, Minn.
KQYN	95.7	Twentynine Palms, Calif.
KQYT	95.5	Phoenix, Ariz.
KQYX	1560	Joplin, Mo.
KQYZ	104.9	Lemoore, Calif.
KQZR	102.5	Craig, Colo.
KRAA	102.3	Volga, S.D.
KRAB	107.7	Seattle, Wash.
KRAE	1480	Cheyenne, Wyo.
KRAI	550	Craig, Colo.
KRAK	1140	Sacramento, Calif.
KRAL	1240	Rawlins, Wyo.
KRAM	1340	Las Vegas, Nev.
KRAN	1280	Morton, Tex.
KRAV	96.5	Tulsa, Okla.
KRAY-FM	103.9	Salinas, Calif.
KRAZ	96.9	Farmington, N.M.
KRBA	1340	Lufkin, Tex.
KRBC	1470	Abilene, Tex.
KRBC-TV	9	Abilene, Tex.
KRBD	105.9	Ketchikan, Alas.
KRBE	1070	Houston, Tex.
KRBE-FM	104.1	Houston, Tex.
KRBI	1310	St. Peter, Minn.
KRBI-FM	105.5	St. Peter, Minn.
KRBK	31	Sacramento, Calif.
KRBM	90.9	Pendleton, Ore.
KRBN	1450	Red Lodge, Mont.
KRBQ	102.3	Red Bluff, Calif.
KRBU	104.9	Pocatello, Id.
KRBU	102.5	Pocatello, Id.
KRCB-TV	22	Cotati, Calif.
KRCC	91.5	Colorado Springs, Colo.
KRCG	13	Jefferson City, Mo.
KRCH	101.7	Rochester, Minn.
KRCK	101.1	Portland, Ore.
KRCL	90.9	Salt Lake City, Utah
KRCO	690	Prineville, Ore.
KRCQ	1400	Indio, Calif.
KRCR-TV	7	Redding, Calif.
KRCS	93.1	Sturgis, S.D.
KRCT	94.3	Ozona, Tex.
KRCU	90.9	Cape Girardeau, Mo.
KRDC-FM	99.3	St. George, Utah
KRDD	1320	Roswell, N.M.
KRDF-FM	98.3	Spearman, Tex.
KRDG	1230	Redding, Calif.
KRDO	93.5	Breckenridge, Tex.
KRDO	1240	Colorado Springs, Colo.
KRDO-FM	95.1	Colorado Springs, Colo.
KRDO-TV	13	Colorado Springs, Colo.
KRDR	1230	Gresham, Ore.
KRDS	1190	Tolleson, Ariz.
KRDU	1130	Dinuba, Calif.
KRDZ	1470	Wray, Colo.
KRDZ	1440	Wray, Colo.
KRDZ	1000	Hayden, Colo.
KRE	1400	Berkeley, Calif.
KRED	1480	Eureka, Calif.
KREE	1360	Ruidoso, N.M.
KREH	900	Oakdale, La.

KREI	800	Farmington, Mo.
KREK	104.9	Bristow, Okla.
KREM	970	Spokane, Wash.
KREM-FM	92.9	Spokane, Wash.
KREM-TV	2	Spokane, Wash.
KREN	43	Reno, Nev.
KREO	92.9	Healdsburg, Calif.
KRER-FM	88.9	Billings, Mont.
KRES	104.7	Moberly, Mo.
KREW	1210	Sunnyside, Wash.
KREW	1230	Sunnyside, Wash.
KREW-FM	96.7	Sunnyside, Wash.
KREX	1100	Grand Junction, Colo.
KREX-FM	92.3	Grand Junction, Colo.
KREX-TV	5	Grand Junction, Colo.
KREY-TV	10	Montrose, Colo.
KREZ-TV	6	Durango, Colo.
KRFD	99.9	Marysville, Calif.
KRFG	93.5	Greenfield, Mo.
KRFM	96.5	Show Low, Ariz.
KRFO	1390	Owatonna, Minn.
KRFO-FM	104.9	Owatonna, Minn.
KRFS	1600	Superior, Neb.
KRFS-FM	103.9	Superior, Neb.
KRGI	1430	Grand Island, Neb.
KRGI-FM	96.5	Grand Island, Neb.
KRGK	104.9	Carthage, Mo.
KRGO	1550	West Valley City, Utah
KRGQ-FM	107.9	Roy, Utah
KRGS	104.9	Spencer, Ia.
KRGT	92.1	Taylor, Tex.
KRGV	1290	Weslaco, Tex.
KRGV-TV	5	Weslaco, Tex.
KRHD	1350	Duncan, Okla.
KRHD-FM	102.3	Duncan, Okla.
KRHS	1000	Bullhead City, Ariz.
KRHS-FM	102.7	Bullhead City, Ariz.
KRIB	1490	Mason City, Ia.
KRIC	90.1	Rexburg, Id.
KRIC	100.5	Rexburg, Id.
KRIG	1410	Odessa, Tex.
KRIJ	92.7	Paradise, Calif.
KRIM	95.1	Winslow, Ariz.
KRIN	32	Waterloo, Ia.
KRIO	910	Mc Allen, Tex.
KRIS-TV	6	Corpus Christi, Tex.
KRIT	96.9	Clarion, Ia.
KRIV-TV	26	Houston, Tex.
KRIX	99.5	Brownsville, Tex.
KRIZ	97.1	Roswell, N.M.
KRJB	97.7	Monte Rio, Calif.
KRJC	95.3	Elko, Nev.
KRJH	1520	Hallettsville, Tex.
KRKA	104.7	Alva, Okla.
KRKC	1490	King City, Calif.
KRKE	610	Albuquerque, N.M.
KRKK	1360	Rock Springs, Wyo.
KRKN	102.1	Anchorage, Alas.
KRKO	1380	Everett, Wash.
KRKS	990	Denver, Colo.
KRKT	990	Albany, Ore.
KRKT-FM	99.9	Albany, Ore.
KRKY	92.1	Castle Rock, Colo.
KRKZ	100.3	Portland, Ore.
KRLA	1110	Pasadena, Calif.
KRLB	580	Lubbock, Tex.
KRLB-FM	99.5	Lubbock, Tex.
KRLC	1350	Lewiston, Id.
KRLD	1080	Dallas, Tex.
KRLG	98.1	Lawton, Okla.
KRLN	1400	Canon City, Colo.
KRLN-FM	103.9	Canon City, Colo.
KRLQ	97.1	Muskogee, Okla.

KRLR	21	Las Vegas, Nev.
KRLS	92.1	Knoxville, Ia.
KRLT	93.9	South Lake Tahoe, Calif.
KRLT	100.1	South Lake Tahoe, Calif.
KRLW	1320	Walnut Ridge, Ark.
KRLX	90.3	Northfield, Minn.
KRLY	93.7	Houston, Tex.
KRMA-TV	6	Denver, Colo.
KRMC	1220	Midwest City, Okla.
KRMD	1340	Shreveport, La.
KRMD-FM	101.1	Shreveport, La.
KRME	1460	Hondo, Tex.
KRMG	740	Tulsa, Okla.
KRML	1410	Carmel, Calif.
KRMO	990	Monett, Mo.
KRMW	700	Silt, Colo.
KRMX	690	Pueblo, Colo.
KRMX-FM	107.1	Pueblo, Colo.
KRNA	93.9	Iowa City, Ia.
KRNB	101.1	Memphis, Tenn.
KRNE-TV	12	Merriman, Neb.
KRNL-FM	89.7	Mt. Vernon, Ia.
KRNN	95.3	Creswell, Ore.
KRNO	106.9	Reno, Nev.
KRNQ	102.5	Des Moines, Ia.
KRNR	1490	Roseburg, Ore.
KRNS	1230	Burns, Ore.
KRNT	1350	Des Moines, Ia.
KRNU	90.3	Lincoln, Neb.
KRNY	1460	Kearney, Neb.
KRNY-FM	98.9	Kearney, Neb.
KROA	95.7	Grand Island, Neb.
KROB	1510	Robstown, Tex.
KROB-FM	99.9	Robstown, Tex.
KROC	1340	Rochester, Minn.
KROC-FM	106.9	Rochester, Minn.
KROD	600	El Paso, Tex.
KROE	930	Sheridan, Wyo.
KROE-FM	94.9	Sheridan, Wyo.
KROF	960	Abbeville, La.
KROG	92.7	Sonora, Calif.
KROI	1270	Sparks, Nev.
KROK	94.5	Shreveport, La.
KRON-TV	4	San Francisco, Calif.
KROP	1300	Brawley, Calif.
KROQ	1500	Burbank, Calif.
KROQ-FM	106.7	Pasadena, Calif.
KROR	1360	Myrtle Creek, Ore.
KROS	1340	Clinton, Ia.
KROW	780	Reno, Nev.
KROX	1260	Crookston, Minn.
KROY	96.9	Sacramento, Calif.
KROZ	92.1	Tyler, Tex.
KRPC	90.5	Owatonna, Minn.
KRPL	1400	Moscow, Id.
KRPL-FM	103.9	Moscow, Id.
KRPM-FM	106.1	Tacoma, Wash.
KRPR	89.9	Rochester, Minn.
KRPT	850	Anadarko, Okla.
KRPT-FM	103.7	Anadarko, Okla.
KRPX	1080	Price, Utah
KRQK	100.9	Lompoc, Calif.
KRQQ	93.7	Tucson, Ariz.
KRQR	97.3	San Francisco, Calif.
KRRA	95.9	Huntsville, Ark.
KRRB	92.1	Dickinson, N.D.
KRRG	98.1	Lared0, Tex.
KRRI	105.5	Boulder City, Nev.
KRRK	1590	East Grand Forks, Minn.
KRRK-FM	103.9	East Grand Forks, Minn.
KRRO	92.1	Ardmore, Okla.
KRRP	950	Coushatta, La.
KRRV	100.3	Alexandria, La.
KRRZ	101.9	Fargo, N.D.
KRSA	580	Petersburg, Alas.
KRSB	103.1	Roseburg, Ore.

KRSC	1400	Othello, Wash.
KRSE	98.3	Yakima, Wash.
KRSH	90.1	Overland, Mo.
KRSI	950	St. Louis Park, Minn.
KRSJ	100.5	Durango, Colo.
KRSL	990	Russell, Kan.
KRSL-FM	95.9	Russell, Kan.
KRSM	88.5	Dallas, Tex.
KRSN	1490	Los Alamos, N.M.
KRSN-FM	98.5	Los Alamos, N.M.
KRSP	1060	South Salt Lake City, Utah
KRSP-FM	103.5	Salt Lake City, Utah
KRSS	1520	Sioux Falls, S.D.
KRST	92.3	Albuquerque, N.M.
KRSW	91.7	Worthington, Minn.
KRSY	1230	Roswell, N.M.
KRTH	101.1	Los Angeles, Calif.
KRTM	88.9	Temecula, Calif.
KRTN	1490	Raton, N.M.
KRTN-FM	94.3	Raton, N.M.
KRTR	1490	Thermopolis, Wyo.
KRTU	91.7	San Antonio, Tex.
KRTV	3	Great Falls, Mont.
KRTZ	96.7	Cortez, Colo.
KRUN	1400	Ballinger, Tex.
KRUN-FM	103.1	Ballinger, Tex.
KRUS	1490	Ruston, La.
KRUX	102.5	Malakoff, Tex.
KRUX	102.5	Lubbock, Tex.
KRUZ	103.3	Santa Barbara, Calif.
KRVC	730	Medford, Ore.
KRVE	95.3	Los Gatos, Calif.
KRVH	90.9	Rio Vista, Calif.
KRVH	101.5	Rio Vista, Calif.
KRVM	91.9	Eugene, Ore.
KRVN	880	Lexington, Neb.
KRVN-FM	93.1	Lexington, Neb.
KRVR	106.5	Davenport, Ia.
KRVS	88.1	Lafayette, La.
KRVS	88.7	Lafayette, La.
KRVZ	1400	Springville, Ariz.
KRWA-FM	103.1	Waldron, Ark.
KRWB	1410	Roseau, Minn.
KRWC	1360	Buffalo, Minn.
KRWG	90.7	Las Cruces, N.M
KRWG-TV	22	Las Cruces, N.M
KRWN	92.9	Farmington, N.M.
KRWQ	100.3	Gold Hill, Ore.
KRWY	11	Rawlins, Wyo.
KRXA	950	Seward, Alas.
KRXK	1230	Rexburg, Id.
KRXL	94.5	Kirksville, Mo.
KRXV	98.1	Yermo, Calif.
KRYK	101.3	Chinook, Mont.
KRYS	1360	Corpus Christi, Tex.
KRZA	88.7	Alamosa, Colo.
KRZE	1280	Farmington, N.M.
KRZI	1580	Waco, Tex.
KRZK	106.3	Branson, Mo.
KRZN	1150	Englewood, Colo
KRZQ-FM	98.3	Wray, Colo.
KRZY	1450	Albuquerque, N.M.
KRZY	1090	Albuquerque, N.M.
KSAA	105.5	Casa Grande, Ariz.
KSAC	580	Manhattan, Kan.
KSAF-TV	2	Sante Fe, N.M.
KSAK	90.1	Walnut, Calif.
KSAL	1150	Salina, Kan.
KSAM	1490	Huntsville, Tex.
KSAN-FM	94.9	San Francisco, Calif.
KSAQ	96.1	San Antonio, Tex.
KSAR	95.9	Salem, Ark.

Call	Freq.	Location
KSAT-TV	12	San Antonio, Tex.
KSAU	90.1	Nacogdoches, Tex.
KSAY	96.1	Clinton, Ia.
KSBC	90.1	Hot Springs, Ark.
KSBI	52	Oklahoma City, Okla.
KSBJ	88.1	Humble, Tex.
KSBQ	1480	Santa Maria, Calif.
KSBR	88.5	Mission Viejo, Calif.
KSBT	96.7	Steamboat Springs, Colo.
KSBW-TV	8	Salinas, Calif.
KSBY-TV	6	San Luis Obispo, Calif.
KSCA	88.7	Santa Barbara, Calif.
KSCB	1270	Liberal, Kan.
KSCB-FM	105.5	Liberal, Kan.
KSCB-FM	107.5	Liberal, Kan.
KSCC	107.1	Berryville, Ark.
KSCG	90.5	St. Peter, Minn.
KSCH	58	Stockton, Calif.
KSCI	18	San Bernardino, Calif.
KSCJ	1360	Sioux City, Ia.
KSCL	91.3	Shreveport, La.
KSCM-FM	99.3	Houston, Mo.
KSCO	1080	Santa Cruz, Calif.
KSCO-FM	99.1	Santa Cruz, Calif.
KSCR	1420	Renton, Wash.
KSCS	96.3	Ft. Worth, Tex.
KSCU	103.3	Santa Clara, Calif.
KSCV	91.3	Kearney, Neb.
KSD	550	St. Louis, Mo.
KSD-FM	93.7	St. Louis, Mo.
KSDB-FM	88.1	Manhattan, Kan.
KSDK	5	St. Louis, Mo.
KSDM	94.3	International Falls, Minn.
KSDN	930	Aberdeen, S.D.
KSDN-FM	94.1	Aberdeen, S.D.
KSDO	1130	San Diego, Calif.
KSDO-FM	102.9	San Diego, Calif.
KSDS	88.3	San Diego, Calif.
KSDW	100.9	Sulphur, Okla.
KSDY	95.1	Sidney, Mont.
KSDZ	95.5	Gordon, Neb.
KSEA	100.7	Seattle, Wash.
KSEC	93.3	Lamar, Colo.
KSEE	24	Fresno, Calif.
KSEI	930	Pocatello, Id.
KSEK	1340	Pittsburg, Kan.
KSEL	950	Lubbock, Tex.
KSEL-FM	93.7	Lubbock, Tex.
KSEM	1470	Moses Lake, Wash.
KSEM-FM	99.3	Moses Lake, Wash.
KSEN	1150	Shelby, Mont.
KSEO	750	Durant, Okla.
KSER	99.3	Searcy, Ark.
KSES	1420	Yucca Valley, Calif.
KSET	1340	El Paso, Tex.
KSET-FM	94.7	El Paso, Tex.
KSEY	1230	Seymour, Tex.
KSEY-FM	94.3	Seymour, Tex.
KSEZ	97.9	Sioux City, Ia.
KSFA	860	Nacogdoches, Tex.
KSFC	91.9	Spokane, Wash.
KSFE	1340	Needles, Calif.
KSFH	90.5	Mountain View, Calif.
KSFI	100.3	Salt Lake City, Utah
KSFM	102.5	Woodland, Calif.
KSFO	560	San Francisco, Calif.
KSFT	105.1	St. Joseph, Mo.
KSFY-TV	13	Sioux Falls, S.D.
KSGL	900	Wichita, Kan.
KSGM	980	Chester, Ill.
KSGM-FM	105.7	Ste. Genevieve, Mo.
KSGN	89.7	Riverside, Calif.
KSGT	1340	Jackson, Wyo.
KSGW-TV	12	Sheridan, Wyo.
KSHA	104.3	Redding, Calif.
KSHB-TV	41	Kansas City, Mo.
KSHE	94.7	Crestwood, Mo.
KSHI	90.9	Zuni, N.M.
KSHO	26	Honolulu, Haw.
KSHO-FM	96.3	Kailua, Haw.
KSHR	630	Coquille, Ore.
KSHR-FM	102.3	Coquille, Ore.
KSHU	89.3	Huntsville, Tex.
KSHY	1370	Cheyenne, Wyo.
KSIB	1520	Creston, Ia.
KSID	1340	Sidney, Neb.
KSID-FM	95.3	Sidney, Neb.
KSIG	1450	Crowley, La.
KSIL	1340	Silver City, N.M.
KSIM	1400	Sikeston, Mo.
KSIN	27	Sioux City, Ia.
KSIQ	96.1	Brawley, Calif.
KSIR	1470	Estes Park, Colo.
KSIS	1050	Sedalia, Mo.
KSIT	104.5	Rock Springs, Wyo.
KSIV	1320	Clayton, Mo.
KSIW	1450	Woodward, Okla.
KSIW-FM	93.5	Woodward, Okla.
KSIX	1230	Corpus Christi, Tex.
KSJB	600	Jamestown, N.D.
KSJC-FM	89.3	Stockton, Calif.
KSJL	760	San Antonio, Tex.
KSJM	93.3	Jamestown, N.D.
KSJN	1330	Minneapolis, Minn.
KSJN-FM	91.1	St. Paul, Minn.
KSJO	92.3	San Jose, Calif.
KSJR-FM	90.1	Collegeville, Minn.
KSJS	90.7	San Jose, Calif.
KSJU	89.1	Collegeville, Minn.
KSJV	91.5	Fresno, Calif.
KSKA	103.1	Anchorage, Alas.
KSKD	105.1	Salem, Ore.
KSKE	106.3	Kremmling, Colo.
KSKG	99.9	Salina, Kan.
KSKI	1340	Hailey, Id.
KSKI-FM	93.5	Sun Valley, Id.
KSKN	22	Spokane, Wash.
KSKO	870	Mc Grath, Alas.
KSKS	1140	Conroe, Tex.
KSKU	102.1	Hutchinson, Kan.
KSKX	1440	Topeka, Kan.
KSKY	660	Dallas, Tex.
KSL	1160	Salt Lake City, Utah
KSL-TV	5	Salt Lake City, Utah
KSLA-TV	12	Shreveport, La.
KSLC	90.3	Mc Minnville, Ore.
KSLE	105.5	Seminole, Okla.
KSLH	91.5	St. Louis, Mo.
KSLL	88.1	Richardson, Tex.
KSLM	1390	Salem, Ore.
KSLO	1230	Opelousas, La.
KSLQ	98.1	St. Louis, Mo.
KSLR	630	San Antonio, Tex.
KSLS	101.5	Liberal, Kan.
KSLT	107.3	Spearfish, S.D.
KSLU	90.9	Hammond, La.
KSLV	1240	Monte Vista, Colo.
KSLY	1400	San Luis Obispo, Calif.
KSMA	1240	Santa Maria, Calif.
KSMB	94.5	Lafayette, La.
KSMC	89.5	Moraga, Calif.
KSME	90.7	Manti, Utah
KSMI-FM	104.9	Donaldsonville, La.
KSMK-FM	95.9	Cottonwood, Ariz.
KSML	1240	Globe, Ariz.
KSMM	1530	Shakopee, Minn.
KSMN	1010	Mason City, Ia.
KSMO	1340	Salem, Mo.
KSMO-FM	95.9	Salem, Mo.
KSMR	90.9	Winona, Minn.
KSMR	92.5	Winona, Minn.
KSMU	91.1	Springfield, Mo.
KSMX	92.1	Ft. Dodge, Ia.
KSNB-TV	4	Superior, Neb.
KSND	93.1	Springfield, Ore.
KSNE	92.1	Broken Arrow, Okla.
KSNF	16	Joplin, Mo.
KSNG	11	Garden City, Kan.
KSNI-FM	102.5	Santa Maria, Calif.
KSNK	8	Mc Cook, Neb.
KSNM	95.5	Santa Fe, N.M.
KSNN	104.7	Los Banos, Calif.
KSNO	1260	Aspen, Colo.
KSNR	99.3	Thief River Falls, Minn.
KSNT	27	Topeka, Kan.
KSNW	3	Wichita, Kan.
KSNY	1450	Snyder, Tex.
KSNY-FM	101.7	Snyder, Tex.
KSO	1460	Des Moines, Ia.
KSOA	1430	Ava, Mo.
KSOH	1050	Little Rock, Ark.
KSOJ	93.9	Flagstaff, Ariz.
KSOK	1280	Arkansas City, Kan.
KSOL	107.7	San Mateo, Calif.
KSON	1240	San Diego, Calif.
KSON-FM	97.3	San Diego, Calif.
KSOO	1140	Sioux Falls, S.D.
KSOP	1370	South Salt Lake City, Utah
KSOP	91.1	Wichita, Kan.
KSOP-FM	104.3	Salt Lake City, Utah
KSOR	90.1	Ashland, Ore.
KSOX	1240	Raymondville, Tex.
KSOX-FM	101.7	Raymondville, Tex.
KSOZ	91.7	Point Lookout, Mo.
KSPA	96.7	Hot Springs, Ark.
KSPB	91.9	Pebble Beach, Calif.
KSPB	91.5	Pebble Beach, Calif.
KSPC	88.7	Claremont, Calif.
KSPD	790	Boise, Id.
KSPG	99.3	El Dorado, Kan.
KSPI	780	Stillwater, Okla.
KSPI-FM	93.9	Stillwater, Okla.
KSPL	1150	Seattle, Wash.
KSPN	97.7	Aspen, Colo.
KSPO	1050	Dishman, Wash.
KSPR	33	Springfield, Mo.
KSPS-TV	7	Spokane, Wash.
KSPT	1400	Sandpoint, Id.
KSPZ	92.9	Colorado Springs, Colo.
KSQU	100.9	Weed, Calif.
KSQY	95.1	Deadwood, S.D.
KSRA	960	Salmon, Id.
KSRA-FM	92.7	Salmon, Id.
KSRB	1570	Hardy, Ark.
KSRC	1290	Socorro, N.M.
KSRD	96.9	Seward, Neb.
KSRE	6	Minot, N.D.
KSRF	103.1	Santa Monica, Calif.
KSRH	88.1	San Rafael, Calif.
KSRM	920	Soldatna, Alas.
KSRN	104.5	Reno, Nev.
KSRO	1350	Santa Rosa, Calif.
KSRQ	90.1	Thief River Falls, Minn.
KSRR	96.5	Houston, Tex.
KSRV	1380	Ontario, Ore.

KSSA	1270	Ft. Worth, Tex.
KSSK	590	Honolulu, Haw.
KSSN	95.7	Little Rock, Ark.
KSSS	740	Colorado Springs, Colo.
KSST	1230	Sulphur Springs, Tex.
KSTA	1000	Coleman, Tex.
KSTA-FM	107.1	Coleman, Tex.
KSTB	1430	Breckenridge, Tex.
KSTC	1230	Sterling, Colo.
KSTC-FM	104.7	Sterling, Colo.
KSTF	10	Scottsbluff, Neb.
KSTG	97.7	Sikeston, Mo.
KSTI	90.1	Springfield, S.D.
KSTK	101.7	Wrangell, Alas.
KSTL	690	St. Louis, Mo.
KSTM	107.1	Apache Jct, Ariz.
KSTN	1420	Stockton, Calif.
KSTN-FM	107.3	Stockton, Calif.
KSTP	1500	St. Paul, Minn.
KSTP-FM	94.5	St. Paul, Minn.
KSTP-TV	5	St. Paul, Minn.
KSTQ	99.3	Alexandria, Minn.
KSTR	620	Grand Junction, Colo.
KSTS	48	San Jose, Calif.
KSTT	1170	Davenport, Ia.
KSTU	20	Salt Lake City, Utah
KSTV	1510	Stephenville, Tex.
KSTW	11	Tacoma, Wash.
KSUB	590	Cedar City, Utah
KSUB-FM	92.5	Cedar City, Utah
KSUC	88.3	Keene, Tex.
KSUD	730	West Memphis, Ark.
KSUE	1240	Susanville, Calif.
KSUE-FM	92.7	Susanville, Calif.
KSUI	91.7	Iowa City, Ia.
KSUL	90.1	Long Beach, Calif.
KSUM	1370	Fairmont, Minn.
KSUN	1400	Phoenix, Ariz.
KSUT	91.3	Ignacio, Colo.
KSUZ-TV	15	Abilene, Tex.
KSVA	1470	Sierra Vista, Ariz.
KSVC	980	Richfield, Utah
KSVN	730	Ogden, Utah
KSVP	990	Artesia, N.M.
KSVR	90.1	Mt. Vernon, Wash.
KSWA	1330	Graham, Tex.
KSWB	930	Seaside, Ore.
KSWC	100.3	Winfield, Kan.
KSWH	91.1	Arkadelphia, Ark.
KSWM	940	Aurora, Mo.
KSWO	1380	Lawton, Okla.
KSWO-TV	7	Lawton, Okla.
KSWS-TV	8	Roswell, N.M.
KSXO	600	Redding, Calif.
KSXT	97.1	Walla Walla, Wash.
KSXX	630	Sandy, Utah
KSYC	1490	Yreka, Calif.
KSYL	970	Alexandria, La.
KSYM-FM	90.1	San Antonio, Tex.
KSYN	92.5	Joplin, Mo.
KSYR-FM	97.5	El Paso, Tex.
KSYS	8	Medford, Ore.
KSYV	96.7	Solvag, Calif.
KSYX	1340	Santa Rosa, N.M.
KSYZ-FM	107.7	Grand Island, Neb.
KSZN	1340	Pampa, Tex.
KTAB-TV	32	Abilene, Tex.
KTAC	850	Tacoma, Wash.
KTAE	1260	Taylor, Tex.
KTAG	97.9	Cody, Wyo.
KTAI	91.1	Kingsville, Tex.
KTAJ	16	St. Joseph, Mo.
KTAK	93.9	Riverton, Wyo.
KTAL-FM	98.1	Texarkana, Tex.
KTAL-TV	6	Shreveport, La.
KTAM	1240	Bryan, Tex.
KTAN	1420	Sierra Vista, Ariz.

KTAP	103.9	Crete, Neb.
KTAR	620	Phoenix, Ariz.
KTAT	1570	Frederick, Okla.
KTAV	92.1	Knoxville, Ia.
KTAW	92.1	College Station, Tex.
KTAZ-FM	100.9	Sierra Vista, Ariz.
KTBA	1050	Tuba City, Ariz.
KTBB	600	Tyler, Tex.
KTBC	92.1	Nacogdoches, Tex.
KTBC-TV	7	Austin, Tex.
KTBN-TV	40	Santa Ana, Calif.
KTBO	14	Oklahoma City, Okla.
KTBS-TV	3	Shreveport, La.
KTBY	4	Anchorage, Alas.
KTCA-TV	2	St. Paul, Minn.
KTCB	1470	Malden, Mo.
KTCC	91.9	Colby, Kan.
KTCH	1590	Wayne, Neb.
KTCH-FM	104.9	Wayne, Neb.
KTCI-TV	17	St. Paul, Minn.
KTCL	93.3	Ft. Collins, Colo.
KTCR	690	Minneapolis, Minn.
KTCR-FM	97.1	Minneapolis, Minn.
KTCS	1410	Ft. Smith, Ark.
KTCS-FM	99.9	Ft. Smith, Ark.
KTCU-FM	88.7	Ft. Worth, Tex.
KTDB	89.7	Ramah, N.M.
KTDL	1470	Farmerville, La.
KTDO	1230	Toledo, Ore.
KTDY	99.9	Lafayette, La.
KTDZ	24	Portland, Ore.
KTEC	89.5	Klamath Falls, Ore.
KTED	96.7	Fowler, Calif.
KTEE	1260	Idaho Falls, Id.
KTEH-TV	54	San Jose, Calif.
KTEI	105.5	Piggott, Ark.
KTEJ	19	Jonesboro, Ark.
KTEK	1110	Alvin, Tex.
KTEL	1490	Walla Walla, Wash.
KTEM	1400	Temple, Tex.
KTEN	10	Ada, Okla.
KTEN-FM	93.3	Ada, Okla.
KTEO	1340	San Angelo, Tex.
KTEP	88.5	El Paso, Tex.
KTEQ	91.3	Rapid City, S.D.
KTER	1570	Terrell, Tex.
KTEZ	101.1	Lubbock, Tex.
KTFA	92.1	Groves, Tex.
KTFC	103.3	Sioux City, Ia.
KTFM	102.7	San Antonio, Tex.
KTFS	1400	Texarkana, Tex.
KTFX	103.3	Tulsa, Okla.
KTGC	21	Negerland, Tex.
KTGO	1090	Tioga, N.D.
KTGR	1580	Columbia, Mo.
KTHE	1240	Thermopolis, Wyo.
KTHI-TV	11	Fargo, N.D.
KTHO	590	South Lake Tahoe, Calif.
KTHS	1480	Berryville, Ark.
KTHV	11	Little Rock, Ark.
KTIB	640	Thibodaux, La.
KTIB	630	Thibodaux, La.
KTIE	63	Oxnard, Calif.
KTIG	100.1	Pequot Lakes, Minn.
KTIL	1590	Tillamook, Ore.
KTIL-FM	104.1	Tillamook, Ore.
KTIM	1510	San Rafael, Calif.
KTIM-FM	100.9	San Rafael, Calif.
KTIN	21	Ft. Dodge, Ia.
KTIP	1450	Porterville, Calif.
KTIS	900	Minneapolis, Minn.
KTIS-FM	98.5	Minneapolis, Minn.
KTIV	4	Sioux City, Ia.
KTIX	1240	Pendleton, Ore.
KTIZ	96.9	Alexandria, La.

KTJA	103.3	Beaverton, Ore.
KTJJ	98.5	Farmington, Mo.
KTJO-FM	88.1	Ottawa, Kan.
KTJS	1420	Hobart, Okla.
KTKC	92.7	Springhill, La.
KTKN	930	Ketchikan, Alas.
KTKR	1310	Taft, Calif.
KTKT	990	Tucson, Ariz.
KTLA	5	Los Angeles, Calif.
KTLB	105.5	Twin Lakes, Ia.
KTLC	1270	Twin Falls, Id.
KTLD	1360	Tallulah, La.
KTLE	1010	Tooele, Utah
KTLE	990	Tooele, Utah
KTLE-FM	92.1	Tooele, Utah
KTLK	1460	Lubbock, Tex.
KTLO	1240	Mountain Home, Ark.
KTLO-FM	98.3	Mountain Home, Ark.
KTLQ	1350	Tahlequah, Okla.
KTLR-FM	107.1	Terrell, Tex.
KTLU	1580	Rusk, Tex.
KTLX	91.9	Columbus, Neb.
KTMA-TV	23	St. Paul, Minn.
KTMC	1400	Mc Alester, Okla.
KTMG	1370	Deer Trail, Colo.
KTMO	98.9	Kennett, Mo.
KTMS	1250	Santa Barbara, Calif.
KTMS-FM	97.5	Santa Barbara, Calif.
KTMT	93.7	Medford, Ore.
KTNC	1230	Falls City, Neb.
KTNC-FM	95.3	Falls City, Neb.
KTNE-TV	13	Alliance, Neb.
KTNL	13	Sitka, Alas.
KTNM	1400	Tucumcari, N.M.
KTNQ	1020	Los Angeles, Calif.
KTNR	92.1	Kennedy, Tex.
KTNT	93.5	Rudioso, N.M.
KTNV-TV	13	Las Vegas, Nev.
KTNW	10	Riverton, Wyo.
KTNX	1080	Anchorage, Alas.
KTOB	1490	Petaluma, Calif.
KTOC	920	Jonesboro, La.
KTOD	88.1	St. Louis, Mo.
KTOD	1330	Conway, Ark.
KTOE	1420	Mankato, Minn.
KTOF	104.5	Cedar Rapids, Ia.
KTOK	1000	Oklahoma City, Okla.
KTOM	1380	Salinas, Calif.
KTON	940	Belton, Tex.
KTON-FM	106.3	Belton, Tex.
KTOO	104.3	Juneau, Alas.
KTOO-TV	3	Juneau, Alas.
KTOP	1490	Topeka, Kan.
KTOQ	1340	Rapid City, S.D.
KTOT	101.7	Big Bear Lake, Calif.
KTOW	1340	Sand Springs, Okla.
KTOX	740	Boise, Id.
KTOX	730	Boise, Id.
KTOY	91.7	Tacoma, Wash.
KTPA	1370	Prescott, Ark.
KTPI	103.1	Tehachapi, Calif.
KTPK	106.9	Topeka, Kan.
KTPR	91.1	Ft. Dodge, Ia.
KTPS	28	Tacoma, Wash.
KTPX	9	Monahans, Tex.
KTQM-FM	99.9	Clovis, N.M.
KTQQ	100.9	Sulphur, La.
KTRB	860	Modesto, Calif.
KTRC	1400	Santa Fe, N.M.
KTRE-TV	9	Lufkin, Tex.
KTRF	1230	Thief River Falls, Minn.
KTRH	740	Houston, Tex.
KTRI-FM	95.9	Mansfield, Mo.
KTRJ	95.9	Ephrata, Wash.
KTRK	13	Houston, Tex.
KTRM	990	Beaumont, Tex.
KTRN	1290	Wichita Falls, Tex.
KTRQ	810	Ephrata, Wash.

Call	Freq.	Location
KTRS	95.5	Casper, Wyo.
KTRT	1400	Truckee, Calif.
KTRU	91.7	Houston, Tex.
KTRV	12	Nampa, Id.
KTRW	97.7	East Wenatchee, Wash.
KTRX	93.5	Tarkio, Mo.
KTRY	730	Bastrop, La.
KTRY-FM	94.3	Bastrop, La.
KTSA	550	San Antonio, Tex.
KTSC	8	Pueblo, Colo.
KTSC-FM	89.5	Pueblo, Colo.
KTSC-FM	89.7	Pueblo, Colo.
KTSD-TV	10	Pierre, S.D.
KTSF-TV	26	San Francisco, Calif.
KTSJ	1220	Pomona, Calif.
KTSM	1380	El Paso, Tex.
KTSM-FM	99.9	El Paso, Tex.
KTSM-TV	9	El Paso, Tex.
KTSP-TV	10	Phoenix, Ariz.
KTSR	90.1	Kansas City, Mo.
KTSU	90.9	Houston, Tex.
KTTC	10	Rochester, Minn.
KTTH	100.9	Naknek, Alas.
KTTI	95.1	Yuma, Ariz.
KTTL	93.9	Dodge City, Kan.
KTTN	1600	Trenton, Mo.
KTTN-FM	92.1	Trenton, Mo.
KTTR	1490	Rolla, Mo.
KTTS	1400	Springfield, Mo.
KTTS-FM	94.7	Springfield, Mo.
KTTT	1510	Columbus, Neb.
KTTT-FM	93.5	Columbus, Neb.
KTTU-TV	2	Fairbanks, Alas.
KTTV	11	Los Angeles, Calif.
KTTX	1280	Brenham, Tex.
KTTY	69	San Diego, Calif.
KTTZ	103.1	Oracle, Ariz.
KTTZ	22	Seattle, Wash.
KTUC	1400	Tucson, Ariz.
KTUE	1260	Tulia, Tex.
KTUF	93.5	Kirksville, Mo.
KTUH	90.3	Honolulu, Haw.
KTUI	1560	Sullivan, Mo.
KTUI-FM	100.9	Sullivan, Mo.
KTUL-TV	8	Tulsa, Okla.
KTUN	1180	Humble, Tex.
KTUO	91.5	Sonora, Calif.
KTUO	99.1	Sonora, Calif.
KTUS	103.9	Snowmas Village, Colo.
KTUU-TV	2	Anchorage, Alas.
KTVA	11	Anchorage, Alas.
KTVB	7	Boise, Id.
KTVC	6	Dodge City, Kan.
KTVE	10	El Dorado, Ark.
KTVF	11	Fairbanks, Alas.
KTVG	12	Helena, Mont.
KTVI	2	St. Louis, Mo.
KTVJ	14	Boulder, Colo.
KTVK	3	Phoenix, Ariz.
KTVL	10	Medford, Ore.
KTVM	6	Butte, Mont.
KTVN	2	Reno, Nev.
KTVO	3	Kirksville, Mo.
KTVP	29	Fayetteville, Ark.
KTVQ	2	Billings, Mont.
KTVR	13	La Grande, Ore.
KTVS	3	Sterling, Colo.
KTVT	11	Ft. Worth, Tex.
KTVU	2	San Francisco, Calif.
KTVV	36	Austin, Tex.
KTVW-TV	33	Phoenix, Ariz.
KTVX	4	Salt Lake City, Utah
KTVY	4	Oklahoma City, Okla.
KTVZ	21	Bend, Ore.
KTWA	92.7	Ottumwa, Ia.
KTWD	106.3	Lonoke, Ark.
KTWO	1030	Casper, Wyo.
KTWO-TV	2	Casper, Wyo.
KTWS	27	Dallas, Tex.
KTWU	11	Topeka, Kan.

Call	Freq.	Location
KTXA	21	Ft. Worth, Tex.
KTXC	1250	Port Arthur, Tex.
KTXF	100.3	Brownsville, Tex.
KTXH	20	Houston, Tex.
KTXJ	1350	Jasper, Tex.
KTXK	91.5	Texarkana, Tex.
KTXL	40	Sacramento, Calif.
KTXN-FM	98.7	Victoria, Tex.
KTXO	1500	Sherman, Tex.
KTXQ	102.1	Ft. Worth, Tex.
KTXR	101.5	Springfield, Mo.
KTXS-TV	12	Sweetwater, Tex.
KTXT-FM	88.1	Lubbock, Tex.
KTXT-TV	5	Lubbock, Tex.
KTXU	99.3	Paris, Tex.
KTXX	1450	Whitefish, Mont.
KTXY	106.9	Jefferson City, Mo.
KTXZ	1560	West Lake Hills, Tex.
KTYD	99.9	Santa Barbara, Calif.
KTYE	99.3	Tye, Tex.
KTYL	1330	Tyler, Tex.
KTYL-FM	93.1	Tyler, Tex.
KTYM	1460	Inglewood, Calif.
KTYN	1430	Minot, N.D.
KTZA	92.9	Artesia, N.M.
KTZO	20	San Francisco, Calif.
KUAC-FM	104.7	Fairbanks, Alas.
KUAC-TV	9	Fairbanks, Alas.
KUAD	1170	Windsor, Colo.
KUAD-FM	99.1	Windsor, Colo.
KUAF	88.9	Fayetteville, Ark.
KUAI	720	Eleele, Haw.
KUAL	103.1	Enid, Okla.
KUAR	89.1	Little Rock, Ark.
KUAT	1550	Tucson, Ariz.
KUAT-FM	90.5	Tucson, Ariz.
KUAT-TV	6	Tucson, Ariz.
KUBA	1600	Yuba City, Calif.
KUBB	96.3	Mariposa, Calif.
KUBC	580	Montrose, Colo.
KUBC-FM	94.1	Montrose, Colo.
KUBE	93.3	Seattle, Wash.
KUBO	90.9	Chualar, Calif.
KUBS	91.5	Newport, Wash.
KUCA	91.3	Conway, Ark.
KUCB-FM	89.3	Des Moines, Ia.
KUCI	89.9	Irvine, Calif.
KUCR	88.1	Riverside, Calif.
KUCU	40	St. Louis, Mo.
KUCV	90.9	Lincoln, Neb.
KUDL	98.1	Kansas City, Kan.
KUDO	93.1	Las Vegas, Nev.
KUDY	1280	Spokane, Wash.
KUED	7	Salt Lake City, Utah
KUEN	900	Wenatchee, Wash.
KUER	90.1	Salt Lake City, Utah
KUET	710	Black Canyon City, Ariz.
KUFM	89.1	Missoula, Mont.
KUFO	97.9	Odessa, Tex.
KUFW	90.5	Woodlake, Calif.
KUGN	590	Eugene, Ore.
KUGN-FM	97.9	Eugene, Ore.
KUGR	1490	Green River, Wyo.
KUGS	89.3	Bellingham, Wash.
KUHF	88.7	Houston, Tex.
KUHL	1440	Santa Maria, Calif.
KUHT	8	Houston, Tex.
KUIC	95.3	Vacaville, Calif.
KUID	91.7	Moscow, Id.
KUID-TV	12	Moscow, Id.
KUIK	1360	Hillsboro, Ore.
KUIN	92.7	Vernal, Utah
KUJ	1420	Walla Walla, Wash.
KUJ-FM	95.7	Walla Walla, Wash.

Call	Freq.	Location
KUKA	1250	San Antonio, Tex.
KUKI	1400	Ukiah, Calif.
KUKQ	1060	Tempe, Ariz.
KUKU	1330	Willow Springs, Mo.
KULA	92.3	Waipahu, Haw.
KULM	98.3	Columbus, Tex.
KULP	1390	El Campo, Tex.
KULR-TV	8	Billings, Mont.
KULY	1420	Ulysses, Kan.
KUMA	1290	Pendleton, Ore.
KUMA-FM	107.7	Pendleton, Ore.
KUMD-FM	103.3	Duluth, Minn.
KUMM	89.7	Morris, Minn.
KUMR	88.5	Rolla, Mo.
KUMU	1500	Honolulu, Haw.
KUMU-FM	94.7	Honolulu, Haw.
KUMV-TV	8	Williston, N.D.
KUNA	96.1	San Luis Obispo, Calif.
KUNC-FM	91.5	Greeley, Colo.
KUNI	90.9	Cedar Falls, Ia.
KUNM	90.1	Albuquerque, N.M.
KUNO	1400	Corpus Christi, Tex.
KUNR	88.7	Reno, Nev.
KUNV	91.5	Las Vegas, Nev.
KUOA	1290	Siloam Springs, Ark.
KUOI-FM	89.3	Moscow, Id.
KUOL	101.7	Mena, Ark.
KUOM	770	Minneapolis, Minn.
KUON-TV	12	Lincoln, Neb.
KUOP	91.3	Stockton, Calif.
KUOR-FM	89.1	Redlands, Calif.
KUOW	94.9	Seattle, Wash.
KUPD-FM	97.9	Tempe, Ariz.
KUPI	980	Idaho Falls, Id.
KUPK-TV	13	Garden City, Kan.
KUPL	1330	Portland, Ore.
KUPL-FM	98.5	Portland, Ore.
KUPS	90.1	Tacoma, Wash.
KUQQ	1540	Ft. Worth, Tex.
KURA	1450	Moab, Utah
KURL	730	Billings, Mont.
KURM	790	Rogers, Ark.
KURO	92.1	Huron, S.D.
KURU	89.1	San Antonio, Tex.
KURV	710	Edinburg, Tex.
KURY	910	Brookings, Ore.
KURY-FM	95.3	Brookings, Ore.
KUSC	91.5	Los Angeles, Calif.
KUSD	690	Vermillion, S.D.
KUSD-FM	89.7	Vermillion, S.D.
KUSD-TV	2	Vermillion, S.D.
KUSF	90.3	San Francisco, Calif.
KUSH	1600	Cushing, Okla.
KUSI	51	San Diego, Calif.
KUSK	7	Prescott, Ariz.
KUSP	88.9	Santa Cruz, Calif.
KUSR	91.9	Ames, Ia.
KUSR	91.5	Ames, Ia.
KUSU-FM	91.5	Logan, Utah
KUT-FM	90.5	Austin, Tex.
KUTA	790	Blanding, Utah
KUTE	101.9	Glendale, Calif.
KUTI	980	Yakima, Wash.
KUTV	2	Salt Lake City, Utah
KUTY	1470	Palmdale, Calif.
KUUK	1250	Wickenburg, Ariz.
KUUL	92.1	Madera, Calif.
KUUT	107.5	Orem, Utah
KUUU	88.1	Neola, Utah
KUUX	1480	Hobbs, N.M.
KUUY	1530	Cheyenne, Wyo.
KUVO	89.3	Denver, Colo.
KUVR	1380	Holdrege, Neb.
KUVR-FM	97.7	Holdrege, Neb.
KUWR	91.9	Laramie, Wyo.

KUXL	1570	Golden Valley, Minn.
KUZN	1310	West Monroe, La.
KUZZ	970	Bakersfield, Calif.
KVAA	910	Volga, S.D.
KVAC	1490	Forks, Wash.
KVAL	13	Eugene, Ore.
KVAN	1550	Vancouver, Wash.
KVAR	104.5	San Antonio, Tex.
KVAS	1230	Astoria, Ore.
KVBC	3	Las Vegas, Nev.
KVBR	1340	Brainerd, Minn.
KVCK	1450	Wolf Point, Mont.
KVCL	1270	Winnfield, La.
KVCL-FM	92.1	Winnfield, La.
KVCM	103.9	Montgomery City, Mo.
KVCO	88.3	Concordia, Kan.
KVCR	91.9	San Bernardino, Calif.
KVCR-TV	24	San Bernardino, Calif.
KVDB	1090	Sioux Center, Ia.
KVDB-FM	94.3	Sioux Center, Ia.
KVEC	920	San Luis Obispo, Calif.
KVEG	1410	Las Vegas, Nev.
KVEL	920	Vernal, Utah
KVEN	1450	Ventura, Calif.
KVEO	23	Brownsville, Tex.
KVET	1300	Austin, Tex.
KVEW	42	Kennewick, Wash.
KVEX	103.9	Smithfield, Utah
KVFC	740	Cortez, Colo.
KVFD	1400	Ft. Dodge, Ia.
KVFG	91.3	Thibodaux, La.
KVGB	1590	Great Bend, Kan.
KVGB-FM	104.3	Great Bend, Kan.
KVGM	930	Yakima, Wash.
KVHP	29	Lake Charles, La.
KVHS	90.5	Concord, Calif.
KVI	570	Seattle, Wash.
KVIA-TV	7	El Paso, Tex.
KVIB	94.3	Mukawao, Haw.
KVIE	6	Sacramento, Calif.
KVII-TV	7	Amarillo, Tex.
KVIJ-TV	8	Sayre, Okla.
KVIK	91.5	Travis A F B, Calif.
KVIL	1150	Highland Park, Tex.
KVIL-FM	103.7	Dallas, Tex.
KVIM	970	Coachella, Calif.
KVIN	1470	Vinita, Okla.
KVIP	540	Redding, Calif.
KVIP-FM	98.1	Redding, Calif.
KVIQ-TV	6	Eureka, Calif.
KVKI	96.5	Shreveport, La.
KVKM	1330	Monahans, Tex.
KVLE	102.7	Gunnison, Colo.
KVLF	1240	Alpine, Tex.
KVLG	1570	La Grange, Tex.
KVLH	1470	Pauls Valley, Okla.
KVLI	1140	Lake Isabella, Calif.
KVLL	1220	Woodville, Tex.
KVLR	95.3	Detroit Lakes, Minn.
KVLU	91.3	Beaumont, Tex.
KVLV	980	Fallon, Nev.
KVLV-FM	99.3	Fallon, Nev.
KVLY	107.9	Edinburg, Tex.
KVMA	630	Magnolia, Ark.
KVMA-FM	107.9	Magnolia, Ark.
KVMC	1320	Colorado City, Tex.
KVML	1450	Sonora, Calif.
KVMR	89.5	Nevada City, Calif.
KVMT	104.7	Vail, Colo.
KVMV	96.9	Mc Allen, Tex.
KVMX	96.7	Eastland, Tex.
KVNE	89.5	Tyler, Tex.
KVNF	90.9	Paonia, Colo.
KVNI	1080	Coeur D' Alene, Id.
KVNJ	15	Fargo, N.D.
KVNM	101.7	Taos, N.M.
KVNO	90.7	Omaha, Neb.
KVNU	610	Logan, Utah
KVOA-TV	4	Tucson, Ariz.
KVOB	1340	Bastrop, La.
KVOC	1230	Casper, Wyo.
KVOD	99.5	Denver, Colo.
KVOE	1400	Emporia, Kan.
KVOF-TV	38	San Francisco, Calif.
KVOI	690	Tucson, Ariz.
KVOK	560	Kodiak, Alas.
KVOL	1330	Lafayette, La.
KVOM	800	Morrilton, Ark.
KVOM-FM	101.7	Morrilton, Ark.
KVON	1440	Napa, Calif.
KVOO	1170	Tulsa, Okla.
KVOP	1400	Plainview, Tex.
KVOR	1300	Colorado Springs, Colo.
KVOS-TV	12	Bellingham, Wash.
KVOU	1400	Uvalde, Tex.
KVOV	1280	Henderson, Nev.
KVOW	1450	Riverton, Wyo.
KVOX	1280	Moorhead, Minn.
KVOX-FM	99.9	Moorhead, Minn.
KVOY	1400	Yuma, Ariz.
KVOZ	1490	Laredo, Tex.
KVPI	1050	Ville Platte, La.
KVPI-FM	93.5	Ville Platte, La.
KVPR-FM	89.3	Fresno, Calif.
KVRA	1570	Vermillion, S.D.
KVRC	1240	Arkadelphia, Ark.
KVRD	1600	Cottonwood, Ariz.
KVRE	1460	Santa Rosa, Calif.
KVRE-FM	101.7	Santa Rosa, Calif.
KVRF	102.3	Vermillion, S.D.
KVRH	1340	Salida, Colo.
KVRH-FM	92.1	Salida, Colo.
KVRN	980	Sonora, Tex.
KVRN-FM	92.1	Sonora, Tex.
KVRO	105.5	Stillwater, Okla.
KVRP-FM	95.5	Haskell, Tex.
KVRS	105.5	Sterling, Colo.
KVSA	1220	Mc Gehee, Ark.
KVSC	88.1	St. Cloud, Minn.
KVSF	1260	Santa Fe, N.M.
KVSH	940	Valentine, Neb.
KVSI	1450	Montpelier, Id.
KVSL	1450	Show Low, Ariz.
KVSO	1240	Ardmore, Okla.
KVSR	97.9	Rapid City, S.D.
KVSV	1190	Beloit, Kan.
KVSV-FM	105.5	Beloit, Kan.
KVTI	90.9	Tacoma, Wash.
KVTT	91.7	Dallas, Tex.
KVTV	13	Laredo, Tex.
KVTX	31	Victoria, Tex.
KVUE-TV	24	Austin, Tex.
KVUU	99.9	Pueblo, Colo.
KVVA	860	Phoenix, Ariz.
KVVC-FM	106.3	Cabool, Mo.
KVVP	105.5	Leesville, La.
KVVQ	103.1	Victorville, Calif.
KVVU	5	Henderson, Nev.
KVWC	1490	Vernon, Tex.
KVWC-FM	102.3	Vernon, Tex.
KVWG	1280	Pearsall, Tex.
KVWG-FM	95.3	Pearsall, Tex.
KVWM	970	Show Low, Ariz.
KVWM-FM	93.5	Show Low, Ariz.
KVYL	1370	Holdenville, Okla.
KVYN	99.3	St. Helena, Calif.
KWAB	4	Big Spring, Tex.
KWAC	1490	Bakersfield, Calif.
KWAD	920	Wadena, Minn.
KWAK	1240	Stuttgart, Ark.
KWAL	620	Wallace, Id.
KWAM	990	Memphis, Tenn.
KWAR	89.1	Waverly, Ia.
KWAS	101.9	Amarillo, Tex.
KWAT	950	Watertown, S.D.
KWAV	96.9	Monterey, Calif.
KWAX	91.1	Eugene, Ore.
KWAY	99.3	Waverly, Ia.
KWAY	1470	Waverly, Ia.
KWBA	12	Pembina, N.D.
KWBC	1550	Navasota, Tex.
KWBE	1450	Beatrice, Neb.
KWBG	1590	Boone, Ia.
KWBG-FM	98.3	Boone, Ia.
KWBI	91.1	Morrison, Colo.
KWBJ	100.1	Payette, Id.
KWBJ	100.3	Payette, Id.
KWBO	97.5	Hot Springs, Ark.
KWBU	107.1	Waco, Tex.
KWBW	1450	Hutchinson, Kan.
KWC-FM	88.1	Ogden, Utah
KWCB	94.3	Floresville, Tex.
KWCH-TV	12	Hutchinson, Kan.
KWCK	1300	Searcy, Ark.
KWCL	1280	Oak Grove, La.
KWCL-FM	96.7	Oak Grove, La.
KWCM-TV	10	Appleton, Minn.
KWCO	1560	Chickasha, Okla.
KWCS	96.7	Bridgeport, Tex.
KWCT	27	Wenatchee, Wash.
KWCW	90.5	Walla Walla, Wash.
KWCX	98.3	Willcox, Ariz.
KWDE	96.1	Montrose, Colo.
KWDG	96.7	Idabel, Okla.
KWDJ	92.7	Riverside, Calif.
KWDM	88.9	West Des Moines, Ia.
KWDX	101.7	Silsbee, Tex.
KWEB	1270	Rochester, Minn.
KWED	1580	Seguin, Tex.
KWED-FM	105.3	Seguin, Tex.
KWEH	97.1	Camden, Ark.
KWEI	1260	Weiser, Id.
KWEI-FM	100.9	Weiser, Id.
KWEL	1070	Midland, Tex.
KWEN	95.5	Tulsa, Okla.
KWES	102.1	Monahans, Tex.
KWET	12	Cheyenne, Okla.
KWEX-TV	41	San Antonio, Tex.
KWEY	1590	Weatherford, Okla.
KWEY-FM	97.3	Weatherford, Okla.
KWEZ	104.1	Monroe, La.
KWFC	97.3	Springfield, Mo.
KWFM	92.9	Tucson, Ariz.
KWFT	620	Wichita Falls, Tex.
KWG	1230	Stockton, Calif.
KWGG	105.5	Harlan, Ia.
KWGH	1290	Big Lake, Tex.
KWGN-TV	2	Denver, Colo.
KWGS	89.5	Tulsa, Okla.
KWHI-FM	106.3	Brenham, Tex.
KWHK	1260	Hutchinson, Kan.
KWHL	106.5	Anchorage, Alas.
KWHN	1320	Ft. Smith, Ark.
KWHO	860	Salt Lake City, Utah
KWHO-FM	93.3	Salt Lake City, Utah
KWHP	14	Boise, Id.
KWHS	91.7	West Sacramento, Calif.
KWHW	1450	Altus, Okla.
KWHW-FM	93.5	Altus, Okla.
KWHY-TV	22	Los Angeles, Calif.
KWIC	107.7	Beaumont, Tex.
KWIK	1240	Pocatello, Id.
KWIL	790	Albany, Ore.
KWIN	97.7	Lodi, Calif.
KWIP	880	Dallas, Ore.
KWIQ	1260	Moses Lake, Wash.
KWIQ	1020	Moses Lake, Wash.
KWIQ-FM	100.3	Moses Lake, Wash.

KWIT	90.3	Sioux City, Ia.
KWIV	1470	Douglas, Wyo.
KWIX	1230	Moberly, Mo.
KWIZ	1480	Santa Ana, Calif.
KWIZ-FM	96.7	Santa Ana, Calif.
KWJJ	1080	Portland, Ore.
KWJM	92.7	Farmerville, La.
KWJS	94.9	Arlington, Tex.
KWK	1380	St. Louis, Mo.
KWK-FM	106.5	Granite City, Ill.
KWKA	680	Clovis, N.M.
KWKC	1340	Abilene, Tex.
KWKH	1130	Shreveport, La.
KWKI	95.3	Big Spring, Tex.
KWKI	95.3	Bayou Vista, La.
KWKK	102.3	Dardanelle, Ark.
KWKQ	107.1	Graham, Tex.
KWKR	99.9	Leoti, Kan.
KWKS	105.5	Winfield, Kan.
KWKT	44	Waco, Tex.
KWKW	1300	Pasadena, Calif.
KWKY	1150	Des Moines, Ia.
KWLA	1400	Many, La.
KWLB-FM	97.7	Marksville, La.
KWLC	1240	Decorah, Ia.
KWLD	91.5	Plainview, Tex.
KWLL	1460	Casa Grande, Ariz.
KWLM	1340	Willmar, Minn.
KWLO	1330	Waterloo, Ia.
KWLS	1290	Pratt, Kan.
KWLV	107.1	Jesup, La.
KWLW	93.9	San Angelo, Tex.
KWMB	1190	Wabasha, Minn.
KWMC	1490	Del Rio, Tex.
KWMJ	103.3	Midland, Tex.
KWMT	540	Ft. Dodge, Ia.
KWMU	90.7	St. Louis, Mo.
KWNA	1400	Winnemucca, Nev.
KWNA-FM	92.7	Winnemucca, Nev.
KWNB-TV	6	Hayes Center, Neb.
KWNC	1370	Quincy, Wash.
KWND	99.9	Saratoga, Wyo.
KWNE	94.5	Ukiah, Calif.
KWNG	105.5	Red Wing, Minn.
KWNK	670	Simi Valley, Calif.
KWNO	1230	Winona, Minn.
KWNR	102.7	Liberal, Kan.
KWNS	104.9	Winnsboro, Tex.
KWOA	730	Worthington, Minn.
KWOA-FM	95.1	Worthington, Minn.
KWOC	930	Poplar Bluff, Mo.
KWOD	106.5	Sacramento, Calif.
KWOK	1530	Wagoner, Okla.
KWON	1400	Bartlesville, Okla.
KWOR	1340	Worland, Wyo.
KWOS	1240	Jefferson City, Mo.
KWOW	1600	Pomona, Calif.
KWOX	101.1	Woodward, Okla.
KWOZ	103.3	Mountain View, Ark.
KWPB	91.9	Liberty, Mo.
KWPC	860	Muscatine, Ia.
KWPM	1450	West Plains, Mo.
KWPM-FM	93.9	West Plains, Mo.
KWRC	940	Woodburn, Ore.
KWRD	1470	Henderson, Tex.
KWRE	730	Warrenton, Mo.
KWRF	860	Warren, Ark.
KWRF-FM	105.5	Warren, Ark.
KWRM	1370	Corona, Calif.
KWRS	90.3	Spokane, Wash.
KWRT	1370	Boonville, Mo.
KWRW	97.7	Rusk, Tex.
KWSB-FM	91.9	Gunnison, Colo.
KWSB-FM	91.1	Gunnison, Colo.
KWSC	91.9	Wayne, Neb.
KWSD	620	Mt. Shasta, Calif.
KWSE	4	Williston, N.D.
KWSH	1260	Wewoka, Okla.

KWSI	96.5	Warm Springs, Ore.
KWSL	1470	Sioux City, Ia.
KWSO	1180	Wasco, Calif.
KWSR	810	Rifle, Colo.
KWSS	94.5	Gilroy, Calif.
KWST	101.7	Carmel, Calif.
KWSU	1250	Pullman, Wash.
KWSU-TV	10	Pullman, Wash.
KWTO	560	Springfield, Mo.
KWTO-FM	98.7	Springfield, Mo.
KWTS	91.1	Canyon, Tex.
KWTV	9	Oklahoma City, Okla.
KWTX	1230	Waco, Tex.
KWTX-FM	97.5	Waco, Tex.
KWTX-TV	10	Waco, Tex.
KWUN	1480	Concord, Calif.
KWUR	90.3	Clayton, Mo.
KWVE	107.9	San Clemente, Calif.
KWVR	1340	Enterprise, Ore.
KWWA	106.9	Bremerton, Wash.
KWWK	96.7	Rochester, Minn.
KWWL	7	Waterloo, Ia.
KWWM	105.7	Stephenville, Tex.
KWWR	95.7	Mexico, Mo.
KWWW	1340	Wenatchee, Wash.
KWWY	13	Rock Springs, Wyo.
KWXI	670	Glenwood, Ark.
KWXI	1470	Glenwood, Ark.
KWXL	94.1	Albuquerque, N.M.
KWXX	94.7	Hilo, Haw.
KWXY	1340	Cathedral City, Calif.
KWXY-FM	98.5	Cathedral City, Calif.
KWYD	105.5	Security, Colo.
KWYK-FM	94.9	Aztec, N.M.
KWYN	1400	Wynne, Ark.
KWYN-FM	92.7	Wynne, Ark.
KWYO	1410	Sheridan, Wyo.
KWYR	1260	Winner, S.D.
KWYR-FM	93.7	Winner, S.D.
KWYS	920	West Yellowstone, Mont.
KWYT-FM	100.7	Salinas, Calif.
KWYX	102.3	Jasper, Tex.
KWYZ	1230	Everett, Wash.
KXA	770	Seattle, Wash.
KXAK	1310	Corrales, N.M.
KXAR	1490	Hope, Ark.
KXAS-TV	5	Ft. Worth, Tex.
KXAX	104.9	St. James, Minn.
KXAZ	93.5	Page, Ariz.
KXBJ	26	Bemidji, Minn.
KXBQ	96.1	Ontario, Ore.
KXCI	91.7	Tucson, Ariz.
KXCL	107.9	Corsicana, Tex.
KXCV	90.5	Maryville, Mo.
KXDD	104.1	Yakima, Wash.
KXEG	1010	Phoenix, Ariz.
KXEL	1540	Waterloo, Ia.
KXEM	1590	Mc Farland, Calif.
KXEN	1010	St. Louis, Mo.
KXEO	1340	Mexico, Mo.
KXES	1570	Salinas, Calif.
KXEW	1600	Tucson, Ariz.
KXEX	1550	Fresno, Calif.
KXEZ	103.9	Yuba City, Calif.
KXFM	99.1	Santa Maria, Calif.
KXGC-FM	96.9	El Campo, Tex.
KXGN	1400	Glendive, Mont.
KXGN-TV	5	Glendive, Mont.
KXGO	93.5	Arcata, Calif.
KXGO	93.1	Arcata, Calif.
KXIC	800	Iowa City, Ia.
KXII	12	Ardmore, Okla.
KXIQ	94.1	Bend, Ore.
KXIT	1240	Dalhart, Tex.
KXIT-FM	95.9	Dalhart, Tex.
KXIX	19	Victoria, Tex.

KXJB-TV	4	Valley City, N.D.
KXJK	950	Forrest City, Ark.
KXJX	103.3	Pella, Ia.
KXKQ	94.1	Safford, Ariz.
KXKS	1190	Albuquerque, N.M.
KXKW	1520	Lafayette, La.
KXKX	106.5	Galveston, Tex.
KXKZ	107.5	Ruston, La.
KXL	750	Portland, Ore.
KXL-FM	95.5	Portland, Ore.
KXLA	990	Rayville, La.
KXLE	1240	Ellensburg, Wash.
KXLE-FM	95.3	Ellensburg, Wash.
KXLF	1370	Butte, Mont.
KXLF-TV	4	Butte, Mont.
KXLI	41	St Cloud, Minn.
KXLO	1230	Lewistown, Mont.
KXLP	93.1	New Ulm, Minn.
KXLS	99.7	Alva, Okla.
KXLT	47	Rochester, Minn.
KXLU	88.9	Los Angeles, Calif.
KXLV-FM	105.5	Cambridge, Minn.
KXLY	920	Spokane, Wash.
KXLY-FM	99.9	Spokane, Wash.
KXLY-TV	4	Spokane, Wash.
KXMB-TV	12	Bismarck, N.D.
KXMC	105.3	Mc Cook, Neb.
KXMC-TV	13	Minot, N.D.
KXMD-TV	11	Williston, N.D.
KXNE-TV	19	Norfolk, Neb.
KXNP	103.5	North Platte, Neb.
KXO	1230	El Centro, Calif.
KXO-FM	107.5	El Centro, Calif.
KXOA	1470	Sacramento, Calif.
KXOA-FM	107.9	Sacramento, Calif.
KXOF	106.3	Bloomfield, Ia.
KXOI	810	Crane, Tex.
KXOJ	1550	Sapulpa, Okla.
KXOJ-FM	100.9	Sapulpa, Okla.
KXOK	630	St. Louis, Mo.
KXOL	1360	Ft. Worth, Tex.
KXON	5	Mitchell, S.D.
KXOR	106.3	Thibodaux, La.
KXOW	1420	Hot Springs, Ark.
KXOX	1240	Sweetwater, Tex.
KXOX-FM	96.7	Sweetwater, Tex.
KXPO	1340	Grafton, N.D.
KXPO-FM	100.9	Grafton, N.D.
KXPR	89.5	Sacramento, Calif.
KXPR	90.9	Sacramento, Calif.
KXQR	790	Clovis, Calif.
KXRA	1490	Alexandria, Minn.
KXRA-FM	92.7	Alexandria, Minn.
KXRB	1000	Sioux Falls, S.D.
KXRC	93.7	Craig, Colo.
KXRK	1580	Davenport, Ia.
KXRM-TV	21	Colorado Springs, Colo.
KXRO	1320	Aberdeen, Wash.
KXRQ	1530	Trumann, Ark.
KXSS	95.3	Lincoln, Neb.
KXTC	1340	Nampa, Id.
KXTP	970	Superior, Wis.
KXTR	96.5	Kansas City, Mo.
KXTV	10	Sacramento, Calif.
KXTX	39	Dallas, Tex.
KXTZ	94.1	Henderson, Nev.
KXVI	1600	Mc Kinney, Tex.
KXVQ	1500	Pawhuska, Okla.
KXVR	99.5	Mountain Pass, Calif.
KXXE	101.3	Forsythe, Mont.
KXXI-FM	102.3	Van Buren, Ark.
KXXK	105.5	Chickasha, Okla.
KXXL	1450	Bozeman, Mont.
KXXN	1290	Santa Barbara, Calif.
KXXR	1440	Spokane, Wash.

Call	Freq.	Location
KXXX	790	Colby, Kan.
KXXX-FM	100.3	Colby, Kan.
KXXY	96.1	Oklahoma City, Okla.
KXYL	1240	Brownwood, Tex.
KXYL-FM	104.1	Brownwood, Tex.
KXYZ	1320	Houston, Tex.
KYA	93.3	San Francisco, Calif.
KYAK	650	Anchorage, Alas.
KYBB	100.9	Tracy, Calif.
KYBE	95.9	Frederick, Okla.
KYBS	97.5	Livingston, Mont.
KYCA	1490	Prescott, Ariz.
KYCN	1340	Wheatland, Wyo.
KYCU-TV	5	Cheyenne, Wyo.
KYDE	1590	Pine Bluff, Ark.
KYDS	91.5	Sacramento, Calif.
KYDZ	90.1	Cody, Wyo.
KYEA	98.3	West Monroe, La.
KYES	950	Roseburg, Ore.
KYET	1450	Payette, Id.
KYEZ	93.7	Salina, Kan.
KYFC	50	Kansas City, Mo.
KYFM	100.1	Bartlesville, Okla.
KYFR	920	Shenandoah, Ia.
KYGO	98.5	Denver, Colo.
KYIN	24	Mason City, Ia.
KYJC	1230	Medford, Ore.
KYJR	104.9	Wenatchee, Wash.
KYKC	1230	Sioux Falls, S.D.
KYKK	1110	Humble City, N.M.
KYKR-FM	93.3	Port Arthur, Tex.
KYKS	105.1	Lufkin, Tex.
KYKX	105.7	Longview, Tex.
KYKZ	96.1	Lake Charles, La.
KYLC	93.5	Osage Beach, Mo.
KYLO	105.5	Davis, Calif.
KYLS	92.7	Ironton, Mo.
KYLT	1340	Missoula, Mont.
KYMC	89.7	Ballwin, Mo.
KYMN	1080	Northfield, Minn.
KYMO	1080	East Prairie, Mo.
KYMS	106.3	Santa Ana, Calif.
KYNE-TV	26	Omaha, Neb.
KYNG	1420	Coos Bay, Ore.
KYNG-FM	105.5	Coos Bay, Ore.
KYNN	1490	Omaha, Neb.
KYNO	1300	Fresno, Calif.
KYNO-FM	95.7	Fresno, Calif.
KYNO-FM	95.5	Fresno, Calif.
KYNT	1450	Yankton, S.D.
KYOC	102.3	Yorkum, Tex.
KYOK	1590	Houston, Tex.
KYOO	1130	Bolivar, Mo.
KYOO-FM	106.3	Bolivar, Mo.
KYOS	1480	Merced, Calif.
KYOT	106.3	Refugio, Tex.
KYOU	1450	Greeley, Colo.
KYRE	97.7	Yreka, Calif.
KYRO	1280	Potosi, Mo.
KYRS	105.5	Chariton, Ia.
KYSC	88.5	Yakima, Wash.
KYSM	1230	Mankato, Minn.
KYSM-FM	103.5	Mankato, Minn.
KYSN	1460	Colorado Springs, Colo.
KYSR	920	El Paso, Tex.
KYSS	930	East Missoula, Mont.
KYSS	930	Missoula, Mont.
KYSS-FM	94.9	Missoula, Mont.
KYST	920	Texas City, Tex.
KYTE	970	Portland, Ore.
KYTN	94.7	Grand Forks, N.D.
KYTT-FM	98.3	Coos Bay, Ore.
KYTV	3	Springfield, Mo.
KYUF	104.9	Uvalde, Tex.
KYUK	580	Bethel, Alas.
KYUK-TV	4	Bethel, Alas.
KYUS-TV	3	Miles City, Mont.
KYUU	99.7	San Francisco, Calif.
KYVA	1230	Gallup, N.M.
KYVE-TV	47	Yakima, Wash.
KYW	1060	Philadelphia, Pa.
KYW-TV	3	Philadelphia, Pa.
KYXE	1020	Selah, Wash.
KYXI	1520	Oregon City, Ore.
KYXS	1140	Mineral Wells, Tex.
KYXS-FM	95.9	Mineral Wells, Tex.
KYXX	920	Odessa, Tex.
KYXY	96.5	San Diego, Calif.
KYYA	93.3	Billings, Mont.
KYYK	98.3	Palestine, Tex.
KYYS	102.1	Kansas City, Mo.
KYYX	96.5	Seattle, Wash.
KYYY	92.9	Bismarck, N.D.
KYYZ	96.1	Williston, N.D.
KYZK	97.1	Crookston, Minn.
KYZZ	92.7	Wolf Point, Mont.
KZAN	97.9	Ogden, Utah
KZAP	98.5	Sacramento, Calif.
KZAY	105.3	Delano, Calif.
KZAZ	11	Nogales, Alta.
KZBQ	1290	Pocatello, Id.
KZBQ	93.7	Pocatello, Id.
KZDO	105.5	Copperopolis, Calif.
KZDQ	96.7	Belgrade, Mont.
KZED	93.5	Wellington, Kan.
KZEE	1220	Weatherford, Tex.
KZEL-FM	96.1	Eugene, Ore.
KZEU	107.9	Victoria, Tex.
KZEV	103.1	Clear Lake, Ia.
KZEW	97.9	Dallas, Tex.
KZEY	690	Tyler, Tex.
KZEZ	93.5	St. George, Utah
KZFM	95.5	Corpus Christi, Tex.
KZFR	103.1	South Lake Tahoe, Calif.
KZFR	102.9	South Lake Tahoe, Calif.
KZIA	1580	Albuquerque, N.M.
KZIA-FM	101.7	Rio Rancho, N.M.
KZIG	89.9	Cave City, Ark.
KZIN-FM	96.3	Shelby, Mont.
KZIO	102.5	Superior, Wis.
KZIP	1310	Amarillo, Tex.
KZIQ	1360	Ridgecrest, Calif.
KZIQ-FM	92.7	Ridgecrest, Calif.
KZKZ	690	Flagstaff, Ariz.
KZLA	1540	Los Angeles, Calif.
KZLA-FM	93.9	Los Angeles, Calif.
KZLE	93.1	Batesville, Ark.
KZLN	60	Harlingen, Tex.
KZLO	100.7	Pueblo, Colo.
KZLS	97.1	Billings, Mont.
KZMK	92.1	Bisbee, Ariz.
KZMK	100.3	Greybull, Wyo.
KZMO	1420	California, Mo.
KZMO-FM	94.3	California, Mo.
KZNG	1340	Hot Springs, Ark.
KZNN	105.3	Rolla, Mo.
KZNS	94.3	Barstow, Calif.
KZOC	92.7	Osage City, Kan.
KZOK-FM	102.5	Seattle, Wash.
KZOM	104.5	Orange, Tex.
KZON	1600	Santa Maria, Calif.
KZOO	1210	Honolulu, Haw.
KZOQ	100.1	Missoula, Mont.
KZOR	94.1	Hobbs, N.M.
KZOT	1460	Marianna, Ark.
KZOZ	93.3	San Luis Obispo, Calif.
KZPR	105.3	Minot, N.D.
KZRK	1540	Ozark, Ark.
KZRK-FM	96.7	Ozark, Ark.
KZRO	104.3	Marshall, Ark.
KZSC	88.1	Santa Cruz, Calif.
KZSD-TV	8	Martin, S.D.
KZST	100.1	Santa Rosa, Calif.
KZSU	90.1	Stanford, Calif.
KZTR	95.9	Camarillo, Calif.
KZTV	10	Corpus Christi, Tex.
KZUL	1380	Parker, Ariz.
KZUM	89.5	Lincoln, Neb.
KZUU	90.7	Pullman, Wash.
KZXL-FM	96.7	Sherman, Tex.
KZYM	1220	Cape Girardeau, Mo.
KZZA	107.1	Glenwood, Minn.
KZZB	95.1	Beaumont, Tex.
KZZC	98.9	Leavenworth, Kan.
KZZI	1510	West Jordan, Utah
KZZK-FM	102.7	Richland, Wash.
KZZL	99.5	Le Mars, Ia.
KZZN	1490	Littlefield, Tex.
KZZP	1310	Mesa, Ariz.
KZZP-FM	104.7	Mesa, Ariz.
KZZQ	94.3	Galliano, La.
KZZX	99.5	Albuquerque, N.M.
KZZY	103.5	Devils Lake, N.D.
KZZZ	94.7	Kingman, Ariz.
PJA-TV	13	Aruba, Ne. Antil.
PJA-10	1330	Aruba, Ne. Antil.
PJA5	1435	Aruba, Ne. Antil.
PJA6	920	Aruba, Ne. Antil.
PJA8	1270	Aruba, Ne. Antil.
PJB	800	Bonaire, Ne. Antil.
PJB2	1380	Bonaire, Ne. Antil.
PJC-TV	8	Curacao, Ne. Antil.
PJC2	855	Curacao, Ne. Antil.
PJC7	1010	Curacao, Ne. Antil.
PJC7A	1500	Curacao, Ne. Antil.
PJD2	1295	St. Martin, Ne. Antil.
PJL	1540	Curacao, Ne. Antil.
PJL3	1230	Curacao, Ne. Antil.
REZT	104.1	Ames, Ia.
TGW	640	Guatemala City, Guatemala
TIRICA	625	San Jose, Costa Rica
VOA	1180	Marathon Key, Fla.
VOAR	1230	St. John's, Nfld.
VOCM	590	St. John's, Nfld.
VOWR	800	St. John's, Nfld.
VPL6	610	Port Of Spain, Trinidad
VP4RD	730	Port Of Spain, Trinidad
WAAA	980	Winston Salem, N.C.
WAAF	107.3	Worcester,
WAAG	94.9	Galesburg, Ill.
WAAK	960	Dallas, N.C.
WAAL	99.1	Binghamton, N.Y.
WAAM	1230	Woodstock, Va.
WAAM	1600	Ann Arbor, Mich.
WAAO	1530	Andalusia, Ala.
WAAQ	102.3	Big Rapids, Mich.
WAAS	1100	Thompson Station, Tenn.
WAAT	40	Wildwood, N.J.
WAAV	1340	Wilmington, N.C.
WAAW	103.7	Murray, Ky.
WAAX	570	Gadsden, Ala.
WAAY	1550	Huntsville, Ala.
WAAY-TV	31	Huntsville, Ala.
WAAZ-FM	104.9	Crestview, Fla.
WABA	850	Aguadilla, P.R.
WABB	1480	Mobile, Ala.

WABB-FM	97.5	Mobile, Ala.
WABC	770	New York, N.Y.
WABC-TV	7	New York, N.Y.
WABD	1370	Ft. Campbell, Ky.
WABD-FM	107.9	Ft. Campbell, Ky.
WABE	90.1	Atlanta, Ga.
WABF	1220	Fairhope, Ala.
WABG	960	Greenwood, Miss.
WABG-TV	6	Greenwood, Miss.
WABI	910	Bangor, Me.
WABI-TV	5	Bangor, Me.
WABJ	1490	Adrian, Mich.
WABK	1280	Gardiner, Me.
WABK-FM	104.3	Gardiner, Me.
WABL	1570	Amite, La.
WABM	101.7	Muskegon Heights, Mich.
WABN-FM	92.7	Abingdon, Va.
WABO	990	Waynesboro, Miss.
WABO-FM	105.5	Waynesboro, Miss.
WABQ	1540	Cleveland, O.
WABR-FM	90.5	Tifton, Ga.
WABR-FM	107.5	Tifton, Ga.
WABS	780	Arlington, Va.
WABT	1360	Madison, Ala.
WABV	1590	Abbeville, S.C.
WABW-TV	14	Pelham, Ga.
WABX	99.5	Detroit, Mich.
WABY	1400	Albany, N.Y.
WABZ-FM	100.9	Albemarle, N.C.
WACB	1380	Kittanning, Pa.
WACC	89.9	Arnold, Md.
WACD	1590	Alexander City, Ala.
WACE	730	Chicopee, Mass.
WACF	98.5	Paris, Ill.
WACG-FM	90.7	Augusta, Ga.
WACK	1420	Newark, N.Y.
WACL	570	Waycross, Ga.
WACL-FM	103.3	Waycross, Ga.
WACM	1490	West Springfield,
WACO	1460	Waco, Tex.
WACQ	1130	Tallassee, Ala.
WACR	1050	Columbus, Miss.
WACR-FM	103.9	Columbus, Miss.
WACS-TV	25	Dawson, Ga.
WACT	1420	Tuscaloosa, Ala.
WACT-FM	105.5	Tuscaloosa, Ala.
WADA	1390	Shelby, N.C.
WADB	95.9	Point Pleasant, N.J.
WADC	1050	Parkersburg, W.V.
WADE	1210	Wadesboro, N.C.
WADI	95.3	Corinth, Miss.
WADJ	1330	Somerset, Pa.
WADK	1540	Newport, R.I.
WADM	1540	Decatur, Ind.
WADM-FM	92.7	Decatur, Ind.
WADO	1280	New York, N.Y.
WADR	1480	Remsen, N.Y.
WADS	690	Ansonia, Conn.
WADX	1420	Trenton, Ga.
WADZ	94.3	Americus, Ga.
WAEB	790	Allentown, Pa.
WAEC	860	Atlanta, Ga.
WAED	90.9	Huntsville, Ala.
WAEL	600	Mayaguez, P.R.
WAEL-FM	96.1	Mayaguez, P.R.
WAEO-TV	12	Rhinelander, Wis.
WAER	88.3	Syracuse, N.Y.
WAES-FM	93.5	Remsen, N.Y.
WAEV	97.3	Savannah, Ga.
WAEW	1330	Crossville, Tenn.
WAEY	1490	Princeton, W.V.
WAEY-FM	95.9	Princeton, W.V.
WAEZ	97.5	Akron, O.
WAFB-FM	98.1	Baton Rouge, La.
WAFB-TV	9	Baton Rouge, La.
WAFC	106.3	Clewiston, Fla.
WAFF	48	Decatur, Ala.
WAFG	90.3	Ft Lauderdale, Fla.
WAFL-FM	97.7	Milford, Del.

WAFM	95.3	Amory, Miss.
WAFR	90.3	Durham, N.C.
WAFT	101.1	Valdosta, Ga.
WAFX	1450	Ft. Wayne, Ind.
WAGA-TV	5	Atlanta, Ga.
WAGC	1560	Centre, Ala.
WAGE	1290	Leesburg, Va.
WAGG	1320	Birmingham, Ala.
WAGI	105.3	Gaffney, S.C.
WAGL	1560	Lancaster, S.C.
WAGM-TV	8	Presque Isle, Me.
WAGN	1340	Menominee, Mich.
WAGQ	104.7	Athens, Ga.
WAGR	580	Lumberton, N.C.
WAGS	1380	Bishopville, S.C.
WAGY	1320	Forest City, N.C.
WAHC	96.7	Oshkosh, Wis.
WAHR	99.1	Huntsville, Ala.
WAHS	89.5	Auburn Heights, Mich.
WAHT	1510	Annville, Pa.
WAIA	97.3	Miami, Fla.
WAIC	91.9	Springfield,
WAID	106.3	Clarksdale, Miss.
WAIF	88.3	Cincinnati, O.
WAIK	1590	Galesburg, Ill.
WAIL	105.3	Slidell, La.
WAIM	1230	Anderson, S.C.
WAIN	1270	Columbia, Ky.
WAIN-FM	93.5	Columbia, Ky.
WAIQ	26	Montgomery, Ala.
WAIR	1340	Winston Salem, N.C.
WAIT	820	Chicago, Ill.
WAIV-FM	96.9	Jacksonville, Fla.
WAJC	104.5	Indianapolis, Ind.
WAJE	1580	Ebensburg, Pa.
WAJF	1490	Decatur, Ala.
WAJK	99.3	La Salle, Ill.
WAJL	1440	Winter Park, Fla.
WAJN	790	Ashland City, Tenn.
WAJP	93.5	Joliet, Ill.
WAJQ	1310	Marion, Ala.
WAJR	1440	Morgantown, W.V.
WAJX	98.3	Titusville, Fla.
WAJY	101.9	New Orleans, La.
WAKE	1500	Valparaiso, Ind.
WAKG	103.3	Danville, Va.
WAKH	105.7	Mc Comb, Miss.
WAKI	1230	Mc Minnville, Tenn.
WAKK	1140	Mc Comb, Miss.
WAKM	950	Franklin, Tenn.
WAKN	990	Aiken, S.C.
WAKO	910	Lawrenceville, Ill.
WAKO-FM	103.1	Lawrenceville, Ill.
WAKQ	101.1	Russellville, Ky.
WAKR	1590	Akron, O.
WAKR-TV	23	Akron, O.
WAKS	1460	Fuquay Springs, N.C.
WAKS-FM	103.9	Fuquay Springs, N.C.
WAKW	93.3	Cincinnati, O.
WAKX-FM	98.9	Duluth, Minn.
WAKY	790	Louisville, Ky.
WALA-TV	10	Mobile, Ala.
WALB-TV	10	Albany, Ga.
WALD	1060	Walterboro, S.C.
WALD	1080	Walterboro, S.C.
WALD-FM	100.9	Walterboro, S.C.
WALE	1400	Fall River, Mass.
WALF	89.7	Alfred, N.Y.
WALG	1590	Albany, Ga.
WALI	1230	Cumberland, Md.
WALK	1370	Patchogue, N.Y.
WALK-FM	97.5	Patchogue, N.Y.
WALL	1340	Middletown, N.Y.
WALO	1240	Humacao, P.R.
WALP	90.5	Corinth, Miss.
WALR-FM	104.9	Union City, Tenn.
WALT	910	Meridian, Miss.
WALV	98.3	Cleveland, Tenn.
WALX	100.9	Selma, Ala.
WALZ	95.3	Machias, Me.
WAMA	860	Clearwater, Fla.

WAMB	1170	Donelson, Tenn.
WAMB	1160	Donelson, Tenn.
WAMC	90.3	Albany, N.Y.
WAMD	970	Aberdeen, Md.
WAME	1480	Charlotte, N.C.
WAMF	90.3	Tallahassee, Fla.
WAMF	90.5	Tallahassee, Fla.
WAMG	1130	Gallatin, Tenn.
WAMH	89.5	Amherst, Mass.
WAMI	860	Opp, Ala.
WAMI-FM	102.3	Opp, Ala.
WAMJ	1580	South Bend, Ind.
WAMK	1410	Brockton, Mass.
WAML	1340	Laurel, Miss.
WAMO	860	Pittsburgh, Pa.
WAMO-FM	105.9	Pittsburgh, Pa.
WAMP-FM	88.3	Toledo, O.
WAMQ	1400	Loretto, Pa.
WAMR	1320	Venice, Fla.
WAMS	1380	Wilmington, Del.
WAMT	1060	Titusville, Fla.
WAMU-FM	88.5	Washington, D.
WAMV	1420	Amherst, Va.
WAMW	1580	Washington, Ind.
WAMX	93.7	Ashland, Ky.
WAMY	1580	Amory, Miss.
WAMZ	97.5	Louisville, Ky.
WANA	1490	Anniston, Ala.
WANB	1580	Waynesburg, Pa.
WANB-FM	103.1	Waynesburg, Pa.
WANC	1350	Aberdeen, N.C.
WAND	17	Decatur, Ill.
WANE-TV	15	Ft. Wayne, Ind.
WANH-FM	90.7	Manchester, N.H.
WANJ	107.5	Wheeling, W.V.
WANM	1070	Tallahassee, Fla.
WANN	1190	Annapolis, Md.
WANO	1230	Pineville, Ky.
WANR	1600	Wheeling, W.V.
WANS	1280	Anderson, S.C.
WANS-FM	107.3	Anderson, S.C.
WANT	990	Richmond, Va.
WANV	970	Waynesboro, Va.
WANX-TV	46	Atlanta, Ga.
WANY	1390	Albany, Ky.
WANY-FM	106.3	Albany, Ky.
WAOA	1520	Opelika, Ala.
WAOB	1280	Winamac, Ind.
WAOC	1420	St. Augustine, Fla.
WAOK	1380	Atlanta, Ga.
WAOP	104.9	Otsego, Mich.
WAOR	95.3	Niles, Mich.
WAOV	1450	Vincennes, Ind.
WAOW-TV	9	Wausau, Wis.
WAPA	680	San Juan, P.R.
WAPA-TV	4	San Juan, P.R.
WAPB	22	Annapolis, Md.
WAPE	690	Jacksonville, Fla.
WAPF	980	Mc Comb, Miss.
WAPG	1480	Arcadia, Fla.
WAPI	1070	Birmingham, Ala.
WAPI-FM	94.5	Birmingham, Ala.
WAPL-FM	105.7	Appleton, Wis.
WAPP	103.5	Lake Success, N.Y.
WAPR	1390	Avon Park, Fla.
WAPS	89.1	Akron, O.
WAPT	16	Jackson, Miss.
WAQE	1090	Rice Lake, Wis.
WAQE-FM	97.7	Rice Lake, Wis.
WAQP	49	Saginaw, Mich.
WAQT	94.1	Carrollton, Ala.
WAQX	95.3	Manlius, N.Y.
WAQY	102.1	Springfield, Mass.
WARA	1320	Attleboro, Mass.
WARB	730	Covington, La.
WARC	90.3	Meadville, Pa.
WARD	1540	Pittston, Pa.
WARE	1250	Ware, Mass.
WARF	1240	Jasper, Ala.
WARG	88.9	Summit, Ill.
WARI	1480	Abbeville, Ala.
WARK	1490	Hagerstown, Md.
WARM	590	Scranton, Pa.
WARO	540	Canonsburg, Pa.
WARR	1520	Warrenton, N.C.
WART	22	Narajito, P.R.

WARU	1600	Peru, Ind.
WARU-FM	98.3	Peru, Ind.
WARV	92.1	Venice, Fla.
WARV	1590	Warwick, R.I.
WARY	88.5	Valhalla, N.Y.
WASA	1330	Havre De Grace, Md.
WASC	1530	Spartanburg, S.C.
WASD	88.1	Exeter, Pa.
WASG	1140	Atmore, Ala.
WASH	97.1	Washington, D. C.
WASK	1450	Lafayette, Ind.
WASK-FM	105.3	Lafayette, Ind.
WASL	100.1	Dyersburg, Tenn.
WASM	102.3	Saratoga Springs, N.Y.
WASP	1130	Brownsville, Pa.
WASR	1420	Wolfeboro, N.H.
WASU-FM	90.5	Boone, N.C.
WASZ	95.3	Ashland, Ala.
WATA	1450	Boone, N.C.
WATD	95.9	Marshfield, Mass.
WATE-TV	6	Knoxville, Tenn.
WATH	970	Athens, O.
WATI	810	Indianapolis, Ind.
WATK	900	Antigo, Wis.
WATL-TV	36	Atlanta, Ga.
WATM	1590	Atmore, Ala.
WATN	1240	Watertown, N.Y.
WATO	1290	Oak Ridge, Tenn.
WATP	1430	Marion, S.C.
WATP-FM	94.3	Marion, S.C.
WATR	1320	Waterbury, Conn.
WATR-TV	20	Waterbury, Conn.
WATS	960	Sayre, Pa.
WATT	1240	Cadillac, Mich.
WATU-TV	26	Augusta, Ga.
WATV	900	Birmingham, Ala.
WATW	1400	Ashland, Wis.
WATW-FM	95.9	Ashland, Wis.
WATX	54	Arelibo, P.R.
WATZ	1450	Alpena, Mich.
WATZ-FM	93.5	Alpena, Mich.
WAUB	1590	Auburn, N.Y.
WAUC	1310	Wauchula, Fla.
WAUD	1230	Auburn, Ala.
WAUK	1510	Waukesha, Wis.
WAUN	92.7	Kewaunee, Wis.
WAUP	88.1	Akron, O.
WAUR	107.9	Aurora, Ill.
WAUS	90.7	Berrien Springs, Mich.
WAVA	105.1	Arlington, Va.
WAVC	105.1	Duluth, Minn.
WAVC	1350	Warner Robbins, Ga.
WAVE-TV	3	Louisville, Ky.
WAVG	970	Louisville, Ky.
WAVI	1210	Dayton, O.
WAVL	910	Apollo, Pa.
WAVM	91.7	Maynard, Mass.
WAVO	1420	Decatur, Ga.
WAVR	102.3	Waverly, N.Y.
WAVS	1190	Ft. Lauderdale, Fla.
WAVT-FM	101.9	Pottsville, Pa.
WAVU	630	Albertville, Ala.
WAVV	95.9	Vevay, Ind.
WAVW	105.5	Vero Beach, Fla.
WAVX	1330	Milton, Fla.
WAVY-TV	10	Portsmouth, Va.
WAVZ	1300	New Haven, Conn.
WAWA	1590	West Allis, Wis.
WAWK	1140	Kendallville, Ind.
WAWK-FM	93.3	Kendallville, Ind.
WAWS-TV	30	Jacksonville, Fla.
WAWZ	1380	Zarephath, N.J.
WAWZ-FM	99.1	Zarephath, N.J.
WAXA	40	Anderson, S.C.
WAXC	92.1	Wapakoneta, O.
WAXE	1370	Vero Beach, Fla.
WAXI	104.9	Rockville, Ind.
WAXL	97.7	Lancaster, W.V.
WAXO	1220	Lewisburg, Tenn.
WAXT	96.7	Alexandria, Ind.
WAXU-FM	103.1	Georgetown, Ky.
WAXX	104.5	Eau Claire, Wis.
WAXY	105.9	Ft. Lauderdale, Fla.
WAYB	1490	Waynesboro, Va.
WAYC	1600	Bedford, Pa.
WAYD	1190	Ozark, Ala.
WAYE	860	Baltimore, Md.
WAYL	93.7	Minneapolis, Minn.
WAYN	900	Rockingham, N.C.
WAYR	550	Orange Park, Fla.
WAYS	610	Charlotte, N.C.
WAYT	1510	Wabash, Ind.
WAYU	93.9	Lewiston, Me.
WAYV	95.1	Atlantic City, N.J.
WAYW	91.9	Worcester, Mass.
WAYX	1230	Waycross, Ga.
WAYY	1150	Chippewa Falls, Wis.
WAYZ	1380	Waynesboro, Pa.
WAYZ-FM	101.5	Waynesboro, Pa.
WAZA	1360	Bainbridge, Ga.
WAZE	92.1	Dawson, Ga.
WAZF	1230	Yazoo City, Miss.
WAZI	95.9	Morristown, Tenn.
WAZL	1490	Hazleton, Pa.
WAZS	980	Summerville, S.C.
WAZU	102.9	Springfield, O.
WAZX	106.3	Georgetown, S.C.
WAZY-FM	96.5	Lafayette, Ind.
WAZZ	101.9	New Bern, N.C.
WBAA	920	West Lafayette, Ind.
WBAB-FM	102.3	Babylon, N.Y.
WBAC	1340	Cleveland, Tenn.
WBAD	94.3	Leland, Miss.
WBAF	1090	Barnesville, Ga.
WBAG	93.9	Burlington, N.C.
WBAI	99.5	New York, N.Y.
WBAK-TV	38	Terre Haute, Ind.
WBAL	1090	Baltimore, Md.
WBAL-TV	11	Baltimore, Md.
WBAM	740	Montgomery, Ala.
WBAM-FM	98.9	Montgomery, Ala.
WBAP	820	Ft. Worth, Tex.
WBAQ	97.9	Greenville, Miss.
WBAR	1460	Bartow, Fla.
WBAS	1330	Crescent City, Fla.
WBAT	1400	Marion, Ind.
WBAU	90.3	Garden City, N.Y.
WBAW	740	Barnwell, S.C.
WBAW-FM	101.7	Barnwell, S.C.
WBAX	1240	Wilkes Barre, Pa.
WBAY-TV	2	Green Bay, Wis.
WBAZ	101.7	Southold, N.Y.
WBBA	1580	Pittsfield, Ill.
WBBA-FM	97.7	Pittsfield, Ill.
WBBB	920	Burlington, N.C.
WBBC	93.5	Blackstone, Va.
WBBE	1580	Georgetown, Ky.
WBBF	950	Rochester, N.Y.
WBBG	1260	Cleveland, O.
WBBH-TV	20	Ft. Myers, Fla.
WBBI	1230	Abingdon, Va.
WBBJ-TV	7	Jackson, Tenn.
WBBK	1260	Blakely, Ga.
WBBK-FM	93.5	Blakely, Ga.
WBBL	1480	Richmond, Va.
WBBM	780	Chicago, Ill.
WBBM-FM	96.3	Chicago, Ill.
WBBM-TV	2	Chicago, Ill.
WBBO	780	Forest City, N.C.
WBBO-FM	93.3	Forest City, N.C.
WBBQ	1340	Augusta, Ga.
WBBQ-FM	104.3	Augusta, Ga.
WBBR	1580	Travelers Rest, S.C.
WBBS-TV	60	West Chicago, Ill.
WBBT	1340	Lyons, Ga.
WBBW	1240	Youngstown, O.
WBBX	1380	Portsmouth, N.H.
WBBY	103.9	Westerville, O.
WBBZ	1230	Ponca City, Okla.
WBCA	1110	Bay Minette, Ala.
WBCB	1490	Levittown, Pa.
WBCE	1010	Wickliffe, Ky.
WBCE	1100	Wickliffe, Ky.
WBCF	1240	Florence, Ala.
WBCG	98.3	Murfreesboro, N.C.
WBCH	1220	Hastings, Mich.
WBCH-FM	100.1	Hastings, Mich.
WBCK	930	Battle Creek, Mich.
WBCL	90.3	Ft. Wayne, Ind.
WBCM	1440	Bay City, Mich.
WBCN	104.1	Boston, Mass.
WBCO	1540	Bucyrus, O.
WBCO-FM	92.7	Bucyrus, O.
WBCR-FM	90.3	Beloit, Wis.
WBCS-FM	102.9	Milwaukee, Wis.
WBCT	43	Bridgeport, Conn.
WBCU	1460	Union, S.C.
WBCV	1550	Bristol, Tenn.
WBCW	1530	Jeanette, Pa.
WBCX	89.1	Gainesville, Ga.
WBCY	107.9	Charlotte, N.C.
WBDC	100.9	Huntingburg, Ind.
WBDG	90.9	Indianapolis, Ind.
WBDJ-FM	97.7	Brazil, Ind.
WBDN	600	Escanaba, Mich.
WBDX	1030	White Bluff, Tenn.
WBDY	1190	Bluefield, Va.
WBDY-FM	106.3	Bluefield, Va.
WBEA	107.3	Elyria, O.
WBEC	1420	Pittsfield, Mass.
WBEC-FM	105.5	Pittsfield, Mass.
WBEE	1570	Harvey, Ill.
WBEJ	1240	Elizabethton, Tenn.
WBEK	88.1	Cherry Hill, N.J.
WBEL	1380	Beloit, Wis.
WBEN	930	Buffalo, N.Y.
WBEN-FM	102.5	Buffalo, N.Y.
WBER	950	Moncks Corner, S.C.
WBES	96.1	Charleston, W.V.
WBET	1460	Brockton, Mass.
WBEU	960	Beaufort, S.C.
WBEV	1430	Beaver Dam, Wis.
WBEX	1490	Chillicothe, O.
WBEY	103.1	Grasonville, Md.
WBEZ	91.5	Chicago, Ill.
WBFC	1470	Stanton, Ky.
WBFD	1310	Bedford, Pa.
WBFF	45	Baltimore, Md.
WBFG	97.7	Effingham, Ill.
WBFH	88.1	Bloomfield Hills, Mich.
WBFJ	1550	Winston Salem, N.C.
WBFL	107.1	Bellows Falls, Vt.
WBFM	98.1	Seneca, S.C.
WBFN	1500	Quitman, Miss.
WBFO	88.7	Buffalo, N.Y.
WBFS-TV	33	Miami, Fla.
WBGA	1440	Brunswick, Ga.
WBGC	1240	Chipley, Fla.
WBGD	91.9	Brick Town, N.J.
WBGL	91.7	Champaign, Ill.
WBGM	98.9	Tallahassee, Fla.
WBGN	1340	Bowling Green, Ky.
WBGO	88.3	Newark, N.J.
WBGR	1440	Paris, Ky.
WBGU	88.1	Bowling Green, O.
WBGU-TV	27	Bowling Green, O.
WBGW	97.1	Bangor, Me.
WBGY-FM	93.3	Tullahoma, Tenn.
WBGY-TV	64	Tullahoma, Tenn.
WBHB	1240	Fitzgerald, Ga.
WBHC	1270	Hampton, S.C.
WBHF	1450	Cartersville, Ga.
WBHI	88.5	Chicago, Ill.
WBHM	90.3	Birmingham, Ala.
WBHN	1590	Bryson City, N.C.
WBHP	1230	Huntsville, Ala.
WBHR	88.7	Bellaire, O.

Call	Frequency/Channel	Location
WBHT	1520	Brownsville, Tenn.
WBIB	1110	Centreville, Ala.
WBIF	105.5	Bedford, Ind.
WBIG	1470	Greensboro, N.C.
WBII	91.5	Watertown, Wis.
WBIL	580	Tuskegee, Ala.
WBIL-FM	95.9	Tuskegee, Ala.
WBIM-FM	91.5	Bridgewater, Mass.
WBIN	1540	Benton, Tenn.
WBIP	1400	Booneville, Miss.
WBIP-FM	99.3	Booneville, Miss.
WBIQ	10	Birmingham, Ala.
WBIR-TV	10	Knoxville, Tenn.
WBIS	1440	Bristol, Conn.
WBIT	1470	Adel, Ga.
WBIW	1340	Bedford, Ind.
WBIX	1010	Jacksonville Beach, Fla.
WBIZ	100.7	Eau Claire, Wis.
WBJA	1540	Guayama, P.R.
WBJB-FM	90.5	Lincroft, N.J.
WBJC	91.5	Baltimore, Md.
WBJW	105.1	Orlando, Fla.
WBJX	94.3	Goose Creek, S.C.
WBJZ	100.9	Olean, N.Y.
WBKB-TV	11	Alpena, Mich.
WBKC	1560	Chardon, O.
WBKE-FM	89.5	North Manchester, Ind.
WBKF	92.1	Mac Clenny, Fla.
WBKH	950	Hattiesburg, Miss.
WBKO	13	Bowling Green, Ky.
WBKR	92.5	Owensboro, Ky.
WBKT	93.3	Brockport, N.Y.
WBKV	1470	West Bend, Wis.
WBKV-FM	92.5	West Bend, Wis.
WBKW	99.5	Beckley, W.V.
WBKY	91.3	Lexington, Ky.
WBLA	1440	Elizabethtown, N.C.
WBLB	1510	Pulaski, Va.
WBLC	1360	Lenoir City, Tenn.
WBLD	89.3	Orchard Lake, Mich.
WBLE	1290	Batesville, Miss.
WBLE	95.9	Batesville, Miss.
WBLF	970	Bellefonte, Pa.
WBLI	106.1	Patchogue, N.Y.
WBLJ	1230	Dalton, Ga.
WBLK-FM	93.7	De Pew, N.Y.
WBLM	107.5	Lewiston, Me.
WBLN	43	Bloomington, Ill.
WBLP	850	Fairview, Tenn.
WBLR	1430	Batesburg, S.C.
WBLS	107.5	New York, N.Y.
WBLT	1350	Bedford, Va.
WBLU	92.1	Hinesville, Ga.
WBLV	90.3	Twin Lake, Mich.
WBLW	810	Royston, Ga.
WBLX	92.9	Mobile, Ala.
WBLY	1600	Springfield, O.
WBLZ	103.5	Hamilton, O.
WBMB	1060	West Branch, Mich.
WBMC	960	Mc Minnville, Tenn.
WBMC-FM	103.9	Mc Minnville, Tenn.
WBMD	750	Baltimore, Md.
WBME	1230	Belfast, Me.
WBMG	42	Birmingham, Ala.
WBMI	105.5	West Branch, Mich.
WBMJ	1190	San Juan, P.R.
WBMK	1430	Knoxville, Tenn.
WBML	900	Macon, Ga.
WBMP	101.7	Elwood, Ind.
WBMR	91.7	Telford, Pa.
WBMT	88.3	Boxford, Mass.
WBMU-FM	91.3	Asheville, N.C.
WBMX	102.7	Oak Park, Ill.
WBNB-TV	10	Charlotte Amalie, V.I.
WBNC	1050	Conway, N.H.
WBNG-TV	12	Binghamton, N.Y.
WBNI	89.1	Ft. Wayne, Ind.
WBNL	1540	Boonville, Ind.
WBNL-FM	107.1	Boonville, Ind.
WBNO-FM	100.9	Bryan, O.
WBNQ	101.5	Bloomington, Ill.
WBNR	1260	Beacon, N.Y.
WBNS	1460	Columbus, O.
WBNS-FM	97.1	Columbus, O.
WBNS-TV	10	Columbus, O.
WBNT	1310	Oneida, Tenn.
WBNT-FM	105.5	Oneida, Tenn.
WBNX	1380	New York, N.Y.
WBNY	91.3	Buffalo, N.Y.
WBNZ	99.3	Frankfort, Mich.
WBOB	1360	Galax, Va.
WBOB-FM	98.1	Galax, Va.
WBOC-TV	16	Salisbury, Md.
WBOD	100.9	Canton, Ill.
WBOK	1230	New Orleans, La.
WBOL	1560	Bolivar, Tenn.
WBOP	980	Pensacola, Fla.
WBOR	91.1	Brunswick, Me.
WBOS	92.9	Brookline, Mass.
WBOW	1230	Terre Haute, Ind.
WBOX	920	Bogalusa, La.
WBOY-TV	12	Clarksburg, W.V.
WBOZ	1090	San German, P.R.
WBPA	1460	Elkhorn City, Ky.
WBPM	94.3	Kingston, N.Y.
WBPR	88.5	Barrington, Ill.
WBPV	90.1	Charlton, Mass.
WBPZ	1230	Lock Haven, Pa.
WBQM	91.7	Decatur, Ala.
WBQN	1160	Barceloneta, P.R.
WBQW	1320	Scranton, Pa.
WBRA-TV	15	Roanoke, Va.
WBRC-TV	6	Birmingham, Ala.
WBRD	1420	Bradenton, Fla.
WBRE-TV	28	Wilkes Barre, Pa.
WBRG	1050	Lynchburg, Va.
WBRH	90.1	Baton Rouge, La.
WBRH	90.3	Baton Rouge, La.
WBRI	1500	Indianapolis, Ind.
WBRJ	910	Marietta, O.
WBRK	1340	Pittsfield, Mass.
WBRL	1400	Berlin, N.H.
WBRM	1250	Marion, N.C.
WBRN	1460	Big Rapids, Mich.
WBRN-FM	100.9	Big Rapids, Mich.
WBRO	1310	Waynesboro, Ga.
WBRQ	97.7	Cidra, P.R.
WBRS	91.7	Waltham,
WBRT	1320	Bardstown, Ky.
WBRU	95.5	Providence, R.I.
WBRV	900	Boonville, N.Y.
WBRW	1170	Somerville, N.J.
WBRX	1280	Berwick, Pa.
WBRY	1540	Woodbury, Tenn.
WBRZ	2	Baton Rouge, La,
WBSA	1300	Boaz, Ala.
WBSB	104.3	Baltimore, Md.
WBSC	1550	Bennettsville, S.C.
WBSD	89.1	Burlington, Wis.
WBSF	91.7	Biddeford, Me.
WBSJ	102.3	Ellisville, Miss.
WBSL	91.7	Sheffield, Mass.
WBSM	1420	New Bedford, Mass.
WBSN-FM	89.1	New Orleans, La.
WBSP	51	Ocala, Fla.
WBSR	1450	Pensacola, Fla.
WBSS	980	Pompano Beach, Fla.
WBST	90.7	Muncie, Ind.
WBST	92.1	Muncie, Ind.
WBSU	88.9	Brockport, N.Y.
WBT	1110	Charlotte, N.C.
WBTA	1490	Batavia, N.Y.
WBTB	1400	Beaufort, N.C.
WBTC	1540	Uhrichsville, O.
WBTE	990	Windsor, N.C.
WBTF	1017	Attica, N.Y.
WBTG	106.3	Sheffield, Ala.
WBTH	1400	Williamson, W.V.
WBTI	64	Cincinnati, O.
WBTM	1330	Danville, Va.
WBTN	1370	Bennington, Vt.
WBTO	1600	Linton, Ind.
WBTR-FM	92.1	Carrollton, Ga.
WBTS	1480	Bridgeport, Ala.
WBTV	3	Charlotte, N.C.
WBTW	13	Florence, S.C.
WBTX	1470	Broadway, Va.
WBTY	105.5	Homerville, Ga.
WBTZ	1080	Oliver Springs, Tenn.
WBUC	1460	Buckhannon, W.V.
WBUD	1260	Trenton, N.J.
WBUD	32	Appleton, Wis.
WBUF	92.9	Buffalo, N.Y.
WBUK	1560	Portage, Mich.
WBUR	90.9	Boston, Mass.
WBUT	1050	Butler, Pa.
WBUX	1570	Doylestown, Pa.
WBUY	1440	Lexington, N.C.
WBUZ	1570	Fredonia, N.Y.
WBVD	1570	Beverly, Mass.
WBVP	1230	Beaver Falls, Pa.
WBWA	105.9	Washburn, Wis.
WBWB	96.7	Bloomington, Ind.
WBWC	88.3	Berea, O.
WBXB	100.1	Edenton, N.C.
WBXL	90.5	Baldwinsville, N.Y.
WBXQ	94.3	Cresson, Pa.
WBYC-FM	94.3	Biddeford, Me.
WBYE	1370	Calera, Ala.
WBYG	99.9	Kankakee, Ill.
WBYO	107.5	Boyertown, Pa.
WBYQ	88.1	Baltimore, Md.
WBYQ	96.7	Baltimore, Md.
WBYS	1560	Canton, Ill.
WBYS-FM	98.3	Canton, Ill.
WBYU	95.7	New Orleans, La.
WBYZ	94.5	Baxley, Ga.
WBZ	1030	Boston, Mass.
WBZ-TV	4	Boston, Mass.
WBZA	1410	Glens Falls, N.Y.
WBZB	1090	Selma, N.C.
WBZI	95.3	Xenia, O.
WBZK	980	York, S.C.
WBZQ	1550	Greenville, N.C.
WBZT	1130	Waynesboro, Pa.
WBZY	1140	New Castle, Pa.
WBZZ	93.7	Pittsburgh, Pa.
WCAB	590	Rutherfordton, N.C.
WCAD	105.7	San Juan, P.R.
WCAE	50	St. John, Ind.
WCAI	1350	Ft. Myers, Fla.
WCAJ	68	Birmingham, Ala.
WCAK	92.7	Catlettsburg, Ky.
WCAL	770	Northfield, Minn.
WCAL-FM	89.3	Northfield, Minn.
WCAM	1590	Camden, S.C.
WCAO	600	Baltimore, Md.
WCAP	980	Lowell, Mass.
WCAR	1090	Livonia, Mich.
WCAS	740	Cambridge, Mass.
WCAT	1390	Orange, Mass.
WCAT	700	Orange, Mass.
WCAU	1210	Philadelphia, Pa.
WCAU-FM	98.1	Philadelphia, Pa.
WCAU-TV	10	Philadelphia, Pa.
WCAV	97.7	Brockton, Mass.
WCAW	680	Charleston, W.V.
WCAX-TV	3	Burlington, Vt.
WCAY-TV	30	Nashville, Tenn.
WCAZ	990	Carthage, Ill.
WCAZ-FM	92.1	Carthage, Ill.
WCBA	1350	Corning, N.Y.
WCBB	10	Augusta, Me.
WCBC	1270	Cumberland, Md.
WCBD	2	Charleston, S.C.
WCBE	90.5	Columbus, O.
WCBF	1010	Tampa, Fla.
WCBG	1590	Chambersburg, Pa.
WCBI	550	Columbus, Miss.
WCBI-TV	4	Columbus, Miss.

WCBK	1540	Martinsville, Ind.
WCBK-FM	102.3	Martinsville, Ind.
WCBL	1290	Benton, Ky.
WCBL-FM	102.3	Benton, Ky.
WCBM	680	Baltimore, Md.
WCBN-FM	88.3	Ann Arbor, Mich.
WCBQ	1340	Oxford, N.C.
WCBR	1110	Richmond, Ky.
WCBR-FM	101.7	Richmond, Ky.
WCBS	880	New York, N.Y.
WCBS-FM	101.1	New York, N.Y.
WCBS-TV	2	New York, N.Y.
WCBT	1230	Roanoke Rapids, N.C.
WCBU	89.9	Peoria, Ill.
WCBW	104.9	Columbia, Ill.
WCBX	1130	Eden, N.C.
WCBY	1240	Cheboygan, Mich.
WCCA	94.1	Mc Comb, Miss.
WCCB	18	Charlotte, N.C.
WCCC	1290	Hartford, Conn.
WCCC-FM	106.9	Hartford, Conn.
WCCD	1470	Athens, Ga.
WCCE	90.1	Buie's Creek, N.C.
WCCF	1580	Punta Gorda, Fla.
WCCG	1130	Camden, S.C.
WCCH	103.5	Holyoke, Mass.
WCCI	100.1	Savanna, Ill.
WCCK	103.7	Erie, Pa.
WCCL	1590	Jackson, Miss.
WCCM	800	Lawrence, Mass.
WCCN	1370	Neillsville, Wis.
WCCN-FM	107.5	Neillsville, Wis.
WCCO	830	Minneapolis, Minn.
WCCO-TV	4	Minneapolis, Minn.
WCCP	1560	Clemson, S.C.
WCCQ	98.3	Crest Hill, Ill.
WCCR	1580	Urbana, Ill.
WCCT-TV	57	Columbia, S.C.
WCCV		Cartersville, Ga.
WCCW	1310	Traverse City, Mich.
WCCY	1400	Houghton, Mich.
WCCZ	1550	New Smyrna Beach, Fla.
WCDB	90.9	Albany, N.Y.
WCDC	19	Adams, Mass.
WCDE	90.3	Elkins, W.V.
WCDJ	1260	Edenton, N.C.
WCDL	1440	Carbondale, Pa.
WCDL-FM	94.3	Carbondale, Pa.
WCDO	1490	Sidney, N.Y.
WCDR-FM	90.3	Cedarville, O.
WCDS	1440	Glasgow, Ky.
WCDT	1340	Winchester, Tenn.
WCEB	91.9	Corning, N.Y.
WCEC	810	Rocky Mount, N.C.
WCED	1420	Du Bois, Pa.
WCEE	13	Mount Vernon, Ill.
WCEF	98.3	Ripley, W.V.
WCEH	610	Hawkinsville, Ga.
WCEH-FM	103.9	Hawkinsville, Ga.
WCEI	1460	Easton, Md.
WCEI-FM	96.7	Easton, Md.
WCEK	1470	Newburyport, Mass.
WCEM	1240	Cambridge, Md.
WCEM-FM	106.3	Cambridge, Md.
WCEN	1150	Mt. Pleasant, Mich.
WCEN-FM	94.5	Mt. Pleasant, Mich.
WCES-TV	20	Wrens, Ga.
WCET	48	Cincinnati, O.
WCEV	1450	Cicero, Ill.
WCEW	90.9	Charleston, S.C.
WCEZ	93.5	Columbia, S.C.
WCFB	1060	Tupelo, Miss.
WCFC-TV	38	Chicago, Ill.
WCFE-TV	57	Plattsburgh, N.Y.
WCFL	1000	Chicago, Ill.
WCFM	91.9	Williamstown, Mass.
WCFR	1480	Springfield, Vt.
WCFR-FM	93.5	Springfield, Vt.
WCFT-TV	33	Tuscaloosa, Ala.
WCFW	105.5	Chippewa Falls, Wis.
WCGA	1050	Conyers, Ga.
WCGB	1050	Juana Diaz, P.R.
WCGC	1270	Belmont, N.C.
WCGC	48	Greenwood, S.C.
WCGL	1360	Jacksonville, Fla.
WCGO	1600	Chicago Heights, Ill.
WCGQ	107.3	Columbus, Ga.
WCGR	1550	Canandaigua, N.Y.
WCGV-TV	24	Milwaukee, Wis.
WCGY	93.7	Lawrence, Mass.
WCHA	800	Chambersburg, Pa.
WCHB	1440	Inkster, Mich.
WCHC	89.1	Worcester, Mass.
WCHE	1520	West Chester, Pa.
WCHI	1350	Chillicothe, O.
WCHJ	1470	Brookhaven, Miss.
WCHK	1290	Canton, Ga.
WCHK-FM	105.5	Canton, Ga.
WCHL	1360	Chapel Hill, N.C.
WCHN	970	Norwich, N.Y.
WCHO-FM	105.5	Washington Court House, O.
WCHQ	1360	Camuy, P.R.
WCHQ-FM	102.9	Camuy, P.R.
WCHR	94.5	Trenton, N.J.
WCHS	580	Charleston, W.V.
WCHS-TV	8	Charleston, W.V.
WCHU	1550	Soddy Daisy, Tenn.
WCHU-FM	102.3	Soddy Daisy, Tenn.
WCHW-FM	91.3	Bay City, Mich.
WCHY	94.1	Savannah, Ga.
WCIA	3	Champaign, Ill.
WCIB	101.9	Falmouth, Mass.
WCIC	91.5	Pekin, Ill.
WCIE	91.3	Lakeland, Fla.
WCIF	106.3	Melbourne, Fla.
WCIG	107.1	Mullins, S.C.
WCII	1080	Louisville, Ky.
WCIK	103.1	Bath, N.Y.
WCIL	1020	Carbondale, Ill.
WCIL-FM	101.5	Carbondale, Ill.
WCIN	1480	Cincinnati, O.
WCIQ	7	Munford, Ala.
WCIR-FM	103.7	Beckley, W.V.
WCIT	940	Lima, O.
WCIU-TV	26	Chicago, Ill.
WCIV	4	Charleston, S.C.
WCIX	6	Miami, Fla.
WCJB	20	Gainesville, Fla.
WCJC	96.7	Madison, Ind.
WCJL	1300	Marinette, Wis.
WCJM	100.9	West Point, Ga.
WCJO	97.7	Jackson, O.
WCJU	1450	Columbia, Miss.
WCJW	1140	Warsaw, N.Y.
WCKA	97.1	Sutton, W.V.
WCKB	780	Dunn, N.C.
WCKC	1490	Milton, Fla.
WCKI	1300	Greer, S.C.
WCKJ	1230	Augusta, Ga.
WCKK	690	Oshkosh, Wis.
WCKL	560	Catskill, N.Y.
WCKM	1250	Winnsboro, S.C.
WCKN-FM	101.1	Anderson, S.C.
WCKO	102.7	Pompano Beach, Fla.
WCKQ-FM	103.9	Campbellsville, Ky.
WCKR	92.1	Hornell, N.Y.
WCKS	101.1	Cocoa Beach, Fla.
WCKV	94.9	Ceredo, W.V.
WCKW	92.3	La Place, La.
WCKY	1530	Cincinnati, O.
WCKZ	1600	Austell, Ga.
WCLA	1470	Claxton, Ga.
WCLA-FM	107.1	Claxton, Ga.
WCLB	1220	Camilla, Ga.
WCLC	1260	Jamestown, Tenn.
WCLD	1490	Cleveland, Miss.
WCLD-FM	103.9	Cleveland, Miss.
WCLE	1570	Cleveland, Tenn.
WCLF	22	Clearwater, Fla.
WCLG	1300	Morgantown, W.V.
WCLG-FM	100.1	Morgantown, W.V.
WCLH	90.7	Wilkes Barre, Pa.
WCLI	1450	Corning, N.Y.
WCLK	91.9	Atlanta, Ga.
WCLL-FM	92.9	Wesson, Miss.
WCLN	1170	Clinton, N.C.
WCLO	1230	Janesville, Wis.
WCLP-TV	18	Chatsworth, Ga.
WCLQ-TV	61	Cleveland, O.
WCLR	101.9	Skokie, Ill.
WCLS	1580	Columbus, Ga.
WCLT	1430	Newark, O.
WCLT-FM	100.3	Newark, O.
WCLU	1320	Covington, Ky.
WCLV	95.5	Cleveland, O.
WCLW	1140	Mansfield, O.
WCLW-FM	105.3	Mansfield, O.
WCLX	93.5	Boyne City, Mich.
WCLZ	98.9	Brunswick, Me.
WCMA	1230	Corinth, Miss.
WCMB	1460	Harrisburg, Pa.
WCMC	1230	Wildwood, N.J.
WCME	96.7	Boothbay Harbor, Me.
WCMF	96.5	Rochester, N.Y.
WCMG	1520	Lawrenceburg, Tenn.
WCMH-TV	4	Columbus, O.
WCMI	1340	Ashland, Ky.
WCML-FM	91.7	Alpena, Mich.
WCML-TV	6	Alpena, Mich.
WCMN	1280	Arecibo, P.R.
WCMN-FM	107.3	Arecibo, P.R.
WCMO	98.5	Marietta, O.
WCMP	1350	Pine City, Minn.
WCMP-FM	92.1	Pine City, Minn.
WCMQ	1220	Miami, Fla.
WCMQ-FM	92.1	Hialeah, Fla.
WCMR	1270	Elkhart, Ind.
WCMS	1050	Norfolk, Va.
WCMS-FM	100.5	Norfolk, Va.
WCMT	1410	Martin, Tenn.
WCMT-FM	101.7	Martin, Tenn.
WCMU-FM	89.5	Mt. Pleasant, Mich.
WCMU-TV	14	Mt. Pleasant, Mich.
WCMV	27	Cadillac, Mich.
WCMW	21	Manistee, Mich.
WCMY	1430	Ottawa, Ill.
WCNB-FM	100.3	Connersville, Ind.
WCNC	1240	Elizabeth City, N.C.
WCND	940	Shelbyville, Ky.
WCNE	88.7	Batavia, O.
WCNF	95.3	Whitehall, Mich.
WCNH	1230	Quincy, Fla.
WCNI	91.1	New London, Conn.
WCNI	91.5	New London, Conn.
WCNL	1010	Newport, N.H.
WCNL-FM	101.7	Newport, N.H.
WCNM	92.1	Lock Haven, Pa.
WCNN	680	Atlanta, Ga.
WCNR	930	Bloomsburg, Pa.
WCNS	1480	Latrobe, Pa.
WCNT	46	Cidra, P.R.
WCNU	1010	Crestview, Fla.
WCNV	107.9	Amherst, Va.
WCNW	1560	Fairfield, O.
WCNX	1150	Middletown, Conn.
WCNY-FM	91.3	Syracuse, N.Y.
WCNY-TV	24	Syracuse, N.Y.
WCOA	1370	Pensacola, Fla.

WCOD-FM	106.1	Hyannis, Mass.
WCOE	96.7	La Porte, Ind.
WCOG	1320	Greensboro, N.C.
WCOH	1400	Newnan, Ga.
WCOJ	1420	Coatesville, Pa.
WCOK	1060	Sparta, N.C.
WCOL	1230	Columbus, O.
WCOM-FM	101.7	Urbana, O.
WCON	1450	Cornelia, Ga.
WCON-FM	99.3	Cornelia, Ga.
WCOR	900	Lebanon, Tenn.
WCOS	1400	Columbia, S.C.
WCOS-FM	97.9	Columbia, S.C.
WCOT	950	Orlando, Fla.
WCOU	1240	Lewiston, Me.
WCOV	1170	Montgomery, Ala.
WCOV-TV	20	Montgomery, Ala.
WCOW	1290	Sparta, Wis.
WCOW-FM	97.1	Sparta, Wis.
WCOX	1450	Camden, Ala.
WCOZ	94.5	Boston, Mass.
WCPA	900	Clearfield, Pa.
WCPB	28	Salisbury, Md.
WCPC	940	Houston, Miss.
WCPC-FM	93.3	Houston, Miss.
WCPE	89.7	Raleigh, N.C.
WCPH	1220	Etowah, Tenn.
WCPH-FM	103.1	Etowah, Tenn.
WCPI	98.7	Wheeling, W.V.
WCPK	1600	Chesapeake, Va.
WCPL	1510	Pageland, S.C.
WCPL-FM	102.3	Pageland, S.C.
WCPM	1280	Cumberland, Ky.
WCPN	90.3	Cleveland, O.
WCPO-TV	9	Cincinnati, O.
WCPQ	1330	Havelock, N.C.
WCPR	1450	Coama, P.R.
WCPS	760	Tarboro, N.C.
WCPX	6	Orlando, Fla.
WCPZ	102.7	Sandusky, O.
WCQO	106.3	Blairsville, Pa.
WCQR	50	Washington, D.C.
WCRA	1090	Effingham, Ill.
WCRB	102.5	Waltham, Mass.
WCRC	95.7	Effingham, Ill.
WCRD	100.1	Bluffton, Ind.
WCRE	1420	Cheraw, S.C.
WCRF	103.3	Cleveland, O.
WCRH	90.5	Williamsport, Md.
WCRI	1050	Scottsboro, Ala.
WCRJ	1530	Jacksonville, Fla.
WCRJ-FM	107.3	Jacksonville, Fla.
WCRK	1150	Morristown, Tenn.
WCRL	1570	Oneonta, Ala.
WCRM	103.9	Dundee, Ill.
WCRN	101.1	Charlotte Amalie, V.I.
WCRO	1230	Johnstown, Pa.
WCRP	88.1	Guayama, P.R.
WCRQ-FM	92.7	Arab, Ala.
WCRR	1170	Cornwall, N.Y.
WCRS	1450	Greenwood, S.C.
WCRT	1260	Birmingham, Ala.
WCRV	1580	Washington, N.J.
WCRW	1240	Chicago, Ill.
WCRX	88.1	Chicago, Ill.
WCSA	1260	Ripley, Miss.
WCSB	89.3	Cleveland, O.
WCSC	1390	Charleston, S.C.
WCSC-TV	5	Charleston, S.C.
WCSD-FM	89.3	Warminster, Pa.
WCSE	92.3	Asheboro, N.C.
WCSG	91.3	Grand Rapids, Mich.
WCSH	970	Portland, Me.
WCSH-TV	6	Portland, Me.
WCSI	1010	Columbus, Ind.
WCSI-FM	101.5	Columbus, Ind.
WCSJ	1550	Morris, Ill.
WCSJ-FM	104.7	Morris, Ill.
WCSK	90.3	Kingsport, Tenn.
WCSL	1590	Cherryville, N.C.
WCSM	1350	Celina, O.
WCSM-FM	96.7	Celina, O.
WCSO	91.5	Signal Mountain, Tenn.
WCSP	1520	Crystal Springs, Miss.
WCSQ	89.3	Central Square, N.Y.
WCSR	1340	Hillsdale, Mich.
WCSR-FM	92.1	Hillsdale, Mich.
WCSS	1490	Amsterdam, N.Y.
WCST	1010	Berkeley Springs, W.V.
WCST-FM	93.5	Berkeley Springs, W.V.
WCSU-FM	88.9	Wilberforce, O.
WCSV	1490	Crossville, Tenn.
WCSW	940	Shell Lake, Wis.
WCSY	940	South Haven, Mich.
WCSY-FM	98.3	South Haven, Mich.
WCTA	1280	Alamo, Tenn.
WCTC	1450	New Brunswick, N.J.
WCTD-FM	107.1	Federalsburg, Md.
WCTE	22	Cookeville, Tenn.
WCTI	12	New Bern, N.C.
WCTL	106.3	Union City, Pa.
WCTM	1130	Eaton, O.
WCTN	950	Potomac, Md.
WCTO	94.3	Smithtown, N.Y.
WCTR	1530	Chestertown, Md.
WCTS-FM	100.3	Minneapolis, Minn.
WCTT	680	Corbin, Ky.
WCTT-FM	107.1	Corbin, Ky.
WCTV	6	Thomasville, Ga.
WCTW	1550	New Castle, Ind.
WCTX	92.1	Palmyra, Pa.
WCTY	97.7	Norwich, Conn.
WCUB	980	Manitowoc, Wis.
WCUC-FM	91.7	Clarion, Pa.
WCUE	1150	Akron, O.
WCUG	850	Cuthbert, Ga.
WCUL	103.1	Culpeper, Va.
WCUP	100.3	Tifton, Ga.
WCUW	91.3	Worcester, Mass.
WCUZ	1230	Grand Rapids, Mich.
WCUZ-FM	101.3	Grand Rapids, Mich.
WCVA	1490	Culpeper, Va.
WCVB-TV	5	Boston, Mass.
WCVC	1330	Tallahassee, Fla.
WCVE-TV	23	Richmond, Va.
WCVF-FM	88.9	Fredonia, N.Y.
WCVH	90.5	Flemington, N.J.
WCVI	1340	Connellsville, Pa.
WCVL	1550	Crawfordsville, Ind.
WCVM	100.9	Middlebury, Vt.
WCVN	54	Covington, Ky.
WCVO	104.9	Gahanna, O.
WCVP	600	Murphy, N.C.
WCVQ	960	Kodiak, Alas.
WCVR	1320	Randolph, Vt.
WCVR-FM	102.3	Randolph, Vt.
WCVS	1450	Springfield, Ill.
WCVT	89.7	Towson, Md.
WCVU	94.5	Naples, Fla.
WCVW	57	Richmond, Va.
WCVY	91.5	Coventry, R.I.
WCWA	1230	Toledo, O.
WCWC	1600	Ripon, Wis.
WCWL	91.3	Stockbridge, Mass.
WCWM	89.1	Williamsburg, Va.
WCWP	88.1	Brookville, N.Y.
WCWS	91.9	Wooster, O.
WCWT-FM	92.1	Centerville, O.
WCWV	92.9	Summerville, W.V.
WCWY	740	Tullahoma, Tenn.
WCXI	1130	Detroit, Mich.
WCXI-FM	92.3	Detroit, Mich.
WCXL	89.3	Dayton, O.
WCXQ	1040	Moca, P.R.
WCXT	105.3	Hart, Mich.
WCYB-TV	5	Bristol, Va.
WCYC	88.7	Chicago, Ill.
WCYJ-FM	88.7	Waynesboro, Pa.
WCYN	1400	Cynthiana, Ky.
WCYN-FM	102.3	Cynthiana, Ky.
WCZY	95.5	Detroit, Mich.
WDAC	94.5	Lancaster, Pa.
WDAD	1450	Indiana, Pa.
WDAE	1250	Tampa, Fla.
WDAF	610	Kansas City, Mo.
WDAF-TV	4	Kansas City, Mo.
WDAI	56	Gary, Ind.
WDAK	540	Columbus, Ga.
WDAM-TV	7	Hattiesburg, Miss.
WDAN	1490	Danville, Ill.
WDAO	107.7	Dayton, O.
WDAQ	98.3	Danbury, Conn.
WDAR-FM	105.5	Darlington, S.C.
WDAS	1480	Philadelphia, Pa.
WDAS-FM	105.3	Philadelphia, Pa.
WDAT	1380	Ormond Beach, Fla.
WDAU-TV	22	Scranton, Pa.
WDAV	89.9	Davidson, N.C.
WDAV	30	Davenport, Ia.
WDAX	1410	Mc Rae, Ga.
WDAX-FM	95.3	Mc Rae, Ga.
WDAY	970	Fargo, N.D.
WDAY-FM	93.7	Fargo, N.D.
WDAY-TV	6	Fargo, N.D.
WDAZ-TV	8	Devils Lake, N.D.
WDBA	107.3	Du Bois, Pa.
WDBC	680	Escanaba, Mich.
WDBD	40	Jackson, Miss.
WDBF	1420	Delray Beach, Fla.
WDBI-FM	101.7	Tawas City, Mich.
WDBJ	7	Roanoke, Va.
WDBK	91.5	Blackwood, N.J.
WDBL	1590	Springfield, Tenn.
WDBL-FM	94.3	Springfield, Tenn.
WDBM	1320	Dothan, Ala.
WDBN	94.9	Medina, O.
WDBO	580	Orlando, Fla.
WDBQ	1490	Dubuque, Ia.
WDBR	103.7	Springfield, Ill.
WDBS	107.1	Durham, N.C.
WDBY	91.7	Duxbury, Mass.
WDCA-TV	20	Washington, D.C.
WDCB	90.9	Glen Ellyn, Ill.
WDCC	90.5	Sanford, N.C.
WDCE	90.1	Richmond, Va.
WDCF	1350	Dade City, Fla.
WDCG	105.1	Durham, N.C.
WDCI	1590	Gorham, Me.
WDCJ	88.1	Lorton, Va.
WDCL	89.7	Somerset, Ky.
WDCN	8	Nashville, Tenn.
WDCO-FM	89.7	Cochran, Ga.
WDCO-TV	15	Cochran, Ga.
WDCR	1340	Hanover, N.H.
WDCS	106.3	Scarborough, Me.
WDCU	90.1	Washington, D.C.
WDCV-FM	88.3	Carlisle, Pa.
WDCX	99.5	Buffalo, N.Y.
WDDC	100.1	Portage, Wis.
WDDD	107.3	Marion, Ill.
WDDD-TV	27	Marion, Ill.
WDDJ	96.9	Paducah, Ky.
WDDO	1240	Macon, Ga.
WDDQ	92.1	Adel, Ga.
WDDT	900	Greenville, Miss.
WDDW	810	Johnston City, Ill.
WDDY	1420	Gloucester, Va.
WDEA	1370	Ellsworth, Me.
WDEB	1500	Jamestown, Tenn.
WDEB-FM	103.9	Jamestown, Tenn.
WDEC	1290	Americus, Ga.
WDEE	1500	Reed City, Mich.
WDEF	1370	Chattanooga, Tenn.
WDEF-FM	92.3	Chattanooga, Tenn.
WDEF-TV	12	Chattanooga, Tenn.

Call	Freq.	Location
WDEH	800	Sweetwater, Tenn.
WDEH-FM	95.3	Sweetwater, Tenn.
WDEK	92.5	De Kalb, Ill.
WDEL	1150	Wilmington, Del.
WDEN-FM	105.3	Macon, Ga.
WDEQ-FM	91.1	De Graff, O.
WDER	1320	Derry, N.H.
WDET-FM	101.9	Detroit, Mich.
WDEV	550	Waterbury, Vt.
WDEX	1430	Monroe, N.C.
WDEY	1530	Lapeer, Mich.
WDEY-FM	103.1	Lapeer, Mich.
WDEZ	101.9	Wausau, Wis.
WDFM	91.1	State College, Pa.
WDFP	95.3	Battle Creek, Mich.
WDGC-FM	88.3	Downers Grove, Ill.
WDGL	1520	Douglasville, Ga.
WDGR	1520	Dahlonega, Ga.
WDGR	1210	Dahlonega, Ga.
WDGS	1290	New Albany, Ind.
WDGY	1130	Minneapolis, Minn.
WDHA-FM	105.5	Dover, N.J.
WDHN	18	Dothan, Ala.
WDHO-TV	24	Toledo, O.
WDHP	96.9	Presque Isle, Me.
WDHR	92.1	Pikeville, Ky.
WDHS	91.1	Gaston, Ind.
WDHS	90.9	Gaston, Ind.
WDIA	1070	Memphis, Tenn.
WDIC	1430	Clinchco, Va.
WDIF	94.3	Marion, O.
WDIO-TV	10	Duluth, Minn.
WDIQ	2	Dozier, Ala.
WDIV	4	Detroit, Mich.
WDIX	1150	Orangeburg, S.C.
WDIZ-FM	100.3	Orlando, Fla.
WDJB	97.7	Windsor, N.C.
WDJC	93.7	Birmingham, Ala.
WDJD	1510	Jackson, Mich.
WDJF	107.9	Westport, Conn.
WDJM-FM	91.3	Framingham, Mass.
WDJQ	92.5	Alliance, O.
WDJS	1430	Mt. Olive, N.C.
WDJW	89.7	Somers, Conn.
WDJW	105.3	Somers, Conn.
WDJZ	1530	Bridgeport, Conn.
WDKA	1240	Cross City, Fla.
WDKD	1310	Kingstree, S.C.
WDKN	1260	Dickson, Tenn.
WDKX	103.9	Rochester, N.Y.
WDKY-TV	56	Danville, Ky.
WDLA	1270	Walton, N.Y.
WDLA-FM	92.1	Walton, N.Y.
WDLB	1450	Marshfield, Wis.
WDLC	1490	Port Jervis, N.Y.
WDLC-FM	96.7	Port Jervis, N.Y.
WDLF	1310	De Land, Fla.
WDLK	1450	Dadeville, Ala.
WDLM	960	East Moline, Ill.
WDLM-FM	89.3	East Moline, Ill.
WDLP	590	Panama City, Fla.
WDLR	1550	Delaware, O.
WDLV	550	Pinehurst, N.C.
WDLW	1330	Waltham, Mass.
WDMA-TV	36	Toledo, O.
WDME	1340	Dover Foxcroft, Me.
WDME-FM	103.1	Dover Foxcroft, Me.
WDMG	860	Douglas, Ga.
WDMG-FM	99.5	Douglas, Ga.
WDMJ	1320	Marquette, Mich.
WDMP	810	Dodgeville, Wis.
WDMP-FM	99.3	Dodgeville, Wis.
WDMS	100.7	Greenville, Miss.
WDMT	107.9	Cleveland, O.
WDMV	540	Pocomoke City, Md.
WDNA	88.9	Miami, Fla.
WDNC	620	Durham, N.C.
WDND	105.5	Wilmington, Ill.
WDNE	1240	Elkins, W.V.
WDNE-FM	99.3	Elkins, W.V.
WDNG	1450	Anniston, Ala.
WDNH	1590	Honesdale, Pa.
WDNH-FM	95.3	Honesdale, Pa.
WDNL	102.1	Danville, Ill.
WDNR	89.5	Chester, Pa.
WDNS	98.3	Bowling Green, Ky.
WDNT	1280	Dayton, Tenn.
WDNX	89.1	Olive Hill, Tenn.
WDNY	1400	Dansville, N.Y.
WDOC	1310	Prestonburg, Ky.
WDOD	1310	Chattanooga, Tenn.
WDOD-FM	96.5	Chattanooga, Tenn.
WDOE	1410	Dunkirk, N.Y.
WDOG	1460	Allendale, S.C.
WDOH	107.1	Delphos, O.
WDOK	102.1	Cleveland, O.
WDOM	91.3	Providence, R.I.
WDOQ	101.9	Daytona Beach, Fla.
WDOR	910	Sturgeon Bay, Wis.
WDOR-FM	93.9	Sturgeon Bay, Wis.
WDOS	730	Oneonta, N.Y.
WDOT	1390	Burlington, Vt.
WDOV	1410	Dover, Del.
WDOW	1440	Dowagiac, Mich.
WDOW-FM	92.1	Dowagiac, Mich.
WDOY	96.5	Fajardo, P.R.
WDPB	64	Seaford, Del.
WDPN	103.1	Columbia, S.C.
WDPS	89.3	Dayton, O.
WDQN	1580	Du Quoin, Ill.
WDQN-FM	95.9	Du Quoin, Ill.
WDRB-TV	41	Louisville, Ky.
WDRC	1360	Hartford, Conn.
WDRC-FM	102.9	Hartford, Conn.
WDRE	99.3	Ellenville, N.Y.
WDRL	97.7	Monmouth, Ill.
WDRM	102.1	Decatur, Ala.
WDRQ	93.1	Detroit, Mich.
WDRV	550	Statesville, N.C.
WDSC	800	Dillon, S.C.
WDSC-FM	92.9	Dillon, S.C.
WDSD	94.7	Dover, Del.
WDSE-TV	8	Duluth, Minn.
WDSG	1450	Dyersburg, Tenn.
WDSI-TV	61	Chattanooga, Tenn.
WDSL	1520	Mocksville, N.C.
WDSM	710	Superior, Wis.
WDSO	89.7	Chesterton, Ind.
WDSO	89.1	Chesterton, Ind.
WDSR	1340	Lake City, Fla.
WDST	100.1	Woodstock, N.Y.
WDSU-TV	6	New Orleans, La.
WDSY	107.9	Pittsburgh, Pa.
WDTB	1170	Dimondale, Mich.
WDTM	1130	Selmer, Tenn.
WDTN	2	Canton, O.
WDTR	90.9	Detroit, Mich.
WDTV	5	Weston, W.V.
WDUB	90.9	Granville, O.
WDUB	91.1	Granville, O.
WDUK	99.3	Havana, Ill.
WDUN	550	Gainesville, Ga.
WDUQ	90.5	Pittsburgh, Pa.
WDUR	1490	Durham, N.C.
WDUV	103.3	Bradenton, Fla.
WDUX	800	Waupaca, Wis.
WDUX-FM	92.7	Waupaca, Wis.
WDUZ	1400	Green Bay, Wis.
WDUZ-FM	98.5	Green Bay, Wis.
WDVA	1250	Danville, Va.
WDVE	102.5	Pittsburgh, Pa.
WDVH	980	Gainesville, Fla.
WDVI	61	Wilmington, Del.
WDVL	1270	Vineland, N.J.
WDVM-TV	9	Washington, D. C.
WDVR	98.3	Ocean City, N.J.
WDWD	990	Dawson, Ga.
WDWN	88.9	Auburn, N.Y.
WDWS	1400	Champaign, Ill.
WDWS-FM	97.5	Champaign, Ill.
WDXB	1490	Chattanooga, Tenn.
WDXE	1370	Lawrenceburg, Tenn.
WDXE-FM	95.9	Lawrenceburg, Tenn.
WDXI	1310	Jackson, Tenn.
WDXL	1490	Lexington, Tenn.
WDXN	540	Clarksville, Tenn.
WDXR	1450	Paducah, Ky.
WDXY	1240	Sumter, S.C.
WDYL	92.1	Chester, Va.
WDYN	89.7	Chattanooga, Tenn.
WDYX	1460	Buford, Ga.
WDZ	1050	Decatur, Ill.
WDZD	93.5	Shallotte, N.C.
WDZK	99.3	Chester, S.C.
WDZL	39	Miami, Fla.
WDZQ	95.1	Decatur, Ill.
WDZZ-FM	92.7	Flint, Mich.
WEAA	88.9	Baltimore, Md.
WEAB	800	Greer, S.C.
WEAC	1500	Gaffney, S.C.
WEAG	1470	Alcoa, Tenn.
WEAI	100.5	Jacksonville, Ill.
WEAK	900	Eddyville, Ky.
WEAL	1510	Greensboro, N.C.
WEAM	1390	Arlington, Va.
WEAN	790	Providence, R.I.
WEAO	49	Akron, O.
WEAQ	790	Eau Claire, Wis.
WEAR-TV	3	Pensacola, Fla.
WEAS-FM	93.1	Savannah, Ga.
WEAT	850	West Palm Beach, Fla.
WEAT-FM	104.5	West Palm Beach, Fla.
WEAU-TV	13	Eau Claire, Wis.
WEAV	960	Plattsburgh, N.Y.
WEAW	1330	Evanston, Ill.
WEAX	88.3	Angola, Ind.
WEAZ	101.1	Philadelphia, Pa.
WEBA-TV	14	Allendale, S.C.
WEBB	88.1	Pittsburgh, Pa.
WEBB	1360	Baltimore, Md.
WEBC	560	Duluth, Minn.
WEBF	95.7	Olean, N.Y.
WEBI	92.1	Sanford, Me.
WEBJ	1240	Brewton, Ala.
WEBN	102.7	Cincinnati, O.
WEBO	1330	Owego, N.Y.
WEBQ	1240	Harrisburg, Ill.
WEBQ-FM	99.9	Harrisburg, Ill.
WEBR	970	Buffalo, N.Y.
WEBS	1110	Calhoun, Ga.
WECA	27	Tallahassee, Fla.
WECI	91.5	Richmond, Ind.
WECI	89.7	Richmond, Ind.
WECK	1230	Cheektowaga, N.Y.
WECL	103.1	Elkhorn City, Ky.
WECM	106.1	Claremont, N.H.
WECO	940	Wartburg, Tenn.
WECP	1080	Carthage, Miss.
WECQ	101.7	Geneva, N.Y.
WECS	90.1	Willimantic, Conn.
WECT	6	Wilmington, N.C.
WECW	88.1	Elmira, N.Y.
WEDA-FM	95.1	Grove City, Pa.
WEDB-TV	40	Berlin, N.H.
WEDC	1240	Chicago, Ill.
WEDH	24	Hartford, Conn.
WEDM	91.1	Indianapolis, Ind.
WEDN	53	Norwich, Conn.
WEDO	810	Mc Keesport, Pa.
WEDR	99.1	Miami, Fla.
WEDU	3	Tampa, Fla.
WEDW	49	Bridgeport, Conn.
WEDY	65	New Haven, Conn.
WEEB	990	Southern Pines, N.C.
WEEC	100.7	Springfield, O.

WEED	1390	Rocky Mount, N.C.
WEEE	89.5	Cherry Hill, N.J.
WEEF	1430	Highland Park, Ill.
WEEI	590	Boston, Mass.
WEEJ	100.1	Port Charlotte, Fla.
WEEK-TV	25	Peoria, Ill.
WEEL	1310	Fairfax, Va.
WEEM	91.7	Pendleton, Ind.
WEEN	1460	Lafayette, Tenn.
WEEP	1080	Pittsburgh, Pa.
WEET	1320	Richmond, Va.
WEEU	850	Reading, Pa.
WEEX	1230	Easton, Pa.
WEEZ	99.3	Heidelberg, Miss.
WEFC	27	Roanoke, Va.
WEFM	95.9	Michigan City, Ind.
WEFT	90.1	Champaign, Ill.
WEGA	1350	Vega Baja, P.R.
WEGG	710	Rose Hill, N.C.
WEGL	91.1	Auburn, Ala.
WEGN	1470	Evergreen, Ala.
WEGN-FM	93.5	Evergreen, Ala.
WEGO	1410	Concord, N.C.
WEGP	1390	Presque Isle, Me.
WEGS	95.3	Gaylord, Mich.
WEHB	89.9	Grand Rapids, Mich.
WEHH	1590	Elmira Heights, N.Y.
WEHT	25	Evansville, Ind.
WEIB	101.1	Marco, Fla.
WEIC	1270	Charleston, Ill.
WEIC-FM	92.1	Charleston, Ill.
WEIF	1370	Moundsville, W.V.
WEIM	1280	Fitchburg, Mass.
WEIQ	42	Mobile, Ala.
WEIR	1430	Weirton, W.V.
WEIS	990	Centre, Ala.
WEIU	88.9	Charleston, Ill.
WEIZ	100.1	Phenix City, Ala.
WEJC	20	Lexington, N.C.
WEJL	630	Scranton, Pa.
WEJY	89.5	Monroe, Mich.
WEKC	710	Williamsburg, Ky.
WEKG	810	Jackson, Ky.
WEKO	930	Cabo Rojo, P.R.
WEKR	1240	Fayetteville, Tenn.
WEKU-FM	88.9	Richmond, Ky.
WEKW-TV	52	Keene, N.H.
WEKY	1340	Richmond, Ky.
WEKZ	1260	Monroe, Wis.
WEKZ-FM	93.7	Monroe, Wis.
WELA	104.3	East Liverpool, O.
WELB	1350	Elba, Ala.
WELC	1150	Welch, W.V.
WELD	690	Fisher, W.V.
WELE-FM	105.9	De Land, Fla.
WELI	960	New Haven, Conn.
WELK	95.3	Elkins, W.V.
WELL	1260	Albion, Mich.
WELL-FM	104.9	Marshall, Mich.
WELM	1410	Elmira, N.Y.
WELO	580	Tupelo, Miss.
WELP	1360	Easley, S.C.
WELP-FM	103.9	Easley, S.C.
WELR	1360	Roanoke, Ala.
WELR-FM	102.3	Roanoke, Ala.
WELR-FM	95.3	Roanoke, Ala.
WELS	1010	Kinston, N.C.
WELV	1370	Ellenville, N.Y.
WELW	1330	Willoughby, O.
WELX	1110	Xenia, O.
WELY	1450	Ely, Minn.
WELZ	1460	Belzoni, Miss.
WEMB	1420	Erwin, Tenn.
WEMC	91.7	Harrisonburg, Va.
WEMI	100.1	Menasha, Wis.
WEMJ	1490	Laconia, N.H.
WEMM	107.9	Huntington, W.V.
WEMP	1250	Milwaukee, Wis.
WEMU	89.1	Ypsilanti, Mich.

WENA	1330	Penuelas, P.R.
WENC	1220	Whiteville, N.C.
WENE	1430	Endicott, N.Y.
WENG	1530	Englewood, Fla.
WENH-TV	11	Durham, N.H.
WENK	1240	Union City, Tenn.
WENN-FM	107.7	Birmingham, Ala.
WENO	1580	Chattahoochee, Fla.
WENR	1090	Englewood, Tenn.
WENS	97.1	Shelbyville, Ind.
WENT	1340	Gloversville, N.Y.
WENU	101.7	Hudson Falls, N.Y.
WENY	1230	Elmira, N.Y.
WENY-TV	36	Elmira, N.Y.
WEOK	1390	Poughkeepsie, N.Y.
WEOL	930	Elyria, O.
WEOS-FM	89.7	Geneva, N.Y.
WEOZ	94.3	Saegertown, Pa.
WEPA	710	Eupora, Miss.
WEPG	910	South Pittsburg, Tenn.
WEPM	1340	Martinsburg, W.V.
WEPR	90.1	Greenville, S.C.
WEPS	90.9	Elgin, Ill.
WEQO	1220	Whitley City, Ky.
WEQR	96.9	Goldsboro, N.C.
WEQX	102.7	Manchester, Vt.
WERA	1590	Plainfield, N.J.
WERB	89.9	Berlin, Conn.
WERC	960	Birmingham, Ala.
WERD	1400	Jacksonville, Fla.
WERE	1300	Cleveland, O.
WERF	56	Hazleton, Pa.
WERG	89.9	Erie, Pa.
WERH	970	Hamilton, Ala.
WERH-FM	92.1	Hamilton, Ala.
WERI	1230	Westerly, R.I.
WERI-FM	103.7	Westerly, R.I.
WERK	990	Muncie, Ind.
WERL	950	Eagle River, Wis.
WERL-FM	94.3	Eagle River, Wis.
WERN	88.7	Madison, Wis.
WERR	104.1	Utuado, P.R.
WERS	88.9	Boston, Mass.
WERT	1220	Van Wert, O.
WERT-FM	98.9	Van Wert, O.
WERU	1190	Sun Prairie, Wis.
WERZ	46	Binghamton, N.Y.
WERZ	107.1	Exeter, N.H.
WESA	940	Charleroi, Pa.
WESA-FM	98.3	Charleroi, Pa.
WESB	1490	Bradford, Pa.
WESC	660	Greenville, S.C.
WESC-FM	92.5	Greenville, S.C.
WESD	89.1	Schofield, Wis.
WESE	95.9	Baldwyn, Miss.
WESH-TV	2	Daytona Beach, Fla.
WESL	1490	East St. Louis, Ill.
WESN	88.1	Bloomington, Ill.
WESO	970	Southbridge, Mass.
WESR	1330	Onley, Va.
WESR-FM	103.3	Onancock, Va.
WESS	90.3	East Stroudsburg, Pa.
WEST	1400	Easton, Pa.
WESU	88.1	Middletown, Conn.
WESX	1230	Salem, Mass.
WESY	1580	Leland, Miss.
WETA-FM	90.9	Washington, D. C.
WETA-TV	26	Washington, D. C.
WETB	790	Johnson City, Tenn.
WETC	540	Zebulon, N.C.
WETD	90.9	Alfred, N.Y.
WETK	33	Burlington, Vt.
WETL	91.7	South Bend, Ind.
WETM-TV	18	Elmira, N.Y.

WETN	88.1	Wheaton, Ill.
WETQ	94.3	Oak Ridge, Tenn.
WETS	89.5	Johnson City, Tenn.
WETT	1590	Ocean City, Md.
WETU	1250	Wetumpka, Ala.
WETV	30	Atlanta, Ga.
WETZ	1330	New Martinsville, W.V.
WEUC	1420	Ponce, P.R.
WEUC	101.1	Ponce, P.R.
WEUP	1600	Huntsville, Ala.
WEVA	860	Emporia, Va.
WEVD	97.9	New York, N.Y.
WEVE	1340	Eveleth, Minn.
WEVE-FM	100.1	Eveleth, Minn.
WEVL	90.3	Memphis, Tenn.
WEVO	89.1	Concord, N.H.
WEVR	1550	River Falls, Wis.
WEVR-FM	106.3	River Falls, Wis.
WEVU	26	Naples, Fla.
WEVV	44	Evansville, Ind.
WEVZ	96.7	Cadillac, Mich.
WEW	770	St. Louis, Mo.
WEWO	1460	Laurinburg, N.C.
WEWS	5	Cleveland, O.
WEWZ	106.7	Ft. Lauderdale, Fla.
WEXA	101.7	Eupora, Miss.
WEXI	1280	Jacksonville, Fla.
WEXL	1340	Royal Oak, Mich.
WEXP	91.5	Gadsden, Ala.
WEXY	1520	Oakland Park, Fla.
WEYI-TV	25	Saginaw, Mich.
WEYQ	94.3	Marietta, O.
WEYS	90.9	Institute, W.V.
WEYY	1580	Talladega, Ala.
WEYZ	1450	Erie, Pa.
WEZB-FM	97.1	New Orleans, La.
WEZC	104.7	Charlotte, N.C.
WEZE	1260	Boston, Mass.
WEZF	92.9	Burlington, Vt.
WEZI	105.1	Coral Gables, Fla.
WEZJ	1440	Williamsburg, Ky.
WEZK	97.5	Knoxville, Tenn.
WEZL	103.5	Charleston, S.C.
WEZN	99.9	Bridgeport, Conn.
WEZO	101.3	Rochester, N.Y.
WEZQ	1300	Winfield, Ala.
WEZR	106.7	Manassas, Va.
WEZS	103.7	Richmond, Va.
WEZV	101.7	Ft. Wayne, Ind.
WEZW	103.7	Wauwatosa, Wis.
WEZX	107.1	Scranton, Pa.
WEZY	1350	Cocoa, Fla.
WEZY-FM	99.3	Cocoa, Fla.
WEZZ	97.7	Clanton, Ala.
WFAA	570	Dallas, Tex.
WFAA-TV	8	Dallas, Tex.
WFAB	1460	Juncos, P.R.
WFAD	1490	Middlebury, Vt.
WFAE	90.7	Charlotte, N.C.
WFAH	1310	Alliance, O.
WFAI	1230	Fayetteville, N.C.
WFAM	91.1	Jacksonville, Fla.
WFAM	90.9	Jacksonville, Fla.
WFAN	102.3	Stonington, Conn.
WFAR	88.5	Danbury, Conn.
WFAR	93.3	Danbury, Conn.
WFAS	1230	White Plains, N.Y.
WFAS-FM	103.9	White Plains, N.Y.
WFAT	19	Johnstown, Pa.
WFAU	1340	Augusta, Me.
WFAV	98.3	Cordele, Ga.
WFAW	940	Fort Atkinson, Wis.
WFAX	1220	Falls Church, Va.
WFBA	1460	San Sebastian, P.R.
WFBC	1330	Greenville, S.C.
WFBC-FM	93.7	Greenville, S.C.
WFBE	95.1	Flint, Mich.
WFBG	1290	Altoona, Pa.

WFBG-FM	98.1	Altoona, Pa.
WFBL	1390	Syracuse, N.Y.
WFBM	1110	Noblesville, Ind.
WFBN	66	Joliet, Ill.
WFBQ	94.7	Indianapolis, Ind.
WFBR	1300	Baltimore, Md.
WFBT	29	Minneapolis, Minn.
WFBZ	1570	Minocqua, Wis.
WFCA	107.9	Ackerman, Miss.
WFCB	94.3	Chillicothe, O.
WFCG	1110	Franklinton, La.
WFCI	89.3	Franklin, Ind.
WFCI	89.5	Franklin, Ind.
WFCJ	93.7	Miamisburg, O.
WFCL	1380	Clintonville, Wis.
WFCL-FM	92.1	Clintonville, Wis.
WFCM	91.9	Orangeburg, S.C.
WFCR	88.5	Amherst, Mass.
WFCS	97.9	New Britain, Conn.
WFCS	90.1	New Britain, Conn.
WFCT	62	Fayetteville, N.C.
WFCV	1090	Ft. Wayne, Ind.
WFDD-FM	88.5	Winston Salem, N.C.
WFDF	910	Flint, Mich.
WFDG	28	New Bedford, Mass.
WFDU	89.1	Teaneck, N.J.
WFEA	1370	Manchester, N.H.
WFEB	1340	Sylacauga, Ala.
WFEC	1400	Harrisburg, Pa.
WFEM	92.1	Ellwood City, Pa.
WFEZ	1390	Meridian, Miss.
WFFF	1360	Columbia, Miss.
WFFF-FM	96.7	Columbia, Miss.
WFFG	1300	Marathon, Fla.
WFFG	1300	Marathon, Fla.
WFFT	55	Ft. Wayne, Ind.
WFFV	99.3	Front Royal, Va.
WFGB	89.7	Kingston, N.Y.
WFGC	63	Palm Beach, Fla.
WFGH	90.7	Fort Gay, W.V.
WFGL	960	Fitchburg, Mass.
WFGM	97.9	Fairmont, W.V.
WFGN	1570	Gaffney, S.C.
WFGW	1010	Black Mountain, N.C.
WFHC	91.5	Henderson, Tenn.
WFHG	980	Bristol, Va.
WFHK	1430	Pell City, Ala.
WFHR	1320	Wisconsin Rapids, Wis.
WFIA	900	Louisville, Ky.
WFIC	1530	Collinsville, Va.
WFID	95.7	Rio Piedras, P.R.
WFIE-TV	14	Evansville, Ind.
WFIF	1500	Milford, Conn.
WFIG	1290	Sumter, S.C.
WFIL	560	Philadelphia, Pa.
WFIN	1330	Findlay, O.
WFIQ	36	Florence, Ala.
WFIR	960	Roanoke, Va.
WFIS	1600	Fountain Inn, S.C.
WFIT	89.5	Melbourne, Fla.
WFIU	103.7	Bloomington, Ind.
WFIV	1080	Kissimmee, Fla.
WFIW	1390	Fairfield, Ill.
WFIW-FM	104.9	Fairfield, Ill.
WFIX	1450	Huntsville, Ala.
WFJA	105.5	Sanford, N.C.
WFJT	1590	Inez, Ky.
WFKN	1220	Franklin, Ky.
WFKX	95.9	Henderson, Tenn.
WFKY	1490	Frankfort, Ky.
WFKZ	103.1	Plantation Key, Fla.
WFLA	970	Tampa, Fla.
WFLB	1490	Fayetteville, N.C.
WFLC	102.3	Canandaigua, N.Y.
WFLD-TV	32	Chicago, Ill.

WFLE	1060	Flemingsburg, Ky.
WFLI	1070	Lookout Mountain, Tenn.
WFLM	103.9	Crown Point, Ind.
WFLN	900	Philadelphia, Pa.
WFLN-FM	95.7	Philadelphia, Pa.
WFLO	870	Farmville, Va.
WFLO-FM	95.7	Farmville, Va.
WFLQ	100.1	French Lick, Ind.
WFLR	1570	Dundee, N.Y.
WFLR-FM	95.9	Dundee, N.Y.
WFLS	1350	Fredericksburg, Va.
WFLS-FM	93.3	Fredericksburg, Va.
WFLT	1420	Flint, Mich.
WFLW	1360	Monticello, Ky.
WFLX	29	West Palm Beach, Fla.
WFLY	92.3	Troy, N.Y.
WFMA	100.7	Rocky Mount, N.C.
WFMB	104.5	Springfield, Ill.
WFMC	730	Goldsboro, N.C.
WFMD	930	Frederick, Md.
WFME	94.7	Newark, N.J.
WFMF	102.5	Baton Rouge, La.
WFMH	1460	Cullman, Ala.
WFMH-FM	101.1	Cullman, Ala.
WFMJ	1390	Youngstown, O.
WFMJ-TV	21	Youngstown, O.
WFMK	99.1	East Lansing, Mich.
WFML	106.5	Washington, Ind.
WFMN	103.1	Newburgh, N.Y.
WFMO	860	Fairmont, N.C.
WFMP	104.5	Fitchburg, Mass.
WFMQ	91.5	Lebanon, Tenn.
WFMR	98.3	Menomonee Falls, Wis.
WFMS	95.5	Indianapolis, Ind.
WFMT-FM	98.7	Chicago, Ill.
WFMU	91.1	East Orange, N.J.
WFMV	106.3	Blairstown, N.J.
WFMW	730	Madisonville, Ky.
WFMX	105.7	Statesville, N.C.
WFMY-TV	2	Greensboro, N.C.
WFMZ	100.7	Allentown, Pa.
WFMZ-TV	69	Allentown, Pa.
WFNC	940	Fayetteville, N.C.
WFNE	100.1	Forsyth, Ga.
WFNM	89.1	Lancaster, Pa.
WFNN	1470	Dunedin, Fla.
WFNX	101.7	Lynn, Mass.
WFNY	92.1	Racine, Wis.
WFOB	1430	Fostoria, O.
WFOB-FM	96.7	Fostoria, O.
WFOF	90.3	Covington, Ind.
WFOG-FM	92.9	Suffolk, Va.
WFOM	1230	Marietta, Ga.
WFON	107.1	Fond Du Lac, Wis.
WFOR	1400	Hattiesburg, Miss.
WFOS	90.3	Chesapeake, Va.
WFOX	97.1	Gainesville, Ga.
WFOY	1240	St. Augustine, Fla.
WFOY-FM	97.7	St. Augustine, Fla.
WFPA	1400	Fort Payne, Ala.
WFPG	96.9	Atlantic City, N.J.
WFPK	91.9	Louisville, Ky.
WFPL	89.3	Louisville, Ky.
WFPR	1400	Hammond, La.
WFPS	92.1	Freeport, Ill.
WFRA	1450	Franklin, Pa.
WFRB	560	Frostburg, Md.
WFRB-FM	105.3	Frostburg, Md.
WFRD	99.3	Hanover, N.H.
WFRE	99.9	Frederick, Md.
WFRI	97.7	Auburn, Ala.
WFRL	1570	Freeport, Ill.
WFRM	600	Coudersport, Pa.
WFRN	104.7	Elkhart, Ind.

WFRO	900	Fremont, O.
WFRO-FM	99.1	Fremont, O.
WFRV-TV	5	Green Bay, Wis.
WFRX	1300	West Frankfort, Ill.
WFRX-FM	97.7	West Frankfort, Ill.
WFSB	3	Hartford, Conn.
WFSC	1050	Franklin, N.C.
WFSE	88.9	Edinboro, Pa.
WFSH	1340	Valparaiso, Fla.
WFSI	107.9	Annapolis, Md.
WFSL	47	Lansing, Mich.
WFSP	90.1	Ft. Myers, Fla.
WFSP	1560	Kingwood, W.V.
WFSR	1470	Harlan, Ky.
WFSS	89.1	Fayetteville, N.C.
WFST	600	Caribou, Me.
WFSU-FM	91.5	Tallahassee, Fla.
WFSU-TV	11	Tallahassee, Fla.
WFTA	101.7	Fulton, Miss.
WFTC	960	Kinston, N.C.
WFTE	1410	Lafayette, Ind.
WFTG	980	London, Ky.
WFTG	1400	London, Ky.
WFTH	1590	Richmond, Va.
WFTL	1400	Ft. Lauderdale, Fla.
WFTM	1240	Maysville, Ky.
WFTM-FM	95.9	Maysville, Ky.
WFTN	1240	Franklin, N.H.
WFTO	1330	Fulton, Miss.
WFTP	1330	Ft. Pierce, Fla.
WFTQ	1440	Worcester, Mass.
WFTR	1450	Front Royal, Va.
WFTS	28	Tampa, Fla.
WFTV	9	Orlando, Fla.
WFTW	1260	Ft. Walton Beach, Fla.
WFTW-FM	96.5	Ft. Walton Beach, Fla.
WFUL	1270	Fulton, Ky.
WFUM	28	Flint, Mich.
WFUN	970	Ashtabula, O.
WFUR	1570	Grand Rapids, Mich.
WFUR-FM	102.9	Grand Rapids, Mich.
WFUV	90.7	New York, N.Y.
WFUZ	93.7	Ocala, Fla.
WFVA	1230	Fredericksburg, Va.
WFVA-FM	101.5	Fredericksburg, Va.
WFWL	1220	Camden, Tenn.
WFWQ	95.1	Ft. Wayne, Ind.
WFWY	43	Syracuse, N.Y.
WFXE	104.9	Columbus, Ga.
WFXI	930	Haines City, Fla.
WFXW	1480	Geneva, Ill.
WFXX	1450	South Williamsport, Pa.
WFXX-FM	99.3	South Williamsport, Pa.
WFXY	1490	Middlesboro, Ky.
WFXZ	100.9	Pinconning, Mich.
WFYC	1280	Alma, Mich.
WFYC-FM	104.9	Alma, Mich.
WFYI	20	Indianapolis, Ind.
WFYN-FM	92.5	Key West, Fla.
WFYR	103.5	Chicago, Ill.
WFYV	104.5	Atlantic Beach, Fla.
WFYZ	39	Murfreesboro, Tenn.
WGAA	1340	Cedartown, Ga.
WGAC	580	Augusta, Ga.
WGAD	1350	Gadsden, Ala.
WGAE	88.3	Girard, Pa.
WGAF	910	Valdosta, Ga.
WGAG-FM	89.3	Orlando, Fla.
WGAI	560	Elizabeth City, N.C.
WGAJ	91.7	Deerfield, Mass.
WGAL-TV	8	Lancaster, Pa.
WGAN	560	Portland, Me.

WGAN-FM	102.9	Portland, Me.
WGAP	1400	Maryville, Tenn.
WGAQ	95.9	Franklin, Ind.
WGAR	1220	Cleveland, O.
WGAS	1420	South Gastonia, N.C.
WGAT	1050	Gate City, Va.
WGAU	1340	Athens, Ga.
WGAW	1340	Gardner, Mass.
WGAY	1050	Silver Spring, Md.
WGAY-FM	99.5	Washington, D. C.
WGBB	1240	Freeport, N.Y.
WGBF	1280	Evansville, Ind.
WGBH	89.7	Boston, Mass.
WGBH-TV	2	Boston, Mass.
WGBI	910	Scranton, Pa.
WGBI-FM	101.3	Scranton, Pa.
WGBM	102.3	Viroqua, Wis.
WGBP-FM	90.1	Green Bay, Wis.
WGBQ	92.7	Galesburg, Ill.
WGBR	1150	Goldsboro, N.C.
WGBS	710	Miami, Fla.
WGBW	91.5	Green Bay, Wis.
WGBX-TV	44	Boston, Mass.
WGBY-TV	57	Springfield, Mass.
WGCA	1450	Charleston, S.C.
WGCB	1440	Red Lion, Pa.
WGCB-FM	96.1	Red Lion, Pa.
WGCB-TV	49	Red Lion, Pa.
WGCD	1490	Chester, S.C.
WGCH	1490	Greenwich, Conn.
WGCI	1390	Chicago, Ill.
WGCI-FM	107.5	Chicago, Ill.
WGCL	98.5	Cleveland, O.
WGCM	102.3	Gulfport, Miss.
WGCO	102.3	Buford, Ga.
WGCS	91.1	Goshen, Ind.
WGCY	106.3	Gibson City, Ill.
WGDL	1200	Lares, P.R.
WGDR	91.1	Plainfield, Vt.
WGEA	1150	Geneva, Ala.
WGEA-FM	93.5	Geneva, Ala.
WGEC	103.9	Springfield, Ga.
WGEE	1360	Green Bay, Wis.
WGEM	1440	Quincy, Ill.
WGEM-FM	105.1	Quincy, Ill.
WGEM-TV	10	Quincy, Ill.
WGEN	1500	Geneseo, Ill.
WGEN-FM	104.9	Geneseo, Ill.
WGER-FM	102.5	Bay City, Mich.
WGET	1320	Gettysburg, Pa.
WGEV	88.3	Beaver Falls, Pa.
WGEZ	1490	Beloit, Wis.
WGFA	1360	Watseka, Ill.
WGFA-FM	94.1	Watseka, Ill.
WGFB	99.9	Plattsburgh, N.Y.
WGFG-FM	100.1	Lake City, S.C.
WGFM	99.5	Schenectady, N.Y.
WGFR	92.1	Glens Falls, N.Y.
WGFS	1430	Covington, Ga.
WGFT	1500	Youngstown, O.
WGFW	1580	Morovis, P.R.
WGGA	1240	Gainesville, Ga.
WGGB-TV	40	Springfield, Mass.
WGGC	95.1	Glasgow, Ky.
WGGF	59	Lebanon, Pa.
WGGG	1230	Gainesville, Fla.
WGGH	1150	Marion, Ill.
WGGL-FM	91.1	Houghton, Mich.
WGGM	1410	Chester, Va.
WGGN	97.7	Castalia, O.
WGGN-TV	52	Sandusky, O.
WGGO	1590	Salamanca, N.Y.
WGGQ	99.3	Waupun, Wis.
WGGR	1240	Hibbing, Minn.
WGGS-TV	16	Greenville, S.C.
WGGT	48	Greensboro, N.C.
WGHB	1250	Farmville, N.C.
WGHC	1570	Clayton, Ga.
WGHN	1370	Grand Haven, Mich.
WGHN-FM	92.1	Grand Haven, Mich.
WGHP-TV	8	High Point, N.C.
WGHQ	920	Kingston, N.Y.
WGHR	102.5	Marietta, Ga.
WGIA	1350	Blackshear, Ga.
WGIB	91.9	Birmingham, Ala.
WGIC	1500	Xenia, O.
WGIG-FM	100.7	Brunswick, Ga.
WGIL	1400	Galesburg, Ill.
WGIQ	43	Louisville, Ala.
WGIR	610	Manchester, N.H.
WGIR-FM	101.1	Manchester, N.H.
WGIT	92.1	Hormigueros, P.R.
WGIV	1600	Charlotte, N.C.
WGKA	1190	Atlanta, Ga.
WGKP	940	Webster, Mass.
WGKR	1310	Perry, Fla.
WGKX	105.9	Memphis, Tenn.
WGKY-FM	105.5	Greenville, Ky.
WGL	1250	Ft. Wayne, Ind.
WGLB	1560	Port Washington, Wis.
WGLB-FM	100.1	Port Washington, Wis.
WGLC	1090	Mendota, Ill.
WGLC-FM	100.1	Mendota, Ill.
WGLD-FM	100.3	High Point, N.C.
WGLE	90.7	Lima, O.
WGLF	104.1	Tallahassee, Fla.
WGLI	1290	Babylon, N.Y.
WGLL	92.1	Mercersburg, Pa.
WGLO	95.3	Pekin, Ill.
WGLQ	97.1	Escanaba, Mich.
WGLR	1280	Lancaster, Wis.
WGLS-FM	89.7	Glassboro, N.J.
WGLT	89.1	Normal, Ill.
WGLU	92.1	Johnstown, Pa.
WGLV	1440	Greenville, S.C.
WGLX	1570	Galion, O.
WGLY	98.3	Goulds, Fla.
WGMA	1520	Spindale, N.C.
WGMB	1470	Georgetown, S.C.
WGMB	97.7	Georgetown, S.C.
WGMC	90.1	Greece, N.Y.
WGMD	92.7	Rehoboth Beach, Del.
WGME	13	Portland, Me.
WGMF	1500	Watkins Glen, N.Y.
WGMK	106.3	Donalsonville, Ga.
WGML	990	Hinesville, Ga.
WGMM	103.1	Gladwin, Mich.
WGMO	95.3	Shell Lake, Wis.
WGMR	101.1	Tyrone, Pa.
WGMS	570	Washington, D. C.
WGMS-FM	103.5	Washington, D. C.
WGMZ	107.9	Flint, Mich.
WGN	720	Chicago, Ill.
WGN-TV	9	Chicago, Ill.
WGNA	107.7	Albany, N.Y.
WGNB	1520	Indian Rocks Beach, Fla.
WGNC	1450	Gastonia, N.C.
WGNE-FM	98.5	Panama City, Fla.
WGNG	550	Pawtucket, R.I.
WGNI	102.7	Wilmington, N.C.
WGNO-TV	26	New Orleans, La.
WGNR	88.9	Grand Rapids, Mich.
WGNS	1450	Murfreesboro, Tenn.
WGNT	930	Huntington, W.V.
WGNU	920	Granite City, Ill.
WGNW	1370	Pewaukee, Wis.
WGNW	1370	Sussex, Wis.
WGNY	1220	Newburgh, N.Y.
WGOC	1090	Kingsport, Tenn.
WGOG	1000	Walhalla, S.C.
WGOH	1370	Grayson, Ky.
WGOJ	105.5	Conneaut, O.
WGOK	900	Mobile, Ala.
WGOL	98.3	Lynchburg, Va.
WGOM	860	Marion, Ind.
WGOS	1070	High Point, N.C.
WGOV	950	Valdosta, Ga.
WGOV-FM	92.9	Valdosta, Ga.
WGOW	1150	Chattanooga, Tenn.
WGPA	1100	Bethlehem, Pa.
WGPC	1450	Albany, Ga.
WGPC-FM	104.5	Albany, Ga.
WGPR	107.5	Detroit, Mich.
WGPR-TV	62	Detroit, Mich.
WGR	550	Buffalo, N.Y.
WGRA	790	Cairo, Ga.
WGRB	34	Campbellsville, Ky.
WGRC	1300	Spring Valley, N.Y.
WGRD-FM	97.9	Grand Rapids, Mich.
WGRE	91.5	Greencastle, Ind.
WGRG	103.9	Greensboro, Ga.
WGRI	1410	Griffin, Ga.
WGRK	1540	Greensburg, Ky.
WGRK-FM	103.1	Greensburg, Ky.
WGRM	1240	Greenwood, Miss.
WGRN	89.3	Greenville, Ill.
WGRN	89.5	Greenville, Ill.
WGRO	960	Lake City, Fla.
WGRP	940	Greenville, Pa.
WGRP-FM	107.1	Greenville, Pa.
WGRQ	96.9	Buffalo, N.Y.
WGRT	107.1	Danville, Ind.
WGRV	1340	Greeneville, Tenn.
WGRY	1590	Grayling, Mich.
WGRZ	2	Buffalo, N.Y.
WGSA	1310	Ephrata, Pa.
WGSE	43	Myrtle Beach, S.C.
WGSF	1220	Arlington, Tenn.
WGSM	740	Huntington, N.Y.
WGSN	900	North Myrtle Beach, S.C.
WGSP	1310	Charlotte, N.C.
WGSQ	94.3	Cookeville, Tenn.
WGSR	1570	Millen, Ga.
WGSS	95.7	Lumberton, N.C.
WGST	920	Atlanta, Ga.
WGSU	89.3	Geneseo, N.Y.
WGSV	1270	Guntersville, Ala.
WGSW	1350	Greenwood, S.C.
WGSX	94.7	Bayamon, P.R.
WGTA	950	Summerville, Ga.
WGTC	92.3	Bloomington, Ind.
WGTD	91.1	Kenosha, Wis.
WGTE-FM	91.3	Toledo, O.
WGTE-TV	30	Toledo, O.
WGTF	96.3	Nantucket, Mass.
WGTH	105.5	Richlands, Va.
WGTL	870	Kannapolis, N.C.
WGTM	590	Wilson, N.C.
WGTN	1400	Georgetown, S.C.
WGTO	540	Cypress Gardens, Fla.
WGTQ	8	Sault Ste. Marie, Mich.
WGTR-TV	66	Marlborough, Mass.
WGTS-FM	91.9	Takoma Park, Md.
WGTU	29	Traverse City, Mich.
WGTV	8	Athens, Ga.
WGTX	1280	De Funiak Springs, Fla.
WGTY	107.7	Gettysburg, Pa.
WGUC	90.9	Cincinnati, O.
WGUD	106.3	Pascagoula, Miss.
WGUF	1130	Gulfport, Miss.
WGUF-FM	96.7	Gulfport, Miss.
WGUL	1500	New Port Richey, Fla.
WGUL-FM	105.5	New Port Richey, Fla.
WGUN	1010	Atlanta, Ga.
WGUS	1380	Augusta, Ga.
WGUS-FM	102.3	Augusta, Ga.
WGUY-FM	100.9	Brewer, Me.
WGVA	1240	Geneva, N.Y.
WGVC	35	Grand Rapids, Mich.

WGVC-FM	88.5	Allendale, Mich.
WGVE	88.7	Gary, Ind.
WGVM	1260	Greenville, Miss.
WGVO	91.7	Greenville, O.
WGVO	91.5	Greenville, O.
WGWG	88.3	Boiling Springs, N.C.
WGWR	1260	Asheboro, N.C.
WGWY	1390	Charlotte, Mich.
WGXA	24	Macon, Ga.
WGXM	97.3	Dayton, O.
WGY	810	Schenectady, N.Y.
WGYL	93.5	Vero Beach, Fla.
WGYV	1380	Greenville, Ala.
WGZS	1170	Waupun, Wis.
WHA	970	Madison, Wis.
WHA-TV	21	Madison, Wis.
WHAB	89.1	Acton, Mass.
WHAD	90.7	Delafield, Wis.
WHAG	1410	Halfway, Md.
WHAG-TV	25	Hagerstown, Md.
WHAI	1240	Greenfield, Mass.
WHAI-FM	98.3	Greenfield, Mass.
WHAJ	104.5	Bluefield, W.V.
WHAK	960	Rogers City, Mich.
WHAL	1400	Shelbyville, Tenn.
WHAM	1180	Rochester, N.Y.
WHAP	1340	Hopewell, Va.
WHAR	1340	Clarksburg, W.V.
WHAS	840	Louisville, Ky.
WHAS-TV	11	Louisville, Ky.
WHAT	1340	Philadelphia, Pa.
WHAV	1490	Haverhill, Mass.
WHAW	980	Weston, W.V.
WHAY	105.5	Aberdeen, Miss.
WHAZ	1330	Troy, N.Y.
WHB	710	Kansas City, Mo.
WHBB	1490	Selma, Ala.
WHBC	91.5	Bristol, Tenn.
WHBC	1480	Canton, O.
WHBC	105.5	Wickenburg, Ariz.
WHBC-FM	94.1	Canton, O.
WHBF	1270	Rock Island, Ill.
WHBF-FM	98.9	Rock Island, Ill.
WHBF-TV	4	Rock Island, Ill.
WHBG	1360	Harrisonburg, Va.
WHBI	105.9	Newark, N.J.
WHBL	1330	Sheboygan, Wis.
WHBN	1420	Harrodsburg, Ky.
WHBN-FM	99.3	Harrodsburg, Ky.
WHBO	1040	Pinellas Park, Fla.
WHBO	1050	Tampa, Fla.
WHBQ	560	Memphis, Tenn.
WHBQ-TV	13	Memphis, Tenn.
WHBT	92.7	Harriman, Tenn.
WHBU	1240	Anderson, Ind.
WHBY	1230	Appleton, Wis.
WHCC	1400	Waynesville, N.C.
WHCE	91.1	Highland Springs, Va.
WHCF	88.5	Bangor, Me.
WHCG	104.9	Metter, Ga.
WHCJ	88.5	Savannah, Ga.
WHCL-FM	88.7	Clinton, N.Y.
WHCN	105.9	Hartford, Conn.
WHCO	1230	Sparta, Ill.
WHCR-FM	90.3	New York, N.Y.
WHCT-TV	18	Hartford, Conn.
WHCU	870	Ithaca, N.Y.
WHCU-FM	97.3	Ithaca, N.Y.
WHDG	103.7	Havre De Grace, Md.
WHDH	850	Boston, Mass.
WHDL	1450	Olean, N.Y.
WHDM	1440	Mc Kenzie, Tenn.
WHEB	750	Portsmouth, N.H.
WHEB-FM	100.3	Portsmouth, N.H.
WHEC-TV	10	Rochester, N.Y.
WHED-TV	15	Hanover, N.H.
WHEE	1370	Martinsville, Va.
WHEI	88.9	Tiffin, O.
WHEL	1240	Knoxville, Tenn.
WHEN	620	Syracuse, N.Y.
WHEO	1270	Stuart, Va.
WHEP	1310	Foley, Ala.
WHER	103.7	Hattiesburg, Miss.
WHEW	101.9	Ft. Myers, Fla.
WHEX	1580	Columbia, Pa.
WHFB	1060	Benton Harbor, Mich.
WHFB-FM	99.9	Benton Harbor, Mich.
WHFC	99.1	Bel Air, Md.
WHFD	95.9	Archbold, O.
WHFH	88.5	Flossmoor, Ill.
WHFL	104.9	Havana, Fla.
WHFM	98.9	Rochester, N.Y.
WHFR	89.3	Dearborn, Mich.
WHFS	99.1	Annapolis, Md.
WHFT	45	Miami, Fla.
WHGC	94.3	Bennington, Vt.
WHGI	1050	Augusta, Ga.
WHGM	103.9	Bellwood, Pa.
WHGR	1290	Houghton Lake, Mich.
WHGW	91.3	Fort Valley, Ga.
WHHB	91.5	Holliston, Mass.
WHHI	91.3	Highland, Wis.
WHHJ	88.9	Dix Hills, N.Y.
WHHL	1190	Pine Castle, Fla.
WHHM	1580	Henderson, Tenn.
WHHO	1320	Hornell, N.Y.
WHHQ	1130	Hilton Head Island, S.C.
WHHR	106.3	Hilton Head Island, S.C.
WHHS	89.3	Havertown, Pa.
WHHV	1400	Hillsville, Va.
WHHY	1440	Montgomery, Ala.
WHHY-FM	101.9	Montgomery, Ala.
WHIC	1520	Hardinsburg, Ky.
WHIC-FM	94.3	Hardinsburg, Ky.
WHIE	1320	Griffin, Ga.
WHII	1570	Bay Springs, Miss.
WHIJ-FM	90.5	Washburn, Wis.
WHIL-FM	91.3	Mobile, Ala.
WHIM	1110	Providence, R.I.
WHIN	1010	Gallatin, Tenn.
WHIO	1290	Dayton, O.
WHIO-FM	99.1	Dayton, O.
WHIO-TV	7	Dayton, O.
WHIP	1350	Mooresville, N.C.
WHIQ	25	Huntsville, Ala.
WHIR	1230	Danville, Ky.
WHIS	1440	Bluefield, W.V.
WHIT	1550	Madison, Wis.
WHIY	1190	Moulton, Ala.
WHIZ	1240	Zanesville, O.
WHIZ-FM	102.5	Zanesville, O.
WHIZ-TV	18	Zanesville, O.
WHJB	620	Greensburg, Pa.
WHJC	1360	Matewan, W.V.
WHJE	91.3	Carmel, Ind.
WHJJ	920	Providence, R.I.
WHJT	93.5	Clinton, Miss.
WHJY	94.1	Providence, R.I.
WHK	1420	Cleveland, O.
WHKC	103.1	Henderson, Ky.
WHKK	100.9	Erlanger, Ky.
WHKP	1450	Hendersonville, N.C.
WHKW	98.1	Fayette, Ala.
WHKY	1290	Hickory, N.C.
WHKY-FM	102.9	Hickory, N.C.
WHKY-TV	14	Hickory, N.C.
WHLA	90.3	La Crosse, Wis.
WHLA-TV	31	La Crosse, Wis.
WHLB	1400	Virginia, Minn.
WHLB-FM	107.1	Virginia, Minn.
WHLD	1270	Niagara Falls, N.Y.
WHLF	1400	South Boston, Va.
WHLG	102.3	Jensen Beach, Fla.
WHLI	1100	Hempstead, N.Y.
WHLM	550	Bloomsburg, Pa.
WHLM-FM	106.5	Bloomsburg, Pa.
WHLN	1410	Harlan, Ky.
WHLO	640	Akron, O.
WHLP	1570	Centerville, Tenn.
WHLP-FM	96.7	Centerville, Tenn.
WHLS	1450	Port Huron, Mich.
WHLT	1300	Huntington, Ind.
WHLW	1170	Lakewood, N.J.
WHLY	106.7	Leesburg, Fla.
WHMA	1390	Anniston, Ala.
WHMA-FM	100.5	Anniston, Ala.
WHMA-TV	40	Anniston, Ala.
WHMB-TV	40	Indianapolis, Ind.
WHMC	23	Conway, S.C.
WHMD	107.1	Hammond, La.
WHME	103.1	South Bend, Ind.
WHME-TV	46	South Bend, Ind.
WHMH-FM	101.7	Sauk Rapids, Minn.
WHMI	1350	Howell, Mich.
WHMI-FM	93.5	Howell, Mich.
WHMM	32	Washington, D. C.
WHMP	1400	Northampton, Mass.
WHMP-FM	99.3	Northampton, Mass.
WHMQ	100.5	Findlay, O.
WHMT	1190	Humboldt, Tenn.
WHMT	1160	Humboldt, Tenn.
WHN	1050	New York, N.Y.
WHNC	890	Henderson, N.C.
WHND	560	Monroe, Mich.
WHNE	1170	Cumming, Ga.
WHNI	1060	Mebane, N.C.
WHNN	96.1	Bay City, Mich.
WHNS	21	Asheville, N.C.
WHNT-TV	19	Huntsville, Ala.
WHNY	1250	Mc Comb, Miss.
WHO	1040	Des Moines, Ia.
WHO-TV	13	Des Moines, Ia.
WHOC	1490	Philadelphia, Miss.
WHOD	1230	Jackson, Ala.
WHOD-FM	104.9	Jackson, Ala.
WHOG	1570	Fernandina Beach, Fla.
WHOK	95.5	Lancaster, O.
WHOL	1600	Allentown, Pa.
WHOM	94.9	Mt. Washington, N.H.
WHON	930	Richmond, Ind.
WHOO	990	Orlando, Fla.
WHOO-FM	96.5	Orlando, Fla.
WHOP	1230	Hopkinsville, Ky.
WHOP-FM	98.7	Hopkinsville, Ky.
WHOS	800	Decatur, Ala.
WHOT	1330	Campbell, O.
WHOU	1340	Houlton, Me.
WHOU-FM	100.1	Houlton, Me.
WHOV	88.3	Hampton, Va.
WHOW	1520	Clinton, Ill.
WHOW-FM	95.9	Clinton, Ill.
WHOY	1210	Salinas, P.R.
WHP	580	Harrisburg, Pa.
WHP-FM	97.3	Harrisburg, Pa.
WHP-TV	21	Harrisburg, Pa.
WHPA	104.9	Hollidaysburg, Pa.
WHPB	1390	Belton, S.C.
WHPC	90.3	Garden City, N.Y.
WHPE-FM	95.5	High Point, N.C.
WHPH	90.5	Whippany, N.J.
WHPI	1340	Herrin, Ill.
WHPK-FM	88.3	Chicago, Ill.
WHPO	100.9	Hoopeston, Ill.
WHPR	88.1	Highland Park, Mich.
WHPW-FM	89.9	Huntington, W.V.
WHPY	1590	Clayton, N.C.
WHQR	91.3	Wilmington, N.C.
WHRB	95.3	Cambridge, Mass.
WHRC	92.1	Port Henry, N.Y.
WHRK	97.1	Memphis, Tenn.
WHRL	103.1	Albany, N.Y.
WHRM	90.9	Wausau, Wis.
WHRM-TV	20	Wausau, Wis.
WHRO-FM	89.5	Norfolk, Va.
WHRO-TV	15	Norfolk, Va.
WHRS	90.7	West Palm Beach, Fla.

WHRS	42	West Palm Beach, Fla.
WHRS-FM	90.7	Boynton Beach, Fla.
WHRT	860	Hartselle, Ala.
WHRW	90.5	Binghamton, N.Y.
WHRZ	97.7	Providence, Ky.
WHSA	89.9	Brule, Wis.
WHSB	107.7	Alpena, Mich.
WHSC	1450	Hartsville, S.C.
WHSD	88.5	Hinsdale, Ill.
WHSI	51	Portland, Me.
WHSK	89.1	Kokomo, Ind.
WHSK	98.9	Kokomo, Ind.
WHSL	97.3	Wilmington, N.C.
WHSM	910	Hayward, Wis.
WHSM-FM	101.7	Hayward, Wis.
WHSN	89.3	Bangor, Me.
WHSR-FM	91.9	Winchester, Mass.
WHSS	89.5	Hamilton, O.
WHSV-TV	3	Harrisonburg, Va.
WHSY	1230	Hattiesburg, Miss.
WHSY-FM	104.5	Hattiesburg, Miss.
WHTB	92.7	Talladega, Ala.
WHTC	1450	Holland, Mich.
WHTF	92.7	Starview, Pa.
WHTG	1410	Eatontown, N.J.
WHTG-FM	106.3	Eatontown, N.J.
WHTH	790	Heath, O.
WHTL-FM	102.3	Whitehall, Wis.
WHTM-TV	27	Harrisburg, Pa.
WHTT	103.3	Boston, Mass.
WHTT	1260	Miami, Fla.
WHTV	24	Meridian, Miss.
WHTX	96.1	Pittsburgh, Pa.
WHTY-TV	12	Wilmington, Del.
WHTZ	100.3	Newark, N.J.
WHUB	1400	Cookeville, Tenn.
WHUB-FM	98.3	Cookeville, Tenn.
WHUC	1230	Hudson, N.Y.
WHUD	100.7	Peekskill, N.Y.
WHUE	1150	Boston, Mass.
WHUE-FM	100.7	Boston, Mass.
WHUG	101.7	Jamestown, N.Y.
WHUH	97.7	Houghton, Mich.
WHUM	1240	Reading, Pa.
WHUN	1150	Huntingdon, Pa.
WHUR-FM	96.3	Washington, D. C.
WHUS	91.7	Storrs, Conn.
WHUT	1470	Anderson, Ind.
WHUZ	103.1	Huntington, Ind.
WHVI-FM	106.1	North Vernon, Ind.
WHVL	1600	Hendersonville, N.C.
WHVN	1240	Charlotte, N.C.
WHVR	1280	Hanover, Pa.
WHVW	950	Hyde Park, N.Y.
WHWB	1000	Rutland, Vt.
WHWB-FM	98.1	Rutland, Vt.
WHWC	88.3	Menomonie, Wis.
WHWC-TV	28	Menomonie, Wis.
WHWE	89.7	Howe, Ind.
WHWH	1350	Princeton, N.J.
WHWK	98.1	Binghamton, N.Y.
WHWL	95.7	Marquette, Mich.
WHYC	88.5	Swan Quarter, N.C.
WHYD	1270	Columbus, Ga.
WHYI	100.7	Ft. Lauderdale, Fla.
WHYL	960	Carlisle, Pa.
WHYM	610	Pensacola, Fla.
WHYN	560	Springfield, Mass.
WHYN-FM	93.1	Springfield, Mass.
WHYP	1530	North East, Pa.
WHYP-FM	100.9	North East, Pa.
WHYT	96.3	Detroit, Mich.
WHYW-FM	96.9	Braddock, Pa.
WHYY-FM	90.9	Philadelphia, Pa.
WHYZ	1070	Greenville, S.C.
WIAA	88.3	Interlochen, Mich.
WIAC	740	San Juan, P.R.
WIAC-FM	102.5	San Juan, P.R.

WIAF	1500	Clarkesville, Ga.
WIAI	99.1	Danville, Ill.
WIAK	96.7	Clifton Park, N.Y.
WIAL	94.1	Eau Claire, Wis.
WIAM	900	Williamston, N.C.
WIAN	90.1	Indianapolis, Ind.
WIBA	1310	Madison, Wis.
WIBA-FM	101.5	Madison, Wis.
WIBB	1280	Macon, Ga.
WIBC	1070	Indianapolis, Ind.
WIBF-FM	103.9	Jenkintown, Pa.
WIBG	1520	Ocean City, N.J.
WIBI	91.1	Carlinville, Ill.
WIBM-FM	94.1	Jackson, Mich.
WIBN	98.3	Earl Park, Ind.
WIBQ	98.7	Utica, N.Y.
WIBR	1300	Baton Rouge, La.
WIBS	97.9	Charlotte Amalie, V.I.
WIBU	1240	Poynette, Wis.
WIBV	1260	Belleville, Ill.
WIBW	580	Topeka, Kan.
WIBW-FM	97.3	Topeka, Kan.
WIBW-TV	13	Topeka, Kan.
WIBX	950	Utica, N.Y.
WIBZ	99.3	Parkersburg, W.V.
WICB	91.7	Ithaca, N.Y.
WICC	600	Bridgeport, Conn.
WICD	15	Champaign, Ill.
WICH	1310	Norwich, Conn.
WICK	1400	Scranton, Pa.
WICN	90.5	Worcester, Mass.
WICO	1320	Salisbury, Md.
WICO-FM	94.3	Salisbury, Md.
WICR	88.7	Indianapolis, Ind.
WICS	20	Springfield, Ill.
WICU-TV	12	Erie, Pa.
WICY	1490	Malone, N.Y.
WICZ-TV	40	Binghamton, N.Y.
WIDA	1400	Carolina, P.R.
WIDA-FM	90.5	Carolina, Pa.
WIDD	1520	Elizabethton, Tenn.
WIDD-FM	99.3	Elizabethton, Tenn.
WIDE	1400	Biddeford, Me.
WIDG	940	St. Ignace, Mich.
WIDO	103.1	Dunn, N.C.
WIDR	89.1	Kalamazoo, Mich.
WIDS	1190	Russell Springs, Ky.
WIDU	1600	Fayetteville, N.C.
WIEL	1400	Elizabethtown, Ky.
WIFC	95.5	Wausau, Wis.
WIFE	1580	Connersville, Ind.
WIFF	1570	Auburn, Ind.
WIFF-FM	105.5	Auburn, Ind.
WIFM-FM	100.9	Elkin, N.C.
WIFO-FM	105.5	Jessup, Ga.
WIFR-TV	23	Freeport, Ill.
WIFX	1000	Jenkins, Ky.
WIFX-FM	94.3	Jenkins, Ky.
WIGC	105.7	Troy, Ala.
WIGG	1420	Wiggins, Miss.
WIGL	106.7	Orangeburg, S.C.
WIGM	1490	Medford, Wis.
WIGM-FM	99.3	Medford, Wis.
WIGO	1340	Atlanta, Ga.
WIGS	1230	Gouverneur, N.Y.
WIGS-FM	95.3	Gouverneur, N.Y.
WIGY	105.9	Bath, Me.
WIHN	96.7	Normal, Ill.
WIHS	104.9	Middletown, Conn.
WIHT	31	Ann Arbor, Mich.
WIIM-TV	8	Iron Mountain, Mich.
WIIN	1450	Atlantic City, N.J.
WIIQ	41	Demopolis, Ala.
WIIS	107.1	Key West, Fla.
WIIZ	1290	Jacksonville, N.C.
WIKB	99.3	Iron River, Mich.
WIKB	1230	Iron River, Mich.
WIKC	1490	Bogalusa, La.
WIKE	1490	Newport, Vt.
WIKI	100.1	Carrollton, Ky.

WIKQ	94.9	Greeneville, Tenn.
WIKS	1450	Parkersburg, W.V.
WIKU	91.3	Pikeville, Tenn.
WIKX	98.3	Immokalee, Fla.
WIKY-FM	104.1	Evansville, Ind.
WIKZ	95.1	Chambersburg, Pa.
WIL	1430	St. Louis, Mo.
WIL-FM	92.3	St. Louis, Mo.
WILA	1580	Danville, Va.
WILD	1090	Boston, Mass.
WILE	1270	Cambridge, O.
WILE-FM	96.7	Cambridge, O.
WILI	1400	Willimantic, Conn.
WILK	980	Wilkes Barre, Pa.
WILL	580	Urbana, Ill.
WILL-FM	90.9	Urbana, Ill.
WILL-TV	12	Urbana, Ill.
WILM	1450	Wilmington, Del.
WILO	1570	Frankfort, Ind.
WILQ	105.1	Williamsport, Pa.
WILS	1320	Lansing, Mich.
WILS-FM	101.7	Lansing, Mich.
WILX-TV	10	Jackson, Mich.
WILY	1210	Centralia, Ill.
WIMA	1150	Lima, O.
WIMG	1300	Trenton, N.J.
WIMI	99.7	Ironwood, Mich.
WIMK	93.1	Iron Mountain, Mich.
WIMO	1300	Winder, Ga.
WIMS	1420	Michigan City, Ind.
WIMT	102.1	Lima, O.
WIMV	104.9	Madison, Fla.
WIMZ	103.5	Knoxville, Tenn.
WINA	1070	Charlottesville, Va.
WINC	1400	Winchester, Va.
WIND	560	Chicago, Ill.
WINE	940	Brookfield, Conn.
WINF	1230	Manchester, Conn.
WING	1410	Dayton, O.
WINI	1420	Murphysboro, Ill.
WINK	1240	Ft. Myers, Fla.
WINK-FM	96.9	Ft. Myers, Fla.
WINK-TV	11	Ft. Myers, Fla.
WINN	1240	Louisville, Ky.
WINQ	97.7	Winchendon, Mass.
WINR	680	Binghamton, N.Y.
WINS	1010	New York, N.Y.
WINT	20	Crossville, Tenn.
WINU	1510	Highland, Ill.
WINW	1520	Canton, O.
WINX	1600	Rockville, Md.
WINY	1350	Putnam, Conn.
WINZ	940	Miami, Fla.
WINZ-FM	94.9	Miami Beach, Fla.
WIOA	97.5	Mayaguez, P.R.
WIOB	99.9	San Juan, P.R.
WIOC	105.1	Ponce, P.R.
WIOD	610	Miami, Fla.
WIOF	104.1	Waterbury, Conn.
WIOG	106.3	Saginaw, Mich.
WIOI	1010	New Boston, O.
WIOK	95.3	Falmouth, Ky.
WION	1430	Ionia, Mich.
WIOO	1000	Carlisle, Pa.
WIOQ	102.1	Philadelphia, Pa.
WIOS	1480	Tawas City, Mich.
WIOT	104.7	Toledo, O.
WIOU	1350	Kokomo, Ind.
WIOV	105.1	Ephrata, Pa.
WIOZ	107.1	Southern Pines, N.C.
WIP	610	Philadelphia, Pa.
WIPB	49	Muncie, Ind.
WIPC	1280	Lake Wales, Fla.
WIPM-TV	3	Mayaguez, P.R.
WIPR	940	San Juan, P.R.
WIPR-FM	91.3	San Juan, P.R.
WIPR-TV	6	San Juan, P.R.

Call	Freq.	Location
WIPS	1250	Ticonderoga, N.Y.
WIQB	102.9	Ann Arbor, Mich.
WIQH	88.3	Concord, Mass.
WIQI	100.7	Tampa, Fla.
WIQO-FM	100.9	Covington, Va.
WIQR	1410	Prattville, Ala.
WIQT	1000	Horseheads, N.Y.
WIRA	1400	Ft. Pierce, Fla.
WIRB	600	Enterprise, Ala.
WIRC	630	Hickory, N.C.
WIRD	920	Lake Placid, N.Y.
WIRE	1430	Indianapolis, Ind.
WIRJ	740	Humboldt, Tenn.
WIRK-FM	107.9	West Palm Beach, Fla.
WIRL	1290	Peoria, Ill.
WIRO	1230	Ironton, O.
WIRQ	90.9	Rochester, N.Y.
WIRT	13	Hibbing, Minn.
WIRV	1550	Irvine, Ky.
WIRX	107.1	St. Joseph, Mich.
WIRY	1340	Plattsburgh, N.Y.
WIS	560	Columbia, S.C.
WIS-TV	10	Columbia, S.C.
WISA	1390	Isabela, P.R.
WISC-TV	3	Madison, Wis.
WISE	1310	Asheville, N.C.
WISH-TV	8	Indianapolis, Ind.
WISK	1390	Americus, Ga.
WISL	1480	Shamokin, Pa.
WISM	1480	Madison, Wis.
WISN	1130	Milwaukee, Wis.
WISN-TV	12	Milwaukee, Wis.
WISO	1260	Ponce, P.R.
WISP	1230	Kinston, N.C.
WISQ	100.1	West Salem, Wis.
WISR	680	Butler, Pa.
WISS	1090	Berlin, Wis.
WISS-FM	102.3	Berlin, Wis.
WIST	94.3	Lobelville, Tenn.
WISU	89.7	Terre Haute, Ind.
WISU-TV	26	Terre Haute, Ind.
WISV	1360	Viroqua, Wis.
WITA	1490	Knoxville, Tenn.
WITB-FM	91.1	Salem, W.V.
WITC	90.9	Cazenovia, N.Y.
WITF-FM	89.5	Harrisburg, Pa.
WITF-TV	33	Harrisburg, Pa.
WITH	1230	Baltimore, Md.
WITI-TV	6	Milwaukee, Wis.
WITL	1010	Lansing, Mich.
WITL-FM	100.7	Lansing, Mich.
WITN	930	Washington, N.C.
WITN-FM	93.3	Washington, N.C.
WITN-TV	7	Washington, N.C.
WITO	107.1	Ironton, O.
WITR	89.7	Henrietta, N.Y.
WITT	93.5	Tuscola, Ill.
WITV	7	Charleston, S.C.
WITY	980	Danville, Ill.
WITZ	990	Jasper, Ind.
WITZ-FM	104.7	Jasper, Ind.
WIUJ	88.9	St. Thomas, V.I.
WIUM	91.3	Macomb, Ill.
WIUP-FM	90.1	Indiana, Pa.
WIUS	88.3	Macomb, Ill.
WIUV	91.3	Castleton, Vt.
WIUW	67	High Point, N.C.
WIVA-FM	100.3	Aguadilla, P.R.
WIVB-TV	4	Buffalo, N.Y.
WIVD	1510	Lajas, P.R.
WIVE	1430	Ashland, Va.
WIVI-FM	99.5	Christiansted, V.I.
WIVK	850	Knoxville, Tenn.
WIVK-FM	107.7	Knoxville, Tenn.
WIVQ	100.9	Peru, Ill.
WIVS	850	Crystal Lake, Ill.
WIVV	1370	Vieques, P.R.
WIVY-FM	102.9	Jacksonville, Fla.
WIXC	1140	Fayetteville, Tenn.
WIXE	1190	Monroe, N.C.
WIXI	1280	Lancaster, Ky.
WIXK	1590	New Richmond, Wis.
WIXK-FM	107.1	New Richmond, Wis.
WIXL-FM	103.7	Newton, N.J.
WIXN	1460	Dixon, Ill.
WIXN-FM	101.7	Dixon, Ill.
WIXQ	91.7	Millersville, Pa.
WIXR	1500	Mt. Pleasant, S.C.
WIXT	9	Syracuse, N.Y.
WIXV	95.3	Front Royal, Va.
WIXV	95.5	Savannah, Ga.
WIXX	101.1	Green Bay, Wis.
WIXY	1600	E. Longmeadow, Mass.
WIXZ	1360	Mc Keesport, Pa.
WIYD	1260	Palatka, Fla.
WIYE	55	Leesburg, Fla.
WIYN	1360	Rome, Ga.
WIYQ	99.1	Ebensburg, Pa.
WIYY	97.9	Baltimore, Md.
WIZD	98.7	Ft. Pierce, Fla.
WIZE	1340	Springfield, O.
WIZM	1410	La Crosse, Wis.
WIZM-FM	93.3	La Crosse, Wis.
WIZN	106.3	Vergennes, Vt.
WIZO	1380	Franklin, Tenn.
WIZO-FM	100.1	Franklin, Tenn.
WIZR-FM	104.9	Johnstown, N.Y.
WIZS	1450	Henderson, N.C.
WIZZ	1250	Streator, Ill.
WJAC	850	Johnstown, Pa.
WJAC-TV	6	Johnstown, Pa.
WJAD	97.3	Bainbridge, Ga.
WJAG	780	Norfolk, Neb.
WJAI	92.9	Eaton, O.
WJAK	1460	Jackson, Tenn.
WJAM-FM	103.9	Marion, Ala.
WJAQ	100.9	Marianna, Fla.
WJAR-TV	10	Providence, R.I.
WJAS	1320	Pittsburgh, Pa.
WJAT	800	Swainsboro, Ga.
WJAT-FM	98.3	Swainsboro, Ga.
WJAX	930	Jacksonville, Fla.
WJAX-FM	95.1	Jacksonville, Fla.
WJAY	1280	Mullins, S.C.
WJAZ	960	Albany, Ga.
WJBB	1230	Haleyville, Ala.
WJBB-FM	92.7	Haleyville, Ala.
WJBC	1230	Bloomington, Ill.
WJBD	1350	Salem, Ill.
WJBD-FM	100.1	Salem, Ill.
WJBF	6	Augusta, Ga.
WJBI	101.7	Clarksdale, Miss.
WJBK-TV	2	Detroit, Mich.
WJBL-FM	94.5	Holland, Mich.
WJBM	1480	Jerseyville, Ill.
WJBM-FM	104.1	Jerseyville, Ill.
WJBO	1150	Baton Rouge, La.
WJBQ	97.9	Portland, Me.
WJBR	1290	Wilmington, Del.
WJBR-FM	99.5	Wilmington, Del.
WJBT	1590	Brockport, N.Y.
WJBU	1080	Port St. Joe, Fla.
WJBW-FM	103.1	Hampton, S.C.
WJBY	930	Gadsden, Ala.
WJCD	1390	Seymour, Ind.
WJCD-FM	93.7	Seymour, Ind.
WJCF	100.9	Westover, W.V.
WJCL	22	Savannah, Ga.
WJCL-FM	96.5	Savannah, Ga.
WJCM	960	Sebring, Fla.
WJCR	92.1	Washington, Pa.
WJCT	7	Jacksonville, Fla.
WJCT-FM	89.9	Jacksonville, Fla.
WJCW	910	Johnson City, Tenn.
WJDA	1300	Quincy, Mass.
WJDB	630	Thomasville, Ala.
WJDB-FM	95.3	Thomasville, Ala.
WJDM	1530	Elizabeth, N.J.
WJDQ	1330	Meridian, Miss.
WJDQ	1240	Marion, Miss.
WJDQ	101.3	Meridian, Miss.
WJDR	98.3	Prentiss, Miss.
WJDW	1550	Corydon, Ind.
WJDX	620	Jackson, Miss.
WJDY	1470	Salisbury, Md.
WJDZ	89.9	Levittown, P.R.
WJEB	1350	Gladwin, Mich.
WJED	1410	Somerville, Tenn.
WJEF	91.9	Lafayette, Ind.
WJEH	990	Gallipolis, O.
WJEJ	1240	Hagerstown, Md.
WJEL	89.1	Indianapolis, Ind.
WJEL	89.3	Indianapolis, Ind.
WJEM	1150	Valdosta, Ga.
WJEP	1020	Ochlochnee, Ga.
WJEQ	103.1	Macomb, Ill.
WJER	1450	Dover, O.
WJER-FM	101.7	Dover, O.
WJES	1190	Johnston, S.C.
WJET	1400	Erie, Pa.
WJET-TV	24	Erie, Pa.
WJEZ	104.3	Chicago, Ill.
WJFC	1480	Jefferson City, Tenn.
WJFD-FM	97.3	New Bedford, Mass.
WJFL	1490	Vicksburg, Miss.
WJFM	93.7	Grand Rapids, Mich.
WJFT-TV	19	Albany, Ga.
WJGA-FM	92.1	Jackson, Ga.
WJGF	91.5	Romney, W.V.
WJGS	98.5	Houghton Lake, Mich.
WJHD	90.7	Portsmouth, R.I.
WJHG-TV	7	Panama City, Fla.
WJHL-TV	11	Johnson City, Tenn.
WJHO	1400	Opelika, Ala.
WJHR	103.1	Jackson, Tenn.
WJHU	88.1	Baltimore, Md.
WJIB	96.9	Boston, Mass.
WJIC	1510	Salem, N.J.
WJIK	1580	Camp Lejeune, N.C.
WJIL	1550	Jacksonville, Ill.
WJIM	1240	Lansing, Mich.
WJIM-FM	97.5	Lansing, Mich.
WJIM-TV	6	Lansing, Mich.
WJIT	1480	New York, N.Y.
WJIV	101.9	Cherry Valley, N.Y.
WJIZ	96.3	Albany, Ga.
WJJA	49	Racine, Wis.
WJJB	97.7	Hyde Park, N.Y.
WJJC	1270	Commerce, Ga.
WJJD	1160	Chicago, Ill.
WJJJ	1260	Christiansburg, Va.
WJJK	1400	Eau Claire, Wis.
WJJL	1440	Niagara Falls, N.Y.
WJJM	1490	Lewisburg, Tenn.
WJJM-FM	94.3	Lewisburg, Tenn.
WJJN	1180	Newburgh, Ind.
WJJQ	810	Tomahawk, Wis.
WJJS-FM	101.7	Lynchburg, Va.
WJJT	1540	Jellico, Tenn.
WJJW	91.1	North Adams, Mass.
WJJY	106.7	Brainerd, Minn.
WJJZ	1460	Mount Holly, N.J.
WJKA	26	Wilmington, N.C.
WJKC	95.1	Christiansted, V.I.
WJKK	1070	Beckley, W.V.
WJKL	94.3	Elgin, Ill.
WJKM	1090	Hartsville, Tenn.
WJKR	103.9	Muncy, Pa.
WJKS-TV	17	Jacksonville, Fla.
WJKW-TV	8	Cleveland, O.
WJKX	1460	Moss Point, Miss.
WJKY	1060	Jamestown, Ky.
WJLA-TV	7	Washington, D. C.
WJLB	97.9	Detroit, Mich.
WJLC-FM	97.5	South Boston, Va.
WJLD	1400	Homewood, Ala.
WJLE	1480	Smithville, Tenn.
WJLE-FM	101.7	Smithville, Tenn.
WJLK	1310	Asbury Park, N.J.
WJLK-FM	94.3	Asbury Park, N.J.
WJLM	93.5	Salem, Va.
WJLQ	100.7	Pensacola, Fla.
WJLS	560	Beckley, W.V.

WJLW	95.9	De Pere, Wis.
WJLY	1550	Braddock, Pa.
WJMA	1340	Orange, Va.
WJMA-FM	96.7	Orange, Va.
WJMB	1340	Brookhaven, Miss.
WJMC	1240	Rice Lake, Wis.
WJMC-FM	96.3	Rice Lake, Wis.
WJMF	88.7	Smithfield, R.I.
WJMG	92.1	Hattiesburg, Miss.
WJMI	99.7	Jackson, Miss.
WJMJ	88.9	Hartford, Conn.
WJML	1110	Petoskey, Mich.
WJML-FM	98.9	Petoskey, Mich.
WJMM	106.3	Versailles, Ky.
WJMN-TV	3	Escanaba, Mich.
WJMO	1490	Cleveland Heights, O.
WJMQ	1170	Norfolk, Mass.
WJMR	1430	Ridgeland, S.C.
WJMS	590	Ironwood, Mich.
WJMT	730	Merrill, Wis.
WJMT-FM	93.5	Merrill, Wis.
WJMU	89.5	Decatur, Ill.
WJMU	89.9	Decatur, Ill.
WJMW	730	Athens, Ala.
WJMW	770	Athens, Ala.
WJMX	970	Florence, S.C.
WJNC	1240	Jacksonville, N.C.
WJNJ	1600	Atlantic Beach, Fla.
WJNL	1490	Johnstown, Pa.
WJNL-FM	96.5	Johnstown, Pa.
WJNO	1230	West Palm Beach, Fla.
WJNR-FM	101.5	Iron Mountain, Mich.
WJNS	1530	Yazoo City, Miss.
WJNS-FM	92.1	Yazoo City, Miss.
WJNZ	94.3	Greencastle, Ind.
WJOB	1230	Hammond, Ind.
WJOI	97.1	Detroit, Mich.
WJOJ	106.3	Picayune, Miss.
WJOK	1150	Gaithersburg, Md.
WJOL	1340	Joliet, Ill.
WJON	1240	St. Cloud, Minn.
WJOS	1540	Elkin, N.C.
WJOT	1260	Lake City, S.C.
WJOY	1230	Burlington, Vt.
WJOZ	1310	Troy, Pa.
WJPA	1450	Washington, Pa.
WJPC	950	Chicago, Ill.
WJPD	1240	Ishpeming, Mich.
WJPD-FM	92.3	Ishpeming, Mich.
WJPJ	1530	Huntingdon, Tenn.
WJPM-TV	33	Florence, S.C.
WJPR	21	Lynchburg, Va.
WJPT	14	Jacksonville, Ill.
WJPW	810	Rockford, Mich.
WJQI	1450	New Bern, N.C.
WJQS	1400	Jackson, Miss.
WJQY	98.3	Chickasaw, Ala.
WJR	760	Detroit, Mich.
WJRB	1430	Madison, Tenn.
WJRC	1510	Joliet, Ill.
WJRD	1150	Tuscaloosa, Ala.
WJRE	92.1	Kewanee, Ill.
WJRH	90.5	Easton, Pa.
WJRI	1340	Lenoir, N.C.
WJRL	1530	Calhoun City, Miss.
WJRM	1390	Troy, N.C.
WJRO	1590	Glen Burnie, Md.
WJRQ	92.1	Williston, Fla.
WJRS	104.9	Jamestown, Ky.
WJRT-TV	12	Flint, Mich.
WJRZ	100.1	Manahawkin, N.J.
WJSA	1600	Jersey Shore, Pa.
WJSB	1050	Crestview, Fla.
WJSC-FM	90.7	Johnson, Vt.
WJSK	102.3	Lumberton, N.C.
WJSL	90.3	Houghton, N.Y.
WJSM	1110	Martinsburg, Pa.
WJSM-FM	92.7	Martinsburg, Pa.
WJSN-FM	97.7	Jackson, Ky.
WJSO	1590	Jonesboro, Tenn.
WJSP-TV	28	Columbus, Ga.
WJSQ	101.7	Athens, Tenn.
WJSR	91.1	Birmingham, Ala.
WJST	94.5	Port St. Joe, Fla.
WJST	93.5	Port St. Joe, Fla.
WJSU	88.5	Jackson, Miss.
WJSV	90.5	Morristown, N.J.
WJSY	104.3	Harrisonburg, Va.
WJTM	45	Winston Salem, N.C.
WJTN	1240	Jamestown, N.Y.
WJTO	730	Bath, Me.
WJTP	1130	Newland, N.C.
WJTT	94.3	Red Bank, Tenn.
WJTV	12	Jackson, Miss.
WJTX-TV	12	Charlotte Amalie, V.I.
WJTY	88.1	Lancaster, Wis.
WJUL	91.5	Lowell, Mass.
WJUN	1220	Mexico, Pa.
WJVL	99.9	Janesville, Wis.
WJVM	94.3	Sterling, Ill.
WJVS	88.3	Cincinnati, O.
WJW	850	Cleveland, O.
WJWF	103.1	Columbus, Miss.
WJWJ-FM	89.9	Beaufort, S.C.
WJWJ-TV	16	Beaufort, S.C.
WJWK	91.5	Jamestown, N.Y.
WJWL	900	Georgetown, Del.
WJWS	1370	South Hill, Va.
WJXL	810	Jacksonville, Ala.
WJXN	1450	Jackson, Miss.
WJXQ	106.1	Jackson, Mich.
WJXT	4	Jacksonville, Fla.
WJXY	1050	Conway, S.C.
WJYA	1080	Marietta, Ga.
WJYE	96.1	Buffalo, N.Y.
WJYF	104.1	La Grange, Ga.
WJYJ	90.5	Fredericksburg, Va.
WJYL	101.7	Jeffersontown, Ky.
WJYM	730	Bowling Green, O.
WJYR	92.1	Myrtle Beach, S.C.
WJYT	960	Quebradillas, P.R.
WJYV	850	Forest, Miss.
WJYW	107.1	Southport, N.C.
WJYY	105.5	Concord, N.H.
WJZ-TV	13	Baltimore, Md.
WJZM	1400	Clarksville, Tenn.
WJZQ	95.1	Kenosha, Wis.
WJZR	99.7	Kannapolis, N.C.
WJZZ	105.9	Detroit, Mich.
WKAA.		Ocilla, Ga.
WKAB-TV	32	Montgomery, Ala.
WKAC	1080	Athens, Ala.
WKAD	100.1	Canton, Pa.
WKAE	104.9	High Springs, Fla.
WKAF	62	Syracuse, N.Y.
WKAI	1510	Macomb, Ill.
WKAI-FM	100.1	Macomb, Ill.
WKAJ	900	Saratoga Springs, N.Y.
WKAK	101.7	Albany, Ga.
WKAL	1450	Rome, N.Y.
WKAL-FM	95.9	Rome, N.Y.
WKAM	1460	Goshen, Ind.
WKAN	1320	Kankakee, Ill.
WKAO	1040	Boynton Beach, Fla.
WKAO	1510	Boynton Beach, Fla.
WKAP	1320	Allentown, Pa.
WKAQ	580	San Juan, P.R.
WKAQ-FM	104.7	San Juan, P.R.
WKAQ-TV	2	San Juan, P.R.
WKAR	870	East Lansing, Mich.
WKAR-FM	90.5	East Lansing, Mich.
WKAR-TV	23	East Lansing, Mich.
WKAS	25	Ashland, Ky.
WKAT	1360	Miami Beach, Fla.
WKAU	1050	Kaukauna, Wis.
WKAU-FM	104.9	Kaukauna, Wis.
WKAX	1500	Russellville, Ala.
WKAY	1490	Glasgow, Ky.
WKAZ	1300	St. Albans, W.V.
WKBA	1550	Vinton, Va.
WKBB	100.9	West Point, Miss.
WKBC	810	North Wilkesboro, N.C.
WKBC-FM	97.3	North Wilkesboro, N.C.
WKBD	50	Detroit, Mich.
WKBI	1400	St. Marys, Pa.
WKBI-FM	94.3	Ridgeway, Pa.
WKBJ	1600	Milan, Tenn.
WKBK	1220	Keene, N.H.
WKBL	1250	Covington, Tenn.
WKBL-FM	93.5	Covington, Tenn.
WKBM-TV	11	Caguas, P.R.
WKBN-FM	98.9	Youngstown, O.
WKBN-TV	27	Youngstown, O.
WKBO	1230	Harrisburg, Pa.
WKBQ	1000	Garner, N.C.
WKBR	1250	Manchester, N.H.
WKBT	8	La Crosse, Wis.
WKBV	1490	Richmond, Ind.
WKBW	1520	Buffalo, N.Y.
WKBW-TV	7	Buffalo, N.Y.
WKBX	630	Savannah, Ga.
WKBY	1080	Chatham, Va.
WKBZ	850	Muskegon, Mich.
WKCA	107.1	Owingsville, Ky.
WKCB	1340	Hindman, Ky.
WKCB-FM	107.1	Hindman, Ky.
WKCC	96.7	Grayson, Ky.
WKCD	93.5	Mechanicsburg, Pa.
WKCE	1230	Harriman, Tenn.
WKCG	101.3	Augusta, Me.
WKCH	43	Knoxville, Tenn.
WKCI	101.3	Hamden, Conn.
WKCJ	105.5	Lewisburg, W.V.
WKCK	1470	Orocovis, P.R.
WKCL	91.5	Ladson, S.C.
WKCM	1140	Hawesville, Ky.
WKCM	1160	Hawesville, Ky.
WKCN	910	North Charleston, S.C.
WKCO	91.9	Gambier, O.
WKCQ	98.1	Saginaw, Mich.
WKCR-FM	89.9	New York, N.Y.
WKCS	106.9	Hagerstown, Md.
WKCS	91.1	Knoxville, Tenn.
WKCT	930	Bowling Green, Ky.
WKCU	1350	Corinth, Miss.
WKCU-FM	94.3	Corinth, Miss.
WKCW	1420	Warrenton, Va.
WKCX	97.7	Rome, Ga.
WKCY	1300	Harrisonburg, Va.
WKDA	1240	Nashville, Tenn.
WKDC	1530	Elmhurst, Ill.
WKDD	96.5	Akron, O.
WKDE	1000	Altavista, Va.
WKDE-FM	105.5	Altavista, Va.
WKDF	103.3	Nashville, Tenn.
WKDJ	100.1	Winchester, Ky.
WKDJ	680	Memphis, Tenn.
WKDK	1240	Newberry, S.C.
WKDN-FM	106.9	Camden, N.J.
WKDO	1560	Liberty, Ky.
WKDO-FM	105.5	Liberty, Ky.
WKDQ	99.5	Henderson, Ky.
WKDR	1070	Plattsburgh, N.Y.
WKDS	89.9	Kalamazoo, Mich.
WKDT	89.3	West Point, N.Y.
WKDU	91.7	Philadelphia, Pa.
WKDW	900	Staunton, Va.
WKDX	1250	Hamlet, N.C.
WKDY	1400	Spartanburg, S.C.
WKDZ	1110	Cadiz, Ky.
WKDZ-FM	106.3	Cadiz, Ky.
WKEA	1330	Scottsboro, Ala.
WKEA-FM	98.3	Scottsboro, Ala.

Call	Freq.	Location
WKED	1130	Frankfort, Ky.
WKEE	800	Huntington, W.V.
WKEE-FM	100.5	Huntington, W.V.
WKEF	22	Dayton, O.
WKEG	1110	Washington, Pa.
WKEI	1450	Kewanee, Ill.
WKEM	1490	Immokalee, Fla.
WKEN	1600	Dover, Del.
WKEQ	910	Burnside, Ky.
WKER	1500	Pompton Lakes, N.J.
WKES	101.5	St. Petersburg, Fla.
WKET	89.5	Kettering, O.
WKEU	1450	Griffin, Ga.
WKEU-FM	97.7	Griffin, Ga.
WKEW	1400	Greensboro, N.C.
WKEX	1430	Blacksburg, Va.
WKEY	1340	Covington, Va.
WKEZ	94.1	Yorktown, Va.
WKFE	1550	Yauco, P.R.
WKFI	1090	Wilmington, O.
WKFM	104.7	Fulton, N.Y.
WKFR-FM	103.3	Battle Creek, Mich.
WKFT	40	Fayetteville, N.C.
WKGA	1260	Grafton, W.V.
WKGB	53	Bowling Green, Ky.
WKGC	1480	Panama City Beach, Fla.
WKGC-FM	90.7	Panama City, Fla.
WKGE	1350	Darlington, S.C.
WKGI	103.9	New Martinsville, W.V.
WKGK	1600	Saltville, Va.
WKGL	92.7	Middletown, N.Y.
WKGM	940	Smithfield, Va.
WKGN	1340	Knoxville, Tenn.
WKGO	106.1	Cumberland, Md.
WKGQ	1060	Milledgeville, Ga.
WKGR	1390	Gainesville, Fla.
WKGW	104.3	Utica, N.Y.
WKGX	1080	Lenoir, N.C.
WKHA	35	Hazard, Ky.
WKHG	104.9	Leitchfield, Ky.
WKHI	99.9	Ocean City, Md.
WKHJ	1440	Holly Hill, S.C.
WKHK	106.7	New York, N.Y.
WKHM	970	Jackson, Mich.
WKHQ	105.9	Charlevoix, Mich.
WKHR	88.3	Bainbridge, O.
WKHS	90.5	Worton, Md.
WKHX	101.5	Marietta, Ga.
WKIC	1390	Hazard, Ky.
WKID	51	Ft. Lauderdale, Fla.
WKIE	1540	Richmond, Va.
WKIG	1580	Glennville, Ga.
WKIG-FM	106.3	Glennville, Ga.
WKIJ	1130	Parrish, Ala.
WKIK	1370	Leonardtown, Md.
WKIN	1320	Kingsport, Tenn.
WKIO	103.9	Urbana, Ill.
WKIP	1450	Poughkeepsie, N.Y.
WKIR	104.1	Jackson, Tenn.
WKIS	740	Orlando, Fla.
WKIT	102.5	Hendersonville, N.C.
WKIX	850	Raleigh, N.C.
WKIZ	1500	Key West, Fla.
WKJA	92.1	Belhaven, N.C.
WKJB	710	Mayaguez, P.R.
WKJB-FM	99.1	Mayaguez, P.R.
WKJC	103.9	Tawas City, Mich.
WKJF	1370	Cadillac, Mich.
WKJF-FM	92.9	Cadillac, Mich.
WKJG-TV	33	Ft. Wayne, Ind.
WKJJ-FM	99.7	Louisville, Ky.
WKJK	900	Granite Falls, N.C.
WKJL	24	Baltimore, Md.
WKJQ	99.3	Jefferson City, Tenn.
WKJR	1520	Muskegon Heights, Mich.
WKJS	1600	Harriman, Tenn.
WKJY	98.3	Hempstead, N.Y.
WKKA	90.9	Cornwall, Conn.
WKKB	92.1	Manitowoc, Wis.
WKKC	89.3	Chicago, Ill.
WKKD	1580	Aurora, Ill.
WKKD-FM	95.9	Aurora, Ill.
WKKE	1180	Pearl, Miss.
WKKI	94.3	Celina, O.
WKKJ	93.3	Chillicothe, O.
WKKL	90.7	West Barnstable, Mass.
WKKM	92.1	Harrison, Mich.
WKKN	1150	Rockford, Ill.
WKKO	860	Cocoa, Fla.
WKKQ	1060	Hibbing, Minn.
WKKQ	1080	Hibbing, Minn.
WKKS	1570	Vanceburg, Ky.
WKKS-FM	104.9	Vanceburg, Ky.
WKKW	106.5	Clarksburg, W.V.
WKKX	1560	Paoli, Ind.
WKKY	104.9	Moss Point, Miss.
WKKZ	92.7	Dublin, Ga.
WKLA	1450	Ludington, Mich.
WKLA-FM	106.3	Ludington, Mich.
WKLB	1290	Manchester, Ky.
WKLC-FM	105.1	St. Albans, W.V.
WKLD	97.7	Oneonta, Ala.
WKLE	46	Lexington, Ky.
WKLF	980	Clanton, Ala.
WKLH	92.1	St. Johns, Mich.
WKLK	1230	Cloquet, Minn.
WKLK-FM	100.9	Cloquet, Minn.
WKLM	980	Wilmington, N.C.
WKLN	92.1	Cullman, Ala.
WKLO	1000	Danville, Ky.
WKLP	1390	Keyser, W.V.
WKLR	99.9	Toledo, O.
WKLS	970	Atlanta, Ga.
WKLS-FM	96.1	Atlanta, Ga.
WKLT	97.7	Kalkaska, Mich.
WKLV	1440	Blackstone, Va.
WKLX	95.9	Plymouth, N.C.
WKLY	980	Hartwell, Ga.
WKLZ	1470	Kalamazoo, Mich.
WKMA	35	Madisonville, Ky.
WKMB	1070	Stirling, N.J.
WKMC	1370	Roaring Spring, Pa.
WKMD	94.3	Loogootee, Ind.
WKMF	1470	Flint, Mich.
WKMG	1520	Newberry, S.C.
WKMI	1360	Kalamazoo, Mich.
WKMJ	68	Louisville, Ky.
WKMK	1000	Blountstown, Fla.
WKMO	106.3	Hodgenville, Ky.
WKMR	38	Morehead, Ky.
WKMS-FM	91.3	Murray, Ky.
WKMT	1220	Kings Mountain, N.C.
WKMU	21	Murray, Ky.
WKMX	106.7	Enterprise, Ala.
WKMY	100.9	Princeton, W.V.
WKMZ	97.5	Martinsburg, W.V.
WKNC-FM	88.1	Raleigh, N.C.
WKND	1480	Windsor, Conn.
WKNE	1290	Keene, N.H.
WKNG	1060	Tallapoosa, Ga.
WKNH	89.1	Keene, N.H.
WKNJ	90.3	Union, N.J.
WKNO-FM	91.1	Memphis, Tenn.
WKNO-TV	10	Memphis, Tenn.
WKNR	1400	Battle Creek, Mich.
WKNS	90.5	Kinston, N.C.
WKNT	1520	Kent, O.
WKNU	106.3	Brewton, Ala.
WKNX	1210	Saginaw, Mich.
WKNY	1490	Kingston, N.Y.
WKNZ	101.7	Collins, Miss.
WKOA	1480	Hopkinsville, Ky.
WKOA-FM	100.3	Hopkinsville, Ky.
WKOC	88.3	Kankakee, Ill.
WKOE	1520	Dayton, Tenn.
WKOH	31	Owensboro, Ky.
WKOI	43	Richmond, Ind.
WKOJ	1310	Hattiesburg, Miss.
WKOK	1070	Sunbury, Pa.
WKOL	1570	Amsterdam, N.Y.
WKOM	101.7	Columbia, Tenn.
WKON	52	Owenton, Ky.
WKOP	1360	Binghamton, N.Y.
WKOR	980	Starkville, Miss.
WKOR-FM	92.1	Starkville, Miss.
WKOS	96.3	Murfreesboro, Tenn.
WKOV	1330	Wellston, O.
WKOV-FM	96.7	Wellston, O.
WKOW-TV	27	Madison, Wis.
WKOX	1190	Framingham, Mass.
WKOY	1240	Bluefield, W.V.
WKOZ	1340	Kosciusko, Miss.
WKOZ-FM	105.1	Kosciusko, Miss.
WKPA	1150	New Kensington, Pa.
WKPC-TV	15	Louisville, Ky.
WKPD	29	Paducah, Ky.
WKPE	104.7	Orleans, Mass.
WKPG	1320	Port Gibson, Miss.
WKPI	22	Pikeville, Ky.
WKPL	107.1	Platteville, Wis.
WKPO	1510	Prentiss, Miss.
WKPQ	105.3	Hornell, N.Y.
WKPR	1420	Kalamazoo, Mich.
WKPT	1400	Kingsport, Tenn.
WKPT-TV	19	Kingsport, Tenn.
WKPX	88.5	Sunrise, Fla.
WKQA	104.9	Pekin, Ill.
WKQB	107.5	St. George, S.C.
WKQE	1410	Tallahassee, Fla.
WKQK	92.7	Eufaula, Ala.
WKQQ	98.1	Lexington, Ky.
WKQS	99.9	Boca Raton, Fla.
WKQT	1010	Garyville, La.
WKQV	92.1	Vineland, N.J.
WKQW	1120	Oil City, Pa.
WKQX	101.1	Chicago, Ill.
WKRA	1110	Holly Springs, Miss.
WKRA-FM	92.7	Holly Springs, Miss.
WKRB	103.1	Brooklyn, N.Y.
WKRC	550	Cincinnati, O.
WKRC-TV	12	Cincinnati, O.
WKRE	1520	Exmore, Va.
WKRE-FM	107.5	Exmore, Va.
WKRG	710	Mobile, Ala.
WKRG-FM	99.9	Mobile, Ala.
WKRG-TV	5	Mobile, Ala.
WKRI	1450	West Warwick, R.I.
WKRK	1320	Murphy, N.C.
WKRM	1340	Columbia, Tenn.
WKRN-TV	2	Nashville, Tenn.
WKRO	1490	Cairo, Ill.
WKRP	1500	Dallas, Ga.
WKRQ	101.9	Cincinnati, O.
WKRS	1220	Waukegan, Ill.
WKRT	920	Cortland, N.Y.
WKRV	107.1	Vandalia, Ill.
WKRX	96.7	Roxboro, N.C.
WKRZ	1340	Wilkes Barre, Pa.
WKRZ-FM	98.5	Wilkes Barre, Pa.
WKSA-FM	101.5	Isabela, P.R.
WKSB	102.7	Williamsport, Pa.
WKSC	1300	Kershaw, S.C.
WKSI	102.3	Eldorado, Ill.
WKSJ	1270	Prichard, Ala.
WKSJ-FM	94.9	Mobile, Ala.
WKSK	580	West Jefferson, N.C.
WKSL	94.3	Greencastle, Pa.
WKSM	104.9	Tabor City, N.C.
WKSN	1340	Jamestown, N.Y.
WKSO	29	Somerset, Ky.
WKSP	1090	Kingstree, S.C.
WKSQ	94.5	Ellsworth, Me.
WKSQ	94.3	Ellsworth, Me.
WKSR	1420	Pulaski, Tenn.
WKSS	95.7	Meriden, Conn.
WKST	1280	New Castle, Pa.
WKSU-FM	89.7	Kent, O.
WKSW	99.5	Cleveland, O.

WKSY	106.3	Columbia City, Ind.
WKSZ	100.3	Media, Pa.
WKTA	106.9	Mc Kenzie, Tenn.
WKTC	104.3	Tarboro, N.C.
WKTE	1090	King, N.C.
WKTG	93.9	Madisonville, Ky.
WKTI	94.5	Milwaukee, Wis.
WKTJ	1380	Farmington, Me.
WKTJ-FM	99.3	Farmington, Me.
WKTK	105.7	Catonsville, Md.
WKTL	90.7	Struthers, O.
WKTM	102.5	Charleston, S.C.
WKTN	95.3	Kenton, O.
WKTR	97.7	Millinocket, Me.
WKTS	950	Sheboygan, Wis.
WKTU	92.3	New York, N.Y.
WKTV	2	Utica, N.Y.
WKTY	580	La Crosse, Wis.
WKTZ	1220	Jacksonville, Fla.
WKTZ-FM	96.1	Jacksonville, Fla.
WKUB	104.9	Blackshear, Ga.
WKUL	1340	Cullman, Ala.
WKUN	1580	Monroe, Ga.
WKUZ	95.9	Wabash, Ind.
WKVA	920	Lewistown, Pa.
WKVE	800	Cave City, Ky.
WKVI	1520	Knox, Ind.
WKVI-FM	99.3	Knox, Ind.
WKVL	1550	Clarksville, Tenn.
WKVM	810	San Juan, P.R.
WKVR-FM	103.5	Huntingdon, Pa.
WKVT	1490	Brattleboro, Vt.
WKVT-FM	92.7	Brattleboro, Vt.
WKWC	90.3	Owensboro, Ky.
WKWF	1600	Key West, Fla.
WKWI	101.7	Kilmarnock, Va.
WKWK	1400	Wheeling, W.V.
WKWK-FM	97.3	Wheeling, W.V.
WKWL	1230	Florala, Ala.
WKWM	1140	Kentwood, Mich.
WKWQ-FM	92.1	Batesburg, S.C.
WKWR	28	Cookeville, Tenn.
WKWX	93.5	Savannah, Tenn.
WKWZ	88.5	Syosset, N.Y.
WKXA	900	Brunswick, Me.
WKXC	1470	New Albany, Miss.
WKXI	1300	Jackson, Miss.
WKXJ	1450	Campbellsville, Ky.
WKXK	100.9	Pana, Ill.
WKXL	1450	Concord, N.H.
WKXL-FM	102.3	Concord, N.H.
WKXN	95.9	Greenville, Ala.
WKXO	1500	Berea, Ky.
WKXV	900	Knoxville, Tenn.
WKXW	101.5	Trenton, N.J.
WKXX	106.9	Birmingham, Ala.
WKXY	1360	Milan, Tenn.
WKXY	930	Sarasota, Fla.
WKY	930	Oklahoma City, Okla.
WKYA	101.9	Central City, Ky.
WKYB	1000	Hemingway, S.C.
WKYC-TV	3	Cleveland, O.
WKYD	920	Andalusia, Ala.
WKYD-FM	98.1	Andalusia, Ala.
WKYE	95.5	Johnstown, Pa.
WKYG	1230	Parkersburg, W.V.
WKYH-TV	57	Hazard, Ky.
WKYK	940	Burnsville, N.C.
WKYM	101.7	Monticello, Ky.
WKYO	1360	Caro, Mich.
WKYO-FM	104.9	Caro, Mich.
WKYQ	93.3	Paducah, Ky.
WKYR	1570	Burkesville, Ky.
WKYS	93.9	Washington, D. C.
WKYT-TV	27	Lexington, Ky.
WKYU-FM	88.9	Bowling Green, Ky.
WKYV-FM	106.7	Vicksburg, Miss.
WKYW	104.9	Frankfort, Ky.
WKYX	570	Paducah, Ky.
WKYZ	105.5	Salisbury, Md.
WKZA	960	Kane, Pa.
WKZB	95.3	Drew, Miss.
WKZC	95.9	Scottville, Mich.
WKZI	800	Casey, Ill.
WKZK	1600	North Augusta, S.C.
WKZL	107.5	Winston Salem, N.C.
WKZM	105.5	Sarasota, Fla.
WKZO	590	Kalamazoo, Mich.
WKZO-TV	3	Kalamazoo, Mich.
WKZQ	101.7	Myrtle Beach, S.C.
WKZR	102.3	Milledgeville, Ga.
WKZS	99.9	Auburn, Me.
WKZT	23	Elizabethtown, Ky.
WKZU	1350	Laconia, N.H.
WKZW	93.3	Peoria, Ill.
WKZX	950	Presque Isle, Me.
WKZZ	100.1	Lynchburg, Va.
WLAC	1510	Nashville, Tenn.
WLAC-FM	105.9	Nashville, Tenn.
WLAD	800	Danbury, Conn.
WLAE-TV	32	New Orleans, La.
WLAF	1450	La Follette, Tenn.
WLAG	1240	La Grange, Ga.
WLAJ	53	Lansing, Mich.
WLAK	93.9	Chicago, Ill.
WLAM	1470	Lewiston, Me.
WLAN	1390	Lancaster, Pa.
WLAN-FM	96.9	Lancaster, Pa.
WLAP	630	Lexington, Ky.
WLAP-FM	94.5	Lexington, Ky.
WLAQ	1410	Rome, Ga.
WLAR	1450	Athens, Tenn.
WLAS	910	Jacksonville, N.C.
WLAT	1330	Conway, S.C.
WLAT-FM	104.1	Conway, S.C.
WLAU	1430	Laurel, Miss.
WLAV-FM	96.9	Grand Rapids, Mich.
WLAW	1360	Lawrenceville, Ga.
WLAX	97.7	Streator, Ill.
WLAY	1450	Muscle Shoals, Ala.
WLAY-FM	105.5	Muscle Shoals, Ala.
WLBA	1130	Gainesville, Ga.
WLBC	1340	Muncie, Ind.
WLBC-FM	104.1	Muncie, Ind.
WLBE	790	Leesburg, Fla.
WLBF	89.1	Montgomery, Ala.
WLBG	860	Laurens, S.C.
WLBH	1170	Mattoon, Ill.
WLBH-FM	96.9	Mattoon, Ill.
WLBI	1220	Denham Springs, La.
WLBJ	1410	Bowling Green, Ky.
WLBJ-FM	96.7	Bowling Green, Ky.
WLBK	1360	De Kalb, Ill.
WLBL	930	Auburndale, Wis.
WLBM	30	Meridian, Miss.
WLBN	1590	Lebanon, Ky.
WLBQ	1570	Morgantown, Ky.
WLBR	1270	Lebanon, Pa.
WLBS	102.7	Mt. Clemens, Mich.
WLBT-TV	3	Jackson, Miss.
WLBZ-TV	2	Bangor, Me.
WLCA	89.9	Godfrey, Ill.
WLCB	1430	Buffalo, Ky.
WLCC	106.3	Luray, Va.
WLCH	88.7	Lebanon, Tenn.
WLCK	1250	Scottsville, Ky.
WLCK-FM	99.3	Scottsville, Ky.
WLCL-FM	107.1	Lowell, Ind.
WLCM	1360	Lancaster, S.C.
WLCN	19	Madisonville, Ky.
WLCO	1240	Eustis, Fla.
WLCS	910	Baton Rouge, La.
WLCT	26	New London, Conn.
WLDM	1570	Westfield, Mass.
WLDR	101.9	Traverse City, Mich.
WLDS	1180	Jacksonville, Ill.
WLDY	1340	Ladysmith, Wis.
WLDY-FM	92.7	Ladysmith, Wis.
WLEA	1480	Hornell, N.Y.
WLEC	1450	Sandusky, O.
WLED-TV	49	Littleton, N.H.
WLEE	1480	Richmond, Va.
WLEF-TV	36	Park Falls, Wis.
WLEJ	1560	Ellijay, Ga.
WLEM	1250	Emporium, Pa.
WLEN	103.9	Adrian, Mich.
WLEO	1170	Ponce, P.R.
WLEQ	95.9	Bonita Springs, Fla.
WLER-FM	97.7	Butler, Pa.
WLES	580	Lawrenceville, Va.
WLET	1420	Toccoa, Ga.
WLET-FM	106.1	Toccoa, Ga.
WLEV	96.1	Easton, Pa.
WLEW	1340	Bad Axe, Mich.
WLEW-FM	92.1	Bad Axe, Mich.
WLEX-TV	18	Lexington, Ky.
WLEY	1080	Cayey, P.R.
WLEZ	92.7	Elmira, N.Y.
WLFA	1590	Lafayette, Ga.
WLFC	88.3	Findlay, O.
WLFE	102.3	St. Albans, Vt.
WLFF	620	Cayce, S.C.
WLFH	1230	Little Falls, N.Y.
WLFI-TV	18	Lafayette, Ind.
WLFJ	89.3	Greenville, S.C.
WLFL-TV	22	Raleigh, N.C.
WLFM	91.1	Appleton, Wis.
WLFQ	103.9	Crawfordsville, Ind.
WLGA	95.9	Valdosta, Ga.
WLGC	105.5	Greenup, Ky.
WLGI	90.9	Hemingway, S.C.
WLGM	1320	Lynchburg, Va.
WLGN	1510	Logan, O.
WLGN-FM	98.3	Logan, O.
WLHI	88.3	Ft. Wayne, Ind.
WLHN	97.9	Anderson, Ind.
WLHQ	96.9	Enterprise, Ala.
WLHS	89.9	West Chester, O.
WLHT	22	Hattiesburg, Miss.
WLIB	1190	New York, N.Y.
WLIC	1540	Adamsville, Tenn.
WLID	98.9	Vieques, P.R.
WLIF	101.9	Baltimore, Md.
WLIG	55	Riverhead, N.Y.
WLIJ	1580	Shelbyville, Tenn.
WLIK	1270	Newport, Tenn.
WLIL	730	Lenoir City, Tenn.
WLIL-FM	93.5	Lenoir City, Tenn.
WLIM	1580	Patchogue, N.Y.
WLIN	95.5	Jackson, Miss.
WLIO	35	Lima, O.
WLIP	1050	Kenosha, Wis.
WLIR	92.7	Garden City, N.Y.
WLIS	1420	Old Saybrook, Conn.
WLIT	950	Steubenville, O.
WLIU	88.7	Oxford, Pa.
WLIV	920	Livingston, Tenn.
WLIW	21	Garden City, N.Y.
WLIX	540	Islip, N.Y.
WLIZ	1380	Lake Worth, Fla.
WLJC	102.3	Beattyville, Ky.
WLJC	65	Beattyville, Ky.
WLJE	105.5	Valparaiso, Ind.
WLJN	1400	Elmwood Twp, Mich.
WLJS-FM	91.9	Jacksonville, Ala.
WLJT-TV	11	Lexington, Tenn.
WLJY	106.5	Marshfield, Wis.
WLKC	93.5	St. Mary's, Ga.
WLKF	1430	Lakeland, Fla.
WLKI	100.1	Angola, Ind.
WLKK	1260	Erie, Pa.
WLKL	89.9	Mattoon, Ill.
WLKM	1510	Three Rivers, Mich.
WLKM-FM	95.9	Three Rivers, Mich.
WLKN	1450	Lincoln, Me.

WLKN-FM	99.3	Lincoln, Me.
WLKR	1510	Norwalk, O.
WLKR-FM	95.3	Norwalk, O.
WLKS	1450	West Liberty, Ky.
WLKW	990	Providence, R.I.
WLKW-FM	101.5	Providence, R.I.
WLKX-FM	95.9	Forest Lake, Minn.
WLKY	32	Louisville, Ky.
WLKZ	104.9	Wolfeboro, N.H.
WLLA	64	Kalamazoo, Mich.
WLLE	570	Raleigh, N.C.
WLLH	1400	Lowell, Mass.
WLLI-FM	96.7	Joliet, Ill.
WLLL	930	Lynchburg, Va.
WLLN	1370	Lillington, N.C.
WLLR	101.3	East Moline, Ill.
WLLS	1600	Hartford, Ky.
WLLS-FM	106.3	Hartford, Ky.
WLLT	94.9	Fairfield, O.
WLLV	107.1	Melbourne, Fla.
WLLX	92.1	Minor Hill, Tenn.
WLLY	1350	Wilson, N.C.
WLLZ	98.7	Detroit, Mich.
WLMC	103.1	Okeechobee, Fla.
WLMD	900	Laurel, Md.
WLMH	89.1	Morrow, O.
WLMJ	1280	Jackson, O.
WLMS	1000	Leominster, Mass.
WLNA	1420	Peekskill, N.Y.
WLNC	1300	Laurinburg, N.C.
WLNE	6	New Bedford, Mass.
WLNG	1600	Sag Harbor, N.Y.
WLNG-FM	92.1	Sag Harbor, N.Y.
WLNH-FM	98.3	Laconia, N.H.
WLNR	106.3	Lansing, Ill.
WLNT	1140	London, Tenn.
WLNV	90.1	Derby, Conn.
WLNX	88.9	Lincoln, Ill.
WLOB	1310	Portland, Me.
WLOC	1150	Munfordville, Ky.
WLOC-FM	102.3	Munfordville, Ky.
WLOE	1490	Eden, N.C.
WLOG	1230	Logan, W.V.
WLOH	1320	Lancaster, O.
WLOI	1540	La Porte, Ind.
WLOJ	97.7	Rensselaer, Ind.
WLOK	1340	Memphis, Tenn.
WLOL	99.5	Minneapolis, Minn.
WLON	1050	Lincolnton, N.C.
WLOO	100.3	Chicago, Ill.
WLOP	1370	Jessup, Ga.
WLOQ	103.1	Winter Park, Fla.
WLOR	730	Thomasville, Ga.
WLOS	99.9	Asheville, N.C.
WLOS-TV	13	Asheville, N.C.
WLOT	97.7	Trenton, Tenn.
WLOU	1350	Louisville, Ky.
WLOV	1370	Washington, Ga.
WLOV-FM	100.1	Washington, Ga.
WLOX	1490	Biloxi, Miss.
WLOX-TV	13	Biloxi, Miss.
WLPA	1490	Lancaster, Pa.
WLPB	27	Baton Rouge, La.
WLPD	910	Mishawaka, Ind.
WLPH	1480	Irondale, Ala.
WLPJ	91.5	New Port Richey, Fla.
WLPM	1450	Suffolk, Va.
WLPO	1220	La Salle, Ill.
WLPQ	980	Pittsburg, Ky.
WLPR	96.1	Mobile, Ala.
WLPW	105.5	Lake Placid, N.Y.
WLPX	97.3	Milwaukee, Wis.
WLQF	99.3	Pleasantville, N.J.
WLQH	940	Chiefland, Fla.
WLQR	101.5	Toledo, O.
WLQV	1500	Detroit, Mich.
WLQY	1320	Hollywood, Fla.
WLRA	88.1	Lockport, Ill.
WLRC	850	Walnut, Miss.
WLRE	26	Green Bay, Wis.
WLRH	89.3	Huntsville, Ala.
WLRN-FM	91.3	Miami, Fla.
WLRN-TV	17	Miami, Fla.
WLRO	1380	Lorain, O.
WLRS	102.3	Louisville, Ky.
WLRV	1380	Lebanon, Va.
WLRW	94.5	Champaign, Ill.
WLRX	100.1	Lincoln, Ill.
WLS	890	Chicago, Ill.
WLS-FM	94.7	Chicago, Ill.
WLS-TV	7	Chicago, Ill.
WLSA	105.5	Louisa, Va.
WLSB	1400	Copper Hill, Tenn.
WLSC	1570	Loris, S.C.
WLSD	1220	Big Stone Gap, Va.
WLSD-FM	93.5	Big Stone Gap, Va.
WLSE	1400	Wallace, N.C.
WLSH	1410	Lansford, Pa.
WLSI	900	Pikeville, Ky.
WLSK	100.9	Lebanon, Ky.
WLSM	1270	Louisville, Miss.
WLSM-FM	107.1	Louisville, Miss.
WLSN	106.5	Greenville, O.
WLSO	92.7	Spencer, Ind.
WLSQ	950	Montgomery, Ala.
WLSR	104.9	Lima, O.
WLST	95.1	Marinette, Wis.
WLSU	88.9	La Crosse, Wis.
WLSV	790	Wellsville, N.Y.
WLSW	103.9	Scottdale, Pa.
WLTC	1370	Gastonia, N.C.
WLTD	106.3	Lexington, Miss.
WLTE	102.9	Minneapolis, Minn.
WLTH	1370	Gary, Ind.
WLTL	88.1	La Grange, Ill.
WLTM	1480	Franklin, N.C.
WLTN	1400	Littleton, N.H.
WLTR	91.3	Columbia, S.C.
WLTT	94.7	Bethesda, Md.
WLTV	23	Miami, Fla.
WLTX	19	Columbia, S.C.
WLTY	95.7	Norfolk, Va.
WLTZ	38	Columbus, Ga.
WLUC-TV	6	Marquette, Mich.
WLUK-TV	11	Green Bay, Wis.
WLUM	102.1	Milwaukee, Wis.
WLUN	95.3	Lumberton, Miss.
WLUP	97.9	Chicago, Ill.
WLUR	91.5	Lexington, Va.
WLUV	1520	Loves Park, Ill.
WLUV-FM	96.7	Loves Park, Ill.
WLUW	88.7	Chicago, Ill.
WLUX	1550	Baton Rouge, La.
WLUY	1300	Nashville, Tenn.
WLUZ	1600	Bayamon, P.R.
WLUZ	7	Ponce, P.R.
WLVA	590	Lynchburg, Va.
WLVC	1340	Ft. Kent, Me.
WLVE	94.9	Baraboo, Wis.
WLVH	93.7	Hartford, Conn.
WLVI-TV	56	Cambridge, Mass.
WLVL	1340	Lockport, N.Y.
WLVN	1080	Luverne, Ala.
WLVO	99.3	Mt. Zion, Ill.
WLVQ	96.3	Columbus, O.
WLVR	91.3	Bethlehem, Pa.
WLVS	94.3	Germantown, Tenn.
WLVT-TV	39	Allentown, Pa.
WLVU	99.9	Erie, Pa.
WLVV	96.9	Statesville, N.C.
WLVW	105.5	Moncks Corner, S.C.
WLVY	94.3	Elmira, N.Y.
WLW	700	Cincinnati, O.
WLWI	92.3	Montgomery, Ala.
WLWL	1500	Rockingham, N.C.
WLWT	5	Cincinnati, O.
WLXI-TV	61	Greensboro, N.C.
WLXI-TV	61	Greeville, N.C.
WLXN	94.1	Lexington, N.C.
WLXR	1490	La Crosse, Wis.
WLXR-FM	104.9	La Crosse, Wis.
WLXX	99.5	Sault Ste. Marie, Mich.
WLYC	1050	Williamsport, Pa.
WLYF	101.5	Miami, Fla.
WLYH-TV	15	Lancaster, Pa.
WLYJ	46	Clarksburg, W.V.
WLYK	107.1	Milford, O.
WLYN	1360	Lynn, Mass.
WLYQ	95.9	Norwalk, Conn.
WLYT	92.5	Haverhill, Mass.
WLYX	89.5	Memphis, Tenn.
WLZZ	1290	Greenfield, Wis.
WMAA	29	Jackson, Miss.
WMAA-FM	91.3	Jackson, Miss.
WMAB	2	Ackerman, Miss.
WMAB-FM	96.7	Mississippi State, Miss.
WMAC	1360	Metter, Ga.
WMAD	92.1	Sun Prairie, Wis.
WMAE	12	Booneville, Miss.
WMAE-FM	89.5	Booneville, Miss.
WMAF	1230	Madison, Fla.
WMAG	99.5	High Point, N.C.
WMAH	19	Biloxi, Miss.
WMAH-FM	90.3	Biloxi, Miss.
WMAJ	1450	State College, Pa.
WMAK-FM	92.1	Hendersonville, Tenn.
WMAL	630	Washington, D. C.
WMAM	570	Marinette, Wis.
WMAN	1400	Mansfield, O.
WMAO	23	Greenwood, Miss.
WMAO-FM	90.9	Greenwood, Miss.
WMAP	1060	Monroe, N.C.
WMAQ	670	Chicago, Ill.
WMAQ-TV	5	Chicago, Ill.
WMAR-FM	106.5	Baltimore, Md.
WMAR-TV	2	Baltimore, Md.
WMAS	1450	Springfield, Mass.
WMAS-FM	94.7	Springfield, Mass.
WMAU	17	Brookhaven, Miss.
WMAU-FM	88.9	Bude, Miss.
WMAV	18	Oxford, Miss.
WMAV-FM	90.3	Oxford, Miss.
WMAW	14	Meridian, Miss.
WMAW-FM	88.1	Meridian, Miss.
WMAX	1480	Kentwood, Mich.
WMAX	1480	Grand Rapids, Mich.
WMAY	970	Springfield, Ill.
WMAZ	940	Macon, Ga.
WMAZ-FM	99.1	Macon, Ga.
WMAZ-TV	13	Macon, Ga.
WMBA	1460	Ambridge, Pa.
WMBB	13	Panama City, Fla.
WMBC	1400	Columbus, Miss.
WMBD	1470	Peoria, Ill.
WMBD-TV	31	Peoria, Ill.
WMBE	1530	Chilton, Wis.
WMBG	740	Williamsburg, Va.
WMBH	1450	Joplin, Mo.
WMBI	1110	Chicago, Ill.
WMBI-FM	90.1	Chicago, Ill.
WMBJ-FM	95.9	Morehead City, N.C.
WMBL	740	Morehead City, N.C.
WMBM	1490	Miami Beach, Fla.
WMBN-FM	96.3	Petoskey, Mich.
WMBO	1340	Auburn, N.Y.
WMBR	88.1	Cambridge, Mass.
WMBS	590	Uniontown, Pa.
WMBT	1530	Shenandoah, Pa.
WMBW	88.9	Chattanooga, Tenn.
WMC	790	Memphis, Tenn.
WMC-FM	99.7	Memphis, Tenn.
WMC-TV	5	Memphis, Tenn.
WMCA	570	New York, N.Y.
WMCD	100.1	Statesboro, Ga.
WMCF-TV	45	Montgomery, Ala.
WMCG	104.9	Milan, Ga.

WMCH	1260	Church Hill, Tenn.
WMCI	90.5	Brockton, Mass.
WMCL	1060	Mc Leansboro, Ill.
WMCM	93.5	Rockland, Me.
WMCN	91.7	St. Paul, Minn.
WMCO	90.7	New Concord, O.
WMCP	1280	Columbia, Tenn.
WMCR	1600	Oneida, N.Y.
WMCR-FM	106.3	Oneida, N.Y.
WMCS	1400	Machias, Me.
WMCT	1390	Mountain City, Tenn.
WMCU	89.7	Miami, Fla.
WMCW	1600	Harvard, Ill.
WMCX	88.1	West Long Branch, N.J.
WMDB	880	Nashville, Tenn.
WMDC	1220	Hazlehurst, Miss.
WMDC-FM	100.9	Hazlehurst, Miss.
WMDD	1480	Fajardo, P.R.
WMDH	102.5	New Castle, Ind.
WMDJ	1440	Martin, Ky.
WMDK	92.1	Peterborough, N.H.
WMDM-FM	97.7	Lexington Park, Md.
WMDO	1540	Wheaton, Md.
WMDT	47	Salisbury, Md.
WMEA	90.1	Portland, Me.
WMEB-FM	91.9	Orono, Me.
WMEB-TV	12	Orono, Me.
WMED	89.7	Calais, Me.
WMED-TV	13	Calais, Me.
WMEE	97.3	Ft. Wayne, Ind.
WMEG-TV	26	Biddeford, Me.
WMEH	90.9	Bangor, Me.
WMEK	980	Chase City, Va.
WMEL	920	Melbourne, Fla.
WMEM	106.1	Presque Isle, Me.
WMEM-TV	10	Presque Isle, Me.
WMEQ	92.1	Menomonie, Wis.
WMER	1440	Westbrook, Me.
WMES	1570	Ashburn, Ga.
WMET	95.5	Chicago, Ill.
WMEV	1010	Marion, Va.
WMEV-FM	93.9	Marion, Va.
WMEW	91.3	Waterville, Me.
WMEX	100.9	Clyde, O.
WMEZ	94.1	Pensacola, Fla.
WMFC	1360	Monroeville, Ala.
WMFC-FM	99.3	Monroeville, Ala.
WMFD	630	Wilmington, N.C.
WMFE-FM	90.7	Orlando, Fla.
WMFE-TV	24	Orlando, Fla.
WMFG	106.3	Hibbing, Minn.
WMFJ	1450	Daytona Beach, Fla.
WMFL	1090	Monticello, Fla.
WMFM	100.9	Gainesville, Fla.
WMFO	91.5	Medford, Mass.
WMFQ	92.7	Ocala, Fla.
WMFR	1230	High Point, N.C.
WMGA	1130	Moultrie, Ga.
WMGC-TV	34	Binghamton, N.Y.
WMGE	107.1	Danville, Ky.
WMGF	96.5	Milwaukee, Wis.
WMGG	95.7	Clearwater, Fla.
WMGK	102.9	Philadelphia, Pa.
WMGL	98.3	Pulaski, Tenn.
WMGM	103.7	Atlantic City, N.J.
WMGN	98.1	Madison, Wis.
WMGO	1370	Canton, Miss.
WMGQ	98.3	New Brunswick, N.J.
WMGR	930	Bainbridge, Ga.
WMGT	41	Macon, Ga.
WMGW	1490	Meadville, Pa.
WMGX	93.1	Portland, Me.
WMGY	800	Montgomery, Ala.
WMGZ	1470	Farrell, Pa.
WMGZ-FM	95.9	Sharpsville, Pa.
WMHB	91.5	Waterville, Me.
WMHB	90.5	Waterville, Me.
WMHC	91.5	South Hadley, Mass.
WMHD-FM	90.5	Terre Haute, Ind.
WMHE	92.5	Toledo, O.
WMHK	89.7	Columbia, S.C.
WMHR-FM	102.9	Syracuse, N.Y.
WMHT	17	Schenectady, N.Y.
WMHT-FM	89.1	Schenectady, N.Y.
WMHW-FM	91.5	Mt. Pleasant, Mich.
WMIA	1070	Arecibo, P.R.
WMIB	1510	Marco Island, Fla.
WMIC	1560	Sandusky, Mich.
WMID	1340	Atlantic City, N.J.
WMIE-FM	91.5	Cocoa, Fla.
WMIK	560	Middlesboro, Ky.
WMIK-FM	92.7	Middlesboro, Ky.
WMIL	106.1	Waukesha, Wis.
WMIM	1590	Mt. Carmel, Pa.
WMIN	1010	Maplewood, Minn.
WMIQ	1450	Iron Mountain, Mich.
WMIR	1550	Lake Geneva, Wis.
WMIS	1240	Natchez, Miss.
WMIT	106.9	Black Mountain, N.C.
WMIX	940	Mt. Vernon, Ill.
WMIX-FM	94.1	Mt. Vernon, Ill.
WMJA	28	Panama City, Fla.
WMJC	94.7	Birmingham, Mich.
WMJD	97.7	Grundy, Va.
WMJI	105.7	Cleveland, O.
WMJJ	96.5	Birmingham, Ala.
WMJK	1220	Kissimmee, Fla.
WMJL	1500	Marion, Ky.
WMJM	1490	Cordele, Ga.
WMJQ	92.5	Rochester, N.Y.
WMJS	92.7	Prince Frederick, Md.
WMJT	1330	Mt. Juliet, Tenn.
WMJW	92.1	Nanticoke, Pa.
WMJX	106.7	Boston, Mass.
WMJY	107.1	Long Branch, N.J.
WMKC	102.9	St. Ignace, Mich.
WMKE	1340	Milwaukee, Wis.
WMKM	105.5	St. Augustine, Fla.
WMKR	1240	Millinocket, Me.
WMKT	54	Muskegon, Mich.
WMKW	30	Memphis, Tenn.
WMKX	95.9	Brookville, Pa.
WMKY-FM	90.3	Morehead, Ky.
WMLA	92.7	Le Roy, Ill.
WMLB	1550	Bloomfield, Conn.
WMLC	1270	Monticello, Miss.
WMLD	96.9	Manati, P.R.
WMLF	1310	Indianapolis, Ind.
WMLI	1250	Bangor, Me.
WMLM	1540	St. Louis, Mich.
WMLN-FM	91.5	Milton, Mass.
WMLO	106.3	Sarasota, Fla.
WMLP	1380	Milton, Pa.
WMLR	1230	Hohenwald, Tenn.
WMLS-FM	98.3	Sylacauga, Ala.
WMLT	1330	Dublin, Ga.
WMLW	94.1	Watertown, Wis.
WMLX	1230	Cincinnati, O.
WMMB	1240	Melbourne, Fla.
WMMG	93.5	Brandenburg, Ky.
WMMH	1460	Marshall, N.C.
WMMJ	96.7	Brattleboro, Vt.
WMMK	92.1	Destin, Fla.
WMMM	1260	Westport, Conn.
WMMN	920	Fairmont, W.V.
WMMQ	92.7	Charlotte, Mich.
WMMR	93.3	Philadelphia, Pa.
WMMS	100.7	Cleveland, O.
WMMT	88.7	Whitesburg, Ky.
WMMW	1470	Meriden, Conn.
WMNA	730	Gretna, Va.
WMNA-FM	106.3	Gretna, Va.
WMNB	1230	North Adams, Mass.
WMNB-FM	100.1	North Adams, Mass.
WMNC	1430	Morganton, N.C.
WMNE	1360	Menomonie, Wis.
WMNF	88.5	Tampa, Fla.
WMNI	920	Columbus, O.
WMNJ	88.9	Madison, N.J.
WMNR	88.1	Monroe, Conn.
WMNS	1360	Olean, N.Y.
WMNT	1500	Manati, P.R.
WMNX	95.9	Tallahassee, Fla.
WMNZ	1050	Montezuma, Ga.
WMOA	1490	Marietta, O.
WMOB	1360	Mobile, Ala.
WMOD	43	Melbourne, Fla.
WMOG	1490	Brunswick, Ga.
WMOH	1450	Hamilton, O.
WMOK	920	Metropolis, Ill.
WMON	1340	Montgomery, W.V.
WMOO	1550	Mobile, Ala.
WMOP	900	Ocala, Fla.
WMOR	1330	Morehead, Ky.
WMOR-FM	92.1	Morehead, Ky.
WMOS	95.3	Bath, Me.
WMOT	89.5	Murfreesboro, Tenn.
WMOU	1230	Berlin, N.H.
WMOV	1360	Ravenswood, W.V.
WMOX	1010	Meridian, Miss.
WMPA	1240	Aberdeen, Miss.
WMPB	67	Baltimore, Md.
WMPC	1230	Lapeer, Mich.
WMPG	90.9	Gorham, Me.
WMPG	91.1	Gorham, Me.
WMPH	91.7	Wilmington, Del.
WMPI	100.9	Scottsburg, Ind.
WMPL	920	Hancock, Mich.
WMPM	1270	Smithfield, N.C.
WMPO	1390	Pomeroy, O.
WMPO-FM	92.1	Middleport, O.
WMPP	1470	Chicago Heights, Ill.
WMPR	90.1	Jackson, Miss.
WMPV-TV	21	Mobile, Ala.
WMPX	1490	Midland, Mich.
WMPZ	1000	Soperton, Ga.
WMPZ-FM	101.7	Soperton, Ga.
WMQM	1480	Memphis, Tenn.
WMQT	107.1	Ishpeming, Mich.
WMRA	90.7	Harrisonburg, Va.
WMRB	1490	Greenville, S.C.
WMRC	1490	Milford, Mass.
WMRE	1510	Boston, Mass.
WMRF	1490	Lewistown, Pa.
WMRF-FM	95.9	Lewistown, Pa.
WMRI	106.9	Marion, Ind.
WMRK	1340	Selma, Ala.
WMRN	1490	Marion, O.
WMRN-FM	106.9	Marion, O.
WMRO	1280	Aurora, Ill.
WMRQ	92.1	Brookhaven, Miss.
WMRT	88.3	Marietta, O.
WMRV	105.7	Endicott, N.Y.
WMRX-FM	97.7	Beaverton, Mich.
WMRY	101.1	East St. Louis, Ill.
WMRZ	1230	Moline, Ill.
WMSA	1340	Massena, N.Y.
WMSB	89.1	Mississippi State, Miss.
WMSC	101.5	Upper Montclair, N.J.
WMSE	91.7	Milwaukee, Wis.
WMSG	1050	Oakland, Md.
WMSI	102.9	Jackson, Miss.
WMSK	1550	Morganfield, Ky.
WMSK-FM	95.3	Morganfield, Ky.
WMSL	1400	Decatur, Ala.
WMSN-TV	47	Madison, Wis.
WMSO	640	Collierville, Tenn.
WMSO	1590	Collierville, Tenn.
WMSP	94.9	Harrisburg, Pa.
WMSQ	104.9	Havelock, N.C.
WMSR	1320	Manchester, Tenn.

WMSR-FM	99.7	Manchester, Tenn.
WMSS	91.1	Middletown, Pa.
WMST	1150	Mt. Sterling, Ky.
WMST-FM	105.5	Mt. Sterling, Ky.
WMSU	88.5	Hattiesburg, Miss.
WMSW	1120	Hatillo, P.R.
WMSY	52	Marion, Va.
WMT	600	Cedar Rapids, Ia.
WMT-FM	96.5	Cedar Rapids, Ia.
WMTA	1380	Central City, Ky.
WMTB-FM	89.9	Emmitsburg, Md.
WMTC	730	Vancleve, Ky.
WMTD	1380	Hinton, W.V.
WMTD-FM	102.3	Hinton, W.V.
WMTE	1340	Manistee, Mich.
WMTF	91.5	Stowe, Vt.
WMTH	88.5	Park Ridge, Ill.
WMTJ	40	Fajardo, P.R.
WMTL	1580	Leitchfield, Ky.
WMTM	1300	Moultrie, Ga.
WMTM-FM	93.9	Moultrie, Ga.
WMTN	1300	Morristown, Tenn.
WMTR	1250	Morristown, N.J.
WMTS	810	Murfreesboro, Tenn.
WMTV	15	Madison, Wis.
WMTW-TV	8	Portland, Me.
WMTY	1090	Greenwood, S.C.
WMTZ	94.3	Martinez, Ga.
WMUA	91.1	Amherst, Mass.
WMUB	88.5	Oxford, O.
WMUC	88.1	College Park, Md.
WMUF	1000	Paris, Tenn.
WMUH	89.7	Allentown, Pa.
WMUK	102.1	Kalamazoo, Mich.
WMUL	88.1	Huntington, W.V.
WMUM	94.3	Marathon, Fla.
WMUR-TV	9	Manchester, N.H.
WMUS	1090	Muskegon, Mich.
WMUS-FM	106.9	Muskegon, Mich.
WMUU	1260	Greenville, S.C.
WMUU-FM	94.5	Greenville, S.C.
WMUW	89.5	Columbus, Miss.
WMUZ	103.5	Detroit, Mich.
WMVA	1450	Martinsville, Va.
WMVA-FM	96.3	Martinsville, Va.
WMVB	97.3	Millville, N.J.
WMVG	1450	Milledgeville, Ga.
WMVI	1170	Mechanicville, N.Y.
WMVN	970	Ishpeming, Mich.
WMVO	1300	Mt. Vernon, O.
WMVO-FM	93.7	Mt. Vernon, O.
WMVQ	97.7	Amsterdam, N.Y.
WMVR	1080	Sidney, O.
WMVR-FM	105.5	Sidney, O.
WMVS	10	Milwaukee, Wis.
WMVT	36	Milwaukee, Wis.
WMVV	90.7	Mcdonough, Ga.
WMVY	92.7	Tisbury, Mass.
WMWA	88.9	Glenview, Ill.
WMWC	91.7	Gardner, Mass.
WMWM	91.7	Salem, Mass.
WMWV	93.5	Conway, N.H.
WMXM	88.9	Lake Forest, Ill.
WMYD	1370	Wickford, R.I.
WMYF	1540	Exeter, N.H.
WMYK	93.7	Elizabeth City, N.C.
WMYL	930	Johnstown, N.Y.
WMYN	1420	Mayodan, N.C.
WMYQ	1410	Newton, Miss.
WMYQ-FM	106.3	Newton, Miss.
WMYR	1410	Ft. Myers, Fla.
WMYS	98.1	New Bedford, Mass.
WMYU	102.1	Sevierville, Tenn.
WMYX	99.1	Milwaukee, Wis.
WMZK	92.1	Traverse City, Mich.
WMZQ	98.7	Washington, D. C.
WNAA	90.5	Greensboro, N.C.
WNAB	1450	Bridgeport, Conn.

WNAE	1310	Warren, Pa.
WNAH	1360	Nashville, Tenn.
WNAK	730	Nanticoke, Pa.
WNAM	1280	Neenah, Wis.
WNAN	106.3	Demopolis, Ala.
WNAP	93.1	Indianapolis, Ind.
WNAR	1110	Norristown, Pa.
WNAS	88.1	New Albany, Ind.
WNAT	1450	Natchez, Miss.
WNAV	1430	Annapolis, Md.
WNAX	570	Yankton, S.D.
WNAZ-FM	89.1	Nashville, Tenn.
WNBB	99.3	Grifton, N.C.
WNBC	660	New York, N.Y.
WNBC-TV	4	New York, N.Y.
WNBF	1290	Binghamton, N.Y.
WNBG	1400	Waynesboro, Tenn.
WNBI	980	Park Falls, Wis.
WNBI-FM	98.3	Park Falls, Wis.
WNBK	93.5	New London, Wis.
WNBR	100.7	Wildwood, N.J.
WNBS	1340	Murray, Ky.
WNBT	1490	Wellsboro, Pa.
WNBT-FM	104.5	Wellsboro, Pa.
WNBX-FM	103.7	Keene, N.H.
WNBY	1450	Newberry, Mich.
WNBY-FM	93.5	Newberry, Mich.
WNBZ	1240	Saranac Lake, N.Y.
WNCA	1570	Siler City, N.C.
WNCC	950	Barnesboro, Pa.
WNCE	101.3	Lancaster, Pa.
WNCI	97.9	Columbus, O.
WNCM-FM	90.9	Traverse City, Mich.
WNCN	104.3	New York, N.Y.
WNCO	1340	Ashland, O.
WNCO-FM	101.3	Ashland, O.
WNCQ	97.5	Watertown, N.Y.
WNCR	1080	St. Pauls, N.C.
WNCS	96.7	Montpelier, Vt.
WNCT	1070	Greenville, N.C.
WNCT-FM	107.9	Greenville, N.C.
WNCT-TV	9	Greenville, N.C.
WNCW	96.7	Paris, Ky.
WNCY	91.1	Springvale, Me.
WNDA	95.1	Huntsville, Ala.
WNDB	1150	Daytona Beach, Fla.
WNDE	1260	Indianapolis, Ind.
WNDH	103.1	Napoleon, O.
WNDI	1550	Sullivan, Ind.
WNDI-FM	95.3	Sullivan, Ind.
WNDN-FM	102.5	Salisbury, N.C.
WNDR	1260	Syracuse, N.Y.
WNDS	50	Derry, N.H.
WNDU	1490	South Bend, Ind.
WNDU-FM	92.9	South Bend, Ind.
WNDU-TV	16	South Bend, Ind.
WNDY	106.3	Crawfordsville, Ind.
WNEA	1300	Newnan, Ga.
WNEB	1230	Worcester, Mass.
WNEC-FM	91.7	Henniker, N.H.
WNED-FM	94.5	Buffalo, N.Y.
WNED-TV	17	Buffalo, N.Y.
WNEG	630	Toccoa, Ga.
WNEG-TV	32	Toccoa, Ga.
WNEK-FM	97.5	Springfield, Mass.
WNEL	1430	Caguas, P.R.
WNEM-TV	5	Bay City, Mich.
WNEO-TV	45	Alliance, O.
WNEP-TV	16	Scranton, Pa.
WNER	1250	Live Oak, Fla.
WNES	1050	Central City, Ky.
WNET	13	New York, N.Y.
WNEV-TV	7	Boston, Mass.
WNEW	1130	New York, N.Y.
WNEW-FM	102.7	New York, N.Y.
WNEW-TV	5	New York, N.Y.
WNEX	1400	Macon, Ga.
WNEZ	99.3	Aiken, S.C.
WNFI	99.9	Palatka, Fla.
WNFL	1440	Green Bay, Wis.
WNFM	104.9	Dayton, Tenn.
WNFT	47	Jacksonville, Fla.

WNGA	1600	Nashville, Ga.
WNGC	95.5	Athens, Ga.
WNGO	1320	Mayfield, Ky.
WNGS	92.1	West Palm Beach, Fla.
WNGZ	104.9	Montour Falls, N.Y.
WNHC	1340	New Haven, Conn.
WNHS	88.7	Portsmouth, Va.
WNHT	21	Concord, N.H.
WNHU	88.7	West Haven, Conn.
WNHV	910	White River Junction, Vt.
WNHV-FM	95.3	White River Junction, Vt.
WNIB	97.1	Chicago, Ill.
WNIC	1310	Dearborn, Mich.
WNIC-FM	100.3	Dearborn, Mich.
WNIK	1230	Arecibo, P.R.
WNIK-FM	106.5	Arecibo, P.R.
WNIL	1290	Niles, Mich.
WNIN	9	Evansville, Ind.
WNIN-FM	88.3	Evansville, Ind.
WNIO	1540	Niles, O.
WNIQ-FM	107.1	Hudson Falls, N.Y.
WNIR	100.1	Kent, O.
WNIS	1350	Portsmouth, Va.
WNIT	34	South Bend, Ind.
WNIU-FM	89.5	De Kalb, Ill.
WNIX	1330	Greenville, Miss.
WNIZ	1500	Zion, Ill.
WNIZ-FM	96.9	Zion, Ill.
WNJB	58	New Brunswick, N.J.
WNJC-FM	88.9	Senatobia, Miss.
WNJM	50	Montclair, N.J.
WNJR	1430	Newark, N.J.
WNJS	23	Camden, N.J.
WNJT	52	Trenton, N.J.
WNJU-TV	47	Linden, N.J.
WNJX-TV	22	Mayaguez, P.R.
WNJY	94.3	Riviera Beach, Fla.
WNKJ	89.3	Hopkinsville, Ky.
WNKJ-TV	51	Hopkinsville, Ky.
WNKO	101.7	Newark, O.
WNKU	89.7	Highland Hgts., Ky.
WNKX	95.3	Clinton, Tenn.
WNKY	1480	Neon, Ky.
WNLA	1380	Indianola, Miss.
WNLA-FM	105.5	Indianola, Miss.
WNLB	1290	Rocky Mount, Va.
WNLC	1510	New London, Conn.
WNLK	1350	Norwalk, Conn.
WNLR	1150	Churchville, Va.
WNLT	1390	Duluth, Minn.
WNMB	105.5	North Myrtle Beach, S.C.
WNMH	91.5	Northfield, Mass.
WNMT	1520	Garden City, Ga.
WNMU-FM	90.1	Marquette, Mich.
WNMU-TV	13	Marquette, Mich.
WNNC	1230	Newton, N.C.
WNNE	31	Hartford, Vt.
WNNJ	1360	Newton, N.J.
WNNN	107.1	Canton, N.J.
WNNO	900	Wisconsin Dells, Wis.
WNNO-FM	107.1	Wisconsin Dells, Wis.
WNNR	990	New Orleans, La.
WNNS	98.7	Springfield, Ill.
WNNT	690	Warsaw, Va.
WNNT-FM	100.9	Warsaw, Va.
WNOE	1060	New Orleans, La.
WNOE-FM	101.1	New Orleans, La.
WNOG	1270	Naples, Fla.
WNOI	103.9	Flora, Ill.
WNOK	1230	Columbia, S.C.
WNOK-FM	104.7	Columbia, S.C.
WNOL-TV	38	New Orleans, La.
WNON	100.9	Lebanon, Ind.

WNOO	1260	Chattanooga, Tenn.
WNOP	740	Newport, Ky.
WNOR	1230	Norfolk, Va.
WNOR-FM	98.7	Norfolk, Va.
WNOU	98.3	Willimantic, Conn.
WNOV	860	Milwaukee, Wis.
WNOW	1250	York, Pa.
WNOX	990	Knoxville, Tenn.
WNPB	24	Morgantown, W.V.
WNPC	1060	Newport, Tenn.
WNPE	16	Watertown, N.Y.
WNPI	18	Norwood, N.Y.
WNPQ	95.9	New Philadelphia, O.
WNPT	1280	Tuscaloosa, Ala.
WNPV	1440	Lansdale, Pa.
WNRC	95.1	Dudley, Mass.
WNRE	1540	Circleville, O.
WNRE-FM	107.1	Circleville, O.
WNRG	940	Grundy, Va.
WNRI	1380	Woonsocket, R.I.
WNRK	1260	Newark, Del.
WNRP	20	Ponce, P.R.
WNRR	92.1	Bellevue, O.
WNRS	1290	Saline, Mich.
WNRV	990	Narrows, Va.
WNSB	91.1	Norfolk, Va.
WNSC-FM	88.9	Rock Hill, S.C.
WNSL	100.3	Laurel, Miss.
WNST	1600	Milton, W.V.
WNST-FM	106.3	Milton, W.V.
WNSV	1310	Newport News, Va.
WNSY-FM	97.3	Newport News, Va.
WNTE	89.5	Mansfield, Pa.
WNTH	88.1	Winnetka, Ill.
WNTI	91.9	Hackettstown, N.J.
WNTN	1550	Newton, Mass.
WNTQ	93.1	Syracuse, N.Y.
WNTS	1590	Beech Grove, Ind.
WNTT	1250	Tazewell, Tenn.
WNTV-TV	29	Greenville, S.C.
WNTY	990	Southington, Conn.
WNUB-FM	89.1	Northfield, Vt.
WNUE	1400	Ft. Walton Beach, Fla.
WNUF	100.7	New Kensington, Pa.
WNUR	89.3	Evanston, Ill.
WNUS	102.1	Belpre, O.
WNUV-TV	54	Baltimore, Md.
WNUZ	1230	Talladega, Ala.
WNVA	1350	Norton, Va.
WNVA-FM	106.3	Norton, Va.
WNVC	56	Fairfax, Va.
WNVI	1460	North Vernon, Ind.
WNVL	1250	Nicholasville, Ky.
WNVR	1380	Naugatuck, Conn.
WNVT	53	Annandale, Va.
WNVY	1230	Pensacola, Fla.
WNVZ	104.5	Norfolk, Va.
WNWC	102.5	Madison, Wis.
WNWI	1080	Valparaiso, Ind.
WNWN	98.5	Coldwater, Mich.
WNWS	790	South Miami, Fla.
WNWZ	1450	Highland Springs, Va.
WNXT	1260	Portsmouth, O.
WNXT-FM	99.3	Portsmouth, O.
WNYC	830	New York, N.Y.
WNYC-FM	93.9	New York, N.Y.
WNYC-TV	31	New York, N.Y.
WNYE	91.5	New York, N.Y.
WNYE-TV	25	New York, N.Y.
WNYG	1440	Babylon, N.Y.
WNYK	88.7	Nyack, N.Y.
WNYM	1330	New York, N.Y.
WNYN	900	Canton, O.
WNYS	1120	Buffalo, N.Y.
WNYS-FM	104.1	Buffalo, N.Y.
WNYT	13	Albany, N.Y.
WNYU-FM	89.1	New York, N.Y.
WNZE	94.3	Plymouth, Ind.
WOAB	104.9	Ozark, Ala.
WOAC	67	Canton, O.
WOAI	1200	San Antonio, Tex.
WOAK	90.9	La Grange, Ga.
WOAM	980	Otsego, Mich.
WOAP	1080	Owosso, Mich.
WOAP-FM	103.9	Owosso, Mich.
WOAS	88.5	Ontonagon, Mich.
WOAY	860	Oak Hill, W.V.
WOAY-TV	4	Oak Hill, W.V.
WOBC-FM	88.7	Oberlin, O.
WOBL	1320	Oberlin, O.
WOBM-FM	92.7	Toms River, N.J.
WOBN	105.7	Westerville, O.
WOBO	88.1	Batavia, O.
WOBR	1530	Wanchese, N.C.
WOBR-FM	95.3	Wanchese, N.C.
WOBS	1570	New Albany, Ind.
WOBT	1240	Rhinelander, Wis.
WOC	1420	Davenport, Ia.
WOC-TV	6	Davenport, Ia.
WOCA	1370	Ocala, Fla.
WOCN	1450	Miami, Fla.
WOCO	1260	Oconto, Wis.
WOCO-FM	107.1	Oconto, Wis.
WOCQ	103.9	Berlin, Md.
WOCR	89.7	Olivet, Mich.
WODB	102.3	Camden, Ala.
WODI	1230	Brookneal, Va.
WODY	900	Bassett, Va.
WOEA	97.7	Rogers City, Mich.
WOEL-FM	89.9	Elkton, Md.
WOES	91.3	Elsie, Mich.
WOEZ-FM	100.9	Milton, Pa.
WOFE	580	Rockwood, Tenn.
WOFF	105.5	Camilla, Ga.
WOFL	35	Orlando, Fla.
WOFM	92.1	Moyock, N.C.
WOFR	1250	Washington Court House, O.
WOGC	90.1	Huntsville, Ala.
WOGO	680	Cornell, Wis.
WOHI	1490	East Liverpool, O.
WOHO	1470	Toledo, O.
WOHP	1390	Bellefontaine, O.
WOHS	730	Shelby, N.C.
WOI	640	Ames, Ia.
WOI-FM	90.1	Ames, Ia.
WOI-TV	5	Ames, Ia.
WOIC	1320	Columbia, S.C.
WOIO	19	Shaker Heights, O.
WOIV	105.1	De Ruyter, N.Y.
WOJB	88.9	Reserve, Wis.
WOJC	93.3	Tampa, Fla.
WOJO	105.1	Evanston, Ill.
WOKA	1310	Douglas, Ga.
WOKA-FM	106.7	Douglas, Ga.
WOKB	1600	Winter Garden, Fla.
WOKC	1570	Okeechobee, Fla.
WOKD	98.3	Arcadia, Fla.
WOKE	1340	Charleston, S.C.
WOKG	1570	Warren, O.
WOKH	96.7	Bardstown, Ky.
WOKI-FM	100.3	Oak Ridge, Tenn.
WOKJ	1550	Jackson, Miss.
WOKK	97.1	Meridian, Miss.
WOKL	1050	Eau Claire, Wis.
WOKM	103.5	New Albany, Miss.
WOKN	102.3	Goldsboro, N.C.
WOKO	1460	Albany, N.Y.
WOKO	104.9	Paxton, Ill.
WOKQ	97.5	Dover, N.H.
WOKR	13	Rochester, N.Y.
WOKS	1340	Columbus, Ga.
WOKT	1270	Newport News, Va.
WOKU-FM	107.1	Greensburg, Pa.
WOKV	600	Jacksonville, Fla.
WOKW	99.9	Cortland, N.Y.
WOKX	1590	High Point, N.C.
WOKY	920	Milwaukee, Wis.
WOKZ	1570	Alton, Ill.
WOL	1450	Washington, D. C.
WOLA	1380	Barranquitas, P.R.
WOLC	102.5	Princess Anne, Md.
WOLD	1330	Marion, Va.
WOLD-FM	102.3	Marion, Va.
WOLE-TV	12	Aguadilla, P.R.
WOLF	1490	Syracuse, N.Y.
WOLO-TV	25	Columbia, S.C.
WOLS	1230	Florence, S.C.
WOMC	104.3	Detroit, Mich.
WOMI	1490	Owensboro, Ky.
WOMP	1290	Bellaire, O.
WOMP-FM	100.5	Bellaire, O.
WOMR	91.9	Provincetown, Mass.
WOMT	1240	Manitowoc, Wis.
WONA	1570	Winona, Miss.
WONA-FM	96.7	Winona, Miss.
WONC	89.1	Naperville, Ill.
WOND	1400	Pleasantville, N.J.
WONE	980	Dayton, O.
WONN	1230	Lakeland, Fla.
WONO	1350	Black Mountain, N.C.
WONT	98.3	Ontonogan, Mich.
WONW	1280	Defiance, O.
WONX	1590	Evanston, Ill.
WONY	90.9	Oneonta, N.Y.
WOOD	1300	Grand Rapids, Mich.
WOOD-FM	105.7	Grand Rapids, Mich.
WOOF	560	Dothan, Ala.
WOOF-FM	99.7	Dothan, Ala.
WOOJ	1440	Lehigh Acres, Fla.
WOOJ-FM	107.1	Lehigh Acres, Fla.
WOOK	100.3	Washington, D. C.
WOOR	97.5	Oxford, Miss.
WOOS-FM	106.9	Canton, O.
WOOT	95.3	Homosassa Springs, Fla.
WOOW	1340	Greenville, N.C.
WOPA	1490	Oak Park, Ill.
WOPC	23	Altoona, Pa.
WOPI	1490	Bristol, Tenn.
WOPP	1290	Opp, Ala.
WOPR	90.3	Oak Park, Mich.
WOQF	39	Greenville, Tenn.
WOQI	93.3	Ponce, P.R.
WOR	710	New York, N.Y.
WOR-TV	9	New York, N.Y.
WOR-TV	9	Secaucus, N.J.
WORA	760	Mayaguez, P.R.
WORA-TV	5	Mayaguez, P.R.
WORB	90.3	Farmington Hills, Mich.
WORC	1310	Worcester, Mass.
WORD	910	Spartanburg, S.C.
WORG	1580	Orangeburg, S.C.
WORG-FM	103.9	Orangeburg, S.C.
WORI	1550	Oak Ridge, Tenn.
WORJ	103.9	Ozark, Ala.
WORJ-FM	107.7	Mt. Dora, Fla.
WORK	107.1	Barre, Vt.
WORL	1270	Orlando, Fla.
WORM	1010	Savannah, Tenn.
WORM-FM	101.7	Savannah, Tenn.
WORO	92.5	Corozal, P.R.
WORT	89.9	Madison, Wis.
WORV	1580	Hattiesburg, Miss.
WORW	91.9	Port Huron, Mich.
WORX	1270	Madison, Ind.
WOSC	1300	Fulton, N.Y.
WOSE	94.5	Port Clinton, O.

WOSH	103.9	Oshkosh, Wis.
WOSM	103.1	Ocean Springs, Miss.
WOSO	1030	San Juan, P.R.
WOSS	90.3	Ossining, N.Y.
WOSU	820	Columbus, O.
WOSU-FM	89.7	Columbus, O.
WOSU-TV	34	Columbus, O.
WOTB	107.1	Middletown, R.I.
WOTT	1410	Watertown, N.Y.
WOTV	8	Grand Rapids, Mich.
WOTW	900	Nashua, N.H.
WOTW-FM	106.3	Nashua, N.H.
WOUB	1340	Athens, O.
WOUB-FM	91.3	Athens, O.
WOUB-TV	20	Athens, O.
WOUC-TV	44	Cambridge, O.
WOUI	88.9	Chicago, Ill.
WOUR	96.9	Utica, N.Y.
WOVI	89.5	Novi, Mich.
WOVO	105.5	Glasgow, Ky.
WOVR	103.1	Versailles, Ind.
WOVV	95.5	Ft. Pierce, Fla.
WOW	590	Omaha, Neb.
WOW-FM	94.1	Omaha, Neb.
WOWD	103.1	Tallahassee, Fla.
WOWE	105.5	Rossville, Ga.
WOWI	102.9	Norfolk, Va.
WOWK	13	Huntington, W.V.
WOWL-TV	15	Florence, Ala.
WOWN	960	Shawano, Wis.
WOWN-FM	99.3	Shawano, Wis.
WOWO	1190	Ft. Wayne, Ind.
WOWQ	102.1	Du Bois, Pa.
WOWT	6	Omaha, Neb.
WOWW	107.3	Pensacola, Fla.
WOXO	1450	South Paris, Me.
WOXO-FM	92.7	Norway, Me.
WOXY	97.7	Oxford, O.
WOYE-FM	94.1	Mayaguez, P.R.
WOYK	1350	York, Pa.
WOYL	1340	Oil City, Pa.
WOZI	101.7	Presque Isle, Me.
WOZK	900	Ozark, Ala.
WOZN	970	Jacksonville, Fla.
WOZO	850	Pennyan, N.Y.
WOZQ	91.9	Northampton, Mass.
WOZW	710	Monticello, Me.
WPAA	91.7	Andover, Mass.
WPAB	550	Ponce, P.R.
WPAC	92.7	Ogdensburg, N.Y.
WPAD	1560	Paducah, Ky.
WPAG	1050	Ann Arbor, Mich.
WPAG-FM	107.1	Ann Arbor, Mich.
WPAJ-FM	107.1	Lancaster, S.C.
WPAK	1490	Farmville, Va.
WPAL	730	Charleston, S.C.
WPAM	1450	Pottsville, Pa.
WPAN	35	Ft. Walton Beach, Fla.
WPAP-FM	92.5	Panama City, Fla.
WPAQ	740	Mt. Airy, N.C.
WPAS	1400	Zephyr Hills, Fla.
WPAT	930	Paterson, N.J.
WPAT-FM	93.1	Paterson, N.J.
WPAX	1240	Thomasville, Ga.
WPAY	1400	Portsmouth, O.
WPAY-FM	104.1	Portsmouth, O.
WPAZ	1370	Pottstown, Pa.
WPBC	92.9	Bangor, Me.
WPBE	100.9	Huntingdon, Tenn.
WPBF-FM	105.9	Middletown, O.
WPBH	90.5	Meriden, Conn.
WPBH	90.5	Middlefield, Conn.
WPBH	90.5	Middlefield, Conn.
WPBH	90.5	Meriden, Conn.
WPBK	1490	Whitehall, Mich.
WPBM	1300	Aiken, S.C.
WPBM-FM	95.9	Aiken, S.C.
WPBN-TV	7	Traverse City, Mich.
WPBO-TV	42	Portsmouth, O.
WPBR	1340	Palm Beach, Fla.
WPBT	2	Miami, Fla.
WPBX	91.3	Southampton, N.Y.
WPBY	33	Huntington, W.V.
WPCB-TV	40	Greensburg, Pa.
WPCC	1410	Clinton, S.C.
WPCD	88.7	Champaign, Ill.
WPCE	1400	Portsmouth, Va.
WPCF	1290	Panama City Beach, Fla.
WPCH	94.9	Atlanta, Ga.
WPCK	1290	West Palm Beach, Fla.
WPCM	101.1	Burlington, N.C.
WPCN	960	Mt. Pocono, Pa.
WPCO	1590	Mount Vernon, Ind.
WPCQ-TV	36	Charlotte, N.C.
WPCR-FM	91.7	Plymouth, N.H.
WPCS	89.3	Pensacola, Fla.
WPCV	97.5	Winter Haven, Fla.
WPCX	106.9	Auburn, N.Y.
WPDC	1600	Elizabethtown, Pa.
WPDE-TV	15	Florence, S.C.
WPDH	101.5	Poughkeepsie, N.Y.
WPDM	1470	Potsdam, N.Y.
WPDQ	1460	Jacksonville, Fla.
WPDR	1350	Portage, Wis.
WPDS-TV	59	Indianapolis, Ind.
WPDX	750	Clarksburg, W.V.
WPDX-FM	104.9	Clarksburg, W.V.
WPDZ	103.1	Cheraw, S.C.
WPEA	90.5	Exeter, N.H.
WPEB	88.1	Philadelphia, Pa.
WPEC	12	West Palm Beach, Fla.
WPED	810	Crozet, Va.
WPED-FM	102.3	Crozet, Va.
WPEG	97.9	Concord, N.C.
WPEH	1420	Louisville. Ga.
WPEH-FM	92.1	Louisville, Ga.
WPEL	1250	Montrose, Pa.
WPEL-FM	96.5	Montrose, Pa.
WPEN	950	Philadelphia, Pa.
WPEO	1020	Peoria, Ill.
WPEP	1570	Taunton, Mass.
WPET	950	Greensboro, N.C.
WPEX	1490	Hampton, Va.
WPEZ	107.9	Macon, Ga.
WPFA	790	Pensacola, Fla.
WPFB	910	Middletown, O.
WPFL	88.9	Winter Park, Fla.
WPFM	107.9	Panama City, Fla.
WPFR	1300	Terre Haute, Ind.
WPFR-FM	102.7	Terre Haute, Ind.
WPFW	89.3	Washington, D. C.
WPGA	980	Perry, Ga.
WPGA-FM	100.9	Perry, Ga.
WPGC	1580	Morningside, Md.
WPGC-FM	95.5	Morningside, Md.
WPGH-TV	53	Pittsburgh, Pa.
WPGM	1570	Danville, Pa.
WPGM-FM	96.7	Danville, Pa.
WPGO	106.3	Shallotte, N.C.
WPGT	90.1	Roanoke Rapids, N.C.
WPGU	107.1	Urbana, Ill.
WPGW	1440	Portland, Ind.
WPGW-FM	100.9	Portland, Ind.
WPHB	1260	Philipsburg, Pa.
WPHC	1060	Waverly, Tenn.
WPHD	103.3	Buffalo, N.Y.
WPHL-TV	17	Philadelphia, Pa.
WPHM	1380	Port Huron, Mich.
WPHP	91.9	Wheeling, W.V.
WPHS	91.5	Warren, Mich.
WPIC	790	Sharon, Pa.
WPID	1280	Piedmont, Ala.
WPIG	95.9	Saco, Me.
WPIK	990	Flomaton, Ala.
WPIO	89.1	Titusville, Fla.
WPIQ	101.5	Brunswick, Ga.
WPIT	730	Pittsburgh, Pa.
WPIT-FM	101.5	Pittsburgh, Pa.
WPIX	11	New York, N.Y.
WPIX-FM	101.9	New York, N.Y.
WPJB-FM	105.1	Providence, R.I.
WPJL	1240	Raleigh, N.C.
WPKE	1240	Pikeville, Ky.
WPKN	89.5	Bridgeport, Conn.
WPKX-FM	105.9	Woodbridge, Va.
WPKY	1580	Princeton, Ky.
WPKY-FM	104.9	Princeton, Ky.
WPKZ	1540	Pickens, S.C.
WPLA	910	Plant City, Fla.
WPLB	1380	Greenville, Mich.
WPLB-FM	107.3	Greenville, Mich.
WPLG	10	Miami, Fla.
WPLJ	95.5	New York, N.Y.
WPLK	1220	Rockmart, Ga.
WPLM	1390	Plymouth, Mass.
WPLM-FM	99.1	Plymouth, Mass.
WPLN	90.3	Nashville, Tenn.
WPLO	590	Atlanta, Ga.
WPLP	570	Pinellas Park, Fla.
WPLR	99.1	New Haven, Conn.
WPLS-FM	96.5	Greenville, S.C.
WPLT	93.9	Plattsburgh, N.Y.
WPLW	1590	Carnegie, Pa.
WPLY	1420	Plymouth, Wis.
WPLZ	99.3	Petersburg, Va.
WPMB	1500	Vandalia, Ill.
WPMH	1010	Portsmouth, Va.
WPMJ	48	Owensboro, Ky.
WPMO	99.1	Pascagoula, Miss.
WPMP	1580	Pascagoula, Miss.
WPMT	43	York, Pa.
WPMW	92.7	Mullens, W.V.
WPNC	1470	Plymouth, N.C.
WPNE	38	Green Bay, Wis.
WPNE-FM	89.3	Green Bay, Wis.
WPNF	1240	Brevard, N.C.
WPNH	1300	Plymouth, N.H.
WPNH-FM	100.1	Plymouth, N.H.
WPNM	106.3	Ottawa, O.
WPNR-FM	90.7	Utica, N.Y.
WPNT	92.9	Pittsburgh, Pa.
WPNX	1460	Phenix City, Ala.
WPOB	88.5	Plainview, N.Y.
WPOC	93.1	Baltimore, Md.
WPOE	1520	Greenfield, Mass.
WPOK	1080	Pontiac, Ill.
WPOK-FM	103.1	Pontiac, Ill.
WPOM	1600	Riviera Beach, Fla.
WPON	1460	Pontiac, Mich.
WPOP	1410	Hartford, Conn.
WPOR	1490	Portland, Me.
WPOR-FM	101.9	Portland, Me.
WPOS-FM	102.3	Holland, O.
WPOW	1330	New York, N.Y.
WPPA	1360	Pottsville, Pa.
WPPC	1570	Penuelas, P.R.
WPPI	1330	Carrollton, Ga.
WPPL	103.9	Blue Ridge, Ga.
WPQR-FM	99.3	Uniontown, Pa.
WPQZ	1400	Clarksburg, W.V.
WPRA	990	Mayaguez, P.R.
WPRB	103.3	Princeton, N.J.
WPRC	1370	Lincoln, Ill.
WPRE	980	Prairie Du Chien, Wis.
WPRE-FM	94.3	Prairie Du Chien, Wis.
WPRI-TV	12	Providence, R.I.
WPRK	91.5	Winter Park, Fla.
WPRM-FM	98.5	San Juan, P.R.
WPRN	1330	Butler, Ala.
WPRN	1240	Butler, Ala.
WPRO	630	Providence, R.I.
WPRO-FM	92.3	Providence, R.I.
WPRP	910	Ponce, P.R.
WPRR	100.1	Altoona, Pa.
WPRS	1440	Paris, Ill.
WPRT	960	Prestonburg, Ky.

WPRT-FM	105.5	Prestonburg, Ky.
WPRW	1460	Manassas, Va.
WPRX	880	Sabana Granda, P.R.
WPRY	1400	Perry, Fla.
WPRZ	1250	Warrenton, Va.
WPSA	89.1	Paul Smith's, N.Y.
WPSD-TV	6	Paducah, Ky.
WPSK	107.1	Pulaski, Va.
WPSR	90.7	Evansville, Ind.
WPST	97.5	Trenton, N.J.
WPSU	89.1	Lehman, Pa.
WPSX-TV	3	Clearfield, Pa.
WPTA	21	Ft. Wayne, Ind.
WPTB	850	Statesboro, Ga.
WPTC	1500	Macon, Ga.
WPTD	16	Dayton, O.
WPTF	680	Raleigh, N.C.
WPTF-TV	28	Durham, N.C.
WPTG	90.3	Lancaster, Pa.
WPTL	920	Canton, N.C.
WPTM	102.3	Roanoke Rapids, N.C.
WPTN	1550	Cookeville, Tenn.
WPTO	14	Oxford, O.
WPTR	1540	Albany, N.Y.
WPTT-TV	22	Pittsburgh, Pa.
WPTV	5	West Palm Beach, Fla.
WPTW	1570	Piqua, O.
WPTW-FM	95.7	Piqua, O.
WPTX	920	Lexington Park, Md.
WPTY-TV	24	Memphis, Tenn.
WPTZ	5	Plattsburgh, N.Y.
WPUB-FM	94.3	Camden, S.C.
WPUL	1130	Bartow, Fla.
WPUM	90.5	Rensselaer, Ind.
WPUR	97.7	Americus, Ga.
WPUT	1510	Brewster, N.Y.
WPUV	1580	Pulaski, Va.
WPVA	1290	Colonial Heights, Va.
WPVA-FM	95.3	Petersburg, Va.
WPVI	6	Philadelphia, Pa.
WPVL	1460	Painesville, O.
WPVR	94.9	Roanoke, Va.
WPWC	1480	Quantico, Va.
WPWR	60	Aurora, Ill.
WPWT	91.7	Philadelphia, Pa.
WPXE	1490	Starke, Fla.
WPXE-FM	106.3	Starke, Fla.
WPXI	11	Pittsburgh, Pa.
WPXY	1280	Rochester, N.Y.
WPXY-FM	97.9	Rochester, N.Y.
WPXZ	1540	Punxsutawney, Pa.
WPXZ-FM	105.5	Punxsutawney, Pa.
WPYB	1130	Benson, N.C.
WPYK	1010	Dora, Ala.
WPYX	106.5	Albany, N.Y.
WQAA	103.9	Luray, Va.
WQAB	92.1	Phillipi, W.V.
WQAC	53	Ft. Walton Beach, Fla.
WQAD-TV	8	Moline, Ill.
WQAL	104.1	Cleveland, O.
WQAM	560	Miami, Fla.
WQAQ	88.3	Hamden, Conn.
WQAQ	98.1	Hamden, Conn.
WQAW	103.1	Parkersburg, W.V.
WQAZ	92.7	Cleveland, Miss.
WQBA	1140	Miami, Fla.
WQBA-FM	107.5	Miami, Fla.
WQBC	1420	Vicksburg, Miss.
WQBE	950	Charleston, W.V.
WQBE-FM	97.5	Charleston, W.V.
WQBH	1400	Detroit, Mich.
WQBK	1300	Rensselaer, N.Y.
WQBK-FM	103.9	Rensselaer, N.Y.
WQBS	630	San Juan, P.R.
WQBX	710	Blacksburg, Va.
WQBZ	106.3	Fort Valley, Ga.
WQCC	1540	Charlotte, N.C.
WQCK	92.7	Clinton, La.
WQCM	96.7	Halfway, Md.
WQCN	1450	Savannah, Ga.
WQCR	98.9	Burlington, Vt.
WQCS	88.3	Ft. Pierce, Fla.
WQCT	1520	Bryan, O.
WQCW	102.5	Waycross, Ga.
WQCY	99.5	Quincy, Ill.
WQDE	1250	Albany, Ga.
WQDI	1430	Homestead, Fla.
WQDK	99.3	Ahoskie, N.C.
WQDQ	1600	Lebanon, Tenn.
WQDR	94.7	Raleigh, N.C.
WQDW	97.7	Kinston, N.C.
WQDY	1230	Calais, Me.
WQDY-FM	92.7	Calais, Me.
WQED	13	Pittsburgh, Pa.
WQED-FM	89.3	Pittsburgh, Pa.
WQEN	103.7	Gadsden, Ala.
WQEQ	103.1	Freeland, Pa.
WQEX	16	Pittsburgh, Pa.
WQEZ	99.3	Ft. Myers, Fla.
WQFL	100.9	Rockford, Ill.
WQFM	93.3	Milwaukee, Wis.
WQFS	90.9	Greensboro, N.C.
WQGL	93.5	Butler, Ala.
WQGN-FM	105.5	Groton, Conn.
WQHJ		Key West, Fla.
WQHK	1380	Ft. Wayne, Ind.
WQHL	98.1	Live Oak, Fla.
WQHQ	104.7	Ocean City, Md.
WQHY	95.5	Prestonburg, Ky.
WQIC	1450	Meridian, Miss.
WQID	93.7	Biloxi, Miss.
WQII	1140	San Juan, P.R.
WQIK	1320	Jacksonville, Fla.
WQIK-FM	99.1	Jacksonville, Fla.
WQIM	95.3	Prattville, Ala.
WQIN	1290	Lykens, Pa.
WQIQ	1590	Chester, Pa.
WQIS	1260	Laurel, Miss.
WQIX	100.9	Horseheads, N.Y.
WQIZ	810	St. George, S.C.
WQKI	710	St. Matthews, S.C.
WQKS	96.5	Williamsburg, Va.
WQKT	104.5	Wooster, O.
WQKX	94.1	Sunbury, Pa.
WQKY	92.7	Emporium, Pa.
WQKZ	96.7	Bolivar, Tenn.
WQLA	104.9	La Follette, Tenn.
WQLI	88.7	Newbury, Mass.
WQLK	96.1	Richmond, Ind.
WQLM-FM	92.7	Punta Gorda, Fla.
WQLN	54	Erie, Pa.
WQLN-FM	91.3	Erie, Pa.
WQLO	98.7	Beaufort, S.C.
WQLR	106.5	Kalamazoo, Mich.
WQLT	107.3	Florence, Ala.
WQLX	102.3	Galion, O.
WQLZ	105.1	Cheboygan, Mich.
WQMA	1520	Marks, Miss.
WQMC	95.3	Charlottesville, Va.
WQMF	95.7	Jeffersonville, Ind.
WQMG	97.1	Greensboro, N.C.
WQMR	1150	Skowhegan, Me.
WQMS	1500	Alabaster, Ala.
WQMT	99.3	Chatsworth, Ga.
WQMU	103.1	Indiana, Pa.
WQMV	98.7	Vicksburg, Miss.
WQNA	89.9	Springfield, Ill.
WQNA	88.3	Springfield, Ill.
WQNS	104.9	Waynesville, N.C.
WQNY	103.7	Ithaca, N.Y.
WQNZ	95.1	Natchez, Miss.
WQOD	93.3	Youngstown, O.
WQOK	1450	Myrtle Beach, S.C.
WQON	100.1	Grayling, Mich.
WQOW-TV	18	Eau Claire, Wis.
WQOX	88.5	Memphis, Tenn.
WQPD	94.3	Lake City, Fla.
WQPM	1300	Princeton, Minn.
WQPM-FM	106.3	Princeton, Minn.
WQPO	100.7	Harrisonburg, Va.
WQPT	24	Moline, Ill.
WQQB	40	Bowling Green, Ky.
WQQQ	99.9	Easton, Pa.
WQQW	1590	Waterbury, Conn.
WQRA	94.3	Warrenton, Va.
WQRB	1150	Burlington, N.C.
WQRC	99.9	Barnstable, Mass.
WQRF-TV	39	Rockford, Ill.
WQRL	106.3	Benton, Ill.
WQRO	1080	Huntingdon, Pa.
WQRP	88.1	West Carrollton, O.
WQRS-FM	105.1	Detroit, Mich.
WQSA	1220	Sarasota, Fla.
WQSB	105.1	Albertville, Ala.
WQSI	1270	Portland, Tenn.
WQSM	98.1	Fayetteville, N.C.
WQST	92.5	Forest, Miss.
WQSU	88.9	Selinsgrove, Pa.
WQTC-FM	102.3	Two Rivers, Wis.
WQTE	95.3	Adrian, Mich.
WQTK	1580	Mt. Dora, Fla.
WQTQ	89.9	Hartford, Conn.
WQTR	99.1	Whiteville, N.C.
WQTU	102.3	Rome, Ga.
WQTV	68	Boston, Mass.
WQTW	890	Latrobe, Pa.
WQTW	1570	Latrobe, Pa.
WQTY	93.5	Linton, Ind.
WQUE	1280	New Orleans, La.
WQUE-FM	93.3	New Orleans, La.
WQUH	103.1	De Funiak Springs, Fla.
WQUS	92.5	Winchester, Va.
WQUT	101.5	Johnson City, Tenn.
WQVR	100.1	Southbridge, Mass.
WQWK	96.7	State College, Pa.
WQWQ-FM	104.5	Muskegon, Mich.
WQXA	105.7	York, Pa.
WQXB	100.1	Grenada, Miss.
WQXE	100.1	Elizabethtown, Ky.
WQXI	790	Atlanta, Ga.
WQXI-FM	94.1	Smyrna, Ga.
WQXL	1470	Columbia, S.C.
WQXM	1560	Gordon, Ga.
WQXM	1120	Gordon, Ga.
WQXM-FM	107.1	Gordon, Ga.
WQXO	1400	Munising, Mich.
WQXO-FM	98.3	Munising, Mich.
WQXR	1560	New York, N.Y.
WQXR-FM	96.3	New York, N.Y.
WQXX	92.1	Morganton, N.C.
WQXX	105.1	Salem, O.
WQXY-FM	100.7	Baton Rouge, La.
WQXZ	860	Taylorsville, N.C.
WQYK-FM	99.5	St. Petersburg, Fla.
WQYX	93.5	Clearfield, Pa.
WQZP-FM	94.1	Keyser, W.V.
WQZY	95.9	Dublin, Ga.
WRAA	1330	Luray, Va.
WRAB	1380	Arab, Ala.
WRAC	103.1	West Union, O.
WRAD	1460	Radford, Va.
WRAF	90.9	Toccoa Falls, Ga.
WRAG	590	Carrollton, Ala.
WRAI	1520	San Juan, P.R.
WRAJ	1440	Anna, Ill.
WRAJ-FM	92.7	Anna, Ill.
WRAK	1400	Williamsport, Pa.
WRAL	101.5	Raleigh, N.C.
WRAL-TV	5	Raleigh, N.C.
WRAM	1330	Monmouth, Ill.
WRAN	1510	Dover, N.J.
WRAP	850	Norfolk, Va.
WRAQ	1380	Asheville, N.C.
WRAR	1000	Tappahannock, Va.
WRAR-FM	105.5	Tappahannock, Va.
WRAS	88.5	Atlanta, Ga.
WRAU-TV	19	Peoria, Ill.
WRAW	1340	Reading, Pa.

WRAX	100.9	Bedford, Pa.
WRAY	1250	Princeton, Ind.
WRAY-FM	98.1	Princeton, Ind.
WRBA	1440	Normal, Ill.
WRBB	104.9	Boston, Mass.
WRBC	91.5	Lewiston, Me.
WRBD	1470	Pompano Beach, Fla.
WRBE	1440	Lucedale, Miss.
WRBH	88.3	New Orleans, La.
WRBI	103.9	Batesville, Ind.
WRBL	3	Columbus, Ga.
WRBN	1600	Warner Robbins, Ga.
WRBN-FM	101.7	Warner Robbins, Ga.
WRBQ	1380	St. Petersburg, Fla.
WRBQ-FM	104.7	Tampa, Fla.
WRBS	95.1	Baltimore, Md.
WRBT	33	Baton Rouge, La.
WRBV	65	Vineland, N.J.
WRBX	1530	Chapel Hill, N.C.
WRC	980	Washington, D. C.
WRC-TV	4	Washington, D. C.
WRCB-TV	3	Chattanooga, Tenn.
WRCC	103.9	Cape Coral, Fla.
WRCD	1430	Dalton, Ga.
WRCG	1420	Columbus, Ga.
WRCH-FM	100.5	New Britain, Conn.
WRCI	93.5	Midland, Mich.
WRCJ	89.3	Reading, O.
WRCK	107.3	Utica, N.Y.
WRCM	92.1	Jacksonville, N.C.
WRCN-FM	103.9	Riverhead, N.Y.
WRCO	1450	Richland Center, Wis.
WRCO-FM	100.9	Richland Center, Wis.
WRCP	1290	Providence, R.I.
WRCQ	910	New Britain, Conn.
WRCR	94.3	Rushville, Ind.
WRCS	970	Ahoskie, N.C.
WRCT	88.3	Pittsburgh, Pa.
WRCU-FM	90.1	Hamilton, N.Y.
WRCW	1060	Canton, O.
WRDB	1400	Reedsburg, Wis.
WRDB-FM	104.9	Reedsburg, Wis.
WRDC	1410	Cleveland, Miss.
WRDG	16	Burlington, N.C.
WRDL	88.9	Ashland, O.
WRDN	1430	Durand, Wis.
WRDN-FM	95.9	Durand, Wis.
WRDO	1400	Augusta, Me.
WRDO-FM	92.1	Augusta, Me.
WRDO-FM	92.3	Augusta, Me.
WRDR	104.9	Egg Harbor, N.J.
WRDS	1500	Sardis, Miss.
WRDW	1480	Augusta, Ga.
WRDW-TV	12	Augusta, Ga.
WRDX	106.5	Salisbury, N.C.
WREB	930	Holyoke, Mass.
WREC	600	Memphis, Tenn.
WRED	1490	Monroe, Ga.
WREG-TV	3	Memphis, Tenn.
WREI	98.3	Quebradillas, P.R.
WREK	91.1	Atlanta, Ga.
WREL	1450	Lexington, Va.
WREN	1250	Topeka, Kan.
WREO-FM	97.1	Ashtabula, O.
WRET-TV	39	Spartanburg, S.C.
WREV	1220	Reidsville, N.C.
WREX-TV	13	Rockford, Ill.
WREY	1440	Millville, N.J.
WREZ	103.3	Montgomery, Ala.
WRFB	101.7	Stowe, Vt.
WRFC	960	Athens, Ga.
WRFD	880	Worthington, O.
WRFE	105.5	Aguada, P.R.
WRFG	89.3	Atlanta, Ga.
WRFK-FM	106.5	Richmond, Va.
WRFM	105.1	New York, N.Y.
WRFN	88.1	Nashville, Tenn.
WRFR	96.7	Franklin, N.C.
WRFS	1050	Alexander City, Ala.
WRFS-FM	106.1	Alexander City, Ala.
WRFT	91.5	Indianapolis, Ind.
WRFW	88.7	River Falls, Wis.
WRFY-FM	102.5	Reading, Pa.
WRGA	1470	Rome, Ga.
WRGB	6	Schenectady, N.Y.
WRGC	680	Sylva, N.C.
WRGI	93.5	Naples, Fla.
WRGS	1370	Rogersville, Tenn.
WRHC	1550	Coral Gables, Fla.
WRHD	1570	Riverhead, N.Y.
WRHI	1340	Rock Hill, S.C.
WRHL	1060	Rochelle, Ill.
WRHL-FM	102.3	Rochelle, Ill.
WRHN	107.9	Rhinelander, Wis.
WRHO	89.5	Oneonta, N.Y.
WRHR	90.5	Henrietta, N.Y.
WRHS	88.1	Park Forest, Ill.
WRHU	88.7	Hempstead, N.Y.
WRIA	101.3	Richmond, Ind.
WRIB	1220	Providence, R.I.
WRIC	540	Richlands, Va.
WRID	1160	Homer City, Pa.
WRIE	1330	Erie, Pa.
WRIF	101.1	Detroit, Mich.
WRIG	1400	Wausau, Wis.
WRIK	98.3	Metropolis, Ill.
WRIN	1560	Rensselaer, Ind.
WRIP	980	Rossville, Ga.
WRIQ	101.7	Radford, Va.
WRIS	1410	Roanoke, Va.
WRIT	92.7	Stuart, Fla.
WRIU	90.3	Kingston, R.I.
WRIV	1390	Riverhead, N.Y.
WRIX	103.1	Honea Path, S.C.
WRJA-FM	88.1	Sumter, S.C.
WRJA-TV	27	Sumter, S.C.
WRJB	98.3	Camden, Tenn.
WRJC	1270	Mauston, Wis.
WRJC-FM	92.1	Mauston, Wis.
WRJH	97.7	Brandon, Miss.
WRJK	40	Bluefield, Va.
WRJL	94.1	Oak Hill, W.V.
WRJN	1400	Racine, Wis.
WRJQ	92.7	Tomahawk, Wis.
WRJS	98.5	Oil City, Pa.
WRJW	1320	Picayune, Miss.
WRJZ	620	Knoxville, Tenn.
WRKA	103.1	St. Matthews, Ky.
WRKB	1460	Kannapolis, N.C.
WRKC	88.5	Wilkes Barre, Pa.
WRKD	1450	Rockland, Me.
WRKF	89.3	Baton Rouge, La.
WRKI	95.1	Brookfield, Conn.
WRKK	99.5	Birmingham, Ala.
WRKL	910	New City, N.Y.
WRKM	1350	Carthage, Tenn.
WRKM-FM	102.3	Carthage, Tenn.
WRKN	970	Brandon, Miss.
WRKO	680	Boston, Mass.
WRKQ	1250	Madisonville, Tenn.
WRKR	1460	Racine, Wis.
WRKR-FM	100.7	Racine, Wis.
WRKS-FM	98.7	New York, N.Y.
WRKT	1300	Cocoa Beach, Fla.
WRKT-FM	104.1	Cocoa Beach, Fla.
WRKX	95.3	Ottawa, Ill.
WRKY	103.5	Steubenville, O.
WRKZ	106.7	Hershey, Pa.
WRLC	91.7	Williamsport, Pa.
WRLD	1490	Lanett, Ala.
WRLH	35	Richmond, Va.
WRLK-TV	35	Columbia, S.C.
WRLO-FM	105.3	Antigo, Wis.
WRLP	32	Greenfield, Mass.
WRLR	106.3	Huntingdon, Pa.
WRLS-FM	92.1	Hayward, Wis.
WRLV	1140	Saylersville, Ky.
WRMB	89.3	Boynton Beach, Fla.
WRMC-FM	91.7	Middlebury, Vt.
WRMF	97.9	Palm Beach, Fla.
WRMG	1430	Red Bay, Ala.
WRMJ	102.3	Aledo, Ill.
WRML	1470	Portage, Pa.
WRMM	99.7	Atlanta, Ga.
WRMN	1410	Elgin, Ill.
WRMR	730	Alexandria, Va.
WRMS	790	Beardstown, Ill.
WRMS-FM	94.3	Beardstown, Ill.
WRMT	1490	Rocky Mount, N.C.
WRMU	91.1	Alliance, O.
WRMV	1420	Herkimer, N.Y.
WRMZ	99.7	Columbus, O.
WRNA	1140	China Grove, N.C.
WRNB	1490	New Bern, N.C.
WRNC	1600	Reidsville, N.C.
WRNG	96.7	Newnan, Ga.
WRNJ	1000	Hackettstown, N.J.
WRNL	910	Richmond, Va.
WRNN	95.3	Clare, Mich.
WRNO	99.5	New Orleans, La.
WRNR	740	Martinsburg, W.V.
WRNS	95.1	Kinston, N.C.
WRNV	89.7	Annapolis, Md.
WRNY	1350	Rome, N.Y.
WRNZ	96.7	Wrens, Ga.
WROA	1390	Gulfport, Miss.
WROB	1450	West Point, Miss.
WROC-TV	8	Rochester, N.Y.
WROD	1340	Daytona Beach, Fla.
WROE	99.3	Neenah, Wis.
WROG	102.9	Cumberland, Md.
WROI	92.1	Rochester, Ind.
WROK	1440	Rockford, Ill.
WROL	950	Boston, Mass.
WROM	710	Rome, Ga.
WRON	1400	Ronceverte, W.V.
WRON-FM	97.7	Ronceverte, W.V.
WROQ	95.1	Charlotte, N.C.
WROR	98.5	Boston, Mass.
WROS	1050	Jacksonville, Fla.
WROV	1240	Roanoke, Va.
WROW	590	Albany, N.Y.
WROW-FM	95.5	Albany, N.Y.
WROX	1450	Clarksdale, Miss.
WROY	1460	Carmi, Ill.
WROZ	1400	Evansville, Ind.
WRPC	95.1	San German, P.R.
WRPI	91.5	Troy, N.Y.
WRPM	1530	Poplarville, Miss.
WRPM-FM	107.9	Poplarville, Miss.
WRPN-FM	90.1	Ripon, Wis.
WRPQ	740	Baraboo, Wis.
WRPR	90.3	Mahwah, N.J.
WRPS	91.5	Rockland, Mass.
WRPT	1050	Peterborough, N.H.
WRQC	92.3	Cleveland Heights, O.
WRQK	98.7	Greensboro, N.C.
WRQN	93.5	Bowling Green, O.
WRQR	94.3	Farmville, N.C.
WRQX	107.3	Washington, D. C.
WRR	101.1	Dallas, Tex.
WRRA	1290	Fredericksted, St. Croi, V.I.
WRRB	107.9	Syracuse, N.Y.
WRRG	88.9	River Grove, Ill.
WRRH	88.7	Franklin Lakes, N.J.
WRRK	97.7	Manistee, Mich.
WRRL	1130	Rainelle, W.V.
WRRL-FM	96.7	Rainelle, W.V.
WRRM	98.5	Cincinnati, O.
WRRN	92.3	Warren, Pa.

WRRO	1440	Warren, O.
WRRR	1570	St. Marys, W.V.
WRRR-FM	101.7	St. Marys, W.V.
WRRZ	880	Clinton, N.C.
WRRZ-FM	107.1	Clinton, N.C.
WRSA	96.9	Decatur, Ala.
WRSB	88.3	Weston, Mass.
WRSC	1390	State College, Pa.
WRSD	94.9	Folsom, Pa.
WRSE-FM	88.7	Elmhurst, Ill.
WRSF	89.9	Miamisburg, O.
WRSG	1540	Sylvester, Ga.
WRSH	91.1	Rockingham, N.C.
WRSI	95.3	Greenfield, Mass.
WRSJ	1560	Bayamon, P.R.
WRSL	1520	Stanford, Ky.
WRSL-FM	95.9	Stanford, Ky.
WRSM	1540	Sumiton, Ala.
WRSP	55	Springfield, Ill.
WRSS	1410	San Sebastian, P.R.
WRST-FM	90.3	Oshkosh, Wis.
WRSU-FM	88.7	New Brunswick, N.J.
WRSV	92.1	Rocky Mount, N.C.
WRSW	1480	Warsaw, Ind.
WRSW-FM	107.3	Warsaw, Ind.
WRTA	1240	Altoona, Pa.
WRTB	96.7	Vincennes, Ind.
WRTC-FM	89.3	Hartford, Conn.
WRTE	89.5	Cahokia, Ill.
WRTH	590	Wood River, Ill.
WRTI	90.1	Philadelphia, Pa.
WRTK	1370	Rochester, N.Y.
WRTL	1460	Rantoul, Ill.
WRTL-FM	95.3	Rantoul, Ill.
WRTM	102.3	Blountstown, Fla.
WRTN	93.5	New Rochelle, N.Y.
WRTR	1590	Two Rivers, Wis.
WRTT	1170	Vernon, Conn.
WRTU	89.7	San Juan, P.R.
WRTV	6	Indianapolis, Ind.
WRUA	1510	Monroeville, Pa.
WRUC	89.7	Schenectady, N.Y.
WRUF	850	Gainesville, Fla.
WRUF-FM	103.7	Gainesville, Fla.
WRUL	97.3	Carmi, Ill.
WRUM	790	Rumford, Me.
WRUN	1150	Utica, N.Y.
WRUS	610	Russellville, Ky.
WRUT	97.1	Rutland, Vt.
WRUV	90.1	Burlington, Vt.
WRUW-FM	91.1	Cleveland, O.
WRVA	1140	Richmond, Va.
WRVG	90.1	Georgetown, Ky.
WRVG	89.9	Georgetown, Ky.
WRVH	106.5	Patterson, N.Y.
WRVI	96.7	Virden, Ill.
WRVK	1460	Mt. Vernon, Ky.
WRVL	88.3	Lynchburg, Va.
WRVM	102.7	Suring, Wis.
WRVO	89.9	Oswego, N.Y.
WRVQ	94.5	Richmond, Va.
WRVR	104.5	Memphis, Tenn.
WRVU	91.1	Nashville, Tenn.
WRVW	93.5	Hudson, N.Y.
WRWC	103.1	Rockton, Ill.
WRWH	1350	Cleveland, Ga.
WRWR	30	San Juan, P.R.
WRXB	1590	St. Petersburg Beach, Fla.
WRXL	102.1	Richmond, Va.
WRXO	1430	Roxboro, N.C.
WRXV	1530	Auburn, Me.
WRXX	95.3	Centralia, Ill.
WRXZ	103.9	Kane, Pa.
WRYM	840	New Britain, Conn.
WRYO	98.5	Crystal River, Fla.
WRZK	1450	Spring Lake, N.C.
WRZQ	107.3	Greensburg, Ind.
WSAC	1470	Ft. Knox, Ky.
WSAE	89.3	Spring Arbor, Mich.
WSAI	1360	Cincinnati, O.
WSAI-FM	94.1	Cincinnati, O.
WSAJ	1340	Grove City, Pa.
WSAJ-FM	89.5	Grove City, Pa.
WSAK	106.3	Sullivan, Ill.
WSAL	1230	Logansport, Ind.
WSAL-FM	102.3	Logansport, Ind.
WSAM	1400	Saginaw, Mich.
WSAN	1470	Allentown, Pa.
WSAO	1140	Senatobia, Miss.
WSAQ	107.1	Port Huron, Mich.
WSAR	1480	Fall River, Mass.
WSAT	1280	Salisbury, N.C.
WSAU	550	Wausau, Wis.
WSAV-TV	3	Savannah, Ga.
WSAW	7	Wausau, Wis.
WSAY-TV	66	Forest City, N.C.
WSAZ-TV	3	Huntington, W.V.
WSB	750	Atlanta, Ga.
WSB-FM	98.5	Atlanta, Ga.
WSB-TV	2	Atlanta, Ga.
WSBA	910	York, Pa.
WSBA-FM	103.3	York, Pa.
WSBB	1230	New Smyrna Beach, Fla.
WSBC	1240	Chicago, Ill.
WSBE-TV	36	Providence, R.I.
WSBF-FM	88.1	Clemson, S.C.
WSBG	93.5	Stroudsburg, Pa.
WSBH	95.3	Southampton, N.Y.
WSBK-TV	38	Boston, Mass.
WSBL	1290	Sanford, N.C.
WSBR	740	Boca Raton, Fla.
WSBS	860	Great Barrington, Mass.
WSBT	960	South Bend, Ind.
WSBT-TV	22	South Bend, Ind.
WSBU	88.3	St. Bonaventura, N.Y.
WSBV	1560	South Boston, Va.
WSBW	100.1	Sturgeon Bay, Wis.
WSBY	960	Salisbury, Md.
WSCA	100.9	Union Springs, Ala.
WSCB	89.9	Springfield, Mass.
WSCC	92.1	Somerset, Ky.
WSCC	90.7	Somerset, Ky.
WSCD-FM	92.9	Duluth, Minn.
WSCG	93.5	Corinth, N.Y.
WSCH	99.3	Aurora, Ind.
WSCI	89.3	Charleston, S.C.
WSCM	1190	Cobelskill, N.Y.
WSCO	14	Suring, Wis.
WSCP	1070	Sandy Creek, N.Y.
WSCQ	100.1	Columbia, S.C.
WSCR	1220	Hamden, Conn.
WSCS	89.5	Sodus, N.Y.
WSCT	56	Melbourne, Fla.
WSCW	1410	South Charleston, W.V.
WSCY	100.9	North Syracuse, N.Y.
WSCZ	96.7	Greenwood, S.C.
WSDC	1490	Hartsville, S.C.
WSDH	91.5	Sandwich, Mass.
WSDL	1560	Slidell, La.
WSDM	990	Clare, Mich.
WSDP	88.1	Plymouth, Mich.
WSDR	1240	Sterling, Ill.
WSDS	1480	Ypsilanti, Mich.
WSDT	1240	Soddy Daisy, Tenn.
WSEA	93.5	Georgetown, Del.
WSEB	1340	Sebring, Fla.
WSEC	103.7	Williamston, N.C.
WSEE	35	Erie, Pa.
WSEG	102.3	Mc Kean, Pa.
WSEI	92.9	Olney, Ill.
WSEK	96.7	Somerset, Ky.
WSEL	1440	Pontotoc, Miss.
WSEL-FM	96.7	Pontotoc, Miss.
WSEM	1500	Donalsonville, Ga.
WSEN	1050	Baldwinsville, N.Y.
WSEN-FM	92.1	Baldwinsville, N.Y.
WSER	1550	Elkton, Md.
WSES	1550	Raleigh, N.C.
WSET-TV	13	Lynchburg, Va.
WSEV	930	Sevierville, Tenn.
WSEW	1240	Selinsgrove, Pa.
WSEX	92.7	Arlington Heights, Ill.
WSEY	96.7	Sauk City, Wis.
WSEZ	93.1	Winston Salem, N.C.
WSFA-TV	12	Montgomery, Ala.
WSFB	1490	Quitman, Ga.
WSFC	1240	Somerset, Ky.
WSFJ	51	Newark, O.
WSFL	106.5	Bridgeton, N.C.
WSFL	106.5	New Bern, N.C.
WSFM	99.3	Harrisburg, Pa.
WSFP-TV	30	Ft. Myers, Fla.
WSFT	1220	Thomaston, Ga.
WSFW	1110	Seneca Falls, N.Y.
WSFW-FM	99.3	Seneca Falls, N.Y.
WSGA	1400	Savannah, Ga.
WSGB	1490	Sutton, W.V.
WSGC	1400	Elberton, Ga.
WSGE	91.7	Dallas, N.C.
WSGI	1190	Springfield, Tenn.
WSGL	97.7	Naples, Fla.
WSGM	93.5	Staunton, Va.
WSGN	610	Birmingham, Ala.
WSGO	1440	Oswego, N.Y.
WSGO-FM	105.5	Oswego, N.Y.
WSGR-FM	91.3	Port Huron, Mich.
WSGS	101.1	Hazard, Ky.
WSGW	790	Saginaw, Mich.
WSHA	88.9	Raleigh, N.C.
WSHC	88.7	Shepherdstown, W.V.
WSHC	93.7	Shepherstown, W.V.
WSHD	91.7	Eastport, Me.
WSHE-FM	103.5	Ft. Lauderdale, Fla.
WSHF	1290	Sheffield, Ala.
WSHH	99.7	Pittsburgh, Pa.
WSHJ	88.3	Southfield, Mich.
WSHL-FM	91.3	Easton, Mass.
WSHN	1550	Fremont, Mich.
WSHN-FM	100.1	Fremont, Mich.
WSHO	800	New Orleans, La.
WSHP	1480	Shippensburg, Pa.
WSHR	91.9	Lake Ronkonkoma, N.Y.
WSHS	91.7	Sheboygan, Wis.
WSHU	91.1	Fairfield, Conn.
WSHV	105.5	South Hill, Va.
WSHW	99.7	Frankfort, Ind.
WSHY	1560	Shelbyville, Ill.
WSHY-FM	104.9	Shelbyville, Ill.
WSIA	88.9	Staten Island, N.Y.
WSIC	1400	Statesville, N.C.
WSID	100.9	Sidney, N.Y
WSIE	88.7	Edwardsville, Ill.
WSIF	94.7	Wilkesboro, N.C.
WSIG	790	Mount Jackson, Va.
WSIL-TV	3	Harrisburg, Ill.
WSIP	1490	Paintsville, Ky.
WSIP-FM	98.9	Paintsville, Ky.
WSIR	1490	Winter Haven, Fla.
WSIU	91.9	Carbondale, Ill.
WSIU-TV	8	Carbondale, Ill.
WSIV	1540	East Syracuse, N.Y.
WSIX	980	Nashville, Tenn.
WSIX-FM	97.9	Nashville, Tenn.
WSIZ	1380	Ocilla, Ga.

WSJC	810	Magee, Miss.
WSJC-FM	107.5	Magee, Miss.
WSJK-TV	2	Sneedville, Tenn.
WSJL	102.3	Cape May, N.J.
WSJM	1400	St. Joseph, Mich.
WSJN	24	San Juan, P.R.
WSJP	1130	Murray, Ky.
WSJR	1230	Madawaska, Me.
WSJS	600	Winston Salem, N.C.
WSJU	18	San Juan, P.R.
WSJV	28	Elkhart, Ind.
WSJW	1510	Woodruff, S.C.
WSJY	107.3	Fort Atkinson, Wis.
WSKB	91.5	Westfield, Mass.
WSKE	1050	Everett, Pa.
WSKE	1040	Everett, Pa.
WSKG-FM	89.3	Binghamton, N.Y.
WSKI	1240	Montpelier, Vt.
WSKP-FM	105.5	Sebring, Fla.
WSKQ	620	Newark, N.J.
WSKR	104.1	Atmore, Ala.
WSKS	96.5	Hamilton, O.
WSKT	1580	Knoxville, Tenn.
WSKV	104.9	Stanton, Ky.
WSKY	1230	Asheville, N.C.
WSKZ	106.5	Chattanooga, Tenn.
WSLA	8	Selma, Ala.
WSLB	1400	Ogdensburg, N.Y.
WSLC	610	Roanoke, Va.
WSLG	1090	Gonzales, La.
WSLI	930	Jackson, Miss.
WSLK	1600	Hyden, Ky.
WSLM	1220	Salem, Ind.
WSLM-FM	98.9	Salem, Ind.
WSLN	91.1	Delaware, O.
WSLQ	99.1	Roanoke, Va.
WSLR	1350	Akron, O.
WSLS-TV	10	Roanoke, Va.
WSLT	106.3	Ocean City, N.J.
WSLU	96.7	Canton, N.Y.
WSLV	1110	Ardmore, Tenn.
WSLW	1310	White Sulphur Springs, W.V.
WSLX	91.9	New Canaan, Conn.
WSLY	99.3	York, Ala.
WSM	650	Nashville, Tenn.
WSM-FM	95.5	Nashville, Tenn.
WSMA	1590	Marine City, Mich.
WSMB	1350	New Orleans, La.
WSMC-FM	90.5	Chattanooga, Tenn.
WSMD	1560	La Plata, Md.
WSME	1220	Sanford, Me.
WSMF	21	Florence, S.C.
WSMG	1450	Greeneville, Tenn.
WSMI	1540	Litchfield, Ill.
WSMI-FM	106.1	Litchfield, Ill.
WSML	1190	Graham, N.C.
WSMN	1590	Nashua, N.H.
WSMQ	1450	Bessemer, Ala.
WSMR	1400	Raeford, N.C.
WSMR	89.3	Dayton, O.
WSMS	91.7	Memphis, Tenn.
WSMT	1050	Sparta, Tenn.
WSMT-FM	105.5	Sparta, Tenn.
WSMU-FM	106.3	Starkville, Miss.
WSMV	4	Nashville, Tenn.
WSMW-TV	27	Worcester, Mass.
WSMX	1500	Winston Salem, N.C.
WSMY	1400	Weldon, N.C.
WSNC	89.3	Winston Salem, N.C.
WSND-FM	88.9	Notre Dame, Ind.
WSNE	93.3	Taunton, Mass.
WSNG	610	Torrington, Conn.
WSNI	1540	Philadelphia, Pa.
WSNI-FM	104.5	Philadelphia, Pa.
WSNJ	1240	Bridgeton, N.J.
WSNJ-FM	107.7	Bridgeton, N.J.
WSNL-TV	67	Smithtown, N.Y.
WSNN	99.3	Potsdam, N.Y.
WSNO	1450	Barre, Vt.
WSNS	44	Chicago, Ill.
WSNT	1490	Sandersville, Ga.
WSNT-FM	93.5	Sandersville, Ga.
WSNW	1150	Seneca, S.C.
WSNY	94.7	Columbus, O.
WSOC	930	Charlotte, N.C.
WSOC-FM	103.7	Charlotte, N.C.
WSOC-TV	9	Charlotte, N.C.
WSOE	89.3	Elon College, N.C.
WSOF-FM	89.9	Madisonville, Ky.
WSOJ	98.3	Jessup, Ga.
WSOK	1230	Savannah, Ga.
WSOL	1370	Elloree, S.C.
WSOM	600	Salem, O.
WSON	860	Henderson, Ky.
WSOO	1230	Sault Ste. Marie, Mich.
WSOQ	1220	North Syracuse, N.Y.
WSOR	95.3	Ft. Myers, Fla.
WSOU	89.5	South Orange, N.J.
WSOX	1240	West Yarmouth, Mass.
WSOX-FM	94.9	West Yarmouth, Mass.
WSOY	1340	Decatur, Ill.
WSOY-FM	102.9	Decatur, Ill.
WSPA	950	Spartanburg, S.C.
WSPA-FM	98.9	Spartanburg, S.C.
WSPA-TV	7	Spartanburg, S.C.
WSPB	1450	Sarasota, Fla.
WSPC	1140	St. Paul, Va.
WSPD	1370	Toledo, O.
WSPF	1000	Hickory, N.C.
WSPI	95.3	Shamokin, Pa.
WSPK	104.7	Poughkeepsie, N.Y.
WSPL	95.9	La Crosse, Wis.
WSPN	91.1	Saratoga Springs, N.Y.
WSPR	1270	Springfield, Mass.
WSPS	90.5	Concord, N.H.
WSPT	97.9	Stevens Point, Wis.
WSPY	107.1	Plano, Ill.
WSQR	1560	Sycamore, Ill.
WSQV	97.7	Jersey Shore, Pa.
WSRA	106.9	Guayama, P.R.
WSRB	91.5	Walpole, Mass.
WSRC	1410	Durham, N.C.
WSRD	101.1	Youngstown, O.
WSRE	23	Pensacola, Fla.
WSRF	1580	Ft. Lauderdale, Fla.
WSRG	1070	Elkton, Ky.
WSRK	103.9	Oneonta, N.Y.
WSRN-FM	91.5	Swarthmore, Pa.
WSRO	1470	Marlboro, Mass.
WSRQ	94.5	Eden, N.C.
WSRS	96.1	Worcester, Mass.
WSRU	90.1	Slippery Rock, Pa.
WSRW	1590	Hillsboro, O.
WSRW-FM	106.7	Hillsboro, O.
WSRZ	102.5	Sarasota, Fla.
WSSA	1570	Morrow, Ga.
WSSB-FM	90.3	Orangeburg, S.C.
WSSC	1340	Sumter, S.C.
WSSD	88.1	Chicago, Ill.
WSSG	1300	Goldsboro, N.C.
WSSH	99.5	Lowell, Mass.
WSSJ	1310	Camden, N.J.
WSSL	100.5	Gray Court, S.C.
WSSL	100.5	Laurens, S.C.
WSSL	1580	Centreville, Miss.
WSSN	102.3	Weston, W.V.
WSSO	1230	Starkville, Miss.
WSSR	91.9	Springfield, Ill.
WSST	800	Largo, Fla.
WSSU	99.1	Superior, Wis.
WSSV	1240	Petersburg, Va.
WSSX-FM	95.1	Charleston, S.C.
WSTA	1340	Charlotte Amalie, V.I.
WSTB	91.5	Streetsboro, O.
WSTC	1400	Stamford, Conn.
WSTE	13	Fajardo, P.R.
WSTG	64	Providence, R.I.
WSTJ	1340	St. Johnsbury, Vt.
WSTL	1600	Eminence, Ky.
WSTM-TV	3	Syracuse, N.Y.
WSTN	106.3	Florence, S.C.
WSTO	96.1	Owensboro, Ky.
WSTP	1490	Salisbury, N.C.
WSTR	1230	Sturgis, Mich.
WSTR-FM	99.3	Sturgis, Mich.
WSTS	96.5	Laurinburg, N.C.
WSTU	1450	Stuart, Fla.
WSTV	1340	Steubenville, O.
WSTW	93.7	Wilmington, Del.
WSTX	970	Christiansted, V.I.
WSUB	980	Groton, Conn.
WSUC-FM	90.5	Cortland, N.Y.
WSUE	101.3	Sault Ste. Marie, Mich.
WSUH	1420	Oxford, Miss.
WSUI	910	Iowa City, Ia.
WSUL	98.3	Monticello, N.Y.
WSUM	1000	Parma, O.
WSUN	620	St. Petersburg, Fla.
WSUP	90.5	Platteville, Wis.
WSUR-TV	9	Ponce, P.R.
WSUS	102.3	Franklin, N.J.
WSUW	91.7	Whitewater, Wis.
WSUX	1280	Seaford, Del.
WSUX-FM	98.3	Seaford, Del.
WSUZ	800	Palatka, Fla.
WSVA	550	Harrisonburg, Va.
WSVC	1190	Dunlap, Tenn.
WSVE	92.7	Green Cove Springs, Fla.
WSVH	91.1	Savannah, Ga.
WSVI	8	Christiansted, V.I.
WSVL	1520	Shelbyville, Ind.
WSVM	1490	Valdese, N.C.
WSVN	7	Miami, Fla.
WSVN-TV	47	Norton, Va.
WSVQ	740	Harrogate, Tenn.
WSVS	800	Crewe, Va.
WSVS-FM	104.7	Crewe, Va.
WSVT	710	Smyrna, Tenn.
WSWB	38	Wilkes Barre, Pa.
WSWG-FM	99.1	Greenwood, Miss.
WSWI	820	Evansville, Ind.
WSWN	900	Belle Glade, Fla.
WSWN-FM	93.5	Belle Glade, Fla.
WSWO	102.3	Wilmington, O.
WSWP-TV	9	Grandview, W.V.
WSWR	100.1	Shelby, O.
WSWS	66	Opelika, Ala.
WSWT	106.9	Peoria, Ill.
WSWV	1570	Pennington Gap, Va.
WSWV-FM	105.5	Pennington Gap, Va.
WSYB	1380	Rutland, Vt.
WSYC-FM	88.7	Shippensburg, Pa.
WSYD	1300	Mt. Airy, N.C.
WSYL	1490	Sylvania, Ga.
WSYR	570	Syracuse, N.Y.
WSYX	106.3	London, O.
WTAB	1370	Tabor City, N.C.
WTAC	600	Flint, Mich.
WTAD	930	Quincy, Ill.
WTAE	1250	Pittsburgh, Pa.
WTAE-TV	4	Pittsburgh, Pa.
WTAF-TV	29	Philadelphia, Pa.
WTAG	580	Worcester, Mass.
WTAI	1560	Melbourne, Fla.
WTAJ-TV	10	Altoona, Pa.
WTAK	1000	Huntsville, Ala.
WTAL	1450	Tallahassee, Fla.
WTAM	1240	Gulfport, Miss.
WTAN	1340	Clearwater, Fla.
WTAO	104.9	Murphysboro, Ill.

WTAP-TV	15	Parkersburg, W.V.
WTAQ	1300	La Grange, Ill.
WTAR	790	Norfolk, Va.
WTAS	102.3	Crete, Ill.
WTAW	1150	College Station, Tex.
WTAX	1240	Springfield, Ill.
WTAY	1570	Robinson, Ill.
WTAY-FM	101.7	Robinson, Ill.
WTAZ	102.3	Morton, Ill.
WTBC	1230	Tuscaloosa, Ala.
WTBF	970	Troy, Ala.
WTBG	95.3	Brownsville, Tenn.
WTBN	560	Brentwood, Tenn.
WTBO	1450	Cumberland, Md.
WTBP	1550	Parsons, Tenn.
WTBQ	1110	Warwick, N.Y.
WTBR-FM	89.7	Pittsfield, Mass.
WTBS	17	Atlanta, Ga.
WTBY	54	Poughkeepsie, N.Y.
WTBZ	95.9	Grafton, W.V.
WTCA	1050	Plymouth, Ind.
WTCC	90.7	Springfield, Mass.
WTCG	1400	Andalusia, Ala.
WTCI	45	Chattanooga, Tenn.
WTCJ	1230	Tell City, Ind.
WTCM	580	Traverse City, Mich.
WTCM-FM	103.5	Traverse City, Mich.
WTCN-TV	11	Minneapolis, Minn.
WTCQ	97.7	Vidalia, Ga.
WTCR	103.3	Huntington, W.V.
WTCR	1420	Kenova, W.V.
WTCS	1490	Fairmont, W.V.
WTCW	920	Whitesburg, Ky.
WTCX	1250	Bay City, Mich.
WTEB	89.5	New Bern, N.C.
WTEL	860	Philadelphia, Pa.
WTEN	10	Albany, N.Y.
WTFM	98.5	Kingsport, Tenn.
WTGA	1590	Thomaston, Ga.
WTGA	95.3	Thomaston, Ga.
WTGC	1010	Lewisburg, Pa.
WTGE	1420	Kalkaska, Mich.
WTGI	103.3	Hammond, La.
WTGL	52	Cocoa, Fla.
WTGN	97.7	Lima, O.
WTGP	88.1	Greenville, Pa.
WTGQ	102.3	Cairo, Ga.
WTGR	1520	Myrtle Beach, S.C.
WTGS	28	Hardeeville, S.C.
WTGV-FM	97.7	Sandusky, Mich.
WTHB	1550	Augusta, Ga.
WTHD	105.7	Columbia, N.C.
WTHE	1520	Mineola, N.Y.
WTHI	1480	Terre Haute, Ind.
WTHI-FM	99.9	Terre Haute, Ind.
WTHI-TV	10	Terre Haute, Ind.
WTHO-FM	101.7	Thomson, Ga.
WTHQ	101.5	South Bend, Ind.
WTHR	13	Indianapolis, Ind.
WTHS-TV	2	Miami, Fla.
WTHU	1450	Thurmont, Md.
WTIB	104.9	Iuka, Miss.
WTIC	1080	Hartford, Conn.
WTIC-FM	96.5	Hartford, Conn.
WTIF	1340	Tifton, Ga.
WTIG	990	Massillon, O.
WTIK	1310	Durham, N.C.
WTIL	1300	Mayaguez, P.R.
WTIM	1410	Taylorville, Ill.
WTIN	14	Ponce, P.R.
WTIP	1240	Charleston, W.V.
WTIQ	1490	Manistique, Mich.
WTIS	1110	Tampa, Fla.
WTIU	30	Bloomington, Ind.
WTIV	1230	Titusville, Pa.
WTIX	690	New Orleans, La.
WTJC	26	Springfield, O.
WTJH	1260	East Point, Ga.
WTJM	106.3	Pineville, Ky.

WTJP	44	Gadsden, Ala.
WTJR	16	Quincy, Ill.
WTJS	1390	Jackson, Tenn.
WTJU	91.3	Charlottesville, Va.
WTJY	92.7	Taylorville, Ill.
WTKC	1300	Lexington, Ky.
WTKK	66	Manassas, Va.
WTKL	1260	Baton Rouge, La.
WTKM	1540	Hartford, Wis.
WTKM-FM	104.9	Hartford, Wis.
WTKN	970	Pittsburgh, Pa.
WTKO	1470	Ithaca, N.Y.
WTKR	3	Norfolk, Va.
WTKS	102.3	Bethesda, Md.
WTKW	16	Key West, Fla.
WTKX	101.5	Pensacola, Fla.
WTKY	1370	Tomkinsville, Ky.
WTKY-FM	92.1	Tomkinsville, Ky.
WTLB	1310	Utica, N.Y.
WTLC	105.7	Indianapolis, Ind.
WTLG	88.3	Starke, Fla.
WTLK	1570	Taylorsville, N.C.
WTLL	63	Richmond, Va.
WTLN	1520	Apopka, Fla.
WTLN-FM	95.3	Apopka, Fla.
WTLO	1480	Somerset, Ky.
WTLQ	102.3	Pittston, Pa.
WTLR	89.9	State College, Pa.
WTLS	1300	Tallassee, Ala.
WTLV	12	Jacksonville, Fla.
WTLW	44	Lima, O.
WTMA	1250	Charleston, S.C.
WTMB	1460	Tomah, Wis.
WTMB-FM	98.9	Tomah, Wis.
WTMB-TV	43	Tomah, Wis.
WTMC	1290	Ocala, Fla.
WTMI	93.1	Miami, Fla.
WTMJ	620	Milwaukee, Wis.
WTMJ-TV	4	Milwaukee, Wis.
WTMP	1150	Tampa, Fla.
WTMR	800	Camden, N.J.
WTMS	96.1	Presque Isle, Me.
WTMT	620	Louisville, Ky.
WTNC	790	Thomasville, N.C.
WTNC-FM	98.3	Thomasville, N.C.
WTND	920	Orangeburg, S.C.
WTNE	1530	Trenton, Tenn.
WTNH-TV	8	New Haven, Conn.
WTNJ	105.9	Mt. Hope, W.V.
WTNL	1390	Reidsville, Ga.
WTNN	1380	Millington, Tenn.
WTNQ	102.3	Dickson, Tenn.
WTNS	1560	Coshocton, O.
WTNS-FM	99.3	Coshocton, O.
WTNT	1270	Tallahassee, Fla.
WTNT-FM	94.9	Tallahassee, Fla.
WTNX	1290	Lynchburg, Tenn.
WTNY	790	Watertown, N.Y.
WTOB	1300	Winston Salem, N.C.
WTOC-TV	11	Savannah, Ga.
WTOD	1560	Toledo, O.
WTOE	1470	Spruce Pine, N.C.
WTOF	98.1	Canton, O.
WTOG	44	St. Petersburg, Fla.
WTOH	105.9	Mobile, Ala.
WTOH	90.5	Mobile, Ala.
WTOK-TV	11	Meridian, Miss.
WTOL-TV	11	Toledo, O.
WTOM-TV	4	Cheboygan, Mich.
WTON	1240	Staunton, Va.
WTOO-FM	98.3	Bellefontaine, O.
WTOP	1500	Washington, D.C.
WTOQ	1590	Platteville, Wis.
WTOS	105.1	Skowhegan, Me.
WTOT	980	Marianna, Fla.
WTOV-TV	9	Steubenville, O.
WTOW	1570	Towson, Md.
WTOX	102.3	St. Andrews, S.C.
WTOY	910	Roanoke, Va.
WTPA-FM	104.1	Harrisburg, Pa.

WTPC	89.7	Elsah, Ill.
WTPL-FM	102.3	Tupper Lake, N.Y.
WTPM	92.9	Aguadilla, P.R.
WTPR	710	Paris, Tenn.
WTPR-FM	105.5	Paris, Tenn.
WTQR	104.1	Winston Salem, N.C.
WTQX	1570	Selma, Ala.
WTRA	16	Mayaguez, P.R.
WTRB	1570	Ripley, Tenn.
WTRC	1340	Elkhart, Ind.
WTRE	1330	Greensburg, Ind.
WTRF-TV	7	Wheeling, W.V.
WTRI	1520	Brunswick, Md.
WTRJ	1510	Troy, O.
WTRL	1490	Bradenton, Fla.
WTRN	1340	Tyrone, Pa.
WTRO	1330	Dyersburg, Tenn.
WTRP	620	La Grange, Ga.
WTRQ	1560	Warsaw, N.C.
WTRS	920	Dunnellon, Fla.
WTRS-FM	102.3	Dunnellon, Fla.
WTRU	1600	Muskegon, Mich.
WTRX	1330	Flint, Mich.
WTRY	980	Troy, N.Y.
WTSA	1450	Brattleboro, Vt.
WTSB	1340	Lumberton, N.C.
WTSC-FM	91.1	Potsdam, N.Y.
WTSF	61	Ashland, Ky.
WTSG	31	Albany, Ga.
WTSJ	1050	Cincinnati, O.
WTSK	790	Tuscaloosa, Ala.
WTSL	1400	Hanover, N.H.
WTSN	1270	Dover, N.H.
WTSO	1070	Madison, Wis.
WTSP-TV	10	St. Petersburg, Fla.
WTSR	91.3	Trenton, N.J.
WTSU	89.9	Troy, Ala.
WTSV	1230	Claremont, N.H.
WTTB	97.7	Bonifay, Fla.
WTTB	1490	Vero Beach, Fla.
WTTC	1550	Towanda, Pa.
WTTC-FM	95.3	Towanda, Pa.
WTTE	28	Columbus, O.
WTTF	1600	Tiffin, O.
WTTF-FM	103.7	Tiffin, O.
WTTG	5	Washington, D.C.
WTTI	1530	Dalton, Ga.
WTTL	1310	Madisonville, Ky.
WTTM	920	Trenton, N.J.
WTTN	1580	Watertown, Wis.
WTTO	21	Birmingham, Ala.
WTTP	1060	Natick, Mass.
WTTR	1470	Westminster, Md.
WTTR-FM	100.7	Westminster, Md.
WTTS	1370	Bloomington, Ind.
WTTT	1430	Amherst, Mass.
WTTU	88.5	Cookeville, Tenn.
WTTV	4	Indianapolis, Ind.
WTTW	11	Chicago, Ill.
WTTX	1280	Appomattox, Va.
WTTX-FM	107.1	Appomattox, Va.
WTUE	104.7	Dayton, O.
WTUF	107.1	Thomasville, Ga.
WTUG	92.7	Tuscaloosa, Ala.
WTUL-FM	91.5	New Orleans, La.
WTUN	100.1	Selma, Ala.
WTUP	1490	Tupelo, Miss.
WTUV	33	Utica, N.Y.
WTVA	9	Tupelo, Miss.
WTVB	1590	Coldwater, Mich.
WTVC	9	Chattanooga, Tenn.
WTVD	11	Durham, N.C.
WTVE	51	Reading, Pa.
WTVF	5	Nashville, Tenn.
WTVG	13	Toledo, O.
WTVH	5	Syracuse, N.Y.
WTVI	42	Charlotte, N.C.
WTVJ	4	Miami, Fla.
WTVK	26	Knoxville, Tenn.
WTVL	1490	Waterville, Me.
WTVL-FM	98.3	Waterville, Me.
WTVM	9	Columbus, Ga.
WTVN	610	Columbus, O.

Call	Freq.	Location
WTVN-TV	6	Columbus, O.
WTVO	17	Rockford, Ill.
WTVP	47	Peoria, Ill.
WTVQ	36	Lexington, Ky.
WTVR	1380	Richmond, Va.
WTVR-TV	6	Richmond, Va.
WTVS	56	Detroit, Mich.
WTVT	13	Tampa, Fla.
WTVU	59	New Haven, Conn.
WTVW	7	Evansville, Ind.
WTVX	34	Ft. Pierce, Fla.
WTVY	4	Dothan, Ala.
WTVY-FM	95.5	Dothan, Ala.
WTVZ	33	Norfolk, Va.
WTWA	1240	Thomson, Ga.
WTWB	1570	Auburndale, Fla.
WTWC	40	Tallahassee, Fla.
WTWE	92.1	Manning, S.C.
WTWG	1220	Birmingham, Ala.
WTWO	2	Terre Haute, Ind.
WTWR	98.3	Monroe, Mich.
WTWX	95.9	Guntersville, Ala.
WTWZ	1150	Clinton, Miss.
WTXI	102.3	Ripley, Miss.
WTXN	910	Lafayette, Ala.
WTXR	94.3	Chillicothe, Ill.
WTXY	1540	Whiteville, N.C.
WTYC	1150	Rock Hill, S.C.
WTYD	100.9	New London, Conn.
WTYJ	97.7	Fayette, Miss.
WTYL	1290	Tylertown, Miss.
WTYL-FM	97.7	Tylertown, Miss.
WTYM	1300	Tampa, Fla.
WTYN	1160	Tryon, N.C.
WTYN	1550	Tryon, N.C.
WTYO	1580	Hammondton, N.J.
WTYS	1340	Marianna, Fla.
WTYX	94.7	Jackson, Miss.
WTZA	23	Kingston, N.Y.
WTZE	1470	Tazewell, Va.
WTZE-FM	100.1	Tazewell, Va.
WTZX	860	Sparta, Tenn.
WUAA	16	Jackson, Tenn.
WUAB-TV	43	Lorain, O.
WUAG	106.1	Greensboro, N.C.
WUAL-FM	91.5	Tuscaloosa, Ala.
WUAT	1110	Pikeville, Tenn.
WUBE-FM	105.1	Cincinnati, O.
WUCF-FM	89.9	Orlando, Fla.
WUCM-TV	19	Bay City, Mich.
WUCO	1270	Marysville, O.
WUDZ	91.5	Sweet Briar, Va.
WUEC	89.7	Eau Claire, Wis.
WUEV	91.5	Evansville, Ind.
WUEZ	1480	Salem, Va.
WUFE	1260	Baxley, Ga.
WUFF	710	Eastman, Ga.
WUFF-FM	92.1	Eastman, Ga.
WUFK	92.1	Ft. Kent, Me.
WUFK	90.3	Ft. Kent, Me.
WUFM	100.1	Lebanon, Pa.
WUFN	96.7	Albion, Mich.
WUFO	1080	Amherst, N.Y.
WUFT	5	Gainesville, Fla.
WUFT-FM	89.1	Gainesville, Fla.
WUGN	99.7	Midland, Mich.
WUGO	102.3	Grayson, Ky.
WUHF	31	Rochester, N.Y.
WUHN	1110	Pittsfield, Mass.
WUHQ-TV	41	Battle Creek, Mich.
WUHS	91.7	Urbana, O.
WUHX	49	Norfolk, Va.
WUIA-TV	42	San German, P.R.
WUIV	1580	Icard Township, N.C.
WUJA	58	Caguas, P.R.
WUJC	88.7	Cleveland, O.
WULA	1240	Eufaula, Ala.
WULF	1400	Alma, Ga.
WULT-TV	20	New Orleans, La.
WUMB-FM	91.9	Boston, Mass.
WUME-FM	95.3	Paoli, Ind.
WUMF-FM	91.9	Farmington, Me.
WUMF-FM	92.3	Farmington, Me.
WUNA	1340	Aguadilla, P.R.
WUNC	91.5	Chapel Hill, N.C.
WUNC-TV	4	Chapel Hill, N.C.
WUND-TV	2	Columbia, N.C.
WUNE-TV	17	Linville, N.C.
WUNF-FM	88.1	Asheville, N.C.
WUNF-TV	33	Asheville, N.C.
WUNG-TV	58	Concord, N.C.
WUNH	91.3	Durham, N.H.
WUNI	1410	Mobile, Ala.
WUNJ-TV	39	Wilmington, N.C.
WUNK-TV	25	Greenville, N.C.
WUNL-TV	26	Winston Salem, N.C.
WUNM-TV	19	Jacksonville, N.C.
WUNN	1110	Mason, Mich.
WUNO	1320	San Juan, P.R.
WUNR	1600	Brookline, Mass.
WUOA	95.7	Tuscaloosa, Ala.
WUOG	90.5	Athens, Ga.
WUOL	90.5	Louisville, Ky.
WUOM	91.7	Ann Arbor, Mich.
WUOT	91.9	Knoxville, Tenn.
WUPE	95.9	Pittsfield, Mass.
WUPI	92.1	Presque Isle, Me.
WUPM	106.9	Ironwood, Mich.
WUPR	1530	Utuado, P.R.
WURD	97.7	Georgetown, O.
WUSB	90.1	Stony Brook, N.Y.
WUSC-FM	90.5	Columbia, S.C.
WUSF	89.7	Tampa, Fla.
WUSF-TV	16	Tampa, Fla.
WUSI-TV	16	Olney, Ill.
WUSL	98.9	Philadelphia, Pa.
WUSM	90.5	North Dartmouth, Mass.
WUSN	99.5	Chicago, Ill.
WUSO	89.1	Springfield, O.
WUSQ	102.5	Winchester, Va.
WUSS	1490	Atlantic City, N.J.
WUST	1120	Washington, D. C.
WUSV	45	Schenectady, N.Y.
WUSY	100.7	Cleveland, Tenn.
WUTA	90.1	Farmville, Va.
WUTC	88.1	Chattanooga, Tenn.
WUTK	90.3	Knoxville, Tenn.
WUTM-FM	90.3	Martin, Tenn.
WUTQ	1550	Utica, N.Y.
WUTR	20	Utica, N.Y.
WUTS	91.5	Sewanee, Tenn.
WUTV	29	Buffalo, N.Y.
WUTZ	88.3	Summertown, Tenn.
WUUN	100.1	Marquette, Mich.
WUUU	102.5	Rome, N.Y.
WUVA	92.7	Charlottesville, Va.
WUVT-FM	90.7	Blacksburg, Va.
WUWF	88.1	Pensacola, Fla.
WUWM	89.7	Milwaukee, Wis.
WUWU	107.7	Wethersfield, N.Y.
WVAB	1550	Virginia Beach, Va.
WVAC	107.9	Adrian, Mich.
WVAF	99.9	Charleston, W.V.
WVAH	23	Charleston, W.V.
WVAI	610	Winchester, Va.
WVAL	800	Sauk Rapids, Minn.
WVAM	1430	Altoona, Pa.
WVAN-TV	9	Savannah, Ga.
WVAP	1510	Burnettown, S.C.
WVAQ	101.9	Morgantown, W.V.
WVAR	600	Richwood, W.V.
WVAS	90.7	Montgomery, Ala.
WVBC	88.1	Bethany, W.V.
WVBF	105.7	Framingham, Mass.
WVBK	1440	Herndon, Va.
WVBR-FM	93.5	Ithaca, N.Y.
WVBS	1470	Burgaw, N.C.
WVBS-FM	99.9	Burgaw, N.C.
WVBU-FM	90.5	Lewisburg, Pa.
WVCA-FM	104.9	Gloucester, Mass.
WVCB	1410	Shallotte, N.C.
WVCC	101.7	Linesville, Pa.
WVCD	97.9	Hazleton, Pa.
WVCF	1480	Ocoee, Fla.
WVCG	1080	Coral Gables, Fla.
WVCH	740	Chester, Pa.
WVCH	1260	Charlottesville, Va.
WVCI	61	Bay City, Mich.
WVCM	107.1	Miami, W.V.
WVCP	88.5	Gallatin, Tenn.
WVCR-FM	88.3	Loudonville, N.Y.
WVCS	91.9	California, Pa.
WVCT	91.5	Keavy, Ky.
WVCY	30	Milwaukee, Wis.
WVCY	107.7	Milwaukee, Wis.
WVDI	570	Port Of Spain, Trinidad
WVEC-TV	13	Norfolk, Va.
WVEE	103.3	Atlanta, Ga.
WVEL	1140	Pekin, Ill.
WVEM	101.9	Springfield, Ill.
WVEN	99.3	Franklin, Pa.
WVEO	44	Aguadilla, P.R.
WVER	28	Rutland, Vt.
WVEU	69	Atlanta, Ga.
WVEZ	106.9	Louisville, Ky.
WVFC	1530	Mc Connellsburg, Pa.
WVFJ	1370	Manchester, Ga.
WVFJ-FM	93.3	Manchester, Ga.
WVFK	95.5	Key West, Fla.
WVFM	94.1	Lakeland, Fla.
WVFR	850	Ridgefield, Conn.
WVGA	44	Valdosta, Ga.
WVGB	1490	Beaufort, S.C.
WVGO	1580	St. Johns, Mich.
WVGR	104.1	Grand Rapids, Mich.
WVGS	107.7	Statesboro, Ga.
WVHF-FM	92.7	Clarksburg, W.V.
WVHG	92.1	Labelle, Fla.
WVHI	1330	Evansville, Ind.
WVHP-FM	90.3	Highland Park, N.J.
WVIA-FM	89.9	Scranton, Pa.
WVIA-TV	44	Scranton, Pa.
WVIC	730	East Lansing, Mich.
WVIC-FM	94.9	Lansing, Mich.
WVID	90.3	Anasco, P.R.
WVII-TV	7	Bangor, Me.
WVIK	90.1	Rock Island, Ill.
WVIM-FM	95.3	Coldwater, Miss.
WVIN	1380	Bath, N.Y.
WVIN-FM	98.3	Bath, N.Y.
WVIP	1310	Mount Kisco, N.Y.
WVIP-FM	106.3	Mount Kisco, N.Y.
WVIR-TV	29	Charlottesville, Va.
WVIS	106.1	Fredericksted, St. Croix, V.I.
WVIT	30	New Britain, Conn.
WVIZ-TV	25	Cleveland, O.
WVJC	89.1	Mt. Carmel, Ill.
WVJP	1110	Caguas, P.R.
WVJP-FM	103.3	Caguas, P.R.
WVJS	1420	Owensboro, Ky.
WVKC	90.5	Galesburg, Ill.
WVKO	1580	Columbus, O.
WVKR-FM	91.3	Poughkeepsie, N.Y.
WVKY	1270	Louisa, Ky.
WVLC	1170	Orleans, Mass.
WVLD	1450	Valdosta, Ga.
WVLE	1220	Stillwater, Minn.
WVLJ	105.5	Monticello, Ill.
WVLK	590	Lexington, Ky.
WVLK-FM	92.9	Lexington, Ky.
WVLN	740	Olney, Ill.

WVLV	940	Lebanon, Pa.
WVLY	1320	Water Valley, Miss.
WVMC	90.7	Mansfield, O.
WVMG	1440	Cochran, Ga.
WVMG-FM	96.7	Cochran, Ga.
WVMH-FM	90.5	Mars Hill, N.C.
WVMI	570	Biloxi, Miss.
WVMR	1370	Frost, W.V.
WVMS	1570	Appleton, Wis.
WVMT	620	Burlington, Vt.
WVMW-FM	91.5	Scranton, Pa.
WVNA	1590	Tuscumbia, Ala.
WVNA-FM	100.3	Tuscumbia, Ala.
WVNF	1400	Alpharetta, Ga.
WVNH	1110	Salem, N.H.
WVNO-FM	106.1	Mansfield, O.
WVNP	89.9	Wheeling, W.V.
WVNR	1340	Poultney, Vt.
WVNY	22	Burlington, Vt.
WVOB	1520	Bel Air, Md.
WVOC	102.9	Columbus, Ga.
WVOE	1590	Chadbourn, N.C.
WVOF	88.5	Fairfield, Conn.
WVOG	600	New Orleans, La.
WVOH	920	Hazlehurst, Ga.
WVOH-FM	93.5	Hazlehurst, Ga.
WVOI	1520	Toledo, O.
WVOK	690	Birmingham, Ala.
WVOL	1470	Nashville, Tenn.
WVOM	1270	Iuka, Miss.
WVOP	970	Vidalia, Ga.
WVOR-FM	100.5	Rochester, N.Y.
WVOS	1240	Liberty, N.Y.
WVOS-FM	95.9	Liberty, N.Y.
WVOT	1420	Wilson, N.C.
WVOW	1290	Logan, W.V.
WVOW-FM	101.9	Logan, W.V.
WVOX	1460	New Rochelle, N.Y.
WVOY	1270	Charlevoix, Mich.
WVOZ	870	San Juan, P.R.
WVOZ-FM	107.7	Carolina, P.R.
WVPB	91.7	Beckley, W.V.
WVPE	88.1	Elkhart, Ind.
WVPG	90.3	Parkersburg, W.V.
WVPH	90.3	Piscataway, N.J.
WVPM	90.9	Morgantown, W.V.
WVPN	88.5	Charleston, W.V.
WVPO	840	Stroudsburg, Pa.
WVPR	89.5	Windsor, Vt.
WVPS	107.9	Burlington, Vt.
WVPT	51	Staunton, Va.
WVPW	88.9	Buckhannon, W.V.
WVRC	1400	Spencer, W.V.
WVRM	89.3	Hazlet, N.J.
WVRS	103.1	Waterbury, Vt.
WVRT	101.7	Reform, Ala.
WVRU	89.9	Radford, Va.
WVRY	104.9	Waverly, Tenn.
WVSA	1380	Vernon, Ala.
WVSB	27	West Point, Miss.
WVSC	990	Somerset, Pa.
WVSC-FM	97.7	Somerset, Pa.
WVSH	91.9	Huntington, Ind.
WVSI	1000	Jupiter, Fla.
WVSI-FM	96.7	Jupiter, Fla.
WVSM	1500	Rainsville, Ala.
WVSP	90.9	Warrenton, N.C.
WVSS	90.7	Menomonie, Wis.
WVSU-FM	91.1	Birmingham, Ala.
WVSV	101.7	Stevenson, Ala.
WVTA	41	Windsor, Vt.
WVTB	20	St. Johnsbury, Vt.
WVTC	90.7	Randolph Center, Vt.
WVTF	89.1	Richmond, Va.
WVTH	89.5	Goodman, Miss.
WVTM-TV	13	Birmingham, Ala.
WVTN	105.5	Gatlinburg, Tenn.
WVTS	100.7	Terre Haute, Ind.
WVTV	18	Milwaukee, Wis.
WVTY	106.3	Holiday, Fla.
WVUA-FM	90.7	Tuscaloosa, Ala.
WVUB	91.1	Vincennes, Ind.
WVUD-FM	99.9	Kettering, O.
WVUE	8	New Orleans, La.
WVUM	90.5	Coral Gables, Fla.
WVUR-FM	95.1	Valparaiso, Ind.
WVUR-FM	89.5	Valparaiso, Ind.
WVUT	22	Vincennes, Ind.
WVVA	6	Bluefield, W.V.
WVVS	90.9	Valdosta, Ga.
WVVV	104.9	Blacksburg, Va.
WVVX	103.1	Highland Park, Ill.
WVWC	92.1	Buckhannon, W.V.
WVWI	1000	Charlotte Amalie, V.I.
WVWR-FM	89.1	Roanoke, Va.
WVWV	103.1	Covington, Ind.
WVXU-FM	91.7	Cincinnati, O.
WVYC	88.1	York, Pa.
WWAB	1330	Lakeland, Fla.
WWAC-TV	53	Atlantic City, N.J.
WWAS	88.1	Williamsport, Pa.
WWAX	840	Mobile, Ala.
WWAY-TV	3	Wilmington, N.C.
WWBA	107.3	St. Petersburg, Fla.
WWBB	1450	Madison, W.V.
WWBC	1510	Rockledge, Fla.
WWBD	790	Bamberg, S.C.
WWBD-FM	92.7	Bamberg, S.C.
WWBR	960	La Follette, Tenn.
WWBR	1350	Windber, Pa.
WWBT	12	Richmond, Va.
WWBZ	1360	Vineland, N.J.
WWCA	1270	Gary, Ind.
WWCB	1370	Corry, Pa.
WWCC	1440	Bremen, Ga.
WWCH	1300	Clarion, Pa.
WWCJ	89.3	Jackson, Miss.
WWCK	105.5	Flint, Mich.
WWCM	1130	Brazil, Ind.
WWCO	1240	Waterbury, Conn.
WWCT	105.7	Peoria, Ill.
WWCU	90.5	Cullowhee, N.C.
WWDB	96.5	Philadelphia, Pa.
WWDC	1260	Washington, D. C.
WWDC-FM	101.1	Washington, D. C.
WWDE-FM	101.3	Hampton, Va.
WWDJ	970	Hackensack, N.J.
WWDL-FM	104.9	Scranton, Pa.
WWDM	101.3	Sumter, S.C.
WWDS	90.5	Muncie, Ind.
WWEB	89.9	Wallingford, Conn.
WWEE	1430	Memphis, Tenn.
WWEL	103.9	London, Ky.
WWES	1270	Hot Springs, Va.
WWET	95.3	Monticello, Ind.
WWEV	91.5	Cumming, Ga.
WWEZ	92.5	Cincinnati, O.
WWFM	89.1	Trenton, N.J.
WWGA	100.9	Waynesboro, Ga.
WWGC	90.7	Carrollton, Ga.
WWGM	1560	Nashville, Tenn.
WWGN	1320	Washington, N.C.
WWGP	1050	Sanford, N.C.
WWGS	1430	Tifton, Ga.
WWHB	107.1	Hampton Bays, N.Y.
WWHC	93.5	Hartford City, Ind.
WWHC	104.9	Hartford City, Ind.
WWHI	91.5	Muncie, Ind.
WWHK	1430	Mt. Clemens, Mich.
WWHS-FM	91.7	Hampden Sydney, Va.
WWHT	68	Newark, N.J.
WWHY	1470	Huntington, W.V.
WWIB	103.7	Ladysmith, Wis.
WWIH	90.3	High Point, N.C.
WWIL	1490	Wilmington, N.C.
WWIN	1400	Baltimore, Md.
WWIN-FM	95.9	Glen Burnie, Md.
WWIS	1260	Black River Falls, Wis.
WWIT	970	Canton, N.C.
WWIW	1450	New Orleans, La.
WWIZ	103.9	Mercer, Pa.
WWJ	950	Detroit, Mich.
WWJB	1450	Brooksville, Fla.
WWJC	850	Duluth, Minn.
WWJD	900	Savannah, Ga.
WWJM	106.3	New Lexington, O.
WWJO	98.1	St. Cloud, Minn.
WWJQ	1260	Holland, Mich.
WWJR	97.7	Sheboygan, Wis.
WWJZ	1400	Sanford, Fla.
WWKA	92.3	Orlando, Fla.
WWKF	99.3	Fulton, Ky.
WWKI	100.5	Kokomo, Ind.
WWKK	105.5	Ft. Knox, Ky.
WWKO	1480	Fair Bluff, N.C.
WWKQ	1500	Battle Creek, Mich.
WWKS	106.7	Beaver Falls, Pa.
WWKT-FM	98.3	Kingstree, S.C.
WWKX	104.5	Gallatin, Tenn.
WWKY	1380	Winchester, Ky.
WWL	870	New Orleans, La.
WWL-TV	4	New Orleans, La.
WWLC	90.3	Lynchburg, Va.
WWLF	680	St. Petersburg, Fla.
WWLH	102.3	Pound, Va.
WWLP	22	Springfield, Mass.
WWLR	91.5	Lyndonville, Vt.
WWLS	640	Norman, Okla.
WWLT	106.7	Gainesville, Ga.
WWLV	94.5	Daytona Beach, Fla.
WWLX	620	Lexington, Ala.
WWMC-FM	98.3	Mifflinburg, Pa.
WWMD	104.7	Hagerstown, Md.
WWMG	1380	New Bern, N.C.
WWMH	95.9	Minocqua, Wis.
WWMJ	95.7	Ellsworth, Me.
WWMN	1570	Flint, Mich.
WWMO	102.1	Reidsville, N.C.
WWMR	96.3	Rumford, Me.
WWNC	570	Asheville, N.C.
WWNH	930	Rochester, N.H.
WWNO-FM	89.9	New Orleans, La.
WWNR	620	Beckley, W.V.
WWNS	1240	Statesboro, Ga.
WWNT	1450	Dothan, Ala.
WWNW	88.9	New Wilmington, Pa.
WWNY-TV	7	Watertown, N.Y.
WWOC	94.3	Avalon, N.J.
WWOD	1390	Lynchburg, Va.
WWOG	88.1	Boca Raton, Fla.
WWOJ	106.3	Avon Park, Fla.
WWOM	100.9	Albany, N.Y.
WWON	1240	Woonsocket, R.I.
WWON-FM	106.3	Woonsocket, R.I.
WWOQ	105.5	Berryville, Va.
WWOW	1360	Conneaut, O.
WWOZ	90.7	New Orleans, La.
WWPA	1340	Williamsport, Pa.
WWPB	31	Hagerstown, Md.
WWPH	107.9	Princeton Junction, N.J.
WWPT	90.3	Westport, Conn.
WWPV-FM	88.7	Colchester, Vt.
WWPZ	1340	Petoskey, Mich.
WWQC	90.3	Quincy, Ill.
WWQI	25	La Crosse, Wis.
WWQM-FM	106.3	Middleton, Wis.
WWRC	88.5	Lawrenceville, N.J.
WWRK	92.1	Elberton, Ga.
WWRL	1600	New York, N.Y.
WWRM	106.7	Gaylord, Mich.
WWRN	94.9	Virginia Beach, Va.
WWRT	1590	Algood, Tenn.
WWRW	103.3	Wisconsin Rapids, Wis.
WWSA	1290	Savannah, Ga.
WWSC	1450	Glens Falls, N.Y.
WWSD	101.7	Quincy, Fla.
WWSE	93.3	Jamestown, N.Y.
WWSG	57	Philadelphia, Pa.

WWSH	106.1	Philadelphia, Pa.
WWSL	102.3	Philadelphia, Miss.
WWSM	105.5	Bay Minette, Ala.
WWSP	89.9	Stevens Point, Wis.
WWSR	1420	St. Albans, Vt.
WWST	960	Wooster, O.
WWSU	106.9	Fairborn, O.
WWSW-FM	94.5	Pittsburgh, Pa.
WWTC	1280	Minneapolis, Minn.
WWTL	39	Marshfield, Wis.
WWTO-TV	35	Lasalle, Ill.
WWTR-FM	95.9	Bethany Beach, Del.
WWTV	9	Cadillac, Mich.
WWUH	91.3	West Hartford, Conn.
WWUP-TV	10	Sault Ste. Marie, Mich.
WWUS	104.7	Big Pine Key, Fla.
WWVA	1170	Wheeling, W.V.
WWVR	105.5	West Terre Haute, Ind.
WWVU-FM	91.7	Morgantown, W.V.
WWWB	1360	Jasper, Ala.
WWWB-FM	102.5	Jasper, Ala.
WWWC	1240	Wilkesboro, N.C.
WWWD	1240	Schenectady, N.Y.
WWWE	1100	Cleveland, O.
WWWF	990	Fayette, Ala.
WWWG	1460	Rochester, N.Y.
WWWJ	103.1	Jackson, O.
WWWK	107.7	Warrenton, Va.
WWWL	93.9	Miami Beach, Fla.
WWWM	93.3	Sylvania, O.
WWWN	1550	Vienna, Ga.
WWWQ	1430	Panama City, Fla.
WWWR	920	Russellville, Ala.
WWWS	107.1	Saginaw, Mich.
WWWT	101.7	Owego, N.Y.
WWWV	97.5	Charlottesville, Va.
WWWW	106.7	Detroit, Mich.
WWWX	1010	Albemarle, N.C.
WWWY	104.9	Columbus, Ind.
WWWZ	93.5	Summerville, S.C.
WWXL	1450	Manchester, Ky.
WWXL-FM	103.1	Manchester, Ky.
WWYN	98.3	Carthage, Miss.
WWYO	970	Pineville, W.V.
WWYZ-FM	92.5	Waterbury, Conn.
WWZD	96.7	Buena Vista, Va.
WWZE	101.7	Central City, Pa.
WWZZ	1280	Sarasota, Fla.
WXAC	91.3	Reading, Pa.
WXAL	1400	Demopolis, Ala.
WXAM	1400	Charlottesville, Va.
WXAN	103.9	Ava, Ill.
WXBA	88.1	Brentwood, N.Y.
WXBM-FM	102.7	Milton, Fla.
WXBQ-FM	96.9	Bristol, Va.
WXBX	1090	Albertville, Ala.
WXCC	96.5	Williamson, W.V.
WXCE	1260	Amery, Wis.
WXCF	1230	Clifton Forge, Va.
WXCF-FM	103.9	Clifton Forge, Va.
WXCI	91.7	Danbury, Conn.
WXCL	1350	Peoria, Ill.
WXCM	1450	Jackson, Mich.
WXCO	1230	Wausau, Wis.
WXCO-FM	107.9	Wausau, Wis.
WXCR	92.1	Safety Harbor, Fla.
WXDR	91.3	Newark, Del.
WXDU	88.7	Durham, N.C.
WXEE	1340	Welch, W.V.
WXEW	840	Yabucoa, P.R.
WXEX-TV	8	Petersburg, Va.
WXFL	8	Tampa, Fla.
WXFM	105.9	Elmwood Park, Ill.
WXGA-TV	8	Waycross, Ga.
WXGC	88.9	Milledgeville, Ga.
WXGI	950	Richmond, Va.
WXGR	1190	Bay St. Louis, Miss.
WXGT	92.3	Columbus, O.
WXIA-TV	11	Atlanta, Ga.
WXIC	1380	Waverly, O.
WXID	94.7	Mayfield, Ky.
WXIE	92.1	Oakland, Md.
WXII	12	Winston Salem, N.C.
WXIK	96.1	Shelby, N.C.
WXIL	95.1	Parkersburg, W.V.
WXIR	98.3	Plainfield, Ind.
WXIS	103.9	Erwin, Tenn.
WXIT	1490	Charleston, W.V.
WXIX-TV	19	Newport, Ky.
WXIY	93.5	Bay Springs, Miss.
WXIZ	100.9	Waverly, O.
WXJC	63	Angola, Ind.
WXKE	103.9	Ft. Wayne, Ind.
WXKG	95.9	Livingston, Tenn.
WXKO	1150	Ft. Valley, Ga.
WXKQ	103.9	Whitesburg, Ky.
WXKS	1430	Medford, Mass.
WXKS-FM	107.9	Medford, Mass.
WXKW	104.1	Allentown, Pa.
WXKZ	96.7	Rochester, N.H.
WXKZ	93.9	Norwich, N.Y.
WXLC	102.3	Waukegan, Ill.
WXLE	94.3	Abbeville, Ala.
WXLI	1230	Dublin, Ga.
WXLK	92.3	Roanoke, Va.
WXLL	1310	Decatur, Ga.
WXLN	103.9	Louisville, Ky.
WXLP	96.9	Moline, Ill.
WXLQ	103.7	Berlin, N.H.
WXLR	103.1	State College, Pa.
WXLT-TV	40	Sarasota, Fla.
WXLV	90.3	Schencksville, Pa.
WXLW	950	Indianapolis, Ind.
WXMC	1310	Parsippany, N.J.
WXMG	103.9	South Bend, Ind.
WXMI	17	Grand Rapids, Mich.
WXNE	25	Boston, Mass.
WXOK	1460	Baton Rouge, La.
WXOL	1450	Cicero, Ill.
WXON	20	Detroit, Mich.
WXOR	1340	Florence, Ala.
WXOS	100.3	Plantation Key, Fla.
WXOW-TV	19	La Crosse, Wis.
WXPN	88.9	Philadelphia, Pa.
WXPQ	1520	Eatonton, Ga.
WXPR	91.7	Rhinelander, Wis.
WXPX	1300	West Hazleton, Pa.
WXQK	970	Spring City, Tenn.
WXQR	105.5	Jacksonville, N.C.
WXQT	1410	Grand Rapids, Mich.
WXRC	95.7	Hickory, N.C.
WXRD	105.5	Woodstock, Ill.
WXRF	1590	Guayama, P.R.
WXRI	105.3	Portsmouth, Va.
WXRL	1300	Lancaster, N.Y.
WXRO	95.3	Beaver Dam, Wis.
WXRQ	1460	Mt. Pleasant, Tenn.
WXRS	1590	Swainsboro, Ga.
WXRS-FM	103.9	Swainsboro, Ga.
WXRT	93.1	Chicago, Ill.
WXTA	1330	Rockford, Ill.
WXTC	96.9	Charleston, S.C.
WXTN	1000	Lexington, Miss.
WXTQ	105.5	Athens, O.
WXTQ-FM	101.7	Pittsfield, Mass.
WXTR-FM	104.1	La Plata, Md.
WXTU	92.5	Philadelphia, Pa.
WXTV	41	Paterson, N.J.
WXTX	54	Augusta, Ga.
WXTX	54	Columbus, Ga.
WXTY	103.9	Ticonderoga, N.Y.
WXTZ	103.3	Indianapolis, Ind.
WXUS	93.5	Lafayette, Ind.
WXUS	92.7	Lafayette, Ind.
WXVA	1550	Charles Town, W.V.
WXVA-FM	98.3	Charlestown, W.V.
WXVI	1600	Montgomery, Ala.
WXVL	99.3	Crossville, Tenn.
WXVQ	1490	De Land, Fla.
WXVT	15	Greenville, Miss.
WXVW	1450	Jeffersonville, Ind.
WXXA	23	Albany, N.Y.
WXXI	21	Rochester, N.Y.
WXXI-FM	91.5	Rochester, N.Y.
WXXQ	98.5	Freeport, Ill.
WXYC	89.3	Chapel Hill, N.C.
WXYQ	1010	Stevens Point, Wis.
WXYV	102.7	Baltimore, Md.
WXYX	100.7	Bayamon, P.R.
WXYY	106.1	Wilson, N.C.
WXYZ	1270	Detroit, Mich.
WXYZ-TV	7	Detroit, Mich.
WYAH-TV	27	Portsmouth, Va.
WYAJ	88.1	Sudbury, Mass.
WYAK	1270	Surfside Beach, S.C.
WYAK-FM	103.1	Surfside Beach, S.C.
WYAL	1280	Scotland Neck, N.C.
WYAN-FM	95.9	Upper Sandusky, O.
WYBC-FM	94.3	New Haven, Conn.
WYBG	1050	Massena, N.Y.
WYBR-FM	104.9	Belvedere, Ill.
WYCA	92.3	Hammond, Ind.
WYCB	1340	Washington, D. C.
WYCC	20	Chicago, Ill.
WYCE	88.1	Wyoming, Mich.
WYCM	1080	Murfreesboro, N.C.
WYCQ	102.9	Shelbyville, Tenn.
WYCR	98.5	Hanover, Pa.
WYCS	91.5	Yorktown, Va.
WYDD	104.7	Pittsburgh, Pa.
WYDE	850	Birmingham, Ala.
WYDK	1480	Yadkinville, N.C.
WYEA	1290	Sylacauga, Ala.
WYEN	106.7	Des Plaines, Ill.
WYEP-FM	91.3	Pittsburgh, Pa.
WYER	1360	Mt. Carmel, Ill.
WYER-FM	94.9	Mt. Carmel, Ill.
WYES-TV	12	New Orleans, La.
WYEZ	100.7	Elkhart, Ind.
WYFC	1520	Ypsilanti, Mich.
WYFE-FM	95.3	Winnebago, Ill.
WYFF-TV	4	Greenville, S.C.
WYFG	91.1	Gaffney, S.C.
WYFI	99.7	Norfolk, Va.
WYFJ	100.1	Ashland, Va.
WYFL	92.5	Henderson, N.C.
WYFM	102.9	Sharon, Pa.
WYGO	1330	Corbin, Ky.
WYGO-FM	99.3	Corbin, Ky.
WYGR	1530	Wyoming, Mich.
WYHY	107.3	Lebanon, Tenn.
WYII	95.9	Williamsport, Md.
WYIS	690	Phoenixville, Pa.
WYKC	1400	Grenada, Miss.
WYKK	98.3	Quitman, Miss.
WYKM	1250	Rupert, W.V.
WYKR	1490	Wells River, Vt.
WYKS	105.5	Gainesville, Fla.
WYKX	104.7	Escanaba, Mich.
WYLD	940	New Orleans, La.
WYLD-FM	98.5	New Orleans, La.
WYLF	95.1	South Bristol, N.Y.

WYLO	540	Jackson, Wis.
WYLQ	1410	Kingston, Tenn.
WYLR-FM	95.9	Glens Falls, N.Y.
WYLS	1350	York, Ala.
WYMB	1410	Manning, S.C.
WYMC	1430	Mayfield, Ky.
WYMJ-FM	103.9	Beaver Creek, O.
WYMS	88.9	Milwaukee, Wis.
WYMX	105.7	Augusta, Ga.
WYNC	1540	Yanceyville, N.C.
WYNE	1150	Kimberly, Wis.
WYNF	94.9	Tampa, Fla.
WYNG	105.3	Evansville, Ind.
WYNK	1380	Baton Rouge, La.
WYNK-FM	101.5	Baton Rouge, La.
WYNN	540	Florence, S.C.
WYNO	1120	Nelsonville, O.
WYNR	790	Brunswick, Ga.
WYNS	1150	Lehighton, Pa.
WYNU	92.3	Milan, Tenn.
WYNX	1550	Smyrna, Ga.
WYNY	97.1	New York, N.Y.
WYNZ-FM	100.9	Westbrook, Me.
WYOU	1550	Tampa, Fla.
WYPC	101.5	Gallipolis, O.
WYPR	970	Danville, Va.
WYRE	810	Annapolis, Md.
WYRK	106.5	Buffalo, N.Y.
WYRL	102.3	Melbourne, Fla.
WYRN	1480	Louisburg, N.C.
WYRQ	92.1	Little Falls, Minn.
WYRS	96.7	Stamford, Conn.
WYRU	1520	Red Springs, N.C.
WYSE	1560	Inverness, Fla.
WYSH	1380	Clinton, Tenn.
WYSL	1400	Buffalo, N.Y.
WYSO	91.3	Yellow Springs, O.
WYSP	94.1	Philadelphia, Pa.
WYSR	1250	Franklin, Va.
WYSR	102.7	Charleston, W.V.
WYST	1010	Baltimore, Md.
WYST-FM	92.3	Baltimore, Md.
WYSU	88.5	Youngstown, O.
WYTH	1250	Madison, Ga.
WYTI	1570	Rocky Mount, Va.
WYTL	1490	Oshkosh, Wis.
WYTM-FM	105.5	Fayetteville, Tenn.
WYTV	33	Youngstown, O.
WYTX	95.3	Washington, Pa.
WYUR-FM	95.9	Ripon, Wis.
WYUS	930	Milford, Del.
WYUT-FM	92.7	Herkimer, N.Y.
WYVE	1280	Wytheville, Va.
WYWY	950	Barbourville, Ky.
WYWY-FM	93.5	Barbourville, Ky.
WYXC	1270	Cartersville, Ga.
WYXI	1390	Athens, Tenn.
WYXX	96.1	Holland, Mich.
WYXY	1000	Cypress Gardens, Fla.
WYXZ	93.5	Allendale, S.C.
WYYD	96.1	Raleigh, N.C.
WYYN	96.3	Jackson, Miss.
WYYY	94.5	Syracuse, N.Y.
WYYZ	1490	Jasper, Ga.
WYZD	1560	Dobson, N.C.
WYZE	1480	Atlanta, Ga.
WYZZ	92.9	Wilkes Barre, Pa.
WZAK	93.1	Cleveland, O.
WZAL	1540	Mc Donough, Ga.
WZAM	1110	Norfolk, Va.
WZAP	690	Bristol, Va.
WZAR	101.9	Ponce, P.R.
WZAT	102.1	Savannah, Ga.
WZBC	90.3	Newton, Mass.
WZBO-FM	102.3	Edenton, N.C.
WZBR	1520	Amory, Miss.
WZBS	1490	Ponce, P.R.
WZBT	91.1	Gettysburg, Pa.
WZDQ	102.3	Humboldt, Tenn.
WZEE	104.1	Madison, Wis.
WZEL	1380	Young Harris, Ga.
WZEN	100.3	Alton, Ill.
WZEP	1460	De Funiak Springs, Fla.
WZEW	92.1	Fairhope, Ala.
WZEZ	92.9	Nashville, Tenn.
WZFM	98.3	Charles Town, W.V.
WZFM	107.1	Briarcliff Manor, N.Y.
WZGC	92.9	Atlanta, Ga.
WZID	95.7	Manchester, N.H.
WZIP	1590	South Daytona, Fla.
WZIR	98.5	Niagara Falls, N.Y.
WZKB	94.3	Wallace, N.C.
WZKX	107.1	Gulfport, Miss.
WZKY	1580	Albemarle, N.C.
WZKZ	106.1	Corning, N.Y.
WZLD	96.7	Cayce, S.C.
WZLE	104.9	Lorain, O.
WZLQ	98.5	Tupelo, Miss.
WZLT	99.3	Lexington, Tenn.
WZLY	91.5	Wellesley, Mass.
WZMB	91.3	Greenville, N.C.
WZND	99.3	Zeeland, Mich.
WZNE	97.9	Clearwater, Fla.
WZNT	93.7	San Juan, P.R.
WZOB	1250	Fort Payne, Ala.
WZOE	1490	Princeton, Ill.
WZOE-FM	98.3	Princeton, Ill.
WZOK	97.5	Rockford, Ill.
WZOL	92.1	Luquillo, P.R.
WZON	620	Bangor, Me.
WZOO	710	Ashboro, N.C.
WZOT	107.1	Rockmart, Ga.
WZOW	97.7	Goshen, Ind.
WZOZ	103.1	Oneonta, N.Y.
WZPL	99.5	Greenfield, Ind.
WZPR	100.3	Meadville, Pa.
WZRA	1450	Chattanooga, Tenn.
WZRD	88.3	Chicago, Ill.
WZRK	93.5	Hancock, Mich.
WZRO	98.3	Farmer City, Ill.
WZST	1410	Leesburg, Fla.
WZTA	105.5	Tamaqua, Pa.
WZTN	1000	Montgomery, Ala.
WZTQ	1080	Hurricane, W.V.
WZTV	17	Nashville, Tenn.
WZUE	102.3	Carlisle, Pa.
WZUU-FM	95.7	Milwaukee, Wis.
WZWZ	93.5	Kokomo, Ind.
WZWZ	92.7	Kokomo, Ind.
WZXI	101.9	Gastonia, N.C.
WZXM	900	Gaylord, Mich.
WZXQ	101.7	Canton, Miss.
WZXR	102.7	Memphis, Tenn.
WZXY	104.9	Kingsport, Tenn.
WZYC	103.3	New Port, N.C.
WZYP	104.3	Athens, Ala.
WZYQ	1370	Frederick, Md.
WZYQ-FM	103.9	Braddock Heights, Md.
WZYX	1440	Cowan, Tenn.
WZYZ	100.9	Fairmont, N.C.
WZZA	1410	Tuscumbia, Ala.
WZZB	104.9	Centreville, Miss.
WZZD	990	Philadelphia, Pa.
WZZE	88.1	Hockessin, Del.
WZZK	104.7	Birmingham, Ala.
WZZM-TV	13	Grand Rapids, Mich.
WZZO	95.1	Bethlehem, Pa.
WZZP	106.5	Cleveland, O.
WZZQ	107.5	Terre Haute, Ind.
WZZR-FM	95.7	Grand Rapids, Mich.
WZZW	103.1	Augusta, Ga.
WZZX	1540	Lineville, Ala.
WZZY	98.3	Winchester, Ind.
WZZZ	1310	West Point, Ga.
XEA	1370	Campeche, Cam.
XEAA	1340	Mexicali, B.C.
XEAB	1400	Santa Ana, Son.
XEABA	1300	Nueva Rosita, Coah.
XEABC	760	Los Reyes, Mich.
XEAC	1400	Aguascalientes, Ags.
XEACA	630	Acapulco, Gro.
XEACB	660	Delicias, Chih.
XEACC	1520	Camargo, Chih.
XEACC	870	Puerto Escondido, Oax.
XEACD	550	Acapulco, Gro.
XEACE	1470	Mazatlan, Sin.
XEACG	1600	Acapulco, Gro.
XEACH	1590	Monterrey, N.L.
XEACM	620	Villahermosa, Tab.
XEAD	910	Mexicali, B.C.
XEAD	1150	Guadalajara, Jal.
XEAE	1600	Ciudad Acuna, Coah.
XEAF	1580	Apaseo El Grande, Gto.
XEAG	1280	Cordoba, Ver.
XEAGA	1590	Aguascalientes, Ags.
XEAGN	910	San Francisco Del Rincon, Gto.
XEAGR	810	Acapulco, Gro.
XEAGV	1360	Ciudad Mendoza, Ver.
XEAH	1330	Juchitan, Oax.
XEAI	1440	Mexico City, D.F.
XEAJ	1080	Saltillo, Coah.
XEAK	1600	Acambaro, Gto.
XEAL	860	Manzanillo, Col.
XEAM	1310	Matamoros, Tams.
XEAMO	870	Irapuato, Gto.
XEAN	790	Ocotlan, Jal.
XEANA	1280	Caborca, Son.
XEAP	1290	Ciudad Obregon, Son.
XEAPM	1380	Apatzingan, Mich.
XEAQ	1490	Agua Prieta, Son.
XEAR	930	Tampico, Tams.
XEARO	1400	Nueva Rosita, Coah.
XEART	1590	Zacatepec, Mor.
XEAS	1410	Nuevo Laredo, Tams.
XEAT	1250	Parral, Chih.
XEATL	1520	Atlacomulco, Mex.
XEATP	1520	Tehuacan, Pue.
XEAU	1090	Monterrey, N.L.
XEAV	580	Guadalajara, Jal.
XEAVR	1540	Alvarado, Ver.
XEAW	1280	Monterrey, N.L.
XEAX	1270	Oaxaca, Oax.
XEAY	1470	Parras, Coah.
XEB	1220	Mexico City, D.F.
XEBA	820	Guadalajara, Jal.
XEBAL	1470	Becal, Cam.
XEBB	600	Acapulco, Gro.
XEBBB	1040	Zapopan, Jal.
XEBBB	1040	Zapopan, Zac.
XEBBC	1470	Tijuana, B.C.
XEBC	990	Ciudad Guzman, Jal.
XEBCC	1340	Carmen, Cam.
XEBD	1100	Perote, Ver.
XEBE	1160	Perote, Ver.
XEBF	1150	San Pedro, Coah.
XEBG	1550	Tijuana, B.C.
XEBH	920	Hermosillo, Son.
XEBI	790	Aguascalientes, Ags.
XEBJ	970	Ciudad Victoria, Tams.
XEBJB	570	Monterrey, N.L.
XEBK	1340	Nuevo Laredo, Tams.
XEBL	710	Culiacan, Sin.
XEBM	920	San Luis Potosi, S.L.P.
XEBN	1240	Delicias, Chih.
XEBO	1330	Irapuato, Gto.
XEBQ	1240	Guaymas, Son.

Call	Freq.	Location
XEBS	1410	Mexico City, D.F.
XEBU	620	Chihuahua, Chih.
XEBV	1100	Moroleon, Gto.
XEBW	1280	Chihuahua, Chih.
XEBX	610	Sabinas, Coah.
XEBY	1340	Tuxpan, Ver.
XEBZ	1590	Meoqui, Chih.
XEC	1310	Tijuana, B.C.
XECA	1430	Ixtepec, Oax.
XECAA	1020	Calvillo, Ags.
XECAL	1270	Tijuana, B.C.
XECAM	1280	Campeche, Cam.
XECAP	790	Zacapu, Mich.
XECAS	1090	Zacatecas, Zac.
XECAV	1470	Durango, Dgo.
XECB	1450	San Luis, Son.
XECC	960	Camargo, Chih.
XECCC	1440	Tonala, Jal.
XECD	1170	Puebla, Pue.
XECE	1240	Oaxaca, Oax.
XECF	1410	Los Mochis, Sin.
XECG	1240	Nogales, Son.
XECGP	1520	Morelia, Mich.
XECH	1490	Toluca, Mex.
XECHG	1130	Chilpancingo, Gro.
XECI	1340	Acapulco, Gro.
XECJ	970	Apatzingan, Mich.
XECJC	1490	Ciudad Juarez, Chih.
XECK	620	Durango, Dgo.
XECL	990	Mexicali, B.C.
XECM	1450	Ciudad Mante, Tams.
XECMQ	1320	Mexico City, D.F.
XECN	1080	Irapuato, Gto.
XECNO	760	Concepcion Oro, Zac.
XECO	1380	Mexico City, D.F.
XECOC	1430	Colima, Col.
XECP	1590	Valladolid, Yuc.
XECPQ	1460	Carillo Puerto, Q.R.
XECQ	920	Culiacan, Sin.
XECR	1340	Morelia, Mich.
XECS	960	Manzanillo, Col.
XECSI	1590	Culiacan, Sin.
XECT	1190	Monterrey, N.L.
XECU	1470	Los Mochis, Sin.
XECUC	840	Campeche, Cam.
XECUS	1020	Muacuspana, Tab.
XECV	610	Ciudad Valles, S.L.P.
XECW	1340	Los Mochis, Sin.
XECX	1040	Tala, Jal.
XECY	1320	Huejutla, Hgo.
XECZ	960	San Luis Potosi, S.L.P.
XED	1050	Mexicali, B.C.
XEDA	1290	Mexico City, D.F.
XEDB	860	Tonala, Chis.
XEDC	1080	Aguascalientes, Ags.
XEDCH	1540	Delicias, Chih.
XEDD	1560	Montemorelos, N.L.
XEDE	1400	Saltillo, Coah.
XEDF	970	Mexico City, D.F.
XEDG	1300	Tuxtla, Chis.
XEDG	1490	Chihuahua, Chih.
XEDGO	760	Durango, Dgo.
XEDH	1340	Ciudad Acuna, Coah.
XEDI	1360	Chihuahua, Chih.
XEDJ	1450	Magdalena, Son.
XEDK	1250	Guadalajara, Jal.
XEDKR	700	Guadalajara, Jal.
XEDKT	1340	Guadalajara, Jal.
XEDL	1250	Hermosillo, Son.
XEDM	1580	Hermosillo, Son.
XEDN	600	Torreon, Coah.
XEDO	1190	Jojutila, Mor.
XEDP	710	Cuahutemoc, Chih.
XEDP	920	Villa Frontera, Coah.
XEDQ	1360	San Andres Tuxtla, Ver.
XEDR	1490	Guaymas, Son.
XEDRD	1540	Durango, Dgo.
XEDS	1470	Colima, Col.
XEDT	1080	Cuahutemoc, Chih.
XEDU	860	Durango, Dgo.
XEDV	1550	El Oro, Mex.
XEDX	1010	Ensenada, B.C.
XEDY	1080	Ciudad Morelos, B.C.S.
XEDZ	580	Cordoba, Ver.
XEE	590	Durango, Dgo.
XEEA	1130	Cuahutemoc, Chih.
XEEB	1010	Esperanza, Son.
XEEC	1440	Tlapacoyan, Ver.
XEED	1490	Ameca, Jal.
XEEF	1050	Compostela, Nay.
XEEG	1280	Panzacola, Tlax.
XEEH	1520	San Luis, Son.
XEEI	1070	San Luis Potosi, S.L.P.
XEEJ	740	Puerto Vallarta, Jal.
XEEL	610	Fresnillo, Zac.
XEEM	880	Rio Verde, S.L.P.
XEEMM	1210	Salamanca, Gto.
XEEN	1540	Chetumal, Q.R.
XEEP	1500	Ensenada, B.C.
XEEP	1450	Gomez Palacio, Dgo.
XEEP	1060	Mexico City, D.F.
XEEQ	760	San Luis Potosi, S.L.P.
XEER	990	Cuahutemoc, Chih.
XEES	1110	Chihuahua, Chih.
XEESC	820	Escarcega, Cam.
XEEU	1170	Papantla, Ver.
XEEV	1330	Izucar De Matamoros, Pue.
XEEW	1420	Matamoros, Tams.
XEEX	1400	Culiacan, Sin.
XEEY	1260	Jalapa, Zac.
XEEZ	970	Caborca, Son.
XEF	1420	Ciudad Juarez, Chih.
XEFA	950	Chihuahua, Chih.
XEFAC	920	Salvatierra, Gto.
XEFAJ	1560	Mexico City, D.F.
XEFB	630	Monterrey, N.L.
XEFB-TV	3	Monterrey, N.L.
XEFBF	1360	Martinez De La Torre, Ver.
XEFC	1330	Merida, Yuc.
XEFCD	1440	Camargo, Chih.
XEFD	590	Rio Bravo, Tams.
XEFE	790	Nuevo Laredo, Tams.
XEFE-TV	2	Nuevo Laredo, Tams.
XEFF	1490	Matehuala, S.L.P.
XEFG	840	Celaya, Gto.
XEFH	1310	Agua Prieta, Son.
XEFI	580	Chihuahua, Chih.
XEFL	1500	Guanajuato, Gto.
XEFM	1010	Veracruz, Ver.
XEFN	1130	Uruapan, Mich.
XEFO	680	Chihuahua, Chih.
XEFP	1290	Jalapa, Zac.
XEFQ	980	Cananea, Son.
XEFR	1180	Mexico City, D.F.
XEFS	1400	Izucar De Matamoros, Pue.
XEFU	630	Cosamaloapan, Ver.
XEFV	1000	Ciudad Juarez, Chih.
XEFW	810	Tampico, Tams.
XEFX	630	Guaymas, Son.
XEFY	950	Cortazar, Gto.
XEFZ	740	Monterrey, N.L.
XEG	1050	Monterrey, N.L.
XEGA	1300	San Andres Tuxtla, Ver.
XEGAJ	1520	Guadalajara, Jal.
XEGB	960	Coatzacoalcos, Ver.
XEGC	1450	Sahuayo, Mich.
XEGD	1400	Parral, Chih.
XEGEM	1600	Toluca, Mex.
XEGF	1420	Gutierrez Zomora, Ver.
XEGG	1490	Ciudad Mante, Tams.
XEGH	620	Rio Bravo, Tams.
XEGI	1160	Tamazunchale, S.L.P.
XEGJ	1190	Arriaga, Chis.
XEGK	770	Tamazunchale, S.L.P.
XEGL	1270	Navojoa, Son.
XEGM	950	Tijuana, B.C.
XEGN	1500	Piedras Negras, Ver.
XEGNK	1370	Nuevo Laredo, Tams.
XEGO	1530	Los Reyes, Mich.
XEGP	1540	Poza Rica, Ver.
XEGR	1040	Coatepec, Ver.
XEGS	610	Guasave, Sin.
XEGT	1490	Zamora, Mich.
XEGTO	600	Arperos, Gto.
XEGU	1450	El Fuerte, Sin.
XEGUZ	550	Ciudad Guzman, Jal.
XEGV	1120	Villa Del Pueblito, Qro.
XEGW	1380	Ciudad Victoria, Tams.
XEGX	1480	San Luis De La Paz, Gto.
XEGY	1070	Tehuacan, Pue.
XEGYS	1560	Guaymas, Son.
XEGZ	790	Gomez Palacio, Dgo.
XEH	1420	Monterrey, N.L.
XEHA	560	Tecate, B.C.
XEHA	1560	Progreso, Yuc.
XEHB	770	San Francisco, Del Oro, Chih.
XEHC	1590	Ensenada, B.C.S.
XEHC	920	Ensenada, B.C.
XEHD	1270	Durango, Dgo.
XEHE	1450	Rio Grande, Zac.
XEHF	1370	Nogales, Son.
XEHG	1370	Mexicali, B.C.
XEHI	1470	Ciudad Miguel Aleman, Tams.
XEHIT	1310	Puebla, Pue.
XEHJ	1310	Petalan, Gro.
XEHK	960	Guadalajara, Jal.
XEHL	1010	Guadalajara, Jal.
XEHL-TV	6	Guadalajara, Jal.
XEHM	1470	Delicias, Chih.
XEHN	1130	Nogales, Son.
XEHO	910	Ciudad Obregon, Son.
XEHOS	1540	Hermosillo, Son.
XEHP	580	Ciudad Victoria, Tams.
XEHQ	590	Hermosillo, Son.
XEHR	1090	Puebla, Pue.
XEHS	1280	Los Mochis, Sin.
XEHT	810	Huamantla, Tlax.
XEHU	1300	Martinez De La Torre, Ver.
XEHV	1310	Veracruz, Ver.
XEHW	1440	Rosario, Sin.
XEHY	1310	Villa De La Corregidora, Qro.
XEHZ	990	La Paz, B.C.S.
XEI	1400	Morelia, Mich.
XEIA	1430	Allende, Coah.
XEIB	1490	Todas Santos, B.C.S.
XEIB	1170	Caborca, Son.
XEIC	1540	Cuernavaca, Mor.
XEID	1230	Alamo, Ver.
XEIE	1450	Matehuala, S.L.P.

XEIG	1430	Iguala, Gro.
XEIH	930	Fresnillo, Zac.
XEIK	1360	Piedras Negras, Coah.
XEIM	810	Saltillo, Coah.
XEIN	810	Cintalapa, Chis.
XEIO	840	Tuxtla, Chis.
XEIP	1480	Uruapan, Mich.
XEIPN-TV	11	Mexico City, D.F.
XEIQ	960	Ciudad Obregon, Son.
XEIR	1410	Ciudad Valles, S.L.P.
XEIRG	1590	Irapuato, Gto.
XEIS	670	Ciudad Guzman, Jal.
XEIT	1070	Carmen, Cam.
XEITC	1200	Celaya, Gto.
XEIU	990	Oaxaca, Oax.
XEIV	1190	Oaxaca, Oax.
XEIW	1160	Uruapan, Mich.
XEIX	1290	Jiquilpan, Mich.
XEIY	1290	Rio Verde, S.L.P.
XEIZ	1240	Monterrey, N.L.
XEJ	970	Ciudad Juarez, Chih.
XEJ-TV	5	Ciudad Juarez, Chih.
XEJA	610	Jalapa, Ver.
XEJAC	1110	Cardenas, Tab.
XEJAQ	1040	Jalpan, Qro.
XEJB	630	Guadalajara, Jal.
XEJC	1340	Cuernavaca, Mor.
XEJCP	1600	Tehuacan, Pue.
XEJD	1450	Poza Rica, Ver.
XEJE	1370	Dolores Hidalgo, Gto.
XEJF	1350	Tierra Blanca, Ver.
XEJH	1460	Jalapa, Ver.
XEJI	1390	Tehuantepec, Oax.
XEJK	1340	Delicias, Chih.
XEJL	1300	Guamuchil, Sin.
XEJM	1450	Monterrey, N.L.
XEJP	1150	Mexico City, D.F.
XEJPM	1510	Cardel, Ver.
XEJPV	1560	Zaragoza, Chih.
XEJQ	1500	Parras, Coah.
XEJR	1490	Parral, Chih.
XEJS	1150	Parral, Chih.
XEJTF	1450	Zacoalco, Jal.
XEJV	1420	Jaltipan, Ver.
XEJX	1250	Queretaro, Qro.
XEJY	1350	El Grullo, Jal.
XEJZ	1320	Jimenez, Chih.
XEK	960	Nuevo Laredo, Tams.
XEKA	1420	San Jose Del Cabo, B.C.S.
XEKB	1410	Encarnacion, Jal.
XEKB	1410	Atemajac, Jal.
XEKC	1460	Oaxaca, Oax.
XEKD	1010	Ciudad Acuna, Coah.
XEKE	980	Navojoa, Son.
XEKF	1360	Iguala, Gro.
XEKG	820	Fortin De Las Flores, Ver.
XEKH	1020	Queretaro, Qro.
XEKI	1510	Navojoa, Son.
XEKJ	1400	Acapulco, Gro.
XEKL	550	Jalapa, Ver.
XEKM	1450	Minatitlan, Ver.
XEKN	1490	Huetamo, Mich.
XEKOK	750	Las Cruces, Gro.
XEKQ	680	Tapachula, Chis.
XEKS	960	Saltillo, Coah.
XEKT	1380	Tecate, B.C.
XEKU	710	Acapulco, Gro.
XEKV	740	Villahermosa, Tab.
XEKW	1300	Morelia, Mich.
XEKX	620	Carillo Puerto, Q.R.
XEKY	1280	Huixtla, Chis.
XEKZ	610	Tehuantepec, Oax.
XEL	1260	Mexico City, D.F.
XELA	830	Mexico City, D.F.
XELAC	1560	Lazaro Cardenas, Mich.
XELB	1090	La Barca, Jal.
XELBL	1350	San Luis, Son.
XELC	980	La Piedad, Mich.
XELCM	930	Lazaro Cardenas, Mich.
XELD	780	Autlan, Jal.
XELE	1300	Tampico, Tams.
XELE	1400	Linares, N.L.
XELEO	1110	Leon, Gto.
XELG	680	Leon, Gto.
XELH	1400	Acaponeta, Nay.
XELI	1580	Chilpancingo, Gro.
XELIA	1140	Morelia, Mich.
XELJ	1030	Lagos, Jal.
XELK	830	Zacatecas, Zac.
XELL	1430	Veracruz, Ver.
XELM	1240	Tuxtla, Chis.
XELMS	1000	Los Mochis, Sin.
XELN	790	Linares, N.L.
XELN-TV	4	Torreon, Coah.
XELO	1010	Chihuahua, Chih.
XELP	1170	La Piedad, Mich.
XELPZ	1310	La Paz, B.C.S.
XELQ	570	Morelia, Mich.
XELS	1360	Armeria, Col.
XELT	920	Guadalajara, Jal.
XELTZ	740	El Puertecito, Ags.
XELTZ	740	Loreto, Zac.
XELU	1340	Cuidad Serdan, Pue.
XELV	680	Hermosillo, Son.
XELW	1510	Ciudad Guzman, Jal.
XELY	870	Morelia, Mich.
XELZ	1600	Torreon, Coah.
XEM	850	Chihuahua, Chih.
XEMA	690	Fresnillo, Zac.
XEMAB	950	Carmen, Cam.
XEMAC	1330	Manzanillo, Col.
XEMAS	1560	Salamanca, Gto.
XEMAU	890	Miguel Auza, Zac.
XEMBA	750	Tacambaro, Mich.
XEMBC	1190	Mexicali, B.C.
XEMC	1480	Salvatierra, Gto.
XEMCA	1480	Ciudad Morelos, B.C.S.
XEMCA	1090	Panuco, Ver.
XEMCH	830	Cheran, Mich.
XEMDA	1170	Monclova, Coah.
XEME	1490	Valladolid, Yuc.
XEMF	1260	Monclova, Coah.
XEMG	1250	Arriaga, Chis.
XEMH	970	Merida, Yuc.
XEMI	1070	Minatitlan, Ver.
XEMIA	850	Tlaquepaque, Jal.
XEMJ	920	Piedras Negras, Coah.
XEMK	930	Huixtla, Chis.
XEML	770	Apatzingan, Mich.
XEMM	960	Morelia, Mich.
XEMMM	800	Tijuana, B.C.
XEMMS	1000	Mazatlan, Sin.
XEMN	600	Monterrey, N.L.
XEMO	860	Tijuana, B.C.
XEMON	1370	Monterrey, N.L.
XEMOS	1130	Los Mochis, Sin.
XEMP	710	Mexico City, D.F.
XEMQ	1240	Merida, Yuc.
XEMR	1140	Monterrey, N.L.
XEMS	1490	Matamoros, Tams.
XEMST	910	Mascota, Jal.
XEMT	1340	Matamoros, Tams.
XEMTJ	1430	Mascota, Jal.
XEMTS	1590	Ciudad Madero, Tams.
XEMTV	1260	Minatitlan, Ver.
XEMU	580	Piedras Negras, Coah.
XEMV	770	Los Mochis, Sin.
XEMV	1000	Matamoros, Tams.
XEMW	1260	San Luis, Son.
XEMY	1000	Merida, Yuc.
XEMY	840	Ciudad Mante, Tams.
XEN	690	Mexico City, D.F.
XENA	1450	Queretaro, Qro.
XENAS	1400	Navojoa, Son.
XENAY	1470	Ahuacatlan, Nay.
XENAZ	1600	Nacozari, Son.
XENB	660	Muacuspana, Tab.
XENC	1540	Celaya, Gto.
XENF	680	Tepic, Nay.
XENG	1240	Huauchinango, Pue.
XENH	870	Mazatlan, Sin.
XENI	1320	Nueva Italia, Mich.
XENK	620	Mexico City, D.F.
XENL	860	Monterrey, N.L.
XENLT	1000	Nuevo Laredo, Tams.
XENM	1320	Aguascalientes, Ags.
XENP	1430	Ocotlan, Jal.
XENQ	1580	Tulancingo, Hgo.
XENR	980	Nueva Rosita, Coah.
XENS	1480	Navojoa, Son.
XENT	790	La Paz, B.C.S.
XENU	1550	Nuevo Laredo, Tams.
XENV	1340	Monterrey, N.L.
XENW	860	Culiacan, Sin.
XENX	1290	Mazatlan, Sin.
XENY	1270	Nogales, Son.
XENZ	570	Culiacan, Sin.
XEO	970	Matamoros, Tams.
XEOA	570	Oaxaca, Oax.
XEOB	1080	Pichucalco, Chis.
XEOBS	1370	Ciudad Obregon, Son.
XEOC	560	Mexico City, D.F.
XEOCE	570	Ojo Caliente, Zac.
XEOD	1090	Boca Del Rio, Ver.
XEOE	810	Tapachula, Chis.
XEOF	1510	Cortazar, Gto.
XEOG	1260	Ojinaga, Chih.
XEOH	1270	Camargo, Chih.
XEOJ	1400	Lazaro Cardenas, Mich.
XEOK	920	Monterrey, N.L.
XEOL	990	Tezultlan, Pue.
XEOLA	1460	Altamira, Tams.
XEOM	1340	Coatzacoalcos, Ver.
XEON	710	Tuxtla, Chis.
XEOO	620	Tepic, Nay.
XEOQ	1110	Rio Bravo, Tams.
XEOR	1390	Reynosa, Tams.
XEORF	950	El Fuerte, Sin.
XEORO	680	Guasave, Sin.
XEOS	1340	Ciudad Obregon, Son.
XEOT	980	San Pedro, Coah.
XEOU	1480	Huajuapan De Leon, Oax.
XEOV	1240	Orizaba, Ver.
XEOX	1430	Ciudad Obregon, Son.
XEOY	1000	Mexico City, D.F.
XEOZ	960	Jalapa, Ver.
XEP	1300	Ciudad Juarez, Chih.
XEPA	1370	Puebla, Pue.
XEPAB	1380	La Paz, B.C.S.
XEPAC	600	Palenque, Chis.
XEPAT	1050	Patzcuaro, Mich.
XEPAV	1540	Panuco, Ver.
XEPB	1400	Hermosillo, Son.
XEPC	1240	Zacatecas, Zac.

XEPD 1460 Nueva Rosita, Coah.
XEPE 1450 Empalme, Son.
XEPE 1600 Nogales, Son.
XEPF 1400 Ensenada, B.C.
XEPG 1400 Veracruz, Ver.
XEPH 590 Mexico City, D.F.
XEPI 1250 Tixtla, Gro.
XEPJ 1370 Tlaquepaque, Jal.
XEPK 1190 Pachuca, Hgo.
XEPL 550 Cuahutemoc, Chih.
XEPLA 860 Pebellon, Ags.
XEPM-TV 2 Ciudad Juarez, Chih.
XEPN 3 Piedras Negras, Coah.
XEPNA 1590 Tepic, Nay.
XEPNK 880 Los Mochis, Sin.
XEPO 1310 San Luis Potosi, S.L.P.
XEPOP 1490 Puebla, Pue.
XEPP 1450 Orizaba, Ver.
XEPQ 710 Muzquiz, Coah.
XEPR 1480 Poza Rica, Ver.
XEPRS 1090 Rosarito, B.C.
XEPRT 1270 Ciudad Madero, Tams.
XEPS 710 Empalme, Son.
XEPT 1590 Misantla, Ver.
XEPU 1110 Monclova, Coah.
XEPV 1270 Papantla, Ver.
XEPVJ 1110 Puerto Vallarta, Jal.
XEPW 1200 Poza Rica, Ver.
XEPX 1340 Puerto Angel, Oax.
XEPY 1450 Merida, Yuc.
XEPZ 1190 Ciudad Juarez, Chih.
XEQ 940 Mexico City, D.F.
XEQ-TV 9 Mexico City, D.F.
XEQA 1600 Autlan, Jal.
XEQAA 560 Chetumal, Q.R.
XEQB 1340 Tulancingo, Hgo.
XEQC 1390 Puerto Penasco, Son.
XEQD 920 Chihuahua, Chih.
XEQE 1340 Escuinapa, Sin.
XEQF 750 Loma Bonita, Oax.
XEQG 980 Queretaro, Qro.
XEQH 1270 Ixmiquilpan, Hgo.
XEQI 1510 Monterrey, N.L.
XEQJ 1400 Tamazula, Jal.
XEQK 1350 Mexico City, D.F.
XEQL 1580 Zamora, Mich.
XEQN 1310 Torreon, Coah.
XEQO 980 Cosamaloapan, Ver.
XEQP 1280 Guadalajara, Jal.
XEQQQ 880 Teapa, Tab.
XEQR 1030 Mexico City, D.F.
XEQS 980 Fresnillo, Zac.
XEQT 1600 Veracruz, Ver.
XEQU 1450 Ojinaga, Chih.
XEQW 550 Merida, Yuc.
XEQX 970 Monclova, Coah.
XEQY 1360 Toluca, Mex.
XEQZ 1560 Cuahutemoc, Chih.
XEQZ 720 Lagos, Jal.
XER 1260 Linares, N.L.
XERA 760 San Cristobal, Chis.
XERAA 1240 Atoyac, Gro.
XERAC 1430 Campeche, Cam.
XERAL 1560 Arandas, Jal.
XERB 1510 Cozumel, Gro.
XERB 1170 Cozumel, Qro.
XERB 1170 Cozumel, Q.R.
XERC 790 Mexico City, D.F.
XERCH 1340 Ojinaga, Chih.
XERCM 1410 Ciudad Victoria, Tams.
XERCP 1600 Purepero, Mich.
XERD 1420 Pachuca, Hgo.
XERE 1290 Salvatierra, Gto.
XERED 1110 Mexico City, D.F.
XEREL 1550 Morelia, Mich.
XEREY 1240 San Blas, Sin.
XERF 1570 Ciudad Acuna, Coah.
XERG 690 Monterrey, N.L.
XERH 1500 Mexico City, D.F.
XERI 810 Reynosa, Tams.
XERIO 1560 Ixtlan, Nay.
XERJ 600 Mazatlan, Sin.
XERK 710 Tepic, Nay.
XERKS 940 Reynosa, Tams.
XERL 710 Colima, Col.
XERLA 930 Santa Rosalia, B.C.S.
XERLK 1340 Atlacomulco, Mex.
XERM 1150 Mexicali, B.C.
XERN 950 Montemorelos, N.L.
XERO 1490 Aguascalientes, Ags.
XEROK 800 Ciudad Juarez, Chih.
XEROO 960 Chetumal, Q.R.
XERP 1330 Ciudad Madero, Tams.
XERPA 1240 Morelia, Mich.
XERPC 790 Chihuahua, Chih.
XERPL 1270 Leon, Gto.
XERPM 660 Mexico City, D.F.
XERPO 710 Oaxaca, Oax.
XERPU 1370 Durango, Dgo.
XERPV 1340 Ciudad Victoria, Tams.
XERRF 1150 Merida, Yuc.
XERS 1380 Gomez Palacio, Dgo.
XERSV 810 Ciudad Obregon, Son.
XERT 1170 Reynosa, Tams.
XERTF 1600 San Martin, Pue.
XERTM 1150 Muacuspana, Tab.
XERU 1310 Chihuahua, Chih.
XERUV 1550 Jalapa, Ver.
XERUY 1390 Merida, Yuc.
XERV 9 Reynosa, Tams.
XERW 1390 Leon, Gto.
XERY 1450 Acapulco, Gro.
XERZ 1240 Leon, Gto.
XES 1240 Tampico, Tams.
XESA 1260 Culiacan, Sin.
XESAC 1580 Saltillo, Coah.
XESAG 1040 Salamanca, Gto.
XESB 820 Santa Barbara, Chih.
XESC 1250 Sabinas, Coah.
XESCT 1230 Ensenada, B.C.
XESD 1530 Silao, Gto.
XESE 1560 Champoton, Cam.
XESF 1320 Montemorelos, N.L.
XESH 1400 Sabinas Hidalgo, N.L.
XESHT 1430 Saltillo, Coah.
XESI 1240 Santiago Ixcuintla, Nay.
XESJ 1250 Saltillo, Coah.
XESK 1490 Ruiz, Nay.
XESL 1340 San Luis Potosi, S.L.P.
XESM 1470 Mexico City, D.F.
XESMR 1380 San Luis Potosi, S.L.P.
XESN 1250 Caborca, Son.
XESO 1150 Ciudad Obregon, Son.
XESOL 1190 Ciudad Hidalgo, Mich.
XESOM 720 Sombrerete, Zac.
XESON 1110 Navojoa, Son.
XESP 1070 Tlaquepaque, Jal.
XESQ 1280 San Miguel Allende, Gto.
XESR 1320 Santa Rosalia, B.C.S.
XESS 1450 Ensenada, B.C.
XEST 1580 Mazatlan, Sin.
XESTN 1540 Santa Catarina, N.L.
XESU 790 Mexicali, B.C.
XESV 1370 Morelia, Mich.
XESW 1300 Ciudad Madero, Chih.
XESX 1390 Tuxtla, Chis.
XESY 1320 Magdalena, Son.
XESZ 1520 Cholula, Pue.
XET 990 Monterrey, N.L.
XET-FM 94.1 Monterrey, N.L.
XET-TV 6 Monterrey, N.L.
XETA 600 Zitacuaro, Mich.
XETAA 920 Torreon, Coah.
XETAB 1410 Villahermosa, Tab.
XETAC 1000 Tapachula, Chis.
XETAK 1100 Tapachula, Chis.
XETAM 1550 Ciudad Victoria, Tams.
XETAP 890 Tapachula, Chis.
XETB 1350 Torreon, Coah.
XETBV 1580 Tierra Blanca, Ver.
XETC 1240 Torreon, Coah.
XETD 1450 Tecuala, Nay.
XETE 1140 Tehuacan, Pue.
XETEP 1450 Pinotepa, Oax.
XETEY 840 Tepic, Nay.
XETF 1250 Veracruz, Ver.
XETG 990 Tuxtla, Chis.
XETGO 1350 Tlaltenango, Zac.
XETH 1290 Palizada, Cam.
XETIA 1310 Guadalajara, Jal.
XETJ 570 Torreon, Coah.
XETK 630 Mazatlan, Sin.
XETKR 1480 Villa De Guadalupe, N.L.
XETL 1390 Tuxpan, Ver.
XETM 1350 Nacozari, Son.
XETN 700 Moroleon, Gto.
XETNC 550 Tepic, Nay.
XETNT 650 Los Mochis, Sin.
XETO 1400 Tampico, Tams.
XETOR 670 Matamoros, Coah.
XETOT 1190 Tampico, Tams.
XETP 1380 Nadlingo, Ver.
XETQ 850 Orizaba, Ver.
XETR 1120 Ciudad Valles, S.L.P.
XETRA 690 Tijuana, B.C.
XETRA-FM 91.1 Tijuana, B.C.
XETRN 690 Progreso, Yuc.
XETS 630 Tapachula, Chis.
XETT 1430 Tlaxcala, Tlax.
XETU 980 Tampico, Tams.
XETUN 1430 Rio Verde, S.L.P.
XETV 6 Tijuana, B.C.
XETVH 1230 Villahermosa, Tab.
XETVR 1150 Tuxpan, Ver.
XETW 860 Tampico, Tams.
XETX 1010 Nuevo Casas Grandes, Chih.
XETY 1390 Tecoman, Col.
XETZ 880 Zapopan, Jal.
XETZI 550 Apatzingan, Mich.
XEU 930 Veracruz, Ver.
XEUA 830 Zacatecas, Zac.
XEUAA 1370 Aguascalientes, Ags.
XEUAS 1150 Culiacan, Sin.
XEUBJ 1400 Oaxaca, Oax.
XEUC 550 Tehuantepec, Oax.
XEUD 1360 Tuxtla, Chis.
XEUE 580 Tuxtla, Chis.
XEUF 610 Uruapan, Mich.
XEUG 970 Guanajuato, Gto.
XEUH 1320 Tuxtepec, Oax.
XEUI 1320 Comitan, Chis.
XEUJ 1460 Carmen, Cam.
XEUK 1470 Caborca, Son.
XEUL 1360 Progreso, Yuc.

XEUM	990	Valladolid, Yuc.
XEUN	860	Mexico City, D.F.
XEUNO	1120	Guadalajara, Jal.
XEUO	1250	Chetumal, Q.R.
XEUP	1310	Tizimin, Yuc.
XEUQ	960	Zihuatenejo, Gro.
XEUR	1530	Mexico City, D.F.
XEURM	1440	Uruapan, Mich.
XEUS	850	Hermosillo, Son.
XEUU	910	Colima, Col.
XEUV	1500	Villahermosa, Tab.
XEUVA	1170	Aguascalientes, Ags.
XEUX	810	Tuxpan, Nay.
XEUY	1580	Las Choapas, Ver.
XEUZ	1330	Martinez De La Torre, Ver.
XEV	1390	Chihuahua, Chih.
XEVA	790	Villahermosa, Tab.
XEVAB	1580	Valle De Bravo, Mex.
XEVAL	1360	Ciudad Valles, S.L.P.
XEVB	1310	Monterrey, N.L.
XEVC	700	Cordoba, Ver.
XEVD	1380	Allende, Coah.
XEVE	1040	Colima, Col.
XEVF	1540	Villa Flores, Chis.
XEVG	650	Merida, Yuc.
XEVH	1450	Valle Hermosa, Tams.
XEVI	1400	San Juan Del Rio, Qro.
XEVJP	570	Villa Juarez, Qro.
XEVK	1010	Torreon, Coah.
XEVM	1240	Piedras Negras, Coah.
XEVMA	1430	Acapulco, Gro.
XEVN	1190	Nogales, Son.
XEVO	1520	San Rafael, Ver.
XEVOX	970	Mazatlan, Sin.
XEVOZ	1590	Mexico City, D.F.
XEVP	1030	Acapulco, Gro.
XEVP	1490	Guasave, Sin.
XEVQ	830	Navolato, Sin.
XEVR	1030	Ixtlan, Nay.
XEVS	1110	Villa De Seris, Son.
XEVSD	1440	Villa Constitucion, B.C.S.
XEVSS	1340	Villa De Seris, Son.
XEVT	970	Villahermosa, Tab.
XEVU	1350	Mazatlan, Sin.
XEVUC	1520	Villa Union, Coah.
XEVV	920	Chiapa De Corzo, Chis.
XEVW	1160	Acambaro, Gto.
XEVX	570	Comalcalco, Tab.
XEVZ	1490	Acayucan, Ver.
XEW	900	Mexico City, D.F.
XEW-TV	2	Mexico City, D.F.
XEW-1	900	Mazatlan, Sin.
XEW-2	900	Queretaro, Qro.
XEWA	540	San Luis Potosi, S.L.P.
XEWA-1	540	Monterrey, N.L.
XEWB	900	Veracruz, Ver.
XEWD	1430	Ciudad Miguel Aleman, Tams.
XEWE	1420	Irapuato, Gto.
XEWF	1420	Cuernavaca, Mor.
XEWG	1240	Ciudad Juarez, Chih.
XEWH-TV	6	Hermosillo, Son.
XEWJ	1420	Tehuacan, Pue.
XEWK	1190	Guadalajara, Jal.
XEWL	1090	Nuevo Laredo, Tams.
XEWM	640	San Cristobal, Chis.
XEWN	1270	Gomez Palacio, Dgo.
XEWO	1020	Chetumal, Q.R.
XEWO-TV	2	Guadalajara, Jal.
XEWP	1420	Sayula, Jal.
XEWQ	1330	Monclova, Coah.
XEWR	1110	Ciudad Juarez, Chih.
XEWS	1010	Culiacan, Sin.
XEWT	1200	Culiacan, Sin.
XEWT-TV	12	Tijuana, B.C.
XEWU	1400	Matehuala, S.L.P.
XEWV	940	Mexicali, B.C.
XEWX	660	Durango, Dgo.
XEX	730	Mexico City, D.F.
XEX-TV	7	Mexico City, D.F.
XEX-1	710	Leon, Gto.
XEXC	1480	Taxco, Gro.
XEXD	1450	Atlixco, Pue.
XEXE	1490	Queretaro, Qro.
XEXF	1140	Leon, Gto.
XEXH	1390	Mixquiahuala, Hgo.
XEXI	1400	Ixtapan De La Sal, Mex.
XEXK	1080	Poza Rica, Ver.
XEXL	1020	Patzcuaro, Mich.
XEXM	1360	Jerez, Zac.
XEXN	1010	Ures, Son.
XEXO	1390	Ciudad Mante, Tams.
XEXP	1150	Tuxtepec, Oax.
XEXQ	1460	San Luis Potosi, S.L.P.
XEXR	1260	Ciudad Valles, S.L.P.
XEXT	980	Tepic, Nay.
XEXU	1480	Villa Frontera, Coah.
XEXV	1300	San Francisco Del Rincon, Gto.
XEXW	1300	Nogales, Son.
XEXX	1420	Tijuana, B.C.
XEXY	780	Ciudad Altimirano, Gro.
XEXZ	1150	Zacatecas, Zac.
XEY	1360	Celaya, Gto.
XEYA	1470	Irapuato, Gto.
XEYAA	740	Peto, Yuc.
XEYB	1380	Cosamaloapan, Ver.
XEYC	1460	Ciudad Juarez, Chih.
XEYD	1410	Francisco I. Madero, Coah.
XEYG	660	Matias Romero, Oax.
XEYH	1170	Hermosillo, Son.
XEYI	580	Cancun, Q.R.
XEYJ	950	Nueva Rosita, Coah.
XEYK	1540	Motul, Yuc.
XEYL	1170	Iguala, Gro.
XEYM	810	Morelia, Mich.
XEYO	560	Huatabampo, Son.
XEYP	1520	El Limon, Tams.
XEYQ	1500	Fresnillo, Zac.
XEYS	1350	Yajalon, Chis.
XEYT	1490	Teocelo, Ver.
XEYV	1180	Huatusco, Ver.
XEYW	1270	Uman, Yuc.
XEYX	1590	Mexicali, B.C.
XEYZ	1450	Aguascalientes, Ags.
XEZ	600	Merida, Yuc.
XEZ-TV	3	Guanajuato, Gto.
XEZA	740	Topolobampo, Son.
XEZAZ	1120	Zacatecas, Zac.
XEZB	950	Oaxaca, Oax.
XEZC	810	Rio Grande, Zac.
XEZD	1350	Camargo, Tams.
XEZE	1340	Santiago Ixcuintla, Nay.
XEZF	850	Mexicali, B.C.
XEZG	1510	Ixmiquilpan, Hgo.
XEZH	1260	Salamanca, Gto.
XEZI	1200	Zacapu, Mich.
XEZJ	1480	Zapopan, Jal.
XEZK	1600	Tepatitlan, Jal.
XEZL	1130	Jalapa, Ver.
XEZM	650	Zamora, Mich.
XEZN	780	Celaya, Gto.
XEZO	1070	Guerrero Negro, B.C.
XEZOL	860	Ciudad Juarez, Chih.
XEZQ	1520	Huimanguillo, Tab.
XEZR	860	Zaragoza, Coah.
XEZS	1170	Coatzacoalcos, Ver.
XEZT	1250	Puebla, Pue.
XEZU	1270	Zacapu, Mich.
XEZV	800	Tlapa, Gro.
XEZW	1380	Hidalgo, Chis.
XEZW	1560	Cerritos, S.L.P.
XEZX	860	Tenosique, Tab.
XEZYB	1530	Oaxaca, Oax.
XEZZ	760	Tonala, Jal.
XEZZZ	590	Hidalgo, Chis.
XHA-TV	10	Durango, Dgo.
XHAA-TV	7	Tapachula, Chis.
XHAB	7	Matamoros, Tams.
XHAD-TV	7	Saltillo, Coah.
XHAE-TV	5	Saltillo, Coah.
XHAH-TV	8	Las Lajas, Ver.
XHAI-TV	10	Las Lajas, Ver.
XHAJ-TV	6	Las Lajas, Ver.
XHAK-TV	12	Chilpancingo, Gro.
XHAK-TV	12	Hermosillo, Son.
XHAN-TV	12	Campeche, Cam.
XHAP-TV	2	Acapulco, Gro.
XHAQ-TV	5	Mexicali, B.C.
XHAW-TV	12	Monterrey, N.L.
XHBC-TV	3	Mexicali, B.C.
XHBL-TV	13	Culiacan, Sin.
XHBN-TV	7	Oaxaca, Oax.
XHBQ-TV	8	Zacatecas, Zac.
XHBR-TV	11	Nuevo Laredo, Tams.
XHBS-TV	4	Los Mochis, Sin.
XHBS-TV	4	Ciudad Obregon, Son.
XHBT-TV	7	Culiacan, Sin.
XHBU-TV	8	Jimenez, Chih.
XHBW	9	Monclova, Coah.
XHBZ-TV	7	Colima, Col.
XHCB-TV	10	Tepic, Nay.
XHCC-TV	5	Colima, Col.
XHCC-TV	5	Hermosillo, Son.
XHCG-TV	12	Los Mochis, Sin.
XHCH-TV	2	Chihuahua, Chih.
XHCV-TV	3	Coatzacoalcos, Ver.
XHD-TV	4	Tampico, Tams.
XHDF-TV	13	Mexico City, D.F.
XHEC-FM	91.9	Sabinas, Coah.
XHEM-FM	103.5	Ciudad Juarez, Chih.
XHFA-TV	2	Nogales, Son.
XHFG-FM	107.3	Tijuana, B.C.
XHFI-TV	5	Chihuahua, Chih.
XHFM-TV	2	Veracruz, Ver.
XHG-TV	4	Guadalajara, Jal.
XHGC-TV	5	Mexico City, D.F.
XHI-TV	2	Ciudad Obregon, Son.
XHIA-TV	2	Torreon, Coah.
XHIS-FM	90.3	Tijuana, B.C.
XHIT-TV	4	Chihuahua, Chih.
XHJC-FM	91.5	Mexicali, B.C.
XHK-TV	10	La Paz, B.C.S.
XHKW-TV	10	Morelia, Mich.
XHL-TV	10	Leon, Gto.
XHLL-TV	13	Villahermosa, Tab.
XHMA-TV	3	Parral, Chih.
XHMC-FM	104.9	Mexicali, B.C.
XHMLS	101.5	Matamoros, Tams.
XHMMP	92.3	Mexicali, B.C.
XHMZ-TV	7	Mazatlan, Sin.

XHNOE	94.1	Nuevo Laredo, Tams.
XHO-TV	11	Torreon, Coah.
XHOW-TV	12	Mazatlan, Sin.
XHP-TV	3	Puebla, Pue.
XHPF-FM	101.9	Mexicali, B.C.
XHQ-TV	3	Colima, Col.
XHQF-FM	98.9	Tijuana, B.C.
XHQQ-FM	93.3	Monterrey, N.L.
XHQS-FM	95.7	Tijuana, B.C.
XHQTV	3	Culiacan, Sin.
XHRE-FM	105.5	Piedras Negras, Coah.
XHRG-FM	95.5	Ciudad Acuna, Coah.
XHRM	92.5	Tijuana, B.C.
XHSG-FM	99.9	Piedras Negras, Coah.
XHSL-FM	99.1	Piedras Negras, Coah.
XHST-TV	13	Merida, Yuc.
XHTA-FM	94.5	Piedras Negras, Coah.
XHTH-TV	10	Hermosillo, Son.
XHTK-TV	11	Ciudad Victoria, Tams.
XHTM-TV	8	Mexico City, D.F.
XHTO-TV	9	Queretaro, Qro.
XHTP-TV	9	Merida, Yuc.
XHTV	4	Mexico City, D.F.
XHTX-TV	8	Tuxtla, Chis.
XHUA	90.1	Chihuahua, Chih.
XHUS-TV	8	Hermosillo, Son.
XHVG-FM	103.3	Mexicali, B.C.
XHX-TV	10	Monterrey, N.L.
XHY-TV	3	Merida, Yuc.
XHZ-TV	6	Guanajuato, Gto.
XRIO-TV	2	Matamoros, Tams.
YNX	750	Managua, Nicaragua
ZAL-TV	10	St. Johns, Anti.
ZBF-TV	8	Hamilton, Bermuda
ZBM-FM	89.1	Hamilton, Bermuda
ZBM-TV	10	Hamilton, Bermuda
ZBM-1	1230	Hamilton, Bermuda
ZBM-2	1340	Hamilton, Bermuda
ZBTV	5	Roadtown, Tortula, Br V I, Virgin Is.
ZBVI	780	Roadtown, Tortula, Br V I, Virgin Is.
ZDK	1100	St. Johns, Anti.
ZFB-F.		Hamilton, Bermuda
ZFB-1	960	Pembroke West, Bermuda
ZGB	885	Plymouth, Montserrat
ZIZ	570	Springfield, St. Kitts
ZNS-TV	13	Nassau, Bahamas
ZNS-1	1540	Nassau, Bahamas
ZNS-2	1240	Nassau, Bahamas
ZQI	720	Kingston, Jamaica
4VA	1080	Port Au Prince, Haiti
4VAA	880	Port Au Prince, Haiti
4VAB	1150	Port Au Prince, Haiti
4VAE	1190	Jeremie, Haiti
4VCD	960	Port Au Prince, Haiti
4VCPS	1000	Port Au Prince, Haiti
4VDS	860	Port Au Prince, Haiti
4VEA	1460	Cap Haitien, Haiti
4VEC	1035	Cap Haitien, Haiti
4VEF	830	Cap Haitien, Haiti
4VF	1120	Port Au Prince, Haiti
4VGM	1430	Port Au Prince, Haiti
4VI	760	Aux Cayes, Haiti
4VIE	780	Jeremie, Haiti
4VJS	930	Les Gonaives, Haiti
4VM	1250	Port Au Prince, Haiti
4VMR	5	Port Au Prince, Haiti
4VOC	1500	Port Au Prince, Haiti
4VRD	1170	Port Au Prince, Haiti
4VS	1380	Port Au Prince, Haiti
4VUE	660	Port Au Prince, Haiti
4VW	1330	Port Au Prince, Haiti

Important Notice

Would you like to be notified when the next edition of the *North American Radio-TV Station Guide* is introduced? If so, please complete the form below and mail to:

Mr. Vane A. Jones
6710 Hampton Drive East
Indianapolis, Indiana 46226

If you change your address after sending in the card, please notify us of your old and new address.

Form sent (date) ______________________________

Address change (date) ___________________________

- -

Please notify me when the sixteenth edition of the *North American Radio-TV Station Guide* is available.

16

Name ____

Current Address ______________________________________

City ____________________ State ____________ Zip Code ________

If change of address, please include old address also.